Louisiana Property Law

Louisiana Property Law

The Civil Code, Cases, and Commentary

SECOND EDITION

Markus G. Puder

THE HONORABLE HERBERT W. CHRISTENBERRY PROFESSOR OF LAW
LOYOLA UNIVERSITY NEW ORLEANS COLLEGE OF LAW

John A. Lovett

DEVAN D. DAGGETT, JR. DISTINGUISHED PROFESSOR OF LAW
LOYOLA UNIVERSITY NEW ORLEANS COLLEGE OF LAW

Evelyn L. Wilson

PROFESSOR EMERITA
SOUTHERN UNIVERSITY LAW CENTER

CAROLINA ACADEMIC PRESS
Durham, North Carolina

ISBN   978-1-5310-1868-9
eISBN   978-1-5310-1869-6
LCCN   2019957126

Carolina Academic Press
700 Kent Street
Durham, NC 27701
Telephone (919) 489-7486
Fax (919) 493-5668
www.caplaw.com

Printed in the United States of America

Contents

Table of Cases

Preface

Property law covers competing claims regarding access to resources, the use and control of resources, the transfer of resources, and it also mediates change in access to, use and control of resources over time. Although a course in property law necessarily covers some dry and abstract technicalities—property titles, boundary markers, classifications of different kinds of things and the like, property law remains one of the most interesting introductory subjects in law school. Our initial goal in this casebook is to share our excitement about that subject. We aim to show you the stakes in a property dispute and help you identify the important societal and economic interests at play in property law. We also strive to reveal that property rules, principles and practices reflect distinct local conditions and cultures.

Because this casebook focuses on property law specific to Louisiana, however, we want to help you appreciate that Louisiana's system of property law is a core part of this state's civilian legal heritage inherited from its days as a French and Spanish colony. As many commentators have observed over the years, property law is one of the principal areas where Louisiana's civil law tradition has been most carefully preserved in the Louisiana Civil Code. It is also an area where important substantive differences between Louisiana civil law and the common law of its sister states still prevail. This book thus opens with an introduction to the history and nature of the civil law tradition and the sources of Louisiana property law. Throughout the rest of book, we refer to historical contexts for current Louisiana law. We also point out, where relevant, how Louisiana property law is different from or similar to property law in common law states and foreign jurisdictions.

A third goal of this casebook is to introduce you to hotly contested areas of property law, including debates about how property law actually functions and how its fundamental purposes and core values affect principles and practice. Understanding these controversies within property law will enrich your understanding of codal provisions, judicial opinions and statutes that form the substantive base of Louisiana property law today.

A final goal of this casebook is to demystify property law so that you can become a proficient property law practitioner. Lawyers who work on property law matters must become efficient problem-solvers. They must be able to develop arguments that are likely to persuade judges and assist clients. Acquiring a firm grasp of basic property law principles is therefore an essential first step to becoming a proficient, practice-ready lawyer who can assist individuals, businesses, not-for-profit organizations and government institutions in a myriad of transactions and disputes.

Property involves actual persons and significant stakes. The contestants include people, corporations, towns, cities, and even the State of Louisiana. Property law decides who has access to things, who can use things, who can exclude or be excluded from things, who can sell, lease or donate things, what terms and limits govern such transfers, and how and when our relationship to things can change over time. In the pages that follow we endeavor to help you sort Louisiana property law into its basic elements and understand its vocabulary, its codal structure and the modes of civilian legal thinking essential to helping actual people—your future clients and constituents—flourish as individuals, as families or in other kinds of associations.

Even if you do not intend to become a Louisiana lawyer, this casebook should still be enlightening. It explores how a mixed jurisdiction like Louisiana has embraced its civilian legal heritage in one important area of private law, nurtured and modified that heritage over the course of two centuries and struggled to make that heritage serviceable in the twenty-first century. We are proud of the many unique contributions made by property law to Louisiana's legal culture. At the same time, we invite you to join us in probing its values, challenging its assumptions, and evaluating the ways it has adapted to fit the diverse needs of modern society.

It is with gratitude that we acknowledge Dean Madeleine M. Landrieu of Loyola University New Orleans College of Law, Professor Dr. Roland Wittmann of the European University Viadrina and Professor Marc Roark of Southern University Law Center for their support in helping us prepare the second edition of this book. We are also grateful to the diligent students in our property classes over the last five years who have asked hard questions and helped us see where improvement was needed. Finally, we give special thanks to research assistants Jerald Andry, Sarah Didlake, Philip Laborde, Sara LaRosa, Gabriel Silva and Andre Stolier, who all made valuable contributions to this edition. We hope that our book will not only offer a helpful resource to learners and practitioners alike, but also bring joy to those interested in the scientific aspect of the study of law. *Sis felix!*

MARKUS G. PUDER
JOHN A. LOVETT
EVELYN L. WILSON

September 2019
New Orleans and Baton Rouge

Louisiana Property Law

Chapter 1

Sources of Louisiana Property Law

This casebook is about *Louisiana* property law. In general, this area of the law is imparted primarily through the Louisiana Civil Code. Because property is a crucial vessel for the preservation of Louisiana's civil law heritage, it is essential to appreciate the nature of civil law in general, its historical origins and its scientific development in Europe before it was transplanted in the soil of Louisiana. In this chapter, we offer some general background material to explain the history of civil law in Europe and codification and revision in Louisiana. Throughout this casebook, we will address questions related to judicial methodology in Louisiana, including the role that various kinds of authority play in the jurisprudence making and the complementary and sometimes competing relationships between judge and legislator.

A. The Civil Law Tradition in Europe: From Justinian to Codification

The civil law derives from Roman law which developed between the middle of the fifth century BCE and the middle of the sixth century CE. Property law was at the core of the enormous body of law assembled by the Romans. We do not present a complete introduction to Roman law but will refer to it when appropriate because of its lasting legacy for our legal heritage in Louisiana.

Today many lawyers mistakenly assert that civil law is simply the law embodied in the civil codes that emerged in Europe at the beginning of the nineteenth century and then spread to Latin American and many parts of the world. As the following reading shows, however, the civil law was already highly developed throughout most of Europe long before the French Civil Code, or any civil code, was ever enacted. Indeed, the civil law was decisively shaped over a period of more than 700 years, beginning with the re-discovery of Roman law in Italy in the late eleventh century.

The following excerpt comes from a law review essay authored by the civil law scholar Peter Stein, who held the Regius Chair of Civil Law at Oxford University for many years. With a Louisiana audience in mind, Stein offers important insights into the evolution of the civil law in Europe and the rise of the codification movement. The essay describes how that legal tradition differs from the common law legal culture that eventually developed in England and throughout the United States.

In his essay, Peter Stein discusses the Roman Emperor **Justinian**. Given the name *Urauda* at his birth in Tauresium, which is located in today's Republic of

Macedonia, Justinian was a native Latin speaker who received a Greek education. In 527, he became Emperor of the Eastern Roman Empire. A very ambitious and active Emperor, Justinian sought to revive the fame and fortune of the greatest days of the Roman Empire. One of his important historical legacies was his effort to recover, restore and reorganize the juristic texts and other writings from the Golden Age of Roman Law.

Justinian left us the *Corpus Iuris Civilis* (the body of the civil law), which Stein refers to as the *Corpus Juris*. This monumental compilation was prepared under the supervision and guidance of the quaestor Tribonianus in the first half of the sixth century in the wake of important discoveries of classical legal source texts. It consists of four parts traditionally discussed in the chronological order of their publication: the *Institutiones* (the instructions or "teaching manual"); the *Digesta* (the folders for the seminal writings of the classical jurists); the *Codex* (the collection of the imperial laws and edicts up to 534—essentially an update of the Theodosian Code of 438); and the *Novellae* (the continuation of the codex for subsequent laws and edicts).

The *Digest* forms the legal core of the Corpus Juris. Between the launch of the project in 530 and publication of the Digest in 533, a commission of academics from Constantinople (modern day Istanbul) and Berytos (Beirut) read, excerpted and redacted 2,000 book rolls with three million lines housing the responses to legal questions, commentaries, notes, epitomes, manuals and monographs authored by the great classical jurists. The final product encompasses 150,000 lines spread over fifty books or *libri*, which are subdivided into titles or *titulos*. Every title further falls into fragments or *leges*. Although it contains writings from a large number of jurists, both known and unknown, most of the Digest is drawn from a relatively small pool of writers. Among these jurists are **Ulpian**, whose writings alone comprise approximately one-third of the *Digest*, and **Paul**, whose contributions constitute about one-sixth of the Digest. The Digest was promulgated on December 16, 533. It went into effect fourteen days later as the law of the Empire.

Recognizing that the Digest was too vast and complicated a work for law students to master, Justinian also commissioned the drafting of a shorter and more coherent law school textbook now known as the *Institutes*. This text was based partially on a work written by the Roman jurist **Gaius** four centuries earlier, which bore the same title. Justinian's *Institutes* follows Gaius' model by dividing the law into three parts: one covering *persones* (persons and family), a second pertaining to *res* (things and property), and a third concerning *actiones* (actions). This Romanist tripartite division of private law influenced the anatomy of the French Code Napoleon of 1804, the Austrian General Civil Code of 1811, and Louisiana's first civil code, the 1808 *Digest of the Laws in Force in the Territory of Orleans*. The current version of the Louisiana Civil Code still follows this same basic structure for three of its four books. The fourth book of Louisiana's code is entitled *Conflict of Laws*. The *Institutes* were given the force of law at the same time as the *Digest*. Unlike the *Digest*, though, the various passages woven together to form the *Institutes* are not attributed to any particular author.

For those interested in learning more about the classical period of Roman law, Justinian's compilation and the subsequent impact of Roman law, we recommend HANS JULIUS WOLFF, ROMAN LAW: AN HISTORICAL INTRODUCTION (1951); BARRY NICHOLS, AN INTRODUCTION TO ROMAN LAW (1962); PETER STEIN, ROMAN LAW IN EUROPEAN HISTORY (1999); AND DAVID JOHNSTON, ROMAN LAW IN CONTEXT (1999), all available in handy, paperback editions.

Peter G. Stein, *Judge and Jurist in the Civil Law: A Historical Interpretation*
46 LA. L. REV. 241, 242–57 (1986)

When we speak of the civil law, there is a tendency to assume that its characteristic feature is that it is codified, in the sense that the whole law is expressed in a coherent, systematic authoritative form. But the earliest modern codes are little more than two hundred years old, and there are still one or two indisputable civil law systems that are uncodified, notably that of the Republic of San Marino.

The civil law was developing for at least five hundred years before the codification movement became fashionable in the eighteenth century, i.e., from the re-discovery of the texts of Justinian in twelfth-century Italy. Surely we can presume that it had found its identity before codification became the vogue.

So it is in the pre-code period that I propose to seek the features of the civil law. This period can be divided roughly into two parts, divided at about the year 1500. The first, from 1100 to 1500, saw the rise of the European common law, *ius commune*, and the second, from 1500 to 1800, saw the adaptation of that law by court practice to the needs of nation-states.

The Period of the *Ius Commune*

The main feature of medieval law in Europe was its pluralism. There was no territorial unity of law within the various principalities. Within the same state, there were different sets of laws for different regions; there were also different sets of laws for different social classes: nobles, peasants, merchants. Additionally, there were different sets of laws for different aspects of life: matters of personal injury would be dealt with by courts of lay judges applying traditional unwritten customs; landholding was governed by feudal law; personal status, marriage, and succession to movables were the province of the canon law of the church.

This plethora of overlapping jurisdictions meant that outside the area of the canon law, which was international, the sources of law were a jumble of local customs and statutes, which often did not provide answers in cases of any complexity. As long as the judges were part-time laymen applying traditional custom, they would make up an appropriate rule according to their sense of justice. Increasingly, however, princes created courts with professional judges whose whole work was the administration of justice. In cases of doubt, these judges drew on their university training.

The medieval university saw as its task the transmission of the learning of antiquity, as recorded in recognized books of authority. In theology these were the Bible and the church fathers; in law they were the *Corpus Juris* of Justinian. The main university for law was Bologna, which had two law faculties, one for the canon law of the church and another for Justinian's law, which was beginning to be called civil law, to distinguish it from the canon law. Students flocked to Bologna from all over Europe, and by the thirteenth century there were over a thousand foreign students enrolled. The system developed there became the model for all European universities. The only laws that were worthy of study in a university were those that transcended national boundaries, that were universal in scope, and the only laws that satisfied that criterion were the canon and the civil. All other laws were excluded, even in the English universities of Oxford and Cambridge.

Justinian's texts are not easy to understand. They are about twice the size of the Bible and except for a small part, the Institutes, the arrangement of the material is very confused. The individual rulings and distinctions between cases show enormous subtlety and technical skill, but their sheer bulk and complexity have intimidated many generations of students. The first law professors at Bologna, the so-called glossators, concentrated on pure exegesis: they cross-referenced the whole Corpus of texts, bringing together those dealing with similar topics, reconciling apparent contradictions, summarizing, and so on. They treated the texts themselves as sacred, so that all exposition was limited by the meaning the texts could in totality bear. But the range of those texts was such that somewhere in the Corpus one could find the answer to any conceivable question of law. Accursius synthesized the work of the glossators in his Great Gloss, and when he asserted categorically, "everything is found in the Corpus Juris," he did not seem to exaggerate. The glossators introduced the idea that what was important in a legal argument was the support of a text from somewhere in the corpus of authorities; it did not have to be from the context of the argument, for Justinian had stated that his compilation was a complete whole, with no contradictions.

The products of this kind of legal training, the *juristae*, became the meritocrats who were recruited by princes to serve their councils and staff their courts. They naturally analyzed legal issues in the way they had been taught. They applied the appropriate local law to those issues, but they interpreted that law according to the techniques of Roman law, and when they found a gap in the local law they applied the Roman rule. Whatever their national origin, the *juristae* shared the same legal culture, based on the same texts, expounded in the universal language of the educated people, Latin. So also they shared their legal experience. For example, in the thirteenth century the city of Lübeck asked the city of Hamburg what rules were applied in Hamburg to a certain question of maritime law. The Head of the Chancery at Hamburg could not find any specific rules in the Hamburg statute book or custom. But since he was university trained, he translated certain passages from Justinian's Digest into German and sent them to Lübeck, stating that they were the law of Hamburg, and thereafter the Roman rules were followed. In this way Roman law infiltrated into local laws.

It was not until the fourteenth century that the so-called commentators began consciously to adapt Roman law. The commentators used manuscripts of the Corpus Juris accompanied by Accursius's Gloss and made no distinction between the two. Without the glossators' explanations and cross-references to analogous texts, Justinian's law was incomplete; so the rule was accepted, "What the Gloss does not recognize, the court does not recognize." As a fifteenth-century commentator, Fulgosius, stated: "In court I would rather have the authority of the Gloss on my side than a text; otherwise it will be said: do you think the Gloss has not seen that text and has not understood it as well as you?" Hence the idea that authoritative juristic comment on a statutory text is itself an authentic source of law.

The commentators, led by Bartolus of Sassoferrato, were faced with problems of the validity of local custom and the conflict between local law and the imperial law of Justinian. The glossators had argued that, if a local custom or statute differed from the Roman law, then the latter, as the imperial law of the whole empire, must prevail, and they cited specific texts to that effect. But local popular feeling, particularly in the fiercely independent Italian city-states, would not tolerate that. Bartolus took a more realistic attitude to the problem than his predecessors.

Justinian's Digest and Code did not lay down broad general rules. They dealt with specific cases, and some of them referred to the existence of local customs that did not contradict the general law. Bartolus built up general rules from these particular case rulings. . . .

. . . But it is important to note that in doing so, he [Bartolus] observed the conventions of Roman law itself. That law provided the grammar for all arguments of general jurisprudence. Such argument only carried authority if it purported to bring out what was latent in the Roman texts, even if it was not so expressed. So Bartolus and his followers created what was effectively a new law out of the old Roman law, and because of its general acceptance, it was called *ius commune*, the common law of Europe. When, for example, a sixteenth-century Scottish statute refers to "the common law," it means this law and not the English common law.

. . .

The Period of the *Usus Modernus*

In the sixteenth century a number of factors appeared which altered the picture with regard both to the role of the courts and to the function of the jurists. On the one hand, the various nation-states began to assert what they called their individual sovereignty. This meant that their supreme courts saw themselves as exponents not of the *ius commune* but of the particular law of the state. They could no longer turn automatically to the Roman law, as adopted by the Bartolists, to fill gaps in the law. The *ius commune* might be received or it might not, depending on the suitability of the rule in question to the needs of the state; and this decision was the courts'.

On the other hand, the academic study of law was affected by the gradual influence of humanist ideas. Humanists were in the first place concerned about the form of law. They showed up Justinian's *Corpus Juris* for what it was, a Byzantine mosaic composed of much more ancient materials, arranged in a confused jumble. The humanists began to rearrange those materials in a more coherent and systematic form. It was at this time that Justinian's Institutes, hitherto regarded as a mere students' nutshell, became the object of special attention as demonstrating how private law could be seen as a system with a relatively simple structure. By stressing the rationality of the civil law as a system, the humanists sought to demystify it.

The humanists also exploited the inherent ambiguity which the word for "law" has in every European language except English. They argued that the subject of a legal system is the Latin *ius* or French *droit*, not in the sense of objective rules, but in the sense of subjective rights attaching to individuals' powers which they could assert through the legal system. But once the legal system is perceived as a set of subjective rights rather than as a set of rules, there is no place in it for procedural rules. Law must now be distinguished from procedure. Substantive law is concerned with rights and duties, and procedure becomes the subject of adjective law.

Thirdly, the humanists stressed the connection, which had been played down by the Bartolists, between the law of the Roman texts and the circumstances of ancient Roman society at different periods. Their main interest was academic, and they were interested in the legal texts primarily for the light they threw on ancient culture. But by this emphasis on the relation between law and a particular society, the humanists supported the argument that Roman law could not be applied *in toto* in their own time and that each nation receives as much or as little of it as is suitable for it.

These trends did not destroy the *ius commune*, or the Bartolist School which created it, but they introduced new uncertainties into the practice of the civil law. It became more difficult to predict how the professional judges of the national supreme courts would react to the arguments put to them. The problem was not a lack of authorities but rather a superabundance of authorities. The Bartolists tried to overcome this problem by developing the doctrine of "the common opinion of the doctors," the lowest common multiple of juristic opinion on the *ius commune*. What everyone wanted to know, however, was whether the judges would follow that opinion. Practitioners needed a guide to the practice of their particular court, and judges needed to show that their judgments were based not on whims but on accepted principles.

To meet these needs, collections of court decisions began to appear, and a whole new genre of legal literature was born, which the recently discovered art of printing was harnessed to disseminate. Until recently legal historians have overlooked the large number of printed series of civil law reports from the sixteenth to the eighteenth centuries, and only now are we appreciating their importance. The earliest reports were made by judges who wanted to show that, despite the official secrecy that surrounded their deliberations, their judgments were rational and based on authority. One of the earliest, Georges Louet, a judge of the *Parlement de Paris*, grouped several decisions together with an accompanying explanation that "the reason was such and such" or that "what we can understand from them, is so and so." Whether the reports were made by judges or by advocates, the overriding motive seems to have been to prove that the court in question adopted a consistent practice—consistent with itself and consistent with a proper choice among relevant authorities.

What was the status of this forensic practice? Should it be regarded as a source of law? To justify its existence, the jurists turned to Bartolus and his doctrine of custom. They argued that each state, when it received as much of the *ius commune* as it deemed appropriate for its needs, created a custom. The only body that could declare authoritatively what a state received and what it did not was its supreme court, so that each court by custom created a different variant of the *ius commune*. In this way what had been a common version of Roman law gave way to Roman-Dutch law, Roman-German law, Roman-Spanish law, and so on. Scholars began to make collections of abrogated or rejected laws of the *Corpus Juris*. The evidence was in the reports.

These reports were, of course, a form of case law, but it is a mistake to regard them as having the same function as reported cases in the common law.

In England the king's court superseded local courts much earlier than elsewhere in Europe. The jurisdictions of the feudal courts and even of the church courts were limited, and in most cases the king's courts offered a common law for every Englishman, wherever he happened to live and whatever his social status. Unlike other customary systems, this law was taught and developed scientifically, not in the English universities, it is true, but in the Inns of Court which effectively functioned as a legal university.

But this law remained in theory unwritten, a set of rules that were gradually revealed as successive generations of judges pulled back the veil under which they had been lurking. They existed, if anywhere, not in the practices of everyday life but in the "bosom of the judges." Because of the procedure which used the jury for fact finding and did not allow appeals from jury verdicts, the number of English judges was small; they became an elite group who assumed the status of father-figures, the oracles of the law. The law they declared was essentially open-ended. It had no existence as a body of material distinct from what the court decided. Academic treatises were of value only in so far as they reflected what went on in court and discerned the direction that the judges were giving to the growth of legal doctrine. That doctrine was still expressed in terms of remedies rather than rights. What a man could do in law was indicated only in terms of the different forms of action available to him.

Since the common law existed only in the decisions of the judges, they could have been free to develop it as they wanted. To prove their consistency, however, they imposed on themselves the doctrine of *stare decisis*. But this doctrine applied only when the relevant facts of the instant case and the precedent case were the same. As a result, the law reports for common law became increasingly pre-occupied with facts, with the assumption that rules to be derived from the decisions are of limited scope, and with the idea that the judges have a personal responsibility for what they decide, which has much to do with their prestige as individuals.

The civil law, on the other hand, was considered to be contained in recognized texts, whose mysteries were expounded by the commentators. It was a recognized body of law, even when it was not reflected in current court practice. There were "elegant" treatises on pure Roman law as well as "'forensic'" treatises on the law in action. It was not the jurists but the judges who were on the defensive; they were expected to prove that their practice, in choosing among the various academic authorities presented to them, was respectable and able to withstand rational scrutiny. What mattered was not so much what they decided but how they approached the legal issue. Thus, civil law reports often did not mention the facts of the case. They functioned as justifications of court practice in light of juristic critique, and they justified decisions by citing the relevant texts and commentators that were utilized to reach them. Since what mattered was what rules the court as a whole adopted, the views of individual judges hardly counted. Civil law judges saw themselves as bureaucrats rather than father-figures, as fungible persons who were readily replaceable.

. . .

Codification

It was the jurists who thus prepared the ground for the codification movement of the eighteenth century. But that movement was, in part at least, inspired by the layman's suspicion both of jurists and of judges and by a popular desire to weaken the power of both groups. The jurists, it was felt, had a vested interest in maintaining the complexity of the sources of law, since only they could indicate the narrow paths between the marshes of conflicting doctrine. The judges, it was believed, exploited the same complexity to justify any decisions they wanted to reach. A code, worded in simple, straight-forward language, would, it was hoped, both eliminate the need for academic commentaries and at the same time reduce the discretionary power of the judges.

. . .

The French Civil Code [of 1804] was drafted in the spirit of the Revolution; it was presented to the world as a new beginning, as marking a clean break with the past. In recently colonial Louisiana, however, the ideology was not the same. Those concerned with the law were hardly in full sympathy with the ideals of the Revolution; they wanted in many respects to maintain the status quo. Fashion and political change demanded an authoritative statement of the law. The first code of 1808 looked like the French Code in style, although it contained some Roman law thought relevant to Louisiana which was not in the French code, such as the rules of public rights on the river banks (articles 452 and 456), the sale of a hope (article 2451), and the action for things thrown onto the street (article 177). In 1817 the Louisiana Supreme Court squashed any radicals who might have thought that their code should be treated as a new beginning by holding that the old law was still in force, unless it was actually inconsistent with the code.

The problem for the developing Louisiana law in the nineteenth century was the absence of jurists who could make it their special concern to monitor the application of the law and keep it on course. There were, of course, capable lawyers such as Edward Livingston, whom my predecessor Sir Henry Maine in 1856 called "the first legal genius of modern times," but, although they drafted legislation, they could not devote the time to the continuous commentaries on its application which were required. Continental commentaries were imported but they gradually became less relevant than they had been in the colonial period. So the commission for the 1825 code back-tracked and added a good deal of detail to flesh out the general rules in the manner of a juristic commentary. Maine described the Louisiana Civil Code of 1825 as "of all republications of Roman law, the one which appears to us the clearest, the fullest, the most philosophical and the best adapted to the exigencies of modern society."

An example is the law of formation of contracts. The French Code, which was followed in the Louisiana Civil Code of 1808, contained nothing about offer and acceptance except a broad rule, derived from Roman law through Pothier, that there must be agreement. Whether or not there is an agreement in a particular case is thus a question of fact, and in principle the French courts are left with wide discretion to find that the parties have agreed or not. When perplexed, they can turn to juristic discussions. The Louisiana Civil Code of 1825, however, contains a number of rules about offer and acceptance. They are mainly taken from Toullier. But these rules look rather like the common law rules relating to the formation of a contract, and that made it easier for judges to turn to those rules for further guidance. After all, jurists such as Sir William Jones were saying that consent is consent the world over and that Pothier's doctrine of contracts was "law at Westminster as well as Orleans."

The compilers of the Louisiana Civil Code of 1825 not only added more detail, they also included explanatory comment. They made it clear what parts of the old law were no longer in force, and they included explanations of the reasoning behind the matter that was retained. The code was no longer addressed to the ordinary citizen, but to advocates and judges; it had become technical. Left to themselves, the judges naturally assumed a more prominent posture. They filled the vacuum left by the absence of jurists and assumed the oracular role of their colleagues in the common law states. The reports began to include judicial dissents which are, in general, alien to the civil law. . . .

Notes

1. Several important personalities have shaped the development of the civil law and reception of Roman law after its re-discovery in Italy. Chief among them was **Irnerius** (1050–1125), the "lantern of the law," who founded the law school at Bologna and became one of the greatest law professors of all times. Indeed, Bologna — one of medieval Europe's first great universities — was to become the epicenter for the percolation of the science of law throughout the Old World. The other important figure is **Francesco Accursius** (1182–1260), who wrote the seminal annotation to the *Corpus Juris*, which came to be known as *The Gloss* ("glossa ordinaria"). The practice of commenting on and explicating the old Roman texts gave rise to the scholarly movement of the **Glossators**.

One important fruit of the work of these scholars was the Spanish *Codigo de las Siete Partidas*, a collection of law narratives produced during the reign of Alfonso X of Castile (1252–1284) by scholars like **Maestro Jacobo** (a pupil of Irnerius), who returned home from Italy deeply steeped in Roman law. This masterwork, which was to become part of Louisiana's legal heritage, principally draws on the Roman law that had been rediscovered and discussed in Europe's medieval universities, but also exhibits influences from Islamic law.

The next wave of scholars, no longer content with passive comments, started to probe the question of how to apply Roman law in contemporary contexts. The leaders of this movement have been called the **Commentators** (or post-glossators). Among them were **Bartolus of Sassoferrato** (1314–1357) and **Baldus de Ubaldis** (1327–1400), whose work ushered in the reign of the *ius commune* — the common law of Europe.

Bartolus was born in Sassoferrato, a small village in Italy. He studied law at Perugia and later at the great medieval law school at Bologna, where he earned his doctorate at the age of twenty-one. Although he served for a time as a judge, Bartolus was principally a law teacher and writer. As Stein indicates in his essay, Bartolus was important because he did more than merely cite his predecessors like other Commentators; he enriched the discourse about Roman law by distilling a workable legal regime that could resolve conflicts common in late medieval society. This became particularly relevant in the context of clashes between the law of the Empire and the increasingly independent Italian city-states, as well as between Roman law and canon law (the law of the Roman Catholic Church). *See generally* Peter Stein, Roman Law in European History 71–73 (1999).

2. After the Peace of Westphalia (1648), which ended the Thirty Years War, the codification process fractured into separate streams, notably French, Germanic, Dutch, and Nordic. In light of our French heritage, you should know about two figures particularly important for the development of Louisiana law who worked in the late pre-codification period discussed in the second half of Stein's essay: **Jean Domat** (1625–1696) and **Robert Joseph Pothier** (1699–1772). Domat was influenced by the natural law movement of the late seventeenth century, which sought

to further rationalize Roman law in light of Christian ethics, and endeavored to identify first principles or maxims from which more specific legal rules could be deduced. His great work, *Les lois civiles dans leur order natural* (The Civil Laws in their Natural Order) (1689–1694), typifies this approach. Several important provisions of the 1825 Louisiana Civil Code that govern obligations owed by property owners to their neighbors and that are still part of the current Civil Code were derived almost *verbatim* from Domat. *Compare* Jean Domat, The Civil Law in its Natural Order §§ 1046–48 (Luther S. Cushing, ed., William Strahan trans., 1853) *with* La. Civ. Code arts. 667–69 (1870, amended 1996).

In the middle of the 1700s, the groundbreaking scholarship of Pothier began to appear; chief among his writings was a re-arrangement and scientific elaboration of classical Roman law. *See* Robert J. Pothier, the Pandectae Justinianae in novum ordinem digestae (Paris & Chartres 1748–1752). Though he began his legal career as a hereditary magistrate in Orleans, Pothier's work introducing, reorganizing and elaborating on Justinian's *Digest* brought him great fame and an appointment as royal professor of French law at the University of Orleans. In another work, *Coutumes d'Olreans* (1761), Pothier ordered and expounded on the customary law of different parts of France. Later, he wrote a series of treatises covering the main branches of private law including, most famously, his *Traité des Obligations*, which, building on Roman law, showed the relationship between general principles and more specific rules used in everyday practice. This work was eventually translated into other languages, including English. It had a significant influence on the development of Anglo-American contract law. The drafters of both the 1808 *Digest of the Laws in Force in the Territory of Orleans* and the 1825 Civil Code relied on Pothier extensively.

3. In civilian jurisdiction the distinction between *private law* and *public law* is of paramount importance. When a civilian lawyer (or a common law lawyer for that matter) speaks about the "private law," she is usually referring to the body of law that governs relationships and transactions among and between private actors. Public law, on the other hand, is usually thought of as the law regulating the relationship between the State (federal, state and local government in the United States) and private persons. Some "purist" civil codes, like the German Civil Code, are careful not to include any rules that might be deemed to fall into the realm of public law.

The subject of this casebook is largely private law. Likewise, the Louisiana Civil Code is concerned almost exclusively with general private law. In practice, the distinction is not always neat because, when the state or one of its political subdivisions acts in its private capacity, it is subject to private law in general and the Louisiana Civil Code in particular. In addition, public law principles (for example, the guarantee of equal protection under the Fourteenth Amendment to the United States Constitution) can permeate transactions between private persons that might otherwise seem to be subject only to private law. We will see examples of this so-called "horizontal impact" of public law and constitutional law principles on private law relationships when we study Building Restrictions.

B. The Civil Law Tradition in Louisiana: A Brief Introduction to Codification and Recodification

As Stein mentions in his essay, Louisiana codified large swaths of the civil law of Europe in the early nineteenth century, following France's example. The story of how Louisiana, alone among the fifty states, came to have a civil code modeled on a European civil code is complex and fascinating. In the following essay, Professor David Gruning summarizes some of the key developments in that process and provides an overview of the architecture of the current version of the Civil Code. Read the following excerpt with your desk copy of the Louisiana Civil Code in hand. Examine the preliminary materials that accompany the desk copy. Peruse its table of contents. Leaf through its pages. Consider especially La. Civ. Code arts. 1–14, 24, 448, 870 and 3515.

David Gruning, *Mapping Society through Law: Louisiana, Civil Law Recodified*
19 Tul. Eur. & Civ. L. Forum 1, 1–12, 14–20, 31–34 (2004)

I. Introduction

Everything ages. Some things (red wine, cheese) improve with age. Others (cream, cut flowers) do not. Still others, while they may lose utility with age, particularly when compared to newer versions of themselves, nevertheless take on a distinct value. Yesterday's astrolabe or compass becomes today's collectible. Civil codes and maps both seem to fall into this third category. The techniques for measuring land improve, or its ownership or its nationality changes; a map of the land must be updated in light of the improvements and alterations.

Likewise, the rules of society change. A civil code that attempts to represent them must also change and adapt so as to remain connected to them. At a point in time difficult to specify, the age of a code or a map renders it less a useful tool or instrument than an object of curiosity that belongs clearly to another epoch. When a map becomes obsolete, one draws a new one and either discards or archives the old. When a civil code becomes obsolete, one must decide whether to remake the code, to recodify. For maps, new techniques effectively free the new drawing from the constraints and limitations of the old. For civil codes, however, this is not the case. Unlike old maps, old codes refuse to retire to the wastebasket or the museum. The old code persists and constrains the new. Indeed, although one can imagine mapping some portion of the earth without looking at any earlier map of it, to recodify civil law necessarily implies beginning with the prior code (or codes, if another code antedates the immediately preceding code), even if only more surely to depart from them.

Sometimes, perhaps even usually, this effort to recodify runs into trouble. France is a notable example where a serious effort to recodify the civil law began not long after World War II but failed to produce a new, comprehensive text. Quebec's recodification went through difficulties of its own but emerged on the other side of them with a new Civil Code. Both France and Quebec, then, opted to redraft and to re-adopt their Codes in a single piece of legislation and after thorough study and discussion. Louisiana, also, has gone through a process of recodification. Unlike France and Quebec, however, Louisiana has revised its civil law not as a whole but in distinct blocks. The pejorative term often used to describe the process is "piecemeal" recodification. Almost all of the 1870 Code has been revised in this fashion.

That recodification is the main subject here. . . .

II. The Louisiana Civil Code: Then and Now

In order to understand the recodification of the Louisiana Civil Code, it may be helpful to recall how, alone of all American states, Louisiana came to have such a code.

French explorers arrived on the American coast of the Gulf of Mexico in 1682. In 1712, the crown decreed that the Custom of Paris would govern the colony, and placed the colony effectively in the hands both of private interests and of a Superior Council. After failure of the private interests, the Crown assumed full control in 1731. In 1762, France transferred Louisiana to Spain. The latter, however, did not achieve effective control until 1769. Thereafter Spain administered Louisiana, perhaps more effectively than had France. Spain established its own system of government, replacing the Superior Council with a Cabildo or city council, and applying Spanish colonial law. Later, in 1800, Napoleon engineered the return of Louisiana to France, but his intentions in the Caribbean having been frustrated, he sold Louisiana to the United States in April 1803. The French flag went up over Louisiana for a few weeks in the fall of that year, being replaced definitively by the American flag by the end of the year. Louisiana had become an American territory.

Now a part of the United States, Louisiana (then the Territory of Orleans) faced the question of what law would be applicable. Claiborne, the territorial governor, initially sought to bring Louisiana's legal system into the American fold. Indeed, for civil procedure, the judicial system, and criminal law, the old law gave way quickly to the new. The lawyerly inhabitants, however, succeeded in maintaining their private law and in keeping the common law out. Accordingly, in 1808 "A Digest of the Civil Laws now in force in the Territory of Orleans" went into effect. That Digest (which lawyers often referred to as a Code) remained in effect when the territory became a state in 1812. In 1817, however, the Louisiana Supreme Court ruled so as to limit the effectiveness of the 1808 Digest: prior law not inconsistent with the Digest was still in force. This confused the sources of law applicable to any case, as through skillful interpretation the civil law outside the Digest, chiefly Spanish law, could be made relevant. But the Spanish sources were difficult to obtain and they were cast in a language not mastered by all lawyers. This problem was partially remedied by a translation of large parts of one of the most influential Spanish texts, the Siete Partidas, in 1820.

The problem was more effectively remedied by the enactment of the Civil Code of 1825. That Code, in article 3521, included an express repeal of the "Spanish, Roman and French" laws in force at the time of the Louisiana Purchase. But article 3521 "repealed" the old law "in every case . . . especially provided in this Code." Based on that phrase, the Louisiana supreme court held that much of the old law had indeed survived the enactment of the 1825 Code. The legislature responded quickly. The Great Repealing Act of 1828 repealed "all the civil laws which were in force before the promulgation of the civil code lately promulgated." Initially, the supreme court accepted that "the whole body" of Spanish law that had survived enactment of the Digest of 1808 had now been repealed. Nevertheless, for that court it was one thing for the legislature to repeal legislation, "the positive, written, or statute laws," whether produced by itself or otherwise. But according to the supreme court the 1828 repealer could not affect the "principles of law . . . established or settled by the decisions of the courts of justice" under the old law. The practical effects of this qualification appear not to have been substantial. The tension between legislation and case law, however, continues as a theme of contemporary recodification.

In large measure, then, the 1825 Code and explicit repeal attained the goal sought. Louisiana civil law achieved substantially complete expression between the covers of a single book.

The 1825 Code was in force through the Civil War. During Reconstruction, the Louisiana legislature enacted the Civil Code of 1870. For a long time, it was accepted that the 1870 Code was no more than the 1825 Code, shorn of the relatively few provisions dealing with slavery and of the French text. More recently, it has been argued that the institution of slavery was more deeply worked into the fabric of the 1825 Code and thus its removal was not a minor operation. An unmistakable difference, however, was that the 1870 Code, unlike the 1825 Code or the 1808 Digest, was published in English only, without the French text.

After the enactment of the 1870 Code, the economy and the culture of Louisiana underwent enormous changes during the decades preceding and immediately following World War I. It is clear that these changes put the law of the Civil Code under serious pressures. For example, the change in language habits (initially a cultural shift only later reflected in statute) undermined the civilian character of the legal system. The use of English in education and the media accompanied a decline in the use of French. For the practicing lawyer who did not master French, this decline put French doctrine out of reach. It also made the use of English authorities more attractive to English-speaking lawyers and judges. There were other pressures in addition to language. Practice techniques, for example, were borrowed from outside the state. Frequently, those techniques were based on institutions not recognized in the Civil Code, and were perceived as deriving from the "common law" even when based on statutes from other jurisdictions. Beyond these influences from the practice of law as such, Louisiana lawyers also adopted more seductive techniques from the common law tradition. From equity, the concept of estoppel became familiar to Louisiana lawyers. Even the common law notion of stare decisis gained acceptance. Substantively, the common law of tort was highly influential.

The net effect of these influences, together with the existence only of a Civil Code in comparison to the classic five codes of the French system, led one professor to claim in 1937 that Louisiana had become a common law state. That claim led to a spirited article defending the civil law in Louisiana. That defense is sometimes seen as the beginning of a renaissance of the civil law in Louisiana. But well before those articles appeared, Louisiana law schools were giving more than lip service to the civil law and to Roman law in their faculty hiring, in their curricula, and in their scholarship. This occurred at a time when legal education in the university was still a relatively new phenomenon on the national scene. At a relatively early point, then, Louisiana legal education opted to commit to the civil law as its hallmark.

The Louisiana legislature's actions during the same decade seem allied with those of the academy. The legislature chartered the Louisiana State Law Institute (LSLI or Law Institute) in 1938. The role of the LSLI was to provide research that would suggest avenues of reform of the law generally. With regard to the civil law, the Law Institute was to provide "studies and doctrinal writings" so as to aid an understanding of the "philosophy" on which it is based.

At about the same time, Louisiana legal scholars were calling for a "comprehensive revision" of the Code. These early recommendations envisaged a revision of the Code as a whole. World War II, of course, interrupted progress, but in 1948 the legislature charged the LSLI "to prepare comprehensive projects" for the revision of both the Civil Code and the Code of Practice. After systematic study and planning, the Louisiana Code of Civil Procedure replaced the Code of Practice in 1960.

The revision as a whole of the Civil Code itself, however, stalled. Although no formal decision seems to have been made, the strategy adopted by the Law Institute was to recommend enactment of portions of the Code as they were revised. Furthermore, particular portions of the 1870 Code confronted serious challenges. In some cases, the judicial application of federal constitutional norms threatened the Code. This was the case notably with matrimonial regimes. Such vulnerable portions of the Code, unless revised quickly, would face virtually certain judicial rejection on constitutional grounds. In other cases, business or economic pressures pushed for quick enactment of up-to-date legislation. Wholesale changes in social attitudes likewise could not be ignored by the legislature while awaiting comprehensive reform of the Code. Such external pressures thus worked against the deliberate pace of Code revision in Louisiana, giving additional impetus to revision block by block. Piecemeal revision may therefore have come about for several reasons, but come about it did. The process of revision, of block-by-block recodification, is now nearly complete, as will be shown in the next section.

III. The Code as Small-Scale Map: Zooming Out

When one reduces its scale, a map takes in more territory and eliminates detail. A measure on the map—a centimeter—represents a large distance (say one hundred kilometers). One pulls back, one zooms out. To the extent one eliminates detail, though, one inevitably distorts or falsifies the object portrayed. Yet unless detail is sacrificed, no design or map is possible. Reducing scale, then, is a key technique in drawing or mapping, and it both represents and distorts. It may represent by distorting. Our initial pass at the Code currently in effect—the "2003" Code—perforce takes place in terms of the Code of 1870.

A. Code Structure: The Lay of the Land and
How the Map Has Changed

The [current version of the Civil] Code maintains the structure of the 1870 Code. That Code used the three-book structure, typical of the French codification tradition. The 1870 Code also included a short Preliminary Title, which the 2003 Code maintains. In continuing this format, the Law Institute ignored suggestions from within the Louisiana legal community to reconsider that structure. It also ignored the example of later codes, such as those of Germany (five books), Italy (six books), the Netherlands (seven books), or Quebec (ten books). On the other hand, once the decision had been made or the practice adopted to revise the Code block by block, the prospect of re-structuring the whole was rendered significantly more difficult, probably impossible. Indeed, if the 2003 Code formally has a four-book structure (plus a preliminary title), with Conflicts of Laws occupying the new fourth book, this is in no small part due to the ease of adding a comparatively small number of articles toward the end.

Substantially all of the Code has now been revised. . . .

. . . Merely showing what remains to be done gives an incomplete image. Left open is the question of the fate of the material in the 1870 Code that has been removed. Some, of course, has simply been deleted. But in many cases portions of the 1870 Code have been placed elsewhere in Louisiana legislation. To show them simply as missing from the Code itself would give an incorrect impression. Matters are more complicated than that.

The beneficiary of the largest quantity of transfers is probably the text known as the Civil Code Ancillaries. [Title 9 of the Louisiana Revised Statutes, "Civil Code—Ancillaries."] By following the same structure as the Civil Code, the Ancillaries house matter complementary to the Civil Code and organize it in parallel with that text. This makes it easier to match the two sets of provisions when they must be construed together. Sometimes, such matter is regulatory in character. Thus, the Ancillaries contain numerous "housekeeping" rules, which to the Louisiana lawyer seem out of place in a Civil Code for several reasons. First, they are of insufficient importance and would not usually be capable of generating other rules; they cannot be *féconds en conséquences* in the sense Portalis famously intended. They are rather the ends of the process of reasoning from the Code. Second, such rules are more likely to require frequent adjustment, just because of their detailed character and their proximity to the application of legal norms in practice. And frequent amendment detracts from its stability. One might call these two motivations purism and pragmatism, respectively.

The Civil Code Ancillaries, however, have attracted some matters that do properly belong in the Civil Code itself. Some of these rules in the Ancillaries that are fundamental in character are located there for reasons practical, political, or both. For example, the Louisiana legislation on trusts is in the Ancillaries, where it is called a trust "Code." Notwithstanding its placement in the Ancillaries, trusts are basic for any lawyer planning a client's estate or handling many, if not most, testate successions. Trusts are also used for inter vivos transfers, to receive the proceeds of insurance policies, for retirement benefits, or a combination of these functions. Thus, trusts are as important as the rules governing donations mortis causa within the Code itself. From the perspective of their importance, then, inclusion of them within the Code itself would make sense and certainly would not be shocking. And there are other civil law jurisdictions with a mixture of common law institutions that have taken this path. At the time of the enactment of the legislation on trusts in the early 1960s, however, there was still some spirited opposition to trusts as not belonging in a civilian system at all. The placement of trusts in the ancillaries seems due thus to both politics and pragmatism. . . .

Sometimes material that would naturally be found within the Civil Code is judged too important for inclusion either in the Ancillaries or in the Civil Code. A good example is The Children's Code. The Children's Code has a distinct designation within the Louisiana Revised Statutes, where it follows the principal codes of Louisiana law: the Civil Code, the Code of Civil Procedure, the Code of Criminal Procedure, and the Code of Evidence. . . .

Business and commercial law also left (or stayed out of) the Civil Code. Perhaps the chief reason for this was that Louisiana did not adopt a commercial code on the French model during the nineteenth century. Nor did Louisiana follow Italy's example and make a deliberate decision to embrace commercial law in its title on Obligations. Once the Uniform Commercial Code was in place, Louisiana enacted all but the provisions on sales and leases. Corporate law took a slightly different path. The 1870 Civil Code in Book I, Title X, did contain several articles on corporation law. Highly abstract, now repealed, they had long since been supplanted by a modern business corporation law.

Thus the current Code, nearly fully revised, maintains the structure of the 1870 Code, but quite a lot of content has been stripped from it. The next two sections of this article describe and attempt to map the way the content of the current Code is distributed.

B. A Rough Count

The articles of the Code still run from 1 to 3556, as under the Civil Code of 1870. Not all of the numbers correspond to legislated text, however. . . .

C. Picturing the Code

Moving from the overview and rough count of the Code, an image can begin to take shape. Simply enumerating the books of the Code adds no information. Listing them in a column is a beginning:

Preliminary Title

BOOK I Of Persons

BOOK II Things and the Different Modifications of Ownership

BOOK III Of the Different Modes of Acquiring the Ownership of Things

BOOK IV Conflict of Laws

One may add another piece of information, the number of articles within each book. The pattern reflects (apart from new Book IV) the pattern of the 1870 Code. As Books I and II are about equal in number, one could adjust the size of the entire line for Book III — making it almost seven times larger — but that would make the map awkward. . . .

The Code thus remains one based on the essential ideas of the bourgeois or business revolutions of the eighteenth and nineteenth centuries. The Code defines who the actors are (persons), what those actors can acquire (things and rights in things) and how the actors may acquire things. Of course, by maintaining the same overall structure the revised Code carries forward some of the awkwardness of the 1870 Code. For example, Book III still includes matrimonial regimes, which more logically belong in Book I. Current society simply does not view marriage as a mode of acquiring the ownership of things in anything like the way Louisiana society did in 1808, 1825, and even in 1870. Likewise, Book III still houses the basic rules on delictual and quasi-delictual liability; again, it seems strange to describe a tort as a mode of acquiring the ownership of things. The same criticism can be leveled at successions and donations, which within the family are methods not so much for acquiring as for the transferring or distributing the ownership of things. An additional book might suitably welcome successions and donations — in which case trusts could at last return from their exile in the Civil Code Ancillaries and be codified together with them in the same place.

This small-scale view of the Code, then, suggests that it remains primarily concerned with arms-length exchanges. If Book III has gained ground and Book II has not lost any, the same cannot be said for Book I. The Code's contribution to the law of persons and family is less, both absolutely and relatively. . . .

V. The Revision Contested

In 1988, Professor Palmer published *The Death of a Code: The Birth of a Digest* [63 Tul. L. Rev. 221 (1988)]. The author argued that there are two ways repeal can occur in Louisiana law. First, repeal may be express, as when the legislature specifically names a particular piece of legislation and "repeals" it by using that word or another word equally unambiguous. Second, repeal may be implied or implicit, as when the legislature enacts new legislation that is so inconsistent with prior legislation that the old cannot continue to be applied without ignoring the new. In that case, the new legislation applies and the prior legislation has suffered implicit (or tacit) repeal.

Next, Palmer canvassed all of the legislation dealing with the revision of the Civil Code. He noted that the legislature in some cases had expressly repealed articles of the 1870 Code. In many other cases, however, the legislature used the formula "amend and re-enact" when putting blocks of the Code into effect. This, Palmer submitted, does not repeal the prior articles explicitly. To decide whether amending and re-enacting has worked an implied repeal, one must compare the language of articles of the revised Code with that of articles of the 1870 Code. With sufficient lawyerly skill (and sufficient client interest), whenever the language differs one may legitimately argue during litigation that the prior law is still in effect. Indeed, when the prior law is not inconsistent with the revised legislation, the lawyer is in fact ethically obligated to present such arguments. Thus, according to Palmer, the 1870 Code in large measure remains arguable in effect.

The final step in Palmer's argument is that the revision of the 1870 Code has therefore turned the Civil Code of 1870 into a digest—the Digest Thesis. That is, the Louisiana Code, in his view, has lost the crucial characteristic of exclusivity. Without an explicit repeal of the prior law, the revised Code is merely the place where one may begin legal research, just as with a digest; but one cannot stop there. The 1870 Code and the jurisprudence and doctrine interpreting it remain relevant sources of the law for deciding disputes and planning legal activities. One's research on a given issue will lead the reader immediately into the thicket of jurisprudence, of case law. This, he concludes, produces a "fragmentation" uncharacteristic of the civil law.

The second part of the argument follows from the first. Further proof that the new Code functions as a digest is the nature of the connection between the text of the Code on the one hand and doctrine and jurisprudence on the other. In fact, this second argument is particularly critical of the role that a certain kind of doctrine plays, namely the comments that accompany each article of the revised Code. For Palmer, the comments have taken on an improper role; they link the new Code to the case law that interpreted the old Code. Palmer finds six separate functions of the comments in this regard. They (1) illustrate the scope of a concept or rule; (2) show the continuity between the source article and the new article; (3) indicate that a jurisprudential ruling is the source for a new article; (4) reject or overrule a line of cases; (5) interpret the new text; and (6) establish a counterrule or exception at variance with the text. Some of the six functions do not seem a fortiori controversial: illustrating the scope of a new article (number 1), connecting a new provision with an old one (number 2), or interpreting a new text (number 5). Likewise, indicating an intent to recognize ("codify") prior case law (number 3) or to reject it (number 4) seem to be fairly ordinary functions of *travaux préparatoires*. These functions, however, do have the disadvantage of drawing attention away from the text down into details of application, with the risk that the revised Code will sacrifice an articulation of rules at a higher level of generality. On the other hand, it is clearly a problem when doctrine arrogates to itself the prerogative to establish rules and exceptions that contradict the text of the Code (number 6). Arguably, the comments discussed here form a separate, seventh category, namely, comments whose function it is to delegate to the courts the authority to resolve an issue that the recodification process confronted but could not resolve. . . .

Notes and Questions

1. Professor Gruning's essay describes the Louisiana Civil Code as it existed in 2003. The vast majority of the provisions in the code do not change from year to year. Since Gruning's essay was published, however, several other significant portions of the code have been revised. Consequently, his observation that the 1870 Civil Code has now been substantially revised and updated through the process of "piecemeal" revision is even more accurate today. Only a relatively small portion of the 1870 Civil Code has yet to be addressed through the piecemeal revision process. Furthermore, the number of blank and repealed articles found in the current version of the Civil Code has likely increased since the publication of Gruning's article.

In the realm of property law, the most significant amendments to the Civil Code in the last ten years have occurred in the law of usufruct (Book II, Title III, Ch. 2). In addition, a small handful of articles concerning attachments to buildings or other constructions permanently attached to the ground and things principal and accessory have been revised. *See* La. Civ. Code arts. 466, 508 (2012). Most of the provisions of the Louisiana Civil Code addressed in this book were revised in the late 1970s and early 1980s. Because Louisiana courts have now had several decades of experience interpreting and applying these provisions, we have a healthy amount of post-revision jurisprudence (or "case law" in common law vernacular) to guide us in understanding and questioning these revised articles.

2. One important question frequently raised by students, particularly if Civil Law Property is their first civil law course, concerns the role of the revision comments found after most codal provisions. As Gruning's essay suggests, this is a subject of considerable academic interest. The official account is that the comments are not law; nor do they represent an official statement of the legislature's intent. They are merely what their name suggests, explanatory comments usually written by the reporter of the particular Law Institute committee charged with drafting the proposed package of revisions for consideration by the Legislature. As such, they are technically considered to be only persuasive, not binding authority.

As you will see when you read judicial opinions, however, judges sometimes give great weight to the revision comments in formulating their opinions. This can create considerable anxiety and confusion when statements in the revision comments are themselves ambiguous or become outdated because of subsequent amendments to the pertinent articles of the Civil Code. We recommend that you always read the revision comments with care. For a more recent exploration of the problematic role of comments in the Louisiana Civil Code, see Melissa T. Lonegrass, *Hidden Law: Taking the Comments More Seriously*, 92 Tul. L. Rev. 265 (2017).

3. Gruning provides a succinct summary of the events leading to the codification of the civil law in Louisiana. Numerous shifts in political sovereignty have shaped Louisiana's legal history. What is now the state of Louisiana experienced two distinct periods of colonial rule prior to its incorporation within the United States. Each change of government left imprints on local law and gave rise to what one might call a pre-codal legal chaos. When French colonists arrived they brought their edicts, ordinances and customs, without regard to the customs of the indigenous peoples. After the cession of Louisiana from France to Spain through the Treaty of Fontainebleau (1762), French laws continued to prevail until Spanish institutions and laws were imposed by Governor Alejandro O'Reilly in 1769. This meant that through the Spanish system of collected and weighted materials the laws of the *Siete Partidas* came to Louisiana. Spain's retrocession of Louisiana to France through the Treaty of San Ildefonso (1800) did not result in a purge of Spanish laws and a restoration of French law because the French enjoyed de facto sovereignty for a mere twenty days before selling Louisiana to the United States in the Louisiana Purchase Treaty (1803).

When the United States acquired Louisiana, the territory witnessed an influx of public officials and attorneys trained and steeped in Anglo-American legal traditions. These actors pushed for Louisiana's assimilation into Anglo-American legal culture. President Thomas Jefferson and his representatives, however, underestimated the resistance of the local political leaders, property owners and lawyers who professed a strong attachment to the French and Spanish civil laws to which they had grown accustomed. Indeed, wealthy Louisianans feared that any change in the substantive law might put their substantial property interests in land and slaves at risk.

After considerable machinations on all sides "The Great Compromise" between the local and federal actors agreed on a design for a new legal system for the Territory of Orleans, which would soon become the State of Louisiana. Public law, civil procedure and criminal law would be Americanized. But much of what we consider private law—that is, the law regulating private affairs and transactions between private persons—would remain civil law regulated by a newly drafted code. **James Brown** and **Louis Casimir Elizabet Moreau Lislet** were commissioned by the territorial legislature to prepare this code, which was supposed to be based on the civil law then currently in force in the territory. The compromise thus paved the way for the promulgation of Louisiana's civil codes of 1808, 1825 and 1870.

4. One of the most enduring academic debates about the early codification period in Louisiana concerns the nature of the Digest of 1808. Was it actually a straightforward restatement of the Spanish law technically in force for a period of more than thirty years before Louisiana became an American territory? Or did it represent a more radical break with Spanish law and therefore, was a codification

of French law based on the new and revolutionary Code Napoleon of 1804? The debate was crystalized in the early 1970s when Professor Rodolfo Batiza published a path breaking study of the 1808 Digest. Batiza contended that the Digest was primarily modeled on French law, that more than seventy percent of its provisions were in fact verbatim or almost verbatim transcriptions of the 1804 French Civil Code or the draft version of that code (the *Projet* of 1800), and that eighty-five percent of the Digest's provisions were French derived. Rodolfo Batiza, *The Louisiana Civil Code of 1808: Its Actual Sources and Present Relevance*, 46 TUL. L. REV. 4 (1971).

Professor Robert Pascal countered Batiza's thesis by arguing that the drafters of the 1808 Digest, Louis Moreau Lislet and James Brown, merely used the language of the French Civil Code to codify the Spanish-Roman law governing the territory up until the eve of the Louisiana Purchase. In support of his claim, Pascal pointed to several examples of conflicts between French and Spanish civil law and noted that the drafters chose to implement Spanish law in these instances. Robert A. Pascal, *Sources of the Digest of 1808: A Reply to Professor Batiza*, 46 TUL. L. REV. 603 (1972). Over the last four decades, adherents of the Batiza and Pascal positions have continued the debate in many law review articles and books. For a summary of recent research exploring the debate as well as consideration of early editions of the 1808 Digest and other historical manuscripts, see VERNON V. PALMER, THE LOUISIANA CIVILIAN EXPERIENCE (2005); John W. Cairns, *The de la Vergne Volume and the Digest of 1808*, 24 TUL. EUR. & CIV. L. F. 31 (2009).

The debate has never been fully resolved. Recent scholarship points to tensions and conflicts that were not vetted in the scholarly tournament between Batiza and Pascal. For example, Professor John W. Cairns has emphasized that: (1) the Spanish doubts as to the validity of the Louisiana Purchase, which was indeed a threat to Spanish territories to the East and West; (2) the influx of French speakers in the wake of the slave revolt on St. Domingue; and (3) the surge of francophone nationalism under the brief French regime preceding the transfer to the United States). Professor Cairns further notes that the accumulated weight of evidence casts doubt on the Pascal thesis. John W. Cairns, *Spanish Law, the Teatro de la legislación universal de España e Indias, and the Background to the Drafting of the Digest of 1808*, 31 TUL. EUR. & CIV. L. F. 79, 79–82 (2017). As Cairns observes, however, the important point is not so much whether Batiza or Pascal will ultimately be declared the winner of their debate but rather that that the drafters of the 1808 Digest were fundamentally eclectic in their approach to codification and not constrained by a modern conception of legal positivism:

> All that one can know for certain is what the redactors in fact did; study of the provisions of the Digest can reveal with some degree of certainty what they considered, rejected and adapted to create the new code. Much, of course, was taken from the *Code Civil des Francais* of 1804, its *projet* of 1800, and territorial legislation, but the redactors also drew on provisions and texts of Castilian law, Roman law, Blackstone's *Commentaries*,

Christian's notes to Blackstone, and even the translation of Blackstone into French. They may even have drawn on other sources as yet unrecognized. In fact, the men who compiled the Digest of the Civil Laws were creative and eclectic in the choices they made in drafting their code, even if they relied on that of France and its *projet*. A hundred years later, F.P. Walton, was jocularly to remark that "codifiers are arrant thieves;" this comment was already applicable to Moreau Lislet and Brown.

Id. at 93. For more detail regarding the legal background to codification in Louisiana and the 1808 Digest of Orleans, see JOHN W. CAIRNS, CODIFICATION, TRANSPLANTS AND HISTORY: LAW REFORM IN LOUISIANA (1808) AND QUEBEC (1866) 39–80 & 427–72 (2015).

5. Other scholars of early Louisiana legal history have focused their attention on another clash of legal cultures. This clash involved the newly arriving, American, common law oriented officials, like territorial Governor W.C.C. Claiborne and his sponsor, President Thomas Jefferson, on one hand, and the native, French speaking, European oriented, "Creole" *anciens inhabitants*, on the other, who owned land and slaves and who were worried that the new American administration would establish a legal system hostile to their interests. A number of books and articles have thoroughly explored this conflict, including GEORGE DARGO, JEFFERSON'S LOUISIANA: POLITICS AND THE CLASH OF LEGAL TRADITIONS (Revised ed. 2009), and VERNON V. PALMER, THE LOUISIANA CIVILIAN EXPERIENCE (2005). Other notable studies of early Louisiana legal history include MARK F. FERNANDEZ, FROM CHAOS TO CONTINUITY: THE EVOLUTION OF LOUISIANA'S JUDICIAL SYSTEM: 1712–1862 (2001); RICHARD H. KILBOURNE, JR., A HISTORY OF THE LOUISIANA CIVIL CODE: THE FORMATIVE YEARS, 1803–1839 (1987).

6. In his essay, Gruning introduces us to Professor Vernon Palmer's critique of the piecemeal revision process in his article *Death of a Code—Birth of a Digest*, 63 TUL. L. REV. 221, 262 (1988). Palmer argued that the piecemeal revision process and the inexact forms of repeal of the older articles accompanying the revision brought Louisiana back almost full circle, to the same state of legal uncertainty that existed between 1808 and 1825. At that time, it was unclear whether the Digest of 1808 had constituted a clean break with the un-codified Spanish law applicable in Louisiana before 1803 or was a "mere Digest"). Palmer generally took the position that a true civil code in the French tradition should repeal all prior law and produce a new legal order that could be discerned within the covers of a single book.

Others took the pragmatist position that a revised Civil Code in a jurisdiction like Louisiana will necessarily require lawyers and judges to read a civil code both prospectively and retrospectively. *Pragmatists* tend to believe that a revised civil code will always, or at least to some extent, require extensive judicial interpretation, which will include consideration of how courts in earlier decisions interpreted older versions of civil code articles that may have been only implicitly repealed. For a detailed discussion of the debate between civil law purists like Palmer and civil law pragmatists, see John A. Lovett, *Another Great Debate?: The Ambiguous Relationship*

Between the Revised Civil Code and Pre-Revision Jurisprudence as Seen Through the Prytania Park Controversy, 48 Loy. L. Rev. 615 (2002).

7. Due to its hybrid legal system Louisiana belongs to the family of mixed jurisdictions. In Louisiana's version public law, criminal law and civil procedure follow Anglo-American common law norms established by either the United States or Britain as the ruling political sovereign, but the bulk of private law retains a civil law orientation established during a period of prior colonial rule by continental European powers such as France, Spain or the Netherlands. *See* Mixed Jurisdictions Worldwide: The Third Legal Family (Vernon V. Palmer, ed., 2001). Other widely recognized "classic" mixed jurisdictions are Quebec, Puerto Rico, the Philippines, South Africa, Scotland and Israel. Except for Scotland and Israel, all follow this same developmental pattern: civil law established as the private law base during an initial period of colonial rule by a Continental European power followed by an overlay of common law procedure, public and criminal law established during an Anglo-American conquest or cession. More recently still, legal systems in places as diverse as Nepal, Macao and Hong Kong have also been described as mixed jurisdictions. *See generally Symposium, Methodology and Innovation in Mixed Legal Systems, Papers from the Third Congress of the World Society of Mixed Jurisdiction Jurists*, 57 Loy. L. Rev. 703 (2012).

8. In Louisiana the rich civilian legal heritage remains relevant to this day. It is helpful not only for explicating hard law but also for informing reform endeavors. For this dual theme, see Markus G. Puder, *Did You Ever Hear of the Napoleonic Code, Stella? A Mixed Jurisdiction Impact Analysis from Louisiana's Law Laboratory!*, 85 Tul. L. Rev. 635 (2011).

Consider, for example, former Article 177 of the Civil Code (1870), which reads:

> The master is answerable for the damage caused to individuals or to the community in general by whatever is thrown out of his house into the street or public road, and inasmuch as the master has the superintendence and police of his house, and is responsible for the faults committed therein.

La. Civ. Code art. 177 (1870).

In *Williams v. Employers Liab. Assurance Corp.*, 296 F.2d 569 (5th Cir. 1961), the court had to resolve the question of whether this provision applied when an invitee sustained injuries in the wake of events occurring inside a building. Judge John Minor Wisdom determined that liability under Article 177 of the 1870 Civil Code only arose for injuries sustained when things were thrown out of a house. His scholarly decision mainly rests on the historical analysis of the law that preceded adoption of Article 177. The judge first noted the identical contents of Article 177 (1870), Article 171 of the 1825 Civil Code and Article 14, Title VI of the 1808 Digest. *Williams*, 296 F.2d at 576. In the French original these provisions read:

> *"Le maître est responsable pour tout ce qu'on jette de sa maison dans la rue ou dans le grand chemin et qui cause du dommage à quelqu'un en particulier,*

ou peut être préjudiciable aux habitans du lieu en général, car le maître a la surintendance de la police de sa maison et est responsable de toutes les fautes qui s'y commettent."

["The master is answerable for the damage caused to individuals or to the community in general, by whatever is thrown out of this house into the street or public road, in as much as the master has the superintendence and police of his house, and is responsible for the faults committed therein."]

1808 Digest art. 14, tl. VI; La. Civ. Code art. 171. Pursuing a reference to Spanish law in the notations accompanying this provision in the DE LA VERGE VOLUME of the 1808 Digest, Judge Wisdom discovered clues to additional sources, which allowed him to identify the source of the principle of such absolute liability in Roman law and then to use the *Siete Partidas* and Domat's work to trace its migration into Louisiana law. *Williams*, 296 F.2d at 578–79. Indeed, the Praetorian Edict "about those who pour anything down or throw anything down" (*de his qui effuderint vel dejecerint*), commented on by the jurist Ulpian in Book 9, Title 3 of Justinian's Digest, reads in part:

> *"Praetor ait de his, qui deiecerint vel effuderint: Unde in eum locum, quo volgo iter fiet vel in quo consistetur, deiectum vel effusum quid erit, quantum ex ea re damnum datum factumve erit, in eum, qui ibi habitaverit, . . . iudicium dabo."*

> ["The Praetor says about those who throw down or pour out [something from a building onto the street]: When into such place where one usually passes through or stops, something is thrown or poured [from a building], I will grant an action against him who dwells there. . . ."]

D.9.3.1.pr. From these various sources in Spanish, French and Roman law, Judge Wisdom crystallized several insights: the linkage of the master's absolute liability to the pursuit of public order and safety; the absence of any requirement of fault to establish liability for things thrown out of a building; and the lack of any support for broadening the scope of liability in this situation. In light of this diagnosis, Judge Wisdom declined to extend the liability formula of Article 177 of the Civil Code to injuries occurring inside a building. Note that Judge Wisdom used translations of the foreign language sources he analyzed. Do you see an open flank to such an approach?

The subtle appreciation for the way codal sources evolve may enhance legal reform deliberations. Eventually, Article 177 of the 1870 Civil Code was repealed by the Louisiana legislature. La. Acts 1990, No. 705, § 1. Sadly, proponents of suppressing the absolute liability principle articulated by the article prevailed with their argument that it was outdated, scarcely litigated and redundant. In contrast, other jurisdictions have chosen to maintain their Romanist roots in this area of law, while also pursuing comprehensive reform, as illustrated by the example of Article 938 of the revised Brazilian Civil Code, which provides:

> *"Aquele que habitar prédio, ou parte dele, responde pelo dano proveniente das coisas que dele caírem ou forem lançadas em lugar indevido."*

["The one who dwells in a building, or a part thereof, answers for the damage originating from the things that fall or are thrown from it into an inappropriate place."]

Cód. Civ. Bras. art. 938 (2002). In light of the above, is it preferable for a civil code to reflect its legal heritage? Or should a modern civil code make a complete break from the past?

9. We leave this initial chapter with an appreciation for the uniqueness of our Civil Code in law and language. Louisiana's early codifications—the Digest of 1808 and the 1825 Civil Code—were originally drafted in French and subsequently translated into English. The English translations were riddled with errors and inaccuracies. In response to the translation issues associated with Louisiana's codal law, the Louisiana Supreme Court developed different harmonization rules. As translation errors that had not previously been caught were reenacted in the unilingual English version of the 1870 Civil Code, some of the legacy errors and inaccuracies continued to linger for many years. In response to the translation issues associated with Louisiana's codal law, the Louisiana Supreme Court developed different harmonization rules. Beyond the translation errors, however, the legal English of the Louisiana Civil Code has proven fully functional in the American Union and offers a powerful bridge into common law and civil law systems around the world.

In recognition of the importance of legal translation for comparative law, two major translation projects have been seen through in Louisiana. A project team under the direction of Professor Olivier Moréteau back-translated the Louisiana Civil Code from English into French. Olivier Moréteau, *The Louisiana Civil Code in French: Translation and Retranslation*, 9 J. Civ. L. Stud. (2016), available at: https:// digitalcommons.law.lsu.edu/jcls/vol9/iss1/11. Meanwhile Professor Markus G. Puder published, in solo work, his translation and bilingual edition of the Louisiana Civil Code into German, along with an introduction to Louisiana civil law. *Markus G. Puder, Das Zivilgesetzbuch von Louisiana—Zweisprachige Erstausgabe mit einer Einleitung* (Nomos Verlagsgesellschaft, Baden-Baden 2017). For the first time in its history, the Louisiana Civil Code is available in the German language. Prof. Puder discusses his discoveries and insights as a legal comparativist and legal translator in a law review article. Markus G. Puder, *Law and Language in Action: Transformative Experiences Associated with Translating the Louisiana Civil Code into German*, in progress.

Chapter 2

Ownership

A. Ownership and Real Rights

1. Ownership

Ownership is one of the most fundamental concepts in property law. A famous legal philosopher once noted that ownership can be understood at its most basic level as *"the greatest possible interest in a thing which a mature system of law recognizes."* Tony Honoré, *Ownership, in* Making Law Bind: Essays Legal and Philosophical 162 (1987) (emphasis in original). In Louisiana law, we think of ownership in much the same way. Near the beginning of Book II, the Louisiana Civil Code provides a classic definition of ownership:

> **Art. 477. Ownership**
>
> A. Ownership is the right that confers on a person direct, immediate, and exclusive authority over a thing. The owner of a thing may use, enjoy, and dispose of it within the limits and under the conditions established by law.

La. Civ. Code art. 477 (1995). Like many seemingly straightforward definitions in the Civil Code, this definition is quite rich in its implications. It deserves careful study and consideration.

Article 477 of the Louisiana Civil Code begins by recognizing ownership as a right that belongs to a person. Under Article 479 "[t]he right of ownership may exist only in favor of a natural person or a juridical person." La. Civ. Code art. 479 (1979). A *natural person* is a human being; a *juridical person* is an entity with a legal personality distinct from that of its members, like a corporation, partnership or private association. La. Civ. Code art. 24 (2012). Note that the State of Louisiana and its political subdivisions can also own things, and, when they do, we need to be careful to consider the capacity in which they own things because this can affect whether we classify a thing as "public" or "private."

Another important characteristic of ownership, not mentioned in Article 477 but implied by Article 481, is that its duration is *potentially perpetual*. This notion has two aspects. First, an owner of a thing cannot lose ownership merely by failing to exercise the rights and privileges of ownership. *See* La. Civ. Code art. 481 (1979) (ownership "may not be lost by nonuse"). In contrast, other real rights, such as personal and predial servitudes, can be lost by the failure to exercise them for a period of time through the prescription of nonuse. La. Civ. Code arts. 621 (1976), 753 (1977), and 3448 (1982). Ownership, however, is lost involuntarily only in two ways: (1) "when acquisitive prescription accrues in favor of an adverse possessor," La. Civ. Code art. 481 (1979), a subject we will study in a subsequent chapter; or (2) when the state, one of its political subdivisions or another entity with expropriation powers takes ownership away from a private person for certain limited public purposes and just compensation is paid to the property owner and due process requirements are satisfied. *See generally* La. Const. art. 1, § 4(B) (1974, amended 2010).

The second aspect of the potentially perpetual nature of ownership is that a person's ownership of a thing can be transferred by either intestate succession or a donation *mortis causa* (through a will) at a natural person's death. We will briefly study this topic in the context of voluntary transfers of ownership. It is important now to realize that the real right of ownership is heritable and transmissible at death, while other property rights, such as usufruct and habitation, automatically terminate at death and, thus, are not heritable. La. Civ. Code arts. 607 & 637–38 (1976).

2. Real Rights versus Personal Rights

Another crucial aspect of Article 477 of the Louisiana Civil Code is that it defines ownership as a "right." Although this might seem like a self-evident assertion, it is an important statement, rich in classificatory implication for the lawyer in general and the civilian in particular. Property law is often said to govern *rights in things*. Real rights are a subcategory of a broader category called *patrimonial rights*. Someone's patrimony includes the total mass of extant and potential rights and liabilities attached to a person for the satisfaction of his or her economic needs. *See generally* A.N. Yiannopoulos, 2 Louisiana Civil Law Treatise: Property § 190 (4th ed. 2011). What then are the characteristics of real rights?

Article 476 of the Louisiana Civil Code, which precedes the codal definition of ownership, is the starting point for our analysis. Consider the text:

Art. 476. Rights in Things

One may have various rights in things:

1. Ownership;

2. Personal and predial servitudes; and

3. Such other real rights as the law allows.

La. Civ. Code art. 476 (1978). This article makes several interesting points, while leaving important questions unanswered. It reveals that ownership is one of the specifically enumerated "real rights" recognized under Louisiana law. The other "real rights" mentioned in the article, personal servitudes and predial servitudes, along with "such other real rights as the law allows," are the subject of subsequent chapters in this casebook.

The last line of Article 476 implies that the Civil Code does not allow for an unconstrained universe of real rights. New real rights cannot be invented or modified randomly by individuals; rather, they must be sanctioned by the legal system in some way. Revision comment (d) to Article 476 suggests, however, that there is some room for parties to exercise contractual freedom and create new kinds of real rights. Property law scholars both in the United States and abroad typically refer to the explicit or implicit limitations imposed on this kind of contractual freedom as the ***numerus clausus* principle**. They have offered many explanations to justify this tendency of legal systems to limit the number of property forms available. Among the most prominent explanations is that limiting the menu of usable property forms promotes economic efficiency by reducing information processing costs for persons who deal with and trade in property or, alternatively, that the *numerus clausus* reveals important, value-based ideals about the kind of human relationships the law should sanction. *See generally* Thomas W. Merrill & Henry Smith, *Optimal Standardization in the Law of Property: The* Numerus Clausus *Principle*, 110 YALE L. J. 1 (2000); John Lovett, *Title Conditions in Restraint of Trade, in* MIXED JURISDICTIONS COMPARED: PRIVATE LAW IN LOUISIANA AND SCOTLAND, 30, 33–41 (Vernon V. Palmer & Elspeth C. Reid, eds. 2009).

Perhaps the most curious aspect of Article 476 of the Louisiana Civil Code is that, although it speaks of real rights, it does not provide a definition of the concept. This task is left to the revision comments, which provide that real rights "confer direct and immediate authority over a thing" and are distinguished from "personal (obligatory) rights that confer merely authority over the person of a certain debtor who has assumed the obligation to allow the enjoyment of a thing by his creditor." La. Civ. Code art. 476 rev. cmt. (b) (1978). What does this rather opaque statement mean? What is a *real* right and how is a real right different from its legal correlative, a *personal* right?

A real right is a *right in a thing* that is *good against the entire world,* whether that thing is immovable or movable. A real right defines a *person's relationship to a thing* and uniquely distinguishes that person's relationship to the thing from all other persons who are not holders of that real right. A real right thus applies against all non-right holders in almost all circumstances.

Consider the following examples. When you purchase a plane ticket, your right to be transported from one place to another is a personal right. If you miss your plane, you might be able to transfer your right to another plane or to another carrier. You may be assigned a seat, but your seat assignment may be changed without your consent. When you exit the plane, the seat can be claimed by someone else. Millions of passengers purchase tickets and travel in airplanes every day.

In contrast, when you purchase a chair, you make all the decisions about the chair. You decide where it will be placed, who will sit on it, for how long someone may sit, whether to keep or give away the chair and when to destroy the chair. Your relationship to the chair is unlike anyone else's relationship to that chair because you have a real right in that chair, more than a personal right to use the chair.

Generally speaking, real rights, unlike personal rights, are not context specific. Once a person acquires a real right in a thing—for example, the right of ownership—that person's rights against the world are largely pre-determined. Although a real right might have come into existence because of some contractual arrangement or as a matter of law based on the relationship between certain individuals at a certain moment in time, once the real right is established, its power is self-executing against all non-owners. Put differently, a real right like ownership is generally not subject to revision or modification with every change in the context of the right holder's interaction with non-right holders. When a person acquires ownership of a tract of land, the new owner acquires a package of rights with respect to that tract, which are enforceable generally against all persons who are not owners of the land. The owner is not required to enter into negotiations with every other non-owner who might come into contact with the tract of land to work out his or her rights as an owner and how non-owners will respect them.

According to some property scholars, it is this special characteristic of real rights—their uniformity and "modularity," the fact that they are constructed in standardized units or dimensions that the rest of the world easily recognizes and must respect—that allows real rights to function as the building blocks of property. Their uniformity or modularity turns real rights into easily exchangeable packages of rights that non-right holders generally recognize and respect without having to spend much time or energy investigating their shape or limits. *See generally* Henry E. Smith, *Property as the Law of Things*, 125 Harv. L. Rev. 1691 (2012); Thomas W. Merrill, *Property as Modularity*, 125 Harv. L. Rev. 151 (2012).

Another crucial characteristic of real rights is that they generally confer a power to exclude others from the object of the right. We will have much more to say about this power in the rest of this chapter. A related but technically different characteristic is that holders of real rights generally have the ability to recover or pursue the thing subject to the right if it is removed from the control of the right holder.

All of these statements about real rights imply a contrast with *personal rights*. What, then, is a personal right? Most fundamentally, a personal right is a right or legal power to demand some particular kind of performance from a particular person or set of persons. It is not a right against the whole world. A personal right usually arises out of some specific contractual or quasi-contractual obligation and is generally case specific and particular, not universal or modular like a real right. Personal rights are, essentially, the subject of the law of obligations, whereas real rights are the subject of the law of property.

Article 1756 of the Civil Code tells us that "an obligation is a legal relationship whereby a person, called the obligor, is bound to render a performance [to give, do, or not do something] in favor of another, called the obligee." La. Civ. Code art. 1756 (1984). A simple contract of sale of a corporeal movable, for example, creates obligations between the purchaser and the seller. The purchaser has an obligation to pay the price and the seller has an obligation to deliver the object of the sale to the purchaser. The right of each party to demand that the other perform a reciprocal obligation creates a "personal right" with respect to the other party. Once the sale is completed and ownership transfers from the seller to the buyer, the new owner will now have a real right in the object of the sale.

Consider several examples to illustrate this crucial distinction between real rights and personal rights. If you buy a parking lot in downtown Baton Rouge from its current owner and your purchase satisfies all of the requirements for a valid transfer of immovable property, you will become the new owner of that parking lot and, consequentially, will acquire the real right of ownership in that lot. As the owner, you can now fence it in and exclude the entire world from that parking lot, assuming there are no conflicting real rights that have been created in that same lot. If someone enters your parking lot without your permission and refuses to leave, you can file a trespass action against the interloper to vindicate your rights as owner. A court may specifically order the interloper to leave and to stay off of the parking lot. The court can even require the sheriff to enforce that order. In general, various forms of *injunctive relief* may be available to protect your rights as owner, even if you have not suffered monetary damages.

Personal rights, however, can also arise in connection with your parking lot. You might, for example, open the parking lot for business and begin to make certain arrangements with people who agree to pay you money for the privilege of parking their cars on your lot. The rights that these individual promisees, your customers, acquire as a result of these arrangements, which will be memorialized through contracts of some kind, will be classified as personal rights, rights that apply against you, as grantor of a specific personal right, but not against the rest of the world. If you violate one of the promises or contractual commitments arising from your arrangement with the customer—for example, by closing the lot earlier than you promised or by giving away the particular parking space you promised to another person—the unhappy customer might sue you and, if successful in his suit, obtain a judgment for breach of the promise. Generally speaking, the remedy the court will award to your customer if you breach one of the personal obligations arising from the parking contract will take the form of *monetary damages*, not injunctive relief. The same will be true if your customer breaches the parking contract—for example, if the customer does not pay the monthly fee owed for the privilege of parking in your lot. You can sue the customer for monetary damages resulting from the breach of the parking contract.

Another personal right that might arise in your customer's favor in connection with the parking lot results from what we call in the civil law "delictual obligations" (*i.e.*, the law of torts). If one of your customers' vehicles is damaged because of your fault or negligence, he will, generally speaking, have the right to recover monetary damages associated with the cost of repairing the vehicle. *See* La. Civ. Code arts. 2315 & 2317.

Any one of these persons—the disappointed parking contract customer, you as the disappointed parking lot operator, or the owner of the damaged car—will become an obligee or creditor and can eventually obtain a judgment against the corresponding obligor or debtor in a court of law. As indicated above, this judgment will typically be satisfied, not by injunctive relief of the kind mentioned in connection with the trespass action or in an action to recover possession, but by a judgment for monetary damages or what we simply call *compensatory relief*. In all of these cases, we are dealing with personal rights, or rights "in personam." These rights are personal, not real, because they define a specific relationship between two persons—the obligor and obligee, the debtor and creditor—that arises because of some particular relationship between the two persons or sets of persons.

In contrast, a real right, we should recall, is universal. The owner of the parking lot, as the holder of the real right of ownership, is the gatekeeper of that lot, within the limits and subject to the conditions established by law (the Civil Code, various statutes and other forms of valid governmental regulation). The owner's real rights as gatekeeper rights are enforceable against the entire world, not just against individuals with whom the owner has a specific contractual or delictual relationship. As gatekeeper, the owner generally gets to decide who enters the lot, the owner generally decides with whom he or she will enter contracts for parking or other purposes, the owner controls the uses to which the lot can be put, and the owner is also free to decide whether and when to transfer ownership of the lot to someone else and who the transferee will be.

Now, think about one of the vehicles parked in the parking lot. The owner of that vehicle also has a real right in the vehicle. If any person other than the owner of the vehicle walks onto the parking lot, that person generally owes a duty to the vehicle owner not to enter the vehicle, take possession of the vehicle or damage it, regardless of who the owner is or how the vehicle came to be in the parking lot. This is true because, once again, real rights are enforceable against the whole world. In short, the term "real right" has nothing to do with whether the object of the right is an immovable or movable.

We should consider the possibility that the owners of the vehicles parked in the lot may have given other persons personal rights in those vehicles. For example, the parking lot contract might give the lot operator the right to move customers' vehicles for its convenience, or it might require the operator to park customers' vehicles once they are deposited with a parking lot attendant. In either case, the parking lot operator may have the right to take physical control of the vehicle for specific purposes and might owe certain duties of care with respect to the vehicles in its control. In either instance, the law of obligations, not property, would govern.

Although distinct from real rights, personal rights might affect real rights in a thing. The owner of one of the vehicles in the parking lot might have borrowed money pursuant to a loan agreement, either to purchase the vehicle or for some other purpose, and created a personal right in the lender to have that debt repaid pursuant to the terms of the loan agreement. If the borrower (the debtor) fails to repay the debt, the lender (the creditor) might eventually obtain a judgment ordering the debtor to pay the debt, and, if that judgment is not satisfied by the debtor, a court might allow the creditor to seize the assets of the debtor, including the vehicle, and have them sold to satisfy the debt. In such a case, we can see how the personal obligations created by the owner of the vehicle as a borrower might eventually lead to termination of the owner's real rights in the vehicle.

In a recent law review article, two commentators elaborated on the expansiveness of the category of real rights in Louisiana law while also drawing attention to two more characteristics that distinguish real rights from personal rights. Consider their observations below.

L. David Cromwell & Chloé M. Chetta, *Divining the Real Nature of Real Obligations*
92 Tul. L. Rev. 127, 133–37 (2017)

Real rights in Louisiana have traditionally included ownership, usufruct and other personal servitudes, predial servitudes, building restrictions, mortgages, and pledges. The Louisiana Mineral Code characterizes all mineral rights as real rights. The rent of lands was a real right under the 1870 Civil Code, but it has been suppressed and replaced by the annuity charge, which, while unquestionably a real right, bears only the faintest resemblance to its predecessor. Some privileges, such as the vendor's privilege on immovables and those privileges arising under the Louisiana Private Works Act, constitute real rights, but the general privileges on immovables and most privileges on movables do not. Antichresis was likely a real right, but it was eliminated by the revision of the law of pledge in 2014. A perfected security interest created under Chapter 9 of the Louisiana Uniform Commercial Code is certainly a real right, even though no provision of the Uniform Commercial Code refers to a security interest as a real right. As in other jurisdictions, there is considerable debate whether the set of real rights in Louisiana is *numerus clausus* (a closed set) or whether parties enjoy contractual freedom to create new forms of real rights.

Real rights have two defining characteristics that distinguish them from most personal rights: the right of preference and the right of pursuit. The operation of these characteristics can readily be seen by contrasting the enforcement of a mortgage of an immovable with the enforcement of a lessor's privilege upon the lessee's movable property. Both the mortgage and the lessor's privilege, by their nature, give rise to a right of preference over other creditors and other persons claiming a right in the thing subject to the mortgage or privilege. The mortgage, if recorded, follows the mortgaged property into whatever hands it may pass and remains enforceable notwithstanding the transfer of ownership of the mortgaged property. In contrast, the lessor's privilege upon movable effects of the lessee is lost if those effects are alienated from the lessee's patrimony. Thus, a mortgage enjoys both the right of preference and the right of pursuit and is, as Civil Code article 3280 proclaims, a real right. The lessor's privilege, however, like most other privileges on movable property, is devoid of a right of pursuit and is consequently not a real right. Privileges on movables are "a simple right of priority between creditors, a permit to come in out of turn in the division of the price."

While real rights entail both a right of preference and a right of pursuit, the converse is not true; not all rights that enjoy these two characteristics are real rights. There are numerous personal contracts that, upon recordation, are given certain real effects, causing them to resemble real rights even though they truly are not. This is largely a result of the public records doctrine, particularly as it was formulated in article 2264 of the 1870 Civil Code: "No notarial act concerning immovable property shall have any effect against third persons, until the same shall have been deposited in the office of the parish recorder, or register of conveyances of the parish where such immovable property is situated." As the Louisiana Supreme Court observed long ago in *Summers & Brannins v. Clark*, the provisions of article 2264 were "negatives pregnant with affirmatives to the effect that contracts 'affecting' or 'concerning' immovables (and therefore leases thereof), will have effect against third persons, if duly recorded." Accordingly, promises of sale, options, rights of first refusal, and other similar agreements become binding on third persons upon recordation, an effect that has prompted some commentators to label these contracts as "quasi-real rights . . ."

It has been held time and again that a contract of lease of an immovable is a mere personal contract that, upon recordation, attains certain real effects. It would be historically inaccurate, however, to attribute this effect to the public records doctrine. The real effect given to a contract of lease originated with the text of the Civil Code, which formerly provided that if the lessor sold the thing leased, the purchaser could not evict the tenant before his lease expired. Thus, under the Louisiana Civil Code of 1870, rather than creating the real effects given to a recorded lease, the public records doctrine actually *limited* the real effects that the Code itself otherwise accorded a contract of lease. . . .

3. The Real versus Personal Rights Distinction and the Subsequent Purchaser Doctrine

In a seminal decision, *Eagle Pipe and Supply, Inc. v. Amerada Hess Corp.*, 79 So.3d 246 (La. 2011), the Louisiana Supreme Court offered a lengthy discussion of the distinction between real rights and personal rights when it was called upon to determine whether the current owner of a tract of land could sue third parties who allegedly caused environmental damage to the land while it was in the possession of a previous owner. A plurality of the court held that the current owner could not sue third parties—oil companies whose oilfield tubing was cleaned on the property, along with trucking companies who transported tubing onto the property—for damages allegedly inflicted upon the land prior to the current owner's acquisition, even though the alleged damage was not apparent of the time of the sale. *Id.* at 278–84. Read Justice Clark's majority opinion and Justice Weimer's dissent. Then decide for yourself whether the distinction between *real rights* and *personal rights* justifies the outcome in this hotly contested case.

Eagle Pipe and Supply, Inc. v. Amerada Hess Corp.,

79 So.3d 246 (La. 2011)

CLARK, Justice. The issue presented in these consolidated matters arises from the sale of land to the plaintiff, who later discovered that the land was allegedly contaminated with radioactive material. The plaintiff filed suit against the former landowners and the oil and trucking companies allegedly responsible for the contamination. In the district court, exceptions of no right of action raised by the oil and trucking companies were granted. The court of appeal initially affirmed this decision, but reversed on rehearing.

We granted writs to determine whether a subsequent purchaser of property has the right to sue a third party for non-apparent property damages inflicted before the sale in the absence of the assignment of or subrogation to that right. After review, we find the fundamental principles of Louisiana property law compel the conclusion that such a right of action is not permitted under the law. Instead, the subsequent purchaser has the right to seek rescission of the sale, reduction of the purchase price, or other legal remedies. For the following reasons, we hold the appellate court on rehearing erred by reversing the district court's granting of the peremptory exceptions of no right of action on behalf of the oil and trucking companies. Accordingly, we reverse the court of appeal's decision on rehearing and reinstate the ruling of the district court.

Factual and Procedural Background

This matter is before the court on an exception of no right of action . . .

On July 15, 2008, Eagle Pipe and Supply, Inc. ("Eagle Pipe" or plaintiff) filed a petition for damages in the Civil District Court for the Parish of Orleans, alleging causes of action for breach of contract, negligence, strict liability, redhibition, fraud and conspiracy in connection with property Eagle Pipe acquired two decades earlier. Named in the petition were four groups of defendants: (1) ten oil companies, collectively referred to as the "Oil Company Defendants;" (2) eight trucking companies, collectively referred to as the "Trucking Company/Transporter Defendants;" (3) Robert Bridges, Patsy Tremble Bridges and Edmund J. Baudoin, Jr., collectively referred to as the "Former Property–Owner Defendants;" and (4) ABC Insurance Company, Inc.

According to the petition, more than twenty years ago, on April 22, 1988, Eagle Pipe purchased property in Lafayette Parish from the Former Property Owner Defendants. For several years before the sale, from 1981 to 1988, the Former Property Owner Defendants allegedly leased the property at issue to Union Pipe and Supply, Inc. ("Union Pipe"), which operated a pipe yard or pipe cleaning facility on the property. In conducting its business, Union Pipe allegedly bought, cleaned, stored and sold used oilfield tubing from the Oil Company Defendants. The Trucking Company/Transporter Defendants allegedly transported the tubing from the Oil Company Defendants to Union Pipe's facilities.

Eagle Pipe asserted that radioactive scale known by the acronym TENORM was removed from the tubing or pipes during Union Pipe's cleaning process and was deposited onto the surface of the pipe yard, contaminating the soil where Eagle Pipe now conducts its business. Eagle Pipe claimed it became aware of the alleged contamination of its property after the Louisiana Department of Environmental Quality ("La. DEQ") conducted a field interview and found Eagle Pipe to be in violation of a number of TENORM exposure regulations. The La. DEQ allegedly found TENORM exposure levels on the property which exceeded the regulatory criteria for unrestricted use of property and posed a health hazard to both Eagle Pipe and the public. Eagle Pipe asserted subsequent testing by La. DEQ prompted the agency to issue an order for the remediation of the property. Sometime thereafter, Eagle Pipe filed its suit.

The petition alleged Eagle Pipe has never cleaned pipe on its premises. Therefore, the plaintiff asserted all of the TENORM allegedly present on the property is the result of Union Pipe's activities in cleaning hazardous and radioactive contaminated pipe from the Oil Company Defendants, which was transported to Union Pipe's facilities by the Trucking Company/Transporter Defendants. Eagle Pipe alleged its property has lost all value and is no longer marketable as a result of the long-standing radioactive contamination.

Eagle Pipe alleged a specific cause of action against the Former Property Owner Defendants for redhibition; the other causes of actions are generally asserted against all of the defendants. Eagle Pipe asserted that its petition made no claims under federal law; the Louisiana Conservation Act (La. R.S. 30:1 *et seq.*); or the Louisiana Environmental Quality Act (La. R.S. 30:2001 *et seq.*).

The defendants filed declinatory, dilatory and/or peremptory exceptions. All of the defendants filed, or joined in, the peremptory exception of no right of action, arguing Eagle Pipe had no right to assert a claim for damage to the property which occurred before Eagle Pipe was its owner. After a hearing on the exceptions, the trial court ruled, *inter alia,* that the defendants' exceptions of no right of action be sustained, dismissing Eagle Pipe's claims with prejudice.

Eagle Pipe filed a motion for new trial seeking, in part, to amend its petition. The trial court denied the motion for new trial. Thereafter, the plaintiff filed an appeal with the Fourth Circuit Court of Appeal. On original hearing, a three-judge panel affirmed the trial court's ruling on the exception of no right of action by a two-to-one vote. On rehearing before a five-judge panel, the court of appeal majority reversed the judgment of the district court with respect to its ruling on the exception of no right of action.

All of the Oil Company Defendants participating in the courts below and all but two of the Trucking Company/Transporter Defendants filed writs in this court.

These applications were consolidated and granted to review the correctness of the court of appeal's decision on rehearing. Leave was granted by the court for the filing of several briefs by *amicus curiae*.

Law and Discussion

Standard of Review

At issue in this matter is the correctness of the trial court's ruling to grant the exceptions of no right of action filed by the Oil Company Defendants and the Trucking Company/Transporter Defendants. We begin our review by acknowledging that an action can be brought only by a person having a real and actual interest which he asserts. La. C.C.P. art. 681. By filing a peremptory exception of no right of action, a defendant challenges whether a plaintiff has such a real and actual interest in the action. La. C.C.P. art. 927(A)(6). . . .

"The function of the exception of no right of action is to determine whether the plaintiff belongs to the class of persons to whom the law grants the cause of action asserted in the suit." *Hood v. Cotter*, 2008–0215, p. 17 (La.12/2/08), 5 So.3d 819, 829. An appellate court reviewing a lower court's ruling on an exception of no right of action should focus on whether the particular plaintiff has a right to bring the suit and is a member of the class of persons that has a legal interest in the subject matter of the litigation, assuming the petition states a valid cause of action for some person. *Id.* . . .

The determination whether a plaintiff has a right to bring an action raises a question of law. A question of law requires *de novo* review. *Holly & Smith Architects, Inc. v. St. Helena Congregate Facility, Inc.*, 2006–0582, p. 9 (La.11/29/06), 943 So.2d 1037, 1045. Applying this standard of review to the instant matter, we will examine the law *de novo* to determine whether a purchaser of property may sue a third person for damage which was not apparent at the time of the sale and which was inflicted on the property before the purchase.

Jurisprudence Constante

The Louisiana Civil Code provides there are only two sources of law: legislation and custom. La. C.C. art. 1; *see Doerr v. Mobil Oil Corp.*, 2000–0947, p. 13 (La.12/19/00), 774 So.2d 119, 128. However, legislation is the superior source of law in Louisiana; custom may not abrogate legislation. La. C.C. art. 3, Revision Comments–1987, (d). "Judicial decisions, on the other hand, are not intended to be an authoritative source of law in Louisiana. . . . our civilian tradition does not recognize the doctrine of *stare decisis* in our state." *Doerr*, 2000–0947, p. 13, 774 So.2d at 128.

Under our civilian tradition, we recognize instead that "a long line of cases following the same reasoning within this state forms *jurisprudence constante*." *Doerr*, 2000–0947, p. 13, 774 So.2d at 128. This concept has been explained, as follows: "[w]hile a single decision is not binding on our courts, when a series of decisions form a 'constant stream of uniform and homogenous rulings having the same reasoning,' *jurisprudence constante* applies and operates with 'considerable persuasive authority.'" *Doerr,* 2000–0947, p. 13–14, 774 So.2d at 128. Thus, "prior holdings by this court are persuasive, not authoritative, expressions of the law." *Doerr,* 2000–0947, p. 14, 774 So.2d at 129.

With these principles in mind, we will examine the general Louisiana rule that a purchaser of property cannot recover from a third party for property damage inflicted prior to the sale, sometimes referred to as the subsequent purchaser rule. In order to make this examination, we will review the property law precepts that support this rule, and the reasoning and development of the rule over more than a hundred years of jurisprudence.

Subsequent Purchaser Rule

The subsequent purchaser rule is a jurisprudential rule which holds that an owner of property has no right or actual interest in recovering from a third party for damage which was inflicted on the property before his purchase, in the absence of an assignment or subrogation of the rights belonging to the owner of the property when the damage was inflicted.

The Oil Company Defendants and the Trucking Company/Transporter Defendants rely upon this rule as the basis of their peremptory exceptions of no right of action. According to the defendants, any alleged damage to the property at issue occurred well before Eagle Pipe became owner. The defendants further assert Eagle Pipe cannot show it was the recipient of an assignment or a subrogation of any rights the Former Property Owner Defendants may have against them as alleged tortfeasors.

Eagle Pipe contends the subsequent purchaser rule does not apply here. According to the plaintiff, the rule applies only where the prior damage to property was overt or apparent at the time of the sale. Here, the plaintiff argues the radioactive contamination of the property at issue was not apparent at the time of its purchase. Moreover, Eagle Pipe has asserted its entitlement to damages as the owner of property which is currently being damaged. Finally, the plaintiff asserts that it was subrogated to all of the property rights of the Former Property Owner Defendants through the sale. Alternatively, Eagle Pipe argues that it is a third-party beneficiary to contracts entered into between Union Pipe and the Oil Company Defendants.

In order to resolve this matter, it is necessary to examine some fundamental principles of Louisiana property law and how those principles differ from the law of obligations.

Principles of Louisiana Property Law

Property law in Louisiana is a distinct branch of the civil law, dealing with the principal real rights that a person may have in things. . . .

The Civil Code provides that a person may have various rights in things. La. C.C. art. 476 describes the various rights in things as: (1) ownership; (2) personal and predial servitudes; and (3) such other real rights as the law allows. Real rights are not defined by the Civil Code, but ownership is. Ownership is defined as "the right that confers on a person direct, immediate, and exclusive authority over a thing." La. C.C. art. 477(A); *see also* La. C.C. art. 476, Revision Comments—1978, (b). The three main elements of ownership are set forth as the rights of use, enjoyment and disposal, within the limits and under the conditions established by law. *Id.*

The owner of a thing may perform a certain number of juridical acts relating to the thing, all consisting of the transfer

> to another, in whole or in part, the right of enjoyment and of consumption that belongs to the owner of the thing. If he transmits all his right, it is said that he alienates the thing; he performs an act translative of ownership. If he grants merely a right of partial enjoyment of the thing, it is said that he dismembers his ownership. He creates upon the thing a real right of usufruct, emphyteusis or servitude. He is still owner but his ownership has been dismembered. Somebody else has a part, more or less important, of his rights upon the thing. [Planiol and Ripert, at No. 2337, p. 384–385]

Furthermore, "[t]he idea must be thoroughly understood that these various juridical acts are carried out, not upon the thing but upon the owner's right." *Id.* Thus, a real right can be understood as ownership and its dismemberments.

The various dismemberments of ownership also confer real rights on the owner or holder of that right. For example, servitudes are of two types—personal and predial—and they each confer a real right on the holder of the servitude. *See* La. C.C. arts. 476, 533. A personal servitude is a charge on a thing for the benefit of a person, and is divided in the Civil Code into three sorts—usufruct, habitation, and rights of use. A predial servitude is a charge on a servient estate for the benefit of a dominant estate, where the two estates belong to different owners, and can be of four types—natural, legal, voluntary, and conventional. La. C.C. art. 654. Mineral rights and building restrictions are further examples of real rights. Some distinguishing features of real rights are that they cannot exist without a determined object, may be asserted against anyone, confer the right of preference and the right to follow, and are susceptible of possession and of abandonment.

This Court has defined a real right as "synonymous with proprietary interest, both of which refer to a species of ownership. Ownership defines the relation of man to things and may, therefore, be declared against the world." *Harwood Oil & Mining Co.,* 240 La. at 652, 124 So.2d at 767, *citing Reagan v. Murphy,* 235 La. 529, 541, 105 So.2d 210, 214 (1958), *superceded by statute on other grounds, recognized in Salvex, Inc. v. Lewis,* 546 So.2d 1309 (La.App. 3 Cir.1989). Commentators have discussed the essential quality of ownership, that which distinguishes ownership from other real rights, as "the power of disposing of the thing, by consuming it, by physically destroying it and by transforming its substance." [Planiol and Ripert, at No. 2332,

p. 380] By contrast, "[a]ll other real rights authorize those in whom they are vested to enjoy the thing of another in a more or less complete manner, but always with the obligation of preserving the substance." *Id.*

The domain of property law in Louisiana is generally distinct from the other main branches of the civil law, including the law of obligations. Because we find the plaintiff urges, and the court of appeal on rehearing held, that certain principles of the law of obligations are applicable to this question of property law, we must also examine some principles of the law of obligations.

Principles of Obligations Law

The law of obligations is found in Book III of the Louisiana Civil Code, and is entitled "Of the Different Modes of Acquiring the Ownership of Things." Whereas property law encompasses the legal relationship which a person has in things, the law of obligations deals with a specific legal relationship between persons. The Civil Code defines an obligation as a "legal relationship whereby a person, called the obligor, is bound to render a performance in favor of another, called the obligee." La. C.C. art. 1756.

Obligations may arise from contracts and other declarations of will. La. C.C. art. 1757. In a contract of sale, for example, the seller is obligated "to deliver the thing sold and to warrant to the buyer ownership and peaceful possession of, and the absence of hidden defects in, that thing. The seller also warrants that the thing sold is fit for its intended use." La. C.C. art. 2475. Specifically, the seller warrants the buyer against redhibitory defects, or vices, in the thing sold, as follows:

> A defect is redhibitory when it renders the thing useless, or its use so inconvenient that it must be presumed that a buyer would not have bought the thing had he known of the defect. The existence of such a defect gives a buyer the right to obtain rescission of the sale.
>
> A defect is redhibitory also when, without rendering the thing totally useless, it diminishes its usefulness or its value so that it must be presumed that a buyer would still have bought it but for a lesser price. The existence of such a defect limits the right of a buyer to a reduction of the price.

La. C.C. art. 2520. Thus, when defects are discovered in a thing sold which were not apparent, or hidden, at the time of the sale, the law of obligations provides to the buyer a cause of action in redhibition and the right to sue for rescission of the sale or for a reduction of the purchase price.

However, the seller owes no warranty for defects in the thing that were known to, or should have been discovered by, a reasonably prudent buyer. La. C.C. art. 2521. When the defects of the thing sold are apparent, the law of obligations does not provide a cause or right of action to the buyer. Thus, the Civil Code makes a distinction between apparent (overt) and non-apparent (hidden) defects in a thing sold, and what rights and causes of action are provided for the buyer/new owner, within the law of obligations.

Obligations may also arise directly from the law, regardless of a declaration of will, in instances such as wrongful acts, the management of the affairs of another, unjust enrichment, and other acts or facts. La. C.C. art. 1757. An example of an obligation that arises as a matter of law is found in La. C.C. art. 2315, which establishes the basis of tort liability and provides: "[e]very act whatever of man that causes damage to another obliges him by whose fault it happened to repair it."

In general, obligations are divided in the Civil Code into "strictly personal," "heritable," and "real." An obligation is strictly personal when its performance can be enforced only by the obligee, or only against the obligor. La. C.C. art. 1766. An obligation is heritable when its performance may be enforced by a successor of the obligee or against a successor of the obligor. La. C.C. art. 1765. A real obligation is a duty correlative and incidental to a real right. La. C.C. art. 1763. Thus, a real obligation does not exist in the absence of a real right.

Real obligations are pertinent to our discussion of the present issue because a real obligation and real right both attach to a thing. La. C.C. art. 1764, Revision Comments—1984, (b). La. C.C. art. 1764 explains the effects of a real obligation:

> A real obligation is transferred to the universal or particular successor who acquires the movable or immovable thing to which the obligation is attached, without a special provision to that effect.

> But a particular successor is not personally bound, unless he assumes the personal obligations of his transferor with respect to the thing, and he may liberate himself of the real obligation by abandoning the thing.

The nature of a real obligation has been thus described:

> Real obligations are always duties incidental and correlative of real rights. They are obligations in the sense that they are duties imposed on a particular person who owns or possesses a thing subject to a real right, and they are real in the sense that, as correlative of a real right, these obligations attach to a particular thing and are transferred with it without the need of an express assignment or subrogation. They are also real in the sense that the responsibility of the obligor may be limited to value of the thing. [Yiannopoulos, at § 212, p. 407]

Both real rights and real obligations may be contrasted with personal rights. The legal right that a person has against another person to demand the performance of an obligation is called a personal right. Distinct from a real right, which can be asserted against the world, a personal right is effective only between the parties. La. C.C. art. 1758. This court has declared that "a personal right . . . defines man's relationship to man and refers merely to an obligation one owes to another which may be declared only against the obligor." *Harwood Oil & Mining Co.*, 240 La. at 651, 124 So.2d at 767, *citing Reagan*, 235 La. at 541, 105 So.2d at 214.

In some instances, a real right and a personal right may appear to be the same, but the underlying nature of the rights distinguishes them. For example,

> [a]ccording to appearances, a usufructuary and a lessee seem to have the use and enjoyment of a house in much the same way. But, technically, the usufructuary has a right in the enjoyment of a house; the lessee has a right against the owner of a house to let him enjoy it. One has a real right and the other a personal right. [Yiannopoulos, at ¶ 201, at p.384]

This court has held "[u]nder the civil law concept, a lease [a contract about property] does not convey any real right or title to the property leased, but only a personal right." *Richard v. Hall,* 2003–1488, p. 17–18 (La.4/23/04), 874 So.2d 131, 145. "That a lease is not a real right under the civil law is well settled." *Reagan,* 235 La. 529, 541, 105 So.2d 210, 214. This concept was further explained:

> The rights of use, enjoyment, and disposal are said to be the three elements of property in things. They constitute the *jura in re:* The right of a lessee is not a real right, *i.e.,* a *jus in re.* In other words, the lessee does not hold one of the elements of property in the thing. His right is a *jus ad rem,* a right upon the thing.

Reagan, 235 La. at 541, 105 So.2d at 214, citing *In Re Morgan R.R. & S.S. Co.,* 32 La.Ann. 371 (1880).

Real rights, and real obligations pass to a subsequent acquirer of the thing to which it is attached without the need of a stipulation to that effect. La. C.C. art. 1764, Revision Comments—1984, (c). A personal right, by contrast, cannot be asserted by another in the absence of an assignment or subrogation. La. C.C. art. 1764, Revision Comments—1984, (d) and (f).

We now examine the jurisprudential rule at issue in light of the principles of property law and the law of obligations.

Subsequent Purchaser Rule and its Development

[In this portion of the judgment, Justice Clark discusses more than 150 years of jurisprudence, including: *Clark v. J.L. Warner Co. et al.,* 6 La.Ann. 408 (1851); *Prados v. South Central Bell Tel. Co.,* 329 So.2d 744 (La.1975); *St. Jude Medical Office Bldg. Ltd. Partnership v. City Glass and Mirror, Inc.,* 619 So.2d 529 (La.1993). Eds.]

Analysis

Although the plaintiff asserts the subsequent purchaser rule applies only when there is apparent damage to property, we think the rationale also extends to the situation where the damage to property is not apparent. Whether this should be called an extension of the subsequent purchaser rule, or simply the way in which the fundamental principles of property law operate, the result is the same. Damage to property may disturb not only the owner's rights of use of, and enjoyment in, the property (the *usus* and *fructus* rights in ownership), but may also disturb his right to alienate the property, or to dispose of the property, completely and without disturbance (the *abusus* right in ownership).

The property owner at the time the damages were inflicted has a personal right of action against the tortfeasor for the disturbance of his real right in the property. When the damage is apparent, the property owner obtains the personal right of action to sue for damages to compensate for a loss of value in the property or an interference with the property's use. This personal right exists during his use and enjoyment while he owns the property. This personal right exists even during and after his disposal of the property, as it is assumed the apparent damage would result in a loss of value to the property which would be reflected in the sale price. Where damage to the property is not apparent, and the property has been sold, the law provides the purchaser with the right to seek rescission of the sale or a reduction in the purchase price. In that instance, the former owner's right to dispose of the property without disturbance has been affected, as the owner must now defend against an action in redhibition or take some other action to repair, remedy or correct the defect.

With apparent damage to property, the law does not provide to the subsequent purchaser a source of profit by allowing him to negotiate a low purchase price based on the condition of the property *and* the right to seek damages from the tortfeasor who is responsible for the property's poor condition. With damage that is not apparent, the law does not provide the subsequent purchaser with both the right to sue for rescission of the sale, or a reduction in the purchase price, *and* the right to sue for damages against the tortfeasor. Instead, whether damage to the property is apparent or not, the personal nature of the right of the landowner at that time does not change, and remains with the landowner unless the right is explicitly assigned or subrogated to another.

We are not unaware of the effects which the rules of discovery and prescription will have on certain fact situations under this analysis, especially where the damage to property occurred in the distant past, where property rapidly changes hands, or where ancestors in title are non-existent. We find the rules of discovery and prescription are deliberate legislative choices which ultimately limit otherwise imprescriptible torts and which maintain certainty in transactions involving immovable property. The legislature, if it chose, could have created a right of action to seek damages against tortfeasors for damage to property which affects current property owners no matter when the damage occurred, or could have made an exception to prescription rules for long-term contamination of property. But such legislation has not been enacted. Instead, the legislature has decided the only addition to current legal remedies is a mechanism for remediating the property.

Nor are we indifferent to criticisms of the remediation procedures of the La. DEQ raised by the plaintiff and *amicus curiae*. However, these assessments of the current legislative scheme for property remediation are also matters best addressed to the legislature. What we discern from the current legislative scheme is a determination by the legislature to remediate property to put it back into use and commerce. In the absence of legislative action, we cannot supply a right of action through jurisprudence which the law does not.

. . . .

For the foregoing reasons, we find the ruling of the court of appeal on rehearing was erroneous. We now turn to our own review of the plaintiff's claims.

Allegations of the Petition

Reviewing the allegations of the petition *de novo*, and assuming the petition states a valid cause of action for some person, we must now determine whether the plaintiff belongs to the class of persons to whom the law grants the causes of action asserted in the suit. In reviewing the causes of action asserted by the plaintiff, we find they fall into two general categories, those arising in tort and those arising under contract.

a. Tort claims

Eagle Pipe raises a tort cause of action, claiming the defendants are strictly liable and liable for their negligence in damaging the property. Eagle Pipe claims a right of action as the current property's owner who is injured by the contamination of the property by TENORM. Although Eagle Pipe argues the distinction between real and personal rights is irrelevant, our analysis shows that this distinction is at the very core of the Louisiana property laws which resolve this dispute.

As we have explained, injury to property must be understood as damage to the real rights in the property. A tortfeasor who causes injury or damage to a real right in property owes an obligation to the owner of the real right. This relationship arises as a matter of law and provides to the owner of the real right a personal right to sue the tortfeasor for damages. In the absence of an assignment or subrogation of this personal right, a subsequent purchaser of the property cannot recover from a third party for property damage inflicted prior to the sale. Insofar as Eagle Pipe claims a right to sue based on the damage to the property which occurred before its ownership, we hold the plaintiff has no right of action to assert as a matter of law.

To the extent the plaintiff claims the damage to the property is continuing, such that Eagle Pipe asserts its own right of action to sue for damages, we find the law is clear that the allegations of the plaintiff's petition cannot constitute a continuing tort. In *Crump v. Sabine River Authority*, 98–2326, p. 7 (La.6/29/99), 737 So.2d 720, 726, this court noted "the theory of continuing tort has its roots in property damage cases and requires that the operating cause of the injury be a continuous one which results in continuous damages." We have held "[a] continuing tort is occasioned by continual unlawful acts and for there to be a continuing tort there must be a continuing duty owed to the plaintiff and a continuing breach of that duty by the defendant." *Id.*, 98–2326, p. 10, 737 So.2d at 728.

The inquiry as to whether there is continuous tortious conduct "is essentially a conduct-based one, asking whether the tortfeasor perpetuates the injury through overt, persistent, and ongoing acts." *Hogg v. Chevron USA, Inc.*, 2009–2632, p. 16 (La.7/6/10), 45 So.3d 991, 1003. In *Hogg*, we cited with approval the following analysis:

> ... courts look[ ] to the alleged injury-producing conduct of the tortfeasors to determine whether that conduct was perpetuated through overt, persistent, and ongoing acts. Where the wrongful conduct was completed, but the plaintiff continued to experience injury in the absence of any further activity by the tortfeasor, no continuing tort was found. *Id.*, 2009–2632, p. 21, 45 So.3d at 1005.

We find the operating cause of the injury claimed in the petition here was the tender of allegedly contaminated oilfield equipment from the Oil Company Defendants and the Trucking Company/Transporter Defendants to Union Pipe, the lessee of the Former Property Owner Defendants. The petition does not claim that there have been continual or ongoing unlawful acts; instead, the petition asserts the alleged tortious acts ceased as of 1988. We also find the continued presence of the alleged contamination, the injury claimed, is simply the continuing ill effect from the original tortious acts. *Crump*, 98–2326, p. 9, 737 So.2d at 727–728. The fact that a subsequent purchaser "discovers" the continuing ill effects of the original tortious acts does not give rise to a new, discrete right of action in tort.

Similarly, to the extent the allegations in the petition could be construed to assert a cause of action under trespass, as alluded to in the plaintiff's brief and urged by *amicus*, we find the law does not extend a right of action to Eagle Pipe under the facts alleged. The plaintiff cites to *McCutchen, supra*, where this court noted in ruling that the current landowner could not recover for damages to the land that occurred prior to purchase that "[t]he exception to this rule (to which the learned counsel calls attention) arises when the entry or taking of land is in the nature of a trespass, and applied to the demand for the value of the land as contradistinguished from the claim for damages incidental to such trespass." 118 La. at 439, 43 So. at 42 (parenthetical in original). However, Eagle Pipe does not include the court's conclusion in *McCutchen*, which found: "[i]n the instant case we find as a fact that the entry was made and the land occupied with the acquiescence of the owner. The case does not, therefore, fall within the exception." *Id.*

A civil trespass is a tort. Even if the facts alleged in the petition could be considered tortious acts which constituted a trespass which caused damage to the property, the principles of Louisiana property law would still provide the owner of the property at the time the injury occurred with a personal right to sue the trespasser for damages, and not the subsequent owner. Moreover, not all trespasses are continuous acts giving rise to successive damages.

In *Hogg*, we observed "the concept of continuing tort finds its origins in trespass and nuisance cases." *Id.*, 2009–2632, p. 16, 45 So.3d at 1003.

> A continuous trespass is a continuous tort; one where multiple acts of trespass have occurred and continue to occur; where the tortious conduct is ongoing, this gives rise to successive damages. . . . That situation, our

courts have cautioned, is to be distinguished from a trespass which causes continuing injury by permanently changing the physical condition of the land. *When a trespass which permanently changes the physical condition of the land is concluded, no additional causes of action accrue merely because the damage continues to exist or even progressively worsens. Id.,* 2009–2632, p. 17, 45 So.3d at 1003 (citation omitted).

Thus, to determine whether a trespass is continuous, a court must use the same inquiry used to determine the existence of a continuing tort. As we have already seen, the injury alleged in the petition was not perpetuated through overt, persistent, and ongoing acts. Consequently, even if the allegations in the petition could be considered as asserting a trespass claim, Eagle Pipe would not have a right of action to assert that claim.

Finally, Eagle Pipe relies upon a Civil Code comment for the proposition that "the obligation . . . to restore the premises to their previous condition is a real obligation, following the immovable into the hands of any acquirer." La. C.C. art. 1764, Revision Comments—1984(f). Although the language used in the comment certainly appears to provide relief for the plaintiff, a closer look at the paragraph in which this statement is made and the authorities cited for the proposition reveal the comment is referring to a real obligation to restore premises correlative and incidental to a predial servitude. *See* Yiannopoulos, *Predial Servitudes,* § 157 (3d ed.2004). The paragraph in which the relied-upon statement appears is a discussion of the effects of real obligations in connection with predial servitudes. Consequently, Eagle Pipe cannot assert a right of action under these provisions.

b. Contract claims

We have already found, absent assignment or subrogation, Eagle Pipe as a subsequent purchaser of the property does not have a right to assert a claim for damages which were inflicted on the property before the sale. Consequently, we must examine the act of sale to determine whether the Former Property Owners Defendants explicitly assigned their personal right to sue for damage to Eagle Pipe. The act of sale was attached to the petition and was offered as an exhibit at the hearing on the exceptions. In pertinent part, the act of sale provides:

> . . . [the sellers] do by these presents sell, transfer and deliver, with full guarantee of title and free from all encumbrances, and with full subrogation to all their rights and action of warranty against previous owners . . .

We find these provisions are substantially similar to those found in [*Prados v. South Central Bell Tel. Co.,* 329 So.2d 744 (La.1975) (on rehearing)], in which we stated the subrogation clause in the act of sale was directed to the rights and actions of warranty against previous owners, and not an express assignment or subrogation of personal rights to the new owner. *Prados,* 329 So.2d at 749–750. Likewise, we find no express assignment or subrogation of the former property owners' personal right to sue for damage in the act of sale at issue here. Consequently, Eagle Pipe has no right of action based on an assignment of personal rights from its vendor.

Eagle Pipe contends that Union Pipe and the Oil Company Defendants entered into contracts, obligations or agreements that provide for the recovery of damages caused to the property. This contention suggests earlier contracts between the lessee and its customers established a real obligation which followed the property. However, a real obligation is correlative and incidental to a real right. Although Union Pipe as lessee had a right against the Former Property Owner Defendants to use and enjoy the property during the term of its lease, Union Pipe did not have a real right in the property. The Former Property Owner Defendants retained the real rights to use and enjoy the property, while the lease provided Union Pipe with a personal right against the owners to allow it to use and enjoy the property. The contracts between Union Pipe and the Oil Company Defendants, therefore, could not involve any real right in the property. It is a fundamental principle that "no one can transfer a greater right than he himself has." If there was no real right involved in the contracts between Union Pipe and the Oil Company Defendants, then there could be established no real obligation which was correlative and incidental to that real right. Instead, the contractual rights and obligations between Union Pipe and the Oil Company Defendants established personal rights between the contracting parties. Eagle Pipe does not have a right of action based on a real obligation established by an earlier contract between a lessee of the property and its customers. . . .

Conclusion

Under the facts alleged in the petition, the law has provided to Eagle Pipe a cause of action in redhibition and the right to sue for rescission of the sale or the reduction of the purchase price. In addition, the legislature has provided a mechanism for Eagle Pipe to obtain remediation of the property. While the law provides Eagle Pipe a contractual remedy, and the legal remedy of remediation, the law is not required to provide Eagle Pipe with *every possible* remedy. *PPG Industries, Inc. v. Bean Dredging*, 447 So.2d 1058, 1061 (La.1984) (". . . the rule of law which prohibits negligent damage to property does not necessarily require that a party who negligently causes injury to property must be held legally responsible to *all* persons for *all* damages flowing in a 'but for' sequence from the negligent conduct.") (emphasis in original). Our *de novo* review of the allegations in the plaintiff's petition shows that Eagle Pipe does not belong to the class of persons to whom the law grants the causes of action asserted in the suit.

Decree

So finding, we reverse the ruling of the court of appeal on rehearing and reinstate the ruling of the court of appeal on original hearing, affirming the trial court's granting of the defendants' exceptions of no right of action.

Reversed.

WEIMER, J., dissenting. I respectfully dissent from the majority opinion insofar as it adopts a bright line rule expanding the application of the jurisprudentially created subsequent purchaser rule to all circumstances, regardless of the facts. In my view, the blanket expansion of the subsequent purchaser rule to include latent conditions on property divorced of any consideration of the particular circumstances out of which those conditions arise has the potential to produce unworkable and inconsistent results at odds with the facts and the law.

This matter comes before the court on an exception of no right of action that simply tests whether the plaintiff has an interest in the action. La. C.C.P. art. 927(A)(6). In other words, the exception asks "whether the plaintiff belongs to the class of persons to whom the law grants the cause of action asserted in the suit." *Hood v. Cotter*, 2008–0215, p. 17 (La.12/2/08), 5 So.3d 819, 829. Adopting a bright line, inflexible approach to this preliminary determination in view of the myriad of factual circumstances that may present themselves is, in my view, unwise and conducive to unjust and inequitable results.

The subsequent purchaser rule is a jurisprudential creation. It recognizes that the right to recover for damage to real property is a personal right belonging to the property owner *at the time the damage occurs;* as such, it does not transfer to a subsequent purchaser absent an express assignment. *See, St. Jude Med. Office Bldg. Ltd. P'ship v. City Glass & Mirror, Inc.,* 619 So.2d 529, 530–531 (La.1993); *Prados v. S. Cent. Bell Telephone Co.,* 329 So.2d 744, 749–751 (La.1976) (on reh'g). Although linked to La. C.C. art. 1764, the rule is not derived from that, or any, codal provision; rather, it finds its roots in the case of *Clark v. J.L. Warner & Co.,* 6 La.Ann. 408 (La.1851).

In *Clark,* the plaintiff purchased a tract of land with a two-story brick house, kitchen and out-houses. *Id.* at 408. After taking possession of the property, he sued the defendant, a lessee of the neighboring property owner, for damages to the house and out-buildings caused by defendant's operation of an ice house. *Id.* The trial court's judgment in favor of the plaintiff was reversed on appeal, with the court noting:

> It is true, that the purchaser of property is presumed to purchase all actions appurtenant to the property, and necessary to its perfect enjoyment; but as to damages actually suffered before the purchase, we know of no other principles governing the case than those referrable to this general provision of the code, that "every act of man that causes damage to another obliges him by whose fault it happened to repair it." It is a mere corollary, that the reparation must be made to him who suffered the injury. And the principle is strikingly illustrated by this case. The plaintiff, after possessing the property twenty months, claims one-third more damages than he gave *Mrs. Springer* for his lot with all the buildings and improvements. This leads to the impression, that the modicity of the price he gave for the premises may, perhaps, be attributed to their dilapidated and dangerous situation, on account of the erection of the ice house and other causes. It is impossible, from the law, to concur with the district court, that these damages, which probably caused the moderate price given for the house and kitchen, should be a source of profit to the purchaser, who had a perfect knowledge of their existence when he purchased.

Clark, 6 La.Ann. at 409.

The rule first announced in *Clark* has been followed consistently in this court's jurisprudence. It is premised on the idea that the purchaser is not the party damaged by the tortious conduct; rather it is the seller who has suffered damage in the form of the reduced price received for the property: "The general principle, we think, is that a buyer is presumed to know the overt condition of the property and to take that condition into account in agreeing to the sales price." *Prados,* 329 So.2d at 751. The subsequent purchaser rule is, therefore, nothing more than the jurisprudence's common sense approach to situations where known or overt conditions of immovable property result in a diminution in value that in turn results in a lower price paid for the property. The jurisprudence recognizes that the purchaser, who receives the benefit of the diminution in value, suffers no loss and, therefore, no damage.

The rule has roots in French civilian tradition. As explained by Aubry and Rau in their discussion regarding what rights transfer in a sale of property:

> There is no doubt that an action for rescission or in damages because of circumstances occurring before the sale such as changes in the premises or an unauthorized assignment of the lease, is not transferred to the buyer. But an action on grounds of excessive deterioration should pass on to the buyer, *at least if this circumstance was not taken into account when the sales price was set.* [Emphasis added; footnotes omitted.]

2 AUBRY & RAU, LOUISIANA CIVIL LAW TRANSLATIONS: DROIT CIVIL FRANCAIS § 176, pp. 76–77 (7th ed.1971). *See also, Id.,* at n.6 ("This solution presupposes that the deterioration has been taken into account when setting the sales price. Otherwise the opposite decision would be justified.")

The majority opinion goes to some length, in tracing the origins of the subsequent purchaser rule, to discount the idea that application of the doctrine hinges on the overt or known characteristic of the damage. Thus, it recites that the rationale of *Clark* does not indicate a requirement that the damage be overt. *Eagle Pipe and Supply v. Amerada Hess Corp.,* 10–C–2267, 10–C–2272, 10–C2275, 10–C–2279, and 10–C–2289, op. at 265–66 (October 2011). However, *Clark* was not a case in which the damage to the property was latent or hidden. As a result, it was unnecessary for the *Clark* court to comment on whether the rule should be extended to cases of latent damage. Had it attempted to do so, its statement in that regard would have been dicta. The majority opinion similarly distinguishes *Prados* on grounds that the presumption that the buyer is aware of the overt condition of the property and takes that condition into consideration in agreeing to the sales price is discussed in a paragraph on accessory rights. *Eagle Pipe,* op. at 272–73. Ultimately, however, this is a distinction without a difference, as the key to the holding in *Prados* is revealed in the single statement, quoted by the majority: "The right to damages accrued to the lessor prior to the sale." *Prados,* 329 So.2d at 751. That right accrued before the sale because before that time the damages were obvious, and their existence interfered with the owner's "use, enjoyment or disposal of the property," in that the owner received a reduced price for the property, and thereby incurred damages.

Given the common sense underpinnings of the subsequent purchaser rule, it is not surprising that it has been applied by this court thus far *only* in cases where the damage to the real property has been overt. There is simply nothing in the rationale underlying the doctrine that supports its extension to hidden or latent injuries to property. Indeed, adoption of the majority's position in this case will result in precisely the situation then-Justice Tate counseled against in his dissent in *Prados:* a former owner with a right of action but no cause of action (because having received full value for the property, the former owner has suffered no damage) and a present owner with damage, and a cause of action, but no right of action. *Prados,* 329 So.2d at 752 (Tate, J., dissenting). This is the seemingly absurd result produced by applying a rule that simply was never contemplated or designed to apply to hidden or latent conditions.

Indeed, on the single prior occasion in which this court has been called upon to answer the precise question presented here, *i.e.,* whether a landowner whose property was damaged as a result of hidden contamination prior to purchase has a right of action against the defendant/tortfeasor to recover for damages to the property, or whether this right belongs solely to the owner of the land at the time of damage and does not transfer to the new owner absent a specific stipulation, the court has answered that issue favorably to the subsequent owner, finding a right of action in favor of the subsequent purchaser. *Hopewell, Inc. v. Mobil Oil Co.,* 00–3280 (La.2/9/01), 784 So.2d 653. While the brief per curiam in *Hopewell* is, admittedly, a bit obtuse, the bottom line is that in the per curiam this court acknowledged a right of action in favor of a subsequent purchaser against a tortfeasor in an action similar to the one asserted here, refusing to extend the subsequent purchaser rule to a case involving latent damage, unknown to either the seller or purchaser.

In my view, the central problem with the majority opinion is the false dilemma on which it is based. According to the majority's reasoning, either the right to recover for damage to immovable property is a personal right, in which case the subsequent purchaser rule applies to deprive the plaintiff in this case of a right of action, or it is a real right that is transferred with the sale of the property. This approach ignores the third approach to the issue, the one adopted by the court of appeal.

In its opinion on rehearing, the court of appeal recognized that the right to recover for damages to immovable property is a personal right belonging to the property owner at the time the damage occurs. However, it examined in the context of La. C.C. art. 2315, the fountainhead of tort responsibility in Louisiana, when injury/damage occurs and a resultant cause of action for property damage arises. This single issue — when the damage occurs and who suffers that damage — holds the key to resolving this case.

Under Louisiana law, for a negligence cause of action to accrue, three elements are required: fault, causation and damages. *Owens v. Martin,* 449 So.2d 448, 450

(La.1984). "Thus, a *sine qua non* for accrual of a cause of action is damages." *Cole v. Celotex Corp.*, 599 So.2d 1058, 1063 n. 15 (La.1992). In Louisiana, "damage" to real property is typically measured by the difference between the value of the property before and after the harm. *Roman Catholic Church of the Archdiocese of New Orleans v. La. Gas Service Co.*, 618 So.2d 874 (La.1993). Consequently, a seller who receives fair market value for real property with a hidden or latent defect is not "damaged" by the condition of the property. This seller has experienced no pecuniary loss. However, pecuniary loss is a necessary predicate to the award of compensatory damages for property damage. *See,* RESTATEMENT (SECOND) OF TORTS § 906 (1979) ("Compensatory damages that will not be awarded without proof of pecuniary loss include compensation for (a) harm to property. . . ."). Therefore, in the context of tortious injury to property, the relevant "injury" is the loss of use and resulting loss of value and this injury is not incurred by the landowner at the time of the tortious conduct, but by the landowner at the moment the injury is (or should be) discovered.

The majority opinion, far from undercutting this idea, actually supports it. According to that opinion, damage to property occurs when there is a disturbance or interference with the owner's right to use, enjoy, or alienate the property. *Eagle Pipe*, op. at 275–76. In the case of hidden damage, which is unknown to either seller or purchaser at the time of a sale, the only landowner who sustains an interference with his use, enjoyment, or alienation of the property is the owner of the property at the time the hidden damage is discovered.

As the majority opinion points out, the civil code draws a distinction between apparent and non-apparent damage. It does so in the context of the redhibition articles, La. C.C. arts. 2520, et seq.; and it does so in the context of prescription, expressly adopting a discovery rule in La. C.C. art. 3493. Indeed, La. C.C. art. 3493 conditions the commencement of prescription on knowledge, and further links that knowledge to the owner of the immovable at the time such knowledge is, or should have been, acquired. In its linkage, the article implies that it is the owner at discovery who possesses the cause and the right of action.

Again, as the majority opinion points out, in Louisiana, there are only two sources of law — legislation and custom — and of the two, legislation is the superior source of law. *Eagle Pipe*, op. at 256, citing La. C.C. arts. 1, 3 and *Doerr v. Mobil Oil Corp.*, 00–0947, p. 13 (La.12/19/00), 774 So.2d 119, 128. Judicial decisions are not intended to be an authoritative source of law. *Doerr*, 00–0947 at 13, 774 So.2d at 128. In the provisions of the civil code can be found broad principles which are intended to be extended and applied to different factual circumstances to formulate a coherent body of law. Louisiana C.C. art. 3493, a written provision of our law, specifically refers to the owner of immovable property and explicitly links the commencement of prescription to knowledge of damage. Implicitly, this article recognizes a right of action in the owner of the immovable at the time damage is or should have been discovered. I believe that it is this codal provision, rather than the expansion of a jurisprudential rule, which must serve as guidance in this case. Drawing upon that codal provision, I believe that it is proper to conclude, as did the court of appeal on rehearing, that in the case of latent or unknown damage to property, the cause of action arises upon actual or constructive knowledge, and the right of action belongs to the property owner at the time of that discovery.

Ultimately, then, the majority's analysis of the issue presented in this case, while exhaustive and detailed, is one with which I must respectfully disagree. I do not believe that the subsequent purchaser rule, which has previously been applied by this court only in cases of overt injury to property where the injury has been accounted for in the reduced price paid for the property, can or should be expanded to cases of latent and unknown injury so as to deprive the subsequent landowner who discovers the injury of a right of action, especially where, in the one case to raise the issue prior to the present one, *Hopewell*, the court refused to do so. . . .

Notes and Questions

1. Identify the contents of the subsequent purchaser rule as articulated in *Eagle Pipe and Supply, Inc. v. Amerada Hess Corp.*, 79 So.3d 246 (La. 2011). How do Justice Clark's majority opinion and Justice Weimer's dissent differ with regard to its operations? Note that both camps rely on the same line of cases. The positions were so entrenched that both Justice Clark and Justice Weimer wrote separately with additional reasons in support of their basic positions. For the terms "assignment" and "subrogation" under Louisiana law, see La. Civ. Code arts. 1827–1830, 1900 (1984). *See also* Saul Litvinoff, *Subrogation*, 50 La. L. Rev. 1143 (1990).

2. A rich body of case law has developed in the wake of *Eagle Pipe*. Initially, a number of courts struggled with a question left open in a footnote stating that the plurality "express[ed] no opinion as to the applicability of [its] holding to fact situations involving mineral leases or obligations arising out of the Mineral Code." *Id.* at 281, n. 80. Taking advantage of this apparent opening, the Louisiana Third Circuit held that because the lease at issue in *Eagle Pipe* was a surface lease, the court's holding had no application to a post-acquisition contamination damage claim brought by a property owner against mineral lessees who allegedly damaged the property at issue when the property owner was owned by a previous owner and during the pendency of the mineral leases. *Duck v. Hunt Oil Co.*, 134 So. 3d 114, 119 (La. App. 3 Cir. 2014). Paradoxically, the court in *Duck* also held that, even though a mineral lease is a classified as a real right under the Louisiana Mineral Code, the right to sue mineral lessees for damages under prior mineral leases did not automatically pass to the plaintiff-subsequent purchaser when he acquired the land at issue. *Id.* at 119–120. The court in *Duck* also remanded for further proceedings finding privity of contract between the property owner and mineral lessee defendants based on a stipulation pour autrui created by the mineral lease. *Id.* at 120–22. In *Global Marketing Solutions, LLC v. Blue Mill Farms, Inc.*, 153 So.3d 1209, 1215 (La. App. 1 Cir. 2014), the Louisiana First Circuit reached the opposite result and held that the subsequent purchase rule from *Eagle Pipe* did apply to bar claims against mineral lessees.

The following year, the Louisiana Third Circuit overruled its decision in *Duck* and, agreeing with the First Circuit in *Global Marketing*, held that the expanded subsequent purchaser rule announced in *Eagle Pipe* does apply in cases involving mineral leases. *Bundrick v. Anadarko Petroleum Corp.*, 159 So.3d 1137, 1143 (La. App. 3 Cir. 2015). That decision thus held that the subsequent purchaser doctrine thus bars a property owner from recovering from a third party mineral lessee for damages allegedly inflicted on the property before the owner purchased the property in the absence of an assignment or subrogation of rights belonging to the previous owner of the property to the subsequent purchaser. *Id.* More recently still, the United States Fifth Circuit Court of Appeal reviewed the state of the law and observed that "a clear consensus has emerged among all Louisiana appellate courts that have considered the issue, and they have held that the subsequent purchaser rule does apply to cases, like this one, involving expired mineral leases." *Guilbeau v. Hess Corp.*, 854 F.3d 310, 313 (5th Cir. 2017). *See id.* at 313–315 (reviewing many subsequent purchaser cases in the Louisiana appellate courts). For a concise critical assessment of *Eagle Pipe* and the case law applying its reaffirmation of the subsequent purchase doctrine, see L. David Cromwell & Chloé M Chetta, *Divining the Real Nature of Real Obligations*, 92 Tul. L. Rev. 127, 210–17 (2017).

3. In light of *Eagle Pipe* and its progeny, an important issue in cases involving alleged contamination of land by third parties now concerns whether the owner at the time of the alleged contamination effectively transferred his personal rights to recover damages to the subsequent purchaser through an assignment or subrogation. In *Catahoula Lake Investments, LLC v. Hunt Oil Co.*, 237 So.3d 585 (La. App. 3 Cir. 2018), the Louisiana Third Circuit found that an effective subrogation had occurred when the contract of sale between the previous owner and the subsequent purchaser stated:

> Vendor expressly subrogates Vendee to all rights, claims and causes of action Vendor may have arising from or relating to any hidden or latent defects in the Property.

The court in *Catahoula Lake* found that "the use of the terms 'hidden or latent defects' [to be] an intentional attempt by the parties to this contract to protect the purchaser of this property by transferring any rights the seller might have against a third party for 'hidden or latent' damages to the property, the very damages at issue in this case," *Id.* at 591. Therefore, the contract did operate to subrogate the subsequent purchaser to the seller's personal rights to seek damages for all hidden, latent defects in the property allegedly caused by former mineral operators. *Id.* at 592.

4. In another important case, *Vekic v. Popich*, 236 So.3d 526 (La. 2017), the Louisiana Supreme Court distinguished *Eagle Pipe* and held that the subsequent purchase doctrine did *not* bar a plaintiff who had acquired an interest in oyster leases through a sublease and option-to-purchase agreement from recovering more than $900,000 in property damages in the wake of the British Petroleum Deepwater Horizon oil spill disaster. In *Vekic*, the court distinguished *Eagle Pipe* and determined that the sublessee-plaintiff was entitled to receive all property damage claim

payments arising from the BP settlement. Crucially, the court observed that the sublease and option-to-purchase agreement effectively transferred not only all of the original lessee's rights and interests in the oyster leases to the sublessee, subject to the requirement that the sub-lessee complete payment of the contemplated $90,000 rent/purchase price for the oyster leases, but also transferred all responsibility and risk of loss related to the oyster leases to the sublessee. In short, the court found that the agreement effectively assigned *all rights to property damage claims* relating to the oyster leases to the sub-lessee. *Id.* at 529–36.

5. The distinction between real rights and personal rights—and, in particular, the difference between a right of use and a lease—can have important consequences for the parties involved. *Sasol North America, Inc. v. Bolton,* 103 So.3d 1267, 1269–70 (La. App. 3 Cir. 2012) (holding that an agreement establishing a right of way for a pipeline created a personal servitude of right of use, not a lease, and that the purported renewal of the right of use after the agreement expired would be a transfer of immovable property subject to the requirement that the agreement be in writing).

4. Exclusivity in Ownership

Returning to the definition of ownership found in Article 477 of the Civil Code, we should briefly focus on another fundamental characteristic of ownership—the centrality of an owner's *exclusive authority* over a thing. Recall that Article 477 defines ownership as a right that confers on a person "direct, immediate, and *exclusive* authority over a thing." La. Civ. Code art. 477(A) (1979) (emphasis added). Also recall the suggestion in the revision comments to Article 476 that real rights "confer direct and immediate authority over a thing." La. Civ. Code art. 476 rev. cmt. (b) (1978).

The drafters of the Civil Code appear to conceptualize ownership as that particular real right, alone among the entire universe of real rights, which furnishes not just "direct and immediate authority" over a thing, but also "exclusive" authority over a thing. In other words, as we will see much more clearly when we study personal and predial servitudes later in this casebook, some very important real rights give their right holders "direct and immediate authority over a thing," but that authority is *not exclusive*. In fact, the authority that personal or predial servitude holders have over things subject to their servitudes can often be intentionally shared or divided in some way. This is not true for owners. Their authority is truly exclusive.

5. The Classic Triad of Ownership Rights

The second sentence of Article 477 of the Civil Code reveals yet another significant lesson about the nature of ownership. The owner of a thing, the article tells us, "may use, enjoy, and dispose of it within the limits and under the conditions established by law." La. Civ. Code art. 477(A) (1979). This sentence suggests that

ownership comprises at least three particular elements, which some property scholars conceptualize as options (or *facultés*) accruing from ownership.

The first element, the right to "use" the thing that is owned (also referred to as
usus), is the most easily recognizable. The right of *usus* refers to the right to physically possess a thing, to put a thing to some direct and immediate usage, to occupy
it, or to exert or exercise some physical control over it. Although the law may impose
limitations on how a thing may be used, the owner's right to use the thing he owns
is fundamental to ownership. A person who has property rights in a thing, without
some right to use or to determine the use of the thing, might enjoy some kind of real
right, but that real right would not be full ownership.

usus

The second element or *faculté* of ownership, the right to "enjoy" something (also
referred to as *fructus*), may seem similar to the right to use a thing. But to civil law
lawyers, and to Louisiana lawyers in particular, the right to enjoy a thing or the
right of *fructus* refers to a very specific right—the right to the natural and civil
fruits of a thing, or more generally, the right to benefit from the thing.

faculté

The right to the natural and civil fruits of a thing is generally governed by the
law of accession, which we will study in Chapter Five. The owner of a pecan tree not
only has the right to exercise physical control over the tree, deciding where it is to be
planted and when and how it should be pruned, but, when the tree produces pecans,
the owner is entitled to claim the pecans—the natural fruits of the tree. La. Civ.
Code art. 483 (1979). Similarly, the owner of a house, in addition to having the right
to physically occupy the house, also generally has the right to the rental income that
can be derived from the house if it is rented out to lessees. In this case, the owner
receives the civil fruits of the house. Finally, the owner of an interest bearing savings
account or a corporate bond has the right to receive the interest payments that are
paid by the bank or by the issuer of the bond. This is another example of civil fruits.

The owner's right to "dispose" of a thing is generally understood in the civil
law to mean the right to alienate things, the right to transfer ownership by sale,
donation or exchange, as well as the right to lease things and encumber things with
mortgages. We often refer to this right as *abusus*. A non-lawyer might think that a
right to dispose entails the right to destroy a thing, to throw it away or abandon it.
And indeed the owner of a thing generally does enjoy such rights, subject once again
to limitations imposed by law. But the right of disposal is broader than this notion
of physical destruction or abandonment. It means the right to alienate or encumber—to transfer ownership, or lease or mortgage a thing.

Dispose

Common law lawyers long ago adopted this typically civilian way of disaggregat-
ing the concept of ownership into some of its constitutive elements and began to
refer to ownership as a "bundle of rights" or even more colloquially as a "bundle of
sticks." Some property law scholars in the United States, as well as prominent judges,
use this bundle metaphor to argue that property rights are not *a priori* rights with
respect to things that have their own objective meaning, but instead describe a set
of malleable and socially constructed legal relationships between people. The most

famous statement of this view is found in Thomas C. Grey, *The Disintegration of Property*, in NOMOS XXII: PROPERTY 69 (J. Roland Pennock & John W. Chapman eds 1980). Whether this conceptualization of property rights in general, and of ownership in particular, is accurate or desirable is a hotly contested issue in property law scholarship today. For a succinct critique of the bundle of rights theory, see Henry E. Smith, *Property as the Law of Things*, 125 HARV. L. REV. 1691, 1694–1700 (2012). For a much more detailed discussion of the bundle of rights debate, see James E. Penner, *The Bundle of Rights Picture of Property*, 43 U.C.L.A. L. REV. 711 (1996).

For present purposes, it is useful to keep the three specific rights that Article 477 identifies in mind. Later in this casebook, we will study how the Civil Code takes these three fundamental ownership rights and allows for their dismemberment or disaggregation into "other real rights," particularly personal servitudes and predial servitudes. We will see then, for example, how, under the law of usufruct, a person called the *usufructuary* can be given the right to use and enjoy a thing (*usus* and *fructus*), while the right of disposal (*abusus*) remains with another person called *the naked owner*. And we will see how, under the law of predial servitudes, one landowner can acquire limited rights to use someone else's land for a particular purpose like crossing that land to reach a public road.

Of course, one can imagine a much longer and more complex list of rights associated with ownership. The legal philosopher Tony Honoré once famously identified eleven "leading incidents" of ownership: the right to possess (which includes the right to exclude), the right to use, the right to manage, the right to the income of the thing (*fructus*), the right to the capital (which includes the right to alienate and the right to consume, waste or destroy), the right to security (an immunity from expropriation except under limited contexts), the rights or incidents of transmissibility and absence of term (heritability at death and potentially infinite duration of ownership), the duty to prevent harm, liability to execution (to satisfy a debt), and the incident of residuarity (the notion that when a lesser interest terminates, the full interest in a thing re-emerges in the owner). TONY HONORÉ, OWNERSHIP, IN MAKING LAW BIND: ESSAYS LEGAL AND PHILOSOPHICAL, 161, 165–179 (1987). *See also* GREGORY S. ALEXANDER AND EDUORDO PEÑALVER, AN INTRODUCTION TO PROPERTY THEORY 4 (2012). How many of these incidents are implied in Article 477 of the Civil Code? Keep this list of incidents of ownership in mind as we proceed through this casebook and consider whether Louisiana property law associates a similar set of rights with its notion of ownership.

6. The Historical Origins of Article 477

The revision comments to Article 477 indicate that the Civil Code's current definition of ownership is derived in part from the commentary of the French jurist **Marcel Planiol (1853–1931)**. Planiol was a distinguished law professor at the University of Paris. He wrote an influential treatise entitled "Traité Élémentaire de Droit Civil," or, in English, "An Elementary Treatise on the Civil Law," a detailed commentary on the French Civil Code of 1804. The first edition of Planiol's treatise was published in 1899. After the publication of the eighth edition, another French jurist, George Ripert, continued to update the treatise and published several more editions. The twelfth edition of this treatise, published in 1939, was eventually translated into English by the Louisiana State Law Institute in 1959. That version of Planiol's treatise, the twelfth edition updated by Ripert, has exerted a profound influence on the development of Louisiana law over the last sixty years. You will see many references to it and to other editions of Planiol and Ripert's work in Louisiana judicial decisions and scholarly commentary.

The revision comments to current Article 477 openly acknowledge Planiol's influence when they state:

> Ownership is the right by virtue of which a thing is subjected perpetually and exclusively, to the acts and will of a person.

La. Civ. Code art. 477 rev. cmt. (b) (quoting 3 PLANIOL ET RIPERT, TRAITÉ PRATIQUE DE DROIT CIVIL FRANÇAIS 220 (2d ed. Picard 1952)). Notice the emphasis on the potentially perpetual nature of ownership, which we pointed out above, and the fundamental characteristic of exclusivity — the gatekeeper right associated with ownership.

Perhaps the first systematic definition of ownership (or *dominium*), however, comes from Bartolus of Sassoferrato, whom we met in Peter Stein's essay in Chapter One. Bartolus described ownership this way:

> What then is ownership? Respond: the right to totally dispose of a corporeal thing unless prohibited by law.

BARTOLUS OF SASSOFERRATO, COMMENTARIA IN PRIMAM DIGESTI NOVI PARTEM, Ad l. Si quis vi; D.41.2.17.1. Moving forward several centuries, Article 544 of the French Civil Code defines ownership, in language quite reminiscent of Bartolus, as "the right of enjoying and disposing of things in the most absolute manner, provided they are not used in a way prohibited by the laws or regulations." C. Civ. 544 (1804).

Planiol found the French Civil Code's definition deficient in several ways. First, it only drew attention to the supposedly "absolute" nature of ownership, without taking sufficient account of other, more specific, attributes — particularly the various specific ownership rights we discussed above. Second, the description of an owner's powers of enjoyment and disposition as "absolute" was misleading because the law in reality was full of restrictions limiting an owner's ability to enjoy or transfer an object of ownership, as the final clause in Article 544 itself implied.

For Planiol, several more specific attributes of ownership were just as, if not more, salient than the simple idea of absoluteness. These attributes included: (1) the *exclusiveness* of ownership, which, as we have seen, the current definition of ownership underscores; (2) the potentially *perpetual* nature of ownership rights; and (3) the theoretically unlimited power of the owner *to dispose* of a thing, by "consuming it, by physically destroying it, and by transforming its substance," powers that are certainly subsumed within the right of *abusus*. Planiol, TREATISE ON THE CIVIL LAW, Vol. 1, Part 2. §§ 2329, 2330, 2332 (La. Law. Inst. Transl., 1959).

One of the essential characteristics of ownership identified previously by Planiol is exclusivity. Even here Planiol was careful to emphasize the limitations of this characteristic. Planiol pointed out that ownership "consists in the attribution of a thing to a given person to the exclusion of all others." Planiol, § 2329. Assessing the physical extent of ownership of a tangible object like land, Planiol observed that the owner of the soil owned everything beneath the surface "usque ad inferos" (to the center of the earth), and all aerial space above the surface "usque ad coelum" (to the heavens). *Id.* But Planiol pointed out that this right of a land owner to exert exclusive dominion over all that was below or above the surface was limited by other laws, for example, regulations concerning mines and aviation rights established by statutes or by courts. *Id.* § 2329A.

When the drafters of the latest revision of the Louisiana Civil Code turned to Article 477, they drew on Planiol's insights as well as elements of Article 491 of the 1870 Civil Code that contained this more nuanced understanding of ownership. The current version of Article 477 provides a clear textual warning that an owner's right to use, enjoy and alienate, though theoretically direct, immediate and exclusive, can nevertheless only be exercised "within the limits and under the conditions established by law." La. Civ. Code art. 477(A) (1979). Hence, the adjective "absolute" found in Article 544 of the French Civil Code is not present in Louisiana's definition of ownership. Many examples of the limits and conditions imposed on ownership under Louisiana law will be considered throughout this casebook.

7. Civil Law "Ownership" versus Common Law "Estates"

What we have learned so far about the concept of ownership in the civil law may seem quite subtle. Interestingly, though, the concept of ownership in common law property is perhaps even harder to pin down. This elusiveness stems from the historical underpinnings of English common law. The excerpt below, from an essay authored by John Merryman, a distinguished comparative law scholar who taught at Stanford University Law School for many years, compares the civil law conception of ownership with the concept of "estates in land" in Anglo-American common law.

The initial Restatement of the Law Property, published in 1936, defined "an estate" in the following terms:

> The word "estate" as it is used in this Restatement; means an interest in land which
>
> (a) is or may become possessory; and
>
> (b) its ownership is measured in terms of duration.

RESTATEMENT (FIRST) PROPERTY: INTRODUCTION AND FREEHOLD ESTATES § 9 (1936). Put simply, an *estate* is a kind of property right in which a person's interest in land is measured in terms of duration. Further, the person who holds this property interest may be able to enjoy possession immediately or may have to wait to take possession until some future event occurs.

The Restatement followed upon its definition of estate by clarifying that an "owner" is "the person who has one or more interests." *Id.* § 10. The comments to Section 10 of the Restatement are slightly more illuminating and bring us closer to the civilian conception of ownership by noting that "[a] person who has the totality of rights, powers, privileges and immunities which constitute complete property in a thing . . . is the 'owner' of the 'thing' or 'owns' the 'thing.'" *Id.* rev. cmt. (b). Notice here in all of these definitional statements both the focus on interests *in land* and the highly abstract nature of the concepts.

Merryman's essay will help you see how the common law developed this land-based and highly technical notion of ownership and estates. Understanding the common law lawyer's vocabulary "of estates" will also help you translate our civilian concept of full ownership into the common law lexicon of "fee simple estates" and other estates in land. Furthermore, grasping how the two legal systems, common law and civil law, approach the foundational issue of how to define the building blocks of property should help you appreciate the formal simplicity and elegance of civilian legal thinking. It may also cause you to begin to make some institutional choice comparisons. Are there any practical advantages or disadvantages to grounding a property law system in "estates" compared to the notion of ownership? Does the civil law create its own version of "estates" through its formal mechanisms for dismembering ownership?

John Henry Merryman, *Ownership and Estate (Variations on a Theme by Lawson)*
48 Tul. L. Rev. 916, 921–25, 927–29 (1974)

. . . The principal relevant concepts of the common law [of property], and hence of American law, are the estates. Neither they nor the legal system of which they are a part existed prior to the Norman Conquest. English society, government, and property law begin together and grow up together, and consequently they share the same history. In this history the law of property plays a very important role, and, although the process of secularization has gone very far, it has never reached the point of effective systematic codification. American lawyers still learn their property law historically, and they usually begin with the victory of Duke William of Normandy at Hastings in 1066.

At Hastings, William decisively defeated the assembled forces of the English barons and became conqueror and undisputed ruler of England. From the strong central power position so established, he instituted reforms that consolidated and strengthened the royal authority and led ultimately to the transformation of English society, government, and law. The most important of these reforms, for present purposes, was that he established, and he and his successors maintained, the theory that all of English land belonged to him by right of conquest. No person owned land except the king; he owned it all. Further, he retained his ownership. When he distributed lands among his retainers and the Church, and when he confirmed the holdings of those English barons who had supported him, William did so on the feudal model. They became, in every case, his tenants; they held the land but did not own it. These, in turn, distributed their holdings among lesser persons in the familiar form of the feudal ladder, sometimes with many rungs. At the top was the king, who was always lord and never tenant. At the bottom was the villein, who occupied and tilled the land, and who was always tenant and never lord. Between were those who were tenants of those above them and lords of those below.

The tenant held the land under certain obligations to his lord, depending on the nature of his tenure, and he could be removed from the land for failure to perform them. The kinds of service he was required to perform varied with the type of tenure, from something as lowly as tilling the land or tending flocks to such exalted functions as furnishing and leading knights in the king's army or filling important positions in government and the royal household. At every level of the feudal scale was a court that combined advisory, legislative, and judicial functions in which the lord presided and his tenants attended, and to whose jurisdiction they were subject.

In this way the land tenure system of feudal England was also the basis of government, of the military system, and of revenue and supply. One's tenure of land determined his wealth, his power, his social status, his career, the court he attended, and the jurisdiction to which he was subject. Even the Church was made to fit into the feudal model; it held its lands as tenant with the obligation to perform services that, however, were hardly burdensome, since at most they involved the exercise of traditional religious functions. Thus, the theory of feudalism was pushed farther under the Norman kings than it ever had been in Anglo-Saxon England or in France, and English land law became the most thoroughly feudal in Europe.

The history of the decay and transformation of this system in succeeding centuries fills many books, and the reader must go to them for an understanding of how these great changes took place. It is enough to say that every branch of the American law of the twentieth century bears the marks of its feudal origins and that nowhere are these marks so obvious and indelible as in the law of property. Of all the legacies of that period, the institution of royal ownership, and hence of universal tenure, of land is the one of most relevance to the present discussion. In it one finds the key to an understanding of that peculiar common law concept, the estate in land.

For the Italian lawyer, however, large periods of history are irrelevant to the field of property law. The work of Justinian is the starting point, and any interest in the development of property institutions in classical and earlier times is at most remote. The vulgar Roman law that developed as the Western Empire decayed and eventually collapsed has left few marks on contemporary Italian property institutions. The subsequent infusion of Germanic principles, particularly under the Holy Roman Empire, and the later development of feudal institutions in the middle ages undoubtedly produced a great body of customary law that was applied, with wide local variations, throughout the peninsula. But, with codification in the nineteenth century, the revived Roman system emerged as the victor in competition with the customary law, and the victory was complete. So far as the land law is concerned, all elements of feudalism and much of customary law were wiped out, leaving no trace. The return to or reception of Roman law was perhaps even exaggerated in emphasis, in reaction to the "undemocratic" character attributed to customary feudal institutions. The contemporary civil law of property is thus the result of a revolution, rather than an evolution. It is based on a rejection of customary law and is a conscious return to Justinian. It does not smell of the dark ages. It has no flavor of feudalism, no scent of Charlemagne, no aroma of Leonardo. . . .

Ownership is, as concepts go, a very powerful one, and those who employ it pay its price. The land law of Italy and other civil law nations, based firmly on Roman law, is a law of individual ownership. It is part of the tyranny of the concept of ownership that it strongly resists fragmentation. To say that I own a thing is to imply that you do not, for if it is yours how can it be mine? Such thinking thus tends to eliminate all intermediate possibilities between ownership and non-ownership. Consequently, when it becomes desirable to equate power over land with more than one person it seems preferable to do so by a device which, at least apparently, avoids dividing ownership. In every transaction ownership must be transferred *in toto* or not at all.

This, although simplified, gives some of the flavor of ownership in the Italian land law. Although its non-legal composition may vary from time to time with social and economic change, legal ownership remains exclusive, single, and indivisible. Only one person can own the same thing at the same time. But, since the requirements of society are such that power over land must frequently be divided between individuals, it becomes necessary to rationalize the dictates of theory and the requirements of practice. If the theory is a powerful one it will resist, and in this way the achievement of practical ends will be retarded.

The inconsistency between ownership and fragmentation can, of course, be exaggerated. Even in the civil law, land can be "owned" simultaneously by two or more persons *in comune*, a form of co-ownership much like our tenancy in common. But a functional division between beneficial and security title, or between legal and equitable title, or a temporal division into present and future estates, simply does not exist. Ownership is, in theory, indivisible in function and time. . . .

The contrast with English theory is remarkable. In England, ownership resided in the king, and the distribution and retention of lands throughout the kingdom was carried out according to the theory of tenure. Those who actually occupied and used the great mass of English land were not owners of it but holders of derivative rights from the king or from the king's tenants, and hence English land law was concerned not with ownership and the rights and duties of owners but with tenure and the rights and duties of tenants. The concept of ownership simply did not come into play.

This basic difference between Romanic ownership and the Anglo-American "estate" or "interest" in land can be illustrated by a simple metaphor. Romanic ownership can be thought of as a box, with the word "ownership" written on it. Whoever has the box is the "owner." In the case of complete, unencumbered ownership, the box contains certain rights, including that of use and occupancy, that to the fruits or income, and the power of alienation. The owner can, however, open the box and remove one or more such rights and transfer them to others. But, as long as he keeps the box, he still has the ownership, even if the box is empty. The contrast with the Anglo-American law of property is simple. There is no box. There are merely various sets of legal interests. One who has the fee simple absolute has the largest possible bundle of such sets of legal interests. When he conveys one or more of them to another person, a part of his bundle is gone.

This basic difference has several possible theoretical consequences. First, tenure seems to be a more flexible concept than ownership. Consequently, it might be expected that the number and variety of institutionalized interests in land will be greater in a tenure than in an ownership property system. In short, improvisation is likely to be inhibited by the theory of ownership and encouraged by that of tenure.

The much greater variety of permissible future interests (vested and contingent remainders, executory interests, powers of appointment, reversions, rights of entry, possibilities of reverter) in the common law than in the civil law (where they really do not exist) supports this prediction. It is further supported by the existence of the trust and the concept of separate legal and equitable interests and by the distinction between security interests and beneficial interests in land, both found in the common law but not in the civil law.

The second consequence is somewhat more subtle, but tends to produce the same effect. The analytical jurist has little difficulty in establishing that, in a certain sense, both ownership and tenure are simply methods by which the law allocates interests among persons with respect to the land. Whatever their source, these interests have legal effect only as they are recognized and enforced by the legal system. To say that one owns land is merely to say he has certain legal relations with respect to it, and analytically this is equally true of tenure. But in less analytical times ownership was not so understood. One said of A that he owned the land, not that the law had fixed certain legal relations between him and others with respect to it.

In England, during the formative period of its property law, the dominance of the tenure concept necessarily made this distinction more obvious. Lawyer and layman alike were compelled to deal with tenure—legal relations having their source in the legal system—and to realize that they were doing so. Thus, the English law began as law about rights with respect to land rather than about ownership of it. The nature and extent of these rights could vary widely, depending in part on the agreement of the parties, in part on custom, and to a large extent on the will of the dominant party—the lord. Eventually, these conventional arrangements became fixed and limited and were given distinctive names. As a group they were called estates, and each kind of estate became to some extent reified—it became a thing that could be "owned." But the initial distinction between ownership and tenure prevented the oversimplification of the relationship between man and land that came so easily to the Roman law. The most that could be said of the Englishman was that he "owned" or "held" or was "seised of" an estate in the land, so that the estate was a legal concept interposed between the tenant and the land.

The estate is a relatively pure legal device. Although Englishmen would fight and romanticize about their estates, still it was not as easy to become concerned in a theoretical way about their nature and origins as was the case with ownership. "Estate" offered no aspect of indivisibility, nor did it hint of divine or natural or socioeconomic justification. It was a tool, not a weapon. Ownership, on the contrary, even as employed by Romanists and Civilists, has always seemed to have a life and vigor of its own. It is easy to speculate about its source and its functions. Speculation of this kind may easily become debate about private property, and this opens the door to the full range of questions about man and the state, man and his nature, and man and God. No culture has successfully freed ownership of such associations. It is a loaded concept.

Thus, the working theoretical unit of the English land law was, in its critical period, a legal abstraction free of the extra-legal associations and the inhibitions imposed by the Roman concept of ownership. This does not, of course, imply any superiority of one to the other; it merely illustrates a fundamental and highly important theoretical difference in legal theory during the formative period of the common law. In later centuries this distinction became, in a sense, less real as power over land moved from the king and the lord to the tenant in possession under an estate. Eventually the practical difference between a tenant in fee simple in England and an owner in Italy became, for some purposes, insignificant. Indeed, it might be said that, in England, a point was reached in which he who was in theory merely a tenant had all the practical advantages of ownership and he who was technically owner had none.

Notes and Questions

1. The excerpt from Professor Merryman's essay connects the notion of "estates" in English property law to the feudal land tenure system introduced after Duke William of Normandy won a decisive victory at Hastings in 1066. English common law (as such) was born under the reign of Plantagenet King Henry II (1133–1189), who elevated and unified the divergent customs in England to the law *common* to the entire country. Lay persons organized in Inns of Court, agencies for the legal education of barristers, mounted a challenge to the monopoly on legal knowledge enjoyed by the clergy. Just after the Magna Carta, **Henry Lord Bracton** (ca. 1210–1268), the Father of Common Law, thoroughly elaborated the English common law system in his work *ON THE LAWS AND CUSTOMS OF ENGLAND*. During the Elizabethan era, the entrenchment of the common law was guided by **Edward Coke** (1552–1634) and **Francis Bacon** (1561–1626). Bracton's work, along with that of Coke and Bacon,

remained the premier sources for legal reference until **William Blackstone** (1723–1780) organized and explicated the entire body of England's common law in his *COMMENTARIES ON THE LAWS OF ENGLAND* (published between 1765 and 1769). The drafters of Louisiana's first Civil Code, the Digest of 1808, along with Louisiana's early nineteenth century judges, were well aware of Blackstone's *COMMENTARIES* and occasionally drew on it in their work.

2. In the United States, the English terminology has survived, but the break with the feudal system in England is eloquently embodied by the second section of the Declaration of Independence (July 4, 1776), which reads: "We hold these truths to be self-evident, that all men are created equal, that they are endowed by their creator with certain inalienable Rights, that among these are Life, Liberty, and the pursuit of Happiness." Scholars have debated the sources of this language. In his *Two Treatises of Government*, **John Locke** (1632–1704) argued that political society was entrusted with the protection of property, which he defined as a person's "life, liberty, and estate." The word "estate" did not carry over into the Declaration of Independence. Rather, the phrase "pursuit of happiness" was chosen, a natural law concept found in the works of Blackstone, **Gottfried Wilhelm Leibniz** (1646–1716), and **Emer de Vattel** (1714–1767).

3. In Louisiana civil law, we also use the term "estate," but in a much narrower sense than in Anglo-American common law. In the law governing predial servitudes, for instance, the term "estate" (from the French *héritage*) refers to a distinct corporeal immovable (for example a tract of land or a building) that is either benefitted or burdened by a servitude. *See* La. Civ. Code arts. 646–47 (1977). A predial servitude is a real right that establishes a charge on a servient "estate" for the benefit of a dominant "estate." La. Civ. Code art. 646 (1977). A simple example of a predial servitude would be a servitude of passage that allows the owner of one tract of land (the dominant estate) to cross over a neighboring estate (the servient estate) at a convenient location to reach a public road. *See* La. Civ. Code art. 705 (1977).

In the Civil Code, the term "estate" is also used in the law of successions. A "succession" means "the transmission of the *estate* of the deceased to his successors." La. Civ. Code art. 871 (1981) (emphasis added). The term "estate" in this context refers to "the property, rights, and obligations that a person leaves after his death, whether the property exceeds the charges or the charges exceed the property, or whether he has only left charges without any property." La. Civ. Code art. 872 (1981). When a person dies, all of the decedent's estate immediately passes to the decedent's successors, whether testate or intestate. La. Civ. Code art. 935 (1997).

4. Which basic building block—the civilian concept of ownership or the common law notion of estates—do you think is a more efficient or flexible platform upon which to build a property law system? In a recent article, two leading scholars explore this subject and argue that the biggest difference between the civil law and common law approaches to property are found in the *style* used to characterize these building blocks of property rather than in any functional or structural differences between the two systems. *See* Yun-chien Chang & Henry E. Smith, *An*

Economic Analysis of Civil versus Common Law Property, 88 Notre Dame L. Rev. 1 (2012). Do you agree that the difference is primarily one of style and not structure?

B. Exclusive Authority and Trespass

1. Immovable Property

As central as the definition of ownership in Article 477 may be in the structure of Louisiana property law, paradoxically few Louisiana judicial opinions interpret or apply the article. Judicial decisions addressing trespass claims will enable us to develop some sense of how an owner's exclusive authority over a thing functions in Louisiana law. While some of the judicial decisions that follow illustrate the centrality of an owner's "direct, immediate, and *exclusive* authority" over a thing, others reveal how the law, as Planiol suggested, establishes limits on the exclusive authority of an owner.

Discussions of trespass in Louisiana often arise in two specific contexts. First, and not surprisingly, they arise in criminal trespass actions. They also appear frequently in delictual actions arising under Article 2315 of the Louisiana Civil Code, which provides that "[e]very act whatever of man that causes damage to another obliges him by whose fault it happened to repair it." La. Civ. Code art. 2315(A). In practice, Louisiana courts have frequently turned to common law tort causes of action, like trespass, to give more specific content to the general principle of delictual responsibility articulated in Article 2315. In Chapter Thirteen we will see how Louisiana courts have used other common law concepts in cases resolving property law disputes among neighbors.

In the first case below, *Lacombe v. Carter*, 957 So.2d 687 (La. App. 3 Cir. 2008), the plaintiff, Lacombe, brings a tort suit seeking monetary damages for the harm he claims to have suffered as a result of the defendants' alleged trespass on his land. In the second case, *Perrin v. Randy Tupper Homes*, 21 So.3d 474 (La. App. 3 Cir. 2009), the plaintiffs, a married couple, bring a tort action against a landowner for injuries they allegedly suffered while they were on the defendant's property. In this case the court discusses a criminal trespass statute in detail.

Lacombe v. Carter

975 So.2d 687 (La. App. 3 Cir. 2008)

DECUIR, Judge. This is a trespass action based on the defendants' refusal to remove duck blinds and other structures from the plaintiff's property.

Facts

Plaintiff, Randy Lacombe, purchased property adjacent to Saline Bayou. A portion of the purchased property is inundated by water due to a control structure built by the State in the 1960s. Prior to Lacombe's purchase, the defendants, Shawn N.

Daze, Brian Mabou, Marvin Carter, Jr., and William L. Smith, had erected duck blinds and a floating boathouse on the property. Subsequently, Lacombe asked the defendants to remove the structures. They refused, and Lacombe filed this suit alleging trespass on the part of the defendants. Defendants then circulated flyers and posted signs stating that Lacombe was endangering hunting and fishing rights in the Saline Bayou area.

D argument →

Subsequently, the defendants answered and filed an exception alleging that the inundated area is a navigable waterway and that the State of Louisiana (State) owns or has a servitude over the property and is, therefore, an indispensable party. The trial court granted the exception, and the State was joined as a party. . . . [The court of appeal ultimately declared defendants' arguments about navigable water bodies to be a "red herring." — Eds.]

Trial Ct. ordered D to vacate

The trial court declared the boundary to be as that presented in evidence, ordered the defendants to vacate Lacombe's property and remove existing structures, and enjoined them from future entry.

D trespassed

In addition, the trial court concluded that the defendants did trespass on Lacombe's property and awarded Lacombe damages of $5,000.00 from each of the defendants.

The defendants, Daze and Mabou, lodged this appeal.

Trespass

D claim -no trespass - excessive damages

The defendants assert that the trial court erred in finding they had committed a trespass and in awarding excessive damages. . . . In the midst of much discussion about boundaries, navigable waterways, and hunting rights, the trial court was faced with a simple action in trespass. Accordingly, we will focus our attention on the tort of trespass.

In discussing trespass, this court has said:

A trespass occurs when there is an unlawful physical invasion of the property or possession of another person. Additionally,

what PL need to show →

In an action for trespass, it is incumbent upon the plaintiff to show damages based on the result or the consequences of an injury flowing from the act of trespass. The damages must be proved by a preponderance of the evidence, and this burden of proof may be met by either direct or circumstantial evidence. One who is wronged by a trespass may recover general damages suffered, including mental and physical pain, anguish, distress, and inconvenience.

Griffin v. Abshire, 04-37, p. 11 (La. App. 3 Cir. 6/2/04), 878 So.2d 750, 757–58, *writ denied,* 04-1663 (La. 10/8/04), 883 So.2d 1018 (citations omitted).

➤ In the case before us, Lacombe is in actual possession of the property in question, and the defendants do not claim ownership in themselves. The appropriate burden of proof for Lacombe is well settled in our law.

Under these circumstances, it is not necessary that plaintiff should show a title perfect in all respects; and, even if there be defects in plaintiff's title, they are not available as a defense to defendant company, a mere trespasser. *JAMISON V. SMITH*, 35 La. Ann. 609. . . .

River & Rail Terminals v. La. Ry. & Nav. Co., 171 La. 223, 236, 130 So. 337, 341 (1930). "A prima facie title is good against trespassers." *Gould v. Bebee*, 134 La. 123, 126, 63 So. 848, 849 (1913).

The question for this court is whether the trial court correctly concluded that the defendants had committed a trespass. The trial court summarized the evidence in its written reasons for judgment as follows:

Mr. Lacombe produced deeds, a survey, official state maps, and testimony showing he has title to the land where the defendants' blinds and floating structures are located. He produced the expert testimony of Jessie Lachney, showing the defendants['] blinds and floating structure are located on land, acquired and included in the 2000 sale. Lachney used a GPS unit to locate the exact position of the blinds and floating structure relative to Lacombe's property line. The State's representative, John P. Evans, Jr., P.L.S. Chief, Titles, Surveys & GIS of the State Land Office, also testified that the defendants['] blinds and floating structure are on Lacombe's land and that the State makes no claim to Lacombe's inundated land.

After reviewing the evidence, it is clear that Lacombe has met his burden of proof with regard to his title and its limits. The defendants have produced no evidence that establishes the boundary is not as agreed by Lacombe and the State and represented in the judgment of the trial court. Moreover, this court has consistently held that a trial court's determination of a boundary location is a finding of fact which will not be disturbed on appeal unless it is manifestly erroneous. *Lamson Petroleum Co. v. Hallwood Petroleum, Inc.*, 99-1444 (La. App. 3 Cir. 5/24/00), 770 So.2d 786, *writ denied*, 00-2568 (La. 11/27/00), 775 So.2d 448. . . . Accordingly, we find no manifest error in the trial court's determination that the defendants committed a trespass on Lacombe's property.

We next turn to defendants' claim that the trial court's damage award was excessive. In an action for trespass, the plaintiff must show damages based on the result or the consequences of an injury flowing from the act of trespass. *Bell v. Sediment Removers, Inc.*, 479 So.2d 1078 (La. App. 3 Cir. 1985), *writ denied*, 481 So.2d 1350 (La. 1986). The damages must be proved by a preponderance of the evidence, and this burden of proof may be met by either direct or circumstantial evidence. *Id.* One who is wronged by a trespass may recover general damages suffered, including mental and physical pain, anguish, distress, and inconvenience. *Ard v. Samedan Oil Corp.*, 483 So.2d 925 (La. 1986). Mental anguish does not result of necessity from a trespass or the encroachment on a person's property. Even though mental anguish may be compensable, it must be proven with sufficient evidence. *Bell*, 479 So.2d 1078. However, mental anguish does not require proof that medical or psychiatric care was required as a result of the incident, but minimal worry and inconvenience should not be compensated. *Phillips v. Town of Many,* 538 So.2d 745 (La. App. 3 Cir. 1989).

In the present case, Lacombe was prevented from using or leasing his property to the fullest extent by the presence of defendants' blinds and floating structure. In addition, the defendants intentionally set out to attack Lacombe's standing in the community by placing flyers naming him as a party seeking to take away the hunting and fishing rights of sportsmen. Lacombe testified that some individuals quit frequenting his hardware business because of the flyers produced by the defendants. Under these circumstances, we do not find the trial court's damage award to be manifestly erroneous. . . .

Decree

For the foregoing reasons, the judgment of the trial court is affirmed. All costs of these proceedings are taxed to defendants Shawn N. Daze and Brian Mabou.

Notes and Questions

1. In *Lacombe v. Carter,* 975 So.2d 687 (La. App. 3 Cir. 2008), the court defines a trespass as "an unlawful physical invasion of the property or possession of another person." Take note that in this standard definition the court is careful to recognize that a claim for trespass can be brought not only by a true owner (someone who has "property" in a thing, as this definition and common law courts often put it), but also by someone who is a mere *possessor* of a thing. This policy of treating owners and possessors similarly for purposes of who is eligible to assert a trespass claim against a third person is significant. In some ways, possessors do function in the law just like owners, and possession is sometimes treated in Louisiana law as a proxy for ownership. We will consider possession and the rights and powers of possessors in later chapters.

In another recent case illustrating the importance of a plaintiff's legal identity in a trespass action, an appellate court affirmed the dismissal of a trespass action because the person bringing the cause of action was neither the owner nor the possessor of the immovable property that had been entered by the defendants without the permission of its owner or possessor. *Richard v. Richard,* 24 So.3d 292, 297–98 (La. App. 3 Cir. 2009). In *Richard,* the court determined that someone could potentially state a trespass action against the defendants for allegedly delivering furniture and belongings and depositing them in a house's driveway without the consent of its then owner (the plaintiff's deceased mother) even if the unlawful entry was unintentional. *Id.* at 296–97. Nevertheless, the court affirmed the granting of a peremptory exception of "no right of action" under Article 927 of the Louisiana Code of Civil Procedure because the plaintiff was neither the owner nor the possessor of the house. As the court observed, the plaintiff did not allege that he had any "real right" in the house; all he contended was that he occupied or resided in his mother's house. *Id.* at 297–98.

2. In *Lacombe*, once the question of whether the defendants had committed a physical invasion of the plaintiff's property was answered in the plaintiff's favor, the court then turned to the question of damages. Notice the court's statement that a plaintiff seeking damages for trespass must prove "damages based on the result or consequences of an injury flowing from the act of trespass." One might interpret this statement to mean that a plaintiff who brings a trespass action in tort under Louisiana law is entitled only to direct, compensatory damages—damages attributable to some physical harm to his property or some directly ensuing economic injury caused by the trespass. This is the approach that some common law jurisdictions in the United States have followed for years. *See Shiffman v. Empire Blue Cross & Blue Shield*, 681 N.Y.S.2d 511 (N.Y. App. Div. 1998) (no punitive damages available when reporters fraudulently gained entrance to a medical clinic because the entry was not motivated by malice). Not all courts agree.

In a much discussed decision, the Wisconsin Supreme Court affirmed a jury's punitive damage award of $100,000 in favor of a couple who owned a farm and against a mobile home distributor that intentionally trespassed across the farm in the middle of winter to deliver a mobile home to a neighboring property owner. *Jacque v. Steenberg Homes, Inc.*, 563 N.W.2d 154 (Wisc. 1997). In *Jacque*, the trespass caused no physical damage or economic harm to the plaintiffs and the jury awarded only $1 in nominal damages. Yet the Wisconsin court affirmed the jury's $100,000 punitive damage award. In general, punitive damages (or "exemplary" damages) are designed to punish a defendant in a civil action and to discourage other persons from engaging in the same kind of wrongful conduct as the defendant. In a subsequent decision, the Wisconsin Supreme Court pointed out that its ruling in *Jacque* was still an exception to the general rule that punitive damages are only available in a tort action when the claimant recovers compensatory damages and that the holding in *Jacque* has not been extended beyond the circumstances of that case. *C & A Investments v. Kelly*, 792 N.W.2d 644, 647 (Wisc. 2010).

In Louisiana tort law, punitive damages are generally disfavored and only allowed in very narrow circumstances. *See e.g.*, La. Civ. Code arts. 2315.3, 2315.4, 2315.7 (allowing exemplary damages in cases involving child pornography, drunk driving and criminal sexual activity with a minor). How does the court in *Lacombe* respond to this limitation? Is the court in *Lacombe* using the concept of "general damages," including "mental anguish," as a substitute for punitive damages? What was Lacombe's real harm that the court wanted to address in this case?

In another recent decision, a Louisiana appellate court *reduced* a general damage award in a case involving a "trespass to chattel" (*i.e.*, an unlawful interference with a person's movable property). *Dubuy v. Luse*, 17 So.3d 425 (La. App. 2 Cir. 2009). There, the defendant, a co-worker of Jacueline Dubuy, maliciously vandalized the plaintiff's car by placing nails and screws in the car's tires on several occasions. The total damage to the plaintiff's car was less than $1,000. *Id.* at 426. The trial court awarded general damages in the amount of $225,000 ($150,000 to Jacqueline and $75,000 to her husband and children). *Id.* The appellate court observed that the defendant had "terrorized" the plaintiff for over three months but reduced the damage award to a total of $75,000 ($50,000 for Jacqueline and $25,000 for her husband and children). *Id*. at 428–29.

In yet another decision, *Williams v. City of Baton Rouge*, 731 So.2d 240, 254 (La. 1999), the Louisiana Supreme Court found that the City of Baton Rouge/Parish of East Baton Rouge trespassed when it entered the land of several property owners against their will, and without, instituting a proper expropriation proceeding, and, accompanied by armed police officers, excavated three large ditches to prevent flooding of a neighborhood. The Court concluded that the property owners were entitled to compensatory and mental anguish damages, even though the City/Parish was acting with a public purpose in mind. *Id*.

Finally, after employees of the Town of Rayville mistakenly demolished a local resident's 1900 square foot building and thus committed trespass, the Louisiana Second Circuit Court of Appeal affirmed a trial court award of $2,500 in actual damages for the value of the building, $2,500 in special damages for the contents of the building. *Moss v. Town of Rayville*, 181 So.3d 809 (La. App. 2 Cir. 2015). The appellate court further affirmed the trial court's *denial* of damages for mental anguish and inconvenience after noting the "deplorable" condition of the building on the date of its accidental destruction, the fact that it was "unsecured and open to vandalism," and the plaintiff's evident "failure to stop the harm" which "demonstrated a lack of genuine concern on his part for any property of value." *Id*.

Perrin v. Randy Tupper Homes

21 So.3d 474 (La. App. 3 Cir. 2009), *writ denied*, 27 So.3d 848 (La. 2010)

COOKS, Judge. Hunter Perrin and his wife, Mary J. Perrin (Plaintiffs), while driving through a developing subdivision on a Sunday afternoon, focused their attention on a town-house nearing completion in Graywood Subdivision, Lake Charles, Louisiana (Graywood). The couple, looking to purchase a new home in Graywood, stopped to take a closer look at the home, observing that it appeared to be near completion and perhaps available for purchase. Although it is disputed whether this town-house had a "for sale" sign posted, it is undisputed and admitted by Defendant Tupper there were no signs, tape, nor barricade warning, preventing, or prohibiting persons from entering upon the premises. Defendants' own exhibit in support of the Motion for Summary Judgment demonstrates there was signage against the exterior wall of the house advertising Tupper Homes posted on the property. The sign included a telephone number and contact names. The development had several homes and town-homes under various stages of construction, many posted with "for sale" signs, as well as many signs advertising various builders, contractors, and construction companies in the subdivision, including Tupper Homes.

There was no concrete or paved walkway leading to the house. Instead, a series of wooden pallets were placed on the damp ground to fashion a makeshift walkway from the street to the garage to allow access to the home. The photograph in evidence depicts such a wooden pallet directly in front of the Tupper Homes sign. Because the ground was "tacky and damp" that day, Plaintiffs decided to use the pallet walkway to get to the town-house from the street. As she walked across the wooden pallets, Mary Perrin fell and allegedly injured her right shoulder. Plaintiffs sued Randy Tupper Homes d/b/a Fantasy Homes, Inc., the general contractor building the town-house, and Employers Mutual Casualty Company (Defendants), its general liability insurer.

Trial Court

The trial court granted summary judgment in favor of Defendants dismissing the case, finding Plaintiffs entered the property without express or implied legal consent from either the owner or the custodian of the property. The trial court ruled from the bench and mentioned in its oral reasons for judgment Plaintiffs did not have implied consent to be on the property and were not on the property "for making a delivery or conducting business or communicating with the owner or custodian." Based on these conclusions, the trial court found Plaintiffs were trespassers in violation of La. R.S. 14:63, despite also finding Plaintiffs had a legitimate reason to "look at the property." Under the provisions of La. R.S. 14:63(H), the trial court found Defendants were immune from suit by such trespassers and for these reasons granted summary judgment dismissing Plaintiffs' suit. Plaintiffs appealed alleging the trial court committed legal error and must be reversed. We agree. The judgment of the trial court is reversed and the case is remanded for further proceedings.

Law and Analysis

Plaintiffs did not commit criminal trespass. The provisions of La. R.S. 14:63(F) provide in pertinent part:

> The following persons may enter or remain upon immovable property of another, *unless specifically forbidden to do so by the owner or other person with authority, either orally or in writing*: (3) Any person making a delivery, soliciting, selling any product or service, conducting a survey or poll, a real estate licensee or *other person who has a legitimate reason for making a delivery, conducting business or communicating with the owner, lessee, custodian or a resident of the immovable property,* and who, immediately upon entry, seeks to make the delivery, to conduct business or to conduct the communication (emphasis added).

La. R.S. 14:63(F)(3).

Defendant Tupper admits there were no signs, warning tape, nor barricades whatsoever on the subject property forbidding anyone to enter upon the premises. The trial court made a factual finding that Plaintiffs had a legitimate reason to be on the property, *i.e.* they were looking at the property as prospective home buyers. Under the express provisions of La. R.S.14:63(F)(3) Plaintiffs were "other persons" who had a "legitimate reason" for conducting business or communicating with the owner or a custodian of the property. Plaintiffs testified they were attracted to the home where the accident occurred because it appeared to be the type of house they were looking to purchase in Graywood. Defendant testified he was the sole contractor building houses on the street where the alleged accident occurred. He also testified there were many of his signs throughout Graywood, and on this street, advertising Tupper Homes/Fantasy Homes. Depicted in Defendants' exhibits are his own photographs of the subject property showing a Randy Tupper Homes Design and Construction sign. Defendant also admits some homes were for sale although this particular home was built for identified owners.

The statute does not define "implied consent" and is not necessary that we fashion a definition nor determine whether Mrs. Perrin had implied consent to walk up to the house nearing completion in a developing subdivision with many newly constructed or partially constructed homes for sale. Nevertheless, it would certainly appear that the area was being actively marketed and was intended to invite and attract prospective home buyers like the Plaintiffs. Be that as it may, the pertinent provisions of La. R.S. 14:63 at paragraph F clearly place the burden on the "owner or other person with authority" to either post a written notice forbidding persons from entering upon the property or to orally forbid access. Clearly, neither prohibition was present here. The statute further authorizes certain persons to "enter or remain" upon immovable property of another when there is no notice forbidding entry. Plaintiffs are included in that list of authorized persons: "Any person. . . . who has a legitimate reason for conducting business or communicating with the owner, lessee, custodian or resident . . . who immediately . . . seeks to conduct business or to conduct the communication." La. R.S. 14:63(F)(3). As the trial court found, Plaintiffs obviously had a legitimate reason for conducting business with or communicating with the owner or custodian of the property. Plaintiffs were prospective buyers, not criminal trespassers.

We agree with Plaintiffs that their behavior, engaged in frequently in all developing subdivisions, was not the sort of behavior criminalized by La. R.S. 14:63. Signs in the area were no doubt meant to attract the attention of prospective buyers or home builders who might logically conclude that they were welcome to stop and examine such homes in various stages of completion. It certainly could come as no surprise to Tupper that Plaintiffs, and no doubt many others, might approach these properties to take a closer look, get information, or attempt to make contact with or to conduct business with any representative of the owner or custodian they might encounter by visiting the property. No doubt, it would be disappointing indeed to Tupper if no one showed any interest in the homes he was building in Graywood or in his work being actively advertised through his products in Graywood.

The trial court erred as a matter of law in basing its ruling on whether Mrs. Perrin had implied consent to be on the property, and in making this erroneous application of law, further erred in applying the immunity provisions of La. R.S. 14:63. Because there were no signs posted on the premises forbidding entry thereon, the Plaintiffs were permitted to enter upon the property for legitimate reasons, in this case for the purpose of conducting business with or communicating with the owner or custodian of the immovable property. La. R.S. 14:63(F)(3).

Because the judgment on appeal is a summary judgment, our review is *de novo,* and we employ "the same criteria that govern the trial court's consideration of whether summary judgment is appropriate, i.e., whether there is a genuine issue of material fact and whether the mover is entitled to judgment as a matter of law." *Supreme Serv. & Specialty Co., Inc. v. Sonny Greer, Inc.,* 06-1827, p. 4 (La.5/22/07), 958 So.2d 634, 638. Under the provisions of La. Code Civ. P. art. 966, Defendants, as movers herein, are entitled to summary judgment only if they prove (1) there are no genuine issues of material fact in dispute and (2) they are entitled to judgment as a matter of law. We find Defendants are not entitled to judgment as a matter of law. Plaintiffs were not criminal trespassers as envisioned by La. R.S.14:63 and the immunity protection Defendants affirmatively rely on as a defense does not extend to any person whose activity falls within the exception expressly made in La. R.S. 14:63(F)(3). The ruling of the trial court is reversed and the case is remanded for further proceedings. All cost of appeal are assessed against Defendants.

Reversed and Remanded

AMY, Judge, dissenting. I respectfully dissent from the majority opinion as I find that an affirmation is warranted and that the circumstances of this case do not implicate La. R.S. 14:63(F)(3).

Rather, La. R.S. 14:63(A) provides that "[n]o person shall enter upon immovable property owned by another without express, legal, or implied authorization." In my opinion, the mere construction of this home in a neighborhood under development did not convey authorization for entry onto this privately owned property. Without such authority, and absent intentional acts or gross negligence, "owners, lessors, and custodians of structures, watercraft, movable or immovable property shall not be answerable for damages sustained by any person who enters upon the structure, watercraft, movable or immovable property . . . [.]" La. R.S. 14:63(H). As there was no evidence of intentional acts or gross negligence, I find that the trial court correctly entered summary judgment.

Notes and Questions

1. In *Perrin v. Randy Tupper Homes,* 21 So.3d 474 (La. App. 3 Cir. 2009), *writ denied,* 27 So.3d 848 (La. 2010), the court had to decide whether the plaintiffs, Hunter and Mary Perrin, were trespassing on the property owned by Randy Tupper Homes to determine whether they were among the class of persons who can bring a tort claim for personal injury damages. Interestingly, the court turns to a criminal statute defining who is a trespasser for purposes of answering this question. Is this an appropriate way to frame this dispute? Are there other ways the court could have framed this question?

2. The disagreement between the trial court judge and dissenting Third Circuit Court of Appeal Judge Marc Amy on one hand and the other judges on the Third Circuit appellate panel on the other largely focuses on the legal significance of signage—in this case the presence of "for sale" signs in the development and a

"Tupper Homes" sign on the house at issue, and the absence of any sign clearly warning people not to approach the house. The majority opinion seems to imply that in a situation like this the landowner and homebuilder must erect a clear sign indicating that members of the public are barred from entering upon the premises to avoid liability for personal injuries sustained by persons while on the property. The trial court and dissenting judge imply that persons who want to examine a house under construction must obtain the consent of the owner/builder first to avoid being characterized as trespassers. Who should have the burden of acting here: a landowner/builder or a prospective purchaser examining new homes under construction?

Discusses Procedural Posture

3. This case also introduces us to the importance of the procedural posture in a case. Notice that the trial judge dismissed the Perrin's lawsuit upon a motion for summary judgment, ruling in effect that there were no genuine issues of material fact in dispute and that the movant, Tupper Homes, was entitled to a *summary judgment* under Article 966 of Louisiana Code of Civil Procedure. Thus, the trial court judge resolved the case without allowing a jury to decide the dispute. On appeal, the majority of the Third Circuit could have simply stated that there were genuine issues of material fact in dispute with regard to the issue of whether the plaintiffs had the implied consent of the defendant to enter on the home construction site or whether they had a "legitimate reason to be on the property" within the meaning of La. Rev. Stat. 14:63(F)(3). The majority opinion goes well beyond this, however, and actually rules that the Perrins' entry onto Tupper Homes' property was not an unlawful trespass under these facts as a matter of law because they had a *legitimate reason* to be on the property in question. Do you think the majority opinion was correct in making such a ruling? Should the question of whether the Perrins had "implied consent" or a "legitimate reason" to be on the property in these circumstances be decided by a judge or by a jury after a trial during which the parties can present evidence on this issue?

4. The controlling legislative authority in this case, Louisiana Revised Statute § 14:63, is not in the Civil Code. Instead, it is found in the portion of the Revised Statutes containing most of Louisiana's criminal statutes. The statute provides in pertinent part:

A. No person shall enter any structure, watercraft or movable owned by another without express, legal or implied authorization.

B. No person shall enter upon immovable property owned by another without express, legal or implied authorization.

C. No person shall remain in or upon property, movable or immovable, owned by another, without express, legal or implied authorization.

D. It shall be an affirmative defense to a prosecution for a violation of Subsection A, B or C of this Section, that the accused had express, legal or implied authority to be in the movable or on the immovable property.

. . . .

H. The provisions of any other law notwithstanding, owners, lessees and custodians of structures, watercraft, movable or immovable property shall not be answerable for damages sustained by any person who enters upon the structure, watercraft, movable or immovable property without express, legal or implied authorization, or who without legal authorization, remains upon the structure, watercraft, movable or immovable property after being forbidden by the owner, or other person with the authority to do so; however, the owner, lessee or custodian of the property may be answerable for damages only upon a showing that the damages sustained were the result of the intentional acts or gross negligence of the owner, lessee or custodian.

La. Rev. Stat. § 14:63.

The statute goes on to enumerate several classes of people who may enter or remain on a structure, watercraft, movable or immovable property of another, including: a law officer performing his official duties, a firefighter fighting a fire, emergency medical personal delivering medical assistance, any government employee or public utility employee responding to an emergency presenting an "imminent danger to human safety or health or to the environment." La. Rev. Stat. § 14:63(E).

Another broad class of persons — including professional land surveyors, persons affiliated with the Louisiana Public Service Commission or the Federal Communication Commission, candidates for political office or persons working on behalf of political candidates, livestock owners or their employees trying to retrieve escaped livestock, and the owners of domestic animals trying to retrieve their animals — are authorized "to enter or remain upon immovable property of another, unless specifically forbidden to do so by the owner or other person with authority, either orally or in writing." La. Rev. Stat. § 14:63(F). This provision and subsection H addressing express or implied authorization to enter property were both at issue in *Perrin*. Should the Louisiana legislature amend this statute to address the particular situation raised in *Perrin*?

5. Would an individual who enters a privately owned rail yard that is entirely surrounded by a chain link fence and razor wire except for one unobstructed entrance and does so without the consent of the rail yard owner be considered a trespasser or someone who has a legitimate reason to be on property within the meaning of La. Rev. Stat. § 14:63 as interpreted by the court in *Randy Tupper Homes*? Would it make a difference if the rail yard was a "common crossing point" for area residents and this fact was known to the owners of the rail yard? *See Williams v. Union Pacific Railroad Co.*, 973 F.Supp.2d 684, 686–88 (W.D. La. 2013).

6. Sometimes individuals or companies will enter into a complex agreement allowing one person or entity to enter another's property for specified purposes, and yet a dispute can still arise as to whether the party that acquired the explicit right of entry exceeded the scope of the agreement or committed trespass. For a recent example, see *Spanish Lake Restoration v. Petrodome*, 186 So.3d 230 (La. App. 4 Cir. 2016).

2. Movable Property

The two decisions presented above concern trespass on immovable property. Anglo-American common law courts have often used the term "trespass" when addressing claims involving interference with chattels (or "movables" in Louisiana) as well. In 2011, the Louisiana Supreme Court addressed a novel question raised in a federal court: whether Louisiana law recognizes a distinct cause of action for trespass to movable things, in this case, an underground cable which had been cut. The defendant argued that the plaintiff's proposed jury instruction for such a cause of action—that a defendant can be liable for an inadvertent trespass to a movable resulting from an intentional act—is not a correct statement of Louisiana law.

MCI Communications Services, Inc. v. Hagan
74 So.3d 1148 (La. 2011)

GUIDRY, Justice. We accepted the certified question presented to this court by the United States Court of Appeals, Fifth Circuit, in *MCI Communications Services, Inc. v. Hagan*, 641 F.3d 112 (5th Cir. 2011). The question is this: "Is the proposed jury instruction in this case, which states that '[a] Defendant may be held liable for an inadvertent trespass resulting from an intentional act,' a correct statement of Louisiana law when the trespass at issue is the severing of an underground cable located on property owned by one of the alleged trespass[e]rs, and the property is not subject to a servitude by the owners of the underground cable but only to the contractual right to keep it, as an existing cable, underneath the property?" For the reasons that follow, we answer this question in the negative.

Facts and Procedural History

We decide this certified question on the facts as presented to us by the Court of Appeals. This case arose out of an incident in which an underground cable owned by MCI Communications Services, Inc. (hereinafter, "MCI"), was allegedly severed. MCI filed suit against Wayne Hagan and James Joubert alleging theories of negligence and trespass. MCI alleged that Joubert was negligently excavating with a backhoe in violation of the Louisiana Damage Prevention Act (Louisiana Underground Utilities and Facilities Damage Prevention Law), La.Rev.Stat. 40:1749.11 *et seq.* MCI alleged Hagan was vicariously liable because Joubert was acting as his agent at the time. The underground cable at issue was buried in part under land owned by Hagan. After a trial in the United States District Court for the Eastern District of Louisiana, the jury found for Hagan and Joubert. The district court awarded attorneys' fees to Hagan and Joubert under La.Rev.Stat. 40:1749.14(F) of the Damage Prevention Act. MCI appealed to the Court of Appeals, Fifth Circuit, asserting four separate grounds, only one of which is relevant to our decision today: MCI contended the district court erred when it refused to give the jury MCI's proposed instruction on trespass.

According to the Court of Appeals, on January 20, 2006, defendant Joubert allegedly severed MCI's underground fiber-optic cable while using a backhoe on defendant Hagan's property. MCI contended at trial that the backhoe was being used to install a concrete boat ramp. Hagan and Joubert contended that in the week prior, the two friends decided to go duck hunting on property owned by Hagan. When hunting together, they typically launched an airboat from a boat ramp into a canal on the property. Joubert alleged that he went to Hagan's property on January 20, 2006, to see if Hagan had cleared driftwood from the canal, which needed to be done before they could launch the airboat. Joubert contended that he then drove Hagan's backhoe onto a concrete boat ramp to clear the driftwood before leaving the property. The defendants returned the next day to hunt and found MCI contractors on the property working on repairing the severed cable.

Hagan had acquired the property in 2004 from Illinois Central Gulf Railroad (hereinafter, "Illinois Central"). MCI alleges that in 1984, its predecessor entered into an agreement with Illinois Central to install and operate a telecommunication system on Illinois Central's property, and that the property in question was added to the agreement in 1985. MCI contends that in Hagan's purchase agreement with Illinois Central, Hagan agreed not to interfere with any previously bargained for rights to continue operating all existing utilities.

As evidence of Hagan's negligence, MCI asserted Hagan had violated the requirements of the Damage Prevention Act. Hagan asserted a counterclaim against MCI for trespass on his property. The district court ruled that MCI had failed to establish that it had a servitude over Hagan's property, but that MCI did have a right to keep its existing cable on Hagan's property due to the contents of the Act of Sale between Hagan and Illinois Central. The district court dismissed Hagan's counterclaim on these grounds. Hagan did not appeal from that ruling. The case was tried to a jury, which returned a verdict finding that Joubert and Hagan were not negligent. No other findings were made, according to the Court of Appeals, because the remaining jury questions submitted were all contingent on a finding of negligence on the part of at least one of the two defendants. The district court awarded attorneys' fees to Hagan and Joubert under the provision in the Damage Prevention Act that allows for such fees if the "excavators" prevail in a suit to enforce the act. La.Rev. Stat. 40:1749.14(F).

During the trial, MCI objected to the district court's refusal to submit to the jury MCI's proposed instruction regarding trespass to the cable. The district court judge responded that he felt "that it's a part of the negligence aspect of the case" and that because MCI did not have a servitude, he thought it was not "an appropriate charge." MCI's requested instruction on trespass reads in relevant part:

> Trespass is an unlawful invasion of the property or possession of another person without consent. Damage to property is a trespass regardless of whether the Defendants intended the damage to the property or were negligent. A Defendant may be held liable for an inadvertent trespass resulting

from an intentional act. Therefore, the basic standard applicable to the Defendants is that they must refrain from taking intentional action that results in harm to the Plaintiff.

According to the Court of Appeals, the evidence presented at trial would, in its view, be sufficient to support a finding that the MCI cable was struck and damaged by movement of the backhoe intentionally made by Joubert as he operated it with Hagan's permission, and on his behalf, although Joubert and Hagan did not intend for the backhoe to strike the underground cable, which they did not see and the precise location of which they did not know. MCI contended the district court erred when it refused to submit to the jury its proposed instruction on trespass and the requisite intent therefor. MCI's view was that Louisiana law defines trespass as an unlawful physical invasion of property in the possession of another, and the only intent required is the trespasser's intent to perform the act which constitutes the trespass.

Because the district court ruled before trial that MCI did not have a servitude, the Court of Appeals found MCI was not entitled to recover for a trespass to land. However, though MCI apparently did not assert as much, the Court of Appeals opined that MCI may be entitled to have the jury instructed on a claim of trespass to chattels, which that court described as a claim for damages to personal property of the plaintiff—the personal property in this case being MCI's underground cable. Because it believed that Louisiana courts have not considered the intent standard applicable to claims of trespass to underground cables, and because it found no clear consensus either within the Fifth Circuit or across all jurisdictions as to whether strict liability in a trespass action is an appropriate standard for damage to underground utilities by excavators, the Court of Appeals declined to determine whether MCI's proposed jury instruction was an accurate statement of Louisiana trespass law as it pertains to damage to underground utilities.

In deciding to invoke the certification privilege granted by Louisiana Supreme Court Rule XII, the Court of Appeals reasoned that, if MCI's requested jury instruction was a substantially correct statement of Louisiana law, then it was reversible error for the trial court not to have given that instruction, and MCI would be entitled to a new trial on the theory of trespass. Otherwise, if the requested jury instruction is not a substantially correct statement of Louisiana law, a new trial on the merits would not be required.

Discussion

Inherent in the Fifth Circuit's question is whether Louisiana law provides for a distinct tort of trespass to movables akin to that of the common law claim of trespass to chattels. As the Fifth Circuit noted, MCI did not cite, nor does it do so in this court, to any Louisiana court cases that deal specifically with the intent standard for trespass to chattels. More pertinently, however, MCI has not cited to any Louisiana case recognizing a tort of trespass to chattels, much less one in the form of a trespass to underground cable, which the Fifth Circuit understandably presumed was a chattel, or a movable under Louisiana law, rather than immovable property. It is this latter issue on which our decision today turns.

In its presentation to this court, MCI makes two arguments. MCI first argues that it has some possessory interest in Mr. Hagan's immovable property by virtue of either the agreement among MCI's and Mr. Hagan's predecessors, which agreement was perpetuated in the Act of Cash Sale, or, as MCI stressed in oral argument, simply because of its cable's physical proximity to and direct contact with the dirt underlying Mr. Hagan's property. MCI thus argues that Hagan and Joubert committed a trespass by unlawfully and physically invading upon MCI's possessory interest in immovable property when the backhoe they were intentionally operating inadvertently came in contact with the cable and the dirt surrounding it. We dispose of this first argument by noting the federal district court already determined that MCI had no servitude over Mr. Hagan's land, and thus, under Louisiana law, MCI had no possessory interest in Mr. Hagan's land. The Court of Appeals accepted the district court's finding; thus, the federal courts have previously found that MCI had merely a contractual right to leave its cable on Mr. Hagan's land at the time of the incident involving the backhoe. Indeed, the Court of Appeals repeatedly pointed out in its opinion that MCI did not have a servitude over Mr. Hagan's property. Consequently, we decline to decide anew or otherwise review a factual and legal determination that was settled in the federal courts.

MCI next argues that it can recover in trespass regardless of whether Hagan and Joubert were negligent so long as they intended to perform the act of operating the backhoe, which resulted in the trespass, i.e., contact with its cable or that portion of Mr. Hagan's land in which MCI had some possessory interest. However, the issue of whether MCI had some possessory interest in the property has already been resolved against MCI.

Essentially, the Fifth Circuit's inquiry is whether Louisiana law recognizes a distinct tort of "trespass to chattels" and, if so, can a "trespass to chattels" be committed inadvertently if it results from an otherwise intentional act. No party has cited to any case or treatise discussing the common law claim of trespass to chattels. Black's Law Dictionary defines trespass to chattels as "[t]he act of committing without lawful justification, any act of direct physical interference with a chattel possessed by another. The act must amount to a direct forcible injury." Black's Law Dictionary, p. 1643 (9th ed. 2009). Some Louisiana commentators have discussed the claim of trespass to chattels. "Trespass to chattels is the *intentional* intermeddling with a chattel (movable) in the possession of another that damages the chattel, reduces its value, or deprives the possessor of the use of the chattel for a significant period of time." Frank L. Maraist and Thomas C. Galligan, Jr., *Louisiana Tort Law*, §2.06[8], p. 2-34 (2004) (emphasis supplied). These commentators note the tort of trespass to movables is generally treated as a conversion in Louisiana. *Id.*, p. 2-35. *See also* 12 William E. Crawford, *Louisiana Civil Law Treatise; Tort Law* (2d ed. 2009) ("The taking or damage of movable property in the possession of another is regarded as a trespass. It happens often when repossession through self-help is exercised."). The Restatement (Second) of Torts explains that a trespass to chattel "may be committed by *intentionally* (a) dispossessing another of the chattel, or (b) using or intermeddling with a chattel in the possession of another." Restatement (Second) of Torts, § 217 (1965) (emphasis supplied). Thus, the common law claim of trespass to chattels appears to require intent to interfere with another's interest in movable property before an action for trespass to chattels may lie.

At any rate, in Louisiana, the victim of an intentional intermeddling with a movable in the possession of another, or even accidental damage to a movable that belongs to another, which is the more apt description under the facts of this case, has an adequate remedy under the law of tort without recourse to the common law trespass to chattels. La. Civ. Code art. 2315(A) provides that "[e]very act whatever of man that causes damage to another obliges him by whose fault it happened to repair it." As we noted in *Dual Drilling Co. v. Mills Equipment Investments, Inc.,* 98-0343 (La. 12/1/98), 721 So.2d 853, 856, in rejecting the adoption of the strict liability remedy of the common law action of conversion, "[o]ur civilian remedies amply protect personal and real rights in movable property and should not be obscured by an application of common law . . . principles." Thus, MCI had available to it, as the owner of a movable allegedly damaged by the fault of another, the delictual action in tort. Moreover, the Louisiana legislature has created specific statutes regarding damage to underground cables in the above-described Damage Prevention Law, placing certain statutory duties upon the excavator. However, a violation of the statute does not result in either strict civil liability or negligence *per se;* instead, the failure of an excavator to detect the presence of an underground utility as required by statute subjects the excavator to delictual liability under the theory of negligence, and any statutory violation is considered in the traditional duty-risk analysis. *See, e.g., Bellsouth Telecommunications, Inc. v. Eustis Engineering Co., Inc.,* 07-865 (La. App. 4 Cir. 12/9/07), 974 So.2d 749. Thus, the federal district court was correct in determining that MCI's "trespass" claim was "part of the negligence aspect of the case — or the claim of negligence."

We therefore answer the question certified to us in the negative: The proposed jury instruction in this case, which states in part that "[a] Defendant may be held liable for an inadvertent trespass resulting from an intentional act," is not a correct statement of Louisiana law when the "trespass" at issue is the severing of an underground cable located on property owned by one of the alleged trespassers, and the property is not subject to a servitude by the owners of the underground cable but only to the contractual right to keep it, as an existing cable, underneath the property.

Decree

We answer the certified question as set forth in this opinion. Pursuant to Rule XII, Supreme Court of Louisiana, the judgment rendered by this court upon the question certified shall be sent by the clerk of this court under its seal to the United States Court of Appeals for the Fifth Circuit and to the parties.

Notes and Questions

1. In a footnote in *MCI Communications v. Hagan,* 74 So.3d 1148 (La. 2011), the Louisiana Supreme Court explains the tort of conversion.

> "'A conversion is committed when any of the following occurs: (1) possession is acquired in an unauthorized manner; (2) the chattel is removed from one place to another with the intent to exercise control over it; (3) possession of the chattel is transferred without authority; (4) possession is withheld from the owner or possessor; (5) the chattel is altered or destroyed; (6) the chattel is used improperly; or (7) ownership is asserted over the chattel.' *Dual Drilling Co. v. Mills Equipment Investments, Inc.,* 98-0343 (La. 12/ 1/ 98), 721 So.2d 853, 857. But, as we explained in *Dual Drilling,* "[t]he conversion action is predicated on the fault of the defendant and directed to the recovery of the movable or, in the alternative, the plaintiff may demand compensation." *Id.* Thus, in *Dual Drilling,* we found that civil law remedies, including a delictual action in tort, effectively protect victims without the necessity of adopting the common law version of conversion. Accordingly, we declined to adopt strict liability, but instead required the plaintiff to prove the fault of the defendant under La. Civ. Code art. 2315. *Id.,* n. 3."

Id. at 1154 n.8.

2. Before reaching the ultimate issue in the case, the Louisiana Supreme Court was careful to reject the argument by MCI that it held some kind of possessory interest or real right in the land where its underground communications cable was damaged by the defendants Hagan and Joubert. Specifically, the court rejected the argument that MCI had acquired a servitude in Hagan's land. In later chapters we will study how an entity like MCI might acquire an immovable property interest (*i.e.,* a real right as opposed to a mere personal or contractual right) in the land of another person through either a predial servitude or a limited personal servitude (right of use). *See* La. Civ. Code art. 639 (1976); *Id.* art. 646 (1977). Had the lawyers for MCI been more careful at the time they originally contracted with Hagan's predecessor in interest, Illinois Central, and established a predial servitude or right of use, the outcome of the case might have been very different.

In Louisiana, liability for trespass to a person's possession or property interest in *land* or some other *immovable property* requires only that the defendant commit an *intentional act,* even if the harm resulting from that act is *accidental or inadvertent.* Consider *Terre Aux Boeufs Land v. J.R. Gray Barge Co.,* 803 So.2d 86 (La. App. 4 Cir. 2001). In that case, an unmanned deck barge broke free from its mooring during a hurricane and was stranded on plaintiff's marshland, 1000 feet away from the nearest navigable water body. The plaintiff landowner sued the barge owner and others under many theories of law, including trespass. Ultimately, however, the court of appeal overturned the trial court's imposition of liability under Louisiana trespass law, observing that although trespass liability can still arise when the harm to the plaintiff is "inadvertent," the plaintiff still must prove that the defendant took "some intentional action that resulted in harm." *Id.* at 95–96. As the court summed up:

> [T]he rule to be drawn from [three previous cases] is that a defendant may be held liable for an **inadvertent** trespass resulting from an **intentional** act; nevertheless, proof that the defendant took an intentional act remains an important element for proving plaintiff's claims in those cases. In the instant case, the defendants took no **intentional** actions that resulted in the stranding of Barge RG 7 on TAB's land. Although the trespass itself might be inadvertent, we find that a defendant generally may not be liable for trespass under Louisiana law in the absence of evidence that the trespass resulted from some intentional act taken by the defendant.

Id. at 96 (emphasis in original). The court in *Terre Aux Boeufs Land* also noted that the defendants could have been liable for trespass, even in the absence of intent, if they had been at fault in causing the trespass. But the court excused the defendants from liability on this ground as well, noting that the record clearly established that the stranding of the barge was caused solely by an Act of God. *Id.*

In *MCI Communications*, the plaintiff MCI sought to have the courts approve a jury verdict for trespass to movables that appears to track the language quoted above in *Terre Aux Boeufs Land*. As we now know, the Louisiana Supreme Court held that such an instruction was inapplicable to a trespass to movables. If MCI had established some property interest in the land at issue, it could well have established trespass liability by proving that Joubert and Hagan committed an intentional act that inadvertently caused harm to MCI's property interest in that land.

3. Notice the emphatic statement toward the end of the opinion in which the court observes, quoting from a prior decision, that "our civilian remedies amply protect personal and real rights in movable property and should not be obscured by an application of common law . . . principles." Why do you think the court goes out of its way to try to fence off any reference to common law principles? Do you believe this kind of warning to avoid application of common law principles will be heeded by other Louisiana courts?

4. It may strike you as strange that the cable owner, MCI, is essentially left without a remedy in *property law* for damage that was caused by the intentional act of Hagan and Joubert excavating the boat ramp with a back hoe without making any inquiries about the possible presence of underground cables. (We note, however, that MCI could have appealed the trial court's finding of no negligence.) The court seems to imply, just as we saw in *Perrin v. Randy Tupper Homes*, that sometimes property owners, even owners of movable property, have a duty to put the rest of world on notice of the existence of their property rights in an object, and of the potential for harm that might result from interacting with that object. Legal scholars often call this the *publicity principle*. We will encounter this notion throughout the casebook.

Frequently, the problem of the sufficiency of notice arises when a landowner grants a juridical person like a pipeline company or cable company a property right less than full ownership in its land — for example, a right of way to establish a pipeline or a telecommunications line — and then the grantor of that right sells the land to a third person. If the pipeline company or cable company wants to be able to assert its property interests in the land against the new owner, it has to be able to prove it acquired some kind of real right in the land, as opposed to a personal right. In *MCI Communications*, we encounter the unusual situation of a cable company seeking to establish a tort claim for damages against an owner of land with respect to movable property in the absence of any kind of property interest in the land. How did this come about? What kind of rights, if any, did MCI acquire in the land at issue when it originally entered into an agreement with Illinois Central Gulf Railroad, the landowner prior to Hagan?

5. In the United States, a powerful system of federal courts coexists with state courts in the fifty states. The structural separation of the two court systems does not automatically mean that federal courts and state courts hear and decide only cases confined to federal law or state law respectively. Rather, the combination of jurisdictional overlaps and law-selection rules in our dual federal and state court systems quite frequently results in "cross-overs" — a complexity frequently under-appreciated in quarters outside the United States. Note that when exercising diversity of citizenship jurisdiction (in lawsuits involving citizens of different states or of a state and a different country) federal courts must apply state substantive law to state-based claims.

This type of federal-state duality raises the question of how to address potential inter-system errors. When a federal court has erroneously interpreted or applied state law, a review of federal decisions in state court is not an option. A federal court may, however, consider two precautionary avenues of cooperative judicial federalism — certification and abstention. Certification, which must be made available by state law, and which was the technique used in *MCI Communications*, enables a federal court to seek from a state's highest court answers to novel or unsettled legal questions deemed dispositive for the outcome of the case. In Louisiana, certification is governed by Louisiana Supreme Court Rule XII, section 1, which reads: "When it appears to the Supreme Court of the United States, or to any circuit court of appeal of the United States, that there are involved in any proceedings before it questions or propositions of law of this state which are determinative of said cause independently of any other questions involved in said case and that there are no clear controlling precedents in the decisions of the supreme court of this state, such federal court before rendering a decision may certify such questions or propositions of law of this state to the Supreme Court of Louisiana for rendition of a judgment or opinion concerning such questions or propositions of Louisiana law. This court may, in its discretion, decline to answer the questions certified to it." La. Sup. Ct. Rule 12 § 1. For more on federal judges and their judicial methodology when handling Louisiana civil law cases, see Markus G. Puder, *Federalism and Mixity in the United*

States: A Survey of Federal Judges Regarding Erie Courts and Louisiana's Civil Law, 77 RABELSZ 251 (2013).

C. Contemporary Perspectives on Ownership and Exclusion

Throughout the introductory portions of this chapter, we have emphasized the linkage between property rights in general and ownership in particular with the notion of exclusion. In recent years, some very prominent judges, lawyers and property law scholars have argued that the right to exclude is, in fact, the most fundamental right in all of property law. If a person does not have the right to exclude, they claim, the person does not really own the property. At times, the U.S. Supreme Court has made statements that seem to support this general proposition. *See e.g., Kaiser Aetna v. United States*, 444 U.S. 164, 176 (1979); *Dolan v. City of Tigard*, 512 U.S. 374, 384 (1994). That proposition, however, has been challenged by other property lawyers who argue that property law in general and ownership in particular is more accurately described in terms of norms of social obligation. The following excerpt from an article written by one of authors of this casebook gives you a sense of the contemporary debate about the centrality of the right to exclude in property law.

John A. Lovett, *Progressive Property in Action: The Land Reform (Scotland) Act of 2003*
89 NEB. L. REV. 739, 743–750 (2011)

The decade of "the noughties" (roughly 2000–09) was an exciting time for American property scholarship. Perhaps one of the most distinctive aspects of the scholarly discussion about property law during this period was the on-going, high level debate between two rival camps of property theorists about the fundamental structure and values of property law in general and over the nature and importance of the right to exclude in particular. This portion of the Article discusses the views of the key protagonists in this debate as well as the views of several theorists who do not fit neatly into either category.

A. Progressive or Social Obligation Theorists

A prominent group of theorists who claim for themselves the moniker "progressive" have contended that property law can and should embrace a social obligation norm designed to promote human flourishing, or at least the basic human capabilities that allow individuals to make reasoned and meaningful decisions about the projects they will undertake in their lives. In a series of influential articles and books, Gregory Alexander, Eduardo Peñalver, Joseph Singer, Eric Freyfogle, and Jedediah Purdy have repeatedly argued that property law is fundamentally about relationships: between neighboring property owners or co-owners, between landlord and tenant, between present possessor and future interest holder, between property owners and non-owners, and between the property owner and the state. Property law in their view must constantly recalibrate the needs and demands of all these parties. Property entitlements matter not so much because of the negative liberty they provide to owners (and especially the shield that property provides from state interference) but because of what they enable people (both owners and non-owners) to become and to do with their lives in practices of social cooperation.

These "progressive" or "social obligation" theorists picture individuals, and by extension property owners, as fundamentally dependent on human community. In moments of conflict, this interdependence requires property law decision makers to determine whether a property owner's interest in autonomy and control over her asset must be sacrificed, sometimes without compensation or strict reciprocity, to satisfy a non-owner's need for access to that asset or the community's interest in control over use or disposition of that asset. In determining the extent of this need for sacrifice, the progressive theorists tell us that property law has nothing to fear from open-textured standards that allow courts to make ex post, fine-tuned, contextualized decisions about the relative needs and interests of competing property owners, owners and non-owners, or owners and the community, even in cases where property rights have traditionally been protected with relatively crystalline, ex ante rules of exclusion.

Further, in making decisions about land use, for instance, courts will have to consider not just how to maximize a parcel of land's market value and the owner's market return, but they will have to (and already do so more than we realize) consider concepts similar to what Peñalver calls "land's complexity" and "land's memory." In addition, some of these theorists, particularly Alexander and Peñalver, insist that property law has much to learn from the Aristotelian tradition of virtue ethics and should not be afraid to test property owner behavior by considering the application of several "land virtues," specifically the virtues of industry, justice, and humility.

At the end of the day, these theorists' key point of agreement is that property law can serve "plural and incommensurable values." Although economic efficiency, generating wealth, and welfare maximization are among these values, they are not, and should not be, the only metrics of analysis. Other equally important values that can serve as polestars of property law decision making include, in addition to human flourishing itself, the promotion of human freedom (and especially the freedom to recruit or be recruited for social projects on grounds of reciprocity, persuasion, and negotiated cooperation), the creation of a free and democratic society in which human beings are treated with equal dignity and respect, and the preservation of our natural and human environment to serve the needs of future generations and even the interests of the non-human world. Throughout the progressive theorists' writing, there is a consistent willingness to discuss virtues and virtuous behavior and to consider how human beings should treat each other. Rather than serving as platforms for self-regarding behavior, property ownership and property law become the place for building community, not merely satisfying personal preferences.

B. Information or Formal Exclusion Theorists

Competing against these progressive theorists is a group that is sometimes referred to as the "information" theorists, who we might also call "formal exclusion" theorists. These theorists contend that at the very core of any properly functioning private property regime is a robust commitment to protecting a property owner's right to exclude everyone else in the world from the object of his ownership. Their justifications for this core commitment to exclusion, to a vision of property as "thing-ownership," are both moral and utilitarian. Currently Thomas Merrill and Henry Smith's versions of this exclusion oriented view of property are the most vital and influential.

In *Property and the Right to Exclude,* a foundational essay that helped launch the exclusion theory debate, Merrill claimed that the right of a property owner to exclude others is not just "one of the most essential" sticks in the bundle that is often seen as comprising property, but is in fact the "sine qua non" of property. As he put it: "Give someone the right to exclude others from a valued resource . . . and you give them property. Deny someone the exclusion right and they do not have property."

For Merrill, the right to exclude is a "necessary and sufficient condition of identifying the existence of property." He claims that this prioritization of the right to exclude can be justified on numerous grounds: (1) its logical utility (*i.e.,* the notion that most of the other attributes of property can be deduced by simply clarifying or modifying the right to exclude); (2) its deep historical and anthropological roots; and (3) its sheer "ubiquity" in mature legal systems. For Merrill, a robust defense of the right to exclude is essential to guard against the disintegrating effects of legal realism and its bundle-of-sticks approach to property, concepts that threaten to strip property of its institutional coherence and social value.

Henry Smith's writings over the past decade have largely corroborated Merrill's insights but have added his distinctive information-processing-cost rationale to the defense of exclusion. In his recent response to Alexander's important article calling for incorporation of a social obligation norm in American property law, Smith takes us to the nub of the debate. Although he acknowledges the intuitive attractiveness of human flourishing as a societal goal, Smith asserts that property law and scholarship cannot afford to become overly concerned with promoting desirable social ends. Rather, it must focus on means, on how property law goes about its business of serving human interests—and especially on what property law does well, at least in comparison to other branches of the law. Smith thus draws us to his (and Merrill's) key insight: that property law's comparative advantage, its exceptionalism, lies in solving problems "wholesale," in coordinating action for a wide range of often anonymous actors. Thus, the essence of property resides in its unique "in rem" quality, its ability to speak in modular and informationally dense ways to those who must deal with property in a complex and heterogeneous world in which most individuals have little prior information about each other.

Property law accomplishes this by providing default packages of rights that decide important questions ex ante for everyone. The *numerus clausus* principle, the strict limitation on the number and type of property ownership forms in both the civil and common law, illustrates this demand for standardization at the macro level. Merrill and Smith's favorite example of such a default package at the level of individual rules is the right-to-exclude principle that underscores the mechanistic and crystalline law of trespass. Yet another, slightly more complex, but still favorite example is the baseline rule in nuisance—namely that a residential property owner is entitled to be free of pollution. The great benefit of these simple, ex ante property rules, according to Smith, is that they reduce information processing costs for those subject to the rules (i.e., duty holders and non-owners), those who might like to acquire property (i.e., other market participants), and the officials who must administer these rules (i.e., judges).

Like Merrill before him, Smith is quick to acknowledge that a property owner's general right to exclude non-owners and to decide the uses to which his property can be put is "not an end in itself, and is far from absolute even as a means." When it confronts a subject of enough importance, or when parties cannot reach bargains easily on their own, or when we simply do not trust bargaining's results, property law will subordinate an owner's simple ex ante exclusion rights to larger social interests. The general pattern that emerges according to Merrill and Smith is "exclusion" at the core—an ex ante rebuttable presumption in favor of the owner's right to exclude non-owners and to determine the use of the property—and "governance" at the periphery. By "governance" Smith does not necessarily imply government regulation; he merely means more carefully tailored, contextualized solutions that openly refer to some collective ends society hopes to achieve—something akin to what the progressive theorists are calling for more generally.

It is not easy to reconcile the approach of these information or formal exclusion theorists with the basic assumptions of the progressive theorists. As Jane Baron has recently observed, both groups of scholars' understanding of property is founded on divergent and "contested commitments." While the information theorists like Merrill and Smith tend to view property metaphorically as an information generating "machine" that produces, on average, good enough outcomes, the progressive theorists see property law as an on-going "conversation" that should be geared toward identifying human values, dislodging unconscious presumptions, improving the quality and character of social relationships, and creating a more just distribution of resources to facilitate more human flourishing. While the information theorists favor simplicity, stability, and predictability, the progressives embrace complexity, contingency, and contextualism. While the information theorists are ambivalent about change within property law, even when change is needed they are nervous about radical revision and prefer for any innovation to emanate from legislatures. The progressives, on the other hand, are more impatient and ready to accept dynamism whatever its institutional source. In short, as Baron has suggested insightfully, the information theorists see themselves as mechanical engineers concerned with promoting functional efficiency within the legal system and the marketplace, whereas progressive theorists see themselves as social engineers aiming to produce a "virtuous, free, or democratic society."

Note

The broader subject of the article involves legislation enacted in Scotland, another mixed jurisdiction like Louisiana. That legislation, known as the *Land Reform (Scotland) Act 2003*, gives members of the public a right of responsible access to privately owned land and water bodies for purposes of non-motorized recreation. It shares some commonalities with earlier legislation, known as the *Countryside and Rights of Way Act 2000*, enacted by the parliament of the United Kingdom and applicable in England and Wales. Here is a short description of the Scottish "right of responsible access" in contrast with the "right to roam" that exists in England and Wales.

John A. Lovett
The Right to Exclude Meets the Right of Responsible Access: Scotland's Bold Experiment in Access Legislation
26 PROBATE & PROPERTY No. 2, 52–55 (2012)

. . . With the enactment of the Countryside and Rights of Way Act, 2000, c. 37 (Eng. & Wales) (CRoW Act), the British Parliament at Westminster established a statutory "right to roam"—a narrowly defined right of pedestrian, recreational access—over certain statutorily defined "access lands" in England and Wales that account for about 8% to 12% of the total land in those countries. Although the CRoW Act's "right to roam" has been noted by a number of American property law commentators over the past decade, few Americans realize that another parliament in the United Kingdom, the recently reopened Scottish Parliament, has enacted an even more sweeping recreational access right in a remarkable piece of legislation known as the Land Reform (Scotland) Act, 2003 (A.S.P. 2) (LRSA). This *right of responsible access* established in the LRSA imaginatively redefines the right to exclude in Scotland, a nation whose contributions to political economy, law, engineering, and philosophy, to say nothing of golf and malt beverages, is well appreciated by many American lawyers. . . .

Where You Can Go

The first distinctive feature of the LRSA, particularly in contrast to the CRoW Act in England and Wales, is the remarkable geographic reach of access rights granted in Scotland. In England and Wales, the "right to roam" applies only to narrowly defined "access lands"—basically what the statute defines as "mapped open country," which in turn comprises "mountain, moor, heath or down"—and a few other narrow categories of land previously reserved for public access. CRoW Act § 1(1)-(2). The right to roam also now applies to "coastal lands" in England, but not to inland waterways. Marine and Coastal Access Act, 2009, c. 23 §§ 296, 303 (Eng.).

Under the LRSA, however, the public is entitled to exercise its statutory access rights almost everywhere in Scotland—in highland glens, on islands, on lochs and rivers, on wooded estates, even on the margins of suburban housing estates. Rather than have government ministers label certain areas as "access land" based on narrowly defined physical characteristics of that land, as in England and Wales, Scotland borrowed from Scandinavian countries what some observers have labeled a "universalist," bottom-up approach to recreational access, under which the basic assumption is that all land and inland water are presumed to be subject to access. LRSA §§ 1(2)(a) & 32; Lovett, supra, at 778, 782.

Where You Cannot Go

The drafters of the LRSA realized, of course, that certain land deserves to be exempt from the public's right of responsible access. These exempt lands include agricultural fields where crops are growing or have been sown, woodlands where "tree seedlings" have been planted, land where a building is located, the curtilage of nonresidential buildings and other improvements, plants and fixed machinery, certain sporting areas (but remarkably the public can access a golf course as long as access is not taken across a green or while a game is under way), school grounds, mines, quarries, and other dangerous facilities, and castles, historic sites, and amusement parks that normally charge admission. LRSA §§ 6(1), 7.

Not surprisingly, the LRSA also excludes from access a certain amount of space around houses and dwellings. But unlike in England and Wales, where land within 20 meters of a dwelling or a "park or garden" surrounding a home is specifically exempted from the "right to roam," CRoW Act, sch. 1(3)-(4), Scotland chose a more indeterminate dwelling exemption. LRSA § 6(1)(b)(iv) provides that the public does not have access rights to land that comprises, in relation to a house or any other shelter, "sufficient adjacent land to enable persons living there to have reasonable measures of privacy in that house or place and to ensure that their enjoyment of that house or place is not unreasonably disturbed." Other than suggesting that this zone of reasonable privacy and enjoyment must be determined in light of "the location and other characteristics of the house or other place," LRSA § 7(5), the act generally leaves the task of defining the scope of this important exclusion to local authorities, landowners, access takers, and, ultimately, the Scottish courts.

What You Can Do

In England and Wales, persons exercising the right to roam are granted a right of "open-air recreation" that is tightly circumscribed. The only permitted access is "on foot," CRoW Act § 2(1), which means that cycling, horseback riding, mountain biking, and cross-country skiing are not allowed. Canoeing, sailing, swimming, and camping also are prohibited. In essence, the right to roam really permits an access taker only to take a walk, have a picnic, and then go home. Lovett, supra, at 785 and authorities cited therein.

In Scotland, the scope of legitimate access activity is much wider. Access takers are permitted to be on land or inland water for most forms of nonmotorized recreational activity, including walking, hiking, running, orienteering, horseback riding, canoeing, sailing, mountain biking, and even "wild camping," and for carrying on an educational activity—for instance studying the natural or cultural heritage of Scotland. LRSA § 1(3)(a)-(b). In addition, people can be engaged in either one of these two initial purposes (recreation or educational activity) in a commercial or for-profit manner. Id. § 1(3)(c). Thus, a paid nature guide or mountain guide can lead a group on non-exempt land. Finally, the public can access non-exempt land simply to cross from one place to another. Id. § 1(2)(b), (4)(b). The LRSA thus provides a general right of nonmotorized passage, too.

What You Cannot Do

There are, of course, a number of restrictions on permissible access taking under the LRSA. The first and most fundamental restriction is the requirement that all access taking be responsibly exercised. LRSA § 2(1). This may sound hopelessly vague to an American ear, but it is vital to the LRSA in three respects. First, in the long process of consensus building that preceded enactment of the LRSA, the promise that broad access rights would be contingent on their responsible exercise assured private landowners and appealed to a Scottish public that has always prided itself on its genteel manners. Lovett, supra, at 776–77. Second, a vision of responsible access also was fleshed out through the drafting and eventual promulgation of the widely circulated *Scottish Outdoor Access Code*, a soft law document that describes responsible and irresponsible access in numerous detailed contexts. Scottish Natural Heritage, *Scottish Outdoor Access Code*, available at www.outdooraccess-scotland.com (last updated Oct. 4, 2011). Although this code does not have official status as law, it is an important guideline that allows landowners and access takers to find solutions to many everyday conflicts. Finally, the duty of access takers to act responsibly has been paired with a duty on the part of land managers to manage their land responsibly for access takers' interests. LRSA § 3(1)-(2). In essence, the LRSA imposes reciprocal duties of mutual, other-regarding behavior on access takers and landowners.

Other restrictions on access are more specific. Access takers cannot enter or cross land in breach of some specific injunction or commit any "offence." If they are accompanied by a dog or other animal, it must be leashed. Access takers cannot use motorized vehicles other than motorized wheelchairs. Finally, they cannot hunt, shoot, or fish. LRSA §§ 2(2)(a)(1), 9. The fishing and hunting ban preserves a land manager's ability to charge fees or grant licenses for activities like deer stalking and grouse hunting, which are important sources of revenue that can be used to keep large estates sustainable.

Notes and Questions

1. Do you think Scotland's approach of creating a general public right of recreational access to private land and inland water bodies could work in Louisiana? Keep this question in mind when we consider a challenging case at the conclusion of Chapter 3, *Cenac v. Public Access Water Rights Ass'n*, 851 So.2d 1006 (La. 2003).

2. The ideas of the social obligation theorists of property described in the initial excerpt above have a civil law analogue, and perhaps a civil law source, in the writing of an early twentieth century French law professor named **Leon Duguit**. Duguit was born near Bordeaux, France in 1859, and became a law professor in the 1880, eventually settling at the University of Bordeaux, where he taught for forty years. In 1911, he travelled to Buenos Aires, Argentina, where he gave a series of lectures on the topic of how the civil law had changed since the adoption of the Code Napoleon in 1804. In the sixth and final lecture, Duguit expounded on the idea that property was becoming less and less a matter of subjective individual rights (*propriété-droit*) and instead was assuming an ever more important "social function" (*propriété-fonction*). By this Duguit meant not so much that property or wealth should be redistributed, but that owners and others who control wealth and resources have an obligation to put their property to productive social uses that serve the needs of society in general. What seemed to bother him were farm lands being left uncultivated, houses being left vacant and unmaintained, and factories not put to productive use. He thought laws should be enacted to address these problems. Duguit's writings influenced how conceptions of property were developed in some subsequent Latin American civil codes and may have exerted an influence on scholars in the United States associated with the movement known as "legal realism" (a school of legal philosophy asserting that legal rules should be based on the interests of society and public policy and should avoid formalism and strict adherence to judicial precedent). *See generally* M.C. Mirow, *The Social Obligation Norm of Property: Duguit, Hayem and Others*, 22 FLA. J. INT'L L. 191 (2010); Sheila R. Foster & Daniel Bonilla, *The Social Function of Property: A Comparative Law Perspective*, 80 FORDHAM L. REV. 101, 102–106 (2011).

Chapter 3

The Division of Things: Of Common, Public and Private Things

Book II of the Louisiana Civil Code ("Things and the Different Modifications of Ownership") consists of seven titles. The first title governs "Things." Somewhat surprisingly, the Civil Code does not define "things." Instead, Article 448, the first provision in Title I, Chapter 1, Section 1 of Book II, divides "things" into a number of categories:

Art. 448. Division of things

Things are divided into common, public and private; corporeals and incorporeals; and movables and immovables.

La. Civ. Code art. 448 (1978). This initial focus on creating classificatory schemes reflects a traditional characteristic of civilian legal thought. As we progress through our study of other sections of the Civil Code, we will encounter other classificatory distinctions. For example, in the law of accession, we will distinguish between "principal" and "accessory" things and between "fruits" and "products." In the law of usufruct, we will study the distinction between "consumable" and "nonconsumable" things and between "ordinary" and "extraordinary" repairs. In several areas of property law, we treat "good faith" and "bad faith" possessors differently.

In this chapter, we focus on the first of the three classificatory distinctions declared by Article 448: the division into common, public and private things. We examine how the Civil Code, Louisiana courts and civilian scholars have defined and deployed these different categories, while noting the degrees of stability and instability in these classification schemes. We also discuss the factors that contribute to the placement of a particular thing in one category or another, including the thing's inherent physical characteristics, legislative policy judgments or judicial interpretations of broad, and sometimes even ambiguous, legal concepts. We observe how the question of proper classification of a thing can be wrapped inside some other area of law, for example obligations, family law, successions, taxation, criminal law or conflict of laws.

A. The Basic Division

1. Common Things

The first classification scheme detailed in Book II of the Louisiana Civil Code divides the world of property into three basic categories of things: common, public and private things. Article 449 provides the definition of common things:

Art. 449. Common Things

Common things may not be owned by anyone. They are such as the air and the high seas that may be freely used by everyone conformably with the use for which nature has intended them.

La. Civ. Code art. 449 (1978).

One way to think about common things is to imagine them as things that cannot be "fenced in" permanently. Consequently, a common thing cannot be held exclusively by any one person. No one can deny others access to a common thing and everyone will ultimately have the opportunity to use it. Air, which denotes the mixture of gases and chemical compounds that surrounds us and comprises the atmosphere, is a classic example of a common thing. No one, practically speaking, can hold onto it more than temporarily, and, therefore, no one can deny others access to it.

While the air is a common thing, legal rights in airspace—the right to occupy or build in the space above a certain parcel of land—are not. *See* La. Civ. Code art. 490 (1979) (declaring that "the ownership of a tract of land carries with it the ownership of everything that is directly above or under it"). The landowner "may make works on, above, or below the land as he pleases, and draw all the advantages that accrue from them, unless he is restrained by law or by rights of others." *Id*. Federal law and municipal zoning regulation provide many of the restraints on the use of airspace alluded to by Article 490.

The Civil Code's other example of a common thing—the high seas—has similar characteristics. Practically speaking, it is impossible for any single person to hold the high seas exclusively or to deny others access to it. Under the 1958 Convention of the High Seas, an international treaty ratified by the United States, the term "high seas" means all parts of the sea that are not included in the territorial sea or in the internal waters of a nation-state. As we will explain in more detail in Part B.3 of this chapter, the state's territorial waters extend three marine leagues (or nine geographic miles) from the coastline. *See generally* La. Rev. Stat. §49:1 (1954, amended 2011); La. Rev. Stat. §49:3.1(2011).

Can you think of other kinds of things that might meet the Civil Code's definition of common things—things "that may not be owned by anyone" and from which no one has the right to exclude anyone else? What about ideas? What about works of literary imagination for which copyright protection has expired? What about scientific inventions for which patents no longer provide the inventor with exclusive control? What about wildlife?

It might be tempting to categorize wild animals, birds and fish, in particular, as things which have no owner. Yet, wildlife is a very special case in Louisiana. On one hand, Louisiana law recognizes that wildlife belongs to the State of Louisiana in "its capacity as a public person" because the state must regulate wildlife for the interests of all its citizens and the public good, just as throughout the rest of the United States. La. Civ. Code art. 3413 rev. cmt. (b) (1982). On the other hand, wild animals, birds, fish and shellfish, while they are in a state of natural liberty, are also said to be "things without an owner." *Id. See also Leger v. Louisiana Dep't of Wildlife and Fisheries*, 306 So.2d 391 (La. App. 3 Cir. 1975). The Civil Code provides a number of detailed rules relating to ownership of wildlife in the law of occupancy under Title XXIII of Book III of the Civil Code.

Under Louisiana's 1870 Civil Code, the category of common things included both running water and the seashore. In the twentieth century, however, the Louisiana legislature reclassified both of these resources as public things owned by the State of Louisiana. *See* La. Rev. Stat. §9:1101 (Acts 1910, No. 258, as amended by Acts 1954, No. 443) (providing for state ownership of "waters of and in all bayous, rivers, streams, lagoons, lakes and bays, and the beds thereof"); La. Rev. Stat. §49:3 (Acts 1938, No. 55) (providing for state ownership of "the waters of the Gulf of Mexico and of the arms of the Gulf and the beds and shores of the Gulf and the arms of the Gulf, including all lands that are covered by the waters of the Gulf and its arms either at low or high tide, within the boundaries of Louisiana"). Why do you suppose the Louisiana legislature moved running water and the seashore into the category of public things? *See* La. Rev. Stat. 49.3.1(B) (Acts 2011, No. 336) (stating that the "unequal gulfward boundaries of Gulf Coast states" established in a 1960 United States Supreme Court decision "have resulted in (1) economic disparity and hardship for Louisiana citizens and entities; (2) economic loss to the state of Louisiana and its political subdivisions . . .").

Case law interpreting the category of common things in Louisiana is scarce as federal regulation and international law provide most of the rules of decision for conflicts regarding the two examples of common things specifically enumerated by Article 449—the air and the high seas. Other things not listed in Article 449 that might be considered common things tend to be regulated by federal law as well.

2. Public versus Private Things

Most of the disputes in Louisiana involving the basic tripartite division into common, public or private things raise the question of whether a particular item falls into the category of **public things** under Article 450 of the Civil Code or **private things** under Article 453 of the Civil Code. This distinction can be slippery and counter-intuitive. First, examine the texts of both articles side by side:

Art. 450. Public Things

Public things are owned by the state or its political subdivisions in their capacity as public persons.

Public things that belong to the state are such as running waters, the waters and bottoms of natural, navigable water bodies, the territorial sea, and the seashore.

Public things that may belong to political subdivisions of the state are such as streets and public squares.

La. Civ. Code art. 450 (1978).

Article 453. Private things

Private things are owned by individuals, other private persons, and by the state or its political subdivisions in their capacity as private persons.

La. Civ. Code art. 453 (1978).

Most people probably conceive of public things as objects that are owned by federal, state or local governments and consider private things as objects owned by natural persons or juridical persons (La. Civ. Code art. 24 (1987)). As Articles 450 and 453 make clear, though, the Civil Code's distinction between public and private things does not hinge on who owns a particular thing. Instead, the Civil Code declares that a certain set of natural resources connected with water and naturally navigable water bodies are, more or less, always going to be public things owned by the state. Another set of things — like the publicly maintained things listed in the third paragraph of Article 450 that tend to be available for public use — "may," depending on the circumstances, be either public things owned by political subdivisions or, as Article 453 indicates, private things that just happen to be owned by a political subdivision of the state.

Consider an automobile. If a private individual buys an automobile for his or her personal use, it will certainly be considered a private thing under Article 453 of the Civil Code. But what happens if a city or parish police department buys the same automobile and paints it with the department's official colors and logo? According to the Civil Code, that automobile will still be a private thing, albeit one owned by the city or parish in its private capacity. It is not a public thing. None of us could walk up to that car, open the door and drive away in it. The same conclusion could be drawn for an automobile that a city buys for its mayor to use, or a copying machine that a state agency buys for its payroll department to use, or an empty lot owned by a city or parish and used as a place to park government owned vehicles. All of these are private things. They are owned by the state or a political subdivision, because they are owned by the state or a political subdivision *in its capacity as a private person*.

In summary, the state or one of its political subdivisions owns a public thing in its capacity as a public person and owns a private thing in its capacity as a private person. In contrast, a private person, whether a natural person or a juridical person, can only own private things. La. Civ. Code art. 453 (1978). As we shall see later in this chapter, however, certain private things owned by private persons can, under certain circumstances, become subject to limited forms of public use as a matter of law, La. Civ. Code art. 456 (1978). Likewise, private things can be dedicated to specific forms of public use by their owners. La. Civ. Code art. 455 (1978).

Some of the most challenging questions concerning the distinction between public and private things arise in connection with things that may not be specifically enumerated in Article 450 but which resemble the things enumerated in that provision. Other questions concern whether the items listed as public things, like streets and roads, should always be considered public things. Can objects move from one category of things to another? If so, on what grounds? And who gets to decide?

Before you proceed, re-read Article 450 carefully. Notice what things are deemed to belong to the state. Rather challenging classification problems are associated with navigable water bodies. Article 450 tells us that a *natural navigable* water body is a public thing owned by the State of Louisiana. But what happens if that water body *ceases* to be *navigable*? What about a *non-natural* or *artificial* navigable water body? Read the lengthy revision comments to Article 450 with care.

Finally, take note of Article 454 of the Civil Code. This article articulates one of the central attributes of private things — that "owners of private things may freely dispose of them under modifications established by law." La. Civ. Code art. 454 (1978). This principle of free alienability of private things is one of the fundamental policy touchstones of property law. Private things are said to be, generally speaking, alienable or capable of being voluntary transferred by their owners. Their owners can sell, donate or exchange them. However, the alienability of private things may be subject to restrictions and modifications by law or convention.

As the first decision below illustrates, when things are characterized as public, their alienation is strictly controlled and sometimes will be prohibited.

In the second decision below, we will see how things that may start out as public things can be re-characterized as private things by the state or political subdivisions and thus become *alienable*, subject to applicable rules and regulations. La. Civ. Code art. 454 rev. cmt. (c) (1978).

Note, however, that the Louisiana Constitution declares two special classes of things to be *forever inalienable* by the state: (1) the beds of navigable water bodies, except in cases of reclamation and (2) mineral rights on property owned by or sold by the state. La. Const. Art. 9, § 3 (1974) (providing that the legislature "shall neither alienate nor authorize the alienation of the bed of a navigable water body, except for purposes of reclamation by the riparian owner to recover land lost through erosion" but allowing for leasing of state lands or water bottoms for mineral or other purposes); La. Const. Art. 9, § 4 (1974) (providing that "mineral rights on property sold by the state shall be reserved," except in certain narrow circumstances).

Now consider the following two judicial opinions:

Band v. Audubon Park Comm'n

936 So.2d 841 (La. App. 4 Cir. 2006)

McKAY, Judge. This is an appeal of the trial court's judgment granting the Audubon Park Commission's motion for summary judgment against David and Ilonka Band. For the reasons set forth below, we affirm.

Affirm

Facts and Procedural History

The Audubon Park Commission (Audubon) operates Audubon Park, the Audubon Zoo, the Aquarium of the Americas, the Louisiana Nature and Science Center and several other related facilities within the City of New Orleans. Historically, on March 16, 1870, the Louisiana State Legislature approved Act 84, "An Act to Establish a Public Park for the City of New Orleans, and to Provide Means Therefore," which created a public body, The Commissioners of the New Orleans Park. The following year the Louisiana State Legislature enlarged the Commissioners' powers and authorized them to purchase additional property in the City of New Orleans, the purpose being to establish a public park in accordance with Act 84. On August 15, 1871, the Commissioners purchased the Park, which was the Foucher Plantation for $ 800,000. This public park was originally named "Upper City Park" but was eventually renamed Audubon Park. By Act 87 of 1887, the legislature abolished the original offices of the Commissioners and transferred all of the powers and duties formerly conferred on the "Park Commission" to the City Council of New Orleans. Accordingly, the City of New Orleans, through the administration of the Audubon Park Commission, is the owner of Audubon Park.

Ilonka Van Der Meulen, wife of/and David Band, Jr. (the Bands), by an Act passed before John H. Norman, Notary Public, dated August 14, 1981, acquired from Thomas A. Oreck property known as 315 Walnut Street. In this Act of purchase, the Bands recognized that there were visible encroachments on this property which intruded onto Audubon Park. There were no substantial buildings on this encroachment. This encroachment consisted of a brick patio and a light metal fence in a 10' by 30' area.

In the year 2003, Audubon began correspondence with the Bands and other residents informing them that their property was encroaching onto Audubon Park property. Audubon presented the homeowners with alternatives including allowing them to sign a lease for the property or to remove the encroachment. All ten of the affected homeowners agreed to one or the other of the alternatives except for the Bands. The Bands declined either alternative and instituted proceedings against Audubon alleging ownership of the property under various theories including acquisitive prescription. Audubon filed a motion for summary judgment in response to the Bands' petition for declaratory judgment.

The trial court granted Audubon's motion for summary judgment finding that Audubon Park was a "public thing" and not susceptible of being acquired through prescription and citing *City of New Orleans v. State of Louisiana*, 443 So.2d 562 (La. 1983), as authority. This case is the essential determinative of all other issues in this matter. We agree with the trial court's reliance on this jurisprudence.

Standard of Review

Appellate courts review summary judgments de novo under the same criteria that govern the district court's consideration of whether summary judgment is appropriate. "Favored in Louisiana, the summary judgment procedure 'is designed to secure the just, speedy, and inexpensive determination of every action' and shall be construed to accomplish these ends." *King v. Parish National Bank*, 2004-0337 (La. 10/19/04), 885 So.2d 540, 545 (quoting La. C.C.P. art. 966(A)(2)).

A summary judgment shall be rendered forthwith if the pleadings, depositions, answers to interrogatories, and admissions on file, together with the affidavits, if any, show that there is no genuine issue as to a material fact, and that the mover is entitled to judgment as a matter of law. La. C.C.P. art. 966. If the court finds that a genuine issue of material fact exists, summary judgment must be rejected. . . . The burden does not shift to the party opposing the summary judgment until the moving party first presents a prima facie case that no genuine issues of material fact exist. At that point, the party opposing the motion must "make a showing sufficient to establish existence of proof of an element essential to his claim, action, or defense and on which he will bear the burden of proof at trial." La. C.C.P. art. 966(C).

Assignments of Error

The single issue, which ultimately controls this case, is a determination of whether or not Audubon Park is a "public thing". Although, the appellants attempt to take this Court on a legal ruse arguing the "academic aspects of property law" we are not motivated to address their novel theories including that Audubon Park is the private property of the City of New Orleans. However, we will address the issue of whether or not Audubon Park is a public thing and the issue of prescription.

Discussion

[handwritten: ☑ Argue]

The appellants argue that they have essentially acquired public property by acquisitive prescription. This particular argument disregards codal and jurisprudential authority, which do not allow landowners encroaching upon public property to acquire ownership rights over the property owned by a municipality and dedicated for public use. This issue is the linchpin for this entire litigation.

[handwritten: Art. 450]

Article 448 of the Louisiana Civil Code provides that things are divided into common, public, and private things. Article 450 specifically states that, "Public things are owned by the state or its political subdivisions in their capacity as public persons." The very definition of a "public thing" prohibits a private person from owning a public thing.

[handwritten: Example]

Article 450 of the Louisiana Civil Code further provides examples of public things which may be owned by a political subdivision, "[s]uch as streets and public squares" to include public parks owned by a political subdivision in its public capacity. *Anderson v. Thomas*, 166 La. 512, 117 So. 573 (1928); *Crick v. Ward Four Recreational Comm.*, 256 So.2d 840 (La. App. 3d Cir. 1972). *Town of Vinton v. Lyons*, 131 La. 673, 60 So. 54. *See also* 2 La. Civ. L. Treatise, § 56 (4th ed.), A.N. Yiannopoulos. Clearly, the City of New Orleans is a "political subdivision" of the State. As such the City may own streets, public squares, and public parks in its public capacity.

The Supreme Court of Louisiana in *The City of New Orleans, et al., v. State of Louisiana, supra*, clearly held that Audubon Park is owned by the City of New Orleans.

Citing Professor Yiannopoulos, the Court also found that Audubon Park is a public thing.

> "A park, which is analogous to a public square, may belong to a political subdivision of the state, such as the City of New Orleans. It is, of course, a public thing owned by the City for the benefit of all persons" [citations omitted].

443 So.2d at 572.

Public things, being insusceptible of private ownership, are inalienable, imprescriptible and exempt from seizure. Vol. 2 *Louisiana Civil Law Treatise, Property, Second Edition*, by Professor A.N. Yiannopoulos. The inalienability of all public things, whether belonging to the State or its political subdivisions, is guaranteed by the Civil Code. La. Civ. Code Art. 450. Unlike the State, there is no constitutional provision declaring that public things belonging to a political subdivision are imprescriptible; however, the imprescriptibility of such a thing is a consequence of their insusceptibility of private ownership under Article 450 of the Civil Code. La. Civ. Code art. 450 and *Vol. 2 Louisiana Civil Law Treatise, Property, Second Edition*, by Professor A.N. Yiannopoulos. While it is possible to acquire things, which are owned by a political subdivision in its private capacity, it is not possible to acquire by acquisitive prescription those things which are owned by a political subdivision in its public capacity. *City of New Orleans et al. v. Salmen Brick Co.*, (La. 1914), 135 La. 828, 66 So. 237.

Audubon Park was purchased in 1871, specifically pursuant to a Louisiana legislative act for a specific purpose to establish a public park for the City of New Orleans. This specific designation for the property was stated in the original act of sale, after the act of sale, and for the last 134 years, the entirety of the area in question has been dedicated and used as a public park for the benefit of all.

The fact that the appellants purchased their property, with knowledge that it was encroaching onto Audubon Park property with constructions such as a lightweight metal fence and a single layer brick patio[,] does not change a public park to private property. The appellants' assertions are untenable. The City has never abandoned this property nor has it ever revoked its dedication as a public park.

Given the law, the evidence, and the applicable jurisprudence, we conclude, as did the trial court, that Audubon Park is public property, as it has been uninterrupted for over 130 years. Audubon Park as a public thing, belonging to the City of New Orleans in its public capacity, assured that the public has a right to unfettered use of the park.

The appellants assert that the fence and the patio meet the requirements of La. C.C. art. 459 and La. R.S. 9:5627. The trial court considered the structures on the encroaching area and determined that the fence and the patio do not meet the requirements of these exceptions. We agree.

Art. 458. Works obstructing the public use

> Works built without lawful permit on public things, including the sea, the seashore, and the bottom of natural navigable waters, or on the banks of

navigable rivers, that obstruct the public use may be removed at the expense of the persons who built or own them at the instance of the public authorities, or of any person residing in the state.

The owner of the works may not prevent their removal by alleging prescription or possession.

Art. 459. Building encroaching on public way

A building that merely encroaches on a public way without preventing its use, and which cannot be removed without causing substantial damage to its owner, shall be permitted to remain. If it is demolished from any cause, the owner shall be bound to restore to the public the part of the way upon which the building stood.

In the case sub judice, the encroaching light weight metal fence and the single bricked patio may fit the description of a building pursuant to art. 459 but in no way can be construed to be merely encroaching upon on a public way, nor can it be said that to remove these encroachments would cause substantial damage to the appellants. This fence and patio ostensibly allows two people to enjoy the use of a public thing to the exclusion of all other members of the public to enjoy the park. Appellants' particular situation does not squarely fit the requirements of art. 459. The appellants are obviously encroaching upon public property and have obstructed public use. They are clearly not entitled to the exception pursuant to art. 459[.] [T]herefore, art. 458 is controlling, and the Audubon Park Commission has the right and the authority to demand the removal of the encroachments at the appellants' expense . . . [The court also rejected the statutory liberative prescription claim under La. R.S. 9:5627 because the statute is based on same requirements as La. Civ. Code art. 459. Eds.]

Appellants further assert that to remove the encroachments would create a security or hazardous living situation as well as affect their property aesthetically, causing a potential decrease in property value. This argument is totally without merit and can in no way be interpreted as "substantial damage" to fit the requirements of La. C.C. art 459. Furthermore, the appellants were well aware that their property was encroaching onto public property when they purchased the property on Walnut Street.

The appellants' encroachments on public property clearly obstruct the public use of the property. The appellants are not entitled to invoke the exceptions found in art. 459 or R.S. 9:5627; therefore, [A]rt. 458 controls. We find no error in the trial court's judgment that the Audubon Park Commission has the right to demand the removal of the encroachments at the appellants' expense.

Appellants also argue that they have acquired property rights in ownership of the encroaching property through a theory of acquisitive prescription or adverse possession as Audubon Park has effectively abandoned the park[']s public use. We disagree.

Acquisitive prescription is a mode of acquiring ownership of immovable property or real rights by possession. La. C.C. art. 3446. Property may be acquired by ten-years possession, with just title and good faith, or by thirty-years possession, without the requirement of just title or good faith. La. C.C. arts. 3473 and 3486. . . .

As discussed above, the purchase of the property, which is now Audubon Park, was a directive of the Louisiana Legislature more than 130 years ago and [the property] has been used as a public park ever since. It has never abandoned its dedication as a public park.

Appellants' assertions primarily rely on the premise that Audubon Park is not a public park but a private property of the City of New Orleans. They have provided neither reliable testimony nor affidavits other than speculation to prove their allegation regarding the boundaries of Audubon Park or the nature of its acquisition. Their argument is unsustainable. We find no merit to their argument concerning the theory of acquisitive prescription.

Conclusion

. . . .

Accordingly, for the above and foregoing reasons we affirm the judgment of the trial court.

AFFIRMED.

Notes and Questions

1. This opinion highlights judicial methodology. Notice the variety of legal sources that Judge McKay draws upon in formulating his opinion for the court. In addition to Louisiana Civil Code articles, he cites to and discusses several of Louisiana's revised statutes, Professor A.N. Yiannopoulos' treatise on property law, and a number of decisions of the Louisiana Supreme Court and the intermediate appellate courts of Louisiana. Which sources does the court utilize first? To which sources does the court appear to give the greatest weight? Is the mix of sources used by the court different from what you might find in a typical opinion by an appellate court in a common law state?

2. Even though parks are not one of the enumerated items that "may belong" to a political subdivision of the state under Article 450, the court in *Band* concludes that Audubon Park is nevertheless a public thing that can only be owned by the state or a political subdivision of the state. What is the basis of that conclusion? What facts suggest a different conclusion?

Based on the court's analysis and the applicable Civil Code articles, what other kinds of things might also be considered public things that belong to a political subdivision? Would a medical clinic or hospital operated by a municipality or parish be a public thing? Would a commercial parking lot operated by a city and available for use by the public for a fee be considered a public thing? How about a municipal airport?

3. Assume for the sake of argument that the Bands had succeeded in convincing the court that Audubon Park was actually a private thing owned by the City of New Orleans in its private capacity. As the court implies in its opinion, this would have rendered the property susceptible of being acquired by "acquisitive prescription." The Civil Code defines acquisitive prescription as a "mode of acquiring ownership or other real rights by possession for a period of time." La. Civ. Code art. 3446 (1982). *See generally* La. Civ. Code arts. 3473, 3475 and 3486 (1982).

4. At one point in his opinion, Judge McKay states that "[u]nlike the State, there is no constitutional provision declaring that public things belonging to a political subdivision are imprescriptible," and therefore, he suggests, the imprescriptibility of public things belonging to a political subdivision must rest on some other ground, namely their status as public, and not private, things. In all likelihood, Judge McKay was referring here to one of two different provisions of the Louisiana Constitution: Article 9, Section 4(b), which, as we saw earlier, provides: "Lands and mineral interests of the State, of a school board, or of a levee district shall not be lost by prescription;" or Article 12, Section 13, which declares that "prescription shall not run against the State in any civil matter, unless otherwise provided in the Constitution or expressly by law." Because political subdivisions (other than school boards and levee districts) are not mentioned in either constitutional text, Judge McKay is surely correct that the Louisiana Constitution alone would *not* render Audubon Park imprescriptible. *See* A.N. YIANNOPOULOS, 2 LOUISIANA CIVIL LAW TREATISE: PROPERTY § 3:10 (5th ed. 2015); *City of Shreveport v. Noel Estate, Inc.* 941 So.2d 66, 80 n. 4 (La. App. 2 Cir. 2006).

5. Now suppose, hypothetically, that the land which now constitutes Audubon Park had initially been acquired by the City of New Orleans for use as a private thing (to build a warehouse to store city equipment and vehicles or as a landfill for the disposal of waste) or that it had been acquired for a public use but had never actually been put to such use. Louisiana case law is clear that in such an instance an individual like David Band could acquire the thing by acquisitive prescription. *Id.*; *City of New Iberia v. Romero*, 391 So.2d 548 (La. App. 3 Cir. 1980); *Louisiana Highway Comm'n v. Raxsdale*, 12 So.2d 631 (La. App. 2 Cir. 1943). Is there anything the City could do in that situation to make its property immune from acquisitive prescription? Consider La. Rev. Stat. § 9:5804 (1926, amended 1950). What would be the effect of municipal action under this statute?

6. Even when property is acquired by a political subdivision to serve some public purpose, the property is not necessarily classified as a public thing. As the revision comments to Article 453 note, political subdivisions can acquire property to serve some public benefit, but that fact alone does not necessarily lead to classification of the property as a public thing. *See, e.g., Anderson v. Thomas*, 117 So. 573, 579 (La. 1928) (noting that "public offices, police and fire stations, markets,

schoolhouses . . . may be dealt with as the municipality sees fit, subject only to the restrictions imposed by the act of sale or by special laws"). *See also* La. Civ. Code art. 453 rev. cmt. (b) (1978).

7. The court in *Band* also rejected the plaintiffs' secondary argument that their fenced-in patio was not a true *obstruction* of a public thing under Article 458, but rather a mere *encroachment* of a public way under Article 459 of the Civil Code. *See* La. Civ. Code arts. 458–59 (1978). If the Bands had voluntarily removed their fence, but left their patio in place, do you think the court would have responded differently to this argument? If so, why?

8. As the opinion above suggests, the Audubon Park Commission offered the Bands and ten similarly situated park neighbors the option of executing leases pursuant to which they would preserve the right to maintain patios, fences and other encroachments on Audubon Park. If, as the court's opinion implies, some of the Bands' neighbors accepted this lease option, could other neighbors or residents of New Orleans have filed suit against the Audubon Park Commission claiming that it has transformed Audubon Park into a private thing in violation of Article 450 of the Louisiana Civil Code? Would your answer depend on the length of the lease? Does the Audubon Park Commission have the authority to make such an offer on its own? As you formulate your answer to these questions, consider the following editorial published in *The Times-Picayune* at the time the dispute between the Bands and the Audubon Park Commission was beginning to take shape.

Audubon Squatters

Walnut Street residents who feel miffed at the Audubon Commission's demand that they stop encroaching on park property should consider how they would feel if the situation were reversed.

If the Audubon Commission were to build a fence, jogging path or a public restroom on part of their backyard, it's a safe bet that those homeowners wouldn't be happy about it.

Homeowners who've built patios, fences and walls on property that belongs to the park shouldn't be surprised, then, that the Audubon Commission isn't going to allow them to continue treating the park's land as their own property.

The commission has notified homeowners that they must remove constructed improvements by April 30. If they don't, the commission will lease them the land at $3.60 per square foot. But the leases won't be indefinite. At the end of 10 years, homeowners will have to clear off park land, and the leases will expire immediately if the property is sold.

That hardly seems unreasonable. Homeowners have options and time to weigh them. But Walnut Street squatters are acting like injured parties.

"It felt like a shakedown," said David Band, who has a fence and patio that extend onto park land. He would have to pay $3,000 a year to leave them in place.

"I resent the idea of having to pay money for something I'm used to," he said.

Jefferson Parker, whose fence is 13 feet into the park, said that he can't imagine that the land in question could be used for anything under the park's master plan.

But those objections completely miss the point. People can't simply take land that doesn't belong to them because they think the owners don't need it. As for Mr. Band's objections, being "used to" something isn't the same as owning it.

The Audubon Commission decided to address this issue because a complaint was raised at a public hearing last year.

"We are a public body with a fiduciary responsibility (to) all the people of New Orleans, not just our neighborhood," said Roger Ogden, a commission member.

That's clearly the right position, and the commission should stick to it.

Walnut Street residents can still enjoy backyards that extend beyond their property line if that's what they want; they just can't have it free of charge.

That's hardly a shakedown. It's a bill that's come due.

Editorial, THE TIMES-PICAYUNE (Jan. 31, 2004).

10. Judge McKay's opinion in *Band* has served as the key jurisprudential authority for the salient portions of another recent decision involving the division of things and Article 450 of the Louisiana Civil Code. *See McGraw v. City of New Orleans*, 215 So. 3d 319 (La. App. 4 Cir. 2017). On December 18, 2015, the Honorable Mitchell J. Landrieu, the Mayor of New Orleans, signed into law an ordinance that provided for the removal from publicly owned property of three monuments depicting General P.G.T. Beauregard, Jefferson Davis, and General Robert E. Lee, in their roles as former leaders of the Confederate States of America. The Beauregard monument was paid for by funds raised and donated by a private association, was donated to the City in 1907 and publicly dedicated in 1915. The Jefferson Davis monument was publicly dedicated in 1911. The Robert E. Lee monument was donated to the City by a private association and publicly dedicated to the memory of General Lee in 1884. In 1991, the monument was placed on the National Register of Historic Places.

On January 27, 2016, Pierre A. McGraw, who is the founder and president of the Monumental Task Committee, filed suit for declaratory and injunctive relief in Civil District Court for the Parish of New Orleans against the City and Mayor Landrieu in an attempt to halt the removal of the statues. McGraw asserted that his property rights were unreasonably restricted as he had invested his own time, money and labor in the upkeep of the monuments. The district court judge denied McGraw's request for a preliminary injunction. On McGraw's appeal, the Fourth Circuit affirmed:

> We now explain why Mr. McGraw has failed to establish that he will suffer irreparable harm. In order to prove that irreparable harm will befall a party from the non-issuance of a preliminary injunction, the petitioning party must show that "money damages cannot adequately compensate for the injuries suffered and that the injuries cannot be measured by pecuniary standards.'". . . .
>
> Article 477 of the Louisiana Civil Code defines ownership as "the right that confers on a person direct, immediate, exclusive authority over a thing." La. C.C. art. 477. Thus, the "owner of a thing may use, enjoy, and dispose of it within the limits and under the conditions established by law." *Id.* The provisions of the Civil Code indicate clearly that the doctrine of negotiorum gestio confers no ownership rights upon the manager who undertakes without authority the administration of another's affairs. . . .
>
> Mr. McGraw's arguments also ignore the fact that the evidence in the record establishes that each of these three monuments are public things that have been dedicated to public use. Article 448 of the Louisiana Civil Code provides that things are divided into common, public, and private things. Article 450 specifically states that, "Public things are owned by the state or its political subdivisions in their capacity as public persons." "The very definition of a 'public thing' prohibits a private person from owning a public thing." *Band v. Audubon Park Comm'n,* 05-0937, p. 5 (La.App. 4 Cir. 7/12/06), 936 So.2d 841, 845. The Jurisprudence has interpreted Article 450, which specifically provides examples of public things which may be owned by a political subdivision "[s]uch as streets and public squares," to also include public parks owned by a political subdivision in its public capacity. *See Id.* We do not hesitate to conclude that the monuments at issue are public things given that the undisputed evidence establishes clearly that they were erected on public property, owned by the City in its public capacity, and subsequently dedicated to the public use.
>
> Equally clear is the fact that the City is a "political subdivision" of the State. As such the City may own streets, public squares, and public parks in its public capacity. *See Band,* 05–0937, p. 6, 936 So.2d at 845. Public things, being insusceptible of private ownership, are inalienable, imprescriptible and exempt from seizure. *See* 2 La. Civ. L. Treatise, Property, sections 3:5, 3:8–3:11 (5th ed.). As the Supreme Court observed in *City of New Orleans v. Carrollton Land Co.,* 131 La. 1092, 1094–1095, 60 So. 695, 696 (1913): "Such property is out of commerce. It is dedicated to public use, and held as a public trust, for public uses. It is inalienable by [municipal] corporations. If the position of the city in this suit be sustained, to the effect that the

property in question is a public square, defendant cannot have acquired title thereto by prescription or otherwise." The inalienability of all public things, whether belonging to the State or its political subdivisions, is guaranteed by the Civil Code. *See* La. C.C. art. 450; *Band*, 05–0937, p. 6, 936 So.2d at 845. While it is possible to acquire things which are owned by a political subdivision in its private capacity, it is not possible for persons to acquire those things which are owned by a political subdivision in its public capacity. *See* Band, 05–0937, pp. 6–7, 936 So.2d at 845. The monuments at suit, therefore, are public things owned by the City in its capacity as a public person. *See* La. C.C. art. 450. And, as we have previously concluded, "the location, the manner and design" of the City's monuments are "within the sound discretion of the governing authorities." *State ex rel. Singelmann v. Morrison*, 57 So.2d 238, 244 (La. App. Orl. Cir. 1952) (holding that the City of New Orleans had the right to permit erection on public property of a privately-funded memorial to the memory of Mother Cabrini).

Id. at 329, 330, 331-32.

11. In addition to being insusceptible of acquisitive prescription by private persons, public things cannot be alienated or appropriated to private use. *See Monumental Task Committee, Inc. v. Foxx*, 157 F. Supp. 3d 573 (E.D. La. 2016) (determining that land on which a confederate monument sat was public land, which could not be alienated or appropriated to private use, and therefore, the City could not have donated it to private entities as asserted by the plaintiff). How does the following case fit in the picture?

Coliseum Square Ass'n v. City of New Orleans

544 So.2d 351 (La. 1989)

ON ORIGINAL HEARING: WATSON, Justice. This case involves the question of whether the City of New Orleans may close a block of a city street which is dedicated to public use and being used by the public, and lease it for sixty years to a private interest.

Facts

Chestnut Street is a narrow traffic artery which runs from Felicity Street in an unbroken line to Joseph Street. At Joseph Street, it falls into an irregular pattern, but it continues past Audubon Park to Broadway. After 1829, the street was developed uptown from Felicity as part of the grid pattern in the Lower Garden District.

The 2100 block in question comprises 14,312.90 square feet and lies between Josephine Street and Jackson Avenue. It includes a bikeway and it is located in the Lower Garden District, an historic and congested area.

Trinity Church owns the property fronting both sides of the 2100 block of Chestnut Street. After Trinity Elementary School was opened twenty-eight years ago, the public street running through the Church's property became a hazard to crossing students. In 1972, the City authorized closure of the block with gates between 10:00 A.M. and 2:30 P.M. Despite this closure, an average of 505 cars a day use the street. Of these, 220 are school related. None of the Trinity students have been injured by the traffic.

In 1985, Trinity Church broached the idea of purchasing the street block from the City and removing it from public use. The obvious advantages were greater safety and security for the school's students. In addition, a larger play area was planned. At some point, a long term lease was proposed in lieu of a sale. Trinity obtained a market value appraisal of $160,300.

The Department of Streets initially opposed the closure because of the inconvenience to vehicles and pedestrians but ultimately acquiesced in the lease proposal.

The City Planning Commission held hearings to consider the effect of closing the 2100 block of Chestnut Street to allow its incorporation into the campus of Trinity School. According to several home owners and residents, the neighbors have no objection to the block being closed during school hours but object to its permanent closure. Concern was expressed about fire and ambulance access to the historic homes in the area. The Planning Commission ultimately recommended "disposing of" the block by closing it and leasing it to Trinity Church on a long term basis.

Apparently recognizing the inalienability of this public block, the City Council elected to lease it for 60 years but did so after finding that it was no longer needed for a public purpose.

The City Council of New Orleans passed Ordinance Number 11,776, which authorized the City of New Orleans to lease "certain immovable property found to be no longer needed for public purposes", to wit, the 2100 block of Chestnut Street, to Trinity Church for 60 years. The rental of $8,040 a year is to increase by ten percent every five years but can be prepaid at a discounted rate for the full term.

Various interested parties filed suit to enjoin closure of the 2100 block of Chestnut Street. The trial court denied plaintiffs' petition for a permanent injunction, concluding that the City Council was not arbitrary and capricious in finding the property no longer needed for public purposes and that the City had authority to lease the property. The court of appeal affirmed [. . .] deciding that the City Council can lease City property under Section 6-307(4) of the Home Rule Charter of the City of New Orleans without finding that the property is no longer needed for public purposes and that the City Council was not arbitrary and capricious in deciding to close and lease the public street. A writ was granted to consider the judgment of the court of appeal.

Law

A street which is being used as a street is a public thing. LSA-C.C. art. 450. Public things cannot be alienated or appropriated to private use. . . . Since streets belong to the community at large, they cannot be the object of a contract of sale while being used by the public. . . .

It is a violation of good faith to the public, and to those who acquired property in reference to the plan of a city with a view to the enjoyment of the use thus publicly granted, to afterwards appropriate a street to private uses. . . . A public street cannot be diverted to an alternate nonpublic use. A municipal corporation has no authority to extinguish public use of public property or divest such property of its public character. . . .

The streets which belong to political subdivisions of the State are owned for the benefit of the public. A political subdivision owns a street subject to public use in its capacity as a public person. Such property, held as a public trust, is inalienable while it is being used by the public. . . . Only if public use terminates can a public street be susceptible of private ownership. "The inalienability of all public things, whether belonging to the state or to its political subdivisions, is guaranteed by the Civil Code." Yiannopoulos, Louisiana Civil Law Treatise, Property, Vol. 2, Section 34, p. 95.

The cases cited in respondent and intervenor's briefs do not support their position. Courts have permitted the sale of a street only when the street was not used by the public. *See Caz-Perk Realty v. Police Jury of Baton Rouge*, 213 La. 935, 35 So.2d 860 (1948) (overwhelming evidence showed that unnamed street was abandoned); *Schernbeck v. City of New Orleans*, 154 La. 676, 98 So. 84 (1923) (street had never been opened to traffic); *Torrance v. Caddo Parish Police Jury*, 119 So.2d 617 (La. App. 2 Cir. 1960) (street was so seldom used it was overrun with brush and only passable in dry weather).

The general laws of the State dealing with the lease of public lands are applicable to the City of New Orleans. . . . Various exceptions to the requirements for lease of public lands are not applicable to this situation. Therefore, even if this block were not dedicated to public use, its lease would be limited to 10 years under LSA-R.S. 41:1217.

Conclusion

A thing may be in use without being necessary in the sense of being essential or indispensable. The use necessary to preserve the public character and therefore prevent alienation must, of course, be substantial and not merely occasional or infrequent. Passage of 500 cars a day (or 300 discounting those on school business) is obviously substantial. A block which forms part of a continuous thoroughfare used by the public is a public thing and being used for a public purpose. While it is possible for the public to utilize alternative streets, this should not be required to further private interests.

original

The City of New Orleans and other political subdivisions can sell idle, vacant and surplus lands. However, a block of a street dedicated to public use and being used by the public is not susceptible of alienation or any other diversion to private use.

Decree

For the foregoing reasons, the judgments of the trial court and the court of appeal are reversed. The closure of the 2100 block of Chestnut Street as no longer needed for public purposes is not within the legal authority of the City Council of the City of New Orleans. The 2100 block of Chestnut Street is not susceptible of alienation or lease because it is dedicated to public use and is being used by the public. Moreover, with certain nonpertinent exceptions, a lease of public property cannot exceed a term of ten years.

Therefore, Ordinance Number 11,776 of the City of New Orleans, adopted April 2, 1987, is null and void and has no legal effect. The plaintiffs' injunction is granted.

Reversed And Rendered.

DENNIS, Justice, dissenting. I respectfully dissent.

The court in today's decision takes a Nineteenth century view of the relationship between state and municipal governments. In doing so, the majority relegates New Orleans and other home rule governments to the class of subordinate legislative creatures and sets itself up as a superlegislature to judge the wisdom or desirability of local government policy. The court's opinion is in serious conflict with the universally recognized intention of the 1974 Louisiana Constitution and with this court's concept of the proper scope of judicial review of legislative action.

Before the present case, this court recognized that Article VI of the 1974 Louisiana Constitution strikes a different balance of power between the state legislature and home rule governments than that which existed under previous constitutions. Article VI section 5 authorizes a home rule government to assume any power or function necessary, requisite or proper for the management of its affairs not denied by general law or inconsistent with the constitution. Consequently, a home rule charter government possesses in affairs of local concern, powers which within its jurisdiction are as broad as that of the state, except when limited by the constitution, or denied by general law. . . .

There is no general law which prohibits a home rule city from closing a public street and leasing or selling its public property formerly dedicated to that purpose. La. C.C. art. 450, the sole article cited in the majority opinion in support of its decision, simply states in pertinent part that "[p]ublic things that may belong to political subdivisions of the state are such as streets and public squares." Conspicuously absent from this and other codal articles is a general prohibition against government entities disposing of public property. Rather, those things which are inalienable and forever insusceptible of private ownership are delineated in the constitution. See, La. Const. art. IX, §§ 3, 4, (1974) prohibiting the alienation of water bottoms and mineral rights, respectively. Neither the Civil Code nor the constitution, therefore, denies the City of New Orleans the power to close public streets and to lease or sell public property formerly dedicated to that purpose. In fact, the legislature has specifically authorized cities of all kinds to sell, lease, exchange, or otherwise dispose of any property which is, in the opinion of the governing authority, not needed for public purposes. La.R.S. 33:4712. . . . In sum, not only is the city empowered by the constitution to direct the management of its streets without interference, but it is also expressly permitted this prerogative by statute.

Ironically, as if to underscore the weakness of its position, the majority opinion relies almost exclusively upon cases decided under state constitutions in effect prior to the 1974 Louisiana Constitution. These decisions are entirely inapposite to an interpretation of a modern home rule government's quasi-sovereign power which cannot be denied except by general law or constitutional provisions.

Because the City's authority to exercise any power or function necessary for the administration of its local affairs (including the leasing of public property for private use) is deeply rooted in our constitution, statutes and jurisprudence, this Court has but one possibly legitimate role in these circumstances: to determine whether the City exercised its authority in an arbitrary or capricious manner. For example, this court has held that it is within the scope of the police power delegated to a local government to determine whether a street is no longer needed for public purposes, and that a court will not interfere with the exercise of this discretionary power unless it has been abused by acting arbitrarily:

> ... when the Legislature delegated to the police juries and municipal corporations of this state full power and authority over the revocation and dedication of streets ... it is necessarily within the scope of the police power thus delegated to these political bodies by the legislature to look into and determine whether the street is abandoned or is no longer needed for public purposes and it is the well settled jurisprudence that courts will not interfere with the functions of ... public bodies in the exercise of this discretion vested in them unless such bodies abuse this power by acting capriciously or arbitrarily. *Caz-Perk Realty v. Police Jury*, 207 La. 796, 22 So.2d 121, 124 (1945).

Furthermore, this court has consistently held that, when an ordinance of even a small village is challenged, the judiciary will not inquire into the motives, policy or wisdom of the municipal legislative body, but will confine their review to a determination of the applicability, legality or constitutionality of laws. . . .

Unless the City's decision regarding the 2100 block of Chestnut Street, an exercise of its duly constituted authority, is shown to be arbitrary and capricious, it should be upheld. Arbitrariness has not been demonstrated. To the contrary, the record reflects that the City's determination was made only after thorough and complete consideration of the relevant evidence. The majority makes no genuine attempt to show that the legislative action in question was taken without due process or that it was arbitrary, capricious or unreasonable. Instead the majority merely substitutes its own judgment for the City's legislative choices by deciding that the street in question should not be closed or alienated because in those justices' opinion the street is in "substantial use."

ON REHEARING, MARCUS, Justice. We granted a rehearing to consider whether the New Orleans City Council (Council) has the legal authority to close the 2100 block of Chestnut Street and lease it to Trinity Episcopal Church (Trinity) and, if so, whether the decision of the Council, finding the property was no longer needed for public purposes, was arbitrary and capricious. . . .

Original

On original hearing, finding that the closure of the 2100 block of Chestnut Street was no longer needed for public purposes was not within the legal authority of the Council, we declared the ordinance null and void and granted plaintiffs' injunction. . . .

La. Const. art. VI, §5(E) provides that a home rule charter "may include the exercise of any power and performance of any function necessary, requisite, or proper for the management of its affairs, not denied by general law or inconsistent with this constitution." There is no general law which prohibits a home rule entity from closing a public street and alienating it for a private purpose. Neither is there a constitutional prohibition. Neither the Civil Code nor the Constitution, therefore, prohibits the city from alienating a public street; in fact, specific authority to sell, lease, exchange or otherwise dispose of public property is authorized by both the home rule charter of New Orleans and the legislative statutes. . . .

The authority of local governmental bodies to alienate public streets has been recognized by our courts. . . . In fact, the City of New Orleans has exercised that authority to lease and sell public streets for many years in an effort to aid economic expansion and development in the city. Hence, we conclude that in the absence of a constitutional prohibition and in view of the express authority granted by the home rule charter and La.R.S. 33:4712(A), the Council possessed the legal authority to enter into a lease of the 2100 block of Chestnut Street with Trinity.

Having determined that the Council has the legal authority to lease the 2100 block of Chestnut Street to Trinity, we must next determine whether the exercise of that authority was proper in the instant case.

In reviewing the decisions of public bodies (the City Council in the instant case), the courts will not interfere with the functions of these bodies in the exercise of the discretion vested in them unless such bodies abuse this power by acting capriciously or arbitrarily. Caz-Perk Realty, Inc. v. Police Jury of Parish of East Baton Rouge, supra. . . .

Generally, "capriciously" has been defined as a conclusion of a commission when the conclusion is announced with no substantial evidence to support it, or a conclusion contrary to substantiated competent evidence. The word "arbitrary" implies a disregard of evidence or of the proper weight thereof. . . .

Plaintiffs contend that the Council's action in closing the street was arbitrary and capricious because the 2100 block of Chestnut Street is presently being used by pedestrian and vehicular traffic during weekdays (except when it is temporarily closed from 10:00 A.M. to 2:30 P.M.) and on weekends. Since the block is presently in use, they argue that the street is "needed"; hence, the decision to close the street "as no longer needed for public purposes" is arbitrary and capricious.

The mere fact that the street is being used by the public does not mean that it is "needed" for public purposes. "Use" and "need" are relative terms and it is the duty of the Council, after reviewing and weighing the evidence presented, to determine whether discontinuance of the present use and any inconvenience resulting therefrom would outweigh whatever benefits would flow from the closure of the street.

The 2100 block of Chestnut Street is presently a one-way street running in the uptown direction and is closed to public use from 10:00 A.M. until 2:30 P.M. five days a week. The traffic impact analysis performed by Urban Systems, Inc. analyzed the effect that the permanent closure of the 2100 block of Chestnut Street would have upon traffic volume and flow in the vicinity of the school. This report established that an average of 505 vehicles used the block each day and out of those vehicles, 220 or about 44% were directly school-related. (This does not include church-related or after school activity-related traffic.) The report further determined that the vehicles that would be re-routed as a result of the closure could be accommodated on existing, adjacent streets without significant negative impacts or reduction in service. The proposed circular driveway on Jackson Avenue for drop-off and pick-up would remove Trinity-related traffic from the narrow one-way streets and also alleviate any potential traffic congestion on Jackson Avenue. The report recommended steps that could be taken to mitigate the impact, including reversing the one-way flow of traffic on Coliseum (the next street running parallel to Chestnut). This change would create a pair of one-way streets (Camp Street going downtown and Coliseum Street going uptown) that would work to the benefit of the neighborhood traffic flow. The relocation of the bike route from Chestnut Street as suggested by the study would simplify the route and improve safety. Implementation of the plan would result in a net increase of about eight parking spaces. Although plaintiffs contended that the closure would damage the historical character of the district by changing the "grid pattern" of the streets, it was the conclusion of the study that the reversal of Coliseum to flow in the uptown direction would preserve the internal grid pattern. The report was reviewed by both the City Planning Commission and the Council in reaching the determination to lease the street.

Trinity presently owns all of the property on both sides of the 2100 block of Chestnut Street. Many past and present Trinity students live in the neighborhood. The permanent closure of the block will not create a dead-end street, will not deprive any property owners of access to their property, and should not impede the access of emergency vehicles to the neighborhood residents.

Proponents contended that some of the benefits that would result from the permanent closure include increased security of the campus and safety of Trinity students as well as various other persons and groups who use the campus facilities on nights and weekends at all times of the year. Trinity has proposed a landscaping plan for the project that will increase the aesthetic quality of the neighborhood. The school's students have had a positive economic impact on the city and fulfillment of the school's long-term goals which include the use of the 2100 block of Chestnut will help the facility maintain its quality educational program. In fact, some residents of the neighborhood with no relationship to Trinity testified that the school's plans for the campus would enhance the value of the neighborhood in addition to increasing the quality of education at this inner city institution.

After weighing the substantial evidence presented to it, the Council determined that the present use made of the 2100 block of Chestnut Street could be served by alternative means and the benefits resulting from the permanent closure of the block outweighed whatever inconvenience the closure would have on the neighborhood in particular and the public in general. Based upon our review of the record, we are unable to say that the Council was arbitrary and capricious in its determination that the 2100 block of Chestnut Street is no longer needed for public purposes and it can be leased to Trinity under the terms and provisions agreed upon by the parties to the lease.

In sum, we find that the Council had the legal authority to close the 2100 block of Chestnut Street and lease it to Trinity and that the decision of the Council that the property was no longer needed for public purposes was neither arbitrary nor capricious. Accordingly, we should not substitute our judgment for that of the Council and will not. Hence, we reverse our judgment on original hearing and affirm the judgments of the courts below.

Decree

For the reasons assigned, the judgment of the court of appeal is affirmed. All costs are assessed against plaintiffs.

DIXON, C.J., respectfully dissents.

WATSON, Justice, dissents, adhering to the view that the City cannot lease public property being used by the public to a private concern under the pretext that the property is no longer needed for public purposes.

Notes and Questions

1. In light of the Louisiana Supreme Court's holding on rehearing in *Coliseum Square Ass'n v. City of New Orleans*, 544 So.2d 351 (La. 1989), and Justice Dennis' concurring dissent in the first hearing, it appears that there are only two kinds of things that can never be converted from public things to private things as the result of a decision by political officials of the State or one of its political subdivisions. Recall what those two things are. *See* La. Const. Art. 9, §§ 3–4 (1974).

2. Why does Justice Watson, in his majority opinion on original hearing, declare the ordinance null and void? Is it for lack of authority? Justice Dennis disagrees. Notice how he sets up his dissent by contrasting "a Nineteenth century view of the relationship between state and municipal governments" with "the universally recognized intention of the 1974 Louisiana Constitution and with this court's concept of the proper scope of judicial review of legislative action." *Coliseum Square Ass'n v. City of New Orleans*, 544 So.2d 351, 355 (La. 1989). Justice Dennis continues:

Before the present case, this court recognized that Article VI of the 1974 Louisiana Constitution strikes a different balance of power between the state legislature and home rule governments than that which existed under previous constitutions. Article VI section 5 authorizes a home rule government to assume any power or function necessary, requisite or proper for the management of its affairs not denied by general law or inconsistent with the constitution. Consequently, a home rule charter government possesses in affairs of local concern, powers which within its jurisdiction are as broad as that of the state, except when limited by the constitution, or denied by general law. . . .

Id. at 355-56. In light of the reasoning on rehearing, is the presence or absence of a home rule charter the decisive criterion?

3. After finding the requisite power to make such decisions (in home rule charter legislation and other special legislation governing municipalities) both Justice Dennis' dissenting opinion and Justice Marcus' opinion on rehearing stress the importance of subjecting municipal decisions about undoing dedication of roads and streets to public use and the underlying question of whether a road or street is *needed* for public use to a standard querying whether the closing of the street was arbitrary and capricious. This type of standard, which is used by the courts to control administrative decisions, gives, by design, great deference to political actors. It applies, for example, when a federal court is asked to hold unlawful and set aside a federal agency's action, findings, and conclusions under the federal Administrative Procedure Act, 5 U.S.C. § 706(2)(A).

Although this standard requires a reviewing court to perform a searching and careful inquiry into the facts to ensure that a decision-maker has considered all factors and has not reached a conclusion that is completely contrary to the evidence or without any logical support, a court is *not* supposed to substitute its own judgment for that of the decision-maker. Do you think this standard of review is appropriate for the determination of whether a street can be transformed from a public thing into a private thing under Louisiana law?

4. Today the 2100 block of Chestnut Street in New Orleans is closed twenty-four hours a day, seven days a week. Compare *Coliseum Square* with *Band* where the leases proposed by the Audubon Park Commission were required to sunset after ten years. Does the public have a greater interest in preserving access to a small corner of Audubon Park or to a public street that is used by motor vehicles more than five hundred times a day?

5. *Terminology.* Louisiana courts have traditionally spoken of public things as "insusceptible of private ownership." The approach favored by Professor Yiannopoulos characterizes public things as "out of commerce" (*hors de commerce*) and private things as "in commerce." A.N. YIANNOPOULOS, 2 CIVIL LAW: PROPERTY § 3:8 (5th ed. 2015). French doctrine has traditionally divided public property into the public domain (*dominalité publique*) or the private domain (*dominalité privée*).

Marcel Planiol & Georges Ripert, Traité Pratique de Droit Civil Français, no. 117 n.1 (2d ed. 1952). This approach was originally adopted by the Louisiana Civil Code of 1870. La. Civ. Code arts. 453, 482(2), 485, 486 (1870). Are these approaches more or less helpful, for purposes of classification, than the current approach?

6. *The Division of Things in other Civilian Legal Systems.* The Civil Code of Puerto Rico offers a tripartite classification similar to that found in the Louisiana Civil Code. P.R. Laws Ann. Tit. 31, §§ 1022–26 (1993). Other civil codes have taken very different approaches.

In the chapter entitled "Kinds of Property," Quebec's Civil Code, for example, divides property, whether corporeal or incorporeal, into immovables and movables, and elaborates on this bifurcation. *See Civil Code of Québec* (C.C.Q.), arts. 899 *et seq.*(1991). The analogues for common things (those "that may not be appropriated") and public things ("property of the State") are found in the chapter entitled "Property in Relation to Persons having rights in it or possession of it." *See* C.C.Q., arts. 913 and 916, 917–920 (1991). Within the domain of the State, a distinction between local and provincial levels is not offered.

In France, in the wake of a revision of its Civil Code, the provisions for property in "the Public Domain" and things belonging to the State—things not owned by private persons—were repealed and moved into special legislation. *See Code général de la propriété des personnes publiques* (General Code for the Property of Public Persons).

The German Civil Code does not govern things considered "out of commerce"— public and common things—either because of their natural characteristics or for reasons provided by law. In Germany, the subject-matter of a legal dispute determines a court's jurisdiction. So while "ordinary courts" exercise jurisdiction over private law matters, public law matters fall into the jurisdiction of the "administrative courts." More detail can be found in the Law on the Organization of the Judiciary (*Gerichtsverfassungsgesetz* or GVG) and the Administrative Procedure Act (*Verwaltungsgerichtsordnung* or VwGO). See § 13 GVG, § 40 VwGO.

Problems

1. Suppose that the City of New Orleans wants to lease or sell Audubon Park to Disney Corporation for development into a private theme park? Can the city do so? What would it have to prove? Outline the steps the city would need to take to justify such a move.

2. Suppose that the City of New Orleans proposes to sell Jackson Square in the French Quarter to Universal Studios for private development. Adjacent merchants are in favor of the proposal because Universal Studios has promised that access to their shops will be guaranteed from 8:00 a.m. to 12:00 p.m. every day of the year, private security details will patrol the adjacent streets, and the streets will be cleaned and maintained to a high standard. Can residents of the French Quarter who do not live in the immediate vicinity of Jackson Square block this proposal? What would

they have to establish? Would the result be any different if Jackson Square was located in the City of Baton Rouge, a city not governed by a home rule charter? *See Landry v. Parish of East Baton Rouge*, 220 So.2d 795 (La. App. 1 Cir. 1979).

3. Imagine a small Louisiana town named Broussard. In 1988, the town purchased some fire-fighting equipment: a 1968 Ford fire truck and the pumping unit of a 1988 Dodge fire truck. Sometime after 1989, the equipment ended up in the possession of a separate entity, known as the Broussard Volunteer Fire Department. There are no official records indicating that the town sold, donated or transferred this equipment to anyone, let alone to the volunteer fire department. The department has maintained possession of the equipment at least since the date of its official incorporation, in 1989, as a non-profit corporation under the laws of the State of Louisiana.

In 2012, the Town of Broussard sued the Broussard Volunteer Fire Department for the return of the fire truck and pumping unit or, in the alternative, for $36,000 in damages. The town claimed that it owns the equipment and that it only loaned the equipment to the volunteer fire department. The fire department responded by claiming that it owns the truck and the pumping unit as the result of ten-year acquisitive prescription. *See* La. Civ. Code art. 3491 (1982). Are the truck and pumping unit, which are movables under Louisiana law, subject to acquisitive prescription?

4. On May 21, 2007, the City of New Orleans purchased a house from a private resident for the purpose of renovating the house into a public library. The renovation of and additions to the building were eventually put out for public bids. In November 2007, the Jones Construction Company began construction on a street and drainage improvement project under a public works contract with the Sewerage and Water Board. During the pile driving and other activities connected with the construction project, the building purchased by the City for use as a public library was damaged. Jones Construction completed the construction work in December 2009.

On March 4, 2011, the city's mayor approaches you for advice. She tells you that the city intends to file a lawsuit seeking monetary relief for the damage to the building that was caused by the construction project. A lawyer for Jones Construction asserts that it considers such proceedings barred by state law.

The Louisiana Civil Code provides that "[d]elictual actions are subject to a liberative prescription of one year." La. Civ. Code art. 3492 (1983, amended 1992). In deviation from the codal prescription, a Louisiana statute provides:

> When private property is damaged for public purposes any and all actions for such damages are prescribed by the prescription of two years, which shall begin to run after the completion and acceptance of the public works.

La. Rev. Stat. § 9:5624 (1950, amended 1987). In both the civil code article and the statute above, the term "prescription" refers to *liberative prescription*—"a mode of barring actions as a result of inaction for a period of time." La. Civ. Code art. 3447

(1982). In other words, both provisions establish a statute of limitations for the filing of a lawsuit. If a party, even one with a valid claim, delays bringing its cause of action beyond the applicable *liberative prescription* period, it will usually be dismissed.

Will the city's action for damages be considered timely filed? Draft a legal memorandum for the mayor providing her with your advice.

B. Defining the Scope of Public Things

Having sketched out the tripartite division of things, we now turn our attention to several public things that are specifically enumerated in the Civil Code. The following sections examine how more specific legislation and case law have combined to define the precise functional and geographic limits of these "public" resources. Articles 450 and 452 of the Civil Code are our initial guideposts.

The starting point for our analysis is the second paragraph of Article 450:

Art. 450. Public Things

Public things that belong to the state are such as running waters, the waters and bottoms of natural, navigable water bodies, the territorial sea and the seashore.

La. Civ. Code art. 450 (1978). Article 452 builds upon Article 450 by providing, in part:

Art. 452. Public things and common things subject to public use

Public things and common things are subject to public use in accordance with applicable laws and regulations. Everyone has the right to fish in the rivers, ports, roadsteads, and harbors, and the right to land on the seashore, to fish, to shelter himself, to moor ships, to dry nets, and the like, provided that he does not cause injury to the property of adjoining owners.

La. Civ. Code art. 452 (1978).

Reading these two provisions *in pari materia* (a statutory construction technique which calls for statutes relating to the same subject matter to be construed together to discern the legislative intent), we conclude that the state owns several key resources associated with water and that members of the public have broad, but not unlimited, rights to use them. These resources include running water, the water and bottoms of natural, navigable water bodies, the territorial sea, and the seashore. The challenge frequently posed in disputes involve defining what these resources are and determining how far their geographic reach extends in any given direction.

1. Running Water

The term *running water*, as used in Article 450 of the Louisiana Civil Code, refers primarily to water flowing on the surface of the earth. It could also be said, however, to refer to water flowing in a natural water body such as a river, stream, bayou or lake. *See* La. Rev. Stat. § 9:1101 (1910, amended 1954) ("The waters of and in all bayous, rivers, streams, lagoons, lakes and bays, and the beds thereof, not under the direct ownership of any person on August 12, 1910, are declared to be the property of the state. There shall never be any charge assessed against any person for the use of the waters of the state for municipal, agricultural or domestic purposes.").

The key point to note here is that the *water* flowing in an inland water body is distinct from the *bed* of that water body. This has important legal consequences if the river, stream or lake at issue is *not* navigable. The bed of an inland, *non-navigable* water body is a private thing and may be owned by a private person or by the state or one of its political subdivisions in its private capacity. *See* La. Rev. Stat. § 9:1115.2(B) (1992) ("Inland non-navigable water beds or bottoms are private things and may be owned by private persons or by the state and its political subdivisions in their capacity as private persons."). The water flowing through a non-navigable, but naturally occurring, stream or bayou, will remain a public thing. Although running water is subject to public use under Article 452, the statement that "[e]veryone has the right to fish in the rivers, ports . . . and harbors" allows fishing only in *natural, navigable* water bodies. The owner of a non-navigable waterway has exclusive rights to occupy the land underneath and the airspace above the waterway, subject to all applicable regulations.

Another set of provisions in the Civil Code, which falls under the heading of "Natural Servitudes," regulates the obligations reciprocally owed by neighboring property owners with respect to surface water and running water that passes through one estate and onto another. *See generally* La. Civ. Code arts. 655–58 (1977). A person who owns land bordering on or containing running water (a person often referred to as a "riparian" landowner), may use the running water passing through or adjacent to her estate to water his estate or for other purposes, La. Civ. Code art. 657 (1977), but the riparian landowner cannot completely block the water or redirect it to another channel as it leaves his property. La. Civ. Code art. 658 (1977). The downstream riparian landowner also has a right to use the running water.

As we noted earlier, prior to 1910, running water in Louisiana was considered a common thing. Today it is classified as a public thing. La. Rev. Stat. § 9:1101 (1910, amended 1954). This change in classification has occasionally created confusion for litigants and courts. Several Louisiana judicial decisions have clarified, for instance, that the mere presence of running water in a natural, *non-navigable* water body such as a small stream or bayou or flooded swampland, or in a navigable, but *non-natural* water body like a private canal, does not require a riparian landowner to permit access to that water. *See Buckskin Hunting Club v. Bayard*, 868 So.2d 266, 274 (La. App. 3 Cir. 2004) (rejecting claims of hunters to gain access to man-made canals); *People for Open Waters, Inc. v. Estate of Gray*, 643 So.2d 415, 418 (La. App. 3 Cir. 1994) (reaching the same conclusion). Rather, the only obligation owed by a riparian landowner to the public or to other riparian landowners is to allow the running water to leave his estate through its natural channel and not unduly diminish its flow. *Buckskin*, 868 So.2d at 274; La. Civ. Code arts. 657–58 (1977). Consequently, members of the public do not have a right to cross private lands merely to avail themselves of running water.

The Civil Code does not address underground water resources. Instead, underground water is regulated—albeit in quite vague terms—by the Louisiana Mineral Code. *See* La. Rev. Stat. § 31:4 (1974) (declaring that the Mineral Code is applicable not only to oil and gas, but also to "rights to explore for or mine or remove from land the soil itself, gravel, shells, *subterranean water,* or other substances occurring naturally in or as part of the soil or geological formations on or underlying the land") (emphasis added). Recognizing the inadequacy of Louisiana's regulatory framework for ground water, especially in light of increasing demands for its use in connection with hydraulic fracturing (or "fracking"), a drilling technique used to increase production from new and old oil and gas wells, the Louisiana Senate has recently directed the Louisiana State Law Institute to create a "Water Code Committee" for the purpose of drafting a comprehensive "Water Code that integrates all of Louisiana's water resources" for consideration by the legislature in the next several years. 2014 La. Acts, Senate Resolution 171. The Institute has meanwhile signed a memorandum of understanding with The Nature Conservancy. It is also working "to bring together a water budget and modeling system for the state that can not only tell what water is available and needed now, but what may be available and needed decades in the future . . . The project will take years to complete and will likely proceed in phases that are tied to current and emerging water management challenges such as those posed by hydraulic fracturing for oil and gas, coastal restoration, and climate change." Tulane Institute on Water Resources Law and Policy, Program Areas, *at* http://www.tulanewater.org /program-areas (Sept. 6, 2018). For early scholarship alerting the academic community to fracking as a law and technology issue of great significance, see Markus G. Puder, *Did the Eleventh Circuit Crack 'Frac?'—Hydraulic Fracturing after the Court's Landmark LEAF Decision*, 18 VA. ENVTL. L.J. 507 (1999).

2. Territorial Sea

In discussing the "high seas," which are classified under Article 449 as a common thing, we noted that the drafters of the Civil Code added the adjective "high" in counter-distinction to other navigable waters, both inland and offshore, which are generally classified as public things belonging to the state. The navigable waters found offshore that are not encompassed by the "high seas" definition fall under the heading of "territorial sea." La. Civ. Code art. 450 (1978). The Civil Code, however, does not define this term.

One Louisiana property scholar summarizes the respective rights of the state of Louisiana and the United States in the following terms:

> . . . The seabottom extending three miles from the coastline, within Louisiana boundaries, belongs to the state, whereas submerged lands beyond the three mile zone seaward belong to the United States. The actual point

of departure for the measurement of the three mile zone has been fixed by court order in the litigation between the United States and Louisiana.

A.N. YIANNOPOULOS, 2 LOUISIANA CIVIL LAW TREATISE: PROPERTY § 4:11, at 153 (5th ed. 2015). The litigation of and legislative responses to the so-called "tidelands controversy" between the United States government and Louisiana and its sister states on the Gulf Coast is detailed below.

In terms of what the "territorial sea" encompasses, we must distinguish between two dimensions of the territorial sea — one international and the other concerning federal-state relations. For purposes of the international law of the oceans, the territorial sea embodies the maritime band closest to the nation-state. In 1988, the United States, consistent with customary international law (as codified by the United Nations Convention on the Law of the Sea, to which the United States is not a State Party), claimed a zone of twelve nautical miles. *See* Proclamation 5928 of Dec. 27, 1988. *Territorial Sea of the United States of America* (54 Fed. Reg. 777 (Jan. 9, 1989)). The United States baselines for measuring this band outward are the mean of the lower water tides as marked on the largest scale National Oceanic and Atmospheric Administration's nautical charts. These baselines are ambulatory as the coastline erodes and accretes.

A nautical mile is a unit of measure used in navigation. It is based on the circumference of the earth. An observer six feet in height standing at sea level can see an object three nautical miles away along the equator before the curve of the earth causes that object to fall below the horizon. A nautical mile is about 1.1508 land miles, and three nautical miles equal one marine league. A geographic mile is one minute of longitude along the equator. A sea mile is one minute of latitude and may vary in length.

In light of the federal makeup of the United States, the other dimension in our discussion of the territorial sea pertains to state claims within that zone. When the State of Louisiana was admitted into the Union, the Gulf of Mexico, inclusive of all islands within "three leagues" of the coast, was identified as its southern border. Victor A. Sachse, *Legislation Defining Louisiana's Coastal Boundaries*, 15 LA. L. REV. 79 (1954).

In 1938, the Louisiana legislature claimed ownership of twenty-seven "marine miles" of submerged lands measured from its coastline gulfward, reasoning that the ancient cannon shot rule of three "marine miles" was out of date. 1938 La. Acts, No. 55, § 1, p. 169 (declaring that (1) the "gulfward boundary of Louisiana is already located in the Gulf of Mexico three leagues distant from the shore, a width of marginal area made greater" by the act leading to the admission of Louisiana to the Union than the "inherent three-mile limit;" (2) that "a State can define its limits on the sea;" and (3) the legislature fixed the gulfward boundary of the state as "a line located in the Gulf of Mexico parallel to the three-mile limit as determined according to said ancient principles of international law, which gulfward boundary is located twenty-four marine miles further out in the Gulf of Mexico than the said three-mile limit."). See also Victor A. Sachse, *Legislation Defining Louisiana's Coastal Boundaries*, 15 LA. L. REV. 79 (1954).

In 1945, President Harry Truman issued a proclamation asserting the Federal Government's interest in offshore sub-seabed wealth. *See* Proclamation 2667 of Sept. 28, 1945. *Policy of the United States with Respect to the Natural Resources of the Subsoil and the Seabed of the Continental Shelf* 10 Fed. Reg. 12303 (Sept. 28, 1945). This proclamation set the stage for the "tidelands controversy" between the United States and the various coastal states.

Litigation began with a trespass complaint by the United States filed in the Supreme Court of the United States against the State of California. Deciding for the United States, the Supreme Court rejected the long-held assumption that individual states had entered the Union with a right to control a three-mile offshore belt of territorial sea. The high court cited the need for the national government to control its territorial sea as a function of external sovereignty. *United States v. California*, 332 U.S. 19 (1947). Three years later, in the first tidelands case initiated by the United States against Louisiana, the Supreme Court gave the federal government sole jurisdiction over the submerged lands adjacent to the Louisiana coast, thus effectively eliminating state claims to title over submerged lands seaward of the low-water mark on the coast. *United States v. Louisiana*, 339 U.S. 699 (1950).

The pendulum, however, swung the other way in 1953, when the Submerged Lands Act and the Outer Continental Shelf Lands Act became federal law. The Submerged Lands Act quitclaimed to the states a maritime belt of three nautical miles measured from the coastline and provided for a special arrangement with the coastal states bordering the Gulf of Mexico. Those states were allowed to prove historical boundaries up to three marine leagues. Thereafter, lawsuits ensued to ascertain the exact nature of the legislative grant as well as the precise location of the states' boundaries.

In 1953, Louisiana's legislature codified as Louisiana's coastline the Inland Water Line adopted by the United States Coast Guard. In 1954, Louisiana set her maritime boundary at nine nautical miles (three marine leagues) from the Coast Guard's "Inland Water Line." This led to an interim agreement between the United States government and the State of Louisiana, which divvied up offshore leasing rights into four zones. In 1960, the Supreme Court decided that the maritime boundary for Louisiana, Mississippi, and Alabama was only three nautical miles, whereas Texas and Florida's boundaries were set at three marine leagues because these states had entered the United States as sovereigns. *United States v. Louisiana, Texas, Mississippi, Alabama, & Florida*, 363 U.S. 1 (1960). The Supreme Court, however, did not address the precise location of the coastline from which to measure the three nautical miles granted to Louisiana.

The location of Louisiana's coastline was not specified until 1969, when the Supreme Court ordered the application of the principles set forth in the *1958 Convention on Territorial Sea and the Contiguous Zone*. A Special Master was appointed for the purpose of locating Louisiana's seaward boundary. *United States v. Louisiana*, 394 U.S. 11 (1969). Six years later, in 1975, the Supreme Court approved the final report of the Special Master. *United States v. Louisiana*, 420 U.S. 529 (1975); *United States v. Louisiana et al.*, No. 9, Orig., 422 U.S. 13 (1975).

Responding to Louisiana's wetlands loss, a 1985 amendment to the Outer Continental Shelf Lands Act immobilized the maritime boundary coordinates established for Louisiana a decade earlier under the final decree of the Supreme Court. The saga, however, has not quite ended. In 2011, the Louisiana legislature amended Title 49 of the Revised Statutes (state administration). Sections 1, 3 and 3.1 now read as follows:

§ 1. Gulfward boundary

A. The historic gulfward boundary of the state of Louisiana extends a distance into the Gulf of Mexico three marine leagues from the coastline. For the purposes of this Part, "three marine leagues" is equal to nine geographic miles or 10.357 statute miles.

B. The coastline of Louisiana shall be the line of ordinary low water along that portion of the coast which is in direct contact with the open sea and the line marking the seaward limit of inland waters, and shall be not less than the baseline defined by the coordinates set forth in United States v. Louisiana, 422 U.S. 13 (1975), Exhibit "A". Under no circumstances shall the coastline of Louisiana be nearer inland than the baseline established by such coordinates.

C. No provision of this Section shall be construed to relinquish any dominion, sovereignty, territory, property, or rights of the state of Louisiana or its political subdivisions otherwise provided by law.

§ 3. Ownership of waters within boundaries

The State of Louisiana owns in full and complete ownership the waters of the Gulf of Mexico and of the arms of the Gulf and the beds and shores of the Gulf and the arms of the Gulf, including all lands that are covered by the waters of the Gulf and its arms either at low tide or high tide, within the boundaries of Louisiana.

§ 3.1. Legislative intent and purpose

A. The gulfward boundary of the state of Louisiana historically consists of three marine leagues, and it is the intent of the Legislature of Louisiana that this historic gulfward boundary be recognized and enforced as law.

B. The unequal gulfward boundaries of Gulf Coast states set forth by the United States Supreme Court in *United States of America v. States of Louisiana, Texas, Mississippi, Alabama, and Florida*, 363 U.S. 1 (1960), have resulted in (1) economic disparity and hardship for Louisiana citizens and entities; (2) economic loss to the state of Louisiana and its political subdivisions; and (3) the inability of the state of Louisiana and its political subdivisions to fully exercise their powers and duties under the federal and state constitutions and state laws and ordinances, including but not limited to protection and restoration of coastal lands, waters, and natural resources, and regulation of activities affecting them.

C. It is the further intent of the Legislature of Louisiana that, in light of the continuing effects of coastal erosion, subsidence, and land loss, the coastline of Louisiana should be recognized as consisting of at least and not less than that coastline defined by the coordinates set forth in *United States v. Louisiana*, 422 U.S. 13 (1975), Exhibit "A".

D. Notwithstanding any provision of law to the contrary, the jurisdiction of the state of Louisiana or any political subdivision thereof shall not extend to the boundaries recognized herein until the U.S. Congress acknowledges the boundary described herein by an Act of Congress or any litigation resulting from the passage of Acts 2011, No. 336 with respect to the legal boundary of the state is resolved and a final non-appealable judgment is rendered.

La. Rev. Stat. §§ 49:1, 3, 3.1 (1954, amended 2011)

Please analyze these statutes. What does the Louisiana legislature seek to accomplish with these statutes? Does it overreach?

3. The Seashore

We now turn to the seashore, one of the resources specifically enumerated in Article 450 as a public thing owned by the state. Article 451 of the Civil Code specifically defines the seashore as "the space of land over which the waters of the sea spread in the highest tide during the winter season." La. Civ. Code art. 451 (1978). This somewhat archaic definition dates back to Justinian's *Corpus Juris*, which provided that "the shore of the sea is as far as the greatest winter wave rolls in." Inst. Lib. 2, t. 1, s. 3; Dig., lib. 50, t. 16, s. 112 (trans. MGP).

In the Mediterranean geography inhabited by the Romans, this definition made sense because the highest tides are usually found in the winter months. But in the Gulf of Mexico, where the highest tides occur in the summer months, its utility is less certain. Nevertheless, the drafters of the Digest of 1808, Moreau-Lislet and Brown, plainly adopted the Roman template. Interestingly, Moreau-Lislet refers to the *Codigo de las Siete Partidas*, a work that he later translated from Spanish into English in light of its significance and operations in Louisiana, as the provision that inspired the definition of seashore in the Digest of 1808. Yet Spanish law, which was compiled in the context of an Atlantic climate in the high Middle Ages, provides that the crucial point from which to measure the seashore is "the highest annual swells, whether in winter or in summer." Louis Moreau Lislet & Henry Carlton, I. The Laws of Las Siete Partidas, which are still in force in the State of Louisiana 336 (1820). As the revision comments and as Louisiana courts have observed, however, the definition of seashore found in Article 451 of the Civil Code is the one we must use until the legislature addresses the subject again. La. Civ. Code art. 451 (1978).

The most important feature of Article 451 lies in its reference to an area of land "over which the waters of the sea spread." This space might at first glance appear to be a fairly wide area. But, as the revision comments to Article 451 explain, Louisiana courts have interpreted the geographic reach of the seashore as "the space of land in the *open* coast that is *directly* overflown by the tides," a zone that may be more limited than the Civil Code's textual definition suggests. La. Civ. Code art. 451 rev. cmt. (b) (1978) (emphasis in original). The revision comments cite the Louisiana Supreme Court decision in *Buras v. Salinovich*, 97 So. 748 (La. 1923), our next case, as its primary source.

What unique circumstances, if any, of the dispute in *Buras* produced this seemingly more narrow and precise definition? Is this judicial definition likely to lead to more or less certainty when disputes erupt between littoral landowners and members of the public attempting to engage in customary hunting, fishing and navigation activities in places they consider to be the seashore?

Buras v. Salinovich

154 La. 495 (La. 1923)

O'NIELL, Chief Justice. The question in this case is whether the conservation laws of the state give to the holder of a license to hunt and trap wild game and fur-bearing animals; the right to hunt and trap on any and all marsh land, even against the protest of the owner of such land, if the land be subject to tidal overflow, unfenced, not in cultivation or used as a pasture, and not set apart as a game preserve.

Plaintiff here owns a tract of marsh land, exceeding 5,000 acres in area, fronting nearly 4 miles on the east bank of the Mississippi river, about 85 miles below New Orleans. The land is not fenced, or cultivated, or used for a pasture; and, excepting the ridge that extends back only a few acres from the river, and the ridges forming the banks of several bayous in the land, it is subject to tidal overflow, and not fit for cultivation.

Each of the six defendants holds a state license, declaring that he 'has paid the license fee required by law, and is entitled to hunt such game birds and game animals, and to catch or trap such animals as are defined under the laws of the state of Louisiana, during the open season, and in such manner and at such times and places as permitted by law.' The defendants, pursuing a custom which had prevailed among the local hunters and trappers from time immemorial, went upon plaintiff's land, without his consent and, for their own profit, engaged in hunting the wild game and in trapping the fur-bearing animals on the land.

The plaintiff had posted notices, printed in bold letters, on boards measuring 18 inches square, along the boundaries of the land and along the banks of the bayous running through the land, forbidding trespassing within the line of stakes, under penalty of the law. The notices and intervening stakes were spaced close enough together to serve their purpose.

Similar notices, describing the land, were published in the two newspapers published in the parish where the land is situated.

Plaintiff also had a man employed patrolling the land, making the rounds regularly through the bayous, warning hunters and trappers against trespassing upon the land. He delivered to each of the defendants personally a written demand that they should quit hunting and trapping on the land. The defendants refused to quit. Thereupon plaintiff brought this suit, alleging the facts which we have stated, and praying for a preliminary injunction, to be eventually made perpetual, forbidding the defendants to go upon the land for the purpose of hunting or trapping.

The district judge issued a rule, ordering the defendants to show cause why the preliminary injunction should not issue.

Answering the petition, and the rule to show cause, the defendants denied that plaintiff was entitled to any relief, on the facts stated, and they set up a reconventional demand for a judgment in their favor, declaring that they had the right to go upon any part of the land described in plaintiff's petition 'for the purpose of trapping, taking, capturing, killing, or removing from the land, any animal, fowl, bird, or quadruped, without the consent or permission of the plaintiff or of any other person, and further condemning the said Manuel Oscar Buras to pay to respondents, as plaintiffs in reconvention, the sum of $3,250, as damages, with legal interest.' etc. The damages claimed were said to be $2,500 for the alleged or approximated value of the fur-bearing animals which, defendants alleged, this suit had prevented their trapping, and $750 for attorneys fees alleged to have been incurred in defending the suit.

Having heard argument on the rule, the district judge refused to issue a temporary injunction. The case was then heard on its merits, resulting in a judgment for the defendants, rejecting the plaintiff's demand for an injunction 'and recognizing the defendants' right to enter upon the premises described in the petition herein, for the purpose of trapping and removing therefrom such wild life and fur-bearing animals as are permitted by state license.' The plaintiff has appealed.

The Civil Code, in article 3415, after declaring that the wild beasts and birds have no owner while they are at large, and that when captured they become immediately the property of their captor, whether he takes them from his own land or from the land of another, says:

> 'But the proprietor of a tract of land may forbid any person from entering it
> for the purpose of hunting thereon.'

The argument of the defendants is twofold. It is contended, first, that this provision of the Code, recognizing the right of any and every landowner to forbid hunting on his land, was repealed by implication, or superseded, by section 20 of the Conservation Law (Act 204 of 1912), as to marsh land, subject to tidal overflow, and not fenced, or in cultivation, or used as a pasture, or set apart as a game preserve. In the alternative, the defendants contend that plaintiff's land, being subject to overflow regularly from the gulf tides, is 'seashore,' according to the definition in the

Civil Code, and is therefore not subject to private ownership. They refer to articles 450, 451, 452 of the Civil Code, viz: . . .

> Art. 451 (442). 'Seashore is that space of land, over which the waters of the sea spread in the highest water, during the winter season. . . .

The district judge, in his written opinion, maintained the defendants' contention that the provision in article 3415 of the Civil Code, recognizing the right of every landowner to forbid hunting on his land, was repealed by implication, or superseded, by section 20 of Act 204 of 1912, in so far at it had applied to marsh land, subject to tidal overflow, and unfenced, and not cultivated or used for a pasture, or set apart as a game preserve. The judge did not maintain that the land was 'seashore,' not subject to private ownership. He must have concluded or assumed that the land was not 'seashore'; otherwise there would have been no occasion for pronouncing judgment upon the repealing effect of section 20 of Act 204 of 1912, as to marsh land that is subject to private ownership.

We concur in the opinion that plaintiff's land should not be classed as 'seashore,' or public property. (The fact that it is subject to tidal overflow does not characterize the land as 'seashore,' under the provisions of the Code.) The statutes providing for disposing of such lands, either by the state or by the federal government, describe them as being subject to tidal overflow. It has never heretofore been supposed that the definition in article 451 of the Civil Code was intended to include in the term 'that space of land over which the waters of the sea spread in the highest water during the winter season,' any and all land that is subject to tidal overflow, however remote from the 'seashore,' as it is generally understood. The waters of the Gulf of Mexico, or the bays or coves behind plaintiff's land, do not 'spread' upon it, during the ordinary high tides, or in the highwater seasons. The tide waters back up into the coves behind the land, and cause the bayous in the land to rise and spread over most of the area. These expressions in the Code 'the sea and its shores,' and 'seashore,' have reference to the gulf coast, and to the lakes, bays and sounds along the coast. The nearest body of water that could reasonably be characterized as a part of the sea, or as having a seashore, in this case, is a small bay nearly a mile away from plaintiff's land.

In the case of *Morgan v. Nagodish*, 40 La. Ann. 246, 3 South. 636, the question presented was whether the plaintiff's marsh land was 'seashore,' under the definition in Article 451 of the Civil Code. The land was situated very much like that of the plaintiff in this case, with relation to the gulf, a small bay, and a bayou penetrating the land, which was subject to tidal overflow. The court's ruling in the case is accurately expressed in the headnotes, thus:

> 'If the salt water ascertained to be in a bayou, lake, cove, or inlet adjacent to, or connected with, an arm of the Gulf of Mexico, does not result from an overflow that is occasioned by high tides flooding its banks, but, in the first instance, enters an arm of the gulf, and thence passes into said bayou, lake, etc., and is there combined with fresh water derived from other

sources, same cannot be considered as an arm of the sea, nor its banks the seashore.

'All that tract of land over which the greatest water flood extends itself is the seashore.

"High seas' mean that portion of the sea which washes the open coast, and do not include the combined salt and fresh waters which, at high tide, flood the banks of an adjacent bay, bayou, or lake" (citing *Waring et al. v. Clarke*, 5 How. 453, 12 L. Ed. 226).

The judgment appealed from, as we have said, is founded upon the proposition that the provision in article 3415 of the Civil Code, allowing any and every landowner to forbid hunting on his land, was repealed by implication, with regard to unfenced and vacant marsh land, by section 20 of Act 204 of 1912, viz. . . .

The judgment appealed from is annulled, and it is now ordered adjudged and decreed that the defendants, Anthony Salinovich, Anthony Scobel, Forest Morgan, Sam Salinovich, August Buras and George Salinovich, are hereby enjoined to quit hunting, trapping, or otherwise trespassing, upon the land of the plaintiff, Manuel Oscar Buras, described as . . . fronting on the east bank of the Mississippi river, in township 20 S., range 18 E., in the parish of Plaquemines. The defendants are to pay the costs of this suit.

Notes and Questions

1. In an omitted portion of *Buras v. Salinovich*, 154 La. 495 (La. 1923), Chief Justice O'Niell rejects the ingenious argument of the defendants that Article 3415 of the 1870 Civil Code (now codified in La. Civ. Code art. 3413), which provided that a proprietor of land may forbid other persons from entering upon his land to hunt on it, was implicitly overruled by Act 204 of 1912, a statute that restricted licensed hunters from hunting on *cultivated* land or *pasture* land without a landowner's written consent. That statute provided in pertinent part:

> **Section 20.** Be it further enacted, etc., That nothing in this act shall be construed to give the holder of a hunting license permission to hunt on the *cultivated or pasture lands* of another person without the written consent of said owner.

1912 La. Acts, No. 204 (emphasis added). The defendants in *Buras* argued that the provisions of this 1912 Act, read carefully, implicitly allowed licensed hunters to hunt on *uncultivated* land and *unfenced* pastureland, even if the landowners withheld their consent and protested.

Although this argument might sound far-fetched today, it was not so far-fetched at the time of the case. In the early nineteenth century, many states, particularly in the South, followed the rule that hunting on uncultivated and unfenced land was generally permissible. A similar rule allowed owners of domestic animals like cattle and pigs to graze their animals on the uncultivated and unfenced lands of others. The rationale behind these rules was that if a landowner wanted his land to be completely off-limits for hunting and grazing, it was up to that owner to fence it in. This practice enabled small, subsistence farmers to enhance their income and food sources by hunting and grazing their animals on the millions of acres of uncultivated and unfenced land in the United States at the time. Over the course of the second half of the nineteenth century, this "open grange" or "open range" approach allowing public access to private land was gradually superseded by statutes allowing landowners to "enclose" uncultivated and unfenced land by merely posting signs. For more on the historical context of the open grange, see generally Brian Sawers, *The Right to Exclude from Unimproved Land*, 83 Temple L. Rev. 665 (2011); Brian Sawers, *The Right to Exclude after Emancipation: A Quantitative Study* (Jan. 16, 2012), *at* http://papers.ssrn.com/sol3/papers.cfm?abstract_id=1986309; Eric Freyfogle, On Private Property: Finding Common Ground on the Ownership of Land 29–57 (2007).

The defendants in *Buras* argued that Section 20 of the 1912 Act preserved this earlier, "open grange" rule in Louisiana. Chief Justice O'Niell, however, rejected this argument, holding that, although the state's conservation laws may regulate hunting and trapping, these laws were not intended to deprive a landowner like Buras of the right to restrict access to his land for hunting and trapping. According to O'Neill's ruling in *Buras*, a landowner needed only to post signs on his land warning hunters and trappers to stay away.

2. The most important aspect of *Buras* for our present purposes is how the Louisiana Supreme Court defines "seashore." The court holds that land impacted by tidal overflow is not always characterized as seashore for purposes of declaring it a public thing and subjecting it to public use. Rather, the court tells us that the land's proximity to the sea is a crucial determining factor. The tidal waters must *directly* spread upon land to make it seashore. Thus, marsh land subject to some indirect tidal overflow, but physically remote from the open sea, like the land at issue in *Buras*, cannot be considered seashore.

Is the court's approach in *Buras* an easy one for subsequent courts to administer? Does it provide adequate guidance in disputes between other landowners and persons seeking to hunt, fish or boat in tidal areas of Louisiana? Do you believe the court should have constructed a test based on regular tidal overflow given the plain language of Article 451 as it existed at the time of the case? Would such a test have been easier to administer?

Regardless of your answer to these questions, the revision comments to Article 451 tell us that "Louisiana jurisprudence interpreting the source provision continues to be relevant." La. Civ. Code art. 451 rev. cmt. (a) (1978). Citing *Buras* and one of the principal decisions relied upon in that opinion, *Morgan v. Negodich*, 3 So. 636 (La. 1888), the comments also tell us that "seashore is the space of land in the *open* coast that is *directly* overflown by the tides." *Id.* rev. cmt. (b) (emphasis in original).

In a 1993 decision, the United States Court of Appeals for the Fifth Circuit relied upon *Buras* to resolve claims of commercial fisherman seeking access to man-made canals and waterways in Lafourche Parish that were, much like the marsh at issue in *Buras*, subject to some tidal influence. *See Dardar v. Lafourche Realty Co.*, 985 F.2d 824, 830–31 (5th Cir. 1993). In that opinion, the court summed up the law this way:

> [T]idelands comprising the seashore or sea bottoms are still owned by the State [of Louisiana].
>
> Tidelands which Louisiana acquired through the equal footing doctrine that are not seashore or sea bottoms, however, may be privately owned. Inland non-navigable water bodies and swamp land subject to indirect tidal overflow, but not direct coastal ebb and flow, may be privately owned under Louisiana law. Accordingly we conclude that the district court properly distinguished "direct" coastal ebb and flow from "indirect" freshwater tidal influence.

Dardar, 985 F.2d at 830.

3. A recent case from California featured a dispute between property owner and billionaire, Vinod Khosla, who had blocked public access to Martins Beach in San Mateo County, California, and Surfrider Foundation, a nonprofit organization dedicated to the protection of world oceans, waves and beaches. Mr. Khosla had erected a locked gate blocking access to a private road leading to the beach, hired a security guard and covered a sign advertising beach access. In 2013, the Surfrider Foundation initiated proceedings to enforce public access to the beach. In California, beaches are public trust resources. Surfirder argued that the right to access was guaranteed by California's Constitution and mandated by California's Coastal Act. The trial court held for Surfrider and provided injunction relief. Mr. Khosla appealed and the court of appeal affirmed the trial court's judgment. It determined that: (1) Mr. Khosla's activities were "development" under California's Coastal Act and therefore, required a Coastal Development Permit; (2) Mr. Khosla's constitutional challenge to the Coastal Act's permitting requirement under the state and federal takings clauses was not ripe for review; and (3) the trial court's injunction was not a per se taking. *Surfrider Found. v. Martins Beach 1, LLC*, 14 Cal. App. 5th 238, 278, 221 Cal. Rptr. 3d 382 (1st Dist. 2017). After the California Supreme Court had declined to review his appeal, Mr. Khosla filed a petition for a writ of certiorari in the U.S. Supreme Court presenting two questions: (1) whether a compulsory public-access easement of indefinite duration is a per se physical taking; and (2) whether applying the California Coastal Act to require the owner of private beachfront property to apply for a permit before excluding the public from its private property, closing or changing the hours, prices, or days of operation of a private business on its private property, or even declining to advertise public access to its private property, violates the Takings Clause, the Due Process Clause, or the First Amendment. On October 1, 2018, the U.S. Supreme Court denied Mr. Khosla's petition. *Martins Beach 1, LLC v. Surfrider Found.*, 2018 U.S. LEXIS 5704. If the facts were to arise in

Louisiana, would members of the public have a right to access the wet sand portion of the beach in front of Mr. Khosla's property from the sea? From a private road crossing the remainder of his property?

Problem

James built a fishing camp on stilts, on the shore of Lake Pontchartrain. James possessed and occupied the camp for eighteen months. The land upon which the camp was situated was covered by the rise and fall of the tides and faced directly onto the open waters of the lake. Peter owned the tract of land that abuts that portion of the lakeshore where James' camp was located. Peter brought a lawsuit to evict James, claiming that James was a trespasser and had no title to the property on which the fishing camp had been erected. Should Peter succeed in this suit?

Note that in a series of cases Louisiana courts have held that Lake Pontchartrain is an "arm of the sea." *See Milne v. Girodeau*, 12 La. 324 (1838); *Zeller v. Southern Yacht Club*, 34 La. Ann. 837 (1882); *Brunning v. City of New Orleans*, 165 La. 511, 115 So. 733 (1928). Thus, land subject to direct tidal overflow from Lake Pontchartrain is seashore.

4. The Equal Footing Doctrine

At this point in our effort to understand how Louisiana's legislature and courts have developed a thick framework of rules to regulate property rights in its often nebulous physical landscape of coasts, rivers and swamps, we must step back and consider the origins of Louisiana's authority to define the ownership of land beneath navigable waters more generally.

At English common law, the King or Crown was deemed to be the owner of all submerged lands, subject to the right of the King's subjects to navigate and to fish. When the original thirteen British colonies declared their independence from the Crown in 1776, the newly formed states were held to succeed to the Crown's rights. Hence, the states owned the land beneath navigable waters, subject to the public's right to navigate and fish. *Martin v. Waddell*, 41 U.S. (16 Pet.) 367 (1842). When new states were added to the union, they were entitled to claim the same rights in submerged lands beneath navigable waters as the original thirteen colonies had been allowed to claim. *Pollard v. Hagan*, 44 U.S. (3 How.) 212, 229 (1845). This principle, known as the "equal footing doctrine," is the basis for Louisiana's constitutional authority to determine ownership of submerged lands beneath navigable waters.

As Joseph Kearney and Thomas W. Merrill explain in the following passage, however, an important distinction emerged between English law and American law with regard to determining state ownership of submerged land:

> In English law, an important distinction was maintained between navigable and non-navigable waters. With respect to navigable waters, the King

was said to own the submerged lands, subject to the rights of all subjects to navigate and to fish. In effect, the land was subject to a public servitude for navigation and fishing. When the American colonies declared their independence, they were held to succeed to the rights of the Crown in this respect. So the state governments were deemed to own the lands beneath navigable waters, again subject to the two historical public rights. In 1845, the Supreme Court held that newly formed states carved out of the federal public domain were entitled to these same rights of ownership with respect to submerged lands beneath navigable waters. This came to be known as the "equal footing" doctrine: the new states stood on an equal footing with the original states in terms of their ownership of submerged lands.

There was a complication. English law, at least as understood by American commentators, defined "navigable waters" to mean waters subject to the ebb and flow of the tides. This made sense in the English context, with its long coastline and short rivers, most of which were tidal in the reaches where commercial traffic was important. So, in England, the Crown was deemed to be the owner of submerged lands beneath tidal waters — but submerged land under rivers, lakes, and ponds not washed by the tides was owned by the abutting riparian landowner to the centerline of the body of water. This set of understandings can be called the "English rule" for ownership of submerged lands under non-navigable waters.

America, unlike England, contained many long rivers and large internal lakes that were not tidal and yet were critical to interstate commerce. So the English definition of navigable waters did not make sense in the American context. The Supreme Court eventually recognized this: it held — initially only for purposes of admiralty jurisdiction — that "navigable" in the United States means navigable in fact. The Court also eventually held that "navigable" means navigable in fact for purposes of the equal footing doctrine. But there was a wrinkle, and it was to contribute to confusion over rights to submerged lands. With respect to waters that were navigable in fact, the equal footing doctrine meant that each state was free to decide for itself how to determine title to land beneath such waters. In effect, each state could choose whether to embrace the English view of submerged land ownership with respect to such lands or, instead, what could be called the American rule, which awarded title to land under waters that were navigable in fact to the state government.

The resulting understanding of the equal footing doctrine has generated a confusing pastiche of rules in the United States about who owns submerged lands. The doctrine means, for example, that where a navigable river forms the boundary between two states, the submerged land on one side of the centerline of the river can belong to the state while on the other side a private party owns title to the submerged land.

Joseph D. Kearney & Thomas W. Merrill, *Contested Shore: Property Rights in Reclaimed Land and the Battle for Streeterville*, 107 N.W. L. Rev. 1057, 1064–66 (2013).

In Louisiana, the equal footing doctrine gave the Louisiana legislature and Louisiana courts the authority to declare that submerged lands would generally be owned by the state itself. It also gave the legislature and our state courts the authority to determine the precise geographic extent of state ownership of the beds and bottoms of navigable water bodies by defining: where the territorial sea ended and private, littoral ownership began; what distinguished an inland navigable water body from an inland non-navigable water body; and whether the banks of inland navigable water bodies would be subject to state ownership, private ownership or some hybrid form of control.

5. Inland Navigable Water Bodies and the Concept of Navigability

Anyone familiar with Louisiana's geography knows that the state is replete with water bodies. There are rivers, lakes, bayous, streams, ponds, swales, canals and inland swamps. Some of these water bodies are navigable. Others are not.

Beginning with the rules offered by the Louisiana Civil Code, we know from Article 450 that "the waters and bottoms of natural, *navigable* water bodies" are public things that belong to the state. La. Civ. Code art. 450 (1979) (emphasis added). Article 506 provides the logical corollary to this proposition:

> **Art. 506. Ownership of beds of nonnavigable rivers or streams**
>
> In the absence of title or prescription, the beds of non-navigable rivers or streams belong to the riparian owners along a line drawn in the middle of the bed.

La. Civ. Code art. 506 (1979). Although the water running through a non-navigable, but naturally occurring, stream or bayou is a public thing under Article 450, the *land beneath* the surface of such a stream or bayou — the *bed* — is, instead, a private thing. Its ownership will usually be apportioned to its riparian owners along a line down the middle of the bed. The bed of a non-navigable stream or bayou can be bought and sold, transferred and donated, and lost by acquisitive prescription just like any other private land.

The revision comments to Article 506 extend the basic principles of the article to non-navigable lakes:

> Non-navigable lakes are private things. Accordingly, they may belong to the state, a political subdivision or a private person.

La. Civ. Code art. 506 rev. cmt. (c) (1979). Thus, a non-navigable lake (what we might simply call a pond, or a swamp, or maybe even a shallow swale) are, just like non-navigable rivers, private things subject to private ownership by private individuals or the state or its political subdivisions in their capacity as private persons. In perhaps the broadest statement of legislative intent imaginable in this area, a statute enacted in 1992 provides that "[i]nland non-navigable water beds or bottoms are private things and may be owned by private persons or by the state and its political subdivisions in their capacity as private persons." La. Rev. Stat. 9:1115.2(B) (1992).

These declarations in the Civil Code and its revision comments as well as the revised statutes suggest that the distinction between a *navigable* and a *non-navigable* water body is crucial. One might expect the Civil Code would provide a definition of navigability. Curiously, though, the Civil Code does not oblige us. Instead, courts have supplied this crucial definition. Consider the following two judicial opinions:

State ex rel. Guste v. Two O'Clock Bayou Land Co., Inc.

365 So.2d 1174 (La. App. 3 Cir. 1978)

WATSON, Judge. Plaintiffs, the State of Louisiana and the Police Jury of the Parish of St. Landry, asked that defendants, Two O'Clock Bayou Land Company, Inc., and its lessee, Creighton James Nall, be enjoined from maintaining a cable across Two O'Clock Bayou. Plaintiffs also sought a declaration that the stream is navigable and subject to public use. The trial court declared the stream navigable and granted the permanent injunction. Defendants have appealed.

The question presented is whether the bayou is navigable, entitling the Parish and the State to enjoin its obstruction by privately owned barriers.[1] LSA-C.C. art. 453; LSA-R.S. 14:96, 97; *Discon v. Saray, Inc.*, 262 La. 997, 265 So.2d 765 (1972).

Two O'Clock Bayou runs roughly north and south through St. Landry Parish in the Atchafalaya Basin Swamp area, crossing sections 14 and 13, T-6-S, R-6-E, and sections 11 and 12, T-6-S, R-7-E. The bayou, at one time, connected with Darbonne Bay on the north and Craft Lake on the south, but dams have now closed off boat access to these areas. Two O'Clock Bayou crosses Cowan Bay and Close Lake. A recent dam was built by a pipeline company roughly halfway between Close Lake and Craft Lake.

In 1808, the bayou appeared on the Darby survey as an unnamed tributary feeding into Bayou De Grasse. Two O'Clock Bayou's northern portion, above Cowan Bay, has apparently moved half a mile to the west. Although it was not meandered by Darby, defendants' expert forester, Lewis C. Peters, admitted that the bayou could in fact have been navigable in 1808. Darby also failed to meander Bayou Courtableau, a primary navigable stream in the area. At times, in the intervening

---

1. Title to the bed of the bayou is not at issue. Obstruction of the bayou can be enjoined if it is navigable, *D'Albora v. Garcia*, 144 So.2d 911 (La. App. 4 Cir. 1962) writ denied; *Discon v. Saray, Inc.*, 262 La. 997, 265 So.2d 765 (1972). Here, in contrast to *Vermilion Corp. v. Vaughn*, 356 So.2d 551 (La. App. 3 Cir. 1978), writ denied 357 So.2d 558 and *National Audubon Society v. White*, 302 So.2d 660 (La. App. 3 Cir. 1974), writ denied 305 So.2d 542 (La., 1975), the bayou is not artificial and its bed does not lie wholly within the confines of defendants' land. See 33 La. Law Review 172.

years, the bed of Two O'Clock has been dry enough to allow germination of cypress trees. The younger trees are approximately 100 years old, showing that the bed was dry 100 years ago. The stumps of the older cypress trees were about four hundred years old when cut in the early nineteen hundreds. Photographs in evidence show large trees and stumps in the bayou, but there is a passage space 10 to 12 feet wide between the old cypress stumps. (TR. 112). The water level at the time the photos were taken was admittedly low.

Creighton James Nall, the lessee, testified in deposition that there are pilings and a trestle at Cowan Bay which he believed to be the remnants of a dummy railroad line used for timbering operations. Nall testified on oral examination that he placed the cable at the northern end of the bayou just south of the old Missouri Pacific right of way to control access by the public. A dam had been built just north of the cable's location some ten years before by Walter Buchanan. Nall said the shallowest portion of the bayou is from 3 [and] 1/2 to 7 feet deep. At the narrowest part of the bayou, where there are old pilings at the abandoned railroad right of way, there is an opening 8 to 10 feet wide. (photograph # 15; TR. 111).

Preston Scruggins testified in deposition that he helped build the railroad trestle at Cowan Bay around 1935, when there was only a foot of water in the bayou. According to Scruggins, Two O'Clock was only suitable for pirogue use at that time.

Joe Elder testified in deposition that he is a lumberman and had a mill at Bayou Close near Lottie in 1931. His company harvested timber around Two O'Clock Bayou, snaked the logs to the bayou and floated them out behind small motor boats. The logs were tied together in rafts or cribs about four feet wide.

Fifteen people attested to their use of Two O'Clock Bayou for fishing over various periods of time, commencing as early as 1930. Emile Miller testified that he had used the bayou for fishing for 26 or 27 years. Ernie Kovack did sport fishing in the bayou, going as far south as Craft Lake in a boat with a two foot draft. A. K. Miller said he had fished the bayou since around 1936 and had seen many commercial fishing boats there.

W. A. Welch has utilized the bayou for fishing since the mid-fifties and has traversed the bayou its entire length beginning at Craft Lake on the south. Welch witnessed use of the bayou by a motion picture company filming "Nevada Smith". The company operated barges on the bayou measuring about 12 feet wide and twenty feet long. Their draft was estimated by Welch at about three feet. According to Welch, the bayou is about three feet deep in the shallowest part of the main channel at low water.

Arthur Roy Shay said he had used the bayou for fishing since 1948, using motors up to 50 horsepower in size. A dam at the northern crossing of old highway 190 and the Missouri Pacific Railroad now obstructs passage into Darbonne Bay on the north. Shay measured a spot 37 feet deep in the bayou where it empties into Close Lake on the south. Another spot at the northern edge of Cowan Bay is twenty feet deep. Shay estimated the average depth of the bayou at nine feet. In his opinion, based on frequent use of a depth finder, the bayou's depth fluctuates three or four feet during periods of high water.

Sherby J. Skrantz testified that he had been familiar with Two O'Clock Bayou since 1949 when he assisted his father in commercial fishing operations there, using a "Joe-boat" four feet wide and fourteen feet long. They caught two to three hundred pounds of fish a night, fishing as far south as Craft Lake. He knew of four other commercial fishermen who used the bayou. Some garfish from Craft Lake weighed in at up to 110 pounds.

In evidence are 1860 patents to sections 14 and 11 and part of section 13 issued by the Louisiana Land Office.

Tax receipts were introduced in evidence to prove that Two O'Clock Bayou Land Company had paid taxes on all of section 13 and 14, T-6-S, R-6-E, without any deduction for a navigable waterway. The land company also paid taxes on the part of section 11, T-6-S, R-7-E, crossed by the bayou, but the tax receipt notes that this W 1/2 of the W 1/2 of section 11 "Includes 13 acres used by the U.S. Government for levee and high level crossing rights-of-way." (TR. 44). Payment of taxes on section 12, T-6-S, R-7-E, where the southern part of the bayou empties into Craft Lake is not claimed by the land company.

Savano Bernard Langlois, an expert surveyor, testified that Two O'Clock Bayou appears in its present location south of Cowan Bay on Darby's 1808 survey notes and the U.S. geodetical map (Exhibit 8) but not north of Cowan Bay. The northern portion of Two O'Clock Bayou is a new stream a half mile to the west. In Langlois' opinion, the 1829 and 1842 maps and surveys indicate that Two O'Clock Bayou was not considered navigable when they were made.

The trial court concluded that the bayou has an average depth of nine feet, and averages 18 to 30 feet in width. The trial court made a factual finding that the bayou is capable of sustaining commerce despite occasional obstructions in its flow.

Navigability is not presumed; the burden of proof rests with the party seeking to establish it. *Johnson v. State Farm Fire and Casualty Company*, 303 So.2d 779 (La. App. 3 Cir. 1974); *Burns v. Crescent Gun & Rod Club*, 116 La. 1038, 41 So. 249 (1906). The trial court concluded that plaintiffs had sustained the burden of proving Two O'Clock Bayou to be a navigable stream.

A body of water is navigable in law when it is navigable in fact. *State v. Jefferson Island Salt Mining Co.*, 183 La. 304, 163 So. 145 (1935) cert. den. 297 U.S. 716, 56 S. Ct. 591, 80 L.Ed. 1001, rehearing denied 297 U.S. 729, 56 S.Ct. 667, 80 L.Ed. 1011. The factual question turns on whether the evidence shows a body of water to be suitable by its depth, width and location for commerce. However, lack of commercial traffic does not preclude a finding of navigability. *State v. Capdeville*, 146 La. 94, 83 So. 421 (1919) cert. den. 252 U.S. 581, 40 S.Ct. 346, 64 L.Ed. 727. A stream, to be navigable, must be usable for commerce in its natural state or ordinary condition. *Madole v. Johnson*, 241 F.Supp. 379 (1965); *The Daniel Ball*, 10 Wall. 557, 19 L.Ed. 999 (1870);

Delta Duck Club v. Barrios, 135 La. 357, 65 So. 489 (1914). Construction of a dam across a bayou does not change its status as a navigable stream. *Beavers v. Butler*, 188 So.2d 725 (La. App. 2 Cir. 1966) writ refused 249 La. 739, 190 So.2d 242. A body of water can be navigable despite natural or man-made obstructions. *Terrebonne Parish School Board v. Texaco, Inc.* 178 So.2d 428 (La. App. 1 Cir. 1965) writ refused 248 La. 465, 179 So.2d 640, cert. den. 384 U.S. 950, 86 S.Ct. 1568, 16 L.Ed.2d 546.

In the instant case it is difficult to determine whether Two O'Clock Bayou was navigable in its ordinary condition because the bayou is not presently in a natural state, having been dammed, bridged and otherwise interfered with over a period of time.

The question of navigability of Two O'Clock Bayou in 1812 is only pertinent to the question of ownership of the bed of the bayou. It has no relevance to the question of whether or not passage on the stream can be obstructed by defendants. *Begnaud v. Grubb & Hawkins*, 209 La. 826, 25 So.2d 606 (1946); *Discon v. Saray, Inc.*, supra. Therefore, the evidence that parts of the bayou bed were dry as recently as 100 years ago does not affect the State's right to enjoin its obstruction if it is in fact a navigable waterway. *Discon v. Saray, Inc.*, supra. Here, unlike the situation in *National Audubon Society v. White*, 302 So.2d 660 (La. App. 3 Cir. 1974) writ denied 305 So.2d 542 (La., 1975) and *Vermilion Corp. v. Vaughn*, 356 So.2d 551 (La. App. 3 Cir. 1978) writ den. La., 357 So.2d 558, the waterway is not privately constructed and does not lie wholly within the confines of the property owned by the defendant land company.

The evidence allows a reasonable inference that Two O'Clock Bayou is navigable in fact, except for various man-made obstructions. It has in the past sustained commercial fishing and logging, which are types of commerce. There is no prescription right to obstruct navigation on a navigable stream. *Ingram v. Police Jury of Parish of St. Tammany*, 20 La. Ann. 226 (1868). The bayou, in its natural state, afforded a channel for navigation although there are now certain difficulties in the form of natural and man-made barriers. The fact that bridges have been built, with or without legal authority, and there is a resulting accumulation of timber, which, to some extent, obstructs and impedes navigation does not preclude a finding that a stream is navigable. Goodwill v. Police Jury, 38 La. Ann. 752 (1886). See the discussion of navigability in fact and law in *D'Albora v. Garcia*, 144 So.2d 911 (La. App. 4 Cir. 1962) cert. den.

The trial court's conclusion that Two O'Clock Bayou is navigable is not manifestly erroneous and therefore must be affirmed.

For the foregoing reasons, the judgment of the trial court herein is affirmed at the cost of defendants-appellants.

AFFIRMED.

Notes and Questions

1. In *State ex rel. Guste v. Two O'Clock Bayou Land Co., Inc.*, 365 So.2d 1174 (La. App. 3 Cir. 1978), what was the most important evidence supporting the court of

appeal's decision that Two O'Clock Bayou was navigable in fact and thus, navigable in law? Was it the initial survey created by William Darby in 1808? The depth and width of the bayou? The presence of cypress trees? The witnesses' testimony observing commercial fishing boats in the bayou? The size of the fish caught in the bayou? The fact that a motion picture was filmed on the bayou?

2. The court in *Two O'Clock Bayou* ultimately defines navigability not in terms of any inherent physical characteristic, such as its width or depth, but in terms of whether the water body is suitable for *commerce* in its natural state or ordinary condition. Why is a water body's suitability for commerce the overriding factor in determining its navigability and thus, its susceptibility to public use? Is the concept of suitability for commerce too elastic or just right? Should navigability depend on the characteristics of the surrounding human community and the kinds of economic and social activity found in the vicinity of the water body?

3. In *Alaska v. United States*, 754 F.2d 851 (9th Cir. 1985), the United States Ninth Circuit Court of Appeals addressed the navigability of a small lake in Alaska, Slopbucket Lake, which was separated from a much larger, navigable water body, known as Lake Iliamna, by a small isthmus of sand beach about 100 feet wide. Because of the absence of roads in much of Alaska, float planes regularly land on lakes there, transporting both people and goods from one part of the state to another. Floatplanes frequently landed on and took off from Slopbucket Lake because of the high winds and rough waters of the nearby Lake Iliamna. The State of Alaska claimed that it had title to Slopbucket Lake under the equal footing doctrine because it was a navigable water body as it formed a part of a highway for commerce, allowing products and people to move from one place to another. The United States opposed Alaska's claim, arguing that the lake was not navigable and thus was federally owned public land that could be transferred to a native Alaskan tribe under the Alaska Native Claims Settlement Act, 43 U.S.C. §§ 1601–1628. *Id.* at 852–53.

The Ninth Circuit acknowledged the traditional suitability-for-commerce test for determining navigability under federal law. It noted that the modes of commerce that can be considered are quite diverse. *Id.* at 854. It observed, though, that the "crux of the test is still the requirement that the body of water be susceptible of use as a highway or channel for commerce *on* water" and that this "necessarily involves the utilization of the waterway as a path between two points." *Id.* at 854 (emphasis added). In the court's words, "the central theme remains the movement of people or goods from point to point *on the water*." *Id.* (emphasis added). Although people landing on Slopbucket Lake in small floatplanes were landing on and taking off from the water body to engage in commerce, the court concluded that the lake was not navigable because the planes were not travelling "on the water" to get from one point to another and the lake was not used as a channel to get from one place to another. *Id.* at 854–55.

4. Observe carefully that in the beginning of its opinion in *Two O'Clock Bayou* the Louisiana appellate court went out of its way to declare that it was not interested in resolving who had "title" to (or who owned) the bed of Two O'Clock Bayou. This

may seem strange given the court's ultimate conclusion that the bayou was navigable in fact. Because the bayou was determined to be a navigable water body, the State of Louisiana will necessarily own its bed, and the entire water body will be subject to public use. *See* La. Civ. Code arts. 450 and 452 (1978).

The court's initial reluctance to delve into the question of who owned the bed of the bayou makes more sense if we consider the possibilities that would have emerged had the court determined that the bayou was not navigable. Then, the bayou would have been a private thing. It might have been owned by one or both riparian landowners, which means that it would then have been potentially alienable and subject to being possibly lost through acquisitive prescription. In the alternative, the bayou could be owned or acquired by the state or a political subdivision in a private capacity. *See* La. Civ. Code art. 506 (1979).

5. In *Two O'Clock Bayou*, the court refers several times to the "Darby survey" and the work of Darby. **William Darby**, geographer and cartographer, and the author of A GEOGRAPHICAL DESCRIPTION OF THE STATE OF LOUISIANA, THE SOUTHERN PART OF MISSISSIPPI, AND THE TERRITORY OF ALABAMA (1817). He was born in Pennsylvania in 1775, settled in the Mississippi Territory in 1799, and, in 1804, left his plantation to become a deputy surveyor in the United States General Land Office. Darby collected information about Louisiana and surrounding states from 1800 until 1814, and published many maps of the area. In addition to Louisiana, Darby prepared maps of most of the states and territories from Maine to Florida and as far west as Ohio and Kentucky. He published those maps in books containing other geological information. Darby's maps were particularly accurate and have been referenced frequently in court decisions concerning property.

In the case featured below, the court reviews a finding that English Bayou is a navigable waterway for purposes of subject matter jurisdiction. Do you agree that English Bayou is susceptible of being used as a highway of commerce?

Trahan v. Teleflex, Inc.
922 So.2d 718 (La. App. 3 Cir. 2006)

PAINTER, Judge. The Defendant, Teleflex, Inc. ("Teleflex"), appeals the trial court's determination that no material issue of fact remains but that English Bayou is a navigable waterway for purposes of admiralty jurisdiction.

Facts

On August 16, 2002, Randy Trahan was riding as a passenger in a seventeen-foot Stratos Outboard water craft, which he owned but which was being operated by his brother, Allen Joseph Trahan. They were going east on English Bayou. After going under the Highway 171 bridge, the steering cable broke causing the boat to make a sharp turn to the right. As a result, Randy Trahan was thrown out of the boat and incurred injuries to his right arm, shoulder, and neck. He filed suit on June 12, 2003, asserting that Teleflex, manufacturer of the steering cable, was liable under maritime products liability and general maritime law.

Teleflex filed exceptions of lack of subject matter jurisdiction and prescription. In its exceptions, it argued that English Bayou is not a navigable waterway so as to give rise to admiralty jurisdiction and that, in the absence of a maritime claim, the matter is prescribed. Randy Trahan filed a motion for partial summary judgment asserting that no genuine issue of fact remained but that English Bayou is a navigable waterway, and that the accident has a maritime nexus.

The trial court, after a hearing, found that "English Bayou in the area where this accident happened, which is very close to where the bridge is, is navigable." As a result, the court denied the exception of lack of subject matter jurisdiction and granted the motion for partial summary judgment. The court, in its oral reasons for judgment, cited evidence of tugboats using the bayou about a half mile downstream from the accident site, a bridge over the bayou designed to open for boat traffic, and the Highway 171 bridge, which has a span of one hundred feet wide and is twenty feet high.

Teleflex appeals.

Subject Matter Jurisdiction

Teleflex asserts that the trial court erred in denying its exception of lack of subject matter jurisdiction.

> Whether a tort action is maritime in nature and governed by admiralty jurisdiction hinges on it satisfying two tests. The first, the locality test, is met *if the tort occurred on navigable waters* or the injury suffered on land was caused by a vessel on navigable waters. *Grubart v. Great Lakes Dredge & Dock Co.,* 513 U.S. 527, 115 S.Ct. 1043, 130 L.Ed.2d 1024 (1995); 46 U.S.C. App. § 740. The second test is met when the tort bears a "significant connection to a traditional maritime activity.". . . .

Conoco, Inc. v. Halter-Calcasieu, L.L.C., 03-136, p. 6 (La. App. 3 Cir. 11/19/03), 865 So.2d 813, 818, *writ denied,* 03-3493 (La.3/12/04), 869 So.2d 822.

The mover has the burden of proof on an exception of lack of subject matter jurisdiction. *Smith v. Gretna Mach. & Iron Works,* 617 So.2d 144, (La. App. 5 Cir. 1993). In the case *sub judice,* Teleflex does not argue that the activity giving rise to the incident does not show a "substantial relationship to traditional maritime activity." *Conoco,* 865 So.2d 813. Rather, it alleges that English Bayou is not navigable at the site of the accident.

> In Louisiana, waterways are navigable in law when they are used or susceptible of being used in their natural and ordinary condition as highways for commerce, over which trade and travel are or may be conducted in the customary modes of trade and travel on the water. *Ramsey River Road Property Owners Association, Inc. v. Reeves,* 396 So.2d 873, 876 (La. 1981). Simply stated, a water course is navigable when by its depth, width and location it is rendered available for commerce. *Shell Oil Company,* 476 So.2d at 1036.

Naquin v. Louisiana Power & Light Co., 98-2270, fn. 4 (La. App. 1 Cir. 3/31/00), 768 So.2d 605, *writ denied,* 00-1741 (La.9/15/00), 769 So.2d 546.

The testimony at the hearing on the exception was as follows. Michael Whitler, Superintendent of Gravity District # 4 of Calcasieu Parish, testified that, for the last eighteen years, he has worked at the pumping station located on English Bayou two miles east of the Highway 171 bridge. He stated that he has never seen barges or tug-boats going up or down the bayou. He works from 6:00 a.m. until 4:30 p.m., Monday through Thursday, and is away from the pumping station about half the time. He admitted that he has seen bass boats engaged in tournament fishing for prize money on English Bayou and knows that it is possible to travel from the pumping station to the Gulf of Mexico on English Bayou. Whitler further admitted that when he is at the pumping station, he is in his office and spends very little time looking at the bayou.

George Bass testified that he worked as an engineer for the Louisiana Department of Transportation and Development, and that, from about 1972, part of his work involved maintaining the bridges over English Bayou. He stated that he never saw the old bridge opened and was not aware of any time when it was opened. He admitted, however, that he did not have anything to do with the old bridge in the course of his work with the DOTD. He stated that he did not know how deep the bayou was at the place the new bridge was built.

Edwin Olmstead testified that twenty-five years previously his uncle towed an old tugboat up the bayou, under the old bridge, scrapped it out, and abandoned it. He admitted that it is possible to go from his shipyard on Contraband Bayou up English Bayou and under the Highway 171 bridge.

Dr. George Castille, III testified that he works doing geoforensics for Coastal Environments, an environmental consulting firm. He was qualified as an expert geographer. He testified that, in the course of his investigation, he traveled up English Bayou to the Highway 397 bridge and that the bayou is between seventy-five and one hundred feet wide and eleven feet deep at that point. He stated that he did not travel further up the bayou because the opening under the bridge at Highway 397 was a little narrow. He testified that he went under the Highway 171 bridge on his way up the bayou and that the central opening of that bridge is about 100 feet wide and that the bridge is about nineteen feet above the water. He admitted that it is possible to travel by water from the Highway 171 bridge on English Bayou all the way into the Gulf of Mexico. He admitted that he had seen evidence of pullboat logging east of the Highway 171 bridge. He further stated that small barges and some types of commercial fishing boats could operate on English Bayou.

Additionally, all of the exhibits attached to the exception and memoranda were introduced into evidence. These consist of maps and photographs of English Bayou filed with the exception. . . . Additionally made part of Trahan's exhibits are U.S. Army Corps of Engineers documents which state that the "bridge will have no adverse affect on present or future navigation for this section of the waterway" and which indicate that the old swing bridge was only opened twenty-five times for passage of navigation between 1945 and 1950 and was not opened thereafter, as well as navigation bulletins notifying mariners about the construction of the new bridge.

Given the evidence before this court in connection with the exception of lack of subject matter jurisdiction, we find that Teleflex failed to carry its burden of showing that English Bayou is not "susceptible of being used in their natural and ordinary condition as highways for commerce, over which trade and travel are or may be conducted in the customary modes of trade and travel on the water." *Naquin*, 768 So.2d 605 at fn. 4. Therefore, we find no error in the trial court's decision to deny the motion.

Summary Judgment

We next consider Teleflex's assertion that the trial court erred in granting Trahan's motion for partial summary judgment with regard to the navigability of English Bayou. . . .

Navigability is a question of fact and must be proven. *Naquin*, 668 So.2d 605, at fn. 4. . . .

Trahan supported his motion with a number of documents. Attached to a memorandum in support of the motion was an excerpt from the deposition of George Castille, III, the Defendant's expert. The excerpt included Castille's testimony that English Bayou is navigable under some definitions, that he saw evidence of commercial pull-boat logging on the bayou, and that pull boat barges are from forty to fifty feet in length. It further includes his testimony that a small barge could float on English Bayou, that some types of commercial fishing can be done in a twenty-foot boat, and that a ferry operated on English Bayou until 1924 when the first bridge was built. Also attached to a supporting memorandum was the affidavit of D. Walter Jessen, a registered land surveyor who made measurements of English Bayou. He noted that the clearance of the Highway 171 bridge is from sixteen to twenty feet depending on the water level of the bayou. He further noted that aerial photos show scars from pull boat barges which pulled logs from points east of the bridge into the bayou to float to mills downstream.

The affidavit of Nola Mae Ross, also attached to Trahan's memorandum, contains her sworn statement that she is an author and historian specializing in the history of southwest Louisiana and Calcasieu Parish. She stated that Native Americans used English Bayou to conduct trade, that in 1819 Jean Lafitte made trips up the Calcasieu River and into English Bayou to the home of Arsene LeBleu, that a ferry existed which took people and livestock across the bayou and that Old Spanish Trail crossed the bayou near the LeBleu property. She further opined that equipment needed for building pumping stations for irrigation in 1902 and 1905 would have been transported by boat up the bayou. She stated that the bayou was used to transport rafts of logs, sometimes measuring more than a mile long, downstream to saw mills in Lake Charles.

. . . .

The affidavit of William G. Castle, Jr. also supported the motion. Mr. Castle attested that his family owned property between English Bayou and Old Town Bay. His family cut timber and floated it down English Bayou to the Calcasieu River and on to lumber mills in Lake Charles. He stated that he has seen large, mostly recreational, cabin cruisers on English Bayou as well as barges of commercial size. He attested that he has personal knowledge of the bayou and opined that it is capable of sustaining commerce.

. . . .

The affidavit of Bradford Mayo, President of Mayo Land Title Co., affirmed that a search was made of the title records in the Calcasieu Parish Clerk of Court's Office which found no claim by a private person or corporation to the beds or bottoms of English Bayou.

Also attached to the memorandum was a copy of the Calcasieu Parish Police Jury Office Emergency Operations Plan which identifies English Bayou as one of "other" waterways which are navigable. Additionally, in support of his motion, Trahan attached a number of Coast Guard Bulletins for mariners containing warnings with regard to the navigability of English Bayou during the building of the Highway 171 bridge, as well as other documents regarding bridge construction.

. . . .

Although the documents submitted in support of Teleflex's opposition to the motion for summary judgment call into question whether English Bayou is currently being used for commerce, they do not contradict the evidence submitted by Trahan which shows that the bayou is *susceptible* to being used as a highway for commerce. After examining the pleadings, depositions, and affidavits, we find it has been established that English Bayou is "susceptible of being used in [its] natural and ordinary condition as [a] highway[ ] for commerce, over which trade and travel are or may be conducted in the customary modes of trade and travel on the water." *Naquin*, 768 So.2d 605 at fn. 4. Accordingly, under the facts of this case, we find that no question of fact remains as to the navigability of English Bayou. Therefore, the trial court correctly granted Trahan's motion for partial summary judgment.

Conclusion

For these reasons, the judgment of the trial court is affirmed. Costs of this appeal are assessed to the Defendant-Appellant, Teleflex, Inc.

AFFIRMED.

Notes and Questions

1. In *Trahan v. Teleflex, Inc.*, 922 So.2d 718 (La. App. 3 Cir. 2006), the court used essentially the same substantive approach to determining navigability as in *State v. Two O'Clock Bayou Land Co., Inc.*, 365 So.2d 1174 (La. App. 3 Cir. 1978). In *Trahan*, however, navigability was important for determining whether the court had subject

matter jurisdiction over the plaintiff's product liability claim under maritime law. Do you think the court's concerns about applying maritime law influenced the court's navigability determination?

2. With regard to the exception of lack of subject matter jurisdiction, the court considered oral testimony taken at a hearing. But when addressing the plaintiff's motion for partial summary judgment, the court limited itself to written documents. Why did the court make this distinction? Were the two sets of evidence similar in their influence on the court? What was the most important evidence supporting the court's determination that English Bayou was navigable?

3. In another relatively recent decision, the Louisiana Second Circuit Court of Appeal affirmed a trial court determination that a water body in the far northeast corner of the state known as Gassoway Lake, which did not exist in 1812 but was subsequently created when the main channel of the Mississippi River shifted its course, was not navigable, even though recreational fishermen and boaters frequently used it and local residents rented boats to visitors. *Walker Lands, Inc. v. East Carroll Parish Police Jury*, 871 So.2d 1258, 1265–66 (La. App. 2 Cir. 2004). In holding that Gassoway Lake was not navigable, the court stressed that it was not directly connected to any other navigable body of water and only received water through a narrow drainage ditch that flowed from the Mississippi River. *Id.* at 1266. It remains to be seen whether other courts will adopt this factor—direct connection to another navigable water body—as an additional requirement for a finding of navigability in fact. On this issue, compare *Walker Lands* to the United States Ninth Circuit Court of Appeals decision in *Alaska v. United States*, 754 F.2d 851 (9th Cir. 1985), discussed above.

This direct connection factor evokes Justice Kennedy's significant nexus test, which he offered with regard to the question of the federal government's power to regulate isolated wetlands under the Clean Water Act:

> [T]he Corps' jurisdiction over wetlands depends upon the existence of a significant nexus between the wetlands in question and navigable waters in the traditional sense. The required nexus must be assessed in terms of the statute's goals and purposes.

Rapanos v. United States, 547 U.S. 715, 789 (2006) (Kennedy, J., concurring). We will revisit Gassoway Lake later in this chapter when we address questions concerning the right of members of the public to fish in this non-navigable body of running water.

4. Compare how Louisiana courts have approached the problem of determining the location and extent of seashore and the question of whether water bodies are navigable. In the first instance (seashore), courts have constructed a test that relies exclusively on physical criteria—primarily the proximity of the land at issue to the open waters and coast of the Gulf of Mexico and the wave action to which the land is subject. In the second instance (navigability), courts take physical characteristics into account but generally examine those characteristics in a socio-economic

context—a water body's suitability for commerce. Why do you suppose courts have taken these different approaches in these two settings?

Consider the following comment by property law scholar Carol Rose who has written about the role that sociability plays in property law decision-making in the context of waterways, roads and beaches and about the socializing effects of what eighteenth century, enlightenment thinkers like Adam Smith called "doux commerce" (sweet commerce):

> "Navigability" has been defined in a variety of ways and for a variety of purposes. For example, "navigable waters" have sometimes been said to include only waters capable of carrying commercial vessels; more generous definitions have included turbulent waters, so long as they could float logs to market, or—even somewhat later—waters that permit use by recreational vessels even as insubstantial as canoes. But the classic measure of navigability has been suitability for commerce, however defined, and commercial use in turn suggests an indefinite and open-ended set of individuals who use the waterway. All these definitions require that the navigable water body have a considerable extent; none would define as "navigable" a waterbody confined within the ownership of one or a few landowners. Like a cul-de-sac, a small body of water is generally confined to a few identifiable users (who presumably can adjust their respective rights by negotiation) and is quite different from a "long thin roadway of water joining regions and communities," as one more modern Pennsylvania case put it.

Carol Rose, *The Comedy of the Commons: Custom, Commerce and Inherently Public Property*, 53 U. CHI. L. REV. 711, 764–65 (1986).

5. *Changes in Navigability over Time:* Determining whether a water body is navigable is important in a number of different contexts. It tells us whether a natural water body is classified as a public thing under Article 450 or as a private thing under Article 506. It also tells us whether a water body is subject to public use under Article 452. If a particular water body was navigable in 1812 (the year Louisiana became a state), and the water body continues to be navigable today, it always was and continues to be a public thing. A.N. YIANNOPOULOS, 2 LOUISIANA CIVIL LAW TREATISE: PROPERTY §4.2 (5th ed. 2015). Similarly, water bodies that were non-navigable in 1812 and are non-navigable today are and always have been private things. *Id.* But what happens when a water body's navigable status changes over time? Two possibilities exist.

First, a water body that was navigable in 1812 might have become non-navigable in subsequent years. In that case, at the moment the water body ceased to be navigable, it also ceased to be a public thing and became a private thing belonging to the state in its private capacity and, thus, being potentially alienable. *Id.* The court may have been worried about this possibility in *State v. Two O'Clock Bayou Land Co., Inc.*, 365 So.2d 1174 (La. App. 3 Cir. 1978).

The more common, and certainly more problematic, issue arises when a water body that was originally non-navigable in 1812 subsequently becomes navigable as the result of some natural phenomenon or as a result of artificial works. In his treatise on Louisiana property law, Professor Yiannopoulos observes that a literal reading of Article 450 of the Civil Code leads to the conclusion that "a body of water, which, though non-navigable in 1812, subsequently became navigable by operation of natural forces, is a public thing." YIANNOPOULOS, *supra*, §4.2. He further warns that this kind of literal application of Article 450 might raise the specter of an unconstitutional taking of property without just compensation under both the United States and Louisiana constitutions. *Id.* Conversely, Professor Yiannopoulos acknowledges a counter argument based on the premise that any person who acquires land in Louisiana, particularly land encompassing a non-navigable water body or marshland near the coast, does so subject to Article 450 and thus, in effect, has been on notice that the land could become a public thing owned by the state if the water body ever became navigable. *Id.*

Professor Yiannopoulos' source for this second interpretation is commentary by another distinguished Louisiana property law scholar who was heavily involved in the drafting and adoption of the Louisiana Constitution of 1974. Lee Hargrave, *"Statutory" and "Hortatory" Provisions of the Louisiana Constitution of 1974*, 43 LA. L. REV. 647, 660–63 (1983). Professor Hargrave summed up *his* views in the following terms:

> Conversely, if a nonnavigable stream becomes navigable, it would cease to be susceptible to private ownership and would become property of the state. The argument that such a change in ownership may be a taking without due process . . . probably falls because such a loss is not caused by the state itself. Rather the loss is part of the natural changes in water bodies. Indeed, if this is a taking without due process, the entrenched institution of loss of land by dereliction and by natural expansion of water bodies to cover more area should be equally unconstitutional.

Id. at 661. Both lines of argument, however, are only applicable to natural changes of water bodies; changes resulting from artificial works should be analyzed in light of principles of delictual liability and *not* Article 450. *Id.*; YIANNOPOULOS, *supra*, §4.2.

For discussion of the narrow exception to the broad prohibition against the alienation of the beds of navigable water bodies in Louisiana when a private riparian landowner seeks to reclaim land lost through erosion, see Hargrave, *supra*, at 662-63 (noting that La. Const. art. IX, sec. 3 does not require that ownership of reclaimed land be transferred to a riparian landowner but only *allows* such a transfer and that when such a reclamation does occur it must be for some "substitute public use").

6. *The Freeze Statute (La. Rev. Stat. 9:1151):* Assume for the sake of argument that Professor Yiannopoulos' second hypothesis described above is correct. A previously non-navigable water body, for example a salt water marsh in one of Louisiana's coastal parishes, becomes so inundated as a result of natural forces like coastal

erosion, subsidence and sea-level rise that it now must be classified as a navigable water body. Indeed, it is now likely part of the territorial sea and thus, a public thing. Consequently, the water bottom, a previously private thing, is now a public thing under Article 450 because any owner of a non-navigable water bottom in Louisiana takes ownership with notice that the water bottom could become a public thing if the water body ever becomes navigable in the future as a result of natural forces.

Because the water bottom now lies beneath a navigable water body, the former private landowner would have lost his ability to use that water bottom for constructions or for other activities like hunting and trapping anyway. But what if the landowner used the land to extract minerals? Does he lose his mineral rights along with his land?

The Louisiana legislature addressed this concern with special legislation, originally enacted in 1952 and amended in 2001. Commonly known as the "Freeze Statute," it provides as follows:

> In all cases where a change occurs in the ownership of land or water bottoms as a result of the action of a navigable stream, bay, lake, sea, or arm of the sea, in the change of its course, bed, or bottom, or as a result of accretion, dereliction, erosion, subsidence, or other condition resulting from the action of a navigable stream, bay, lake, sea, or arm of the sea, the new owner of such lands or water bottoms, including the state of Louisiana, shall take the same subject to and encumbered with any oil, gas, or mineral lease covering and affecting such lands or water bottoms, and subject to the mineral and royalty rights of the lessors in such lease, their heirs, successors, and assigns; the right of the lessee or owners of such lease and the right of the mineral and royalty owners thereunder shall be in no manner abrogated or affected by such change in ownership.

La. Rev. Stat. 9:1151 (1952, amended 2001).

This statute deserves careful scrutiny. On one hand, its scope is broad. It deals not only with water bottoms of formerly non-navigable water bodies, but also with formerly dry lands subsequently inundated to such a degree that they now underlie a navigable water body. The 2001 amendments broadened the statute's reach by adding references to "erosion" and "subsidence" and to the "sea or arm of the sea" in response to the widespread phenomenon of coastal erosion and wetland loss in much of Louisiana. On the other hand, the statute seems to address only the consequences of natural, not artificial, changes to water bodies resulting from course changes or from "accretion, dereliction, erosion, subsidence, or other condition."

When natural changes cause a non-navigable water body to become navigable or cause formerly dry land to be inundated to the extent that it now forms a navigable water body, the statute implies that changes in ownership are anticipated, including shifting ownership to the state of Louisiana. Importantly, though, the statute preserves the pre-existing rights of parties to a mineral lease, including those of mineral lessors and lessees, and mineral royalty owners other than the surface owners. The statute appears designed to reflect the practical fact that once previously swampy land or dry land becomes inundated to such a degree that it now forms a navigable water body, mineral rights are probably the only concern of the original landowners or mineral interest holders. After all, what else can be done with land that is now completely submerged to the extent that it lies underneath a navigable water body?

The Freeze Statute does not offer any protection to a landowner whose land has been inundated and transformed into a navigable water body when the land was not leased for mineral development or when separate mineral rights had not been previously established in the land. *See Cities Service Oil and Gas Corp. v. State*, 574 So.2d 455 (La. App. 2 Cir. 1991) (stating that the Freeze Statute is only applicable if a change of ownership occurs and a mineral lease is in effect covering lands or water bottoms at issue, but noting that mineral production from leased land is not required for the mineral lease protection to be effective). For a more recent decision applying the Freeze Statute, see *Plaquemines Parish Government v. State*, 826 So.2d 14 (La. App. 4 Cir. 2002). Does this statute help answer the questions raised by Professor Yiannopoulos about the ownership of a water body that was non-navigable in 1812 but has subsequently become navigable?

7. Continuing Controversy over Recently Submerged Lands near the Coast: Over the last several years, controversy has continued to simmer over who owns and who has access to lands that have recently become submerged beneath arms of the sea or the open territorial waters of the State of Louisiana as a result of natural or artificial causes. These include sea-level rise, natural subsidence, and erosion of marshland due to factors such as salt-water intrusion through man-made pipeline and navigational canals and introduction of non-native species (such as nutria). During the 2018 Regular Session of the Louisiana Legislature, House Bill No. 391 was introduced in an attempt to establish public navigation rights over running waters of the State, including those that are navigable by registered motorboats and "[those] passing over any privately owned water bottom which has a direct natural or man-made inlet or outlet to a state-owned water bottom that is subject to the ebb and flow of the tide of the Gulf of Mexico and the tidally influenced arms and tributaries passing through the coastal areas of this state." H.B. No. 391 (La. 2018 Reg. Sess.). H.B. 391, however, also stated it did not seek "to establish a change in ownership of the bottoms and banks of any privately owned waterway." *Id*. H.B. 391 caused great controversy and failed to achieve passage in the House of Representatives by a vote of 59-37.

After the demise of H.B. 391, the Louisiana Senate established by concurrent resolution a Public Recreation Access Task force with the charge to "study the conditions, needs and issues relative to potential recreation access on the navigable waters of the state and to make recommendations to the legislature." Sen. Conc. Res. No. 99 (La. 2018 Reg. Sess.). The task force is comprised of representatives of landowners groups, recreational sportsmen, conservation organizations, the oil and gas industry and the Louisiana State Law Institute. The following excerpt from a student comment published in the *Louisiana Law Review* sets the scene for the debates that are likely to occur before the Public Access Recreation Task Force and in the legislature for years to come.

Jacques Mestayer, *Saving Sportsman's Paradise: Article 450 and Declaring Ownership of Submerged Lands in Louisiana*
76 LA. L. REV. 889 (2016)

Introduction

Louisiana is Sportsman's Paradise-home to some of the most sought-after hunting, fishing, and nature-viewing opportunities in the world. Seeking to net the best catch, sportsmen and commercial fishermen scour Louisiana's coast. Due to the current legal landscape and Louisiana's constantly morphing coastal environment, however, these fishermen often find that lawfully using Louisiana's coastal waters is impossible.

Unlike most other coastal states, the vast majority of Louisiana's coastal lands are private. These lands are swiftly submerging, as Louisiana loses the equivalent of a football field of coastal land every hour. Under the current practice in Louisiana, many of these large tracts of coastal land remain in private hands after they submerge. As a result, even to the trained eye, the line between public and private coastal property is often indiscernible.

In 2006, the Louisiana Legislature realized that permitting private ownership of some submerged lands made the public's utilization of state lands and water bottoms difficult. As a result, the legislature commissioned the State Lands Office to use an interactive mapping system to determine the ownership of Louisiana's lands and water bottoms. As the State Lands Office began reviewing Louisiana's coast, it found that large areas of submerged land were formerly private land. Believing that, under article 450 of the Louisiana Civil Code, ownership of these lands reverted to the State once the land became submerged, Louisiana informally claimed title to the lands through the State Lands Office review. Prominent private landowners strongly opposed these title claims and began lobbying the State Lands Office not to take formal action. Apparently overlooking that article 450 may dictate that many submerged lands belong to the State, the State Lands Office officials decided that a further assertion of State ownership would lead to an onslaught of litigation that the State could not afford. In the absence of a legislative solution to the problem, and in an effort to minimize litigation, the State Lands Office opted to classify most of the submerged land as "claimed by the state and the adjoining property owner" and cautioned citizens to enter at their own risk. Instead of clearing up titles, this classification clouded title to vast areas of submerged land. Although any state's failure to declare that it owns certain areas of submerged land would be problematic, that failure is especially problematic for Louisiana because Louisiana's coastal environment is submerging faster than any other landmass in the United States.

Between 1932 and 2000, Louisiana lost over one million acres of coastal land to the Gulf of Mexico's inescapable grasp. Due to a variety of natural processes, over a million more acres of land will likely submerge within the next 50 years. By then, Louisiana's total land loss will be roughly equivalent to two times the entire land-mass of Delaware. Though some mitigating measures are in place, severe land loss will continue unless the state or federal government subsidizes drastic corrective action.

As time passes, a combination of natural and manmade forces will submerge larger quantities of Louisiana's coast, thereby creating an underwater labyrinth riddled with tracts of private land. Thus, promptly declaring the ownership of submerged lands is imperative to give Louisiana's citizens some valuable direction regarding what lands are public. The legislature should take note of the current and future issues regarding submerged lands and formally declare ownership over them. Until then, Louisiana's citizens remain deprived of not only valuable property rights, but also significant revenue from mineral transactions that accompany State-owned submerged lands. . . .

II. The History, Doctrine, and Jurisprudence Pertaining to Submerged Land Ownership in Louisiana

Due to the vast economic and sentimental value of Louisiana's submerged coastal marshlands, declaring that the State owns certain submerged coastal lands is vitally important to the people of Louisiana. Examining the history of Louisiana's coastal environment elucidates how such a significant mass of submerged land found its way into private hands in the first place.

A. Tracing the Origin of Louisiana's Privately Owned Coastal Marshlands

Currently, most of Louisiana's coastal marshlands are private. This private ownership is an anomaly, as most states have a broad reach with respect to coastal land ownership. This abnormality in Louisiana is largely attributable to the Swamp Land Grant Acts of 1849 and 1850, which gave Louisiana an estimated nine million acres of "swamp and overflowed lands" that were unfit for cultivation. The collective purpose of these grants was to permit Louisiana to sell these lands and use the proceeds to protect valuable agricultural lands near the banks of the Mississippi River. In furtherance of this objective, Louisiana began passing legislation permitting the alienation of a vast amount of coastal swamplands. In particular, the legislature passed Act 75 of 1880 that seemingly extended the alienability of Louisiana's lands beyond the original scope of the Swamp Land Grants. Although those federal grants gave Louisiana "swamp and overflowed lands," Act 75 allowed the alienation of "sea marsh or prairie, subject to tidal overflow." As noted by Professor A.N. Yiannopoulos:

> This Act was destined to create confusion [because] it seemed to obliterate the difference between lands "subject to the ebb and flow of the tide[,]" [otherwise known as lands subject to tidal overflow] that Louisiana acquired from the United States under the equal footing doctrine, and "swamp lands

subject to overflow" that Louisiana acquired from the United States under the Swamp Land Grant Acts.[47]

Indeed, after the passage of Act 75, courts began jumbling land descriptions by classifying "sea marsh and sea prairie subject to tidal overflow" separately from "lands within the tidewaters of the sea." Thus, all sea marsh and sea prairie subject to tidal overflow became alienable, thereby permitting private ownership of vast areas of land highly susceptible to submersion. As a result, 80% of Louisiana's coastal marshlands are now private.

Most of these private coastal marshlands either are submerged or will become submerged in the near future. Avoiding those lands when navigating, fishing, or hunting near Louisiana's coast is a formidable task, which has become even more difficult since the passage of House Bill 667 in 2003. That bill removed the requirement that landowners place signs indicating that their land is private. Declaring that the State owns all submerged lands within the scope of Louisiana Civil Code article 450 would allow Louisiana's sportsmen to utilize many coastal areas without subjecting themselves to liability for trespassing. Further, this declaration would align with the explicit language in article 450. . . .

III. Louisiana Owns All Submerged Land Fitting Under Article 450 Regardless of When That Land Submerged

Under article 450, the State owns several different types of land, including seashore, sea bottoms, and the beds and bottoms beneath Louisiana's navigable waters. But consider a tract of private marshland that, in 1820, was located five miles inland from the Gulf of Mexico. As the Gulf waters rose, or as the land subsided, that tract became submerged under ten feet of water. Adhering to Louisiana's public policy, Constitution, Civil Code, and the jurisprudential reasoning of many Louisiana courts, this tract of submerged marshland must fall within the scope of article 450 and therefore be owned by the State. Although no cases or doctrine direct a court's analysis on this particular issue, seashore, sea bottoms, and navigable water bottoms created after state alienation are public things insusceptible of private ownership.

A. The State Owns Submerged Land That Bordered Natural Navigable Water Bodies

As private land abutting a natural navigable water body erodes into that body, that land becomes part of the water body's bottom, and, consequently, its ownership is transferred to Louisiana under article 450. According to the Louisiana Supreme Court in *Miami Corp.* [173 So. 315 (La. 1936)], public policy and sound logic necessitate this result. In that case, Miami Corporation sought a declaration that it was

---

47. *See* A.N. Yiannopoulos, Property §66, in 2 Louisiana Civil Law Treatise 125 (4th ed. 2001); cf. *Pollard v. Hagan*, 44 U.S. (3 How.) 212, 218 (1845) (distinguishing between waters subject to the ebb and flow of the tide and swamplands, and noting that tidelands "between the low and high" tide that are covered by the ebb and flow of the tide belong to the State).

the owner of an eroded area forming a portion of Grand Lake's bed. The court noted that "[i]t appears to be the rule that where the forces of nature . . . have operated on the banks of a navigable body of water . . . the submerged area becomes a portion of the bed and is insusceptible of private ownership." If the rule in *Miami Corp.* was not the law, the entire rim of land surrounding a public lake could erode and become private submerged land, thereby preventing public use of the lake. Thus, taking policy considerations into account, submerged land that formerly abutted a natural navigable water body must be a public thing under article 450.

B. The State Owns the Bottoms of Natural Navigable Water Bodies Created After State Alienation

Analyzing Louisiana's jurisprudence that addresses the ownership of the bottoms of natural navigable water bodies created after state alienation proves to be quite difficult. No case directly presents the issue, and the courts that tangentially address the issue only provide a framework that might lead to improper interpretation. [*See Vermilion Bay Land Co. v. Phillips Petroleum Co.*, 646 So. 2d 408, 410–12 (La. Ct. App. 1994) (noting that previous cases only dealt with water bodies navigable in 1812, and, subsequently, answering the question as to water bodies that were non-navigable in 1812 but became navigable before severance). Eds.] Fortunately, Louisiana's public policy, interpretative maxims, and the Louisiana Constitution — despite the lack of guidance from Louisiana's jurisprudence — lead to the conclusion that all navigable water bottoms should be State owned, regardless of when they became navigable.[130]

Capturing the essence of Louisiana's public policy, Chief Justice Fournet, in his dissent in *California Co. v. Price*, stated that a land grant including navigable water bottoms was "equivalent to a patent to air, or to the water running through the Mississippi river on its way to the sea." [*Cal. Co. v. Price*, 74 So. 2d 1, 16 (La. 1953) (Fournet, J., dissenting).] Chief Justice Fournet further explained that "[a]n arm of the sea is one of those things which all men may freely use conformable with the use for which it is intended by nature, and is among those things that are insusceptible of private ownership." [*Id.* (internal citations omitted).] Courts consistently interpret this public policy to mean that Louisiana does not permit private control over the bottoms of channels of commerce; thus, those courts consistently find that navigable water bottoms existing in 1812 or created prior to state alienation are insusceptible

---

130. *See Gulf Oil Corp. v. State Mineral Bd.*, 317 So. 2d 576, 590 (La. 1974) ("It has been the public policy of the State of Louisiana at all times since its admission into the Union that all navigable waters and the beds of same within its boundaries are common or public things and insusceptible of private ownership . . ." (quoting La. Rev. Stat. Ann. § 1107 (1954))); *but see Delacroix Corp. v. Jones-O'Brien, Inc.*, 597 So. 2d 65, 69-70 (La. Ct. App. 1992) (implying that the public policy discussed in Gulf Oil does not apply to inland navigable lakes). A landowner's right of reclamation — the right to apply for a permit that allows a landowner to reclaim land that he has lost due to erosion by essentially rebuilding the land — is the only exception to the prohibition on private ownership of Louisiana's natural navigable water bottoms. *See* La. Const. art. IX, § 3. Louisiana's submerged coastal environment remains privately owned, or at the very least, privately claimed.

of private ownership.[133] Those courts did not address the ownership of water bodies that become navigable in fact after state alienation, however. "[P]rivately owned land does not become part of a navigable body of water" and thus does not become insusceptible of private ownership "when a nearby navigable body of water over-flows its normal bed and temporarily covers the property." [*Walker Lands, Inc. v. E. Carroll Parish Police Jury*, 871 So. 2d 1258, 1264 (La. Ct. App. 2004) (emphasis added).] But several sound reasons exist, in addition to strong public policy, for why land should be insusceptible of private ownership when that land indefinitely becomes the bottom of a navigable water body.

A literal interpretation of article 450 dictates that these lands become public by operation of law. Article 450 does not distinguish between the bottoms of water bodies that became navigable in fact before severance from state ownership and water bodies that become navigable in fact after state alienation. The article simply states that the bottoms of natural navigable water bodies are public things. Obeying the maxim "where the law does not distinguish, courts should not distinguish," the ownership of the bottoms of newly navigable water bodies should revert to the State.

The Louisiana Constitution also supports this conclusion. Article IX, section 3 provides that "[t]he legislature shall neither alienate nor authorize the alienation of the bed of a navigable water body, except for purposes of reclamation by the riparian owner to recover land lost through erosion." In ratifying this provision, Louisiana's voters expressed their desire to keep these water bottoms out of private ownership. Thus, "if a non-navigable stream" or other body of water "becomes navigable, it would cease to be susceptible of private ownership and would become property of the state." Further, nothing in the Louisiana Constitution, the Civil Code, or the jurisprudence suggests that a privately owned thing cannot become a public thing by operation of law. As such, as private land submerges beneath seawater or natu-rally navigable waterways, that private land becomes public by operation of law.

Lastly, if the bottoms of water bodies that become naturally navigable after state alienation were susceptible of private ownership, then the bottoms of a body of water large enough to support substantial commercial activity could be private. If such a water body could be private, the owner could possibly interfere with trade. That result is impermissible because, under Article 450, the public domain indef-initely retains the right to use Article 450 waters and bottoms without private inter-ference. Considering Louisiana's strong public policy opposing the alienation of

---

133. *See, e.g., Gulf Oil Corp.*, 317 So. 2d at 582 ("[N]avigable water bottoms other than rivers are public things insusceptible of private ownership."); *State v. Barras*, 615 So. 2d 285, 287 (La. 1993) ("The beds of navigable waters are insusceptible of private ownership."); Miami Corp., 173 So. at 326 ("But, in order to reach this conclusion, the court had to go counter to the long-established sound principles of public policy in our jurisprudence-that the title to the bottoms of navigable bodies of water belong to the State as a result of its inherent sovereignty and are insusceptible of private ownership."); see also Vermilion Bay Land Co., 646 So. 2d at 410–12 (noting that previous cases only dealt with water bodies navigable in 1812 and, subsequently, answering the question as to water bodies that were non-navigable in 1812 but became navigable before severance).

navigable water bottoms from the State, the effects of a law that allows the private ownership of navigable water bottoms leads to absurd results that Louisiana's legal regime should not tolerate. Therefore, as a principle of law and public policy, Louisiana must own land that becomes the bottom of a natural navigable water body after state alienation.

C. The State Owns Sea Bottoms and Seashores Created After State Alienation

As with the bottoms of natural navigable water bodies, sea bottom and seashore created before state alienation is clearly insusceptible of private ownership. But whether land that transformed into sea bottom and seashore after state alienation is susceptible of private ownership remains undecided. Several courts have implied that the bottoms and shores of arms of the sea and the Gulf of Mexico are always State owned; however, some older jurisprudence suggests otherwise.

Citing this older jurisprudence, Professor Yiannopoulos suggests that private individuals may own portions of sea bottom. Still, Louisiana law only permits sea bottom ownership in extremely rare cases where the State issued patents to the sea bottom prior to 1921. Those patents' validity is a consequence of a line of controversial jurisprudence, which further casts doubt on the legitimacy of private ownership of sea bottom and seashore. As to sea bottoms created since 1921, however, Louisiana law is unequivocal: "[W]hen the water bottom in question lies . . . under the sea or an arm of the sea, it is explicitly included among the inalienable things vested in the State." Thus, submerged land that becomes sea bottom or seashore after state alienation is a public thing that the State owns.

The Louisiana Constitution of 1974, the Louisiana Civil Code, and the Louisiana Revised Statutes dictate that natural navigable water bottoms, sea bottoms, and seashore are insusceptible of private ownership. None of these sources indicate that exceptions exist or that this rule should not apply to lands that, after state alienation, submerge due to natural forces. Rather, jurisprudence and legal scholarship suggest that classifying newly navigable water bottoms, newly created sea bottoms, and newly created seashore as public things under article 450 is reasonable. Further, reading article 450 in light of the majority view of Louisiana's public policy leads to the conclusion that those newly submerged lands fall within the scope of article 450. Thus, all submerged land exhibiting the characteristics of the water bodies explicitly included under article 450, regardless of when they began to exhibit those characteristics, are public things that the State owns. . . . . .

Notes and Questions

1. Notice that Mestayer provides a useful and succinct explanation of how most of Louisiana's coastal swamplands and marshlands became privately owned. As Mestayer explains, the federal government transferred to the State of Louisiana millions of acres of "swamp and overflowed lands" unfit for cultivation in the Swamp Land Grant Acts of 1849 and 1850. In subsequent decades, Louisiana passed legislation

that allowed the state to alienate much of this coastal swampland and marshland. Thus, private individuals and companies acquired ownership of this largely wet land which was crisscrossed by navigable and non-navigable water bodies. In recent decades, this former swampland and marshland, which was alienated by the state and became privately owned, is now in many cases fully submerged beneath navigable water bodies, including the Gulf of Mexico and arms of the sea. This history explains why Mestayer frames his legal analysis in terms of the contested ownership of coastal swamplands and marshlands that have become submerged beneath navigable water bodies either after 1812 or "after state alienation."

2. According to Mestayer, the law is clear that all previously dry land, swampland, marshland or dry land that featured a non-navigable water body of some sort and that has become submerged beneath a navigable water body as a result of natural forces either after Louisiana became a state in 1812 or after alienation by the state is now, as matter of law, a public thing owned by the state? Are you convinced by this proposition? If Mestayer is correct that ownership of these water bottoms has now become vested in the state, is the state obligated to compensate the former landowners for the loss of ownership under the Fifth Amendment to the United States Constitution and Article 1, Section 4 of the Louisiana State Constitution? Those constitutional provisions and topical case law and jurisprudence will be further explored in Chapter 6, Part B.

C. Private Things Subject to Public Use

Having explored several examples of public things specifically enumerated in Article 450 of the Civil Code, we now complicate our understanding of the tripartite division of things by yet another category of things. Article 455 announces what amounts to a hybrid category:

La. Civ. Code art. 455. Private things subject to public use

Private things may be subject to public use in accordance with law or by dedication.

La. Civ. Code art. 455 (1978). This article was inserted into the revised Civil Code largely for didactic purposes—to help lawyers and judges avoid the mistake of labeling those private things that happen to be subject to some form of public use as "public things." *Id.* rev. cmt. (b).

As we shall see, certain private things can nevertheless still be subjected to public use—either by direct legislative declaration or by an act of the owner dedicating these things to public use. Below we examine the primary example of a private thing subjected to public use through the express directive of the Civil Code—banks of navigable rivers. We then discuss how the legislature and courts have developed the notion of a private dedication to public use.

1. Banks of Navigable Rivers

Before examining our primary Civil Code text, first recall that both the water in a natural, navigable river or stream *and* the bed or bottom of such a water body are *public things* pursuant to Article 450 of the Civil Code. As indicated earlier, Article 452 merely amplifies Article 450 by describing some of the activities that members of the public can undertake in connection with public things, including, *inter alia*, the right to fish in rivers. Article 456 of the Civil Code, however, addresses a third element in the geographic space typically associated with rivers—their banks. The provision offers a very specific rule of law for this specific zone:

Art. 456. Banks of navigable rivers or streams

The banks of navigable rivers or streams are private things that are subject to public use.

The bank of a navigable river or stream is the land lying between the ordinary low and the ordinary high water stage of the water. Nevertheless, when there is a levee in proximity to the water, established according to law, the levee shall form the bank.

La. Civ. Code art. 456 (1978).

Article 456 boldly declares that a thing inherently classified as private is, by legislative fiat, subject to public use. The policy justification for declaring river banks to be private things and yet subject to some form of public use is ancient. Rivers have always been important avenues of transportation and commerce. In Louisiana this was particularly true in the colonial era and the early statehood period because almost all of the early settlements took place on the banks of navigable rivers and bayous and because transportation was so difficult over the swampy or heavily wooded terrain elsewhere. In addition, the most highly elevated and often the most fertile land was found on the banks of rivers and bayous as this is where sedimentary deposits resulting from hundreds or thousands of years of annual spring flooding had produced natural "levees" comprised of rich soil. It made sense that all the lands immediately adjacent to navigable rivers and bayous should be susceptible to private ownership to encourage their commercial and agricultural development.

At the same time, though, it was important that members of the public should have some right of access to the land bordering these important avenues of commerce. If that were not the case, any person traveling upon a navigable river or bayou would have to seek and obtain permission from private riparian landowners any time the traveler needed to stop during his journey. The transaction costs involved in having to negotiate for such permission in advance of or during each journey along a navigable river or bayou would have been quite high.

Just like its predecessors, current Article 456 aims to strike a balance between these two policy goals of promoting the commercial and agricultural development of banks of navigable rivers and furnishing access to the river-going public to avoid wasteful transaction costs. Article 455 of the 1870 Civil Code, based on similar provisions in the 1808 Digest and the 1825 Civil Code, expressed the nature of this policy compromise even more explicitly than current Article 456. That article provided:

> **Art. 455 [1870]**
>
> The use of the banks of navigable rivers or streams is public; accordingly everyone has a right freely to bring his vessels to land there, to make fast the same to trees which are there planted, to unload his vessels, to deposit his goods, to dry his nets, and the like.
>
> Nevertheless the ownership of the river banks belongs to those who possess the adjacent lands.

La. Civ. Code art. 455 (1870).

Interestingly, unlike many other provisions of the 1808 Digest or 1825 Civil Code, the source provisions of Article 455 (1870) had no counterpart in the Napoleonic Code which provided that navigable rivers and streams, as well as their banks, were part of the public domain. C. Civ. art. 538 (1804). Thus, Louisiana's legislative decision to place the banks of navigable rivers in a hybrid legal status—private things that are nevertheless subject to public use—connects Louisiana law to ancient concepts of the public ownership of rivers and the public's right to use the banks of rivers that are rooted, as Justinian's *Institutes* make clear, in the law of nations found in Roman law:

> Also, the public use of the banks of rivers, as of the river itself, is part of the law of nations: and, so anyone is free to bring to land a ship, to tie ropes to the trees naturally growing thereon, to place in these any cargo, just as to navigate the river itself. But the ownership of the bank is in those to whom the adjoining estates belong: and for this reason, the trees, which are naturally growing on these, also belong to them.

Inst. 2.1.2 & 4 (Translation Markus G. Puder). Louisiana embraced this Roman approach to regulating banks of navigable rivers to serve the state's particular economic and social needs.

Until the enactment of current Article 456 of the Civil Code, numerous Louisiana decisions attempted to define the geographic space denoted by the terms "bank" and "batture," which is also important for understanding the scope of the state's so called "levee servitude" under Article 665 of the Civil Code. *See* John A. Lovett, *Comment, Batture, Ordinary High Water and the Louisiana Levee Servitude*, 69 Tul. L. Rev. 561, 568–75 (1994) (describing early Louisiana cases defining the terms "bank" and "batture"). Revised Article 456 builds upon Article 457 of the 1870 Civil Code in providing a relatively precise geographic definition of the "bank." As the revision comments indicate, the definition of a river's "bank" as the land "between the ordinary low and ordinary high stage" of the water is derived from Article 457 of the 1870 Civil Code and from the Louisiana Supreme Court decision *Wemple v. Eastham*, 90 So. 637, 638 (La. 1922); La. Civ. Code art. 456 rev. cmt. (d) (1978).

Visualize the relationship between the bed of a navigable river or stream (a public thing) and its bank (a private thing subject to public use) under Article 456 of the Louisiana Civil Code. The key point to remember is that the *ordinary low water* stage or mark establishes the boundary between the purely public sphere, comprised of the river and the river bed or bottom, on one hand, and the partially private and partially public sphere, comprised of the bank, on the other. The *ordinary high water* stage or mark separates the bank from the rest of the riparian tract, which is classified as a private thing and which may be owned by a private person or the state or a political subdivision in its private capacity. The ordinary low and high water stages of rivers are determined by examining evidence relating to both the physical characteristics of the bank and statistical evidence of water stages maintained by levee districts and the United States Army Corps of Engineers, among others. Lovett, *Batture*, 69 Tul. L. Rev. at 582–607.

If the river is bounded by a levee in proximity to the water, the levee forms the landward boundary of the bank. The statement in Article 456 that the geographic reach of a bank will be delimited by the presence of a levee when a levee is in proximity to the water offers another element of uncertainty. When exactly is a levee in enough proximity to the water to supplant the ordinary high water mark as the landward boundary of a navigable river bank? The following decision and the notes thereafter highlight how state and federal courts have grappled with this and other questions relating to the physical extent of the bank of a navigable river.

The revision comments to Article 456 suggest that "ordinarily" the same person or entity that owns the bank will own the rest of the riparian tract. La. Civ. Code art. 456 rev. cmt. (c) (1978). Yet it is certainly possible that the owner of a riparian tract—the riparian "proprietor" in the language of the revision comments—might subdivide his riparian tract and alienate only the portion that consists of the bank while retaining the rest of the tract. The riparian owner could also do the reverse and retain the bank, while alienating the rest of the riparian tract. In addition, it is possible that either the bank or non-bank portion of a riparian tract might be acquired by another person through acquisitive prescription. In sum, it is entirely conceivable that one person might own the bank, while another person owns what remains of the original riparian tract.

The final issue in connection with Article 456 involves the scope of the public's right to use the bank of a navigable river or stream, however widely or narrowly delimited that physical space may be. Statements in the revision comments to Article 456, written at the time of the 1978 Civil Code revision, have proven to be very influential. In light of the following decisions, have the courts appropriately defined the substantive scope of the public's right to use the banks of a navigable river?

Warner v. Clarke

232 So.2d 99 (La. App. 2 Cir. 1970)

DIXON, Judge. This is a suit to enjoin the district attorney and the sheriff of East Carroll Parish from prosecuting the plaintiffs for trespass under R.S. 14:63. One plaintiff is domiciled in East Carroll Parish; the other three are domiciled in West Carroll Parish. Plaintiffs allege that they have been arrested by the sheriff of East Carroll Parish and threatened with prosecution.

The lands involved lie adjacent to the Mississippi River south of the Arkansas line and include the levee and land between the levee and the river. There are various bodies of water located on this land which are, or have been, navigable.

The petition alleges that considerable quantities of fish and game abound in the area involved, and that petitioners hold hunting and fishing licenses, and desire to hunt and fish on the lands involved. Their arrest, and threatened prosecution by the district attorney, they allege, will result in irreparable harm by loss of their alleged right to use the lands involved, or by wrongful prosecution.

The answer does not contradict any of the allegations of the petition, except for the petitioners' claimed right to hunt. An 'Agreed Stipulation of Facts' is included in the record. No oral testimony was adduced. The case was submitted on the pleadings and the stipulation.

It was stipulated that the lands are owned by private individuals or corporations, and that the vast majority of the owners or lessees of the land have posted it in accordance with the requirements of R.S. 14:63. There are roads on the levee, constructed with public funds, but not open to the public.

The stipulation concluded with an agreement that the following are the issues to be decided by the Court:

'(a) Does the riparian servitude in favor of the public affecting the banks of navigable streams, give the public the right to freely enter upon riparian lands, particularly the lands described in Exhibit A, for the purpose of hunting and fishing thereon when: (1) entering by navigable streams or lakes?; (2) entering otherwise. . . .'

There was judgment in the trial court for the defendants, rejecting the demands of the plaintiffs. In a scholarly and impressive opinion, the trial judge decided that the plaintiffs did not have a right to go upon the levees and the lands of others that lay between the levee and the river for the purpose of hunting and fishing.

The appellants claim that their rights to the land come from provisions of the Civil Code. Article 455 of the Civil Code declares that the use of the banks of navigable rivers is public. Article 453 states that public things are those, the property of which is vested in a whole nation, and the use of which is allowed to all the members of the nation. Article 457 says that the levees form the banks on the borders of the Mississippi River. Plaintiffs claim that although the land between the levee and the river is subject to private ownership, that ownership is imperfect, according to Article 490.

The statutory basis for the plaintiffs' claimed right to hunt and fish on the levee and the land between the levee and the river is Article 455 of the Civil Code:

'The use of the banks of navigable rivers or streams is public; accordingly everyone has a right freely to bring his vessels to land there, to make fast the same to the trees which are there planted, to unload his vessels, to deposit his goods, to dry his nets, and the like.

'Nevertheless the ownership of the river banks belongs to those who possess the adjacent lands' (emphasis added).

The prayer of the petition is for judgment 'decreeing that the lands *** are subject to a servitude in favor of the public or, that is, subject to public use' and for an injunction against the arrest and prosecution of the plaintiffs when hunting, fishing or walking on the lands described. . . .

[The court discussed its power to issue a declaratory judgment in the absence of indispensable parties and the propriety of enjoining a criminal prosecution in the absence of a claim that the trespass statute, La. R.S. 14:63, was unconstitutional or in the absence of any allegation of a presently pending prosecution. Eds.]

Regardless of the doubt that may exist about the propriety of an injunction in a case where it is not contended that the penal statute complained of is unconstitutional, it seems clear that the plaintiffs here have no right to an injunction because they do not possess a property right threatened with invasion.

Whatever Article 455 once meant about the use of banks of navigable rivers, subsequent legislation has made it apparent that the legislature did not intend to maintain a right in these plaintiffs or in the general public to hunt and fish upon the levees and the land that lies between the levees and the Mississippi River. R.S. 14:63 defines 'criminal trespass' as follows:

(2) The unauthorized and intentional entry upon any:

(a) Plot of immovable property in excess of one acre which is posted but not enclosed, unless said property is situated in an open range area; or

(b) Plot of immovable property which is posted and enclosed, including property situated in open range areas; or

(c) Posted lands belonging to public institutions; or ***.

Where an entry is made from a waterway for emergency purposes the party in distress may use the banks of said waterway without violating the provisions of Paragraph 2. . . . [omitting definitions contained in 14:63(B). Eds.]

Louisiana's trespass statute has been frequently amended and reenacted (see Act 458 of 1960 and Act 497 of 1964). Article 665 of the Civil Code provides that problems related to public servitudes are regulated by 'laws or particular regulations.'

Our courts have repeatedly held that the riparian servitudes are not subject to a broad and liberal construction, as contended by the plaintiffs, but exist 'only for that which is incident to the nature and the navigable character of the stream washing the land of such proprietor.' Hebert v. T. L. James & Company, Inc. et al., 224 La. 498, 70 So.2d 102, 106 (1953), quoting from Carollton R. Company v. Winthrop, 5 La. Ann. 36 (1850); Lake Providence Port Commission v. Bunge Corporation, La. App., 193 So.2d 363.

It does not seem that a fair interpretation of C.C. 455, which gives everyone the right to land his vessel and tie up to trees on the banks, and there 'to dry his nets, and the like' could construe that article to grant to the public the right to hunt and fish upon the lands and waters between the river and the levee. The right to hunt and fish on these lands seems unrelated to the nature and the navigable character of the Mississippi River. . . .

Since we find no property right in these plaintiffs which enables them to hunt and fish between the river and the levee, they are not entitled to an injunction. Consequently, the judgment of the district court is affirmed, at the cost of the appellants.

Notes and Questions

1. Notice how the court in *Warner v. Clarke*, 232 So.2d 99 (La. App. 2 Cir. 1970), frames the ultimate question as one of whether the plaintiffs, the hunters and fishermen who were prosecuted by the sheriff and district attorney of East Carroll Parish, have a "property right" in the area described by the court as lying between the Mississippi River and the levee—the river bank. The court acknowledges that members of the public have some right of access to the bank of navigable rivers by virtue of what it calls "the riparian servitudes." But it also asserts that this right only relates to "the nature and navigable character" of the river. According to the court, this right does not give hunters and fishermen the right to engage in their pursuits, despite the ideal conditions for hunting and fishing that exist when the lands at issue are submerged by annual floodwaters.

The court relies on just three prior decisions in reaching this conclusion. The first, *Hebert v. T.L. James & Co., Inc.*, 70 So.2d 102 (La. 1953), concerned the scope of Article 665 of the Civil Code, which provides the public with a servitude over riparian tracts for the purposes of construction and repair of levees and roads, in connection with the state highway department's efforts to improve and widen a public highway crossing the plaintiff's riparian tract. That decision, however, did not address the codal predecessors to Article 456 at all.

Another decision cited by the court, *Lake Providence Port Comm'n v. Bunge Corp.*, 193 So.2d 363 (La. App. 2 Cir. 1966), involved the authority of local levee districts to control development on the banks of navigable rivers and obstructions of the public's access to such banks under Articles 458 and 459 of the Civil Code. Once again, that decision did not concern the scope of the public servitude under the codal predecessors of Article 456.

Only the third authority cited, *Carrollton R. Company v. Winthrop*, 5 La. Ann. 36 (1850), arguably concerned the scope of the public's right to access navigable river banks under Article 456 or its predecessors. That decision involved a dispute between a riparian landowner that had leased a portion of its river bank to persons operating a wood yard on the premises. The lessees failed to pay rent for various reasons and, after their lease was cancelled, refused to surrender possession. *Id.* at 36. They argued that they occupied a public servitude and that their former landlords held only a naked ownership of the land. In an opinion authored by Justice Rost, the Louisiana Supreme Court held that the defendants could *not* rely upon the public's servitude over the bank of a navigable river under Article 446 of the 1825 Civil Code, a predecessor to Article 455 (1870) and current Article 456, for their possession. Any private use of the land must inure to the benefit of its owners. *Id.* at 36–37:

> The conversion of a portion of the batture in front of the town of Carrollton into a wood yard, is not one of those uses [sanctioned by Article 446 (1825)]. It is a private destination of property which, so long as it continues, must inure to the benefit of the owner of the soil. If the corporation had the right to establish wood yards, they would have an equal right to establish brick yards and saw mills; and by refusing to advance the present line of the levee they could enjoy forever, as owners the property of the plaintiffs.

Carrollton R. Co. v. Winthrop, 5 La. Ann. 36, 37 (1850). Are the factual circumstances in *Carrollton R. Co.* similar to or distinguishable from those presented in *Warner*?

Now consider another decision rendered the same year as *Warner* that analyzes the public's right of access to the levee adjacent to the Mississippi River in a different context.

Tenneco, Inc. v. Oil, Chemical & Atomic Workers Union, Local 4-522

234 So.2d 246 (La. App. 4 Cir. 1970)

CHASEZ, Judge. Tenneco, Inc., plaintiff-appellant (Tenneco herein), is a corporation operating an oil refinery and bulk terminal in St. Bernard Parish, Louisiana. Its property is located in the Chalmette area of that Parish, with its northern boundary near Louisiana Highway No. 39, its eastern boundary adjacent to Paris Road and its southern boundary on the Mississippi River.

Tenneco's refinery employees are represented by the defendant-appellee, the Oil, Chemical & Atomic Workers Union, Local 4-522 (OCAW herein).

When the labor agreement between Tenneco and OCAW expired at the end of 1968, OCAW commenced a strike of Tenneco's Chalmette Refinery. . . . The picketing was attended by violence, intimidation, and mass picketing of such proportions as to cause Tenneco to institute this suit against OCAW, Local 4-522, and certain of their officers for a temporary restraining order and an injunction.

The district court issued a temporary restraining order on January 8, 1969, and after extensive hearings issued a preliminary and permanent injunction on January 27, 1969, which prohibited any picketing on Tenneco's property, any picketing that obstructed free ingress and egress to Tenneco's property, and prohibited any acts of intimidation or molestation.

The judgment, however, excepted from these prohibitions the part of Tenneco's property which constituted the levee of the Mississippi River.

Tenneco has appealed from the ruling by the district judge that picketing on the levee of a navigable stream in furtherance of a labor dispute was a public use within the meaning of Civil Code Article 455.

. . . .

As previously stated, the injunction prohibited any picketing on Tenneco's property with the exception of that portion which constituted the levee of the Mississippi River.

In his reasons for judgment the trial judge explained the exception in this manner:

> In the opinion of the Court public usage of the levee for passage, for recreational purposes and related activities, for viewing the magnificence of the broad expanse of the Mississippi River, and for any other uses which are not destructive to the primary purpose of a levee are permitted within the purview of Civil Code Article 455. Accordingly, to recognize these rights and to deny defendants the use of said levee for the purpose of peaceful picketing, a right guaranteed to them under the Louisiana Constitution and under the First and Fourteenth Amendments of the United States Constitution, would indeed be a trespass on defendants.

We cannot agree with the court a quo. The pertinent Articles of the Civil Code are as follows: . . .

. . . The servitude of public use described in the above Articles [Articles 455, 457 and 665 of the 1870 Civil Code] has been defined as a use which is incidental to the river, for example, commerce or navigation.

In Hebert v. T. L. James & Co., 224 La. 498, 70 So.2d 102 (1953), the Supreme Court stated that 'the servitude so imposed by the codal articles on property bordering a navigable stream was not intended to serve the public for any purpose other than that which is incident to the nature, navigable character, or use of the stream.'

In Lyons v. Hinckley, 12 La. Ann. 655 (1856), the Supreme Court stated:

> The character of the servitude which is due from the proprietors of the soil is here described, and instead of being for the use of the public at large for all purposes, is only for that which is incident to the nature and the navigable character of the stream washing the land of such proprietor. (Carrollton R. Co. v. Winthrop) 5 (La.) Ann. 36.

Finally, in State v. Richardson (1916), 140 La. 329, 72 So. 984 at 988, our Supreme Court made the following statement:

> The ownership of the banks of a navigable river, as recognized by C.C. art. 455, and of the alluvion which is formed "to any soil situated on the shore of a river or stream," as recognized by C.C. art. 509, is qualified by the conditions imposed by those articles, and hence the right of use, in both instances, is in the public; but that right is also qualified by the terms in which it is reversed. The use must not only be a public use, but it must be the particular public use specified in the reservation, being, in the one case, that which is incidental to the navigable character of the stream and its use as an avenue of commerce, and, in the other, that "which is required by law for the public use," and which, where the stream is nonnavigable, is perhaps more restricted. And, save to the extent that it is so qualified, the ownership is as perfect as law can make it.

We do not think that Article 455 encompasses picketing on the levee—a decidedly private use—and one not incidental to navigation or commerce on the river.

For the foregoing reasons, we conclude that the trial court erred in that part of its judgment which excepted the crown of the levee of the Mississippi River from Tenneco's private property. We hold that picketing on the levee is a private use by one not the riparian owner of the property and not incidental to commerce or navigation on the river and is, therefore, not protected by Articles 455, 457 and 665 of the Civil Code. That portion of the trial court's judgment is reversed and judgment herein is rendered in favor of Tenneco, Inc. and against the defendants, Oil, Chemical & Atomic Workers Union, Local 4-522, et al. All costs of this appeal to be paid by defendants-appellees.

Reversed and rendered.

REDMANN, Judge. (dissenting). Plaintiff sued for an injunction against a labor union's picketing during a strike which is now over. Plaintiff was, in part, denied the injunction. In my opinion the plaintiff's entitlement to obtain an *injunction* is no longer (if ever) existent. This question is as moot as if plaintiff had never sued until after the strike was ended. No injunction should issue at this stage from a trial court nor from this court.

However, plaintiff might be entitled to a declaratory judgment, as a proper judgment which this court ought to render on appeal, LSA-C.C.P. 2164, and we therefore need not dismiss the appeal as moot.

The servitude in favor of the public for use of the navigable river bank (including the levee, LSA-C.C. art. 457) is limited by C.C. art. 455 to purposes accessory to using the river.

But it appears to me that a union of maritime employees ought to be entitled under the servitude to picket on the banks of the river where their employer moors his vessels, deposits his goods, etc. Surely while engaged in mooring and unloading the *employer's* vessels, depositing *his* goods, drying *his* nets, 'and the like', the employees are not mere trespassers because the vessel and goods etc. are not their own. Presumably a would-be employee could properly go to the river bank to seek employment with a shipper, and bargain for its terms, as an included exercise of the servitude. In my opinion the employees would not suddenly become trespassers because they have a dispute as to the terms of their employment. It appears to me the peaceful picketing by such employees on the river bank ought, in simple fairness and in administration of justice without partiality, La. Const. art. 1 s 6, to be considered a lawful exercise of the servitude.

At the opposite extreme, I think it clear that employees whose employment and employer are utterly unconnected with the use of a navigable river are not entitled to picket on its banks, because the servitude is only granted for purposes related to some use of the river.

The defendant union is not in either extreme position. Its members are not longshoremen or the like. Yet their employer is using the river, and its banks, in conducting the very business in which they are employed.

The employer may be said not to be exercising the public servitude, since it occupies the position of landowner. Still the principle is the same as if the employer itself were exercising the servitude: if picketing is an exercise of the servitude when done by employees of a company using the servitude in its business, then picketing is still an exercise of the servitude when done by employees of another company which is doing the exact same business on the bank, but happens to be the landowner (whose title, after all, is subject to the servitude).

In my opinion the use by an employer of the navigable river and its bank for the purposes of C.C. art. 455, whether merely as servitude-exerciser or as owner, entitles the employer's employees to be present on the bank and to peacefully picket there in the exercise of the servitude as an adjunct to the use of the navigable river and its bank. The servitude is not in favor of shipowners only, but of the entire public.

(And I might note the servitude is not for public uses, but for use by the public for limited private purposes. Picketing may be a private use, but the shipowner's unloading his ship is also a private use.)

Under the circumstances of this case, the employees are entitled to picket on the levee as an exercise of the public servitude of use of navigable river banks for purposes related to use of the river itself.

The trial court's refusal to enjoin peaceful picketing on the levee should be affirmed.

Notes and Questions

1. Judge William Redmann was a respected Louisiana jurist who taught at Loyola University New Orleans College of Law. He wrote several influential articles about Louisiana property law. With respect to Article 455 of the 1870 Civil Code, which opinion is more persuasive: Judge Chasez's majority opinion or Judge Redmann's dissent?

2. The battle over the rights of recreational fishermen, hunters and boaters to access the occasionally submerged banks of major navigable rivers in Louisiana, including the Mississippi River, reached a fever pitch in the dispute which the following opinion resolved. The land at issue in *Parm v. Shumate*, 513 F.3d 135 (5th Cir. 2007), is similar to the land at issue in *Warner*. It is situated between the levee and the main channel of the Mississippi River in East Carroll Parish, Louisiana. As the Fifth Circuit Court of Appeals explains below, the land in *Parm* is between the ordinary low water mark and the ordinary high water mark of the river. It includes a body of water known as Gassoway Lake, which the plaintiffs considered an ideal venue for recreational fishing. The lake is located three and half miles from the ordinary low water mark of the main river channel. It is connected to the river by a drainage ditch. During the spring, the lake is typically submerged under the Mississippi River's floodwaters. Recall that in another case, a Louisiana appellate court classified Gassoway Lake as a non-navigable waterbody. *Walker Lands, Inc. v. East Carroll Police Jury*, 871 So. 2d 1258, 1265-66 (La. App. 2 Cir. 2004).

Parm v. Shumate

513 F.3d 135 (5th Cir. 2007)

KING, Circuit Judge. Plaintiffs-appellants Normal Parm, Jr., Harold Eugene Watts, Roy Michael Gammill, William T. Rogers, and Robert Allen Balch ("Plaintiffs"), recreational fishermen, appeal the district court's denial of their summary judgment motion and the grant of the cross-motion for summary judgment by defendant-appellee East Carroll Parish Sheriff Mark Shumate ("Sheriff Shumate"). Plaintiffs brought their claims against Sheriff Shumate under 42 U.S.C. § 1983, alleging that they were falsely arrested for trespass when they refused to cease fishing on waters covering ordinarily dry, private property (the "Property") owned by Walker Cottonwood Farms, L.L.C., successor-in-title to Walker Lands, Inc. (collectively "Walker"). Plaintiffs argue that Sheriff Shumate lacked probable cause to arrest them for fishing on the Property because the public has a federal and state right to fish on the Property when it is submerged under the Mississippi River. Because we disagree, we AFFIRM the district court's judgment.

I. Factual and Procedural Background

The underlying dispute in this case began over a decade ago, and the facts have been considered in various forms by multiple courts, including this one. Plaintiffs are lifelong boaters, hunters, and fisherman who fish on the Mississippi River in East Carroll Parish and other river parishes in northeast Louisiana. The water levels of the Mississippi River fluctuate seasonally. In East Carroll Parish, the normal low water mark is seventy-seven feet above mean sea level. Yet during the spring season the river floods well beyond its normal channel—as a result of increased rainfall and snow melt in the North—and the river regularly rises to as high as one hundred and twelve feet above mean sea level. It is normal for the river to remain at this level for at least two months.

The Property is located in East Carroll Parish. On its eastern side, the Property is bound by the Mississippi River, and on its western side, it is bound by the Mississippi River's levees. Buildings, crop lands and forests, with trees as tall as one hundred and forty feet, are located on the Property. In addition, waterways known as Gassoway Lake, Little Gassoway Lake, and other bodies of water are contained within its boundaries. Gassoway Lake, which Plaintiffs consider the most ideal venue for fishing on the Property, is located on the Property's western side, nearly three-and-a-half miles from the ordinary low water mark of the Mississippi River and its channel. Gassoway Lake is connected by a man-made drainage ditch to Bunch's Cutoff, which, in turn, flows into the Mississippi River. When the river floods in the spring, Gassoway Lake, along with the rest of the Property, is submerged under its waters.

Plaintiffs have fished the waters of Gassoway Lake when it was flooded by the Mississippi River, even though they knew that Walker objected to their presence. In 1996, Walker began filing complaints with Sheriff Shumate against boaters fishing on Gassoway Lake. Sheriff Shumate responded by arresting Plaintiffs, and others found on the Property, for trespass. While admitting that they did not have Walker's permission, Plaintiffs claimed that they were entitled to fish on the Property when it was flooded because Gassoway Lake was either: (1) owned by the State of Louisiana on behalf of the public; or (2) subject to state and federal servitudes.

The Attorney General for the State of Louisiana agreed with Plaintiffs' position and issued Louisiana Attorney General Opinion No. 96-206, concluding that channels of the Mississippi River traversed the Property and were "river bed" owned by the State. His opinion stated that "Lake Gassoway is a naturally navigable body of water under both State and Federal law and actually supports navigation for such purposes as hunting, fishing, [and] trapping. . . ." He also determined that the Property was subject to a public servitude. Notwithstanding this opinion, Sheriff Shumate continued to arrest fishermen found on the Property. However, the East Carroll Parish District Attorney, James "Buddy" Caldwell, informed Sheriff Shumate that he did not intend to prosecute any of the Plaintiffs for trespass until the ownership and public servitude issues were resolved. To this day, Plaintiffs have not been prosecuted.

. . . .

II. Discussion

. . . . The key issue, therefore, is whether Plaintiffs have either a federal or state right to fish on the Property in the spring during the Mississippi River's normal flood stage. If they do not, Sheriff Shumate had probable cause to arrest them for trespass and was entitled to prevail on summary judgment.

A. Federal Rights

Plaintiffs argue that they have a federal right to fish on the Property when it is covered by the Mississippi River's waters because the Mississippi River is a navigable waterway of the United States. They contend that a federal navigational servitude burdens the Property, creating a public right to fish there. Plaintiffs also assert that there is a corresponding federal common law right to fish on the navigable waters of the United States. . . .

It is well established that the Commerce Clause of the United States Constitution gives the federal government a "dominant servitude" over the navigable waters of the United States. *United States v. Cherokee Nat. of OKLA.*, 480 U.S. 700, 704, 107 S. Ct. 1487, 94 L.Ed.2d 704 (1987) (citation omitted). The so-called navigational servitude extends "laterally to the entire water surface and bed of a navigable waterway, which includes all the land and waters below the ordinary high water mark." 33 C.F.R. § 329.11(a); *see also United States v. Rands,* 389 U.S. 121, 123, 88 S.Ct. 265, 19 L.Ed.2d 329 (1967). A river's ordinary high water mark is set at "the line of the shore established by the fluctuations of water. . . ." 33 C.F.R. § 329.11(a)(1). It is ascertained by "physical characteristics such as a clear, natural line impressed on the bank; . . . changes in the character of the soil; destruction of terrestrial vegetation; . . . or other appropriate means that consider the characteristics of the surrounding areas." *ID.* The navigational servitude does not burden land that is only submerged when the river floods. *Oklahoma v. Texas,* 260 U.S. 606, 632, 43 S.Ct. 221, 67 L.Ed. 428 (1923); *United States v. Harrell,* 926 F.2d 1036, 1041–43 (11th Cir. 1991); *United States v. Claridge,* 416 F.2d 933, 934 (9th Cir. 1970).

As implied by its very name and the constitutional provision from which it arises, the federal navigational servitude is concerned with *navigational* rights and *commerce. See Montana v. United States,* 450 U.S. 544, 551, 101 S.Ct. 1245, 67 L. Ed.2d 493 (1981) ("The State's power over the beds of navigable waters remains subject to only one limitation: the paramount power of the United States to ensure that such waters remain free to interstate and foreign commerce."); *Kaiser Aetna v. United States,* 444 U.S. 164, 177, 100 S.Ct. 383, 62 L.Ed.2d 332 (1979) ("The navigational servitude . . . gives rise to an authority in the Government to assure that such streams retain their capacity to serve as continuous highways for the purpose of navigation in interstate commerce.") . . . Neither navigation nor commerce encompass recreational fishing. *See Phillips Petroleum Co. v. Mississippi,* 484 U.S. 469, 482–84, 108 S.Ct. 791, 98 L.Ed.2d 877 (1988) (noting that fishing is not related to navigability); *George v. Beavark, Inc.,* 402 F.2d 977, 981 (8th Cir. 1968) ("Although the rule on navigability has been at times liberalized, to our knowledge none of the authoritative cases has liberalized the rule so as to indicate that mere pleasure fishing on a stream of water is such usage as would constitute navigability."). Accordingly, the navigational servitude does not create a right to fish on private riparian land.

Moreover, Plaintiffs' claim to a federal right ignores "the 'general proposition [that] the law of real property is, under our Constitution, left to the individual States to develop and administer.'" *Phillips Petroleum,* 484 U.S. at 484, 108 S.Ct. 791 (citation omitted). Louisiana took title to all lands below navigable waters in its boundaries when it was admitted to the Union. *Dardar,* 985 F.2d 824, 826–27 (citation omitted). . . . It has broad authority to regulate public trust lands, including the

Property, as it sees fit. *See Phillips Petroleum*, 484 U.S. at 482–84, 108 S.Ct. 791. . . . In any event, as things now stand, the right to fish on public trust lands is governed by Louisiana law, and there is no reason for us to displace that law by adopting a federal rule of decision in this context. *See Wallis v. Pan Am. Petroleum Corp.*, 384 U.S. 63, 68, 86 S.Ct. 1301, 16 L.Ed.2d 369 (1966) (stating that it is for Congress to decide whether latent federal power should be exercised to displace state law).

B. State Navigational Servitude

Plaintiffs argue that a state servitude burdens the Property and grants them the right to fish upon it when it is flooded. Plaintiffs assert that this right exists in the Louisiana Constitution, which provides that the freedom to hunt, fish, and trap wildlife is a valued natural heritage that will be forever preserved. *See* LA. CONST. art. I, § 27. They also find support in the Louisiana Civil Code, which provides that everyone has the right to fish in the State's rivers. . . . Finally, they contend that the Property is burdened by the State for the public's use because Louisiana owns all of the running waters in the State. . . . In response, Sheriff Shumate argues that the right to fish in Louisiana is explicitly limited to public lands and does not extend to private riparian property. Moreover, he argues that the Second Circuit Court of Appeal, while failing to hold that the Property is free of a state servitude because the issue was not properly raised, left a "guide post" for this court by noting in passing that the public does not have a right to fish on private lands. We agree with Sheriff Shumate.

First, the Louisiana Constitution, far from creating a private right to fish on the Property, explicitly reserves to private property owners the right to refuse consent to fishermen's entry on their land. The article Plaintiffs rely on reads:

> The freedom to hunt, fish, and trap wildlife, including all aquatic life, traditionally taken by hunters, trappers and anglers, is a valued natural heritage that shall be forever preserved for the people. . . . Nothing contained herein shall be construed to authorize the use of private property to hunt, fish, or trap without the consent of the owner of the property.

See LA. CONST. art. I, § 27.6 When the article is read in full, it is plain that the right to fish is circumscribed and does not extend to waters on private property.

Second, the Louisiana Civil Code does not create a right to fish upon the Property, even if we assume that the Property in its entirety is a bank of the Mississippi River. Under Louisiana law, the "banks of navigable rivers are private things that are subject to public use." LA. CIV. CODE ANN. art. 452; *see also Buckskin Hunting Club v. Bayard*, 868 So.2d 266, 275–76 (La.Ct.App. 2004). The public use, however, is limited to use for navigational purposes. *Walker Lands*, 871 So.2d at 1268 n. 6 (citations omitted); *Buckskin Hunting Club*, 868 So.2d at 276 (citation omitted). As stated in the comments to article 456, "[a]ccording to well-settled Louisiana jurisprudence, which continues to be relevant, the servitude of public use under this provision is not 'for the use of the public at large for all purposes' but merely for purposes that are 'incidental' to the navigable character of the stream and its enjoyment as an avenue of commerce." LA. CIV. CODE ANN. art. 45[6] cmt. b (citations omitted). The Second Circuit Court of Appeal noted, in the parallel state proceeding, that fishing on the banks of the Mississippi River does not meet the definition of a navigational use. *Walker Lands,* 871 So.2d at 1268 n. 6 (citations omitted). We agree. *See, e.g., State v. Barras,* 602 So.2d 301, 305 (La.Ct.App. 1992) (holding that fishing was not incidental to navigation); *Edmiston v. Wood,* 566 So.2d 673, 675–76 (La.Ct.App. 1990) (same).

Finally, we reject Plaintiffs' argument that they have the right to fish on the Property when it is submerged under the Mississippi River because "running waters" are public things owned by the State. Under Louisiana law, "public things" belong to the State, and "public things" include "running waters." LA. CIV. CODE ANN. art. 45[0]. Plaintiffs argue that the public has a right to fish on the running waters of the State based on *Chaney v. State Mineral Bd.,* 444 So.2d 105 (La. 1983). In that case, the Louisiana Supreme Court stated that the running waters over non-navigable streams are preserved for the general public. *Id.* at 109. This court has since determined that claims to the use of waterways based on *Chaney* have "failed to carry the day in Louisiana courts." *Dardar,* 985 F.2d at 834 (citation omitted). We have no reason to deviate from that holding. To the contrary, the Third Circuit Court of Appeal of Louisiana recently stated that although an owner must permit running waters to pass through his estate, Louisiana law "does not mandate that the landowner allow public access to the waterway." *Buckskin Hunting Club,* 868 So.2d at 274.

III. Conclusion

For the reasons stated above, we AFFIRM the district court's judgment.

Notes and Questions

1. In light of *Parm v. Shumate,* 513 F.3d 135 (5th Cir. 2007), it now appears as if the legal conflict between recreational fishermen, hunters and boating enthusiasts on one hand and private owners of banks of navigable rivers on the other has been resolved in favor of the latter. Do you believe the Louisiana legislature should revisit this issue on public policy grounds? Do riparian landowners suffer any harm when fishermen and boaters engage in their recreational pursuits on flooded riverbanks? Can you imagine any alternative policy solutions? Consider the discussion of recreational access rights in Scotland at the end of this chapter.

2. *Access to banks of navigable rivers from places other than the water:* Can a member of the public gain access to the bank of a navigable river for purposes incidental to navigation by crossing over the landward side of a riparian tract without the permission of the intervening riparian landowner? This issue was addressed by the Louisiana Supreme Court in a difficult-to-parse decision, *Pizannie v. Gautreaux,* 138 So. 650 (La. 1931). There the court held that a member of the public does *not* have an unlimited right to cross privately owned riparian property from an adjacent public road for the purpose of taking advantage of the servitude of public use on the bank of a navigable river. *Id.* at 652.

The court in *Pizannie*, however, appeared to approve the trial court's finding that the defendant (a merchant who sold oil and gas to persons engaged in the fishing business and other maritime activities) could not be enjoined from gaining access to a wharf constructed by the plaintiff (the owner of the relevant portion of the river bank) as long as the defendant remained on a portion of the wharf controlled by one of the plaintiff's lessee's, an ice and coal company, which did not object to the defendant's presence. *Id.* at 651–52. Presumably, the defendant would be free to use this portion of the wharf as long as he gained access to it by some means other than crossing over the rest of the plaintiff's riparian tract. The decision in *Pizannie* thus implies that the public's only guaranteed means of access to the bank of a navigable river or stream for purposes of enjoying the public servitude under Article 456 is from the navigable river or stream itself.

3. *Articles 458–460 and Constructions on the Banks of Navigable Rivers*: In the first judicial decision featured in this chapter, *Band v. Audubon Park Comm'n*, 936 So.2d 841, 846 (La. App. 4 Cir. 2006), the court briefly addressed a claim by the plaintiffs (the Bands) that they should be allowed to keep a patio and fence located on land adjacent to their house that was actually part of Audubon Park in New Orleans because under Civil Code Article 459 the patio and fence merely *encroached* on a public way and removal of these features would cause the plaintiffs substantial damage. The court rejected this argument, concluding that the patio and fence constituted a full-fledged *obstruction* of the public's use of a public thing and that it had been built without a lawful permit. Therefore, the patio and fence had to be removed at the plaintiffs' expense. *Band*, 936 So.2d at 846.

In a 1966 decision, the Louisiana Second Circuit Court of Appeal applied the same distinction between obstructions of public use and mere encroachments under Articles 861–862 of the 1870 Civil Code in the context of the public servitude over the banks of navigable rivers. *See Lake Providence Port Comm'n v. Bunge Corp.*, 193 So.2d 363 (La. App. 2 Cir. 1966). The court held that a port commission vested with regulatory authority over the banks of the Mississippi River in East Carroll Parish could not, relying on Articles 861 through 863 of the 1870 Civil Code, prevent a riparian land owner from constructing a grain elevator on the bank of the Mississippi River, as long as the elevator did not obstruct or prevent public use of the bank. *Id.* at 367–68.

Because the proposed grain elevator did not obstruct or prevent public use of the bank, the court concluded that the defendant could proceed with its construction. *Id.* The court explained that even though the Port Commission had the authority, under Article 863 of the Civil Code (the predecessor to current Article 460) and under the Louisiana Constitution, to build wharves and similar permanent structures on its portions of the bank, none of the authorities cited by the Port Commission gave it a right to prohibit the reasonable use of other property, simply because it was situated on land classified as the bank of the Mississippi River. *Id.* at 368.

For more statutory authority and case law relevant to Articles 458 through 460, see La. Rev. Stat. 9:1102.1; *Kliebert Educational Trust v. Watson Marine Services, Inc.*,

454 So.2d 855, 858 (La. App. 5 Cir. 1984) (stating that (1) a riparian owner has the right to erect buildings and other improvements on the bank of a navigable river if required for commerce, navigation or other public purposes, as long as the owner obtains a permit from the port commission; and (2) a port commission must grant such a permit unless it can prove that denial serves the best interest of the public in light of safety or other accepted navigation regulations).

4. *Cottonport Bank v. Garrett*: In this dispute between two adjacent riparian land owners, one landowner, Cottonport Bank, alleged that the other, Garrett, limited its access to a navigable water body known as False River by constructing a T-shaped pier extending from Garrett's property out into the water and arguably obstructing access to Cottonport's property. *Cottonport Bank v. Garrett*, 111 So.3d 431, 434 (La. App. 1 Cir. 2012). Cottonport Bank asked the trial court to order the removal of the obstructing portion of the pier. The trial court concluded that "the portion of the pier at issue was constructed on state property," and not Cottonport's property, and therefore, the pier was allowed to "'remain as constructed.'" *Id.* Cottonport Bank appealed the trial court decision and asserted that Garrett's pier should be removed as it constituted a violation of Garrett's obligations of neighborhood under Articles 667 and 668 of the Civil Code and constituted an abuse of right. *Id.* at 434–35.

The appellate court dismissed Cottonport Bank's claims, holding that Articles 667 and 668 do not apply to constructions on state-owned land. It affirmed the trial court's holding that the abuse of rights doctrine was inapplicable absent any contractual or fiduciary relationship between the parties. *Id.* at 435. On its own motion, however, the appellate court remanded the case to the trial court for consideration of whether Garrett's pier obstructed the public's right to use natural navigable water bodies under Article 458 of the Civil Code and should therefore be removed, provided removal would not cause substantial harm to Garrett. The court reasoned as follows:

> Citizens of this state have a right of action coincidental with that of the governing authority to sue for the removal of a structure which physically obstructs the citizens' right of use of public land. *Worthen v. DeLong*, 99-1149, p. 5 (La. App. 1 Cir. 6/23/00), 763 So.2d 820, 824. . . .
>
> Cottonport has not asserted that the entirety of the pier obstructed public use. Rather, Cottonport urged that the portion of Mr. Garrett's pier's westerly extension in front of its lot has limited Cottonport's access to False River and has caused it damage. An owner of land adjacent to public property has been recognized as possessing a right, separate from the ordinary citizen, to sue to remove encroachments on public property which cause harm peculiar to him. *Giardina v. Marrero Furniture Co., Inc.*, 310 So.2d 607, 610–11 (La. 1975). Thus, under the reasoning in *Giardina*, it is clear that Cottonport had a right to bring an action. Moreover, the remedy sought herein is limited to that portion of the pier that extends over the imaginary boundary line between the two properties. . . .

We note that a private citizen can only avail himself of LSA-C.C. art. 458 when he can show there is a physical obstruction of the citizen's right of use of public land. *See Giardina*, 310 So.2d at 612. Moreover, a building that merely encroaches on a public way without preventing its use, and which cannot be removed without causing substantial damage to its owner, shall be permitted to remain. LSA-C.C. art. 459.

In the instant case, although Cottonport introduced evidence regarding how Mr. Garrett's pier impacted the plans for its waterfront property, there is scant evidence in the record regarding how Mr. Garrett's pier obstructed Cottonport's and/or [the] public's right of use of False River. Additionally, should it be proven that the pier is merely an encroachment that does not prevent use, nothing in the record reflects whether the portion of the pier at issue could be removed without causing substantial damage to Mr. Garrett. Therefore, under the particular facts of this case, we conclude that a remand is appropriate to afford the parties an opportunity to address these issues.

Cottonport Bank, 111 So.3d 431, 436–37. What is the most important aspect of the court's discussion in this case? Notice the court's reading of the textual language in Article 458(1).

2. Dedication of Private Property to Public Use

As we have just learned, private things may become subject to public use in accordance with law. La. Civ. Code art. 455 (1978). The other way to make a private thing subject to public occurs through dedication by a private owner. *Id.* Under Louisiana law there are several ways that a private thing can become subject to public use through some action or inaction on the part of the owner of the thing. The doctrine of dedication to public use either transfers ownership to some public authority or furnishes a servitude giving members of the public the right to use specific property for certain purposes even as the property remains under private ownership. Article 457 of the Civil Code is the only codal authority directly addressing this subject. It notes that although a public road is subject to public use, the public "may own the land on which the road is built or *merely have the right to use it*." La. Civ. Code art. 457 (1978) (emphasis added). This part of Article 457 contemplates a private landowner dedicating a portion of his land to public use for purposes of a road, but reserving ownership of the underlying land to himself.

The public rights created as a result of the doctrine of dedication to public use are *irrevocable* in the sense that once the dedication takes place the private owner cannot demand to have the public rights terminate at will. Although the public use rights resulting from the dedication might terminate one day because of the occurrence of a condition imposed at the time of the dedication or because of the public's non-use of the servitude, the dedication to public use does not terminate merely because the grantor changes his or her mind. This is what makes a dedication to public use different from what happens when a private owner gives the public some kind of *revocable* (or terminable) rights to specific property through the grant of a temporary *license* or some informal concession in favor of the public.

The Louisiana legislature has not enacted a comprehensive framework for the law of dedication. As noted above, the Civil Code barely addresses dedication to public use. Instead, the four distinct methods of dedication in Louisiana are based on a wide-ranging set of statutory and jurisprudential authorities.

The first of the four modes of dedication to public use is called **formal dedication**. It occurs when a private owner formally donates a thing or its use to the public for some designated public purpose. A formal dedication can result in the transfer of ownership of the property to some public authority. If the owner expressly or implied reserves ownership, however, a formal dedication will result in the transfer of a servitude in favor of the public. *Clement v. City of Lake Charles*, 52 So.3d 1054, 1058 (La. App. 3 Cir. 2010); A.N. YIANNOPOULOS, 2 LOUISIANA CIVIL LAW TREATISE: PROPERTY § 6:8 (5th ed. 2015). In a relatively recent decision, the Louisiana Second Circuit Court of Appeal held that when land owners dedicated some of their land to Caddo Parish for the purpose of establishing public roads, when the parish used pre-printed forms that stated "I . . . do hereby dedicate to the public use, for a public road, the following described land" and "The said property to be used for public road purposes only," when there was no language dedicating "fee title" to Caddo Parish, when no compensation was given, and when "the dedications had been historically treated as servitudes," the formal dedications only resulted in the grant of a servitude to the parish. *Webb v. Franks Investment Co.*, 105 So.3d 764, 767, 771 (La. App. 2 Cir. 2012).

In theory, a formal dedication should comply with the formal requisites for completing a gratuitous donation — an authentic act executed by the donor and written acceptance by some public authority. *See* La. Civ. Code arts. 1541, 1544 (2008). Courts have accepted less by insisting only upon a written juridical act, such as an act under private signature, a showing of clear intent on the part of the private owner to dedicate the thing to public use, and subsequent use or maintenance by the public or public authorities. *Vernon Parish Police Jury v. Buckley*, 829 So.2d 610, 612–15 (La. App. 3 Cir. 2002); *Stelly v. Vermillion Parish Police Jury*, 482 So.2d 1052, 1055 (La. App. 3 Cir. 1986).

A second form of dedication is called **statutory dedication**. It requires substantial, though not strict, compliance with La. Rev. Stat. § 33:5051, which provides as follows.

> A. Whenever the owner of any real estate desires to lay off the same into squares or lots with streets or alleys between the squares or lots and with the intention of selling or offering for sale any of the squares or lots, he shall, before selling any square or lot or any portion of same:
>
> > (1) Cause the real estate to be surveyed and platted or subdivided by a licensed land surveyor into lots or blocks, or both, each designated by number.

(2) Set monuments at all of the corners of every lot and block thereof.

(3) Write the lot designation on the plat or map, and cause it to be made and filed in the office of the keeper of notarial records of the parish wherein the property is situated and copied into the conveyance record book of such parish, and a duplicate thereof filed with the assessor of the parish, a correct map of the real estate so divided.

B. The map referenced in Subsection A of this Section shall contain the following:

(1) The section, township, and range in which such real estate or subdivision thereof lies according to government survey.

(2) The dimensions of each square in feet, feet and inches, or meters.

(3) The designation of each lot or subdivision of a square and its dimensions in feet, feet and inches, or meters.

(4) The name of each street and alley and its length and width in feet, feet and inches, or meters.

(5) The name or number of each square or plat dedicated to public use.

(6) A certificate of the parish surveyor or any other licensed land surveyor of this state approving said map and stating that the same is in accordance with the provisions of this Section and with the laws and ordinances of the parish in which the property is situated.

(7) A formal dedication made by the owner or owners of the property or their duly authorized agent of all the streets, alleys, and public squares or plats shown on the map to public use.

C. Formal dedication of property as a road, street, alley, or cul-de-sac shall impose no responsibility on the political subdivision in which the property is located until:

(1) The dedication is formally and specifically accepted by the political subdivision through a written certification that the road, street, alley, or cul-de-sac is in compliance with all standards applicable to construction set forth in ordinances, regulations, and policies of the political subdivision, which certification may be made directly on the map which contains the dedication; or

(2) The road, street, alley, or cul-de-sac is maintained by the political subdivision.

La. Rev. Stat. Ann. § 33:5051 (1962, amended 1988, 1995).

Statutory dedication is most often used when a developer, who is subdividing land to create a new subdivision or development, wants to dedicate certain portions of the land for use as streets, alleys or public squares. In such situations, a developer is required to file in the public records of the parish in which the immovable property is located (both in the conveyance records and with the assessor) a map (often called a "plat") prepared by a surveyor that shows the numbered blocks and lots in the proposed development.

As long as the developer *substantially* complies with the essential statutory requisites, Louisiana courts have held, relying in part on common law authorities, that the developer's intent to dedicate to the public is presumed, even despite some technical failures in complying with the statute's detailed rules. *Parish of Jefferson v. Doody*, 174 So.2d 798, 801–03 (La. 1965); *Metairie Park, Inc. v. Currie*, 122 So. 859, 861–62(1929). As the Louisiana Supreme Court has explained in a leading decision:

> Thus, it is seen that the Court has not regarded essential a detailed compliance with the requirements of Act 134 of 1896 [La. Rev. Stat. §33:5051] in order to effect a statutory dedication but, rather, that failure of the owner and subdivider to follow strictly the mandate of the law only renders him amenable to prosecution for the penalty therein prescribed. And this is the realistic and common sense view of the statute. For we can think of no plausible reason for deducing that an owner, who seeks to subdivide and sell his land as a commercial enterprise and has filed a plan in the recorder's office (showing the squares, lots and abutting streets, alleys or walks) under which he proposes to develop the subdivision, has not validly dedicated the streets, alleys and walkways to the public use merely because he has failed to observe detailed requirements which were inserted in the statute solely for the benefit and protection of the land purchasers. And if the owner must be held to have effected a dedication, a fortiori, trespassers (like defendants herein) upon such public ways find themselves in no position to oppose the claims of the parish authorities seeking to have them evicted therefrom.

Parish of Jefferson v. Doody, 174 So.2d 798, 803 (1965).

Louisiana courts have yet to develop a precise test for the determination of whether a developer's actions amount to statutory dedication. A.N. YIANNOPOULOS, 2 LOUISIANA CIVIL LAW TREATISE: PROPERTY § 6:10, at 245 (5th ed. 2015). However, in *Doody*, the Louisiana Supreme Court held that the failure of the parish surveyor to sign the recorded subdivision plat and the failure of the plat to identify the section, township and range of the dedicated property did not prevent recognition of a statutory dedication. *Doody*, 174 So.2d at 803. In contrast, a complete failure to record subdivision plans in the applicable conveyance records or assessor's records will preclude a finding of statutory dedication. *Vinson v. Levy*, 372 So.2d 694, 698–99 (La. App. 1 Cir. 1979). Further, the mere fact that a map containing language referring to a public dedication is submitted to public authorities at the time of a land transfer time does not by itself establish a statutory dedication. *See Himel v. Bourque*, 185 So.3d 42, 45-46 (La. App. 1 Cir. 2015) (rejecting statutory dedication where inclusion of dedication language on a map showed only a portion of road but that map was not submitted to parish authorities in conjunction with subdivision approval request, was not signed by landowner, and only displayed a bordering extant road). Nevertheless, if a plat is recorded in substantial compliance with La.

Rev. Stat. § 33:5501, and that plat specifies certain portions of the affected land to be dedicated for purposes such as streets, alleys, parks or squares, courts will find that the land has in fact been so dedicated despite any technical deficiencies in complying with the act.

Unlike formal dedication, statutory dedication does not require formal acceptance by the public. Instead, the only requirement is the recordation of the subdivision plat (or map) containing the description of the streets, alleyways or other locations slated to be dedicated to public use in the public records. A.N. YIANNOPOULOS, 2 LOUISIANA CIVIL LAW TREATISE: PROPERTY § 6:10 (5th ed. 2015). Courts recognize that a statutory dedication will normally vest ownership of the land at issue in some public authority. *Walker v. Coleman*, 540 So.2d 983, 985 (La. App. 2 Cir. 1989). The person performing the dedication, however, can define the interest he intends to convey to the public more narrowly and reserve ownership to himself, while vesting the public only with a servitude or a specifically designated right.

Unlike formal dedication which results in the transfer of ownership to the public unless the owner *expressly or impliedly* reserves ownership, "in statutory dedication the public acquires title to the property 'unless the subdivider *expressly reserves* ownership of streets *and* grants the public only a servitude of use.'" *Clement v. City of Lake Charles*, 52 So.3d 1054, 1058 (La. App. 3 Cir. 2010) (emphasis added) (quoting *Stonegate Homeowners Civic Ass'n v. City of Baton Rouge/Parish of East Baton Rouge*, 836 So.2d 440, 442 (La. App. 1 Cir. 2002)); *see also* YIANNOPOULOS, PROPERTY § 6:10. As the court explained in *Clement*, there are policy reasons for a stronger presumption in favor of a transfer of ownership in the case of statutory dedication than with formal dedication:

> Statutory dedication and formal dedication are two different modes of dedication. *See* YIANNOPOULOS, PROPERTY § 97 (4th ed. 2001). A landowner who ordinarily sells his land may never formally dedicate anything to the public use. On the other hand, a landowner who divides his property into lots with streets or alleys between them and then sells the lots must, in addition to performing other duties, dedicate to public use all the streets, alleys, and public squares or plats. La.R.S. 33:5051. Because in formal dedication the act of dedication is voluntary, there is a greater need to guard against a landowner's inadvertent mistakes. Thus, the landowner may impliedly retain ownership of the dedicated land without any specific reservation. *S. Amusement*, 871 So.2d 630; YIANNOPOULOS, PROPERTY § 97 (4th ed. 2001).

> On the other hand, when the landowner dedicates his land under the compulsion of La. R.S. 33:5051, there is a greater need for the public to acquire ownership of the land for the reasons expressed previously in this opinion. Thus, if, after considering all the legal implications of ownership, the owner indeed desires to retain ownership of the dedicated land, he must not only grant a servitude to the public, but also expressly reserve the ownership in the act of dedication.

Clement, 52 So.3d at 1058. In *Clement*, the court held that a developer transferred ownership of a street in a subdivision to a municipality when the developer used the term "servitudes" for the use of utilities and drainage and dedicated a "right of way of streets . . . to the perpetual use of the public," without otherwise expressly reserving ownership of the land. *Id.* at 1059–60. The importance of classifying the nature of the property interest acquired as the result of formal and statutory dedication was on display in *Chesapeake Operating, Inc. v. City of Shreveport*, 132 So.3d 537, 542-45 (La. 2 Cir. 2014). In this case, the Second Circuit Court of Appeal held that when the City of Shreveport annexed land from Caddo Parish, it obtained *ownership* of land underneath public roads and roadbeds that had previously been formally and statutorily dedicated to the parish and therefore, the city had authority over the mineral rights in the land underlying the disputed roads and the right to receive resulting mineral production.

A third form of dedication is ***tacit dedication***. This mode arises pursuant to another statute, La. Rev. Stat. § 48:491.B. It applies only to streets or alleyways. Tacit dedication to public use occurs after some public authority (for example, a town, city, or parish) maintains a street or alley for a period of three years and the land owner concerned was afforded either actual or constructive knowledge of the maintenance activities. Actual or constructive knowledge is presumed if the public body performing the maintenance sends the last known adjoining landowner written notice prior to or during the work in question. Actual or constructive knowledge is *conclusively* presumed after the public authority has maintained the street or alley for a period of four years. La. Rev. Stat. § 48:491. B.(1)(c).

Although tacit dedication occurs pursuant to a statute, it differs from statutory dedication in several respects. First, it only applies to streets and alleyways and not to other places. Second, the public acquires rights in a street or alley because a landowner has allowed a public entity to maintain the street or alley for a sufficient period of time, not because of an intentional act by the landowner. Finally, tacit dedication only results in the establishment of a servitude in favor of the public; it does not effectuate a change of ownership. If public use terminates on the land subject to a tacit dedication for any reason, the land is freed from the encumbrance. For more on tacit dedication, see A.N. YIANNOPOULOS, 2 LOUISIANA CIVIL LAW TREATISE: PROPERTY § 6:11 (5th ed. 2015).

The amount of maintenance activity necessary to establish tacit dedication depends on the circumstances of the case. *Compare Scott v. Chustz*, 135 So.3d 766, 770–771 (La. App. 1 Cir. 2013) (finding evidence that one parish employee trimmed branches in the early 1980s and another placed gravel near area once is insufficient to establish the requisite maintenance for tacit dedication, especially where landowners denied knowledge of these acts), *with Himel v. Bourque*, 185 So.3d 42, 47-48 (La. App. 1 Cir. 2015) (finding tacit dedication of both paved and unpaved portions of a road occurred when landowners requested public maintenance, the parish performed maintenance by paving gravel road with asphalt, other acts of maintenance occurred for six to seven years, and the parish used unpaved portion, all without any objection by landowners).

A final method of dedication, *implied dedication*, has been created exclusively by the courts. This type of dedication comes to Louisiana from the common law and for that reason, it has sometimes been referred to as "common law" dedication. A.N. YIANNOPOULOS, 2 LOUISIANA CIVIL LAW TREATISE: PROPERTY § 6:9 (5th ed. 2015). An implied dedication requires a plain and positive intent on the part of the private owner to dedicate her property to public use and an equally plain and positive intent on the part of the public to accept the dedication. *Id.* Courts have frequently emphasized that the owner's intent to dedicate, even though implied, must still be objectively demonstrated in some conduct on the part of the owner and cannot be buried in her heart. *Richard v. City of New Orleans*, 197 So. 594, 599–600 (1940).

Courts have most frequently found an implied dedication when the owner of a tract of land subdivides the land into lots, designates streets, roads or some other public place on a plat, but does not substantially comply with La. Rev. Stat. 33:5051, and then sells portions of other land with reference to the plat. In such a case, implied dedication can produce public rights to specific property in the absence of statutory dedication. As *White v. Kinberger*, 611 So.2d 810 (La. App. 3 Cir. 1992) exemplifies, courts have determined the presence of statutory dedication and implied dedication in the same instance.

Just as with tacit dedication, implied dedication only results in the establishment of a servitude in favor of the public. It does not result in a change of ownership. YIANNOPOULOS, 2 LOUISIANA CIVIL LAW TREATISE: PROPERTY § 6.9 (5th ed. 2015).

The first decision below, *St. Charles Parish School Board v. P & L Investment Corp.*, 674 So.2d 218 (La. 1996), provides an example of a court considering claims of all four forms of dedication recognized under Louisiana law. In the second decision, *White v. Kinberger*, 611 So.2d 810 (La. App. 3 Cir. 1992), the court addresses the relationship between statutory and implied dedication.

St. Charles Parish School Board v. P & L Investment Corp.

674 So.2d 218 (La. 1996)

MARCUS, Justice. The issue in this case is whether a private road is subject to public use.

P & L Investment Corporation (P & L) owned 45 acres of land abutting Highway 90 in St. Charles Parish. In November 1972, the St. Charles Parish School Board (School Board) purchased 35 of the 45 acres for construction of a new high school leaving P & L with a small parcel of land fronting Highway 90, a 50 foot wide strip of land along the western boundary of the School Board's property, and a small parcel of land in back of the School Board's property. The 50 foot wide strip of land was approximately 1,700 feet long and connected P & L's two small parcels. The School Board began construction of the new Hahnville High School on its thirty-five acres.

Two public streets, First Street and Second Street, provided access to the School Board's property from Highway 90. The builders of the high school used Second Street to reach the School Board's property during construction.

In March 1973, the St. Charles Parish Police Jury (Police Jury) exchanged Second Street, a dedicated roadway, for a comparable strip of land which abutted Highway 90 and was owned by P & L. The strip of land connected Highway 90 to the 50 foot wide strip of land owned by P & L along the western boundary of the School Board's property. The strip of land the Police Jury received in the exchange became a dedicated roadway known as Tiger Drive. When the Police Jury built and paved Tiger Drive with asphalt, the Police Jury also paved at least 200 feet of the strip of land still owned by P & L. P & L did not protest the paving by the Police Jury of this portion of its fifty foot wide strip of land. The parish then placed shells on a further 500 feet of the strip of land owned by P & L and placed shells in the parking area of Hahnville High School, which was on School Board property. The School Board refers to the dedicated roadway and the continuation of the road on P & L's property as Tiger Drive. After school officials installed a gate across Tiger Drive at the property line where P & L's strip of land began, P & L asked the School Board not to lock the gate because P & L wanted access to its property in the back.

In 1977, the Police Jury or the School Board paved an additional 500 feet of P & L's property with concrete when the parking lot for Hahnville High School was paved. The shells, which had covered the road and the parking lot prior to the paving, were relocated from the parking lot and Tiger Drive to a portion of the fifty foot wide strip which remained unpaved. The concrete paving and placement of the shells on the fifty foot strip were done with the consent of P & L. Thus, 700 feet of P & L's 50 foot wide strip were partially paved with either asphalt or concrete and the remaining 1000 feet were partially covered with shells.

Although P & L intended to dedicate its portion of Tiger Drive, it never formally dedicated the strip of land to the public or sold the strip to the School Board. School officials were aware that the strip of land along the western boundary of the campus was not school property, but thought that the School Board had an agreement with P & L that the school would have access to its parking lot from Tiger Drive. From 1975 to the early 1980s, St. Charles Parish maintained the asphalt portion of Tiger Drive including the section owned by P & L. The School Board performed maintenance on the concrete and shell portions of Tiger Drive.

In 1990, P & L claimed ownership of 1,700 feet of Tiger Drive in a letter to the St. Charles Parish School Board. In the letter, P & L demanded that the School Board cease using the portion of Tiger Drive owned by P & L and informed the School Board that it planned to run sewer and water lines down the middle of Tiger Drive. The School Board then filed suit seeking a declaration that Tiger Drive was a public street and an injunction to prevent P & L from interfering with the public's use of Tiger Drive. The School Board contended that P & L's portion of Tiger Drive had been dedicated to public use. After a trial on the merits, the trial judge declared Tiger Drive to be the property of P & L and denied the School Board's petition for an injunction. The court of appeal affirmed finding that P & L had not dedicated its portion of Tiger Drive. Upon the School Board's application, we granted certiorari to review the correctness of that decision.

The issue presented for our review is whether the portion of Tiger Drive owned by P & L is subject to public use.

A road may be either public or private. La. Civ. Code art. 457. A public road is one that is subject to public use. *Id.* The public may own the land on which the road is built or may only have the right to use it (a servitude of passage). *Id.* When a private person owns the land on which a public road is built and the public merely has the right to use it, the land is a private thing subject to public use. A.N. YIANNOPOU-LOS, PROPERTY § 96, at 206 (2 LOUISIANA CIVIL LAW TREATISE 3d ed. 1991). The public may acquire an interest in the land on which a road is built or in the use of a road through purchase, exchange, donation, expropriation, prescription or dedication. YIANNOPOULOS, PROPERTY § 96, at 207.

Neither the School Board nor the Police Jury ever purchased the fifty foot wide strip of land from P & L. The Police Jury exchanged property with P & L creating ownership in the public of only the front portion of Tiger Drive. P & L did not donate its portion of Tiger Drive to the Police Jury or School Board. No public entity ever expropriated P & L's portion of Tiger Drive.

The School Board did not obtain a servitude of passage on P & L's portion of Tiger Drive through acquisitive prescription. A servitude of passage, an apparent servitude, may be acquired through acquisitive prescription. La. Civ. Code arts. 707, 742. An apparent servitude may be acquired by peaceable and uninterrupted possession of the right for ten years in good faith and by just title; it may also be acquired by uninterrupted possession for thirty years without title or good faith. La. Civ. Code art. 742. The School Board does not have thirty years possession of the right of passage over P & L's portion of Tiger Drive. The School Board does have ten years possession of the right, but does not have just title. Just title is a juridical act sufficient to transfer ownership or another real right. It must be written, valid in form, and filed for registry in the conveyance records of the parish in which the immovable is situated. La. Civ. Code art. 3483. The "boilerplate language" included in the deed of sale ["A CERTAIN PORTION OR TRACT OF GROUND, together with the improvements thereon, and all rights, ways, privileges, servitudes and advantages thereunto"] for the thirty-five acres from P & L to the School Board is too ambiguous and imprecise to establish a servitude of passage over the fifty foot wide strip of land. *Palomeque v. Prudhomme*, 95-0725 (La. 11/27/95); 664 So. 2d 88. For a servitude to be created by title, the instrument must be express as to the nature and extent of the servitude. Therefore, the public did not acquire an interest in the use of P & L's portion of Tiger Drive through prescription. The only remaining method by which the public could have acquired an interest in the land or in the use of the street is dedication.

Louisiana has never enacted a comprehensive scheme of dedication to public use. *Garrett v. Pioneer Production Corporation*, 390 So.2d 851, 854 (La. 1980). However,

Louisiana courts have recognized four modes of dedication: formal, statutory, implied, and tacit. A landowner may make a formal dedication of a road by virtue of a written act, such as a deed of conveyance to the police jury of the parish. *Frierson v. Police Jury of Caddo Parish*, 160 La. 957, 107 So. 709 (1926). The written act may be in notarial form or under private signature. YIANNOPOULOS, PROPERTY § 95, at 204–205. A formal dedication transfers ownership of the property to the public unless it is expressly or impliedly retained. YIANNOPOULOS, PROPERTY § 95, at 208–209. If the landowner retains ownership of the property, the public acquires a servitude of public use.

Statutory dedication occurs when a landowner subdivides real estate in accordance with the requirements of La. R.S. 33:5051. In order to effect a statutory dedication, complete and detailed compliance with the statute is not required; substantial compliance will suffice. *Garrett*, 390 So. 2d at 856. La. R.S. 33:5051 provides for the subdivision of real estate into squares or lots with named streets and for the dedication to public use of all streets, alleys, and public squares on the map. A statutory dedication vests ownership in the public unless the subdivider reserves ownership of streets and public places and grants the public only a servitude of use. *Arkansas-Louisiana Gas Co. v. Parker Oil Co. Inc.*, 190 La. 957, 183 So. 229, 238 (1938) (on rehearing).

Implied dedication is a common law doctrine recognized by the courts of this state. *Ford v. City of Shreveport*, 204 La. 618, 16 So. 2d 127, 128 (1943). A dedication by implication consists of the assent of the owner, use by the public, and maintenance by the municipality. *WYATT v. HAGLER*, 238 La. 234, 114 So. 2d 876, 878 (1959). Because implied dedication lacks the formalities and safeguards of formal or statutory dedication, courts have required "a plain and positive intention to give and one equally plain to accept." *Carrollton Rail Road Co. v. Municipality No. Two*, 19 La. 62, 71 (1841). Courts have also found an implied dedication when the owner of a tract of land subdivides it into lots, designates streets or roads on a map, and then sells the property or any portion of it with reference to the map. *James v. Delery*, 211 La. 306, 29 So. 2d 858, 859 (La. 1947). An implied dedication establishes a servitude of public use. *Arkansas-Louisiana Gas Co. Inc.*, 183 So. at 240; *Becnel v. Citrus Lands of Louisiana, Inc.*, 429 So. 2d 459 (La. App. 4th Cir.), *writ denied*, 437 So. 2d 1147 (La. 1983). *See, Missouri Pacific Railroad Co. v. City of New Orleans*, 46 F.3d 487 (5th Cir. 1995).

A tacit dedication of a strip of land for use as a public road occurs when the requirements of La. R.S. 48:491 are met. La. R.S. 48:491 provides, in pertinent part,

> B. (1)(a) All roads and streets in this state which have been or hereafter are kept up, maintained, or worked for a period of three years by the authority of a parish governing authority within its parish, or by the authority of a municipal governing authority within its municipality, shall be public roads or streets, as the case may be, if there is actual or constructive knowledge of such work by adjoining landowners exercising reasonable concern over their property.

If a road is maintained for a period of three years by authority of the parish govern-ing authority, the public acquires a servitude of passage by tacit dedication. *Robinson v. Beauregard Parish Police Jury*, 351 So. 2d 113, 115 (La. 1977). Token maintenance or an occasional brushing up of a road is insufficient to establish a tacit dedication for public use. *Robinson*, 351 So. 2d at 115.

Of the four modes of dedication, formal dedication and statutory dedication clearly do not apply. In February of 1976, the president of P & L, Richard Warren Landry, wrote to the Administrative Assistant for Operations of the St. Charles Par-ish School Board and indicated P & L's intention to formally dedicate to the Police Jury the fifty foot street along the western property line of the new Hahnville High School. The Police Jury accepted a recommendation from the St. Charles Parish Planning and Zoning Commission to accept the dedication. Although the Police Jury asked its attorney to prepare a formal act of dedication for P & L, no formal act of dedication of P & L's portion of Tiger Drive to the public was executed.

Statutory dedication of P & L's portion of Tiger Drive did not occur. P & L did not subdivide its land in compliance with La. R.S. 33:5051.

Implied dedication also does not apply. While the public has used the road and the parish has maintained the road, the owner has not assented to the dedication of the road. Warren Landry testified at trial that P & L would have agreed to dedicate its portion of Tiger Drive only if the parish had paved the entire strip of land. Nor does the second type of implied dedication apply. While the 1972 Collier survey indicates a fifty foot street along the western boundary of P & L's land prior to the sale to the School Board, P & L was not subdividing its land into lots and did not sell the land with reference to the Collier survey. Furthermore, the School Board knew that the strip of land belonged to P & L and had not been dedicated to public use at the time of the sale.

Finally, we must determine whether P & L made a tacit dedication to public use of its portion of Tiger Drive under La. R.S. 48:491. From the testimony of school officials, it appears that the School Board filled both its land and part of P & L's land in order to build the high school and to provide a base for the road. The parish then delivered five or six truck loads of shells to Hahnville High School to build up the street. After the exchange of property between the Police Jury and P & L in 1973, the Police Jury paved the public portion of Tiger Drive and 200 feet of P & L's portion of Tiger Drive with asphalt. A few years later, either the School Board or the Police Jury paved the parking lot of Hahnville High School and an additional 500 feet of Tiger Drive with concrete. Eventually, shells were placed along the unpaved portions of Tiger Drive. P & L does not claim to have participated in or funded any of these road construction activities on its land.

After Hahnville High School and Tiger Drive were built, the parish opened, cleaned out, and drained ditches along the street. Larry Sesser, St. Charles Parish School Board's Chief of Physical Plant Operations, testified that the parish repaired potholes on the asphalt section of Tiger Drive from the fall of 1975 until the early

1980s. The foreman of the blacktop crew for the parish testified that his crew performed maintenance on Tiger Drive by overlaying the street with blacktop. School Board employees repaired and maintained the shell portion of Tiger Drive by using a tractor to grade the road and fill potholes. Although the School Board maintained the shell and concrete portions of Tiger Drive rather than the Police Jury, the School Board was operating under the authority of the Police Jury and was using public funds.

P & L had actual knowledge of the construction and maintenance of Tiger Drive by the Police Jury and School Board. Warren Landry testified by deposition that the School Board, not P & L, had maintained the paved portion of Tiger Drive. P & L used Tiger Drive to access its parcel of land in back of the school. P & L never claimed to have performed its own maintenance on the portion of Tiger Drive that it owned. Because P & L's portion of Tiger Drive was built, maintained, and worked by authority of the parish governing authority for a period of at least three years with P & L's actual knowledge of such work, we find that P & L tacitly dedicated the asphalt, concrete, and shell roadway located on P & L's property under La. R.S. 48:491. The portion of Tiger Drive owned by P & L is a private street dedicated to public use. The trial judge was clearly wrong in holding otherwise. The court of appeal erred in affirming the judgment of the trial court. Accordingly, we must reverse.

Decree

For the reasons assigned, the judgment of the court of appeal is reversed. Judgment is rendered in favor of the St. Charles Parish School Board and against P & L Investment Corporation, Angelo Puglise, Salvadore Puglise and Richard Warren Landry declaring the asphalt, concrete, and shell roadway located on P & L's property and commonly known as Tiger Drive to be a private street dedicated to public use, as per survey by Roland P. Bernard, surveyor, dated October 4, 1990, attached and made a part of this opinion. All costs are assessed against defendants.

Notes and Questions

1. The court in *St. Charles Parish School Board* found a tacit dedication of the strip of land in dispute because P & L allowed the School Board and the parish to maintain the road for more than three years. The court also noted two possible methods of implied dedication, but rejected both. For one of those methods, the court listed three requirements: (1) the assent of the owner, (2) use by the public, and (3) maintenance by the municipality. For the other, the court asked if P & L had subdivided its property and sold lots pursuant to a plan that exhibited an implied dedication of the road.

2. In the decision featured below, *Cenac v. Public Access Water Rights Association*, 851 So.2d 1006 (La. 2003), the Louisiana Supreme Court revisited the three requirements for the first path to implied dedication. It held that while public maintenance is a *factor* that may be considered in determining whether implied dedication has

occurred, it is not required for a finding of implied dedication. *Id.* at 1011–12. In *White v. Kinberger*, 611 So.2d 810 (La. App. 3 Cir. 1992), the case below, identify the test the court deploys to find an implied dedication.

White v. Kinberger

611 So.2d 810 (La. App. 3 Cir. 1992)

KNOLL, Judge. This appeal concerns a determination of whether a vacant 4.053 acre tract of undeveloped land in the Charles Park Addition Subdivision in Alexandria, Louisiana (the City) was dedicated to public use as a park. On defendants' motion for summary judgment, the trial court held that the City owned the property as a public thing by virtue of an implied dedication.

The plaintiffs (collectively referred to as "the Whites"), were attempting to develop the disputed property. They contend on appeal that the trial court erred in: (1) finding that the property was impliedly dedicated to the public by virtue of the filing of the plat of subdivision; (2) finding that the property was a public thing owned by the City in its capacity as a public person by virtue of the implied dedication; and, (3) failing to find that the renunciation of servitude executed by the Red River, Atchafalaya, and Bayou Bouef Levee District (Levee District) on March 27, 1985, was valid. Finding the recording of a plat with a vacant tract marked "PARK", and the sale of lots according to the plat, constitutes an irrevocable dedication to the public use, we affirm.

Facts

In January of 1977, Charles N. White, Inc. recorded a plat of the Charles Park Addition Subdivision. Although the plat showed many other lots, Charles Park Addition was identified as the lots numbered 316 through 326 on the plat. In addition to delineating lots, streets, and utility easements, the plat also referenced an undeveloped tract across Wycliff Way, the main street through the subdivision, that was labeled "PARK." This undeveloped tract labeled "PARK" forms the basis of this dispute. The plat contained language dedicating the streets and utility easements to public use, but it failed to include a specific reference to the tract labeled "PARK." Lots in the subdivision were then sold which referenced the recorded plat.

In December of 1982, Charles N. White sold the disputed property with warranty to Paul D. White, Sr., who in turn sold the property in December of 1985 to the Whites, the plaintiffs herein.

In 1989, the Whites applied for permission from the Rapides Area Planning Commission to develop this property as a residential subdivision. Their request was denied after the neighboring landowners and the City claimed that the property was dedicated to public use as a park in 1977. The Whites then filed this possessory action against the eight adjoining landowners, the City, and the Levee District, all defendants herein, alleging that the actions of defendants and the recordation of certain documents amounted to a disturbance of their peaceable possession of the property. . . .

The trial court concluded that the City owned the property by virtue of an implied dedication. Because of the trial court's ruling on the dedication issue, it regarded the issue of renunciation of the Levee District's servitude moot. The Whites bring this appeal.

Dedication of Park

The Whites contend that the trial court erred in its determination that there was a dedication of the park to public use in 1977.

A statutory dedication is effected when an owner of real estate files a subdivision plat that substantially complies with the requirements of LSA-R.S. 33:5051. The intent to dedicate is generally presumed from the act of filing the subdivision plan. *Parish of Jefferson v. Doody*, 247 La. 839, 174 So.2d 798 (1965). A statutory dedication may exist even though there is no language in the plat formally dedicating lands to public use. *Morris v. Parish of Jefferson*, 487 So.2d 647 (La. App. 5th Cir. 1986).

Nevertheless, the intention to dedicate must be clearly established. *Banta v. Federal Land Bank of New Orleans*, 200 So.2d 107 (La. App. 1st Cir. 1967), writ denied, 251 La. 46, 202 So.2d 657 (1967). If the fact of dedication is doubtful, the court must look to the surrounding circumstances to determine whether there was an intent to dedicate. *Pioneer Production Corp. v. Segraves*, 340 So.2d 270 (La. 1976). When a rational construction of the record negates an intent of a landowner to dedicate a particular piece of land, the fact that reference to the land appears on a map does not effect a statutory dedication. *Hailey v. Panno*, 472 So.2d 97 (La. App. 5th Cir. 1985).

An implied dedication results when there has been no substantial compliance with the statute but the property owner has nevertheless sold property by reference to a recorded plat. *James v. Delery*, 211 La. 306, 29 So.2d 858 (1947).

In the present case, the Whites rely upon *O'Quinn v. Burks*, 231 So.2d 660 (La. App. 2nd Cir. 1970), to support their claim that the property was not dedicated to public use. In *O'Quinn*, the developer filed a subdivision plat in substantial compliance with LSA-R.S. 33:5051. The appellate court found that the developer did not intend to dedicate a tract designated as a "Proposed Park" on the plat where the plat contained language dedicating streets and utility easements, but not a park.

The landowner defendants assert that *Town of Vinton v. Lyons*, 131 La. 673, 60 So. 54 (1912), is dispositive of the issue before us. *Vinton* held that the word "Park" inscribed on a recorded plat manifested the developer's clear intent to dedicate the land to the public, and that an implied dedication became binding when the developer sold subdivision lots with reference to the plat. In *Vinton*, the plat did not contain any formal dedicatory language.

After carefully reviewing the record, we find that the *Vinton* case better addresses the issue before us. In *O'Quinn*. the developer only stated that the park was proposed, and his intent was not proven by a preponderance of the evidence. In *Vinton*, although there was no dedicatory language, the developer's intent was clear: the undeveloped land was designated, not simply proposed, as a park, and his intent to leave the land undeveloped was established.

In the present case, although the dedicatory language did not refer to the park, the undeveloped land was designated, just as in *Vinton*, as a park. Likewise, the developer's intent was established with his statement that "[the property was to remain] for the use and benefit of the owners of lots located in Charles Park." On this basis, we find that the *Vinton* case is more analogous to the present case.

Moreover, we are further convinced of the correctness of the trial court ruling when we consider the developer's recordation of the plat of survey, and its references to the plat in the sales to the lot owners. In *Vinton*, the Louisiana Supreme Court stated at page 678:

> "The word 'park' written on a block at the instance of the owner in a plat, subdividing a tract of land into lots and blocks for the purpose of founding a town, is as significant of the dedication of such block to the public for a park, as the word 'street' on such plat is of a dedication for a public street....It would be contrary to equity and justice to hold that a real estate company could plat a town, make provisions for a park, sell lots from the plat after filing it for recordation and after the purchasers had built homes on their lots, and after the company no doubt received a better consideration for those lots, or many of them, because of the dedication, to then withdraw the dedication and make a sale of the property to a private individual."

We find that when a plat is filed of public record with an inscription, like "PARK", and lots are sold pursuant thereto, the subdivider should not profit at the expense of the purchasers who bought lots referenced to such a plat.

The *O'Quinn* case, relied upon by the Whites, was criticized by Professor A.N. Yiannopoulos in a case comment in The Work of the Appellate Courts for the 1969–1970 Term, 31 La.L.Rev. 202 (1971). The article questioned *O'Quinn* in light of recent cases which "tend to purport to protect the interests of persons buying property in a subdivision by finding a statutory dedication upon substantial compliance with the terms of the statute and by dispensing with the requirement of intention to dedicate." *Id.* citing *Chevron Oil Company v. Wilson*, 226 So.2d 774 (La. App. 2nd Cir. 1969), cert. denied, 254 La. 849, 227 So.2d 593 (1969). In *Chevron Oil Company*, the appellate court stated at page 777: "'Where a plat is made and recorded and lots are sold with reference thereto, the requisite intention is generally indisputable.'" In like manner, we find it unjust in the case *sub judice* not to hold the original subdivider to the designations made on the plat, especially when he stated that it was his original intent to leave the disputed property undeveloped for use by the lot owners as a park.

The Yiannopoulos comment also questioned *O'Quinn* for its holding that "a dedication may be either statutory or implied but that it cannot be both." Addressing this conclusion, Professor Yiannopoulos pointed out, "There is no reason why the statutory dedication of streets and servitudes should exclude the possibility of this third dimension of dedication." Our holding further conflicts with *O'Quinn* in this regard. In the present case, the subdivision plat complies with the requirements necessary for a statutory dedication, and we have found that the inclusion of the word, "PARK", at least constitutes an implied dedication. Thus, it may be said that this case sanctions the inclusion of a statutory and implied dedication in the same recorded document. We cannot discern a reason for making these forms of dedication mutually exclusive. . . .

Since we have maintained the trial court judgment, the issue of the Levee District's conventional and/or legal servitude need not be reached.

For the foregoing reasons, the judgment of the trial court is affirmed. Costs of this appeal are assessed to the Whites.

AFFIRMED.

DOMENGEAUX, Chief Judge, dissenting. The developer in the instant case filed a plat of survey with language expressly dedicating the streets and utility easements shown on the plat to public use but with no mention of an undeveloped tract that was labeled "Park." These facts are almost identical to those presented in *O'Quinn v. Burks*, 231 So.2d 660 (La. App. 2d Cir. 1970). Whether the tract was shown as a "Park" or a "Proposed Park" is unimportant. What is important is that in both cases the formal language of dedication did not include any reference to the undeveloped tract. *Inclusio unis est exclusio alterius.* A "park" or a "proposed park" is not a street or a utility easement.

The intent to dedicate must be established, whether the dedication is statutory or implied. If the fact of dedication is doubtful, the court must look to the surrounding circumstances to determine whether there was an intent to dedicate. *Howard v. Louisiana Power and Light Co.*, 583 So.2d 503 (La. App. 5th Cir. 1991). When a rational construction of the record negates an intent to dedicate a particular piece of land, the fact that a reference to the land appears on a map does not, of itself, effect a dedication to public use. *Pioneer Production Corp. v. Segraves*, 340 So.2d 270 (La. 1976).

In an affidavit, the original developer stated that he intended the property to remain undeveloped "for the use and benefit *of the owners of lots located in Charles Park*" (emphasis added). This statement convinces me that the developer never intended to dedicate the disputed tract *to public use*. Lack of intent to dedicate is further found in the developer's subsequent sale of the property, with warranty, to the plaintiffs' ancestor in title.

The plat in *Town of Vinton v. Lyons*, 131 La. 673, 60 So. 54 (1912), contained the original layout of a proposed town. The tract involved was bisected by a railroad right of way, and there seemed to be no question that the area involved was meant to be a public park. In the instant case, a public park seems incongruous with the residential area depicted on the plat. Do the residents of Wyclyffe Way really want a park open to all across the street from their homes? The disputed tract has never been used as a park, either public or private, and the City of Alexandria has required the plaintiffs (the record owners) to maintain the property.

If the plat in this case contained no formal words of dedication, then this case would be governed by *Town of Vinton,* supra. However, that language is present. The result reached by the majority requires us to either ignore the developer's express intent or to, in effect, say that a street "is a park." Other cases cited by the defendants, such as *Parish of Jefferson v. Doody,* 247 La. 839, 174 So.2d 798 (1965) and *Garrett v. Pioneer Production Corp.,* 390 So.2d 851 (La. 1980), hold only that the *absence* of a formal dedication clause will not defeat a statutory dedication *of the streets and alleys* shown on a recorded plat. The instant case is distinguishable in that (1) here, a formal dedication is present, and (2) the language of dedication does not include any reference to a valuable, undivided tract. I respectfully suggest that the majority opinion is based upon equitable considerations rather than an application of the law.

For the above reasons, I would reverse the action of the trial court.

I respectfully dissent.

Notes and Questions

1. What facts or interests do you think tipped the scales to lead Judge (later Justice) Knoll to interpret the ambiguous statements on the plat as effecting at least an implied dedication in *White v. Kinberger,* 611 So.2d 810 (La. App. 3 Cir. 1992)? Do you believe the maxim of statutory and contract interpretation, *inclusio unius est exclusio alterius* (the inclusion of one is the exclusion of the other), relied upon by Judge Domingeaux, should have been the decisive methodological tool to resolve the case? Is Judge Domingeaux correct to suppose that the surrounding neighbors would be more troubled by use of the undeveloped tract in question as a park "open to all across the street from their homes" rather than for more residential development?

2. The court recognized that an implied dedication created a park in the Charles Park Addition Subdivision. Who may use the park: only residents of the subdivision or any person?

3. Note that the trial court held in *White* that the city of Alexandria owned the property in dispute by virtue of an implied dedication. *White,* 611 So.2d at 811–12. Professor Yiannopoulos, among others, has observed that implied dedication can only result in the transfer of a servitude in favor of the public. A.N. YIANNOPOULOS, 2 LOUISIANA CIVIL LAW TREATISE: PROPERTY § 6.9 (5th ed. 2015). In her majority opinion in *White,* however, Judge Knoll, after finding that "the inclusion of the word, 'PARK', at least constitutes an implied dedication," affirmed the trial court judgment without reservation. *White,* 611 So.2d at 814. Does this mean that a statutory dedication also occurred? What other reasons might Judge Knoll have had for recognizing a transfer of ownership, rather than a mere servitude, in this case?

3. Private Canals and Dedication to Public Use

In the final part of the chapter we visit yet another kind of navigable water body—privately owned canals—and examine how the doctrine of dedication to public use has affected the public's right of access to such canals.

In a series of decisions, Louisiana courts have repeatedly held that a man-made canal, built entirely with private funds on privately owned land, remains a private thing, even though the canal may be navigable in fact and thus could be suitable for commerce. *See, e.g., Ilhenny v. Broussard,* 135 So. 669 (La. 1931); *National Audubon Society v. White,* 302 So.2d 680 (La. App. 3 Cir. 1974); *Vermillion Corp. v. Vaughn,* 356 So.2d 551 (La. App. 3 Cir. 1978); *affirmed in part, vacated in part, Vaughn v. Vermillion Corp.,* 444 U.S. 206, 100 S.Ct. 399 (1979); *People for Open Waters, Inc. v. Estate of Gray,* 643 So.2d 415 (La. App. 3 Cir. 1994); *Buckskin Hunting Club v. Bayard,* 866 So.2d 266, 273–75 (La. App. 3 Cir. 2004).

In some of these decisions, parties have argued that private owners of man-made canals should permit public use because the physical suitability for commerce of these canals makes them just like public highways of commerce. Courts have rejected this argument reasoning that canals built with private funds on privately owned land *that have not been dedicated to public use by their owners* are not like public highways at all. Rather, they are analogous to private roads under Civil Code Article 457, which, though capable of use by many kinds of vehicles, nevertheless remain private things *unless they have been dedicated to public use. Vaughn,* 866 So.3d at 555; *White,* So.2d at 667–68.

Another argument occasionally raised in support of public rights of access to privately constructed water bodies is based on the principle of federal law that gives the federal government the right to regulate, prevent obstructions, and control access to the waters of the United States as determined under admiralty law. 33 U.S.C. § 403 (2018). Members of the public have argued that privately constructed, artificial water bodies which effectively divert water from and destroy previously natural, navigable water bodies, have, in effect, substituted the private water body for the previously public water body. Consequently, members of the public may claim a public right of access to the artificial water body.

Although the Louisiana Third Circuit Court of Appeal rejected this argument in *Vermillion Corp. v. Vaughn,* 356 So.2d 551, 556 (La. App. 3 Cir. 1978), the United States Supreme Court later reversed that decision holding that an artificial navigable water body built by a private person on private land with private funds (something like a private canal), but constructed by *altering, improving, or destroying* a previously extant natural navigable water body, *can be burdened by a federal navigational servitude* and, thus, can become subject to public use without the requirement of paying just compensation to the landowner. *Vaughn v. Vermillion Corp.,* 444 U.S. 206, 208 (1979). Such a water body will then be subject to federal regulation for use and maintenance. *Id.* On remand, the Louisiana Third Circuit determined that the individuals seeking access to the private canals at issue had not properly plead their destruction or diversion theory in the trial court and thus, were not entitled to raise it as a defense to a trespass action despite the United States Supreme Court's validation of the theory. *Vermillion Corp. v. Vaughn*, 387 So.2d 698, 700–02 (La. App. 3 Cir. 1980). The Louisiana Supreme Court eventually reversed that decision, holding that the owner of the private canals was not entitled to summary judgment based on the pleadings. *Vermillion Corp. v. Vaughn*, 397 So.2d 490, 493–94 (La. 1981).

After *Vaughn*, litigants have occasionally asserted access claims based on its "destruction or diversion" exception. So far, though, there are no reported cases in which litigants have been able to establish the scientific evidence necessary to prove the level of diversion and destruction sufficient to warrant subjecting a privately built canal to the federal navigational servitude. *See, e.g., Buckskin Hunting Club v. Bayard*, 866 So.2d 266, 273 (La. App. 3 Cir. 2004) (denying plaintiff's claim under the diversion and destruction theory of *Vaughn* on the basis of insufficient expert testimony).

As Louisiana courts have rejected almost all other arguments for subjecting private canals to some form of public use, it should come as no surprise that a community of boaters and fishermen who had relied on navigational access to a privately owned canal for many years might assert that the owners of the canal had subjected it to public use under the doctrine of implied dedication. Consider the following decision.

Cenac v. Public Access Water Rights Ass'n
851 So.2d 1006 (La. 2003)

KIMBALL, Justice. In this case, we are asked to determine whether a privately owned boat launch and navigable canal have been impliedly dedicated to public use such that the property is now burdened with a servitude of use in favor of the public. After considering the evidence presented at trial, we conclude the evidence establishes only that the property has been used for a long period of time by the public with the permission of the owners. We find this evidence is insufficient to establish the requisite intent required for an implied dedication. For this reason, we affirm the judgment of the court of appeal.

Facts and Procedural History

On April 4, 2000, Arlen B. Cenac, Jr. ("Cenac") purchased from the Gheens Foundation ("the Foundation") a large tract of land known as Golden Ranch Plantation in Lafourche Parish. The tract included a portion of a canal, called Company Canal, and an adjacent boat launch and parking area. The canal connects Bayou Lafourche and Bayou Des Allemands and can be used to access Lake Salvador.

On October 19, 2000, Cenac filed a petition for injunction and damages against Public Access Water Rights Association ("PAWRA"), a local community association that seeks to preserve the fishing and water rights of the Gheens community, and several individuals, alleging that on October 10, 11, and 17, 2000, he attempted to erect a security fence on his property and that PAWRA and the named individuals (hereinafter referred to collectively as "PAWRA") trespassed upon his property and prevented him from erecting the fence. Cenac requested a permanent injunction prohibiting PAWRA from engaging in acts that interfere with his use and enjoyment of the property.

Shortly thereafter, on November 22, 2000, Melva Cressionie ("Cressionie"), a resident of the Gheens community in Lafourche Parish, filed a petition for possession and injunctive relief against Cenac, claiming that she had possession of a real right in the form of a servitude of right of way and use to cross Cenac's property, park her vehicles on the area surrounding the boat launch, and use the boat launch to launch boats into Company Canal. Cressionie alleged she had consistently and peacefully used the boat launch and the area surrounding it for several years without objection from anyone. Cressionie further alleged that Cenac's attempt to erect a security fence around the boat launch and parking area prevented her from enjoying her real right. Cressionie requested that she be maintained in her possession and enjoyment of the real right and that an injunction be issued ordering Cenac to refrain from interfering with her access to the boat launch and parking area. . . . [Subsequently, the trial court granted a motion filed by Cenac to consolidate the two cases. Eds.]

After a bench trial, the trial court entered judgment declaring Cenac the owner of the property in dispute. Furthermore, the trial court rendered judgment in favor of Cenac on the issue of the use of the boat launch and parking area and issued a permanent injunction barring Cressionie, PAWRA, and anyone acting on their behalf from launching, parking, or otherwise using the boat launch. Finally, on the issue of the use of the canal, the trial court rendered judgment in favor of Cressionie and PAWRA, declaring that Cenac's ownership of the canal is burdened by a servitude of use in favor of the public at large by virtue of implied dedication.

All parties appealed portions of the trial court's judgment to the court of appeal. The court of appeal affirmed the judgment of the trial court granting a permanent injunction as to the boat launch, but reversed the judgment of the trial court declaring that the canal was dedicated to the public use by implied dedication. *Cenac v. Public Access Water Rights Ass'n*, 01-1859 (La. App. 1 Cir. 9/27/02), 835 So.2d 560. Specifically, the court of appeal found that PAWRA and Cressionie failed to establish the plain and positive intent of the landowners to dedicate the canal and boat launch to public use. *ID.* at p. 14, 835 So.2d at 568.

We granted certiorari to examine the issue of implied dedication. *Cenac v. Public Access Water Rights Ass'n*, 02-2660 (La. 1/31/03), 836 So.2d 78.

Discussion

The trial court's judgment declaring Cenac the owner of the boat launch [and its surrounding area, including the parking lot] and canal has not been objected to and is not before us. Cressionie and PAWRA concede they have not acquired a servitude over the property at issue by acquisitive prescription. Moreover, they agree that the only method of dedication applicable to this case is that of implied dedication. Thus, the sole issue presented for our review is whether the boat launch and/or the canal were impliedly dedicated to public use such that Cenac's property is burdened with a servitude of use in favor of the general public.

Our legislature has never enacted a comprehensive scheme governing dedication to public use. *St. Charles Parish Sch. Bd. v. P & L Inv. Corp.*, 95-2571, p. 4 (La.5/21/96), 674 So.2d 218, 221; *Garrett v. Pioneer Prod. Corp.*, 390 So.2d 851, 854 (La. 1980). The subject has thus been a controversial one. *Garrett*, 390 So.2d at 854. In the absence of such a comprehensive scheme, our courts have recognized four modes of dedication to public use: (1) formal, (2) statutory, (3) implied, and (4) tacit. *P & L Inv. Corp.*, 95-2571 at p. 4-5, 674 So.2d at 221. Only implied dedication is at issue in this case.

Implied dedication is a common law doctrine, but it has been recognized by Louisiana courts since the nineteenth century. *See id.* at p. 5, 674 So.2d at 222. *See also Municipality No. 2 v. Orleans Cotton Press*, 18 La. 122 (1841) (citing *City of Cincinnati v. White's Lessee*, 31 U.S. (6 Pet.) 431, 8 L.Ed. 452 (1832)). No particular formalities are required to effectuate an implied dedication. 2 A.N. YIANNOPOULOS, LOUISIANA CIVIL LAW TREATISE, PROPERTY § 98, at 214 (4th ed. 2001). Traditionally, because implied dedication lacks the formalities and safeguards of the other modes of dedication, the two indispensable elements of implied dedication required by the courts are "a plain and positive intention to give and one equally plain to accept." *P & L Inv. Corp.*, 95-2571 at p. 5, 674 So.2d at 222 (quoting *Carrollton Rail Rd. Co. v. Municipality No. Two*, 19 La. 62, 71 (1841)). *See also Humphreys v. Bennett Oil Corp.*, 195 La. 531, 197 So. 222 (1940); *Bomar v. City of Baton Rouge*, 162 La. 342, 110 So. 497 (1926); *DeGrilleau v. Frawley*, 48 La. Ann. 184, 19 So. 151 (1896); *Town of Carrollton v. Jones*, 7 La. Ann. 233 (1852); YIANNOPOULOS § 98, at 214. Thus, implied dedication requires an unequivocally manifested intent to dedicate on the part of the owner and an equally clear intent to accept on the part of the public.

While traditionally the only requirements for implied dedication are the owner's plain intent to dedicate and the public's clear intent to accept, the additional requirement of maintenance by the municipality has sometimes erroneously been engrafted onto the concept of implied dedication. . . .

. . . The jurisprudence suggesting that maintenance by the municipality is required before an implied dedication can be made is an aberration in our law. As explained above, all that has traditionally been required for an implied dedication is an unequivocally manifested intent to dedicate on the part of the owner and an equally clear intent to accept on the part of the public. While maintenance by the municipality might be a factor in determining whether an implied dedication has in fact been made, it is not required. Any language in our prior cases suggesting such a requirement is erroneous and hereby repudiated.

The weight of authority establishes that an implied dedication gives rise to a servitude of public use and does not transfer ownership. . . . *See also* YIANNOPOULOS § 98, at 217; 11A EUGENE MCQUILLIN, THE LAW OF MUNICIPAL CORPORATIONS § 33.68 (3rd ed. 2000).

The burden of proving the implied dedication falls upon the party asserting the dedication. *Jones*, 7 La. Ann. at 235; *Drabik v. Town of East Lyme*, 234 Conn. 390,

662 A.2d 118 (1995). . . . The question of intent to dedicate to public use is one of fact. *Donaldson's Heirs v. City of New Orleans,* 166 La. 1059, 1063, 118 So. 134, 135 (1928). . . . The factual findings of a trial court should not be set aside by a court unless they are manifestly erroneous or clearly wrong. *Arceneaux v. Domingue,* 365 So.2d 1330 (La. 1978).

In the instant case, Cenac argues PAWRA is prevented from acquiring a servitude of use over the boat launch and canal by the provisions of La. R.S. 9:1251. PAWRA, on the other hand, contends the provisions of the statute do not apply to prohibit a landowner from creating a servitude of use by implied dedication. The trial court found the statute applied to prohibit the creation of a public servitude of use over the boat launch, but did not apply to the canal.

Entitled "Passage to or from waters or recreational sites; servitudes or rights of way or passage not acquired," La. R.S. 9:1251 provides:

A. Any other provisions of the laws of this state to the contrary notwithstanding, whenever any land owner voluntarily, whether expressly or tacitly, permits passage through or across his land by certain persons or by the public, solely for the purpose of providing a convenience to such persons in the ingress and egress to and from waters for boating, or for the purpose of ingress and egress to and from any recreational site, neither the public nor any person shall thereby acquire a servitude or right of passage, nor shall such passage become a public road or street by reason of upkeep, maintenance, or work performed thereon by any governing authority.

B. The provisions of this section shall not be construed to:

(1) prohibit land owners from entering into enforceable contracts specifically granting servitudes or rights of way or passage;

(2) prohibit land owners from specifically dedicating roads, streets or passages to the public use;

(3) repeal any laws relative to expropriation or appropriation of land or servitudes or laws authorizing the legislature or governing authorities to open, lay out or appoint public roads or streets; nor

(4) repeal any laws creating servitudes along rivers, streams or other waters.

This statute was enacted in 1958 by Act No. 463 and has not been amended since its enactment.

We agree with the trial court that La. R.S. 9:1251 applies to the boat launch, but not to the canal. By its own terms, the statute applies to land used as a passage to reach waters for boating. It does not apply to prevent the acquisition of a servitude over the waters of the canal. The clear language of subsection (A) prohibits the public from acquiring a servitude when the owner voluntarily permits the public to pass through or across his land for convenient access to and from a recreational site or a body of water for boating. Subsection (B)(2), however, makes it clear that subsection (A) shall not prohibit land owners from specifically dedicating passages to public use. Thus, if the owner has unequivocally manifested an intent to dedicate his land used to access waters for boating and the public has clearly accepted, then the provisions of La. R.S. 9:1251(A) do not apply to prevent the public from acquiring a servitude over the owner's land.

Like the boat launch, the canal is owned by Cenac. It is a private thing subject to dedication to public use, as are roads and streets. YIANNOPOULOS § 79. Although the canal is navigable, this fact alone does not render it public. *Id.; Brown v. Rougon*, 552 So.2d 1052 (La. App. 1 Cir. 1989), *writ denied*, 559 So.2d 121 (La. 1990); *National Audubon Soc'y v. White*, 302 So.2d 660 (La. App. 3 Cir. 1974), *writ denied*, 305 So.2d 542 (La. 1975). In this case, the uncontroverted evidence reveals that when the canal was built, it did not divert any natural stream or water body. Thus, the privately owned canal is burdened with a servitude of public use only if Cressionie and PAWRA prove the existence of an implied dedication.

Taking all of the above into consideration, we find that if the boat launch has been impliedly dedicated to public use, then La. R.S. 9:1251 does not prevent the public from acquiring a servitude over the boat launch. Likewise, because the terms of La. R.S. 9:1251 do not apply to the canal, if the canal has been impliedly dedicated to public use, then the public has acquired a servitude over that portion of Cenac's property. The sole question presented, then, is whether the boat launch and canal have been impliedly dedicated to public use such that the public has acquired a servitude of use over Cenac's property.

The plain and positive intent to dedicate must be shown by language or acts so clear as to exclude every other hypothesis but that of dedication. *Bomar*, 162 La. at 347, 110 So. at 499 (quoting *Shreveport v. Drouin*, 41 La. Ann. 867, 6 So. 656 (1889)); *DeGrilleau v. Frawley*, 48 La. Ann. at 195, 19 So. at 157. The proof needed to establish an implied dedication has been accurately stated as follows:

> Ownership of land once had is not to be presumed to have been parted with, but the acts and declarations relied on to show a dedication should be unequivocal and decisive, manifesting a positive and unmistakable intention, on the part of the owner, to permanently abandon his property to the specific public use. If they are equivocal, or do not clearly and plainly indicate his intention to permanently abandon the property to the public, they are not sufficient to establish a dedication. The intention to dedicate must clearly appear, though such intention may be shown by deed, by words, or acts. If by words, the words must be unequivocal, and without ambiguity. If by acts, they must be such acts as are inconsistent with any construction, except the assent to such dedication. *Brusseau v. McBride*, 245 N.W.2d 488 (S.D.1976) (quoting *Cole v. Minnesota Loan & Trust Co.*, 17 N.D. 409, 117 N.W. 354 (1908)).

While recognizing that a plain and positive intent to dedicate must be proved, Cressionie and PAWRA assert that the owner's mere toleration or acquiescence of continuous use on the part of the public is sufficient to establish an intent to dedicate. Louisiana jurisprudence does contain some language suggesting that long use by the public is sufficient to establish an implied dedication. *See e.g. Emery v. Orleans Levee Bd.,* 207 La. 386, 21 So.2d 418 (1945). These cases, however, have been criticized by the doctrinal writers and are contrary to the majority of decisions handed down by both Louisiana and common law courts. The majority of our cases establish the principle that continuous use by the public alone is insufficient to establish the requisite intent. *See e.g. Kohn v. Bellott,* 169 La. 352, 125 So. 269 (1929); *Donaldson's Heirs,* 166 La. at 1063, 118 So. at 135; *Bomar v. City of Baton Rouge,* 162 La. at 346, 110 So. at 499; *Torres v. Falgoust,* 37 La. Ann. 497 (1885). Professor Yiannopoulos, a leading commentator, has explained:

> [D]ecisions establishing an implied dedication by the toleration of public use are extremely rare and may be explained on other grounds, such as estoppel vis-à-vis the public authorities. The jurisprudence is well settled that immemorial use by the public does not alone establish dedication.

YIANNOPOULOS § 98, at 215 (footnotes omitted).

Common law jurisdictions similarly reject the idea that mere toleration or acquiescence on the part of the owner is sufficient to establish intent to dedicate. . . .

. . . We therefore conclude an owner's toleration of and acquiescence in long and continuous public use of his land, without more, is insufficient to establish a plain and positive intent to dedicate.

The evidence adduced at trial in the instant case showed that the public had been using both the boat launch and the canal for at least 60 years. During this time period, the prior owners of the canal, Mr. and Mrs. Gheens and, later, the Gheens Foundation, had knowledge of the public's use and never interfered when the public used the boat launch and the canal for passage into Lake Salvador. Melva Cressionie, one of the parties who lives across the highway from the boat launch, testified she never asked permission to use the boat launch and the canal because she thought they were public. She also testified that Mr. Taylor, a general manager of Golden Ranch Plantation, told her the boat launch was public. Other members of the public testified regarding their long use of the boat launch and canal and their understanding that the property was public. There was also testimony that the sheriff's office, the fire department, and an ambulance used the launch and canal in emergency situations.

Cressionie and PAWRA also presented evidence regarding maintenance of the boat launch and canal. Evidence was presented that some members of the community performed minor acts of maintenance around the boat launch such as placing shells in the holes made by vehicles using the launch, picking up trash, and installing steel cleats used to tie up boats. Additionally, evidence was presented that the Army Corps of Engineers sprayed the canal to keep it free of aquatic vegetation that would prohibit navigation. Ray Blouin, an inspector for the Army Corps of Engineers, testified the Corps was maintaining the canal when he began his job there in 1975. He also testified that the canal was generally sprayed from March or April through December of every year. A document was entered into evidence that showed the Corps sprayed the canal 27 times from August 1995 through May 1999. Mr. Blouin testified that he knew of no objection to the spraying by the owners. Finally, Mr. Blouin testified that while it is not the practice of the Corps to spray private canals, if the public used the canal, the Corps would spray it unless it was gated under lock and key. The parties stipulated that Mr. Russell Savoie, if called to testify, would state that he worked for the Parish of Lafourche and had done some spraying in the canal in the course of his employment.

Finally, testimony was presented that the parking area around the boat launch had been enlarged by the owners because they had liability concerns about the cars parking on the side of the highway when the parking area was full.

Cenac offered evidence and testimony purporting to show the owners' efforts to maintain the launch and canal as private. The record contains evidence that the previous owners placed signs at the boat launch and canal indicating that the property was "private" and "posted." Mr. Herman Robichaux, former general manager of Golden Ranch Plantation, testified he began working for the Gheens family in 1963 and posted and maintained private property signs at the boat launch and canal beginning around 1968. He testified the canal itself, including its points of entry and exit, were posted with private property signs. Mr. Robichaux stated he was always instructed by the owners to maintain the boat launch and canal as private. Mr. Robichaux testified his standing orders were that no public funds be spent on the property. He also testified that he ejected trespassers, commercial fisherman, and hunters from the canal. Criminal proceedings were sometimes instituted against people to keep them out of the canal. Mr. Robichaux testified the Foundation received a permit from the Army Corps of Engineers to conduct a marsh management project on the north side of the canal and spent about $120,000 completing the project. The Corps did not contribute any money to the project. Mr. Robichaux further testified that Foundation employees maintained the boat launch.

Additionally, Mr. Lanny Ledet, the property manager employed by Cenac, testified he recalled seeing signs asserting the private nature of the property around the boat launch and canal since his employment in 1987. Mr. Forrest Travirca, a security agent for Golden Ranch Plantation, also testified he saw the signs posted along the boat launch and canal. Because of the signs, he asked for and was granted permission to use the launch to reach his camp on Lake Salvador and, later, for use by his scout troop. He initially sought permission from the general manager, Mr. Taylor, but was told it was more appropriate to ask Mrs. Gheens directly for permission to use the property.

Mr. Donald Doyle, Vice-President of the Gheens Foundation and former attorney of Mr. and Mrs. Gheens, testified that both Mr. and Mrs. Gheens were very strict "relative to any use of the property that might in any way compromise their ownership or their right to exclusive use of the property." Mr. Doyle stated that the

Gheens were against governmental work being done on the property without their permission and his instructions were that the parish should not be allowed to put shells at the launch. He testified that the public was given permission to use the boat launch and canal in an effort to be neighborly, but there was never any intention to grant the public any rights in the property. He also testified that when the Foundation sold the property to Cenac, it was the Foundation's intent to transfer the boat launch and canal to him free of any servitudes or right of public use.

Finally, evidence was presented to show that Mr. and Mrs. Gheens and the Foundation entered into various hunting leases with members of the public and allowed those persons to use the boat launch and canal in connection with the leases. Testimony at trial indicated that when large hunting groups were using the property, those groups were given a key to the "private boat launch" across the canal as the launch at issue was too crowded. Additionally, a letter purporting to show a draft of an agreement between Golden Ranch Plantation and the Gheens Jaycees was admitted into evidence. The letter indicated an agreement "for operation of the boat ramp," which provided that the Jaycees would keep the launch area clean, complete minor maintenance, and "monitor the use of the boat launch, prohibit use by the general public, insure availability of the facilities for the local community, and inform the Golden Ranch of any conflicts." The proposed agreement ended with the statement that Golden Ranch "reserves the right to prohibit anyone from using the facilities."

After considering the above evidence, the trial court found there was no evidence that anyone ever interfered with the public's use of the boat launch or canal. The trial court found the evidence showed the signs posting the property as private had been there for at least 30 years. The trial court determined that the Gheens family and the Foundation granted the community permission to use the launch and this permission has existed for at least 50 years. With regard to maintenance, the trial court found the Corps had done some spraying, but had not spent overwhelming amounts of money maintaining the canal. The trial court stated, "The evidence of maintenance is sketchy and in this case, I don't think significant." The trial court concluded the Gheens family did not allow hunting from the canal or its banks and did not allow air boats in the canal. With regard to the navigable canal, the trial court found tolls were charged for its use in its early years of existence. The trial court found there were never any written acts dedicating the canal or the launch to the public. Finally, the trial court found that the possession of the public has always been with the permission of the owner, or precarious.

. . . .

With regard to the canal, the trial court concluded the central question to be determined was the purpose for which the canal was built. Because it found the canal was built for navigation and has been used for navigation by the public for many years, it found the canal was impliedly dedicated to public use. The trial court did not, however, make any finding regarding the intent of the owners to dedicate the canal to public use. The trial court therefore legally erred in that it applied the wrong test to determine whether, in fact, an implied dedication of the canal had been established.

After reviewing the evidence presented in this case, we find the trial court was reasonable in concluding there is no evidence that any owner prior to Cenac interfered with the public's use of the boat launch and canal and that the canal was built for navigation and has been used by the public for many years. This evidence of mere toleration or acquiescence on the part of the owners, however, is not by itself sufficient to support a finding of implied dedication to public use. Because the trial court erroneously failed to consider whether the previous owners unequivocally manifested a plain and positive intent to dedicate the boat launch to public use after 1958 and whether the requisite intent was present with respect to the canal, we must review the record to determine whether such an intent was proved by Cressionie and PAWRA.

After a thorough review of the record and after considering the findings of fact made by the trial court, we find Cressionie and PAWRA failed to prove a plain and positive intent to dedicate by language or acts so clear as to exclude every other hypothesis but that of dedication. The evidence reveals that Mr. and Mrs. Gheens, and, later, the Foundation, took pains to ensure the property at issue remained private property not subject to any rights in favor of the public. While maintenance by the public is a factor in determining whether an implied dedication has been made, we agree with the trial court that the amount of maintenance provided by the public was somewhat "sketchy" considering the long period of time over which the property was used by the public. The record revealed that although the public provided minor maintenance, the owners did not turn over the maintenance of the property to the public, but continuously retained the responsibility to maintain the property. They gave instructions to their employees that no public funds were to be spent on their property. The minor maintenance provided by the public in this case is, by itself, insufficient to establish a plain and positive intent on the part of the owners to dedicate their property to public use.

The testimony of former employees of Mr. and Mrs. Gheens and the Foundation and that of the vice-president of the Foundation shows that the boat launch and canal were considered private by the owners and that they had no intention of dedicating any portion to the public. They posted signs at the launch and the canal, including its points of entry and exit, asserting the private nature of the property. They gave explicit permission to use the boat launch and canal to those who requested it. Although they gave the public permission to use the launch and canal, the evidence reveals they intended to retain the ability to revoke this permission and exercised this ability when people used the canal in an unapproved manner. The fact that the owners enlarged the parking area around the boat launch and repaired the launch itself is not inconsistent with their private ownership of the property and their decision to allow the public to use the property as long as their permission was given. Furthermore, the Foundation made no attempt to acknowledge any right of the public to the boat launch and canal when it sold the property to Cenac, although other servitudes were mentioned. Mr. Doyle testified that it was the Foundation's attempt to transfer ownership of the property free of any servitudes of use in favor of the public.

In light of the above, we find Cressionie and PAWRA have not presented evidence sufficient to show a plain and positive intent to dedicate by actions so clear as to exclude every other hypothesis but that of dedication. Instead, the evidence presented shows that the public was allowed to use the boat launch and canal for the purpose of traveling to other bodies of water for many years with the permission of the owners. This permissive use does not establish a plain intent on the part of the owners to permanently abandon the property to public use. Thus, like the court of appeal, we find neither the boat launch nor the canal is burdened with a servitude of public use established by implied dedication.

Decree

The judgment of the court of appeal, which affirmed the judgment of the trial court granting a permanent injunction as to the boat launch and reversed the judgment of the trial court declaring the canal to be dedicated to the public use by implied dedication, is affirmed.

AFFIRMED.

WEIMER, Justice, concurring in part and dissenting in part. This matter involves a unique set of facts.

The small community of Gheens is located in an isolated area of a rural portion of Lafourche Parish. There is but one highway serving the community. One cannot drive through Gheens destined for anywhere else.

For decades and generations, the Company Canal provided the only navigable waterborne artery of ingress and egress to the area. The Company Canal was built by a joint public/private endeavor specifically for the purpose of navigation. Although the canal became private and tolls were charged at certain locations in the distant past, the record is clear that the portion of the Company Canal which connected the area where the community of Gheens is located was always utilized by the public as a waterborne thoroughfare.

In 1929 and 1930, C.E. Gheens purchased the Golden Ranch Plantation, which included the portion of the Company Canal at issue. Upon his death, his widow acquired title to the plantation. When she died in 1982, the Gheens Foundation became the owner of the plantation, including the canal and the land surrounding the canal. The evidence is clear the Gheenses always allowed the public to use the canal for travel. Prior to highways, waterways were virtually the only means of travel. The Gheenses apparently had a symbiotic, paternal relationship with the community that bore their name. So long as individuals used the canal as a means of transportation, that use was acceptable. Hunting, fishing, air boat use, and docking vessels in the canal were not tolerated; but navigation through the canal was not just permitted, it was encouraged. The encouragement did not come only in the form of allowing use of the canal. The Gheenses also built a boat launch, referred to as the "public boat launch," for the use of the public and later enlarged the boat launch, which further encouraged the use of the canal. In sharp contrast to this public boat launch is the so-called "private boat launch," located directly across the canal, that the Gheenses built for their own use.

At issue in this matter is whether there exists an implied dedication in favor of the public to use the canal and the boat launch. As explained by Professor Yiannopoulos, "[A]fter much litigation, it became settled that dedication to public use may be accomplished without any express or written act. This mode of dedication came to be known, in contradistinction with formal dedication, as 'implied dedication.'" 2 A.N. YIANNOPOULOS, LOUISIANA CIVIL LAW TREATISE: PROPERTY § 98 at 210 (1999). . . .

While I am extremely reluctant to engraft a so-called common law concept such as implied dedication into our civil law system, it is clear that this concept has been fully adopted by the jurisprudence. *See* YIANNOPOULOS at 210 n. 6. Sanctioned by the experience of ages, the common law doctrine of implied dedication rests on public convenience. 26 C.J.S. *Dedication* § 2, at 280 (2001), *citing Jack v. Fontenot*, 236 So.2d 877 (La. App. 3 Cir. 1970). The doctrine is based on public policy and good faith, securing to the public only rights it has honestly enjoyed or depended upon, but taking nothing from the landowner that was not intended to be given. 26 C.J.S. *Dedication* § 2, at 280. . . .

Further, despite its long history of being jurisprudentially recognized, the legislature has not abrogated the concept of implied dedication except in a limited situation. That situation involves a landowner allowing the use of his property to enable the public to get to a waterway. To encourage a landowner to allow such use, the legislature has expressed that such permissive use does not result in the establishment of a servitude. *See* LSA-R.S. 9:1251. I agree with the trial judge, the court of appeal, and the majority that LSA-R.S. 9:1251 acts to prevent a servitude from being established at the boat launch despite the public's use of the boat launch. For the public to acquire such a right of use, the landowner must specifically grant a servitude of passage or such must be purchased or acquired through expropriation. However, I believe a different result is compelled with respect to the canal.

From a civil law perspective, the concept of an implied dedication merely gives force and effect to the will of the parties based on the grantor's offer to donate and the grantee's acceptance of that offer. *See* LSA-C.C. art. 454; *See also* LSA-C.C. art. 455 and comments. The acts of the donor manifest an intent to dedicate. 26 C.J.S. *Dedication* § 58, at 358.

Mr. Cenac and amicus on behalf of the Louisiana Landowners Association, Inc. express concern that the benevolence of a landowner, who tolerates use by the general public, should not be punished with the loss of ownership rights to his property. I agree. Mere tolerance of use by the general public is not enough to result in the loss of ownership rights. There must be an intent to give on the part of the benefactor.

The law is not insensitive to the rights of property owners and recognizes that a servitude, being a restraint on the use of property, is generally not favored. *See, Brown v. Rougon,* 552 So.2d 1052, 1058 (La. App. 1 Cir. 1989), *writ denied,* 559 So.2d 121, (1990), *citing* LSA-C.C. art. 730, cmt. (b). However, in this case, there was enough evidence for the trial judge to find an intent to dedicate a right of use. This matter does not involve a taking of private property for public use. Rather, this matter involves voluntarily relinquishing rights. A private landowner should not have his property taken simply because he benevolently allows the public to use his property. However, a landowner can intentionally transfer a right of use. . . .

The critical issue regarding the canal is whether there was adequate proof of a positive intent to dedicate. Mr. and Mrs. Gheens are no longer living, so their intent cannot be questioned directly. Rather, we must evaluate their acts to determine their intent. Particular acts of an owner which may be admitted in evidence as manifesting an intent to dedicate property to public use include making a canal through the property for general use and allowing maintenance at public expense. 26 C.J.S. *Dedication* § 58, at 358. However, as the court of appeal noted in the instant case, silence or acquiescence alone is generally insufficient to establish the unequivocal and positive intent necessary to find an offer to dedicate to public use. *Cenac v. Public Access Water Rights Association,* 2001-1859, p. 10 (La. App. 1 Cir. 9/27/02), 835 So.2d 560, 565.

Not one shred of evidence indicates that the Gheenses ever closed or intended to close the canal to waterborne traffic other than restricting the use of air boats. To the contrary, the evidence establishes they took steps to promote the use of the canal, even expanding the boat launch when it became overcrowded. I suggest the evidence indicates Mr. and Mrs. Gheens would not tolerate depriving their rural neighbors, who had used the Company Canal for generations as a means of travel to reach public waterways to fish, hunt, trap, and provide for their families, of the use of this canal.

Additionally, the canal was sprayed with herbicides at public expense to prevent the growth of water hyacinths. While maintenance by the public is not a requisite for implied dedication, it is a factor to be considered. *See* 26 C.J.S. *Dedication* § 58, at 358; *compare,* LSA-R.S. 48:4915. At trial, Ray Blouin, an Army Corps of Engineers inspector in the aquatic growth control unit, testified the Corps has sprayed the portion of the canal at issue in this case to keep it free from aquatic vegetation. Spraying was done from March or April through December of each year. He estimated that the canal had been sprayed by the Corps "in-house" for at least twenty years prior to 1995 when the Corps began contracting with private contractors to do the actual spraying. One such contract indicated the canal had been sprayed approximately 27 times from 1995–1999. The Corps maintains waterways that are used by the public to keep the waterways unclogged and navigable. Although the trial judge acknowledged the canal had been sprayed by the Corps, he indicated the expense to the public had not been monetarily significant. However, the evidence established that the maintenance was substantial and occurred over a long period of time. Without this spraying, which the evidence indicated had occurred numerous times, the canal would have long ago become clogged and non-navigable. The evidence established that the owners of the canal knew about the spraying.

Members of the Gheens community testified that for generations the canal was used by them and their ancestors. No one ever sought permission to use the canal; their use of the canal was never restricted. Understandably, they believed a right to use the canal had been established.

Two witnesses associated with the Gheenses testified no one was denied use of the canal so long as it was used as a thoroughfare. . . .

When questioned as to whether there was ever any intent on behalf of Mr. Gheens to dedicate either the canal or the boat launch to public use, Donald Doyle, the attorney for Mr. and Mrs. Gheens and the Gheens Foundation, testified as follows:

> There was a feeling that within the community of Gheens, which was a small community at the time. There were people who did trapping on the property and there were some families that owned camps out on Lake Salvador. *And that there was no reason why, as long as they obeyed the general rules about maintaining the property and not throwing trash, and debris, and garbage in it, that they could use it to go to their camps* [emphasis added].

Doyle further testified it was his understanding the people using the boat launch and canal were using it with the permission of the owners. On cross examination, Doyle responded, "[T]he type of use that we did not object to and thought that it was a perfectly neighborly thing for us to do was to accord to the community the right to use the canal." He also acknowledged on cross examination that there had been no objection to the spraying of the canal done by the Corps.

The learned trial judge heard the evidence and observed the witnesses. Although he did not make a specific finding regarding the intent to dedicate, his judgment was that the canal remain open to the public for navigation. The trial judge found "the canal is subject to an implied dedication to public use." In reasons for judgment, the trial judge stated:

> . . . .
>
> If there's one thing that the facts in this case show, that cannot be contradicted or avoided, is that the canal was built for navigation. And the difference between this case and all of these other cases cited on the issue of the canal is that it was built for navigation. There is no evidence that the state or any of the owners in this case have ever attempted to block the canal or interfere with it[s] use. Even though over a period of time the canal has gone through periods where it may have been silted up in spots, where they didn't know who the owner was, where the owner was bankrupt, or the owner was a wealthy person, Mr. Barrow, who nobody liked. None of that has anything to do with the use for which the canal was built or the use to which it has been put for the 100 plus years that it has been in existence. . . .

> [I]f any case fit[s] the implied dedication of public use for a canal, if the facts of any case fit it, it is this case. Because the facts in this case are overwhelming about why it was dug, why it was built, and the use for which it was put. So my finding in this case is that there has been over a period of time, even if you take the period of years from the time that the Gheens family took ownership, that there has been an implied dedication to use of this canal by the owners that affects the title of Mr. Cenac. And as a result of that, there has been created a servitude of use in favor of the public to the Company Canal.

In civil cases, the appropriate standard for appellate review of factual determinations is the manifest error-clearly wrong standard which precludes the setting aside of a trial court's finding of fact unless those findings are clearly wrong in light of the record reviewed in its entirety. *Rosell v. ESCO*, 549 So.2d 840 (La. 1989). A reviewing court may not merely decide if it would have found the facts of the case differently, the reviewing court should affirm the trial court where the trial court judgment is not clearly wrong or manifestly erroneous. *Ambrose v. New Orleans Police Department Ambulance Service*, 93-3099, 93-3110, 93-3112, p. 8 (La.7/5/94), 639 So.2d 216, 221. . . .

The trial judge did not find the right of passage exists merely because the canal was navigable. The trial judge found "an implied dedication to use of this canal by the owners. . . . [T]here has been created a servitude of use in favor of the public to the Company Canal." There was no evidence to contradict the fact that the canal was always intended to be used for navigation. The evidence clearly establishes that no one was ever prevented from using the canal so long as the canal was used as a highway for travel.

The evidence indicates the canal provided a link to other navigable waterways used for commercial as well as recreational purposes. The canal has a long history of being an artery of commerce. The Gheenses never intended the closure of the canal to the public which would have a detrimental effect on the lives of the residents of this small community of Gheens and the public at large.

As stated in the beginning, this matter involves a unique set of facts. Because of the unique facts of this case, I believe there is sufficient evidence to establish that the trial judge was correct in his assessment that a limited servitude of passage was established.

I do not agree that the trial court committed legal error in applying the wrong test to determine whether an implied dedication of the canal has been established or that the trial court was manifestly erroneous in its findings of fact. I would reverse the decision of the court of appeal and reinstate the judgment of the trial court.

Notes and Questions

1. In *Cenac v. Public Access Water Rights Ass'n*, 851 So.2d 1006 (La. 2003), the court rejected the defendants' implied dedication claim even though public authorities

(in particular the United States Army Corps of Engineers) had expended public resources maintaining the canal. If the defendants had asserted a right of public access based on tacit dedication, would they have been successful?

2. What concerns appear to have been most important to Justice Kimball in her majority opinion in *Cenac*? If the court had determined that the action and inaction on the part of the Gheens' family and their successors resulted in an implied dedication of the canal to public use, how might other private canal owners react in the future?

3. In his dissenting opinion, Justice Weimer notes that the trial court judge, Jerome J. Barbera, III, who listened to all of the direct testimony and received all of the other evidence, and who apparently knew the community of Gheens from personal experience, concluded:

> If any case fits the implied dedication of public use for a canal, if the facts of any case fit it, it is this case. Because the facts in this are overwhelming about why it was dug, why it was built, and the use for which it was put.

Cenac, 851 So.2d at 1023.

Should other members of the Louisiana Supreme Court have been more deferential to the factual findings of the trial court, as Justice Weimer suggests? Or, do you agree with the majority opinion that the trial court judge misapprehended the applicable law and used the wrong legal test, thus justifying the court in subjecting his decision to *de novo* review on appeal?

4. Are the conclusions reached by the majority opinion and Justice Weimer based on different interpretations of the same underlying facts or on a divergent understanding of the law? What can explain why members of the same court disagree so strongly about the meaning of what seem to be essentially uncontroverted facts?

5. After *Cenac*, in what kinds of factual scenarios, if any, will it be possible for a court to find the existence of an implied dedication? Would a factual situation like that which unfolded in *White v. Kinberger* lead to a finding of implied dedication after *Cenac*?

6. Recall the excerpt from Professor Lovett's article describing the Land Reform (Scotland) Act 2003 at the conclusion of Chapter 2. John A. Lovett, *The Right to Exclude Meets the Right of Responsible Access: Scotland's Bold Experiment in Access Legislation*, 26 PROB. & PROP. No. 2, 52-55 (2012). If the facts in *Cenac* had arisen in contemporary Scotland, would the Land Reform Scotland Act (2003) have required a ruling in favor of members of the public seeking recreational or navigational access to a privately constructed canal located on privately owned land?

Chapter 4

Classification of Things: Of Movables and Immovables, Corporeals and Incorporeals

A. The Primary Classifications

This chapter turns to two more fundamental sets of classifications. Every civil law based property system draws a clear distinction between **movable** and **immovable** things. In Louisiana, immovables are tracts of land with their component parts, buildings and standing timber, and things incorporated into immovables, attached to immovables, or declared to be immovable. *See generally* La. Civ. Code arts. 462–67 (1978). Everything else is categorized as a movable thing. La. Civ. Code art. 475 (1978). The common law similarly distinguishes between personal property (chattels) and real property (real estate).

A second crucial distinction observed involves **corporeal** things and **incorporeal** things. In Roman law, things that could be felt or touched were called "corporeals." In contrast, things that did not have any physical existence but were nevertheless valuable and perceivable as distinct things were described as "incorporeals." In common law the terms "tangible" and "intangible" describe the same intuitive distinction between these two categories of things. Article 461 of the Louisiana Civil Code builds upon the Romanist categorization when it provides:

Art. 461. Corporeals and Incorporeals

Corporeals are things that have a body, whether animate or inanimate, and can be felt or touched.

Incorporeals are things that have no body, but are comprehended by the understanding, such as rights of inheritance, servitudes, obligations, and rights of intellectual property.

La. Civ. Code art. 461 (1978). As we study movables and immovables, we must be mindful of the distinction between corporeal and incorporeal things.

Why Classification Matters. The distinction between movables and immovables is fundamental in the civil law for several reasons. First, it provides a systemic pillar in the overall framework of property law. Civil law or mixed jurisdictions typically formalize the divide between movables and immovables through codal definitions. Second, the civil law tends to maintain the distinction between movables and immovables quite rigorously throughout the private and public law orders. Finally, the classification is important because so many significant legal consequences flow from it.

A first legal consequence involves the formalities governing the transfer of property. In the civil law, parties who seek to transfer *immovable* property must comply with rigorous formal requisites. This is undoubtedly attributable to the fact that for many centuries immovable property was the most important source of wealth in society. Requiring compliance with highly formal requirements for the transfer of immovables served two functions — one precautionary and the other evidentiary. It helped assure that the parties were fully aware of the significance of the transaction. In addition, it provided reliable evidence of the particular nature of the transaction and that the parties actually intended the transaction to take place. The imposition of rigid formalities upon certain kinds of transactions has been present since Roman law distinguished between "res mancipi" (things of greater value requiring the formal and solemn process of "mancipatio" for their transfer) and "res nec mancipi" (other movable things that were amenable to transfer by delivery). The insistence upon strict formalities for the transfer of immovable property has remained important in the civil law throughout the centuries.

Today the Louisiana Civil Code continues this tradition by subjecting all voluntary transfers of immovable property to strict formalities. Several of the most important articles on this subject are found in Book III of the Civil Code. Article 1839 is a particularly important provision:

Art. 1839. Transfer of immovable property

A transfer of immovable property must be made by authentic act or by act under private signature. Nevertheless, an oral transfer is valid between the parties when the property has been actually delivered and the transferor recognizes the transfer when interrogated under oath.

An instrument involving immovable property shall have effect against third persons only from the time it is filed for registry in the parish where the property is located.

La. Civ. Code art. 1839 (1984). Article 1839 illustrates one consequence of classifying a thing as an immovable. Any person seeking to make a voluntary transfer of immovable property must use one of two written forms: (1) an authentic act, a writing executed before a notary public, or a similarly authorized person, in the presence of two witnesses and signed by each party who executed it, by each witness and by each notary public before whom it was executed, La. Civ. Code art. 1833(A) (1984, amended 2003); or (2) or an act under private signature, a written act signed by the parties to the transaction, La. Civ. Code art. 1837 (1984). Absent either kind of written act, a voluntary transfer of immovable property will be valid between the parties only if the property has been actually delivered and the transferor recognizes the transfer when interrogated under oath, La. Civ. Code art. 1839 (1984), a burden that is not easy for a purported transferee to satisfy. *See, e.g., Langevin v. Howard*, 363 So.2d 1209 (La. App. 2 Cir. 1978). These Article 1839 requirements serve both the precautionary and evidentiary functions traditionally associated with formal requirements for the transfer of immovable property.

The second paragraph of Article 1839 is equally important. A transfer of immovable property will be *effective as to third parties*—it will bind persons who were not a party to the original transfer and give constructive notice to them—only when the instrument effecting the transfer is filed for registry in the parish where the immovable property is located. *See* La. Civ. Code art. 1839 (1984). This rule is so important that it is repeated, albeit in a slightly different form, in several other places in the Civil Code. *See, e.g.,* La. Civ. Code art. 517 (1979, amended 2005); La. Civ. Code art. 3338 (2005). This rule is one of the cornerstones of what is called the **Louisiana Public Records Doctrine**. We will revisit the doctrine on numerous occasions in this casebook.

In contrast, the ownership of *movable* property may, generally speaking, be voluntarily transferred between the owner and a transferee as soon as a contract that purports to transfer the ownership has been formed, without any requirement for a writing. La. Civ. Code art. 518 (1979, amended 1984). Moreover, such a transfer will be effective as to third parties upon mere delivery of the object to the transferee. *Id.*

When the underlying transfer is a donation, however, additional rules of formality come into play. Whereas donations of *corporeal movables* can be made by mere delivery of the thing to the donee, donations of other things—immovables and *incorporeal movables*—will generally require authentic acts or compliance with other specific rules. *Compare* La. Civ. Code art. 1543 (2008) *with* La. Civ. Code arts. 1541 and 1550 (2008). Just as with immovables, Louisiana law generally insists upon a greater degree of formality for the transfer of *incorporeal* rights in movable things than it does for *corporeal* movable things that we can feel, touch and manually deliver.

A second consequence of classifying a thing as a movable or immovable arises in the context of the acquisition of ownership through means *other than* a voluntary transfer. The law of occupancy, for instance, which provides a method of acquiring ownership of objects not owned by others through taking up possession, applies only to corporeal movables. La. Civ. Code art. 3412 (1982). In the law of acquisitive prescription, which allows persons to acquire ownership of things by possessing them for specified periods of time, the prescriptive periods differ depending upon whether the thing is movable or immovable. Generally speaking, longer periods of possession are required to attain ownership of immovables. *Compare* La. Civ. Code arts. 3473 and 3486 (1982) (establishing ten and thirty year acquisitive prescription for immovables), *with* La. Civ. Code arts. 3489–91 (1982) (establishing three and ten year acquisitive prescription for movables).

The distinction between movable and immovable things also surfaces when a person transfers or encumbers immovable property and the parties to the transaction do not clearly specify whether they intend things connected to the immovable in some manner to be subject to the transfer or encumbrance. The parties to the transfer or encumbrance or interested third parties may ask, for instance, whether a transfer of land includes the trees or buildings found on the land or whether a mortgage on a house applies to its light fixtures, appliances or gutters. Louisiana law has developed a detailed set of legal rules to answer these questions in the absence of an express agreement by the parties. These rules fall under the heading of accession — a body of property law that concerns questions about the ownership of things that are produced or united with other things, either naturally or artificially. *See generally* La. Civ. Code arts. 482–516. Many rules of accession law turn on this basic distinction between movables and immovables.

Other areas of law entirely outside of the realm of property also implicate the distinction between movable and immovable things. For example, sometimes a dispute between a local taxing authority and a property owner will hinge on whether a particular object is classified as a movable or immovable (or a corporeal or incorporeal for that matter). *See e.g., Bridges v. National Financial Systems, Inc.*, 960 So.2d 202 (La. App. 1 Cir. 2007); *Willis-Knighton Medical Center v. Caddo-Shreveport Sales and Use Tax Comm'n*, 903 So.2d 1071 (2005). The same can be true in lawsuits involving the rights of contractors and workmen who have not been paid for work they have completed, *P.H.A.C. Services v. Seaways Int'l*, 403 So.2d 1199 (La. 1981), in tort cases involving liability for personal injury, *Coulter v. Texaco, Inc.*, 117 F.3d 909, 916–18 (5th Cir. 1997), or for environmental contamination. *United States Environmental Protection Agency v. New Orleans Public Service*, 826 F.2d 351 (5th Cir. 1987). Finally, as we will see in one of the featured decisions below, classification of a thing belonging to a deceased persons' succession can determine in which jurisdiction the succession must be opened. *In re Howard Marshall Charitable Remainder Trust*, 709 So.2d 662 (La. 1998).

Historical Classification of Immovables: The general principles used to distinguish between movables and immovables in Louisiana have shifted over time. In the 1870 Civil Code, Louisiana continued the tripartite division of immovable property inherited from the Code Napoléon. The 1870 Civil Code first created the category of ***immovables by their nature***, which included tracts of land, buildings and other constructions, La. Civ. Code art. 464 (1870), but also included a lengthy list of items such as wire screens, water pipes, gas pipes, radiators, light fixtures, lavatories, closets, sinks, furnaces and others, when they were "actually connected with or attached to the building by the owner for the use or convenience of the building." La. Civ. Code art. 467 (1870).

The category of ***immovables by destination*** included things placed on a tract of land for its service or improvement. La. Civ. Code art. 468 (1870). This category included items as diverse as cattle, agricultural implements, seeds, plants, fodder and manure, pigeons in a pigeon house, beehives, and sugar mills. *Id*. Also included in this category were any "movables as the owner has *attached permanently* to the tenement or building." *Id*. (emphasis added). The Civil Code elaborated on this final subset of movables that became immovable by destination through permanent attachment by explaining that "[t]he owner is supposed to have attached to his tenement or building forever such movables as are affixed to the same with plaster, or mortar, or such as cannot be taken off without being broken or injured, or without breaking or injuring the part of the building to which they are attached." La. Civ. Code art. 469 (1870). *Immovables by their object*, the last category of immovables, referred to rights and actions pertaining to immovable things, or what we now call incorporeal immovables. La. Civ. Code art. 470 (1870).

The 1978 Revision of the Civil Code suppressed the French tripartite classification of immovables and simplified the law by adopting just two basic categories of immovables—*corporeal immovables*, La. Civ. Code arts. 461–62 (1978), and *incorporeal immovables*. La. Civ. Code art. 470 (1978). The drafters of the revised Civil Code also adopted a concept known in German civil law as "essential component parts" (*wesentliche Bestandteile*) and made it a sub-category of things that fall under the general umbrella of immovables. Despite their legislative repeal, some of the old categories continue to appear in Louisiana property scholarship and jurisprudence. They have also resurfaced in the actual text of the revised Civil Code. *See* La. Civ. Code art. 466 (2008) (partially reviving the notion of immovables by their nature established in Article 468 of the 1870 Civil Code by defining component parts as things that "serve to complete a building of the same general type" or that "serve" the "principal use" of a construction other than a building).

In the following sections we will construct a general model for the classification of movables and immovables as well as corporeals and incorporeals. We will see how these categorizations relate to one another to create what is in essence a four part classification scheme which consists of corporeal movables and corporeal immovables, incorporeal movables and incorporeal immovables. A simple visualization of the scheme looks like this:

CORPOREAL MOVABLES	CORPOREAL IMMOVABLES
• Things that have a body and can be felt or touched, **Art. 461**, and that normally move or can be moved from one place to another. **Art. 471**.	• Tracts of land, with their component parts. **Art. 462**.
INCORPOREAL MOVABLES	INCORPOREAL IMMOVABLES
• Things that have no body but are comprehended by the understanding such as rights and obligations, **Art. 461**; rights, obligations and actions that apply to a movable thing; for example, bonds, annuities and interests or shares in entities possessing juridical personality. **Art. 473**.	• Things that have no body but are comprehended by the understanding such as rights and obligations, **Art. 461**; rights and actions that apply to immovable things; for example, personal servitudes established on immovables, predial servitudes, mineral rights, petitory and possessory actions. **Art. 470**.

As we move forward, we will explore each box.

B. Corporeal Movables

We begin our classification analysis by examining corporeal movables. Article 461 of the Civil Code defines "corporeals" as "things that have a body, whether animate or inanimate, and can be felt or touched." La. Civ. Code art. 461 (1978). Article 471 of the Civil Code adds that "corporeal movables" are "things, whether animate or inanimate, that normally move or can be moved from one place to another." La. Civ. Code art. 471 (1978). The revision comments to Article 471 explain that the "[d]efinition of corporeal movables is made, on principle, in accordance with notions of physical mobility." *Id.* rev. cmt. (a). The 1870 Civil Code similarly emphasized the portability of movables when it declared:

> Things movable by their nature are such as may be carried from one place to another, whether they move by themselves, as cattle, or cannot be removed without an extraneous power, as inanimate things.

La. Civ. Code art. 473 (1870). The current version of this article carries this broad definition forward by including in the category of movables both "animate" things, which can move on their own, and "inanimate" things, which require extraneous force to be moved. La. Civ. Code art. 471 (1978).

A synthesis of these definitions leads to the conclusion that corporeal movables are things with some physical embodiment that a person can feel or touch (or otherwise perceive through other senses as we will see below) *and* that can "normally" be moved around from one place to another. A motor vehicle, a bicycle, a watch, a piece of jewelry, an animal, a printed book—all these things would be classified as corporeal movables.

Many things that clearly fall into the category of corporeal movables can lose their identity as corporeal movables and become "immobilized" through their incorporation into an immovable, La. Civ. Code art. 465 (1978), through their attachment to and service to an immovable, La. Civ. Code art. 466 (2008), or when an owner declares a certain thing to be a component part of an immovable by filing a statement in the appropriate public records and placing the thing on the immovable for its service and improvement. La. Civ. Code art. 467 (1978). Thus, for example, hot water heaters, electric fans, construction materials, antique chandeliers, and even expensive factory equipment shipped to a factory from overseas can all shed their initial legal classification as corporeal movables and become fully immobilized component parts of an immovable.

For some items, though, we can quickly imagine complications. Is a mobile home placed on concrete pillars, connected to local utility services, and serving as a person's home or office for a long period of time still a movable? Is an "E-Book" distributed and enjoyed entirely through electronic media still a corporeal thing?

Before we explore the answers to these questions more fully, take note of one other important codal directive. The Civil Code makes the category of movables the residual category for all things "that the law does not consider as immovable."

La. Civ. Code art. 475 (1978). In other words, if doubt exists as to whether a particular thing should fall into the category of immovables or movables, Article 475 instructs that we must resolve that doubt in favor of classifying the thing as a *movable*. Notice, however, that the Civil Code does not put its thumb on the scale in cases questioning whether a thing is corporeal or incorporeal. The resolution of this question is left to the courts.

In the decision below, *South Central Bell Telephone Co. v. Barthelemy*, 643 So.2d 1240 (La. 1994), the Louisiana Supreme Court confronted the question of whether computer software programs that can be transported, viewed and used electronically with the aid of a computer are corporeal movables for purposes of local sales and use taxes. Do you find the court's reasoning persuasive?

South Central Bell Telephone Co. v. Barthelemy
643 So.2d 1240 (La. 1994)

HALL, Justice. We granted writs in this case to decide whether certain computer software constitutes tangible personal property taxable under the sales and use tax imposed by the City of New Orleans pursuant to Section 56 of the City Code. The district court classified the two types of computer software at issue—switching system and data processing software—as intangible, nontaxable property, and thus granted partial summary judgment in favor of the taxpayer, South Central Bell Telephone Co. (Bell). The court of appeal affirmed. We classify computer software as tangible, taxable property, and thus reverse and remand.

I.

During the pertinent taxing periods, January 1, 1986 through April 30, 1990, Bell operated a telephone system in Orleans Parish. As part of its system, Bell set up in the parish sixteen telephone central offices. Each telephone central office is a system, in and of itself, as well as part of the larger telephone system. Simply put, each central office is a place where the caller's telephone line is connected to the line of the person being called, if that person is served by the same central office, or, if not, to a line connected to another telephone central office. Depending upon the location of the person being called, a given call may pass through multiple central offices.

Each central office consists of, among other things, switching equipment. Switching equipment includes computer processors that are directed and operated by computer software programs. Each central office is unique; consequently, each central office requires specifically tailored software designed to meet that office's operations.

During the pertinent taxing periods, Bell licensed specific switching system software programs for use in specific central offices pursuant to license agreements confected out of state with three vendors, AT&T Technologies, Inc., Northern Telecomm and Erickson. Under these license agreements, Bell acquired the limited right to use such switching system software programs; the license agreements limited

Bell's right to use designated switching system software to designated switches in designated telephone central offices. More particularly, the license agreements prohibited Bell's transfer of such software to any switch other than the designated one; prohibited Bell's sublicense, assignment, sale or transfer of the programs; prohibited Bell's use of the programs after the license expired; and required that Bell maintain strict confidentiality with regard to the programs. The license agreements also reserved to the vendors ownership of, and proprietary rights in, the switching system software programs.

The vendors delivered the switching system software programs to Bell via magnetic tapes. Once received, the software programs were loaded onto Bell's switching system processors, and the magnetic tapes were either used or discarded. The vendors either billed Bell for City taxes on the magnetic tapes, or Bell automatically accrued such taxes on the magnetic tapes. Bell was neither billed by the vendors, nor accrued such taxes on the switching system software itself, however. The switching system software is thus one of the two types of software at issue in this case.

The second type of software at issue in this case is data processing software. This software guides the functions of the computers located in Bell's data processing center in Orleans Parish. Bell's data processing center handles basic accounting functions, including processing customer billings and payments, storing and managing customer data and maintaining a voucher and disbursement system. Bell acquired the right to use the data processing software through its affiliate, BellSouth Services, Inc. (BellSouth). BellSouth entered into a master license agreement regarding the software out of state. BellSouth also tested, evaluated and adapted the software out of state. BellSouth then transmitted the software electronically via telephone lines to Bell's modem in Orleans Parish. As with the switching system software, the license agreements limited Bell's rights to use the software and reserved to the vendors ownership of, and proprietary rights in, the data processing software. Bell also acquired certain maintenance services in relation to both types of software. Those services consisted of updating, enhancing and reformatting the software, and advising Bell with respect to certain usages of the software.

The taxes at issue in this case are use taxes levied by the City on Bell's use of the two types of software programs under § 56-21 of the City Code, and sales taxes levied by the City on Bell's payment for the related maintenance services under §§ 56-21 and 56-15(7) of the City Code.

In October 1990, following an audit, the City notified Bell of a proposed tax deficiency assessment for, among other things, Bell's use of the two types of computer software and Bell's payment for maintenance services for such software during the pertinent taxable period. Bell paid the full amount of the proposed tax deficiency under protest. Thereafter, in November 1990, Bell commenced the instant action, seeking to recover the taxes paid under protest and contending that the items at issue were not taxable under the pertinent provisions of the City Code.

Each party filed cross-motions for summary judgment. After a hearing on the motions, the trial court denied the City's motion and granted Bell's motion in part, finding that the sale/use tax of the City of New Orleans is not applicable to the licensing of the data processing software or to the switching software. In written reasons for judgment, the district court stated that under the essence of transaction test neither type of software at issue was taxable. Bell then filed a motion for amended judgment. Granting Bell's motion, the district court found that the sale/use tax of the City of New Orleans is not applicable to the maintenance of software, and granted judgment in favor of Bell for the sum of taxes paid under protest.

Affirming, the court of appeal reasoned that computer software does not fall within the definition of tangible personal property; rather, it falls within the definition of incorporeal property as it constitutes intellectual property. In support of the latter conclusion, the court cited jurisprudence from other jurisdictions holding that computer software is intangible because the essence of the transaction is the acquisition of intangible information or knowledge. South Cent. Bell Tel. Co. v. Barthelemy, 631 So. 2d 1340, 1343 (La. App. 4th Cir. 1/27/94). Likewise, the court found that since the maintenance services related to such intangible property and did not constitute repairs, such services were not subject to the City's sales tax. Id. at 8–9, 631 So. 2d at 1344–45.

On the City's writ application, we granted certiorari to consider the correctness of that decision. 94-0499 (La. 4/29/94), 637 So.2d 451.

II.

The city use tax is imposed by § 56-21 of the Code of the City of New Orleans:

> There is hereby levied, for general municipal purposes, a tax upon the sale at retail, the use, the consumption, the distribution and the storage for use or consumption in the city of each item or article of tangible personal property, upon the lease or rental of such property and upon the sale of services within the city. . . .

Tangible personal property is defined in § 56-18 of the City Code as follows:

> Personal property which may be seen, weighed, measured, felt or touched, or is in any other manner perceptible to the senses. The term tangible personal property shall not include stocks, bonds, notes or other obligations or securities.

Construing this provision, we held in *City of New Orleans v. Baumer Foods, Inc.*, 532 So. 2d 1381 (La. 1988), that the term 'tangible personal property' in the City Code's use tax is synonymous with corporeal movable property as used in the Louisiana Civil Code. 532 So. 2d at 1383. . . . The application of property law concepts in this tax context is an exception to the general rule that tax laws are sui generis, B. Oreck, Louisiana Sales & Use Taxation § 2.2 (1992) (hereinafter Oreck). The reasoning behind applying property concepts in such a tax context is that the use of the common law term tangible personal property by the legislature, or by the various political subdivisions, was not intended to import the common law into Louisiana for purposes of sales and use tax law, nor to require the development of an entirely new body of property law for sales and use tax purposes only, but rather, the term was intended to be interpreted consistently with our civilian property concepts embodied in the Civil Code. *Baumer Foods, Inc.*, 532 So. 2d at 1383, n.4 (citing *Exxon Corp.*, 353 So. 2d at 316–17); *Westside Sand Co.*, 454 So.2d at 456; *Stauffer Chem. Co.*, 506 So.2d at 1258.

The pertinent Civil Code provisions are Louisiana Civil Code articles 461, 471 and 473. Article 461 distinguishes between corporeals and incorporeals, providing:

> Corporeals are things that have a body, whether animate or inanimate, and can be felt or touched.

> Incorporeals are things that have no body, but are comprehended by the understanding, such as the rights of inheritance, servitudes, obligations, and right of intellectual property.

Article 471 further defines corporeal movables as things, whether animate or inanimate, that normally move or can be moved from one place to another. Article 473 further defines incorporeal movables as rights, obligations, and actions that apply to a movable thing. . . . Movables of this kind are such as bonds, annuities, and interests or shares in entities possessing juridical personality.

As a noted property law scholar has observed, under Roman law, "Material objects that could be felt or touched were given as illustrations of corporeal things. Incorporeal things were abstract conceptions, objects having no physical existence but having a pecuniary value. The illustrations given were rights of various kinds. . . ." A. N. Yiannopoulos, Louisiana Civil Law Treatise, Property § 25 (3d Ed. 1991) (hereinafter Yiannopoulos). The Louisiana Civil Code departed from the narrow Roman law conception that only tangible objects were corporeal; instead, the Louisiana Civil Code of 1870 declared that perceptibility by any of the senses sufficed for the classification of a material thing as corporeal. Yiannopoulos, § 26. While the 1978 revision to the property articles used slightly different language, the official comments indicate that it was not intended to change the law. La. Civ. Code art. 461, 1978 Official Revision Comment (a). The word 'felt' in [Article 461] refers to perceptibility by any of the senses. Yiannopoulos, § 26.

Planiol points out that corporeals are things and that incorporeals are rights. 1 M. Planiol, Treatise on the Civil Law, No. 2174 (12th Ed. La. State Law Inst. Trans. 1939) (hereinafter Planiol). Planiol goes on to state that corporeal movables comprise all things (physical objects) which are not immovable and that incorporeal movables are rights. 1 Planiol, Nos. 2238 and 2244. As illustrative of incorporeal movables, Planiol cites literary, artistic and industrial ownership, stating that the temporary monopoly of exploitation which the law grants to authors and inventors is also tantamount to a right of ownership. 1 Planiol, No. 2248. Hence, the civilian concept of corporeal movable encompasses all things that make up the physical world; conversely, incorporeals, i.e., intangibles, encompass the non-physical world of legal rights.

The term tangible personal property set forth in the City Code, and its synonymous Civil Code concept corporeal movable, must be given their properly intended meaning. Physical recordings of computer software are not incorporeal rights to be comprehended by the understanding. Rather, they are part of the physical world. For the reasons set out below, we hold the computer software at issue in this case constitutes corporeal property under our civilian concept of that term, and thus, is tangible personal property, taxable under § 56-21 of the City Code.

III.

The taxation of computer software has only been addressed once by Louisiana appellate courts. *United Companies Life Ins. Co. v. City of Baton Rouge*, 577 So. 2d 195 (La. App. 1st Cir. 1991), held that certain canned computer software was tangible property subject to sales taxation by the Parish of East Baton Rouge. That decision, however, was premised primarily on the taxpayer's attempt to invoke a prior exemption from taxation provided for by the Louisiana Department of Taxation's administrative regulations for certain computer software and did not rest on an analysis of tangibility versus intangibility. That decision is thus inapposite, and needs no further discussion.

The taxation of computer software has, however, been considered by numerous courts across the country. These courts have split on the issue and have employed various analyses in reaching their decisions. The first case generally recognized as addressing the tangibility of computer software for tax purposes was *District of Columbia v. Universal Computer Assoc., Inc.*, 151 U.S. App. D.C. 30, 465 F.2d 615 (D.C. Cir. 1972), which held computer software to be intangible, and therefore not taxable. The cases following soon thereafter, likewise held computer software to be intangible for sales, use and property tax purposes. See e.g. *State v. Central Computer Serv., Inc.*, 349 So. 2d 1160 (Ala. 1977); *County of Sacramento v. Assessment Appeals Bd. No. 2*, 32 Cal. App. 3d 654, 108 Cal. Rptr. 434 (1973); *First Nat'l Bank of Springfield v. Dep't of Revenue*, 85 Ill. 2d 84, 421 N.E.2d 175, 51 Ill. Dec. 667 (1981); *Greyhound Computer Corp. v. State Dep't of Assessments & Taxation*, 271 Md. 674, 320 A.2d 52 (Md. 1974); *Commerce Union Bank v. Tidwell*, 538 S.W.2d 405 (Tenn. 1976); *First Nat'l. Bank of Fort Worth v. Bullock*, 584 S.W.2d 548 (Tex. Civ. App. 1979).

However, as computer software became more prevalent in society, and as courts' knowledge and understanding of computer software grew, later cases saw a shift in courts' attitudes towards the taxability of computer software, and courts began holding computer software to be tangible for sales, use and property tax purposes. This trend began with two cases decided just one day apart—*Comptroller of the Treasury v. Equitable Trust Co.*, 296 Md. 459, 464 A.2d 248 (Md. 1983) and *Chittenden Trust Co. v. King*, 143 Vt. 271, 465 A.2d 1100 (Vt. 1983). The trend continued throughout the 1980s, see e.g. *Citizens & S. Sys., Inc. v. South Carolina Tax Comm'n*,

280 S.C. 138, 311 S.E.2d 717 (S.C. 1984); . . . *Northeast Datacom, Inc. v. City of Wallingford*, 212 Conn. 639, 563 A.2d 688 (1989).

The issue has also been the subject of numerous articles in various legal periodicals. Most commentators agree that computer software is tangible for sales, use and property tax purposes, and thus taxable, at least to some degree. See e.g. Paul P. Hanlon, *Computer Software and Sales Taxes: New Cases Take an Old Direction*, 2: 4 J. St. Tax'n 315 (1984); John M. Shontz, *Computer Software: Time to Pay a Fair Share*, Taxes — The Tax Magazine, Feb. 1990, at 162; Richard D. Harris, *Note, Property Taxation of Computer Software: Northeast Datacom, Inc., v. City of Wallingford*, 23 Conn. L. Rev. 161 (1990); Robert D. Crockett, *Comment, Software Taxation: A Critical Reevaluation of the Notion of Intangibility*, 1980 B.Y.U. L. Rev. 859 (1980); Robert L. Cowdrey, Note, *Software and Sales Tax: The Illusory Intangible*, 63 B.U. L. Rev. 181 (1983).

In addition, computer software has generally been held to constitute goods under the Uniform Commercial Code. See, e.g., *Schroders, Inc. v. Hogan Sys., Inc.*, 137 Misc. 2d 738, 522 N.Y.S.2d 404 (Sup. 1987). . . . See also *Note, Computer Programs as Goods Under the UCC*, 77 Mich. L. Rev. 1149 (1979); Bonna Lynn Horovitz, *Note, Computer Software as a Good Under the Uniform Commercial Code: Taking a Byte Out of the Intangibility Myth*, 65 B.U. L. Rev. 129 (1985); Shontz, *supra*, at 171–72.

Although interesting and helpful as background, the extensive jurisprudence and writings from other jurisdictions are not determinative or controlling of the issues presented in this case. We return to a discussion of the characteristics of computer software and classification thereof as tangible or intangible under Louisiana law.

IV. A.

To correctly categorize software, it is necessary to first understand its basic characteristics. In its broadest scope, software encompasses all parts of the computer system other than the hardware, i.e., the machine; and the primary non-hardware component of a computer system is the program. Horovitz, *supra*, at 183; Kurt Stohlgren, *Note, The Nature and Taxability of Computer Software*, 22 Washburn L. J. 103, 104 (1982); 77 Mich. L.Rev.at 1152 n. 17 (1979) (defining software expansively as the obverse of 'hardware'). In its narrowest scope, software is synonymous with program, which, in turn, is defined as a complete set of instructions that tells a computer how to do something. D. Tunick and D. Schechter, *State Taxation of Computer Programs: Tangible or Intangible?*, Taxes — The Tax Magazine, Jan. 1985, at 54, 56. Thus, another definition of software is a set of instructions or a body of information. Shontz, supra, at 162, 167.

When stored on magnetic tape, disc, or computer chip, this software, or set of instructions, is physically manifested in machine readable form by arranging electrons, by use of an electric current, to create either a magnetized or unmagnetized space. Donald H. Sanders, *Computers Today*, 229, 233 (1988); Schontz, *supra*, at 162 n.2; Stohlgren, *supra*, at 105. The computer reads the pattern of magnetized and unmagnetized spaces with a read/write head as on and off, or to put it another way,

0 and 1. This machine readable language or code is the physical manifestation of the information in binary form. Sanders, *supra*, at 167, 233; Stohlgren, *supra*, at 105.

Ordinarily, at least three program copies exist in a software transaction: (i) an original, (ii) a duplicate, and (iii) the buyer's final copy on a memory device. 77 Mich. L.Rev.at 1154 n. 27. More basically, "[A] program copy is developed at the seller's computer. To deliver a copy to the buyer, the seller duplicates the program copy on software, and transports the duplicates to the buyer's computer. The duplicate is read into the buyer's computer and copied on a memory device." 77 Mich.L.Rev.at 1154 n. 27.

B.

South Central Bell argues that the software is merely knowledge or intelligence, and as such is not corporeal and thus not taxable. We disagree with South Central Bell's characterization. The software at issue is not merely knowledge, but rather is knowledge recorded in a physical form which has physical existence, takes up space on the tape, disc, or hard drive, makes physical things happen, and can be perceived by the senses. See e.g. Crockett, *supra*, at 869–72; Cowdrey, *supra*, at 189–90. As the dissenting judge at the court of appeal pointed out, In defining tangible, 'seen' is not limited to the unaided eye, 'weighed' is not limited to the butcher or bathroom scale, and 'measured' is not limited to a yardstick. 93-1072, at p. 8–9, 631 So.2d at 1348 (dissenting opinion). That we use a read/write head to read the magnetic or unmagnetic spaces is no different than any other machine that humans use to perceive those corporeal things which our naked senses cannot perceive. See Crockett, *supra*, at 871–72; Shontz, *supra*, at 168; Cowdrey, *supra*, at 198–99.

The software itself, i.e. the physical copy, is not merely a right or an idea to be comprehended by the understanding. The purchaser of computer software neither desires nor receives mere knowledge, but rather receives a certain arrangement of matter that will make his or her computer perform a desired function. This arrangement of matter, physically recorded on some tangible medium, constitutes a corporeal body.

We agree with Bell and the court of appeal that the form of the delivery of the software — magnetic tape or electronic transfer via a modem — is of no relevance. However, we disagree with Bell and the court of appeal that the essence or real object of the transaction was intangible property. That the software can be transferred to various media, i.e., from tape to disk, or tape to hard drive, or even that it can be transferred over the telephone lines, does not take away from the fact that the software was ultimately recorded and stored in physical form upon a physical object. See Crockett, *supra*, at 872–74; Shontz, *supra*, at 168–70; Cowdrey, *supra*, at 188–90. As the court of appeal explained, and as Bell readily admits, the programs cannot be utilized by Bell until they have been recorded into the memory of the electronic telephone switch. 93-1072, at p. 6, 631 So.2d at 1343. The essence of the transaction was not merely to obtain the intangible knowledge or information, but rather, was to obtain recorded knowledge stored in some sort of physical form that Bell's computers could use. Recorded as such, the software is not merely an incorporeal idea to be comprehended, and would be of no use if it were. Rather, the software is given physical existence to make certain desired physical things happen.

One cannot escape the fact that software, recorded in physical form, becomes inextricably intertwined with, or part and parcel of, the corporeal object upon which it is recorded, be that a disk, tape, hard drive, or other device. Crockett, *supra*, at 871–72; Cowdrey, *supra*, at 188–90. That the information can be transferred and then physically recorded on another medium is of no moment, and does not make computer software any different than any other type of recorded information that can be transferred to another medium such as film, video tape, audio tape, or books.

The court of appeal rejected the analogy of computer software to such media as motion pictures, books, video tape, audio tape, etc . . . , which are taxable. Like the court of appeal, the earlier jurisprudence from other states uniformly rejected the analogy to such other artistic works, finding computer software distinguishable in several respects. More recent jurisprudence from other states, however, has recognized the appropriateness of such analogy, as have numerous commentators. The court of appeal distinguished the purchase of these types of storage devices, such as books, films, video and audio tapes, etc . . . , which hold stories, ideas, information and knowledge in physical form, by reasoning that the true essence of such transactions is the purchase of the tangible medium, not the intangible property (the artist's expressions) contained in that medium, and that without the specific tangible medium, the artist's expressions are useless, whereas computer software is separable from the tangible object upon which it is recorded. This distinction simply does not exist . . .

Once the software is reduced to physical form and has come to rest in the City of New Orleans, be it on tape, disk, hard drive, or other device the use tax attaches . . .

C.

The court of appeal found that computer software constitutes intellectual property and thus classified such software as an incorporeal under Louisiana Civil Code article 461. In so doing, the court of appeal relied on a line of out of state jurisprudence holding that intangible information stored on magnetic tapes or punch cards is not taxable. That line of jurisprudence is premised on the notion that a computer software program constitutes intangible knowledge or information . . .

We find this line of reasoning flawed and inconsistent with our civilian property concepts outlined above. As the dissenting court of appeal judge in this case perceptively pointed out, this reasoning confuses the corporeal computer software copy itself with the incorporeal right to the software. Explaining this often confused distinction, the dissenting judge noted that the incorporeal right to software is the copyright, which in this case, as is typical in such license agreements, was reserved to the vendors. 93-1072, at p. 2, 631 So.2d at 1345 (dissenting opinion). What Bell acquired, and what the City was attempting to tax, was not the copyright to the software, but the copy of the software itself. It was not the copyright that operated the telephone central office switching equipment, but rather the physical copy of the software . . .

We likewise decline to adopt the canned versus custom distinction invoked by a few state legislatures, commentators and courts. Canned software is software which has been pre-written to be used by more than one customer, or mass marketed; custom software is specially designed for exclusive use by one particular customer. Oreck, *supra*, § 2.2[1](a); Schontz, *supra*, at 164 n.10, 12; Richard Harris, *supra*, at 171–72. Under the canned versus custom distinction, canned programs are classified as taxable on the theory that the buyer acquires an end product; whereas, custom programs are classified as non-taxable services on the theory that the buyer acquires professional services. See e.g. Hanlon, *supra*; Robert W. McGee, *Recent Developments in the Taxation of Computer Software*, 19 Golden Gate U. L. Rev. 265, 272–74 (1989) . . .

In sum, once the information or knowledge is transformed into physical existence and recorded in physical form, it is corporeal property. The physical recordation of this software is not an incorporeal right to be comprehended. Therefore we hold that the switching system software and the data processing software involved here is tangible personal property and thus is taxable by the City of New Orleans . . .

Decree

For the foregoing reasons, we conclude that the court of appeal erred in affirming the trial court's judgment granting Bell's motion for partial summary judgment, with respect to the taxability of the software, and accordingly reverse the judgments of the lower courts in this regard. With respect to the taxability of the maintenance services, we affirm the court of appeal judgment. The case is remanded to the trial court for further proceedings consistent with this opinion.

AFFIRMED IN PART, REVERSED IN PART, AND REMANDED.

WATSON, Justice, concurring in part and dissenting in part. The software at issue was transmitted by two methods: (1) encoded on magnetic tape; or (2) electronically transferred via telephone wires and modems. The ordinary definition or generally prevailing meaning (C.C. art. 11) of tangible personal property would not cover either type of software. However, state jurisprudence gives the phrase an altered meaning which may be extended to cover the taped software. Applying the expansive reasoning of the jurisprudence, the lynch pin of holding the software to be tangible personal property seems to be that it is on a floppy disc, a tape or a compact disc and the value of the software is included in the price of the disc, tape or CD. The simplest example of this type of taxation is the purchase of a software program (such as WordPerfect, Windows or Excel) at a local computer store. Who can argue that only the value of the floppy discs and the manual may be taxed and not the program?

On the other hand, subscribers to bulletin boards can use modems and telephone connections to download software programs without being taxed. The analysis of software being taxed because it is bought on a tape or disc cannot be stretched logically to include data transmitted by modems and telephone wires.

I respectfully concur on taxing the South Central Bell software purchased on tapes, but dissent as to software received electronically.

Notes and Questions

1. Since *South Central Bell Telephone Co. v. Barthelemy*, 643 So.2d 1240 (La. 1994), was decided in 1994, the substance of the tax law in New Orleans has not changed. The tax trigger and the definition of tangible personal property is currently found in Sections 150-576 and 150-441 of the New Orleans City Code of Ordinances. As Justice Hall observed, "tangible personal property" is common law vernacular, which he directly translates into our codal category of corporeal movables. He hastens to emphasize that no substantive difference exists between these terms. This is not the first time we have seen the use of common law terminology. Does it matter that this is a tax case based on a city ordinance? Or should any "contamination" of the civilian language be avoided?

2. How does Justice Hall set up the analysis? Note that the majority explicates the law in Articles 471 and 473 of the Civil Code by elaborating upon its historical origins. In lieu of directly referencing Justinian's Institutes, Justice Hall relies upon Professor Yiannopoulos' treatise, which emphasizes that a corporeal is a thing perceivable by any of our senses. Justice Hall then turns to the French scholar Marcel Planiol. He condenses topical passages from Planiol's treatise to juxtapose corporeal things and incorporeal rights. Justice Hall omits, however, Planiol's observation that the Roman distinction between corporeals (*res corporales*) and incorporeals (*res incorporales*) made sense then because corporeals could only be acquired "in special ways" (*mancipatio, traditio*) which were inapplicable to rights" and because "the domain[s]" of property and contract were more sharply delineated than they are today. 1 Marcel F. Planiol, Treatise on the Civil Law, No. 2178 (12th ed. La. State Law Inst. Trans. 1959).

In any event, what does Justice Hall consider to be the decisive criterion of a corporeal thing? Why does the court reject the plaintiff's submission that software is mere knowledge or intelligence? Make a list of the factors assembled by the court. Do you agree or disagree? In his concurring and dissenting opinion, Justice Watson focuses on the "method of transmission" as the decisive criterion for determining whether the software should be classified as corporeal or incorporeal. Is this any more or less convincing than Justice Hall's approach?

3. Although the *South Central Bell* decision is more than 25 years old, its premise is still applicable in Louisiana. In 2014, the Court of Appeal for the Fifth Circuit used the analytical framework created in *South Central Bell* but determined that the trial court did not err when it found that video on demand (VOD) and pay per view (PPV) programming did *not* constitute "computer software" and was, therefore, *not* tangible "personal property" for purposes of local sales and use taxation. *Normand*

v. Cox Communications Louisiana, 167 So.3d 156, 159–62 (La. App. 5 2014). In *Normand*, officials who worked for Cox Communications testified that VOD and PPV programming are real-time data streams in a digital format that must be interpreted by software or "firmware." *Id.* at 160. As a result, these data streams are not amenable to storage on physical tape and, indeed, disappear as soon as they reach a customer's television. *Id.* at 160–61. What about cloud computing? Does it rely on (tangible) software? Does the location of the server (internet, local network, user's personal hard drive) matter? *See* Eric Griffith, *What is Cloud Computing*, PC Mag. (May 3, 2016), https://www.pcmag.com/article2/0,2817,2372163,00.asp (Sept. 13, 2018).

4. As the Louisiana Supreme Court acknowledged in *South Central*, courts in other states have employed various tests to determine whether software is tangible or intangible. Some have focused on the end product of a computer software transaction—the transmission of knowledge—and thus classified software as intangible. *Commerce Union Bank v. Tidwell*, 538 S.W.2d 405, 408 (Tenn. 1976). Other courts employ an "essence of the transaction" test, which looks to the essence of what is purchased. Since software is knowledge, despite the tangible magnetic strip often present in software transactions, it classifies as intangible. *Cache County v. Property Tax Div. of Tax Comm'n*, 922 P.2d 758, 768 (1996) (classifying custom software as intangible); *First Nat'l Bank v. Bullock*, 584 S.W.2d 548, 550 (Tex. Civ. App. 1979) (finding canned software to be intangible because the essence of the transaction was for intangible knowledge that could be delivered electronically); *Compuserve, Inc. v. Lindley*, 535 N.E.2d 360, 365–66 (Ohio App. 3 1987) (finding custom software was intangible and thus non-taxable). Some courts have classified software as either a good (taxable) or a service (not taxable). Other courts have analogized software to other taxable property such as films, books, and audio cassettes. Christine E. Reinhard, *Tangible or Intangible—Is That The Question? Conflict in the Texas Tax Classification System of Computer Software*, 29 St. Mary's L.J. 871, 895–905 (1997–1998).

In *Gilbreath v. General Elec. Co.*, 751 So.2d 705 (Fla. App. 5 Dist. 2000), a Florida District Court of Appeal held that customized computer software was *intangible personal property* and thus not capable of being subject to ad valorem property taxes by local governments in that state and specifically addressed the Louisiana Supreme Court's decision in *South Central Bell*. The crucial portion of that court's reasoning follows:

> While no appellate court in Florida has addressed the issue, the courts of our sister states have spoken with some frequency. The vast majority of cases cited by the parties and located by the Court have concluded that software is not tangible personal property. See, e.g., *District of Columbia v. Universal Computer Associates, Inc.*, 465 F.2d 615 (D.C. Cir. 1972); *Computer Associates International, Inc. v. City of East Providence*, 615 A.2d 467 (R.I. 1992); *Northeast Datacom v. City of Wallingford*, [212 Conn. 639,]563 A.2d 688 (1989); *Protest of Strayer*, [239 Kan. 136,]716 P.2d 588 (1986); *Honeywell Information Systems, Inc. v. Maricopa County*, [118 Ariz. 171,]575 P.2d 801 (1977); *Matter of Western Resources, Inc.*, [22 Kan. App. 2d 593,] 919 P.2d 1048 (1996).

The court in *Dallas Central Appraisal District v. Tech Data Corp.*, 930 S.W.2d 119 (Tex. App. 1996), nicely summarizes the theory. In holding that computer application software was not tangible personal property subject to local taxation, the appellate court noted that "the 'imperceptible binary impulses' that make up computer application software are not capable of being 'seen, weighed, measured, felt or otherwise perceived by the senses.'" It noted that the essence of the property is the software itself, and not the tangible medium on which the software might be stored.

The Florida Legislature obviously agreed. In amending Section 192.001(19), it made a sharp distinction between the information, program or routine (the "imperceptible binary impulses"), and the medium on which the information, program or routine is carried. That is to say, as the court interprets this amendment, the Legislature determined that the disk or tape itself was tangible personal property, but the information, program or routine was not. The remainder of the statute clearly indicates that the information, program or routine is not subject to local taxation, because it "does not increase the value of the computer or computer-related peripheral equipment, or any combination thereof."

The most significant case holding to the contrary comes out of the State of Louisiana. In *South Central Bell v. Barthelemy*, 643 So.2d 1240 (La. 1994), the Supreme Court of Louisiana held that software was tangible personal property, and therefore subject to local taxation. Unlike the Florida Legislature and the other courts cited above that have considered the issue, the view of the Louisiana court was that under its civil law system software consisted of knowledge recorded in a physical form. As those physical forms—discs, tapes, hard drives, etc.—have a physical existence, take up space, and make things happen, they are tangible and taxable.

The court disagrees, and concludes that the views expressed in the other cited cases are more persuasive. Perhaps the Supreme Court of Connecticut stated it most succinctly. In *Northeast Datacom, Inc. v. City of Wallingford*, [212 Conn. 639,]563 A.2d 688 (1989), the court determined that the physical components of software—the same discs, tapes, hard drives, etc.—discussed by the Louisiana court, are only "tangential incidents" of the program. It noted that "the fact that tangible property is used to store or transmit the software's binary instructions does not change the character of what is fundamentally a classic form of intellectual property."

Accordingly, based on the evidence presented, and the authorities cited, the software components of the two prototype simulators were intangible personal property and not properly taxed by the Property Assessor.

Gilbreath, 751 So.2d at 708–09. *See also Nikolitis v. Verizon Wireless Personal Communications, L.P.*, 9 So.3d 690, 693–94 (Fla. App. 4 Dist. 2009) (following *Gilbreath*).

For an analysis of additional case law addressing the question of whether *customized* computer software is taxable as tangible personal property, see Patricia Kussmann, *Applicability of State Sales and Use Tax Exemptions for Custom Programs Prepared to Special Order of Customer*, 50 A.L.R.6th 261 (2009). For commentary on *South Central Bell*, see Suzanne Bagert, South Central Bell v. Barthelemy: *The Louisiana Supreme Court Determines That Computer Software is Tangible Personal Property*, 69 Tul. L. Rev. 1367, 1376 (1994–1995) (praising the Louisiana Supreme Court's technological sophistication in focusing its analysis on the tangible nature of the computer readable code rather than on the diskette itself); Alia Susann Zohur, *Acknowledging Information Technology under the Civil Code: Why Software Transactions Should Not Be Treated as Sales*, 50 Loy. L. Rev. 461 (2004) (asserting that software is intellectual property, which is intangible and incorporeal, but does not fit within the Louisiana Civil Code's classification of things).

5. *What about canned software programs?* Some states make the distinction between canned software, which is mass-produced for numerous consumers and can be purchased from retail stores or vendors, from custom software, which is personalized for a particular customer's computer system and often involves expert assistance. The courts which make this distinction generally classify canned software as tangible property and customized software as a service and thus intangible. Christine E. Reinhard, *Tangible or Intangible — Is That the Question? Conflict in the Texas Tax Classification System of Computer Software*, 29 St. Mary's L.J. 871, 892–94 (1998). *See also Maccabees Mut. Life Ins. Co. v. State, Dep't of Treasury, Revenue Div.*, 332 N.W.2d 561, 564 (Mich. App. 1983).

6. Money in the form of cash is certainly a corporeal movable. A.N. Yiannopoulos, 2 Civil Law Treatise: Property § 148, n. 2 at 342 (4th ed. 2001). But what about funds withdrawn from a savings account? *See Succession of Miller*, 405 So.2d 812, 818 (La. 1981) (on rehearing). Or funds derived from a mineral lease bonus and deposited in a court registry? *See Steinau v. Pyburn*, 229 So.2d 153 (La. App. 2 Cir. 1969).

7. How would you classify the federal Low Income Housing Tax Credit (LIHTC), which offers an indirect federal subsidy to finance the construction and rehabilitation of low-income affordable rental housing? *See Williams v. The Muses. Ltd. 1*, 203 So.3d 558 (La. App. 4 Cir. 2016) (determining that LIHTC is "an intangible benefit flowing to investors on affordable housing developments" and therefore, an "incorporeal movable, . . . which is exempt from ad valorem taxes under La. Const., art. VII, § 21(18)").

C. Corporeal Immovables

With an understanding of corporeal movables in place, we now examine the category of corporeal immovables under Louisiana law. Rather than provide a clear definition as it does with corporeal movables, the Civil Code approaches this category *indirectly* by listing numerous sub-classes of corporeal things that fall within the general category of immovables. Classifying a thing as immovable turns not so much on the thing's inherent physical characteristics, but on a legislative determination that a particular species of things will fall within the general category of immovables. Immovability "in fact" is not in itself a prerequisite to immovability "in law." *P.H.A.C. Services, Inc. v. Seaways International, Inc.*, 403 So.2d 1199, 1203 (La. 1981). Thus, things that are physically capable of being moved from place to place, or are designed to be moved, might, nonetheless, be classified as immovable.

1. Tracts of Land

Article 462 of the Civil Code provides that "[t]racts of land, with their component parts, are immovables." La. Civ. Code art. 462 (1978). Pursuant to codal directive, tracts of land will *always* be classified as corporeal immovables. Unlike corporeal movables that can lose their original movable status and become immobilized, tracts of land can never lose their immovable status. But what does the Civil Code mean by "land"?

The revision comments to Article 462 state that "[l]ands may be defined as portions of the surface of the earth" and then adds that "ownership of land carries, by accession, the ownership of 'all that is directly above and under it.'" La. Civ. Code art. 462 rev. cmt. (c) (1978) (quoting La. Civ. Code art. 505 (1870)). Article 490 of the Civil Code restates the second maxim—one of the primary rules of the law of accession—in almost identical language: "Unless otherwise provided by law, the ownership of a tract of land carries with it the ownership of everything that is directly above or under it." La. Civ. Code art. 490 (1979).

Article 462, however, does not directly address the following problem. Current technology makes it possible to scoop up large amounts of soil and other material from one tract of land and deposit it onto another. When is such material considered a corporeal movable and when will it remain an inseparable part of a tract of land and thus a corporeal immovable? Consider the following decision.

Landry v. LeBlanc
416 So.2d 247 (La. App. 3 Cir. 1982)

DOUCHET, Judge. Plaintiff-lessor brought suit to recover damages allegedly occasioned by defendant-leasee's removal of topsoil from the leased premises. Defendant asserted plaintiff's agent had authorized him to remove and haul away the soil, and presented parol evidence in support thereof, over plaintiff's objection, which was admitted. The trial judge held that lessor had not sustained her burden of proof and dismissed plaintiff's demands. Plaintiff appeals. We reverse.

The parties entered into a verbal farm lease for 8 [and] 1/2 acres in 1976. The lessee, Adley LeBlanc, maintained the farm lease for the first year and the lease was thereafter verbally renewed for 1977 and 1978. Immediately after the third renewal period commenced, on or about April 1, 1978, lessee made arrangements with R. J. Thibodeaux Shell Yard, Inc. to remove the headland comprising the southeast portion of the property allegedly without lessor's permission. Thereafter, the lessor, Adelaide L. Landry, notified the lessee that the lease would not be renewed. Lessor additionally requested that the land be returned to its original condition by replacing the soil which had been removed earlier that year. Suit followed wherein the lessor claimed lessee's failure to return the property to its original condition resulted in damage to the property consisting of cost of returning the property to its original condition. The lessee filed an exception of prescription which was overruled. At trial on the merits, the lessee claimed that he received permission to remove the soil from one Lucien Landry, brother of plaintiff and lessor's alleged agent. Tommy Thibodeaux, whose father owned property adjacent to plaintiff's, testified that he excavated the unplowed land at the end of the plowed furrow on the leased premises at defendant's request and that the removal thereof improved the drainage of both fields. Plaintiff denied any authorization to alter the property.

The trial judge was of the opinion that the lessor failed in her burden of proof and rendered judgment in favor of lessee. Plaintiff-lessor appeals alleging that . . . the trial judge erred in admitting parol evidence relative to the alleged agent's authorization for defendant to remove the soil.

Plaintiff alleged in her pleadings that she owned the property involved herein; that the property was leased to defendant; that defendant removed the soil without her permission; that the lessee was informed that the lease would terminate; that defendant was instructed to cease his actions and return the soil, and as a result of lessee's refusal thereof plaintiff suffered damages, to-wit: loss in property value, drainage and erosion problems. Defendant answered asserting the affirmative defense of mandate, alleging plaintiff's brother, Lucien Landry, as agent of lessor, had granted authority for removal of the topsoil. Our review of the record discloses that plaintiff substantiated her allegation that defendant breached the verbal lease. The only matter seriously disputed is whether lessee's removal of the soil was authorized. Thus resolution of the dispute turns on whether defendant established the affirmative defense of mandate.

Topsoil is immovable as tracts of land with their component parts are immovables. LSA-C.C. Art. 462. Comment (c) to Art. 462 provides: "Lands may be defined as portions of the surface of the earth. The ownership of land carries, by accession, the ownership of 'all that is directly above and under it.' C.C. Art. [490]." Related thereto is the Louisiana Mineral Code Section listing substances to which the code applies: "The provisions of this Code are applicable to . . . rights to explore for or mine or remove from the land the soil itself. . . ." LSA-R.S. 31:4. The right to minerals is an incorporeal immovable. LSA-R.S. 31:18. Thus, whether Civil Code or Mineral Code articles are applied, the result remains the same that the interest asserted herein is to an immovable. Cf: LSA-R.S. 31:2. Plaintiff-owner's topsoil did not become movable by its placement in trucks to be hauled away.

As the property involved was immovable, any transfer of ownership thereto was required to be in writing. LSA-C.C. Art. 2275. Indeed any dealing with realty, onerous or gratuitous, must be in writing unless the adverse party admits under oath that he made a contract affecting realty. *Williams v. Alexander*, 193 So.2d 94 (La. App. 1st Cir. 1966). Mineral leases are subject to this requirement of writing. *Bills v. Fruge*, 360 So.2d 661 (La. App. 3rd Cir. 1978), writ denied 362 So.2d 792. As there was no such admission under oath, the verbal sale of immovable property was null. LSA-C.C. Art. 2440. That the parties admittedly had a preexisting lease agreement is of no consequence as the oral lease did not effect (sic) an ownership transfer of the immovable topsoil. In this regard it should be noted that we are not concerned with defendant's use of the immovable property per se, to which the parol evidence prohibition would not apply, but rather the transfer thereof. It is the rights to immovables acquired under a lease which cannot be established by parol evidence. *Noble v. Plouf*, 154 La. 429, 97 So. 599 (1923); *Landis v. Agnew*, 154 La. 435, 97 So. 601 (1923); *Slay v. Smith*, 368 So.2d 1144 (La. App. 3rd Cir. 1979); *Guy Scroggins, Inc. v. Emerald Exploration*, 401 So.2d 680 (La. App. 3rd Cir. 1981), *writ denied* 404 So.2d 1257.

Likewise, parol evidence could not be received to prove an agency to buy or sell immovable property, *McKenzie v. Bacon*, 40 La. Ann. 157, 4 So. 65 (1888). A contract to sell affecting title to immovable property is required to be in writing and any mandate authorizing Lucien Landry to dispose of such property must have been express, special, and also in writing. LSA-C.C. Art.2997; *Tchoupitoulas, Inc. v. McCullough*, 349 So.2d 346 (La. App. 4th Cir. 1977), writ denied 351 So.2d 166. None of the above formalities were followed. In fact, Lucien Landry testified at trial that he did not authorize lessee-LeBlanc to remove the soil. The trial judge erred in admitting parol evidence concerning Landry's alleged mandate.

Considering all admissible evidence we conclude that the trial judge was clearly wrong in finding plaintiff had failed to establish her claim by a preponderance of evidence. Accordingly we turn to the issue of damages. Clarence Thibodeaux, a civil engineer accepted as an expert in said field, estimated that 287 cubic yards of soil had been removed from the headland. According to Miller Lewis, Jr., who was accepted as a "dirt hauling" expert, the cost of a seven yard load, or truck full, of dirt was $ 59.20 and testified that forty (40) loads would be required to fill the excavation in question. Clarence Begnaud, a motor grader operator expert, testified that the cost to level the dirt is $ 100.00. Defendant offered no testimony to controvert these figures. Therefore we find that the sum required to return the property to its original condition to be Two Thousand, Four Hundred Sixty-Eight ($ 2,468.00) Dollars and hereby award plaintiff this sum as damages with legal interest from the date of judicial demand. . . .

For the reasons set forth above the judgment appealed is reversed and set aside. It is now ordered, adjudged and decreed that there be a judgment herein in favor of the plaintiff, Adelaide L. Landry, and against the defendant, Adley LeBlanc, for the sum of $ 2,468.00, together with legal interest thereon from date of judicial demand until paid, and all costs, both in the trial court and of this appeal.

REVERSED AND RENDERED.

Notes and Questions

1. In *Landry v. LeBlanc*, 416 So.2d 247 (La. App. 3 Cir. 1982), the court was required to address two basic issues. The first concerned the classification of the topsoil itself. Had it become movable because the defendant/lessee, Adley Leblanc, placed it in trucks and hauled it away, or was it an immovable component part of the land? Once the court determined that, at the time LeBlanc removed the topsoil from the land, it was a component part of the land, the court analyzed whether the defendant was authorized to remove the topsoil by the plaintiff/lessor, Adelaide Landry, or by her brother and purported agent, Lucien Landry. Crucially, the defendant did not have any written evidence to support his argument that the removal of the topsoil was authorized. Instead, he relied on purported oral communications.

As we stated in the beginning of this chapter, Article 1839 of the Civil Code generally requires that any transfer of immovable property be made by authentic act or act under private signature, unless the transferee can prove the existence of a transfer by interrogating the transferor under oath. La. Civ. Code art. 1839 (1984). This insistence upon some kind of writing to establish a transfer of immovable property is consistent with the principle previously embodied in Article 2275 of the 1870 Civil Code, as the opinion in *Landry* notes, and is also consistent with another important provision, Article 1832 of the Civil Code. That article provides:

Art. 1832. Written form required by law

When the law requires a contract to be in written form, the contract may not be proved by testimony or by presumption, unless the written instrument has been destroyed, lost, or stolen.

La. Civ. Code art. 1832 (1984). As its revision comments explain, the principal idea is that "where a writing is required for the validity of an act," *e.g.*, for the transfer of immovable property or to establish a mandate to transfer immovable property as in *Landry*, "that act may not be proved by any other means." *Id.* rev. cmt. (b). So, for example, oral testimony about the parties' intentions would be theoretically inadmissible to prove the *existence* of a contract to transfer immovable property unless one of the exceptional circumstances mentioned in the end of the article is present.

Closely related to Article 1832 is Article 1848 of the Civil Code, which focuses on the admissibility of what lawyers often call "parole evidence" to "negate or vary" the contents of a written act. That article provides that "[t]estimonial or other evidence may not be admitted to negate or vary the contents of an authentic act or an act under private signature," but, just like article 1832, goes on to list several situations in which parole evidence can be admitted to challenge a written act. La. Civ. Code art. 1848 (1984). *See also* La. Civ. Code art. 2276 (1870).

2. Note that a lease, a contract that does not transfer ownership, is not subject to such strict rules of formality. *See* La. Civ. Code art. 2668 *et seq.* (2004). The Civil Code defines a lease as a contract "by which one party, the lessor, binds himself to give to the other party, the lessee, the use and enjoyment of a thing for a term in exchange for the rent that the lessee binds himself to pay." La. Civ. Code art. 2668 (2004). Unlike a transfer of ownership of immovable property, a lease, even if it involves immovable property, may be made orally or in writing. *See* La. Civ. Code art. 2681 (2004). Did the oral lease confected by Landry as lessor and Leblanc as lessee authorize Leblanc to remove the topsoil? Consider La. Civ. Code art. 2683(3) (2004).

3. Consult the codal provisions governing the contract of mandate. *See* La. Civ. Code arts. 2989–3032 (1997). Article 2989 defines the mandate as a contract through which one person (the principal) confers authority on another person (the mandatary) for purposes of transacting affairs for the principal. While Article 2993(1) of the Civil Code declares that the mandate is not subject to any particular form requirement, Article 2993(2) of the Civil Code, when viewed in conjunction with Article 1839 of the Civil Code, determines the outcome of *Landry*.

Problem

Imagine yourself in a Garden Center. You locate the stacks of thirty-pound bags labeled *topsoil*, purchase several bags and go home. How would you classify the topsoil inside the thirty-pound bags? At home, you spread the topsoil in your garden. How would you classify the topsoil now spread in your garden? Would a transfer of your land include the topsoil that you just purchased? Assume, instead, you use a shovel to fill up several bags with soil from your garden. Has the classification of the soil changed? What if, prior to removing the soil, you mortgage your land to a bank or credit union? *See* La. Civ. Code art. 468 (1978).

2. Component Parts of Tracts of Land

Recall that Article 462 of the Civil Code provides that "[t]racts of land, with their component parts, are immovables." La. Civ. Code art. 462 (1978). Article 463 of the Civil Code provides the next crucial subject of analysis by defining component parts.

Art. 463. Component parts of tracts of land

Buildings, other constructions permanently attached to the ground, standing timber, and unharvested crops or ungathered fruits of trees, are component parts of a tract of land when they belong to the owner of the ground.

La. Civ. Code art. 463 (1978). The last clause of this article, "when they belong to the owner of the ground," is critical to understanding component parts. At first glance Article 463 appears just to list items that fall into the category of "component parts of tracts of land" when they happen to "belong to the owner of the land," that is, when there is *unity of ownership* between a thing found on the land and the land itself. Read Article 463 in conjunction with Article 464, and Article 474:

Art. 464. Buildings and standing timber as separate immovable

Buildings and standing timber are separate immovables when they belong to a person other than the owner of the land.

La. Civ. Code art. 464 (1978).

Art. 474. Movables by anticipation

Unharvested crops and ungathered fruits of trees are movables by anticipation when they belong to a person other than the landowner. When encumbered with security rights of third persons, they are movables by anticipation in so far as the creditor is concerned.

The landowner may, by act translative of ownership or by pledge, mobilize by anticipation unharvested crops and ungathered fruits of trees that belong to him.

La. Civ. Code art. 474 (1978).

Reading all of these articles together, we can see that **buildings** and **standing timber** will *always be* considered immovables. When they are owned by the owner of the land, that is, when there is unity of ownership, they are simply component parts of the land under Article 463. When they are owned by *someone other than the owner of the land* upon which they are found, that is, when there is no unity of ownership, they are classified as "separate immovables" under Article 464. Put differently, as the revision comments note, "buildings separated in ownership from the land on which they stand are distinct immovables for all purposes." La. Civ. Code art. 464 rev. cmt. (b) (1978). Likewise, "standing timber segregated in ownership from the land on which it stands is a separate immovable." *Id.* rev. cmt. (c).

Articles 463, 464, and 474 thus suggest that it is possible for the ownership of land and the ownership of things found growing from or attached to the land to be legally *segregated* from the land. *See also* La. Civ. Code art. 491 (1979). This so-called *horizontal segregation,* in which one person owns the land and another person owns something else located on top of it, departs from the old Roman adage *superficies solo cedit,* which treated a tract of land and what was attached to it as a unit. This notion of horizontally separated ownership contradicts the intuitive, default rule of accession in relation to immovables found in Article 490 of the Civil Code. *See* La. Civ. Code art. 490 (1979) ("Unless otherwise provided by law, the ownership of a tract of land carries with it the ownership of everything that is directly above or under it."). But the possibility of horizontal segregation of ownership permits the extensive use of contractual freedom to facilitate the development and exploitation of land and resources associated with land. By classifying buildings and standing timber as *separate immovables* when they are owned by someone other than the owner of the land, the Civil Code also assures that the rules of formality required for the transfer of immovable property are applicable to transfers of these kinds of things even when their ownership has been horizontally segregated from the land.

With regard to the other two categories listed in Article 462 — "other constructions permanently attached to the ground, unharvested crops and ungathered fruits" — different sets of rules apply. Consider *other constructions permanently attached to the ground* first. What kinds of things are we talking about? A water tower, an electrical tower, an advertising sign, railroad tracks, or an oil drilling rig, or a stop sign, a telephone exchange box or light pole would all be *other constructions permanently attached to the ground*. If these *other constructions permanently attached to the ground* are *owned by the same person as the owner of the ground*, we classify them as "component parts of the land" under Article 463, consistent with our baseline rule of accession found in Article 490 of the Civil Code. La. Civ. Code art. 463 (1978).

It is possible, however, for these kinds of things to be owned by someone other than the owner of the ground. In that case, we do *not* classify them as component parts of an immovable. Instead, we classify them as *movables*. La. Civ. Code art. 464 rev. cmt. (d) (1988). If some otherwise corporeal movable thing is only *loosely* or *temporarily*, but not "permanently," attached to the ground, it is not eligible for this analysis at all. In that case the item is simply a corporeal movable.

In the absence of separate ownership of **unharvested crops** and **ungathered fruits,** we fall back upon the default rule established in Article 463 and classify these things as component parts of the land. La. Civ. Code art. 463 (1978). But when unharvested crops or ungathered fruits are *owned by someone other than the owner of the land*, as when a tenant farmer leases a farm or orchard and the terms of the lease provide for the tenant to keep the crop harvested from the land or the fruits gathered from the orchard, the unharvested crops or ungathered fruits are classified as *movables by anticipation*. La. Civ. Code art. 474 (1978).

When the things enumerated in Article 463 are classified as a component part of an immovable, they can be swept into a transfer or encumbrance of the land under Article 469 of the Civil Code, unless they are specifically excluded. *See* La. Civ. Code art. 469 (1978) ("The transfer or encumbrance of an immovable includes its component parts."). But when segregation of ownership exists, then separate immovables, other constructions permanently attached to the ground classified as movables, and movables by anticipation are *not included* in a transfer or encumbrance of the underlying immovable unless the terms of the transfer or encumbrance specifically call for them to be included.

Equally significant, under the law of accession, all of the items listed in Article 463 — buildings, other constructions permanently attached to the ground, standing timber, and unharvested crops or ungathered fruits — are generally presumed to be owned by the owner of the ground. La. Civ. Code art. 491 (1979). This presumption can be overcome, however, if an instrument attesting to separate ownership (a lease, an act of sale, an act of donation) is filed in the registry of the conveyance records of the parish where the immovable property is located. *Id.* The instrument will give notice to the world, and to third parties in particular, that a horizontal separation of ownership exists. In some cases, though, particularly when third parties are *not* involved, the presumption of unified ownership can be overcome through other means, including oral testimony or written evidence that is not found in any public registry. *See, e.g., Marcellous v. David,* 252 So.2d 178 (La. App. 3 Cir. 1971).

Consider our tenant farmer above. If the terms of his lease provide that both the tenant and the landowner each get a portion of the crops and fruits, the crops and fruits are both immovable property and movables by anticipation. The portion owned by the landowner is a component part of his immovable, while the tenant's portion is movable by anticipation. When the lease is filed in the conveyance records, this separation of ownership will be effective vis-à-vis third parties.

a. Buildings

Nowhere does the Civil Code offer a definition of the term "building." Its plain meaning suggests a structure with a roof and walls intended for permanent human occupation or habitation. But many important questions remain. How permanent must the structure be? Must it be attached to the surface of the earth through some kind of foundation? How large must the structure be? Do people have to be present in the building or make use of it all year or all day? If the structure can be moved from one place to another without causing substantial damage to the structure, should it still be classified as a building? Must the structure be intended to be stationary to be a building?

In the following two decisions, courts attempt to develop criteria to distinguish between structures that should be classified as "buildings," "other constructions," or perhaps just corporeal movables. Are the approaches documented below consistent with one another? Could other factors be influencing the court's classification conclusions in these cases?

P.H.A.C. Services, Inc. v. Seaways International, Inc.

403 So.2d 1199 (La. 1981)

DIXON, Justice. This is a suit instituted by two unpaid subcontractors who supplied labor and materials for the construction of an offshore drilling platform living quarters unit; defendants are the general contractor and the owner. The primary issue is what, if any, privileges are available to these plaintiffs. The unit involved in this litigation is a three story steel structure which was built on blocks at a construction site in St. Mary Parish. It was then transported by the owner, Pennzoil Company and Pennzoil Producing Company, and attached to an offshore drilling platform located in the Gulf of Mexico off the coast of Texas.

Pennzoil contracted with Seaways International, Inc. for construction of the unit. This contract was not recorded and no bond was required of Seaways as contractor. Seaways contracted with P.H.A.C. Services, Inc. for installation of plumbing, heating and air conditioning in the unit, and with Acoustical Spray Insulators, Inc. for labor and acoustical materials for the unit.

It is uncontested that P.H.A.C. and Acoustical performed their work in accordance with their subcontracts with Seaways, and that they have not been paid. They have timely filed lien affidavits, and have instituted suit to enforce their privileges.

Three statutes are relied upon by plaintiffs: R.S. 9:4801 et seq. (Private Works Act); R.S. 9:4861 (dealing with privileges on oil, gas, and water wells), and, in the alternative, R.S. 9:4502 (dealing with privileges on movables). The trial court ruled that the only privilege available to the plaintiffs is that granted by R.S. 9:4861 et seq. The Court of Appeal disagreed, and held that that only the Private Works Act, R.S. 9:4801 et seq. is applicable. . . . This court granted writs on application of all parties. . . .

[The court's analysis of La. Rev. Stat. § 9:4861 et seq., which creates a privilege in favor of certain persons who perform work in connection with the exploration for oil, gas or water, and why it did not afford the plaintiffs any privilege on the living quarters, is omitted. Eds.]

The Private Works Act, R.S. 9:4801 et seq. confers a privilege to certain persons who supply labor or materials "for the erection, construction, repair, or improvement of immovable property." R.S. 9:4801. The parties agree that the act applies if the living quarters unit is an immovable.

The Civil Code articles on the classification of thing were recently amended. 1978 La. Acts. No. 728, amending the Civil Code of 1870 articles 448–87. Because the revision became effective in 1979, and the operative facts leading to this litigation occurred in 1978, the rights of the parties are governed by the articles as they existed prior to the revision. Nonetheless, examination of the revision provides guidance and insight into a proper interpretation of the pre-amendment articles.

The Civil Code of 1870 divided immovables into three categories: immovables by nature, immovables by destination and immovables by the object to which they are applied. C.C. of 1870 art. 463. The Code attempted to define immovables by nature as things which "cannot move themselves or be removed from one place to another." C.C. of 1870 art. 462. This definition was followed by a listing of those things considered to be immovables by nature.

This definition was deleted from the Code by the 1978 revision, because, as explained by the revision's redactors:

> "This analytical scheme—definition and illustrations—contradicts reality. Contemporary mechanical means make possible the relocation of immense quantities of earth, timber, buildings, and various kinds of constructions. It appears, therefore, that immovability by nature under present Louisiana law is a legal fiction based partly on practical considerations and partly on inherent characteristics of things. In the light of contemporary conceptions the only immovables by nature are tracts of land, i.e., portions of the surface of the earth individualized by boundaries." Exposé des Motifs of Act 728, 1978 La. Acts, Vol. II, p. 1908.

Immovability is a legal concept and not merely an inherent quality of a thing. Whether a thing is classified as an immovable depends upon whether the legislature has accorded to that thing the preferred status of immovability. Immovability "in fact" is not itself a prerequisite to immovability "in law," and things regarded as immovables by the law might be moved through the application of extraordinary mechanical means. To determine whether this living quarters unit is an immovable by nature, the Code articles listing the things which are immovables by nature should be considered.

The 1870 Code classified as immovables by nature buildings and other constructions. Although the Code did not define these terms, it did provide that buildings and other constructions are immovables regardless of "whether they have their foundations in the soil." C.C. of 1870 art. 464. Integration with the soil was not a prerequisite to immovability under former article 464, and the courts have properly classified as immovables things whose foundations rested upon blocks or posts. See *Prevot v. Courtney*, 241 La. 313, 129 So.2d 1 (1961) (tractor shed and poultry house); *Lafleur v. Foret*, 213 So.2d 141 (La. App. 3d Cir. 1968) (beagle and chicken brooders); *Vaughn v. Kemp*, 4 La. App. 682 (2d Cir. 1926) (small wooden frame garage).

Nor did former article 464 require unity of ownership as a prerequisite to immovability. Buildings and other constructions erected by persons other than the owner of the land are nonetheless immovables by nature under the 1870 Code. *Buchler v. Fourroux*, 193 La. 445, 190 So. 640 (1939); *Lighting Fixture Supply Co. v. Pacific Fire Insurance Co. of New York*, 176 La. 499, 146 So.35 (1932); *Scardino v. Maggio*, 15 La. App. 444, 131 So.217 (1st Cir. 1930); *Vaughn v. Kemp*, supra.

The 1978 revision effects several changes. Constructions other than buildings are now classified as movables unless they are component parts of a tract of land. To be a component part of a tract of land, a construction must meet two requirements: it must be permanently attached to the ground, and it must belong to the owner of the ground. C.C. 463, as amended by 1978 La. Acts, No. 728.

The 1978 legislation made no changes in the classification of buildings. Under the revision, buildings which belong to the owner of the ground are considered component parts of a tract of land, C.C. 463, as amended by 1978 La. Acts, No. 728, and, when there is no unity of ownership, the building is considered a separate immovable. C.C. 464, as amended by 1978 La. Acts, No. 728. Thus, under the revision, as under the 1870 Code, buildings are always classified as immovables.

The trial court concluded that the living quarters unit was not a building because it "was not being used as a building; rather it was set upon wooden blocks while it was under construction." The Court of Appeal reversed, correctly noting that there is no codal requirement that a building have its foundation in the soil. Additionally, the trial court's reasoning would frustrate the purpose of the Private Works Act, which is to protect the claims of laborers and workmen. Many lien claimants perform work for the erection of new structures which naturally are not placed into use until completion. If classification must await actual use, then these lien claimants would find themselves unprotected by the act.

We agree with the conclusion of the Court of Appeal that this living quarters unit is a building. As the picture of the unit demonstrates, the facts speak eloquently for themselves. This is a three story high permanent steel structure with a helicopter landing pad constructed above it, built at a cost of over $400,000. It is designed to house offshore workers. Under prevailing notions, such a structure is a building and is therefore classified as an immovable.

Pennzoil maintains that the unit should not be classified as an immovable because the unit was intended to be moved offshore. The fact that the unit is capable of being moved by a powerful crane does not defeat classification of that thing as an immovable, for, as mentioned earlier, immovability is a legal concept and not an inherent quality of a thing.

Implicit in Pennzoil's position is the concept that classification of a thing as an immovable by nature is somehow contingent upon the owner's intentions. We do not believe the Code granted the owner such flexibility, nor do we believe that immovability by nature should hinge upon such a subjective factor as the owner's intentions. Such a contention may have been meritorious in connection with the 1870 Code's category of immovables by destination, but is not applicable to immovables by nature. As this court has previously explained:

"... there is a vast distinction between immovables by destination and immovables by nature. The status of an immovable by destination can be changed by an act of the landowner, but there is no provision of law that we are aware of, and none has been cited to that effect, that the act of the landowner, or any other person, can change the status of an immovable by nature.... The status of an immovable by nature is never changed by any act of the owner, while the status of an immovable by destination changes according to its use by the owner.... In the instant case, the status of the property could not be changed by the intention or act of the landowner because its status is fixed by law and does not depend upon its use." *Buchler v. Fourroux*, 193 La. at 477–78, 190 So. at 650–51.

The legislature has determined that a building is an immovable regardless of whether its foundation is integrated with the soil. This three story high permanent steel structure qualifies as a building and therefore is an immovable, and subject to the laws governing immovables. Consequently, the Private Works Act (including R.S. 9:4812) applies to this case.

For the foregoing reasons, the judgment of the Court of Appeal is affirmed, at the cost of defendants.

MARCUS, Justice (concurring). I agree with the majority's conclusion at La. R.S. 9:4861 is not applicable here. Moreover, La. Civ. Code art. 464 (under old law prior to amendment effective January 1, 1979) provided: "Lands and buildings or other constructions, whether they have their foundations in the soil or not, are immovable by their nature." Clearly, the living quarters unit was a building whose foundation was not in the soil. Hence, it was an immovable by its nature. Accordingly, I respectfully concur.

Notes and Questions

1. In *P.H.A.C. Services, Inc. v. Seaways International, Inc.*, 403 So.2d 1199 (La. 1981), the classification of the offshore drilling platform living quarters unit as immovable or movable determined the availability of the privilege (a statutory lien) claimed by two unpaid subcontractors under the Private Works Act (La. Rev. Stat. §9:4801 et seq.) with respect to the installation of plumbing, heating, air conditioning and acoustical works for the unit. The parties to the lawsuit did not dispute the facts. They agreed that the subcontractors would have a privilege on the living quarters unit if it was characterized as an immovable. *See* La. Rev. Stat. §9:4802(B) (specifying that "claims against the owner shall be secured by a privilege on the *immovable* on which the work is performed") (emphasis added). A subcontractor's privilege allows the subcontractor to require that the applicable immovable (here the living quarters) be seized and sold to satisfy its claims as creditor unless the owner of the immovable (in this case Pennzoil) pays the subcontractor for the labor or material supplied. *See* La. Civ. Code art. 3186 (1870) (defining a privilege as "a right, which the nature of a debt gives to a creditor, and which entitles him to be preferred before other creditors, even those who have mortgages"). In effect, when a subcontractor obtains an effective privilege, the immovable to which the privilege attaches can no longer be sold or encumbered by the owner, and the owner will be forced to address the subcontractor's claims or risk losing ownership of the immovable.

Note that Pennzoil would have immunized itself from liability in this case if it had required its general contractor, Seaways International, to post a surety bond guaranteeing that the work would be completed and that all claims against the general contractor for work performed under the contract would be satisfied, and if Seaways had recorded the contract and surety bond. La. Rev. Stat. §§9:4802(c), 4811, 4812. As the court observed, however, the construction contract was not recorded in this case and "no bond was required of Seaways as contractor." *P.H.A.C. Services v. Seaways Int'l, Inc.*, 403 So.2d 1199 (La. 1981). Pennzoil either overlooked these standard precautions or sought to save money on the construction contract by not requiring its general contractor to take these steps.

In any event, Pennzoil sought to avoid the plaintiffs' privilege under the Private Works Act by asserting that the living quarters unit was not an immovable because the structure could be moved from one place to another (and in fact was designed for this purpose), its foundations were not connected to the ground, and its owner did not intend the unit to be stationary. How does the court respond to these contentions?

2. Article 11 of the Civil Code distinguishes between the "generally prevailing meaning" (read "plain meaning") of a word used in a law and "words of art" or "technical terms," which "must be given their technical meaning when the law involves a technical matter." La. Civ. Code art. 11 (1987). How does Article 11 impact the court's classification analysis in *P.H.A.C. Services*? Why does the court consider only whether the unit is classified as a "building"? If the court had classified the unit as an "other construction permanently attached to the ground," would the plaintiffs have been able to assert a privilege against the unit under the Private Works Act?

3. Identify the test deployed by the court and the factors that it deems *not* relevant to determining whether a structure is a building. Did the court look only at "permanence" or at something else? Is the court's conclusion convincing? Consider that an offshore drilling platform, to which a living quarters unit like the one at issue in *P.H.A.C. Services* is designed to be attached, can be either affixed to the sea floor or floating. Crews are typically flown to the platform by helicopter. Workers eat, sleep, and spend their free time on the platform for a fortnight working twelve-hour shifts. At the end of its service life, which can span decades, a drilling platform is decommissioned.

Problem

Imagine you are a legislator and have been asked to consider a proposed amendment to the Private Works Act that would allow subcontractors and suppliers like the plaintiffs in *P.H.A.C. Services* to obtain privileges for work performed on large structures that are *not* technically classified as *immovables* under the Civil Code. Would this be a good idea? Should the privilege that subcontractors and suppliers enjoy to make sure they are paid for work done and materials supplied depend on whether the structure at issue is classified as an immovable under the Civil Code? If the privilege could apply to structures other than immovables, where would contractors and suppliers be required to record the privilege? Could you imagine a better way to define eligibility for a privilege under the Private Works Act?

Bridges v. National Financial Systems, Inc.
960 So.2d 202 (La. App. 1 Cir. 2007)

McCLENDON, Judge. This is an appeal of a partial summary judgment in which the trial court determined that modular banking units are corporeal movables and, therefore, the leases of such structures are taxable transactions. For the reasons that follow, we affirm.

Facts and Procedural History

The facts of this matter are not in dispute. The defendant, National Financial Systems, Inc. (NFS), is a non-Louisiana corporation, licensed to do business in the State of Louisiana. It is in the business of leasing modular banking units to banks and federally insured financial institutions desiring to open branch locations in rural and urban areas of Louisiana. The Louisiana Department of Revenue (Department) conducted a sales and use tax compliance audit of NFS's books and records, which revealed that during the period from January 1, 1998, through December 31, 2000, NFS received $165,132.68 in lease payments on its units that were used in Louisiana, and that NFS neither collected nor remitted any taxes on these leases.

As a result of the audit, Cynthia Bridges, Secretary of the Department of Revenue, State of Louisiana (the State) instituted the present action against NFS to collect the lease taxes, asserting that NFS is indebted to the State for the tax period January 1, 1998, through December 31, 2000, in the amount of $24,605.31 in taxes, $6,151.34 in delinquent penalties, plus applicable interest. NFS answered the petition, generally denying its allegations and asserting that no taxes were due. NFS alleged that the State incorrectly classified the structures as "tangible personal property" and, therefore, incorrectly claimed the leases of such structures were subject to a lease tax.[1]

Thereafter, on January 3, 2005, the State moved for summary judgment, asserting that it was entitled to judgment as a matter of law for the lease taxes. Following a hearing, on November 14, 2005, the trial court granted partial summary judgment in favor of the State, having determined that the lease transactions at issue were taxable. The trial court, finding no just reason for delay, designated the judgment as a final judgment. Judgment to this effect was signed on December 15, 2005. Following the denial of its motion for a new trial, NFS appealed. . . .

Discussion

. . . NFS contends that the trial court erred in finding that the modular banking units are "tangible personal property" for purposes of lease taxes. NFS contends that the "buildings" are immovable during the lease period and, therefore, such leases are exempt from the Louisiana lease tax. On the other hand, the Department asserts that NFS and its bank customers contracted, in clear and unambiguous terms, that the modular banking units would remain movable property, and that the structures are in fact movable property, with such leases being subject to the lease tax.

Louisiana law imposes a tax upon the lease or rental within the state of tangible personal property. LSA-R.S. 47:302(B). According to LSA-47:301(16)(a), "'[t]angible personal property' means and includes personal property which may be seen, weighed, measured, felt or touched, or is in any other manner perceptible to the senses."

"Tangible personal property" is a common law term, but Louisiana courts have found it synonymous with the Civil Code concept of "corporeal movable property." *South Central Bell Telephone Co. v. Barthelemy*, 94-0499 (La. 10/17/94) 643 So.2d 1240, 1243; *City of New Orleans v. Baumer Foods, Inc.*, 532 So.2d 1381, 1383 (La. 1988) . . . .

---

1. Throughout these proceedings, NFS has referred to these structures as "buildings" and uses the term "modular building" in its leases. The Department, however, has refused to characterize these banking structures as "buildings." For the purposes of this opinion, we shall refer to these structures as "modular banking units."

The parties agree that the lease tax applies if modular banking units are movable property, but that leases involving the modular banking units are exempt from taxation if the structures are immovable property. Accordingly, resolution of the taxation issue in this matter depends on the classification of the structures, as set forth in the Civil Code. Thus, our analysis must begin with a review of pertinent Civil Code articles governing movable and immovable property, as follows:

Art. 462. Tracts of Land

Tracts of land, with their component parts, are immovables.

Art. 464. Buildings and standing timber as separate immovables

Buildings and standing timber are separate immovables when they belong to a person other than the owner of the ground.

Art. 471. Corporeal movables

Corporeal movables are things, whether animate or inanimate, that normally move or can be moved from one place to another.

Art. 475. Things not immovable

All things, corporeal or incorporeal, that the law does not consider as immovables, are movables.

NFS has consistently argued that the modular banking units, when in place and when lease payments are being received by NFS, are buildings, and thus are separate immovables under Civil Code article 464. [NFS contends that the timing of the receipt of the lease payments is critical in this matter. The lease agreements provide that the monthly rental payments begin on the date that the lessee requests that the modular banking units be delivered on site. Thus, NFS argues, at all times during the lease, when lease payments were received by NFS, the structures were set up and "permanently" attached to the land at their particular location.] The Department contends that these structures were built to be moved, were movables according to the lease terms, and clearly are movable property.

In support of its motion for summary judgment, the Department offered NFS's responses to the Department's discovery, as well as examples of lease agreements between NFS and banking institutions. NFS also offered discovery responses by the Department, together with the deposition testimony of Mr. Raymond Tangney, the Department's senior sales tax policy consultant, and the affidavit of NFS's president and CEO, Don G. Gordon.

The Department has pointed to language in the lease agreements that the modular banking units are "portable" and "temporary in nature" in support of its argument that the structures are movable property. NFS asserts that whether or not the structures were intended to be moved, or could be moved and transported, is irrelevant, because the structures are "buildings" and, therefore, separate immovables under the Civil Code, making leases of them exempt from taxation.

Although our supreme court has not specifically addressed the issue before us, it has made several observations as to what constitutes a "building" for the purpose of imposing delictual responsibility upon the owner under LSA-C.C. art. 2322. An inherent requirement is that there be a structure of some permanence. *Olsen v. Shell Oil Co.*, 365 So.2d 1285, 1289 (La. 1978); *Mudd v. Travelers Indemnity Co.*, 309 So.2d 297, 300–01 (La. 1975). In the context of the Louisiana Civil Code, a "building" is a type of permanent construction that would be classified as an immovable. *Olsen*, 365 So.2d at 1290.

In this matter, Mr. Gordon stated the following in his affidavit, in part:

> [T]he modular bank buildings range in size from 14 feet wide by 70 feet long, to 28 feet wide by 70 feet long, and weigh several tons. The buildings are built on steel frames to support the additional weight of bank equipment (i.e.: safes, depositories, automatic teller machines, and vaults). Each building has one drive-up teller window which also includes access to a night depository and, if requested by the bank, an automatic teller machine. In most cases an architect or state certified engineer is hired by the bank to ensure structural integrity of the building, proper drainage, and compliance with all local, state, and national building codes.

> The building is placed upon a concrete slab foundation at least five (5) inches thick. The building is attached to the slab with tow plate, tie down strap, or hurricane strap, and connected to the slab with an expansion bolt. Concrete curbing is then poured at the drive-up window and for any additional drive-up windows the bank has requested. A canopy over all drive-up windows is built to connect to the building and to attach to the concrete islands of each drive-up lane. A vestibule over the front door is also constructed on site as well as an ADA ramp. The utilities are connected by plumbers, electricians, and telephone technicians.

> Before a building can be removed upon termination of the lease period, the canopy over the drive-up lanes, the vestibule, and the ADA ramp must be removed. The concrete curbing, islands for the additional drive-up lanes, and support posts for the drive-up canopies must be removed. This includes jack-hammering out those items which are concrete. The plumbing, water, and sewer are disconnected by a plumber, electricians disconnect the power, and landscaping is stripped away. The moving crew must lift the building with hydraulic jacks, place wheels, axles, and tongue under the building, and a tractor will pull the building from the slab.

Mr. Gordon further stated that the terms of the leases are typically one to two years. The lease examples reflect that in addition to the monthly rental amount and the security deposit, NFS also charged a transportation fee, setup fee, and a removal fee. Further, upon termination of the leases, NFS agreed to remove the modular banking unit within thirty days. NFS also admitted that upon termination of a lease and the return of the modular banking unit, NFS would attempt to lease the modular banking unit to another client.

The trial court determined that the modular banking units were movables according to the terms of the lease contracts. We agree with the trial court that the modular banking units are movables. However, we disagree with the reasoning of the trial court. Although NFS and its customers may have contracted between themselves that the property would remain movable (i.e., for purposes of ownership, security interests, etc.), that designation does not answer the question of whether the modular banking units are movable for tax purposes. The Department was not a party to the lease transactions at issue. The trial court erred in looking only at the contracts between NFS and its customers to conclude that the structures are movables. In the context of this tax dispute, contractual agreements cannot dictate the classification of a thing under the Civil Code. However, because we review summary judgments de novo, we reach the same result, based upon the determination that these structures are movables under the Civil Code property articles.

Although arguably the structures at issue herein have some degree of permanency once they are set in place, they are not permanent, nor are they intended to be permanent. Rather, they are designed and intended to be used for a specified period of time and then moved, and they are moved. The normal and intended use of these modular banking units is to be moved from one place to another. They are used as temporary units until a permanent structure can be put into place.

We find the present case to be distinguishable from *P.H.A.C. Services, Inc. v. Seaways International, Inc.*, 403 So.2d 1199 (La. 1981), cited by NFS. In the *P.H.A.C.* decision, the supreme court determined that a three-story high permanent steel structure, designed to house offshore oil workers, qualified as a building and therefore, was an immovable for purposes of the Private Works Act. . . . In *P.H.A.C.*, although the structure was built at a construction site and then moved offshore, it was designed to be permanent. *P.H.A.C.*, 403 So.2d at 1203–04. In this matter, when moved onto a leased site, the modular banking units are not meant to stay at that location permanently, but only for the term of the lease.

We also do not find the facts before us analogous to those in *Graffagnino v. Lifestyles, Inc.*, 402 So.2d 742 (La. App. 4 Cir. 1981), wherein the ownership of a structure called an O'Dome was at issue. The modular banking units herein are designed to be moved without losing their identity, whereas the O'Dome in *Graffagnino* had to be disassembled in order to be moved. *Graffagnino*, 402 So.2d at 744.

Accordingly, we determine that the modular banking units at issue herein are corporeal movables "that normally move or can be moved from one place to another." LSA-C.C. art. 471. As such, they are tangible personal property, and the lease of this property in Louisiana subjects the lease to taxation under LSA-R.S. 47:302(B).

Conclusion

For the foregoing reasons, the partial summary judgment in favor of Cynthia Bridges, Secretary of the Department of Revenue, State of Louisiana, determining that the lease transactions at issue in this matter are taxable, pursuant to LSA-R.S. 47:302(B) and related statutes, is affirmed. Costs of this appeal are assessed against National Financial Services, Inc.

AFFIRMED.

Notes and Questions

1. In *Bridges v. National Financial Systems, Inc.*, 960 So.2d 202 (La. App. 1 Cir. 2007), the court of appeal decided that modular banking units are corporeal movables subject to a Louisiana lease tax. Just as in *P.H.A.C. Services*, the parties in *Bridges* were largely in agreement with regard to the facts of the case and agreed that the lease tax applied to "tangible personal property." Note how much effort Judge McClendon expends to support his claim that common law vernacular must be interpreted in consonance with the codal classification scheme. Does Judge McClendon succeed in setting the tone for a neutral analysis by referring to "units"?

2. Notice that although the court of appeal affirmed the trial court's decision that the modular banking units were corporeal movables, it disagreed with the trial court's rationale. The trial court's classification of the units as movables appears to have been based largely on how the units were described in the lease contracts executed between the defendant, National Financial Systems, Inc. (NFS), and its banking customers. Those contracts described the units as movables for purposes of determining who owned the units and security interests in them. Why does the court declare that the classification agreed to by NFS and its banking customers is not dispositive, or, as the court put it, "contractual agreements cannot dictate the classification of a thing under the Civil Code"? *Bridges v. National Financial Systems, Inc.*, 960 So.2d 202, 208 (La. App. 1 Cir. 2007). Using the language of civilian analysis, when, if ever, can the classification of a thing as a movable or immovable be considered a suppletive matter? In other words, when is the classification of a thing amenable to alteration by parties to a contract? *See* La. Civ. Code arts. 467–68 (1978); La. Civ. Code art. 491 (1979).

3. Judge McClendon identifies two classification alternatives for the units. They could be buildings classified as "separate immovables" under Article 464 of the Civil Code or as corporeal movables. Review the rules reproduced by the court. Why is Article 463 of the Civil Code not among them?

4. In the end, the court in *Bridges* focuses its classification analysis on the criterion of whether the structure was intended to be used in one place or to be moved from place to place, and to a lesser extent on the need, or lack of need, for the structure to be disassembled to be moved. Is this focus on intended permanency and need for disassembly consistent with the Louisiana Supreme Court's analysis in *P.H.A.C. Services, Inc. v. Seaways International, Inc.*, 403 So.2d 1199 (La. 1981)?

Note the care taken by the court in *Bridges* to distinguish the result here from that in *P.H.A.C. Services*. Why is it fairly common practice for a Louisiana judge interpreting the Civil Code to "distinguish" a case—a classic common law technique of judicial decision making? Is it likely that an intermediate level appellate court in Louisiana would disagree with a Louisiana Supreme Court precedent?

5. Do you agree with the court's conclusion in *Bridges* that these modular structures, which are pre-built and fully contained facilities that can be dispatched to a specified locale for immediate business use, are corporeal movables? Notice the affidavit submitted by Mr. Gordon, the CEO of NFS, who was trying to convince the court that the units were separate immovables and thus not subject to the state lease tax. He describes the specifications of the "modular bank buildings" in terms of their size, length and weight, their placement on concrete slab foundations, their engineering and safety certification, and the process involved in removing them at the termination of a lease. If the units were the subject of longer-term leases or sales, should the classification result be any different?

6. *Mobile Homes*: How are mobile homes classified in Louisiana? The short answer is that they are generally considered to be movables under Louisiana law, unless the owner of the home takes specific steps to immobilize them under a statute known as the Louisiana Manufactured Home Property Act, La. Rev. Stat. § 9:1149.1 et seq. (1982). The Act applies to any "manufactured home," including a "mobile home," which is defined to mean a "factory assembled structure or structures transportable in one or more sections, with or without a permanent foundation, and includes the plumbing, heating, air conditioning, and electrical systems contained therein." La. Rev. Stat. § 9:1149.2(2)-(3).

Section 4 of the Act allows a landowner who owns a manufactured home located on an immovable to immobilize the home by filing in the applicable conveyance or mortgage records an authentic act, sale or mortgage declaring the owner's or mortgage holder's intention that the manufactured home be permanently attached to a particular lot or tract of land described in the instrument. Otherwise, under section 3 of the act, "when any manufactured home shall be moved and located in or upon any immovable property, or installed therein or thereon in a manner which, under any law, might make the manufactured home an immovable or component part thereof, the manufactured home shall be and will remain a movable. . . ." La. Rev. Stat. § 9:1149.3. Could the modular banking units at issue in *Bridges* have been considered manufactured homes under the Act?

Problem

Assume that the owner of the living quarter unit in *P.H.A.C. Services* sells it to an oil and gas drilling company. Assume likewise that NFS sells a modular banking unit to one of its lessees. The next day the sellers of the respective structures have a change of heart after learning that the actual market value of these structures is more than twice the selling prices they received. They ask you whether Article 2589 of the Civil Code will allow them to bring an action to rescind the respective sales for lesion. What is your advice? *yes b/c its classified as an immovable*

b. Other Constructions Permanently Attached to the Ground

The next category of component parts listed in Article 463, *other constructions permanently attached to the ground*, is not defined in the Civil Code either. Recall that unlike buildings and standing timber, which are always classified as separate immovables, whether or not they are owned by the owner of the ground, La. Civ. Code art. 464 (1978), the presence or absence of unity in ownership will determine whether other constructions permanently attached to the ground are considered component parts of a tract of land or, instead, corporeal movables. La. Civ. Code art. 463 (1978). If the other construction is owned by the owner of the ground, it will be a component part of the land and thus immovable. *Id.* If it belongs to someone else, however, the other construction will be considered a separately owned movable. La. Civ. Code art. 464 rev. cmt. (d) (1978). As we will see in the following decision, classifying an object as an "other construction permanently attached to the ground" can have significant legal consequences, particularly when the ownership of the ground changes hands.

Examples of "other constructions permanently attached to the ground" listed in the revision comments include a tractor and poultry house, a canal, a cistern, a brick pit, a corn mill, a gas tank, a railroad track, and an advertising sign embedded in a concrete foundation. La. Civ. Code art. 463 rev. cmt. (c) (1978). A derrick erected by a farm lessee for the purpose of drilling a waterwell, however, has been held to be a movable, even though the pump used to operate the well was held to be an immovable by destination. *Jones v. Conrad*, 98 So. 397, 398 (1924). One important criterion for distinguishing between movables and "other constructions permanently attached to the ground" is their degree of connection with the soil. In the following decision, discover whether the court identifies any other relevant criteria.

Bayou Fleet Partnership v. Dravo Basic Materials Co., Inc.
106 F.3d 691 (5th Cir. 1997)

POLITZ, Chief Judge. Bayou Fleet Partnership, plaintiff, and Dravo Basic Materials Company, Inc. and Dravo Corporation, defendants, both appeal a judgment against Dravo Basic for $25,000 in damages caused by Dravo's unauthorized removal of limestone working bases from Bayou Fleet's property. We conclude that under controlling provisions of the Louisiana Civil Code the limestone working bases were a component part of the immovable property belonging to Bayou Fleet. For the reasons assigned, we reverse and render judgment in favor of Bayou Fleet.

Background

From 1989 to 1993, pursuant to an oral lease, Dravo operated an aggregate yard in Hahnville, Louisiana on a tract of Mississippi River batture property owned by

Neal Clulee. Dravo established the aggregate yard to store, stockpile, and sell lime-stone extracted from quarries in Illinois and Kentucky and transported down the Mississippi River to the yard.

Dravo established three stockpiles of limestone on the Clulee property, each of which was placed on a foundation made from hardened limestone commonly called a "working base." The working bases were formed by putting a fabric liner on the batture and placing large quantities of loose, saleable, limestone thereon until the weight compressed the batture and the limestone became compacted. Once formed, tons of loose limestone could be stored on the working bases.

On August 13, 1992, the Sheriff of St. Charles Parish seized the Clulee property and on January 27, 1993 sold it at a sheriff's sale. Bayou Fleet acquired ownership and intended to continue to lease to Dravo or some other aggregate yard operator. Bayou Fleet and Dravo could not reach a lease agreement and Dravo determined to vacate the premises but did not do so until the weekend of March 6–8, 1993.

On March 6, 1993[,]Dravo began to remove the limestone from the property, utilizing a Cat 225 Excavator, a backhoe, a bulldozer, front end loaders, and dump trucks. Over the weekend Dravo removed all of the loose stockpiles of limestone as well as the three working bases. In all, Dravo removed approximately 26,000 tons of limestone. On March 9, 1993 Bayou Fleet learned that Dravo had removed the stockpiles and the working bases.

Dravo filed a declaratory judgment action in state court seeking to be declared the owner of the limestone removed from the property. Bayou Fleet then filed this action for damages and removed Dravo's state court action to federal court. The two actions were consolidated and tried to the bench. The district court found that Dravo was entitled to remove a majority of the limestone in the working bases. Dravo was held liable, however, for the excavation of the portion of the working bases that had become a component part of the property. The court stated that Dravo's surreptitious removal of the limestone was "unusual and unbusiness like," and it held Dravo liable for $ 25,000 in damages caused by its trespass on Bayou Fleet's property. Both Bayou Fleet and Dravo timely appealed.

Analysis

Issue

The sole issue presented by this appeal is whether Dravo had the right to remove the limestone working bases and the loose stockpiles of limestone from Bayou Fleet's property. The resolution of this issue turns on the classification of the limestone as either movable or immovable under Louisiana property law. Findings of fact are upheld unless clearly erroneous. . . . The classification of the limestone is a matter of law which we review *de novo*. *Equibank v. United States Internal Revenue Service*, 749 F.2d 1176 (5th Cir. 1985).

The Civil Code classifies things as either movable or immovable. La. Civ. Code art. 448. An immovable is defined as a tract of land with its component parts. La. Civ. Code art. 462. Article 463 of the Civil Code provides that component parts of a tract of land include, among other things, other constructions that are permanently attached to the ground. The Civil Code does not, however, specifically define what qualifies as an "other construction" under Article 463; that determination is left to the judiciary giving due consideration to prevailing societal notions. *Bailey v. Kruithoff*, 280 So.2d 262 (La. App. 1973); *Benoit v. Acadia Fuel & Oil Distributors, Inc.*, 315 So.2d 842 (La. App.), *writ refused*, 320 So.2d 550 (1975). Louisiana courts have found "other constructions" to include a cistern, corn mill, gas tank, barbed wire fence, outdoor advertising sign, and a railroad track. See *Polhman v. De Bouchel*, 32 La. Ann. 1158 (1880); *Bigler v. Brashear*, 11 Rob. 484 (1845); *Monroe Auto & Supply Co. v. Cole*, 6 La. App. 337 (La. App. 1927); *Bailey; Industrial Outdoor Displays v. Reuter*, 162 So. 2d 160 (La. App.), *writ refused*, 164 So. 2d 352 (1964); *American Creosote Co. v. Springer*, 257 La. 116, 241 So.2d 510 (1970). We now conclude that the limestone working bases at issue herein can and properly should be classified under Article 463 as other constructions permanently attached to the ground.

In determining whether an object is an "other construction" within the meaning of Article 463, Louisiana courts generally rely on three criteria: the size of the structure, the degree of its integration or attachment to the soil, and its permanency. If there is a failure of any of these criteria, an object will not be deemed to be an immovable. See, e.g., *McNamara v. Electrode Corp.*, 418 So. 2d 652 (La. App.), *writ denied*, 420 So. 2d 986 (1982) (holding that anodes that were small in size and could be removed in 15 minutes were movable because they lacked the required size and degree of permanency); *Telerent Leasing Corp.* (holding that an alarm system, a public address system, and a background music system which were easily removed were all movable because they lacked the necessary degree of permanency).

The limestone working bases were massive in size. The volume of the limestone excavated by Dravo was 26,628.98 cubic yards and approximately 46,721.5 cubic yards of dirt would be required for fill to restore the land to its prior condition. The working bases were capable of supporting the weight of tons of loose limestone, dump trucks, tractor-trailers, and other heavy equipment used in the operation of the aggregate yard.

The limestone working bases were attached firmly to the property. The weight of the limestone working bases compressed the batture property and, having done so, actually formed the surface level of the property. To remove the working bases Dravo had to dig them out of the ground, using heavy equipment, including a Cat 225 Excavator, to break loose the compacted limestone.

Finally, the limestone working bases achieved the necessary degree of permanency, having been placed on the Clulee property in 1989 and continuing thereon undisturbed until Dravo's action. In its regular course of business Dravo did not remove any of the limestone from the working bases; only loose limestone from the stockpiles on top of the working bases was sold to customers.

We conclude that the size, degree of attachment, and permanence of the limestone working bases, all combine to establish beyond peradventure that the limestone working bases of the aggregate yard were other constructions permanently attached to the ground within the intendment of Article 463. The loose stockpiles of limestone were not; nor do they qualify as an immovable under any other applicable provision of the Civil Code. Although the stockpiles were massive in size, they were neither attached to the ground nor permanent.

The classification of the working bases as other constructions does not, however, end our inquiry. The ownership of the working bases must be determined by reference to Civil Code articles concerning accession in relation to immovables. La. Civ. Code arts. 490–506. Other constructions, such as the limestone working bases, may belong to a person other than the owner of the ground to which they are attached. They are presumed, however, to belong to the owner of the ground unless separate ownership is evidenced properly by a recorded document. Absent such a public recordation, other constructions are considered to be component parts of the land and are transferred with it. See La. Civ. Code art. 491; Yiannopoulos, § 141, p. 312.

Dravo was the original owner of the materials composing the working bases, but it recorded no evidence of its ownership. It could have protected its interest in the limestone working bases by recording its lease with Clulee. *American Creosote*. This was not done and Bayou Fleet acquired the immovable property free and clear of any claim Dravo may have had to the land or any constructions thereon. La. Civ. Code art. 498.

Ownership of the working bases transferred to the purchaser at the sheriff's sale. *Central Oil & Supply Corp. v. Wilson Oil Co.*, 511 So. 2d 19 (La. App. 1987), *writ denied*, 535 So. 2d 747 (1989) (holding that a purchaser at a sheriff's sale became the owner of equipment that had become incorporated into immovable property). Dravo had no right to remove the working bases and is thus liable for their reasonable replacement cost. *Bailey* (holding that lessee who removed a fence which had become a component part of the land was liable to purchaser of land for the reasonable replacement cost of the fence). Uncontroverted expert testimony in the record establishes that it would cost $263,222.22 to restore the property to its former condition.

We therefore REVERSE the judgment of the district court and RENDER judgment in favor of Bayou Fleet and against Dravo Basic Materials Company, Inc. and Dravo Corporation in that amount. We defer to the district court on the matter of interest and return this matter for entry of an appropriate judgment.

Notes and Questions

1. *Bayou Fleet Partnership v. Dravo Basic Materials Co., Inc.*, 106 F.3d 691 (5th Cir. 1997) addresses the ownership of two different items: stockpiles of limestone and limestone working bases. It involves three parties with three distinct interests: an owner of a tract of land who executed a lease giving the lessee the right to make improvements on the leased property; a lessee who made the improvements with the landowner/lessor's consent; and a third person who acquired ownership of the land from the original landowner/lessor and decided to terminate the rights of the

original lessee. This last person is called the "third party" because he is not one of the original parties to the initial contractual arrangement between the lessor and lessee. This tripartite relationship is common in property law disputes, so it is important that you see it clearly. You might want to draw a triangular-shaped diagram to visualize the relationship.

At one corner of the triangle we have Neal Clulee, the original owner of the tract of land, located on the "batture," or the bank, of the Mississippi River, upriver from New Orleans in St. Charles Parish. At another corner of the triangle we have Dravo Basic Materials Company (Dravo), Clulee's lessee. Dravo leased Clulee's land to operate an aggregate yard. Crucially, the lease contract between Clulee and Dravo was oral. It is not clear whether Clulee and Dravo anticipated what would happen to the limestone working bases erected on the premises by Dravo at the termination of the lease.

As Judge Politz's opinion explains, the lease between Clulee and Dravo came to an end because Clulee lost ownership of his tract of land. He lost it *involuntarily* when it was seized and sold by the sheriff of St. Charles Parish, presumably to satisfy a judgment against Clulee arising out of an unpaid debt. At the sheriff's sale, another company purchased the land, but, pursuant to a prior agreement, that company promptly transferred the land to Bayou Fleet. *Id.* at 692, n. 1. The effective purchaser of Clulee's property at the sheriff's sale—the third person in our triangle—is Bayou Fleet.

Once Bayou Fleet acquired ownership of the land, it and Dravo might have reached an agreement for the disposition of the limestone working bases or Bayou Fleet could have agreed to continue the lease arrangements that had existed between Clulee and Dravo. As we learn from Judge Politz's opinion, however, negotiations between Bayou Fleet and Dravo broke down. Then, over one long weekend, Dravo removed from the batture what it believed to be its property, both the loose stockpiles and the limestone working bases. Bayou Fleet contended that the limestone working bases were a component part of the land and therefore, Dravo had no authority to remove them because ownership of the bases had been transferred to it, along with the land, at the sheriff's sale.

It may be useful to consider how things might have turned out had the facts been a little different. First, if the lease between Clulee and Dravo had come to an end of its own terms and Clulee had remained the owner of the land, a dispute about the disposition of the limestone working bases might still have arisen, but the dispute would have been resolved entirely by the law of lease. The rights and obligations of a lessor and lessee with respect to "attachments, additions, or other improvements made to the leased thing by the lessee" are provided by Article 2695. La. Civ. Code art. 2695 (2004). Consult this article and decide for yourself who would have the right to claim the limestone working bases.

Alternatively, Clulee and Dravo could have entered into a written lease specifically giving Dravo, as lessee the right to remove all improvements and attachments to the leased premises at the termination of the lease. They could have then recorded the lease in the conveyance records of St. Charles Parish. What result would you expect then after Bayou Fleet acquired Clulee's land at the sheriff's sale? Consider how Articles 491, 2695 and 3338 of the Civil Code would affect the outcome of the dispute between Dravo and Bayou Fleet. Under these circumstances, would it matter whether the limestone working bases are characterized as movables or other constructions permanently attached to the land?

2. Because neither of the possible circumstances described above actually occurred, the classification of the limestone working bases became the threshold issue in *Bayou Fleet*. If the court had determined that the working bases were movables, then Dravo would have been justified in removing them after the negotiations for the renewal of the lease broke down. The court, however, classified the limestone working bases as component parts of the land under Article 463. Why? Their component part status meant that the limestone working bases were included in the transfer of the underlying land at the sheriff's sale. *See* La. Civ. Code art. 469 (1978) ("The transfer or encumbrance of an immovable includes its component parts."); *see also* La. Civ. Code art. 491 (1979).

What should Dravo have done to protect its interests in the limestone working bases from the outset? How could Dravo have taken advantage of either Article 491 or Article 2695 of the Civil Code? If Dravo had consulted a lawyer before removing the working bases and the lawyer told Dravo it had nothing to worry about in removing the working bases, would that lawyer have anything to worry about?

3. Suppose for the sake of argument that Clulee and Dravo had executed a lease which provided that Dravo would own and have the right to remove the limestone working bases at the end of the lease. But also suppose that this lease was never recorded in the conveyance records of St. Charles Parish. Suppose Bayou Fleet was told about the lease and the provision regarding the limestone working bases before it purchased the batture land at the sheriff's sale. Would this change your analysis regarding the disposition of the working bases? Consult Articles 3338 and 3343 of the Civil Code.

4. Chief Judge Politz developed a three-pronged test to determine whether the limestone stockpiles and working bases were "other constructions permanently attached to the ground." Does his test make sense to you? Should Judge Politz have incorporated other factors into his test? Note that the actual portability of the limestone working bases did not prevent them from being considered component parts of the land and thus, immovable. Conversely, some of the individual limestone blocks in the limestone stockpiles may have been quite large, but all of the loose stockpiles were deemed movable. What does this teach us?

5. In light of *Bayou Fleet*, the U.S. Court of Appeals for the Fifth Circuit affirmed in *Sundown Energy, L.P. v. Haller*, 773 F.3d 606 (5 Cir. 2014) the district court's finding that a loading platform was not immovable:

The district court correctly found that the loading platform at issue is not immovable. Although the platform is substantial in size and was only moved after litigation commenced between the parties, the platform was not permanently attached to the property. Rather, it "was simply placed over two pilings." Moreover, Sundown was able to remove it by lifting the platform from the pilings. In fact, the platform did not lose any of its utility after Sundown moved it; Sundown used the platform at another location. The pilings were dug into the ground; however, that fact does not demonstrate sufficient attachment to classify the platform as immovable. Ultimately, Defendants have failed to demonstrate that the district court clearly erred in its factual findings.

Id. at 616.

6. Sometimes, the legislature may have reasons to designate a substantial structure that is well integrated into the soil and intended to remain there for a long period of time as a movable. *See, e.g.,* La. Rev. Stat. § 9:1106 (1954) (designating storage tanks for butane, propane, liquefied gas and liquid fertilizer, among other substances, as movable when placed on the land by a person "other than the owner of the land" and specifying that ownership of such tanks "shall not be affected by the sale, either private or judicial, of the land on which they are placed"). Conversely, if substantial, well integrated and apparently permanent gas storage tanks are placed on land *by the owner of the land,* they could be characterized as other constructions permanently attached to the grounds and thus would be classified as component parts of the land. What kind of duties does R.S. 9:1106 create for sellers and buyers of land sporting gas storage tanks?

c. Standing Timber

Under the 1870 Civil Code, trees not yet cut down were considered immovable by nature and thus an inseparable part of the land. La. Civ. Code art. 465(1) (1870). Courts and commentators recognized, however, that trees not yet cut down — unharvested trees — could also be sold separately from the land. In this situation they were classified as movables by anticipation, just like unharvested crops or ungathered fruits today. A.N. Yiannopoulos, 2 Louisiana Civil Law Treatise: Property § 133 (2001 4th ed.); *see also* La. Civ. Code art. 474 (1978).

In the beginning of the twentieth century, the Louisiana legislature declared that standing timber would henceforth be considered an immovable even when it was owned separately from the land. La. Acts 1904, No. 188. This significant policy change was motivated by the recognition that standing timber is an extremely valuable asset; so valuable that, frequently, the unharvested timber on a tract of land is worth more than the land itself. In some parts of Louisiana, timber companies and railroads were amassing complex contractual and property rights in thousands of acres of standing timber. *See, e.g., Louisiana & Arkansas Railway Co. v. Winn Parish Lumber Co.,* 59 So. 403 (La. 1912). The desire to make these transactions more

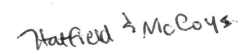

certain by requiring them to comply with the strict rules of formality associated with immovable property further supported the change in classification.

The current version of the Civil Code has preserved this classification structure for standing timber. As we have already seen, Article 463 declares that standing timber is a component part of a tract of land when owned by the owner of the land upon which the trees are growing. La. Civ. Code art. 463 (1978). When standing timber is owned by someone other than the landowner, Article 464 provides that, just like a building, the standing timber remains a separate immovable. La Civ. Code art. 464 (1978).

The Civil Code does not define standing timber. The term "timber" seems to be more narrow than "trees"—the term used in nineteenth-century French and Louisiana civil law. Revision comment (c) to Article 562 of the Civil Code, which defines the rights and obligations of a usufructuary with respect to "timberlands," offers the following definition:

> Timber may be defined as trees, which, if cut, produce lumber for building or manufacturing purposes. This includes trees that could be cut for economic gain, such as pulp wood, pines, hardwoods or building lumber. This would be equivalent to the definition of 'merchantable timber' as used in Louisiana law.

La. Civ. Code art. 562 rev. cmt. (c) (1976). The revision comments to Article 551 of the Civil Code, which define different kinds of fruits in the context of the law of usufruct, describe trees in the following terms:

> Trees are born and reborn of the soil, but they are ordinarily considered to be capital assets rather than fruits on account of their slow growth and high value. See Harang v. Bowie Lumber Co., 145 La. 96, 81 So. 769 (1919). However, trees in a tree farm or in a regularly exploited forest may be regarded as fruits, because they are produced according to the destination of the property and without diminution of its substance. See Yiannopoulous, Personal Servitudes § 27 (1968).

La. Civ. Code art. 551 rev. cmt. (b) (1976). We will examine whether trees should be classified as capital assets or fruits when we study the usufruct of "timberlands." *See* La. Civ. Code art. 562 (1976). For now, we should focus on how a separate timber estate can be created through the horizontal separation of the interests of a surface owner and those a standing timber owner as well as the consequences of such a separation.

Once trees are cut down they become movables, "whether carried off or not." La. Civ. Code art. 463 rev. cmt. (d) (1978). Conversely, "[t]rees and plants in nurseries, though destined to be *transplanted*, have been held to be part of the immovable." *Id.* (emphasis added). Would this cover potted trees?

Consider the following decision and trace the separate ownership interests in the land and the standing timber estate. Identify the means by which the separate ownership interest in the timber estate was preserved.

Brown v. Hodge-Hunt Lumber Co., Inc.

110 So. 886 (La. 1929)

THOMPSON, Justice. This suit is for the value of timber cut and removed from a certain tract of land claimed by the plaintiff and fully described in the petition.

The plaintiff's title to the land has its origin in a deed from the defendant company to G.A. Woods, of date December 4, 1906.

The ownership of the timber is claimed by virtue of a tax sale in the name of the estate of said Woods for the taxes of 1918.

The defendant denied that the plaintiff was the owner of either the land or timber, asserted ownership of the timber itself, with the right to cut and remove the timber at any time, and further pleaded the prescription of one year against any demand for timber cut and removed more than a year prior to the filing of the suit.

The trial judge recognized plaintiff as the owner of the land and timber, and gave plaintiff judgment for $750, being the value of 300,000 feet of timber cut and removed after plaintiff's purchase of the land. Both parties have appealed.

The land, with the timber thereon, was originally owned by the Huie-Hodge Lumber Company. By an amendment to the charter the name of the company was changed to that given in the title of the case. On December 4, 1906, the then owner (Huie-Hodge Lumber Company) sold the land to G.A. Woods, reserving unto said company all of the merchantable timber on the land, together with right of way for railroad, wagons, etc., for the removal of the timber. There was no time limit fixed in the deed for the removal of the timber, and no application was ever made to the court to have the timber cut and removed within a fixed and definite period.

The reservation of the timber in the sale of the land was clearly a segregation of ownership of the timber from the land and created two separate and distinct estates—one to the land in Woods, and the other to the timber in the lumber company. This is so well settled since Act No. 188 of 1904 as to need no citation of authorities. It is equally well settled that the failure to fix a time limit in the deed for the removal of the timber does not affect the validity of the transfer of the timber, since the omission may be supplied by application to the courts, and until such a period is fixed the right to remove the timber remains in the grantee (in this case the owner of the timber) indefinitely. *Kavanaugh v. Frost-Johnson Lbr. Co.*, 149 La. 972, 90 So. 275.

Some time after his purchase of the land, Woods died, and in 1919 the land was sold for the taxes of 1918, under an assessment in the name of the estate of G.A. Woods. At this sale Dr. W.S. Jones bought the land, and a year thereafter sold the same to the present plaintiff. On September 17, 1921, the present plaintiff sold the land to T.H. Brown, but repurchased the same on March 24, 1923. . . .

It does not appear that the timber was included in the assessment and valuation of the land as a basis for the tax sale. The timber is not specially mentioned, either in the assessment or the tax deed. The value placed on the land for taxing purposes would seem to indicate that it was not intended to include the timber.

From the allegations of plaintiff's petition and the proof in the record, the timber on the land was worth more than eight times the value of the land without the timber.

The same may be said in reference to all of the deeds to the land subsequent to the tax deed. In none of these deeds was any reference made to the timber on the land, and price stated in the deeds indicates very clearly, we think, that the sale was not to include the timber.

The plaintiff concedes, and very properly so, that since Act No. 188 of 1904, where timber has been segregated in ownership from the land, there should be separate assessments; that the land should be assessed to its owner, and the timber to its owner.

This was not true prior to the act of 1904.

In *Williams v. Triche, Shff.*, 107 La. 92, 31 So. 926, decided February 3, 1902 it was held that as long as the then legal ownership of trees standing upon land remains in the owner of the land they must be assessed with the land as forming part of it, and that assessors were not warranted in separating, for the purpose of assessment, the trees from the land, and making the trees the direct object of direct taxation, as corporeal movables distinct from the land to which they are attached.

This is still the law, so long as the trees remain the property of the owner of the land on which they are standing. But, where the trees and the land have been segregated into two distinct estates, they become separate and distinct immovables, and should be so assessed for purposes of taxation.

It appears that the timber was not assessed to the lumber company for the year 1918, the year for which the land was sold for taxes, and it is contended that the owner of the timber, by failing to have it assessed, waived any rights it had to the timber, and that the timber then reverted to the owner of the land, and was covered by the assessment of the land and the tax sale thereof.

The argument is specious and has no real foundation.

It presents a novel species of forfeiture of ownership, unknown to our law and jurisprudence.

The only authority relied on in support of the contention that the timber was a part of the land is article 465 of the Civil Code, which provides, among other things, that trees before they are cut down are immovable, and are considered as a part of the land to which they are attached.

This article has no application to the question here presented since the passage of the act of 1904, which retained the immovable character of standing timber, but classified it as a separate and distinct estate from that of the land, when segregated in ownership from the land by the act of the owner, who held the title to the combined estate of timber and land.

Our conclusion is that the timber in question was reserved to the defendant in the original sale of the land to Woods; that the title to the timber never vested in Woods, was not covered by the assessment of the land to the estate of Woods, and did not pass under the tax sale, nor any of the subsequent sales of the land.

Our further conclusion is that the failure of the lumber company to assess the timber did not have the effect of a forfeiture of the title to the timber, nor did such timber thereby revert to the owner of the land and become part of the land for purposes of taxation or otherwise. . . .

The judgment appealed from is reversed and set aside, and plaintiff's demand is rejected, with costs.

Notes and Questions

1. In *Brown v. Hodge-Hunt Lumber Co., Inc.*, 110 So. 886 (La. 1926), Justice Thompson determined that the defendant, Hodge-Hunt Company, retained the right to sever the timber from the land last owned by Brown because the title to the timber never vested in the purchaser of the land, G.A. Woods, nor in anybody who acquired it subsequently. What are the factual and legal bases for this determination?

2. Take a closer look at the events on December 4, 1906. What happened when Hodge-Hunt Company, which owned the land and the timber, sold the land but held on to the timber? Is such a reservation the only way to effectuate a separation between the estates? Must the person reserving a standing timber interest do anything to make that interest known to third parties potentially acquiring the land?

3. Given that standing timber can be owned separately from the land, an important question to consider is whether a separate timber estate can last in perpetuity. In other words, if an instrument creating a separate timber estate does not establish a time period during which the standing timber must be cut down, can the owner of the timber interest refuse to cut down the timber forever? Notice that in *Hodge-Hunt Lumber* Justice Thompson advises that "[i]t is equally well settled that the failure to fix a time limit in the deed for the removal of the timber does not affect the validity of the transfer of the timber, since the omission may be supplied by application to the courts, and until such a period is fixed the right to remove the timber remains in the grantee (in this case the owner of the timber) indefinitely." *Brown v. Hodge-Hunt Lumber Co., Inc.*, 110 So. 886 (La. 1926).

Consider the following decision to determine whether the owner of a timber estate — a separate immovable — can at some point in time be compelled to harvest the timber and effectively terminate the standing timber interest.

Willetts Wood Products Co. v. Concordia Land and Timber Co.
124 So. 841 (La. 1929)

THOMPSON, Justice. This is a suit to have the court fix a term within which the timber on certain described lands situated in Concordia parish should be removed and in default of such removal to have plaintiff, owner of the land, decreed to be the owner of the timber.

After certain exceptions were filed and overruled, the case was put at issue and tried, resulting in a judgment in favor of plaintiff fixing a term of four years to run from the date of the judgment, and providing that all timber not removed within the time fixed shall revert to the plaintiff.

Issue.

There is no dispute as to the facts except on the question as to what is a reasonable time in which to remove the timber. The legal controversy results from the interpretation sought to be given by counsel for defendant to the many decisions of this court in which the precise question here involved was at issue. The defendant was at one time the owner of both the land and timber, and some time during 1917 or 1918 granted a mortgage in favor of the Continental & Commercial Trust & Savings Bank and Frank H. Jones, trustees. The mortgage debt not having been paid, foreclosure proceedings were brought in the federal court, as a result of which the land was sold to Roy H. Goddard. From Goddard the land passed to the Black River Lumber Company, and from the latter to the present plaintiff. In each and every one of the sales mentioned the timber on the land described in paragraph 2 of plaintiff's petition was expressly excepted, and hence remained the property of the defendant.

One of the contentions of defendant is that there was no contractual relation between the defendant and the plaintiff and its authors in title with reference to the removal of the timber, and for that reason the court was without authority to order the removal within any fixed time.

But the defendant gave a mortgage on the land and consented that the land be sold in default of the payment of the debt. The defendant remained silent, permitted the land to be sold separately from the timber, and acquiesced therein, and now claims to own the timber while admitting that the land belongs to the plaintiff. The defendant by its conduct placed it in the power of, and made it possible for, the mortgagee to sell the land separately from the timber and thereby to bring about the creation of two separate estates. Hence there were created two separate estates as perfectly and completely as if the defendant had made a conventional sale of the land and reserved to itself the timber. The plaintiff therefore occupies the same position towards the defendant with respect to the timber as it would have occupied if it had purchased the land from the defendant. Whatever contractual relations existed between the defendant and its mortgagee with regard to the timber passed to the present plaintiff, owner of the land.

The further contention is made that, when separated in ownership from the land on which it stands, the timber becomes an immovable possessing equal rank and dignity with the land, and that the owner of the land has no more inherent right to compel the owner of the timber to sell his timber than the owner of the timber has to compel the owner of the land to sell the land. The contention amounts to a legal heresy, and is contrary to numerous decisions of this court. It is true there may be created under the statute two separate estates, and the title to the land rested in one person and that of the timber in another, but it was never intended and will not do to say that the respective titles are of equal rank and dignity, in the sense that the owner of the timber can require that the timber be permitted to remain on the land in perpetuity without any right in the owner of the land to cause the timber to be removed. No such impossible situation was ever intended or contemplated. Statutes must be construed, if possible, so as to make them practicable, and to hold that the owner of the land must subordinate the use of the land to the will and pleasure of the owner of the timber would effectually put the land out of commerce. It is further contended that this court has never fixed a time limit for the removal of timber in a case where the contract between the parties is silent on the subject, and that any expressions that the court might in some cases fix such a limit, are purely obiter. The very cases which counsel cite in support of this contention hold to the contrary.

In *Savage v. Wyatt Lbr. Co.*, 134 La. 627, 64 So. 491, the court fixed six months from the date the judgment became final in which to remove the timber, and decreed that at the end of such time the defendant should have no claim to any timber remaining on the land. In the case of *Woods v. Union Saw Mill Company*, 142 La. 554, 77 So. 280, the court fixed two years from the date the judgment became final within which to remove the timber, and decreed that all timber remaining on the land at the expiration of the two years shall belong to the owner of the land. In the two cases cited there was a time limit fixed by consent, but was qualified by the stipulation that, if the timber was not removed within the time fixed, the owner of the timber should have further time to remove the timber on paying the taxes. After the fixed period had expired, the contract stood as though no time had been fixed, and the court so treated it, and held that the right to remove the timber could not be continued indefinitely, and that the owner of the land had the legal right to have the time definitely fixed. Many cases might be cited, but the question is so well and uniformly settled that it would seem a waste of time to quote from or either cite the cases.

We will say, however, as said in one of the very latest cases, *Ward v. Hayes-Ewell Co.*, 155 La. 15, 98 So. 740, 741, "that this court has always held, *** that standing timber was property subject to be acquired separately from the land on which it grows; but that when sold it must be cut and removed within the period agreed upon by the parties or fixed by the court in default of agreement; otherwise said timber reverts to the owner of the land."

The only remaining question is as to the time allowed for the removal of the timber. The evidence is somewhat conflicting, but we think that the great preponderance of the evidence supports the finding of the trial judge. Indeed his ruling could not be said to be manifestly wrong if he had fixed a shorter period than four years. The date should, however, be fixed to run from the finality of the judgment. That seems to be the ruling of this court in such cases.

We have not overlooked the plea of estoppel, and only mention it to say that it has no merit.

The judgment appealed from is amended by making the term for the removal of the timber to commence from the date this judgment becomes final. In all other respects the judgment is affirmed, at the cost of defendant in both courts.

Notes and Questions

1. In *Willetts Wood Products Co. v. Concordia Land & Timber Co.*, 124 So. 841 (La. 1929), the Louisiana Supreme Court emphatically rejects the argument that a separate timber estate is "equal in rank and dignity" to the property interest of the landowner, even though a separate timber estate was validly created and preserved in the conveyance records and even though standing timber is classified under the Civil Code as a separate immovable. The court's primary justification for this holding is the fear that treating a timber estate with equal rank and dignity as the surface owner's interest in the land would effectively put the land "out of commerce."

Would allowing a separate timber estate to be perpetual really take the encumbered land out of commerce? As we will see later, other kinds of property interests *less than* full ownership in land — namely predial servitudes and rights of use — are potentially perpetual. What makes a separate timber estate different than, say, a predial servitude of passage established for purposes of allowing vehicular or pedestrian access across a tract of land?

2. Do you think the court's holding in a case like *Willetts Wood Products* would be any different if the separate timber estate had been acquired by a conservation organization, like the Sierra Club, the Nature Conservancy, or the Trust for Public Lands? Would it make sense for such an organization to acquire an ownership interest in standing timber if the landowner could demand that the organization cut down its standing timber within some judicially determined period of time? How would you advise a conservation organization if it wanted to secure a perpetual interest in standing timber, not for the purpose of harvesting it, but for ecological preservation? Does Louisiana law offer any alternatives? *See* La. Rev. Stat. § 9:1271 *et seq.* (Louisiana Conservation Servitude Act) (1986).

3. Is the court in *Willetts Wood Products* effectively forcing an owner of immovable property — albeit a separate immovable — to liquidate its property interest involuntarily? Does this amount to a judicial taking of property in violation of the Fifth or Fourteenth Amendments to the United States Constitution? Does it matter that all of the persons who purchased the land subject to the timber estate had notice of the separate timber estate reserved by Concordia Land & Timber? Similarly, does it matter if all of these subsequent landowners had acquired the land at a reduced price because the timber estate burdened the land? Or, is it likely that the sales price of the land factored in the likelihood that a court would ultimately have the power to set a harvest date for the standing timber?

4. Sometimes an unrecorded timber estate can still be enforceable against a third person. In *Bradley v. Sharp*, 793 So.2d 500 (La. App. 2 Cir. 2001), the owners of a 159-acre tract of land sold the standing pine timber on the land to plaintiff Bradley,

a professional logger, and then two days later sold the land, along with the hardwood timber, to defendant Sharp. Sharp, however, recorded his title to the land and hardwood timber first, some two weeks before Bradley recorded his timber deed. Bradley eventually harvested a significant portion of the pine trees on the tract. After a dispute arose between Bradley and Sharp about damage to some of the hardwood trees and a cemetery on the property, Sharp prevented Bradley from gaining access to the land and completing the harvest of the pine trees. Bradley eventually sued and obtained a judgment awarding him over $50,000 in damages for the remaining pine trees he was prevented from harvesting.

At trial and on appeal, the principal argument of the landowner Sharp, was that because he recorded his deed to the property thirteen days before Bradley's timber deed was recorded, he was a third party purchaser protected by the **Louisiana Public Records Doctrine**. Sharp argued that even though his purchase agreement and his deed to the land both acknowledged the existence of Bradley's timber deed, he acquired ownership of the land unencumbered by the timber deed because he did not expressly assume the obligations of the timber deed. The court of appeal disagreed and affirmed the trial court. After quoting Articles 464, 469, 1839, and the predecessor of current Articles 3338 *et seq.*, the court reasoned as follows.

> The Civil Code recognizes that standing timber may be a separate immovable belonging to a person other than the owner of the land. However, the ownership of both immovables, the land and the standing timber, are interrelated and are not of equal rank in a manner which is analogous in many respects to the ownership of predial servitudes. *Willetts Wood Products Co. v. Concordia Land & Timber Co.*, 169 La. 240, 124 So. 841 (La. 1929), *cert. denied*, 281 U.S. 742, 50 S.Ct. 348, 74 L.Ed. 1156 (1930). For example, the owner of the land must subordinate the use of the land to the timber owner's dominant rights to grow and eventually harvest the timber. This horizontal division of land ownership gives rise to duties that are attached to the land, which are similar to those owed by the owner of a servient estate to the owner of a predial servitude. *See* La. C.C. art. 651. Likewise, our supreme court has said that a timber owner's dominant rights are not perpetual so as to burden the full ownership and use of the land indefinitely and "put the land out of commerce." *Willetts*, 124 So. at 842. Therefore, the subordination of the landowner's use of the property is for a term fixed in the timber deed or set by a court. *Id.; see also,* A. N. Yiannopoulos, *Property* § 135, in 2 *Louisiana Civil Law Treatise*, 302–303 (3d ed. 1991). This rule serves a purpose similar to that of the prescription of non-use which frees the ownership of the servient estate from the burden of the predial servitude. *See,* La. C.C. art. 753.

> The Civil Code articles on ownership make clear that Bradley acquired a real right in immovable property through the Timber Deed. La. C.C. arts. 476 and 477. Furthermore, Bradley's real right of ownership of the standing timber burdened the ownership of the land, thereby giving rise to real

obligations or duties attached to the land. La. C.C. art. 1763 ["A real obligation is a duty correlative and incidental to a real right"]. Those real obligations, as discussed above, made the Browns' ownership of the land subject to Bradley's rights to continue to grow the pine timber and to access the property to harvest the pine timber.

La. C.C. art. 1764 describes the effects of real obligations when the land burdened by such obligations is transferred:

> A real obligation is transferred to the universal or particular successor who acquires the movable or immovable thing to which the obligation is attached, without a special provision to that effect.

> But a particular successor is not personally bound, unless he assumes the personal obligations of his transferor with respect to the thing, and he may liberate himself of the real obligation by abandoning the thing.

From this article, it can be seen that Sharp could acquire the land from the Browns and be subject to the real obligations arising from the Timber Deed, without assuming any personal obligations under the Timber Deed, such as the Browns' personal obligation of warranty of title. Therefore, the fact that Sharp's deed to the property did not employ language assuming the personal obligations of the timber contract is not dispositive.

The evidence at trial overwhelmingly revealed that Sharp and the Browns intended to recognize Bradley's ownership of the standing timber. In two written contracts, the purchase agreement and the cash sale deed, Sharp effectively acknowledged that his acquisition of the land would be subject to the real obligations flowing from Bradley's ownership of the timber. To that extent, the jurisprudence cited below indicates that under the public records doctrine, Sharp is not considered to be in the position of a protected third party purchaser who can acquire ownership of the land free from the unrecorded document evidencing Bradley's ownership rights. Just as the public records doctrine is unnecessary to protect Bradley's ownership rights in the timber *vis-à-vis* the Browns, the doctrine is likewise inapplicable to afford Sharp protection, since the Browns contractually required Sharp to recognize Bradley's ownership rights as a burden or real obligation on the land which he was acquiring.

In *Stanley v. Orkin Exterminating Co., Inc.,* 360 So.2d 225 (La. App. 1st Cir. 1978), the purchaser of commercial property executed a purchase agreement acknowledging that the property was to be sold subject to a lease. At the time of execution of the deed to the property, however, there was no mention of the lease in the sale. When the purchaser sued to evict the tenant, the court determined that the apparent intent of the parties throughout the entire sales transaction was for the property to be sold subject to the lease. Thus, the purchaser's reliance upon the public records doctrine was rejected because of his contractual agreement to purchase the property burdened with the lease.

In the present case, the contractual intent was evidenced in the three written agreements pertaining to the sale of the land to Sharp: the prospectus, the purchase agreement, and the cash sale deed. Therefore, we reject as irrelevant Sharp's legal argument that he did not assume any personal obligation under the Timber Deed. We hold that Bradley's failure to timely obtain protection from the proper recordation of the Timber Deed was unnecessary because of Sharp's contractual acknowledgment of Bradley's rights. Sharp acquired the land subject to the real obligations owed to the owner of the pine timber.

Bradley, 793 So.2d at 504–06. What is the primary lesson of *Bradley*? What is the court's decision in *Bradley* telling us about the supposedly strict, crystalline nature of the Louisiana Public Records Doctrine?

5. Further evidence of the degree to which Louisiana law considers standing timber a particularly valuable asset can be found in special legislation dealing with theft of timber—sometimes called "timber piracy" or "timber trespass." Timber theft carries hefty criminal sanctions, La. Rev. Stat. § 14:67.12 (2008), and perhaps even more important, can trigger substantial civil damages, even for the good faith violator. Consider the following statute:

Section 3:4278.1. Trees, cutting without consent; co-owners and co-heirs; penalty

A.(1) It shall be unlawful for any person to cut, fell, destroy, remove, or to divert for sale or use, any trees, or to authorize or direct his agent or employee to cut, fell, destroy, remove, or to divert for sale or use, any trees, growing or lying on the land of another, without the consent of, or in accordance with the direction of, the owner or legal possessor, or in accordance with specific terms of a legal contract or agreement.

(2) It shall be unlawful for any co-owner or co-heir to cut, fell, destroy, remove, or to divert for sale or use, any trees, or to authorize or direct his agent or employee to cut, fell, destroy, remove, or to divert for sale or use, any trees, growing or lying on co-owned land, without the consent of, or in accordance with the direction of, the other co-owners or co-heirs, or in accordance with specific terms of a legal contract or agreement. The provisions of this Paragraph shall not apply to the sale of an undivided timber interest pursuant to R.S. 3:4278.2.

B. Whoever willfully and intentionally violates the provisions of Subsection A of this Section shall be liable to the owner, co-owner, co-heir, or legal possessor of the trees for civil damages in the amount of three times the fair market value of the trees cut, felled, destroyed, removed, or diverted, plus reasonable attorney fees and costs.

C. Whoever violates the provisions of Subsection A of this Section in good faith shall be liable to the owner, co-owner, co-heir, or legal possessor of the trees for three times the fair market value of the trees cut, felled, destroyed, removed, or diverted, if circumstances prove that the violator should have been aware that his actions were without the consent or direction of the owner, co-owner, co-heir, or legal possessor of the trees.

D. If a good faith violator of Subsection A of this Section fails to make payment under the requirements of this Section within thirty days after notification and demand by the owner, co-owner, co-heir, or legal possessor, the violator shall also be responsible for the reasonable attorney fees and costs of the owner, co-owner, co-heir, or legal possessor. . . .

G. Notwithstanding any other provision of law to the contrary, a civil action pursuant to provisions of this Section shall be subject to a liberative prescriptive period of five years.

La. Rev. Stat. § 3:4278.1 (1974, amended 2011). *See also* La. Rev. Stat.§ 3:4278.2 (establishing the so called "eighty percent rule" by which a buyer of timber may not buy and remove timber from a tract owned by more than one owner without obtaining the consent of co-owners representing more than eighty percent of the ownership interest).

In recent years, several cases involving the interpretation of the timber piracy statute and its intersection with Louisiana law of co-ownership were decided and attracted critical attention. *See e.g., Sullivan v. Wallace*, 51 So.3d 702 (La. 2010). For a detailed analysis of these controversies and their resolution in Act 226 of 2010, see Mirais M. Holden, *Timber Piracy, Statutory Interpretation and Legislative Intent: The Louisiana Supreme Court's Decision in* Sullivan v. Wallace, 21 San Joaquin Ag. L. Rev. 103 (2012).

In another recent case, a court held that owners of a residential lot in Baton Rouge could *not* recover treble damages under the timber piracy statute from two sets of neighbors who cut down thirty-three, very large and tall camellia bushes growing near the boundaries of the plaintiffs' lot because the camellias were "shrubs," and "not trees," and because the defendants were not "loggers," but merely neighbors "who wrongfully trimmed the plaintiffs' camellias on several occasions because the owners would not property maintain their lot." *Kahl v. Luster*, 110 So.3d 1101, 1105 (La. App. 1 Cir. 2012). In *Kahl*, however, the trespassing neighbors were held liable for the reasonable restoration value of the camellias ($14,850) and other trespass damages ($5,000). *Id*. at 1106–07.

d. Unharvested Crops and Ungathered Fruits of Trees

Louisiana's treatment of the category of unharvested crops and ungathered fruits, whether grown for subsistence or profit, follows the traditional French pattern. When unharvested crops and ungathered fruits are owned by the landowner, they are considered component parts of the land and thus immovable. La. Civ. Code art. 463 (1978). This rule comports with the default rule of accession that we have encountered previously. *See* La. Civ. Code arts. 490–91 (1979).

Like standing timber, buildings and other constructions, unharvested crops and ungathered fruits can be subject to the horizontal segregation of ownership. When unharvested crops or ungathered fruits are owned by "a *person other than the landowner*," even while growing in the landowner's soil or attached to a tree or plant, they are considered "movables by anticipation." La. Civ. Code art. 474 (1978) (emphasis added). Moreover, when unharvested crops or ungathered fruits are encumbered with security rights of a third person—someone other than the owner of the land or the person who planted the crop or tended the plants or trees bearing the fruits—they are considered movables by anticipation "as far as the creditor is concerned." *Id.*

The last paragraph of Article 474 suggests that this process of turning unharvested crops or ungathered fruits into movables by anticipation, typically occurs in one of two ways: through execution of a farm lease granting the lessee an ownership interest in all or some of the crops or fruits grown on the farm; or when a farmer grants a security interest in his crops to a bank that has lent him money to fund his farming operations. La. Civ. Code art. 474 (1978). An arrangement in which a landowner grants a tenant farmer an ownership interest in a portion of the crop that the farmer produces may make economic sense for a landowner who lacks the expertise or interest to produce a crop on his own or for a farmer who lacks sufficient capital or credit to purchase his own land. By granting a farmer an ownership interest in an unharvested crop or ungathered fruit, the farm lease can align both parties' interests and provide the farmer with an incentive to produce a good crop.

Similarly, a farmer's ability to grant a security interest in the unharvested crops or ungathered fruits she has sown may enable the farmer to increase the amount of capital available to improve the quality of the soil or to purchase new farming equipment. In either case, it will be essential for the person who is not a landowner but who claims an interest in the unharvested crops or unfathered fruits to be able to point to an act of mobilization that has been recorded in the appropriate public records registry. La. Civ. Code art. 474 rev. cmt. (c) (1978). The public records doctrine protects the separate ownership interests of farmers and security- interest holders only when notice of those interests is recorded in the appropriate public records.

In the following decision, we see a contemporary example of how both methods of mobilizing unharvested crops described above—a farm lease that splits, or appears to split, the ownership of unharvested crops between the lessor and lessee *and* a security interest in unharvested crops granted to a bank—can intersect to create an unanticipated legal problem for the owner of the land. In this case, pay special attention to the issue of where an instrument establishing an interest in unharvested crops must be recorded for that interest to be effective against third parties.

Meyhoeffer v. Wallace

792 So.2d 851 (La. App. 2 Cir. 2001)

PEATROSS, Judge. This appeal arises out of a dispute over the proceeds from the sale of crops grown in 1998 by farmer David Wallace on farm land located in Franklin Parish that Mr. Wallace leased from Dr. Klaus Meyhoeffer. Winnsboro State Bank & Trust Co., Inc. ("the Bank") had a security interest in the crops and crop proceeds granted to it by Mr. Wallace, under which it took possession of the entire 1998 crop proceeds. Dr. Meyhoeffer filed suit against Mr. Wallace and the Bank asserting his lessor's privilege and seeking the 1998 rental payment. The case was submitted on stipulated facts and the trial court held that the Bank's perfected security interest in the crop proceeds was superior to Mr. Meyhoeffer's lessor's privilege. Mr. Meyhoeffer's suit was, therefore, dismissed and he now appeals. For the reasons stated herein, we affirm.

Facts

On January 27, 1993, David Wallace leased 530 acres of farm land in Franklin Parish from Dr. Klaus Meyhoeffer. The lease agreement stated the annual rental as "one-fifth (1/5th) of the [annual] crop or $32,000.00, whichever is greater." The lease was recorded in the conveyance records of Franklin Parish on January 31, 1995. In 1998, Mr. Wallace obtained a loan from the Bank, for which he granted a security interest in the crops and crop proceeds of the leased farm land. The Bank perfected its security interest by filing a financing statement (UCC 1F) in the Louisiana Agricultural Central Registry ("LACR"), as required by La. R.S. 3:3654. A UCC search revealed security interests in the crops (and proceeds therefrom), and various equipment belonging to Mr. Wallace, beginning with filings dated February 28, 1995, and continuing through February 17, 1998. The lease from Dr. Meyhoeffer was not filed in the LACR. When Mr. Wallace could not meet his obligation to the Bank and pay rent to Dr. Meyhoeffer in 1998, the Bank took possession of the proceeds from the 1998 crops and applied them to Mr. Wallace's debt.

Action of The Trial Court

Dr. Meyhoeffer sued for 1998 rentals in the amount of $32,000, arguing that his lessor's privilege was superior to the Bank's security interest. The trial court disagreed and held that, since the Bank had taken the necessary steps to perfect its security interest in the crops and crop proceeds where Dr. Meyhoeffer had not (he did not file a financing statement or the lease in the LACR-only in the conveyance records of Franklin Parish), the Bank's interest in the property outranked Dr. Meyhoeffer's interest. Specifically, the trial court concluded that Dr. Meyhoeffer did not avail himself of the protection of La. R.S. 9:4521, which provides that the lessor's privilege outranks a perfected security interest only when the lessor's privilege is properly filed and maintained in accordance with the central registry provisions of La. R.S. 3:3651, et seq. As such, the trial court concluded that the Bank's perfected security interest outranked Dr. Meyhoeffer's lessor's privilege; and he was not, therefore, entitled to collect the rent for 1998 from the crop proceeds.

Discussion

At the outset, we note that, in his petition, Dr. Meyhoeffer asserted a lessor's privilege on the "crops produced," and the proceeds therefrom, to secure payment of the rent. He further alleged that the Bank had constructive notice of the privilege and, therefore, should not have taken possession of the entire proceeds from the 1998 crops and should not have applied the entire crop proceeds to Mr. Wallace's loan. Nowhere in his petition did Dr. Meyhoeffer assert *ownership* of any portion or share of the crops or their proceeds.

After the trial court's ruling regarding the ranking of the interests, however, Dr. Meyhoeffer changed his argument for purposes of appeal, now asserting *ownership* of 1/5th of the crops under the lease. According to Dr. Meyhoeffer, since he retained ownership of 1/5th of the crops, Mr. Wallace did not have the authority to encumber this portion by granting a security interest in the same to the Bank and the Bank's retention of the proceeds from "his" 1/5th of the crops was improper. We acknowledge that this argument may have merit under certain circumstances; however, under the facts of this particular case and the terms of this particular lease agreement, as executed by the parties, we find Dr. Meyhoeffer's argument is without merit.

The lease

After careful examination of the lease, we conclude that Dr. Meyhoeffer did not retain ownership of 1/5th of the crops under the terms of the lease. First, the lease is the standard form Farmers Home Administration's ("FmHA") "Crop-Share Farm Lease." The standard provisions of the form lease seem to contemplate joint ownership of crops between lessor and lessee, as evidenced by sections B(7) and (8), which provide space for the parties to add agreements as to the buying and selling of "jointly owned property" and provide for the division of such jointly owned property on termination of the lease. The form lease also provides space for the parties to define the "place of sale or delivery" of a portion of the crops due lessor as rent under section D(1), regarding the sharing of costs and returns and, specifically, defining rental rates. It is not, however, the blank standard form lease we are called upon to examine.

In this case, we find that the parties intended for the rental on the farm land to be a cash sum rather than the physical "delivery" of 1/5th of the crops to Dr. Meyhoeffer as rent. We draw this conclusion from several provisions of the lease. First, in section B(7), which provides for the buying and selling of "jointly owned property," the parties have written in that "[t]enant sell at his choice." Second, in section B(8), regarding the division of jointly owned property on termination of the lease, the parties have written in "N/A," indicating that this section is not applicable to the parties' intentions or agreement. Third, in section D(1), where the rental rate is specified, the parties failed to provide a "place for sale or delivery" of any portion of the crops to the lessor, which indicates that the lessor did not intend to own or to ever take possession of any part of the crops. Finally, the rental rate itself states that the "[r]ent due after [h]arvest 1/5th (sic) or $32,000 whichever greatest." We believe that it was only "after harvest" that the lessee was obligated to pay rent and that, after the lessee exercised its right to harvest and after the crops were sold by lessee, the lessor was left with a claim for cash rent specified in the lease. Stated another way, we find that this agreement reveals that the parties intended that there be a cash payment to Dr. Meyhoeffer of at least $32,000 per year, to be made after the fall's harvest. In the event that 1/5th of the crop proceeds exceeded $32,000, Dr. Meyhoeffer was entitled to a cash payment of the value of 1/5th of the crop proceeds. If 1/5th of the crop proceeds was less than $32,000, Dr. Meyhoeffer was still entitled to $32,000 cash payment as rent. In this regard, we also find telling that, in his original petition, Dr. Meyhoeffer characterized the rental agreement between him and Mr. Wallace as follows:

> Under the terms of said lease, [Dr. Meyhoeffer] was entitled to rent in the amount of $32,000 at the very least, and in a greater amount if one-fifth (1/5) of the crops produced on the leased premises exceeded $32,000.

No provision of this lease contemplates physical possession or ownership of 1/5th of the crops by Dr. Meyhoeffer; and, according to the allegation in his petition, he intended to always receive a cash rent payment. Moreover, the practice of the parties supports this conclusion as well. Since the inception of this lease arrangement between Mr. Wallace and Dr. Meyhoeffer, the practice was that Mr. Wallace would sell the entirety of the crops (which the lease specifically authorizes him to do) and would then pay Dr. Meyhoeffer cash rent.

Dr. Meyhoeffer relies on three sources for support of his position that he retained ownership of 1/5th of the crops: section F(7)(b) of the lease; La. R.S. 9:3204; and *Guaranty Bank and Trust Company of Alexandria v. Daniels*, 399 So.2d 790 (La. App. 3d Cir. 1981). First, section F(7)(b) of the lease provides as follows:

> Landlord subordination.—In consideration of loan(s) to be made by the Farmers Home Administration (FmHA) the landlord hereby subordinates in favor of the FmHA any lien the landlord now has or may acquire in or on: . . . (b) the crops, livestock increase and livestock products of the tenant (*except a lien on such property produced in any year for that year's rent*); . . . . (emphasis ours).

Dr. Meyhoeffer argues that this provision, in which the lessor refuses to subordinate his lien on crop proceeds produced for rent, indicates that the lessee does not have the right to encumber that portion of the crops or proceeds. The fatal flaw in this logic, however, is that, if the lessor retains *ownership* of 1/5th of the crops, then the lessor would not have a lien on the crops to subordinate—he would own them. It is axiomatic that one does not have a lien on something one owns. To the contrary, we read this provision to apply to cases such as this, where the lessor does not retain ownership of the crops, but, rather, has a lien on the proceeds for the payment of rent. In this particular case, the lessor was not the only party with a security interest in the proceeds, hence, the ranking issue, which will be addressed later in this opinion. In summary, we find no support for Dr. Meyhoeffer's position in section F(7), or any other section, of this lease.

Second, in light of our conclusion regarding ownership of the crops, we find La. R.S. 9:3204 inapplicable to this case. That statute provides:

3204. Lessor's part of crop considered his property; disposition penalty.

In a lease of land for part of the crop, that part which the lessor is to receive is considered at all times the property of the lessor.

The lessee or any person acting with his consent who sells or disposes of the part of the crop belonging to the lessor shall be fined not more than one thousand dollars, or imprisoned for not more than one year, or both.

By its terms, 9:3204 applies to leases wherein a part of the crop is to be "received" by the lessor. As discussed above, the lease in the case *subjudice,* does not so provide, nor has such been the practice of the parties. We find, therefore, that the protection of 9:3204 is not available to Dr. Meyhoeffer.

We reach a similar conclusion regarding Dr. Meyhoeffer's reliance on *Guaranty Bank v. Daniels, supra.* In that case, the bank sued the tenant farmer under certain promissory notes secured by a pledge of crops. The landowners intervened and the court ultimately found that the tenant farmer did not have authority to pledge the crops because the lease made it clear that the landowners retained ownership of a portion of the crops. The rental rate under the lease read as follows: "LESSEE agrees to pay LESSOR a total rental of Twenty-five (25%) of all the crop or $150,000 whichever is more." Significantly, however, the lease in *Guaranty Bank v. Daniels* also had other provisions which indicated the landowners' retention of ownership, such as an agreement that the lessee could not in any way encumber or place a crop lien on the 25% of the "crop due LESSOR" and that lessor could sell his 25% at any time. As previously discussed, there are no similar provisions in the lease before us; and, therefore, we find *Guaranty Bank v. Daniels* to be clearly distinguishable from the present case.

As such, we find that Mr. Wallace owned all of 1998 crops and had the authority to sell and/or encumber all of the crops. We have already noted that the lease expressly gave Mr. Wallace the authority to sell the crops, as was his practice for all previous crop years. Further authority is found in the civil code in La. C.C. art. 474, Movables by anticipation, which provides as follows:

Unharvested crops and ungathered fruit of trees are movables by anticipation when they belong to a person other than the landowner. When encumbered with security rights of third persons, they are movables by anticipation insofar as the creditor is concerned.

The landowner may, by act translative of ownership or by pledge, mobilize by anticipation unharvested crops and ungathered fruits of trees that belong to him.

Under this article, the 1998 crops were movables by anticipation which Mr. Wallace, as owner of the crops, was entitled to encumber. In addition, the crops were movables by anticipation insofar as the Bank was concerned once Mr. Wallace granted the Bank a security interest in the crops.

Notwithstanding our conclusion that Dr. Meyhoeffer did not retain ownership of 1/5th of the crops or the proceeds therefrom, we agree with him and the trial court that he did, however, enjoy a statutory lessor's privilege on the same. Our conclusions thus far, therefore, are (1) Dr. Meyhoeffer did not retain ownership of 1/5th of the crops or proceeds, but did enjoy a statutory privilege on the same and (2) Mr. Wallace had the authority to sell and encumber all of the 1998 crops. We will now address the trial court's conclusion regarding the ranking of Dr. Meyhoeffer's lessor's privilege and the Bank's perfected security interest in the crop proceeds.

Lessor's privilege and ranking of interests

The dispute in the case *sub judice* is over 1/5th of the cash proceeds from the sale of the 1998 crops and not the actual crops. In 1998, consistent with his usual practice, Mr. Wallace harvested and sold the crops. Thereafter, the Bank seized the proceeds of the crops and applied them to Mr. Wallace's indebtedness. La. C.C. art. 3217(3) establishes a lessor's privilege on "the crops of the year" for "[t]he rents of immovables," which clearly gave Dr. Meyhoeffer a lessor's privilege on the crops for payment of rent due. Further, La. C.C. art. 3218 elevates that privilege to a right, allowing the lessor to seize and detain the crops until the lessor is paid. . . .

Louisiana law provides that the lessor must exercise his privilege while the crops are still on the lessee's premises or within 15 days after they have been removed from the premises, provided the crops still remain in the lessee's possession. La. C.C. art.2709; *Carroll v. Bancker,* 43 La. Ann. 1078, 43 La. Ann. 1194, 10 So. 187 (La. 1891); *Bayou Pierre Farms v. Bat Farms Partners, III,* 95-1669 (La. App. 3d Cir. 5/29/96), 676 So.2d 643, *aff'd,* 96-2826 (La. 5/20/97), 693 So.2d 1158. We cannot discern from the record before us the exact dates of harvest and sale of the crops or the date on which Dr. Meyhoeffer made demand for the 1998 rent. In any event, we find that, since Dr. Meyhoeffer did not assert his privilege by seizing the unharvested or harvested crops within the required 15 days, his lessor's privilege over the *crops* was lost.

Assuming arguendo, without specifically deciding, that Dr. Meyhoeffer enjoyed a privilege on the *proceeds* of the sale of the 1998 crops which survived his failure to timely assert his right of pledge and detention over the *physical crops,* we agree with the trial court that the only means by which Dr. Meyhoeffer could have had a viable claim for the 1998 rent was if he had complied with the filing requirements of La. R.S. 9:4521. Filing would, in effect, have rendered him a secured party with a perfected security interest in the crop proceeds. See *Bayou Pierre Farms v. Bat Farms Partners, III, supra.* The issue presented in such situation would be whether Dr. Meyhoeffer's right in the proceeds of the crops outranked the Bank's security interest in the same.[3]

---

3. The Bank had a security interest in the crops and the proceeds therefrom by virtue of the security instrument executed by Mr. Wallace which expressly extended the security rights of the

Recall that the lease was recorded in the conveyance records of Franklin Parish, but was not filed in the LACR. The Bank argues that, since it is undisputed that Dr. Meyhoeffer did not take the necessary steps required for his lessor's privilege to outrank the Bank's security interest, the trial court was correct in ruling that the Bank's security interest was superior. We agree.

La. R.S. 9:4521, Rank of privileges and security interests in crops, provides as follows:

> As a specific exception to R.S. 9:4770 and R.S. 10:9-201, the following statutory privileges and perfected security interests as affecting unharvested crops shall be ranked in the following order of preference, provided that such privileges and security interests have been properly filed and maintained in accordance with the central registry provisions of R.S. 3:3651 et seq.:
>
> (1) Privilege of the laborer, the thresherman, combineman, grain drier, and the overseer.
>
> (2) Privilege of the lessor.
>
> (3) Perfected security interests under Chapter 9 of the Louisiana Commercial Laws in the order of filing, as provided by R.S. 3:3651 et seq.
>
> (4) Privilege of the furnisher of supplies and of money, of the furnisher of water, and of the physician.

The statute expressly provides that the lessor's privilege is superior to a Chapter 9 security interest, "provided that such privilege . . . ha[s] been properly filed and maintained in accordance with the central registry provisions of R.S. 3:3651 et seq." In other words, to enjoy the superior ranking provided by 9:4521, Dr. Meyhoeffer had to have filed his lessor's privilege in the LACR; and it is undisputed that Dr. Meyhoeffer did not do so. Accord *Henry v. Pioneer Sweet Potato Co., Inc.,* 614 So.2d 853 (La. App. 2d Cir. 1993); *Howard v. Stokes,* 607 So.2d 868 (La. App. 2d Cir. 1992). It is also undisputed that the Bank properly perfected its security interest by so filing. Again, if Dr. Meyhoeffer retained a privilege over the proceeds in this case, we see no error in the trial court's conclusion that the Bank's perfected security interest would outrank that lessor's privilege.

Conclusion

For the foregoing reasons, the judgment of the trial court in favor of Daniel E. Wallace and Winnsboro State Bank & Trust Co., Inc. and dismissing Dr. Klaus Meyhoeffer's suit is affirmed. Costs are assessed to Dr. Klaus Meyhoeffer.

AFFIRMED.

Bank to the sale proceeds of the crops. See also La. R.S. 10:9-203(3) which provides that, "[u]nless otherwise agreed a security agreement gives the secured party the rights to proceeds provided by R.S. 10:9-306." La. R.S. 10:9-306(2) provides, in pertinent part, that "a security interest continues in collateral notwithstanding sale, exchange, or other disposition thereof unless the disposition was authorized by the secured party. . . ."

Notes and Questions

1. The court's reasoning in *Meyhoeffer v. Wallace*, 792 So.2d 851 (La. App. 2 Cir. 2001), can be broken down into three main branches. First, the court was required to determine how the 1993 farm lease between the landowner, Dr. Meyhoeffer, and the farmer, David Wallace, allocated ownership of the unharvested crop that Wallace would grow each year on the 530-acre farm in Franklin Parish. To resolve this issue, the court carefully examined the language of the lease.

The court concluded that the landowner did *not* retain an ownership interest in one-fifth of the crop, but only the right to receive rent in money at an annual rate of $32,000 per year *or* one-fifth the value of the total crop, *whichever was greater. Id.* at 854–55. This meant that the landowner, Meyhoeffer, had only a lessor's *lien on the proceeds* to be realized from the sale of the crop in the amount of rent owed under the lease. *Id.* at 855. Put differently, Meyhoffer had only a personal right to receive payment in money and nothing more. Meanwhile, the farmer, Wallace, owned the entire unharvested crop each year as movables by anticipation under Article 474 of the Civil Code. *Id.* at 856. As a corollary, Wallace had a right to grant a security interest to Winnsboro State Bank on the entire unharvested crop he owned.

For similar reasons, the court explained that La. Rev. Stat. 9:3204, which provides that "[i]n a lease of land for part of the crop, that part which the lessor is to receive is considered at all times the property of the lessor," was inapplicable because the lease at issue never required any portion of the crop to be actually "received" by Meyhoeffer. Instead, as the court concluded, the lease here anticipated that "Mr. Wallace owned all of the 1988 crops and had the authority to sell and/or encumber all of the crops." *Meyhoeffer*, 792 So.2d at 856.

Note that in 2004, the legislature added the following article in its revision of the law of lease:

Art. 2677. Crop Rent

When the parties to an agricultural lease agree that the rent will consist of a portion of the crops, that portion is considered at all times the property of the lessor.

La. Civ. Code art. 2677 (2004). The revision comments to this article, however, indicate that it was intended merely to reproduce the first sentence of La. Rev. Stat. 9:3204 and not to change the law. *Id.* rev. cmt. If the facts of *Meyhoeffer* were to occur today, would the result be the same in light of Article 2677? Did the parties in *Meyhoeffer* agree that rent would "consist of a portion of the crops"? If Meyhoeffer wanted to retain an ownership interest in some portion or all of the unharvested crop, how should he (or his lawyer) have written the lease?

2. The second branch of the court's reasoning in *Meyhoeffer* concerns the relative priority and ranking of the landowner's and the bank's liens on the unharvested crops. Meyhoeffer retained a lien and privilege on the unharvested crops—a preference and

priority vis-à-vis other creditors. Relying on articles 3217(3), 3218 and 2709 of the 1870 Civil Code, the court concluded that Louisiana law granted the lessor a *privilege* to take physical control of unharvested or harvested crops and hold them until the rent is paid, while they are on the lessor's premises or within fifteen days after they have been removed from the premises, provided the crops are still in the lessee's possession,. *Meyhoeffer*, 792 So.2d at 857. Since Meyhoeffer did not assert this privilege by seizing the crops within the fifteen day period, this privilege was lost.

3. The third branch of the court's analysis addressed the possibility that, having lost his lessor's privilege, Meyhoeffer might have retained a privilege vis-à-vis other creditors on the *proceeds* realized from the sale of the crop if he had recorded an instrument establishing such a privilege in the appropriate public registry. Here, the court implied that the lease itself would have been sufficient to establish such a privilege had it been timely recorded in the appropriate registry. Meyhoeffer did record the lease in the conveyance records of Franklin Parish, but this was to no avail. Where should Meyhoeffer have recorded the lease? If Meyhoeffer had retained a lawyer to assist him in his dealings with Wallace, would the lawyer face any malpractice liability in a case like this?

4. With the exception of Article 3217(3), the articles of the 1870 Civil Code cited by the court in *Meyhoeffer* were repealed in 2004 and replaced with Articles 2707 and 2710 of the Civil Code, as amended, without any significant change in the law. *See* La. Civ. Code arts. 2707 & 2709 rev. cmts. (2004).

5. For a detailed analysis of security interests in crops and the rights of a lessor to a share of the crops in an agricultural lease, see David Cromwell, *Secured Interests in Louisiana Crops: The 2010 Legislative Session*, 71 La. L. Rev. 1176, 1214–16 (2011). Note that La. Rev. Stat. 9:4521, also cited in *Meyhoeffer*, was repealed in 2010. *See* Cromwell, *Secured Interests*, 71 La. L. Rev. at 1193.

3. Component Parts through Incorporation, Attachment, and Declaration

Articles 465, 466 and 467 of the Civil Code describe three mechanisms by which corporeal movables can become component parts of a tract of land, a building or other construction permanently attached to the ground. All three articles contemplate some form of physical connection with the base thing, although with diminishing degrees of physical integration:

Art. 465. Things incorporated into an immovable

Things incorporated into a tract of land, a building, or other construction, so as to become an integral part of it, such as building materials, are its component parts.

La. Civ. Code art. 465 (1978).

Art. 466. Component parts of a building or other construction

Things that are attached to a building and that, according to prevailing usages, serve to complete a building of the same general type, without regard to its specific use, are its component parts. Component parts of this kind may include doors, shutters, gutters, and cabinetry, as well as plumbing, heating, cooling, electrical, and similar systems.

Things that are attached to a construction other than a building and that serve its principal use are its component parts.

Other things are component parts of a building or other construction if they are attached to such a degree that they cannot be removed without substantial damage to themselves or to the building or other construction.

La. Civ. Code art. 466 (1978, amended 2005, 2006, 2008).

Art. 467. Immovables by declaration

The owner of an immovable may declare that machinery, appliances, and equipment owned by him and placed on the immovable, other than his private residence, for its service and improvement are deemed to be its component parts. The declaration shall be filed for registry in the conveyance records of the parish in which the immovable is located.

La. Civ. Code art. 467 (1978).

After incorporation, attachment or declaration, the movable becomes subject to the rules governing immovables. Movables that become component parts of an immovable pursuant to Article 465 (incorporation) and Article 466 (attachment) are generally considered to "belong to the owner of the immovable." La. Civ. Code art. 493.1 (1984). In certain cases, however, a person who loses ownership in a movable when it becomes a component part of an immovable through incorporation or attachment may assert claims against the owner of the immovable under the laws of accession (Articles 494 through 497 of the Civil Code) or against third persons, if that person's rights in the former movable are reflected in an instrument recorded in the appropriate conveyance or mortgage records of the parish in which the immovable property is located. La. Civ. Code art. 498 rev. cmt. (b) (1979). Because of the frequency with which movables are turned into component parts of immovables in everyday life, there is considerable interest in this subject among homeowners, home sellers, realtors, banks, lessors, lessees, insurers, tax authorities and other concerned actors.

Other jurisdictions refer to things that we describe as "component parts" under Articles 465–467 as "fixtures." Black's Law Dictionary defines a fixture as "[a]n article in the nature of personal property which has been so annexed to the realty that it is regarded as a part of the real property." Black's Law Dictionary (6th ed. 1990). Another definition provides that a fixture is "a thing which, although originally a movable chattel, is by reason of its annexation to, or association in use with land, regarded as a part of the land." RAY ANDREWS BROWN, THE LAW OF PERSONAL PROPERTY 698 (1955).

Louisiana's commercial laws addressing security interests in movables define "fixtures" in reference to Louisiana's concept of component parts by providing:

> 'Fixtures' means goods, other than consumer goods and manufactured homes, that after placement on or incorporation in an immovable have become a component part of such immovable as provided in Civil Code Articles 463, 465, and 466, or that have been declared to be a component part of an immovable under Civil Code Article 467.

La. Rev. Stat. Ann.§ 10:9-102(a)(41) (West Supp. 2013). Although Louisiana's concept of component parts is not radically dissimilar from the common law notion of fixtures, it is not identical.

Before delving into the often contentious subject of how movables can become component parts of buildings or other constructions under Article 466, we first examine how movables become component parts under Article 465 (incorporation) and Article 467 (declaration). These means of immobilization have generally not been controversial.

a. Incorporated Items and Building Materials (Articles 465 and 472)

When things are "incorporated into a tract of land, a building or other construction, so as to become an integral part of it" under Article 465 of the Civil Code, they lose their separate identity as corporeal movables and become part and parcel of the larger object. La. Civ. Code art. 465 rev. cmt. (c) (1978). For example, when a farmer spreads fertilizer or topsoil on her land, the fertilizer or topsoil becomes integrated into and indistinguishable from the land. When a homeowner works various kinds of building materials like nuts, bolts, lumber, tiles and drywall into his house, these elements combine together to form the house and no longer have a separate identity as corporeal movables.

The application of Article 465 has not given rise to much controversy. It establishes a rule that is consistent with most people's intuitive expectations about how common building materials are classified when incorporated into the land, a building or other construction.

Article 472 of the Civil Code is a close cousin of Article 465. It also provides two logical rules that are consistent with common notions of building materials:

Art. 472. Building Materials

Materials gathered for the erection of a new building or other construction, even though deriving from the demolition of an old one, are movables until their incorporation into the new building or other construction.

Materials separated from a building or other construction for the purpose of repair, addition, or alteration to it, with the intention of putting them back, remain immovable.

La. Civ. Code art. 472 (1978).

The first paragraph tells us that brand new building materials that have not yet been physically incorporated into land, a building or other construction remain corporeal movables. The drywall and two by fours that will become the building are movables until they are attached to the ground, building or other construction, even if the materials were derived from the demolition of an old building. La. Civ. Code art. 472(1) (1978). In Louisiana, it is common to reuse bricks, shudders, mill-work or old cypress floorboards derived from a demolished house and incorporate these into a new or renovated structure. When this happens, the building materials from the old building do not become "integrated parts" of the new structure under Article 465 until the moment of incorporation. Brand new building materials that have not yet been physically incorporated into land, a building or other construction remain, not surprisingly, corporeal movables until their physical incorporation occurs. La. Civ. Code art. 472 rev. cmt. (b) (1978).

The second paragraph of Article 472 creates a small exception to this general rule. It explains that when parts of a building or other construction are temporarily separated from that building or other construction, the separated parts remain component parts of the immovable, as long as they are intended to be put back into the same building or other construction. La. Civ. Code art. 472(2) (1978). If a homeowner, in the process of painting his house, removes some boards to repair them, the boards do not become movables if the owner intends to reinstall them in the house. Unlike the situations contemplated in Articles 465 and 472(1), physically separating the building materials from the base thing does not change their classification to corporeal movables. Rather, if they have been removed from a building or other construction and the owner intends to re-incorporate them, they will retain their status as component part immovables.

b. Immovables by Declaration (Article 467)

Article 467 of the Civil Code authorizes the owner of non-residential property to immobilize "machinery, appliances and equipment" by placing these items on the immovable property "for its service and improvement" and recording an instrument declaring the intent of the owner of the immovable to immobilize the items in the conveyance records of the parish where the immovable property is located. La. Civ. Code art. 467 (1978). Unlike immobilization established through integration under Article 465, immobilization under Article 467 does not require any kind of physical transformation of the movable. The physical attachment to the base immovable may be no more significant than that the movable is located on a tract of land or placed in a building or other construction. Instead, classification changes merely because the movable is placed on an immovable for *its service or improvement* and the act declaring the intent to immobilize the movable is recorded.

A farmer could immobilize a tractor or combine harvester by following the procedures of Article 467. Similarly, the owner of a convenience store could immobilize large refrigerator units, a cash register, shelving or display cases. The owner of a factory could immobilize industrial machinery, forklifts or conveyor belts. But note that "service and improvement" does not include placement of a movable on an immovable for storage.

There are several limitations to Article 467 immobilization by declaration. First, immobilization under Article 467 differs substantially from the older French concept of "immovables by destination" in the 1870 Louisiana Civil Code. Under that category, movables as diverse as cattle, pigeons, beehives and other industrial implements, dedicated to the "service and improvement" of a tract of land, were immobilized by mere placement on the tract without any requirement of recordation. La. Civ. Code art. 468 (1870). Under current Article 467, by contrast, immobilization is not accomplished unless and until an instrument declaring the intent to immobilize has been registered in the appropriate public records.

Second, immobilization by declaration is not allowed if the base immovable is a private residence. Thus, a homeowner cannot immobilize a refrigerator or washer-dryer through an act of declaration under Article 467, but the owner of a multi-unit apartment building could immobilize these things if they are placed in an apartment building for the building's service and improvement.

Next, immobilization by declaration is available only when there is unity of ownership of the movable and the base thing. Thus, the owner of a factory or warehouse could not immobilize a piece of loading equipment or machinery rented from a supplier. Similarly, machinery, appliances or equipment subject to a "chattel mortgage" in favor of "mortgage creditor" under Louisiana commercial law cannot be immobilized by declaration. La. Civ. Code art. 467 rev. cmt. (d) (1978). Accordingly, a factory owner who purchases expensive equipment but grants a lender a security interest in the equipment to secure the loan will not be able to take advantage of immobilization by declaration under Article 467.

Finally, in *City of New Orleans v. Baumer Foods, Inc.*, 532 So.2d 1381 (La. 1988), the Louisiana Supreme Court strictly construed current Article 467 to require that all four conditions for immobilization by declaration be satisfied before a corporeal movable will be considered a component part of an immovable: (1) the owner of the base immovable must be the owner of the thing being immobilized; (2) the underlying immovable must be non-residential property; (3) the movable must be actually placed and *actually used* on the immovable for its service and improvement; and (4) the declaration must be registered in the public records. *Id.* at 1384.

In *Baumer*, the defendant purchased conveyor line equipment for its food production plant in New Orleans from an out-of-state supplier, had the equipment shipped to New Orleans, and then filed an authentic act in the public records declaring the machinery to be an immovable under Article 467. Because some time elapsed after the equipment had come to rest in New Orleans but before it was actually put into service in the plant because electrical hook-ups and other preparatory work had to be completed, the City of New Orleans claimed that the city use tax applied to the machinery.

The city taxes any "tangible personal property" (a common law term roughly equivalent to corporeal movable property) that comes to rest in the city. The defendant sought to convert the movable property purchased outside of the city to immovable property to avoid the tax. The Louisiana Supreme Court sided with the city, holding that the movables remained movable and subject to taxation until all the requirements of immobilization by declaration were met. *Baumer*, 532 So.2d at 1384. *See also Farmer's Export Co. v. McNamara*, 515 So.2d 629, 630–31 (La. App. 1 Cir. 1987) (holding that immobilization by declaration does not take place until *placement* of items on an immovable; hence at least 200 items purchased by the owner of a grain elevator for its service and improvement were movable at the time of the sale and subject to local sales tax and subsequent immobilization was immaterial).

Planiol, doubting the utility of the source concept of immovables by destination long before *Baumer Foods*, called the concept "perhaps the most useless creation in modern law." Marcel Planiol, Traité Élémentaire de Droit Civil, No. 2213, at 306 (Louisiana St. L. Inst. trans. 1959). Do you believe the drafters of current Article 467 shared Planiol's view? As we will see in Chapter Six when we study accession in relation to mobile homes and manufactured homes, the concept of immobilization by declaration has important echoes elsewhere in Louisiana property law.

c. Component Part Attachments (Article 466)

Immobilization through attachment under Article 466 of the Civil Code occurs in contexts when the degree of physical integration of the former corporeal movable thing into the building or other construction to which it is attached is weaker than in the case of incorporation under Article 465. Nevertheless, the Civil Code allows immobilization to take place in the situations contemplated by Article 466 because enough of a physical connection or unification of purpose exists between the attached thing and the building or other construction to warrant component part status.

Under the current version of Article 466, which was enacted in 2008, three separate categories of component parts of buildings or other constructions resulting from attachment exist. Recall the entirety of the revised article:

Art. 466. Component parts of a building or other construction

Things that are attached to a building and that, according to prevailing usages, serve to complete a building of the same general type, without regard to its specific use, are its component parts. Component parts of this kind may include doors, shutters, gutters, and cabinetry, as well as plumbing, heating, cooling, electrical, and similar systems.

Things that are attached to a construction other than a building and that serve its principal use are its component parts.

Other things are component parts of a building or other construction if they are attached to such a degree that they cannot be removed without substantial damage to themselves or to the building or other construction.

La. Civ. Code art. 466 (2008).

The most straightforward category of Article 466 component parts is offered in the third paragraph. Things attached to either a building or other construction will be considered a component part of the base thing "if they are attached to such a degree that they *cannot be removed without substantial damage to themselves or to the building or other construction.*" La. Civ. Code art. 466(3) (2008) (emphasis added). This category of component parts has a long tradition in Louisiana. Not only did the 1978 revision of the Civil Code contain it, but the 1870 Civil Code included the same basic notion, though it was expressed in more antique language. *See* La. Civ. Code art. 466(2) (1978) and La. Civ. Code art. 469 (1870) ("The owner is supposed to have attached to his tenement or building forever such movables as are affixed to the same with plaster, or mortar, or such as can not be taken off without being broken or injured, or without breaking or injuring the part of the building to which they are attached.").

The question of how much damage is "substantial" is always one of degree. A substantial damage analysis allows a trier of fact to take into account the context of a particular case. While several thousand dollars of damage resulting from the removal of an attachment to a modest shotgun house might well be substantial, the same amount of damage resulting from the removal of an attachment from an industrial facility, a hospital or a commercial shopping center might be insignificant. This aspect of Article 466 has never been especially problematic. The bigger question has concerned whether this should be the only test for determining the presence or absence of attachments.

If substantial damage were the only pertinent criterion for component part status, corporeal movables that are routinely attached to buildings or other constructions but that can be easily removed without causing substantial damage to either the movable or the base thing would not qualify as component parts. Several of the examples listed in the first paragraph of Article 466 readily fit into this category. Doors, shutters, gutters, cabinetry, water heating units, plumbing fixtures all can be, and routinely are, removed from buildings and other constructions and then re-attached to the same or other buildings or other constructions without causing substantial damage to the movables or the buildings or other constructions. The problem has been how to classify what we might call *loosely connected movables* that nevertheless serve important functions associated with a building or other construction.

The current version of Article 466 of the Civil Code solves this problem by returning in part to an idea previously embedded in the 1870 Civil Code. As noted earlier, Article 467 of the 1870 Civil Code offered a lengthy list of items; for example, "water pipes, gas pipes, sewerage pipes, heating pipes, . . . lighting fixtures, bathtubs, lavatories," and specified that these items "when actually connected with or attached to the building by the owner for the *use or convenience* of the building are immovable by their nature." La. Civ. Code art. 467 (1870) (emphasis added). Current Article 466 resuscitates this notion by specifying that certain loosely attached items that "serve to complete a building of the same general type" or serve the "principal use" of other constructions are component parts. Hence, the following statement in the first paragraph of Article 466:

> Things that are attached to a building and that, according to prevailing usages, *serve to complete a building of the same general type, without regard to its specific use,* are its component parts. Component parts of this type may include doors, shutters, gutters, and cabinetry, as well as plumbing, heating, cooling, electrical and similar systems.

La. Civ. Code art. 466(1) (Rev. 2008) (emphasis added).

This part of the article offers examples, as did the 1870 code article, but goes further to provide a key operating principle to determine when a corporeal movable that is loosely attached to a building (one that is not a component part under the substantial damage test of paragraph three) is, nonetheless, a component part of the immovable. The inquiry is then whether the movable "serves to complete a building of the same general type." As the 2008 revision comments advise, a shutter or gutter attached to a house will be considered a component part of the house, even if the house might have stood without the shutter or gutter for the past fifty years and even if the shutter or gutter is not essential for the structure to function as a house, because, according to prevailing usages, it makes the structure more complete as a house. La. Civ. Code art. 466 rev. cmt. (e) (2008). Similarly, a light fixture installed inside a commercial building such as a hospital will be considered a component part because any light fixture "that illuminates the interior of a commercial building . . . serves to complete the building in its quality as a commercial building." La. Civ. Code art. 466 rev. cmt. (f) (2008). A more exotic attachment like a "nuclear camera" (a very sophisticated and expensive imaging machine) could not be said to complete a generic commercial building, even though it would be useful to have in a commercial building used as a hospital. *Id.* Here, you will notice that the revision comments draw heavily on decisions by the Louisiana Second Circuit Court of Appeal and the Louisiana Supreme Court in a controversial tax case. *See Willis-Knighton Medical Center v. Caddo-Shreveport Sales and Use Tax Comm'n,* 862 So.2d 358 (La. App. 2 Cir. 2003), *affirmed* 903 So.2d 1071(La. 2005).

The phrase "prevailing usages" used in the first paragraph of Article 466 is not meant to open the door to a wide-ranging, judicial search for "societal expectations." As the revision comments indicate, this phrase is included to remind us that the determination of whether a particular thing serves to complete a building cannot be fixed at one moment in time; rather the determination must be made in light of contemporary uses of the kind of building at issue at the time the attachment was made. La. Civ. Code art. 466 rev. cmt. (d) (2008). Also note that the enumeration of things in the first paragraph that may satisfy this completion-of-a-building test is "merely illustrative." *Id.* Other kinds of loosely attached corporeal movables may fit into this category of completing attachments.

With regard to corporeal movables attached to "other constructions," the current version of Article 466 shifts away from the notion of *completing* a structure of the same general type and focuses instead on the notion of serving the primary function of the other construction. It provides that "[t]hings that are attached to a construction other than a building and that *serve its principal use* are its component parts." La. Civ. Code art. 466(2) (2008) (emphasis added). Rather than include a list of this kind of attachment in the article's text, as in the first paragraph, the drafters illustrate the operative principle in the article's second paragraph with a lucid negative example in the revision comments: a cellular telephone antenna attached to a water tower is not a component part of the water tower. La. Civ. Code art. 466 rev. cmt. (g) (2008). For jurisprudence, see *Chesney v. Entergy Louisiana, LLC.* 166 So.3d 1204, 1212–13 (La. App. 2 Cir. 2015), *writ denied*, 236 So. 3d 1262 (2018) (classifying a power cable as a component part of a landfill's power system because it served the principal use of 26 power poles, which themselves were "construction(s) other than a building" and were an integral part of the landfill power system).

In summary, distinct corporeal movables that are so loosely attached to a building that they can be removed without substantial damage to themselves or to the building to which they are attached are nevertheless component parts of the building when they *serve to complete a building of the same general type*. Likewise, corporeal movables loosely attached to other constructions will be component parts if they *serve the principal use of the other construction*. In short, *serving to complete* and *serving principal use* are the touchstone considerations in Article 466.

Disputes over the 1978 Version of Article 466: Between 1999 and 2008, Article 466 of the Civil Code was the subject of a furious controversy among property scholars, judges and practitioners. *Willis-Knighton Medical Center v. Caddo-Shreveport Sales and Use Tax Comm'n*, 903 So.2d 1071 (La. 2005) raised the issue of whether nuclear cameras placed in a hospital were subject to a city sales and use tax paid on maintenance and repair of corporeal movables ("tangible real property"). If the nuclear cameras were found to be component parts of the hospital's buildings, and thus *immovable*, maintenance and repair of the cameras would *not* be subject to the sales and use tax. Conversely, if the nuclear cameras were deemed *movables*, the work on them would be subject to taxation. At the time of the decision, Article 466 read:

Art. 466. Component parts of an immovable

Things permanently attached to a building or other construction, such as plumbing, heating, cooling, electrical or other installations, are its component parts.

Things are considered permanently attached if they cannot be removed without substantial damage to themselves or to the immovable to which they are attached.

La. Civ. Code art. 466 (1978). This article required all component parts to be permanently attached to a building or other construction and added the second paragraph, which, according to the revision comments, was intended to reproduce the substance of Article 469 of the 1870 Civil Code ("The owner is supposed to have attached to his tenement or building forever such movables as are affixed to the same with plaster, or mortar, or as such cannot be taken off without being broken or injured. . . .") with a broad test of substantial damage upon removal.

The debate about when a movable became immobilized by attachment under Article 466 revolved around two questions. The first was whether the two paragraphs of the provision had to be read together ("conjunctively") or each on their own terms ("disjunctively") to determine whether a distinct corporeal movable had become a component part of a building or other construction. Pursuant to the *conjunctive* analysis, the probability of substantial damage upon removal (paragraph 2) furnished the standard for determining whether an item met the overarching requirement of permanent attachment (paragraph 1). Under this conjunctive analysis, only one category of component parts existed: things *similar to* those enumerated in the first paragraph of Article 466 of the Civil Code that were sufficiently permanently attached to the structure to meet the substantial damage test.

In contrast, the *disjunctive* analysis posited that the two paragraphs of Article 466 housed two separate and distinct tests and categories of component parts. The first test under this approach hinged on the functional similarity of a thing to the items enumerated in the first paragraph. It established a category of component parts as a matter of law. The other test and category was keyed to the substantial damage test in the second paragraph.

The second and separate question was whether a "societal expectations" test had a proper place in the application of Article 466 of the Civil Code, in particular under the first prong of the disjunctive analysis. This test, developed in pre-revision jurisprudence and continued in the post-revision jurisprudence after *Equibank v. United States Internal Revenue Service*, **749 F.2d 1176 (5th Cir. 1999)**, addressed whether non-listed items could be fitted into the catchall set of "other installations" mentioned in the first paragraph of Article 466 (1978). This test invoked "prevailing notions" in society and the economy for purposes of determining if a thing was a component part of an immovable without regard to the factual question of substantial damage upon removal. Practically, speaking it was used as a substitute for the unstated intentions of the parties in acts of sale, mortgages, or similar types of instruments.

In *Willis-Knighton*, the justices of the Louisiana Supreme Court divided in their answers to the questions identified above. Writing for a plurality, Justice John L. Weimer embraced the conjunctive analysis and rejected the societal expectations test. His opinion followed the path charted by Judge Jacques L. Wiener, Jr. in *Prytania Park Hotel, Ltd. v. General Star Indemnity Co.,* **179 F.3d 169 (5th Cir. 1999)**. Two main arguments drove Justice Weimer's analysis. First, civilian methodology looks foremost to legislation as the expression of the supreme will of the legislator. In the case of Article 466 of the Civil Code (1978), the plain codal text suggested that both paragraphs were interwoven. Second, considerations of uncertainty and unpredictability counseled against deploying what a court might perceive to be the prevailing currents in society. Due to the ease with which the nuclear cameras could be removed, Justice Weimer concluded that the nuclear cameras were not permanently attached and, therefore, did not qualify as component part attachments. *Willis-Knighton*, 903 So.2d at 1078–92. In reaching its conclusion, Justice Weimer's plurality opinion quoted and relied upon a law review article by one of the co-authors of this book. *See* John A. Lovett, *Another Great Debate?: The Ambiguous Relationship Between the Revised Civic Code and Pre-Revision Jurisprudence as Seen Through the* Prytania Park *Controversy*, 48 Loy. L. Rev. 615 (2002).

Justice (later Chief Justice) Kimball's partial dissent in *Willis-Knighton* contended that the legislative text was not so clear and unambiguous as suggested by the plurality. *Willis-Knighton*, 903 So.2d at 1097–98 (Kimball, J., dissenting). She offered that Article 466 houses two separate tests for component part attachments—one test for plumbing, heating, cooling and other like installations; and another test for those fixtures permanently attached to a building. Moreover, she argued, the history and spirit of the law supported the continued relevance of societal expectations when it came to making the determination as to whether a fixture fitted into "other installations." Justice Kimball directed the inquiry under the societal expectations test to the specific building to which a particular fixture was attached. In this case, she asked whether or not society would expect to see a sophisticated imaging machine in a full service hospital (as opposed to a building in general). She therefore concluded that the nuclear cameras qualified as component part attachments. *Willis-Knighton*, 903 So.2d at 1097–1101.

On June 22, 2005 the Louisiana Supreme Court issued its per curiam opinion on rehearing. *Willis-Knighton Medical Center v. Caddo-Shreveport Sales and Use Tax Comm'n*, 903 So.2d 1071, 1107–10 (La. 2005). It had granted the rehearing for the sole purpose of considering the retroactive effect of its *Willis-Knighton* decision on the proper interpretation of Article 466 of the Civil Code and its definition of a component part attachment to an immovable. The Supreme Court adhered to its original opinion eschewing a disjunctive reading of the two paragraphs in Article 466 of the Civil Code and rejecting the societal expectations test. Although emphasizing that its original opinion did not change the law, the Supreme Court determined to equip it with prospective effect only. Does this strike you as contradictory? Identify some factors that counsel for giving the article prospective effect only or retrospective effect as well.

While *Willis-Knighton* was pending on rehearing, the legislature injected itself into the fray and passed legislation to revise Article 466 of the Civil Code. On June 29, 2005, the Governor signed the legislation into law. 2005 La. Acts, No. 301 changed Article 466 of the Civil Code to read:

Art. 466. Component parts of an immovable

Things permanently attached to an immovable are its component parts.

Things such as plumbing, heating, cooling, electrical or other installations, are component parts of an immovable as a matter of law.

Other things are considered to be permanently attached to an immovable if they cannot be removed without substantial damage to themselves or to the immovable or if, according to prevailing notions in society, they are considered to be component parts of an immovable.

La. Civ. Code art. 466 (2005). In the words of Section 4 of Act No. 301, the revision was "intended to clarify and re-confirm interpretation of Louisiana Civil Code Article 466, including the 'societal expectations' analysis, that prevailed prior to the decision in *Willis-Knighton*. . . ." Are such "legislative fixes" good policy? Should the legislature and the judiciary stay out of each other's business?

Section 3 of Act No. 301 offered an explication of the law in the wake of the revision. It reset the law in favor of the approach advocated by Professor Yiannopoulos who served as the Reporter on the Property Committee of the Louisiana State Law Institute.

"According to legislative intent, the two Paragraphs of Article 466 contemplate distinct tests for the classification of things as component parts of building or other constructions. The things that are indicatively enumerated in the first Paragraph of Article 466 are component parts as a matter of law. All other things are considered to be permanently attached and, therefore, component parts of a building or other construction under the second Paragraph of Article 466, if they cannot be removed without substantial damage to themselves or to the immovable. Further, Louisiana courts have correctly superimposed on the two Paragraphs of Article 466 the realistic test of 'societal expectations.' Things attached to an immovable may be component parts of the immovable or may remain movables depending on societal expectations, namely, prevailing notions in society and economy concerning the status of those things."

La. Acts 2005, No. 301.

The "466 Saga" continued to unfold. Effective August 15, 2006, 2006 La. Acts, No. 765 limited the application of Article 466 to buildings or other constructions, rather than to all immovables. A clause giving the law retroactive effect raised serious constitutional concerns. Broader dissatisfaction with the substance of the revised Article 466 led to yet another overhaul. Effective July 1, 2008, 2008 La. Acts, No. 632 endeavored to offer a "fresh start." The current version of Article 466 of the Civil Code, introduced at the beginning of this section, is the fruit of that fresh start.

One question frequently raised by students and practitioners concerns the continuing relevance, if any, of jurisprudence that interpreted the 1978 version of Article 466, including particularly the now famous decision in *Equibank v. United States Internal Revenue Service*, 749 F.2d 1176 (5th Cir. 1985). Note that the current version of the article uses the phrase "prevailing usages" but not "societal expectations." Revision comment (h) invokes *Equibank* and its statement that common household appliances merely plugged into an electrical outlet are not component parts to illustrate that this kind of attachment would still be insufficient to satisfy the degree of physical attachment necessary for component part status under the current article. *See* La. Civ. Code art. 466 rev. cmt. (h) (2008) ("[a]ttachment consisting solely of the insertion of an electrical plug into an outlet is too ephemeral and insubstantial to satisfy the requirements of this article. Mere placement of movables upon an immovable for its service and improvement, without physical attachment, does not suffice to make them component parts of the immovable under this Article, though they may be susceptible of immobilization by declaration made in accordance with Civil Code Article 467 (Rev. 1978)"). Does this mean that *Equibank* and its "societal expectations" test is still good law?

In light of the many twists and turns in the debate over Article 466, do you consider its new version to be a "fresh start" as the revision comments proclaim? La. Civ. Code art. 466 rev. cmt. (a) (2008). Is the new law likely to increase uncertainties? Note that verb "attached" in paragraph 1 is no longer accompanied by the adverb "permanently." Will an assessment of the modicum of physical attachment referenced in revision comment (h) require case by case jurisprudential interpretation? Is this healthy or problematic? Note that the list of examples of component parts provided in paragraph 1 is gauged in non-mandatory terms, as signaled by the word "may." Are traditional component part attachments, such as electrical systems, now subject to ad hoc assessments of physical attachment, completion of a building or serving the principal use of other constructions?

Finally, recall from our study of Article 463 that not every other construction permanently attached to the ground is itself an immovable. If the other construction is owned by someone other than the owner of the ground, it will be classified as a movable. Strictly speaking, then, current Article 466 does not apply to immobilize an item that serves the principal use of other constructions owned by someone other than the owner of the ground. Nevertheless, the same general principle is used in revised Article 508 of the Civil Code to determine whether an item attached to a movable construction is an accessory of that construction. *See* La. Civ. Code art. 466 rev. cmt. (i) (2008); La. Civ. Code art. 508(2) (2008).

In the following unreported decision, a federal district court used the revised version of Article 466 in a dispute between a bank and another secured creditor. The bank had asserted that its earlier mortgage over a residential, retail and entertainment complex in Baton Rouge applied to an integrated security and information system installed in the complex because the system was a "component part." The other creditor had subsequently filed a security interest arising out of a lease. The collateral for that security interest specifically included the security and information system. Consequently, the key issue in dispute was whether the system was a component part of the complex. If it was, the bank's mortgage applied to the system and primed the subsequently filed security interest arising out of the lease. Is revised Article 466 fulfilling its promise?

De Lage Landen Financial Services, Inc. v. Perkins Rowe Associates, Inc.

2011 WL 1337381 (M.D. La. 2011)

BRADY, Judge. This matter is before the Court on cross motions for summary judgment. Plaintiff De Lage Landen Financial Services ("De Lage") has filed a motion for summary judgment to which KeyBank National Association ("KeyBank") and Jones Lang LaSalle Americas, Inc. ("JLLA") (collectively, "Intervenors") filed an opposition. KeyBank and JLLA filed a motion for summary judgment to which DeLage filed an opposition. There is no need for oral argument. This Court's jurisdiction exists pursuant to 28 U.S.C. § 1332. For the reasons stated here in the Court DENIES both motions.

Background

I. Facts

This case arises out of the alleged failure of Defendants to pay Plaintiff De Lage for the construction an integrated security and informational System ("the System") for the Perkins Rowe Development ("the Development"), a mixed residential, retail and entertainment complex.

The following facts are undisputed. On July 21, 2006, Defendants Perkins Rowe and Perkins Rowe Associates II, LLC, executed a mortgage ("the Mortgage") with KeyBank. Under the terms of the Mortgage, KeyBank retained a security interest in "[a]ll buildings, structures, component parts, other constructions and improvements now located on or later to be constructed on the premises". The Mortgage was recorded with the Clerk of Court and Recorder of Mortgages of East Baton Rouge Parish on July 21, 2006.

On October 3, 2007, Perkins Rowe executed a master lease agreement ("the Lease") with Cisco Systems Capital Corporation ("Cisco") for the System. On November 20, 2007, a UCC-1 Financing Statement was filed and recorded covering the collateral described in the Lease, including the System's equipment. On or about December 11, 2007, Cisco assigned its rights under the Lease to De Lage, at which point De Lage began acquiring equipment, software and services necessary to complete and operate the System.

The System was to be installed for the purpose of controlling the Development's security, fire safety, lighting, music, etc., from a central location. The System is comprised of individual units which are bolted to large black racks which are themselves bolted to the floors of various buildings in the Development. The units' wires run throughout the walls and ceilings of the Development's buildings and through underground conduits in between buildings. Removing the system would require unbolting the units from the racks and pulling the wires from the holes through which they were connected to the individual units. If the System were to be removed, the security, fire safety, lighting, music, etc., would continue to function, but could not be centrally controlled. In addition, questions remain as to how much damage would result from removing the system.

II. Procedural History

On November 19, 2009, De Lage filed suit against Defendants to recover the almost $1.5 million due under the October-2007 Lease. In its complaint, De Lage seeks to enforce its alleged security interest in the System under the Lease. On April 20, 2010, KeyBank and JLLA intervened to protect their alleged security interest in the Development under the Mortgage. KeyBank asserts that the System is a component part of the Development, subject to the July-2006 Mortgage, and that its security interest is superior to De Lage's security interest under the Lease, which was perfected no earlier than October 2007.

On January 20, 2011, De Lage filed its Motion for Summary Judgment. De Lage asserts that its security interest under the Lease is superior to Intervenors security interest under the Mortgage because the System is not a component part of the Development, and is therefore not covered by the Mortgage.

On January 20, 2011, Intervenors filed their Motion for Summary Judgment. Intervenors assert that . . . even if De Lage's lease is valid and its security interest is perfected, Intervenors' security interest is superior because the Mortgage encumbering the Development was filed before the Lease, and the System is a component part of the Development.

Standard of Review

A motion for summary judgment should be granted when the pleadings, depositions, answers to interrogatories, and admissions on file, together with the affidavits, show that there is no genuine issue as to any material fact and that the moving party is entitled to a judgment as a matter of law. . . .

Discussion

. . . .

Under Louisiana Law, an encumbrance on an immovable, such as a mortgage, includes the immovable's component parts. La. Civ. Code art. 469. Under Louisiana Law, "[t]hings incorporated into a tract of land, a building, or other construction, so as to become an integral part of it, such as building materials, are its component parts." La. Civ. Code. art. 465. "Incorporation is a question of fact to be determined by the trier of facts." La. art. 465. There are two tests for determining whether a particular thing is a component part. La.. art. 466. Under first test, "[t]hings that are attached to a building and that, according to prevailing usages, serve to complete a building of the same general type, without regard to its specific use, are its component parts." La.. art. 466. Under the second test, things are component parts if "they are attached to such a degree that they cannot be removed without substantial damage to themselves or to the building or other construction." La.. art. 466. The United States Court of Appeals for the Fifth Circuit has stated that items such as "central heating and air conditioning, . . . built-in public address and alarm systems, . . . interior, physically attached light fixtures, exterior lighting, . . . and like electrical equipment" are component parts under Louisiana Law. *Equibank v. U.S. I.R.S.,* 749 F.2d 1176, 1179 (5th Cir. 1985).

The Court finds that there are genuine issues of material fact. KeyBank's Mortgage granted a security interest in the debtor's "Property" which was defined as including the buildings comprising the Development and their component parts. The processes that the System centrally controlled can still be controlled without the System in place, however, KeyBank has introduced evidence suggesting that doing so would be inappropriate and likely impracticable, especially with regards to lighting and fire safety. That is, the evidence suggests that such a System "completes" a large mixed-use complex "under prevailing usages." The Court finds that this testimony creates genuine issues of material fact as to whether the System is a component part under Louisiana Civil Code article 466.

The Court also finds that there are genuine issues of material fact as to whether removing the System would cause substantial damage to the System itself or the Development. Plaintiff states that removing the system would require nothing more than unbolting the individual units and pulling the wires from the ceilings, walls and conduits through which they run. According to Plaintiffs, the only "damage" that will occur is that the holes into which the units were bolted and through which the wires ran will be exposed. Intervenors claim that (1) it is impossible to tell what wires are related to the System—and could be removed—and which are not; and (2) removing the System may also damage these other wires. Because there are no "as built" drawings of where the various wires are located, Intervenors are not certain whether these "other" wires even exist and state that an electrician will need to be hired to determine their presence and/or location.

Because resolution of both parties' motions require the Court to determine whether the System is a component part of the Development, the Court will DENY both Motions for Summary Judgment.

Conclusion

Accordingly, the Court hereby DENIES Plaintiff De Lage's Motion and Third-Party Plaintiffs KeyBank and JLLA's Motion for Summary Judgment.

Notes and Questions

1. In light of the factual uncertainty that still exists as to whether an unusual but valuable security and information system like the one at issue in *De Lage Landen Financial Services, Inc. v. Perkins Rowe Associates, Inc.,* 20111 WL 1337381 (M.D. La. 2011), will be considered a component part of a building, what steps should a lender take before lending substantial sums for the construction of a major commercial complex? What precautions should be taken by a party like Cisco, or its assignee, De Lage, who grants a lease of valuable equipment that will be installed in a major commercial complex?

2. In *De Lage*, the trial court did not resolve whether the security and information system was a component part of the complex under Article 466. At a trial on the merits, what would you expect the court to decide based on these facts? What additional facts would you like to know if you were deciding the issue?

3. Subsequent to the last revision of Article 466 of the Louisiana Civil Code, the legislature amended the tax laws by enacting R.S. 47:301(16)(q), which reads:

> [f]or purposes of sales and use taxes imposed by the state, any statewide taxing authority, or any political subdivision, the term 'tangible personal property' shall not include any property that would have been considered immovable property prior to the enactment on July 1, 2008, of Act No. 632 of the 2008 Regular Session of the Legislature.

2009 La. Acts No. 442, §2, eff July 1, 2009. The stated purpose of this act was to "restore the prior definition of a component part for sales tax purposes consistent with [2005 La. Acts, No. 301] and [2006 La. Acts, No. 594]." 2009 La. Acts No. 442, §3. Moreover, the enactment of the new provision was declared to be "remedial, curative, and procedural and therefore [to] be applied retroactively as well as prospectively, and shall [be applied] to all transactions occurring on or after the enactment of [2008 La. Acts, No. 632]." 2009 La. Acts, No. 442, §5. What does this mean for purposes of sales taxes? For a decision summarizing the developments surrounding Article 466 and the *Willis Knighton* litigation in the taxation context, see *Hitachi Medical Systems of America, Inc. v. Bridges*, 2015 La. App. Unpub. LEXIS 496, 2015 0658 (La. App. 1 Cir. 2015), *writ denied*, 187 So.3d 1004 (2016) (addressing subject matter jurisdiction of the court below).

4. Deimmobilization

Now that we have reviewed immobilization, we need to briefly consider the converse situation. When can component parts lose their status and become corporeal movables again? Article 468 of the Civil Code, a provision accompanied by comments dense with citations to older case law, provides three pathways to deimmobilization.

Deimmobilization may first result from some physical transformation — usually some event like a fire or hurricane or perhaps just neglect which "so damage[s] or deteriorate[s] [the component parts] that they can no longer serve the use of the lands or buildings." La. Civ. Code art. 468(1) (1978). The most important attribute of this first pathway to deimmobilization is that it takes effect regardless of the interests of third parties like mortgage holders. *Id.* rev. cmt. (b). For an exposition of the rationales and a detailed discussion of French authority supporting this form of deimmobilization as a matter of law, see *Folse v. Triche*, 37 So. 875 (La. 1904). As discussed earlier, note that under Article 472 of the Civil Code, building materials that are temporarily separated from a building for the purpose of repair, addition or alteration of the building are not considered to be deimmobilized as long as the owner intends to put them back. La. Civ. Code art. 472(2) (1978).

The second route to deimmobilization occurs when the owner of the underlying immovable transfers ownership of the component part to a third person through "an act translative of ownership" and delivers the item to an "acquirer in good faith." La. Civ. Code art. 468(2) (1978). If an owner accomplishes these two steps, then the thing will be deimmobilized, even though a third party might have had an interest in the deimmobilized items. If a third party, like a mortgagee, fears that an owner of an immovable may attempt a deimmobilization of component parts by transfer and delivery, that person can seek injunctive relief to prevent the transfer and delivery. In addition, special rules governing home appliances covered by a mortgage on immovable property also protect against this kind of deimmobilization. *See generally* La. Civ. Code art. 468 rev. cmt. (c) (1978). Typically, residential and commercial mortgage documents also contain "waste" provisions that protect mortgagees and penalize mortgagors who engage in activities that tend to diminish the value of mortgaged property serving as collateral for the repayment of loans. *See* John A. Lovett, *Doctrines of Waste in a Landscape of Waste*, 72 Mo. L. Rev. 1209, 1220–27 (2007). This kind of deimmobilization thus may be more theoretical than real.

The third kind of deimmobilization arises in situations when third persons do not have rights in the underlying immovable — for example, when the owner of a house has paid off his mortgage note and owns it "free and clear" of any encumbrances. In this situation, the owner may deimmobilize a component part of his home by simply detaching and removing the item. La. Civ. Code art. 468(3) (1978). When detachment occurs in this context, the detached thing reacquires the status of a corporeal movable. *Id*. rev. cmt. (d).

D. Incorporeal Immovables and Movables

Now that we have fully explored the classification of corporeal movables and immovables, we turn to the distinction between the two classes of incorporeal things, incorporeal immovables and incorporeal movables, which we placed at the bottom of the table introduced earlier.

In contrast to corporeal things, which "have a body, whether animate or inanimate, and can be felt or touched," incorporeals are "things that have no body, but are comprehended by the understanding, such as the rights of inheritance, servitudes, obligations, and right of intellectual property." La. Civ. Code art. 461(2) (1978). As we saw in *South Central Bell Telephone Co. v. Barthelemy*, 643 So.2d 1240 (La. 1994), the Louisiana Supreme Court has interpreted the language in Article 461 defining corporeals as things that can be felt or touched quite liberally to include anything perceptible by the senses. *Id*. at 1244. There is a large universe of things that cannot be perceived by the senses and can only be comprehended by understanding. The interpretative challenge is to distinguish between those that are incorporeal *immovables* and those that are incorporeal *movables*.

Articles 470 and 473 are our guideposts here and provide us with a number of specific examples of each kind of thing.

Art. 470. Incorporeal immovable

> Rights and actions that apply to immovable things are incorporeal immovables. Immovables of this kind are such as personal servitudes established on immovables, predial servitudes, mineral rights, and petitory or possessory actions.

La. Civ. Code art. 470 (1978). This article employs a didactic technique of introducing a simple definition followed by illustrative examples. With the exception of mineral rights, we will study each of these classic kinds of incorporeal immovable things in this book.

The list of incorporeal immovables in Article 470 is merely illustrative. A mortgage is a "nonpossessory right created over property to secure the performance of an obligation." La. Civ. Code art. 3278 (1991). Thus, a mortgage encumbering an immovable is an incorporeal immovable thing. If the mortgagor (for example, a borrower who has pledged immovable property to secure a loan) fails to perform the obligation that the mortgage secures (for example, if the borrower fails to repay the loan) the mortgage gives the mortgagee (the lender who makes the secured loan), "the right to cause the property to be seized and sold in the manner provided by law and to have the proceeds applied toward the satisfaction of the obligation in preference to claims of others." La. Civ. Code art. 3279 (1991). This powerful right of a mortgagee to force a sale of the mortgaged property and claim the proceeds of the sale ahead of the obligee's other creditors is an *incorporeal immovable* right because the collateral—the mortgaged property—is an immovable thing. When a security interest is granted over a movable thing to secure the performance of an obligation, however, the security interest will be classified as an *incorporeal movable*. A.N. YIANNOPOULOS, 2 LOUISIANA CIVIL LAW TREATISE: PROPERTY § 7:47, at 395 (5th ed. 2015).

Many kinds of property interests that a person can acquire in immovable property are not corporeal. They are intangible interests that give the right holder a particular set of rights with respect to the immovable property. The rights of a buyer or seller under a contract to purchase and sell immovable property are further examples of incorporeal immovable rights.

Now let us consider Article 473. It defines incorporeal movables:

Art. 473. Incorporeal Movables

> Rights, obligations, and actions that apply to a movable thing are incorporeal movables. Movables of this kind are such as bonds, annuities, and interests or shares in entities possessing juridical personality.

Interests or shares in a juridical person that owns immovables are considered as movables as long as the entity exists; upon its dissolution the right of each individual to a share in the immovables is an immovable.

La. Civ. Code art. 473 (1978). Just as with incorporeal immovables, the classification of the underlying object determines the classification of the intangible interest related to it. Thus, as noted above, a security interest granted over a movable thing would be classified as an incorporeal movable. Likewise, a cause of action to vindicate the ownership of a movable would be considered an incorporeal movable. A cause of action for the recovery of a sum of money would similarly be considered an incorporeal movable because the object, money, is a corporeal movable. *Id.* rev. cmts. (b) and (c).

Note that Article 473 provides a detailed rule for the classification of interests in things that have a distinct juridical personality separate from the natural persons or other juridical persons who may own the beneficial interests in the entity; for example, a corporate shareholder's interest in a corporation. If a natural person owns 500 shares in a corporation, whether publicly traded or privately held, that person enjoys a number of specific personal rights against the corporation or its board of directors and officers. These may include rights to receive a proportionate share of the corporation's profits in the form of dividends, to participate in the election of the board of directors of the corporation, or to vote on changes in the governing rules of the corporation.

Paragraph two of Article 473 instructs that while a juristic entity such as a corporation is a going concern, the interests or shares of persons in that entity are always considered *incorporeal movables*, regardless of the classification of the things owned by that entity. Thus, even if a corporation's only asset is a tract of land or a building (immovables), the shareholders' interests in that corporation will be classified as *incorporeal movables*. Once such a juristic entity is dissolved, however, the residual rights of each former interest holder to the entity's assets will be classified according to the nature of those assets. Thus, after dissolution of the corporation, the former shareholder's interests in the former corporation's immovable property will be classified as interests in immovable things. *See* La. Civ. Code art. 473 rev. cmt. (e) (1978). If the former corporation also owned movables, the former shareholder's interests in that property would be movable. *Id.*

1. Classification of Interests in Trusts

Trusts play an important role in many aspects of contemporary society, including family wealth transfers, the work of charitable, religious and educational institutions, and complex financial transactions. Because of their ubiquity, entire law courses are devoted to the subject of trusts. The institution of trust hails from the common law, but numerous civil law as well as mixed law jurisdictions meanwhile recognize the trust or trust-like devices in their legal systems. *See generally* EDWARD E. CHASE, JR., 11 LOUISIANA CIVIL LAW TREATISE: TRUSTS (2d ed. 2009). For recent comparative scholarship addressing the assimilation into civilian milieus of the common law's split of ownership, which allocates, at the same time, trust ownership to the trustee and beneficial ownership to the beneficiary, see Markus G. Puder & Anton D. Rudokvas, *How Trust-Like Is Russia's Fiduciary Management? Answers from Louisiana*, 79 La. L. Rev. 1071 (2019) (offering that Louisiana has found a living arrangement with the trust even absent a formal embrace of equitable interests); François du Toit, *Trusts in Mixed Jurisdictions—Aspects of the Louisiana and South African Trusts Compared*, 33 Tul. Eur. & Civ. L.F. 2 (2018) (finding that "in Louisiana uncertainty remains regarding whether the trustee or the principal beneficiary actually owns the property); Ronald J. Scalise, *Some Fundamentals of Trusts: Ownership or Equity in Louisiana?*, 92 Tul. L. Rev. 53, 125 (2017) (concluding that "Louisiana adopted the common law trust and, in doing so, adopted a system in which both the trustee and the beneficiary have real rights in the trust property").

For our purposes, however, it is only necessary to distinguish the various persons involved in a trust and to recognize that a trust is a legal relationship that creates distinct rights and obligations among these various persons. A trust under the Louisiana Trust Code of 1964, La. Rev. Stat. § 9:1721 *et seq.*, is the relationship resulting from the transfer of title to property to a person to be administered by him as a fiduciary for the benefit of another. *Id.* § 9:1731. In a typical trust, there are three crucial players. First, the **trustee** is "the person to whom title to the trust property is transferred to be administered by him as a fiduciary." *Id.* § 9:1781. Different kinds of persons can serve as a trustee, including natural persons or juridical persons like a bank or a non-profit corporation. *Id.* § 9:1731. The person on whose behalf the trust is created and administered is called a **beneficiary**. *Id.* § 1801. Natural persons or juridical persons can be beneficiaries as long as they have the capacity to receive property. *Id.* A person entitled to receive income or the "beneficial use" of the property of the trust during the existence of a trust is called an **income beneficiary**. *Id.* § 1725(2). A person entitled to receive what is left of the property in the trust after the trust's termination and "distribution" of the trust assets is called a **principal beneficiary**. *Id.* § 1725(4). Finally, the person who establishes a trust by transferring property to the trust is called the **settlor**. *Id.* § 1761. The law allows a settlor to establish a trust in which the settlor will be a beneficiary of principal or income or both. *Id.* § 1804. Moreover, the trustee may be someone who is the settlor, the beneficiary or both. *Id.* § 1783.

Over the years, some controversy has surfaced in the case law over how to interpret Articles 470 and 473 in the context of interests in trust. A key case preceding the 1978 revision concerned how to classify a beneficiary's interest in a trust when the underlying assets held by the trust (often referred to as the "principal" or "corpus" of the trust) consisted of immovable property: mineral leases and mineral servitudes. *St. Charles Land Trust v. St. Amant*, 217 So.2d 385 (La. 1968). The majority opinion authored by Justice Sanders ultimately classified "the principal beneficiary's interest in the trust" as "an incorporeal immovable for Louisiana inheritance tax purposes" because the things held by the trustee for the beneficiary were immovables—mineral leases and servitudes. *Id.* at 390.

Dissenting in *St. Charles Land Trust*, Justice Barham contended that the court should have classified the beneficiary's interest in the trust as an incorporeal movable for two reasons: (1) Article 475 of the 1870 Civil Code treated all things which are not clearly defined as immovable as movables, thus making movables the "residual" classification category; and (2) a trust enjoys independent juridical personality just like a corporation or partnership. *Id.* at 391 (Barham, J., dissenting). On the latter point, Justice Barham asserted that by classifying a beneficiary's interest in a trust according to the nature of the principal (the property held by the trust), "the majority has destroyed the entity of a trust, which is the only and real 'object' of the beneficiary's interest, and has incorrectly treated the mineral leases owned by the trust as the 'object' of the beneficiary's interest." *Id.* For additional commentary, *see* A.N. Yiannopoulos, 2 Louisiana Civil Law Treatise: Property § 7:50 (5th ed. 2015).

In the following decision, the Louisiana Supreme Court had occasion to revisit the tricky question of how to classify a beneficiary's interest in a trust. In this case, the beneficiary's interest requiring classification was that of an *income* beneficiary, not a *principal* beneficiary as in *St. Charles Land Trust*. Pay careful attention to the implications of this fact.

In re Howard Marshall Charitable Remainder Annuity Trust
709 So.2d 662 (La. 1998)

KNOLL, Justice. We granted writs in the instant case to determine whether Louisiana has jurisdiction over the succession of a Texas domiciliary, whose only property at the time of his death consisted of undisbursed income from two Louisiana *inter vivos* trusts. For the following reasons, we determine that Louisiana does not have jurisdiction over the succession of J. Howard Marshall, II.

Facts and Procedural History

Decedent, J. Howard Marshall, II, (Mr. Marshall) was an extremely wealthy attorney and businessman who was domiciled in Houston, Texas. He died on August 4, 1995. In the years preceding his death, Mr. Marshall transferred all of his personal assets into a series of *inter vivos* trusts in an attempt to avoid the necessity for probate. The vast majority of Mr. Marshall's assets were transferred to the J. Howard Marshall, II, Living Trust (Living Trust). In addition, Mr. Marshall created a second trust, the Howard Marshall Charitable Remainder Annuity Trust (Charitable Trust) to fund his charitable pledges and donations. The Charitable Trust was funded by an interest bearing note in the amount of $2,950,000, payable to J. Howard Marshall, II, by his son, E. Pierce Marshall.

Mr. Marshall was an income beneficiary under the terms of both trust agreements. The Living Trust provided: "During and throughout [Mr. Marshall's] lifetime, Trustee shall pay over to [Mr. Marshall] sufficient income to maintain [Mr. Marshall's] standard of living." The Charitable Trust states:

The Trustee shall pay to J. Howard Marshall, II (sometimes referred to as *the Recipient*) in each taxable year of the Trust during the Recipient's life an annuity in the amount of One Hundred Ninety-four Thousand Seven Hundred Dollars ($194,700).

Both trusts contained a provision authorizing the trustee to invade the corpus or principal of the trust if necessary to maintain the income streams provided for in the trusts.

The instant dispute concerns the distribution of the principal of the Charitable Trust. By the terms of the trust agreement, following the death of Mr. Marshall the principal was to be distributed as follows:

DISTRIBUTION TO CHARITY. Upon the death of the Recipient, the Trustee shall distribute all of the then principal and income of the trust (other than any amount due Recipient or Recipient's estate under 2 and 3, above) to Haverford College, Haverford Pennsylvania, George School, Bucks County, Pennsylvania, and Yale University, New Haven, Connecticut (hereinafter referred to as *the Charitable Organizations*) in the following proportions:

Haverford College	40.678%
George School	25.424%
Yale University	33.898%

Provided, however, that if any charitable pledge from the Donor exists to any of the Charitable Organizations, the Trustee shall make the distribution in such a manner to satisfy that pledge or pledges with the balance distributed in the proportions specified.

Following Mr. Marshall's death, the trustee of the Charitable Trust, Finley L. Hilliard, a resident of Lake Charles, Louisiana, took preliminary measures to distribute the corpus of the trust to the Charitable Organizations. Mr. Hilliard contacted the Charitable Organizations in an attempt to determine the extent of outstanding pledges, if any, which were due each organization by Mr. Marshall. George School responded that Mr. Marshall owed pledges in excess of $1.1 million dollars at the time of his death, and Haverford College reported between $3.8 and $5.3 million in outstanding pledges. Yale University responded that Mr. Marshall owed no outstanding pledges to that organization. The combined pledges of George School and Haverford College easily exceed the corpus of the charitable trust.

Mr. Hilliard then filed a "Petition for Instructions" in the 14th Judicial District Court in Calcasieu Parish, denying that the Charitable Trust was legally bound to George School and Haverford College for the claimed pledges. In his petition, Mr. Hilliard requested that the corpus of the Charitable Trust be distributed in accordance with the stated percentages without any privilege to the alleged pledges made by Mr. Marshall to Haverford College and George School. Mr. Hilliard further stated that it was Mr. Marshall's intention that the corpus of the trust would fully extinguish any and all pledges he had made to the Charitable Organizations.

George School, Haverford College, and Yale University responded to Mr. Finley's petition. Haverford College asserted that its pledges were valid, and further responded that under the provisions of the trust, the outstanding pledges should be paid first, with only the remainder, if any, to be distributed according to the percentages. Haverford College further expressly reserved the right to enforce any pledges not extinguished by payment against Mr. Marshall's estate. Similarly, George School responded by averring the validity of its pledges, and by reserving the right to pursue the unpaid balance of remaining pledges against Mr. Marshall's estate. George School and Yale University did not oppose the distribution of the trust corpus in accordance with the percentages provided in the Charitable Trust.

In addition to the Charitable Organizations, Mr. Hilliard had named as a party defendant "The Succession of J. Howard Marshall, II, a succession being administered in Calcasieu Parish Louisiana in the 14th Judicial District Court docket number 32,699." (Louisiana Succession). The Louisiana Succession had been opened when E. Pierce Marshall and Finley L. Hilliard, co-executors, filed a "Petition for Probate of Foreign Testament and Codicil" on August 8, 1995. The executors averred that Mr. Marshall owned property in Calcasieu Parish at the time of his death, and that the 14th Judicial District Court therefore had jurisdiction to open Mr. Marshall's succession under La. Code Civ. P. art. 2811. The executors filed a detailed descriptive list of the property owned by Mr. Marshall at the time of his death. Because Mr. Marshall had allegedly transferred all of his property to his *inter vivos* trusts, the descriptive list stated that the only property in Mr. Marshall's estate consisted of the following income earned by the trusts, but undisbursed at the time of his death:

PROPERTY SITUATED IN CALCASIEU PARISH LOUISIANA

1. Accrued but unpaid income due from the J. Howard Marshall, II, Living Trust, a Trust in the Parish of Calcasieu, State of Louisiana: $142,613.62

2. Accrued but unpaid income due from the Howard Marshall Charitable Remainder Annuity Trust, a Trust in the Parish of Calcasieu, State of Louisiana: $17,481.73

The Louisiana Succession responded to Mr. Hilliard's petition for instructions, supporting the position taken by Mr. Hilliard and denying any liability to the Charitable Organizations for outstanding pledges. The Louisiana Succession further asserted that, in the event that J. Howard Marshall, II, made any charitable pledges to the Charitable Organizations, such pledges were solely to be discharged by the assets of the Charitable Trust, and were not liabilities of the Louisiana Succession. The Louisiana Succession then prayed for declaratory relief, requesting that the court issue a judgment specifically enumerating the rights of George School and Haverford College with respect to both the Charitable Trust and the Louisiana Succession.

Both Haverford College and George School responded to the answer of the Louisiana Succession by filing, among other exceptions, a declinatory exception of lack of jurisdiction, asserting that Louisiana had no jurisdiction to open the succession of J. Howard Marshall, II, a Texas domiciliary. The exception to jurisdiction was denied by the trial court and the Third Circuit Court of Appeal denied writs. This Court granted the George School's application for supervisory writs and remanded to the Third Circuit for briefing and opinion on the issue of jurisdiction. *In re: Howard Marshall Charitable Remainder Annuity Trust*, 96-CC-2372 (La. 12/06/96), 684 So.2d 404.

In an unpublished opinion, the Third Circuit affirmed the trial court's denial of the exception of jurisdiction, and held that jurisdiction was proper under La. Code Civ. P. art. 2811. From this judgment, George School applied for writ of certiorari which was granted by this Court. *In re: Howard Marshall Charitable Remainder Annuity Trust*, 97-CC-1718 (La. 10/17/97), 701 So.2d 1349.

Law & Analysis

Jurisdiction is the legal power and authority of a court to hear and determine an action or proceeding involving the legal relations of the parties, and to grant the relief to which they are entitled. La. Code Civ. P. art. 2811 provides for jurisdiction in succession proceedings as follows:

A proceeding to open a succession shall be brought in the district court of the parish where the deceased was domiciled at the time of his death.

If the deceased was not domiciled in this state at the time of his death, his succession may be opened in the district court of any parish where:

(1) Immovable property of the deceased is situated; or,

(2) Movable property of the deceased is situated, if he owned no immovable property in the state at the time of his death.

It is undisputed that Mr. Marshall was a domiciliary of Harris County, Texas at the time of his death. Furthermore, it is undisputed that the only basis for Louisiana's jurisdiction over Mr. Marshall's succession is the alleged existence of undisbursed income from the Louisiana Trusts of which he was a beneficiary. Therefore, the linchpin issue in the instant case is whether the undisbursed trust income listed in the descriptive list is movable or immovable property of the deceased situated in Calcasieu Parish for purposes of establishing the proper jurisdiction for Mr. Marshall's succession.

We initially note that the lower courts erroneously focused their determination of jurisdiction on the basis that the *trusts* were sited in Louisiana. . . .

There can be no doubt that Louisiana has jurisdiction over the *trust* at issue in the instant case. Nevertheless, the fact that the trust is sited in Louisiana does not necessarily mean that Mr. Marshall's *succession* was properly opened in Louisiana. Put simply, the property held by the *trust* of which the decedent was merely an income beneficiary is not relevant for purposes of jurisdiction, while the property owned by the *decedent* at the time of his death is. Therefore, the nature of Mr. Marshall's alleged property interest in the two trusts bears exploration.

As noted by this Court in *St. Charles Land Trust v. St. Amant*, 253 La. 243, 217 So.2d 385 (1969), the classification of the beneficiary's interest in a trust in terms of recognized property concepts raises difficult questions. This classification has been the subject of much controversy in the common law, as well as in the courts of this state. This Court has had considerable discussion on the issue of whether beneficiaries have a property interest in the corpus of the trust or merely an incorporeal right to enforce the terms of the trust. See *Reynolds v. Reynolds*, 388 So.2d 1135 (La. 1979).

The respondent, Louisiana Succession, cites this Court's holding in *St. Charles Land Trust v. St. Amant*, 253 La. 243, 217 So.2d 385 (1969), in support of its position that the undisbursed income is immovable property owned by Mr. Marshall, given that the corpus of the Living Trust is composed of mineral leases. The Third Circuit also cited *St. Charles Land Trust* for the proposition that the interest of a beneficiary of a trust which holds title to immovables is also an immovable.

In *St. Charles Land Trust* we held that the principal beneficiary's interest in a trust whose corpus was composed of immovable property is an incorporeal immovable for Louisiana inheritance tax purposes. Nevertheless, that case is easily distinguished from the instant case. The beneficiary's interest in *St. Charles Land Trust* concerned the nature of the interest of a *principal* beneficiary, while Mr. Marshall's interest was that of an *income* beneficiary.

The principal interest in a trust is the right to receive the corpus of the trust itself, at a future time, in accordance with the provisions of the terms of the trust. If the corpus of the trust is composed of immovable property, the principal interest therefore could be fairly characterized as a future right to immovable property. As a result, *St. Charles Land Trust* classified the principal beneficiary's interest in a trust composed of immovables as immovable property under La. Civ. Code arts. 470 and 471. The interest of an income beneficiary, however, is significantly different. An income beneficiary has no future or present interest in the corpus of the trust, instead having only an interest in the income generated by the corpus, and subsequently disbursed under the terms of the trust. The income beneficiary has only a future interest in income, regardless of whether the corpus of the trust is immovable property, such as a mineral royalty, or whether it is movable property, such as a financial instrument.

The distinction between a principal beneficiary and an income beneficiary is important in that the legal effects which flow from the two interests form the basis for the classification of those interests as either incorporeal movables or incorporeal immovables. The principal beneficiary's interest in a trust which holds immovable property was classified as an incorporeal immovable because it was a future right to an *immovable* thing. Generally, under La. Civ. Code art. 470, "rights and actions that apply to immovable things are incorporeal immovables." An income beneficiary, on the other hand, has no right to immovable property. In short, the interest of an income beneficiary does not apply to immovable property under Article 470, and it is therefore properly classified as an incorporeal movable under La. Civ. Code art. 475, which provides:

> All things, corporeal or incorporeal, that the law does not consider as immovables, are movables.

Additionally, we note that the legal effect that flows from the interest of an income beneficiary is a right to income, or money, which is movable property. Accordingly, we find that the interest of an income beneficiary is properly characterized as an incorporeal movable under La. Civ. Code art. 473, which provides:

> Rights, obligations, and actions that apply to a movable thing are incorporeal movables. Movables of this kind are such as bonds, annuities, and interests or shares in entities possessing juridical personality.
>
> Interests or shares in a juridical person that owns immovable are considered as movables as long as the entity exists; upon its dissolution, the right of each individual to a share in the immovables is an immovable.

We note that while a trust is not a "juridical person" in the strict sense of the word, the first paragraph of Article 473 is plainly illustrative rather than exclusive. We find that the interest of an income beneficiary is analogous to a bond or annuity, in that the stream of payments are made pursuant to the terms of an agreement, in the instant case, the trust instrument.

The entire purpose for Mr. Marshall's creation of the trusts was to divest himself of any ownership interest in the property of the trust corpus. Mr. Marshall had only the right to receive an income stream from the two trusts. He had no independent property interest in the immovables constituting the trust corpus itself. Although the *trustee* could liquidate a portion of the corpus of the trust to insure the income stream guaranteed by the trust, this was not a right vested in the beneficiary.

Furthermore, in *St. Charles Land Trust*, this Court was concerned with the transfer of the beneficiary's interest to her heirs. In the instant case, we note that any beneficiary interest that Mr. Marshall had in the two trusts terminated at the moment of his death, and his interest as a continuing income beneficiary could not be passed to his estate. La.R.S. 9:1964. Put simply, Mr. Marshall's continuing beneficiary interest itself did not form a part of his succession. All that remains in Mr. Marshall's patrimony is the incorporeal movable right to receive the income which accrued while his rights as an income beneficiary still existed.

Undisbursed Income

While the right to receive the undisbursed income had vested in Mr. Marshall and subsequently in his heirs, title to the funds at issue has remained with the trustee. The undisbursed income merely represents an obligation that the trustee owed Mr. Marshall, both as result of his fiduciary status as trustee, and his obligations under the terms of the trust itself. La.R.S. 9:2061. Whether or not these funds actually exist, in trust accounts or otherwise, is irrelevant. Until the funds were disbursed in accordance with the trust code and the provisions of the trusts, they were not the property of Mr. Marshall. In *Reynolds, supra,* this Court noted:

> Title to the property vested in the trustee. LSA-R.S. 9:1731. The undistributed income from the trust was under the control and dominion of the trustee. It accrued to the trustee during the term of the trust as a civil fruit unseparated from the corpus of the trust. LSA-C.C. art. 489 and former art. 499. Ms. Reynolds had no right to this money until the trustee decided to distribute it. The undistributed income did not fall into the community.

Reynolds, supra at 1142 (footnotes omitted). . . .

Similarly, in the instant case, we hold that Mr. Marshall did not have an independent property right, or real right, to the undisbursed income. See La. Civ. Code art. 476, comment (b). His incorporeal rights to the undisbursed income existed only in contrast to the trustee's fiduciary obligations under the Louisiana Trust Code and the terms of the trusts. See La. Civ. Code art. 1757. In short, when he died, Mr. Marshall did not own $160,000 in Calcasieu Parish. Mr. Marshall had merely a limited right to require the trustee to perform his obligation under the terms of the trust. This credit-right was an incorporeal movable which formed a part of Mr. Marshall's patrimony. La. Civ. Code art. 473, 475. Under Louisiana law, the patrimony is a coherent mass of existing or potential rights and liabilities attached to a person for the satisfaction of his economic needs. The patrimony, as a universality of rights and obligations, is ordinarily attached to a person until termination of personality. Yiannopoulos, Louisiana Civil Law Treatise, Property § 194, 195 (1991). Accordingly, until the instant of his death, the right to collect income under the terms of the trust agreement attached to the person of Mr. Marshall in Harris County, Texas. While it could be argued that Mr. Hilliard's obligation to perform under the terms of the trust was situated in Calcasieu Parish, *such obligation belonged to the patrimony of Mr. Hilliard, not Mr. Marshall.*

We find that the concept of *mobilia sequuntur personam, immobilia situa* ("movables follow the person, immovables their locality") is useful in determining the situs of the incorporeal movable rights held by Mr. Marshall. The above phrase means simply that movable property is regarded as being located at the legal domicile of its owner. Although merely a legal fiction, this concept is particularly applicable to incorporeal movables, whose very nature makes the determination of their location problematic . . .

Mobilia sequuntur personam has been held applicable to incorporeal movables by Louisiana courts. In *United Gas Corp. v. Fontenot,* 129 So.2d 748, 241 La. 488 (1961), this Court explained:

> . . . Thus, under this fiction, identification and association in the mind of intangibles with their owners (as in the case of movable tangibles and personalty) gave them, in the law, a 'situs' at the legal domicile of the owner.

United Gas Corporation, supra at 753 (emphasis original). See also, *Sugar v. State Through Collector of Revenue,* 142 So.2d 401, 243 La. 217 (1962); *Campbell v. Bagley,* 276 F.2d 28 (5th Cir. 1960).

The concept of *mobilia sequuntur personam* is well suited to determining the situs of incorporeal movables for succession purposes. Initially, we note that although not controlling for jurisdictional purposes, La. Civ. Code art. 3532 provides that the succession of movables is governed by the law of the decedent's domicile. The policy behind this rule is noted in comment (c) of that article: "the domiciliary rule recognizes the obvious, which is that, of all the states potentially involved in a multistate succession, the last domicile of the testator has a more legitimate claim to have its law applied than either the state where the movable property was located at the time of death or, even less, the state where the testament was made." As noted by Professor Symeonides, in his comprehensive article on conflicts of succession law:

> Whatever their other differences, most systems on both sides of the Atlantic agree on at least one point — that succession to movables should be governed by the personal law of the deceased at the time of death. This is an old rule which, nevertheless, has withstood the test of time. . . .

Symeonides, *Exploring the "Dismal Swamp": The Revision of Louisiana's Conflicts Law on Successions,* 47 La. Law Rev. 1029 (1987).

Similarly, this Court recognizes that, in the context of a succession, policies of comity among our sister states are persuasive. In choosing between the domicile of the decedent and the location of the decedent's debtors, who may be spread across multiple jurisdictions, we find that the maxim *mobilia sequuntur personam* properly places the situs of an incorporeal movable at the domicile of the decedent. Accordingly, we hold that where a decedent held incorporeal movable property at the time of his death, the situs of the incorporeal movable property for purposes of La. Code Civ. P. art. 2811 is the decedent's domicile. . . .

Conclusion

For the foregoing reasons, we find that Mr. Marshall owned no property, movable or immovable, which was situated in Calcasieu Parish. Accordingly, we hold that the Louisiana Succession was improperly opened in a court which lacked jurisdiction under La. Code Civ. P. art. 2811. The judgment of the district court, overruling the exception of lack of jurisdiction is reversed, and set aside, and this case is remanded to the district court for further proceedings consistent with this opinion.

REVERSED AND REMANDED.

Notes and Questions

1. *The Life of J. Howard Marshall*: J. Howard Marshall II attended George Preparatory School, Haverford College and Yale Law School, where he graduated *magna cum laude*. After law school he worked as an associate in a New York law firm before

accepting a position at Yale Law School where he taught, among other courses, Wills and Trusts, and served as Assistant Dean. While at Yale, Marshall's scholarship included an article written with future United States Supreme Court Justice William Douglas in support of legal realism. William O. Douglas & J. Howard Marshall, *A Factual Study of Bankruptcy Administration and Some Suggestions*, 32 Colum. L. Rev. 25 (1932). During this time, Marshall also co-authored two influential articles addressing oil and gas law. *Legal Planning of Petroleum Production*, 41 Yale L. J. 33 (1931–32); 42 Yale L. J. 702 (1932–33). Marshall then worked in the Roosevelt Administration, serving as Assistant Solicitor of the Department of the Interior. During World War II, Marshall became Solicitor of the Petroleum Administration for War and helped to develop America's emerging energy policy.

Marshall began his career in the oil industry as special counsel to Standard Oil Company (now Chevron). Marshall then became President of Ashland Oil and Refining Company (now Marathon Oil) and later worked as Executive Vice President of Signal Oil and Gas and of Allied Signal (now Honeywell). After his semi-retirement, Marshall was one of the founders of the Great Northern Oil Company and founded Marshall Petroleum. Along with others, he helped found Koch Industries, Coastal Corporation, Independent Refinery and International Oil and Gas.

Marshall's first marriage produced two sons, E. Pierce Marshall, and J. Howard Marshall III, and ended in divorce after thirty years. His second marriage ended with his second wife's death. During this second marriage, Marshall had a significant love affair with an exotic dancer, Lady Walker. Marshall bestowed numerous financial gifts on Lady Walker, amounting to millions of dollars. Because he did not pay taxes on those gifts, and purportedly deducted them from his personal taxes, Marshall required legal assistance to avoid an action by the IRS. When Lady Walker died in her fifties, Marshall referred to her death as the great tragedy of his life. Later, at age eighty-nine, Marshall married Vickie Lynn Marshall, also known as Anna Nicole Smith.

Marshall died fourteen months after his marriage to Vickie Lynn (Anna Nicole). He was survived by his two sons and Vickie Lynn. Substantial litigation followed. Neither Vickie Lynn Marshall nor J. Howard III were left anything in J. Howard Marshall's last will. They both asserted claims against E. Pierce Marshall. J. Howard III was apparently disinherited due to a financial disagreement with his father regarding Koch Industries. Disputes over J. Howard Marshall's estate were litigated in Texas and California courts, and appeals were heard twice by the United States Supreme Court. *See Marshall v. Marshall*, 547 U.S. 293 (2006); *Stern v. Marshall*, 131 S. Ct. 2594 (2011). For a detailed account of J. Howard Marshall's life see *In re Marshall*, 275 B.R. 5 (C.D. Cal. 2002); and J. Howard Marshall II, Done in Oil: An Autobiography (Robert L. Bradley, Jr. ed. 2000).

2. In the case before the Louisiana Supreme Court, *In re J. Howard Marshall Charitable Remainder Annuity Trust*, 709 So.2d 662 (La. 1998), why did the George School and Haverford College resist the attempt of Finley L. Hilliard, a resident of

Lake Charles, Louisiana, and the trustee of Marshall's Charitable Trust, to resolve outstanding issues surrounding the distribution of the trust assets in the 14th Judicial District Court in Calcasieu Parish? Why would those two institutions have preferred to have their claims against the trust resolved in a court in Houston, Texas, where Marshall was domiciled at his death? Note that probate proceedings for Marshall had been opened both in Calcasieu Parish and in Harris County, Texas.

3. Why would J. Howard Marshall decide to place a substantial amount of his vast wealth into a trust? What goals might he have been attempting to accomplish by making himself an income beneficiary of a charitable trust, in which his various alma maters were the principal beneficiaries?

4. In his dissent to the Supreme Court's refusal to grant rehearing Justice Lemmon offered that the debtor's domicile was the relevant situs for purposes of triggering jurisdiction over an ancillary succession. *In re: Howard Marshall*, 709 So.2d at 670–71 (1998) (J. Lemmon dissenting) (basing his determination on the revision comments to Article 8 of the Louisiana Code of Civil Procedure).

5. How should a mineral lease bonus be classified? According to industry practice, a mineral lease bonus is a sum of money paid by a would-be mineral lessee to induce a would-be mineral lessor to execute a mineral lease. Is such a bonus a corporeal movable because money is generally classified as a corporeal movable? *See Traigle v. AMI, Inc.*, 280 So.2d 558, 860 (La. App. 3 Cir. 1973) (holding that the right to receive rental payments arising out of the lease of immovable property was an incorporeal movable right not subject to the laws of registry and to which the recordation statute is inapplicable). Or should the payment be considered an incorporeal immovable thing. Note that the Louisiana Mineral Code provides that "[a] mineral right is an incorporeal immovable." La. Rev. Stat. § 31:18 (1974).

Problem

A number of checks drawn on the checking account of IHS, Inc., a local business, were fraudulently cashed at Abe's grocery store by an employee of IHS. Abe's grocery store carries a commercial general liability policy provided by ABC Insurance Company. The policy insures against damage to "tangible property." Is the insurance clause under Abe's insurance policy triggered so as to provide coverage to IHS? Or, put differently, should the fraudulently cashed checks drawn on IHS's checking account be classified as corporeal movable property, and thus tangible property under the insurance policy, or as the right to use funds, an incorporeal movable? *See Innovative Hospitality Systems, Inc. v. Abraham*, 61 So.3d 740 (La. App. 3 Cir. 2011).

→ unsign check

Chapter 5

Accession

A. Introduction

Accession is a means of establishing ownership of things by operation of law. The etymology of the word *accession* reflects its Roman law heritage. "The word *accessio* means properly an increase or addition, *sc.* of something formerly belonging to us [and] is also used to denote the mode in which this increase or addition becomes our property." GORDON CAMPBELL, A COMPENDIUM OF ROMAN LAW FOUNDED ON THE INSTITUTES OF JUSTINIAN 37 (1878).

Following the Roman law adage that "the accessory shares the legal fate of the principal" (*accessio cedit principali*), the accessory, a new thing, will generally belong to the owner of the principal, the more prominent thing. This close, intuitively appealing connection between the accessory and the principal produces one of the basic modes for the acquisition of ownership in most legal systems.

Accession, which brackets resources into one economic unit based on a physical relationship of proximity and connection, produces significant practical benefits for a property law system. Prominent law and economics scholars have observed that accession serves the *internalization function* of property. By assigning "the gains and losses associated with the management of resources" to "the owner of the most prominently connected property," accession tends to "assign resources to those likely to be competent managers of the resource." Thomas W. Merrill, *Accession and Original Ownership*, 1 J. LEGAL ANALYSIS 459, 461 (2009). Restated, if an owner of a farm is generally allocated the ownership of crops and fruits produced on the farm, the owner will have a strong incentive to manage the resources of the farm to maximize gains and minimize losses.

The basic accession rules are generally straightforward and easily understood. But like all simple rules, accession can sometimes produce puzzling and problematic results — windfall gains to an owner of the principal thing that may not be attributable to a wise or energetic management of resources, or losses or liabilities that were not attributable to poor planning or lack of labor on the part of the owner of the principal thing. To temper these results, another legal principle — that of unjust enrichment — often circulates just beneath the surface of accession rules. When we use the term "unjust enrichment" in this chapter, we are not referring specifically to the cause of action provided by Civil Code article 2298: "A person who has been enriched without cause at the expense of another person is bound to compensate that person." La. Civ. Code art. 2298 (1995). Rather, we are referring to the broader principle in civil law, dating as far back as the Roman jurist Pomponious, who said "by the law of nature it is right that nobody should be unjustly enriched at another's expense." D. 50.17.206 (Pomp. 9 ex var. lect.) (transl. from DAVID JOHNSON & REINHARD ZIMMERMAN, EDS. UNJUSTIFIED ENRICHMENT: KEY ISSUES IN COMPARATIVE PERSPECTIVE 3 (2002)).

We will see how the unjust enrichment principle intersects with the principle of accession most dramatically when we study the rights of possessors with regard to fruits and products created on or yielded by immovable property belonging to another person, La. Civ. Code arts. 485–89 (1979), and with regard to buildings, other constructions, plantings and other works made by non-owners in possession of immovable property belonging to another person. La. Civ. Code arts. 493–98 (1979).

Because the basic accession rules are generally intuitive and easily understood by non-lawyers, they also serve to reduce disputes and transaction costs when new things emerge in proximity to other things whose ownership is clear. Yet, as we shall see, the law provides exceptions that allow someone else to claim ownership of a new thing in certain circumstances, particularly when the parties contract for a different result or when equity concerns relating to unjust enrichment or unjust impoverishment are present.

The civil codes of the nineteenth century offer specific accession regimes. In the French and Spanish civil codes, accession rules appear under *droit d'accesion* and *derecho de accesión*, respectively. The Austrian Civil Code speaks of *Zuwachs*, which denotes increase. Although almost absent in the contemporaneous Anglo-American property literature until quite recently, the term *accession* appears in works of English commentators as diverse as Henricus de Bracton, David Hume and William Blackstone.

In the Louisiana Civil Code, the general principle of accession is announced in Title 2 of Book II as one of the foundational principles associated with the concept of ownership:

Art. 482. Accession

The ownership of a thing includes by accession the ownership of everything that it produces or is united with it, either naturally or artificially, in accordance with the following provisions.

La. Civ. Code art. 482 (1979).

A typical accession problem will usually involve four basic ingredients: (1) some accessional force, either natural, artificial or mixed; (2) a new thing, often called the *accessory* thing; (3) another more prominent thing that the accessory is united with or connected to in some fashion, often called the *principal* thing; and (4) at least two interested persons, the owner of the principal thing and the person whose labor or efforts are somehow responsible for the creation of the accessory thing. Accession will often arise in revendicatory proceedings in which either the owner of a principal thing or the creator or producer of the accessory thing claims ownership of the accessory thing. It will also arise in eviction proceedings when an owner evicts a possessor who has taken fruits or products (accessories) from the land (the principal thing).

When faced with competing claims of ownership, a court must allocate ownership of the new thing to one of the interested persons and then determine if the other party is entitled to any compensation. The evicted person, if it is the creator or producer of the new thing, may claim reimbursement for expenses incurred in producing the new thing. As suggested above, the rationale for such a remedy is often one of equalization or unjust enrichment. Sometimes courts have looked beyond the law of accession, and even beyond the principle of unjust enrichment, as, for example, when the owner of a tract of land asserted that she was saddled with an unwanted construction made by a good faith possessor that diminished the value of her land. *See Britt Builders Inc. v. Brister,* 618 So.2d 899 (La. App. 1 Cir. 1993) (turning to the law of delict, specifically trespass, to compensate the landowner).

Most of the rules of the law of accession are **suppletive** in nature; they can be altered by a contract between the parties involved. Take, for example, the case of an improvement to leased premises made by a lessee. A typical lease agreement can provide that the lessor will own any improvements to the leased premises made by the lessee and that the lessee may not remove them upon termination of the lease without the lessor's consent. Conversely, the lessor and lessee might contract for the lessee to have the right to remove improvements upon termination of the lease under specific conditions. Alternatively, a lease could provide that the lessor will retain the improvements but must compensate the lessee for their value or for the cost of making the improvements. One important skill new lawyers must learn is to identify situations where the law of accession allocates ownership of new things — accessories — in ways that might deviate from a client's expectations. A lawyer who can anticipate these situations can help a client contract for a different, perhaps more favorable, outcome.

The Louisiana Civil Code identifies four distinct regimes within the law of accession: (1) a relatively concise set of rules (Articles 483 through 489) that address ownership of natural and civil fruits and concern accessory objects such as the offspring of animals, crops or fruits of trees; (2) a more complex set of rules (Articles 490 through 498) that concern accession *in relation to immovables,* when both the principal thing and the accessory thing are either immovables or their component parts; (3) another set of rules (Articles 499 through 506) that govern accession in relation to land formed in connection with changes in navigable water bodies; and (4) a set of rules (Articles 507 through 516) that cover accession when both the principal and accessory thing are movables. In this chapter, we address all four accession regimes.

B. Ownership of Fruits or Natural Accession: Articles 483–489

1. Basic Terms: Fruits and Products; Good Faith and Bad Faith Possessors

Fruits are defined as things produced by or derived from another thing without diminishing its substance. La. Civ. Code art. 551 (1976); La. Civ. Code art. 483 rev. cmt. (b) (1979). Fruits are subdivided into natural fruits and civil fruits. La. Civ. Code art. 551 (1976). *Natural fruits* are products of the earth or of animals. *Id.* Examples include crops and newborn animals. These things are fruits because the thing that produced them, the land or the mother animal, can continue to produce new things even after a crop is harvested or one set of offspring is produced. *Civil fruits* are "revenues derived from a thing by operation of law or by reason of a juridical act." *Id.* Examples of civil fruits include rent, dividends and interest earned on money deposited in a savings account. *Id.* These revenues are civil fruits because the apartment building that produced the rent, the corporate stock that produced the dividend and the money invested in the savings account can, in theory at least, continue to produce the revenue month after month, year after year, without diminution of the building, the stock or the principal sum of money invested in the savings account.

In contrast to fruits, *products* are derived from another thing, the substance of which is inherently diminished by the act of production. La. Civ. Code art. 488 (1979). Examples of products include topsoil, sand, solid minerals such as coal or granite, fugacious minerals such as oil and natural gas, and standing timber. Removing a tree, topsoil, or a solid mineral leaves a deficit in the long-term capital value of the land. Depleting an underground pool of fugacious minerals such as oil or gas likewise diminishes the value of the surface of the land, even if the surface of the land is not permanently scarred after the drilling and production is complete.

Occasionally Louisiana law treats as fruits certain things that would normally be classified as products. A usufructuary, for example, is entitled to the revenues derived from mineral production if those revenues are generated from a mine or quarry that was open at the commencement of the usufruct, even though minerals are normally classified as products rather than fruits under the law of usufruct. *Compare* La. Min. Code art. 190 [La. Rev. Stat. 31:190] ("open mine doctrine"), *with* La. Civ. Code art. 551, rev. cmt (c) ("Mineral substances extracted from the ground and the proceeds of mineral rights are not fruits, because their production results in depletion of the property."). Similarly, a usufructuary is entitled to trees growing in a managed tree farm or regularly exploited forest or trees classified as "timberlands," even though trees are "ordinarily considered to be capital assets rather than fruits on account of their slow growth and high value." La. Civ. Code art. 551 rev. cmt. (b) (1976), La. Civ. Code art. 562 (1976). Despite this occasional blurring, the distinction between fruits and products is critical in the law of accession. Possessors who are responsible for the production of new things on land will be entitled to different ownership and reimbursement rights depending on whether the new thing is classified as a fruit or product.

The other key distinction necessary for understanding many accession articles involves the status of the person who is not the owner of the base or prominent thing but who is responsible for the creation of the accessory thing. The first crucial distinction is between a true possessor or adverse possessor, on one hand, and a precarious possessor, on the other. A **true** or **adverse possessor** is someone who possesses a thing with the intent to become its owner. La. Civ. Code art. 3424 (1982) ("To acquire possession, one must intend to possess as owner and must take corporeal possession of the thing."); La. Civ. Code art. 481 (1979) ("Ownership is lost by acquisitive when prescription accrues in favor of an adverse possessor."). Thus, a true possessor is someone who physically detains or exercises corporeal control of a thing *and* does so with the intent to become its owner. La. Civ. Code arts. 3421, 3424 (1982). Conversely, a person who only has the physical detention or control of a thing without the intent to become its owner is not a possessor in a legal sense. We call such a person a *precarious possessor*. *See* La. Civ. Code art. 3437 (1982) ("The exercise of possession over a thing with the permission of or on behalf of the owner or possessor is precarious possession."). The most common example of a precarious possessor is a lessee. A person who leases a motor vehicle or a house, for example, has physical control over the vehicle or house, but only with the permission of the lessor—the owner. As the lessee does not possess with the intent to become an owner, that person is only a precarious possessor. The articles on accession treat precarious possessors differently than true or adverse possessors.

The general category of adverse possessors, however, is further subdivided into two important categories. An adverse possessor can be either a *possessor in good faith* or a *possessor in bad faith*. In its rules governing accession, the Civil Code offers a specific definition of the good faith possessor:

Art. 487. Possessor in good faith; definition

For purposes of accession, a possessor is in good faith when he possesses by virtue of an act translative of ownership and does not know of any defects in his ownership. He ceases to be in good faith when these defects are made known to him or an action is instituted against him by the owner for the recovery of the thing.

La. Civ. Code art. 487 (1979). In addition to emphasizing that it applies only in the context of accession, this definition specifies two necessary elements. First, the possessor must possess by virtue of "*an act translative of ownership,*" that is, an act that could have transferred ownership had it originated from the true owner. A good faith possessor must have acquired possession by virtue of some act—a sale, exchange or donation—that on its face would have been sufficient to transfer ownership had it been executed by the true owner or had not the title been "null or annullable on account of defects of substance or form." *Id.* rev. cmt. (d). Unless the possessor acquires his possession of the thing by virtue of an act *translative of ownership*, he cannot be a good faith possessor.

The second requirement for being a good faith possessor is that the possessor must not have knowledge of "any defects in his ownership." La. Civ. Code art. 487 (1979). Note that Article 487 does not specify whether the possessor's lack of knowledge must be reasonable given the circumstances. It merely states, in the words of the revision comments, that the possessor must be "ignorant of the defects of his title." *Id.* rev. cmt (b). This appears to leave open the possibility that someone could be a good faith possessor if the possessor has an act translative of ownership and believes that his title is derived from the true owner, no matter how naïve or foolish that belief may be.

For purposes of the law of acquisitive prescription, the determination of whether a possessor is ignorant of defects in his title, and thus in good faith, is subject to more rigorous scrutiny. Article 3480 of the Civil Code provides that "[f]or purposes of acquisitive prescription, a possessor is in good faith when he reasonably believes, *in light of objective considerations*, that he is owner of the thing he possesses." La. Civ. Code art. 3480 (1982) (emphasis added). In making an *objective* determination as to whether a possessor is in good faith, a court must determine not only that the possessor actually believed at the time his possession commenced that he had acquired ownership from the previous owner, but also that his belief was reasonable as measured by what other reasonable persons in objectively similar circumstances would believe. Article 3480, thus mandates a two-step inquiry: (1) did the possessor subjectively believe he was acquiring ownership; and (2) whether that belief was reasonable. Article 487, by contrast, appears to require only the first step.

Perhaps the explanation for the difference between Article 487 and 3480 is that the articles were revised at different times (Article 487 in 1979 and Article 3480 in 1982), and the inconsistency was merely an oversight of the drafters. Alternatively, Article 487 may intentionally impose a less burdensome test for good faith because the stakes in accession disputes are typically not as high as in acquisitive prescription controversies when an owner can lose ownership, not just of fruits and accessories, but of the actual base thing itself.

A possessor's status as a good faith possessor immediately comes to an end for purposes of accession at the moment the "defects [in his title] are made known to him or an action is instituted against him by the owner for the recovery of the thing." La. Civ. Code art. 487 (1979). By contrast, a possessor's status as a good faith possessor for purposes of acquisitive prescription continues even after he becomes aware of defects in his title. *See* La. Civ. Code art. 3482 (1982) ("It is sufficient that possession has commenced in good faith; subsequent bad faith does not prevent the accrual of prescription of ten years."). Perhaps the enduring effect of good faith possession for purposes of acquisitive prescription explains why the Civil Code insists upon a more rigorous inquiry into whether possession begins in good faith.

For purposes of accession, a bad faith possessor lacks an act translative of title or is aware of defects in his ownership. A bad faith possessor, however, is not simply a willful but temporary trespasser—a person who temporarily enters upon another person's property unlawfully. Rather, a bad faith possessor is someone who physically controls or detains something *with the intent to become its owner*, even though the possession is not coupled with an act translative of ownership or with good faith. La. Civ. Code art. 488 rev. cmt. (e) (1979). Although not explicitly stated in Article 487, good faith is presumed for purposes of accession, just as it is for acquisitive prescription. Thus, a challenger has the burden to rebut the presumption that an accession possessor is in good faith. La. Civ. Code art. 487 rev. cmt. (e) (1979).

For a detailed discussion of how the Civil Code and Louisiana courts distinguish between good faith and bad faith possessors in both the law of accession and the law of acquisitive prescription, see generally John A. Lovett, *Good Faith in Louisiana Property Law*, 78 La. L. Rev. 1162, 1200–1218 (2018). For a discussion of how Louisiana law identifies precarious possessors, see John A. Lovett, *Precarious Possession*, 77 La. L. Rev. 617 (2017).

2. Ground Rules for Allocating Fruits and Products

Article 483 of the Civil Code offers the basic ground rule for allocating ownership of natural and civil fruits.

Art. 483. Ownership of fruits

In the absence of rights of other persons, the owner of a thing acquires the ownership of its natural and civil fruits.

La. Civ. Code art. 483 (1979). This article articulates a nearly universal principle of accession in almost all legal systems. The owner of a thing from which civil or natural fruits are produced will be considered the owner of the fruits as well. Thus, the owner of the fruit producing thing—whether it is land or a share of corporate stock—will have the right to reclaim fruits from another person who has taken possession of them or to obtain injunctive relief to prevent another person from taking possession of them.

The phrase "[i]n the absence of rights of others" at the beginning of Article 483 signals, however, that this base line rule of accession can give way to exceptions in certain circumstances and can be modified by an agreement of the relevant parties. In some settings, a person other than the owner will have the right to retain the fruits of a thing as a matter of law—for example, when fruits have been gathered by a good faith possessor. La. Civ. Code art. 485 (1979). A person who holds a usufruct over the producing thing also has the right to retain fruits as a matter of law. *See generally* La. Civ. Code arts. 550–56. As we saw in *Meyhoeffer v. Wallace*, 792 So.2d 851 (La. App. 2 Cir. 2001), certain lessees—for example, a farm lessee—can acquire the right to retain fruits pursuant to a contract. *See also* La. Civ. Code art. 483 rev. cmt. (c) (1979).

Article 484 of the Civil Code provides an illustration of the general principle of accession in relation to one specific kind of natural fruit—the offspring of animals.

It provides that the "young of animals belong to the owner of the mother of them." La. Civ. Code art. 484 (1979). Virtually all legal systems follow this bright line rule known as the *doctrine of increase* in common law jurisdictions. Although other rules for this scenario are conceivable (the offspring could be assigned to the person who first takes possession), Article 484 assigns the new resource, the offspring, to the person owning the thing with the most salient connection to it—the newborn's mother. That biological maternity usually coincides with physical proximity between the mother and the offspring helps reinforce the intuitive appeal of the rule. Thomas W. Merrill, *Accession and Original Ownership*, 1 J. Leg. Analysis 459, 465 (2009).

Article 485 of the Civil Code provides another general rule applicable when fruits are produced by a person other than the owner of the principal thing, whether a good or bad faith possessor or a consensual possessor.

Art. 485. Fruits produced by a third person; reimbursement

> When fruits that belong to the owner of a thing by accession are produced by the work of another person, or from seeds sown by him, the owner may retain them on reimbursing such person his expenses.

La. Civ. Code art. 485 (1979). Article 485 provides a general rule of reimbursement based on the principle of unjust enrichment; it does not address ownership of fruits. Under Article 485, it is assumed that ownership of a thing's fruits will be allocated under the baseline rule provided by Article 483—the owner of the producing thing will own the fruits in the absence of rights of other persons. Article 485 illustrates how the unjust enrichment principle operates as a counter current through the law of accession. That someone other than the owner of the producing thing, for instance a lessee, contributed to the production of natural fruits does not change how ownership of the fruits is allocated in the absence of a contrary provision of law or contract. But it does give the producer a modest right to be reimbursed for production expenses so that the owner of the producing thing will not receive too much of a windfall at the hands of the person who actually produced the fruits.

Notice two more things about Article 485. First, it does not tell us what is intended by the term "production expenses." Do such expenses include only expenses paid to third persons or do they include the value of the producer's labor? Other provisions of the Civil Code distinguish between these two kinds of expenses in disputes over fruits and products. *Cf.* La. Civ. Code art. 798 (1991) (providing that when "fruits and products are produced by a co-owner, other co-owners are entitled to their share of the fruits or products after deduction of the costs of production"); *Id.* rev. cmt. (c) (but noting that under Article 798 a producing "co-owner does not have the right to claim compensation for his own labor or services"). Second, Article 485 does not distinguish between different kinds of producers of fruits. Accordingly, both *good faith* and *bad faith possessors*, as well as *precarious possessors* and even *trespassers,* are all entitled to the production expense reimbursement right established by this article.

Article 486 provides a finely nuanced rule for the allocation of fruits and reimbursement rights. In contrast to the general presumption of Article 483 that the owner of a thing acquires its natural and civil fruits, this provision establishes ownership rights of persons other than the owner of the producing thing in the case of producers who are good faith possessors while relegating another class of producers—bad faith possessors—to the residual unjust enrichment-based reimbursement right provided in Article 485.

Art. 486. Possessor's rights to fruits

A possessor in good faith acquires the ownership of fruits he has gathered. If he is evicted by the owner, he is entitled to reimbursement for expenses for fruits he was unable to gather.

A possessor in bad faith is bound to restore the owner the fruits he has gathered, or their value, subject to the claim for reimbursement of expenses.

La. Civ. Code art. 486 (1979). Notice that this article gives a member of a particular class of producers—a good faith possessor as defined in Article 487 of the Civil Code—an ownership right in the fruits the good faith possessor has produced and gathered before eviction by the owner of the principal thing. If the producer actually believed he was the owner of the principal thing (for instance a tract of land) and was relying on an act translative of ownership, it seems fair that the Civil Code allows him to keep the fruits that his labor and effort produced. If the true owner of the principal thing evicts the good faith possessor before the fruits of his labor are gathered, Article 486 puts the good faith possessor in at least as good a position as he would have been in under Article 485; that is, he is entitled to reimbursement for expenses incurred with regard to the ungathered fruits.

The second paragraph of Article 486 places the bad faith possessor—someone more than a temporary trespasser but who lacks one or the other of the two requisites for good faith under Article 487—in a much less favorable position, but not completely without remedy. The bad faith possessor whose efforts and expenses have yielded natural or civil fruits must first "restore to the owner the fruits he has gathered, or their value." La. Civ. Code art. 486 (1979). The general presumption of Article 483 is not reversed for the bad faith possessor because he will still lose ownership of fruits he has gathered or must account for their value to the owner of the principal thing. Further, the bad faith possessor will also relinquish any claim to ungathered fruits. Consistent with the unjust enrichment principle embedded in Article 485, however, Article 486 entitles the bad faith possessor to reimbursement of his expenses incurred in connection with the fruits he has gathered. La. Civ. Code art. 486(2) (1979).

It may seem strange that the Civil Code would reward a bad faith possessor with even this modest reimbursement right. But consider this: The true owner of the principal thing, who allowed a bad faith possessor enough time in possession to produce and gather fruits from the principal thing, presumably would have incurred production costs himself had he been the producer of the fruits. The true owner can reclaim the fruits, or be reimbursed for their value, but will not be entitled to the additional windfall of benefitting from the bad faith possessor's production expenses. The Civil Code allows both the good faith and bad faith possessor to retain possession of the principal thing until these production expenses are reimbursed. La. Civ. Code art. 529 (1979).

When a person other than the owner of the principal thing is entitled to the fruits of the thing during a specified period of time only, the fruits must be apportioned between that person and the owner. Under Article 489 of the Civil Code, the producer acquires "the ownership of natural fruits gathered during the existence of his right and a part of the civil fruits proportionate to the duration of his right." La. Civ. Code art. 489 (1979). Thus, a good faith possessor may keep the natural fruits he gathers while he believes he is the owner of the principal thing, but once he becomes aware of defects in his ownership or an action is instituted against him by the owner for the recovery of the principal thing, he no longer has the right to keep the natural fruits he gathers. Civil fruits yielded by the principal thing must also be split proportionally between the good faith possessor and the true owner as of the date the possessor learns that he is no longer in good faith or an action is instituted against him.

Article 488 addresses accession in relation to *products* and provides rules more favorable to the owner of the principal thing.

Art. 488. Products; reimbursement of expenses

Products derived from a thing as a result of diminution of its substance belong to the owner of that thing. When they are reclaimed by the owner, a possessor in good faith has the right to reimbursement of his expenses. A possessor in bad faith does not have this right.

La. Civ. Code art. 488 (1979). Article 488 provides a simple corollary to Article 483. The first sentence instructs that products *always* belong to the owner of the principal thing, which makes sense given that the removal of products always, by definition, reduces the value of the principal thing. If things like timber or minerals are removed from land, thus diminishing the land's value permanently or for a long period of time, the owner of the principal thing should be entitled to claim those products or demand that the person who removed them account for their value if the products cannot be restored. The second sentence of Article 488, like Article 486, provides a modest unjust enrichment based reimbursement right for the good faith possessor. It allows a good faith possessor to recover any production expenses from the owner of the principal thing. The third sentence denies a bad faith possessor any reimbursement rights whatsoever.

Application of Article 488 requires two separate inquiries: (1) whether the accessory at issue is a product rather than a fruit; and (2) if the accessory is a product, whether the person responsible for the removal of the product is a good faith or bad faith possessor. Keep in mind that Article 488 does not preclude application of other rules of delictual (or even criminal) liability. Thus, Louisiana's revised statutes addressing timber piracy, *e.g.*, La. Rev. Stat. §3:4278.1, are not preempted by this article. La. Civ. Code art. 488 rev. cmt. (e) (1979).

Problems Feb 14 Lecture

1. Johanna comes to your office for advice. She shares with you the following story. "I am the owner of a tract of fenced-in crop land in Evangeline Parish. A week ago I discovered two animals on my land: a black cow with a white-mottled face, muley-headed, approximately five years old; and a white-faced calf, not even a week old. Yesterday my neighbor Jimmy told me that a pregnant cow was missing from his herd."

Johanna asks you the following questions: Does she have any legal basis to claim ownership of the cow and the calf? Would it matter if the cow was inseminated by her prized bull?

2. Four years ago, on January 1, Vladimir, the owner of Greenacre, departed for an extended stay in the Russian Federation. Vladimir's friend, Ludmila, took advantage of Vladimir's absence by moving into the farm house situated on Greenacre, changing the locks on the front gate and generally carrying on as if she owned Greenacre. A little more than two years later, Ludmila executed an act of sale purporting to convey Greenacre to David, who promptly recorded the act of sale in the conveyance records of the parish where Greenacre was located and took possession of Greenacre.

David promptly cleared Greenacre of all pine trees and sold the harvested timber for $100,000. In a portion of the cleared land, David planted and harvested a crop of strawberries, which he then sold for $30,000. He spent $5,000 on seeds, fertilizer and other production expenses associated with the strawberry crop. David also leased thirty acres in the southwestern corner of the property to Helma for $2,000 per month, "due and payable in advance" on the first day of the month. Helma made these rental payments regularly. David had his trusted lawyer prepare the lease for a fee of $1,500. Finally, having learned of large natural gas deposits in the shale substrata straddling Greenacre, David executed a mineral lease in favor of ABC Exploration Company, which in turn drilled several wells and began to recover natural gas at an average flow rate of 600 cubic meters of gas per day. ABC Exploration has paid David $190,000 in royalties and bonus payments pursuant to the mineral lease.

On January 1 of this year, Vladimir returned to Louisiana and discovered David in possession of Greenacre. One week later, Vladimir filed a petitory action to evict David from Greenacre. In December of this year, the court issued a final judgment finding Vladimir to be the true owner of Greenacre and evicting David. Describe the parties' respective rights and remedies with respect to the following: (1) The strawberry crop planted and harvested by David; (2) the pine trees cut and sold by David; (3) the rent payments under the lease executed by David and Helma; (4) the mineral royalties and bonus payments paid by ABC Exploration Company. How would your analysis change if we assume that David took possession of Greenacre from Ludmila without a written act of sale? Can Vladimir recover from Ludmila the money David paid to Ludmila for the purchase of Greenacre? Who gets the crops Helma grew on the land she leased?

C. Accession in Relation to Immovables: Artificial Accession

1. The Presumption of Unified Ownership and the Possibility of Horizontal Segregation of Ownership (Articles 490–492)

The first sentence of Article 490 of the Civil Code provides that "[u]nless otherwise provided by law, the ownership of a tract of land carries with it the ownership of everything that is directly above or under it." La. Civ. Code art. 490 (1979). This rule—generally known as the *ad coelum* doctrine at common law—is consistent with the general accession principle stated in Article 482 of the Civil Code: "The ownership of a thing includes by accession the ownership of everything that it produces or is united with it, either naturally or artificially, in accordance with the following provisions." La. Civ. Code art. 482 (1979). As a general matter, if something is attached to, placed on top of, or buried underneath a tract of land, assigning ownership of the accessory object to the owner of the principal thing—the land—seems logical both as a matter of intuition and as an efficient information processing shortcut. Most persons coming across an object placed on top of or buried beneath a tract of land will probably assume that the object is owned by the owner of the tract of land.

We discussed natural accession earlier in this chapter. Crops growing on land and fruit growing on land are presumed to belong to the owner of the land. While separate ownership is permitted, the presumption will govern in the absence of proof to the contrary. Similarly, artificial additions to land are presumed to belong to the landowner. With this understanding in mind, consider Article 491 of the Civil Code and observe how it complicates what we know about accession:

Art. 491. Buildings, other constructions, standing timber and crops

Buildings, other constructions permanently attached to the ground, standing timber, and unharvested crops or ungathered fruits of trees may belong to a person other than the owner of the ground. Nevertheless, they are presumed to belong to the owner of the ground, unless separate ownership is evidenced by an instrument filed for registry in the conveyance records of the parish in which the immovable is located.

La. Civ. Code art. 491 (1979). Article 491 builds on the bedrock accession principle articulated in Article 490 but refines it in three ways.

First, Article 491 unmistakably authorizes horizontal separation of ownership with regard to the enumerated items that are otherwise classified as component parts of land under Article 463 of the Civil Code when they are owned by the owner of the land. *See* La. Civ. Code art. 491 rev. cmt. (b) (1979). Recall that all four of the categories of items listed in the first sentence of Article 491 — buildings, other constructions permanently attached to the ground, standing timber, and unharvested crops or ungathered fruits — can lose their component part status and become either separately owned immovables (in the case of buildings and standing timber), separately owned movables (in the case of other constructions), or movables by anticipation (in the case of unharvested crops or ungathered fruits). *See* La. Civ. Code arts. 464, 474 (1978); La. Civ. Code art. 491 rev. cmt. (b) (1979). Article 491 thus confirms what we learned in Chapter Four: Even things that are permanently classified as immovables (buildings or standing timber) or have some direct physical connection with the ground (other constructions permanently attached to the ground, unharvested crops or ungathered fruits) can be owned by someone other than the owner of the ground.

Second, Article 491 articulates a rebuttable presumption of unified ownership between the owner of the principal thing — the land — and the enumerated accessory objects. At the same time, however, Article 491 expressly indicates one mechanism for overcoming this rebuttable presumption of unified ownership — recordation — and instructs that this mechanism must be used to make a horizontal separation of ownership effective as to third parties. *Id.* rev. cmt. (c) (noting that, in the absence of recordation, "third persons are entitled to assume that these things are component parts of the ground"). Article 491 does not address whether and how the rebuttable presumption of ownership may be overcome in the absence of third parties.

Now, consider the following two decisions. Can you explain their seemingly contradictory results? Why in the first decision, *Marcellous v. David*, 252 So.2d 178 (La. App. 3 Cir. 1971), was a person who placed a building on the land of another without recording any instrument establishing separate ownership allowed to remove the building over the landowner's objection? Why in the second case, *Graffagnino v. Lifestyles Inc.*, 402 So.2d 742 (La. App. 4 Cir. 1981), was a person who placed a building on the land of another with the landowner's consent found not to have any rights in the building or any remedies when the building was willfully destroyed by a subsequent owner of the land?

Marcellous v. David

252 So.2d 178 (La. App. 3 Cir. 1971)

CULPEPPER, Judge. This is a suit for the return of a building and for damages caused by its wrongful removal from plaintiff's land. The district judge found the building was owned by the defendant, Coralie David, and hence rejected plaintiff's demand for return of the building and damages. However, the court awarded plaintiff his actual expenses of $245 for moving the house to his land and painting it, under the equitable principle of unjust enrichment. Plaintiff appealed. Defendants answered the appeal, contending the award to plaintiff of $245 is improper.

This litigation arises out of an unusual set of circumstances. The defendant, Mrs. Coralie David, who is 80 years of age, was living alone in a house in the country and desired to move to the town of Breaux Bridge. Her only income was from Welfare and her only possession was this house. She proposed to various members of her family that if one of them would buy a lot in Breaux Bridge and pay for the expense of moving the house to the lot and installing a cess pool and then let her live there rent free for the remainder of her life, she would execute a will leaving the house to the owner of the lot. This proposal was finally accepted by defendant's niece, Gloria Jones Marcellous, wife of the plaintiff, George Marcellous. Plaintiff also agreed to the proposition and purchased two lots in Breaux Bridge to which the house was moved. It was placed on brick pillars, a cess pool was installed and attached to the plumbing, and George Marcellous painted the building. At about the same time, Coralie David executed a will leaving all of her property to plaintiff's wife.

Coralie David lived in the house rent free for almost two years. During this time she made improvements to the building at a cost of about $1200. In 1969, difficulties arose between Coralie David and her niece. Finally, Mrs. David contacted her brother, Alex Lewis Jean, and requested that he help her move her house from plaintiff's lot. Alex purchased a lot, about two doors away, and had the house moved to it. This suit followed.

Essentially, plaintiff contends that he became the owner of the house when it was moved onto his lot, and that he can recover for its wrongful removal without his consent. On the other hand, defendant, Coralie David, contends she never lost her ownership of the house and had the right to move it.

The first issue to which we will address ourselves is plaintiff's contention that when the house was moved to his lot in Breaux Bridge, installed on brick pillars and a cess pool constructed and connected to the plumbing, it became immovable by nature and its ownership passed to the owner of the lot. Plaintiff cites LSA-C.C. Articles 464 and 506 and the case of *Lighting Fixture Supply Company Inc. v. Pacific Fire Insurance Company of N. Y.*, 176 La. 499, 146 So.35 (1933), for the proposition that buildings are immovable by nature and not susceptible of ownership separate from the land.

The issue is discussed in detail in Yiannopoulos, Civil Law of Property, Sections 43, 46 and 93. Under traditional civilian concepts, the ownership of land was not susceptible of horizontal division. However, Article 506 of the Civil Code of 1870 states that "All the constructions, plantations and works, made on or within the soil, are supposed to be done by the owner, and at his expense, and to belong to him, *unless the contrary be proved.* ***" (emphasis supplied). This language clearly contemplates the ownership of buildings separate from the land. Buildings are presumed to belong to the owner of the soil, but a person claiming the ownership of a building on the land of another can overcome that presumption by proof to the contrary, *Ouachita Parish School Board v. Clark*, 197 La. 131, 1 So.2d 54 (1941);

Meraux v. Andrews, 145 So.2d 104 (La. App. 4th Cir. 1962); and *Haney v. Dunn*, 96 So.2d 243 (La. App. 1957).

The next question is whether Coralie David has sustained her burden of proving that she owned the house which was located on plaintiff's lot. Since she owned the house before it was moved to plaintiff's lot, she remained the owner unless she conveyed it to plaintiff. Plaintiff contends ownership of the house was transferred by an oral donation inter vivos. But buildings are immovable by nature, whether they belong to the owner of the ground or not, *Cloud v. Cloud*, 145 So.2d 331 (La. App. 3rd Cir. 1962); *Meraux v. Andrews, supra*; *Buchler v. Fourroux*, 193 La. 445, 190 So. 640 (1939); Yiannopoulos, Civil Law of Property, Section 46. Under LSA-C.C. Article 1536, every donation inter vivos of immovable property must be by an act passed before a notary public and two witnesses. In the present case, there was no written instrument whatever and hence there was no donation inter vivos of this house. The only thing in writing was the will executed by Coralie David leaving all property of which she died possessed to her niece, Gloria Marcellous. Of course, the will did not take effect since Coralie David is still alive, and, furthermore, the will could be changed by the testatrix at any time before her death, LSA-C.C. Article 1469.

Plaintiff also contends this is an onerous donation and that the rules peculiar to donations inter vivos do not apply, since in this case the value of the object given did not exceed by one-half that of the charges and services rendered by the donee, LSA-C.C. Article 1526. Even assuming that there was an onerous donation, and that Civil Code Article 1523, requiring an act before a notary and two witnesses, does not apply, there remains the fact that the object given in this case was an immovable, the transfer of which must be in writing, LSA-C.C. Article 2275. There was no written transfer of the house.

We conclude the evidence shows the ownership of the house remained in Coralie David while it was located on plaintiff's lot. In consequence, Coralie David had the right to move the house from plaintiff's lot and his demand for its return and damages must be rejected.

It is noteworthy that the present litigation involves the parties to the transaction and not a third person relying on the public records. *Prevot v. Courtney*, 241 La. 313, 129 So.2d 1 (1961). Furthermore, plaintiff does not assert in these proceedings any rights which he may have under LSA-C.C. Article 508.

Defendant filed an answer to the appeal, contending the district court erred in awarding plaintiff the sum of $245, representing his actual cost for moving the house to his lot and painting it. Apparently, this award was made under LSA-C.C. Article 1965, which states the equitable principle that "no one ought to enrich himself at the expense of another." We agree this equitable principle supports the award. Plaintiff actually expended this amount to move the house to Breaux Bridge and paint it. Of course, Coralie David consented to these expenditures and benefited from them. Counsel for Coralie David argues there is a presumption that services rendered by and between relatives are gratuitous. We think it is clear in the present case that these services furnished by plaintiff were not intended to be gratuitous. The parties intended that plaintiff would ultimately be compensated by becoming the owner of the house under Coralie David's will, but of course this event did not occur. We conclude the award of $245 is justified.

For the reasons assigned, the judgment appealed is affirmed. All costs of this appeal are assessed against the plaintiff appellant.

Affirmed.

Graffignino v. Lifestyles, Inc.
402 So.2d 742 (La. App. 4 Cir. 1981)

BARRY, Judge. The trial judge's reasons for judgment present the factual background of this litigation and the basis for judgment which provides in pertinent part:

"This litigation began on August 22, 1974, when A. J. Graffagnino and Donald G. Perez, owners of the property at the corner of 8th Street and Causeway Boulevard in Metairie, filed a petition to enjoin the defendants, Lifestyles, Inc. and Murray P. Holmes, an officer of Lifestyles, from removing or disassembling a structure on the land. The defendants then answered, alleging that the structure is an "O'Dome", a dome-like building on a wooden platform supported by pilings and hooked up to electrical and water connections. The defendant, Murray, later testified at trial that the former owner of the property, Leeand, Inc., had allowed Lifestyles to place this demonstration model of the type of building it sells in return for keeping the grass cut. The defendants further alleged that the building is designed to be portable and therefore movable and its ownership did not pass when ownership of the land passed to the plaintiffs on December 20, 1973. Defendants also alleged that Leeand had agreed in its arrangement with Lifestyles that it would retain ownership of the O'Dome and the right to remove it at the end of the lease and had informed the plaintiffs of this agreement before plaintiffs had bought the property.

The defendant also reconvened against the plaintiffs for damages to the structure, which is now destroyed, in the amount of $ 15,000.00. The defendants also third-partied the former owner, Leeand and its president, Folse Roy, alleging that if the third party defendants had failed to notify the original plaintiffs, specifically the ownership of the structure separate from the land, then the third party defendants are liable to defendants for the amount of their reconventional demand.

The original plaintiffs' petition for an injunction has become moot since the building has subsequently been destroyed. The only issues now before this court concern the defendants' demands.

The written act of sale by which Leeand conveyed the land to the plaintiffs on December 20, 1973, describes the property conveyed as "Six certain lots of ground, together with all the buildings and improvements thereon . . ." The property is described in the same manner in the mortgage and conveyance certificates. Art. 2276 of the La. Civil Code provides that "neither shall parol evidence be admitted against what is beyond what is contained in the acts nor on what may have been said before, or at the time of making them, or since." Other than in an action for reformation for mutual mistake, the sole exception to this general rule excluding parol evidence is that uncertain ties or ambiguities in the language may be clarified by parol evidence. *Liberty Mutual Ins. Co. v. Ads, Inc.*, 357 So.2d 1360 (4th Cir. 1978). In this case the wording of the contract of sale between Leeand and the plaintiffs is clear and unambiguous. Ownership of all buildings and improvements transferred with the land. The terms of the verbal agreement between Leeand and Lifestyles cannot be introduced to vary the terms of the contract of sale.

It is agreed by all parties that Lifestyles did own the O'Dome and did lease the land from Leeand in July of 1973. Nevertheless, this lease was not recorded and the plaintiffs were not parties to it, so the plaintiffs acquired the property and buildings and improvements thereon free of obligations of the unrecorded lease regardless of the plaintiffs' actual knowledge of the situation. Art. 2276; *McDuffie v. Walker*, 125 La. 152, 51 So. 100 (La., P. 100); *Benoit v. Acadia Fuel & Oil Distributors, Inc.*, 315 So.2d 842 (3rd Cir. 1975), *writ refused*, 320 So.2d 550 (La. 1975); *American Creosote Co., Inc. v. Springer*, 257 La. 116, 241 So.2d 510 (La. 1970)."

Therefore, ownership of the O'Dome passed to the plaintiffs in the act of sale if it was a "building or improvement," i.e., an immovable. The Court believes that it is an immovable, a "building or other construction" according to La.C.C. Art. 464 (now C.C. Art. 463, as revised by acts of 1978, No. 728), and the jurisprudence of this state.

In *Ellis v. Dillon*, 345 So.2d 1241 (1st Cir. 1977), the court held that a mobile home, sitting on its axle, hooked up to electrical wires and water pipes, was an immovable by nature. See the court's reasoning, at p. 1243.

In *Bailey v. Kruithoff*, 280 So.2d 262 (2nd Cir. 1975), the court held that a fence was immovable by nature because it was embedded in the ground and because, unlike a movable, it had no identity as a fence when moved; it had identity only when constructed. See the court's reasoning, p. 264.

While the O'Dome is designed to be portable, it is also designed to withstand storms and high winds. Therefore, when it is in use, it is designed to have a degree of permanency.

The structure involved in this case was situated on a platform integrated into the ground with pilings. The structure remained so situated on the property for over a year in all kinds of weather, as the defendant, Holmes, testified that it was designed to do. It could be and was designed to be disassembled and transported easily, but it would lose its identity as a result. Furthermore, as the court held in *Ellis v. Dillon, supra,* the courts must determine what is a building or other construction qualifying as an immovable under Art. 464 (now Art. 463, revised by Acts 1978, No. 728) in light of the social needs of the time. The O'Dome is designed to be easily portable, yet it is intended to be used as a dwelling. When used as a dwelling it is integrated with the soil and stationary. It is a movable only when disassembled, i. e., not in use. The O'Dome on the plaintiff's property was therefore an immovable and therefore ownership of it passed to the plaintiffs along with the land it occupied in the act of sale of December 20, 1973.

Therefore, the court will dismiss Lifestyles' demands against A. J. Graffagnino and Donald G. Perez.

The court is of the opinion that Leeand, Inc. was well aware of the fact that it did not own the building when it sold the land. Therefore, the court will order Leeand, Inc. to pay to Lifestyles, Inc., $ 8,000.00 representing the value of the building. The court bases this recovery on the fact that Leeand, Inc. would be unjustly enriched if it was allowed to sell a building that was not their own and keep all the proceeds."

We agree that plaintiffs' petition for injunctive relief is moot and we fail to find abuse of discretion in the trial judge's determination that the O'Dome structure was immovable. Further, Leeand's lease with Lifestyles was not recorded and plaintiffs were not privy to the lease, therefore, title to the immovable structure was legally transferred to plaintiffs at the time of the sale with Leeand.

We have difficulty with the lower court's holding that Leeand owes damages to Lifestyles because the O'Dome structure was transferred to plaintiffs when the sale was passed. The record shows that Leeand notified one of the plaintiffs in writing prior to the sale that Lifestyles owned the O'Dome structure, and it is abundantly clear that all parties to this litigation were aware that the O'Dome structure was owned by Lifestyles. Most importantly, Lifestyles was put on notice that Leeand was selling its property to the plaintiffs.

The act of sale included the standard verbage ". . . , together with all the buildings and improvements thereon, . . ." and Leeand's only fault, if it be considered a fault, was in not noticing this language in the sale nor noting or requesting that the O'Dome structure be specifically excluded in the sale. However, Lifestyles had knowledge that the sale was pending, certainly was aware that its lease with Leeand was not recorded, yet did nothing to protect its acknowledged ownership of the structure. Lifestyles' apparent options included recordation of its written lease, or removal of the structure prior to the sale, or working out an agreement with the plaintiffs. We feel that Lifestyles' failure to protect itself constituted negligence and was the proximate cause for its subsequent loss and conclude that the district court judgment to the contrary was manifest error.

Accordingly, the judgment of the district court awarding damages in favor of Lifestyles, Inc. is reversed and set aside and in all other respects the judgment is affirmed. Costs of this appeal are to be paid by Lifestyles, Inc.

REVERSED IN PART, AFFIRMED IN PART, AND RENDERED

Notes and Questions

1. In *Marcellous v. David*, 402 So.2d 742 (La. App. 4 Cir. 1981), Coralie David was able to rebut the presumption of unified ownership of land and a building placed upon the land established by Article 491 of the Civil Code, even though she had not filed any instrument for registry in the public records in St. Martin Parish where George Marcellous' two lots were located. How did she overcome the presumption of unified ownership established in Article 491?

2. In *Graffagnino v. Lifestyles, Inc.*, 402 So.2d 742 (La. App. 4 Cir. 1981), the two third parties (A.J. Graffagnino and Donald J. Perez) appear to have had actual knowledge that Leeand, Inc., the previous owner of a tract of land in Jefferson Parish, and another juridical entity, Lifestyles, Inc., which placed a construction known as an "O'Dome" on that land, had agreed that Lifestyles would retain the right to remove this construction at the end of their relationship. Why, then, did Lifestyles, a consensual improver, find itself without a remedy when the new owners, Graffignino and Perez, tore down the O'Dome?

3. The trial court in *Graffagnino* believed that Lifestyles was treated unfairly and pointed to unjust enrichment principles to justify its $8,000 damage award against Leeand and in favor of Lifestyles. Was the trial court ruling justified? Or was the court of appeal correct in finding that Lifestyles bore responsibility for the loss of its O'Dome? Consider carefully the effect of Article 498 of the Civil Code on the potential claims of a consensual improver, such as Lifestyles, Inc., that has lost the ownership of a large-scale or small-scale improvement it has made on the land of another person:

Art. 498. Claims against third persons

One who has lost the ownership of a thing to the owner of an immovable may assert against third persons his rights under Articles 493, 493.1, 494, 495, 496, or 497 when they are evidenced by an instrument filed for registry in the appropriate conveyance or mortgage records of the parish in which the immovable is located.

La. Civ. Code art. 498 (1979). Also take note of the admonition found in revision comment (e) to that article:

The transfer or encumbrance of an immovable includes its component parts. In the absence of a recorded instrument, the third person's or good faith possessor's rights in constructions, plantings, or works that he may have made on the land of another are lost in case of alienation of the land. . . . In such a case, the third person is relegated to a personal action for reimbursement from the former landowner. . . . In order to protect his interest against any owner of the land, a person who constructs improvements should record 'his title to those improvements.'

Id. rev. cmt. (e) (citations omitted). Although these comments were written after *Graffagnino* was decided, what conclusions can you draw?

4. *The O'Dome*: The improvement at the heart of the dispute in *Graffagnino* was a rather odd construction called an "O'Dome." Structures like this, reminiscent of geodesic domes, were more common in the 1970s than they are today. Do you agree with the trial court and court of appeal's characterization of the O'Dome as a building? Had it been labeled a corporeal movable temporarily located on Leeand's land, like the modular banking units in *Bridges v. National Financial Systems, Inc.*, 960 So.2d 202 (La. App. 1 Cir. 2007), the result in *Graffagnino* would have been very different. Do you see why? What result if the O'Dome had been characterized as an "other construction permanently attached to the ground"?

5. *The Manufactured Home Property Act:* In 1982, one year after the decision in *Graffagnino*, the Louisiana legislature enacted the Manufactured Home Property Act, La. Rev. Stat. § 9:1149.1 *et seq.* Consider the following provisions of the Act and determine whether their application to the facts in *Graffagnino* would produce a different outcome:

9: 1149.2: Definitions

In this Chapter, the following words and phrases shall have the meaning ascribed to them unless the content or subject matter clearly indicate otherwise. . . .

(2) "Manufactured home" means a mobile home or residential mobile home.

(3) "Mobile home" means a factory assembled structure or structures transportable in one or more sections, with or without a permanent foundation, and includes the plumbing, heating, air conditioning, and electrical systems contained therein.

. . .

(10) "Residential mobile home" means a manufactured home designed to be used as a dwelling, and may include a mobile home or a residential mobile home that has been declared to be a part of the realty as provided in R.S. 9:1149.4.

. . .

9: 1149.3: Classification

Except as otherwise provided in R.S. 9:1149.4, when any manufactured home shall be moved to and located in or upon any immovable property, or installed therein or thereon in a manner which, under any law, might make the manufactured home an immovable or component part thereof, the manufactured home shall be and will remain a movable subject to the provisions of Chapter 4 of Title 32 of the Louisiana Revised Statutes of 1950 governing its mortgage or sale and subject to the provisions of Chapter 9 of Title 10 of the Louisiana Revised Statutes. . . . Title to the vehicle shall not pass the by sale of the immovable property to which it has been actually or fictitiously attached, whether such sale be conventional or judicial. No sale or mortgage of or lien upon the immovable shall in any manner affect or impair the rank or privilege of a chattel mortgage or security interest under Chapter 9 of the Louisiana Commercial Laws on such manufactured home, or the remedies of the holder thereof for its enforcement.

9: 1149.4: Immobilization

A. A manufactured home placed upon a lot or tract of land shall be an immovable when there is recorded in the appropriate conveyance or mortgage records of the parish where the said lot or tract of land is situated an authentic act or a validly executed and acknowledged sale or mortgage or sale with mortgage which contains a description of the manufactured home as described in the certificate of title or manufacturer's certificate of origin and a description of the lot or tract of land upon which the manufactured home is placed, and contains a declaration by owner of the manufactured home and, when applicable, the holder of a mortgage or security interest under Chapter 9 of the Louisiana Commercial Laws on the manufactured home, that it shall remain permanently attached to the lot or tract of land described in the instrument.

. . .

9: 1149.6: Deimmobilization

A. The owner may deimmobilize a manufactured home by detachment or removal. However, to affect third persons, an authentic act or sale or mortgage or sale with mortgage containing a description of the manufactured home as described in the previous certificate of title or manufacturer's certificate of origin, a description of the lot or tract of land upon which the manufactured home has been placed, a statement of intent by the owner that he no longer intends the manufactured home to be an immovable and a description of the document by which the manufactured home was immobilized, including the recording information, must be filed in the in the appropriate conveyance or mortgage records of the parish where the said lot or tract of land is situated.

. . .

C. Upon the issuance of a certificate of title by the commissioner, the manufactured home shall be deemed a movable, and shall be subject to all laws concerning movable property.

To determine how the Act might (or might not) change the outcome of a case like *Graffagnino*, answer the following questions: (a) Would the O'Dome be a "manufactured home" that falls within the scope of Section 1 of the Act? (b) If so, what is the effect of Sections 3, 4 and 6 of the Act on the classification of the O'Dome? (c) If you were advising a company today in the same position as Lifestyles, what recommendations, if any, might you give in light of the Act to protect the company's interests in something like an O'Dome?

For an illustrative example of the pitfalls that can arise in complying with the Manufactured Home Property Act, see *Hunt v. McNamara*, 494 So.2d 1279, 1281 (La. App. 2 Cir. 1986) (holding that although unity of ownership of land and a manufactured home is not required for compliance with the Act, immobilization will only occur if the "present owner" of the manufactured home, rather than the vendor, completes and records the declaration of immobilization).

6. *Town of Arcadia v. Arcadia Chamber of Commerce* — The Veterans Memorial Controversy: A dispute between a small town and a local chamber of commerce concerning a veterans memorial has recently required Louisiana courts to return to basic principles of accession. In 1999, the town's local chamber of commerce, a non-profit organization comprised of local business people, decided it wanted to build a memorial to honor veterans from the town and surrounding parish. The chamber of commerce raised funds for the project by obtaining small donations from local residents and used those funds to pay for the acquisition of four granite panels. The town supported the project and allowed the granite panels to be installed on a concrete slab on a tract of land owned by the town next to a museum. No written agreement addressed the ownership of the panels, but a formal dedication ceremony was held in December 1999, and memorial plaques commemorating the donations covered almost all of the panels. For the next fourteen years, the town mowed and maintained the grass around the panels, replaced the flag that adorned the memorial, washed the panels, and paid the electric bill for the lighting of the wall. In late 2013, however, the chamber of commerce suddenly, and without consulting town officials, moved the four panels comprising the memorial to the grounds of the new Bienville Parish Courthouse. Soon enough litigation ensued between the town and the chamber of commerce regarding the ownership of the memorial wall. See *Town of Arcadia v. Arcadia Chamber of Commerce*, 195 So.3d 23 (La. App. 2 Cir. 2016). How should the memorial wall be classified? Is it a component part of the land on which it was originally placed? Is it a separately owned movable or a separately owned immovable? Who owns the wall: the town or the chamber of commerce? What Civil Code articles will be decisive in resolving this dispute?

7 . Article 492 of the Civil Code, a close cousin of Article 491, presents a specialized accession rule allowing discrete units within a building, such as a floor, apartment or even a single room, to be separately owned from the rest of the building, as long as this separation of ownership is established by a "juridical act of the owner of

the entire building when and in the manner expressly authorized by law." La. Civ. Code art. 492 (1979). This provision opens the door to the complex but important regime of condominium regulation under the Louisiana Condominium Act, La. Rev. Stat. § 1121.101 *et seq.* Note the observation in the revision comments to Article 492 that "separate ownership of a floor or of an apartment of a building may not be established by acquisitive prescription . . ." *Id.* rev. cmt. (a). Why would the Civil Code prohibit acquisition of a floor or apartment inside a building by acquisitive prescription?

2. Improvements Made by Precarious and Adverse Possessors (Articles 493–498)

One well-known legal scholar described Articles 493 through 498 of the Civil Code as "a pile of 'cans of worms.'" Symeon Symeonides, *Developments in the Law, Property*, 47 La. L. Rev. 429, 451 (1986). Other scholars have observed how frequently these articles have been misinterpreted by courts and by commentators. *See* A.N. Yiannopoulos, 2 Louisiana Civil Law Treatise, Property § 116.10 (4th ed. 2013–14 Pocket Part). One of these articles, Article 493, has been prominently revised but still creates confusion. *Id.*, n. 9 (criticizing *Broussard v. Compton*, 36 So.3d 376 (La. App. 3 Cir. 2010)). Despite the misery that this suite of articles seems to have spawned in the Louisiana legal community, the articles themselves persist.

To illuminate how these articles might be deployed more fruitfully, we offer an analytical approach to the four most frequently cited articles — Articles 493, 495, 496 and 497 — which draws attention to the kind of possessor each article addresses and to the particular improvement at issue. These articles sort out the ownership rights of the improver and the owner of the underlying immovable. They also address the remedies available when either the precarious possessor loses the right to remain on or in the immovable or the owner of an immovable evicts an adverse possessor.

Rather than memorize the detailed and sometimes confusing sets of rights and remedies that each of the articles establishes, we recommend that you focus initially on the kind of possessor and the kind of improvement each article addresses. We visualize this approach by a set of funnels. Each funnel represents one of the four primary articles in this series. The **Article 493** funnel applies to a category of improvements we call *large-scale improvements by a precarious possessor.* The **Article 495** funnel applies to what we call *small-scale improvements by a precarious possessor.* **Article 496** creates a set of rules to regulate the rights of *good faith possessors* who make improvements or "constructions," to use the language of the article, on or to an immovable owned by another person, regardless of the size of the improvement. And finally **Article 497** regulates the rights of *bad faith possessors* and the owner of the underlying immovable, without regard to the size of the possessor's improvement or construction.

a. Article 493 and Large Scale Improvements

To understand how Article 493 functions today, one must break the article into discrete parts. Article 493's first paragraph provides:

Art. 493. Ownership of Improvements

> Buildings, other constructions permanently attached to the ground, and plantings made on the land of another with his consent belong to him who made them. They belong to the owner of the ground when they are made without his consent.

La. Civ. Code art. 493(1) (1979). The first sentence of this paragraph recognizes what we have seen already in Article 491 — namely that the large scale things enumerated in the article, which are presumed to be component parts of a tract of land under Article 463 of the Civil Code, can be separately owned by the person who created them. The crucial phrase in the first sentence is the proviso that separate ownership of these large-scale improvements exists only if the improver *obtained the consent* of the owner of the land. This sentence thus applies only when the landowner agrees to the addition of the improvements.

The second sentence in the first paragraph of Article 493 establishes the inverse corollary to the first sentence by providing that the large-scale improvements enumerated in the first sentence "belong to the owner of the ground when they are made *without his consent*." La. Civ. Code art. 493(1) (1979) (emphasis added). If the precarious possessor does not obtain the consent of the landowner before erecting large-scale improvements, the improvements he makes belong to the owner of the ground. The first two sentences of Article 493 thus imply that this provision was originally designed to deal with large-scale improvements made by precarious possessors such as the holder of a predial or personal servitude, a co-owner, a purchaser under a contract to purchase and sell immovable property, or a lessee, *see* La. Civ. Code art. 493 rev. cmt. (b)(1979), rev. cmt. (b)(1984), and to distinguish improvements made with the landowner's consent from those made without the landowner's consent.

The remainder of Article 493 returns to the situation envisioned by the article's first sentence — a large-scale improvement erected by a precarious possessor. It further establishes the rules governing the interests of the precarious possessor and the landowner when the former loses the consent to keep his improvement on the landowner's property. Thus, it dictates the results when a predial servitude has terminated but constructions remain on the servient estate, when a contract to buy and sell immovable property fails and a transfer of ownership of the immovable property is never consummated, or when a co-owner withdraws his consent for a fellow co-owner to maintain an improvement on co-owned land.

This second paragraph of Article 493 of the Civil Code has proven to be one of the most controversial provisions in the Civil Code's chapters on accession. The problem stems from the fact that the article, as originally drafted in 1979, and then as amended in 1984, created a curious predicament: a person who constructs a large and perhaps ultimately value destroying or even dangerous "improvement" on the land of another person *with that landowner's consent* could, in time, abandon that "improvement" and leave it to deteriorate, reducing the value of the underlying land and creating a hazard to public health and safety.

This problem first became apparent in *Guzzetta v. Texas Pipeline Co.*, 485 So.2d 508, 511 (La. 1986). In that decision, an oil and gas pipeline company abandoned a pipeline it had buried on another person's land pursuant to a pipeline servitude, and the servitude terminated. The court held that the ownership of the abandoned pipeline reverted to the owner of the land once the pipeline company refused to remove the pipeline within ninety days of a written demand issued by the landowner. *Id.* at 510–11. Moreover, the court held, the underlying landowner had no right under the then governing version of Article 493 either to demand that the pipeline company remove its pipeline or to recover the costs necessary to remove the unwanted pipeline. *Id.* at 511.

The so-called *Guzzetta* problem has now been remedied in part by the 2003 amendment to Article 493, which added the final sentence of the second paragraph of the article. *See* 2003 La. Acts, No. 751.

The second paragraph of Article 493 establishes a *three stage* sequence once it is determined that a precarious possessor no longer has the consent of the landowner to keep his large scale improvements on the land of another person. In *stage one*, the article gives the "owner of the buildings, other constructions permanently attached to the ground, or plantings," who "no longer has the right to keep them on the land of another," the right to "remove them subject to his obligation to restore the property to its prior condition." La. Civ. Code art. 493(2) (1984).

This initial right of the precarious possessor to remove his large scale improvement makes perfect sense. If a landowner is willing to let someone else erect a building or other construction on the land or make plantings on the land, and the landowner does not negotiate to keep those improvements for his own benefit, the law assumes that the landowner expected the precarious possessor to retain ownership of the improvements, to remove them at the termination of their consensual arrangement, and to restore the land to its previous condition. Article 493 thus establishes an intuitively appealing default rule warning landowners who give other persons consent to make significant improvements on their land that they should negotiate for ownership in advance if they want to claim ownership of these improvements at the end of the consensual period.

In *stage two*, the next sentence of Article 493 creates rights for the landowner if the precarious possessor does not take advantage of his initial right to remove large scale improvements at the end of the consensual period. In pertinent part, it provides:

> If he [the improver] does not remove them [the improvements] within ninety days after written demand, the owner of the land may, after the

ninetieth day from the date of mailing the written demand, appropriate ownership of the improvements by providing an additional written notice by certified mail, and upon receipt of the certified mail by the owner of the improvements, the owner of the land obtains ownership of the improvements and owes nothing to the owner of the improvements.

La. Civ. Code art. 493(2) (1984). This sentence creates what might be called the landowner's right of *free appropriation*. If the improvement is really a desirable thing—a valuable building, construction or set of plantings—the landowner will certainly try to take advantage of this part of Article 493. It allows the landowner to obtain the ownership of valuable large-scale improvements by making an initial written demand for the improver to remove the improvements, waiting ninety days, and then sending another written notice by certified mail of an intent to appropriate ownership. After these three requisites have been satisfied, ownership of the improvements vests immediately in the landowner. Furthermore, and crucially, the landowner owes nothing to the improver in compensation.

This landowner's right of free appropriation is also intuitively appealing. If a precarious possessor is careless enough to erect a valuable, large-scale improvement on another person's land without negotiating for some kind of extended removal rights or reimbursement rights *and, further,* neglects to remove his improvement after receiving ninety days written notice, why should the law allow the precarious possessor any compensation? After all, the precarious possessor could have negotiated for and obtained contractual rights to receive compensation from the landowner at the outset of the consensual period. Furthermore, the precarious possessor can always take advantage of the ninety-day period to remove his improvements. If he neither negotiated for reimbursement rights nor takes advantage of his removal right, the law assumes the precarious possessor does not want to keep his improvements after the consensual period comes to an end.

In *stage three*, the final sentence of the second paragraph of Article 493, added pursuant to 2003 La. Acts, No. 715, § 1, deals with the predicament revealed by the *Guzetta* decision described above: the unwanted or undesirable improvement. Quite logically and fairly, it provides that if the consensual improver does not take advantage of his initial right of removal *and* if the underlying landowner does not seek to take advantage of his right of free appropriation, "the improvements shall remain the property of he who made them and he [the improver] shall be solely responsible for any harm caused by the improvements." La. Civ. Code art. 493 (2003). Thus, if a precarious possessor erects buildings, other constructions or plantings on the land of another person that could eventually harm the land, decrease its value or, even more importantly, create conditions that put the general public or neighbors' health and safety at risk, the precarious possessor should be responsible for the potential liability that results from his failure to remove this unwanted or undesirable "improvement." In the end, although the landowner may not be able to compel the precarious possessor to remove the unwanted improvement or obtain removal costs from the precarious possessor, the potential liability that the precarious possessor faces under this part of Article 493 should motivate the precarious possessor to remove the undesirable or dangerous improvement. This rule shifts to the precarious possessor the social costs of a failure to remove the improvement.

In 2006, the Louisiana Supreme Court addressed Article 493 in another case that revealed the crucial role this article can play in disputes concerning unwanted improvements. In *Giorgio v. Alliance Operating Corp.*, 921 So.2d 58 (La. 2006), two boaters suffered serious injuries in 1998 when, in the middle of the night, their recreational fishing boat collided with pilings that were adjacent to an unlit, orphaned oil production platform in Breton Sound. The boaters filed suit for damages arising from their personal injuries and for the loss of their boat. They named as defendants both the oil and gas companies that had erected the production platform and associated pilings and the State of Louisiana, which owned the navigable water bottom upon which the platform and pilings were constructed and which had granted a mineral lease allowing the erection of the platform and pilings. After the oil and gas company defendants settled with the plaintiffs, a trial proceeded against the State of Louisiana. The trial court and court of appeal found the State one hundred percent liable for the harm caused by the unlit, orphaned structure.

The Louisiana Supreme Court reversed, holding, in pertinent part, that the State did not own the abandoned oilfield production platform and the associated pilings because it had never issued a written demand to remove the structures to the mineral lease holders who had constructed the platform and pilings pursuant to Article 493. *Id.* at 73–75. Consider this portion of the court's analysis in *Giorgio*:

> . . . . we find the clear and unambiguous language of La. Civ. Code art. 493 as written in 1997 specifically required written notice or demand prior to the transfer of ownership. La. Civ. Code art. 9.
>
> In the present case, the platform and pilings attached to the land subject to State Lease 8342 were made on the land with the consent of the State. Therefore, upon the termination and release of all rights to the water bottom under State Lease 8342, all the rights in and to the water bottom reverted back to the owner, the State of Louisiana, and according to article 493 as written in 1997, the ownership of the platform and pilings as constructions permanently attached to the ground remained with him who made them, the lessee. The ownership so remains until failure of the lessee to remove the platform and pilings within ninety days of written notice. In the present case, the record contains no evidence of written notice of removal, and accordingly, the ownership of the constructions belongs to him who made them. Ownership has not reverted to the State. . . .

Giorgio v. Alliance Operating Corp., 921 So.2d 58, 75 (La. 2006).

The ruling in *Giorgio* implies that if a landowner (like the State) does not want to acquire ownership of ultimately undesirable improvements it allowed to be constructed on its land, it must *not* demand their removal within ninety days because such a demand, coupled with a refusal by the precarious possessor to remove the structure, would lead to ownership of the "improvement" vesting in the owner of the land. The 2003 revision of Article 493 provides for a similar, but easier to understand and arguably more fair, result directly in the final sentence of the article's second paragraph. Under that provision, the owner can demand removal of the improvement, but if the improver does not remove the improvement, the landowner does not necessarily become owner of the improvement until the landowner appropriates the improvement through the second phase of written demand procedures detailed above (the issuance of the ninety-day appropriation notice). La. Civ. Code art. 493(2) (1979, amended 2003) ("Until such time as the owner of the land appropriates the improvements, the improvements shall remain the property of he who made them and he shall be solely responsible for any harm caused by the improvements.").

Note that the incident that gave rise to the dispute in *Giorgio* occurred in 1998, before the current last sentence of the second paragraph was added. If that sentence had been part of the codal text at the time of the incident, it would have made clear that ownership of the production platform and pilings remained with the oil and gas company defendants, absent an express appropriation of the structures by the State through the ninety-day written demand and subsequent notice of intent to appropriate.

The effective scope of Article 493 has been considerably narrowed by the addition of current revised Article 2695 of the Civil Code, which provides detailed rules governing the fate of improvements created pursuant to a lease. *See* La. Civ. Code art. 2695 (2004).

b. Article 495 and Small Scale Improvements by Precarious Possessors

The next major funnel created by the series of accession articles addressing improvements applies to what we call small scale improvements. It is established by Article 495 of the Civil Code:

> **Art. 495. Things incorporated in, or attached to, an immovable with the consent of the owner of the immovable**
>
> One who incorporates in, or attaches to, the immovable of another, with his consent, things that become component parts of the immovable under Articles 465 and 466, may, in the absence of other provisions of law or juridical acts, remove them subject to his obligation of restoring the property to its former condition.
>
> If he does not remove them after demand, the owner of the immovable may have them removed at the expense of the person who made them or elect to keep them and pay, at his option, the current value of the materials and of the workmanship or the enhanced value of the immovable.

La. Civ. Code art. 495 (1979). We label the improvements targeted by this article "**small-scale**" because they consist of things that are incorporated in or attached to an immovable owned by another person "that become component parts of the immovable under Articles 465 and 466." La. Civ. Code art. 495 (1979). Rather than actual buildings, other constructions permanently attached to the ground, or plantings, which are the subject of Article 493, the type of improvements at issue here are relatively smaller things that are incorporated in or attached primarily to buildings or other constructions, though also potentially to a tract of land. As we saw in Chapter Four, such items include not only building materials addressed under Article 465, but many kinds of loosely attached items that "serve to complete a building of the same general type" or that "serve the principal use" of some "other construction" under Article 466. Just as with Article 493, however, the improvements addressed by Article 495 must have been created by a person who is occupying the property with the "consent" of the owner of the building, other construction, or tract of land, and hence is also a precarious possessor.

Just as with Article 493 and large-scale improvements, Article 495 assigns to the improver the initial option to remove the small-scale improvement "subject to his [the improver's] obligation of restoring the property to its former condition." La. Civ. Code art. 495 (1979). The assumption behind this default rule is that if the owner of a building or other construction wanted to claim ownership of these small-scale improvements after the consensual period ends, he could have, and should have, bargained for this right before he gave the improver consent to make the improvements. Indeed, the phrase "in the absence of other provisions of law or juridical acts" emphatically reminds us of the suppletive nature of Article 495's default rule. *Id.*

Today, Article 2695 of the Civil Code, which addresses improvements made by a lessee, is the most commonly applicable "other provision of law" that will modify the initial default rule created by Article 495. Similarly, a written lease is the most commonly relevant "juridical act" that would create rights deviating from Article 495. The first paragraph of Article 2695, however, mirrors Article 495 in assigning to the lessee the initial option, at the termination of the lease, to remove improvements and additions made to the leased thing by the lessee in the absence of a contrary agreement. *See* La. Civ. Code art. 2695 (2004) ("In the absence of contrary agreement, upon termination of the lease . . : (1) The lessee may remove all improvements that he made to the leased thing, provided that he restore the thing to its former condition."). Thus, Article 2695 contains the same default rule as Article 495 and underscores its suppletive nature.

In the event an improver does not remove his small scale consensual improvements after receiving a demand from the owner of the underlying thing to remove them (presumably when the consensual period has come to an end), Article 495 now gives the owner of the underlying thing two options. First, the owner of the principal thing can have the improvements removed at the expense of the improver. Alternatively, the owner can elect to "to keep them [the improvements] and pay, at his option, the current value of the materials and of the workmanship or the enhanced value of the immovable." La. Civ. Code art. 495(2) (1979). If the improvement made by the improver adds value to the underlying building, other construction or tract of land, it is likely that the owner will not seek to enforce the removal option but will instead seek to employ what we call the *compensated appropriation* option (in contrast to the *free appropriation* option under Article 493). Why, though, would the Civil Code require the owner of a principal thing—a building, other construction or tract of land—to reimburse the small scale, consensual improver either for the cost of creating the small scale improvements or for the increased value of the principal thing, while it does not impose any reimbursement obligation in the case of large scale improvements under Article 493?

We believe the answer lies in the consensual nature of the relationship between the improver and the owner of the principal thing. Given the consensual origin of the relationship, the redactors must have tipped the scales *in favor* of the owner of the principal thing with respect to *large-scale* improvements because they believed that a person erecting a building or other construction or major plantings on the land of another should appreciate the significance of his investment and contract accordingly. With regard to small scale improvements (Article 465 and 466 component parts), however, the redactors must have assumed that the typical precarious possessor/improver would have less reason to be aware of the risk that he might lose his investment in the improvements upon termination of the original consensual relationship. Further, the redactors might reasonably have assumed that the typical owner of a principal thing covered by Article 495, for example, a commercial landlord who leases space in an office building or shopping center, is likely to be a repeat player in these type of transactions and thus should have the experience and bargaining power to know that he must negotiate for a "free appropriation" outcome with respect to small scale improvements if he wants to avoid the default rule imposed by Article 495 of the Civil Code.

Article 495 of the Civil Code may reflect the redactors' desire to impose what is often called a **penalty default rule** in favor of the small-scale improver. A penalty default rule puts the burden on the party negatively affected by the rule to affirmatively bargain for an outcome that deviates from the penalty default setting. It thus forces the penalized party to disclose to the other party a preference for an outcome that may be unfavorable to the party protected by the default position. *See generally* Ian Ayers and Robert Gertner, *Strategic Contractual Inefficiency and Optimal Choice of Legal Rules*, 101 YALE L. J. 729 (1992). Although the penalized party may or may not have sufficient contractual leverage to bargain for the result it seeks, the benefitted party will more fully appreciate the stakes in the contract drafting process because of the disclosure. To offset the effect of Article 495, the owner of the principal thing must signal, while bargaining or in express contract language, that he expects to own small-scale improvements at the end of the consensual relationship without having to compensate the improver for them. Article 493 establishes the opposite kind of penalty default rule in favor of the owner of the underlying immovable that effectively puts the large-scale improver on notice of the need to negotiate for an outcome other than free appropriation.

Article 495 does not always create an easily recoverable reimbursement award for the value of a precarious possessor's small scale improvements at the end of a consensual relationship. In *Smith v. State DOTD*, 899 So.2d 516, 532 (La. 2005), the Louisiana Supreme Court held that a lessee of a commercial building was not entitled to reimbursement for the value of small scale improvements that fell within the scope of Article 495 because the building owner never made a demand upon the lessee to remove the improvements and, therefore, the remedies of Article 495 were not triggered. Further, the court noted in *Smith* that the lessee never attempted to remove any of the improvements for which he later sought reimbursement from the lessor, even though he had been given ample time to remove any improvements he wished prior to termination of the lease. Here is how the court in *Smith v. State* summed up its interpretation of Article 495:

> Article 495 provides a mechanism for a person to retain those items of value he incorporates or attaches to the property of another. Further, the article provides a mechanism for the landowner to have those improvements removed from his property, if he so desires, by demanding their removal. *Id.* If upon demand the improver fails to remove, the owner may remove the items or elect to keep them and then pay the value of the items to the improver. *Id. However, Article 495 does not appear to contemplate a situation where the improver abandons his improvements, then makes a demands to be compensated for their value. See Riggs v. Lawton*, 231 La. 1019, 93 So. 2d 543 (La. 1957) (applying the pre-revision La. C.C. art. 2726 regarding lessor-lessee obligations relating to improvements). *Thus, Article 495 does not require a lessor to pay for improvements to a lessee if the lessee abandons the improvements upon the termination of the lease. Pylate v. Inabnet*, 458 So. 2d 1378, 1391 (La. App. 2 Cir. 1984) (citing *Riggs v. Lawton*, supra). Furthermore, use of one's property, and other acts of ownership, which necessarily result in the use of improvements placed upon the premises by a lessee who does not remove the improvements upon termination of the lease, but rather abandons them, does not constitute an election within the contemplation of Article 495. *See id.* However, denying a lessor the right to remove improvements upon termination of the lease could be construed as an election, as required by Article 495.

Smith, 899 So.2d at 533 (emphasis added). Under the current Civil Code, Article 2695 would be used to analyze the situation presented in *Smith v. State*, but the outcome would be the same if the lessor made a demand upon the lessee to remove the improvements and the lessee refused to remove them within a reasonable time. Study Article 2695(2)(b) and see if you understand why.

Article 495 of the Civil Code only discusses things incorporated into an immovable *with the owner's consent*. What happens to small-scale improvements made without the landowner's consent? Two short articles added to the chapter on "Accession in Relation to Immovables" in 1984 answer that question.

Article 493.1 of the Civil Code provides that "[t]hings incorporated in or attached to an immovable so as to become its component parts under Articles 465 and 466 belong to the owner of the immovable." La. Civ. Code art. 493.1 (1984). Although this statement was originally found in the first version of revised Article 493 adopted in 1979, it was dropped from that article. It logically follows from Articles 465 and 466, however, and needs to be read in conjunction with Article 495.

Absent the rights of third parties, when a corporeal movable thing is incorporated into or attached to a tract of land, building or other construction in such a way that it can be considered a component part of that thing under the terms of either Article 465 or 466, the owner of the tract of land, building or other construction also owns the component part. La. Civ. Code art. 493.1 (1984). However, when the person who makes Article 465 and 466 improvements is someone other than the owner of the immovable and he makes them with the consent of the owner, Article 495, and potentially Article 2695, will govern the respective rights and remedies between the owner and the improver.

Civil Code article 493.2 was also adopted in 1984, not to create any new substantive rules, but for didactic purposes. It provides that "[o]ne who has lost the ownership of a thing to the owner of an immovable may have a claim against him or against a third person in accordance with the following provisions." La. Civ. Code art. 493.2 (1984). This article points out that the general purpose of Articles 495 through 498 is to regulate the claims of improvers, whether consensual or non-consensual, to some kind of unjust enrichment based remedy in the event they lose ownership of improvements.

c. Articles 496–497 and Improvements by Adverse Possessors

The last two funneling articles in our artificial accession suite, Articles 496 and 497, address the rights and obligations of persons who make improvements on immovable property owned by another without initially obtaining the consent of the owner to occupy the immovable. Because the improvers contemplated by these articles possess with the intent to be the owners themselves, and without the consent of the owners of the underlying immovables, we call them *"adverse possessors."* See La. Civ. Code art. 481 (1979) (using the term "adverse possessor"). Their interest in possessing the immovable is adverse to the interest of the owner of the immovable.

Notice here, though, that the articles do not distinguish between large or small scale improvements. They apply to "constructions, plantings or works," regardless of whether they are Article 465 or 466 component parts of buildings or other constructions or buildings or other constructions themselves situated on a tract of land. La. Civ. Code arts. 496–97 (1979). The key distinction that affects the rights and obligations available to the improver and the immovable owner is whether the improver was a "good faith" or "bad faith" possessor at the time he made the improvement. *Id.*

The consequences of characterizing the improver as one or the other kind of possessor are significant. The **good faith possessor** is, not surprisingly, accorded significant protection. Although he will lose ownership of all the improvements he has made, the good faith possessor enjoys a right to reimbursement. *See* La. Civ. Code art. 496 rev. cmt. (c) (1979). The good faith possessor will be entitled to reimbursement for either (1) "the cost of the materials and of the workmanship" attributable to the creation of the improvement, (2) the "current value" of the improvements, or (3) "the enhanced value of the immovable." La. Civ. Code art. 496 (1979). The owner of the immovable can choose the least expensive reimbursement option, depending on the circumstances, but generally cannot avoid paying some amount of compensation to the good faith possessor. Significantly, under Article 496, the good faith possessor does not have an affirmative duty to remove the improvement or to pay the expenses of removal.

The **bad faith possessor**, on the other hand, is placed in a less advantageous position under Article 497. Not only is he potentially liable for the costs of demolition and removal of the improvements should the owner demand this, but the bad faith possessor is also potentially liable for any additional damages that his improvements may have caused to the owner of the immovable. La. Civ. Code art. 497 (1979). Further, if the owner of the immovable does not demand the demolition and removal of the constructions, plantings or works made by the bad faith possessor, the owner only owes reimbursement to the bad faith possessor for "separable improvements" that he elects to keep. Separable improvements are things that are not merged with the soil, like homes, barns, garages and fences. *Id.* rev. cmt. (c).

With regard to "inseparable improvements" made by the bad faith possessor, like drainage ditches, artificial ponds or ground leveling, the owner of the immovable owes no reimbursement at all, except in the very limited circumstance in which the bad faith possessor might claim a set off against a landowner's claim for the return of natural or civil fruits under Articles 485 and 486. La. Civ. Code art. 497 rev. cmt. (d) (1979). When reimbursement is due from the landowner, the landowner may choose to pay either the current value of the materials and of the workmanship of the improvements, or the enhanced value of the immovable. La. Civ. Code art. 497 (1979).

The next decision presents an example of a court confronting a situation in which the categories and remedial options found in the accession articles described above did not seem to provide an equitable solution to a dispute between a person who was undeniably a good faith improver at the time of construction of the "improvement" and the owner of the underlying land. Consequently, the court turned to the law of delict, and specifically the law of trespass, for an alternative solution. Do you believe the court's approach makes sense?

Britt Builders, Inc. v. Brister

618 So.2d 899 (La. App. 1 Cir. 1993)

CHIASSON, Judge Pro. Tem. This is a devolutive appeal from a judgment denying claims for continuing trespass on a reconventional demand. The trial court rendered judgment in favor of the defendant/plaintiff in reconvention, Maureen Brister, and against the plaintiff/defendant in reconvention, James D. Britt. The trial court further dismissed Britt's main demand and ordered that he pay Ms. Brister $3,500 for damage to her property. Ms. Brister filed this appeal.

Facts

Maureen Johnson Brister bought Lot 201 of Woodlands Subdivision, Baton Rouge, Louisiana, on March 1, 1984. Title to the lot was recorded on March 2, 1984. Ms. Brister bought this lot because it had an unusual shape and a large oak tree. She financed this purchase by paying $5,000 down and promised to pay $251.22 a month for ten years. Total purchase price of the lot was $20,500. On June 25, 1984, Britt Builders, Inc., a Louisiana corporation owned by James Britt, entered into a purchase agreement for Lot 201 with Five L Development Corporation, the same company that sold the lot to Ms. Brister. A title search was conducted by H. Matthew Chambers who did not discover that the lot was owned by Ms. Brister. Soon after Britt was told that the title was clear, he removed the large oak tree, poured a concrete slab for a residence, and began framing the walls. Cost of this work was $10,179.76

On July 10, 1984, Britt first learned that Ms. Brister owned the lot. Ms. Brister was immediately contacted, all work on the lot was stopped, and negotiations began to mitigate damages. Two weeks later Britt filed suit against Ms. Brister seeking $12,000 in damages for the enhanced value to her lot. She answered and filed a reconventional demand, seeking damages associated with the cost of her lot, damages for trespass, mental anguish, and attorney's fees.

Trial was held on May 24, 1991. At trial several experts in real estate appraisal testified. Marvin R. McDaniel, II said that a treed lot should bring $2,000 to $2,500 more than an untreed lot. He estimated that the cost of removing the concrete slab was $8,000 to $10,000 and the lot had a present value of $14,000 to $15,000 with the slab on it. He said that anyone purchasing the lot and planning to use the slab would have the problem of no warranty and few people would want the lot with a slab on it.

Jim Wilson, a general contractor, testified that he gave Ms. Brister an estimate of $9,168 to remove the slab. He said that there was no salvage value to the slab and the job would require use of four or five trucks all day to remove the debris.

H. Matthew Chambers, the real estate lawyer who did the title search for Britt, said that he was hired June 20, 1984, to close the sale. He stated that a week to two weeks after he said the title was clear, he learned that Ms. Brister, and not the corporation which sold the lot to Britt, was the owner of Lot 201.

James Britt was accepted by the court as an expert in residential construction. He testified that he started building homes in 1965. He said that he did not know about the defect in the title before he began construction and he spent $400 to $500 to have the tree removed. He added that he bought the lot next to 201 hoping to negotiate a settlement and he was paid $8,816 by Chambers for the materials used in constructing the slab on Ms. Brister's lot.

Maureen Brister was the last witness. She said she had financed the purchase of the lot and she selected this lot because it was pie-shaped, on a curve, and had a large tree which she envisioned next to her bedroom. She and her family had prepared the lot for construction by cutting down five trees, hauling off debris, and mowing the grass. She had spent $1,630 clearing the lot. She said that she had spent the last seven years having to keep the lot clear because of liability and complaints by her neighbors. She also stated that she had no idea that construction began on her lot until Chambers told her, that she had asked Britt to remove the slab, and she could not understand why Britt was suing her for something he had put on her property. She claimed that her life has been on hold waiting for a resolution of her damages.

The court dismissed Britt's demands for $12,000 and assigned him costs of the trial. On the reconventional demand, the court awarded Ms. Brister $3,500, plus legal interest, for the destruction of the tree and clean-up of the lot. From that decision, Ms. Brister filed this appeal.

Determination of Good Faith Possession and Failure to Award Full Measure of Damages for Trespass

(Assignments of error numbers 1, 2 and 3)

Ms. Brister argues that the court erred when it determined that Britt was a good faith possessor when he constructed the slab on her lot. She contends that she should not be fully precluded from her damages in trespass because these damages resulted solely from Britt's actions. She maintains that the construction of the slab on her lot, removal of the tree, and placement of debris and construction materials by Britt constituted legal trespass.

In his brief to this court Britt argues that he was in good faith when he bought Lot 201 and began construction. He contends that he enhanced the value of the lot by constructing $12,000 worth of improvements on it and he should be entitled to restitution for these improvements. However, this Court cannot consider changing the trial court's ruling against Britt because he neither appealed nor answered Ms. Brister's appeal. See La.C.C.P. art. 2133; *Lamousin v. Ankesheiln*, 560 So. 2d 459, 461 (La. App. 1st Cir. 1990).

Possession is the detention or enjoyment of a corporeal thing, movable and immovable, that one holds or exercises by himself or by another who keeps or exercises it in his name. La.C.C. art. 3421. A possessor is considered provisionally as owner of the thing he possesses until the right of the true owner is established. La.C.C. art. 3423. To acquire possession, one must intend to possess as owner and must take corporeal possession of the thing. La.C.C. art. 3424. Corporeal possession is the exercise of physical acts of use, detention, or enjoyment over a thing. La.C.C. art. 3425.

One is presumed to intend to possess as owner unless he began to possess in the name of and for another. La.C.C. art. 3427. Possession is lost when the possessor manifests his intention to abandon it or when he is evicted by another by force or usurpation. La.C.C. art. 3433. Good faith is presumed. Neither error of fact nor error of law defeats this presumption. This presumption is rebutted on proof that the possessor knows, or should know, that he is not owner of the thing he possesses. La.C.C. art. 3481.

Buildings, other constructions permanently attached to the ground, and plantings made on the land of another with his consent belong to him who made them. They belong to the owner of the ground when they are made without his consent. La.C.C. art. 493. When constructions, plantings, or works are made by a possessor in good faith, the owner of the immovable may not demand their demolition and removal. He is bound to keep them and at his option to pay to the possessor either the cost of the materials and of the workmanship, or their current value, or the enhanced value of the immovable. La.C.C. art. 496.

When constructions, plantings, or works are made by a bad faith possessor, the owner of the immovable may keep them or he may demand their demolition and removal at the expense of the possessor, and, in addition, damages for the injury that he may have sustained. If he does not demand demolition and removal, he is bound to pay at his option either the current value of the materials and of the workmanship of the separable improvements that he has kept or the enhanced value of the immovable. La.C.C. art. 497.

In his ruling the trial court determined that Britt was a good faith possessor in light of *Phillips v. Parker*, 483 So. 2d 972 (La. 1986) and that Civil Code Article 496 governed the outcome concerning the slab. By so ruling, the court concluded that Ms. Brister would have been bound to pay, at her option, either the cost of the materials and of the workmanship, or their current value, or the enhanced value of her immovable. However, because Britt failed to present adequate proof of the amounts, the court refused to award him damages under Article 496.

This Court agrees with the determination that Britt was a good faith possessor. In *Phillips* our Supreme Court held that good faith is presumed and when an erroneous title search is made, the possessor who relied on that search should not be precluded from the same status given a good faith possessor who conducts no search. *Phillips v. Parker*, 483 So. 2d at 978–979. Britt was similarly situated when he placed reliance on a faulty title search and acted upon the advice of his attorney.

However, this Court's inquiry does not end simply because Britt was a good faith possessor under La.C.C. art. 496. The article itself speaks of enhanced value and Comment (c) to this article refers to improvements made to another's property. This comment states in pertinent part that all improvements made by a possessor in good faith on another's immovable belong to the owner of the immovable. The wording in both suggests that Article 496 is intended to apply to buildings, other constructions, and plantings that improve and enhance the value of an immovable. The article does not speak of partial constructions that actually diminish the value of an immovable.

In the instant case the record reveals that the only person likely to benefit from the slab was Britt. He poured the slab to fit the configuration of his house plans. For Ms. Brister and any potential buyer of the lot, it would be necessary to use an unwanted and unwarranted slab that has no utility until a house is built on it or else spend eight to ten thousand dollars to remove the slab. The testimony clearly established that the slab diminished the value of the lot.

Therefore, this Court believes that the redactors of our Civil Code envisioned application of Article 496 when the owner of the immovable would be unjustly enriched by the efforts of a good faith possessor. They did not intend that the owner be burdened with partial constructions and unwanted works on his property that actually diminished its value. Further recourse is available to an owner in a situation such as this.

Article 2315 of the Civil Code provides in pertinent part that every act whatever of man that causes damage to another obliges him by whose fault it happened to repair it. The tort of trespass has long been recognized by courts throughout this state as a means to correct the damage caused when an owner is unjustly deprived of the use and enjoyment of his immovable.

The tort of trespass is defined as the unlawful physical invasion of the property or possession of another. *Dickie's Sportsman's Centers, Inc. v. Department of Transportation and Development*, 477 So. 2d 744, 750 (La. App. 1st Cir.), writ denied, 478 So. 2d 530 (La. 1985). A trespasser is one who goes upon the property of another without the other's consent. *Williams v. J. B. Levert and Company, Inc.*, 162 So. 2d 53, 58 (La. App. 1st Cir.), writ refused, 162 So. 2d 574 (La. 1964).

A person injured by trespass is entitled to full indemnification for the damages caused. Where there is a legal right to recovery but the damages cannot be exactly estimated, the courts have reasonable discretion to assess same based upon all of the facts and circumstances. Damages are recoverable even though the tort-feasor acts in good faith. *Versai Management, Inc. v. Monticello Forest Products Corporation*, 479 So. 2d 477, 484 (La. App. 1st Cir. 1985).

Damages for dispossession are regarded as an award of compensatory damages for violation of a recognized property right and are not confined to proof of actual pecuniary loss. Anguish, humiliation, and embarrassment are appropriate considerations. OWENS V. SMITH, 541 So. 2d 950, 955 (La. App. 2nd Cir. 1989). Damages are recoverable for unconsented activities performed on the property of another, based on physical property damage, invasion of privacy, inconvenience, and mental and physical suffering. *Beacham v. Hardy Outdoor Advertising, Inc.*, 520 So. 2d 1086, 1091 (La. App. 2nd Cir. 1987).

In the instant case Britt did not dispute that he erected the concrete slab on Ms. Brister's property without her permission, nor does Britt claim to be owner of the property. Britt only occupied the lot as owner for two weeks, but the slab has remained on the lot seven years. Furthermore, the continued presence of the slab deprived Ms. Brister of the use and enjoyment of her property and diminished its value to her or other potential owners.

For the reasons herein stated, this Court concludes that under the circumstances of this case the trial court erred by determining that Article 496 of the Civil Code precluded full payment of damages resulting from a tort of trespass. Accordingly, the first and third assignments of error pertaining to trespass have merit.

Quantum

Ms. Brister claimed the following damages:

(1) Cost of removing the slab and repairing the lot	$9,168.00
(2) Interest paid on lot loan	13,000.00
(3) Destruction of tree	2,500.00
(4) Out of pocket lot expenses	1,630.00
(5) Inconvenience, invasion of privacy, mental anguish and emotional trauma (7 years at $ 2,000.00 per year for the continuing nature of the trespass)	14,000.00
(6) Loss of use of down payment ($ 5,000.00) on lot loan for 7 years at 6% per year	2,100.00
TOTAL	
plus legal interest and court costs	$42,398.00

In his oral reasons for judgment, the trial judge awarded Ms. Brister damages of $1,000 for trespass for cleanup of materials left on her lot when Britt constructed another house and $2,500 for removal of the tree. These awards are affirmed. However, the court committed error when it denied Ms. Brister's claims for the continuing trespass caused by the slab remaining on her lot. Accordingly, Ms. Brister is awarded an additional $9,168 for the removal of the slab. No other damages were sufficiently proven in the record.

Decree

For the foregoing reasons, the judgment of the trial court rejecting Ms. Britt's claim for the cost of removing the slab as a continuing trespass is reversed. The awards for $1,000 for cleanup of construction materials and $2,500 for removal of the tree are affirmed. Judgment is rendered in favor of Ms. Brister and against James D. Britt for an additional $9,168 as damages in trespass for removal of the concrete slab, for a total award of $12,668, with legal interest thereon from date of judicial demand until paid. Mr. Britt is cast for all costs.

AFFIRMED IN PART; REVERSED IN PART AND RENDERED.

Notes and Questions

1. In *Britt Builders, Inc. v. Brister*, 618 So.2d 899 (La. App. 1 Cir. 1993), the court created a remedial scheme for an accession situation not clearly contemplated by

the Civil Code's accession articles: a good faith possessor made a construction on land owned by another person that arguably diminished the value of the land. Even though the plaintiff, Britt Builders, Inc., was indisputably a good faith possessor at the time it constructed the concrete slab on Maureen Brister's lot, the court found a way to avoid application of Article 496 of the Civil Code. What would have been the consequences of characterizing Britt Builders as a bad faith possessor? Could Britt Builders have been characterized as a consensual improver to justify application of Article 493? Do you believe the court's delict-based solution to this dispute was sound? Would Britt Builders ultimately have been better off if it had completed the home it started on Maureen Brister's lot instead of leaving the concrete slab?

2. *Necessary and Useful Expenses*: One more remedial scheme that can come into play in situations involving good faith and bad faith possessors is found in Book II, Title II, Chapter 4: "Protection of Ownership." In particular, Articles 527 and 528 provide evicted possessors the right to be reimbursed for certain necessary or useful expenses incurred in relation to the thing from which they are evicted. These articles apply when owners of land have lost possession of their property but later reclaim possession through what are called real actions. We will study real actions in greater depth when we learn more about possession and acquisitive prescription.

For now, it is enough to note that a good faith possessor is, once again, favored by these articles. The good faith possessor is allowed to recover not just "necessary expenses incurred for the preservation of the thing and for the discharge of private or public burdens," La. Civ. Code art. 527 (1979), but also "useful expenses to the extent that they have enhanced the value of the thing." La. Civ. Code art. 528 (1979). Meanwhile, a bad faith possessor can only recover necessary expenses incurred for preservation of the thing and for the discharge of private or public burdens. La. Civ. Code art. 527–28 (1979). Neither kind of possessor can recover expenses "for ordinary maintenance and repairs." *Id*. The revision comments to these articles are replete with examples of each kind of expense.

Problem

Several years ago, a married couple, Peter and Patsy, constructed a house on land owned by Patsy's mother, Theta. Theta contributed $32,000 to the cost of constructing the house. The house contained a bedroom designated for Theta to use for the rest of her life if she desired. Theta promised Peter and Patsy that she would eventually donate the land on which the house was constructed to them. Peter and Patsy have lived in the house ever since its construction. Theta never fulfilled her promise to donate the land to Peter and Patsy. Instead, Theta donated the land to Patsy's brother and sister, Woodrow and Elva.

When Peter and Patsy found out about Theta's donation of the land to Woodrow and Elva, they filed suit seeking to force Theta to renounce the donation, to honor "her contract," and, in the alternative, for reimbursement for the value of the house now owned by Patsy's siblings. It is undisputed that the current value of the house, separate and apart from the land, is $220,000.

Who owns the house? Are Peter and Patsy entitled to revoke Theta's donation or to enforce their "contract" with Theta? If not, are they entitled to any reimbursement from Theta and Woodrow and Elva? Which accession article, if any, provides the remedies applicable in this situation? *See Broussard v. Compton*, 36 So.3d 376 (La. App. 3 Cir. 2010).

D. Accession in Relation to Land Adjacent to Navigable Water Bodies

The next set of accession rules addresses the rights of owners of land adjacent to natural navigable water bodies. At the end of the section on Accession in Relation to Immovables, the Civil Code provides several detailed rules for ownership rights in land that is gradually formed or appears suddenly adjacent to natural water bodies.

1. The General Rule: Accretion Belongs to the Riparian Landowner

When new land appears gradually on the bank of a river or stream, whether that land results from gradual sedimentary deposits or a gradual lowering of the water level, the Civil Code awards the new land to the owner of the most prominent nearby thing, the bank, subject to the rights of use afforded to the public under Civil Code Article 456 for activities incidental to navigation. The Civil Code could have declared that such newly formed land is subject to the claims of the first person to find it or possess it. Alternatively, it could have allotted this new land to the state, at least in the case of navigable rivers or streams, whose beds are owned by the state already. But, in Louisiana, as in most legal systems, under general principles of accession, newly formed land along rivers and streams is allotted to the owner of the other prominent thing in proximity to the river or stream—the bank of the river or stream.

This general rule, known in the common law as the Doctrine of Accretion, is found in Article 499:

Art. 499. Alluvion and dereliction

Accretion formed successively and imperceptibly on the bank of a river or stream, whether navigable or not, is called alluvion. The alluvion belongs to the owner of the bank, who is bound to leave public that portion of the bank which is required for public use.

The same rule applies to dereliction formed by water receding imperceptibly from a bank of a river or stream. The owner of the land situated at the edge of the bank left dry owns the dereliction.

La. Civ. Code art. 499 (1979). This rule is particularly significant in Louisiana because, as we have noted earlier, Louisiana has many navigable rivers and streams which have seen their banks augmented with considerable amounts of new land—particularly in the form of alluvion. One of the most famous early legal controversies in Louisiana history was fought over several acres of alluvion that had built up on the banks of the Mississippi River in what is now downtown New Orleans. The chief protagonists included none other than Edward Livingston, one of the drafters of the 1825 Civil Code, and Thomas Jefferson, President of the United States. For a discussion of the famous "Batture Controversy," see ARI KELMAN, A RIVER AND ITS CITY: THE NATURE OF LANDSCAPE IN NEW ORLEANS 19–49 (2003), and GEORGE DARGO, JEFFERSON'S LOUISIANA: POLITICS AND THE CLASH OF LEGAL TRADITIONS 133–182 (Rev. ed. 2009).

Article 501 of the Civil Code does not alter the basic principle of accretion found in Article 499, but it provides a rule for the allocation of alluvion when new land is formed on the bank of two or more separately owned riparian tracts. The article, which is based on equitable principles, instructs that new land formed on the bank of a navigable river or stream should be awarded to several owners in proportion to each respective property owner's "frontage" on the river or stream prior to the alluvion's formation as well as the total amount of new "acreage" formed by the alluvion. La. Civ. Code art. 501 (1979). The reference to the term "relative values" in this provision means, for instance, that when river frontage has little economic significance, apportionment should focus more on total area. Conversely, if frontage has great economic significance in a particular situation, that factor should be given greater weight. Article 501's approach to apportioning alluvion codified prior jurisprudence. *Id.* rev. cmt. (b) (citing *Jones v. Hogue*, 129 So.2d 194 (1960)).

2. Exceptions to the General Rule

The Civil Code makes two exceptions to the general rule regarding ownership of new land formed by accretion or dereliction in Article 499. They are both articulated by Article 500, which provides that "[t]here is no right to alluvion or dereliction on the shore of the sea or lakes." La. Civ. Code Art. 500 (1979).

a. Seashore

It is fairly easy to understand why the owners of land next to seashore should not acquire newly formed alluvial land. *See* La. Civ. Code art. 501 (1979). The seashore itself is a public thing, owned by the state in its sovereign or public capacity, La. Civ. Code arts. 450–51 (1978). The Code therefore awards alluvion formed by the sea to the state. The approach taken under revised Civil Code Article 501 is the same as under the 1870 Civil Code and prior jurisprudence. *See Zeller v. Southern Yacht Club*, 1882 WL 8688 (La. 1882) (holding that there is no right of accretion on the shore of Lake Ponchartrain as it is an "arm of the sea").

b. Lakes

By expressly denying accretion and dereliction rights to the owners of land adjacent to lakes, Article 501 of the revised Civil Code clarifies an issue that was ambiguous under the 1870 Civil Code. But why exempt newly formed land adjacent to navigable lakes from the general principle of accession found in Article 499? After all, lakes, rivers and streams are all inland water bodies. Just like rivers, lakes can be used as avenues of commerce or for recreational purposes. Why not reward lakeside property owners with new land formed gradually and imperceptibly just as we do with navigable rivers and streams? If lakes can be as dynamic as rivers and streams, why not give the owner of the most prominent nearby private thing, the land beside the lake, the right to claim its natural fruit?

One answer to these questions may lie in the legal fact that, unlike with rivers or streams, the state owns the beds *and* banks of navigable lakes all the way to their ordinary high water mark in 1812. Thus shores of navigable lakes are public things, not private things subject to public use. A.N. YIANNOPOULOS, 2 LOUISIANA CIVIL LAW TREATISE: PROPERTY § 80, at 164 (4th ed. 2001). This begs the question, though. Why should the owners of land adjacent to rivers and streams own the banks of these water bodies — that is, the land between the ordinary low and ordinary high water mark — while owners of land adjacent to lakes have no rights in the lakeshore, the land between the ordinary low and ordinary high water line of a lake? Why shouldn't a lakeside landowner be able to claim new land that permanently rises above the lake bed?

Consider the following decision that addresses the question of how to determine whether a particular water body is a river or a lake. As you analyze this decision, be cognizant that in denying accretion and dereliction rights to the owners of land adjacent to lakes, Louisiana law is granting the state, the owner of the beds of all natural, navigable water bodies, including lakes, the right to claim ownership of newly formed alluvion or dereliction along the shores of lakes.

State v. Placid Oil Co.

300 So.2d 154 (La. 1973) (On Rehearing)

SANDERS, Chief Justice. We granted a rehearing in this case because of the importance of the legal issues to the people of the State of Louisiana. Although the bare controversy between the State and defendants is the ownership of a tract of land located below the high-water mark of Grand Lake-Six Mile Lake in St. Mary Parish, the decision has far-reaching consequences, affecting that State's natural resources, ecology, and the public fisc.

For the purposes of rehearing, the facts set forth in the original opinion may be summarized. The State of Louisiana, joined by Gulf Oil Corporation, its lessee, seeks to be declared the owner of an area of land, on which several oil wells are located, lying below the high-water mark of a large body of water known as Grand Lake-Six Mile Lake in St. Mary Parish, adjacent to Sections 49, 50, and 88, Township 15 South, Range 11 East. In 1812, when Louisiana was admitted into the Union, Grand Lake-Six Mile Lake was navigable. The areas in dispute are referred to as the Woodland Tract, Barnetts Cove, and The Island area. As found on original hearing, the Woodland tract is part of the bank of the water body. The record discloses that the remaining area was as late as 1935 a part of the bottom of Grand Lake. During the ensuing years, however, sedimentary deposits caused a buildup, transforming the area into alluvion lying below the ordinary high-water mark. A fair inference, we think, is that the sedimentary deposits were accelerated by the channeling and dredging performed by governmental agencies as part of an extensive water-resource program.

Although State-Gulf makes a most persuasive argument that the land formation in the Barnett and Island areas is not alluvion, we accept the findings of the lower courts that it is alluvion, that is, accretions formed successively and imperceptibly on the shore. See LSA-C.C.Art. 509.

As correctly noted in our original opinion, the State of Louisiana upon its admission to the Union acquired title to all lands within its boundaries below the ordinary high-water mark of navigable bodies of water, with the power to determine the rights of riparian owners. *Shively v. Bowlby*, 152 U.S. 1, 14 S. Ct. 548, 38 L. Ed. 331 (1894); *State v. Richardson*, 140 La. 329, 72 So. 984 (1916).

Through statutory provisions, the State of Louisiana has defined the rights of riparian owners.

As to navigable rivers and streams, the State holds in its sovereign capacity all the land that is covered by water at its ordinary low state. The bank belongs to the owner of the adjacent land, subject to public use. LSA-C.C.Arts. 455, 457; *Wemple v. Eastham*, 150 La.247, 90 So. 637 (1922). As to lakes, the State has never ceded, and still holds, the land below the ordinary high-water mark. See LSA-C.C.Art. 455; *State v. Aucoin*, 206 La. 786, 20 So.2d 136 (1944); *State v. Bozeman*, 156 La. 635, 101 So. 4 (1924); *State v. Capdeville*, 146 La. 94, 83 So. 421 (1919); *Milne v. Girodeau*, 12 La. 324 (1838).

Article 509 of the Louisiana Civil Code, regulating the ownership of alluvion, provides: (Layers)

> "The accretions, which are formed successively and imperceptibly to any soil situated on the shore of a river or other stream, are called alluvion.

> "The alluvion belongs to the owner of the soil situated on the edge of the water, whether it be a river or stream, and whether the same be navigable or not, who is bound to leave public that portion of the bank which is required by law for the public use."

By its terms, the foregoing article applies only to rivers and other streams. Thus, alluvion formed on the shores of rivers or streams belongs to the adjacent landowners. The principle of accretion, however, is inapplicable to lakes. As to lakes, the adjacent landowners have no alluvial rights. *Esso Standard Oil Company v. Jones*, 233 La. 915, 98 So. 2d 236 (1957); *Amerada Petroleum Corporation v. Case*, 210 La. 630, 27 So.2d 431 (1946); *Zeller v. Southern Yacht Club*, 34 La. Ann. 837 (1882).

The crucial determination is whether at the time of Louisiana's admission to the Union, Grand Lake-Six Mile Lake was a stream or lake. If it was a stream, the banks belong to the riparian owners, and the law of accretion applies. Thus, the disputed land would belong to the adjacent landowners. If, on the other hand, it was a lake, the banks are state-owned and accretion is inapplicable. Thus, the disputed land would belong to the State in its sovereign capacity.

On original hearing, in holding that Grand Lake-Six Mile Lake was a stream, as distinguished from a lake, we stated:

> "[A] body of water through which a current flows or runs with such capacity and velocity and power as to form accretions is characterized as a river or stream, depending upon all attending circumstances, for the purpose of applying the rules of accretion and dereliction set forth in Articles 509 and 510 of the Civil Code."

We now think we erred in holding the body of water to be a stream, primarily because of two basic errors:

> (1) In holding that *Amerada Petroleum Corporation v. State Mineral Board*, 203 La. 473, 14 So.2d 61 (1943) overruled *State v. Erwin*, 173 La. 507, 138 So. 84 (1931).

> (2) In giving undue weight to the existence of water current capable of forming accretions as a basis of classification.

In *State v. Erwin*, supra, this Court was concerned with the classification of Calcasieu Lake in Cameron Parish as a lake, river, or stream. That body of water was 18 miles long and varied in width from 4-1/2 to 14 miles. The Calcasieu River traversed the water body from north to south, then continued its flow toward the Gulf of Mexico. At times, there were perceptible currents in the water, and it was affected by tides.

In holding that the water body was a lake rather than a stream on original hearing, this Court stated:

> "In our opinion, however, the better view — with reference to the laws, governing alluvion and dereliction — is to regard such a vast expanse of water as Calcasieu Lake as being in fact a lake, although a river empties into the sea through it." (138 So. at 86)

On rehearing, the Court adhered to the holding that the body of water was a lake.

In *Miami Corporation v. State*, 186 La. 784, 173 So. 315 (1937), this Court dealt with the stream-lake classification of Grand Lake in Cameron Parish. The Court described it as a "navigable body of running water." It was about ten miles long and from three to nine miles wide. The Mermentau River flowed into and out of the lake. There was sufficient current to carry sediment. The Court overruled *State v. Erwin*, *supra*, as to a point not pertinent here. In holding the body of water to be a lake, however, it reaffirmed the *Erwin* lake classification, stating: "Grand Lake, like Calcasieu Lake, was a navigable lake, when Louisiana was admitted to the Union in 1812." (173 So. at 319). . . .

First Amerada makes only one reference to *State v. Erwin, supra.* That reference is not to overrule, but to distinguish. . . .

Our examination of *First Amerada* convinces us that it accomplished no overruling of *State v. Erwin*. Rather, it considered the characteristics of the particular water body, bearing no resemblance to that involved in *Erwin*, and classified it as a flowing stream or river. . . .

We conclude, contrary to our first impression, that the holding of *State v. Erwin* as to the classification of lakes has not been overruled.

It is true that sectors of the Court's language in several of the above cases focus strongly upon the existence of accretion-forming current in the water body. When these decisions are read as a whole, however, it is evident that the Court considered, not one, but several characteristics of the water body in making its classification. Our synthesis of these cases yields a conclusion that the existence of accretion-forming current is not, by itself, decisive of a stream classification. As noted in the dissenting opinion on original hearing, a holding that accretion-forming current alone is determinative that the water body is a stream would mean that all alluvion on all water bodies accrues to the riparian owners, contrary to the intent of Article 509, the formal expression of legislative will.

In our opinion, the jurisprudence, as well as the expert testimony, supports a multiple-factor test for classifying a water body as a lake or a stream. A judgment must be based upon a consideration of pertinent characteristics. Among these are the size, especially its width as compared to the streams that enter it; its depth; its banks; its channel; its current, especially as compared to that of streams that enter it; and its historical designation in official documents, especially on official maps. . . .

Considering these factors in the present case, we find that Grand Lake-Six Mile Lake is one of the five largest water bodies in Louisiana. From earliest times, it has been designated on official maps as a lake. In 1812, at the time Louisiana was admitted to the federal union, the body was also known as Lake Chetimaches or Lake Sale (Salt Lake). It was about 30 miles long by 3 to 10 miles wide. It had a "Thalweg depth of only 8 feet."

The water body was subject to the ebb and flow of the tide. Because of the tidal action, the water was brackish and populated by salt water fish.

The record reflects that Grand Lake is about 20 times wider than the Atchafalaya River, which enters it; that currents are reduced substantially in the lake; that 75% of the sedimentation is deposited in the lake, and only 25% is carried out.

Holding

In summary, Grand Lake-Six Mile Lake is a wide, irregularly shaped body of water of great size, relatively shallow in depth, with a current substantially slower than that of the inflowing river. In its main characteristics, it is similar to Lake Pontchartrain and Lake Calcasieu. Historically, it has always been designated as a lake.

We hold that it was a lake in 1812, when Louisiana was admitted to the Union. Accordingly, it must now be classified as such. It follows under the principles already announced that the State owns its banks and that the accretion rule of Louisiana Civil Code Article 509 is inapplicable to it. . . .

Consistent with the views expressed, we hold that the State of Louisiana owns the disputed areas, located below the ordinary high-water mark of Grand Lake-Six Mile Lake, subject to the rights of its mineral lessee, Gulf Oil Corporation.

For the reasons assigned, the judgment of the Court of Appeal, insofar as it decreed the defendants to be the owners of the area hereinafter described, is reversed. Judgment is rendered in favor of plaintiffs, State of Louisiana and Gulf Oil Corporation, against Placid Oil Company, J. Ray McDermott & Co., Inc., and all other defendants decreeing the State of Louisiana to be the owner of the property covered by State Lease 2963, dated April 18, 1956, to Gulf Oil Corporation.

. . . .

SUMMERS, Justice (dissenting). In 1964 we approved a finding that Six Mile Lake in St. Mary Parish was a stream. *State v. Cockrell*, 162 So. 2d 361 (La. App. 1964), *cert. denied*, 246 La. 343, 164 So. 2d 350. . . . Ten years later, by this decision, on the same facts, we change the rule of law and hold that the same body of water is now a lake. Not only is this the identical body of water, the accretion involved here is in close proximity to the accretion in the Cockrell Case. The strange paradox resulting from the decision gives defendant's neighbors in the Cockrell Case a short-distance upstream title to the accretion and denies a like accretion to defendants.

To accomplish this result, the Court has held that the 1931 decision of *State v. Erwin*, 173 La. 507, 138 So. 84, was not supplanted by a series of cases which followed. These later cases established the rule of law applied in the *Cockrell* Case to classify Six Mile Lake as a stream. See *Amerada Petroleum Corporation v. State Mineral Board*, 203 La. 473, 14 So. 2d 61 (1943), later recognized in *Amerada Petroleum Corporation v. Case*, 210 La. 630, 27 So. 2d 431 (1946) and *Esso Standard Oil Company v. Jones*, 233 La. 915, 98 So. 2d 236 (1957). In effect the Court has resurrected the Erwin Case from the ineffective status to which it was assigned by later rulings.

The wells involved in this case were located and drilled on the faith of the principles of property law announced and applied in the first *Amerada* Case and fully recognized in the other cited cases. The return to the *Erwin* rule brings about a retroactive change in the law which was unpredictable in terms of relevant precedents. As a result, defendants have been deprived of their property without due process of law; and this decision results in the taking of private property for public use without compensation, all in violation of the Fifth and Fourteenth Amendments to the Constitution of the United States and Article I, Section 2 of the Constitution of Louisiana.

In setting aside our original decision, the Court asserts that undue weight was given "to the existence of water current capable of forming accretions as a basis for classification." This holding despite the fact that water currents are the natural phenomena of all streams and their most dominant characteristic.

In reviving and applying the *Erwin* rule, the Court cast aside the established jurisprudence of this State for a period in excess of thirty years and reached a decision in direct conflict with the doctrine of accretion long recognized by Articles 455, 509 and 510 of the Civil Code. To reach its result the Court leaned heavily on broad considerations of ecology, environment and the public fisc, matters not at issue in the case and concerning which there are no findings of fact supported by this record.

The so-called "multiple factor test" adopted by the Court for classifying water bodies is in effect a statement of the rule of the *Erwin* Case. In my view the classification of Six Mile Lake as a "Lake" under that test was erroneous and invalid for several reasons.

The finding by the trial court and the Court of Appeal and this Court on original hearing that Six Mile Lake annually carries off a substantial portion of the tremendous volume of water flowing to the sea through the Atchafalaya River has not been changed on rehearing. This determination remains the principal and crucial factual finding of this case. The official state map dramatically illustrates that Six Mile Lake forms an integral part of the dynamic water system of the Atchafalaya Basin, vividly underscoring its capacity as a body of running water of tremendous force.

The laws of accretion were intended to have particular application to water bodies capable of carrying and depositing sedimentary loads and capable of changing their shorelines. Bodies of running water fit into that category, and the history of our Code articles support this rationale.

In classifying Six Mile Lake as a lake the Court disregards the most important characteristic of a water body for the purpose of classification under Civil Code Article 509, that is, a moving or running body of water principally endowed with the capacity for change. Instead the Court has emphasized other physical features which are either not supported by the record or which have pertinence only in the limited fields of geology or cartography. And this notwithstanding the fact that the State expressly admitted in its application for writs that the issue before the Court was the classification of the water body under our laws relating to accretion and dereliction.

This reasoning of the Court is based upon the erroneous premise that if the capacity to form accretions is the test for classification, a minimal amount of accretion in any type of water body would satisfy the requirements of Article 509 of the Civil Code because the presence of accretions proves up the capacity to form them. This overly simplistic approach is irrelevant to the facts of this case. It disregards the admitted fact that Six Mile Lake is a dynamic body of water carrying a substantial portion of the waters of the Atchafalaya Basin to the Gulf. This approach requires classification of Six Mile Lake as a placid or immobile body of water having no real capacity for undergoing physical change. Nothing could be further from the facts. The characteristics of Six Mile Lake are otherwise.

The Court's opinion is also based upon erroneous factual findings. The finding that Six Mile Lake has a thalweg of only eight feet is contrary to the Cathcart finding that immediately after Statehood the water body had a channel of four and one-half fathoms, or twenty-seven and one-half feet.

A finding that Six Mile Lake is subject to tidal action and has brackish water does not detract from its classification as a stream when it is noted that the Mississippi River at New Orleans is also subject to tidal action and has brackish water. It is also error to compare Six Mile Lake to Lake Pontchartrain and Lake Calcasieu. Six Mile Lake has a different shape, configuration, watershed and the dynamics of its water system are strikingly dissimilar. While the Court's finding that Six Mile Lake is one of the five largest water bodies in Louisiana, many times larger than the river that enters it and that it has been designated as a lake on official maps may be correct, these considerations do not detract from the fact that it is a body of running water with capacity to form accretions, characteristics which make it, in natural and legal contemplation, a stream. . . .

I respectfully dissent.

Notes and Questions

1. In *State v. Placid Oil Co.*, 300 So.2d 154 (La. 1973), Justice Sanders and Justice Summers reached two very different conclusions about the proper methodology courts should use to determine whether an inland, natural navigable water body is a river or stream or a lake. Which approach do you think makes more sense: the multi-factor approach favored by Justice Sanders or Justice Summer's proposed analysis that focuses primarily on a water body's "capacity for change," and especially its capacity to generate alluvion or dereliction?

2. In **Miami Corp. v. State**, 173 So. 315 (La. 1936), one of the decisions discussed by the court in *State v. Placid Oil*, the Louisiana Supreme Court addressed a dispute that arose between the state and owners of land adjacent to a navigable lake when natural events caused the shore of the lake to erode or disappear, leaving previously dry land permanently submerged beneath the lake's waters. The court had to decide who owned the eroded or subsided land which had previously been dry land but was now a part of the lake's bed: the state or the owner of the land adjacent to the lake. The Louisiana Supreme Court ruled in favor of the state, holding that eroded or submerged lands that become part of the bed or bottom of a navigable lake belong to the state and are insusceptible of private ownership. *Id.* at 327.

3. **Synthesis:** Today we know that the Freeze Statute, La. Rev. Stat. 9:1151 (1952, amended 2001), discussed in Chapter Three, would protect a landowner's interests in pre-erosion or pre-subsidence mineral leases presented in the situation in *Miami Corp.* But the implications of *Miami Corp.* are still significant. Combined with current Article 500, the court's holdings in *Miami Corp v. State* and *State v. Placid Oil* establish that any land that has ever been below or falls below the ordinary high water mark of a lake belongs to the state. Put differently, the 1812 high water mark

of a lake establishes the minimum of what the state will own with respect to a lake. Although the state may gain new water bottoms as the result of erosion or subsidence of land on the shore of lakes, once this land is submerged below the waters of a navigable lake it can never be lost through alluvion or dereliction. Why has the Louisiana Supreme Court, with the legislature's apparent blessing, chosen to allow the state's claims to land adjacent to navigable lakes to be so much more expansive than its claims to land near navigable rivers? *See* A.N. YIANNOPOULOS, 2 LOUISIANA CIVIL LAW TREATISE: PROPERTY §4:19, at 183–85 (5th ed. 2015) (criticizing majority decision in *State v. Placid Oil* for confusing the notions of public things and things subject to public use).

4. Another large, ambiguous water body, this one found in northwest Louisiana, known as Lake Bistineau, has been the subject of litigation involving fascinating legal disputes for more than one hundred years. *See e.g., Sapp v. Frazier,* 26 So. 378, 380–81 (La. 1899) (addressing a dispute over rights to graze cattle and cut grass in the bed of Lake Bistineau when water levels receded in the low water season and holding that there was no permanent accretion or dereliction in the lake bed when the waters receded and that the lake bed was a public commons for all to enjoy and use in the low water season); *Lake Bistineau Preservation Society, Inc. v. Wildlife and Fisheries Comm'n,* 895 So.2d 821, 826–27 (La. App. 2 Cir. 2005) (holding that the state's Department of Wildlife and Fisheries acted within its discretion in lowering the water level in Lake Bistineau to enhance the lake's ecology and properly balanced the environmental costs and benefits of the drawdown plan against the economic interests of adjacent property owners and others who use the lake for recreational or commercial purposes). *See also* Jen DeGregorio, *Gas-Rich Lake Is at Stake in Legal Feud,* Times-Picayune, E-1 (Nov. 23. 2008) (reporting on a dispute between the state and the United States Department of Interior, which claimed that Lake Bistineau was not navigable in 1812 and thus not owned by the state).

5. It once seemed that disputes concerning the distinction between rivers and lakes were a thing of the past in Louisiana, but a recent controversy concerning a large body of water located in east central Louisiana known as Catahoula Lake proves otherwise. In 2007, the Third Circuit Court of Appeal addressed what kind of evidence can be used to determine the level of the ordinary high water mark of that water body. *See Sanders v. Dep't of Natural Resources,* 973 So.2d 879, 882–87 (La. App. 3 Cir. 2007) (holding that evidence of physical characteristics, such as effects of lake water on vegetation and bedrock, could be used to determine this "intermittent" lake's ordinary high water mark and that the trial court's reliance on testimonial evidence regarding gauge readings of tributaries and distributaries was manifestly erroneous in this instance). More recently, a different panel of the same appellate court determined that the *Sanders* decision did not resolve whether Catahoula Lake was, in fact, a lake or a river or stream and, therefore, remanded the case to the trial court to determine the proper classification of that water body. *Crooks v. State Dep't of Natural Resources,* 81 So.3d 47, 49 (La. App. 3 Cir. 2011).

After lengthy proceedings, the 9th Judicial District Court, Rapides Parish, determined that Catahoula Lake and its entire basin is actually a "one of a kind" geographic feature formed by the channel of the Little River and, moreover, found that in 1812 the area known as Calcasieu Lake constituted the banks of Little River. *Crooks v. State ex rel. Dep't of Natural Res.*, 263 So.3d 540 (La. App. 3 Cir. 2018). The Louisiana Third Circuit Court of Appeal affirmed this ruling in the following decision:

Crooks v. State ex rel. Dept. of Natural Res.

263 So. 3d 540 (La. App. 3 Cir 2018), aff'd in part and rev'd in part
on other grounds, ___ So. 3d ___ (La. 2020)

SAVOIE, Judge: ... After a bench trial on the merits, the trial court issued written reasons for judgment and provided the following description of the Catahoula Basin, the area known as Catahoula Lake, and Little River (alteration in original):

The unique characteristics of Catahoula Lake and indeed the Basin itself cannot be overemphasized since it is truly a "one of a kind," geographic area. The Catahoula Basin is an area of very flat land located in the parishes of Rapides, Grant, and LaSalle that forms a platter extending outward from the channel of Little River. Because of the unusual topography of the basin, the slope of the river's bank is extremely gradual. A description of Catahoula Lake can be found in the "Catahoula Lake Area Report" presented to Governor Kennon and the Louisiana Legislature by the Louisiana Department of Public Works in 1954:

The lake bed proper has a length of about 14 miles and an average width of 3 miles covering an area of some 42 square miles or about 27,000 acres. The western Louisiana uplands adjoin the lake bed on the west and northwest. To the south and southeast of the lake bed lies alluvial area. The lowest portion of the lake's bed of any appreciable extent is at elevation 27 feet m.s.l. ... The principal tributary to the lake is Little River which enters the lake at its southwest end. It traverses the lake in a relatively wide and shallow channel to the northeast end of the lake, a total distance of about 15 miles. Outflow from the lake is principally through French Fork and Old River which join at Lavaca forming Little River down which the flow is carried to Black River at Jonesville. One other principal outlet or distributary of the lake, which serves mostly for flood flows, is Big Saline Bayou which emerges from the lake near its southwest end meandering southeasterly to join Red River. Other outlets for flood waters are Sandy, Indian, Muddy, Cypress and Big Bayous, all of which lead off in a southeastern direction through either Saline Lake or Larto Lake to Red River.

. . . .

A watershed area of 2,672 square miles contributes to the lake. The area is composed principally of upland hilly timbered area and extends generally northwestward from the lake to Ruston and the vicinity of Arcadia, an airline distance of some 80 miles with an average width of about 33 miles. Little River drains an area of 2,555 square miles above its entry into the lake.

Ultimately, the trial court found in favor of the Plaintiffs. First, the trial court concluded that, in 1812, the area known as Catahoula Lake constituted the banks of Little River. Therefore, the trial court declared the Lake Plaintiffs to be the owners of the area known as Catahoula Lake according to Louisiana's laws of riparian ownership. In turn, the trial court further held that the Lake Plaintiffs are entitled to the royalties received by the State for oil, gas, and mineral activities that took place in the area known as Catahoula Lake between May 2003 and the date of trial.

Discussion

Ownership of the Area Known as Catahoula Lake

. . . .

We now move on to the State's argument that the trial court erred in finding that, in 1812, the area known as Catahoula Lake was a permanent river that seasonally overflowed and covered its banks. The trial court made the following factual conclusions on this issue:

> A summary of the entirety of the evidence introduced at trial conclusively established, confirmed and reaffirmed the following inescapable conclusions, to-wit: (1) that the Little River channel in 1812 completely traversed the entire Catahoula Basin; (2) that Little River was a permanent, as opposed to a temporary body of water: (3) that during the wet season, Little River would seasonally overflow its channel and cover the surrounding low-lands in the Catahoula Basin; and (4) that annually at other times of the year, these low-lands were totally dry and clothed in luxuriant vegetation. Therefore, in 1812, there was only one permanent body of water, Little River, in the Catahoula Basin whose waters seasonally overflowed its channel and covered its banks, the extensive adjacent low-lying lands.

The trial court determined that "a temporary water body created when a river seasonally overflows its channel or a temporary body of water cannot qualify as a lake."

In reaching that outcome, the trial court found:

> The court was faced with widely divergent views among the plaintiffs' and defendant's experts on the determinative issue in this case, that is, whether the so-called Catahoula Lake is a river or a lake. The significance of the historical evidence cannot be overstated for a proper analysis of that evidence is critical for the proper determination of the issue at hand. With that in mind, a careful analysis of the expert testimony offered in this case, together with the entirety of the evidence, causes the court to arrive at the following conclusions as to certain experts.

A complete and thorough analysis of the evidence dictates the court's conclusion that the testimonies of plaintiffs' expert witnesses, Dr. Suhayda and Dr. Flowers, are credible, reliable, based on sound methodology, and much more persuasive with regard to the ultimate opinion in this case. For the reasons assigned herein, the court has credited their testimonies over that of Dr. Willis.

Dr. Joseph Suhayda was tendered and accepted as an expert in hydrology, including the movement of water and flooding, who spent thirty years as a professor at Louisiana State University. He testified that the hydraulic characteristics of a certain body of water determine its classification as a river or lake. Dr. Suhayda further testified that the historical records provide the best evidence about a body of water's hydraulic characteristics in 1812. Dr. Suhayda concluded that, based on his extensive review of the historical records, the area at issue was a river.

Next, Dr. George Flowers testified. He was tendered and accepted as an expert in the fields of geology, geography, and hydrogeology. Dr. Flowers also relied on historical records for his opinions and reached the same conclusion. Specifically, he testified that, based upon the definition of a lake from the Glossary of Geology, "a lake is a standing body of water." He stated that Catahoula Lake is not a permanent body of water "because it drains." Dr. Flowers also testified that, after a review of the historical records, "it became clear that early on, extending into the 20th Century, there was an opinion that was repeated over and over again that the water body in the Catahoula Basin was indeed a river."

The State argues that the trial court erred by ignoring the historical documentation recognizing the water body in the Catahoula Basin as a "lake." The Lake Plaintiffs counter that "the overwhelming trial evidence confirmed it would be bad science to determine the classification of a water body based on its name."

The trial court relied on *Schoeffler v. Drake Hunting Club*, 05-499 (La.App. 3 Cir. 1/4/06), 919 So.2d 822. In *Schoeffler*, members of the general public filed a declaratory action seeking to fix the boundary between the state-owned bed of a navigable river and the privately owned banks. The case was dismissed on exceptions of no cause of action and no right of action. The third circuit affirmed, finding persons who hunt and fish on land that is inundated by waterways belonging to the State do not have a right of action to fix boundaries between the State and a private landowner. The trial court in the present case found that "[t]he Third Circuit correctly observed that a temporary body of water that is seasonally inundated a high river stages cannot be a real lake, and therefore cannot be public property."

The trial court refused to apply *State v. Placid Oil Co.*, 300 So.2d 154 (La.1973). In its written reasons, the trial court stated the following:

> [I]n this court's view, *Placid Oil*, does not nor was it ever intended to apply to mere temporary bodies of water created when a river seasonally overflows its channel. In view of extensive and exhaustive research into Louisiana jurisprudence, the court is convinced that no such jurisprudence exists

holding that a temporary body of water can legally be classified as a lake. Nor has any party to this litigation come forward with any such case. Thus, the court is convinced that the factors in that decision [were] intended to address permanent bodies of water — not temporary ones.

After a complete review of the record and the trial court's written reasons for judgment, we cannot say that the trial court was manifestly erroneous in finding that, in 1812, the area in contention was "a permanent river that seasonally overflowed and covered its banks." *" so clearly wrong.*

Questions

1. Do you agree with the appellate court's characterization of the test developed in *State v. Placid Oil* as one applicable only to permanent, as opposed to, temporary bodies of water?

2. In a subsequent decision, the Louisiana Supreme Court affirmed in part and reversed in part the decision of the Third Circuit Court of Appeal in *Crooks*. *Crooks v. Dep't of Natural Resources*, ___ So.3d ___ 2020 (La. 2020). Reviewing the evidence in the record, the supreme court found that the trial court had not committed manifest error in determining that: (1) "the body of water in the Catahoula Basin in 1812 was a permanent river that seasonally overflowed and covered its banks;" (2) the riparian landowners therefore owned "the land between the ordinary low and ordinary high water mark of the river's bank;" and (3) man-made structures installed in and around the Catahoula Basin by the State of Louisiana and the U.S. Army Corps of Engineers "caused significant flooding of both the riparian and overflow lands, which obstructed the natural servitude of drain." *Id.* at ___. The supreme court, however, reversed the trial court's inverse condemnation award in favor of the riparian landowners and against the State of Louisiana. It concluded that the State of Louisiana, and not the United States, was the primary actor and responsible party in the navigation project that produced inundation and appropriation of the riparian lands, and thus the landowners' inverse condemnation claims against the state had prescribed under the three-year liberative prescriptive period for such claims established by La. Rev. Stat. § 13:5111, as those claims accrued when the landowners or their ancestors in title became aware, or should have become aware, of increased inundation of their lands no later than 1973 when water levels failed to subside seasonally as they had in the past. *Id.* at ___.

3. Variations on the General Rule

a. Islands in Rivers

Two articles in the Civil Code's suite of articles addressing accession in the context of navigable water bodies create rules for the allocation of islands that form in a navigable river or stream. The first, Article 503, conforms to the general principles of accession discussed above.

Art. 503. Island formed by river opening a new channel

When a river or stream, whether navigable or not, opens a new channel and surrounds riparian land making it an island, the ownership of that land is not affected.

La. Civ. Code art. 503 (1979). The physical process of forming a new channel is sometimes described as a "chute cut-off." *Walker Lands, Inc. v. East Carroll Parish Policy Jury*, 871 So.2d 1258, 1262 (La. App. 2 Cir. 2004). For a story and photographs of a recent chute cut-off from the Mississippi River called the Mardi Gras Pass and its potential ecological benefits, see: http://www.mississippiriverdelta.org/blog/2012/03/21/mardi-gras-pass-a-new-diversion-on-the-mississippi-river-springs-to-life/.

The rule expressed by Article 503 is consistent with Article 499 because the key factual assumption generating the outcome is that the land at issue, formerly dry land or the bank of a river or stream, was a private thing before the cut-off occurred. The fact that a river *suddenly and unexpectedly* surrounds this land as the result of a change in the river's course should not change the ownership of the land. The policy underlying Article 503 is to preserve the continuity of land ownership, particularly the ownership of the surrounded land.

Article 505 of the Civil Code, however, provides a different result when an island is formed in the midst of a river bed, rather than by a river forming another branch entirely.

Art. 505. Islands and sandbars in navigable rivers

Islands, and sandbars that are not attached to a bank, formed in the beds of *navigable* rivers or streams, belong to the state.

La. Civ. Code art. 505 (1979) (emphasis added). Although this article assigns ownership of a new island or sandbar to the state, rather than a riparian landowner, this result remains consistent with the general principles of accession and dereliction found in Article 499. In this situation, the newly formed land, unlike a previous bank or riparian land surrounded by a river as a result of an Article 503 chute cut-off, emerges out of the bed of a navigable river or stream; that is, directly out of land owned by the state. Article 505 thus awards the new thing—the emerging island or sandbar—to the state, the owner of the most prominent nearby thing, the bed of the navigable river or stream.

b. Avulsion and Abandoned River Beds

Articles 502 and 504 of the Civil Code both address unexpected changes in the courses of rivers and streams. Article 502 provides for the situation that the common law and Roman law both describe as "avulsion."

Art. 502. Sudden Action of Waters

If a sudden action of the waters of a river or stream carries away an identifiable piece of ground and unites it with other lands on the same or on the opposite bank, the ownership of the piece of ground so carried away is not lost. The owner may claim it within a year, or even later, if the owner of the bank with which it is united has not taken possession.

La. Civ. Code art. 502 (1979). The rule created by Article 502 contradicts the general principle of accretion stated in Article 499 in the sense that new land that becomes physically united to the bank of a river or stream is not assigned to the owner of the most prominent nearby thing—the bank to which it is now attached. The rationale for this deviation is related to the preference for historical continuity of landownership when the land can be identified. It would be unfair to take ownership of an identifiable tract of land away from an upstream riparian owner and transfer it to a downstream riparian owner because a natural but sudden and violent avulsive event caused the dislocation. Conversely, when land is lost through a gradual and imperceptible process, the land cannot be identified. The Louisiana legal community eagerly awaits a case that would call upon a court to apply Article 502.

Article 504 of the Civil Code provides a rule designed to address a geological phenomenon that does arise from time to time in the context of Louisiana's meandering rivers and streams.

Art. 504. Ownership of abandoned bed with river changes course

When a navigable river or stream abandons its bed and opens a new one, the owners of the land on which the new bed is located shall take by way of indemnification the abandoned bed, each in proportion to the quantity of land lost.

If the river returns to the old bed, each shall take his former land.

La. Civ. Code art. 504 (1979).

Several details distinguish this article from all of those studied above. Unlike Article 503, which contemplates an enlarged channel surrounding an island, Article 504 contemplates the emergence of an entirely new bed of a navigable river or stream, which will, by operation of Article 450, presumably belong to the state. The unique innovation of Article 504 is that, in recognizing that a riparian landowner will lose ownership of her land to the state as the result of the opening of a new river bed, it compensates that landowner for the loss of her land by giving her the ownership of the old, abandoned bed of the river or stream, regardless of (1) whether that old bed remains a navigable water body or not and (2) whether the affected landowner had been a riparian landowner along the old bed. In other words, despite the basic principle articulated in Article 450 that the bottoms of natural, navigable water bodies are public things that belong to the state, Article 504 creates the possibility that ownership of a remnant bed of a navigable river or stream, usually in the form of what we call an "ox-bow lake," might be lawfully claimed by a private person, even though the water body remains otherwise navigable.

Consider the following decision, *State v. Bourdon*, 535 So.2d 1091, 1097 (La. App. 2 Cir. 1988), writ denied, 536 So.2d 1223 (1989), to see how the court resolved the apparent conflict between Article 504 and Article 450.

State v. Bourdon

535 So.2d 1091 (La. App. 2 Cir. 1986)

MARVIN, Judge. In this petitory action to determine ownership of the bed of an oxbow lake created in this century by Red River near the Grand Bayou community in Red River Parish, the State appeals a judgment rejecting its demands and decreeing that the 123-acre bed of the lake is privately owned by defendants by virtue of 30 years acquisitive prescription.

We affirm on the authority of C.C. Art. 504; *Dickson v. Sandefur*, 259 La. 473, 250 So.2d 708 (1971); *Stephens v. Drake*, 134 So.2d 674 (La. App. 2d Cir. 1961), cert. denied, and *Verzwyvelt v. Armstrong-Ratterree, Inc.*, 463 So.2d 979 (La. App. 3d Cir. 1985). This appeal is a belated sequel to *Strohecker v. Robinson*, 147 La. 652, 85 So. 627 (1920), the plaintiffs there being the ancestors in title of the private landowner-defendants here.

The Red River at Stallings Bend

From *Strohecker*, supra, and plats and exhibits in this record, we glean some facts about the Red River and its meanderings during the past 150 years in sections 23–26, T13N, R11W. Our composite plat, roughly to scale, will illustrate some of the history of the dispute which involves the oxbow lake bed in the peninsula once existing that was known as Stallings Bend Plantation in the latter part of the 19th century.

The river created the peninsula sometimes before the 1830s and cut it off in 1902 before meandering easterly to its present location. Except for the oxbow lake, the former peninsula is not identifiable in an aerial photograph made in the 1980s. We reproduce the composite plat to illustrate the factual circumstances:

The earliest government surveys were completed in the 1830s. We shall assume, as the State contends, that the course of Red River around the peninsula was not grossly changed between 1812 when Louisiana became a State and the 1830s when the government surveys were completed.

Stallings owned the peninsula in sections 23 and 26 and established the peninsula lands as a plantation in 1857. Kennedy owned the lands in sections 23 and 24 north of the westerly flowing river. Robinson owned the lands in section 25 and 26 south of the easterly flowing river.

. . . .

The peninsula at its narrowest point, north to south, in the 1830s was some 1,300 feet. By the end of that century the river on the north and on the south had eroded the narrowest point of the peninsula to about 500 feet. In 1902, this distance shrunk to about 20 feet before completely caving in and washing away about a quarter mile

of river frontage. This 1,300-foot break through the peninsula allowed the west-
bound river on the north to unite with the eastbound river on the south and temporarily made an island of the high ground in the west end of the former peninsula.

. . . .

The new river immediately after the break was 1,300 feet wide and gradually
moved eastward.

. . . .

The levee across the former peninsula yet exists, being shown on the aerial photo
and plats in the record, and is about 2,000 feet from the SW corner of section 23.
The gradual eastward recession of the river continued after 1902. The aerial photo
made in the 1980s shows the river, once only about 2,000 feet east of the SW corner
of section 23, to have meandered more than 8,000 feet east of that corner.

The *Strohecker v. Robinson* controversy was resolved by the Supreme Court of
Louisiana 18 years after the river cut off the peninsula in 1902. Strohecker and Wilson, successors to Stallings and ancestors to defendant landowners here, unsuccess-
fully claimed 29 acres of alluvion vs. Robinson and 62 acres of alluvion vs. Kennedy.

. . . .

A 1945 plat tracks the detail of a 1914 plat and lends some understanding to the
Strohecker explanation of what occurred during and after the 1902 break and unit-
ing of the river. The sand bars or batture shown surrounding the higher "land"
of the island that temporarily existed following the 1902 break, apparently then
formed and connected west of the levee to stop the flow of the river and to create
the oxbow lake. The river meandered eastward, leaving derelicted lands east of the
levee. In any event before 1920, the river had abandoned its former bed and created
a new bed which meandered eastward. We reproduce the 1945 plat which effectively
tracks the 1914 plat that shows the relationship of the oxbow lake to the levee and to
section lines [above].

Accretions that formed on the Robinson and Kennedy lands *before* the break were
also at issue in *Strohecker*. That court noted that plaintiffs "virtually conceded" the
ownership of those accretions to Robinson and Kennedy, whose lands increased in
depth by the accretions at least 400 feet. *Strohecker* reserved to its plaintiffs "whatever right they may have for accretion or alluvion that has formed since the river
bank caved in, in December 1902." The bed of the oxbow lake that was formed was
not at issue in *Strohecker*.

. . . .

The State's Contentions

The State contends that the oxbow lake, from 1812 until 1902, was the bed of Red
River, "navigable in law," and a "public thing" not susceptible of private ownership
under C.C. Art. 450. We have assumed this contention to be true, notwithstanding
that the State has not shown where the bed of Red River was in 1812.

The State contends that a water body, navigable in 1812, is deemed navigable thereafter. In the broad and general sense, we assume this contention is correct.

The State acknowledges C.C. Art. 504

> When a navigable river or stream abandons its bed and opens a new one, the owners of the land on which the new bed is located shall take by way of indemnification the abandoned bed, each in proportion to the quantity of land that he lost . . .

but argues that the phrase *abandoned bed* should not be deemed to include the bed of a newly-formed, navigable oxbow lake because the redactors did not use phrases such as "abandoned river" or "abandoned lake," and did not intend to deprive the public of the right to use a natural navigable water body which was previously enjoyed.

The State says that because the owner who loses land when a meandering river makes a new bed may not be a "riparian owner" of lands surrounding the newly formed oxbow lake, our affirmance of the judgment would deprive the owners of land around a newly formed oxbow lake the "alluvion and dereliction" rights that are provided riparian owners by the Code.

The State suggests that the "correct" way we should interpret the phrase "abandoned bed" in Art. 504, in the light of Art. 499 (the article granting alluvial and dereliction rights), especially where the landowner who "loses" to the new bed of the meandering river is a "riparian owner" around the newly formed oxbow lake, is to reason that the accretion and dereliction rights afforded the losing landowner "compensates" and indemnifies him for the loss of land to the river.

The State, however, does not cite us any authority to support its argument and does not discuss or attempt to distinguish the authorities to the contrary, the more pertinent of which we have cited in paragraph two of this opinion. The landowners, of course, rely on authorities, including the ones we have cited.

The phrase "abandoned bed" in Art. 504 is not ambiguous and does not require a strained interpretation.

. . . ..

The Law

. . . ..

Art. 450 speaks of a *natural navigable water body* as being a public thing. The bed of an oxbow *lake*, navigable in 1812, remains a public thing after 1812. The bed of the river that formed a navigable oxbow lake before 1812 is a public thing. The oxbow lake in question here, even according to the State, did not exist in 1812, but was created, as we have described, in 1902. Before 1902, the oxbow lake was merely Stallings Bend in Red River, the bed of the river being a public thing under CC Art. 450, even though meandering.

Once the break in the peninsula occurred Stallings Bend of the river only temporarily remained a public thing. When the river thereafter abandoned the Stallings Bend bed and moved eastward, creating the oxbow lake and opening a new bed, the private owners of the land on which the new bed was located were privileged to "take" or claim the abandoned bed of the river, now the oxbow lake that was created from the Stallings Bend.

The foregoing principle is clearly expressed in CC Art. 504 and is not contingent upon the abandoned bed being wet, dry, navigable or non-navigable in fact or in law, but simply arises out of a navigable river abandoning its bed for a new one *after 1812.*

> When a navigable river or stream abandons its bed and opens a new one, the owners of the land on which the new bed is located shall take by way of indemnification the abandoned bed, each in proportion to the quantity of land that he lost. If the river returns to the old bed, each shall take his former land.

CC ART. 504.

This article is not ambiguous and makes no exceptions in conferring private ownership of the abandoned river bed on those whose land has been taken by the new channel. *Stephens,* supra, 134 So.2d at 677.

Whether the river abandons its course abruptly, or gradually and slowly, the private landowner who loses to the new bed, takes the abandoned bed as indemnification. It is not required that there be a cut-off. The losing landowner "takes" the old bed no matter how far removed it is from his property, and without need for him to have been a riparian owner along the old river bed. Riparian ownership plays no part in the application of this article. *Dickson,* supra, 250 So.2d. at 720.

The abandoned bed of a navigable river that changes its bed or course may remain, *in fact,* a natural navigable water body, as the State contends. If, however, the change in the river bed occurs *after* 1812, the abandoned bed, even though an oxbow lake that is navigable in fact, as a matter of policy or law for more than 175 years under the specific provisions of Art. 504, loses its identity as a public thing and becomes privately owned. The specific provisions of Art. 504 control the general declaration of Art. 450 in such circumstances.

Decree

Under the specific provisions of CC Art. 504, the bed of the oxbow lake known as Wilson Lake is susceptible of private ownership. The State did not otherwise contest the judgment or the legal sufficiency or duration of defendants' acts of possession for more than 30 years. Under these circumstances, the judgment of the trial court is therefore, at appellant's cost.

AFFIRMED.

Notes and Questions

1. As interpreted by the court in *State v. Bourdon*, 535 So.2d 1091 (La. App. 2 Cir. 1986), Article 504 effectuates a kind of forced ownership exchange between the owner of the former private land covered by a new bed of a navigable river or stream and the owner of the old bed (the state). Article 504 thus establishes a noteworthy exception to the general rule that all natural navigable water bodies are public things owned by the state. Is this exception justified by the principle of unjust enrichment?

2. After the river broke through the 1,300 feet of land between the west-flowing and east-flowing parts of the Red River in *State v. Bourdon*, who owned the land area west of the new river bed and east of the oxbow lake? Who owns the oxbow lake?

3. In 1975, the Louisiana Legislature enacted a statute to address the ownership of a particularly large oxbow lake called False River.

§ 1110. Ownership of land adjacent to False River

The title of the owners of land adjacent to that body of water in Pointe Coupee Parish known as False River shall extend to fifteen feet above mean sea level. The boundary line formed at fifteen feet above mean sea level marks the division between land owned by the state and land owned by private persons along the banks of False River.

La. R.S. 9:1110 (1975). What rule would apply in the absence of this statute? Why do you think the legislature enacted this statute?

4. In another property dispute involving a sudden change in the course of the Red River in Caddo Parish, lots in an existing subdivision were inundated by the river when a new levee was constructed and a manmade cut redirected the river, causing a lake to form over the lots. *Hamel's Farm, L.L.C. v. Muslow*, 988 So.2d 882, 885 (La. App. 2 Cir. 2008). In that case, the court held Article 504 was inapplicable because the plaintiff could not prove "what land it had lost due to the change in the course of the river or that the disputed property constitutes the abandoned bed of a river to which it would be entitled." *Id.* at 893.

E. Accession with Regard to Movables

We finish our chapter on the law of accession with a brief discussion of accession between corporeal movables. This area of the law has not yielded much litigation, except for some jurisprudence covering motor vehicles and industrial equipment. Nevertheless, accession between movables, which comes to us from Roman law, is based on the same philosophical and economic underpinnings as accession in relation to immovables. Most of these provisions date back to the 1825 Civil Code when the redactors borrowed heavily from Toullier's commentary on the Code Napoleon, *Droit civil français*. You will note that the current revised version of these articles goes to great lengths to capture all conceivable settings.

Article 507 of the Civil Code tells us that, absent other provisions of law or contractual arrangements, Articles 508 through 516 of the Civil Code furnish the applicable legal framework. Again, we note the suppletive nature of accession rules.

The Civil Code distinguishes three different categories of accession between movables: (a) Adjunction under Article 510 of the Civil Code; (b) Manufacture under Articles 511 and 513 of the Civil Code; and (c) Mixture under Article 514 of the Civil Code. We will introduce each in turn.

1. Adjunction

Adjunction, the classical Roman *accessio*, which is governed by Article 510 of the Civil Code, is defined as the physical union of two corporeal movables, which results in a composite thing whereby each movable can be distinctly recognized. This type of accession only arises if a "principal" and an "accessory" are joined to form a new "whole." Thus, we must first categorize each of the two things as either the principal thing or the accessory.

The Civil Code offers a definition of accessory in Article 508 and two interpretive guides in Article 509. Under Article 508(1), an "accessory is a corporeal movable that serves the use, ornament, or complement of the principal thing." La. Civ. Code art. 508 (1979). When it is not clear which movable is the principal thing and which is the accessory, Article 509 first tells us that the more valuable of the two objects is the principal thing. La. Civ. Code art. 509 (1979). If the two things are of nearly equal value, then the bulkier object is the principal thing. *Id.*

Once the two movables have been assigned to their respective categories, Article 510 continues the analysis by providing that when the two movables have been "[so] united [as] to form a whole, and one of them is an accessory to the other, the whole belongs to the owner of the principal thing." La. Civ. Code art. 510 (1979). Unjust enrichment, however, comes into play and affords the owner of the accessory thing some reimbursement rights. Specifically, "[t]he owner of the principal thing is bound to reimburse the owner of the accessory its value." *Id.* Moreover, "[t]he owner of the accessory may demand that it be separated and returned to him, although the separation may cause some injury to the principal thing, if the accessory is more valuable than the principal and has been used without his knowledge." *Id.*

An example of this proposition involves automobile tires. One might say that the physical attachment between a motor vehicle and its tires is rather loose. Yet, as a matter of prevailing notions, motor vehicles are expected to come with tires. *See McVay v. McVay,* 318 So.2d 660 (La. App. 3 Cir. 1975). A motor vehicle is the principal thing; its tires are accessories. Tires united with an automobile belong to the owner of the automobile, who owes to the former owner of the tires their value.

In a case of an engine connected to a pump, one court denied adjunction, holding that an engine did not become merged with a pump simply because it might have been mounted upon the same drilling platform and connected by a custom tailored drive device. *Aetna Business Credit Corp. v. Louisiana Machinery Co., Inc.*, 409 So.2d 1304 (La. App. 4 Cir. 1982). In that case, the uniter had rented the pump and then purchased a costly engine to use with the pump. From the perspective of the uniter, the court found, the relationship between the engine and the pump was too temporary or tenuous to lead to adjunction. *Id.*

When the principal thing has been used without its owner's knowledge, the owner of the principal thing who does not wish to own the thing, can choose to have the owner of the accessory deliver to him "materials of the same species, quantity, weight, measure, and quality [as that of the principal thing] or their value." La. Civ. Code art. 515 (1979), rather than claim ownership under Article 514 of the Civil Code. This replacement choice under Article 515 of the Civil Code accrues only if the principal thing has been used without its owner's knowledge. In addition, Article 516 of the Civil Code grants the owner of the principal thing a claim for damages against the owner of the accessory when the latter has used the principal thing without its owner's knowledge. La. Civ. Code art. 516 (1979).

The person who loses ownership of the accessory has a claim against the person who takes ownership of it for reimbursement of the value of the accessory under the general rule of Article 510 of the Civil Code. However, if the accessory is the more valuable asset and its adjunction occurred without its owner's knowledge, Article 510 offers an exception. The owner of the accessory may demand separation (even when injurious to the principal thing). La. Civ. Code art. 510 (1979). The owner of the accessory would then have a claim for damages under Article 516 of the Civil Code. La. Civ. Code art. 516 (1979).

2. Manufacture

Manufacture, the classical Roman *specificatio*, is defined as the production of a completely new thing from materials belonging to another. For example, when Xena applies a dye to color Selma's silk, we will look to adjunction. When Hugo uses Selma's silk to create a designer dress, we have a case of manufacture. But when Cornelius merely cleans Selma's silk, this type of handling is neither adjunction nor manufacture.

The Civil Code offers two variants of manufacture — that of a new thing with materials of another under Article 511, and that of a new thing with partly one's own materials and partly materials of another pursuant to Article 513. Article 511 of the Civil Code, which governs the first manufacture variant, contemplates a setting where the maker applies her labor to the materials owned by someone else without furnishing any materials of her own. The general rule allocates the new thing to the owner of the original materials regardless of whether the materials can be returned to their former state. La. Civ. Code art. 511 (1979). However, when the value of the labor expended by the manufacturer "substantially exceeds" the value of the original materials, the manufacturer becomes owner of the new thing. *Id.* Yet, if the manufacturer exhibited bad faith, the court may award ownership to the owner of the materials. La. Civ. Code art. 512 (1979). The party losing ownership then has a reimbursement claim. La. Civ. Code art. 511 (1979). Moreover, Article 515 of the Civil Code, allowing a demand for replacement, and Article 516 of the Civil Code, allowing a claim for damages, remain applicable.

Article 513 of the Civil Code, which governs the second manufacture variant, contemplates a labor-plus-capital setting where the maker applies his efforts to materials, only some of which are owned by him. Before allocating ownership of the new thing, the parties must determine whether the materials can be conveniently separated and returned to their respective owners. La. Civ. Code art. 513 (1979). If this proves impossible, the materials' owners become co-owners in indivision. *Id.* Their undivided shares are calculated in proportion to the value of labor plus capital furnished by the maker and the value of the materials belonging to the other person. *Id.* No reimbursement remedy is needed, but Article 515 of the Civil Code (replacement) and Article 516 of the Civil Code (damages) again remain applicable.

3. Mixture

Article 514 of the Civil Code speaks of mixture (*mélange*) to describe what happens when a maker (mixer) brings together two mixable movables (mixants) belonging to different owners. In this setting, the mixer does not have to provide any of the materials. Note that South Africa follows classical Roman law and distinguishes between mingling of liquids (Latin *confusio*), for example wine from different owners, and mixing of solids (Latin *commixtio*), for example, grains of corn from different owners. Under the Roman law of *confusio*, where the components have lost their separate identity, each owner had an action for the division of common property. In the case of *commixtio*, the components have as such not lost their separate identity. Either owner could claim their solids, albeit doing so will be quite difficult in practice.

As in Article 513, the rules housed in Article 514 of the Civil Code require a tiered approach. Before allocating ownership, parties must address the threshold question of separation. As Article 514(1) of the Civil Code explains, when "none of [the materials of the different owners] may be considered as principal, an owner who has not consented to the mixture may demand separation if it can be conveniently made." La. Civ. Code art. 514 (1979). Only when separation is not available do we move into the allocation of ownership and remedies (if any).

The owners of the mixants become co-owners in indivision with respect to the new thing, and their shares track their contributions according to the values of their mixants. La. Civ. Code art. 514 (1979). However, when one mixant is "far superior in value" its owner has the prerogative to claim ownership of the new thing. *Id.* In that case, the owner of the less valuable mixant has a claim for reimbursement. *Id.* Note that Article 515 of the Civil Code (replacement) and Article 516 of the Civil Code (damages) remain applicable.

Let us look at a couple of examples. Antonius blends his cheap wine with ten times more expensive wine that belongs to Cornelia. Who owns the wine? What remedies does Cornelia have?

Now assume a recording combining the voice of a famous singer (say Bob Dylan) and the contributions by the musicians and technicians paid by another. Is this a mixture? If yes, how would you resolve ownership and remedies absent any contractual agreements?

Chapter 6

Voluntary and Involuntary Transfers of Ownership

Book III of the Civil Code provides that "[t]he ownership of things or property is acquired by succession either testate or intestate, by the effect of obligations, and by the operation of law." La. Civ. Code art. 870 (1981, amended 2001). Thus, ownership may be transferred voluntarily, involuntarily or by the operation of law.

In the law of property Louisiana provides for three direct modes of acquiring ownership *by the operation of law*. The first mode is *accession*, a doctrine which enables the owner of a thing to become the owner of other things that it produces or other things that are united with the principal thing in some manner. *See generally* La. Civ. Code arts. 482, 490–516 (1979). We studied accession in Chapter Five. The second mode of acquisition of ownership by operation of law is through *occupancy*. A person who takes possession of a corporeal movable that does not belong to anyone becomes the owner of that thing immediately through occupancy. *See generally* La. Civ. Code arts. 3412–20 (1982). We will study occupancy in Chapter Seven. The third method of acquiring ownership by operation of law is through *acquisitive prescription*. A person who takes possession of a thing with the intent to become its owner and possesses the thing for the requisite period of time can become its owner. The required period of possession will vary depending on whether the thing is a movable or an immovable and whether a "just title" and "good faith" are present. *See generally* La. Civ. Code arts. 3421–91 (1982). We will study acquisitive prescription in Chapter Nine. This chapter covers voluntary and involuntary transfers of ownership.

A. Voluntary Transfers of Ownership

The Louisiana Civil Code governs three types of voluntary transfer of ownership: the donation, the sale and the exchange. In the following narratives and cases we introduce some of the basic principles for understanding these contracts translative of ownership.

1. Transfer of Ownership through Sale, Exchange and Donation

As previously stated, one of the rationales for the sharp distinction between movables and immovables in Louisiana law relates to the voluntary transfer of ownership. Articles 517 and 518 of the Civil Code provide the general rules governing voluntary transfers of immovable and movables respectively:

Art. 517. Voluntary transfer of ownership of an immovable

The ownership of an immovable is voluntarily transferred by a contract between the owner and the transferee that purports to transfer the ownership of the immovable. The transfer of ownership takes place between the parties by the effect of the agreement and is not effective against third persons until the contract is filed for registry in the conveyance records of the parish in which the immovable is located.

La. Civ. Code art. 517 (1979, amended 1985).

Art. 518. Voluntary transfer of the ownership of a movable

The ownership of a movable is voluntarily transferred by a contract between the owner and the transferee that purports to transfer ownership of the movable. Unless otherwise provided, the transfer of ownership takes place as between the parties by the effect of the agreement and against third persons when the possession of the movable is delivered to the transferee.

When possession has not been delivered, a subsequent transferee to whom possession is delivered acquires ownership provided he is in good faith. Creditors of the transferor may seize the movable while it is still in his possession.

La. Civ. Code art. 518 (1984).

Both articles start with essentially the same sentence: "The ownership of [an immovable or a movable] is voluntarily transferred by a contract between the owner and the transferee that purports to transfer the ownership of [the immovable or movable]." Note that, generally, only the owner of a thing can transfer ownership. Persons with rights other than ownership may convey those rights, but they cannot convey ownership. The parties involved in a transfer of ownership are called the transferor and the transferee. When a transferee receives ownership of a thing from the true owner, the transferee becomes the new owner. She can then transfer ownership to another transferee or she can retain ownership.

As we will see later, several special rules contradict these principles to protect the rights of purchasers of lost or stolen corporeal movables and corporeal movables that a transferor acquired by fraud. Under the "good faith purchaser doctrine" certain transferees can acquire ownership even though the transferor was not the actual owner. *See generally* La. Civ. Code arts. 521–25 (1979).

Under Articles 517 and 518 of the Civil Code, a transfer of ownership requires a ***contract*** purporting to transfer the thing from the transferor to the transferee. A contract is defined as "an agreement by two or more persons whereby obligations are created, modified, or extinguished." La. Civ. Code art. 1906 (1984). Entering into an agreement requires contractual capacity. All persons except unemancipated minors, interdicts, and persons deprived of reason at the time of contracting enjoy this capacity. La. Civ. Code art. 1918 (1984). "A contract is formed by the consent of the parties established through offer and acceptance." La. Civ. Code art. 1927 (1984). This consent must be free of vices. *See generally* La. Civ. Code arts. 1948 *et seq.* (1984).

The three major contracts translative of ownership are the sale, the exchange and the donation. We tend to think of contracts most frequently in the context of sales, but not every contract is a sale. A *sale* is a contract whereby a person transfers ownership of a thing to another for a price in money. La. Civ. Code art. 2439 (1933). There is no sale unless a purchase price is fixed by the parties as a sum certain or is determinable. The price may be left to the determination of a third person or, under certain circumstances, it may be determined by the court. *See* La Civ. Code arts. 2464–66 (1993). The parties can agree that the seller will surrender ownership rights in the property to the buyer in exchange for the immediate payment of the purchase price or for a promise to pay some, or all, of the price at a future date. Note that in a sale the "price must not be out of all proportion with the value of the thing sold." La. Civ. Code art. 2464(2) (1993). The special remedy of rescission for *lesion beyond moiety* is available to the seller of a corporeal immovable "when the purchase price is less than one half of the fair market value of the immovable." *See* La. Civ. Code arts. 2589 *et seq.* (1993). We will study an example of lesion beyond moiety later in this chapter in *Joiner v. Abercrombie*, 968 So.2d 1184 (La. App. 2 Cir. 2007).

When the contract transferring ownership rights in property is not for money but for ownership rights in another thing, it is called an *exchange*. La. Civ. Code art. 2660 (2010). In general, the contract of exchange is governed by the rules of the contract of sale. La. Civ. Code art. 2664 (2010).

A *donation* differs from a sale and an exchange as it offers the exclusive method of disposing of property gratuitously. La. Civ. Code art. 1467 (2008). In a donation, the donor agrees to give something to another person without expecting anything in return except gratitude. *Cf.* La. Civ. Code arts. 1526–27 (2008) (providing for onerous and remunerative donations).

Louisiana law distinguishes between two basic kinds of donations: donations inter vivos and donations mortis causa. The *donation inter vivos* is a "contract by which a person, called the donor, gratuitously divests himself, at present and irrevocably, of the thing given in favor of another, called the donee." La. Civ. Code art. 1468 (2008). Donations inter vivos must conform to detailed form requisites. *See* La. Civ. Code arts. 1541–51 (2008). The donation inter vivos is a unilateral contract because the donee does not take on a reciprocal obligation. La. Civ. Code art. 1907 (1984). It is a bilateral juridical act because the donee must accept the donation. Recall that we have seen echoes of this bilateral consent requirement as it pertained to donations when we considered dedications to public use.

In this chapter we will study two cases featuring donations inter vivos. *Malone v. Malone*, 77 So.3d 1040 (La. App. 2 Cir. 2011), illustrates the importance of the classification of things and the consequences of the much more onerous formalities required to effectuate donations of incorporeal movables. *Manichia v. Mahoney*, 45 So.3d 618 (La. App. 4 Cir. 2010), involves an important substantive limit on the validity of a donation inter vivos prohibiting a donor from divesting himself of so much of his property that he does not retain enough for his own subsistence.

The other kind of donation is the **donation mortis causa**, which the Civil Code defines as "an act to take effect at the death of the donor by which he disposes of the whole or a part of his property." La. Civ. Code art. 1469 (2008). Because a will (technically called a "testament" in Louisiana) containing a donation mortis causa does not take effect until the death of the donor, it is revocable during the lifetime of the donor. *Id.* We saw a dramatic illustration of this simple rule in *Marcellous v. David*, 252 So.2d 178 (La. App. 3 Cir. 1971). In many cases involving disputed donations mortis causa, the testamentary capacity of the donor presents the crucial issue. We will study such a dispute in *Succession of Cooper*, 830 So.2d 1087 (La. App. 2 Cir. 2002).

Finally, regardless of whether the contract purporting to voluntarily transfer ownership is a sale, exchange or donation, Articles 517 and 518 of the Civil Code require that the parties identify the property and the terms of the transfer. The agreement must evidence the intent of one party to transfer ownership to the other. A court will not find a voluntary transfer of ownership when the parties have not manifested this intent.

2. Effectiveness of a Voluntary Transfer of Ownership; The Louisiana Public Records Doctrine

a. As between the Parties

The determination as to when the transfer of ownership becomes effective—is considered to have taken place—depends on a crucial bifurcation. As between the original transferor and the transferee under a contract transferring the ownership of an immovable or a movable, ownership transfers *immediately* by the effect of the agreement, unless the parties agree otherwise.

The principle that an agreement is all we need for the transfer to occur as between the parties comes from French law where it is known as the *principe du consensualisme*. Once the parties have agreed to the terms for the transfer of ownership, they are bound and the transfer will be effective *inter se*—*as between the parties*—from that moment in time. Nothing more is required La. Civ. Code arts. 517(cl.2) & 518(2) (1979, amended 2005). Take note, however, of the phrase "[u]nless otherwise provided" in Article 518, which indicates that the parties to a voluntary transfer of a movable can agree among themselves that the actual transfer of ownership will take place at a time other than the formation of the agreement. Although Article 517 does not contain this phrase, the same principle of contractual freedom applies to contracts for the transfer of immovable property as well.

Indeed, a buyer and seller will often reach an agreement on the terms of an eventual sale (either of a movable or an immovable) but will specifically agree that the actual transfer of ownership will take place at a later time, upon the happening of a condition or upon the performance of some obligation. *See* La. Civ. Code art. 2623 (1993). Such a contract, called a "bilateral promise of sale or contract to sell" in the Civil Code, *Id.*, or sometimes more colloquially "a purchase and sale agreement" or an "executory contract," must be distinguished from the actual "contract of sale." *Compare* La. Civ. Code art. 2623 (1993), *with* La. Civ. Code art. 2439 (1993). The subtle distinctions between these two different types of contracts and the various remedies available for their enforcement are the subject of a course on the Louisiana law of sales. Note that Articles 517 and 518 are capacious enough to encompass both types of contracts because they provide that transfers of ownership of either movables or immovables will take place between the parties "by the effect of the agreement." The parties can thus select the date the transfer of ownership will take place.

Other civil codes do not follow the French principle of consensualism. Austria follows the *principle of separation*, which requires two distinct juridical acts to accomplish the transfer of ownership — a "causal" transaction in the planning stage (*titulus*) and a "real" transaction act (*modus*) in the execution stage, which depends on the existence of a valid causal title. Under Austrian law, the transferee acquires ownership of a movable if the transferor is owner or authorized to transact, the title (for example, a sale or donation) is valid, and the transferee takes the thing delivered by the transferor. The German *principle of abstraction* takes this one step further by keeping the validity of the real transaction and the underlying causal transaction independent from one another so that the real transaction exists independently (or "abstractly") from a causal transaction. Under German law, the transferee acquires ownership of a movable if the transferor is the owner or is authorized to transact, the transferor delivers the thing to the transferee, and the transferor and transferee are in agreement that ownership shall transfer. These variations among civil codes stem from divergent receptions of Roman law.

b. As to Third Parties

With regard to a ***third party*** (someone other than the original transferor and transferee), the moment when a voluntary transfer of ownership becomes effective differs for immovables and movables. Under Article 517, the voluntary transfer of ownership of an **immovable** "is not effective against third persons until the contract is filed for registry in the conveyance records of the parish in which the immovable is located." La. Civ. Code art. 517 (1979, amended 2005). Article 1839 reiterates the same principle. La. Civ. Code art. 1839(2) (1984) ("An instrument involving immovable property shall have effect against third persons only from the time it is filed for registry in the parish where the immovable property is located."). Article 2442 of the Civil Code also declares that an "act of sale or promise of sale of immovable property," is "not effective against third parties until it is filed for registry according to the laws of registry." La. Civ. Code art. 2442 (1993). Finally, Article 3338 of the

Civil Code provides that an instrument that "transfers an immovable or establishes a real right in or over an immovable" is "without effect as to a third person unless the instrument is registered by recording it in the appropriate mortgage or conveyance records. . . ." La. Civ. Code art. 3338 (2005). All of these provisions carry the same basic message: a voluntary transfer of ownership of immovable property or real rights in an immovable has no effect *against third parties* unless evidence of the transfer is recorded in the appropriate public records.

This is the essence of the **Louisiana Public Records Doctrine**—a subject to which we repeatedly return throughout this casebook. Under the public records doctrine, a party is only entitled to rely upon the absence of something reflecting an interest in a piece of property.

Each parish in Louisiana has "an office for the recording of mortgages and privileges and one for the recordation of conveyances and transfer of immovables." La. Rev. Stat. 44:71 (A). "The clerks of the several district courts throughout the state are ex officio parish recorders of conveyances, mortgages, and other acts." La. Rev. Stat. 44:71 (B). Note that the appropriate conveyance records are those kept by the clerk of court in the parish where the immovable property at issue is located. When the transaction involves property located in two parishes, the instrument purporting to transfer ownership should be filed in both parishes. *See* La. Civ. Code art. 3341 (2005) ("The recordation of an instrument: . . . (4) Is effective only with respect to immovables in the parish where the instrument is recorded."). In addition, the Louisiana Revised Statutes impose a duty on notary publics to record "all acts of sale, exchange, donation, and mortgage of immovable property passed before them." La. Rev. Stat. § 35:199A (2006, amended 2008, 2010). Notary publics who fail to record these acts of transfer are subject to a fine of $200. La. Rev. Stat. § 35:199C.

To see how recordation (or the lack thereof) affects third parties, suppose that Alice owned a tract of land in Avoyelles Parish. Alice agreed to sell her land to Bob. On January 1, 2013, Alice and Bob signed the act of sale. As of January 1, 2013, the date on which the act of sale was signed, ownership of the land passed from Alice to Bob *as between those two parties*.

Suppose that for some reason neither Alice nor Bob *filed* the act of sale in the conveyance records of Avoyelles Parish. The next day, January 2, 2013, Alice sold the exact same tract of land to Cathy. Both Alice and Cathy signed the act of sale that day. Although as between the original parties, Alice and Bob, the transfer of ownership took place on January 1, 2013, and is effective between them, the transfer of ownership is "without effect" or "not effective" vis-à-vis Cathy, who is a third party. La. Civ. Code art. 3338 (2005); La. Civ. Code art. 517 (1979, amended 2005). Further, if Cathy promptly files the act of sale transferring the land from Alice to Cathy before Bob records his act of sale, Cathy will be considered the owner of the land, even if Cathy had actual knowledge of Alice's prior sale to Bob.

This principle was enunciated by the Louisiana Supreme Court in its decision, *McDuffie v. Walker*, 51 So. 100 (La. 1910). It has since been consistently upheld in numerous decisions. Bob may have grounds to file a lawsuit against Alice for her double dealing and for breach of her obligations under their contract of sale. *See especially* La. Civ. Code art. 2503 (1993) (providing that a "seller is liable for an eviction that is occasioned by his own act, and any agreement to the contrary is null."). But Bob will be without remedy against Cathy. Under the Public Records Doctrine, Cathy will be recognized as the owner of the land because Bob's interest remained unrecorded at the time she, Cathy, acquired and recorded her interest in the immovable property.

In the language of Louisiana judicial decisions, Cathy can rely upon *the absence* of any indication in the public records of any rights or obligations in the immovable property at issue that must be recorded to be effective against a third party. La. Civ. Code art. 3338 (2005). The Public Records Doctrine is described as a "negative doctrine" because it "does not create rights, but, rather, denies the effect of certain rights unless they are recorded." *Cimarex Energy Co. v. Mauboules*, 40 So.3d 931, 944 (La. 2010). *See also Longleaf Investments, L.L.C. v. Tolintino*, 108 So.3d 157, 160 (La. App. 2 Cir. 2012). For detailed examinations of the Public Records Doctrine, see William V. Redmann, *The Louisiana Law of Recordation: Some Principles and Some Problems*, 39 Tul. L. Rev. 491 (1965); Michael Palestina, *Comment, Of Registry: Louisiana's Revised Public Records Doctrine*, 53 Loy. L. Rev. 989 (2007).

The primary purpose of the Public Records Doctrine is to protect third persons from unrecorded interests. *Cimarex*, 40 So.3d at 944. The strict nature of the Public Records Doctrine has the salutary effect of creating strong incentives for anyone who acquires an interest in immovable property to record that interest promptly. This, in turn, leads to more complete and informative public records and lower transaction costs for anyone who uses the public records system.

As harsh as the Public Records Doctrine seems, it is perhaps not surprising that courts in Louisiana have recognized a number of exceptions to the general principle that instruments transferring or concerning immovable property will have effect against third persons only from the moment they are filed for registry in the appropriate public records. One exception from the operations of the Public Records Doctrine involves the rights of heirs and legatees. *Long v. Chailan*, 187 La. 507, 525, 175 So. 42 (1937) ("where the plaintiff has a title by inheritance, it is sufficient that his ancestor's title is a recorded title"). Courts have likewise construed an exception in cases involving community property interests of spouses. *Succession of James*, 147 La. 944, 952, 86 So. 403 (1920) ("one cannot acquire a title to the interest of a deceased wife . . . by a purchase from the surviving husband, even though the title to the entire property stands in his name").

A third party who has participated in fraud also cannot rely on the Public Records Doctrine. *See, e.g., Owen v. Owen*, 336 So.2d 782, 788 (La. 1976) (observing that a "third party purchaser can rely on the public records so long as he does not participate in fraud," even though the third party knew of a preceding transfer which should have made him suspicious of the validity of the deed). A purchaser who bases his own interest on the slender reed of a quitclaim deed granted in suspicious, but not necessarily fraudulent, circumstances also may not be able to rely on the Public Records Doctrine. *Simmesport State Bank v. Roy*, 614 So.2d 265, 267–68 (La. App. 1 Cir. 1993) (refusing to apply the Public Records Doctrine to a quitclaim deed recorded earlier than a sale to a prior purchaser of the property, because both the seller and the buyer under the quitclaim deed knew that the seller had lost her ownership in bankruptcy and was no longer able to convey ownership). A recently decided case illustrates the occasional refusal by the courts to apply the Public Records Doctrine when suspicious circumstances exist.

In *Longleaf Investments, L.L.C. v. Tolintino*, 108 So.3d 157, 159 (La. App. 2 Cir. 2012), Sharon Tolintino entered into a purchase and sale agreement on December 6, 2005, with Longleaf Investments respecting certain tracts of land in Bossier Parish. Longleaf paid Tolintino $1,000 as a down payment. About a month later, on January 17, 2006, Tolintino conveyed one of the tracts of land subject to the purchase and sale agreement, Section 3, to two other individuals, Yolanda Williams and Zishun Moore, via a quitclaim deed, in exchange for $1,800. Alvin Williams, Tolintino's "sometime chauffeur and longtime family friend" and the father of Yolanda and Zishun, signed the deed on behalf of his minor son Zishun. This quitclaim deed was recorded in the public records of Bossier Parish on January 24, 2006. On February 22, 2006, Longleaf Investments finally got around to recording its purchase and sale agreement with Tolintino. *Id.* at 158–59. Later in May, 2006, Tolintino purported to convey the rest of the Bossier Parish property to Zishun Moore by another quitclaim deed.

Under the Public Records Doctrine, Longleaf Investments would have been out of luck with respect to Section 3 because, at the time that Tolintino conveyed the tract to Yolanda Williams and Zishun Moore, the purchase and sale agreement with Longleaf was not recorded. No interests in Section 3 other than Tolintino's ownership were recorded. Once Yolanda and Zishun filed their quitclaim deed for registry, they would have been owners of Section 3.

In this case, however, both the trial and appellate courts found that Yolanda and Zishun were *not* entitled to rely on the Public Records Doctrine. Their quitclaim deeds were deemed "invalid" by the courts because they participated in a fraud against Longleaf Investments that had been confected by Tolintino and Alvin Williams. *Id.* at 160–61. The court of appeal explained its reasoning as follows:

> Because it does not create rights but rather denies the effect of certain rights unless they are recorded, the public records doctrine is referred to as a negative doctrine. *Carr, supra.* The public records doctrine provides that an instrument involving immovable property shall be effective against third persons only from the time it is filed for registry in the parish where the property is located. See La. C.C. art. 1839; La. C.C. art. 3338. Third persons are deemed to have constructive knowledge or notice of the existence and contents of recorded instruments affecting immovable property. *Carr, supra.*

A third party purchaser can rely on the public records so long as he does not participate in fraud. *Owen v. Owen*, 336 So.2d 782 (La. 1976); *Kinchen v. Kinchen*, 244 So.2d 316 (La. App. 1 Cir. 1970), *writ not considered*, 257 La. 854, 244 So.2d 608 (La. 1970), 257 La. 854, 244 So.2d 608. . . .

Although Alvin's title search on the property failed to produce a recordation from Longleaf, the evidence indicates that he had knowledge of the Agreement and conspired with Tolintino to fraudulently convey the property through bogus quitclaim deeds. Tolintino even admitted that she had discussed the [purchase and sale] Agreement with her friend, Alvin. Additionally, Young [the managing member of Longleaf Investments] testified that Alvin drove Tolintino to his office for discussions leading up to the Agreement.

Id. at 160–61. The tendency of courts to create equitable, standard based exceptions to otherwise strict or "crystalline" rules in property law has long been observed by scholars. For the most famous articulation of the eternal conflict between "crystalline" rules and "muddy" standards in the context of property law, *see generally* Carol M. Rose, *Crystals and Mud in Property Law*, 40 Stan. L. Rev. 477 (1992). For an exploration of this conflict in the context of the Louisiana Civil Code, see John A. Lovett, *Love, Loyalty and Louisiana Civil Code, Rules, Standards and Hybrid Discretion in a Mixed Jurisdiction*, 72 La. L. Rev. (2012).

We will revisit the Public Records Doctrine in the context of the law of acquisitive prescription, especially when we study the leading case of *Phillips v. Parker*, 483 So.2d 972 (La. 1986). For now it is enough to recognize that the doctrine makes its first appearance in the Civil Code in Article 517 of Book II and that its seemingly harsh effects are sometimes softened by ex post judicial decision-making.

Problem

Teddy owned a 1500-acre tract of land in West Baton Rouge Parish and wanted to sell it. He placed an advertisement in the Sunday Advocate that read: "Prime piece of real estate located in a good area for $100,000." James saw the advertisement and immediately contacted Teddy. The two held a meeting where a contract of sale was properly executed. James, excited about the new purchase, moved onto the property right away. However, James did not have the contract filed for recordation in the conveyance records of West Baton Rouge Parish.

Teddy, without notifying James, sold the same 1500-acre tract to Rob, who also had seen the advertisement. A contract of sale was properly executed between Teddy and Rob and, thereafter, recorded in the conveyance records of East Baton Rouge Parish.

Teddy, without notifying James or Rob, sold the same 1500-acre tract to Sandra. A contract of sale was properly executed between Teddy and Sandra and, thereafter, recorded in the conveyance records of West Baton Rouge Parish.

Teddy then leaves the country with the money. Who owns the property? James, Rob or Sandra?

3. Transfer of Movables

a. Corporeal Movables and Tradition

In contrast to immovables, recordation is not required for a voluntary transfer of ownership of **movables** to be effective against third persons. According to Article 518 of the Civil Code, the transfer of ownership of a corporeal movable is effective "against third persons when the possession of the movable is delivered to the transferee." La. Civ. Code art. 518 (1984). Hence, the delivery or "tradition" (from the Latin *traditio*) serves the function of putting third parties on notice.

In the case below, the plaintiff, Cameron Equipment Co., Inc., purchased two diesel engines from one of the defendants, Petroleum Services, Inc. The plaintiff, however, did not immediately take physical possession of the engines. Instead, the engines sat for two years at a storage site operated by another party. Read the opinion to discover the legal consequences of the buyer's failure to take possession of the engines.

Cameron Equipment Co., Inc. v. Stewart and Stevenson Services, Inc.

685 So.2d 696 (La. App. 3 Cir. 1996)

KNOLL, Judge. In this revendicatory action against the seller and subsequent purchasers of two diesel engines, Cameron Equipment 1987, Inc. d/b/a/ Cameron Equipment appeals the judgment of the trial court. We affirm.

Facts

On June 12, 1987, Cameron Equipment purchased two used General Motors EMD-12-645-E-1 diesel engines from Petroleum Services, Inc. The two engines were purchased along with other used oil field equipment for a total price of $73,000. At the time of this sale, the two diesel engines were located in the equipment yard of Power Rig Drilling Company in Scott, Louisiana.

For two years following the sale, Cameron Equipment left the engines where they were at Power Rig. The engines were not removed from the yard or marked as property of Cameron Equipment.

On June 12, 1989, Petroleum Services sold the engines to another company, Power International, Inc. for $38,000. Power International immediately resold the engines to American General Transportation Co., Inc. for $60,000. On June 14, 1989, American General brokered the engines to Stewart & Stevenson Services, Inc. for $75,000. Stewart & Stevenson needed the engines for use in a towboat it had contracted to build.

On June 15, 1989, American General removed the engines from the Power Rig yard and transported them to Stewart & Stevenson's facility in Harvey, Louisiana. Coincidentally, Cameron Equipment arrived to remove the engines from the Power Rig yard just hours after they had been taken by American General.

On August 10, 1989, Cameron Equipment filed suit against Stewart & Stevenson and Travis Ward, the president and sole shareholder of Petroleum Services, Inc. In its petition, Cameron sought the return of the engines and damages for their conversion. Eventually, Petroleum Services, American General, and Power International (the subsequent purchasers) were added as defendants.

A bench trial on the merits was held on October 18–27, 1994. The trial court rendered judgment in favor of Cameron Equipment and against Petroleum Services for conversion in the amount of $50,000, which the court determined to be the fair market value of the engines at the time of the second sale. The trial court denied Cameron Equipment's claims against the subsequent purchasers, finding that since Cameron Equipment never took possession of the engines, La. Civ. Code art. 518 operated in favor of the subsequent purchasers, whom it determined were in good faith. The trial court refused to pierce the corporate veil and hold Travis Ward personally liable for the conversion damages awarded against his company, Petroleum Services.

Cameron Equipment appeals, assigning as error the trial court's determination that it did not take possession of the engines following the initial sale, the trial court's application of La. Civ. Code art. 518 in favor of the subsequent purchasers, and the trial court's failure to pierce the corporate veil.

Civil Code Article 518

The trial court held that Power International, American General, and Stewart & Stevenson were superior in title to Cameron Equipment under La. Civ. Code art. 518, which states:

> The ownership of a movable is voluntarily transferred by a contract between the owner and the transferee that purports to transfer the ownership of the movable. Unless otherwise provided, the transfer of ownership takes place as between the parties by the effect of the agreement and against third persons when the possession of the movable is delivered to the transferee.

> When possession has not been delivered, a subsequent transferee to whom possession is delivered acquires ownership provided he is in good faith. Creditors of the transferor may seize the movable while it is still in his possession.

This appeal raises two questions with regard to Article 518: first, whether possession was delivered to Cameron Equipment sufficient to perfect the sale with regard to third parties, and second, whether Article 518 vested the subsequent purchasers with title superior to Cameron Equipment's.

Possession

The 1979 Revision comments to Article 518 indicate that "possession" contemplates both actual delivery and constructive delivery. La. Civ. Code art. 2477 provides the following methods for making delivery with regard to movables:

> Delivery of a movable takes place by handing it over to the buyer. If the parties so intend delivery may take place in another manner, such as by the seller's handing over to the buyer the key to the place where the thing is stored, or by negotiating to him a document of title to the thing, or even by the mere consent of the parties if the thing sold cannot be transported at the time of the sale or if the buyer already has the thing at that time.

Cameron Equipment first asserts that it took actual possession of the engines when Baker Littlefield, the owner of Power Rig, possessed the engines as Cameron Equipment's agent. The record reflects that the engines were originally purchased in 1986 as a joint venture between Petroleum Services and Baker Littlefield. Soon thereafter, Petroleum Services bought out Baker Littlefield's interest in the engines, but Littlefield continued to store the engines at Power Rig on behalf of Petroleum Services.

Baker Littlefield never agreed to store the engines on behalf of anyone other than Petroleum Services. He testified that had he known the engines had been sold by Petroleum Services, he would have told the new owner to remove them from his yard. Travis Vollmering, an agent for Cameron Equipment, knew that Baker Littlefield would not allow the engines to remain at Power Rig if he was aware of the sale. The record evidence clearly indicates that Baker Littlefield did not take possession of the engines as an agent of Cameron Equipment.

Cameron Equipment alternatively asserts that it took constructive possession of the engines under La. Civ. Code art. 2477. Cameron Equipment asserts that Petroleum Services "handed over the keys" to the building where the engines were kept when Petroleum Services made arrangements with Baker Littlefield to store the engines indefinitely at Power Rig. In effect, Cameron Equipment asserts that Petroleum Services transferred its storage agreement with Baker Littlefield incident to the sale. This assertion is also without merit. Petroleum Services had limited access to the Power Rig yard, extended only as a courtesy by Baker Littlefield. As noted above, Baker Littlefield was kept in the dark about the sale to Cameron Equipment, and he never agreed to store the engines at Power Rig for Cameron Equipment. The record amply reflects that Baker Littlefield would not have allowed the engines to remain in the Power Rig yard if they belonged to anyone other than Petroleum Services. We find the record supports the trial court's conclusion that there was no act between Cameron Equipment and Baker Littlefield which would equate to "handing over the keys," or that would put a third party on notice that Cameron Equipment was owner of the engines.

Cameron Equipment asserts that because of the enormous size and weight of the engines, they were insusceptible of transport at the time of the sale. Cameron

Equipment therefore alleges that possession of the engines was transferred by the mere consent of the parties under La. Civ. Code art. 2477. The record clearly shows that although the engines were very heavy, they were susceptible of transport. We note with significance that after American General sold the engines to Stewart & Stevenson it took only one day to transport the engines from the Power Rig yard in Scott, Louisiana to Stewart & Stevenson's yard in Harvey, Louisiana. We find that because the engines were susceptible of transport, ownership could not be transferred by mere consent of the parties under La. Civ. Code art. 2477.

Cameron Equipment never took possession of the engines, and its purchase of the engines was never perfected with respect to third parties. Petroleum Services was never divested of possession and Baker Littlefield continued to store the engines for Petroleum Services. Ownership of the engines was never transferred *vis a vis* third parties, and any third party in good faith was entitled to assume that Petroleum Services, who never lost possession, was still owner of the engines.

Cameron Equipment argues that Power International, American General, and Stewart & Stevenson are not entitled to the protection of Article 518 because they each purchased from a vendor who was not in possession of the engines at the time of the sale. Cameron Equipment argues that it already was the owner of the engines and cites the provision contained in La. Civ. Code art. 2452 that: "the sale of a thing belonging to another person is null" to support its superior title to the engines.

Cameron Equipment's argument and reliance on Article 2452 are misplaced. In *Frey v. Amoco Production Co.*, 603 So. 2d 166 (La. 1992), the Supreme Court stated:

> We also note one need not own a thing in order to perfect a sale. The sale of a thing belonging to another is not absolutely null, but only relatively so, and such nullity is in the interest of the purchaser. See La. Civ. Code art. 2452; *Wright v. Barnes*, 541 So. 2d 977 (La. App. 2d Cir. 1989); S. Litvinoff, [2]Obligations § 36.

Frey, 603 So. 2d at 177.

The sale of a corporeal movable without tradition of the movable is insufficient to transfer ownership. Until he receives possession of the movable, the purchaser only has the right to require delivery of the thing from the seller upon payment of the price. See Litvinoff, Obligations, 7 Louisiana Civil Law Treatise § 75, at 126 (1975). In the case *sub judice*, Cameron Equipment merely had the right to require delivery, it did not acquire ownership with regard to third parties. In the same fashion, the subsequent purchasers acquired the right to require delivery of the engines from Petroleum Services. While the sale of the engines alone was insufficient to transfer ownership to the subsequent good faith purchasers, the sale combined with the subsequent good faith purchasers' corporeal possession of the engines was sufficient to transfer ownership. The subsequent purchasers were able to acquire full ownership of the engines when they purchased them in good faith and subsequently took possession.

Accordingly, we find that Cameron Equipment never took possession of the engines and that the subsequent good faith purchasers were entitled to the protection of La. Civ. Code art. 518. . . .

For the foregoing reasons, the judgment of the trial court is affirmed. Costs of this appeal are assessed to Cameron Equipment 1987, Inc.

AFFIRMED.

Notes and Questions

1. Consider the different methods of *tradition*, or "handing over" a movable to the buyer. They are listed in Article 2477 of the Civil Code. Under what circumstances would you use each of those methods?

2. When Cameron Equipment invoked Article 2452, which provides that "[t]he sale of a thing belonging to another does not convey ownership," the Louisiana Supreme Court responded by citing one of its previous decisions stating that "[t]he sale of a thing belonging to another is not absolutely null, but only relatively so. . . ." *Cameron Equipment Co., Inc. v. Stewart and Stevenson Services, Inc.*, 685 So.2d 696 (La. App. 3 Cir. 1996) (quoting *Frey v. Amoco Production Co.*, 603 So.2d 166 (La. 1992)). When is a sale a sale and when is a sale not a sale? Did Petroleum Services, the original vendor, own the engines when it sold them to Power International? Or, did Cameron Equipment, the first vendee, own the engines at that moment in time? If Cameron Equipment did not own the engines when Petroleum Services sold them to Power International, what did Cameron Equipment purchase for $73,000?

3. Consider the second paragraph of Article 518:

> When possession has not been delivered, a subsequent transferee to whom possession is delivered acquires ownership provided he is in good faith. Creditors of the transferor may seize the movable while it is still in his possession.

La. Civ. Code art. 518 (1979, amended 1984). Article 523 in turn defines good faith in the context of this chapter in the following terms:

Art. 523. Good Faith; definition

> An acquirer of a corporeal movable is in good faith for purposes of this Chapter unless he knows, or should have known, that the transferor was not the owner.

La. Civ. Code art. 523 (1979). Was Power International a good faith purchaser? How about American General? Stewart & Stevenson? Did the court in *Cameron Equipment* address any of these questions?

Be careful to note that this is just the second of several definitions of "good faith" we will study in this case book. Other definitions of good faith applicable to property law are found elsewhere in the Civil Code. *See* La. Civ. Code art. 487 (1979) (defining good faith for accession); *Id.* art. 3480 (1982) (defining good faith for acquisitive prescription).

4. Cameron Equipment sued Travis Ward, the President and sole shareholder of Petroleum Services, Stewart & Stevenson, Petroleum Services, and American General and Power International, claiming damages for conversion of the engines. Cameron Equipment argued that it was the owner of the engines and that Stewart & Stevenson had purchased *stolen* property.

Consider Articles 521 and 524 in this chapter of Book II of the Civil Code which govern lost or stolen things:

Art. 521. Lost or stolen thing

One who has possession of a lost or stolen thing may not transfer its ownership to another. For purposes of this Chapter, a thing is stolen when one has taken possession of it without the consent of its owner. A thing is not stolen when the owner delivers it or transfers its ownership to another as a result of fraud.

La. Civ. Code art. 521 (1979).

Art. 524. Recovery of lost or stolen things

The owner of a lost or stolen movable may recover it from a possessor who bought it in good faith at a public auction or from a merchant customarily selling similar things on reimbursing the purchase price.

The former owner of a lost, stolen, or abandoned movable that has been sold by authority of law may not recover it from the purchaser.

La. Civ. Code art. 524 (1979). How does each article support or refute the argument advanced by Cameron Equipment? Can the engines at issue be fairly characterized as "lost or stolen things"?

5. Article 522 of the Civil Code provides that a "transferee of a corporeal movable in good faith and for fair value retains the ownership of the thing even though the title of the transferor is annulled on account of a vice of consent." La. Civ. Code art. 522 (1979). A typical vice of consent is fraud. *See* La. Civ. Code arts. 1953–58 (1984). Does Article 522 offer any help for Cameron Equipment?

6. Do you think the Civil Code rules for vendees in the position of Cameron Equipment are fair? What fairness interests support the judgment in favor of the defendants, Power International, American General and Stewart and Stevenson? Note that the trial court judgment in favor of Cameron Equipment and against Petroleum Services for conversion in the amount of $50,000 was not appealed, but that the court refused to pierce the "corporate veil" of Petroleum Services and hold Travis Ward, its President and sole shareholder, personally liable for the conversion damages. What does this suggest about the ability of Petroleum Services to satisfy the judgment against it?

Who do you think is the most "culpable" party in this sad tale? Note that later in its opinion, the court observed:

> After a thorough review of the record, we find that the elements of fraud necessary to hold Travis Ward personally liable are simply not present. . . . The record reflects that Travis Ward was unaware that the engines had been sold to Cameron Equipment at the time of the second sale. Travis Ward executed the second sale of the engines only in his representative capacity as President of Petroleum Services.

Cameron Equipment, 685 So.2d at 701. Which party could have avoided this trouble with the least cost and effort? Such a person is often called *"the least cost avoider"* by law and economics scholars. Did the court leave the real loss with this party in the end?

7. The voluntary transfer of ownership of an immovable requires a contract to transfer ownership as between the parties and recordation of that contract to be effective vis-à-vis third parties. The voluntary transfer of ownership of a movable requires a contract to transfer ownership as between the parties and tradition or a handing over of the movable to be effective against third parties. The transfer of ownership of a movable may also be accomplished by "the *assignment of the action* for recovery of that movable." La. Civ. Code art. 519 (1979) (emphasis added).

Suppose that you purchased a lawn tractor from someone in your neighborhood and paid that person the agreed upon price. Because you did not own a truck, you went home to call a friend who owned a truck to see if he would assist you in picking up the tractor and transporting it to your house. When you returned to the vendor's house with your friend and his truck, you found that the vendor had left for a month-long vacation and that the lawn tractor was locked in his shed. Since your lawn needs to be cut badly, you purchase another lawn tractor from another source. Your friend with the truck would like to acquire the lawn tractor locked in the shed at the price you paid. You can now sell your friend your "right to require delivery of the thing from the seller upon payment of the price." *Cameron Equipment Co., Inc. v. Stewart and Stevenson Services, Inc.*, 685 So.2d 696, 700 (La. App. 3 Cir. 1996). After purchasing from you the right to require delivery, your friend can require your neighbor to deliver the lawn tractor to him. You have transferred your ownership rights to your friend by assigning to him the right to recover the lawn tractor from your neighbor.

8. Note that Article 520 was repealed by Acts 1981, No. 125, § 1. The Editor's Note for the Thomson Reuter 2018 Edition of the Louisiana Civil Code offers the following observations:

> Prior to its repeal, article 520 provided that "[a] transferee for good faith and for fair value acquires the ownership of a corporeal movable, if the transferor, though not owner, has possession with the consent of the owner, as pledgee, lessee, depositary, or other person of similar standing." In the words of the revision comments, article 520 established a "broad exception

to the principle that no one can transfer a greater right than he himself has." See La. C.C. art. 520 cmt (a) (repealed). See also La. C.C. art 2452. Moreover, former article 520 stood as a centerpiece of Chapter 3 of Title II of Book II of the Civil Code. In 1981, at the behest of special interests, article 520 was repealed by La. Acts 1981, No. 125. The repeal, which left in place articles 521–525, has been characterized as "half-hearted" and likely to "deprive Louisiana courts of . . . guidance." See Yiannopoulos, Property § 13.9 (5th ed. 2015; Comment, The Transfer of Ownership of Movables, 47 La. L.Rev. 841 (1987). The characterizations of the repeal of article 520 have proved prescient, as courts have struggled in addressing situations previously covered by former article 520. See, e.g., *Louisiana Lift & Equipment, Inc. v. Eizel*, 770 So. 2d 859 (La. App. 2 Cir. 2000).

Editor's Note to La. Civ. Code art. 520. In light of this repeal, how does Louisiana private law balance the competing interests of protecting ownership and securing the certainty of transactions?

9. Suppose Alberto has loaned his property law casebook to Bob for a couple of weeks. Instead of returning it to Alberto, Bob sold the book to Claudia, who, at the time of the transaction, had no reason to suspect that Bob was not the owner of the book. Alberto now brings a revendicatory action against Claudia. Is Alberto entitled to recover the book from Claudia? Consider Articles 524, 526, and 530 of the Civil Code. Does the principle articulated in current Article 2452 of the Civil Code and the repeal of Article 520, considered together, suggest that Alberto should prevail? Could the doctrine of equitable estoppel support Claudia's position? How so? Do the presumptions in Article 530 work in favor of Alberto or Claudia? Does your answer depend on a particular conception of theft when compared to that of Article 521?

10. For more detail with regard to the "faithless pledgee, lessee, or depositary," see John A. Lovett, *Good Faith in Louisiana Property Law*, 78 La. L. Rev. 1163, 1193–1200 (2018) (reviewing jurisprudence and concluding that, "even in the absence of Article 520, courts appear to revert to their default good faith analysis" and "always inquire about the honesty and carefulness of the good faith purchaser claimant and often widen their inquiry to investigate the potential carelessness of the original owner who put its movable in the hands of another person").

b. Incorporeal Movables

The voluntary transfer of ownership of a movable requires a contract and tradition, or a handing over of the movable. La. Civ. Code art. 518 (1984). Yet it is difficult to "hand over" an incorporeal movable. For this reason, stricter formalities are required to effectuate a valid transfer of incorporeal movable property. For example, in the law of donations, a manual gift, such as depositing cash in someone's savings account, is not subject to any formality because it satisfies the requirements of giving corporeal movable effects, accompanied by delivery. La. Civ. Code art. 1543 (2008). In contrast, the donation of an entire savings account requires a writing because the account is an incorporeal movable. La. Civ. Code art. 1550 (2008). The

Civil Code classification scheme for property plays an important role in ascertaining the legal consequences of acts intending to transfer ownership.

In the next case, consider whether there was sufficient evidence of a mother's intent to transfer one share of stock in a closely held, family corporation to her two sons. Carefully trace the consequences of classifying the share of stock as incorporeal movable property.

Malone v. Malone

77 So.3d 1040 (La. App. 2 Cir. 2011)

STEWART, Judge. At issue in this appeal by the plaintiff, Kenneth D. Malone ("Ken"), is the validity of a donation of one share of stock in Winnsboro Equipment, Inc. ("WEI"), a closely held, family-owned corporation that operates as a John Deere franchise dealership. Upon finding the purported donation by Doris Malone to her two sons, Ken and James G. Malone, Jr. ("Greg"), to be invalid, the trial court dissolved a temporary restraining order against WEI and dismissed Ken's petitions for injunctive relief, writ of quo warranto, and writ of mandamus with prejudice. Ken now appeals. Finding no error in the trial court's judgment, we affirm.

Facts

This matter stems from a dispute between brothers Ken and Greg, who are the majority shareholders in WEI. When their father, James G. Malone, Sr., died in 2007, Ken and Greg each owned 849 shares of WEI, and their father owned two shares. In accordance with a judgment of possession rendered in Mr. Malone's succession proceedings on April 13, 2009, Doris Malone, the surviving spouse, was recognized as owner of one share as part of her one-half interest in the community property, and Ken and Greg each received one-half of the other share as legatees. Thereafter, Greg and Ken each owned 849.50 shares, and Doris owned one share.

Sometime in the latter half of 2009, just prior to undergoing surgery, Doris executed a document purporting to donate her one share to Ken and Greg with each receiving a one-half share and each then owning 850 shares. The act of donation, which is not dated, was signed by Doris, Ken, Greg, and two witnesses. It was drawn up in the form of a notarial act but was not notarized. Though the act of donation states that Doris, contemporaneously with signing the document, delivered the property to Greg and Ken and that they accepted the donation and received the property, there is no evidence that a stock certificate was in fact transferred between them by endorsement and delivery.

Greg, who managed WEI, and Ken, who worked in sales, had different ideas about what to do with the business. Ken wanted to sell. Greg did not. In April 2010, around the time he ceased working at WEI, Ken requested some documents from WEI's attorney, Gene Cicardo. On April 29, 2010, Cicardo sent a fax to Ken which included the act of donation. Cicardo wrote on the cover sheet of the fax that the documents needed to be redone because they had not been notarized. Ken did not act on this information.

It appears from the record that Greg already knew that there was a problem affecting the validity of the act of donation. He testified that when he sent the original documents to Cicardo, he found out they were not good. Greg testified that he told Cicardo to wait on doing anything more because Doris came out of surgery okay and because of "the way that things were coming down around the John Deere store." Greg did not share with Ken his knowledge about the problem with the act of donation.

On November 18, 2010, Ken filed a shareholder derivative action against Greg. Around this same time, Ken received a notice from Greg of an annual shareholders meeting to be held on December 14, 2010. Prior to the shareholders meeting, Greg obtained from Doris her "Irrevocable Proxy" allowing him to vote any share held by her.

On December 14, 2010, Greg, acting as secretary-treasurer of WEI, certified the stock register. The register listed outstanding shares from 1987 through April 13, 2009, the date of the judgment of possession when Doris received one share and the other was divided between Greg and Ken. A document from WEI's books shows that the certificates representing the shares transferred by the judgment of possession were not issued until November 12, 2010; however, the certificates were apparently backdated to April 13, 2009. Greg also prepared a certified list of shareholders documenting [that] he and Ken each owned 849.5 shares and Doris owned one.

The result of the December 14, 2010, shareholders meeting was that Greg was elected president of WEI and his wife, Phyllis, was elected secretary-treasurer. Ken, whom the record indicates may have been vice-president, lost his position as an officer though he remains a member of the board. Thereafter, Ken filed three actions on December 22, 2010.

First, Ken filed a petition for a temporary restraining order and injunctive relief against Greg, Phyllis, and WEI to enjoin them from making executive decisions pertaining to WEI, particularly regarding the alienation or encumbrance of any property. He also sought a judgment declaring himself and Greg owners of 50% of WEI each and declaring the actions taken at the shareholders meeting to be null and void. The trial court granted a temporary restraining order as prayed for in the petition.

Second, Ken filed a petition for a writ of quo warranto against Greg, Phyllis, and Doris demanding that they show by what authority they claim to be directors or officers of WEI.

Third, Ken filed a petition for a writ of mandamus against Greg and Phyllis seeking to have them recognize the donation by Doris of her share of stock, to have the transfer recorded on the books of WEI and reflected on the certified list of shareholders, and to have new certificates issued.

These three actions were consolidated by agreement of the parties at the start of the hearing on January 6, 2011. The threshold question before the trial court was whether the donation by Doris of her one share of WEI stock to Ken and Greg had been properly confected. . . . In short, the trial court found that the act of donation was not in the form of an authentic act as required for a donation inter vivos under La. C.C. art. 1541, that it was not in a form provided for donations of certain incorporeal movables under La. C.C. art. 1550, and that it was not in compliance with certain requirements of WEI's articles of incorporation. The trial court also determined that the "irrevocable proxy" obtained by Greg from Doris could be revoked. In accordance with its written reasons, the trial court rendered a judgment on January 31, 2011, dissolving the temporary restraining order, dismissing with prejudice the three consolidated petitions, and holding the proxy to be revocable. Costs were assessed equally between Ken and Greg. The trial court noted in its reasons for judgment that neither brother has "clean hands" in this dispute.

Ken now appeals. He assigns as error the trial court's findings that the donation was invalid, that the donation had not been completed and accepted because there was no endorsement and delivery of the stock certificate, and that Louisiana's stock transfer laws apply under the second paragraph of La. C.C. art. 1550. He also assigns as error the trial court's failure to find that the proxy had no effect and the denial of the claims for injunctive relief and writs of mandamus and quo warranto. Whether the donation was valid as to form is the core issue in these assignments of error.

Discussion

A donation inter vivos is a contract by which the donor divests himself, at present and irrevocably, of a thing in favor of the donee, who accepts it. La. C.C. art. 1468; *Thomson v. Thomson*, 34,353 (La. App. 2d Cir. 1/24/01), 778 So. 2d 736. As provided by La. C.C. art. 1541, a donation inter vivos shall be made by authentic act. The act of donation at issue was not notarized and is not in the form of an authentic act. Thus, it is not a valid donation under La. C.C. art. 1541.

A share of stock in a corporation is an incorporeal movable. La. C.C. art. 473. Donations of certain incorporeal movables may be made in a form provided by La. C.C. art. 1550, which states:

> The donation or the acceptance of a donation of an incorporeal movable of the kind that is evidenced by a certificate, document, instrument, or other writing, and that is transferable by endorsement or delivery, may be made by authentic act or by compliance with the requirements otherwise applicable to the transfer of that particular kind of incorporeal movable.

> In addition, an incorporeal movable that is investment property, as that term is defined in Chapter 9 of the Louisiana Commercial Laws, may also be donated by a writing signed by the donor that evidences donative intent and directs the transfer of the property to the donee or his account or for his benefit. Completion of the transfer to the donee or his account or for his benefit shall constitute acceptance of the donation.

This article is new and was added by Acts, No. 204, § 1, effective January 1, 2009, as part of the revision of the law on donations. Because the act of donation was signed sometime in the latter half of 2009, La. C.C. art. 1550 was in effect and is applicable to determine whether the donation was done in a proper form.

Statutory interpretation is subject to a de novo review on appeal. *Harrah's Bossier City Inv. Co., LLC v. Bridges*, 2009-1916 (La. 5/11/10), 41 So. 3d 438. Discernment of the legislative intent is the goal of statutory interpretation. . . . When a law is clear and unambiguous and its application does not lead to absurd consequences, it shall be applied as written with no further interpretation made in search of the legislative intent. La. C.C. art. 9. If the language is susceptible of different meanings, it must be interpreted to have the meaning that best conforms to the purpose of the law. La. C.C. art. 10. Moreover, laws on the same subject matter must be interpreted in reference to each other. La. C.C. art. 13.

The legislative history of La. C.C. art. 1550 indicates that it was not intended to change the prior law (former C.C. article 1536), which required a notarial act for donations of incorporeal movables such as rents, credits, rights, or actions. Rather, article 1550 was drafted to further provide that donations of incorporeal movables evidenced by a certificate, document, instrument or other writing could be donated by authentic act or as provided in special rules applicable to the particular type of movable. See Louisiana Bill Digest, 2008 Reg. Sess. H.B. 527. Prior to the enactment of La. C.C. art. 1550, jurisprudence held that a donation of shares of stock may be made without the formalities of an authentic act so long as the shares of stock are transferred pursuant to Louisiana's stock transfer laws. *Primeaux v. Libersat*, 322 So. 2d 147 (La. 1975); *Champagne v. Champagne*, 2007-1078 (La. App. 1st Cir. 6/27/08), 992 So. 2d 1072; *Moncrief v. Succession of Armstrong*, 2005-1584 (La. App. 3d Cir. 9/27/06), 939 So. 2d 714; *Succession of Payne v. Pigott*, 459 So. 2d 1231 (La. App. 1st Cir. 1984); *Succession of Hall*, 198 So. 2d 511 (La. App. 2d Cir. 1967), app. denied, 250 LA. 974, 200 So. 2d 664 (La. 1967). We find that La. C.C. art. 1550 codifies this jurisprudential holding.

Ken does not argue that the donation was made in a form approved under the first paragraph of La. C.C. art. 1550. It is clear that it was neither in the form of an authentic act nor in compliance with the requirements applicable to the transfer of shares of stock, La. R.S. 10:8-101 et seq., of the Louisiana Commercial Laws. There was no delivery or indorsement as required under La. R.S. 10:8-301 or 10:8-304 for the transfer of securities. As such, the donation was not completed in a form authorized under the first paragraph of La. C.C. art. 1550.

As to the second paragraph of La. C.C. art. 1550, the legislative history reveals that its purpose was to provide for donations of "investment property" by a document directing the transfer of such property in favor of the donee or for his benefit. . . . Based on its review of the definition of "security" set forth at La. R.S. 10:8-102(a)(15), the trial court found the share at issue to be investment property. This finding is not challenged on appeal. Moreover, whether the share at issue is a security, and thereby considered "investment property," is answered by La. R.S. 10:8-103(a), which states, "A share or similar equity interest issued by a corporation, business trust, joint stock company, or similar entity is a security." Uniform Commercial

Code Comment No. 2 to this provision clarifies that ordinary corporate stock, including shares of closely held corporations, are securities.

Ken argues that the form of the donation satisfied the requirements of the second paragraph of La. C.C. art. 1550 and that the trial court erred in finding otherwise. He asserts that the trial court ignored the words "for his benefit" and the fact that the second paragraph provides a form of donation that is "in addition" to that provided in the first paragraph of the article. He also asserts that the proper analysis under the second paragraph is not whether a stock certificate was indorsed or delivered but whether it was transferred for the donee's benefit. He quotes language from the act of donation stating that Doris does "irrevocably give, grant, alienate, confirm, and donate" her one share of stock to her sons and that she "contemporaneously with the signing" of the act "delivered said property" to them. He also refers to that part of the act which states that he and Greg "do hereby acknowledge to have received from donor the property" and declare their acceptance. Ken argues that this language shows there was completion of the transfer to him for his benefit.

We are not persuaded by Ken's arguments. In general, any donation can be said to be for the benefit of the donee. However, the words "for his benefit" have a specific meaning under La. C.C. art. 1550. As explained in Comment (b) of the 2008 Revision Comments of article 1550, the words "for his benefit" are intended "to cover situations when the transfer may not be directly to the donee's account, but would be used to pay something for his benefit, as for example, if the transfer is made to a bank to pay off a child's debt." The record does not show that the purported donation was made for Ken's benefit as intended by La. C.C. art. 1550. Considering the definition of investment property, we find that the second paragraph of article 1550 was intended to facilitate the gratuitous transfer of such property, which would generally be held in bank or brokerage accounts, by the donor directing in writing that the property be transferred to "the donee or his account or for his benefit" and then by the completion of the transfer.

Even if, as found by the trial court, the writing signed by Doris directed the transfer of the share to Ken and Greg, the transfer was not completed as required by La. C.C. art. 1550. We agree with the trial court that completion of the donation (or transfer) of the WEI share would require compliance with the stock transfer law. Regardless of the language used in the writing signed by the parties, the record shows there was no delivery or indorsement as required by La. R.S. 10:8-301 or R.S. 10:8-304 for transfer of the one share.

Under Ken's interpretation, any signed writing that expresses donative intent and states there has been delivery and acceptance would suffice to constitute a donation of a security or other investment property even though such an act would lack the indicia of reliability provided by either an authentic act or by compliance with requirements for completing transfers of the specific investment properties. Nothing in the legislative history or the article indicates that it was intended to allow a writing that is not in the form of an authentic act to effect a transfer of "investment property" without fulfillment of the specific requirements to complete the transfer of such property.

From our review of the record we find no error of law in the trial court's interpretation of La. C.C. art. 1550 and no manifest error in its factual findings regarding the invalidity of the donation. The record shows that both Ken and Greg knew there were questions as to whether the donation had been properly done. However, both acted for months as though the donation was proper. Neither took action to investigate the validity of the donation or to complete the transfer of the share. Also, Doris testified that in October 2010 she signed a copy of the donation that was marked "void" after learning there had been a problem with the donation. She did not seek to complete the donation or to properly confect a new act of donation. As of the time of trial she still owned the one share of WEI.

We agree with the trial court's finding that the donation was invalid. It was not in the form of an authentic act or in compliance with La. C.C. art. 1550. Because the donation was invalid as to form, we need not address the alleged lack of compliance with WEI's articles of incorporation as they pertain to the transfer of shares. The petitions for injunctive relief, writ of mandamus, and writ of quo warranto were also properly denied. These claims were based upon the assertions that the donation was valid, that the proxy given by Doris to Greg and the actions taken on December 14, 2010, were invalid, and that Ken owned fifty percent of the shares in WEI. In the absence of a valid donation, Greg properly obtained Doris's proxy and had the majority shares at the December 14, 2010, shareholder's meeting. Because the donation was determined to be invalid, the trial court correctly dissolved the temporary restraining order and denied the request for injunctive relief and the petitions for writ of mandamus and quo warranto. These claims are not supported by the evidence in the record.

Conclusion

For the reasons explained, we affirm the judgment of the trial court. Costs of this appeal are assessed against the appellant, Kenneth D. Malone.

AFFIRMED.

Notes and Questions

1. What do you think was the intent of Doris, Greg and Ken's mother, in *Malone v. Malone*, 77 So.3d 1040 (La. App. 2 Cir. 2011)? Did she want to give control of the family business to one son or did she intend for her two sons to have equal control? What is the significance of the "irrevocable proxy" she gave to Greg after the purported donation but before the annual shareholder's meeting? Is the court's holding here consistent with your view of Doris' probable intent?

2. Should our *ex post* (after the fact) impression of a donor's intent be relevant in a case like this? Or, is the lesson here that if parties are dealing with assets like shares of corporate stock (even just one share of stock in a closely held corporation), they must be especially careful to comply *ex ante* (in advance) with all of the technical rules applicable to effectuate a transfer of this kind of property. Article 1550 of the Civil Code, which is quoted in full in *Malone*, seems to demand ex ante

compliance with the rules governing the transfer of incorporeal movable property rather than an ex post search for the parties' actual intent. Why do you suppose the Civil Code makes this policy choice? Contrast Article 1550 with the second sentence of Article 1839. Can you explain this contradiction?

3. Note that the trial court held that Doris' grant of a proxy to her son Greg was potentially revocable. *Malone*, 77 So.3d at 1043. The appellate court did not address this point. Did Doris' failure to revoke the proxy she had previously given to Greg imply that she intended to give him control of the family business on a permanent basis? Or was her failure to revoke the proxy irrelevant? Could she give her proxy to another shareholder at a future shareholders meeting? Can you see the importance of complying with strict formalities for the donation of shares in a closely held, family business?

4. Transfer of Immovables

a. Formalities Required for the Transfer of Real Rights in Immovables

As we already know from studying the principal consequences of classifying a thing as immovable, its transfer is subject to the requirements of Article 1839 of the Civil Code. A transfer of immovable property must be made by authentic act or by act under private signature, unless the property has been delivered and the transferor recognizes the transfer under oath. La. Civ. Code art. 1839(1) (1984). The instrument is effective against third parties only if filed for registry in the parish where the property is located. La. Civ. Code art. 1839(2) (1984). We also studied the distinction between a *real right*, a right in a thing, whether movable or immovable, that is good against the world, and a *personal right*, a right or legal power to demand some kind of performance from another person that arises out of some contractual or quasi-contractual obligation.

In the following decision, a court draws on both sets of rules to determine whether an ambiguous agreement establishing a right of way for a pipeline created a real right in immovable property or a personal right under the contract of lease. If the pipeline right of way agreement contemplated a right of use, *i.e.*, a real right in an immovable, the extension of the relationship between the landowner and the pipeline builder would trigger Article 1839 of the Civil Code. In contrast, if the parties intended a lease, the renewal could be accomplished by oral agreement. This decision also provides us with some useful vocabulary for the rest of our study of Louisiana property law.

Sasol North America, Inc. v. Bolton

103 So.3d 1267 (La. App. 3 Cir. 2012)

PICKETT, Judge. Pipeline owner appeals the trial court's grant of summary judgment in favor of the defendants, arguing the judgment was improperly granted because the defendants offered and it accepted an oral offer to renew the pipeline right of way at issue for thirty years. For the following reasons, we affirm the judgment.

Facts

In 1979, Betty Ann Bolton, M.B. Bolton, Jr., and Continental Oil Company entered into a right of way agreement for the construction of a pipeline across a portion of the Boltons' property in Calcasieu Parish. The right of way agreement expired pursuant to its terms in February 2009. Thereafter, Mrs. Bolton[1] and Sasol North America, Inc. (Sasol), which had acquired Continental Oil Company's rights under the right of way agreement, began negotiating an extension of the servitude. They did not finalize an agreement, however, and Sasol filed suit in 2011. Sasol asserted that Mrs. Bolton had made an oral offer to extend the right of way an additional thirty years for $50,000, which it accepted, but she refused to consummate their agreement. It sought a judgment declaring an oral contract existed between it and Mrs. Bolton and ordering the Boltons to fulfill the terms of the contract. The Boltons answered Sasol's petition, denying they offered to renew the right of way and averring requests by Sasol for a renewal had been rejected.

Pointing to La. Civ. Code art. 1839, the Boltons filed a Motion for Summary Judgment, arguing Sasol failed to prove it has a valid pipeline right of way. Article 1839 requires that transfers of immovable property be in writing. It also acknowledges the validity of oral transfers if possession of the property is actually transferred and the transfer is acknowledged under oath by the transferor. The Boltons supported the motion with excerpts of Mrs. Bolton's deposition testimony and an affidavit in which she denied that she agreed to renew the right of way for $50,000.

Sasol opposed the motion, arguing that Mrs. Bolton orally offered to renew the right of way for thirty years in exchange for $50,000, if it built a fence enclosing the pipeline and repaired damages on the right of way caused by third parties. Sasol asserted that it accepted Mrs. Bolton's terms and that their agreement satisfied the requirements of a lease as provided in La. Civ. Code art. 2668.

After a hearing, the trial court granted the judgment. Sasol filed a motion for new trial which was denied; it appealed.

Issue Presented for Review

The pleadings and the parties' arguments on the merits of the trial court's judgment present one issue for our review: Did the trial court err in granting summary judgment in favor of the Boltons?

. . . .

---

1. Mr. Bolton had died, and pursuant to a Judgment of Possession issued in 1994 in his succession, Mrs. Bolton is the owner of an undivided fifty percent interest in the property on which the pipeline is situated and usufructuary of the remaining fifty percent interest in the property; the Boltons' two sons are naked owners of that remaining fifty percent interest.

Discussion

The Boltons argue in their motion for summary judgment that Sasol is seeking to enforce a predial servitude as provided in La. Civ. Code art. 708 and, therefore, must satisfy the requirements of La. Civ. Code art. 1839. Article 1839 requires that a transfer of immovable property be in writing. The Boltons contend, therefore, that Sasol's claim of an enforceable oral contract between it and Mrs. Bolton is without merit and that they are entitled to summary judgment dismissing Sasol's suit.

There are two types of servitudes. Predial servitudes exist in favor of a dominant estate on a servient estate. La. Civ. Code art. 646. There is no evidence that the right of way at issue is a predial servitude because Sasol has not been shown to be the owner of a dominant estate. The facts in the record indicate the right of way is a personal servitude rather than a predial servitude. For purposes of this case, however, the differences between personal and predial servitudes have no bearing on our consideration of the Boltons' motion.

A right of way is a personal servitude of right of use that "confers in favor of a person a specified use of an estate less than full enjoyment"; it may be established in favor of a legal entity. La. Civ. Code arts. 639, 641. Rights of use are incorporeal immovables. La. Civ. Code art. 470. Accordingly, they are subject to the writing requirement of La. Civ. Code art. 1839. *See Richard v. Hall,* 03-1488 (La.4/23/04), 874 So.2d 131. If no writing exists, an oral transfer of immovable property can only be proved "when the property has been actually delivered and the transferor recognizes the transfer when interrogated on oath." La. Civ. Code art. 1839.

Sasol opposes the Boltons' motion, arguing that Mrs. Bolton offered to renew the right of way for a period of thirty years in exchange for the payment of $50,000 and that it accepted her terms. Sasol contends that while the Agreement could be a personal servitude, it also satisfies the requirements of Article 2668 and is not subject to the requirements of Article 1839.

Article 2668 provides that a lease is an agreement between a lessor and a lessee in which the lessee is given "the use and enjoyment of a thing for a term in exchange for a rent." Article 2668 further provides, however, "The consent of the parties as to the thing and the rent is essential but not necessarily sufficient for a contract of lease." Pertinent to this latter provision, Revision Comment (d) to Article 2668 (emphasis added) explains:

> Without an agreement as to the thing and the rent, there cannot be a contract of lease. On the other hand, the existence of such an agreement does not necessarily mean that a contract of lease has come into existence if the parties did not so intend. For example, if, despite agreement on the thing and the rent, it is understood that the parties will not be bound until they agree on other terms of the contract, then there is no lease until these terms are agreed upon. Similarly, **even if the parties intended to be bound upon their agreement as to the thing and the "rent," the resulting contract may or may not be one of lease, depending again on the intent of the parties.**

For example, if the right intended to be conveyed has the attributes of a real right such as a personal servitude or a limited personal servitude of use, then the contract is not a lease, even though the parties used terms like "rent" or "lease." *Cf.* C.C. Art. 730 (Rev.1977).

Sasol attached to its Petition a copy of the Right of Way Agreement (the Agreement) it prepared and submitted to Mrs. Bolton for her to sign. The Agreement states that Mrs. Bolton grants Sasol "an easement and servitude" and the terms "right of way" and "Right of Way Agreement" are used throughout it. The Agreement also provides that if the pipeline ceases operation for a period of twenty-four months or more, all rights "terminate and the land covered by this servitude shall revert to Owner, its successors and/or assigns." Notably, the Agreement does not use either of the terms "rent" or "lease," and it appears as though Sasol only began using these terms in response to the Boltons' Motion for Summary Judgment.

Notwithstanding the fact that a right of way may be the subject of a lease as Sasol argues, the quoted terminology shows Sasol considered the right of way it sought to renew with Mrs. Bolton to be a "servitude" as contemplated by Revision Comment (b) to Article 2688. For these reasons, we find no error with the trial court's conclusions that La. Civ. Code art. 1839 governs the issues presented by Sasol's Petition.

Sasol has not presented evidence that a genuine issue of material fact exists which prohibits summary judgment in favor of the Boltons. Specifically, Sasol has not shown that the Agreement was reduced to writing, and it has not controverted Mrs. Bolton's deposition testimony and affidavit that she did not offer and/or agree to renew the right of way for thirty years for the sum of $50,000. Accordingly, we find no error with the trial court's grant of summary judgment.

Disposition

The judgment of the trial court is affirmed. All costs are assessed to Sasol North America, Inc.

AFFIRMED.

Notes and Questions

1. The decision in *Sasol North America, Inc. v. Bolton*, 103 So.3d 1267 (La. App. 3 Cir. 2012), previews one of the important subjects of this casebook: how to recognize different kinds of servitudes—in particular a *predial servitude* and a *personal servitude of right of use*; and how to distinguish these two real rights less than full enjoyment from a lease. *See* La. Civ. Code arts. 730–34 (1977).

2. In this case, should the lawyers for Continental Oil Company and later Sasol North America have realized that they were dealing with a personal servitude of right of use and not a lease? What particular facts made the 1979 agreement between the Boltons and Continental Oil Company ambiguous? Recall that one of the primary characteristics of real rights other than usufruct and the right of habitation is that they are potentially perpetual. Consider also Article 773 of the Civil Code,

which declares that the expiration of time or happening of a condition extinguishes a predial servitude established for a term or under a resolutory condition. La. Civ. Code art. 773 (1977). Why did Continental agree to a term of thirty years for its personal servitude of right of use in 1979?

3. Now that the decision in *Sasol* is final, what recourse does the company have? How can it acquire a right of way if the Boltons refuse to negotiate or demand an unreasonable price?

4. **Oral Transfers of Immovable Property (*Harter v. Harter*):** As noted at the beginning of this section, in the absence of an authentic act or act under private signature, an oral transfer of immovable property can exceptionally be effective between the parties if "the property has been actually delivered" and "the transferor recognizes the transfer when interrogated on oath." La. Civ. Code art. 1839 (1984). In a recent decision, a Louisiana appellate court upheld an oral transfer of twenty-five percent working interests in mineral leases among several siblings under the terms of Article 1839 of the Civil Code. *Harter v. Harter*, 127 So.3d 5 (La. App. 2 Cir. 2013).

The court in *Harter* found that the working interests in the mineral leases, which the court characterized as incorporeal immovables under Article 470 of the Civil Code, were actually delivered. The defendant placed the plaintiffs in possession of the working interests by amending internal company records to show the plaintiffs as owners, making payments of interest revenues to the plaintiffs, and delivering owner expense and billing reports to the plaintiffs. *Id.* at 11. Further, the court held that the defendant confessed the transfer under oath when he admitted the acts of delivery described above, even though he ultimately denied that a transfer of ownership of the working interests had occurred. *Id.* at 11–12.

b. Public Policy Limits on the Sale of Immovables: Lesion beyond Moiety

From its inception in 1808, the Louisiana Civil Code has continued the French tradition of protecting a party to a commutative contract from harm suffered "if he receives less than an equivalent in exchange for his own commitment." DIAN TOOLEY-KNOBLETT & DAVID W. GRUNING, 24 LOUISIANA CIVIL LAW TREATISE: SALES § 13:2 (1st ed. 2012). This is known as "lesion." Pursuant to Article 1965 of the Civil Code, a "contract may be annulled on the ground of lesion only in those cases provided by law." La. Civ. Code art. 1965 (1984). In Louisiana, lesion may be invoked in sale, exchange and partition. The law of lesion is found in rescripts dating back to the reign of Emperor Diocletian but may have its origins in Rabbinic and Mesopotamian law. *See* Raymond Westbrook, *The Origin of Laesio Enormis*, 55 REVUE INTERNATIONALE DES DROITS DE L'ANTIQUITÉ 39 (2008).

The next case introduces Rescission for Lesion Beyond Moiety in the context of sales. The applicable rules are stated in Chapter 12 of Title VII in Book III of the Civil Code. La. Civ. Code arts. 2589–2600 (1993). In a nutshell, when the purchase price is less than one half the fair market value of the immovable, the vendor is given a right, for a limited period of time, to demand rescission of the sale. As you study the case, consider the consequences of the Civil Code's protection for vendors who sell their immovable property for prices that turn out to be quite low in comparison to their actual market value. Is this policy of allowing courts to take an ex post facto view of voluntary transfers of ownership for purposes of ensuring that they comport with objective considerations of fairness a sound one? Are the legal directives involved in rescission for lesion beyond moiety crystalline rules or muddy standards or a combination of both?

Pay attention to the multiple roles that the lawyer Bruce Hampton played in the transaction. Did the lawyer take too much risk in this transaction? Did he violate any ethical duties? To whom did he owe his primary obligation as an attorney?

Joiner v. Abercrombie

968 So.2d 1184 (La. App. 2 Cir. 2007)

BROWN, Chief Judge. On February 18, 2004, plaintiff, Luzon Joiner, an elderly World War II veteran, sold a 198-acre tract of land located on Highway 33 in Union Parish to defendants, Robert S. Abercrombie and Brenda Kay Hobson Abercrombie, for $110,000. Robert Abercrombie, a timber buyer and manager, had bought and cut timber on this tract from Joiner in the past. The deed was drafted and notarized by attorney Bruce Hampton. Within one month of the sale, on March 17, 2004, defendants transferred the property by an exchange deed to Pinoak Investments, LLC, which developed and sold the property as a residential area. Attorney Hampton, one of the owners of Pinoak, signed the exchange deed as the duly authorized manager of Pinoak. Exactly what Pinoak paid for the property is at issue in this action for damages. Plaintiff alleges lesion beyond moiety, contending that the sale price of his transfer to the Abercrombies was less than one-half of the value of the property. The trial court found that plaintiff did not prove lesion and dismissed his lawsuit. We reverse and render judgment in favor of plaintiff.

Discussion

Lesion beyond moiety is a sale of a corporeal immovable for which the buyer paid less than one-half of its fair market value. Lesion can be claimed only by the seller. La. C.C. art 2589. Fair market value is defined as the amount a willing and informed buyer would pay a willing and informed seller for a particular piece of property, with neither being under any compulsion to buy or sell. *Cook v. Mixon*, 29,491 (La. App. 2d Cir. 08/22/97), 700 So. 2d 1264, *writ denied*, 97-2443 (La. 01/09/98), 705 So. 2d 1101; *Mullins v. Page*, 457 So. 2d 64 (La. App. 2d Cir. 1984), *writ denied*, 459 So. 2d 538 (La. 1984). The immovable sold must be evaluated according to the state in which it was at the time of the sale. La. C.C. art. 2590.

When the sale price is lesionary, the buyer may elect to either return the immovable to the seller or keep the property and pay the seller a supplement equal to the difference between the price paid and the fair market value. La. C. C art 2591. However, when the buyer has sold the immovable, the seller may not bring an action in lesion against a third person. In such a case, the seller may recover whatever profit the buyer realized from the sale, not to exceed the supplement the seller would have received had the buyer kept the property. La. C.C. art. 2594. The seller carries the burden of proving lesion. *Mullins, supra; Caillouet v. Zwei Bruderland*, 99-590 (La. App. 3d Cir. 11/03/99), 746 So. 2d 752. The trial court's determination of fair market value is a finding of fact and is reviewed on appeal under the manifest error standard. *Id.*

Attorney Client Privilege

In *In re Eddie Douglas*, 06-0630 (La. 11/29/06), 943 So. 2d 341, the supreme court recognized the potential for confusion when an attorney wears a multitude of hats.

In this case, Bruce Hampton drafted the deed transferring the property from plaintiff to the Abercrombies. He also handled the closing with the bank that loaned the money to the Abercrombies for the purchase. Thereafter, Pinoak, an LLC, which was owned by Attorney Hampton and Joel Kent Antley, bought the property from the Abercrombies. Hampton acted as manager of the LLC which immediately developed the property for residential use and had successfully sold all of the lots by the time this case went to trial.

The trial court ruled in a pre-trial motion to compel that there was an attorney-client relationship between the Abercrombies and Bruce Hampton and that their discussions concerning these transactions were privileged.

Rules of Professional Conduct Rule 1.8 provides:

(a) A lawyer shall not enter into a business transaction with a client or knowingly acquire an ownership, possessory, security or other pecuniary interest adverse to a client unless:

(1) the transaction and terms on which the lawyer acquires the interest are fair and reasonable to the client and are fully disclosed and transmitted in writing in a manner that can be reasonably understood by the client;

(2) the client is advised in writing of the desirability of seeking and is given a reasonable opportunity to seek the advice of independent legal counsel on the transaction; and

(3) the client gives informed consent, in a writing signed by the client, to the essential terms of the transaction and the lawyer's role in the transaction, including whether the lawyer is representing the client in the transaction.

Obviously, an attorney-client relationship existed between Hampton and the Abercrombies when they purchased the property and borrowed the purchase price from the bank. If Hampton was representing the Abercrombies when Hampton purchased the property for Pinoak, then he may have been in violation of the rules of professional conduct. The record does not disclose if Hampton complied with the requirements of Rule 1.8. It is our belief that Hampton was wearing another hat when he purchased the property for Pinoak and acting as a land developer.

Therefore, the trial court was in error in denying Joiner the right to examine Hampton about the details of the transaction and in particular, the structuring of the purchase price between the LLC and the Abercrombies.

The Purchase Price

This lesion case arises from the sale of 198 acres on Highway 33 between Farmerville and Ruston, by plaintiff, Luzon Joiner, to defendants, Robert and Brenda Abercrombie. Robert Abercrombie had bought and cut the timber on this tract and had the trust of Joiner. The Abercrombies, without obtaining an appraisal, purchased the land for $110,000 on February 18, 2004.

Approximately one month after purchasing the property from Joiner, the Abercrombies sold the land to Pinoak Investment, LLC. The purchase price paid by Pinoak is in conflict. The Abercrombies contend that they sold the property to Pinoak for $155,000 cash and the exchange of a 22-acre tract of property worth $55,000. Thus, the price was $210,000 and not lesionary.

This price, however, does not include the $90,000 timber management agreement that Robert Abercrombie entered into with Pinoak. The $90,000 was considered an advance, and it bound Robert Abercrombie to provide timber management services to Pinoak for either 35 years or until Pinoak ceased to own the subject property, whichever occurred first.

Three things cause this court to seriously question the propriety and actual purpose of the timber management agreement. First, Larry Culp testified that he offered the Abercrombies $300,000 for the entire tract, but that Robert Abercrombie informed him that he was selling it to Bruce Hampton for more. Second, Robert Abercrombie testified that he has been in the timber business for 12 years and, as far as he knows, he has never heard of or seen anyone getting paid in advance for timber management services. Finally, Pinoak immediately started developing and selling the subject property as residential, with all of the lots being sold before the case went to trial. Once all of the property was sold, Robert Abercrombie's agreement to manage the timber terminated. In fact, the "timber management" agreement terminated without Abercrombie ever going onto the property or performing any service after he sold it to Pinoak.

It is clear that the timber management agreement was a sham, designed to conceal the true purchase price received by the Abercrombies, which was $300,000. We again note that the trial court disallowed Joiner's attorney's attempts to question Bruce Hampton or the Abercrombies about their dealings on the Pinoak purchase. This was error.

Fair Market Value

At trial Robert Horton and William Maxwell testified as experts in the area of real estate appraisal and valuation, respectively. Horton valued the property at $237,500 as of February 2004, and Maxwell valued the property at $2,500 per acre. However, John Messina, an expert in real estate appraisal testifying by oral deposition for the defense, determined that the fair market value of the property was $134,000.

Testifying by oral deposition, Joel Kent Antley was tendered by plaintiff as an expert in real estate valuation. Defendants, however, objected to his being accepted as an expert and the trial court never ruled on the objection. Antley testified that he believed that the property was worth $300,000 because that was what he thought Pinoak, in which he and Bruce Hampton were partners, paid for the tract of land.

The Abercrombies contend that Joiner failed to prove the fair market value of the property through clear and convincing evidence. Moreover, the Abercrombies assert that Joiner's, as well as his experts', valuations of the property were speculative, as they were based on the property being classified as residential and not cutover timberland. To support this assertion, the Abercrombies cite *Valley Land Corp. v. Fielder*, 242 So.2d 358 (La. App. 2d Cir. 1971), in which this court found that in lesion cases, evaluations may not be based on conjecture, possibility or speculation.

In *Valley Land Corp., supra*, the plaintiff's experts concluded that the highest and best use of the property in question was for the development of a residential subdivision. While noting that the highest and best use of property may be considered, along with other evidence of value, to show the value of the property at the time of the sale, this court found that to evaluate that particular piece of property as a residential subdivision would be indulging in speculation. *Id.*

Based upon our finding in *Valley Land Corp., supra*, the Abercrombies argue that for this court to value the property based upon its highest and best use, *i.e.* residential, would require us to indulge in speculation. We, however, do not agree with this argument as the property currently at issue and the property at issue in *Valley Land Corp., supra*, are different. In *Valley Land Corp.*, this court found that the disputed land was "not suitable for a subdivision" and that "there were no residential areas within miles." The property in the instant action, however, is located in an area with rapid residential growth, is propitiously situated between Ruston and Farmerville, and has a large amount of road frontage. Furthermore, three out of four experts testified that the highest and best use of the property was residential.

In an attempt to invalidate the experts' conclusion that the highest and best use of the property was residential, the Abercrombies posit that at the time of the sale the property was cutover timberland and that Joiner had no intentions of using the property for residential purposes. Thus, the Abercrombies conclude, to value the property based on the possibility that it could be used as residential is speculative and does not show the value of the property in the condition it was in at the time of the sale.

After reviewing the jurisprudence, we find that there is no rule of law restricting the application of the highest and best use, when determining fair market value in a suit for lesion, to the actual use of the property at the time of the sale. This court previously stated in *Mullins, supra* at 72:

[T]he plaintiff in a lesion suit may present proof of the highest and best use of the property rather than solely the actual use of the property at the time of the sale. Such proof *may* be considered along with all the other evidence of property value provided that it tends to show the value of the property at the time of the sale.

See also Nation v. Wilmore, 525 So. 2d 1269 (La. App. 3d Cir. 1988).

We find that the trial court's reliance solely on the appraisal of the one expert who evaluated the property as cutover timberland without considering the testimony of the three experts who concurred that, inasmuch as the property in question was ideally located and in an area with a burgeoning residential market, its highest and best use was residential was clear error. Further, within a month of the sale, the land was bought and developed as residential property.

Having found that the property should have been evaluated as residential, we must now determine the fair market value of the property at the time Joiner sold it to the Abercrombies. As we have found, within one month of the sale from petitioner to the Abercrombies the property was sold for $300,000 for residential development. Larry Culp testified that the Abercrombies were asking $300,000 before they purchased the property and that he offered $300,000 for the property. This price is supported by the valuations determined by the three experts who considered the property as residential rather than cutover timber.

Louisiana Civil Code art. 2594 states:

When the buyer has sold the immovable, the seller may not bring an action for lesion against a third person who bought the immovable from the original buyer.

In such a case the seller may recover from the original buyer whatever profit the latter realized from the sale to the third person. That recovery may not exceed the supplement the seller would have recovered if the original buyer had chosen to keep the immovable.

Finding the fair market value to be $300,000 and that the profit realized by the Abercrombies was $190,000, we find that Joiner is entitled to damages in the amount of $190,000.

Conclusion

For the foregoing reasons, the judgment of the trial court dismissing Luzon Joiner's petition for lesion is hereby reversed and judgment is rendered in favor of plaintiff in the amount of $190,000, together with interest from the date of judicial demand. Costs are assessed to defendants, Robert and Brenda Abercrombie.

Notes and Questions

1. Do you believe the court in *Joiner v. Abercrombie*, 968 So.2d 1184 (La. App. 2 Cir. 2007), should have taken into account the value of the land for residential development at the time Joiner sold it to the Abercrombies, even though Joiner was

only using the property as cutover timberland at the time of the sale? Should courts be allowed to re-evaluate the fairness of a voluntary transfer between consenting adults who, as far as we know, had an undiminished mental capacity for contracting at the time their agreement was confected?

2. Was it significant here that Joiner had previously sold timber to Robert Abercrombie and that Joiner may have placed his trust in Abercrombie? Would the outcome have been different if Joiner and Abercrombie had been complete strangers to one another?

3. The Civil Code does not allow sellers to rescind sales of immovable property for lesion beyond moiety indefinitely. Article 2595 provides that the action for lesion "must be brought within a peremptive period of one year from the time of the sale." La. Civ. Code art. 2595 (1993). Unlike a prescriptive period, a peremptive period cannot be tolled, even if the party affected, here the vendor, was prevented from realizing he had a cause of action for reasons beyond his control. Why would the Civil Code impose this very short peremptive period on an action to rescind a sale for lesion beyond moiety? Note that the pre-revision law called for a liberative prescription period of four years. Dian Tooley-Knoblett & David W. Gruning, 24 Louisiana Civil Law Treatise: Sales§ 13:24 (1st ed. 2012).

4. Why is rescission for lesion beyond moiety limited to corporeal immovables? Should it apply to corporeal movables as well? Incorporeal immovables?

5. What basic options does the law of lesion make available and who may exercise these options? *See* La. Civ. Code arts. 2589, 2591 (1993). What happens if the buyer has granted a right on the immovable to a third party? *See* La. Civ. Code art. 2596.

6. The law of lesion has been on the retreat in other mixed jurisdictions. For the Republic of South Africa, see for example, H.R. Hahlo & Ellison Kahn, *Good-Bye Laesio Enormis,* 69 SALJ 392 (1952).

7. What are the alternatives to lesion rules? Consider section 2-302 of the Uniform Commercial Code, which provides that "[i]f the court as a matter of law finds the contract or any clause of the contract to have been unconscionable at the time it was made the court may refuse to enforce the contract, or it may enforce the remainder of the contract without the unconscionable clause, or it may so limit the application of any unconscionable clause as to avoid any unconscionable result." U.C.C. § 302 (2002). Official Comment 1 explains that the purpose of policing against unconscionable contracts is to prevent oppression and unfair surprise (*Cf. Campbell Soup Co. v. Wentz,* 172 F.2d 80 (3rd Cir. 1948) and not to disturb the "allocation of risks because of superior bargaining power." U.C.C. § 302, Comment 1.

5. Substantive Limits on Donations Inter Vivos: The Donation *Omnium Bonorum*

Just as the Civil Code's provisions on lesion beyond moiety impose a substantive limit on the sale of an immovable, Article 1498 of the Civil Code imposes a significant substantive limit on donations inter vivos: the donor cannot divest himself of all of his property; he must reserve enough to provide for his own subsistence. La. Civ. Code art. 1498 (1996). If this rule is violated, a donation inter vivos can be nullified by the donor. Consider the following opinion and evaluate the court's attitude toward the donor's attempt to invalidate his own donation inter vivos.

Manichia v. Mahoney

45 So.3d 618 (La. App. 4 Cir. 2010)

LOMBARD, Judge. Plaintiff/appellant, Theodore Louis Manichia, appeals a granting of summary judgment in favor of defendants/appellees, Carole L. Garell Mahoney and Lanny Joseph Garell, dismissing all remaining claims against them in Mr. Manichia's suit to nullify a donation *inter vivos* of immovable property. For the reasons provided herein, the decision of the district court to grant appellees' motion for summary judgment is affirmed.

Factual and Procedural History

Appellant, Theodore Louis Manichia, executed a document dated June 30, 2005 which stated that he "does by these presents, irrevocably donate inter vivos, give, grant, transfer, set over" a tract of land, including "all the buildings and improvements thereon, rights ways, privileges and appurtenances thereto," and bearing the address of 6913 Highway 39 in Braithwaite, Louisiana, in Plaquemines Parish, to his niece, Carol L. Garell Mahoney and his nephew, Lanny Joseph Garell. This donation *inter vivos* was executed via authentic act and was notarized by Charles A. Arceneaux, and witnessed by Kathy Lutz and Kim Toupe.

In February of 2006, Mr. Manichia executed a document in which power-of-attorney status over his personal and financial affairs was granted to Kathleen Becnel Burmaster, who would serve as his "agent" in all matters related to Mr. Manichia's finance, property, donations, and medical decisions. At this time appellant also drafted a Last Will and Testament in which Ms. Burmaster would be the recipient of his estate.

On August 1, 2008, Mr. Manichia filed suit against Mr. Mahoney and Ms. Garell, seeking to declare the donation *inter vivos* of June 30, 2005 null and void . . .

On September 11, 2009, plaintiff . . . alleged a cause of action under La. Civ. Code art. 1498, which raises that a donation *inter vivos* shall not divest if the donor did not reserve for himself enough for subsistence. . . . [T]he trial court issued a written judgment on October 20, 2009 . . . and granted summary judgment in favor of defendants on all remaining claims. Plaintiff then brought forth this timely appeal.

Assignments of Error

. . . Plaintiff's assignments of error all pertain to his sole remaining claim that the donation *inter vivos* of June 30, 2005 is a nullity as a *donation omnium bonorum* under La. Civ. Code art. 1498, because it left him without enough for subsistence. In particular, plaintiff argues that the trial court erred in failing to determine plaintiff's donative intent and amount of property and money at the time of the donation. . . .

Law and Analysis

A donation *inter vivos* is a contract by which a person, called the donor, gratuitously divests himself, at present and irrevocably, of the thing given in favor of another, the donee, who accepts it. La. Civ. Code art. 1468. Capacity to donate *inter vivos* must exist at the time the donor makes the donation. La. Civ. Code art. 1471. A donation *inter vivos* shall be made by authentic act under the penalty of absolute nullity, unless otherwise expressly permitted by law. La. Civ. Code art. 1541. Because we do not find any evidence in the record that the plaintiff did not reserve to himself enough for subsistence, upon *de novo* review, we affirm the decision of the trial court's granting of summary judgment.

Plaintiff/appellant does not raise as assignments of error the determination of the trial court that the donation *inter vivos* instrument of June 30, 2005 was not valid as to form, or that it was lacking his signature. Appellant does argue, though, that he did not have requisite intent to donate his immovable property to appellees. However, "[a]n authentic act constitutes full proof of the agreement it contains, as against the parties, their heirs, and successors by universal or particular title." La. Civ. Code. art. 1835. Therefore, appellant's first assignment of error as to donative intent at the time of the donation is without merit.

Appellant's first and remaining assignments of error mainly involve his primary assertion on appeal, which is that the donation at issue is an absolutely null donation *omnium bonorum* under La. Civ. Code art. 1498. Art. 1498 pertains to the nullity of a donation *inter vivos* that divests a donor's entire patrimony, and provides as follows in pertinent part:

> The donation *inter vivos* shall in no case divest the donor of all his property: he must reserve to himself enough for subsistence. If he does not do so, a donation of a movable is null for the whole, and a donation of an immovable is null for the whole unless the donee has alienated the immovable by onerous title, in which case the donation of such immovable shall not be declared null on the ground that the donor did not reserve to himself enough for his subsistence, but the donee is bound to return the value of the immovable at the time the donee received it (emphasis added).

Where a donation is sought to be annulled on the ground that he would have divested himself of all of his property without enough for his subsistence, the burden of proof rests upon the plaintiff to prove that the donor has not reserved enough for his subsistence. *C.B. Lamkin, et al. v. Hanna*, (La. App. 2 Cir. 1961), 135 So.2d 659, 661; *see also Abshire v. Levine*, 87-1236 (La. App. 3 Cir. 8/28/89), 546 So.2d 642, 643 ("[t]he party seeking to avoid a donation as a donation *omnium bonorum* has the burden of proving that the donor did not retain enough for his subsistence.")

Plaintiff argues that his current monthly income amounts to approximately $306.00, but that his monthly expenses are $3,536.57. Plaintiff also raises questions regarding his ability to *currently* pay utilities, insurance, and other expenses. Essentially, plaintiff would have us make this subsistence determination on circumstances arising well after the making of the donation. However, La. Civ. Code art. 1498 requires that the determination of whether the donor (the plaintiff in this case) reserved enough property for his subsistence must be made from the circumstances existing at the time the donation was made. *LeBourgeois v. Yeutter*, 88-661 (La. App. 3 Cir. 10/4/89), 550 So.2d 314, 316, *rehearing denied*, November 17, 1989. The Louisiana Supreme Court addressed this issue long ago in *Succession of Quaglino*, 232 LA. 870, 95 So. 2d 481 (La. 1957), holding:

> Appellants' argument on this point seems to be that by conveying the real estate and the 46 shares of stock to his sons Philip Quaglino divested himself of all his property and did not reserve to himself enough for subsistence because when he died there were more debts than assets in his estate. Even if these conveyances were donations, which we have found they were not, there is no evidence in this record to show that **at the time these conveyances were made** the father did not reserve enough property for his subsistence.

Id., 232 La. at 888, 95 So.2d 481.

The current financial and property status of a donor is not at issue when considering whether a donor left enough for his own subsistence. Appellant did not raise the issue of donation *omnium bonorum* until after defendants' motion for summary judgment, and he did not present any genuine issue of material fact that he was left without enough for his subsistence **at the time of the donation.** In order to attack such a donation successfully, the plaintiff generally must prove conclusively that the donation divested the donor of all of his or her property. *Owen v. Owen*, (La. 1976), 336 So.2d 782, 786.

In their motion for summary judgment, appellees provided ample evidence regarding the validity of the donation instrument. Plaintiff's claim for nullity under La. Civ. Code art. 1498 was not raised until well after defendants' motion, but at the hearing on defendants' motion for summary judgment, plaintiff admitted on record to having nearly $170,000 in certificates of deposit (CD's) at the time of the donation at issue. The trial record also contains written confirmation from plaintiff and Ms. Burmaster that various certificates of deposit were in his possession on December 21, 2005. Appellant again attested to having as much in CD's as of December 2005 in his failed motion to proceed with this appeal *in forma pauperis*. Therefore, appellant's remaining assignments of error are without merit.

Conclusion

While a *pro se* litigant may be afforded some leeway or patience in the form of liberally construed pleading, plaintiff, as the party with the burden of proof on his claim for nullity under Art. 1498 at trial, has not presented a genuine issue of material fact in response to the defendants' pointing out that he clearly had enough for his own subsistence at the time of the donation. La. Code Civ. Proc. art. 966(B). As such, defendants are entitled to judgment as a matter of law on the plaintiff's sole remaining issue on appeal.

Because the defendants have pointed out to the court that there is a clear absence of factual support of plaintiff's claim that he is entitled to have the donation *inter vivos* of June 30, 2005 nullified under La. Civ. Code art. 1498, the decision of the trial court to grant their motion for summary judgment is affirmed.

AFFIRMED.

Notes and Questions

1. In *Manichia v. Mahoney*, 45 So.3d 618 (La. App. 4 Cir. 2010), note how the court addressed Theodore Manichia's first argument that he did not have the requisite intent to donate his immovable property to his niece and nephew. Referring to Article 1835 of the Civil Code, the court observed that Manichia signed the act of donation before two witnesses and a notary public. According to the court, this act was sufficient evidence of his donative intent. Compare the court's analysis of donative intent in *Manichia* to the analysis of testamentary capacity and undue influence in *Succession of Cooper*, 830 So.2d 1087 (La. App. 2 Cir. 2002). In which case did the court engage in more searching scrutiny?

2. Do you agree with the Civil Code's policy that prohibited Manichia from changing his mind about donating so much of his property to his niece and nephew? Under what circumstances would you allow someone like Manichia to undo a donation?

3. Do you agree with the policy underlying Article 1498 that would allow Mr. Manichia to recover his donated property if, at the time of his donation, he had not reserved enough property for his own subsistence?

4. Can a donation omnium bonorum be nullified by someone other than the donor or a forced heir? For the proposition that this right is personal, see, for example, *Succession of Moran v. Moran*, 25 So.2d 302, 303 (La. App. 1 Cir. 1946). A third party to the donation, such as a creditor of the donor, would need to explore alternative routes, including the revocatory action. *See* La. Civ. Code arts. 2936–2043 (1984).

5. Compare the policy reasons supporting the limit on donations inter vivos under Article 1498 of the Civil Code to the right of a vendor of immovable property to rescind a sale for lesion beyond moiety? Which substantive limit on the effect of voluntary transfers is more justifiable in your view? Are they both equally justified?

6. Testate Successions

In the Civil Code, the term "succession" means "the transmission of the estate of the deceased to his successors." La. Civ. Code art. 871 (1981). In Louisiana, we distinguish two kinds of successions. *Testate succession* results from the will of the deceased person contained in a *valid testament* that disposes of all the deceased's property at death, executed in a form prescribed by law. La. Civ. Code art. 874 (1981). Persons whose right to inherit is established in a testament are called *legatees*, La. Civ. Code art. 876 (1981). In contrast, *intestate succession* results when a person dies without a valid testament or when the testament does not dispose of all of the decedent's property at death, La. Civ. Code art. 880 (1981). The person has died "intestate" and the succession "results from provisions of law in favor of certain persons, in default of testate successors." La. Civ. Code art. 875 (1981). Persons identified by law as entitled to inherit some or all of the decedent's estate through intestate succession are called *heirs*, La. Civ. Code art. 876 (1981).

The term *"estate"* in this context means "the property, rights, and obligations that a person leaves after his death, whether the property exceeds the charges or the charges exceed the property, or whether he has only left charges without any property." La. Civ. Code art. 872 (1981). When a person dies, all of the decedent's estate immediately passes to the decedent's successors, whether testate legatees or intestate heirs. La. Civ. Code art. 935 (1997).

A decedent's property will be distributed in accordance with the directives in the testament, if: (1) the decedent has properly executed a testament that directs to whom the decedent's property should pass upon death; (2) the estate is sufficiently solvent; (3) the provisions of the testament do not contravene any statute or provision of the Civil Code; and (4) the legatees who are to receive the property have capacity to receive gifts at the time of the decedent's death. Again, a succession transmits ownership from the decedent to the legatees at the time of the decedent's death.

When a person dies without a valid will in effect or leaves a will that does not dispose of all of the decedent's property, intestate succession distributes the decedent's estate or the undisposed property according to provisions of law which allocate the decedent's estate according to the specific relationship of the decedent to potential heirs. *See* La. Civ. Code arts. 880–902. Generally speaking, descendants— like children, grandchildren—inherit the decedent's estate ahead of other relatives when the decedent dies intestate. La. Civ. Code art. 888 (1981). If a decedent's child dies before the decedent, the deceased child's children will be said to "represent" the predeceased child. La. Civ. Code art. 882 (1981, amended 1990, 1996).

The children and grandchildren of the decedent inherit the decedent's separate property in full ownership. La. Civ. Code art. 888 (1981). This is consistent with the principle of Louisiana matrimonial property law which provides that "[t]he separate property of a spouse is his exclusively." La. Civ. Code art. 2341 (1979). Descendants inherit community property of the decedent, subject to a usufruct held by the decedent's surviving spouse. *See* La. Civ. Code art. 890 (1981, amended 1982, 1990, 1996). Community property, which includes property acquired by the spouses during their marriage, is co-owned by each spouse who holds a present undivided one-half interest in the property. La. Civ. Code arts. 2336, 2338 (1979). We will study the usufruct, which is generally defined as a real right of limited duration on the property of another, when we discuss dismemberment of ownership.

When the decedent has no descendants, other rules apply. The surviving spouse inherits all of the community property in full ownership; and the surviving parents and surviving siblings or their descendants inherit the decedent's separate property. *See* La. Civ. Code arts. 889, 891–93 (1981, amended 2004). The spouse, the decedent's ascendants, then collateral relatives of the decedent take the decedent's separate property, in that order, when the decedent leaves neither children or their descendants, siblings or their descendants, or parents. La. Civ. Code arts. 894–96 (1981). In the unlikely event that a person dies intestate without blood or adopted relatives, or a spouse not judicially separated, the deceased's estate will devolve to the state. La. Civ. Code art. 902 (1981).

You can further explore all of the detailed rules when you study successions. Consider the following opinion in light of its two themes: testamentary capacity as one of the essential prerequisites for a valid will; and undue influence as one of the most common ways for disappointed heirs to challenge a will when the decedent had testamentary capacity.

Succession of Cooper

830 So.2d 1087 (La. App. 2 Cir. 2002)

KOSTELKA, Judge. The three adult children of Quitman Thomas Cooper, Jr. ("Mr. Cooper") appeal the trial court's grant of a motion for involuntary dismissal which served to dismiss the childrens' claims to annul the probate of Mr. Cooper's testament. For the following reasons, we affirm.

Facts

Mr. Cooper died on July 26, 2000 following a stroke in October, 1999 and months of illness. His adult children, Edwina Cooper Black ("Edwina"), Gary Cooper ("Gary"), and Patsy Cooper Lewis ("Patsy") (collectively, "appellants") sought to annul a notarial testament executed by their father on November 2, 1999, wherein he left virtually the entirety of his estate to his wife, Juanita Cooper ("Juanita").

Mr. Cooper had previously been married for approximately forty years to the appellants' mother until her death in 1981. After his wife's death, Mr. Cooper began seeing Juanita. Although the appellants reportedly enjoyed a good relationship with their father, there was apparently some early tension over his relationship with Juanita; however, it seems that as time passed, the tension eased and the appellants came to accept Juanita.

In September, 1999, Mr. Cooper was hospitalized with pneumonia. During his hospitalization, he suffered a stroke and remained hospitalized until late October. Appellants allege that the effects of the stroke were significant and that their father was taking several medications. They further claim that Mr. Cooper's communication skills were particularly impacted by the stroke, alleging that he suffered from aphasia—a language disorder caused by damage to the language centers of the brain resulting from the stroke.

When Mr. Cooper was discharged, Juanita cared for him in his home. On the evening of October 27, 1999, without the knowledge of the appellants, Mr. Cooper and Juanita were married by a justice of the peace at Mr. Cooper's home.

A few days later, Gary, who lived out-of-town, returned to Monroe, Louisiana, where Mr. Cooper lived. Appellants claim that Gary became concerned about his father's ability to handle his own finances when he allegedly noticed some unpaid medical bills. Years before, Mr. Cooper had opened a joint bank account with Gary, so Gary and Patsy went to the bank to inquire if Mr. Cooper was having financial problems. Instead, they discovered that their father had a checking account and money market accounts with combined balances of over $30,000. The appellants claim that at that time, Gary opened two new accounts in both his and his father's names, transferring most of the money into these accounts.

That very day, Juanita presented herself at the same bank with her and Mr. Cooper's marriage license, asking that her name be placed on all of Mr. Cooper's accounts. The bank officer telephoned Patsy to inform her of the situation. Later, Gary and Patsy returned to the bank, and the bank officer informed them that she had instructed Juanita a power of attorney would be necessary to change the names on the accounts. At that point, Gary and Patsy transferred the funds to an account in their names only.

Subsequently, Robert Curry ("Mr. Curry"), a Monroe attorney, was contacted to prepare a testament for Mr. Cooper.[1] Mr. Curry prepared a notarial testament and on November 2, 1999 brought it to Mr. Cooper's home with two employees from his firm to act as witnesses, and the testament was duly executed. In this testament, Mr. Cooper left everything to his wife, Juanita, save $1 to each of his children. Wendell L. Black, Jr. ("Black"), Mr. Cooper's grandson (who was also married to Juanita's daughter), was named executor.

In December, 1999, Mr. Cooper was admitted to the hospital. His condition worsened and he remained hospitalized until March, 2000. He was able to go home for a short time but soon was re-hospitalized until his death on July 26, 2000.

After Mr. Cooper's death, appellants became aware that their father had executed the testament in favor of Juanita. In August, 2000, they filed a Petition for Notice and Opposition to Probate of Testament and learned that it had already been probated. Subsequently, appellants filed a rule to show cause and this action proceeded to a three-day trial to annul the probate. At the close of appellants' case, the appellees, Black and Juanita, moved for an involuntary dismissal, which the trial court granted. This appeal ensued.

---

1. Mr. Curry had also prepared a power of attorney for Mr. Cooper in favor of Juanita, which had been executed the day prior to the testament.

Discussion

Lack of Capacity

By their first assignment of error, the appellants submit that the trial court erred in its determination that Mr. Cooper had the capacity to execute the November, 1999 testament, arguing that as a result of his stroke, Mr. Cooper was unable to read the testament presented to him. The burden of proving Mr. Cooper's lack of testamentary capacity is a heavy one for the appellants.

All persons have capacity to give and receive donations inter vivos and mortis causa, except as expressly provided by law. La. C.C. art. 1470. There is a presumption in favor of testamentary capacity. *Cupples, supra, citing Succession of Lyons*, 452 So.2d 1161 (La. 1984); *Succession of Kilpatrick*, 422 So.2d 464 (La. App. 2d Cir. 1982), *writ denied*, 429 So.2d 126 (1983). Testamentary capacity means the donor must "be able to comprehend generally the nature and consequences of the disposition that he is making." La. C.C. art. 1477; *Succession of Lyons, supra*; *Succession of Dodson*, 27,969 (La. App. 2d Cir. 02/28/96), 669 So.2d 642.

A party alleging lack of testamentary capacity must overcome the presumption of capacity by clear and convincing evidence. La. C.C. art. 1482. To prove a matter by "clear and convincing" evidence means to demonstrate that the existence of a disputed fact is highly probable, that is, much more probable than its nonexistence. *Mack v. Evans*, 35,364 (La. App. 2d Cir. 12/05/01), 804 So.2d 730, *writ denied*, 2002-0422 (La. 04/19/02). . . .

Here, the appellants argue that their father, as a result of his stroke, was incapable of reading the testament prepared for him by Mr. Curry, and, thus, lacked the capacity to execute the testament in its given form. To support their claim that Mr. Cooper was mentally unable to read, the only expert witness offered by the appellants was Allison Drost, a speech therapist who had worked with Mr. Cooper while he was both in and out of the hospital. She stated that as a result of Mr. Cooper's stroke, he suffered from aphasia, a disorder affecting the language centers of the brain. She explained that Mr. Cooper experienced both expressive aphasia, impeding his ability to express himself via speech and/or gestures, and mild auditory aphasia, impeding his ability to understand the spoken word. Ms. Drost acknowledged that the ability to understand the written word differed from the ability to understand the spoken word. She also stated that a person does not have to be able to speak in order to understand. Finally, Ms. Drost admitted that Mr. Cooper understood 90 percent of the time the words he was reading. There was no other medical testimony regarding the effects of the stroke on Mr. Cooper, and the only other witnesses bearing on Mr. Cooper's alleged inability to read were the appellants.

On the other hand, Mr. Curry, the attorney who drafted the testament, as well as notarized it, stated that he felt "very comfortable" with Mr. Cooper's capacity to execute the testament in the form it was presented to him. Although Mr. Curry noted that Mr. Cooper had not instructed him personally as to the contents of the testament prior to its being drafted, he testified that he would not have notarized it had he felt uncomfortable with Mr. Cooper's capacity. Mr. Curry also stated that at the time of execution, Mr. Cooper appeared to read the testament in his presence while Mr. Curry went over the pertinent provisions, specifically the bequests made. Significantly, Mr. Curry stated that upon concluding his review of the testament with Mr. Cooper, Mr. Cooper started to sign it but was stopped by Mr. Curry. Such action by Mr. Cooper indicates that he understood what Mr. Curry had explained, and that the explanation had concluded. Thus, by implication, it appears that Mr. Cooper had read the testament and understood its contents as well. Mr. Curry had to interrupt Mr. Cooper from executing the testament to ask him to state whether the document, as presented, was his last will and testament, to which Mr. Cooper answered yes. Then, Mr. Curry allowed Mr. Cooper to execute the testament, which Mr. Cooper did unassisted. In addition to Mr. Curry, the trial court also heard testimony from the two individuals employed by Mr. Curry's law firm who had witnessed the execution of the testament, both of whom opined that Mr. Cooper appeared to understand fully his actions. Significantly, one of the witnesses to the testament had also been a witness to the power of attorney the day before and had entered into some discourse with Mr. Cooper at that time.

After hearing the evidence presented by the appellants, the trial court upheld Mr. Cooper's testament and rejected the appellants' claim that their father lacked testamentary capacity. Appellants argue this was error. Resolution of conflicts in testimony and credibility determinations in succession proceedings are within the province of the trial court. *Succession of Fletcher*, 94-1426 (La. App. 3d Cir. 04/05/95), 653 So.2d 119, writ denied, 95-1105 (La.06/16/95), 655 So.2d 338. Although the trial court, in its reasons for judgment, made no explicit statement as to the issue of Mr. Cooper's ability or inability to read, the court noted that it was not satisfied that the appellants had proved their father was legally incapable of making his testament, specifically determining that the appellants had failed to carry their required burden of proof. On this record, it does not appear that the trial court was manifestly erroneous in its factual finding, and the dismissal of the appellants' claim on this issue was proper.

Undue Influence

Having determined that the trial court correctly determined the appellants' failure to prove Mr. Cooper's incapacity, we can turn to the issue of whether his testament was the result of undue influence, as also alleged by the appellants.[3] In their second assignment of error, the appellants argue that the trial court erred in its determination that the testament in favor of Juanita could not have been the product of undue influence because of her marriage to Mr. Cooper. Appellants urge that the trial court's legal error interdicted its fact-finding process on their claim of undue influence by Juanita.

---

3. The capacity of a donor must be assured before a claim of undue influence may be addressed. See, La. C.C. art. 1479, Comment (b).

Prior to 1991, evidence of undue influence was limited in Louisiana. Subsequently, in 1991, the Louisiana Legislature enacted provisions in connection with the redefinition of Louisiana's laws on forced heirship. Louisiana C.C. art. 1479 states:

> A donation inter vivos or mortis causa shall be declared null upon proof that it is the product of influence by the donee or another person that so impaired the volition of the donor as to substitute the volition of the donee or other person for the volition of the donor.

La. C.C. art. 1483 sets forth the applicable burden of proof for claims of undue influence, stating:

> A person who challenges a donation because of fraud, duress, or undue influence, must prove it by clear and convincing evidence. However, if, at the time the donation was made or the testament executed, a relationship of confidence existed between the donor and the wrongdoer and the wrongdoer was not then related to the donor by affinity, consanguinity or adoption, the person who challenges the donation need only prove the fraud, duress, or undue influence by a preponderance of the evidence.

Although Article 1483 does lessen the burden for those in a relationship of confidence with the donor to a "preponderance of the evidence" standard, the article does not relax the burden for those confidantes who are related by marriage (i.e., "affinity"). Thus, as Mr. Cooper and Juanita were married at the time his testament was executed, the appellants are required to prove undue influence by "clear and convincing evidence." Such issues involve questions of fact, and the trial court's determination will not be disturbed unless clearly wrong. *Succession of Anderson*, 26,947 (La. App. 2d Cir. 05/10/95), 656 So.2d 42, *writ denied*, 95-1789 (La. 10/27/95), 662 So.2d 3; *Succession of Hamiter*, 519 So.2d 341 (La. App. 2d Cir. 1988), *writ denied*, 521 So.2d 1170 (La. 1988).

The concept of undue influence in our case law has been inexact. As a subjective standard, it is difficult to define, and thus prove. Article 1479 states that undue influence requires a showing that the "volition" or free will of the donor was replaced by the will of someone else. "Mere advice, or persuasion, or kindness and assistance, should not constitute influence that would destroy the free agency of a donor and substitute someone else's volition for his own." See, Comment (b) to La. C.C. art. 1479.

The appellants point to the trial court's oral reasons for judgment, urging that the trial court mistakenly relied upon and misinterpreted *Succession of Reeves*, 97-20 (La. App. 3d Cir. 10/29/97), 704 So.2d 252, *writ granted*, 98-0581 (La. 05/01/98), 805 So.2d 185.[4] Appellants argue that the trial court erroneously interpreted *Reeves* to stand for the proposition that a spouse cannot be guilty of undue influence, and such mistaken reliance led to the court's erroneous determination that Juanita had not exercised undue influence on Mr. Cooper. Appellants maintain that the trial

---

4. *Reeves* was dismissed by the parties prior to being considered by the Louisiana Supreme Court.

court's mistaken reliance on *Reeves* constituted legal error and interdicted its fact-finding process. However, our reading of the trial court's reasons for judgment, as well as other statements of the court, do not indicate an erroneous interpretation of *Reeves*. Instead, the trial court noted that an opponent to a testament has a heavy burden to prove undue influence. Such a statement, in light of La. C.C. arts. 1479 and 1483, is correct, and the trial court properly assessed the evidence before it in determining that the appellants failed to meet the requisite burden of proof for an undue influence claim.

Specifically, appellants claim that Juanita exercised undue influence and manipulation over their father, resulting in his bequeathing the entirety of his estate to her. The appellants argue that because Juanita was with Mr. Cooper for much of the time he was hospitalized, she was able to convince him the appellants wanted to place him in a nursing home. They further claim Juanita had persuaded Mr. Cooper that his children had stolen his money when they transferred the funds to new accounts. Appellants maintain that Juanita purposefully leveled such accusations against them to Mr. Cooper, clearly influencing him to execute his testament in her favor.

At trial, the appellants had the burden to prove by clear and convincing evidence that Juanita exercised undue influence on Mr. Cooper to execute his testament in her favor, which they failed to do. Although appellants put forth allegations claiming to be evidence of Juanita's undue influence over their father, particularly in connection with her repeated declarations that Gary and Patsy had stolen Mr. Cooper's money, that evidence, at best, is circumstantial, if not mere assumption. The fact that Juanita may have made accusatory statements to the appellants might show her state of mind but does not necessarily prove that she imposed her opinion on Mr. Cooper. On the other hand, we note that Mr. Cooper and Juanita were not newly acquainted. They had been in a relationship with one another for almost twenty years when they married in October, 1999. The testimony throughout the trial consistently showed that Mr. Cooper and Juanita loved one another, and that Juanita nursed Mr. Cooper during his extended illness. There is no evidence that Juanita exerted physical coercion or duress over Mr. Cooper. Further, from the evidence presented at trial, it is just as reasonable to suppose that Mr. Cooper simply made a decision to provide for Juanita, his companion and wife, when he saw his life nearing an end as opposed to the claims that he was unduly influenced to do so by her.

The trial court did not misapply the proper legal standards stated in the applicable statutory law or jurisprudence; moreover, considering the evidence presented at trial, the trial court's finding of fact that Juanita did not unduly influence Mr. Cooper was not manifestly wrong. This assignment of error is without merit.

Conclusion

For the foregoing reasons, the judgment in favor of Wendell L. Black Jr., executor of the Succession of Quitman Thomas Cooper, Jr., and Juanita I. Cooper is hereby affirmed at the appellants' costs.

AFFIRMED.

Notes and Questions

1. In *Succession of Cooper*, 830 So.2d 1087 (La. App. 2 Cir. 2002), what facts were important to the court's determination that Quitman Cooper had the capacity to execute a valid testament in November 1999? Who would have inherited his property if the court had found that Cooper lacked capacity to execute the will? Consult La. Civ. Code arts. 881–82, 885, and 888 (1981).

2. In addition to challenging their father's testamentary capacity to make a will, Quitman Cooper's three adult children asserted that the will should be annulled because their father was subject to undue influence by Juanita Cooper. Articles 1479 and 1483 of the Civil Code provide the most important rules governing allegations of undue influence. What test for undue influence does this court apply?

3. As was the case in *Succession of Cooper*, undue influence claims are often paired with challenges to the testamentary capacity of a testator. Undue influence is not easy to prove, but challenges have become more common in recent years as Louisiana has weakened the rights of children to inherit, as a matter of law, a "forced portion" of their parents' estate. For a detailed discussion of this trend, see John A. Lovett, *Love, Loyalty and the Louisiana Civil Code: Rules, Standards and Hybrid Discretion in a Mixed Jurisdiction*, 72 La. L. Rev. 924, 981–95 (2012).

4. For a discussion of the controversial appellate court decision in *Succession of Reeves*, 704 So.2d 252, 259 (La. App. 3 Cir. 1997) (holding that a claim of undue influence against a surviving spouse can succeed only if the challenger shows evidence of physical or emotional abuse, fraud, deceit, or criminal conduct), see Lovett, *supra*, 987–90; Katherine Shaw Spaht, *The Remnant of Forced Heirship: The Interrelationship of Undue Influence, What's Become of Disinherison, and the Unfinished Business of the Stepparent Usufruct*, 60 La. L. Rev. 637, 649–54 (2000) (criticizing *Reeves* for: (1) erroneously grafting onto the Civil Code additional requirements for a successful challenge against a testator's spouse because of undue influence; and (2) undermining the protections that the undue influence law was designed to provide for vulnerable descendants at risk of disinherison at the hands of strangers and stepparents).

5. A topical succession controversy discussed widely in Louisiana and elsewhere involved Tom Benson, self-made billionaire and owner of the New Orleans Saints and New Orleans Pelicans. Late in his life, Benson apparently altered his succession plans in favor of his then current wife, Gayle Benson, and withdrew legacies in favor of his daughter, Renee, and her children Rita and Ryan. Benson's daughter and grandchildren went to court contending that Benson had become mentally unfit to manage his own affairs. Civil District Court Judge Kern Reese, however, found that Benson suffered only from "mild cognitive impairment," not untypical for his age range, and was therefore still competent at the time he made the changes to his estate plans.

On March 15, 2018, at the age 90, Benson died. Before his death, Benson arranged for his wife, Gayle, to have the sole voting power over the NFL and NBA franchises.

His last will leaves his estate to a Revocable Trust, the terms of which are not public record. In the event this trust does not exist at his death, Benson's will leaves his estate to another trust, the terms of which are set forth in his will. According to these terms, Gayle will receive the income from the trust until she dies. Upon her death, the principal in the trust will devolve one-half to her estate and one-half to his charitable foundation. The will leaves no inheritance to his daughter and grandchildren. What type of challenges could these disappointed heirs mount? What burden of proof would they need to discharge? For a link to Benson's will and additional background, see Ramon Antonio Vargas, Tom Benson's Last Will Makes Clear Who Was In, Out of His Inner Circle Late in his life, The Advocate (Mar. 16, 2018), *at* https://www.theadvocate.com/new_orleans/news/courts/article _cdd2e754-2997-11e8-97f6-ab67a9092c3e.html (Sept. 25, 2018).

B. Involuntary Transfers of Ownership

At the beginning of this chapter, we observed that ownership can be transferred from one owner to another either voluntarily or involuntarily. Involuntary transfers can be broken down into four general categories.

In one broad category of involuntary transfers, creditors exercise their legal authority to force a sale of the debtor's property. This sale results in the transfer of ownership from one private owner to another. A vast body of Louisiana law addresses this subject. Book IV (execution of judgments) and Book V (summary and executory proceedings) of the Louisiana Code of Civil Procedure, Titles XX (Security), XX-A (Pledge), XXI (Privileges), XXII (Mortgages) of the Louisiana Civil Code, along with Chapter 9 of Louisiana's Commercial Laws (Secured Transactions, La. Rev. Stat. § 10:9.101 *et seq.*) and Federal Bankruptcy law are all relevant to understanding how these kinds of involuntary transfers take place and what limits and safeguards the law will impose. In Chapter Four, we saw an example of this kind of involuntary transfer of ownership in *Bayou Fleet Partnership v. Dravo Basic Materials Co.*, 106 F.3d 691 (5th Cir. 1997).

The second broad category of involuntary transfers involves the transfer of ownership from a private person to the government (either the U.S. Government, the State of Louisiana, or one of the state's political subdivisions) and occasionally to a private company that serves as a common carrier. Under the United States Constitution, the Louisiana Constitution, and various state statutes, government entities and common carriers like railroads, utilities and pipeline companies may exercise this power of *expropriation* in pursuit of certain public purposes as long as just compensation is paid to the property owner and due process requirements are satisfied. *See* U.S. Const. Amend. V; La. Const. art. 1, §4(B) (1974, amended 2010). Many common law states use the term "eminent domain" to describe a state's general power to acquire private property for public purposes and use the technical term "expropriation" to refer to the actual acquisition of title under the broad eminent domain power. In Louisiana, the term expropriation has the same general meaning as eminent domain.

A final category of involuntary transfers involves "private takings." *See generally* Abraham Bell, *Private Takings*, 76 UNIV. CHI. L. REV. 517 (2009). These involve instances in which Louisiana law allows ownership or other real rights to be transferred from one person to another as a result of specific private relationships between two property owners who are often neighbors. For example, a property owner who constructs a building that encroaches on his neighbor's property, may under certain circumstances, acquire a predial servitude on his neighbor's property that will allow the encroaching building to remain in place. La. Civ. Code art. 670 (1977). Moreover, the owner of an enclosed or "landlocked" estate may obtain a servitude of passage over his neighbor's property to gain access to the nearest public road or utility upon compensating the neighbor for the right of passage and indemnifying the neighbor for any damage. In other circumstances, the enclosed estate owner can acquire such a servitude without paying any compensation at all. La. Civ. Code arts. 689–696.1 (1977, amended 2012).

This chapter will focus on the second category of involuntary transfers — expropriation of private property by the state or its political subdivisions and to a lesser extent expropriation by common carriers.

1. Eminent Domain: Rationales and Federal Constitutional Limits

. . . nor shall private property be taken for public use, without just compensation.

U.S. Constitution, Amendment V (1791).

Even before the founding of the United States, it was generally understood in English and European law that the state enjoyed broad powers to acquire private property for certain kinds of public ends without the consent of the property owner. This power to take private property — also called eminent domain — was "conditioned on the requirement that the state could pay some form of compensation to the property owner" for the loss of his property.

Influential natural law thinkers in Continental Europe had differing views on what kinds of public ends could justify the exercise of eminent domain. Some writers, such as Samuel von Pufendorf, took the view that the state could only exercise its power of eminent domain in cases of urgent or strict necessity such as to construct a fort or to build a road around some natural obstacle in the landscape. Others, such as Hugo Grotius, took a broader view, arguing that the state should be able to take private property to promote the general public welfare for projects such as public markets, universities, or other public works. *See generally* DAVID DANA AND THOMAS MERRILL, PROPERTY: TAKINGS 20–21 (2002). This debate as to whether the valid justifications for the exercise of eminent domain should be viewed narrowly or broadly has become particularly important in the wake of the decision by the

United States Supreme Court in *Kelo v. City of New London*, 545 U.S. 469 (2005), which is featured below. For a rich discussion of the contemporary constitutional debate, see ILYA SOMIN, THE GRASPING HAND, *KELO V. CITY OF NEW LONDON* AND THE LIMITS OF EMINENT DOMAIN 35–111 (2015).

After the approval of the U.S. Constitution at the Philadelphia Convention on September 17, 1778, and its submission to the States for ratification, most of the state conventions urged that a bill of rights should be added. Interestingly, although many specific proposed amendments surfaced during this period, none of the amendments contained anything resembling the Takings Clause of the Fifth Amendment. Instead, we now know that the Takings Clause was added to the Bill of Rights because of James Madison's intervention. Madison proposed an initial version declaring that no person "be obliged to relinquish his property, where it may be necessary for public use, without a just compensation." A select committee, including representatives from each state, reworked Madison's initial proposal into its current form: "nor shall private property be taken for public use without just compensation." Unfortunately, history has not availed us of the committee's deliberations. It appears that the Takings Clause was approved without any further debate or discussion. Madison's primary motivation for adding the Takings Clause to the Constitution might very well have been to protect property owners from physical expropriations carried out by hostile political majorities who sought to redistribute wealth and property to their political supporters. William Michael Treanor, *The Original Understanding of the Takings Clause and the Political Process*, 95 COLUM. L. REV. 782 (1995).

In any event, when the Bill of Rights was submitted to the States for ratification, the Takings Clause appears to have remained non-controversial as there is little record of contemporaneous discussions and none as to any opposition. DANA AND MERRILL, *supra*, 9–14. One of the few contemporary references merely mentions that the clause "was probably intended to restrain the arbitrary and oppressive mode of obtaining supplies for the army, and other public uses, by impressment, as was too frequently practiced during the revolutionary war, without any compensation whatsoever." 1 ST. GEORGE TUCKER, BLACKSTONE'S COMMENTARIES: WITH NOTES OF REFERENCE TO THE CONSTITUTION AND LAWS OF THE FEDERAL GOVERNMENT OF THE UNITED STATES AND OF THE COMMONWEALTH OF VIRGINIA 305–06 (orig. ed. 1803, reprinted 1996), quoted in DANA AND MERRILL, *supra*, 12. Perhaps the main lesson that we can glean from this brief history is that "the Takings Clause simply codified the established practice [in England and the American colonies] of providing compensation when property was condemned or appropriated for public uses." *Id*. at 15–16.

If the government's power to take private property for a public use was so well understood, one preliminary question remains: why was compensation required at all? Two rationales were offered at the time of the framing of the Constitution and Bill of Rights. One explanation stems from the notion of "*horizontal equity*," which was conceived by natural law thinkers such as von Pufendorf and Vattel. Compensation is required when the government takes property for a public use or purpose to preserve a measure of equity and fairness among property owners in the community. If one property owner were forced to relinquish his property to serve some public end without receiving compensation from the public fisc, this property owner would be harmed while other property owners who were untouched by the taking would receive a windfall. Just compensation is thus required to make sure that each property owner in a community receives his "just share" and that all similarly positioned property owners are required to make the same contribution in support of the workings of government and public welfare. Dana and Merrill, *supra*, at 21–22 (citing William Stoebuck, *A General Theory of Eminent Domain*, 47 WASH. L. REV. 553, 584 (1972)). This notion of "horizontal equity" among property owners still remains a powerful idea, especially since it has received explicit endorsement from the United States Supreme Court. *See Armstrong v. United States*, 364 U.S. 40, 49 (1960) ("The Fifth Amendment's guarantee that private property shall not be taken for a public use without just compensation was designed to bar Government from forcing some people alone to bear public burdens which, in all fairness and justice, should be borne by the public as a whole."); William Michael Treanor, *The Armstrong Principle, The Narratives of Takings, and Compensation Statutes*, 38 WM. & MARY L. REV. 1151 (1997).

A second, and perhaps complimentary, rationale for compensation focuses on the preservation of "*vertical equity*," which pertains to the relationship between the state as sovereign and the individual property owner as subject. Blackstone offers a particularly powerful introduction of this notion into contemporary American discourse:

> [T]he public good is in nothing more essentially interested, than in the protection of every individual's private rights, as modeled by the municipal law. In this, and similar cases the legislature can, and indeed frequently does, interpose, and compel the individual to acquiesce. But how does it interpose and compel? Not by absolutely stripping the subject of his property in an arbitrary manner, but by giving him a full indemnification and equivalent for the injury thereby sustained. *The public is now considered as an individual, treating with an individual for an exchange.* All the legislature does is to oblige the owner to alienate his possessions for a reasonable price; and even this is an exertion of power, which the legislature indulges with caution, and which nothing but the legislature can perform.

1 WILLIAM BLACKSTONE, COMMENTARIES ON THE LAW OF ENGLAND *135 (1768) (emphasis added). Notice Blackstone's two-part argument here. First, if the government wants the property of one of its constituents, it must act with express legislative authority. Second, when it acts in this manner, it must at least enter the marketplace and transact with the property owner just as if it were another market participant. This means that it could only require the condemned property owner to give up his property for a fair price—just compensation. DANA & MERRILL, *supra*, at 23–24.

Modern property law scholarship has shed more light on the question of when the government should or should not be able to exercise its power of eminent domain. Authors in this field have focused on the nature of the market facing the government when it seeks to acquire a particular resource. When the market for the resource desired by the government is "thick"—when there are many potential sellers or suppliers of the resource—the government should be able to acquire the resource just like any other market participant by entering the marketplace to shop for and negotiate for the best price it can obtain. Thus, when a local school district needs to buy paper, pencils and books for students, the government should act like any other private person and buy what it needs from suppliers willing to sell to the government at prices set by the market.

However, when the market for a particular resource is unusually "thin"—when, for instance, there is only one possible seller of the resource sought by the government and there are no substitute resources available—the seller will have a monopoly. In those situations of "bilateral monopoly" the government's use of eminent domain appears more readily justified.

One of the most common examples of such a bilateral monopoly arises when the government needs to acquire a long, linear tract of land to construct and operate a public road. Suppose, for instance, the State of Louisiana decides that it needs to build a new state highway from Opelousas to Ville Platte. The State Department of Transportation and Development (DOTD) studies the topography between the two cities and determines the most practical, safest and direct route, given the natural features of the land, such as bayous and swamps, and existing manmade constructions, such as railroads and towns. The State could start acquiring the land it needs to build the highway along that route. If it succeeds in reaching agreements with 45 out of the 50 property owners whose land was crossed by the announced route, any of the last five property owners, realizing that they held the last parcels needed to complete the highway, could "holdout" for a payment that far exceeded the normal fair market value of the property. In the absence of eminent domain, these property owners, or even the very last property owner, might be able to demand an extraordinary ransom-like payment from the State before agreeing to sell those final pieces of land necessary to complete the highway. This could dramatically raise the costs of the public project, burden taxpayers, and possibly give these last property owners an opportunity to obtain windfall prices far in excess of the sums of money received by the other property owners who voluntarily negotiated with the State earlier on. This kind of situation can likewise arise in common carrier contexts, for instance, when railroads or pipeline companies need to acquire long, linear tracts of land.

Eminent domain may be needed by governments to acquire non-linear parcels as well. Suppose the government wants to build a new public airport, military installation, public park or monument. In all of these situations, there may be just one location suitable for the project. In the absence of eminent domain, the government would find itself facing a monopoly situation in which the "transaction costs" and the final purchase price for the property could be so high that the project will never be undertaken.

Of course, there will always be borderline cases in which there might not be a single location suitable or a single seller of the resource, but the market for the particular recourse at issue might be *relatively thin*. These borderline cases simply return us to the debates among the natural law thinkers of Continental Europe who argued over whether eminent domain could be justified only when necessity was strict or urgent or whether promotion of the general public welfare was all that was required to justify eminent domain.

Over the last six decades, there has been an explosion in commentary exploring the rationales for the takings clause in all of its dimensions and for the compensation requirement in particular. For a useful overview, see generally Dana & Merrill, 32–57, 169–190. For another succinct account, see CHRISTOPHER SERKIN, THE LAW OF PROPERTY 243–79 (2d ed. 2016). Among the most prominent and influential commentaries are Frank I. Michelman, *Property, Utility, and Fairness: Comments on the Ethical Foundations of "Just Compensation" Law*, 80 HARV. L. REV. 1165 (1967); Joseph L. Sax, *Takings and the Police Power*, 74 YALE L.J. 36 (1964); Joseph L. Sax, *Takings, Private Property and Public Rights*, 81 YALE. L.J. 149 (1971); RICHARD A. EPSTEIN, TAKINGS: PRIVATE PROPERTY AND THE POWER OF EMINENT DOMAIN (1985).

It should be noted that many of these commentaries focus on another question posed by the Takings Clause: when does the clause disable government regulation of property that restricts what a property owner can do with her property unless compensation is payed to the property owner? This body of law is known as the *regulatory takings doctrine*. It has its conceptual origins in Justice Oliver Wendel Holmes majority opinion in *Pennsylvania Coal Co. v. Mahon*, 260 U.S. 393, 415 (1922), in which he observed that "while property may be regulated to a certain extent, if regulation goes too far it will be recognized as a taking." Although the regulatory takings doctrine is a rich and fascinating subject, we will leave it aside as it is usually covered in courses covering public land use regulation and zoning.

Now consider the United State Supreme Court's decision in *Kelo v. City of New London*, 545 U.S. 469 (2005). This is easily the most controversial and best known decision in the last fifty years addressing the "public use" limitation found in the Takings Clause.

Kelo v. City of New London
545 U.S. 469 (2005)

JUSTICE STEVENS. In 2000, the city of New London approved a development plan that, in the words of the Supreme Court of Connecticut, was "projected to create in excess of 1,000 jobs, to increase tax and other revenues, and to revitalize an economically distressed city, including its downtown and waterfront areas." 268 Conn. 1, 5, 843 A.2d 500, 507 (2004). In assembling the land needed for this project, the city's development agent has purchased property from willing sellers and proposes to use the power of eminent domain to acquire the remainder of the property from unwilling owners in exchange for just compensation. The question presented is whether the city's proposed disposition of this property qualifies as a "public use" within the meaning of the Takings Clause of the Fifth Amendment to the Constitution.

The city of New London (hereinafter City) sits at the junction of the Thames River and the Long Island Sound in southeastern Connecticut. Decades of economic decline led a state agency in 1990 to designate the City a "distressed municipality." In 1996, the Federal Government closed the Naval Undersea Warfare Center, which had been located in the Fort Trumbull area of the City and had employed over 1,500 people. In 1998, the City's unemployment rate was nearly double that of the State, and its population of just under 24,000 residents was at its lowest since 1920.

These conditions prompted state and local officials to target New London, and particularly its Fort Trumbull area, for economic revitalization. To this end, respondent New London Development Corporation (NLDC), a private nonprofit entity established some years earlier to assist the City in planning economic development, was reactivated. In January 1998, the State authorized a $5.35 million bond issue to support the NLDC's planning activities and a $10 million bond issue toward the creation of a Fort Trumbull State Park. In February, the pharmaceutical company Pfizer Inc. announced that it would build a $300 million research facility on a site immediately adjacent to Fort Trumbull; local planners hoped that Pfizer would draw new business to the area, thereby serving as a catalyst to the area's rejuvenation. After receiving initial approval from the city council, the NLDC continued its planning activities and held a series of neighborhood meetings to educate the public about the process. In May, the city council authorized the NLDC to formally submit its plans to the relevant state agencies for review. Upon obtaining state-level approval, the NLDC finalized an integrated development plan focused on 90 acres of the Fort Trumbull area.

The Fort Trumbull area is situated on a peninsula that juts into the Thames River. The area comprises approximately 115 privately owned properties, as well as the 32 acres of land formerly occupied by the naval facility (Trumbull State Park now occupies 18 of those 32 acres). The development plan encompasses seven parcels. Parcel 1 is designated for a waterfront conference hotel at the center of a "small urban village" that will include restaurants and shopping. This parcel will also have marinas for both recreational and commercial uses. A pedestrian "riverwalk" will originate here and continue down the coast, connecting the waterfront areas of the development. Parcel 2 will be the site of approximately 80 new residences organized into an urban neighborhood and linked by public walkway to the remainder of the development, including the state park. This parcel also includes space reserved for a new U.S. Coast Guard Museum. Parcel 3, which is located immediately north of the Pfizer facility, will contain at least 90,000 square feet of research and development office space. Parcel 4A is a 2.4–acre site that will be used either to support the adjacent state park, by providing parking or retail services for visitors, or to support the nearby marina. Parcel 4B will include a renovated marina, as well as the final stretch of the riverwalk. Parcels 5, 6, and 7 will provide land for office and retail space, parking, and water-dependent commercial uses. App. 109–113.

The NLDC intended the development plan to capitalize on the arrival of the Pfizer facility and the new commerce it was expected to attract. In addition to creating jobs, generating tax revenue, and helping to "build momentum for the revitalization of downtown New London," *id.,* at 92, the plan was also designed to make the City more attractive and to create leisure and recreational opportunities on the waterfront and in the park.

The city council approved the plan in January 2000, and designated the NLDC as its development agent in charge of implementation. See Conn. Gen.Stat. § 8–188 (2005). The city council also authorized the NLDC to purchase property or to acquire property by exercising eminent domain in the City's name. § 8–193. The NLDC successfully negotiated the purchase of most of the real estate in the 90–acre area, but its negotiations with petitioners failed. As a consequence, in November 2000, the NLDC initiated the condemnation proceedings that gave rise to this case.

II

Petitioner Susette Kelo has lived in the Fort Trumbull area since 1997. She has made extensive improvements to her house, which she prizes for its water view. Petitioner Wilhelmina Dery was born in her Fort Trumbull house in 1918 and has lived there her entire life. Her husband Charles (also a petitioner) has lived in the house since they married some 60 years ago. In all, the nine petitioners own 15 properties in Fort Trumbull—4 in parcel 3 of the development plan and 11 in parcel 4A. Ten of the parcels are occupied by the owner or a family member; the other five are held as investment properties. There is no allegation that any of these properties is blighted or otherwise in poor condition; rather, they were condemned only because they happen to be located in the development area.

In December 2000, petitioners brought this action in the New London Superior Court. They claimed, among other things, that the taking of their properties would violate the "public use" restriction in the Fifth Amendment. After a 7–day bench trial, the Superior Court granted a permanent restraining order prohibiting the taking of the properties located in parcel 4A (park or marina support). It, however, denied petitioners relief as to the properties located in parcel 3 (office space). App. to Pet. for Cert. 343–350.

After the Superior Court ruled, both sides took appeals to the Supreme Court of Connecticut. That court held, over a dissent, that all of the City's proposed takings were valid. It began by upholding the lower court's determination that the takings were authorized by chapter 132, the State's municipal development statute. See Conn. Gen. Stat. § 8–186 *et seq.* (2005). That statute expresses a legislative determination that the taking of land, even developed land, as part of an economic development project is a "public use" and in the "public interest." 268 Conn., at 18–28, 843 A.2d, at 515–521. Next, relying on cases such as *Hawaii Housing Authority v.*

Midkiff, 467 U.S. 229, 104 S.Ct. 2321, 81 L.Ed.2d 186 (1984), and *Berman v. Parker,* 348 U.S. 26, 75 S.Ct. 98, 99 L.Ed. 27 (1954), the court held that such economic development qualified as a valid public use under both the Federal and State Constitutions. 268 Conn., at 40, 843 A.2d, at 527. . . .

We granted certiorari to determine whether a city's decision to take property for the purpose of economic development satisfies the "public use" requirement of the Fifth Amendment. 542 U.S. 965, 125 S.Ct. 27, 159 L.Ed.2d 857 (2004).

III

Two polar propositions are perfectly clear. On the one hand, it has long been accepted that the sovereign may not take the property of *A* for the sole purpose of transferring it to another private party *B,* even though *A* is paid just compensation. On the other hand, it is equally clear that a State may transfer property from one private party to another if future "use by the public" is the purpose of the taking; the condemnation of land for a railroad with common-carrier duties is a familiar example. Neither of these propositions, however, determines the disposition of this case.

As for the first proposition, the City would no doubt be forbidden from taking petitioners' land for the purpose of conferring a private benefit on a particular private party. See *Midkiff,* 467 U.S., at 245, 104 S.Ct. 2321 ("A purely private taking could not withstand the scrutiny of the public use requirement; it would serve no legitimate purpose of government and would thus be void"); *Missouri Pacific R. Co. v. Nebraska,* 164 U.S. 403, 17 S.Ct. 130, 41 L.Ed. 489 (1896). Nor would the City be allowed to take property under the mere pretext of a public purpose, when its actual purpose was to bestow a private benefit. The takings before us, however, would be executed pursuant to a "carefully considered" development plan. 268 Conn., at 54, 843 A.2d, at 536. The trial judge and all the members of the Supreme Court of Connecticut agreed that there was no evidence of an illegitimate purpose in this case. Therefore, as was true of the statute challenged in *Midkiff,* 467 U.S., at 245, 104 S.Ct. 2321, the City's development plan was not adopted "to benefit a particular class of identifiable individuals."

On the other hand, this is not a case in which the City is planning to open the condemned land—at least not in its entirety—to use by the general public. Nor will the private lessees of the land in any sense be required to operate like common carriers, making their services available to all comers. But although such a projected use would be sufficient to satisfy the public use requirement, this "Court long ago rejected any literal requirement that condemned property be put into use for the general public." *Id.,* at 244, 104 S.Ct. 2321. Indeed, while many state courts in the mid–19th century endorsed "use by the public" as the proper definition of public use, that narrow view steadily eroded over time. Not only was the "use by the public" test difficult to administer (*e.g.,* what proportion of the public need have access to the property? at what price?), but it proved to be impractical given the diverse and always evolving needs of society. Accordingly, when this Court began applying the Fifth Amendment to the States at the close of the 19th century, it embraced the broader and more natural interpretation of public use as "public purpose." See, *e.g.*, *Fallbrook Irrigation Dist. v. Bradley*, 164 U.S. 112, 158–164, 17 S.Ct. 56, 41 L.Ed. 369 (1896). Thus, in a case upholding a mining company's use of an aerial bucket line to transport ore over property it did not own, Justice Holmes' opinion for the Court stressed "the inadequacy of use by the general public as a universal test." *Strickley v. Highland Boy Gold Mining Co.*, 200 U.S. 527, 531, 26 S.Ct. 301, 50 L.Ed. 581 (1906). We have repeatedly and consistently rejected that narrow test ever since.

The disposition of this case therefore turns on the question whether the City's development plan serves a "public purpose." Without exception, our cases have defined that concept broadly, reflecting our longstanding policy of deference to legislative judgments in this field.

In *Berman v. Parker*, 348 U.S. 26, 75 S.Ct. 98, 99 L.Ed. 27 (1954), this Court upheld a redevelopment plan targeting a blighted area of Washington, D. C., in which most of the housing for the area's 5,000 inhabitants was beyond repair. Under the plan, the area would be condemned and part of it utilized for the construction of streets, schools, and other public facilities. The remainder of the land would be leased or sold to private parties for the purpose of redevelopment, including the construction of low-cost housing.

The owner of a department store located in the area challenged the condemnation, pointing out that his store was not itself blighted and arguing that the creation of a "better balanced, more attractive community" was not a valid public use. *Id.*, at 31, 75 S.Ct. 98. Writing for a unanimous Court, Justice Douglas refused to evaluate this claim in isolation, deferring instead to the legislative and agency judgment that the area "must be planned as a whole" for the plan to be successful. *Id.*, at 34, 75 S. Ct. 98. The Court explained that "community redevelopment programs need not, by force of the Constitution, be on a piecemeal basis—lot by lot, building by building." *Id.*, at 35, 75 S.Ct. 98. The public use underlying the taking was unequivocally affirmed:

> "We do not sit to determine whether a particular housing project is or is not desirable. The concept of the public welfare is broad and inclusive. . . . The values it represents are spiritual as well as physical, aesthetic as well as monetary. It is within the power of the legislature to determine that the community should be beautiful as well as healthy, spacious as well as clean, well-balanced as well as carefully patrolled. In the present case, the Congress and its authorized agencies have made determinations that take into account a wide variety of values. It is not for us to reappraise them. If those who govern the District of Columbia decide that the Nation's Capital should be beautiful as well as sanitary, there is nothing in the Fifth Amendment that stands in the way." *Id.*, at 33, 75 S.Ct. 98.

In *Hawaii Housing Authority v. Midkiff*, 467 U.S. 229, 104 S.Ct. 2321, 81 L.Ed.2d 186 (1984), the Court considered a Hawaii statute whereby fee title was taken from lessors and transferred to lessees (for just compensation) in order to reduce the concentration of land ownership. We unanimously upheld the statute and rejected the Ninth Circuit's view that it was "a naked attempt on the part of the state of Hawaii to take the property of A and transfer it to B solely for B's private use and benefit." *Id.,* at 235, 104 S.Ct. 2321 (internal quotation marks omitted). Reaffirming *Berman's* deferential approach to legislative judgments in this field, we concluded that the State's purpose of eliminating the "social and economic evils of a land oligopoly" qualified as a valid public use. 467 U.S., at 241–242, 104 S.Ct. 2321. Our opinion also rejected the contention that the mere fact that the State immediately transferred the properties to private individuals upon condemnation somehow diminished the public character of the taking. "[I]t is only the taking's purpose, and not its mechanics," we explained, that matters in determining public use. *Id.,* at 244, 104 S. Ct. 2321. . . .

Viewed as a whole, our jurisprudence has recognized that the needs of society have varied between different parts of the Nation, just as they have evolved over time in response to changed circumstances. Our earliest cases in particular embodied a strong theme of federalism, emphasizing the "great respect" that we owe to state legislatures and state courts in discerning local public needs. See *Hairston v. Danville & Western R. Co.,* 208 U.S. 598, 606–607, 28 S.Ct. 331, 52 L.Ed. 637 (1908) noting that these needs were likely to vary depending on a State's "resources, the capacity of the soil, the relative importance of industries to the general public welfare, and the long-established methods and habits of the people"). For more than a century, our public use jurisprudence has wisely eschewed rigid formulas and intrusive scrutiny in favor of affording legislatures broad latitude in determining what public needs justify the use of the takings power.

IV

Those who govern the City were not confronted with the need to remove blight in the Fort Trumbull area, but their determination that the area was sufficiently distressed to justify a program of economic rejuvenation is entitled to our deference. The City has carefully formulated an economic development plan that it believes will provide appreciable benefits to the community, including — but by no means limited to — new jobs and increased tax revenue. As with other exercises in urban planning and development, the City is endeavoring to coordinate a variety of commercial, residential, and recreational uses of land, with the hope that they will form a whole greater than the sum of its parts. To effectuate this plan, the City has invoked a state statute that specifically authorizes the use of eminent domain to promote economic development. Given the comprehensive character of the plan, the thorough deliberation that preceded its adoption, and the limited scope of our review, it is appropriate for us, as it was in *Berman,* to resolve the challenges of the individual owners, not on a piecemeal basis, but rather in light of the entire plan. Because that plan unquestionably serves a public purpose, the takings challenged here satisfy the public use requirement of the Fifth Amendment.

To avoid this result, petitioners urge us to adopt a new bright-line rule that economic development does not qualify as a public use. Putting aside the unpersuasive suggestion that the City's plan will provide only purely economic benefits, neither precedent nor logic supports petitioners' proposal. Promoting economic development is a traditional and long-accepted function of government. There is, moreover, no principled way of distinguishing economic development from the other public purposes that we have recognized. In our cases upholding takings that facilitated agriculture and mining, for example, we emphasized the importance of those industries to the welfare of the States in question, see, *e.g., Strickley,* 200 U.S. 527, 26 S.Ct. 301; in *Berman,* we endorsed the purpose of transforming a blighted area into a "well-balanced" community through redevelopment, 348 U.S., at 33, 75 S.Ct. 98; in *Midkiff,* we upheld the interest in breaking up a land oligopoly that "created artificial deterrents to the normal functioning of the State's residential land market," 467 U.S., at 242, 104 S.Ct. 2321; and in *Monsanto,* we accepted Congress' purpose of eliminating a "significant barrier to entry in the pesticide market," 467 U.S., at 1014–1015, 104 S.Ct. 2862. It would be incongruous to hold that the City's interest in the economic benefits to be derived from the development of the Fort Trumbull area has less of a public character than any of those other interests. Clearly, there is no basis for exempting economic development from our traditionally broad understanding of public purpose.

Petitioners contend that using eminent domain for economic development impermissibly blurs the boundary between public and private takings. Again, our cases foreclose this objection. Quite simply, the government's pursuit of a public purpose will often benefit individual private parties. For example, in *Midkiff,* the forced transfer of property conferred a direct and significant benefit on those lessees who were previously unable to purchase their homes. In *Monsanto,* we recognized that the "most direct beneficiaries" of the data-sharing provisions were the subsequent pesticide applicants, but benefiting them in this way was necessary to promoting competition in the pesticide market. 467 U.S., at 1014, 104 S.Ct. 2862. The owner of the department store in *Berman* objected to "taking from one businessman for the benefit of another businessman," 348 U.S., at 33, 75 S.Ct. 98, referring to the fact that under the redevelopment plan land would be leased or sold to private developers for redevelopment. Our rejection of that contention has particular relevance to the instant case: "The public end may be as well or better served through an agency of private enterprise than through a department of government—or so the Congress might conclude. We cannot say that public ownership is the sole method of promoting the public purposes of community redevelopment projects." *Id.,* at 33–34, 75 S.Ct. 98.

It is further argued that without a bright-line rule nothing would stop a city from transferring citizen *A*'s property to citizen *B* for the sole reason that citizen *B* will put the property to a more productive use and thus pay more taxes. Such a one-to-one transfer of property, executed outside the confines of an integrated development plan, is not presented in this case. While such an unusual exercise of government power would certainly raise a suspicion that a private purpose was afoot, the hypothetical cases posited by petitioners can be confronted if and when they arise. They do not warrant the crafting of an artificial restriction on the concept of public use.

Alternatively, petitioners maintain that for takings of this kind we should require a "reasonable certainty" that the expected public benefits will actually accrue. Such a rule, however, would represent an even greater departure from our precedent. "When the legislature's purpose is legitimate and its means are not irrational, our cases make clear that empirical debates over the wisdom of takings—no less than debates over the wisdom of other kinds of socioeconomic legislation—are not to be carried out in the federal courts." *Midkiff*, 467 U.S., at 242–243, 104 S.Ct. 2321. Indeed, earlier this Term we explained why similar practical concerns (among others) undermined the use of the "substantially advances" formula in our regulatory takings doctrine. *See Lingle v. Chevron U.S.A. Inc.*, 544 U.S. 528, 544, 125 S.Ct. 2074, 2085, 161 L.Ed.2d 876 (2005) (noting that this formula "would empower— and might often require—courts to substitute their predictive judgments for those of elected legislatures and expert agencies"). The disadvantages of a heightened form of review are especially pronounced in this type of case. Orderly implementation of a comprehensive redevelopment plan obviously requires that the legal rights of all interested parties be established before new construction can be commenced. A constitutional rule that required postponement of the judicial approval of every condemnation until the likelihood of success of the plan had been assured would unquestionably impose a significant impediment to the successful consummation of many such plans.

Just as we decline to second-guess the City's considered judgments about the efficacy of its development plan, we also decline to second-guess the City's determinations as to what lands it needs to acquire in order to effectuate the project. "It is not for the courts to oversee the choice of the boundary line nor to sit in review on the size of a particular project area. Once the question of the public purpose has been decided, the amount and character of land to be taken for the project and the need for a particular tract to complete the integrated plan rests in the discretion of the legislative branch." *Berman*, 348 U.S., at 35–36, 75 S.Ct. 98.

In affirming the City's authority to take petitioners' properties, we do not minimize the hardship that condemnations may entail, notwithstanding the payment of just compensation. We emphasize that nothing in our opinion precludes any State from placing further restrictions on its exercise of the takings power. Indeed, many States already impose "public use" requirements that are stricter than the federal baseline. Some of these requirements have been established as a matter of state constitutional law, while others are expressed in state eminent domain statutes that carefully limit the grounds upon which takings may be exercised. As the submissions of the parties and their *amici* make clear, the necessity and wisdom of using eminent domain to promote economic development are certainly matters of legitimate public debate. This Court's authority, however, extends only to determining whether the City's proposed condemnations are for a "public use" within the meaning of the Fifth Amendment to the Federal Constitution. Because over a century of our case law interpreting that provision dictates an affirmative answer to that question, we may not grant petitioners the relief that they seek.

The judgment of the Supreme Court of Connecticut is affirmed.

JUSTICE KENNEDY, concurring. I join the opinion for the Court and add these further observations.

This Court has declared that a taking should be upheld as consistent with the Public Use Clause, U.S. Const., Amdt. 5, as long as it is "rationally related to a conceivable public purpose." *Hawaii Housing Authority v. Midkiff,* 467 U.S. 229, 241, 104 S.Ct. 2321, 81 L.Ed.2d 186 (1984); see also *Berman v. Parker,* 348 U.S. 26, 75 S.Ct. 98, 99 L.Ed. 27 (1954). This deferential standard of review echoes the rational-basis test used to review economic regulation under the Due Process and Equal Protection Clauses, see, *e.g., FCC v. Beach Communications, Inc.,* 508 U.S. 307, 313–314, 113 S.Ct. 2096, 124 L.Ed.2d 211 (1993); *Williamson v. Lee Optical of Okla., Inc.,* 348 U.S. 483, 75 S.Ct. 461, 99 L.Ed. 563 (1955). . . .

A court applying rational-basis review under the Public Use Clause should strike down a taking that, by a clear showing, is intended to favor a particular private party, with only incidental or pretextual public benefits, just as a court applying rational-basis review under the Equal Protection Clause must strike down a government classification that is clearly intended to injure a particular class of private parties, with only incidental or pretextual public justifications. See *Cleburne v. Cleburne Living Center, Inc.,* 473 U.S. 432, 446–447, 450, 105 S.Ct. 3249, 87 L.Ed.2d 313 (1985); *Department of Agriculture v. Moreno,* 413 U.S. 528, 533–536, 93 S.Ct. 2821, 37 L.Ed.2d 782 (1973). As the trial court in this case was correct to observe: "Where the purpose [of a taking] is economic development and that development is to be carried out by private parties or private parties will be benefited, the court must decide if the stated public purpose—economic advantage to a city sorely in need of it—is only incidental to the benefits that will be confined on private parties of a development plan." App. to Pet. for Cert. 263. See also *ante,* at 2661–2662.

A court confronted with a plausible accusation of impermissible favoritism to private parties should treat the objection as a serious one and review the record to see if it has merit, though with the presumption that the government's actions were reasonable and intended to serve a public purpose. Here, the trial court conducted a careful and extensive inquiry into "whether, in fact, the development plan is of primary benefit to . . . the developer [*i.e.,* Corcoran Jennison], and private businesses which may eventually locate in the plan area [*e.g.,* Pfizer], and in that regard, only of incidental benefit to the city." App. to Pet. for Cert. 261. . . .

The trial court concluded, based on these findings, that benefiting Pfizer was not "the primary motivation or effect of this development plan"; instead, "the primary motivation for [respondents] was to take advantage of Pfizer's presence." *Id.,* at 276. Likewise, the trial court concluded that "[t]here is nothing in the record to indicate that . . . [respondents] were motivated by a desire to aid [other] particular private entities." *Id.,* at 278. See also *ante,* at 2661–2662. Even the dissenting justices on the Connecticut Supreme Court agreed that respondents' development plan was intended to revitalize the local economy, not to serve the interests of Pfizer, Corcoran Jennison, or any other private party. 268 Conn. 1, 159, 843 A.2d 500, 595 (2004) (Zarella, J., concurring in part and dissenting in part). This case, then, survives the meaningful rational-basis review that in my view is required under the Public Use Clause.

Petitioners and their *amici* argue that any taking justified by the promotion of economic development must be treated by the courts as *per se* invalid, or at least presumptively invalid. Petitioners overstate the need for such a rule, however, by making the incorrect assumption that review under *Berman* and *Midkiff* imposes no meaningful judicial limits on the government's power to condemn any property it likes. A broad *per se* rule or a strong presumption of invalidity, furthermore, would prohibit a large number of government takings that have the purpose and expected effect of conferring substantial benefits on the public at large and so do not offend the Public Use Clause.

My agreement with the Court that a presumption of invalidity is not warranted for economic development takings in general, or for the particular takings at issue in this case, does not foreclose the possibility that a more stringent standard of review than that announced in *Berman* and *Midkiff* might be appropriate for a more narrowly drawn category of takings. There may be private transfers in which the risk of undetected impermissible favoritism of private parties is so acute that a presumption (rebuttable or otherwise) of invalidity is warranted under the Public Use Clause. Cf. *Eastern Enterprises v. Apfel,* 524 U.S. 498, 549–550, 118 S.Ct. 2131, 141 L. Ed.2d 451 (1998) (KENNEDY, J., concurring in judgment and dissenting in part) (heightened scrutiny for retroactive legislation under the Due Process Clause). This demanding level of scrutiny, however, is not required simply because the purpose of the taking is economic development.

This is not the occasion for conjecture as to what sort of cases might justify a more demanding standard, but it is appropriate to underscore aspects of the instant case that convince me no departure from *Berman* and *Midkiff* is appropriate here. This taking occurred in the context of a comprehensive development plan meant to address a serious citywide depression, and the projected economic benefits of the project cannot be characterized as *de minimis.* The identities of most of the private beneficiaries were unknown at the time the city formulated its plans. The city complied with elaborate procedural requirements that facilitate review of the record and inquiry into the city's purposes. In sum, while there may be categories of cases in which the transfers are so suspicious, or the procedures employed so prone to abuse, or the purported benefits are so trivial or implausible, that courts should presume an impermissible private purpose, no such circumstances are present in this case.

JUSTICE O'CONNOR, with whom THE CHIEF JUSTICE, JUSTIC SCALIA, and JUSTICE THOMAS join, dissenting. . . . While the Takings Clause presupposes that government can take private property without the owner's consent, the just compensation requirement spreads the cost of condemnations and thus "prevents the public from loading upon one individual more than his just share of the burdens of government." *Monongahela Nav. Co. v. United States,* 148 U.S. 312, 325, 13 S.Ct. 622, 37 L.Ed. 463 (1893); see also *Armstrong v. United States,* 364 U.S. 40, 49, 80 S. Ct. 1563, 4 L.Ed.2d 1554 (1960). The public use requirement, in turn, imposes a more basic limitation, circumscribing the very scope of the eminent domain power: Government may compel an individual to forfeit her property for the *public's* use, but not for the benefit of another private person. This requirement promotes fairness as well as security. Cf. *Tahoe–Sierra Preservation Council, Inc. v. Tahoe Regional Planning Agency,* 535 U.S. 302, 336, 122 S.Ct. 1465, 152 L.Ed.2d 517 (2002) ("The concepts of 'fairness and justice' . . . underlie the Takings Clause").

Where is the line between "public" and "private" property use? We give considerable deference to legislatures' determinations about what governmental activities will advantage the public. But were the political branches the sole arbiters of the public-private distinction, the Public Use Clause would amount to little more than hortatory fluff. An external, judicial check on how the public use requirement is interpreted, however limited, is necessary if this constraint on government power is to retain any meaning. See *Cincinnati v. Vester,* 281 U.S. 439, 446, 50 S.Ct. 360, 74 L. Ed. 950 (1930) ("It is well established that . . . the question [of] what is a public use is a judicial one").

Our cases have generally identified three categories of takings that comply with the public use requirement, though it is in the nature of things that the boundaries between these categories are not always firm. Two are relatively straightforward and uncontroversial. First, the sovereign may transfer private property to public ownership—such as for a road, a hospital, or a military base. See, *e.g., Old Dominion Land Co. v. United States,* 269 U.S. 55, 46 S.Ct. 39, 70 L.Ed. 162 (1925); *Rindge Co. v. County of Los Angeles,* 262 U.S. 700, 43 S.Ct. 689, 67 L.Ed. 1186 (1923). Second, the sovereign may transfer private property to private parties, often common carriers, who make the property available for the public's use—such as with a railroad, a public utility, or a stadium. See, *e.g., National Railroad Passenger Corporation v. Boston & Maine Corp.,* 503 U.S. 407, 112 S.Ct. 1394, 118 L.Ed.2d 52 (1992); *Mt. Vernon–Woodberry Cotton Duck Co. v. Alabama Interstate Power Co.,* 240 U.S. 30, 36 S.Ct. 234, 60 L.Ed. 507 (1916). But "public ownership" and "use-by-the-public" are sometimes too constricting and impractical ways to define the scope of the Public Use Clause. Thus we have allowed that, in certain circumstances and to meet certain exigencies, takings that serve a public purpose also satisfy the Constitution even if the property is destined for subsequent private use. See, *e.g., Berman v. Parker,* 348 U.S. 26, 75 S.Ct. 98, 99 L.Ed. 27 (1954); *Hawaii Housing Authority v. Midkiff,* 467 U.S. 229, 104 S.Ct. 2321, 81 L.Ed.2d 186 (1984).

This case returns us for the first time in over 20 years to the hard question of when a purportedly "public purpose" taking meets the public use requirement. It presents an issue of first impression: Are economic development takings constitutional? I would hold that they are not. We are guided by two precedents about the taking of real property by eminent domain. In *Berman,* we upheld takings within a blighted neighborhood of Washington, D.C. The neighborhood had so deteriorated that, for example, 64.3% of its dwellings were beyond repair. 348 U.S., at 30, 75 S. Ct. 98. It had become burdened with "overcrowding of dwellings," "lack of adequate streets and alleys," and "lack of light and air." *Id.,* at 34, 75 S.Ct. 98. Congress had determined that the neighborhood had become "injurious to the public health, safety, morals, and welfare" and that it was necessary to "eliminat[e] all such injurious conditions by employing all means necessary and appropriate for the purpose," including eminent domain. *Id.,* at 28, 75 S.Ct. 98 (internal quotation marks omitted). Mr. Berman's department store was not itself blighted. Having approved of Congress' decision to eliminate the harm to the public emanating from the blighted neighborhood, however, we did not second-guess its decision to treat the neighborhood as a whole rather than lot-by-lot. *Id.,* at 34–35, 75 S.Ct. 98; see also *Midkiff,* 467 U.S., at 244, 104 S.Ct. 2321 ("[I]t is only the taking's purpose, and not its mechanics, that must pass scrutiny").

In *Midkiff,* we upheld a land condemnation scheme in Hawaii whereby title in real property was taken from lessors and transferred to lessees. At that time, the State and Federal Governments owned nearly 49% of the State's land, and another 47% was in the hands of only 72 private landowners. Concentration of land ownership was so dramatic that on the State's most urbanized island, Oahu, 22 landowners owned 72.5% of the fee simple titles. *Id.,* at 232, 104 S.Ct. 2321. The Hawaii Legislature had concluded that the oligopoly in land ownership was "skewing the State's residential fee simple market, inflating land prices, and injuring the public tranquility and welfare," and therefore enacted a condemnation scheme for redistributing title. *Ibid.*

In those decisions, we emphasized the importance of deferring to legislative judgments about public purpose. Because courts are ill equipped to evaluate the efficacy of proposed legislative initiatives, we rejected as unworkable the idea of courts' "'deciding on what is and is not a governmental function and . . . invalidating legislation on the basis of their view on that question at the moment of decision, a practice which has proved impracticable in other fields.'" *Id.,* at 240–241, 104 S. Ct. 2321 (quoting *United States ex rel. TVA v. Welch,* 327 U.S. 546, 552, 66 S.Ct. 715, 90 L.Ed. 843 (1946)); see *Berman, supra,* at 32, 75 S.Ct. 98 ("[T]he legislature, not the judiciary, is the main guardian of the public needs to be served by social legislation"); see also *Lingle v. Chevron U.S.A. Inc.,* 544 U.S. 528, 125 S.Ct. 2074, 161 L. Ed.2d 876 (2005). Likewise, we recognized our inability to evaluate whether, in a given case, eminent domain is a necessary means by which to pursue the legislature's ends. *Midkiff, supra,* at 242, 104 S.Ct. 2321; *Berman, supra,* at 33, 75 S.Ct. 98.

Yet for all the emphasis on deference, *Berman* and *Midkiff* hewed to a bedrock principle without which our public use jurisprudence would collapse: "A purely private taking could not withstand the scrutiny of the public use requirement; it would serve no legitimate purpose of government and would thus be void." *Midkiff,* 467 U.S., at 245, 104 S.Ct. 2321; *id.,* at 241, 104 S.Ct. 2321 ("[T]he Court's cases have repeatedly stated that 'one person's property may not be taken for the benefit of another private person without a justifying public purpose, even though compensation be paid'" (quoting *Thompson v. Consolidated Gas Util. Corp.,* 300 U.S. 55, 80, 57 S.Ct. 364, 81 L.Ed. 510 (1937))); see also *Missouri Pacific R. Co. v. Nebraska,* 164 U.S. 403, 417, 17 S.Ct. 130, 41 L.Ed. 489 (1896). To protect that principle, those decisions reserved "a role for courts to play in reviewing a legislature's judgment of what constitutes a public use . . . [though] the Court in *Berman* made clear that it is 'an extremely narrow' one." *Midkiff, supra,* at 240, 104 S.Ct. 2321 (quoting *Berman, supra,* at 32, 75 S.Ct. 98).

The Court's holdings in *Berman* and *Midkiff* were true to the principle underlying the Public Use Clause. In both those cases, the extraordinary, precondemnation use of the targeted property inflicted affirmative harm on society—in *Berman* through blight resulting from extreme poverty and in *Midkiff* through oligopoly resulting from extreme wealth. And in both cases, the relevant legislative body had found that eliminating the existing property use was necessary to remedy the harm. *Berman, supra,* at 28–29, 75 S.Ct. 98; *Midkiff, supra,* at 232, 104 S.Ct. 2321. Thus a public purpose was realized when the harmful use was eliminated. Because each taking *directly* achieved a public benefit, it did not matter that the property was turned over to private use. Here, in contrast, New London does not claim that Susette Kelo's and Wilhelmina Dery's well-maintained homes are the source of any social harm. Indeed, it could not so claim without adopting the absurd argument that any single-family home that might be razed to make way for an apartment building, or any church that might be replaced with a retail store, or any small business that might be more lucrative if it were instead part of a national franchise, is inherently harmful to society and thus within the government's power to condemn.

In moving away from our decisions sanctioning the condemnation of harmful property use, the Court today significantly expands the meaning of public use. It holds that the sovereign may take private property currently put to ordinary private use, and give it over for new, ordinary private use, so long as the new use is predicted to generate some secondary benefit for the public—such as increased tax revenue, more jobs, maybe even esthetic pleasure. But nearly any lawful use of real private property can be said to generate some incidental benefit to the public. Thus, if predicted (or even guaranteed) positive side effects are enough to render transfer from one private party to another constitutional, then the words "for public use" do not realistically exclude *any* takings, and thus do not exert any constraint on the eminent domain power.

There is a sense in which this troubling result follows from errant language in *Berman* and *Midkiff.* In discussing whether takings within a blighted neighborhood were for a public use, *Berman* began by observing: "We deal, in other words, with what traditionally has been known as the police power." 348 U.S., at 32, 75 S.Ct. 98.

From there it declared that "[o]nce the object is within the authority of Congress, the right to realize it through the exercise of eminent domain is clear." *Id.,* at 33, 75 S.Ct. 98. Following up, we said in *Midkiff* that "[t]he 'public use' requirement is coterminous with the scope of a sovereign's police powers." 467 U.S., at 240, 104 S. Ct. 2321. This language was unnecessary to the specific holdings of those decisions. *Berman* and *Midkiff* simply did not put such language to the constitutional test, because the takings in those cases were within the police power but also for "public use" for the reasons I have described. The case before us now demonstrates why, when deciding if a taking's purpose is constitutional, the police power and "public use" cannot always be equated.

The Court protests that it does not sanction the bare transfer from A to B for B's benefit. It suggests two limitations on what can be taken after today's decision. First, it maintains a role for courts in ferreting out takings whose sole purpose is to bestow a benefit on the private transferee—without detailing how courts are to conduct that complicated inquiry. *Ante,* at 2661–2662. For his part, Justice KENNEDY suggests that courts may divine illicit purpose by a careful review of the record and the process by which a legislature arrived at the decision to take—without specifying what courts should look for in a case with different facts, how they will know if they have found it, and what to do if they do not. *Ante,* at 2669–2670 (concurring opinion). Whatever the details of Justice KENNEDY's as-yet-undisclosed test, it is difficult to envision anyone but the "stupid staff[er]" failing it. See *Lucas v. South Carolina Coastal Council,* 505 U.S. 1003, 1025–1026, n. 12, 112 S.Ct. 2886, 120 L.Ed.2d 798 (1992). The trouble with economic development takings is that private benefit and incidental public benefit are, by definition, merged and mutually reinforcing. In this case, for example, any boon for Pfizer or the plan's developer is difficult to disaggregate from the promised public gains in taxes and jobs. See App. to Pet. for Cert. 275–277.

Even if there were a practical way to isolate the motives behind a given taking, the gesture toward a purpose test is theoretically flawed. If it is true that incidental public benefits from new private use are enough to ensure the "public purpose" in a taking, why should it matter, as far as the Fifth Amendment is concerned, what inspired the taking in the first place? How much the government does or does not desire to benefit a favored private party has no bearing on whether an economic development taking will or will not generate secondary benefit for the public. And whatever the reason for a given condemnation, the effect is the same from the constitutional perspective—private property is forcibly relinquished to new private ownership.

. . . The Court rightfully admits, however, that the judiciary cannot get bogged down in predictive judgments about whether the public will actually be better off after a property transfer. In any event, this constraint has no realistic import. For who among us can say she already makes the most productive or attractive possible use of her property? The specter of condemnation hangs over all property. Nothing is to prevent the State from replacing any Motel 6 with a Ritz–Carlton, any home with a shopping mall, or any farm with a factory. Cf. *Bugryn v. Bristol,* 63 Conn. App. 98, 774 A.2d 1042 (2001) (taking the homes and farm of four owners in their 70's and 80's and giving it to an "industrial park"); *99 Cents Only Stores v. Lancaster Redevelopment Agency,* 237 F.Supp.2d 1123 (C.D.Cal.2001) (attempted taking of 99 Cents store to replace with a Costco); *Poletown Neighborhood Council v. Detroit,* 410 Mich. 616, 304 N.W.2d 455 (1981) (taking a working-class, immigrant community in Detroit and giving it to a General Motors assembly plant), overruled by *County of Wayne v. Hathcock,* 471 Mich. 445, 684 N.W.2d 765 (2004) . . . .

The Court also puts special emphasis on facts peculiar to this case: The NLDC's plan is the product of a relatively careful deliberative process; it proposes to use eminent domain for a multipart, integrated plan rather than for isolated property transfer; it promises an array of incidental benefits (even esthetic ones), not just increased tax revenue; it comes on the heels of a legislative determination that New London is a depressed municipality. See, *e.g., ante,* at 2667 ("[A] one-to-one transfer of property, executed outside the confines of an integrated development plan, is not presented in this case"). Justice KENNEDY, too, takes great comfort in these facts. *Ante,* at 2670 (concurring opinion). But none has legal significance to blunt the force of today's holding. If legislative prognostications about the secondary public benefits of a new use can legitimate a taking, there is nothing in the Court's rule or in Justice KENNEDY's gloss on that rule to prohibit property transfers generated with less care, that are less comprehensive, that happen to result from less elaborate process, whose only projected advantage is the incidence of higher taxes, or that hope to transform an already prosperous city into an even more prosperous one.

Finally, in a coda, the Court suggests that property owners should turn to the States, who may or may not choose to impose appropriate limits on economic development takings. *Ante,* at 2668. This is an abdication of our responsibility. States play many important functions in our system of dual sovereignty, but compensating for our refusal to enforce properly the Federal Constitution (and a provision meant to curtail state action, no less) is not among them.

It was possible after *Berman* and *Midkiff* to imagine unconstitutional transfers from A to B. Those decisions endorsed government intervention when private property use had veered to such an extreme that the public was suffering as a consequence. Today nearly all real property is susceptible to condemnation on the Court's theory. In the prescient words of a dissenter from the infamous decision in *Poletown,* "[n]ow that we have authorized local legislative bodies to decide that a different commercial or industrial use of property will produce greater public benefits than its present use, no homeowner's, merchant's or manufacturer's property, however productive or valuable to its owner, is immune from condemnation for the benefit of other private interests that will put it to a 'higher' use." 410 Mich., at 644–645, 304 N.W.2d, at 464 (opinion of Fitzgerald, J.). This is why economic development takings "seriously jeopardiz[e] the security of all private property ownership." *Id.,* at 645, 304 N.W.2d, at 465 (Ryan, J., dissenting).

Any property may now be taken for the benefit of another private party, but the fallout from this decision will not be random. The beneficiaries are likely to be those citizens with disproportionate influence and power in the political process, including large corporations and development firms. As for the victims, the government now has license to transfer property from those with fewer resources to those with more. The Founders cannot have intended this perverse result. "[T]hat alone is a *just* government," wrote James Madison, "which *impartially* secures to every man, whatever is his *own*." For the National Gazette, Property (Mar. 27, 1792), reprinted in 14 Papers of James Madison 266 (R. Rutland et al. eds.1983).

I would hold that the takings in both Parcel 3 and Parcel 4A are unconstitutional, reverse the judgment of the Supreme Court of Connecticut, and remand for further proceedings.

JUSTICE THOMAS, dissenting. Long ago, William Blackstone wrote that "the law of the land . . . postpone[s] even public necessity to the sacred and inviolable rights of private property." 1 Commentaries on the Laws of England 134–135 (1765) (hereinafter Blackstone). The Framers embodied that principle in the Constitution, allowing the government to take property not for "public necessity," but instead for "public use." Amdt. 5. Defying this understanding, the Court replaces the Public Use Clause with a "'[P]ublic [P]urpose'" Clause, *ante,* at 2662–2663 (or perhaps the "Diverse and Always Evolving Needs of Society" Clause, *ante,* at 2662 (capitalization added)), a restriction that is satisfied, the Court instructs, so long as the purpose is "legitimate" and the means "not irrational," *ante,* at 2667 (internal quotation marks omitted). This deferential shift in phraseology enables the Court to hold, against all common sense, that a costly urban-renewal project whose stated purpose is a vague promise of new jobs and increased tax revenue, but which is also suspiciously agreeable to the Pfizer Corporation, is for a "public use."

I cannot agree. If such "economic development" takings are for a "public use," any taking is, and the Court has erased the Public Use Clause from our Constitution, as Justice O'CONNOR powerfully argues in dissent. *Ante,* at 2671, 2675–2677. I do not believe that this Court can eliminate liberties expressly enumerated in the Constitution and therefore join her dissenting opinion. Regrettably, however, the Court's error runs deeper than this. Today's decision is simply the latest in a string of our cases construing the Public Use Clause to be a virtual nullity, without the slightest nod to its original meaning. In my view, the Public Use Clause, originally understood, is a meaningful limit on the government's eminent domain power. Our cases have strayed from the Clause's original meaning, and I would reconsider them. . . .

The disagreement among state courts, and state legislatures' attempts to circumvent public use limits on their eminent domain power, cannot obscure that the Public Use Clause is most naturally read to authorize takings for public use only if the government or the public actually uses the taken property.

Our current Public Use Clause jurisprudence, as the Court notes, has rejected this natural reading of the Clause. *Ante,* at 2662–2664. The Court adopted its modern reading blindly, with little discussion of the Clause's history and original meaning, in two distinct lines of cases: first, in cases adopting the "public purpose" interpretation of the Clause, and second, in cases deferring to legislatures' judgments regarding what constitutes a valid public purpose. Those questionable cases converged in the boundlessly broad and deferential conception of "public use" adopted by this Court in *Berman v. Parker,* 348 U.S. 26, 75 S.Ct. 98, 99 L.Ed. 27 (1954), and *Hawaii Housing Authority v. Midkiff,* 467 U.S. 229, 104 S.Ct. 2321, 81 L.Ed.2d 186 (1984), cases that take center stage in the Court's opinion. See *ante,* 2663–2664. The weakness of those two lines of cases, and consequently *Berman* and *Midkiff,* fatally undermines the doctrinal foundations of the Court's decision. Today's questionable application of these cases is further proof that the "public purpose" standard is not susceptible of principled application. This Court's reliance by rote on this standard is ill advised and should be reconsidered. . . .

The "public purpose" test applied by *Berman* and *Midkiff* also cannot be applied in principled manner. "When we depart from the natural import of the term 'public use,' and substitute for the simple idea of a public possession and occupation, that of public utility, public interest, common benefit, general advantage or convenience . . . we are afloat without any certain principle to guide us." *Bloodgood v. Mohawk & Hudson R. Co.,* 18 Wend. 9, 60–61 (N.Y.1837) (opinion of Tracy, Sen.). . . .

For all these reasons, I would revisit our Public Use Clause cases and consider returning to the original meaning of the Public Use Clause: that the government may take property only if it actually uses or gives the public a legal right to use the property. . . .

The consequences of today's decision are not difficult to predict, and promise to be harmful. So-called "urban renewal" programs provide some compensation for the properties they take, but no compensation is possible for the subjective value of these lands to the individuals displaced and the indignity inflicted by uprooting them from their homes. Allowing the government to take property solely for public purposes is bad enough, but extending the concept of public purpose to encompass any economically beneficial goal guarantees that these losses will fall disproportionately on poor communities. Those communities are not only systematically less likely to put their lands to the highest and best social use, but are also the least politically powerful. If ever there were justification for intrusive judicial review of constitutional provisions that protect "discrete and insular minorities," *United States v. Carolene Products Co.,* 304 U.S. 144, 152, n. 4, 58 S.Ct. 778, 82 L.Ed. 1234 (1938), surely that principle would apply with great force to the powerless groups and individuals the Public Use Clause protects. The deferential standard this Court has adopted for the Public Use Clause is therefore deeply perverse. It encourages "those citizens with disproportionate influence and power in the political process, including large corporations and development firms," to victimize the weak. *Ante,* at 2677 (O'CONNOR, J., dissenting).

Those incentives have made the legacy of this Court's "public purpose" test an unhappy one. In the 1950's, no doubt emboldened in part by the expansive understanding of "public use" this Court adopted in *Berman,* cities "rushed to draw plans" for downtown development. B. Frieden & L. Sagalyn, Downtown, Inc. How America Rebuilds Cities 17 (1989). "Of all the families displaced by urban renewal from 1949 through 1963, 63 percent of those whose race was known were nonwhite, and of these families, 56 percent of nonwhites and 38 percent of whites had incomes low enough to qualify for public housing, which, however, was seldom available to them." *Id.,* at 28, 75 S.Ct. 98. Public works projects in the 1950's and 1960's destroyed predominantly minority communities in St. Paul, Minnesota, and Baltimore, Maryland. *Id.,* at 28–29, 75 S.Ct. 98. In 1981, urban planners in Detroit, Michigan, uprooted the largely "lower-income and elderly" Poletown neighborhood for the benefit of the General Motors Corporation. J. Wylie, Poletown: Community Betrayed 58 (1989). Urban renewal projects have long been associated with the displacement of blacks; "[i]n cities across the country, urban renewal came to be known as 'Negro removal.'" Pritchett, The "Public Menace" of Blight: Urban Renewal and the Private Uses of Eminent Domain, 21 Yale L. & Pol'y Rev. 1, 47 (2003). Over 97 percent of the individuals forcibly removed from their homes by the "slum-clearance" project upheld by this Court in *Berman* were black. 348 U.S., at 30, 75 S.Ct. 98. Regrettably, the predictable consequence of the Court's decision will be to exacerbate these effects.

... I would reverse the judgment of the Connecticut Supreme Court.

Notes and Questions

1. *The Anti-Kelo Backlash*: To say that the majority decision in *Kelo* was controversial is an understatement. Few recent Supreme Court decisions have sparked as much controversy and criticism in newspaper editorial pages, state legislatures and even Congress. Ilya Somin, The Grasping Hand, Kelo v. City of New London and the Limits of Eminent Domain (2016). Justice John Paul Stevens, the author of the majority opinion in *Kelo,* may not have been entirely displeased with this reaction. Recall that towards the end of his opinion, he wrote:

> We emphasize that nothing in our opinion precludes any State from placing further restrictions on its exercise of the takings power. Indeed, many States already impose "public use" requirements that are stricter than the federal baseline. Some of these requirements have been established as a matter of state constitutional law, while others are expressed in state eminent domain statutes that carefully limit the grounds upon which takings may be exercised.

Kelo v. City of New London, 545 U.S. 468, 488 (2005).

For detailed accountings of the scope of the anti-*Kelo* responses in state legislatures and in the courts, see Somin, 135–203; Illya Somin, *The Limits of Backlash: Assessing the Political Response to Kelo*, 93 Minn. L. Rev. 2100, 2102 (2009); Marc Mihaly & Turner Smith, *Kelo's Trail: A Survey of State and Federal Legislative and Judicial Activity Five Years Later*, 38 Ecology L.Q. 703, 707 (2011). Ten years after the decision, one critic of *Kelo*, who also served as counsel for the property owners contesting the City of New London's condemnation, observed that thirty states had tightened their definitions of public use or public purpose, eleven states specifically gave property owners whose property is condemned a right of first refusal to repurchase property not used for the originally stated purpose, and nine states shifted the burden of proof in condemnation proceedings to the government. Dana Berliner, *Looking Back Ten Years After Kelo*, 125 YALE L.J. F. 82 (2015). Some details of that reaction follow.

2. *State Constitutional Changes*: In response to *Kelo*, a number of states amended their constitutions to place narrower restrictions on public use than were recognized in *Kelo*. Michigan, whose Supreme Court had already signaled a willingness to rethink a broad interpretation of the "public use" concept in *County of Wayne v. Hatchcock*, 684 N.W.2d 765 (Mich. 2004), amended its state constitution to prohibit the "taking of private property for transfer to a private entity for the purpose of economic development or enhancement of tax revenues." Mich. Const. art. X, § 2 (2006). North Dakota enacted a similar amendment. N.D. Cont. art. I, § 16 (2006) (excluding the "increase in tax base, tax revenues, employment, or general economic health" from the meaning of public use or public purpose). Nevada changed its constitution to state that "[p]ublic use shall not include the direct or indirect transfer of any interest in property taken in an eminent domain proceeding from one private party to another private party." Nev. Const. art. I, § 22 (2008). New Hampshire enacted a similar amendment providing that "no part of a person's property shall be taken by eminent domain and transferred, directly or indirectly, to another person if the taking is for the purpose of private development or other private use of the property." N.H. Const. Pt. 1, art. 12a (2006).

Texas amended its constitution to state that "public use does not include the taking of property . . . for transfer to a private entity for the *primary* purpose of economic development or enhancement of tax revenues". Tex. Const. art. I, § 17 (2009) (emphasis added). Virginia similarly amended its constitution to provide that a taking is not for public use "if the *primary* use is for private gain, private benefit, private enterprise, increasing jobs, increasing tax revenue, or economic development, except for the elimination of a public nuisance existing on the property". Va. Const. art. I, § 11 (2013). If a city in Texas condemned property that it claimed was blighted and then transferred that property to a third-party developer, would that condemnation violate the Texas State Constitution? What about a similar condemnation in Virginia?

South Carolina amended its constitution to provide that "[p]rivate property must not be condemned by eminent domain" for "the purpose or benefit of economic development, unless the condemnation is for public use". S.C. Const. art. I, § 13 (2007). What does this limitation accomplish?

As we will see below, Louisiana enacted its own detailed set of constitutional amendments after *Kelo*.

3. *State Statutes Limiting Public Use*: A number of states took the less drastic step of amending or passing statutory provisions that address the power of eminent domain. These statutory responses take several common forms. Some states, such as Arizona, define public use and then exclude as relevant considerations factors such as the "public benefits of economic development" or other factors such as "an increase in tax base, tax revenues, employment or general economic health." Ariz. Rev. Stat. Ann. § 12-1136(5) (2006); Del. Code Ann. tit. 29, § 9501A (2009) (defining public use and excluding "generation of public revenues, increase in tax base, tax revenues, employment or economic health, through private land owners or economic development").

Several states limit the power of eminent domain to prevent the transfer of property to another private person for economic development purposes and then list exceptions to the rule. Alaska Stat. Ann. § 09.55.240(d) (2006, amended in 2009 and 2015); Colo. Rev. Stat. Ann. § 31-25-105.5 (2004) (listing exceptions to the acquisition of private property by eminent domain for subsequent transfer to a private party); Kan. Stat. Ann. § 26-501a (2006) (prohibiting, subject to exceptions, "the taking of private property by eminent domain for the purpose of selling, leasing or otherwise transferring such property"); Me. Rev. Stat. tit. 1, § 816 (2006) (limiting, subject to exceptions, the power of eminent domain for purposes of private development, enhancement of tax revenue or transfer to another individual); Mo. Ann. Stat. § 523.271 (2006) (preventing the taking of private property through the power of eminent domain "for solely economic development purposes" and defining the scope of economic development); 26 Pa. Cons. Stat. Ann. § 204(a) (2006) (prohibiting, subject to exceptions, "the power of eminent domain to take private property in order to use it for private enterprise").

Some states allow room for condemnations that will serve traditional police power justifications such as elimination of blight. Wyoming's statute, for instance, excludes from public purpose "the taking of private property by a public entity for the purpose of transferring the property to another private individual or private entity," but makes an exception for "protecting the public health and safety." Wyo. Stat. Ann. § 1-26-801(c) (2007). Other states, such as Florida, more drastically limit the scope of public purpose by excluding as a legitimate justification the elimination of a public nuisance and elimination of slum or blight conditions, "notwithstanding any other provision of law." Fla. Stat. Ann. § 73.014 (2006). Which approach do you think will most sharply reduce the use of eminent domain for purposes of economic development? What is the best approach in your view?

4. *Judicial Interpretations of Public Use*: In the wake of *Kelo*, several state courts have resisted the proposition that economic development alone is sufficient to satisfy the public use requirement either because of the existence of state provisions limiting the scope of public use or because of the application of a more stringent standard of review. *See Norwood v. Horney*, 853 N.E.2d 1115 (Ohio 2006) (holding that economic or financial benefit alone is insufficient to satisfy the public-use requirement); *Bd. of Cty. Comm'rs of Muskogee Cty. v. Lowery*, 136 P.3d 639 (Okla.

2006) (holding that "takings for the purpose of economic development alone not in connection with the removal of blighted property do not constitute public use or public purpose"); *Gallenthin Realty Development, Inc. v. Borough of Paulsboro*, 924 A.2d 447 (N.J. 2007) (rejecting the idea that private property can be expropriated according to state statute because the property can be put to a higher economic use); *Salt Lake City Corp. v. Evans Dev. Group, LLC*, 369 P.3d 1236 (Utah 2016) (invalidating a taking under the state's eminent domain statutes because the alleged public use was being accomplished by a third party rather than the condemning authority); *Missouri ex rel. Jackson v. Dolan*, 398 S.W.3d 472 (Mo. 2013) (holding that the taking of private property violated a statute prohibiting the port authority from using the power of eminent domain for solely economic development purposes); *Middletown Township v. Lands of Stone*, 939 A.2d 331 (Pa. 2007) (invalidating the taking because the true purpose did not primarily benefit the public). In one way or another, all of these decisions express a concern that in the context of economic development takings, the power of eminent domain is being used primarily to benefit one private party's interests, as opposed to those of the public at large. Do you think this concern is valid? Should local governments be able to decide when a condemnation that will result in a third party transfer will provide sufficiently wide public benefits?

Not all state courts have reacted negatively to the use of eminent domain for economic development purposes. New York courts continue to employ an expansive view of public use. They continue to defer to local development agencies' decisions to use eminent domain for economic development unless the alleged public use is irrational or baseless. *See Goldstein v. New York State Urban Development Corp.*, 921 N.E.2d 164 (N.Y. 2009); *Kaur v. New York State Urban Development Corp.*, 933 N.E.2d 721 (N.Y. 2010); *Rocky Point Realty LLC v. Town of Brookhaven*, 828 N.Y.S.2d 197 (App. Div. 2007).

5. **In Defense of *Kelo***: Not all commentators were displeased with the majority decision in *Kelo*. For a defense of the majority decision and an alternative explanation of the limited reach of the *Kelo* backlash, see Bethany Berger, *Kelo and Constitutional Revolution that Wasn't*, 48 Conn. L. Rev. 1429 (2016). Berger writes:

> Land Assembly for economic development in cities is necessary precisely to help troubled cities, like New London, deserted by white flight to the suburbs and jobs overseas, and trying to provide employment and services for the people left behind. . . . The decision in Kelo . . . means that cities can try to create economic development to help those who cannot flee to the suburbs, and need not target their worst-off residents in doing so.

Id. at 1438. For a defense of the majority decision authored by the City of New London's appellate counsel before the United States Supreme Court, see Wesley W. Horton & Brendon P. Levesque, *Kelo is Not Dred Scott*, 48 Conn. L. Rev. 1405 (2016). For a defense of *Kelo* offered by the author of a prominent article cited by Justice Thomas in his dissent, see Wendell Pritchett, *A Solution in Search of a Problem*: Kelo *Reform over Ten Years*, 48 Conn. L. Rev. 1483 (2016).

After retiring from the Supreme Court, Justice John Paul Stevens made an interesting confession about his views as to whether the Fourteenth Amendment to the U.S. Constitution "incorporated" the Fifth Amendment so that it applied to the states. He then offered a defense of the ultimate decision in *Kelo* on alternative grounds. Justice John Paul Stevens (Ret.), *Kelo, Popularity and Substantive Due Process*, 63 ALA. L REV. 941 (2012).

6. *Undercompensation and Community Empowerment*: For many years, legal scholars influenced by the law and economics movement have focused their attention on the public use limitation of eminent domain expressing skepticism as to its ability to meaningfully restrain government power. *See especially* Lawrence Berger, *The Public Use Requirement in Eminent Domain*, 57 OR. L. REV. 203 (1978); Thomas W. Merrill, *The Economics of Public Use*, 72 CORNELL L. REV. 61 (1986). Berger and Merrill argue that property owners whose land and buildings are acquired by eminent domain for public projects are often undercompensated, particularly because their subjective interests — personal attachments to property, social capital, ties to jobs, homes and community — are not sufficiently accounted for by the standard "fair market valuation" metric used by most states and courts to calculate the amount of compensation a condemnee will receive for the involuntary transfer of property. As a solution to this problem, Berger and Merrill recommend more exacting judicial scrutiny when governments exercise eminent domain, particularly for projects that will not result in either the government or a common carrier owning the condemned property.

One group of scholars has proposed to remedy the problem of undercompensation by requiring increased or premium compensation awards for certain kinds of takings. *See, e.g.,* Richard Epstein, Takings: Private Property and the Power of Eminent Domain, 174–75, 183–84 (1985) (recommending bonus compensation awards set at 50% above fair market value); Lawrence Berger, *The Public Use Requirement in Eminent Domain* 57 OR. L. REV. at 236–37 (same) James E. Krier & Christopher Serkin, *Public Ruses* 2004 MICH. ST. L. REV. 859, 868–73 (recommending that courts use projections about the economic benefits predicted to flow from a proposed project when they determine just compensation for condemnations, particularly for those justified by supposed gains in economic development).

Another group of scholars has responded to concerns about undercompensation by recommending that property owners be allowed to determine the value of their own property and to assert their own community interests through innovative self-assessment and property owner empowerment strategies. *See, e.g.,* Lee Anne Fennell, *Taking Eminent Domain Apart*, 2004 MICH. ST. L. REV. 957, 995-1002 (suggesting that property owners be allowed to opt-in to condemnation at the assessed fair market value of their property in exchange for a property tax break, with the amount decreasing if they select a compensation award at various percentages above the fair market value); Michael Heller & Rick Hills, *Land Assembly Districts*, 121 HARV. L. REV. 1465 (2008) (recommending the formation of democratically managed, quasi-governmental entities called Land Assembly Districts (LADS) to represent a neighborhood targeted for condemnation and negotiate with developers seeking to use eminent domain for economic development purposes); James J. Kelly, Jr. *"We Shall Not Be Moved": Urban Communities, Eminent Domain and the Socioeconomics of Just Compensation*, 80 St. John's L. Rev. 923 (2006) (urging formation of Homestead Community Consent (HCC) requirements and establishment of a Community Residency Entitlement (CRE) to accomplish replacement housing in a redeveloped district after an economic development taking). For a fascinating comparative account of these debates and approaches to eminent domain in Germany, the rest of Europe, the United States, Taiwan and Korea, see Iljoong Kim, Hojun Lee and Ilya Somin, Eminent Domain: A Comparative Perspective (2017). What do you think is the best way to address the problem of undercompensation of property owners who lose their property as the result of a condemnation? Should the law provide more generous compensation for homeowners, as opposed to owners of commercial property or undeveloped property that is held solely for investment purposes?

7. *Eminent Domain and Blight Takings*: As Justice O'Conner's dissenting opinion in *Kelo* noted, cities and municipal redevelopment agencies have often used eminent domain to acquire and redevelop blighted properties or even entire "blighted" neighborhoods. These "blight takings" have often been upheld by the courts, even when the condemned property is later handed over to private developers, on the ground that the condemnation serves the important public purpose of eliminating a distinct public harm — the targeted blight. *See especially Berman v. Parker*, 348 U.S. 26 (1954). However, many commentators have noted that state statutes and municipal ordinances often contain vague definitions of "blighted" property or "blighted" neighborhoods that could be easily manipulated by an expropriating authority. For a particularly influential and critical historical account of the use of eminent domain in urban renewal projects in major U.S. cities, see Wendell E. Pritchett, *The "Public Menace" of Blight: Urban Renewal and the Private Uses of Eminent Domain*, 21 Yale Law & Policy Rev. 1 (2003). For more recent critical assessments, see Somin, Grasping Hand, *supra* 84–90, Ilya Somin, *Let There Be Blight, Blight Condemnations in New York After Goldstein and Kaur*, 38 Fordham Urb. L.J. 1193 (2011); Andrew Tutt, *Blightend Scrutiny*, 47 U. Cal. Davis L. Rev. 1807 (2014).

Other voices in the literature have offered that when economic development takings focus on vacant or abandoned urban parcels, they tend not to be controversial and are less likely the subject of challenges by community activists or political officials because of the perceived lack of investment by the property owners whose property is characterized as blighted and because of the diagnosis that the condemnation protects the investments of nearby property owners who have maintained their property. *See, e.g.,* Debbie Becher, Private Property and Eminent Domain, 7, 9–10 (2014). Should state constitutions or state statutes allow condemnations for the purposes of eliminating blight even if they result in the transfer of the condemned property to private parties? If so, should they narrowly or broadly define blight?

2. Limits on Expropriation in the Louisiana Constitution

Just like every other state's constitution, the Louisiana Constitution also contains a provision that provides protection for the property rights of its citizens. In the summer of 2006, the Louisiana legislature responded to *Kelo* with a number of constitutional amendments that were approved by the voters of the state in the fall. 2006 La. Acts 851 (amending La. Const. Art. I, §§ 4(B), 21(A) and adding Art. VI, § 21 (D)); 2006 La. Acts 859 (adding La. Const. Art. I, § 4(H)). Ironically, these constitutional amendments were passed at the same time that Louisiana began to confront the challenge of rebuilding in the wake of Hurricanes Katrina and Rita, which had hit the state in the late summer of 2005. For a critique of the 2006 amendments in light of the need to rebuild Southeast Louisiana, see Frank S. Alexander, *Louisiana Land Reform in the Storm's Aftermath*, 53. LOY. L. REV. 759 (2007). For additional commentary, see Shelby C. Stone, *Two Tales of One City: Eminent Domain Post-Katrina and a Response to Kelo*, 53 LOY. L. REV. 115 (2007); J. Miller, *Saving Private Development: Rescuing Louisiana from its Reaction to Kelo*, 68 LA. L. REV. 631 (2008). Thereafter, further amendments were made to the Louisiana Constitution.

Before considering the decision below in *St. Benard Port Harbor & Terminal District v. Violet Dock Port, Inc.*, 239 So.3d 243 (La. 2018), read the entire text of Article 1, Section 4 of the Louisiana Constitution in its current, amended form. The opinion in *St. Bernard Port* explains some of the provisions. Others will make sense in light of *Kelo*.

Louisiana Constitution, Article 1

Section 4. (A) Every person has the right to acquire, own, control, use, enjoy, protect, and dispose of private property. This right is subject to reasonable statutory restrictions and the reasonable exercise of the police power.

(B)(1) Property shall not be taken or damaged by the state or its political subdivisions except for public purposes and with just compensation paid to the owner or into court for his benefit. Except as specifically authorized by Article VI, Section 21 of this Constitution property shall not be taken or damaged by the state or its political subdivisions: (a) for predominant use by any private person or entity; or (b) for transfer of ownership to any private person or entity.

(2) As used in Subparagraph (1) of this Paragraph and in Article VI, Section 23 of this Constitution, "public purpose" shall be limited to the following:

(a) A general public right to a definite use of the property.

(b) Continuous public ownership of property dedicated to one or more of the following objectives and uses:

(i) Public buildings in which publicly funded services are administered, rendered, or provided.

(ii) Roads, bridges, waterways, access to public waters and lands, and other public transportation, access, and navigational systems available to the general public.

(iii) Drainage, flood control, levees, coastal and navigational protection and reclamation for the benefit of the public generally.

(iv) Parks, convention centers, museums, historical buildings and recreational facilities generally open to the public.

(v) Public utilities for the benefit of the public generally.

(vi) Public ports and public airports to facilitate the transport of goods or persons in domestic or international commerce.

(c) The removal of a threat to public health or safety caused by the existing use or disuse of the property.

(3) Neither economic development, enhancement of tax revenue, or any incidental benefit to the public shall be considered in determining whether the taking or damaging of property is for a public purpose pursuant to Subparagraph (1) of this Paragraph or Article VI, Section 23 of this Constitution.

(4) Property shall not be taken or damaged by any private entity authorized by law to expropriate, except for a public and necessary purpose and with just compensation paid to the owner; in such proceedings, whether the purpose is public and necessary shall be a judicial question.

(5) In every expropriation or action to take property pursuant to the provisions of this Section, a party has the right to trial by jury to determine whether the compensation is just, and the owner shall be compensated to the full extent of his loss. Except as otherwise provided in this Constitution, the full extent of loss shall include, but not be limited to, the appraised value of the property and all costs of relocation, inconvenience, and any other damages actually incurred by the owner because of the expropriation.

(6) No business enterprise or any of its assets shall be taken for the purpose of operating that enterprise or halting competition with a government enterprise. However, a municipality may expropriate a utility within its jurisdiction.

(C) Personal effects, other than contraband, shall never be taken.

(D) The following property may be forfeited and disposed of in a civil proceeding, as provided by law: contraband drugs; property derived in whole or in part from contraband drugs; property used in the distribution, transfer, sale, felony possession, manufacture, or transportation of contraband drugs; property furnished or intended to be furnished in exchange for contraband drugs; property used or intended to be used to facilitate any of the above conduct; or other property because the above-described property has been rendered unavailable.

(E) This Section shall not apply to appropriation of property necessary for levee and levee drainage purposes.

(F) Further, the legislature may place limitations on the extent of recovery for the taking of, or loss or damage to, property rights affected by coastal wetlands conservation, management, preservation, enhancement, creation, or restoration activities.

(G) Compensation paid for the taking of, or loss or damage to, property rights for the construction, enlargement, improvement, or modification of federal or non-federal hurricane protection projects, including mitigation related thereto, shall not exceed the compensation required by the Fifth Amendment of the Constitution of the United States of America. However, this Paragraph shall not apply to compensation paid for a building or structure that was destroyed or damaged by an event for which a presidential declaration of major disaster or emergency was issued, if the taking occurs within three years of such event. The legislature by law may provide procedures and definitions for the provisions of this Paragraph.

(H)(1) Except for the removal of a threat to public health or safety caused by the existing use or disuse of the property, and except for leases or operation agreements for port facilities, highways, qualified transportation facilities or airports, the state or its political subdivisions shall not sell or lease property which has been expropriated and held for not more than thirty years without first offering the property to the original owner or his heir, or, if there is no heir, to the successor in title to the owner at the time of expropriation at the current fair market value, after which the property can be transferred only by competitive bid open to the general public. After thirty years have passed from the date the property was expropriated, the state or political subdivision may sell or otherwise transfer the property as provided by law.

(2) Within one year after the completion of the project for which the property was expropriated, the state or its political subdivision which expropriated the property shall identify all property which is not necessary for the public purpose of the project and declare the property as surplus property.

(3) All expropriated property identified as surplus property shall be offered for sale to the original owner or his heir, or, if there is no heir, to the successor in title to the owner at the time of expropriation at the

current fair market value, within two years after completion of the project. If the original owner, heir, or other successor in title refuses or fails to purchase the surplus property within three years from completion of the project, then the surplus property may be offered for sale to the general public by competitive bid.

(4) After one year from the completion of the project for which property was expropriated, the original owner or his heir, or, if there is no heir, the successor in title to the owner at the time of expropriation may petition the state or its political subdivision which expropriated the property to have all or any portion of his property declared surplus. If the state or its political subdivision refuses or fails to identify all or any portion of the expropriated property as surplus, the original owner or the successor in title may petition any court of competent jurisdiction to have the property declared surplus.

Notes and Questions

1. Which provisions in Article 1, Section 4 of the Louisiana Constitution were added in response to *Kelo*? Can you imagine any situation in which the state or a political subdivision might face significant difficulties in seeking to promote economic development in light of the detailed provisions of Article 1, Section 4? What about the problem of responding to wide scale blight and devastation in the wake of a major hurricane?

In *New Orleans Redevelopment Authority v. Burgess*, 16 So.3d 569, 571–74 (La. App. 4 Cir. 2009), the court faced precisely this question. It held that a municipal redevelopment agency could exercise the power of expropriation to acquire blighted property with the intent to transfer the property to a private party, Habitat for Humanity. The court declined, on justiciability grounds, however, to address the applicability of Article 1, subsection 4(H)(1), as it was then in effect, which had granted a property owner who suffered an expropriation a right of first refusal to reacquire the expropriated property before it could be sold to a third party or, in the alternative, required a public auction before a post-expropriation transfer could occur. *Id*. In 2010, the Legislature addressed the question left open in *Burgess* by adopting another constitutional amendment, which was subsequently approved by the voters of the state. The new amendment expressly exempted property acquired through expropriation to remedy blight from the onerous right of first refusal and public auction requirements of Article 1, subsection 4(H)(1). *See* La. Acts 2010, No. 1052, amending La. Const. art. 1, § 4(H)(1).

2. For a detailed account of all the post-*Kelo* amendments to Article 1, Section 4, including the 2010 amendments, and the challenges posed in the course of redeveloping Southeast Louisiana after Hurricane Katrina, see John A. Lovett, *Somewhat at Sea: Public Use and Third-Party Transfer Limits in Two U.S. States*, in Bjorn Hoops et. al., Rethinking Expropriation Law I: Public Interest in Expropriation,

93, 114–123 (2015), https://papers.ssrn.com/sol3/papers.cfm?abstract_id=2685860 (Oct. 26, 2018).

3. Two other provisions of the Louisiana Constitution address the power of expropriation. One provision recognizes the power of political subdivisions of the state to acquire property by a variety of means, including expropriation. See La. Const. art. VI, § 23 (1974). ("Subject to and not inconsistent with this constitution and subject to restrictions provided by general law, political subdivisions may acquire property for any public purpose by purchase, donation, *expropriation*, exchange, or otherwise.") (emphasis added).

The second provision raises interesting interpretative challenges. In the interest of promoting industrial developmewnt, regional economic development, and the development of public ports, Article 4, Section 21 of the Louisiana Constitution allows the legislature to authorize certain entities, including a "political subdivision, public port commission, or public port, harbor, and terminal district to . . .

> (b) acquire, through purchase, donation, exchange, *and expropriation*, and improve industrial plant buildings and industrial plant equipment, machinery, furnishings, and appurtenances, including public port facilities and operations which relate to or facilitate the transportation of goods in domestic and international commerce; and

> (c) sell, lease, lease-purchase, or demolish all or any part of the foregoing.

La. Const. art. VI, § 21 (1974, amended 2006) (emphasis added).

Taking advantage of this broad power, the Legislature has, in fact, granted many of the entities listed in the provision, including public ports and port, harbor and terminal districts, expansive expropriation power. *See e.g.*, La. Rev. Stat. §§ 34:1-336.1 (establishing multiple public port authorities with the power of expropriation throughout the state). Do Article 1, Section 21, and the subsequent statutes establishing port authorities and granting them broad powers of expropriation, create a potential conflict with the provisions of Article 1, Section 4(B) that seek to narrow the permissible justifications for expropriation?

4. Now read the decision in *St. Bernard Port Harbor & Terminal District v. Violet Dock Port, Inc.*, 239 So.3d 243 (La. 2018), which involves all of these constitutional provisions. Do not overlook the excerpts from Justice Weimer's dissenting opinion and the subsequent decision of the Louisiana Fourth Circuit Court of Appeal on remand from the Louisiana Supreme Court. Has the majority opinion properly deferred to the policy decision of the public port plaintiff to expropriate the defendant's private property for a legitimate public purpose? Alternatively, did the public port, as Justice Wiemer contends, exceed or abuse its expropriation power in violation of Article, Section 4(B)(6) of the Louisiana Constitution or in violation of the Fifth Amendment of the United States Constitution? Assuming the expropriation was constitutional, did the Fourth Circuit reach the correct result in determining the amount of just compensation payable to the defendant?

St. Bernard Port Harbor & Terminal Dist. v. Violet Dock Port Inc.

239 So.3d 243 (La. 2018), *cert. denied*, 2018 U.S. LEXIS 6129

CRICHTON, Justice: Although the Louisiana Constitution generally restricts the government from expropriating private property, it provides broad exceptions for public port authorities. To Louisiana's maritime industry, public ports are critical. Due to market demands and increasing global competition, public ports must expand in order to compete. The Louisiana Constitution therefore provides that the government can expropriate property for "[p]ublic ports . . . to facilitate the transport of goods or persons in domestic or international commerce." La. Const. art. I, §4(B)(2)(b)(vi).

We granted the writ in this matter to determine whether St. Bernard Port, Harbor & Terminal District's (the "Port") expropriation of property owned by Violet Dock Port, Inc., L.L.C. ("Violet") on the Mississippi River satisfies the "public purpose" requirement of art. I, §4(B)(1) of the Louisiana Constitution and, further, whether it violates the business enterprise clause of art. I, §4(B)(6) of the Louisiana Constitution. For the reasons that follow, we find that the record demonstrates that the Port's expropriation was for the public purpose "to facilitate the transport of goods or persons in domestic or international commerce" and not for the constitutionally prohibited purpose of operating Violet's enterprise or halting competition with a government enterprise. We therefore affirm the court of appeal holding that the expropriation was constitutional. However, we also find the trial court made a legal error in setting the just compensation due to Violet under art. I, §4(B)(1), and further find that the court of appeal failed to correct that error. We therefore remand this matter to the court of appeal solely for the purpose of fixing the amount of just compensation based on the evidence in the record and in accordance with the principles set forth in this opinion.

Background

Maritime trade is a primary mode of transport for national and international commerce. In the last century, the maritime industry has expanded and modernized. This includes advancements such as containerization and other improvements that have ushered in super tankers and mega ships. In other words, more and larger ships now transport greater amounts of cargo. Such advancements have made public ports, like the St. Bernard Port, a virtual necessity. To accommodate these changes, ports must expand and adapt.

The Port, a public cargo facility in St. Bernard Parish, has consistently experienced an increased demand for cargo handling since at least 2001. Through a lease with a Marine Terminal Operator ("MTO"), Associated Terminals, the Port handles several types of cargo, and has remained one of the busiest ports in the country. For example, from 2007–2009, the Port's cargo included 37% of all the ferro alloys imported into the United States, 37% of the barite, 10% of the urea, and 3% of the potash. However, the Port began experiencing a shortage of space, and its customers requested both additional space and a liquid cargo facility. Ultimately, by 2008, the

Port was operating at near capacity, and determined that if it could not meet its customers' demands, its operations would suffer. As a result, the Port sought to expand in order to meet these growing needs.

To support its expansion, the Port identified approximately 75 acres of land along the Mississippi River (the "Property"). The Port began, as early as 1985, the arduous process of locating suitable property. Seven or eight different sites were investigated, and factors such as having a nearby railroad and land for ingress and egress of trucks were paramount. Compared to other sites along the river, the Property had many of these critical attributes. The Port determined that the Property's relatively straight segment and deep water could handle large cargo ships better than other sites. Further, there was enough land between the nearby levee and the existing rail line for the Port to place a cargo facility. At other sites, the levee was too close to the rail line, which would require the Port to relocate the rail line in order to build a cargo facility. According to a representative from Associated Terminals, the Port's MTO, there was no other space in St. Bernard Parish where a bulk terminal facility could be constructed on the river.

Violet, a limited liability company, owned the Property. At the date of the expropriation, the Property had five berths, which were used for berthing and mooring vessels (*i.e.*, what a Violet representative described as a "parking lot for ships") and topside repairs. Violet also had a contract with the Military Sealift Command, a civilian branch of the United States Navy (the "Navy"), to layberth and service oceangoing ships. In the ten years before the expropriation, Violet's cargo operations were described as "negligible."

A five-member Board of Commissioners, appointed by the Governor, makes decisions for the Port. In 2007, the Port offered $10 million to purchase the Property, which Violet rejected. In 2008, the parties tentatively agreed to a sale of the property for $14 million. Based on this agreement, in order to purchase and develop the property, the Port applied for funding to the Louisiana Department of Transportation & Development's Port Priority Program. In 2010, the Port was awarded a $15 million grant to acquire the Property.

The Port then had the Property reappraised and, as a result, informed Violet it would pay the newly appraised fair market value of $16 million. Violet rejected the Port's offer, and instead sought $35 million. After this, negotiations failed, and the Port initiated the expropriation proceedings.

Procedural History

The Port initiated this expropriation on December 22, 2010, under the quick-take expropriation provisions of La. R.S. 19:141, *et seq.* and deposited $16 million into the registry of the district court. According to the petition, the expropriation was for the purpose of expanding the Port's current port facilities to handle dry-bulk and liquid-bulk commodities. The petition stated the construction of development of the Property would occur in three phases and take approximately eight to ten years to complete. During that time, the petition stated the Port intended to "enter into a new contract with [the Navy] for its continued use of the Violet Port during Phase I of the acquisition and development of the [Property]." The petition further stated the expropriation would "create jobs and benefits to the citizens of St. Bernard Parish."

Violet thereafter removed the case to federal court and moved to dismiss the petition for expropriation. . . .

The federal court remanded the case to state court. *Id.* at 538.

Following remand, the trial court held a hearing to consider the public purpose of the expropriation. The trial court heard testimony, reviewed the evidence, and evaluated the credibility of the witnesses. At the hearing, Violet again argued that the Port's true purpose in expropriating the Property was to take over the Navy lease. The Port contended otherwise. According to the Executive Director of the Port: "As far as the lease with the Navy . . . it's an afterthought. . . . [T]hat's certainly not one of our goals." Similarly, a representative from Associated Terminals, the Port's MTO, stated: "[T]he best news for [us] is that the Navy would leave, because we want the use of the berth to handle cargo, and that's the best berth, the one that they're [the Navy] presently tied to." He further stated: "We're not in the ship berthing business. We're in the cargo business." In contrast, Violet's representative stated that in the decade before the expropriation it had handled "probably no cargo. . . . There may have been some negligible cargo."

After the hearing, the trial court rejected Violet's argument that the expropriation was for the purpose of taking the Navy lease. In granting the Port's petition, the trial court stated that the Port took the Property to "build and operate a terminal to accommodate transport of liquid and solid bulk commodities into national and international commerce to and from St. Bernard." This judgment was based on the trial court's firsthand credibility determinations after hearing testimony from various witnesses. Among these was of the Port's Executive Director, who testified about the Port's need for space. According to his testimony, the Port's cargo tonnage in the previous ten years had grown sevenfold. Consistent with this evidence, the trial court also stated the expropriation was a "logical extension of port services in St. Bernard." From this ruling, Violet applied for writs of certiorari. Both the Fourth Circuit Court of Appeal and this Court denied Violet's writ applications. *St. Bernard Port, Harbor & Terminal Dist. v. Violet Dock Port, Inc., LLC,* 12–0417 (La. App. 4 Cir. 5/16/12); 12-1122 (La. 5/30/12), 90 So.3d 419.

The case proceeded to a trial on valuation. The trial court found just compensation to be $16 million. At trial, the Port's experts testified that the highest and best use of the Property was continued layberthing plus limited aggregate operations, valuing the Property at $16 million. Violet's experts maintained that the highest and best use of the Property was as a cargo facility. Violet argued that it should be compensated between $51 million and $67 million. The trial court rejected the highest and best use and valuation opinions of Violet's experts, citing physical limitations that it alleged rendered the Property unsuitable for very large-scale cargo use, including: (a) water depth at the docks; (b) proximity to school and residential areas; (c) limited amount of uplands available for cargo; and (d) configuration of the Property. Consequently, the trial court found just compensation to be $16 million.

On appeal, a divided court of appeal panel affirmed. As to the Port's petition for expropriation, the majority stated: "Although the authority granted to the ports of Louisiana in the expropriation of private property is exceptionally broad, it is supported by the constitution and statutes of the State." *St. Bernard Port, Harbor & Terminal Dist. v. Violet Dock Port, Inc., LLC*, 16–96, 16–262, 16–331, p.7 (La. App. 4 Cir. 12/14/16) ("*St. Bernard Port I*"), 229 So.3d 626. In affirming the trial court's just compensation award, the majority found the record supported the trial court's ruling. *Id.* at p.10. It further noted that '[w]here there are two permissible views of the evidence, the factfinder's choice between them cannot be manifestly erroneous or clearly wrong." *Id.* One judge dissented, finding that the expropriation was unconstitutional. *Id.* at p.15 (Lobrano, J., dissenting). After Violet sought rehearing, the court of appeal denied the request. *St. Bernard Port, Harbor & Terminal Dist. v. Violet Dock Port, Inc., LLC*, 16–96, 16–262, 16–331, p. 7 (La. App. 4 Cir. 2/8/17), ——— So.3d——— ("*St. Bernard Port II*"), 2017 WL 526160.

This Court granted Violet's writ application. 17-0434 (La. 5/26/17), 221 So.3d 853.

Discussion

Authorization for expropriations by a government body—and important limitations placed upon those authorizations—are found in both the federal and state constitutions. *See South Lafourche Levee Dist. v. Jarreau*, 16–0788, 16-0904, p. 8–9 (La. 3/31/17), 217 So.3d 298, 305, *cert. denied*, ——U.S.——, 138 S.Ct. 381, 199 L. Ed.2d 279 (10/31/17). More specifically, the Fifth Amendment of the United States Constitution, made applicable to the states pursuant to the Fourteenth Amendment, provides: "No person shall . . . be deprived of life, liberty or property without due process of law; nor shall private property be taken for public use, without just compensation." Likewise, the Louisiana Constitution provides "[p]roperty shall not be taken or damaged by the state or its political subdivisions except for public purposes and with just compensation . . ." La. Const. art. I, § 4(B)(1). Therefore, under both Constitutions, any expropriation must be for a "public purpose" *and* provide "just compensation."

To review these determinations, we start with the constitutional provisions at issue. *Arrow Aviation Co., L.L.C. v. St. Martin Parish Sch. Bd. Tax Sales Dept.*, 16-1132, p.4 (La. 12/6/16), 218 So.3d 1031, 1035 ("When a constitutional provision is plain and unambiguous and its application does not lead to absurd consequences, its language must be given effect."). We then review the record to determine whether the trial court's factual findings were manifestly erroneous. *See Exxon Mobil Pipeline Co. v. Union Pac. R. Co.*, 09-1629, p.12 (La. 3/16/10), 35 So.3d 192, 200 ("Whether the expropriator's purpose is public and necessary is a judicial determination that will not be reversed on appeal absent manifest error.").

Public Purpose

In 2005, the United States Supreme Court decided the case *Kelo v. City of New London*, 545 U.S. 469, 125 S.Ct. 2655, 162 L.Ed.2d 439 (2005) which expressly upheld a taking for economic development purposes. Following *Kelo*, in 2006, voters of Louisiana approved a constitutional amendment enumerating permissible "public purposes" for a political subdivision to expropriate private property. As amended, art. I, § 4 provides, in pertinent part:

> Section 4. . . .
>
> (B)(1) Property shall not be taken or damaged by the state or its political subdivisions except for public purposes and with just compensation paid to the owner or into court for his benefit. Except as specifically authorized by Article VI, Section 21 of this Constitution property shall not be taken or damaged by the state or its political subdivisions: (a) for predominant use by any private person or entity; or (b) for transfer of ownership to any private person or entity.
>
> (2) As used in Subparagraph (1) of this Paragraph and in Article VI, Section 23 of this Constitution, "public purpose" shall be limited to the following:
>
> * * *
>
> (b) Continuous public ownership of property dedicated to one or more of the following objectives and uses:
>
> * * *
>
> (vi) *Public ports and public airports to facilitate the transport of goods or persons in domestic or international commerce.*
>
> * * *
>
> (6) No business enterprise or any of its assets shall be taken for the purpose of operating that enterprise or halting competition with a government enterprise. . . .

(Emphasis added.)

In other words, the Louisiana Constitution expressly includes "public ports" as an enumerated "public purpose." Specifically, a public purpose is defined as "[p]ublic ports . . . to facilitate the transport of goods or persons in domestic or international commerce." La. Const. art. I, § 4(B)(2)(b)(vi).

Consistent with the authority given to public ports to expropriate property, the trial court made a factual determination that the Port's purpose for expropriation was to "build and operate a terminal to accommodate transport of liquid and solid bulk commodities into national and international commerce to and from St. Bernard." This purpose falls squarely within the constitutional definition of "public purpose" for public ports. La. Const. art. I, § 4(B)(2)(b)(vi). Based on the record before us, we cannot say that the trial court's finding was manifestly erroneous, and we therefore affirm the finding that this expropriation was for a public purpose. We also find that this expropriation satisfies the broad definition of public purpose under federal law. *See Kelo*, 545 U.S. at 479, 125 S.Ct. 2655 ("Without exception, our cases have defined that concept broadly, reflecting our longstanding policy of deference to legislative judgments in this field.").

Business Enterprise Clause

Violet also argues that, even if there was a "public purpose" here, the expropriation violates La. Const. art. I, §4(B)(6), known as the "business enterprise clause." The legislature did not change this provision as part of the 2006 amendments. La. Const. art. I, §4(B)(6) states:

> (6) No business enterprise or any of its assets shall be taken *for the purpose of* operating that enterprise or halting competition with a government enterprise. However, a municipality may expropriate a utility within its jurisdiction.

> (Emphasis added.)

The business enterprise clause requires the court to determine if the expropriation was "for the purpose of" operating an enterprise or halting competition with a government enterprise. On this point, the court of appeal majority held that the trial court was not manifestly erroneous in holding that the business enterprise clause does not apply here from a *factual* standpoint. Violet contests this holding, contending that the Port's expropriation was either to take Violet's revenue stream from the Navy lease or to halt competition with Violet's cargo operations, which it suggests were growing.

First, Violet argues that the purpose of the Port's expropriation was to take over Violet's revenue stream from the Navy lease. Yet testimony at trial was that the Navy lease was "an afterthought." Testimony further indicated that the "best news" for the Port's operation would be to use the Navy berth to further expand cargo operations. Our conclusion is buttressed by the fact that the lower courts and the federal court rejected similar arguments. *See St. Bernard Port I*, 229 So.3d at 632 ("Violet Dock argues that the real purpose for the taking was so the Port could continue to operate its layberthing and cargo facility and obtain the Navy contracts in violation of La. Const. art. I, §4(B)(6) . . . We disagree."); *St. Bernard Port II*, 2017 WL 526160, at *1 (on rehearing) ("[W]e found that the facts and circumstances presented by this case simply did not satisfy the requirements of the restrictions of La. Const. art. I, §4(B)(6)."); *St. Bernard Port Federal*, 809 F.Supp.2d at 531 ("Nor has Violet submitted anything, other than its own characterization, to suggest that acquisition of the [Navy] property was the primary motivating cause of this 70 acre expropriation."). We likewise do so here.

Second, Violet argues that the purpose of the Port's expropriation was to halt competition. Though Violet argues its cargo operations were growing, the record shows that Violet's cargo operations were "negligible" and that it did not compete with the Port. Instead, generally speaking, the businesses of Violet and the Port were not comparable. Violet was in the layberthing business; the Port was in the cargo business. The record supports the trial court's conclusion that the Port experienced an increasing demand for maritime cargo operations, was at capacity, and sought to expand its cargo operations.

To review the judgment we examine the entire record, but we will not set aside the trial court's judgment in absence of manifest error. *Rosell v. ESCO*, 549 So.2d 840, 844 (La. 1989). Here, the trial court's judgment followed an evidentiary hearing, where the trial court examined evidence, evaluated the credibility of multiple witnesses, and weighed the probative value of these assertions. As this Court has stated:

> It is well settled that a court of appeal may not set aside a trial court's or a jury's finding of fact in the absence of "manifest error" or unless it is "clearly wrong," and where there is conflict in the testimony, reasonable evaluations of credibility and reasonable inferences of fact should not be disturbed upon review, even though the appellate court may feel that its own evaluations and inferences are as reasonable.

Id. at 844.

Based upon our consideration of the record before us, we do not find the trial court's judgment to be manifestly erroneous or clearly wrong. We therefore affirm the lower court's judgment granting the Port's petition to expropriate.

Just Compensation

As noted above, the Louisiana Constitution provides that any expropriation must be for a "public purpose" *and* provide "just compensation." La. Const. art. I, § 4(B)(1). It further states: "In every expropriation or action to take property pursuant to the provisions of this Section, ..., the owner shall be compensated to the full extent of his loss." La. Const. art. I, § 4(B)(5). There is no specific formula set forth by the Legislature to aid courts in determining the "full extent of loss." The Constitution states only: "Except as otherwise provided in this Constitution, the full extent of loss shall include, but not be limited to, the appraised value of the property and all costs of relocation, inconvenience, and any other damages actually incurred by the owner because of the expropriation." *Id.*

La. R.S. 19:9 provides limited guidance as to how to determine the "full extent of the loss." It states that the basis of the assessment of value of the property to be expropriated "shall be the value which the property possessed before the contemplated improvement was proposed, without deducting therefrom any general or specific benefits derived by the owner from the contemplated improvement or work." La. R.S. 19:9(A). *See also Exxon Pipeline Co. v. Hill*, 00–2535, 00-2559, p.7 (La. 5/15/01), 788 So.2d 1154, 1159–60. The legislature and courts have developed rules that accept fair market value of the property as a relevant consideration in determining just compensation. *Id. See also West Jefferson Levee Dist. v. Coast Quality Constr. Corp.*, 93-1718 (La. 5/23/94), 640 So.2d 1258, 1277, *cert. denied*, 513 U.S. 1083, 115 S. Ct. 736, 130 L.Ed.2d 639 (1995). Fair market value, in turn, has consistently been defined as the price a buyer is willing to pay after considering all of the uses that the property may be put to where such uses are not speculative, remote or contrary to law. *Id.* In assessing the fair market value of an expropriated property, the Court considers the most profitable use to which the land can be put by reason of its location, topography, and adaptability. *Exxon Pipeline*, 00–2535, 00–2559, p.8, 788 So.2d at 1160. This is known as the "highest and best use" doctrine. *Id.*

Determining the "highest and best use" of land in expropriation cases involves several factors, including scarcity of the land available for that use and the use to which the property was being put at the time of the taking. *Id.* (setting forth various factors for courts to consider). *See also State, through the Dept. of Highways v. Bitterwolf*, 415 So.2d 196, 199 (La. 1982), *State, through the Dept. of Highways v. Constant*, 369 So.2d 699, 702 (La. 1979). It is "well established" that the current use of the property is presumed to be the highest and best use and the burden of overcoming that presumption by proving the existence of a different highest and best use based on a potential, future use is on the landowner. *Exxon Pipeline*, 00–2535, 00–2559, p.8, 788 So.2d at 1160. Where a landowner overcomes the presumption, the landowner is entitled to compensation based on a potential use of the property, even though the property is not being so utilized at the time of the taking, provided he can show it is reasonably probable the property could be put to this use in the "not too distant future." *West Jefferson Levee Dist.*, 640 So.2d at 1273.

In summary, in this case, the use to which Violet was putting the Property at the time of the expropriation—here, layberthing—is presumed to be the Property's highest and best use. Violet may overcome this presumption by demonstrating, by a preponderance of the evidence, that the property could be used in a different, more valuable way, that the potential use is not speculative, and that it could be undertaken in the "not too distant future." *Exxon Pipeline*, 00–2535, 00–2559, p.8–9, 788 So.2d at 1160–61; *West Jefferson Levee Dist.*, 640 So.2d at 1273. Here, the trial court found that Violet did not overcome that presumption.

Turning to the standard by which we review the trial court's findings, in an expropriation proceeding, the trial court's factual determination as to the value of the property will not be disturbed in the absence of manifest error. *West Jefferson Levee Dist.*, 640 So.2d at 1277. "However, where one or more trial court legal errors interdict the fact-finding process, the manifest error standard is no longer applicable, and, if the record is otherwise complete, the appellate court should make its own independent *de novo* review of the record and determine a preponderance of the evidence." *Evans v. Lungrin*, 97-0541 (La. 2/6/98), 708 So.2d 731, 735. *See also West Jefferson Levee Dist.*, 640 So.2d at 1278. Legal errors occur when a trial court applies incorrect principles of law and those errors are prejudicial; when such a prejudicial legal error occurs, the appellate court is required to review the record and determine the facts *de novo*. *Evans*, 708 So.2d at 735.

Here, we find the trial court used the incorrect standard for evaluating experts' valuation testimony. Explaining why it accepted the Port's expert testimony rather than Violet's, the court stated: "It is the opinion of this Court that it does not have the discretion to 'split the baby' and arrive at a valuation somewhere in between" the two expert opinions. This is erroneous. A trier of fact is not required to make a binary choice and accept one side's testimony in its entirety, but is instead empowered to weigh strengths and weaknesses of expert testimony. To the extent the trial court held otherwise, this is legal error. *See West Jefferson Levee Dist.*, 640 So.2d at 1277 ("The opinions of experts regarding valuation are advisory and are used only to assist the court in determining the amount of compensation due in an expropriation case."). *See also, e.g., State, Dep't of Transp. & Dev. v. Schwegmann Westside Expressway, Inc.*, 95-1261, p. 6–7 (La. 3/1/96), 669 So.2d 1172, 1176 ("[A] trier of fact does not have to accept in toto the testimony of any one group or group witnesses."). Further, this error was prejudicial to Violet insofar as the trial court set just compensation in the exact amount put forward by the Port's experts.

The court of appeal compounded this error by failing to identify it and conduct a *de novo* review. *St. Bernard Port I*, 229 So.3d at 634–35 (noting that "we cannot find that the trial court was manifestly erroneous or clearly wrong in its ruling that $16,000,000 was just compensation for the property"). Instead, the court of appeal noted the general proposition that a factfinder has "broad discretion" in determining weight to be given to expert testimony. *Id.* While this is, of course, a correct statement of the law, it overlooks that the trial court was apparently operating under an incorrect belief about the extent of its ability to exercise that broad discretion.

In summary, we find that the lower courts erred in the determination of just compensation. We therefore remand this matter to the court of appeal solely for the purpose of fixing the amount of just compensation based on the evidence in the record and in accordance with the principles set forth in this opinion. *See Gonzales v. Xerox Corp.*, 254 La. 182, 320 So.2d 163, 165 (1975) (remand to appellate court, rather than trial court, is appropriate when the appellate court has all the facts before it); *Buckbee v. United Gas Pipe Line Co.*, 561 So.2d 76, 87 (La. 1990). *See also Exxon Pipeline*, 00–2535, 00–2559, p.18, 788 So.2d at 1166 (Knoll, J., concurring) ("[V]aluation of property in expropriation cases is an open question and each case should be judged on its own under its individual facts and circumstances. Inadequate and inaccurate valuations run rampant and we must strive to find valuations that serve the purpose of protecting property rights while allowing public interests to be served."). Although this Court, like the court of appeal, has appellate jurisdiction of both law and fact and may perform an independent review and render judgment on the merits, *see* La. Const. art. V, § 5 (C), we prefer that the court of appeal perform the first appellate review of the entire record under the correct rule of law. *Buckbee*, 561 So.2d at 87.

Conclusion

We affirm the court of appeal's holding that the expropriation was constitutional. However, we reverse the court of appeal's holding on the amount of just compensation due to Violet under art. I, § 4(B)(1), after finding that the trial court made a legal error in its determination of just compensation and the court of appeal failed to correct that error. We therefore remand this matter to the court of appeal solely for the purpose of fixing the amount of just compensation based on the evidence in the record and in accordance with the principles set forth in this opinion.

AFFIRMED IN PART, REVERSED IN PART, AND REMANDED.

WEIMER, J., dissenting. With all due respect, I find the majority opinion unfortunately eviscerates the long, significant history the citizens of Louisiana have embodied within La. Const. art. I, § 4(B)(6) to protect private business from takeover by the government. The majority opinion thereby subjects business interests across Louisiana to increased risk of government takeovers, which has the effect of thwarting private business from initiating economic development that competes with governmental enterprises. While agreeing that the determination of whether the St. Bernard Port, Harbor & Terminal District ("the Port") expropriated the property and port facilities owned by Violet Dock Port, Inc., LLC ("Violet") for the purpose of operating that port facility or halting competition with the Port is, to an extent, fact-based, I find that legal errors committed by the district court interdicted the fact-finding process, necessitating *de novo* review. I additionally find that the perfunctory and, in the end, erroneous, manifest error review compounds the legal error of the district court, exposing to serious erosion the conscious, concerted efforts to protect private business enshrined in our constitution. Therefore, I respectfully dissent from the majority opinion.

Historical Background

While the resolution of this case centers around the meaning and application of a singular provision in the constitution, the historical context should be considered in evaluating this *res nova* issue.

The citizens of Louisiana have long maintained, through the constitutional provisions they ratified, that the situations in which the government can expropriate private property are greatly limited. Providing a guarantee prominently positioned in the second section of the Bill of Rights, the 1921 Constitution indicates: "Except as otherwise provided in this Constitution, private property shall not be taken or damaged except for public purposes and after just and adequate compensation is paid." La. Const. 1921 art. I, § 2.

With the enactment of the most recent constitution, this protection was enhanced. Under the 1974 Constitution, expropriation requires not merely a "public purpose," but a "public and necessary purpose." La. Const. 1974 art. I, § 4(B). In addition, the amount of compensation owed is not limited to "just and adequate compensation," as in the 1921 Constitution, but expanded to encompass compensation to "the full extent of [the owner's] loss." *Id.* Furthermore, in a provision specifically directed to the issue at hand, a third protection was added. See *id.*

While prohibitions against government engaging in commercial enterprise had been enshrined in constitutions dating back over one-and-a-quarter centuries (see the 1879 Constitution), the 1974 Constitution, consistent with its intent to provide increased protection to private interests from governmental takings, added a new prohibition, currently found in La. Const. art. I, § 4(B)(6). This prohibition, which

I refer to as the "private business enterprise protection clause," provides in relevant part:

> No business enterprise or any of its assets shall be taken for the purpose of operating that enterprise or halting competition with a government enterprise.

The clause represents "the first provision in any state constitution to prohibit the government from seizing the means of production," Louis Woody Jenkins, *The Declaration of Rights*, 21 Loy. L. Rev. 9, 24 (1975), and evidences a clear and unambiguous choice by the electorate to curtail government efforts to take business property or the business itself.

With the above-detailed protections added to and enshrined in Article I, § 4, the 1974 Constitution "goes beyond other state constitutions, including our 1921 Constitution, and the federal constitution in limiting the power of government to regulate private property." State v. 1971 Green GMC Van, 354 So.2d 479, 486 (La. 1977).

However, the citizens of Louisiana did not stop there, demonstrating an adamant and emphatic determination to protect private business from government takeover. When property rights protected by the federal constitution were seemingly eroded by the United State Supreme Court's ruling in Kelo v. City of New London, Connecticut, 545 U.S. 469, 125 S.Ct. 2655, 162 L.Ed.2d 439 (2005), the Louisiana electorate responded by enshrining additional protections in our state constitution. See 2006 La. Acts 851, § 1 (approved September 30, 2006). These protections include a prohibition from taking property "for predominant use by" or "transfer of ownership to any private person," and the inclusion of a more "limited" definition of "public purpose." See La. Const. art. I, § 4(B)(1)(a) and (b); Id., § 4(B)(2). Furthermore, in a rejection of the core holding of Kelo, the Louisiana electorate added the following prohibition: "Neither economic development, enhancement of tax revenue, or any incidental benefit to the public shall be considered in determining whether the taking or damaging of property is for a public purpose. . . ." La. Const. art. I, § 4(B)(3).

As evidenced by the above, Louisiana has a long and storied history of protecting private property interests from undue governmental interference. Nowhere is that strong interest more evident than in the protections extended under La. Const. art. I, § 4(B)(6), protections unique to Louisiana, but entirely consistent with the core principles underlying Louisiana's interest in protecting private property rights.

It is the meaning and application of La. Const. art. I, § 4(B)(6) that is ultimately at issue in this case, an issue which is *res nova* in this court, but not without guidance for its resolution. Foremost among the guiding principles is the dictate that the starting point in interpreting constitutional provisions is the language of the provision itself and that, when the language of a constitutional provision is clear and unambiguous, that language must be given effect. Louisiana Department of Agriculture and Forestry v. Sumrall, 98-1587, pp. 4–5 (La. 3/2/99), 728 So.2d 1254, 1258. In this case, no party contends that the language of Article I, § 4(B)(6) is ambiguous or susceptible to multiple interpretations. Therefore, to evaluate the provision, it is not necessary to look behind its clear language. However, for the purpose of placing the constitutional provision in its historical context, it is relevant to note that secondary sources confirm the clear intent behind the words of the enactment.

As explained by Delegate Jenkins, the co-author and floor sponsor of Section 4(B)(6), the provision "was clearly intended to counter what delegates perceived as excessive interference by government in the economy and the growing possibility that government would attempt to take over certain business enterprises." Jenkins, *The Declaration of Rights*, 21 Loy. L. Rev. at 24. Given this purpose, "the provision should be broadly interpreted to prevent both direct and indirect efforts to seize any private industry." *Id.*

Of course, as acknowledged by Delegate Jenkins and as evidenced in its language, the prohibition contained in Section 4(B)(6) is not absolute, and certain expropriations may have the effect of terminating a business enterprise, as, for example, when a highway right-of-way results in the taking of property belonging to a grocery store, causing it to go out of business. *Id.*, 21 Loy. L. Rev. at 25. In such cases, *the purpose of the expropriation is crucial. Id.* Pursuant to Section 4(B)(6), "[a]ny effort to use the power of eminent domain to take over an existing business or seize its assets in order to create a similar government enterprise or to put an enterprise out of business in order to improve the competitive advantage of a government enterprise is unconstitutional." *Id.*

The Litigation

With this historical context in mind, it is appropriate to turn to the instant case in which, using the "quick-take" provisions of La. R.S. 19:141, *et seq.*, the Port expropriated Violet's privately owned port facility. Violet filed a motion to dismiss the petition for expropriation, arguing, among other things, that the taking violated La. Const. art. I, §4(B)(6). Following an evidentiary hearing, the district court denied the motion to dismiss based on a finding that the taking served a public purpose. In a per curiam issued in connection with that ruling, the district court reasoned:

> Export of goods and commodities through the port is one of the basic industries of St. Bernard Parish. The acquisition of the Violet terminal would be a logical extension of port services in St. Bernard. The port would acquire heavy duty docks and forty two hundred (4200 LF) linear feet of Mississippi River frontage available for immediate use. Thirty eight (38) acres of presently undeveloped uplands would be available for cargo storage. The contemplated construction and use of the property would bring needed revenues into the community which is still recovering from the effects of the 2005 hurricanes and provide needed employment to its citizens. The predominant use for the property would be by the public, not for use by, or for transfer of ownership to any private person or entity. The Court is apprised that the expropriation will not affect the use by MSC ["Military Sealift Command"] for its vessels should MSC elect to continue that use.

Standard of Review

The majority opinion maintains that the district court's per curiam represents a determination "that the business-enterprise clause does not apply here from a *factual* standpoint" and, thus, the district court's ruling is subject to manifest error review. St. Bernard Port, Harbor & Terminal District v. Violet Dock Port, Inc., L.L.C., 17-0434, op. at 251, 252 (La. 1/30/18) (emphasis in original). I respectfully disagree, believing that a more careful analysis in light of the historical context or "a deeper look at the [district] court's reasons for ruling . . . reveals an error in [the] legal analysis, requiring this court to conduct a *de novo* review of the record." See Bridges v. Nelson Indus. Steam Co., 15-1439, p. 4 (La. 5/3/16), 190 So.3d 276, 279.

Even a cursory review of the district court's per curiam reveals that it contains no factual findings or legal determination regarding the primary reason cited by Violet for its contention that the taking is unconstitutional—that it violates La. Const. art. I, §4(B)(6)'s prohibition against the taking of a business enterprise or any of its assets for the purpose of operating that enterprise or halting competition. Indeed the per curiam makes no mention of the private business enterprise protection clause or any factual findings relating thereto. Instead, the per curiam focuses solely on considerations prompted by Section 4(B)(1); *i.e.*, whether the taking is for the predominant use or transfer of ownership to any private entity. Furthermore, it focuses on economic factors—needed revenues and employment—that are expressly prohibited from consideration in determining public purpose by Section 4(B)(3).

"The manifest error standard of review assumes that the trier of fact applied the correct law in arriving at its conclusion." Winfield v. Dih, 01-1357, p. 8 (La.App. 4 Cir. 4/24/02), 816 So.2d 942, 948. That assumption is not warranted in this case where the district court's reasons reflect that the court's decision was guided by principles that are either irrelevant to the question of whether the taking violated the private business enterprise protection clause, *i.e.*, whether the taking is for the predominant use or transfer of ownership to a private entity; or expressly prohibited from consideration in connection therewith; *i.e.*, whether port expansion will add revenues and jobs to the local community. Because, as was the case in Bridges, the district court's reasons focus on factors which are irrelevant to the question presented and (in the instance of economic benefits) prohibited from consideration by the constitution itself, an error in the court's legal analysis is exposed, requiring *de novo* review. See Bridges, 15–1439 at 4, 190 So.3d at 279.

By focusing on La. Const. art. I, §4(B)(1), and its admonition that, except as specifically authorized by La. Const. art. VI, §21, no property shall be taken for predominant use or transfer of ownership to any private entity, the district court elevated the general language of that provision over the specific language of Article I, §4(B)(6), making *no* findings with respect to the central issue presented here— whether the taking violates the private business enterprise protection clause. The majority opinion, I believe, falls into similar error. In focusing on the provisions of Article I, §4(B)(2)(vi), which define a "public purpose" to include expropriation by public ports to facilitate the transport of goods in commerce, the majority opinion elevates this broad general expropriatory authority over the specific qualifying limitation embodied in Section 4(B)(6), in effect untethering the Port's taking authority from the limitation of the private business enterprise protection clause. However, Section 4(B)(6) is a limitation on the "public purpose" definition of Section 4(B) (2)(vi), and it specifically counsels that the taking of a business enterprise for the purpose of operating or halting competition with that enterprise is not a legitimate "public purpose."

As Delegate Jenkins' comments indicate, the purpose of the expropriation is crucial to the determination of whether there is an unconstitutional taking within the meaning of Section 4(B)(6). In assessing whether the taking is for a purpose consistent with the constitutional strictures of this provision, certain principles of interpretation apply. Because "expropriation proceedings are in derogation of the right of individuals to own property, the law governing these proceedings must be strictly construed against the expropriating authority." State v. Estate of Davis, 572 So.2d 39, 42 (La. 1990). This strict construction against the expropriating authority is consonant with the broad interpretation of Section 4(B)(6) urged by Delegate Jenkins, given that Section 4(B)(6) has as its similar aim the protection of private business enterprise against excessive government interference. In addition, "every clause in a written constitution is presumed to have been inserted for some useful purpose, and courts should avoid a construction which would render any portion of the constitution meaningless." Succession of Lauga, 624 So.2d 1156, 1166 (La. 1993).

In this case, to the extent it can be argued that the district court made a factual finding with respect to the "purpose" for the expropriation, it appears the court simply accepted at face value the Port's stated reason for expropriating Violet's property without considering the effect of that taking. Such an analysis is constitutionally deficient, as the myopic focus on the Port's stated reason for the expropriation without any examination of the effect of the taking would allow the Port, or any expropriating authority, virtually unfettered authority to expropriate property as long as it professed an ostensible proper motive for the taking. This would be true even if the stated purpose also had the effect of enabling the expropriating authority to take over and operate a private enterprise, or halt private competition, rendering Section 4(B)(6) meaningless.

It is precisely this type of analysis of Section 4(B)(6) that Delegate Jenkins cautioned against when he offered as an example of a taking prohibited by Section 4(B) (6), the expropriation of apartments or rental homes for the purpose of constructing public housing. See Jenkins, *The Declaration of Rights*, 21 Loy. L. Rev. at 25. The parallels to that example are evident in this case. Here, pointing to La. Const. art. I, § 4(B)(2)(b)(vi), which defines "public purpose" to include continuous public ownership of property by public ports "to facilitate the transport of goods ... in domestic or international commerce," the Port seeks to expropriate for the stated purpose of enhancing and expanding its role as a market participant in the port service industry, property belonging to a private participant (Violet) in the same industry. However, this type of taking runs squarely afoul of Section 4(B)(6) and the protection of private enterprise from fear of governmental takeover that this constitutional provision was intended to promote.

Undeniably, public ports have been granted expropriation powers under the constitution to facilitate the transport of goods in commerce. Unquestionably, public ports are significant economic engines, that work to support trade, enable Louisiana's energy and agricultural industries to further enhance the economy, and provide employment and business opportunities to local, regional, and the state's economies. However, private enterprise does likewise. Ports are granted substantial authority to operate, but ports cannot take over an on-going private business to operate that business or to end competition. In Section 4(B)(6), the people of this state have made a conscious decision to limit governmental interference with private enterprise, and that limitation must be respected. Moreover, it can only be respected (and effectuated) by an examination not only of the stated reasons for expropriation, but of the effect of that taking as well.

De novo review

The ultimate question presented in this case is one that is directed by the language of Section 4(B)(6): whether Violet's business enterprise or any of its assets was taken by the Port for the purpose of operating that enterprise or halting competition with the Port enterprises. At the hearing on the motion to dismiss, Violet contended that the Port's taking runs afoul of both prongs of Section 4(B)(6). According to Violet, the Port took its property for the purpose of operating its layberthing enterprise and also for the purpose of operating its docks for bulk cargo in the future (a venture in which Violet had engaged and into which it was expanding), thereby halting competition from Violet. The testimony and evidence on this point was extensive, with both sides presenting opposing views and conflicting testimony. Nevertheless, at the conclusion of the process, certain facts were undisputed.

Violet owned one mile of the ten miles of river-front property within the Port's jurisdiction on which it had constructed a facility consisting of five docks and related infrastructure. For decades, Violet had contracted with the United States Military Sealift Command ("the Navy") to layberth and service ocean-going Navy ships. While layberthing for Navy (and some commercial) vessels was Violet's primary operation, it did perform some repair and cargo operations at its docks.

In 2006, due to a growing demand for cargo services, the Port found itself operating at capacity and in need of expansion. The Port identified Violet's property as being best suited for its expansion needs and contacted Violet to discuss purchasing its property. In 2007, the parties tentatively agreed on a purchase price. To facilitate the purchase, the Port applied for funding through the Louisiana Department of Transportation and Development's Port Priority Program. A Port Priority Application ("PPA") was submitted in 2008 seeking the maximum grant of $15 million to purchase the property. In its application, the Port represented that the Violet property was best and ideally suited for the transfer and storage of dry and liquid bulk commodities, and that development of the property for this purpose would take place in three phases. In a letter submitted in connection with the application, the Port identified the Navy contract and represented to DOTD that "the [P]ort will derive from this proposed project a lease with the Navy/MARAD in the approximate amount of $550,000 per year for Navy/MARAD ships occupying the berths," that it will "continue to compete for these MARAD/Navy contracts," and that "the annual net revenue from the Navy contracts at the Violet site has averaged $550,000 [and] [f]uture contracts are expected to be in that same . . . range." In essence, the Port represented that the Navy contract could be figured in to DOTD's required rate of return for funding the project. Based on the Port's representations, DOTD awarded it the requested funding.

Ultimately, the negotiations for the sale of the property were unsuccessful. In the interim, however, Violet continued to operate and commenced efforts to expand its own cargo operations at its facility, obtaining permits to allow more cargo operations and constructing a new berth for cargo use. Violet also entered into an option agreement with Vulcan Materials for lease of the new berth and ten adjoining acres to transload and store aggregate bulk cargo.

In December 2010, the Port filed its petition for expropriation. In that petition, the Port averred that the property was necessary and suitable for bulk cargo operations. It described the plans for the Violet facility as taking place in three phases. The petition identifies the Navy contract and avers that during Phase I of the development, "[t]he St. Bernard Port intends to enter into a new contract with the Military Sealift Command for its continued use of the Violet Port."

Violet filed a motion to dismiss the expropriation proceeding, challenging its public purpose. At the hearing on the motion, the Port offered testimony that Violet's property was the only property in the area suitable for handling large-scale bulk cargo operations. It offered its Port Priority submissions and testimony related thereto. The Port acknowledged that it intended to take over the Navy contract and continue to service the Navy ships on the property for at least 8 to 10 years, although it contended that the contract was an "afterthought" and "not one of our goals." The Port reiterated its three-phase plan for development of the Violet facility, but acknowledged that Phase I, the only phase that was actually funded, was simply to acquire the property and enable Associated Terminals, its Marine Terminal Operator, to occupy and use the site for stevedoring operations.

The district court denied Violet's motion to dismiss the expropriation proceeding, and the case moved to the just compensation trial. By the time of this trial, the Port had contracted with the Navy for continued layberthing at the former Violet site. Ironically, it contended, and the district court found, that the highest and best use of the property was not for large-scale cargo operations, as the Port had previously contended when taking the property, but that the highest and best use of the property was layberthing coupled with a limited intermodal container terminal — essentially, a continued use of the property as it was being used by Violet.

Whether viewed at the granular level (focusing on the scope of Violet's layberth-ing and cargo operations) or at a broader level (focusing on the role of both the Port and Violet as operators of riverfront port facilities), it appears from the foregoing undisputed facts that the Port's taking in this case is unconstitutional within the meaning of La. Const. art. I, §4(B)(6). The facts establish that the Port obtained $15 million from the state to facilitate the purchase of Violet's property and that it planned to take and use Violet's assets and existing customer revenue (the Navy contract) as interim financing to fund the expansion of cargo operations. The facts likewise establish that while Violet's cargo operations were "negligible," they were not non-existent, and Violet was making its own efforts to expand into the cargo handling arena, in competition with the Port. The PPA, the petition for expropria-tion, and the testimony at trial all establish that the Port intended to enter into a contract with the Navy for its continued use of the Violet port during Phase I of its port development plan. Thus, while the Port maintains that it was and is not in the layberthing business, the facts disclose that layberthing the Navy ships was an inte-gral part of its plan, it effectuated that plan, and it is still performing layberthing services today, which include the Navy contract.

When a governmental entity takes and uses private business property or assets to generate revenue in ways similar to a private enterprises's prior operations, or when a governmental entity necessarily will use the property or assets as part of its own business plans, that taking is one "for the purpose of operating that enter-prise" within the meaning of Section 4(B)(6). Furthermore, when the taking will necessarily allow a governmental entity to increase its market share and prevent a growing or potential competitor from entering into the market or expanding its business, the taking is for the purpose of "halting competition with a government enterprise."

Under the facts in this case, reviewed *de novo*, the district court erred in denying Violet's motion to dismiss the petition for expropriation, as that taking is unconsti-tutional under Section 4(B)(6).

Manifest Error Review

As indicated, ports are extremely important economic engines for the state; this fact is undeniable. However, the people of this State have made a conscious, con-certed commitment, at every opportunity (particularly when Section 4(B)(6) was adopted in 1974 and again in 2006 when further restrictions were imposed post-Kelo), to protect private ownership against government takeover of the means of pri-vate production. It is this longstanding, fundamental constitutional principle that is at stake in this case. Furthermore, while I remain convinced that *de novo* review is warranted due to the errors in the district court's legal analysis, even should the manifest error rule be applied to the factual findings (that the district court clearly did not make), I would find any "factual" determination that the taking in this case was not for the purpose of operating Violet's port facility or eliminating competi-tion from Violet is manifestly erroneous. . . .

In this case, the uncontradicted *objective* evidence demonstrates the pretextual nature of the Port's *subjective* contention that the taking was not for the purpose of assuming Violet's layberthing operations with the Navy, and that layberthing operations were an "afterthought." This objective evidence—in a nutshell—is found in the Port's PPA submitted to DOTD (in which it represented that the Navy contract could be figured into DOTD's required rate of return for extending funding to the Port), in the petition for expropriation (in which the Port avers that it "intends to enter into a new contract with the Military Sealift Command for its continued use of the Violet Port"), and in the fact that the Port, after the quick-taking, entered into a contract with the Navy and continues to this date to perform the same layberthing operations once conducted by Violet.

The same analysis holds true for the Port's contention that the taking was not for the purpose of eliminating competition from Violet because Violet's cargo operations were "negligible" and the Port was not in the "layberthing" business and thus did not compete with Violet. The objective facts demonstrate that while the Port contends the expropriation was motivated solely by its need to expand its cargo operations, and that the Violet property was the only property suitable for expansion and creation of a liquid cargo facility, once the taking was effected and valuation was at issue, the Port "flipped the script" and argued that the highest and best use of the property was not for large-scale cargo operations, as it had previously contended, but for layberthing coupled with a limited intermodal container terminal—essentially, a continued use of the property exactly as it was being used by Violet. The *subjective* contention that the taking was not for the purpose of taking over Violet's business enterprise is belied by the *objective* reality of what has occurred.

The facts, as acknowledged in the majority opinion, establish that while Violet had historically not been engaged in large-scale cargo operations, Violet was actively expanding into that area, having constructed a new berth that would handle cargo and having entered into an option contract with Vulcan Materials for lease of the new berth and ten adjoining acres to transload and store bulk cargo. In other words, the facts establish that while Violet had not been an active competitor for bulk cargo in the past, it had—like the Port—recognized and acted on the expanding market need for bulk cargo operations, bringing it into competition with the Port, a competition which was effectively "nipped in the bud" and eliminated through the taking. Again, the *subjective* contentions of the Port are contradicted by the *objective* reality of what has occurred. . . .

While I sympathize with sentiments that this case should be limited to its facts, one cannot ignore the legal ramifications that arise from application of those facts. Will the Port (or another public port) next argue that it can expropriate a private port engaged in liquid cargo storage operations because the Port does not currently engage in liquid cargo storage operations and, thus, does not "compete" with a port engaged in such? Will it be able to argue that its "primary" purpose is not to assume the liquid cargo operations, but to expand its bulk cargo operations at that location? Any parsing here ignores what actually, objectively occurred. The Port took the Violet property and assumed its operations while ending competition, violating both the letter and spirit of Section 4(B)(6). . . .

The people of Louisiana repeatedly made judgments that shield private business from the government's entry into the marketplace by taking over an ongoing business or ending competition. The people of Louisiana effectively provided a safeguard for private ownership and for the means of production in the fundamental law of this state. The Port is not without a remedy. If the government wants to enter the marketplace and take over an ongoing business, it must act like any other business; it must purchase the ongoing business at a mutually agreeable price. The constitution is clear—the government cannot simply take a private business to operate the business or to end competition.

For these reasons, I respectfully dissent.

St. Bernard Port Harbor & Terminal Dist. v. Violet Dock Port Inc.
255 So.3d 57 (La. App. 4 Cir. 2018)

Judge Roland L. Belsome: This matter was remanded from the Louisiana Supreme Court for the determination of just compensation for the Violet Dock Port's expropriated property. . . .

After a trial on the issue of just compensation, the trial court found that $16,000,000 was just compensation for the expropriated property. In so finding, the trial court indicated it did not have the authority to "split the baby" and thus had to choose which party's expert he was going to rely on. The trial court chose to adopt the valuation presented by the Port, which was the amount that had been deposited in the registry of the court. Reviewing that ruling under a manifest error/clearly wrong standard, this Court affirmed. The Supreme Court found that the trial court had made its ruling under an erroneous interpretation of the law. More specifically, the Supreme Court opined that the trial court was not bound by any one expert's opinion in its entirety. Accordingly, this Court's affirmation of just compensation was reversed. On remand, we have been directed to conduct a *de novo* review of the evidence in the record to arrive at a valuation of just compensation.

VDP has maintained throughout its appeals that the principles set forth by the Supreme Court in *State, Dept. of Highways v. Constant*, should guide the Court in determining just compensation. *Constant* recognized that the full extent of loss is not always satisfied by the market value analysis based upon comparable sales or other alternate methods that are used in place of fair market value. In *Constant*, the landowner was operating a marina business at the time that the highway department expropriated a portion of his land. The expropriated portion of land represented the entire loading and parking area of the business. It was established that the loading and parking area was indispensible to the landowner's marina business.

The Court noted that the property was unique because the barge slip and adjacent area was the only site available for the commercial loading of heavy equipment servicing the oil industry. The Court reasoned that the property was unique in nature; and the loading and parking area was indispensible to the business's operations. Therefore, the loading and parking area had to be reproduced at another location to maintain the marina business. Accordingly, the Court found that awarding replacement value was the only way to fully compensate the landowner even though that amount exceeded the market value of the land.

In accordance with *Constant,* if a landowner establishes that the location of the expropriated property or some physical feature of it is unique and indispensably related to the success of the landowner's business, just compensation requires the court to award replacement value. Since *Constant,* several courts considering those factors have determined that some landowners can only be fully compensated by replacement cost.

Likewise here, the evidence elicited at trial established that: 1) the Property is unique due to its location and its improvements; and 2) the Property was indispensable to VDP's business. The Property is located in Violet, Louisiana and has one mile of frontage along the Mississippi River and similar frontage on St. Bernard Highway and Norfolk Southern railroad, which gives the site access over land, road, rail, and water. It is zoned industrial and is located on a straight, self-dredging bank line making it an ideal location for river navigation. The Port's Executive Director, Dr. Robert Scafidel testified that the other potential locations along the river in St. Bernard Parish were not as desirable for the Port because they were positioned where the river bends, which would impede river traffic. He represented to the State that VDP's property presented a unique opportunity to greatly expand the Port's ability to handle bulk cargo.

Through the years, VDP had constructed a fully operational, private port facility with five steel and concrete docks. Three of the berths were certified by the Navy for lay berthing ocean-going ships. VDP had held contracts for providing services to the Navy for decades. To fulfill the needs of the Navy, VDP had renovated the Property by installing transformers, a potable water supply, six telephone lines per ship, and a boiler for steam necessary for the ships to be poised for immediate deployment. In addition to the mechanical support for the ships, VDP had also constructed landside improvements to comply with Navy specifications.

The Port highlighted the uniqueness of the Property in its application to the Louisiana Port Construction and Development Program. The Port wrote:

> [t]he best attribute of this site is that it features three sturdy docks designed to berth some of the largest cargo ships in the world. These docks can be easily modified to support cargo handling operations similar to those currently taking place at the Chalmette Slip, such as ship or barge to truck or rail or to storage. The reverse movement is also available.

The application went on to state that:

> [t]he opportunity to acquire three active docks on the Mississippi River with available uplands and access to highway and rail, for only $14 million, is an opportunity that does not happen very often, if ever.

Similarly, the Port's Strategic Business Plan stated that the Property "should be considered a national asset for transportation and manufacturing." The Port conceded that the site was one of the last major properties on the Mississippi River that is suitable for cargo with highway, rail, and deep water access on a straight section of the river. Riverfront property is limited in St. Bernard Parish and property with these attributes is nonexistent. The Port relied on the uniqueness of the Property to secure a $15,000,000 grant from the State and to support its public purpose argument.

Here, as in *Constant*, the Property was also indispensable for the operation of VDP's business. The appraisals in the record repeatedly recognized that the facility and business operations were highly specialized. That is further evident by the fact that the Port is now servicing the Navy contracts once held by VDP. The Port expropriated the Property because it is unique in nature and location. As a result of the expropriation VDP's business has ceased to exist. Thus, we find that the record supports a finding that the Property was unique in nature and location while also being indispensable to the landowners' business operations requiring just compensation to be calculated by assessing the replacement cost of the land and improvements.

At trial, VDP's experts presented reports and testimony suggesting that full replacement cost for the land and improvements would be $73,148,000 without taking into account depreciation. Alternatively, if the land and improvements were to be depreciated, the replacement value would be $50,930,000. Using numbers derived by the Port's experts, full replacement cost without depreciation amounts to $41,084,000, and with depreciation the amount was determined to be $28,764,685.

The most significant reason for the vast discrepancy in the values is due to the experts' differing opinions on the highest and best use of the Property. VDP's experts' calculations were based on the Property being used as a multimodal bulk cargo facility, while the lower calculations were based on layberthing with a limited cargo operation. Multiple factors are considered when determining the highest and best use of land in an expropriation. However, generally, "the current use of the property is presumed to be the highest and best use."

The Port's expert appraiser, Bennett Oubre testified extensively as to his review of the appraisal reports offered by VDP's and the Port's experts. In reviewing the testimony regarding the rationale for the differing appraisals, we find Mr. Oubre's testimony realistically evaluated the character of the Property. Mr. Oubre acknowledged how specialized the Property was while also taking into account the attributes that were problematic. During his testimony, he explained various flaws within VDP's experts' appraisals. The most significant criticism Mr. Oubre had was the use of "extraordinary assumptions." Those "extraordinary assumptions" included zoning and permitting issues as well as the water depth of the docks and its proximity to non-industrial areas. Thus, his testimony supports the highest and best use of the Property to be the layberthing operations that VDP was using the Property for at the time of expropriation. We find his assessment of the condition of the property to be representative of and consistent with the evidence presented as a whole. During his testimony, he relied on estimates from the Port's expert engineer, Patrick Flowers and his own appraisal of the land value to formulate a depreciated value of improvements of $23,515,404 and land value of $3,962,000. Although Mr. Oubre stated that in his opinion this valuation was high, we find it is a reasonable estimation for the purpose of determining just compensation. However, when valuing the improvements one of the docks had been omitted. Based on Dr. Ragas' valuation, the depreciated value of the omitted dock was $667,406.

Using the estimates discussed above, we find the record supports an estimated replacement cost after depreciation, of $28,764,685. Based on the record, we find this to be a credible and accurate valuation of the Property. Accordingly, the trial court's award of just compensation is increased to $28,764,685, together with interest and attorneys' fees as provided for by law. The matter is remanded for further proceedings.

AFFIRMED AS AMENDED AND REMANDED

Jenkins, J., Dissenting: For the reasons that follow, I disagree with the foundation of the majority's conclusion that the "highest and best use" of the Property is for layberthing, rather than use as a multimodal bulk cargo facility. This decision, obviously, greatly impacts the valuation of the Property. My concern is not necessarily about the result reached on that issue, but about the shortfalls in reaching that result. . . .

In *State v. Bitterwolf*, 415 So.2d 196 (La. 1982), the Supreme Court explained that the legislature and the courts have developed rules which accept the fair market value of the property as a relevant consideration in determining just compensation for purposes of expropriation. Fair market value has consistently been defined as the price a buyer is willing to pay after considering all of the uses that the property may be put to where such uses are not speculative, remote or contrary to law. *West Jefferson Levee Dist. v. Coast Quality*, 93-1718 (La. 5/23/94), 640 So.2d 1258. In determining fair market value of the land taken in an expropriation case, consideration is to be given to the most profitable use to which the land can be put by reason of its location, topography, and adaptability. *City of Shreveport v. Abe Meyer Corp.*, 219 La. 128, 52 So.2d 445, 447 (1951), *affirmed as amended*, 223 La. 1079, 67 So.2d 732 (1953); *State, Dep't of Highways v. Rapier*, 246 La. 150, 164 So.2d 280 (1964). This theory, of taking the latter factors into consideration, is commonly known as the "highest and best use" doctrine. The highest and best use of land in expropriation cases involves several factors. Factors which may be considered include:

- market demand;
- proximity to areas already developed in a compatible manner with the intended use;

- economic development in the area;
- specific plans of business and individuals, including action already taken to develop the land for that use;
- scarcity of the land available for that use; negotiations with buyers interested in the property taken for a particular use; absence of offers to buy the property made by the buyers who put it to the use urged; and
- the use to which the property was being put at the time of the taking.

State, through the Dept. of Highways v. Constant, 369 So.2d 699, 702 (La. 1979).

It is "well established" that the current use of the property is presumed to be the highest and best use and the burden of overcoming that presumption by proving the existence of a different highest and best use based on a potential, future use is on the landowner. *Exxon Pipeline*, 00–2535, 00–2559, p. 8, (La. 5/15/01), 788 So.2d 1154, 1160. Where a landowner overcomes the presumption, the landowner is entitled to compensation based on a potential use of the property, even though the property is not being so utilized at the time of the taking, provided he can show it is reasonably probable the property could be put to this use in the "not too distant future." *West Jefferson Levee Dist.*, 640 So.2d at 1273.

In this case, the use to which Violet was putting the Property at the time of the expropriation—layberthing with a limited cargo operation—is presumed to be the Property's highest and best use. Violet, however, may overcome this presumption by demonstrating, by a preponderance of the evidence, that the property could be used in a different, more valuable way, that the potential use is not speculative, and that it could be undertaken in the "not too distant future." *Exxon Pipeline*, 00–2535, 00–2559, pp. 8–9, 788 So.2d at 1160–61; *West Jefferson Levee Dist.*, 640 So.2d at 1273.

The majority's failure to provide a complete analysis of the "highest and best use" gives me pause. As stated above, the current value of the Property is presumed to be the highest and best use, and the burden of overcoming that presumption by proving the existence of a different highest and best use based on a potential, future use is on Violet, the landowner. The majority fails to provide any substantive discussion of Violet's expert's analysis of the factors supporting the "highest and best use" of the Property as a multimodal bulk cargo facility, so as to satisfy Violet's burden. Instead, the majority addresses only the conclusions of the Port's expert that the attributes of the Property were "problematic," and that Violet's experts used "extraordinary assumptions" and a "flawed" rationale. There is no express finding that Violet failed to overcome the presumption, and why.

Although I do not, at this time, challenge the majority's conclusion with respect to the "highest and best use" of the Property, I cannot support it, as I find the majority's analysis of this issue provides an incomplete roadmap for reaching its decision.

I respectfully dissent.

Notes and Questions

1. Does the majority opinion authored by Justice Crichton defer appropriately to the factual determination of the trial court regarding the actual purpose for the Port's expropriation of Violet Dock Port's riparian land and the improvements on the land? Or is it, as Justice Weimer argues in his dissenting opinion, too deferential? Do the differing viewpoints about judicial scrutiny of expropriation actions between Justice Chrichton and Justice Weimer's opinion in *St. Bernard Port* mirror the differences in opinion espoused by Justice Stevens and Justice O'Conner and the other dissenting justices of the United States Supreme Court in *Kelo*? Is it a good idea for judges to be making decisions about the legitimacy of the ostensible public purposes offered by the state and political subdivisions of the state when it comes to expropriation or eminent domain, as long as just compensation is provided to the property owner?

2. *History of Business Enterprise Clause*: The Business Enterprise Clause found in Article 1, Section 4(B)(6) of the Louisiana Constitution arose out of the Louisiana Constitutional Convention in 1973. One of the sponsors of the new provision, former Louisiana Representative Louis "Woody" Jenkins, affirmed that "no other state constitution places such extensive limitations on the power and authority of government to regulate or expropriate private property." Louis Woody Jenkins, *The Declaration of Rights*, 21 Loy. L. Rev. 9, 19 (1975). These limitations were disputed to solve three main concerns expressed by the legislature.

> The [s]ection resulted from a concern that legislative bodies and regulatory agencies have seriously eroded private property rights, while the courts have refused to use constitutional protections, such as the due process clause, to invalidate even the most irrational and demagogic regulatory schemes. Delegates also believed that both public and private entities authorized by law to expropriate have abused that power. Finally, delegates expressed the fear that there were few constitutional safeguards against the expropriation or nationalization of major industries and business concerns which ha[d] occurred in other countries.

Id. at 20. Do you think the Louisiana Legislature had valid concerns? Did the Legislature have to act to prevent nationalization of major industries and businesses in Louisiana?

3. Some would argue that political checks, such as elections and public protest, will be sufficient to guard against abuse of the expropriation power by elected officials. Do you agree? Does it matter that in a case like *St. Bernard Port*, the Commissioners of the St. Bernard Port, Harbor, and Terminal District are not elected but appointed by local political leaders? *See* La. Rev. Stat. § 34:1702 (providing that the Governor, acting upon the recommendation of a majority of the legislative delegation from St. Bernard Parish, shall appoint the five members of the district).

4. In *St. Bernard Port*, the primary source of funds used to acquire the property of Violet Dock Port was a $15 million grant from the State of Louisiana, Department

of Transportation and Development. Do you believe Port officials would have initially been as willing to exercise the Port's power of expropriation if the funds for the acquisition of Violet Dock Port's property were generated by imposing taxes on local property owners in St. Bernard Parish? For an insightful analysis of another noteworthy case involving eminent domain and economic development and posing this precise issue, see William A. Fischel, *The Political Economy of Public Use in Poletown: How Federal Grants Encourage Excessive Use of Eminent Domain*, 2004 MICH. ST. L. REV. 929.

5. In its decision on remand, did the Louisiana Fourth Circuit Court of Appeal appropriately determine the amount of just compensation owed to Violet Dock Port? Recall the court's conclusion that the "highest and best use" for Violet's property was to serve as a "layberthing" facility, with a limited cargo operation, and not as a "multimodal bulk cargo facility." Is that conclusion consistent with the Louisiana Supreme Court's majority opinion with regard to the actual purpose for the Port's expropriation? Did the court make up for any apparent inconsistency by determining that the appropriate method for valuing Violet Dock Port's property was to determine the property's "replacement value," as opposed to its "fair market value" based on comparable sales or other appraisal techniques? What factors drove the court's decision to forecast the "replacement value" of the property? Do you agree with Judge Jenkins' contention in his dissent that the Fourth Circuit's analysis of the "replacement value" of Violet Dock's property should have more carefully considered the *potential* highest and best use of the property *in the future*, particularly in light of the Port's assertion that its ultimate goal in acquiring the property was to create an expanded bulk-cargo operation facility?

6. In its revised statutes, Louisiana law also provides detailed rules governing:

(a) the kinds of property that are subject to expropriation, La. Rev. Stat. § 19:1 ("immovable property, including servitudes and other rights in to or immovable property");

(b) the kinds of property that are *not* subject to expropriation, La. Rev. Stat. § 19:1 (graveyards, cemeteries, mortgages);

(c) the governmental and non-governmental entities that enjoy the power of expropriation generally, La. Rev. Stat. § 19:2(1)-(12) (the state, political subdivisions, private corporations or entities created for or engaged in the construction of "railroads, tollroads, navigation canals, . . . street railways, urban railways, inter-urban railways, . . . water works, filtration and treatment plants, or sewerage plants to supply the public with water and sewerage, . . . the piping and marketing of natural gas . . . transmitting intelligence by telegraph or telephone . . . transmitting or distributing electricity and steam for power, lighting, heating or other such uses" and various other common carriers of substances such as carbon dioxide and liquid or gaseous hydrocarbons);

(d) procedural requirements for a valid expropriation, La. Rev. Stat. § 19:2 (duty to negotiate in good faith), and La. Rev. Stat. § 19:2.1-2.2 (petition requirements, detailed notice requirements);

(e) the right to a trial by jury to determine compensation, La. Rev. Stat. § 19:4; and

(f) detailed rules with regard to the measure of compensation to determine the property owner's loss. La. Rev. Stat. § 19:9.

The last of these provisions is set forth below.

La. R.S. 19:9 (1974, amended 2012)

A. In determining the value of the property to be expropriated, and any damages caused to the defendant by the expropriation, the basis of compensation shall be the value which the property possessed before the contemplated improvement was proposed, without deducting therefrom any general or specific benefits derived by the owner from the contemplated improvement or work.

B. The defendant shall be compensated to the full extent of his loss. The court shall include in its consideration the difference between the rate of interest of any existing mortgage on an owner-occupied residence and the prevailing rate of interest required to obtain a mortgage on another owner-occupied residence of equal value.

Other revised statutes provide similar sets of rules when it comes to: (1) expropriations conducted by municipal corporations, La. Rev. Stat. §§ 19:101-116; (2) granting the powerful "quick-take" expropriation mechanism used in the *St. Bernard Port* case to Louisiana State University, port commissions, port authorities, and the state's Department of Public Works, La. Rev. Stat. § 19:141 *et seq.*; and (3) tailored provisions applicable to particular expropriating authorities. La. Rev. Stat. § 19:121 *et seq.* Why has the Louisiana legislature enacted so many detailed expropriation regimes?

7. In the future, the public demand for expansion of public utility rights of way to transport newly reachable deposits of oil and natural gas as well as electricity created by renewable energy resources such as wind turbines and vast solar power generation plants may cause further controversy concerning eminent domain, expropriation and public use. For detailed accounts of the complex regulatory and constitutional questions that these new energy sources and their transportation will create for expropriation law, see James W. Coleman & Alexandra B. Klass, *Eminent Domain and Energy Transport* (forthcoming); Alexandra B. Klass, *Takings and Transmission*, 91 N.C. L. Rev. 1079 (2013); Alexandra B. Klass, *The Frontier of Eminent Domain*, 79 Col. L. Rev. 651 (2008).

Chapter 7

Acquisition of Ownership through Occupancy

Occupancy is a possession-based mode of acquiring ownership of a corporeal movable that does not belong to anyone. La. Civ. Code art. 3412 (1982). A person who acquires ownership of a thing through occupancy—the occupant—acquires ownership immediately, at the very instant his or her possession begins. *Id.*

Like accession, occupancy can be described as an "original" mode of acquisition of ownership because the occupant does not derive his or her ownership from a previous owner. Unlike accession, which allows a person to acquire ownership of an accessory thing because of its physical or functional relationship to a principal thing, occupancy enables a person to acquire ownership of a thing that it is not owned by anyone else through the occupant's mere act of taking possession.

Occupancy is firmly rooted in the civilian tradition. Roman law made occupancy (*occupatio*) available as a function of natural reasoning (*ratione naturali*). Similarly, in the common law, "first possession" embodies the most basic mode of acquiring original ownership of a thing. Article 3412 of the Civil Code, which closely tracks Pothier's definition of occupancy, defines occupancy as "the taking of possession of a corporeal movable that does not belong to anyone." La. Civ. Code art. 3412 (1982).

We will learn more about possession in Chapter Eight. For now, we note that a person acquires possession of a thing when two elements are satisfied. First, the person claiming possession must exercise sufficient physical control of the object. We call this *corpus*. As Article 3421 of the Civil Code explains:

Art. 3421. Possession

Possession is the detention or enjoyment of a corporeal thing, movable or immovable, that one holds or exercises by himself or by another who keeps it or exercises it in his name.

La. Civ. Code art. 3421 (1982). *See also* La. Civ. Code art. 3425 (1982) (defining "corporeal possession" as "the exercise of physical acts of use, detention, or enjoyment over a thing"). Second, physical detention or enjoyment must be coupled with a particular state of mind. We call this *animus*. The codal source of this *animus* element is expressed in Article 3424:

Art. 3424. Acquisition of possession

To acquire possession, one must intend to possess as owner and must take corporeal possession of the thing.

La. Civ. Code art. 3424 (1982). Hence, a person acquires possession of a thing by assuming actual dominion over it (*corpus*), coupled with the intent of becoming owner (*animus*).

The quality of the physical control over the object must be carefully determined in each individual case. Absent sufficient control over the thing, the would-be occupant does not meet the corpus requirement. For example, suppose two persons, Sally and Harry, are walking along the seashore—a public thing under Article 451 of the Civil Code. Sally notices a precious stone and declares it to be her own. But Harry actually picks up the precious stone and puts it in his pocket. Sally has not acquired ownership of the stone through occupancy unless Harry was acting on Sally's behalf when picking up the stone and storing it his pocket. Could Harry claim ownership of the stone through occupancy? Did he have the requisite animus? Although Harry appears to have the requisite physical control of the stone, we do not know enough about his state of mind to determine whether he has the requisite animus—the intent to possess as owner—to acquire ownership of the stone through occupancy. Is there a presumption available?

Not every kind of thing can be subject to acquisition of ownership through occupancy. First of all, the thing must be amenable to appropriation through physical possession as the scope of things subject to occupancy is confined to *corporeal* things. Second, one cannot gain ownership of an incorporeal thing, like an annuity or shares in a corporation, through occupancy. Although immovable things, like tracts of land or buildings, are subject to appropriation through lengthy periods of possession (that is, through ten and thirty year acquisitive prescription), the Civil Code limits the immediate acquisition of ownership through occupancy to *movable* things. Hence, as Article 3412 declares, only *corporeal movable* things can be acquired by occupancy.

Finally, acquisition of ownership of a thing through occupancy supposes that the thing does "not belong to anyone," which means that it must not have an owner. Article 3412 revision comment (d) speaks to this central idea by observing that "[a]ccording to traditional civilian conceptions, occupancy applies to *res nullius*, that is, things that are not owned by anyone, such as wild animals and abandoned things." La. Civ. Code art. 3412 rev. cmt. (d) (1982). The Roman phrase *res nullius* is translated as *sans maître* in French and *herrenlos* in German. These terms suggest that the thing is "without a master." Taking possession of a thing that belongs to someone else could be characterized as larceny or theft.

If the object at issue is only lost, and not abandoned, a person who takes possession of it may ultimately acquire ownership of that thing, but his ownership is not immediate. He must meet additional requirements before acquiring ownership and continue in possession for a period of time. *See* La. Civ. Code art. 3419 (1982) (specifying that a person who finds a corporeal movable that is lost may acquire ownership of it if he makes "a diligent effort to find its owner or possessor and to return the thing" and if "the owner is not found within three years"). Thus, lost things are not *res nullius.*

The law of occupancy is applicable in two primary instances. Corporeal movable things that have never before been owned by any person can be acquired by occupancy. Examples include wild animals that have never before been deprived of their natural liberty, or fugitive minerals, such as oil, gas and subterranean water. La. Civ. Code art. 3412 rev. cmts. (d), (e) and (g) (1982); La. Civ. Code art. 3413 (1982). In addition, things that . . . may have been *previously* owned but are *no longer owned by anyone*, like abandoned things or wild animals that might have been enclosed or tamed at one point but that have subsequently recovered their natural liberty, are likewise subject to acquisition through occupancy.

A. Occupancy and Wild Animals

Article 3413 of the Civil Code addresses an important category of things in the law of occupancy—"wild animals, birds, fish, and shellfish in a state of natural liberty." La. Civ. Code art. 3413 (1982). The Civil Code draws a clear distinction between these sorts of "wild animals," which are potentially subject to occupancy, and domestic animals, which are usually "privately owned" and thus "not subject to occupancy." La. Civ. Code art. 3417 (1982). If a domestic animal is abandoned by an owner, who relinquishes possession with the intent to give up ownership, such an animal, as well as its offspring, may be subject to occupancy.

In the revision comments to Article 3417, the drafters draw on common law sources to distinguish between domestic and wild animals. Domestic animals, we are told, "include those which are tame by nature, or from time immemorial have been accustomed to the association of man, or by his industry have been subjected to his will, and have no disposition to escape his dominion." La. Civ. Code art. 3417 rev. cmt. (d) (1982). Examples of domestic animals include cats, dogs and cows. In contrast, wild animals are those which "because of habit, mode of life, or natural instinct, are incapable of being completely domesticated and which require the exercise of art, force, or skill to keep them in subjection." *Id.*

In the civilian tradition, wild animals are sub-divided into those which are tamed and those which are not tamed. *Id.* Like domestic animals, "[t]amed wild animals and birds are privately owned," and are not subject to occupancy, "as long as they have the habit of returning to their owner" (*consuetudo revertendi*). La. Civ. Code art. 3416 (1982). If they have lost the habit of returning to their owner (that is, when they do not return within a reasonable time), they are "considered to have recovered their natural liberty" and become subject to occupancy, "unless their owner takes immediate measures for their pursuit and recapture." *Id.*

As noted above, wild animals, birds, fish and shellfish can all be acquired by occupancy. La. Civ. Code art. 3413 (1982). This is true even when they are captured on the land of another who has prohibited hunters and others from entering. *Id*. The landowner may have delictual and other kinds of claims against a trespasser who captures wild animals on his property, but the landowner will not be able to claim ownership of the animals. *Id*. rev. cmt. (c).

Article 3414 adds a curious twist to the rule of capture found under the previous article. It provides that if wild animals, birds, fish or shellfish that have been previously captured, "recover their natural liberty," then "the captor loses ownership unless he takes immediate measures for their pursuit and recapture." La. Civ. Code art. 3414 (1982). The Civil Code does not define, however, what kind of measures would be sufficient to prevent an owner in this situation from losing ownership.

Article 3415 provides two more rules applicable to wild animals. First, it describes a situation that is easy enough to imagine — "[w]ild animals, or birds within enclosures, fish or shellfish in an aquarium or other private waters." It then declares that such animals are "privately owned." La. Civ. Code art. 3415 (1982). For example, the wild animals kept in the Audubon Zoo in New Orleans or found in a privately owned, fenced safari park are not subject to occupancy. In a recent decision, the Louisiana Third Circuit Court of Appeal had occasion to apply Article 3415 and basic principles of the law of accession. It found that a tenant farmer who enjoyed a one year lease that granted him rice and soybean farming rights and, secondarily, "crawfishing rights," was entitled to the crawfish he harvested during the term of the lease but did not have any property rights in crawfish harvested after the expiration of the lease by a subsequent tenant. *Hunter v. Lafayette Consol. Gov't*, 177 So.3d 811, 813–15 (La. App. 3 Cir. 2015).

Article 3415 also tells us that when pigeons, bees, fish and shellfish physically move into the pigeon house, hive or pond of another, they belong to the second person, provided that the migration was not effectuated by inducement or artifice. *Id*. In the days when pigeon houses and bee hives were a common feature of farms and plantations in Louisiana, this rule might have been more commonly applied. The article does not explicitly address the phenomenon of swarming bees — those who exit the hive and follow a new queen to form another bee population. Unless immediately pursued, these bees are deemed ownerless and amenable to occupancy by capture.

The State of Louisiana has asserted ownership over a variety of wildlife species in their state of natural liberty, as Article 3413 recognizes, thus moving their classification from things without an owner to things that are owned by the state in its capacity as a public person. The assertion of state ownership has important ramifications. Article 3413 declares that a person seeking to take possession of a wild animal must comply with all applicable state laws and regulations.

Section 3 of Title 56 of the Revised Statutes offers an example of the kind of carefully tailored legislation designed to reflect the state's responsibility for the conservation of natural resources for the common benefit of the people of Louisiana:

La. Rev. Stat. § 56:3. Ownership of wild birds, quadrupeds, fish, aquatic life, water bottoms, oysters, and shellfish

A. The ownership and title to all wild birds, and wild quadrupeds, fish, other aquatic life, the beds and bottoms of rivers, streams, bayous, lagoons, lakes, bays, sounds, and inlets bordering on or connecting with the Gulf of Mexico within the territory or jurisdiction of the state, including all oysters and other shellfish and parts thereof grown thereon, either naturally or cultivated, and all oysters in the shells after they are caught or taken therefrom, are and remain the property of the state, and shall be under the exclusive control of the Wildlife and Fisheries Commission except as provided in R.S. 56:4.

B. Wild birds, quadrupeds, fish, other aquatic life, and the beds and bottoms of rivers, streams, bayous, lagoons, lakes, bays, sounds, and inlets bordering on or connecting with the Gulf of Mexico, within the territorial jurisdiction of the state, including all oysters and other shellfish and parts thereof grown thereon, either naturally or cultivated, and all oysters in the shells after they are caught or taken therefrom, shall not be taken, sold, or had in possession except as otherwise permitted in this Title; and the title of the state to all such wild birds, quadrupeds, fish, and other aquatic life, even though taken in accordance with the provisions of this Title, and the beds and bottoms of rivers, streams, bayous, lagoons, lakes, bays, sounds, and inlets always remains in the state for the purpose of regulating and controlling the use and disposition thereof. . . .

La. Rev. Stat. § 56:3 (1985).

Despite the state's ownership of wild animals detailed in the revised statute above, delictual causes of action for damages to private property otherwise available under Article 2321 of the Civil Code against the owner of an animal that causes damages are not available when caused by wild animals owned and harbored by the State of Louisiana in its capacity as a public person. *See Leger v. Louisiana Dep't of Wildlife and Fisheries*, 306 So.2d 391, 394–95 (La. App. 3 Cir. 1975), *writ denied*, 310 So.2d 640 (1975) (holding that the State of Louisiana was not liable in tort under the former Article 2321 of the Civil Code with regard to a sweet potato crop eaten by wild deer even though state regulations prevented the farmer from killing the deer which were fleeing a flooded river plain).

The following opinion is from the Superior Court (*Cour Supérieur*) of Québec, a mixed jurisdiction like Louisiana with a Civil Code largely derived from the French Civil Code of 1804. The opinion highlights the challenges involved in discerning when a wild animal has been captured for purposes of applying the law of occupancy. Observe the close parallels between Quebec law and Louisiana law in this area.

Tremblay et Autres v. Boivin et Autres

[1960] C.S. 235 (Translation from the French original by Dr. Markus G. Puder)

Action for damages ($1,600).

Judgment: The present lawsuit is the result of a conflict between two groups of hunters who attribute to themselves, respectively, the merit of having killed the same moose.

The evidence for the plaintiffs is summarized in the testimony of the claimant Philippe Tremblay who states that he left on October 21, 1958, to hunt at Club des Canots, together with his companions, Maltais and Bilodeau. All three had the right to hunt for moose on these premises, within the short time interval when moose hunting is allowed, that is between October 11 and 22.

On October 21st, the three claimants walked about the club premises until nightfall, without encountering any game. The next day they set out again into the forest around 9 o'clock in the morning, and, after having crisscrossed the paths of the premises for about half an hour, witness Bilodeau was the first to catch sight of a moose, to which he drew the attention of his companion Philippe Tremblay who alone held a large caliber rifle in his hands. The animal was about 100 feet away from the group. Philippe Tremblay fired a first bullet, which, so he says, must have hit the animal so that it fell on its back part. Phillippe Tremblay immediately fired off four more shots aiming at the head, which shots meant to stop the animal completely and allow it to be finished off by a blow with an axe.

The plaintiffs rushed to bleed off the moose, and were in the process of disemboweling it, when, roughly 20 minutes after the first rifle shot, defendant Olivier Boivin arrived on the scene. He asserted a right to the moose, arguing that he had first seen and shot the moose. To settle this claim, the plaintiffs offered a quarter of the moose to Boivin. While this appeared to satisfy defendant Olivier Boivin, he, nonetheless, reserved the right to go and consult with his father, who, at this moment, was at Camp du Brûlé.

After Olivier Boivin's departure, the plaintiffs continued to work on the animal which they dragged towards the lake where they planned to load it onto a small boat.

While plaintiffs Tremblay and Maltais embarked on a search for a small boat, and plaintiff Bilodeau cleared a path up to the lake to transport the moose, the defendants turned up at the scene to claim the moose. When the plaintiffs returned, the defendants asserted vehemently that the moose belonged to them and that they would not let go of it, unless they were given one half of the moose plus the head. The plaintiffs ignored the defendants' demand and continued to prepare the moose until the defendants stepped in violently by shoving the plaintiffs, by cutting the rope used to drag the animal, and by threatening them, if they did not relinquish the moose.

To avoid further violence, which could have had grave consequences, the plaintiffs left the scene, instructing the defendants to leave the moose where it lay while they searched for competent officials to bring back to the scene to settle the question.

When the plaintiffs returned, with or without the officials, the moose had been removed by the defendants who had taken full possession of it, to the detriment of the plaintiffs who now have to vindicate their rights by way of the present action.

This version of plaintiff Tremblay is mostly corroborated by the testimony of his companions Maltais and Bilodeau who confirm having seen the moose which strolled around roughly 75 feet from them before falling on its back part as a result of the first bullet fired off by Tremblay. The other bullets had the effect of completely knocking it down so that they could move near it and finish it off with a blow of an axe.

Here now is the defendants' version narrated by defendant, Olivier Boivin, who hunted with his father, Léonce Boivin, and his brother, Guy.

They set out on the morning of October 22, around 8 o'clock, from St-Fulgence, to reach Club Brûlé and hunt for moose. They were unable to cross Lake des Canots by row-boat, given that it was iced over, and so they had to go around it passing near Camp de Nil Tremblay, where the plaintiffs were located. They had to pass over the premises of Club des Canots to reach the cottage of their club.

Heading together towards their camp, they caught sight of moose tracks which crossed the path in the direction of their camp. Theses traces were fresh from the morning. The defendants resolved that Olivier should follow these tracks while the others would carry on towards the camp, which was about ¾ of a mile from there. Olivier Boivin says that, after having followed the tracks for ¼ of a mile, he caught sight of a moose at which he attempted to fire, but to no avail, because the bullet was not in place but stuck in the magazine. Due to the noise, the moose set off in the opposite direction. However, he managed to go around it and cause it to flee in the direction where his father and brother were, closer to Lake Brûlé. Then, a few minutes later, at about 150 feet ahead of him, he caught sight of a male moose accompanied by a female; he fired in its direction and, so he says: "the moose made a half turn to pass ahead again, when I fired another blow towards its head;" then yet another one in consequence of which the animal fell, but it was able to lift itself up to set off again.

Olivier Boivin affirms that he hit the moose on the backside with his third shot. After this, he embarked upon the pursuit of the moose, towards Lake des Canots, following its tracks, in which he saw drops of blood here and there. Roughly 20 minutes thereafter, he heard five rifle shots, which he believed had been fired by his father. He continued to follow the trails in this fashion until he caught sight of the three plaintiffs next to the felled moose, roughly six to seven minutes after having heard the five rifle bursts.

Olivier Boivin maintains that the moose had been mortally wounded by him, that of the three bullets he had fired, one ought to have caught the animal in the jaw, and another one in the rear part. He concedes that there could have been a distance of 1.5 miles between the location where he himself fired at the animal and where he saw it in the hands of the plaintiffs, and he concedes that roughly one-half hour must have transpired between his last rifle shot and his encounter with the plaintiffs.

If he saw some drops of blood in the snow, by the same token he did not see any blood coming out of the wounds that he ought to have inflicted by his own bullets, which he did not find in the body of the animal either. When chopping it up, he found the marks of three bullets, which hit the animal, one of which at the head and the other at the rear.

Defendant Léonce Boivin confirms the version of Olivier, as to his contemporaneous knowledge, and says that, shortly before encountering the plaintiffs on the scene, he saw drops of blood in the snow. At the location, where the animal had to have been felled by Tremblay, little fir trees were marked by the bullets fired by Tremblay, no bullet was found in the body of the animal, but he added that there were marks indicating that an explosive bullet had hit the animal at the rear.

Guy Boivin confirms the version of the two testifying before him, and Roger Guibault, the son-in-law of Léonce Boivin, says that he examined the guts of the animal and that he found pieces of lead, which, however, he does not enter into the record. He says that he followed the tracks of the moose, for one-half mile, and later when he returned to the grounds of the club, he caught sight of drops of blood there.

Maurice Boivin, another son, who went out to the scene with Guibault, says that he found the guts of the animal all broken, what indicated that there must have been an explosive bullet in the stomach.

Here they are: the important facts as they were presented by the witnesses, and which must serve as the basis for making the determination of which group of hunters had acquired the ownership of the killed game.

The right to hunt may be defined as the right to acquire wild animals by a taking up of possession. This is then a right which belongs to all and which makes the one who is the first to seize a wild animal its owner.

That the animal may have been captured on the land of another does not affect the right of ownership in the animal; and thus, the fact that our moose may have been killed on the grounds of Club Brûlé or on the grounds of Club des Canots does in no way affect the decision in the present case.

A hunter who hunts on land where the hunt is to him forbidden can be sued for interference. He can even be convicted as trespasser or to pay for damages which he may have caused. But, nonetheless, he remains owner of the game that he seizes. This is however subject to the hunting laws, which decree the confiscation of the game in cases of certain offenses against the law. This is to say that the game, as long as it is in liberty does not belong to anybody, or rather, if one may say so, it is owned by the State.

The fact that the moose came across the grounds of Club des Canots is not at all something that could affect the rights of the Boivins to the animal.

The objects which have not yet been submitted to private appropriation, like wild animals, are acquired by the first who lays hand on them; and in this case, the right of ownership, which results from taking up possession, cannot be contested against him by any prior right of ownership, which does not exist. To say that the game belongs to the owner of the ground or yet to the one who has the right to hunt on some premises, would mean committing an error because ownership presupposes that one has the power of its disposition, that one can enjoy it, use it, or recover it if it escapes from us. Now, it is impossible to maintain that one is the owner of a flying partridge or of a running moose, since one cannot dispose of it. Game which enjoys its natural liberty is then not a thing of anybody, and it can be acquired by means of occupancy.

A person, who undertakes on his land an act of occupancy with regard to a wild animal, can go and remove this animal from the land of his neighbor. It is such that the Boivins, by proving an act of occupation sufficient with regard to the moose, on the premises of Club Brûlé, could without doubt go and remove the moose, and even pursue it, on the premises of Club des Canots.

Yet, they had to be in a position to prove a real and sufficiently achieved taking up of possession. In their case, the taking up of possession can result from a mortal wound through the shots fired by Olivier Boivin or even by a sufficiently serious wound, which would allow Olivier Boivin to assume immediate and certain capture. One must then ask oneself which of the two groups wounded or strained the moose to the point that it could no longer escape.

If it were proven that the bullets fired by Olivier had mortally wounded the moose or even had rendered the moose unable to escape from his pursuit, there is no doubt that the defendants would prevail in their case because their taking up of possession would then be earlier than that of the plaintiffs.

Messrs Tremblay, Maltais and Bilodeau have shown the actual, certain taking up of possession; and it falls to the Boivins to prove that they had prior but certain possession. The fact of having established, according to the plaintiffs, the peaceful taking up of possession creates in their favor a presumption. The defendants could only rebut this presumption by strong evidence, sufficient to convince the tribunal that, through the bullets fired by Olivier, the moose had previously been mortally wounded or, at least, completely disabled from escaping. If the evidence of the defendants does not rebut this presumption, the tribunal must accept the laying of hands of the plaintiffs as being the first with regard to an animal, which, at that moment, did not belong to anybody.

This is not a case where two groups of hunters have simultaneously fired at an animal, without the possibility of determining whether it was the bullets of one group or the other that killed the animal; then a division of the product between the parties should have taken place, but the tribunal does not believe that the present difficulty should be resolved in this fashion.

The wounds inflicted by Olivier Boivin were deadly or they were not. Was the moose wounded to the point that it could not escape from the pursuits of Olivier? This is the question.

There appears no doubt that the moose was in the first place wounded by Olivier Boivin; the drops of blood sighted in the tracks followed by him establish this; however, the evidence is far from revealing that the wound was mortal. The moose walked normally when it was sighted by the plaintiffs and it had gained a good distance on Olivier who pretended to be on its pursuit, but who, nevertheless, had lost sight of the animal for almost half an hour.

One has to assume that, if an explosive bullet hit the animal at a vital place, it would have been impossible for it to run a mile and one-half and find itself still in good enough a condition to flee at the moment when it came under Tremblay's bullets.

Olivier Boivin admits that roughly half an hour transpired between his first rifle shot and the moment when he saw the animal again after it was felled. This indicates that he followed the animal from quite far; and it is highly probable that, if the moose had not been felled by Tremblay, it would have escaped from Boivin's pursuit.

Under these circumstances, the tribunal is of the opinion that the presumption remains favorable to the plaintiffs, and that it has not been rebutted by the evidence advanced by the defendants. The defendants suppose that the moose was mortally wounded by an explosive bullet, but their assertion is not sustained by any particular fact.

They do not adduce any piece of metal or lead that they assert having found in the organs. They did not see any large spill of blood at the location just where Olivier must have fired. If the animal, half an hour after having been wounded, still walked normally, one must assume that it would have continued its flight and avoided the capture by Olivier Boivin, who did not succeed in getting closer to the moose in flight.

The presumption thus remains favorable to the plaintiffs, and it is far from being contradicted by the evidence of the defendants who were wrong to use violence in order to seize the moose which the plaintiffs had already acquired by their taking up of peaceful possession.

The plaintiffs have jointly pursued and for the three of them claimed from the defendants, against whom they demand a solidary condemnation, damages in the amount of $1,600.

The plaintiffs have alleged the usage and etiquette among hunters who form a group is to divide up the products of their hunts into equal parts. They have confirmed this implied understanding by claiming all three jointly; and the tribunal is persuaded to award damages to each of them. However, the claim of $1,600 is surely exaggerated.

An amount of $500 is in the first place claimed for the value of the meat of the moose, which weighed more than 500 pounds. In the course of the hearing, the parties came to the understanding to fix the value of the moose at the sum of $325.

In addition, the plaintiffs claim $400 for the deprivation of the pleasure to make certain presents to relatives and friends, as such is the usage upon the return from a hunting trip. This claim bears a certain analogy with damages at times claimed as *solatium doloris*; this does not constitute a real loss which the plaintiffs would have incurred, nor a material gain of which they would have been deprived. They have been deprived of the moral pleasure of giving.

The deprivation of such pleasure cannot be evaluated so as to constitute a measure of damages. The jurisprudence up to now has always refrained from granting such damages for mental pain. By the way, given that the full value of their moose has been granted to the plaintiffs, there would be double compensation, if they were awarded beyond the value to which they themselves have agreed. In effect, they would then be compensated for the pleasure of giving while at the same time retaining the present.

Another amount of $400 is claimed for the deprivation of bringing back and showcasing the trophy of a beast that is difficult to hunt down; this also is another type of damage, difficult to estimate, which also bears a certain analogy with *solatium doloris*, and the tribunal cannot award it. Here also, one can say that the evaluation set at $325 covers all the material gastronomical and moral benefit, which the plaintiffs could draw from their hunt.

A last amount of $300 is claimed for compensating the expenses made for maintaining the hunting permits on the premises, and for transportation and food. These expenses would have been incurred regardless of whether the plaintiffs killed a moose or not. They are neither proximately nor remotely the consequence of the defendants' conduct.

Considering that the plaintiffs became the owners of the moose through occupancy on October 22, 1958;

Considering that the defendants have not proven that any of them had wounded the moose mortally or to the point of preventing it from escaping their pursuit, before the occupancy by the plaintiffs;

Considering that it was incumbent on the defendants to establish on their part a certain and peaceful taking of possession before the violent taking of possession, which they undertook with regard to the animal when it was in the hands of the plaintiffs;

Considering that the plaintiffs have proven their ownership of the moose which was taken away from them without right by the defendants;

Considering that the proven damages come to the sum of $325, and must be awarded to the plaintiffs jointly;

Considering that the defendants have committed an offense by taking away from the plaintiffs, by way of threats, the possession of the moose, and that they are jointly and severally responsible;

On these grounds, the tribunal condemns the defendants to pay to the joint plaintiffs the sum of $325 with interest from the award and the costs; jointly and severally.

Notes and Questions

1. In *Tremblay v. Boivin*, [1960] C.S. 235, two groups of hunters, who had hunting privileges in two distinct, but neighboring camps, claimed to have acquired ownership of the moose subject to the dispute through occupancy. As you read the case, observe the Superior Court's great care in assembling the factual record.

The case illustrates the centrality of possession in the law of occupancy: the occupant's possession must be real and sufficiently achieved. This involves a highly fact-sensitive determination in each case. In hunting cases, the bright line, according to the Quebec Superior Court, is crossed when the wild animal is mortally wounded or disabled from escaping. The first person who successfully achieves this *prise de possession* becomes the owner of the wild animal.

2. In *Tremblay v. Boivin*, the Quebec Superior Court emphasized that the location where this mortal wounding occurs and where the wild animal ultimately dies is immaterial for the vesting of ownership by occupancy. If a person takes ownership of a wild animal through occupancy on the land of another person without having obtained the right to hunt on the land, the landowner in Quebec is relegated to pursuing the remedy of trespass against the hunter. For the same idea: that occupancy of wild animals is decoupled from land ownership *ratione soli*, *see* La. Civ. Code art. 3413(2) (1982).

3. If a person kills a wild animal, a strong presumption of occupancy arises and any challengers must prove that they would have achieved certain possession were it not for the intervention of the one who killed the animal. In *Tremblay v. Boivin*, although the defendants fired the first shot, they were unable to rebut the presumption running in favor of the plaintiffs because the moose managed to escape from the defendants and continue its flight. Note also that throughout its possession analysis the Superior Court emphasizes the attribute of peacefulness.

4. After finding that the defendants unlawfully usurped the possession of the moose despite final occupancy by the plaintiffs, the Superior Court analyzes the question of damages in the final portion of its judgment. It awards damages in the amount of the value of the moose but rejects damages for moral prejudice (*solatium*

doloris), that is, being deprived of the pleasure of giving, and for the loss of the pleasure to display a trophy of their successful hunt. If the facts of *Tremblay* had transpired in Louisiana, would a Louisiana court be more receptive to the plaintiffs' claims for these kinds of damages. *See Lacombe v. Carter*, 975 So.2d 687 (La. App. 3 Cir. 2008).

5. *Tremblay v. Boivin* is similar to *Pierson v. Post*, 3 Cai. R. 175, 2 Am. Dec. (N.Y. 1805), a canonical illustration of the principles of first possession in courses covering common law property. Under the common law of first possession, ownership of wild animals (*ferae naturae*) accrues on the basis of the rule of capture. But how close must the final occupant be to taking up possession?

In *Pierson*, the plaintiff, Post, and his hunting party were in hot pursuit of a fox on a "beach" (a public thing) on Long Island in New York. In full knowledge of the plaintiff's chase and just as Post was closing in on the fox, defendant Pierson intercepted the fox, killed it, and carried it off. Post brought an action of "trespass on the case," a common law form of action for recovery of damages resulting from wrongful acts unaccompanied by direct or immediate force against the plaintiff's person or property. Post won in the trial court, but Pierson, the defendant, appealed and won a reversal.

In writing for the majority on New York's Supreme Court of Judicature, Judge Tompkins held that a hunter only establishes a property right in a wild animal by actually killing or capturing it, or at least by inflicting such mortal wounds, while not abandoning pursuit, so as to bring it under the hunter's control. Here is how Judge Tompkins phrased his holding, which synthesizes a number of illustrious European civil law sources.

> That is to say, that actual bodily seizure is not indispensable to acquire right to, or possession of wild beasts; but that, on the contrary, the mortal wounding of such beasts, by one not abandoning his pursuit, may with the utmost propriety, be deemed possession of him; since, thereby, the pursuer manifests an unequivocal intention of appropriating the animal to his individual use, has deprived him of his natural liberty, and brought him within his certain control. So also, encompassing and securing such animals with nets and toils, or otherwise intercepting them in such a manner, as to deprive them of their natural liberty, and render escape impossible, may just be deemed to give possession of them to those persons, by their industry and labor, have used such means of apprehending them.

Pierson, 3 Cai. R. at 178. In addition to rationalizing his rule as a reward to hunters for their industry and labor in pursuing and apprehending wild animals, Judge Tompkins argued that his bright line rule of capture requiring killing, mortal wounding or complete entrapment was justified because it discouraged conflicts and litigation.

In contrast, Judge Livingston's dissenting opinion in *Pierson* siding with the plaintiff Post contended that property rights in wild animals could be acquired without bodily seizure, provided the pursuer was in reach or had a reasonable prospect of taking what he has discovered and provided the pursuer exhibited an intent to capture the animal for his own use. *Pierson*, 3 Cai R. at 180–82. Judge Livingston, too, argued that his version of the rule of capture would encourage hunters like Post to pursue a "wily quadruped" while protecting these hunters from a "saucy intruder" like Pierson. *Id.* at 181. The judge further asserted that the best way to resolve disputes like this would be to submit contested claims to the "the arbitration of sportsmen," who could apply local customs and norms to resolve these kind of disputes. *Id.* at 180. In sum, the majority's rationale invokes rule clarity and ease of administration, whereas the dissent's rationale serves to promote fairness and cohesion among communities of hunters.

For those interested in learning more about the historical context of the famous case of *Pierson v. Post*, see Bethany R. Berger, *It's Not about the Fox: The Untold Story of Pierson v. Post*, 55 Duke L. J. 1089 (2006); Andrea McDowell, *Legal Fictions in Pierson v. Post*, 105 Mich. L. Rev. 735 (2007); and Angela Fernandez, *The Lost Record of Pierson v. Post: The Famous Fox Case*, 27 L. & Hist. Rev. 167 (2009).

6. In *Popov v. Hayashi*, No. 400545, 2002 WL 31833731, Cal. Sup. Ct. Dec. 18, 2002), which could be dubbed the *Pierson* of baseball, the court confronted two competing claims advanced by the litigants with regard to a record setting home run ball hit in their direction. When the ball went into the arcade it landed in the upper portion of the webbing of a softball glove worn by Plaintiff Popov, without it being clear that the ball was secure in his hand. A crowd tackled Plaintiff Popov and the ball became loose. Defendant Hayashi picked it up and secured it in his pocket, only to show it once he was on camera. Plaintiff Popov sued for conversion asserting that he had achieved sufficient possession of the abandoned ball. In its decision the court fashioned rules and remedies anchored in equity. Firstly, according to the court, "[w]here an actor undertakes significant but incomplete steps to achieve possession of a piece of abandoned personal property and the effort is interrupted by the unlawful acts of others, the actor has a legally cognizable pre-possessory interest in the property [which] constitutes a qualified right to possession." *Id.* at 15–16. Conversely, the court hastened to add, Defendant Hayashi had "done everything necessary to claim full possession of the ball." *Id.* at 17. These actions, the court held, led to a situation where both had "a superior claim against the world" but "a claim of equal dignity as to the other." *Id.* at 18. In search of a middle ground, the court deployed the concept of equitable division. *Id.* at 18–21. This means that the property is sold and the proceeds are split evenly between the claimants. For the seminal law review article in this regard, see Richard H. Helmholz, *Equitable Division and the Law of Finders*, 52 Fordham L. Rev. 313 (1983).

How does this decision jibe with *Pierson*? Should possession not be awarded to either the plaintiff or the defendant? Would you recommend that Major League Baseball change its practice and claim ownership of all baseballs used during a game? Patrick Stoklas, Popov v Hayashi, *A Modern Day* Pierson v. Post: *A Comment on What the Court Should have Done with the Seventy-Third Home Run Baseball Hit by Barry Bonds*, 34. Loy. U. Chi. Int'l L. Rev. 901 (2003). How would you decide the case if the item under scrutiny were Mardi Gras beads thrown from a carnival float tenuously caught by one, turned loose and subsequently secured by another? Would equitable division have worked in *Tremblay*? Would it be helpful for cases involving purported possession of immovables?

7. How would you reconcile Louisiana Civil Code Article 481 ("Ownership exists independently of any exercise of it and may not be lost by nonuse.") with Article 3414 ("If wild animals, birds, fish, or shellfish recover their natural liberty, the captor loses his ownership unless he takes immediate measures for their pursuit and recapture.")? Does Article 3418 of the Civil Code ("A thing is abandoned when its owner relinquishes possession with the intent to give up ownership") provide any answers?

8. In *Harrison v. Petroleum Services, Inc.*, 80 So.2d 154 (La. App. 1 Cir. 1955), landowners sought to recover damages from a petroleum surveyor who unintentionally trespassed on and damaged land that was an ideal habitat for muskrats (medium-sized semiaquatic fur-bearing rodents native to North America, which produce litters of two to four kittens each month, burrow underground and live in nests). The surveyor had entered the plaintiffs' land on marsh buggies and set off seismic explosions without the landowners' consent as a result of an honest surveying error. The landowners asserted that their land was capable of producing 100 muskrats per year prior to the trespass, the defendant's operations completely crushed a special variety of "3-cornered grass" which sustained the muskrats and made the plaintiffs' land an ideal muskrat habitat, and these grasses would not recover to their pre-trespass state for eight to fifteen years. *Id.* at 155–56. In its chief legal defense, the surveyor urged the absence of a cause of action because the landowners did not have a property interest in the muskrats on the plaintiffs' land. They were wild animals in their state of natural liberty. *Id.* at 157.

Writing for the Louisiana First Circuit Court of Appeal, Judge Albert Tate rejected this defense, holding that, even though the landowners did not own the muskrats found on their land, they did have the exclusive right to reduce them to possession. The landowners suffered damages to their muskrat lands as a result of the trespass by the defendant company. *Id.* at 158. In determining the amount of compensable damages, the court considered the potential of the land to yield muskrats (100 muskrats per year), the number of muskrat trapping seasons lost (eight) and the value of a muskrat (57 cents). The court awarded the landowners $456 in damages. *Id.* at 158. Is this outcome consistent with La. Civ. Code art. 3413(2) (1982)?

Albert Tate, Jr., known for his leadership of the legal profession, served sixteen years on the Louisiana First and Third Circuit Courts of Appeal, and ten years on the Louisiana Supreme Court, before being nominated by President Jimmy Carter to serve on the United States Fifth Circuit Court of Appeals. A graduate of Yale Law School, Tate also received a law degree from the LSU Law School in 1948. Tate took an active role in promoting legal and court reforms and wrote more than sixty articles on legal topics. He was chairman of the style and drafting section of the

Louisiana Constitutional Convention of 1973. Tate authored many landmark judicial opinions and is considered by many to be the most influential jurist in Louisiana's so called *Civilian Renaissance*. For samples of Tate's juristic writing, see Albert Tate, Jr., *The Role of the Judge in Mixed Jurisdictions: the Louisiana Experience*, in THE ROLE OF JUDICIAL DECISIONS IN CIVIL LAW AND IN MIXED JURISDICTIONS 23 (Joseph Dainow, ed. 1974); Albert Tate, Jr., *Civilian Methodology in Louisiana*, 44 TUL. L. REV. 673 (1970); Albert Tate, Jr., *The Law Making Function of the Judge*, 28 LA. L. REV. 211 (1968); Albert Tate, Jr., *Techniques of Judicial Interpretation in Louisiana*, 22 LA. L. REV. 727 (1962).

B. Occupancy and Fugitive Minerals

As we noted above, another important group of objects subject to being acquired by occupancy consists of fugitive (or fugacious) minerals. La. Civ. Code art. 3412 rev. cmt. (g) (1982). Codifying a theory first articulated by the Louisiana Supreme Court in *Frost-Johnson Lumber Co. v. Sallings Heirs*, 91 So. 207 (1922), Article 6 of the Louisiana Mineral Code now offers the applicable rules for fugitive minerals.

R.S. 31:6. Right to search for fugitive minerals; elements of ownership of land

Ownership of land does not include ownership of oil, gas, and other minerals occurring naturally in liquid or gaseous form, or of any elements or compounds in solution, emulsion, or association with such minerals. The landowner has the exclusive right to explore and develop his property for the production of such minerals and to reduce them to possession and ownership.

La. Rev. Stat. § 31:6 (1974). The provision first clarifies that fugitive minerals are not automatically owned by the landowner who owns the land where the reservoir is found. In this sense, fugitive minerals are not owned by anyone. However, the Mineral Code gives a landowner the exclusive right to explore and develop her land for the production of fugitive minerals. The landowner thus has the prerogative to reduce these minerals to possession and ownership. John M. McCollam, *A Primer for the Practice of Mineral Law under the New Louisiana Mineral Code*, 50 TUL. L. REV. 729, 739–40 (1976). Compare Louisiana Civil Code Article 3413, which addresses the rights of landowners with respect to wild animals found on their land, with Article 6 of the Mineral Code.

Under this example of a rule of capture, one landowner could use advanced drilling techniques to draw oil, gas or other fugacious minerals from a common subterranean pool extending beneath the land of multiple landowners. In order to prevent waste and avoid the unnecessary drilling of wells, Louisiana law offers a complex regulatory regime for what is called "forced pooling" or "unitization" administered by the Commissioner of Conservation. *See* La. Rev. Stat. § 30:1 *et seq.* (1950). Louisiana law allows the Commissioner of Conservation to establish drilling units for

Katsinam, or friends . . . represent the spirit of deceased ancestors, animals, natural features and events, and various deities [and t]hey are used . . . in connection with prayers and ceremonies in which Hopi religious leaders perform their trust obligation to protect the world." Letter from LeRoy N. Shingoitewa (The Hopi Tribe) to Gilles Néret-Minet (Apr. 4, 2013).

Prior to the auction, a French tribunal rejected the interim relief (*référé*) sought by the human rights organization *Survival International France* to suspend the proposed sale of the objects. The court decided that the petition was unfounded. It noted that neither the American Indian Religious Freedom Act of 1978 nor the United Nations Declaration on the Rights of Indigenous Peoples of 13 September 2007 provided the proper legal basis for interim relief in France and therefore, the petitioner did not show the manifest infringement of an applicable law or a general principle of substantive law. Finding that the masks could not be assimilated to human bodies or elements of bodies of humans who exist or existed, the court determined that the masks would not be protected by general principles of substantive law nor by Article 16-1 of the French Civil Code. This provision declares that everyone has the right to have his or her body respected, that the human body is inviolable, and that the human body, its elements and products cannot be the object of a patrimonial right. This led the court to conclude that the manifestly unlawful disturbance or the imminent damage required for judicial intervention into the planned auction was not met.

What kinds of arguments are the parties likely to have exchanged? Do you agree with the position attributed to Monsieur Néret-Minet: "When objects are in private collections, even in the United States, they are desacralized"?

D. Quasi-Occupancy: Lost Things and Treasure

Occupancy applies to things without an owner and furnishes ownership immediately when the occupant takes possession of the thing. In contrast, the last two articles found in Chapter 1 of Title 23 (Articles 3419 and 3420) provide means of acquiring ownership of two additional categories of things: lost things and treasure. Strictly speaking, these things do have an owner. In the case of lost things, the Civil Code requires a finder to satisfy several additional requirements before he can acquire ownership. With regard to treasure, ownership can vest immediately in the finder, but classifying the object as treasure requires a complex factual inquiry. Moreover, ownership may be shared with the owner of the thing where the treasure is found. For these reasons, we suggest that Articles 3419 and 3420 of the Civil Code create what we call quasi-occupancy.

Lost Things. Unlike the German Civil Code, which dedicates nineteen provisions to lost things, Louisiana's Civil Code offers a single, quite compact provision. Article 3419, which does not have a source provision in the French Civil Code, imposes two conditions for the accrual of ownership of a lost corporeal movable in the finder. The finder must first embark upon a diligent effort to locate the owner or possessor for the purpose of returning the thing to her. If this diligent effort is made and the owner does not materialize after three years, then the finder acquires ownership of the lost thing at the end of three years. La. Civ. Code art. 3418 (1982).

While the contours of the rule appear straight forward, Article 3419 leaves many questions unanswered. Most fundamentally, the article does not define "lost thing." In civilian doctrine a thing is lost when it is not in the possession of the owner or of a precarious possessor, and the possession has ended without the owner intending to relinquish ownership. In this light, things jettisoned or left behind in a shipwreck or other accident are lost but not abandoned. *See* La. Civ. Code art. 3419 rev. cmt. (e) (1982) (discussing La. Civ. Code art. 3424 (1870)).

What of things lost on land? How can a finder know that a thing is "lost," and, therefore, that he must make a diligent search to locate the owner and then wait three years before he acquires ownership? How can a finder know that a thing is "abandoned" and, therefore, subject to occupancy immediately? Relevant factors may include the value and condition of the found thing and the location and circumstances of the discovery. A key chain, wallet or diamond bracelet found in a parking lot, one might reasonably surmise, is lost. An old, scuffed up piece of furniture found on the street curb on the afternoon before garbage pick-up occurs is likely abandoned.

Because a finder of a lost thing is not, strictly speaking, an owner until he satisfies the requirements for becoming an owner under Article 3419 of the Civil Code, a finder cannot transfer ownership of a lost thing until his three year period of possession is complete. This helps explain the statement in the first sentence of Article 521 of the Civil Code: "One who has possession of a lost or stolen thing may not transfer its ownership to another." La. Civ. Code art. 521 (1979).

Curiously, Article 3419 does not define what constitutes a "diligent effort" to locate a lost thing's true owner. The "diligent effort" required to claim ownership after three years may differ depending on the thing found and where it was found. Activities that might be sufficient "involve publishing or advertising in newspapers, posting notes, or notifying public authorities." La. Civ. Code art. 3419 rev. cmt. (d) (1982). Other civil codes typically require that notification be given to a competent public authority.

Article 3419 does not address certain questions posed by the three year waiting period. Does this period begin after the first diligent effort to locate is made or does it begin to run from the moment the lost thing is found? How long must the diligent effort to locate the original owner be sustained: for the entire three year waiting period or just at the beginning of the waiting period?

Louisiana's Civil Code does not offer special rules for things found on the premises of a public authority (for example, city hall offices, corridors, stair cases) or in means of public transportation (for example, buses). Under German law, the finder cannot acquire ownership of such things but must return them without delay. She will then receive a finder's reward in the amount of half the value of the thing.

How would you decide the following case? The plaintiff—a soldier who stays in a requisitioned house owned but not occupied by the defendant—finds, in a crevice on the top of a window frame, a brooch the owner of which is unknown. Assume that the police cannot ascertain its rightful owner. *See Hannah v. Peel*, 1 K.B. 509 (King's Bench 1945).

Treasure. The Civil Code defines a treasure as a movable hidden in another thing (movable or immovable) for such a long time that the owner cannot be determined. La. Civ. Code art. 3420 (1982). A treasure is not a lost thing, nor an abandoned thing, nor a thing without an owner. *Id.* rev. cmt. (c). It is simply "a thing hidden in another thing by someone who cannot prove his ownership." *Id.* Many reasons might exist as to why the person who hid the thing cannot prove his ownership. He might be deceased. He may be far away and unaware that his belonging has been discovered by someone else. He might be in jail.

Unlike former Article 3423 of the Louisiana Civil Code of 1870, the current definition of treasure does not require discovery by chance (thus permitting a deliberate search by means of a metal detector), antiquity (thus including things more recently hidden), or burial in the earth (thus qualifying as treasure a cache of gold concealed behind the walls of a building, in the fuselage of an airplane, or in the trunk of a car).

The rules for allocating ownership of treasure bifurcate according to where the treasure is found. If the treasure is found in a thing belonging to the finder or in a thing without an owner, then the finder of the treasure immediately becomes the owner. If the treasure is found in a thing owned by another, then the finder and the owner of the thing where the treasure has been hidden become co-owners. La. Civ. Code art. 3420 (1982). This idea of equalization between competing interests with respect to treasure dates back to the Roman Emperor Hadrian (117–138 AD).

The next case features the discovery of gold certificates worth $22,200 in a mattress sold after the death of its owner. The heirs of the decedent derived their claim from the law governing lost things, while the purchasers of the mattress invoked the law governing treasure. At the time of the case, the relevant provisions of the Civil Code read as follows:

La. Civ. Code art. 3422 (1870):

If he, who has found a movable thing that was lost, having caused it to be published in newspapers, and having done all that was possible to find out the true owner, can not learn who he is, he remains master of it till he, who was the proper owner, appears and proves his rights; but if it be not claimed within ten years, the thing becomes his property, and he may dispose of it at his will.

La. Civ. Code art. 3423 (1870):

Although a treasure be not of the number of the things which are lost or abandoned, or which never belonged to anybody, yet he who finds it on his own land, or on land belonging to nobody, acquires the entire ownership of it; and should such treasure be found on the land of another, one-half of it shall belong to the finder and the other half to the owner of the soil.

A treasure is a thing hidden or buried in the earth, on which no one can prove his property, and which is discovered by chance.

La. Civ. Code arts. 3422–23 (1870). For purposes of comparison, note that Article 716 of the French Code Civil provides:

La propriété d'un trésor appartient à celui qui le trouve dans son propre fonds: si le trésor est trouvé dans le fonds d'autrui, il appartient pour moitié à celui qui l'a découvert, et pour l'autre moitié au propriétaire du fonds.

Le trésor est toute chose cachée ou enfouie sur laquelle personne ne peut justifier sa propriété, et qui est découverte par le pur effet du hasard.

Ownership of a treasure trove belongs to him who discovers it on his own land; when the treasure trove is discovered on another's land, one half of it belongs to him who discovered it, and the other half to the owner of the land.

The treasure trove is any hidden or buried thing of which nobody can prove ownership and which is discovered by mere chance.

C. Civ. art. 716.

United States v. Peter

178 F. Supp. 854 (E.D. La. 1959)

WRIGHT, District Judge. The setting of this drama is the Lemmon Mattress Works, Hammond, Louisiana. Miss Emily Baron, a local recluse, died in 1957 at the age of 82. A year later her mattress, after being locked up in her room since her death, is sold and sent to the Mattress Works for renovation. After the mattress ticking is removed and the cotton contents processed through the chopping machine, they are placed in the deodorizer box. There the cotton is subjected to an air blast which blows into the air $22,200 in gold certificates.

Emily Baron was one of three children of Lucian Sebastian Baron, a wealthy resident of south Louisiana. Mr. Baron died in 1928. Up to the time of his death he was taken care of by his spinster daughter, Emily. A short time after her father's death, Emily moved in with her brother in his family home near New Orleans. She bought a mattress, the mattress in suit. She used the mattress in her brother's home until 1932 when she and her brother's family moved to Covington, Louisiana. She took the mattress with her.

Emily had built on her brother's acreage in Covington a separate house for her occupancy 30 feet from the home in which her brother and his family lived. In addition to the usual locks on the doors of this house, Emily also had a special lock placed on the door of her bedroom, for it was in that bedroom she kept the mattress.

Emily seldom left her little house and she allowed no one to enter her bedroom except she be present. She ordered her clothes by catalog and kept dormant bank accounts in several banks. As the years went by, Emily gradually lost her sight until at the end she was totally blind. On her death she left no will. Her bedroom was searched and $ 26,000 in Government bonds and $ 2,000 in cash was found in scattered places around the room. No one looked in the mattress.

Emily's legal heirs, one set of claimants here, were judicially placed in possession of all property of which she died possessed. In disposing of her property of little value, her mattress was sold for $ 2.50 to Mr. and Mrs. John E. Cleland, another set of claimants in these proceedings. It was the Clelands who had the mattress picked up from the bedroom of Emily's old house and brought to the Mattress Works. They never saw their purchase. At the Mattress Works the mattress ticking was stripped off and the cotton contents processed as heretofore described. The gold certificates were found by Mr. John H. Lemmon, in charge of Lemmon's Mattress Works. Mr. Lemmon refused to make a claim for the gold certificates. He testified that they do not belong to him and that he does not want them.

The United States has brought this interpleader action [28 U.S.C. § 1345], claiming the gold certificates, but agreeing to pay the rightful owner thereof their face value. *See* 31 C.F.R. 53.1. Only the heirs of Emily Baron and the Clelands have made a claim. The Clelands originally contended that when they purchased the mattress for $ 2.50, ownership of the $ 22,200 in gold certificates contained therein was transferred to them. When it appeared that this contention was obviously without merit, the Clelands decided that the gold certificates were in fact a treasure trove, and that, since the treasure was found in their property, it belonged to them. As authority for this lately conceived contention they cite LSA-Civil Code, Article 3423. The heirs of Emily Baron rely on LSA-Civil Code, Article 3422, maintaining that the certificates were merely lost chattels belonging to their Aunt Emily and that, as her heirs, they own them.

The law of treasure trove has been the subject of much exhilarating conjecture but very little use. Under the early English common law, treasure belonged to the finder. 1 Bl. Comm. (Cooley's 4th ed. 1899) 296. The king soon took care of this detail, however, by promulgating a statute declaring that all treasure belonged to the royal sovereign. 4 Edw. I, c. 2, 1 Pick. Stat. at L. 112 (1276). No subsequent sovereign has seen fit to have the law changed, so even today discovered treasure belongs to the monarch. *See* Emden, *The Law of Treasure Trove, Past and Present*, 42 L. Q. Rev. 368, 379 (1926). The Code Napoleon, 1804, Article 716, on which Louisiana Civil Code is largely based, provides that: "The ownership of a treasure belongs to the person who finds it ***." But that same article provides further that: "A treasure is a thing hidden or buried in the earth, on which no one can prove his property, ***." The treasure trove article in the LSA-Civil Code, Article 3423, is but a restatement of the Code Napoleon. While the language may be garbled to some extent in translation, it is clear that under Louisiana Civil Code as well as under the Code Napoleon the finder of treasure did not own it. He became the owner only if no one could prove that the treasure was his property.

The other Louisiana Civil Code article of relevance is Article 3422 which is entitled 'Finding lost things,' which provides that the finder of a lost article, the ownership of which is unknown, "remains master of it till he, who was the proper owner, appears and proves his right; ***." This article has no counterpart in the Code Napoleon. No useful purpose will be served by distinguishing situations intended to be covered by this article from those under Article 3423, because it is clear to this Court that these gold certificates belonged to Aunt Emily and can now be rightfully claimed by her legal heirs under either article.

While ownership of the gold certificates in Emily Baron has not been proved to a mathematical certainty, the preponderance of the evidence shows that in all probability it was Emily who opened the mattress covering sufficiently to insert the certificates inside and crudely sewed the opening up. Emily coveted this mattress, as she did all of her possessions, from the time she first purchased it. When she first came to live with her brother after her father's death, there was a child in diapers in the family. At the time the air blast blew the gold certificates out of the deodorizer box, it also blew bits of diaper into the air, indicating the possibility that the diaper, before being chopped in the chopping machine, was the wrapper on the certificates. Not long after Emily presumably placed the certificates in the mattress, it became illegal to have gold certificates in one's possession. 33 C.F.R. 53.1. This may explain why Emily allowed her cache to remain in the mattress. It is also conceivable that as the years went on she forgot where she placed the certificates or perhaps even that she had them.

It is true that much of the above appears to be speculation. But considering all the circumstances of this case, and the obviously credible testimony of the members of the Baron family, carefully delineating the eccentricities of this recluse, this Court has the abiding conviction that the certificates did belong to Emily Baron and that her rightful heirs are entitled to their currency equivalent.

Judgment accordingly.

Notes and Questions

1. The proceeding in this case is an interpleader. This is a form of equity action allowing a plaintiff—the United States—to initiate a lawsuit and compel the two named defendants—the legal heirs of Emily Baron and the Clelands who purchased the mattress—to litigate their competing claims to the property at issue. The United States claimed the actual gold certificates because, at the time, it was illegal for private parties to hold gold certificates, but it nevertheless agreed to pay their value to the prevailing claimant.

2. The opinion in *U.S. v. Peters*, 178 F. Supp. 854 (E.D. La. 1959), is authored by **Judge James Skelly Wright**, a 1934 graduate of Loyola University New Orleans School of Law, who served fifteen years on the bench of the Eastern District of Louisiana before he was nominated by President John F. Kennedy to become a judge on the Court of Appeals for the District of Columbia Circuit, where he served for twenty-five years. Deeply committed to equality as the bedrock of our constitutional system, he famously issued many orders aimed at desegregating New Orleans area public schools and the bus and streetcar system in 1956 and 1957. Prior to his departure from New Orleans to Washington D.C., he attempted to desegregate Tulane University in 1962. While on the D.C. Circuit, he issued important opinions in environmental law, occupational safety and health as well as landlord and tenant law, among other areas, that made him one of the most well-known and at times controversial judges of his time.

3. In *Peters*, Judge Wright refused to apply the law governing treasure to the Clelands' claim to the gold certificates. At one point, he stated:

> . . . it is clear that under [the] Louisiana Civil Code as well as under the Code Napoleon the finder of treasure did not own it. He became the owner only if no one could prove that the treasure was his property.

U.S. v. Peters, 178 F.Supp. at 856. What is the implication of this statement? Why couldn't the Clelands prevail by arguing that the gold certificates were treasure?

4. Note that the gold certificates in *Peters* were placed in a mattress as opposed to being buried in the earth. Under Article 3423 of the Civil Code of 1870, was it a requirement that treasure be buried in the earth? In *Peters*, Judge Wright did not seem concerned with this issue. Why? Note that the term "hidden" in the 1870 article was ambiguously separated from the phrase "buried in the earth" by the word "or," but that in Article 716 of the Code Napoleon, a treasure is any "hidden or buried thing" (*"Le trésor est toute chose cachée ou enfouie . . ."*), which seems to indicate two categories of treasure — one concealed in the earth, the other not. *Compare* La. Civ. Code art. 3423 (1870), *with*, C. Civ. art. 716 (1804). In any event, the 1982 revision of the Civil Code removed any doubt by explicitly aligning Louisiana law with German and Greek civil law. This is why today, under Article 3420 of the Louisiana Civil Code, a treasure can also be hidden in a movable. La. Civ. Code art. 3420 rev. cmt. (b) (1982).

5. How does Judge Wright chart the path to his determination that the certificates were lost and that ownership was ascertainable? Does the preponderance of evidence point to Emily? Even if Emily was the original owner, could it be argued that the contract of sale between Emily's heirs and the Clelands included the certificates sown up in the mattress? Could Article 2451 of the Louisiana Civil Code have any bearing on the outcome of this dispute?

Chapter 8

Possession and the Possessory Action

A. Introduction: Possession in the Civil Code

Having explored ownership — its fundamental characteristics and effects as well as the modes of acquiring it — we now turn to possession. Quite frequently, the abstract right of ownership is confused with the factual relation between a person and a thing, which we call possession. The Civil Code is quite clear that ownership exists independent of any exercise of the rights associated with it. La. Civ. Code art. 481 (1979). Moreover, ownership of a thing cannot be lost by nonuse. *Id.* It can, however, be lost to another person through acquisitive prescription, a mode of acquisition of ownership which accrues in favor of person that the Civil Code calls "an adverse possessor." *Id.*

Often a person who holds the *real right of ownership* in a thing also has factual *possession* of that thing. But this is not always the case. As we will see in many of the decisions featured below, the person who is the actual possessor of a thing may not hold the real right of ownership. It is therefore crucial to examine what rights flow from the fact of possession. Two important French jurists once observed that possession denotes a set of specific facts, which gives the possessor "the physical, actual, and exclusive capacity with regard to a thing to carry out the acts of use, enjoyment, or transformation." Aubry & Rau, Droit Civil Français, Property, An English Translation by the Louisiana Law Institute § 177, 82 (1966). Conversely, these jurists also diagnosed that "the exercise of legal acts of administration or disposal of a thing does not require necessarily the fact of possession . . . [as t]he owner of a thing can sell or lease it even if it is occupied by or in the possession of a third party." *Id.*

Understanding the fact of possession is challenging in Louisiana because the Civil Code and the Code of Civil Procedure use the words "possess" or "possession" in different ways. At the beginning of Chapter 2 of Title XXIII of Book III, the Civil Code defines possession in several articles that must be read together.

First, the person claiming possession must exercise some physical control of the object. We call this objective element *corpus*. Physical control alone, however, is not sufficient to establish someone as an adverse possessor under Louisiana law. Two additional articles make this abundantly clear. Consider both of those articles now:

Art. 3421. Possession

Possession is the detention or enjoyment of a corporeal thing, movable or immovable, *that one holds or exercises by himself or by another who keeps it or exercises it in his name.*

The exercise of a real right, such as a servitude, *with the intent to have it as one's own* is quasi-possession. The rules governing possession apply by analogy to the quasi-possession of incorporeals.

La. Civ. Code art. 3421 (1982) (emphasis added).

Art. 3424. Acquisition of possession

To acquire possession, one *must intend to possess as owner* and must take corporeal possession of the thing.

La. Civ. Code art. 3424 (1982) (emphasis added). These two articles reveal that, in addition to the physical detention or enjoyment of a thing, a person must also have a particular state of mind in order to qualify as an adverse possessor. We call this subjective element *animus*. In Article 3421, this is expressed through the requirement that a possessor "holds or exercises" possession "by himself or by another who keeps it or exercises it in his name," La. Civ. Code art. 3421 (1982); that is, not on behalf of or with the permission of another person. *Cf.* La. Civ. Code art. 3437 (1982). Even more important is the requirement in Article 3424 that a possessor "must intend to possess as owner," not for some other purpose or for the benefit of another person. La. Civ. Code art. 3424 (1982).

Note here that the state of mind required to be an adverse possessor is independent of notions of good faith and bad faith. The intent to possess as owner can be based on a reasonable, good faith belief that one is the owner of the thing corporeally possessed, as when a person pays a fair price for a thing believing that he has purchased it from its previous owner. But it can also exist without a reasonable basis, as when a person takes corporeal possession of a thing knowing that it does not belong to him and that he has no right to keep it in his custody.

A person acquires possession when that person combines both *corpus* and *animus*. Both are necessary for the acquisition of possession. La. Civ. Code arts. 3421, 3424 (1982). When one exercises a real right other than ownership, such as a servitude, with the intent "to have it as one's own," we speak of "quasi-possession," rather than possession, because the object is an incorporeal. La. Civ. Code art. 3421 (1982).

If a person merely detains a thing, but clearly lacks the requisite intent to possess as owner, this person is not an adverse possessor. Accordingly, Article 3437 of the Louisiana Civil Code defines the exercise of possession with the permission of or on behalf of another as *precarious* possession. La. Civ. Code art. 3437 (1982). Other legal systems refer to this person as a mere detainer rather than a precarious possessor.

Finally, Article 3422 of the Louisiana Civil Code declares that possession is a matter of fact. Ca. Civ. Code art. 3422 (1982). When possession is sustained for more than one year, however, an important additional legal right accrues—the ***right to possess***. La. Civ. Code art. 3422 (1982). This Louisiana invention is particularly important when it comes to managing possessory actions—proceedings designed to maintain or restore possession in immovables or real rights therein.

Art. 3422. Nature of possession; right to possess

Possession is a matter of fact; nevertheless, one who has possessed a thing for over a year acquires the right to possess it.

La. Civ. Code art. 3422 (1982). *See* La. Civ Code art. 3422 rev. cmt. (b) (1982); *Liner v. Louisiana Land and Exploration Co.*, 319 So.2d 766, 782–83 (La. 1975) (Tate, J., concurring in denial on rehearing). Even before the right to possess accrues, however, a possessor acquires important legal rights as some of the cases below will illustrate. Most importantly, a possessor will be "considered provisionally as the owner of a thing he possesses until the right of the true owner is established." La. Civ. Code art. 3423 (1982). *See also* La. Civ. Code art. 530 (1979) ("The possessor of a corporeal movable is presumed to be its owner.").

The following case gives us a first practical exposure to the proposition that possession cannot be acquired absent the requisite intent to possess as owner. It also showcases how crucial a claimant's testimony may be when it comes to determining the presence or absence of this element of possession.

Harper v. Willis

383 So.2d 1299 (La. App. 3 Cir. 1980)

STOKER, Judge. This is a possessory action. It was dismissed in the trial court on a motion for summary judgment brought by the defendant-appellee, Ray Preston Willis. Plaintiff, Leroy Harper, seeks to be maintained in the possession of immovable property consisting of a rectangular tract of open land measuring 323.6 feet by 435.6 feet. The plaintiff asserts he "possessed" the land by grazing his cattle on it and doing certain other acts upon the land. Plaintiff alleges he has been disturbed in his possession by the recordation of a document which purports to convey the property to defendant Willis. The motion for summary judgment, and the judgment granting it, are based solely on a deposition given by plaintiff.

In our opinion the sole issue in this matter is whether plaintiff ever had the intent to acquire possession as required by Article 3436 of the Louisiana Civil Code. That article reads:

Art. 3436. Essentials of possession

To be able to acquire possession of property, two distinct things are requisite: essential

1. The intention of possessing as owner.

2. The corporeal possession of the thing.

For the purpose of determining whether the trial court was justified in dismissing the possessory action, we may assume that plaintiff could establish the corporeal possession of the land in question requisite number two of LSA-C.C. art. 3436 quoted above. We may so assume because, even if plaintiff can establish that required element of the article, he gave testimony in his deposition in which he specifically negatived any "intention of possessing as owner". The concept of "possessing as owner" is the crux of this case and will be discussed later in this opinion.

In order to better follow the principles to be discussed it is appropriate here to set forth briefly certain facts related by plaintiff-appellant, Leroy Harper, in his deposition. It appears that the property in question is part of what was created several decades ago as the Old Pecan Orchard Subdivision. . . . The whole property consisted of two sections of land one mile by two miles. . . . Apparently the subdivision venture encountered difficulty of some nature, and in the early 30s some of the lots began to be sold for taxes. . . . In the beginning a caretaker, a Mr. Crowe, looked after the property. . . . By 1946 or 1947 the caretaker gave up this job, and the property was left untended. . . . None of the lot purchasers ever occupied or used the lots acquired by them, and Mr. Crowe did not look after these lots. . . . Plaintiff-appellant had begun to run cattle on the whole two-section tract in about 1939 and continued thereafter to do so. At some time, perhaps about 1947, plaintiff-appellant began to acquire lots through tax redemptions, or he acquired an interest with others. . . . At some time before Mr. Crowe abandoned his caretaker responsibilities, he gave plaintiff-appellant permission to run his cattle on the land without payment of rent by Harper if Harper would look after the property, keep the fire out and the brush down. . . . Harper testified he took over the property in 1947. . . . By 1952, plaintiff-appellant had acquired sufficient interest in lots in the subdivision that whatever he did for the whole property he considered to be for his own interests. . . . From 1952, some clearing took place year by year. . . . In 1952, this property was overgrown in thickets. . . . Through purchases at tax sales and from individuals, plaintiff-appellant continued to acquire lots in the subdivision. . . . At some time not clear, plaintiff-appellant became interested in the property subject of this law suit. He was interested in purchasing it, but it was sold to defendant-appellee, Willis. . . . The property apparently consists of three lots. . . . Plaintiff-appellant testified there has never been a fence around the three lots in question, but there was a fence around the entire two sections of land. . . .

The facts set forth above are taken entirely from the deposition given by plaintiff-appellant on which the motion for summary judgment of defendant-appellee is founded. Mr. Harper never testified that he acquired the property subject of this possessory action by any species of title. The action is strictly a possessory action based upon his alleged possession quietly and without interruption for more than a year prior to the recordation of the conveyance to Willis.

The critical testimony given by Leroy Willis [sic — Eds.] himself which establishes the actual subjective intention of plaintiff-appellant regarding the tract purchased by Willis, beginning on transcript page 33, is as follows:

> Q. As to those lots that you have not bought from someone either by tax sale or otherwise has it ever been your intention of acquiring ownership of these people's lots that you didn't buy?
>
> A. If I can.

Q. How?

A. Buying them. I've never tried to beat anybody out of anything.

Q. Alright. You never tried to just take their property did you?

A. No, sir. No.

Q. You never just claimed it as your own without buying it, did you?

A. No.

Q. In fact, you've always, right up to this time, tried to buy people out of any of these lots.

A. If they want to sell it.

Q. So, the possession that you have had of this property that Mr. Willis has the deed to now, you never have possessed that property as the owner of that property, have you the lots Mr. Willis has the deed to?

A. No.

Q. Alright. You knew all along you didn't own that lot

A. Yeah.

Q. Alright. Well, then, less than a year, but before Mr. Willis bought the property, you did call Mrs. Kuentz and again offer to buy the property from her did you not?

A. Right.

Q. You do admit, though, that you never have contended that you own this property that we're talking about in this lawsuit.

A. Well, how could I do that?   - break

Q. Well, I want to know what was in your mind. Were you intending to go out and claim this property just by taking it?

A. No, sir. I told you that awhile ago.

Q. Alright, sir. Now, I'd like to show you a copy of a letter, March 7th, 1960, to Mrs. Kuentz which reportedly was written by you and you say you are writing to her in regard to a lot she owned in Elizabeth. If she ever decides to sell her lot, you'd like to buy it. And you go on to say "I will keep the lots in good shape, keep the bushes down, and the fire out so that it will always look good."

Q. That does appear to be your handwriting and your signature, does it not?

A. Yeah.

Q. Yes. Alright. So, I think you've already said that all along, you never contended you owned this property and these letters would verify that, is that correct? Your answer is yes?

A. My answer is yes.

Q. Did you ever tell Mrs. Bert or Mrs. Kuentz or anyone else that you were claiming the lots involved in this lawsuit as your lots?

A. No.

Q. That you had somehow laid claim to them?

A. No, sir. I did not.

Q. Alright. And you didn't tell anyone that because in truth and fact you never had laid claim to their property had you?

A. Right.

The foregoing excerpts from plaintiff's deposition show that plaintiff, testifying very candidly, has completely destroyed the foundation for his possessory action. As stated above we have assumed, for the purposes of this appeal, that plaintiff can establish the necessary corporeal possession. We focus on his intent. We find that plaintiff did not have the requisite intent to maintain this possessory action. We affirm the trial court action.

INTENT AS REQUIRED BY CIVIL CODE ARTICLE 3436

We will discuss in some detail the requirement of LSA-C.C. art. 3436 that to "acquire possession of property" one of the "two distinct things (which) are requisite" is "(1) The intention of possessing as owner." We are prompted to do so by the suggestion that a possessory action may be maintained without the necessity of possessing as owner. We are also prompted to do so because some question appears to exist as to whether the provisions relating to real actions of the Code of Civil Procedure, particularly articles 3655 through 3660, may conflict with, and govern, to the exclusion of the Civil Code (Article 3436).

At the outset we recognize that a possessor in bad faith may maintain a possessory action. LSA-C.C. arts. 3450, 3452, 3454 and LSA-C.C.P. art. 3660. Article 3660 of the Code of Civil Procedure provides, not only that a bad faith possessor may maintain a possessory action, but "even a usurper," may do so. *See Hill v. Richey*, 221 La. 402, 59 So.2d 434 (1952).

No matter in what quality a person professes to be a possessor, whether in good faith or otherwise, it is clear that the person who asserts that he is a possessor must have had the intention of possessing as owner. The matter is aptly stated in the case of *Buckley v. Dumond*, 156 So. 784 (La. App. 1st Cir. 1934). A possessory action was brought by Buckley. Plaintiff had title to the area in dispute, but the defendant, Dumond, had none. Plaintiff prevailed in the possessory action and the Court of Appeal reasoned as follows:

We find that Dumond's claim to have had possession, as owner, of any part of the land, called for in plaintiff's title, is not well founded, because in the beginning and all along since then, in entering on the land, he did not have "the intention of possessing as owner," but hunting and looking after his cattle and hogs ranging thereon was his only purpose in view. Dumond is not to be regarded as an occupant of the land, but as indicating the importance of intent in a matter of taking possession, we refer to the Civil Code, arts. 3412 and 3413. Under these articles, occupancy is not a mode of acquiring the possession, except when it is retained by the acquirer with the intention of keeping it as his own property. And on the subject of possession, the Code, art. 3436, provides that: "To be able to acquire possession of property, two distinct things are requisite: 1. The intention of possessing as owner. 2. The corporeal possession of the thing." There must be a positive intention to take and commence a possession, as owner, in order that possession, as owner, may be created and commenced.

In typical litigation in which possession is the issue, whether it be a possessory action, a petitory action, or whether it concerns some other question resting on possession, the usual inquiry involves a determination of the subjective intent of the party who claims to be a possessor by reference to objective facts. In Humble v. Dewey, 215 So.2d 378 (La. App. 3rd Cir. 1968), this court stated the proposition as follows in a petitory action:

> In some cases, we think the intention to possess as owner may be inferred from the surrounding facts and circumstances. We believe, however, that ordinarily the intent to possess as owner should not be inferred unless the actions of the possessor or the surrounding facts and circumstances are sufficient to reasonably apprise the public, and the record title owner of the property, of the fact that the possessor has the positive intent to possess as owner.

The concept stated in *Humble v. Dewey*, supra, was recently reiterated in *Wm. T. Burton Industries, Inc. v. McDonald*, 346 So.2d 1333 (La. App. 3rd Cir. 1977). However, the need to infer intent from facts and circumstances is not present in the case before us. The plaintiff, out of his own mouth, has denied any intent to possess as owner. In his deposition he stated, without any equivocation, that he did not possess as owner. . . .

From the foregoing it is clear that if someone, without legal claim or intention to possess as owner, uses the property in any manner, it is without legal significance or detriment to the true owner. . . .

Conclusion

. . . .

It is clear that the intent to possess as owner has to do with the subjective intent of one who professes to possess and does not mean that the possessor must pretend to have valid title rights. The possessor may actually have title, but in the possessory action that factor is significant only in determining intent. The intent may exist without title to the knowledge of the possessor, for as shown above, even our codes permit a person in bad faith or a usurper to maintain the possessory action. LSA-C.C. arts. 3450, 3452, and 3454 and LSA-C.C.P. art. 3660. Inasmuch as the corporeal possession required as a predicate to a possessory action is the same as that required for acquisitive prescription of 30 years, the corporeal possession must be open and notorious and adverse or hostile to the true owner and everyone else.

In the case before us Mr. Leroy Harper has affirmed in every way possible that he intended no adverse claim to the property in question. While we have assumed that Mr. Harper could prove corporeal possession (although he may very well not be able to), none of those acts show in themselves a claim of rights to the land hostile to the true owners. Harper makes no pretense of title. He has acknowledged that he does not own the property. He has also acknowledged that his corporeal possession (if such it be) was not with the intention of possessing it as owner. . . .

This case is before us on appeal from the action of the trial court which dismissed plaintiff-appellant's possessory action on a motion for summary judgment. Among his reasons for judgment the trial court observed: "From a reading of (plaintiff's) deposition it appears that plaintiff's case must fail because he does not contend that he possessed as owner. . . ." We agree with that holding and affirm the judgment of dismissal.

. . . .

The costs of this appeal shall be borne by plaintiff-appellant.

AFFIRMED.

Notes and Questions

1. Do you think that the court properly determined the state of mind of the plaintiff, Leroy Harper, in *Harper v. Willis*, 383 So.2d 1299 (La. App. 3 Cir. 1980)? Did he or did he not intend to possess the land as owner? Should the state of mind of someone in actual possession of a tract of land for such a long period of time matter? What were the purported true owner, Willis, and his ancestors in title doing with the land during Leroy Harper's possession? Should the true owner's apparent indifference to the land affect the outcome in a case like this?

2. Notice the kind of lawsuit that the plaintiff, Harper, brought — a possessory action. Later in this chapter, we will study the specific rules applicable to a possessory action. For now it is enough to appreciate that Harper was not seeking to establish his ownership of the two lots in question. He only sought to have his possession recognized in light of the recordation of a document purporting to be a juridical act transferring ownership to the defendant, Willis. At the time of the case, a precarious possessor was not permitted to bring a possessory action. If this case were to arise today, would the result be the same in light of La. Civ. Code art. 3440 (1982)?

3. In the nineteenth century, the analysis of the constituent elements of possession was the subject of a famous controversy between the German jurists **Friedrich Carl von Savigny** and **Rudolf von Jhering**. Savigny argued that the *animus possidendi* was the crucial criterion differentiating possession from the mere detention or holding of a thing. Friedrich Carl Von Savigny: Das Recht Des Besitzes: Eine Civilistische Abhandlung (The Law of Possession: A Civilian Treatise)

(1803). In Savigny's view, the intent to possess as owner was all that mattered to identify possession. Physical possession without the intent to own is mere detention. Savigny's approach came to be known as the *subjectivist* theory.

Jhering contended that for a person to be in possession of a thing, the person had to exercise at least one of the powers inherent in ownership. RUDOLF VON JHERING, DER BESITZWILLE (THE INTENT TO POSSESS) (1889). According to Jhering's *objectivist* theory, possession arises whenever physical power is voluntarily exercised over a thing. Intent is implied in this exercise, and therefore, animus is not the decisive criterion for distinguishing between possession and detention. For Jhering, the distinction between possession and detention is driven by the reason (*causa*) for this exercise of ownership powers. Take the example of a lease or deposit where the lessee or depositary holds the thing for a third party. The underlying reason for the lessee or depositary's detention is one destructive of possession. The *causa possessionis* becomes a *causa detentionis*. Because the lessee or depositary holds for another, neither can intend to possess as owner. For a discussion of the Savigny-Jhering debate in a Louisiana context, see A.N. Yiannopoulos, *Possession*, 51 La. L. Rev. 523 (1991). The French jurist Raymond Saleilles took yet a different approach to possession, viewing it as the conscious and voluntary economic appropriation of a thing. RAYMOND SALEILLES, ÉTUDE SUR LES ÉLÉMENTS CONSTITUTIFS DE LA POSSESSION (STUDY ON THE CONSTITUTIVE ELEMENTS OF POSSESSION) (1894).

We mention this theoretical debate because it helps explain the sometimes conflicting treatment of precarious possessors under Louisiana law. As noted above, precarious possessors, although not actual possessors, are now entitled to bring possessory actions against all but the persons for whom they possess. La. Civ. Code art. 3440 (1982). However, as case law will demonstrate, precarious possessors cannot claim any of the other benefits of possession.

4. In addition to being provisionally deemed owner, a possessor harvests numerous other legal effects. Thus, her possession can ripen into ownership. As occupant she becomes owner instantaneously. Under the law of acquisitive prescription, a possessor over time becomes full owner. Next, a possessor receives delictual protection. Finally, a possessor is granted certain ownership and reimbursement rights under the law of accession.

5. Why does possession play such a strong and prominent role in the Civil Code? At least three reasons come to mind. First, given that the possessor is so often actually the owner of a thing, focusing the legal system on the question of possession often provides a handy shortcut to determining ownership. If the law generally recognizes a possessor as a provisional owner of a thing, then non-owners who want to enter transactions concerning property can often safely deal with a possessor, without demanding stringent proof that a possessor is actually the owner of a thing. This conserves resources and can make transactions more efficient. Second, treating possession as a proxy for ownership encourages non-owners to be respectful and careful of things in someone else's possession, thus discouraging waste and preventing needless conflict. Finally, because possession requires physical detention,

use and enjoyment of a thing, possession helps keep ownership of property economically vibrant and dynamic. If an owner does not engage in active, physical possession of a thing and allows someone else to usurp his or her possession through acts of detention, use and enjoyment, then the owner risks losing not just possession but ownership itself. In short, by privileging possession, the legal system encourages owners to be active resource users or at least vigilant minders of their property.

* * *

The following case illustrates some of the important legal protections afforded to a possessor, including delictual protection. Recall again though that possession and ownership are distinct. La. Civ. Code art. 481 (1979).

Peloquin v. Calcasieu Parish Police Jury

367 So.2d 1246 (La. App. 3 Cir. 1979)

FORET, Judge. Plaintiff, Robert Peloquin, filed suit on behalf of himself, his wife and their two minor children against Mr. and Mrs. Joseph A. Linscomb and the Calcasieu Parish Police Jury for damages for conversion of their pet cat, "George", for the value of the cat, and for mental anguish, inconvenience, and humiliation suffered due to the alleged actions of the defendants.

Mrs. Linscomb, a neighbor of the plaintiffs, borrowed an animal trap from the Calcasieu Parish Animal Control Center, an agency of the Calcasieu Parish Police Jury, placed it in her yard, and eventually succeeded in trapping a cat, allegedly "George". After trapping the cat, Mr. and Mrs. Linscomb returned the trap with the enclosed cat to the Calcasieu Parish Animal Control Center where it was destroyed. The defendants deny that the cat disposed of was in fact, the plaintiffs' cat.

Prior to trial on the merits, defendants filed exceptions of no right of action and no cause of action on the grounds that as the plaintiffs had no ownership interest in George they had no legal grounds to sue for damages for mental anguish, etc. occasioned by his alleged conversion at the hands of defendants. These exceptions were maintained by the trial court, leaving plaintiffs the right to sue for only the worth of the cat, which the court determined was less than the statutorily required amount necessary for a jury trial and thus also denied plaintiffs' request for same. Plaintiffs have appealed dismissal of this part of their claim; the remainder has not been tried in the district court. . . .

Turning to the merits of the appeal, it is initially obvious that the exception of no cause of action maintained by the trial court must be overturned. The exception of no cause of action is to raise the question of whether any remedy is afforded by law. The exception of no right of action is to raise the question of whether a remedy afforded by law can be invoked by a particular plaintiff. . . .

"An exception of no cause of action must be determined in the light of the well pleaded averments of plaintiff's petition, all of which must be accepted as true." *Barnett v. Develle*, 289 So.2d 129 (La. 1974); *Haskins v. Clary*, supra.

The plaintiffs allege their ownership of George and their subsequent dispossession of him by acts of the defendants. This in itself is sufficient to state a cause of action. The judgment of the trial court maintaining this exception is reversed.

We now turn to the exception of no right of action which was also maintained by the trial court. In addition to the facts hereinabove recited, it is stipulated by the parties that:

(1) appellants did not purchase the cat nor did they receive it as a gift;

(2) the Peloquins had possessed the cat for more than seven years since Mrs. Peloquin found it as a kitten in or near her yard;

(3) the Peloquins did not advertise the finding of the kitten in the newspaper or make other attempts to locate the owner except to ask their neighbors.

The trial court, citing Civil Code Article 3422, held that the Peloquins were not the owners of the cat and as mere possessors, did not have the right to sue for mental anguish, etc. suffered as a result of George's alleged demise at the hands of the defendants but could sue only for any actual damages (the worth of the cat). . . .

Article 3422 is contained in the chapter of the Louisiana Civil Code entitled "Occupancy", which is defined in Article 3412: . . .

Further examination of this chapter reveals that property, subject to occupancy, may be acquired by possession of it for different periods of time, depending on the prior ownership status of the property. Article 3421 allows a person who acquires a movable that has been abandoned to immediately become its "master". Article 3415 allows the captor who reduces to possession a wild animal to immediately become the owner of the captured creature.

Mrs. Peloquin stated that approximately seven years prior to the disappearance of George, she had found him as a kitten while putting her children on a school bus. After first asking her neighbors if they had lost a kitten, the Peloquins raised George as a family pet. In applying Article 3422, the trial court must have determined that George was "lost" when taken in by the Peloquins; however, from the record this appears to be a factual determination that the jury should have had a chance to consider. It is at least as likely that George was either abandoned by his prior owner or perhaps never had an owner (a wild beast or animal?). Cursory observation of the streets of our cities reveals many "alley cats" which exist by their wiles without being owned by any person.

As an alternative argument, plaintiffs cite Louisiana Civil Code Article 3506, three year prescriptive period to acquire ownership of a movable. This Article is contained in the same Book III, Title XXIII of the Civil Code as the aforecited articles on occupancy; it is however contained in a different chapter than occupancy. . . .

Article 3506 establishes the prescriptive period to acquire a movable possessed in good faith and with a Just title as owner; while we are unsure what would suffice as a "just title" to such an animal as George, the mere taking possession of the creature is insufficient to constitute the required transfer of title. Such three-year prescriptive period might successfully be urged if the Peloquins had purchased or been given George by a person who claimed ownership of him but was not in fact such.

However, we do not decide this appeal on these grounds as we are persuaded by plaintiffs' further alternative argument that they should be allowed to sue for all claimed damages because of their status as George's possessor. Article 3450 of the Civil Code recognizes possession as a fact as well as a right and Civil Code Article 3454 provides:

> "Art. 3454. Rights which are common to all possessors in good or bad faith are:
>
> 1. That they are considered provisionally as owners of the thing which they possess as long as it is not reclaimed by the true owner or the person entitled to reclaim it, and even, after such reclamation until the right of the person making it is established. . . .

It would thus appear that even as possessor the plaintiffs have the right to maintain their action against any but the true owner (if there is one) of the cat.

We are supported in this holding by a study of the tort of conversion upon which the plaintiffs' claims are based. Despite being a common law action, conversion has been recognized in Louisiana law under Civil Code Article 2315 for many years. *Edward Levy Metals, Inc. v. New Orleans Public Belt RR*, 243 La. 860, 148 So. 2d 580 (1963) . . . *Lincecum v. Smith*, 287 So. 2d 625 (La. App. 3 Cir. 1973), writ refused, 290 So. 2d 904 (La. 1974) . . .

The Restatement of Torts, Second, explicitly recognizes that the person who converts the chattel may be liable to the possessor of the chattel. § 224 A. Liability to Person in Possession As stated in the comments to that section:

> For a conversion the actor is subject to liability to another who was at the time in possession of the chattel.
>
> A. This Section states the rule as to liability to the possessor of a chattel for a conversion, committed as stated in § 223. The converter may also be liable to a person entitled to the immediate possession of the chattel as stated in § 225, or to one entitled to future possession of the chattel as stated in § 243.
>
> B. It is immaterial that the one in possession of the chattel is not entitled to retain possession as against some third person, or that he has obtained possession wrongfully. See § 895.

In his discussion on conversion, Prosser states:

> . . . the man in possession recovers the full value of the chattel, although he may not be the full owner or any owner at all.

Law of Torts, 4th Ed., pg. 95.

Prosser notes that the reason for this lies in ". . . the convenience of treating the possessor as the owner, in the encouragement to peace and security expected to result from the protection of any possession against a wrongdoer with no rights at all". Ibid, pg. 95.

Prosser also notes that in the common law, the procedural method used is to disallow the defendant in a conversion action to set up as a defense the claim of a third party to the chattel, superior to that of the plaintiff, unless the defendant can connect himself with that claim (the "jus tertii"). Ibid, pg. 94.

In French law, Aubry & Rau Property state:

> The possession of corporeal things creates in favor of the possessor a presumption that he has legal title which the possession manifests. More precisely it has the following effects:

> (f) A simple possessor or even a precarious holder of a movable of whose possession he is deprived can recover it against a third party simple possessory in all cases in which the owner of the thing could do so.

Droit Civil Francais, pg. 105, Vol. II, 7th Ed., Civil Law Translations 2 (1966).

We conclude that a possessor has the same rights as an owner of a movable to sue for damages for conversion thereof by the defendant, and those damages may include awards for mental anguish, humiliation, etc. as well as special and/or actual damages. *Lincecum*, supra; *Brown v. Crocker*, 139 So.2d 779 (La. App. 2 Cir. 1962). *Lincecum* involved a puppy and Brown involved a mare. Both of these cases awarded damages for mental anguish, etc. as a result of injury to the animals involved. Admittedly these two cases involved owners of the animals, but we view the legal principle as the same. If plaintiffs can prove possession, and that they suffered provable and compensable damages as a result of the conversion of the cat involved, we are of the opinion that they are entitled to recover for these damages.

Whether plaintiffs in this case owned the cat in question, whether they possessed the cat in question as owner, and proving all other facets of their case, if they can prove damages, they are entitled to recover, unless defendant has a valid defense that would justify denial of recovery to the plaintiffs. All of these factors are properly questions for the trier of fact, be it judge or jury, and the case should be remanded for trial in accordance with the views above expressed.

Accordingly, we reverse the judgment of the trial court, and overrule the exceptions of no right of action and no cause of action, and remand the case for further proceedings.

Costs of this appeal are assessed against the defendants. Costs in the trial court must await final outcome of this matter.

REVERSED AND REMANDED.

Notes and Questions

1. The court in *Peloquin v. Calcasieu Police Jury*, 367 So.2d 1246 (La. App. 3 Cir. 1979), distinguishes between two different pre-trial motions filed by the defendants—an exception of no cause of action and an exception of no right of action. Both exceptions originate in the Louisiana Code of Civil Procedure. *See* La. Code Civ. Proc. art. 425 (1960, amended 1976, 1977). They are roughly equivalent to motions to dismiss "for failure to state a claim upon which relief can be granted." Fed. R. Civ. P. 12(b)(6).

Note first the court's impatience with the defendants' exception of no cause of action and the court's use of the well-pleaded complaint rule ("An exception of no cause of action must be determined in the light of the well pleaded averments of plaintiff's petition . . ."). *Peloquin*, 367 So.2d at 1248. The court quickly, and with little analysis, found that the plaintiffs' allegations of ownership of the cat and dispossession of him by the defendants were sufficient for *some person* to *state a cause of action*, whether or not these plaintiffs were the proper parties to bring the action.

2. The exception of no right of action is designed to ascertain whether the particular claimant is in fact the party to whom the defendant named in a lawsuit owes a duty. The appellate court was most interested in this exception and went out of its way to address the trial court's finding that "the Peloquins were not the owners of the cat and *as mere possessors did not have the right to sue for mental anguish* etc. suffered as a result of George's alleged demise at the hands of the defendants." *Peloquin*, 367 So.2d at 1249 (emphasis added).

Notice the court's methodology here. First, the court considered whether the Peloquins could prove that they were the owners of the cat under any of the various modes of acquiring ownership recognized under the Civil Code but found all of them wanting. The Peloquins stipulated that they did not acquire the cat from a previous owner through a voluntary transfer of ownership because they did not acquire it by sale, exchange or donation.

Next, the court observed that the Peloquins could not prove that they acquired the cat through acquisitive prescription because they had not possessed the cat for three years in good faith and under a just title, La. Civ. Code art. 3506 (1870). Moreover, in the absence of good faith and just title, they had not satisfied the requirement of possession over ten years. La. Civ. Code art. 3509 (1870). For the contemporary rules on acquisitive prescription with respect to movables, see La. Civ. Code arts. 3489–91 (1982).

The court then signaled that George might be classified as a "lost" movable under Article 3422 of the Civil Code of 1870 and therefore, the Peloquins might have acquired ownership of him after three years if they had placed advertisements in newspapers and "done all that was possible to find out the true owner." La. Civ. Code art. 3422 (1870); *cf.* La. Civ. Code art. 3419 (1982) (requiring a finder of a lost thing to make a diligent effort to locate the owner or possessor and return the lost thing before the finder becomes owner). According to the court in *Peloquin*, this was a question for a jury to decide.

Finally, the court further indicated that classifying George for purposes of the law of occupancy raised even more questions. Although the trial court concluded that George had been lost, the appellate court wrote:

> It is at least as likely that George was either abandoned by his prior owner or perhaps never had an owner (a wild beast or animal?). Cursory observation of the streets of our cities reveals many 'alley cats' which exist by their wiles without being owned by any person.

Peloquin, 367 So.2d at 1249. As the court's tone suggests, determining whether the Peloquins acquired ownership of George through any of these modes of acquiring ownership would have required a great deal of speculation at best and may not have been provable. In any event, the trial court should have allowed the Peloquins to present evidence in support of their assertions and therefore, it was in error to sustain the exception of no right of action.

Further rejecting the defendants' exception of no right of action, the court considered the Peloquins' alternative argument. Even absent ownership, the possessor of a thing is treated provisionally as an owner. This enables the possessor to sue for mental anguish damages just like an owner can. *Peloquin*, 367 So.2d at 1250 (citing La. Civ. Code art. 3454 (1870)). A possessor has all the rights of an owner, except for the right to transfer ownership. Because the Peloquins could prove that they possessed the cat for more than a year with the intent to be its owners, the Peloquins were entitled, provisionally at least, to all the rights that an owner of the cat could enjoy, including the right to sue for mental anguish if the cat was destroyed unlawfully by another person.

3. Observe the blend of classic common law and civil law sources the court cited in the concluding paragraphs of its opinion. The practice of treating a possessor as a provisional owner until the true owner emerges has deep roots in both common law and civil law property systems. The common law captures the idea under the doctrine of relativity of title. Until a true owner establishes his right to a movable thing like a cat, the law will presume that its possessor is the owner. Thus, the possessor will be able to defend his possession against all other persons, besides the true owner, who might interlope and try to convert the movable thing to their possession or benefit.

The classic example of this doctrine in the common law is *Armory v. Delamarie*, 1 Strange 505 (K.B. 1722), where the court held that a chimney sweeper's boy who found a jewel and took it to a goldsmith's shop, whereupon the goldsmith's apprentice refused to return it, was entitled to recover it from the goldsmith because "the finder of a jewel, though he does not by such finding acquire an absolute property or ownership, yet he has such a property as will enable him to keep it against all but the rightful owner, and consequently may maintain trover." *Id. See also Jeffries v.*

The Great Western Railway, 119 Eng. Rep. 680 (Q.B. 1856) (observing that "a person possessed of goods has a good title against every stranger, and that one who takes them from him, having no title in himself, is a wrongdoer, and cannot defend himself by showing that there was a title in some third person; for against a wrongdoer possession is title").

The Civil Code captures the idea of possession as a proxy for title in the following provision, which was enacted in the same year that *Peloquin* was decided:

Art. 530. Presumption of ownership of movable

The possessor of a corporeal movable is presumed to be its owner. The previous possessor of a corporeal movable is presumed to have been its owner during the period of his possession.

These presumptions do not avail against a previous possessor who was dispossessed as a result of theft or fraud.

La. Civ. Code art. 530 (1979).

4. After the Peloquins' lawsuit was remanded to the trial court, a jury eventually determined that "the animal trapped by the Linscombs was not the plaintiffs' cat, George, but was a different one." *Peloquin v. Calcasieu Parish Police Jury*, 378 So.2d 560, 561 (La. App. 3 Cir. 1979). After this dramatic revelation, the court of appeal affirmed a judgment in favor of the defendants dismissing the Peloquins' claims. *Id.*

B. Forms of Possession

Adverse possession can be corporeal or civil. The fiction of constructive possession helps ascertain how much land the corporeal or civil possessor possess. In contrast to adverse possession, precarious possession lacks the element of *animus*.

1. Corporeal, Civil and Constructive Possession

Corporeal possession is the strongest form of possession. Article 3425 of the Civil Code declares:

Art. 3425. Corporeal possession

Corporeal possession is the exercise of physical acts of use, detention, or enjoyment over a thing.

La. Civ. Code art. 3425 (1982). As the revision comments to this article explain, one possesses a thing "corporeally, for example, by residing in a house, cultivating land, or using a movable." *Id.* rev. cmt. (b). The acts of possession required vary with the nature of the land. For developed areas (for example, agricultural lands) more is required when compared to undeveloped areas (for example, swamplands or woodlands). *Madden v. L.L. Golson*, Inc., 222 So.3d 1286 (La. App. 2 Cir. 2017), *writ denied*, 230 So.3d 218 (2017).

The Civil Code does not contemplate that a possessor who has acquired corporeal possession, in person or through another, with the intent to possess as owner must physically occupy the thing at all times. Instead, a possessor maintains her possession by her animus even when she no longer is in corporeal possession. This possession by mere will is called *civil possession*. The following provision states this principle in its modern form:

Art 3431. Retention of possession; civil possession

Once acquired, possession is retained by the intent to possess as owner even if the possessor ceases to possess corporeally. This is civil possession.

La. Civ. Code art. 3431 (1982). If you leave your apartment to go law school and leave behind some of your belongings — books, clothes, other personal belongings — you expect those things to be in your apartment when you return. Similarly, if you own a house and take a two week vacation, you want your house to be ready for you to occupy when you return. In both of these situations, you were in corporeal possession of these things at one time and then you relinquished your direct physical control for some period of time by leaving those things unattended. Nevertheless, you expect that your possession will be continued. Civil possession fulfills these reasonable expectations.

The concept of civil possession is so integral to the law of possession that a possessor is presumed to retain the intent to possess absent clear proof of a contrary intention. La. Civ. Code art. 3432 (1982). A possessor's intent to preserve his civil possession can be shown by acts such as paying taxes on immovable property, executing leases or engaging in acts of maintenance and preservation. La. Civ. Code art. 3431 rev. cmt. (d) (1982). Although a possessor is presumed to intend to retain possession as long as his possession is not lost to another person, a possessor can evidence his intent to retain possession by returning to the thing he possesses and engaging in acts of corporeal possession. *See* La. Civ. Code art. 3443 (1982) ("One who proves that he had possession at different times is presumed to have possession during the intermediate period."). Conversely, possession is only lost when the possessor "manifests his intention to abandon it or when he is evicted by another by force or usurpation." La. Civ. Code art. 3433 (1982). Civil possession continues until possession is lost.

Now that we know that possession is acquired by corporeal possession and can be maintained by civil possession, we must address another important concept in the law of possession with respect to immovables — **constructive possession**. It is defined in the following terms:

Art. 3426. Constructive possession

One who possesses a part of an immovable by virtue of a title is deemed to have constructive possession within the limits of his title. In the absence of title, one has possession only of the area he actually possesses.

La. Civ. Code art. 3426 (1982). A person who possesses only a portion of the land described in what this article calls a "title" is deemed to be in possession of the entirety of the tract bounded by that title.

Take careful note, however, that the word "title" as used in Article 3426 does not refer to a certificate or document issued by a government official that declares a particular person (or persons) to be the owner(s) of a tract of land. A title in this context is nothing like a title to a motor vehicle issued by a state's department of motor vehicles which lists the actual owner of a particular vehicle. Rather, "a title," as used in Article 3426 and throughout the Civil Code provisions dealing with immovable property, refers to some kind of juridical act that purports to transfer ownership of immovable property from one owner (or set of owners) to another. It could be an act of sale, exchange or donation. The "title" transfers ownership because the transferor owns all of the immovable property he or she purports to transfer. But sometimes a title does not transfer ownership. For various reasons, the purported transferor may not own all of the immovable property that is purportedly transferred. In other cases, he may not own any of it.

Constructive possession, as defined in Article 3426, comes into play by allowing a possessor to extend his claim of possession to all the land bounded by "his title," even though the possessor is not in corporeal possession of all the immovable property described in the title, and even when that title has not transferred ownership to the possessor. A possessor without any semblance of "a title" must prove that he has had corporeal possession of each part of the land he claims to possess—either inch by inch or within enclosures. La. Civ. Code art. 3426 rev. cmt. (d) (1982). In short, only a possessor with "a title" can take advantage of constructive possession. For the classic formulation relative to possession within enclosures, see *Hill v. Richey*, 221 La. 402, 59 So.2d 434, 440 (1952) ("What the court means by 'enclosures', as that term is used in the numerous cases found in the jurisprudence, is that the land actually, physically, and corporeally possessed by one as owner must be established with certainty, whether by natural or by artificial marks; that is, that they must be sufficient to give definite notice to the public and all the world of the character and extent of the possession, to identify fully the property possessed, and to fix with certainty the boundaries or limits thereof."). For a recent case invoking this language as the crucial standard in disputes over possession, see *Mitchem v. Soileau*, 222 So.3d 143, 148 (La. App. 3 Cir. 2017) (affirming dismissal of possessory action on ground that claimants only presented one survey performed by an expert who had previously surveyed property and whose testimony did not support claim regarding possession to old fence no longer on the property).

Suppose that Anne pays money to purchase ten acres of land. The act of sale executed by her and her vendor declares her to be the owner of the ten acres and identifies and describes the ten acres of land. The ten acres include two acres occupied by a house, a driveway, and a garden, and eight acres occupied by dense woods. Anne moves into the house, regularly uses the driveway and cultivates the garden, but she does not venture into the woods at all. She does not cut down any trees or fence in any of the rest of the property. In this example, Anne has taken corporeal possession of the house, garden and driveway. When she is away from her home, Anne can maintain civil possession by her intent to possess as owner.

With regards to the wooded area, Ann has not exercised any acts of corporeal possession. Yet, since the woods are included in the ten acres of land described in her act of sale, along with the house, the garden and the driveway, Ann is in constructive possession of the woods. Her corporeal possession of part of the property—the house, the garden, and the driveway—allows her to claim constructive possession of the whole property bounded by her title, including the woods. Constructive possession, supported by title, embodies a form of true possession, but it can be trumped by the adverse corporeal possession of another, as we will see in the following case.

Now consider the famous case of *Ellis v. Prevost*, 19 La. 251 (1841). The opinion of Justice Simon illustrates how these rules of possession can be applied and how the Louisiana Supreme Court early on extended the concept of civil possession by allowing parties who acquire interests in property from others to rely on the acts of corporeal possession of their predecessors to establish subsequent civil possession.

Ellis v. Prevost

19 La. 251 (1841)

SIMON, Justice. . . . The record shows, that on the 28th of June, 1836, plaintiff purchased from one John Hutchings, by a notarial act, a tract of land, containing thirty-six arpents in front, by forty in depth, on the east side of bayou Grand Caillou, and eleven arpents and one-third in front, by forty in depth on the west side of the said bayou; and that Hutchings had acquired the same from P. S. Cocke, by an act of sale executed on the 6th of February, 1829. That in the years 1829 or 1830, Hutchings took possession of the tract as owner, and put an overseer and seven hands upon it, who lived on and cultivated the place for about twenty-two months, built some cabins, girdled the trees on about one hundred and fifty arpents on the east side, raised a crop on said land, nearly opposite where Madame Prevost then and now lives, and that two individuals also cultivated the said land at different times by the permission of Hutchings. The plaintiff never resided there, and after his purchase, he abandoned the improvements made by his vendor.

It is also established, that the defendants and their ancestors resided for a long time on the west side of the bayou, and that they occupied and cultivated at different periods an inconsiderable part of the land in controversy on both sides; it is not shown however, that the portions thus cultivated and which were unenclosed, were ever possessed by metes and bounds, but there is proof resulting from the testimony of the witnesses and from the plat returned by the surveyor, that their enclosures around the house on the west side have existed for a long time, and contain a small tract of four arpents in front, by two arpents and a half in depth, which is the spot which the defendants and their father have actually occupied for a certain number of years before the institution of this suit. The evidence further shows, that about eighteen months previous to the first trial of this suit, (in March, 1838; the suit was brought in February, 1837,) two persons named Champagne and Daspit, came to reside on the land on the east side, with Madame Prevost's permission; the spot by them occupied is shown on the plat to be five arpents in front, by two and a half in depth.

Under the legal principles established in the former decision of this cause, which however we are not ready to adopt to the same extent, it is clear, that the plaintiff had a right to institute an action of possession against the defendants by virtue of his civil possession, based on the previous actual and corporeal possession of his vendor. This doctrine, so far as it requires the civil possession to be preceded by an actual and corporeal detention of the thing, and as it allows to the plaintiff the benefit of the previous corporeal possession of his author, appears to us to be correct, and we are not disposed to controvert it; but we cannot accede to the proposition, that our laws recognize but one kind of possession, and that a civil possession will suffice in all cases. We are aware, that the distinction between natural and civil possessions is peculiar to the Roman law, and among the French commentators of the highest authority on the Napoleon Code, there are several who consider it as having no sense or direct meaning. *Troplong, prescription, No. 239*, says: *Ces appellations de possession civile et de possession naturelle sont restées si vagues pour les modernes, que peut-être aujourd'hui encore l'on est indécis sur leur veritable sens.*

But we are not able to say, that with us it is *a distinction without a difference:* it is evident from the different provisions contained in our system of legislation, that our laws, on this subject, too clear and too explicit to be disregarded, recognize two species of possession, natural and civil: natural possession, which may be called possession in fact, is, when a man detains a thing corporeally, as by occupying a house, cultivating a field; and civil possession, or possession in right, is, when a person ceases to reside in the house or on the land which he occupied, but without intending to abandon the possession. *La. Code, articles* 3390, 3391, 3392 [3421, 3425, 3431.]

Another difference is established by *Pothier, on possession, No. 55;* which, it seems to us, explains clearly the object and meaning of the distinction made under our laws between natural and civil possession; it is this: *Pour acquérir la possession d' une chose, la seule volonté ne suffit pas; il faut une préhension corporelle de la chose ou par nous mêmes, ou par quelqu'un qui l'appréhende pour nous et en notre nom. Au contraire, lorsque nous avons acquis la possession d'une chose, la seule volonté que nous avons de la posséder suffit pour nous en faire conserver la possession, quoique nous ne détentions pas cette chose corporellement, ni par nous-mêmes, ni par d'autres.* This distinction, therefore, is very obvious: possession is acquired by the actual and corporeal detention of the property; this is the *natural possession* or possession in fact; and it is preserved and maintained by the mere will or intention to possess; and this is the *civil possession* or possession in right.

Now, in order to acquire prescription by the possession of ten years, founded on a just title, it is necessary, among other requisites, that the possessor should have held the thing in fact and in right as owner, (*ait possédé la chose naturellement et civilement,*) and yet, to complete a possession already begun, the civil possession shall suffice, provided it has been preceded by the corporeal detention of the thing. *La.*

Code, art. 3453 [3476]. So it is with regard to the right of possession: "*When a person has once acquired possession of a thing, by the corporeal detention of it, the intention which he has of possessing, suffices to preserve the possession in him, although he may have ceased to have the thing in actual custody, either himself or by others.*" La. *Code, articles* 3405, 3406 and 3407 [3431]. Thus, if after having abandoned the corporeal possession of my house, or the cultivation of my field, I continue to possess it civilly; the intention which I have of possessing, will preserve the possession in me; unless a third person has usurped or taken such possession from me, during the time required by law . . . and if in the meantime, I am disturbed in my possession, I have the right before the expiration of one year, and by virtue of my civil possession, founded on my previous and anterior corporeal and actual possession of the property, to institute a possessory action to recover it.

This is undoubtedly the meaning of the art. 49 of the Code of Practice, which must be construed in relation to the articles of the Louisiana Code on the subject of possession; this article says: "In order that the possessor may be entitled to bring a possessory action, it is required: 1st, that he should have had the real and actual possession of the property *at the instant when the disturbance occurred:* a mere civil or legal possession is not sufficient." Now we understand the expressions, *real and actual possession,* contained in this law, as used in contradistinction with the possession which is purely civil and legal, that is to say, with the possession which is entirely devoid of the quality of having its source in or being derived from a previous actual and corporeal one; such possession is not sufficient; but when it has been preceded by the corporeal enjoyment of the thing, and the possessor has not ceased to exercise such enjoyment for ten years, the actual possession previously acquired is preserved and maintained, and it continues in the same manner and with the same effect as if the thing had always been actually and corporally possessed. . . .

It is clear, therefore, that if the article 49 of the Code of Practice was to be construed strictly and according to its literal meaning, there would follow the absurdity, that if a person was to absent himself temporarily, and leave his house unoccupied for a certain lapse of time, he could not on his return bring a possessory action against an intruder who would have taken possession of it during his absence, and would be obliged to resort to the petitory action his adversary would always successfully oppose to him the plea, in the words of the Code of Practice, that he was not in the real and actual possession of the house *at the instant when the disturbance occurred.* This cannot have been the intention of the lawgiver; and such an interpretation is too absurd to be for a moment countenanced at our hands. We must consequently conclude, that the possession acquired by the plaintiff's vendor, which possession is shown to have existed really and actually for more than one year, according to the extent and under the limits exhibited by the acts of sale, ought to enure to the benefit of said plaintiff; and that having not failed to exercise the said natural possession for ten years, the same was preserved in his favor by the civil possession, and was sufficient to entitle him to bring and maintain the present action.

With this view of the question, the plaintiff, under the evidence, would have a right to recover the whole tract, unless he is shown to have suffered a year to elapse after the disturbance, without bringing his possessory action, and unless the defendants have succeeded in establishing an adverse possession to it or to any part thereof during the period prescribed by law. *C. of Pr.*, art. 59; *La. Code*, art. 3419 [3465]. It is true, that the defendants have, at various times, occupied and cultivated, for a certain number of years, different inconsiderable parts of the land in dispute; but they have shown no possession according to metes and bounds of the land which was unenclosed, and the testimony is so vague and uncertain as to the extent of the several spots, which they have successively occupied, and of the limits of the fields which they may have cultivated, that it would be impossible to ascertain and indicate the fractions of the plaintiff's land, upon which they may have exercised their alleged acts of possession. "*On ne peut pas posseder la partie incertaine d'une chose;*" *Troplong, prescription, Vol. 1, No. 250.*

In the case of *Prevost's Heirs* vs. *Johnson*, 9 *Mart.* 123, this court held, that when a person claims by possession alone, without showing any title, he must show an adverse possession by enclosures, and his claim will not extend beyond such enclosures. In the case of *Bernard* vs. *Shaw*, 1 Mart. N.S. 480, the facts proved established the plaintiff's right of possession, (as in this case,) to the whole body of land sued for; the defendant, however, gave in evidence his possession and cultivation of a field of fifteen arpents, but neither the pleadings, nor the evidence ascertained the particular spot where this possession was exercised; and the defendant's pretensions were disregarded. In the case of *M'Donough* vs. *Childress et al.*, 15 La. 556, we said, that it was necessary, in an action of possession, not only to show acts of limited and restricted possession, but also to establish by legal evidence the extent and full limits of the property so possessed. These principles are clearly applicable to the present case; and as the defendants have not shown their adverse possession to extend, by metes and bounds, with any degree of certainty, beyond the enclosure of the spot shown on the surveyor's map, to contain four arpents in front, by two arpents and a half in depth, and as the evidence fully establishes their actual and continued possession for a number of years to the quantity of arpents of land comprised within their said enclosures, we are of opinion, that the said defendants should be maintained in their said possession of the said tract of four arpents in front, by two and a half in depth, on the west side of the bayou Grand Caillou; and that the plaintiff should recover the possession of the balance of the whole tract to the extent and limits described in his petition.

With regard to the parcel of land possessed by Champagne and Daspit, with the permission of the defendants, on the east side of the bayou; it is clear from the evidence, that they had not been in possession of it for one year, at the time of the institution of this suit, and that consequently, the defendants cannot derive any benefit from their said possession.

It is therefore ordered, adjudged and decreed, . . . that the plaintiff and appellant do recover and be maintained in the possession of the tract of land described in his petition; except, however, of that portion of the said tract on the west side of the bayou Grand Caillou, shown in the surveyor's map to contain four arpents in front, by two arpents and a half in depth; and that the defendants and appellees be maintained in their possession of the said small tract according to the metes and bounds designated in the said surveyor's map; the costs in both courts to be borne by the said defendants.

Notes and Questions

1. As you review *Ellis v. Prevost*, 19 La. 251 (1841), trace Ellis' chain of title—all the juridical acts purporting to transfer ownership from one person to another—as far back as you can. Identify when the corporeal possession of Ellis or his predecessors in interest began? When did they move into civil possession? When were they in constructive possession?

2. One of the most significant lessons of *Ellis v. Prevost* is that a person like Ellis, who may have never taken corporeal possession of the tract of land, is nevertheless allowed to claim civil possession of the tract if the person from whom he acquired possession had been in corporeal possession, whether through his own physical presence or through a precarious possessor. In this case, Ellis claimed civil possession of the land on both sides of Bayou Grand Caillou because his vendor (Hutchings) had previously taken corporeal possession of the tract. Hutchings only took corporeal possession of a part of that tract, but he was deemed to be in constructive possession of the remainder of the tract described by his title. Thus, both civil possession and constructive possession were used to bolster Ellis's possessory action.

3. Study Article 3431 of the Civil Code and its comments carefully. Can you see that this article represents a codification of the holding in *Ellis v. Prevost*? *See* La. Civ. Code art. 3431 rev. cmt. (c) (1982). Here is the English translation of topical passages from Pothier quoted by Justice Simon: "In order to acquire the possession of a thing, mere will does not suffice; there must be a corporeal control of the thing—either by ourselves or by someone who takes control of it on our behalf and in our name. In contrast, once we have acquired the possession of a thing, the mere will that we have to possess it suffices for us to conserve the possession of it, although we do not corporeally detain this thing—neither by ourselves nor by others." See Markus G. Puder, *Romans Reloaded and Comparativists Charged—Living Law in Louisiana: The Case of Civil Possession* 54 Loy. L. Rev. 571, 594 (2008).

4. Although the court in *Ellis v. Prevost* held that Ellis was entitled to bring a possessory action to evict Madame Prevost and her precarious possessors, Champagne and Daspit, from much of the land described by Ellis' title, the court nevertheless determined that Ellis could not use a possessory action to evict Madame Prevost from the four by two and a half arpent enclosed tract on the west side of the bayou that she was occupying. What was the court's reason for ruling in favor of Madame Prevost with respect to this portion of the land in dispute?

5. What about the five by two and a half arpent tract of land occupied by Champagne and Daspit on the east side of the bayou? Why was Ellis able to evict the

defendants from this tract? What was the problem with Champagne and Daspit's possession of this land? Was it that they resided on this land with Madame Prevost's permission? Or was the length of their possession too brief?

6. *Ellis v. Prevost* demonstrates that adverse corporeal possession can displace both civil and constructive possession. Hence, landowners must continually keep watch over their property to make sure that adverse possessors have not taken up unchallenged possession for a sufficiently long period of time to establish their own right to possess.

7. *Ellis v. Prevost* identifies a "possessory action" as the proper procedural mechanism available to a person who has a right to possess immovable property to protect that right in the face of disturbances and usurpations by others. The possessory action is the subject of our next section.

2. Precarious Possession

The Civil Code provides a definition for precarious possession:

Art. 3437. Precarious Possession

The exercise of possession over a thing with the permission of or on behalf of the owner or possessor is precarious possession.

La. Civ. Code art. 3437 (1982). A precarious possessor is not possessing as owner, but rather on behalf of or with the permission of the person who claims to be the owner. Precarious possession can be helpful to someone who possesses with the intent to become owner (let us call him Alberto) but who relies on the acts of physical detention of another person (let us call her Claudia). Alberto can possess through Claudia, who is a precarious possessor. Precarious possession, however, can also frustrate someone who may be unaware that his corporeal acts of control do not constitute adverse possession in a legal sense but are merely precarious possession.

One of the advantages of precarious possession is that a true possessor—someone who acquires corporeal possession and retains the intent to become owner—can acquire as well as maintain possession through another. *See* La. Civ. Code arts. 3428–29 (1982). For example, when a possessor leases a house to a tenant or loans a car to a friend, the tenant or borrower will each possess, not as owner, but as precarious possessor. In both examples, the lessor or lender is in possession of the house or the vehicle. The lessor and lender' possession through the lessee or borrower puts each on track towards acquiring the right to possess or acquiring ownership through prescription. Note that a juridical person like a corporation can acquire and continue its possession of a thing through the activities of its representatives. La. Civ. Code art. 3430 (1982).

But the advantages of precarious possession generally remain with the person on whose behalf the precarious possessor is acting. As a precarious possessor possesses for and in the name of someone other than himself, the possession of a person who occupies land or who holds a movable as a precarious possessor benefits the person for whom he possesses. A precarious possessor gains no rights for himself.

Two important presumptions reinforce the narrow scope of a precarious possessor's rights. First, the Civil Code provides that a person in possession is "presumed to intend to possess as owner, unless he began to possess in the name of and for another," that is, as a precarious possessor. La. Civ. Code art. 3427 (1982). Conversely, the Civil Code provides that "[a] precarious possessor, such as a lessee or a depositary, is presumed to possess for another although he may intend to possess for himself." La. Civ. Code art. 3438 (1982). Therefore, a precarious possessor cannot prescribe unless she gives notice to the true owner that she has begun to possess for herself with the intent to become owner. La. Civ. Code arts. 3439, 3478 (1982).

These two presumptions tell us that certain types of physical possession are generally presumed to be precarious. The valet at a restaurant or hotel who parks your car does not take possession of the car with the intent to become its owner and is, therefore, just a precarious possessor. A dry cleaning establishment does not take possession of your clothes as owner but merely as a depositary, a kind of precarious possessor. A residential tenant does not take possession of a rental apartment as owner but as a precarious possessor. The law presumes that these persons are precarious possessors since they are not possessing with the intent to own. They acquire no rights to the things other than those delineated in the agreement that permits and circumscribes the precarious possession. As the case below highlights, these rules can lead to disappointment for precarious possessors.

Falgoust v. Innes

163 So. 429 (La. App. Orl. 1935)

WESTERFIELD, Judge. Plaintiff is the owner of a tract of land in the Vacherie Settlement, St. James Parish, La. On September 1, 1932, she gave John William Inness, who was married to her adopted daughter, permission to erect a building for the purpose of operating a garage and filling station on a part of her land adjacent to the public road. Inness constructed a garage and operated it until the 12th day of June, 1933, when she caused written notice to vacate to be served upon him through her attorney. Inness refused to comply with her demand, and this suit was instituted on September 2, 1933, for the purpose of compelling him to vacate the property and remove all buildings which he had erected thereon, and for the sum of $10 per month as rental beginning June 12, 1933, the date on which the notice to vacate was served and continuing as long as plaintiff occupies the property and fails to remove the buildings.

After interposing exceptions of vagueness and of no right or cause of action, which were overruled, the defendant answered admitting practically all the allegations of the plaintiff's petition and averring that he had been given a verbal permission to occupy the land for a period of five years. He reconvened and claimed the sum of $1,823.58 as the cost of the building which he had constructed, the stock which he had on hand, the profits which he expected to earn, and the enhanced value of the plaintiff's land resulting from the improvements which he had erected thereon.

There was judgment below in favor of plaintiff on the main demand ordering the defendant to vacate the property within forty days, and, in the event of his default or neglect to do so, the sheriff for the parish of St. James was ordered to demolish the buildings erected by defendant. Plaintiff's claim for rent was rejected as was defendant's reconventional demand. From this judgment, defendant has appealed.

It is suggested in brief and in argument that plaintiff's reason for her desire to evict the defendant grows out of the fact that the marital relations between defendant and plaintiff's foster daughter were unpleasant, and it has been proven that two days before the institution of this suit his wife, plaintiff's adopted daughter, instituted proceedings against him for separation from bed and board. The explanation of the reason for the litigation seems to us plausible, but immaterial, the important consideration being her legal right to dispossess defendant.

In so far as the main demand is concerned, the only disputed question of fact relates to the character of the oral permission given by plaintiff to defendant to erect a building on plaintiff's property plaintiff claiming that it was indefinite, and defendant that it was for a definite period of five years, and on this point plaintiff must prevail because of the defendant's failure to establish his claim concerning the five-year term.

The contention of the defendant is that he is a possessor in good faith, and that, under the appropriate provisions of the Civil Code, he cannot be dispossessed without reimbursement of the value of the materials and workmanship used in the improvements placed upon the property. . . .

It is apparent from a consideration of the articles we have quoted, the defendant is not a possessor in good faith, and, in fact, not a possessor at all, in the sense of the articles of the Code, because he does not possess as owner, and whatever may be the status of his claim, it involves the recognition of the ownership and legal possession of the plaintiff through whom he holds.

The best that can be said for the defendant is that he had been given the right to erect his garage building on the plaintiff's property and to keep it there for a reasonable period of time. Before this judgment can become final he will have been in possession for more than three years, a period which we consider reasonable.

The claim for rent was properly rejected below. The reconventional demand will be dismissed.

For the reasons assigned, the judgment appealed from is affirmed.

Notes and Questions

1. The court in *Falgoust v. Inness*, 163 So. 429 (La. App. Orl. 1935), determined that the defendant, John Inness, could not be considered a possessor in good faith

or a possessor at all. What specific reasons support the court's conclusions on these two counts?

2. Given the court's conclusion that Inness was not a good faith possessor, what provision in the Civil Code would a court use today to determine the remedies for Inness with respect to the improvements he made on Mrs. Falgoust's land—the garage and filling station? What remedies, if any, would be available to Mrs. Falgoust under that provision?

C. The Possessory Action

In light of the importance of possession in Louisiana, it should come as no surprise that Louisiana establishes a specific action—the possessory action—to protect a person's right to possess immovable property. The Louisiana Civil Code generally cedes the detailed regulation of possessory actions to the Louisiana Code of Civil Procedure. Article 3444 of the Civil Code specifies that "[p]ossession of immovables is protected by the possessory action as provided in Articles 3655 through 3671 of the Code of Civil Procedure," while "[p]ossession of movables is protected by the rules of civil procedure that govern civil actions." La. Civ. Code art. 3444 (1982). The possessory action is thus one of the *nominate* (named) actions for the protection of immovable property interests in Louisiana, while *innominate* (unnamed) actions are deployed to protect property interests in movable property. Louisiana lawyers sometimes use the term "revendicatory action" to describe a proceeding brought to recover possession of a movable. *See e.g., Songbyrd. v. Bearsville Records, Inc.,* 104 F.3d 773 (5th Cir. 1997).

Definition, Purpose and Limits: Article 3655 of the Code of Civil Procedure offers a thumbnail sketch of the essential ingredients of a possessory action:

La. Code Civ. Proc. art. 3655. Possessory action

The possessory action is one brought by the possessor of immovable property or of a real right therein to be maintained in his possession of the property or enjoyment of the right when he has been disturbed, or to be restored to the possession or enjoyment thereof when he has been evicted.

La. Code Civ. Proc. art. 3655 (1960, amended 1981). The action is designed either (1) to enable a person who is in possession of a corporeal immovable or in quasi-possession of a real right (such as a personal or predial servitude) to "be maintained in his possession" or "in the enjoyment" of his real right, "when he has been disturbed" in his possession or enjoyment; or (2) to enable a person who has been evicted from his possession or quasi-possession "to be restored" to possession or enjoyment. Consequently, the possessory action protects possession and quasi-possession of immovables.

The possessory action is *not*, however, used to protect ownership of immovable property or of a real right therein. In this light, Article 3661 specifically limits the admissibility of evidence in regards to ownership or title:

Art. 3661. Same; title not at issue; limited admissibility of evidence of title

In the possessory action, the ownership or title of the parties to the immovable property or real right therein is not at issue.

No evidence of ownership or title to the immovable property or real right therein shall be admitted except to prove:

(1) The possession thereof by a party as owner;

(2) The extent of the possession thereof by a party; or

(3) The length of time in which a party and his ancestors in title have had possession thereof.

La. Code Civ. Proc. art. 3661 (1960, amended 1981). The provision declares that "ownership or title of the parties to immovable or real right therein" cannot be the ultimate issue in a possessory action. It does, however, allow a plaintiff to offer evidence of "ownership or title" to the property under consideration, but only for *ancillary* purposes. This may include proving that the plaintiff has the requisite intent to possess as owner, rather than as a precarious possessor; showing the physical extent of a plaintiff's claimed constructive possession; or demonstrating how long the possessor has maintained his corporeal or civil possession. *See Haas Land Co. Ltd. V. O'Quin*, 187 So. 2d 208, 211 (La. App. 3 Cir. 1966) ("where the pleadings show that as a whole and especially the prayer show that possessory and not petitory relief is sought").

Anti-Cumulation Principle for Plaintiff and Conversion of Possessory into Petitory by Defendant: Article 3657 of the Code of Civil Procedure, which reflects the separation between the protection of possession through the possessory action and the protection of ownership through the petitory action, contains the operative rules for the plaintiff and the defendant in a possessory action:

Art. 3657. Same; cumulation with petitory action prohibited; conversion into or separate petitory action by defendant

The plaintiff may not cumulate the petitory and the possessory actions in the same suit or plead them in the alternative, and when he does so he waives the possessory action. If the plaintiff brings the possessory action, and without dismissing it and prior to judgment therein, institutes the petitory action, the possessory action is abated.

When, except as provided in Article 3661(1)-(3), the defendant in a possessory action asserts title in himself, in the alternative or otherwise, he thereby converts the suit into a petitory action, and judicially confesses the possession of the plaintiff in the possessory action.

If, before executory judgment in a possessory action, the defendant therein institutes a petitory action in a separate suit against the plaintiff in the possessory action, the plaintiff in the petitory action judicially confesses the possession of the defendant therein.

La. Code Civ. Proc. art. 3657 (1960). If the *plaintiff* asserts both possession and ownership at the same time—if he pleads a possessory action and petitory action alternatively in the same lawsuit or if he asserts a possessory action and petitory action in two separate, but simultaneous lawsuits—Article 3657 declares that the possessory action is "waived" or "abated." This anti-cumulation rule, which contradicts modern notions of notice pleading used elsewhere in federal and Louisiana civil procedure, allows a court to find that the plaintiff who "cumulates" a possessory and petitory action may only proceed under the petitory action. For a recent example of the consequences of this rule, see *Hooper v. Hero Lands Co.*, 216 So.3d 965, 973 (La. App. 4 Cir. 2016) (finding on *de novo* review that: (1) the plaintiffs "improperly cumulated their possessory action with a petitory action, demonstrated by their assertions of ownership by title and by prescription, and their request to fix the boundary;" and (2) the plaintiffs had to prove a better title to the property than the defendant).

In another lengthy, multi-round dispute, Louisiana courts struggled with the question of whether a plaintiff in a possessory action violated the anti-cumulation rule when it asserted that the execution, recordation, registration and existence of what the plaintiff considered a fraudulent act of sale obtained by the defendant amounted to a disturbance in law. *On Leong Chinese Merchs. Ass'n v. AKM Acquisitions*, 185 So.3d 80, 81–84 (La. App. 5 Cir. 2015). Initially, the Louisiana Supreme Court held that the "[p]laintiff in this matter has carefully not asserted title or pleaded the petitory action" and instead "claims possession and alleges its possession has been disturbed by the filing in the public records of an Act of Sale which it alleges should not be given legal effect." *On Leong Chinese Merchs. Ass'n v. AKM Acquisitions, L.L.C.*, 137 So.3d 1205, 1205–06 (La. 2014). Accordingly, the court determined that the plaintiff was entitled to have its possessory action heard on the merits and therefore, reversed the judgment of the court of appeal which had dismissed the possessory action. *Id.* at 1206.

In a subsequent opinion, the Louisiana Court of Appeal for the Fifth Circuit again found that "[a]lthough plaintiff carefully worded its petition as one for disturbance of possession, it is clear that in its petition [plaintiff] seeks nullification of the recorded Act of Sale that transferred ownership of the property from [plaintiff to defendant] which necessarily requires a determination of the validity of the title to the property." *On Leong Chinese Merchs. Ass'n v. AKM Acquisitions*, 185 So.3d 80, 84 (La. App. 5 Cir. 2015). That court further reasoned that "[o]nly if the court found that the Act of Sale, and therefore title to the property, was fraudulently obtained, could it annul the Act of Sale and return possession of the immovable property in question." *Id.* Because it believed this claim required a determination as to the "validity of title" in the possessory action, the appellate court again affirmed the trial court's dismissal of the possessory action. *Id.* at 84–85.

The saga continued when the Louisiana Supreme Court vacated the portion of the appellate court opinion affirming dismissal of the possessory action with prejudice. It remanded the case to the district court ordering it to give the plaintiff a reasonable opportunity to amend its petition to remove the objection. *On Leong Chinese Merchs. Ass'n v. AKM Acquisitions*, 188 So.3d 1041, 1041 (La 2016). One justice dissented, observing:

> As has been noted in the jurisprudence, litigants in a possessory action must walk a fine line to avoid invoking a petitory action. . . .When the courts recognize 'implicitly' or 'in essence' a claim not specifically made, they do the litigants and property law in general a disservice. . . .This will deprive the plaintiff of its argument that its possession has been disturbed in law. If defendants wish to rely on the Act of Sale to prove ownership, they should have the burden of proof. By forcing plaintiff to now assert the petitory action in order to avoid dismissal, the courts have wrongfully shifted the burden of proof on ownership from defendants to plaintiffs.

Id. at 1041 (J. Hughes, dissenting)

Conversely, if the *defendant* in a possessory action asserts his ownership of the immovable or real right therein, he converts the possessory action into a petitory action. For jurisprudence, see, for example, *Goal Props. v. Pestridge*, 177 So.3d 126 (La. App. 3 Cir. 2015). Moreover, the defendant who asserts ownership in a possessory action also judicially confesses that the other party (the plaintiff in the possessory action) is "in possession" of the property. Consequently, when the defendant attempts to bring a petitory action to establish his ownership against the successful plaintiff in the possessory action, that person will now face a stringent burden of proof to show that he or she acquired ownership from a previous owner or by acquisitive prescription. La. Civ. Code art. 531 (1979); La. Code Civ. Proc art. 3653(1) (1960, amended 1981); *Pure Oil Co. v. Skinner*, 294 So.2d 797 (La. 1974). For the proposition that the issue of judicial confession, even if not raised or briefed by any party, may be considered on its merits by the appellate court, see *Littleton v. Saline Lakeshore, LLC*, 178 So.3d 274, 280 (La. App. 3 Cir. 2015) (invoking the applicable standard of review and Article 2164 of the Louisiana Code of Civil Procedure).

Why does Louisiana law insist on this rigid separation of actions to protect possession from actions to establish ownership? Why does it insist that the possessory action be resolved first unless either party is willing to confess the lack of possession of the property at issue? The answers are both historical and practical. The historical explanation involves the complex interaction of French and Spanish causes of action for the protection of possession under Louisiana's Code of Practice before the adoption of the modern Code of Civil Procedure in 1960. For details of that history, see A.N. YIANNOPOULOS, 2 LOUISIANA CIVIL LAW TREATISE: PROPERTY § 12:33 (5th ed. 2015). The practical explanation is that the anti-cumulation principle preserves scarce judicial resources and allows parties to bifurcate the litigation of each interest. Because the right to possess immovable property can often be resolved more expeditiously than the more technical question of ownership (which may involve detailed examination of title and succession records or other kinds of evidence offered to address alleged facts that may have occurred many decades earlier), this procedural distinction between possession and ownership can lead to a quicker disposition of many property conflicts.

Hypothetical (Valerie v. Thomas): Test your understanding of the rules so far with the following example. Valerie, who believes she owns land and a home at 123 Water Street, has lived on the property for many years. When she decides to take a vacation, she authorizes automatic drafts for all of her bills and charges in connection with her property. On January 2, Valerie leaves for an extended vacation in Madrid. Her neighbor Thomas, who knows of Valerie's plans, takes advantage of her departure. He waits until Valerie's taxi disappears over the horizon, gains access to the lot and house, switches out all the locks, and notifies the utility providers to have the billing service changed to his name. In addition, he cleans up the yard, mows the grass, plants rose bushes and azalea flowers, builds a new fence around the land, and locks the gate. On March 2, Valerie returns and finds herself locked out of her property. What is Valerie's recourse? Should she file a possessory action to reclaim possession of her house and lot and seek damages for trespass, or should she assert ownership?

Parties and Venue: Article 3656 of the Code of Civil Procedure describes the parties to the possessory action. The plaintiff in a possessory action is most commonly one who possesses "for himself" as owner. La. Civ. Code art. 3656 (1960). A person who possesses "for himself" includes a person who enjoys quasi-possession of a real right in immovable property, such as the holder of a predial servitude or a usufructuary. *Id.* Under the strict terms of Article 3656, it appears that a person such as a lessee, who possesses for and in the name of someone else (his lessor), is not authorized to bring a possessory action. But this limitation has now been legislatively overruled by the adoption of Article 3440 of the Civil Code, which authorizes "a precarious possessor, such as a lessee or depository," to assert a possessory action "against anyone except the person for whom he possesses." La. Civ. Code art. 3440 (1982). This useful change in the law allows a lessee whose lessor is not onsite to bring a possessory action against a third party disturbing his possession, without having to wait for the lessor to act.

The defendant in a possessory action is the person who allegedly caused the disturbance at issue. In appropriate situations, the defendant may reconvene with his own possessory action. Because the possessory action only considers possession, however, the defendant should not assert ownership as a defense in a possessory action unless he is willing to see the proceeding converted into a petitory action in which he will have the heightened burden of proving ownership.

The proper venue for a possessory action is either the parish where the immovable property at issue is located or the parish where the defendant is domiciled. La. Code Civ. Proc. art. 3656, (1960, amended 2010); La. Code Civ. Proc. art. 80(A)(1) (1960, amended 1984, 1989).

Requisites for Relief: Article 3658 of the Code of Civil Procedure sets forth the four essential elements of a successful possessory action:

La. Code Civ. Proc. art. 3658. Same; requisites

To maintain the possessory action the possessor must allege and prove that:

(1) He had possession of the immovable property or real right therein at the time the disturbance occurred;

(2) He and his ancestors in title had such possession quietly and without interruption for more than a year immediately prior to the disturbance, unless evicted by force or fraud;

(3) The disturbance was one in fact or in law, as defined in Article 3659; and

(4) The possessory action was instituted within a year of the disturbance.

La. Code Civ. Proc. art. 3658 (1960, amended 1981). Before we discuss each requisite in turn, note that the procedural law governing the possessory action simply invokes "possession," without making a distinction between possession and the right to possess, which accrues after one year of possession. As we will see, this lack of precision in Article 3658 required the courts and later the legislature to pay more attention to this crucial distinction.

Disturbance in Fact or in Law. The third requisite listed in Article 3658 is a logical place to begin our analysis because a possessor will have no reason to initiate a possessory action in the first place unless there is some kind of disturbance of possession as detailed in Article 3659 of the Code of Civil Procedure. This latter article distinguishes between two types of disturbances—those "in fact" and those "in law":

Art. 3659. Same; disturbance in fact and in law defined

Disturbances of possession which give rise to the possessory action are of two kinds: disturbance in fact and disturbance in law.

A disturbance in fact is an eviction, or any other physical act which prevents the possessor of immovable property or of a real right therein from enjoying his possession quietly, or which throws any obstacle in the way of that enjoyment.

A disturbance in law is the execution, recordation, registry, or continuing existence of record of any instrument which asserts or implies a right of ownership or to the possession of immovable property or of a real right therein, or any claim or pretension of ownership or right to the possession thereof except in an action or proceeding, adversely to the possessor of such property or right.

La. Code Civ. Proc. art. 3659 (1960, amended 1981). A disturbance in fact involves a physical act. It prevents the possessor from the peaceful use and enjoyment of his possession. If a challenger completely usurps the possession of the plaintiff or evicts the plaintiff as a matter of fact, the plaintiff must either regain physical possession of the property in some way or bring the possessory action to be "restored to the possession or enjoyment" of the property within one year of this kind of disturbance. *See* La. Code Civ. Proc. art. 3658(4) (1960, amended 1981). Valerie, in the hypothetical above, must bring her possessory action against Thomas within one year of Thomas' acts of possession.

Sometimes, however, a physical disturbance only temporarily inhibits a possessor's use and enjoyment. For instance, a challenger might temporarily block a road, tear down a fence or go hunting without the permission of the possessor. These types of relatively minor disturbances might justify an award of compensatory damages in a trespass action. They might even lead to a possessory action initiated by the possessor who seeks to be "maintained in his possession." But, importantly, these mere disturbances do not result in a possessor losing physical control of the property and thus do not affect what Article 3422 of the Civil Code identifies as the *right to possess*—the status required to bring a possessory action under Article 3658(2) of the Code of Civil Procedure. The right to possess is acquired after the passage of one year of quiet and uninterrupted possession. When a physical disturbance interfering with a landowner's use of his land amounts to an eviction, the possessor should initiate the possessory action to be "restored" in her possession. This distinction between an eviction or usurpation and a mere disturbance is a question of degree.

In our example (*Valerie v. Thomas*), if Thomas had entered onto Valerie's property to pick some flowers without Valerie's permission, Thomas' entry could be characterized as a trespass and a disturbance under Articles 3658 and 3659. But it certainly would not result in an eviction of Valerie or a usurpation of her possession. Thomas would not be able to claim that Valerie's possession was being significantly challenged or that he began acquiring the right to possess. On the other hand, Thomas' activities of fencing off Valerie's lot and changing the locks of the house completely shut out Valerie and prevented her from using and enjoying the property. The magnitude of these disturbances amounts to an eviction and usurpation that would be sufficient not only to trigger a possessory action but, if they go unchallenged for more than a year, could result in Valerie's loss of the right to possess and the acquisition of the right to possess by Thomas.

A disturbance in law arises in the wake of the execution, recordation, registration, or continuing existence of any instrument asserting or implying a property interest (ownership or possession) in the immovable at issue as well as a claim or pretension of a property right adverse to the incumbent possessor. Note that a disturbance in law is, by its very nature, always a mere disturbance and never an eviction. In practice, cases involving a disturbance in law have been relatively infrequent. Nevertheless, as one of the major innovations in the 1960 Code of Civil Procedure, a possessor has the right to institute a possessory action when confronted with a more or less intangible disturbance in law. Thus, a possessor who has acquired the right to possess can force an adverse claimant who is asserting a legal claim to the immovable based on a written instrument to file a petitory action to prove the basis of that claim within sixty days of the conclusion of the possessory action. *See* La. Code of Civ. Proc. art. 3662(2) (1960, amended 1981).

Should an oral, but not written, proclamation of ownership suffice for a disturbance in law? In our example (*Valerie v. Thomas*), presume that Valerie had not left her home and Thomas had not occupied the property. Instead, Valerie leased her premises to Ben. Despite knowing better, Thomas approached Ben and told him that he is the true owner of the property. Would Thomas' statement be a sufficient disturbance to allow Valerie to seek relief in the form of a possessory action? Would it matter if Thomas' declaration took the form of a letter written by Thomas's lawyer? Would it matter that the letter was not recorded?

Possession at the Time of the Disturbance. Article 3660 of the Code of Civil Procedure defines what it means to be "in possession" of immovable property or of a real right for purposes of satisfying the first element of Article 3658. The plaintiff in the possessory action can rely upon corporeal possession, the strongest form of possession, or civil possession, as long as it is preceded by corporeal possession exercised by either the plaintiff himself or by one of his ancestors in title. We also know that the plaintiff may claim constructive possession within the limits of her title, as long as some portion of the property has been corporeally possessed. The only other requirement is that the possessor must intend to possess, either corporeally or civilly, for himself. Here is the text of Article 3360:

Art. 3660. Same; possession

A person is in possession of immovable property or of a real right therein, within the intendment of the articles of this Chapter, when he has the corporeal possession thereof, or civil possession thereof preceded by corporeal possession by him or his ancestors in title, and possesses for himself, whether in good or bad faith, or even as a usurper.

Subject to the provisions of Articles 3656 and 3664, a person who claims the ownership of immovable property or of a real right therein possesses through his lessee, through another who occupies the property or enjoys the right under an agreement with him or his lessee, or through a person who has the use or usufruct thereof to which his right of ownership is subject.

La. Code Civ. Proc. art. 3660 (1960, amended 1980). We have already learned that courts must be very careful when characterizing possession. True possession always requires *animus* (the intent to possess as owner), which is presumed pursuant to Article 3427 of the Civil Code. The presence or absence of good faith, bad faith, and even usurpation is immaterial in the context of Article 3660 of the Code of Civil Procedure.

The extent to which the immovable property is developed affects the level of activity required to establish corporeal possession. *See, e.g., Buckley v. Dumond*, 156 So. 784, 786, 790 (La. App. 1 Cir. 1934) (holding that a possessor's acts trapping and executing an exclusive trapping lease were sufficient to establish possession of uncultivable and uninhabitable marshland). So, for instance, sustained acts like planting, cultivating, and harvesting crops or grazing cattle might be required to establish corporeal possession of farmland or ranch land, but seasonal hunting, trapping or marking of trees may be sufficient for undeveloped swamp lands or woodlands. Corporeal possession can also be established through the activities of a precarious possessor, such as a lessee or a servitude holder, who possesses for or on behalf of the person claiming possession. *See, e.g., Manson Realty Co., Inc. v. Plaisance*, 196 So.2d 555, 557 (La. App. 4 Cir. 1967) (activities of holder of a right of use in laying and maintaining a gas pipeline are sufficient to establish possession on behalf of the grantor of the right of use).

Recall the special case of constructive possession, which furnishes a conceptual means to extend corporeal possession if a possessor is possessing with a title—an act purporting to transfer ownership. La. Civ. Code art. 3426 (1982). In the absence of a sufficiently clear title that establishes the boundaries of the property at issue, courts will insist that a plaintiff in a possessory action establish her possession "inch-by-inch" or within natural or artificial enclosures. Activities like surveying or blazing and painting a boundary line can create an enclosure when the land at issue is rural and wooded. *Antulovich v. Whitley*, 289 So.2d 174, 176 (La. App. 1 Cir. 1973).

Finally, note that all species of possession (corporeal, civil and constructive) may be usurped when the challenger sets up adverse corporeal possession. In such contexts, adverse corporeal possession trumps civil possession, constructive possession or another corporeal possession that is not restored. Thus, constructive possession by one party cannot defeat adverse corporeal possession by another party; nor can it oust adverse constructive possession of another party under an earlier title. *Whitley v. Texaco*, Inc., 434 So.2d 96, 104–06 (La. App. 5 Cir. 1983).

In our example (*Valerie v. Thomas*), Valerie exercised corporeal possession of her property until leaving for her vacation. After her departure, she retained civil possession. This sequencing of possession qualifies her as "in possession" to satisfy the requirements of Article 3658(1) of the Code of Civil Procedure. In a trial, Valerie could establish her original corporeal possession through her own oral testimony and that of her neighbors. She could offer physical evidence such as photographs and dates on mail. She could further support her intent to continue to possess as owner (for civil possession) by producing her draft authorizations for payment of her utility bills and her return tickets.

Quiet and Uninterrupted Possession for More Than One Year Prior to the Litigated Disturbance. The second requirement of Article 3658 has been interpreted to mean that the plaintiff in a possessory action must have acquired the *right to possess;* that is, the plaintiff must have possessed the immovable peacefully for at least one full year prior to the litigated disturbance. *See* La. Civ. Code art. 3422 rev. cmt. (b) (1982); *Liner v. Louisiana Land and Exploration Co.*, 319 So.2d 766, 782–83 (La. 1975) (Tate, J., concurring in denial of rehearing). Pursuant to Article 3422 of the Civil Code, a person earns the right to possess after one year of possession coupled with the intent to own. La. Civ. Code art. 3422 (1982); La. Civ. Code art. 3424 (1982).

A possessor's possession is "quiet" within the meaning of Article 3658(2) of the Code of Civil Procedure when it is *not* violent. Violence is a vice of possession that renders the possession without any legal effect. La. Civ. Code art. 3435 (1982). According to the Civil Code, "[p]ossession is violent when it is *acquired or maintained* by violent acts." La. Civ. Code art. 3436 (1982) (emphasis added). The Civil Code goes on to state that "[w]hen the violence ceases, the possession ceases to be violent." *Id.* What result if a possessor takes possession of a tract of land by cutting down a fence and scaring off the prior possessor with force of arms and then rebuilds the fence and packs away his weapons? Professor Yiannopoulos takes the following position:

> One's possession is freed of the vice of violence, even if the possession was acquired and maintained by violent acts, when the violence ceases. From that moment acquisitive prescription commences to run, and one year later the possessor acquires the right to possess.

A.N. Yianopoulos, 2 Civil Law Treatise: Property § 12:16 (5th ed. 2015). Do you agree?

Finally, note the exception to the one year of possession requirement under Article 3658(2) of the Code of Civil Procedure for possessors evicted by force or fraud. Such possessors may bring a possessory action no matter how short was the length of their possession preceding the litigated disturbance. One rationale for this exception is that violently displaced possessors should have quick access to court to preserve public peace and dissuade them from engaging in their own violent acts of self-help. 3 Planiol & Ripert, Traité pratique de droit civil français 794 (2d ed. Picard 1952).

Institution of the Possessory Action within One Year of the Disturbance. The final requirement for a successful possessory action under Article 3658(4) of the Code of Civil Procedure functions like a statute of limitations or a liberative prescription period that runs forward in time from the moment of the disturbance, rather than backward in time like the requirement of one year of quiet and uninterrupted possession prior to the disturbance. Whether the disturbance at issue is one in fact or one in law will determine when the one year time period begins to run.

In the case of a disturbance in fact, the one year time period begins to run with the onset of the disturbance. *See, e.g., Richmond v. McArthur*, 157 So.3d 1139 (La. App. 3 Cir. 2015) (identifying the date the one year period set forth in Article 3658(2) began to run as the day a real estate agent placed "For Sale" signs on the property at the direction of a record owner who had acquired it by virtue of a sheriff's deed). In our example (*Valerie v. Thomas*), the period began to run on January 3, the day after Thomas usurped Valerie's possession by taking physical control of her house and property. If Valerie brings her possessory action immediately upon her return two months later, Article 3658(4) will not bar her possessory action. If Valerie waits until January 4 of the following year, her possessory action will be barred and Thomas will have gained the right to possess.

When the disturbance complained of is one at law (for example when a lease is recorded that has been executed by someone claiming to be owner of the property), courts have been quite lenient in considering the fact of recordation to be a continuing disturbance, rather than a disturbance that occurred only on the date of recordation. *Boneno v. Lasseigne*, 514 So.2d 276, 279 (La. App. 5 Cir. 1987); *Roy O. Martin Lumber Co. v. Lemoine*, 381 So.2d 915, 919 (La. App. 3 Cir. 1980). This interpretation allows a possessor complaining of a disturbance at law to satisfy Article 3658(4) by bringing the possessory action at any time after the instrument has been recorded in the public records. For a case not involving the public records, however, see *Kilpatrick v. Saline Lakeshore L.L.C.*, 185 So.3d 350 (La. App. 3 Cir. 2016) (holding that the one year prescription of Article 3658(2) had not run in the case of a letter threatening eviction, but specifically stating that no action would be taken until a certain date because the plaintiff had brought the action within a year from that date, after which any proposed action could have interfered with the plaintiffs' possession).

Pursuant to Article 3433 of the Civil Code, possession itself, but not the right to possess, is lost the moment the possessor manifests the intention to abandon possession or when the possessor is "evicted by force or usurpation." La. Civ. Code art. 3433 (1982). Article 3434(1) of the Civil Code explains that a possessor will lose the right to possess if he either (1) abandons possession or (2) is evicted and does not recover possession within a year of the eviction. La. Civ. Code art. 3434 (1982). Article 3434(2) of the Civil Code adds that "when the right to possess is lost, possession is interrupted." La. Civ. Code art. 3434 (1982). Maintaining the right to possess is crucial for any possessor. If a possessor loses the right to possess, he will not be able to bring a possessory action.

Returning to our example (*Valerie v. Thomas*) yet again, note that Valerie has lived on the property for many years. One year after she acquired corporeal possession with the intent to own, she acquired the right to possess. If her predecessor in title had been in corporeal possession of the property for more than a year with the intent to own, Valerie would have acquired the right to possess immediately upon the purported transfer of ownership from her predecessor because her predecessor's possession would have been transferred to her. *See* La. Civ. Code art. 3433 rev. cmt. (b) (1982); La. Civ. Code art. 3442 (1982). Finally, as there is no indication that Valerie has lost possession in the year preceding her eviction by Thomas, Valerie would be entitled to bring a possessory action and obtain all the forms of relief set forth in Articles 3662 to 3663 of the Code of Civil Procedure. If, however, Valerie took no action for a full year after Thomas evicted her and usurped her possession, Valerie would lose her right to possess. Her loss of the right to possess would coincide with Thomas gaining that same right one year after his usurpation.

Forms of Relief Available in a Possessory Action: Article 3662 of the Code of Civil Procedure describes the relief that can be granted to a successful plaintiff in a possessory action.

Art. 3662. Same; relief which may be granted successful plaintiff in judgment; appeal

A. A judgment rendered for the plaintiff in a possessory action shall:

(1) Recognize his right to the possession of the immovable property or real right therein, and restore him to possession thereof if he has been evicted, or maintain him in possession thereof if the disturbance has not been an eviction;

(2) Order the defendant to assert his adverse claim of ownership of the immovable property or real right therein in a petitory action to be filed within a delay to be fixed by the court not to exceed sixty days after the date the judgment becomes executory, or be precluded thereafter from asserting the ownership thereof, if the plaintiff has prayed for such relief; and

(3) Award him the damages to which he is entitled and which he has prayed for.

La. Code Civ. Proc. art. 3662 (1960, amended 1981, 2010). A judgment in a possessory action will first and foremost recognize the plaintiff's right to possess the immovable property or real right at issue and either restore the plaintiff to possession of the property if the plaintiff has been evicted or maintain him in possession if the disturbance did not lead to an actual eviction. La. Code Civ. Proc. art. 3662(A)(1) (1960, amended 1981, 2010).

Second, and just as important, the successful plaintiff in a possessory action is entitled to have the court order the defendant to assert in a petitory action whatever adverse claim of ownership he may have within sixty days after the possessory action judgment becomes final. If the defendant does not assert his ownership in this time frame, the defendant will be precluded from claiming ownership forever. La. Code of Civ. Proc. art. 3662(A)(2) (1960, amended 1981, 2010). This powerful remedy solves a problem that existed under French law, which did not make available any mechanism to force a losing defendant in a possessory action—even one who had slandered the plaintiff's title by asserting a claim of ownership publicly—to prove his claim of ownership. This meant that a possessor's only response to slanderous claims of ownership asserted by other persons not in possession of immovable property or of a real right was to bring the so-called "jactitory action," which originated in Spanish law. *Id.* rev. cmt. (a); see also A.N. Yiannopoulos, 2 Louisiana Civil Law Treatise: Property § 322 (4th ed. 2001).

The relief now available under Article 3662(A)(2) of the Code of Civil Procedure solves this problem by allowing a successful plaintiff in a possessory action to clear a cloud on his title by requiring that the losing defendant prove his ownership or else give up his pretended claim. Note, though, that the plaintiff in a possessory action must specifically ask for this relief. La. Code Civ. Proc. art. 3662(2) rev. cmt. (b) (1960, amended 1981). A successful defendant in a possessory action cannot require the losing plaintiff to bring a petitory action. *Gill v. Henderson*, 269 So.2d 571, 573 (La. App. 1 Cir. 1972).

A successful plaintiff in a possessory action may also obtain damages resulting from a defendant's disturbance of the plaintiff's possession. La. Code Civ. Proc. art. 3662(A)(3) (1960, amended 1981, 2010). These include damages for pecuniary loss and mental anguish, but not attorney fees.

Returning to our example above, Valerie will first ask the court to restore her to possession of her house and lot. Since Thomas is a usurper, she might consider asking the court to compel him to bring a petitory action, a burden he is unlikely to undertake given his lack of any title whatsoever. Valerie can further pray for damages relative to any physical harm to her property, other monetary losses and mental anguish and suffering.

Article 3663 of the Code of Civil Procedure allows a plaintiff in a possessory action to obtain injunctive relief to restore or protect his possession while the action is pending or at its conclusion if he or his ancestors in title have possessed the property for more than a year. La. Code Civ. Proc. art. 3663 (1960, amended 1981). A plaintiff in a possessory action can also obtain a sequestration of the property under the same provision if the plaintiff can show that the defendant may dispose of all or part of the property in dispute or cause some other irreparable harm to the property—for example by extracting minerals or changing the physical structure of a building. *Id. See also* La. Code Civ. Proc. art. 3571 (1960, amended 1989).

* * *

Now consider what is undoubtedly the most important judicial decision interpreting the law of possession and the possessory action in the modern era of Louisiana jurisprudence. This lawsuit prompted Louisiana Supreme Court Justice Albert Tate to coin in his concurring opinion the phrase, "the right to possess," Louisiana's unique contribution to the law of possession. It led to revisions in the law of possession distinguishing possession from the right to possess. *See* La. Civ. Code arts. 3422, 3434 (1982).

Liner v. Louisiana Land and Exploration Co.

319 So.2d 766 (La. 1975)

DIXON, Justice. This possessory action was brought by Oliver Liner against Louisiana Land and Exploration Company as a result of conflicting claims to marshlands in Terrebonne Parish. Liner's land, he claims, lies in Sections 30, 31 and 32 of Township 20 South, Range 16 East, and in Sections 25 and 36 of Township 20 South, Range 15 East, all in Terrebonne Parish. The portion in dispute is the western end, west of the range line which separates Range 15 from Range 16. Liner's title, in the record before us, includes only land in Range 16. Louisiana Land and Exploration Company's record title covers all that portion of Liner's claim lying in Range 15.

All the land involved is marshland. It forms, roughly, a parallelogram 2909 feet on the easterly side, 6823 feet on the northerly side and 7036 feet along the southerly side. Liner claims that the westerly boundary of his property is the easterly bank of Bayou Dufrene (also known as Ash Point Bayou). Defendant claims Liner's westerly boundary is the line dividing Ranges 15 and 16.

The portion in dispute, which Liner claims that he and his family have possessed as owner for over one hundred years, is bounded on the west side by the east bank of Bayou Dufrene, and is adjacent to Liner's land in Range 16 East. The northern boundary of the disputed claim is about 580 feet in length and runs from Bayou Dufrene easterly through the marsh to the range line. The range line forms the easterly boundary of the disputed tract for about 3000 feet. The south line of the disputed tract runs about 2100 feet between the range line and the east bank of Bayou Dufrene.

The trial court gave judgment in favor of the plaintiff, finding that the evidence strongly supported his claim of possession. The Court of Appeal reversed (303 So.2d 866 (1974)), holding that the construction in the year 1956 and the continued operation of the Tennessee Gas Transmission Company's 24 inch gas pipeline disturbed Liner's possession, and that the disturbance was continuing and uninterrupted, a "usurpation" permitted by Liner for a period in excess of one year.

We granted writs in this case because it appeared that the construction of the pipeline across Liner's claim was with his permission, and not such a usurpation (C.C. 3449) as would result in the loss of possession by Liner. See also C.C. 3490.

Oliver Liner's contention is that he and his family have possessed the land involved since the acquisition of a tract of land by Jacob Liner, Oliver's grandfather, in 1869. The description of the property acquired by Jacob Liner was: "A certain tract of land situated on both sides of the Bayou DuLarge in this parish of Terrebonne and described on the plan of said land on file in this office for reference as Lots Nos. 45 and 46 in Township 20 S. Range 16 E. measuring Fourteen arpents and Eighty-Three feet front on both sides of said Bayou with the depth of survey on confirmation, bounded as shown on said plan afore-referred to."

The plan, or survey, referred to in the deed is apparently no longer in existence.

Jacob Liner's widow sold the land to Pleasant Liner in 1910 by the same description, except that the description was enlarged to say that the tract was located "about 28 miles below the town of Houma" and was said to be bounded "above by land of est. A. St. Martin or assigns, and below by land of est. A. St. Martin or assigns . . ."

Oliver Liner's deeds of acquisition of undivided interests from his kinsmen in 1928 contained the same description.

In spite of having no record title to land in Range 15, the Liner family, from earliest times, occupied and used all the land which lay between Bayou Dufrene and Bayou DuLarge, treating Bayou Dufrene as the western boundary of the Liner tract. Unlike the defendants in *Buckley v. Dumond and Theriot*, 156 So. 784 (La. App. 1934), which involved neighboring swampland, the Liner family possessed as owners.

Oliver Liner was seventy-seven years old at the time of the trial in 1973. For fifty-six years, he testified, he had occupied this land, trapping, raising cattle, and raising his family. For three or four months of each year, during the trapping season, the family would occupy a "camp" constructed on the bank of Bayou DuLarge.

Before 1909, his grandfather and an aunt lived in houses constructed on the bank of Bayou DuLarge. That part of the property used as a farm lay on the westerly side of Bayou DuLarge, and was fenced on the north and south sides between Bayou DuLarge and Bayou Dufrene. These houses and the fence were destroyed by a devastating storm in 1909. Oliver Liner and his family were also living on his grandfather's place in 1909.

Oliver's grandfather planted cotton, pecan trees and orange trees on the farm, and raised cattle. Liner testified that he helped his father replace the fences on the upper end after the storm of 1909, and some fence remained along the northern boundary until about twenty years before the trial. The southerly boundary was marked with stakes after the fence was destroyed, and the stakes along the property line were continually maintained by Liner and his family. One engineer who surveyed the property found evidence of old stakes and markers beneath the water line at almost every place where one of Liner's markers was located.

Each year Oliver Liner followed a practice of burning the marsh—the beneficial nature of which practice is not explained by the record. (There was some testimony that this practice made the disputed tract "too poor to trap.") Although the burning sometimes destroyed some of the property line stakes, they were replaced, indicating continuing activity on the part of the Liners in inspecting and replacing the boundary stakes.

The quality of the marshland deteriorated after the 1909 storm. Liner, however, continued to make his living on the land, using it all for the purposes of trapping and for raising cattle. The Liner boundaries, as staked by Jacob Liner, were recognized by other trappers in the area, even those employed by agents of Louisiana Land and Exploration Company. Oliver Liner and his family occupied the camp on the property every trapping season, for the purpose of tending the traps. Oliver Liner himself only missed the season preceding the trial of this case, having suffered a stroke; and during that season his unmarried son, Randolph, who lived with Oliver Liner, trapped the land involved in this litigation.

Liner's cattle raising activities consisted of running a herd of cattle of between one hundred fifty to two hundred head along the banks of Bayou DuLarge for about ten miles, having made some arrangement with the owners of adjoining tracts.

The only source of income for Oliver Liner disclosed by the record during his entire life is the land which he thought he owned. There is no evidence in this record of any occurrence which might have cast any doubt upon the extent of Liner's ownership until a survey of Louisiana Land and Exploration Company properties in 1952. As a result of that survey, Louisiana Land and Exploration Company set two concrete markers and two iron pipes with Louisiana Land and Exploration Company signs along the 3000 feet of the range line which Louisiana Land and Exploration Company claims is the boundary between its land and Oliver Liner's. The concrete markers were located at a section corner and a quarter section corner along the range line.

In February of 1956 Oliver Liner granted Tennessee Gas Transmission Company a pipeline right-of-way over land described as follows:

> "A Certain tract of land, situated on both sides of Bayou du Large, in the Parish of Terrebonne, and described as lots #45 & 46 in T. 20 S., R. 16 E., measuring 14 Arpents and 83 Feet front on both sides of said Bayou, with the depth of survey or confirmation."

The record leaves no doubt but that Oliver Liner intended to grant a pipeline right-of-way across all the land he owned. Contrary to the finding of the Court of Appeal, there was no loss of possession "against his consent." The pipeline canal and the pipeline which crossed Liner's land were constructed with his knowledge and consent.

In 1958 Louisiana Land and Exploration Company undertook to mark the boundaries of its holdings in this area with a ditch, monuments and signs. The ditch was originally 6 feet wide and 4 feet deep, but had been somewhat widened by subsequent maintenance operations.

Oliver Liner testified that when he found the ditch on his land he did not know who had dug it, and saw no other activity. Therefore, he appropriated the ditch to himself, constructing bulkheads with planks at two points in the ditch. The purpose of the bulkheads was to minimize the intrusion of salt water with the tidal flow, and to maintain a source of fresh water for his cattle. These bulkheads remained in place until removed by Louisiana Land and Exploration Company in 1971. When removed, they were replaced by the Liners.

Several seismograph crews crossed the disputed area from 1958 to 1965, with permission from Louisiana Land and Exploration Company, only.

Louisiana Land and Exploration Company retracted its survey lines in 1965, following Hurricane Hilda, and undertook to clean out the boundary ditch. There was testimony by an engineer for Louisiana Land and Exploration Company that some of the Liner stakes were pulled up during this process.

In 1971 when Louisiana Land and Exploration Company again undertook to clean its boundary ditch with an amphibious dragline, Liner's stakes were noticed by Louisiana Land and Exploration Company employees. On August 2, 1971 the boundary stakes were removed by the amphibious dragline. By August 17 it was reported that stakes were again in place along the Liner claim. On September 24

Louisiana Land and Exploration Company employees again removed the boundary stakes. On September 30 they returned and removed the remaining stakes. There was a confrontation with one of the Liners. On October 25 Louisiana Land and Exploration Company employees again removed the obstructions from the ditch and the Liner boundary markers.

On August 20, 1971 and on October 1, 1971 Oliver Liner's attorneys notified Louisiana Land and Exploration Company that their employees had reportedly removed Liner's boundary stakes. Louisiana Land and Exploration Company was requested to assist in the termination of such activities, in order to avoid legal proceedings. The defendant did not answer the letters, and no further action came to Liner's attention until February of 1972. On that occasion a Louisiana Land and Exploration Company crew, with deputies for protection, again removed Liner' boundary markers. Suit followed on February 9 — a possessory action alleging the February 3, 1972 incident as the disturbance of plaintiff's possession.

Defendant advances two main reasons for affirming the Court of Appeal. The first is that plaintiff has failed to prove possession within enclosures; the second reason is that the extensive activities of Louisiana Land and Exploration Company on the disputed property during the year preceding February of 1972 prevented a finding that plaintiff was in peaceful possession for the time required to maintain the possessory action. . . .

C.C.P. 3658 requires the possessor to prove that he had possession at the time of the disturbance; that his quiet, uninterrupted possession shall have existed more than a year prior to the disturbance; that suit was instituted within a year of the disturbance. . . .

The concept of possession is neither simple nor precise. See Riseman, Elementary Considerations in the Commencement of Prescription on Immovable Property, 12 Tul. L. Rev. 608 (1938). The quality of possession required in a particular case depends not only on its classification as good faith or bad faith possession, but also on the type of land in dispute.

> ". . . Obviously the corporeal possession requisite in the case of agricultural land should not be the same as that in the case of wood land or swamp land, and it is submitted that the courts, in deciding whether the possession has been sufficient to commence prescription, first of all observe the type of land with which they are dealing.
>
> [This suggestion seems obvious enough. Certainly more possession should be required in the case of farm land than in the case of wood land, and more possession in the case of wood land than in the case of swamp land. In the case of swamp lands and certain types of wood lands, very little can be done which might indicate the taking of possession, and if the courts were to require as much corporeal possession in the case of this type of land as in the case of other types of land, it is submitted that the former could never be prescribed. . . . 12 Tul. L. Rev. 608, 610–611.]

The possession required to bring a possessory action has been treated as being the same required to commence the running of prescription. . . .

Oliver Liner's possession of the disputed property satisfies all requirements for bringing the possessory action. The nature of the possession changed as the character of the marsh changed. From 1909, when the land was fenced and subject to some cultivation, the land deteriorated until the north boundary fence was abandoned after 1920. But the fence lines were continually marked. The camp was occupied each year. Trapping continued over the entire claim. Other trappers recognized Liner's boundaries. Hunters and fishermen used Liner's property only with his permission. He burned the prairie marsh every year. He ran his heard of cattle on the land.

Liner's claim continued to have visible boundaries until Louisiana Land and Exploration Company destroyed them. His possession had been preserved by "external and public signs" (C.C. 3501) recognized by neighbors.

Nor did Louisiana Land and Exploration Company's "acts of possession" dispossess Liner. The 1952 survey did not. The boundary ditch was appropriated by him to his own use. The water control structure on Bayou Dufrene extended only to the east bank of that stream, which Liner claimed as his westerly boundary. The seismic explorations, although an act of possession, did not serve to end the possession of Liner nor to evict him. The Tennessee Gas Transmission Company's pipeline ditch was dug with Liner's consent—not against it.

Defendant's second argument is based on subparagraph (2) of C.C.P. 3658 which requires the possessor to allege and prove that he "had such possession quietly and without interruption for more than a year immediately prior to the disturbance, unless evicted by force or fraud." Defendant would interpret the article literally, and maintains its actions for the year before February 3, 1972 prevent any conclusion that Oliver Liner had the quiet uninterrupted possession. The activities relied on by Louisiana Land and Exploration Company are: the August 2, 1971 cleaning of the property line ditch; the August 4, 1971 pulling of Liner's stakes and the continued cleaning of the ditch; the use of an air horn to communicate between the dragline and the marsh buggy while cleaning the ditch; the presence of no trespassing signs along the ditch; the August 17, 1971 removal of the stakes Liner had used to replace those previously removed by Louisiana Land and Exploration Company; the awareness by Liner of the August 17 operation; the September 24 and September 30, 1971 removal of Liner's property line stakes, and Liner's awareness shown by his attorney's letter to the defendant; the October 25, 1971 removal of stakes and obstructions in the property line ditch; and, finally, the February 3, 1972 operation which precipitated the suit.

The redactors' comments make it clear that no additional requirements for bringing the possessory action were intended by the revision in 1960. "This article makes no change in the law" is the first sentence in the redactors' comment under C.C.P. 3658 and is the first clause in the comment under C.C.P. 3660. The intention is obvious that the redactors (as has the court, for more than a century, see *Ellis v.*

Prevost, 19 La. 251 (1841)) correlated the possessory action of the Code of Practice and the Code of Civil Procedure with the Civil Code articles relating to the right of a possessor to maintain himself in possession or to regain possession. C.C. 3454.

The evidence in this case leaves no doubt but that Oliver Liner had the corporeal possession of the property here in dispute for many years. The quality of his possession was that of owner. It extended to visible boundaries. It was neither precarious, clandestine, violent nor ambiguous. Aubry & Rau, Civil Law Translations, Vol. 2, § 180 (1966). One having acquired the corporeal possession of an immovable does not thereafter lose it against his consent except in the manner prescribed by law. "Possession," say Aubry & Rau, *supra*, § 179, "is not necessarily lost just because a third person has occupied the immovable. It is lost only if he remains occupied for a year (Art. 2243). If the former possessor lets this period elapse without any act of enjoyment or any claim for return of possession, he is considered as having lost it, whether he did or did not know of the adverse occupancy."

Our Civil Code provisions make it clear that one who has acquired corporeal possession continues in possession until he transfers it or abandons it, or until another expels him from it, or until he permits the estate to be usurped and held for a year without doing any act of possession or without interfering with the usurper's possession. . . .

We must conclude then that the words "quietly and without interruption" do not mean that a possessor who suffers a "disturbance" on several occasions in the year preceding the suit has lost his right to bring the possessory action. The possessor may suffer disturbances throughout the year preceding the filing of the possessory action, and unless his possession comes to an end in such a way that he cannot show that he was in possession for more than a year prior to the disturbance complained of, he has the right to bring the action within a year of the disturbance.

A disturbance might interrupt possession. It might bring a corporeal possession to an end. (If, however, the disturbance results in an eviction by force or fraud, the one year possession requirement is eliminated). A disturbance may be an eviction, but it might also be "any other physical act which prevents the possessor of immovable property or of a real right from enjoying his possession quietly, or which throws any obstacle in the way of that enjoyment." C.C.P. 3659.

The acts of Louisiana Land and Exploration Company for the year preceding February 3, 1972 did constitute a disturbance of Liner's possession. However, he was not evicted. He and his son continued to trap on the disputed property. He continued to replace the boundary stakes removed by Louisiana Land and Exploration Company. Liner protested the August and September "invasions" by Louisiana Land and Exploration Company employees. Liner was not expelled, nor did he acquiesce in a usurpation. C.C. 3449.

C.C.P. 3658(2) cannot, without adding a new requirement to the possessory action, be read literally. It cannot mean that there must be no adverse claim for a year before the disturbance. "Quietly" appears in C.P. 49 and may be compared to "peaceably" in C.C. 3454, subd. 2, and in contrast to the violence referred to in C.C. 3491:

> "A possession by violence, not being legal, does not confer the right of prescribing.
>
> That right only commences when the violence has ceased."

As stated in Aubry & Rau, *supra*, § 180:

> "Possession is marred by violence, that means it is not peaceful, if it was acquired and continued by acts accompanied by physical or psychological violence. . . .
>
> The defect of violence presupposes that the possession is acquired by active means. If the possession originates peacefully, it does not become defective if troubles related to it are caused by third persons; but there must be no natural interruption of the possession. . . ."

Consequently, we interpret the requirement of C.C.P. 3658(2) to mean that there must have been no interruption of the possession for one year, prior to the disturbance which caused the suit.

Oliver Liner has proven each of the requisite elements of the possessory action set out in C.C.P. 3658. He is entitled to a judgment of possession.

For these reasons, the judgment of the Court of Appeal is reversed and that of the district court is reinstated, at the cost of defendant-respondent.

On Application for Rehearing

PER CURIAM. Our original opinion has adequately disposed of the contentions advanced by the application for rehearing. However, a strong argument has been made that we have misapplied La.C.Civ.P. art. 3658(2). This provision states, that, to maintain the possessory action, the plaintiff possessor must allege and prove that: "He and his ancestors in title had such possession *quietly and without interruption* for more than a year immediately prior to the disturbance, unless evicted by force or fraud ***."

The applicant points out that in our opinion we pointed out several acts by which the defendant Louisiana Land disturbed the plaintiff Liner's "quiet" possession during the year prior to the February 3, 1972 disturbance alleged as the basis for this suit.

The defendant correctly points out that each of these acts was a disturbance of possession which would entitle Liner to bring this possessory action, just as did the February 3, 1972 disturbance. Thus, Louisiana Land contends, due to these late 1971 disturbances, plainly Liner did not possess "quietly and without interruption" during the year preceding the February 3, 1972 disturbance upon which this suit is based.

This contention overlooks that the term to possess "quietly and without interruption", as used in the Louisiana Code of Civil Procedure (and by Article 49(2) of the Louisiana Codes of Practice of 1825 and 1870 preceding it), is equated with its traditional meaning in the Louisiana Civil Code. There, as a substantive right of possession, the Code recognizes the right of a possessor for a year or more who has possessed "peaceably and without interruption" to bring a possessory action against one who disturbs his possession. Louisiana Civil Code of 1808, art. 23, p. 478; Louisiana Civil Code of 1825, art. 3417(2); Louisiana Civil Code of 1870, art. 3454(2). See Art. 3454, La.C.C.Comp.Ed. in West's LSA-C.C., pp. 656–57 (1972).

Under the Civil Code, possession is not interrupted when it is merely disturbed. A possessor does not lose possession against his consent unless he is forcibly expelled or unless the disturber usurps possession and holds it for more than a year. . . .

Thus, an interruption of possession for purposes of the possessory action coincides with an interruption of acquisitive prescription under Article 3517 of the Civil Code. (Moreover, if so interpreted, the loss of the right to possess under Article 3449(2) of the Civil Code coincides with the acquisition of right to possess by another under Articles 3454(2) and 3456 of the Civil Code.)

We therefore conclude that one may possess quietly and without interruption for more than a year so as to be entitled to bring a possessory action, La.C.Civ.P. art. 3658(2), even though during that year disturbances in fact or law have occurred, La.C.Civ.P. art. 3659.

The application for a rehearing is denied.

Rehearing denied.

TATE, Justice (concurring in denial). The writer subscribes to the majority opinion and to the denial of rehearing. The additional sources and analysis are set forth below for what aid they may be in study for future applications of the article.

The Louisiana Civil Code and the Louisiana Code of Civil Procedure draw a distinction between a disturbance in fact that results in eviction and such a disturbance that falls short of eviction. In the first case, the possessor is evicted, and the person who caused the disturbance may commence to possess for himself. In the second case, the disturbance merely questions or places an obstacle to the enjoyment of quiet possession. Civil Code Article 3454 (2); La.C.Civ.P. arts. 3655, 3658(4), 3659.

Under the facts before us, as the majority states, Louisiana Land's acts clearly amounted to no more than a disturbance. They did not amount to an eviction. Nevertheless, whether an eviction or a disturbance, the possessor must within a year bring the possessory action. La. C.Civ.P. art. 3658(4).

The underlying issues, however, concern when a disturbance of possession constitutes an eviction and when an eviction is of sufficient magnitude or duration as to terminate the original possessor's undisturbed possession.

I

According to Article 3658(2) of the Louisiana Code of Civil Procedure, the plaintiff in a possessory action must allege and prove that he and his ancestors in title had possession of the immovable property or real right *"quietly and without interruption . . .* for more than a year immediately prior to the disturbance, unless evicted by force or fraud (Italics mine.) This provision was derived from Article 49(2) of the Codes of Practice of 1825 and 1870. This prescribed that the plaintiff in the possessory action ought to have possession *"quietly and without interruption . . .* for more than a year previous to his being disturbed," unless he had been evicted by force or fraud (Italics mine). An official comment under Article 3658 of the Louisiana Code of Civil Procedure indicates that "this article makes no change in the law."

The redactors of Article 49(2) of the Code of Practice used the words "without interruption" to convey the same idea as in Article 3417(2) of the Louisiana Civil Code of 1825, corresponding with Article 3454(2) of the 1870 Code. There, possessory protection is available to every person "who has possessed an estate for a year, or enjoys *peaceably and without interruption* a real right, and is disturbed in it" (Italics added). The provision reflects language used in Article 23, p. 478, of the Louisiana Civil Code of 1808, taken almost verbatim from the text of Pothier. See Pothier, Traité de la Possession, Chapter VI, No. 83, 9 Oeuvres de Pothier 291 (ed. Bugnet 1861). There is no corresponding provision in the French Civil Code.

II

In drafting Article 23, p. 478 of the 1808 Code, however, the redactors were aware of Article 38, p. 482, which corresponds with Article 2229 of the French Civil Code. Article 38 declared: "Prescription requires a continued, *uninterrupted, peaceable,* public and unequivocal possession; it is also required that the person claiming the prescription shall have possessed animo domini, that is, as master or proprietor" (Italics added). This provision was amended in 1825, and eventually in substance became Article 3487 of the 1870 Code.

In speaking of interruption of prescription (rather than of possession), Article 3517 of the Louisiana Civil Code of 1870 declares that "a natural interruption is said to take place when the possessor is deprived of the possession [enjoyment] of the thing during more than a year, either by the ancient proprietor or even by a third person".

The relevant issue is: Should the same concept be applied to the interruption of possession? Is possession interrupted when the possessor is evicted or only when he has been evicted and stayed out of possession for a full year?

III

Possession is not interrupted when it is merely disturbed. Possession is interrupted when possession is lost. See 3 Planiol et Ripert, Traité pratique de droit civil francais 170 (2d ed. Picard 1952). . . .

IV

The proper interpretation of Article 3449 of the Louisiana Civil Code of 1870, quoted above, raises the question: Does this article establish two modes of loss of possession or just one? . . . .

Pothier and the redactors of the Louisiana Civil Code of 1825 seem to have had in mind two distinct matters: on the one hand, loss of possession as loss of physical control; on the other, loss of the right to possess. Indeed, much confusion has resulted in Louisiana from the use of the word "possession" in the Civil Code and in the jurisprudence to denote both physical control and the right to possess. . . .

V

We may now return to the interpretation of Article 3658(2) of the Louisiana Code of Civil Procedure.

Does this provision contemplate interruption of possession by an eviction of any duration or only by an eviction that has lasted for more than a year?

In other words, does this provision contemplate interruption of possession by the loss of physical control (Civil Code Article 3449(1)), or only interruption of possession by the loss of the right to possess (Civil Code Article 3449(2))? In the final analysis, the question is open to either interpretation and must be resolved in the light of policy considerations.

If possession is interrupted within the meaning of Article 3658(2) of the Louisiana Code of Civil Procedure by the mere loss of physical control at sometime during the period of one year immediately preceding the disturbance, consider the following illustration. A is disturbed in his possession by eviction or otherwise on January 4, 1974. He must bring the possessory action within one year and he must allege and prove that he was in possession on January 4, 1974, and that he was *not evicted at all* during the period between January 4, 1973, and January 4, 1974.

If possession is interrupted within the meaning of Article 3658(2) of the Louisiana Code of Civil Procedure by the loss of the right to possess during the period of one year immediately preceding the disturbance, consider the following illustration. A is disturbed in his possession, by eviction or otherwise, on January 4, 1974. He brings a possessory action on January 3, 1975, meeting the requirement of C.C.P. art. 3658(4). He must also allege and prove that he was in possession on January 4, 1974, and that he *did not lose the right to possess* during the period between January 4, 1973 and January 4, 1974. If he was evicted, at any time, for less than a year and recovered possession prior to January 4, 1974, he may still bring the possessory action. If he was evicted for more than a year but recovered possession prior to January 4, 1973, again he may still bring the possessory action. The possessory action is barred to him only if he recovered possession during the period from January 4, 1973 to January 4, 1974, after having been out of possession for more than a year, namely, if he was evicted prior to January 4, 1972, and his eviction lasted for more than a year.

The second interpretation is preferable. Under this interpretation, an interruption of possession for purposes of the possessory action coincides with an interruption of acquisitive prescription under Article 3517 of the Civil Code. Moreover, under this interpretation, the loss of the right to possess under Article 3449(2) of the Civil Code coincides in time with the acquisition of the right to possess by another under Articles 3454(2) and 3456 of the Civil Code.

This preferred interpretation accords with the apparent intent of the redactors of the Code of Practice and of the Code of Civil Procedure. The redactors intended to accord possessory protection to a person who acquired the right to possess under Civil Code Articles 3449(2), 3454(2), and 3487.

Thus, the legislative intent of the provisions of Article 49(2) of the Code of Practice and 3658(2) of the Code of Civil Procedure seems to be that possessory protection is available to anyone who has previously acquired the right to possess and did not lose it in the year immediately preceding the disturbance.

VI

Finally this interpretation also accords with French tradition, legislation, doctrine and jurisprudence. . . .

Thus, under both the text of the French Code of Civil Procedure and relevant doctrine, possessory protection in France is available unless possession was lost by interruption for a period in excess of one year prior to the disturbance. *See also* 3 Planiol et Ripert, Traité pratique de droit civil francais 1970 (2d ed. Picard 1952). The interpretation of the Louisiana code provisions as declaring to the same effect is thus in accord with the doctrinal sources of our law and with the pertinent general scheme of our own Civil Code.

Notes and Questions

1. Because possession cases are fact intensive, one should always take great care to chronicle the activities of the actors—in this case, Oliver Liner, his predecessors and challengers. Be careful to note the nature and use of the disputed land. Did the use change over time? Make a list of the various acts of possession, if any, of the contestants in the 1950s, 1960s, and in 1971 and 1972. Identify the act that prompted Oliver Liner, and his attorney at the time, Stanwood Duval (who served as U.S. District Judge for the Eastern District of Louisiana between 1997 and 2017), to file a possessory action.

2. Explain why the intermediate appellate court determined that Liner's possession was interrupted. What factors weigh against this determination?

3. Did Oliver Liner have "record title" to the land in Range 15? (By "record title" the court probably means some juridical act purporting to grant Liner ownership of the land in Range 15 or some juridical act recognizing his ownership in that area.) Does this matter for purposes of a possessory action? What would happen if the Louisiana Land and Exploration Company asserted ownership based on its purported record title?

4. Justice Dixon, the author of the original opinion in *Liner v. Louisiana Land & Exploration Co.*, 319 So.2d 766 (La. 1975), characterizes Liner's possession as "neither precarious, clandestine, violent nor ambiguous." *Id.* at 774. When possession is beset by any of these vices, it does not have any legal effect. La. Civ. Code arts. 3435–36 (1982). It is noteworthy that the court found that Liner's possession originated in the absence of violence and was never afflicted by violence. Do you agree?

5. In the central portion of the original opinion, Justice Dixon holds that Liner had uninterrupted possession during the year before the litigated disturbance. He reasons that none of the various acts by the Louisiana Land and Exploration Company amounted to an eviction because they were not vigorous or sustained enough to expel or seriously challenge Liner's possession. Do you agree? Does it help to understand the original opinion better if one were to call these disturbances "mere" disturbances, as opposed to "interruptive" disturbances, as the per curiam opinion on application for rehearing suggests? See *Liner*, 319 So.2d at 778.

6. In his well-known concurrence in the denial of rehearing, Justice Tate agrees that Liner had uninterrupted possession during the entire year before the litigated disturbance. He further explains that Liner had acquired the *right to possess* and had not lost it within the year preceding the disturbance. Therefore, according to Justice Tate, Liner satisfied the requirement of quiet and uninterrupted possession under Article 3658(2) of the Code of Civil Procedure. Would you say that the invention of the *right to possess* stabilizes matters in contested possessory settings? You might consider characterizing the actions and counter actions of Liner and the Louisiana Land and Exploration Company as a series of evictions and counter evictions.

* * *

The right to possess, as conceptualized by Justice Tate, has frequently been the central battleground in Louisiana possessory actions. Consider the following case, which offers a particularly careful analysis of the right to possess.

Mire v. Crowe

439 So.2d 517 (La. App. 1 Cir. 1983)

CARTER, J. This is a possessory action involving a triangular piece of property located in St. Tammany Parish.

Karl Mire instituted this possessory action on December 10, 1981, against Levi L. Crowe, Jr. claiming that the defendant had disturbed his possession by advising plaintiff's lessee that Crowe claimed ownership of a portion of the property. After trial on the merits, judgment was rendered in favor of plaintiff and defendant perfected this appeal.

On March 16, 1968, Karl Mire bought from Levi L. Crowe, Jr. property located in Slidell, Louisiana described as follows:

> "A certain tract or parcel of land, together with all the buildings and improvements thereon, and all rights, ways, advantages, and appurtenances thereunto belonging or in anywise appertaining situated in St. Tammany Parish, Louisiana, and more particularly described as Lot Six (6) of Section Eighteen (18) in Township 8 South, Range 15 East, of the St. Helena Meridian Louisiana, containing two (2) acres and sixteen hundredths of an acre, according to the official plat of survey of the said lands, in file in the General Land Office."

Prior to passage of this act of sale, Mire and Levi Crowe, Jr. walked the boundaries of the property to be conveyed. The area pointed out to Mire by Crowe included an area in Lot 7, which could be generally described as lying east of Lot 6 and bounded on the north and south by an extension of the north and south lines of Lot 6 and on the east by Langston's Bayou.

Crowe does not question Mire's possession of Lot 6. Crowe claims, however, that Mire's title is limited to Lot 6 and does not cover any property in Lot 7. Both parties assert ownership of the disputed land, although the only issue on this appeal is whether Mire is entitled to be maintained in possession of the property. Crowe did not reconvene for possession of the property, but simply denied plaintiff's possession.

Mire's Acts of Possession

Upon acquisition of Lot 6 in 1968, Mire immediately took possession of the disputed property. Mire employed a surveyor and had the property surveyed. Mire and his nephews then walked the property and placed stakes for construction of a fence. A new fence was built along the northern boundary of the property to Langston Bayou and along the southern boundary to a point referred to as the "gully". No fence was erected through the "gully" because the area was under water during parts of the year. Mire also maintained and repaired the fences.

Hunting and fishing activities were also conducted on the disputed area. Family members and friends of Karl Mire often used a portion of the disputed property known as the "hill" to conduct these activities, with Mire's permission.

Several of Mire's nephews (with Mire's consent) raised hogs in the area west of the gully and allowed cattle to graze over the entirety of the area, including the "hill".

Mire erected a barn on the disputed area west of the gully and maintained a garden for several years in the general vicinity of the barn. Grass was clipped and maintained by Mire on the disputed tract.

In July, 1981, Mire leased the property to John Buttrey for the purpose of housing and maintaining horses on the premises.

Crowe's Acts of Possession

Crowe lived on the property in dispute as a child and conducted various activities on the property prior to the sale to Mire in 1968. Crowe now owns a campsite south of and adjacent to the Mire property. The Crowe camp is bounded on the north by the disputed "hill", on the east by Langston Bayou, and on the west by other Mire property. Crowe and his friends have used the disputed tract on several occasions to get to his camp.

The Trial Court's Judgment

The trial court found that Mire was entitled to be maintained in possession of the disputed area and stated:

". . . since acquisition of the property, Mr. Mire has been in actual, physical, open, public, unequivocal continuous, and uninterrupted possession of the property with the intent to possess as owner. The Court is also convinced by the evidence that upon execution of the act of sale on March 16, 1968, Mr. Crowe terminated his prior possession of the disputed area. Mire was in possession at the time of Crowe's disturbance and had been so without interruption for more than a year prior to the disturbance. Crowe's disturbance was a disturbance in fact, and the possessory action was instituted by Mire well within a year of the disturbance. The few trespasses upon the property by Crowe and his friends, without knowledge of Mire, are of no significance. These trespasses are inadequate to establish possession by Crowe or his usurpation of the property in dispute. These disturbances— unknown to Mire—are not strong enough to interrupt Mire's right to possess. These activities would in no way bring home to Mire the realization that his possession and control of the property is being challenged by Crowe. . . ."

Defendant has appealed the trial court judgment, contending that the trial judge erred in finding that the plaintiff maintained the necessary possession of the area in dispute.

The Law

This action is governed primarily by LSA-C.C.P. art. 3658, which provides:

"To maintain the possessory action the possessor must allege and prove that:

(1) He had possession of the immovable property or real right therein at the time the disturbances occurred;

(2) He and his ancestors in title had such possession quietly and without interruption for more than a year immediately prior to the disturbance, unless evicted by force or fraud;

(3) The disturbance was one in fact or in law, as defined in Article 3659; and

(4) The possessory action was instituted within a year of the disturbance."

Although Article 3658 lists four requirements for bringing the possessory action, the battle lines are often drawn over the question posed by paragraph (2): Who has the right to possess? This question, in turn, is often decided by a determination of whether any acts of the defendant have sufficiently interrupted the plaintiff's possession so as to strip the plaintiff of his right to possess.

How the Right is Acquired

A person acquires the right to possess immovable property by possessing the property quietly and without interruption for more than a year. LSA-C.C.P. art. 3658(2); LSA-C.C. art. 3454(2), now repealed; *see also* LSA-C.C. arts. 3449(2), now LSA-C.C. art. 3434, and 3487, now LSA-C.C. arts. 3435, 3436 and 3476. The species of possession required to acquire the right to possess is either corporeal possession or civil possession preceded by the corporeal possession of the plaintiff or his ancestors in title. LSA-C.C.P. art. 3660. In all cases, a person must possess as owner and for himself. Thus, to acquire the right to possess, "one must combine the intention of possessing as owner with the corporeal detention of the thing." *Norton v. Addie*, 337 So.2d 432, 436 (La. 1976). *Pitre v. Tenneco Oil Co.*, 385 So.2d 840 (La. App. 1st Cir. 1980), *writ denied* 392 So.2d 678 (La. 1980) . . . .

The Louisiana law of possession and the jurisprudence interpreting it also provide that a person who possesses property in good faith under a deed translative of ownership is considered to possess to the extent of his title, provided he has corporeally possessed part of the property described in the deed. In such a case, the person is considered to be in constructive possession of the entire tract. However, when one possesses without title, he is required to show an adverse possession by enclosures. *Hill v. Richey, supra.* Corporeal possession required to maintain a possessory action when one has no title contemplates actual possession within enclosures sufficient to establish the limits of possession with certainty, by either natural or artificial marks, giving notice to the world of the extent of possession exercised. *Hill v. Richey, supra; Gaulter v. Gennaro, supra.* . . .

Once it is established that a person has possessed property, as required by law, quietly and without interruption for more than a year, he has proven his right to possess. There is no need to show he acquired this right in the year immediately preceding suit, but only that he obtained the right at one time and that he has not lost it prior to the disturbance. *Liner v. Louisiana Land and Exploration Company*, 319 So.2d 766 (La. 1975).

How the Right is Lost

A person loses the right to possess immovable property either voluntarily, by transferring or abandoning the property; or involuntarily, by being evicted or expelled for more than a year or by acquiescing in a third party's usurpation of the property for more than a year. LSA-C.C. arts. 3447, 3448, 3449, now LSA-C.C. art. 3433. *Pitre v. Tenneco Oil Co., supra.*

A question often arises as to what type of activity by an adverse party will sufficiently interrupt a person's right to possess so as to usurp his possession and strip him of his right upon passage of more than a year's time. Not every disturbance is strong or long enough to interrupt another's right to possess. Disturbances which do not interrupt another person's right to possess may be challenged in court and the disturber cast for appropriate damages and other appropriate relief. But such minor disturbances will be insufficient, even if unchallenged within a year's time, to strip the right to possess from the person who presently has that right. *See Liner, supra*, particularly the per curiam opinion on rehearing, 319 So.2d at 778; *Pitre v. Tenneco Oil Co., supra; Plaisance v. Collins, supra; Richard v. Comeaux*, 260 So.2d

350 (La.App. 1st Cir. 1972); *Yiannopoulous, 2 Louisiana Civil Law Treatise, Property,* § 217, page 582 (2d Ed. 1980); and *Work of the Appellate Court — 1974–1975, Property,* 36 La.L.Rev. 354 (1976).

Louisiana courts have indicated that for a disturbance to be sufficient to interrupt another's right to possess, the disturbance must bring home to the actual possessor the realization that his dominion is being seriously challenged. *Pittman v. Bourg,* 179 La. 66, 153 So. 22 (1934); *Souther v. Domingue,* 238 So.2d 264 (La. App.3rd Cir. 1970), writ refused 256 La. 891, 239 So.2d 544 (1970); *Hebert v. Chargois,* 106 So.2d 15 (La.App. 1st Cir. 1958). In addition, the person with the right to possess must acquiesce in the interruption for more than a year without conducting any act of possession or without interfering with the usurper's possession. LSA-C.C. art. 3449(2), now LSA-C.C. art. 3434.

The single rule of law that can be fashioned from the foregoing is that the plaintiff, to win a possessory action, must show that he at one time acquired the right to possess and that he has not lost the right prior to the disturbance. Stated another way, "possessory protection is available to anyone who has previously acquired the right to possess and did not lose it in the year preceding the disturbance." *Yiannopoulous, supra,* § 215, page 580; see also Tate, J., concurring in denial of rehearing in *Liner, supra,* 319 So.2d 779, 782. In all cases, of course, suit must be filed within a year of the disturbance. LSA-C.C.P. art. 3658(4). A person who proves that he had the right to possess and that he has not lost it in the year prior to the disturbance has proved, concomitantly, that he is in possession of the property as required by LSA-C.C.P. art. 3658(1). See *Liner, supra,* and *Plaisance v. Collins, supra,* at 613.

Did Mire have the Right to Possess?

The facts that the trial court found, and we agree, prove that Karl Mire acquired the right to possess. For some fourteen years, Mire, his family, and his friends have performed various acts of corporeal possession on the disputed tract. Upon purchasing Lot 6 in 1968, Mire moved onto the property, had the property surveyed, and erected visible boundaries which complemented natural boundaries. Other acts of corporeal possession were conducted on the property, each act corresponding to the different kinds of property involved. Certain cleared areas were used to build a barn and plant a garden. The more wooded areas were utilized for walking and hunting. The areas which were partially covered by water were used for fishing. The disputed property was also used to graze cattle and raise hogs. Mire also granted a lease to a portion of the disputed tract. Those areas on which no corporeal activities were conducted were enclosed within the natural and the artificial boundaries established by Mire.

The record is also clear that when Mire took possession of Lot 6 and the disputed portion of Lot 7 in 1968, Crowe, who had previously conducted activities on the property, abandoned his use of the property, as owner, until August, 1981.

Did Mire Lose the Right to Possess?

Having found that Mire acquired the right to possess, and actually possessed, we must now determine whether any acts of Crowe were of sufficient strength to interrupt Mire's possession or usurp Mire's right to possess.

Unquestionably, Crowe committed a number of trespasses on the property. Crowe crossed Mire's property to get to his own camp, primarily because Crowe had enclosed his camp by selling the surrounding property which fronted roads. These trespasses, however, seem not to have been made with Mire's permission.

Crowe may also have conducted several disturbances, each of which would have entitled Mire to bring a possessory action, as Crowe hunted and fished on the disputed tract through the years. These isolated acts were insufficient to dispossess Mire, especially in light of the fact that Crowe had prior to the sale pointed out the now disputed area to Mire as being sold to Mire. *See Plaisance v. Collins, supra* at 616, where sporadic trapping, chicken farming, hunting, and leasing a house in the vicinity were held to be insufficient acts to dispossess the plaintiff.

Additionally, when plaintiff's lessee, John Buttrey, was advised by Crowe on August 16, 1981, that he must cease building a corral and developing the "hill", plaintiff instituted this possessory action on December 10, 1981, clearly within a year of the disturbance.

We are simply not convinced that any of the activities conducted on the disputed tract prior to the disturbance in August, 1981, interrupted the quiet and peaceable possession of Mire. Mire possessed the property as owner and conducted numerous activities which were consistent with the nature of the property in question. He never acquiesced in Crowe's claims to the property, and he brought this action when it became apparent that Crowe claimed ownership of the "hill". The trial court correctly determined that Mire proved his right to possession of the disputed area and that he did not lose this right in the year immediately preceding this suit. The requisites for the possessory action were clearly established, and Mire is entitled to be maintained in possession.

Therefore, for the foregoing reasons, the judgment of the trial court is affirmed. Appellant is to pay all costs.

AFFIRMED.

Problem

Peter and Dennis own contiguous properties. Peter's property is immediately south of Dennis' property. Their dispute involves a strip of land thirty-six feet wide and 210 feet long located along the common boundary.

Peter acquired his one-acre tract of land by an act of sale on November 1, 1971. At the time of purchase, a wire fence was located thirty-six feet further north than the northern boundary of his property as described in the act of sale. After he acquired his tract, Peter began to mow the grass in the additional strip of land bounded by the wire fence, and he and his wife planted and tended a flower garden there.

Dennis acquired his property in 1998. At that time, there was no visible boundary line between the two properties because the wire fence had been torn down in 1997. In May 2001, Dennis had his land surveyed and, pursuant to this survey, built a chain link fence across the southern boundary of his property. His fence encompassed the thirty-six foot strip of land where Peter had mowed the grass and where he and his wife had tended the flower garden.

Peter and his wife continued to water the flowers in the flower garden with the aid of a garden hose but never went onto the disputed strip of land again. The flowers north of the chain link fence continued to grow until July 2002, when Dennis replaced the chain link fence with a barbed wire fence at the same location. Soon after this fencing change, Dennis destroyed the flowers north of the fence and allowed his cattle to graze that area. Peter filed a possessory action in September 2002.

Will Peter's possessory action be successful? Why or why not?

D. Possessory Actions against the State

The possessory action protects the possession of corporeal immovables (such as land and buildings) as well as incorporeal immovables (such as servitudes and mineral rights) when those things are private things owned by individuals and other private persons. Public things, however, which are necessarily owned and possessed by the state or by its political subdivisions, will not be the subject of possessory actions.

As we learned earlier, private things can also be owned by the state or its political subdivisions in their private capacity. La. Civ. Code art. 453 (1978). Recall also that, although private things owned by a political subdivision are susceptible to acquisitive prescription, private things belonging to the state are exempt from acquisitive prescription according to state constitutional mandates. *Id.* rev. cmt. (b); La. Civ. Code art. 3485 rev. cmt. (b) (1982); *cf.,* La. Rev. Stat. 9:5804. Given that private things owned by the state are imprescriptible, should an individual or other private person be allowed to assert a possessory action against the state with respect to immovable property classified as a private thing?

After a lengthy debate, the Louisiana Supreme Court concluded that, yes, a possessory action may be maintained against the State of Louisiana when the object of the possessory action is a private thing owned by the state. *See Todd v. State,* 474 So.2d 430 (La. 1985) (on second rehearing). However, the state cannot be forced to assert ownership within sixty days or be silent forever. The "right to possess" recognized by the court in *Todd* protects the possessor from eviction by other private persons, but it does not prevent the state from asserting its ownership at any time. Study the following opinion to understand the rationales offered by the court to support its conclusions.

Todd v. State Dep't of Natural Resources

474 So.2d 430 (1985) (on second rehearing)

CALOGERO, Justice. The troubling issue in this case, whether a possessory action may be brought against the State of Louisiana, has produced contrary opinions in this Court originally and on first rehearing. Plaintiffs, who won in the lower courts, and who with minor exceptions prevailed in this Court on original hearing, only to lose on first rehearing, were granted a rehearing by this Court, the first that they have had reason to seek.

In an opinion written for the Court by this same author, rendered on November 28, 1983, we determined that a possessory action may be maintained against the state. However, we concluded that the successful plaintiff's right under La. Code Civ. Pro. art. 3662(2) to have the judge require that the losing defendant file a petitory action within a period not to exceed sixty days (where plaintiff has prayed for such relief) is not constitutionally permissible when the state is the loser in the possessory action.

After we granted a rehearing sought by the state, a differently constituted majority, with three dissents, reversed our earlier judgment and the judgments of the district court and the Court of Appeal and held that "one does not have a cause of action to maintain a possessory action against the state." That majority's reasons can be summarized as follows:

1) The purpose of the possessory action is to protect the presumption of ownership as acquisitive prescription accrues.

2) However, since state property can never be acquired by prescription,

3) it would be a useless exercise to give judicial recognition to a plaintiff's right to possess against the state which would never be sufficient to acquire ownership.

4) Furthermore, the strong public policy of the state to protect the wealth of its lands and minerals would not be served by distinguishing between public things and private things and permitting the possessory action against the state as relates to private things.

5) Also, other remedies are available to the owner to protect the peaceful possession of his property whether disturbed by the state or by any other person.

6) Therefore, one does not have a cause of action to maintain a possessory action against the state.

Rehearing applicants have in brief countered a number of the underlying premises on which the majority relied on first rehearing. We now conclude that our original opinion was correct and should be reinstated; that a possessory action may be maintained against the state where the object of possession is a private rather than public thing.

Our reasons are more fully stated in our original opinion. *Todd v. State, Dept. of Natural Resources*, 456 So.2d 1340 (La. 1983) reversing 422 So.2d 1353 (La. App. 1st Cir. 1982). Those reasons are adopted herein with one minor exception.

The fallacy of our opinion on first rehearing lies in the assertion that the purpose of the possessory action is simply to facilitate a continued possession while acquisitive prescription accrues, and in rendering a judgment based largely upon an ascertained or presumed public policy of the state, rather than appropriate constitutional and legal principles. We also conclude that the first rehearing majority's assertion that there are other adequate remedies available to an owner to protect the peaceful possession of his property is in some measure misleading.

Purpose of the Possessory Action

The purpose of a possessory action is to protect possession. It is part of the well conceived and long-standing system of real actions for the protection of possession and ownership of immovable property, adopted by the Legislature and recognized by the courts of this state. The concept of possession, established by our Civil Code, is designed as a first step in protecting ownership, whether acquired by acquisitive prescription, title, or otherwise. The series of real actions set forth in our Code of Civil Procedure has been carefully structured to establish an orderly procedure by which questions concerning possession, and subsequently ownership, can be determined. Thereunder, the status quo is maintained in order to promote peace and stability and to avoid resort to self-help when disputes arise as to ownership and possession of property.

Accordingly, a presumption is established by the Civil Code that a possessor is the provisional owner of the object of his possession until the true owner establishes his right. La. Civ. Code Ann. art. 3423. Should his possession be disturbed, he is entitled, by means of the possessory action, to be either maintained in or restored to his possession. La. Code Civ. Pro. Ann. art. 3655. The legislative reasoning in adopting this approach to the resolution of disputes over property is self-evident. In most cases, those in possession of land are the owners, not squatters attempting to acquire ownership through acquisitive prescription. Rather than requiring these rightful owners to carry the heavy burden of proof, and expense, in establishing ownership, the Legislature allows one who is disturbed in his possession and who claims ownership to bring a possessory action against any person who evicts him or disturbs his possession. La. Code Civ. Pro. Ann. art. 3658. Because of the difficulty of proving ownership, the law permits a person in possession (normally the owner) to set aside disturbances of that possession simply upon proof of the right to possess rather than upon proof of ownership.

We did of course note in our opinion on original hearing that:

> the 'intent to possess' in a possessory action has been found to be similar in nature to that required of a person seeking to acquire property by prescription. *City of New Orleans v. New Orleans Canal, Inc.*, 412 So.2d 975 (La. 1982); *Norton v. Addie*, 337 So.2d 432 (La. 1976); *Liner v. Louisiana*

Land and Exploration Company, 319 So.2d 766 (La. 1975); Note, 49 Tul. Law Review 1173 (1975). Admittedly, too, the possessory action is oftentimes but the "skirmishing ground for the impending contest as to ownership." *Writ System in Real Actions*, 22 Tul. Law Review 459 at 467 (1948). *However, the fact that one action may in the usual course precede another does not mean that availability of the latter is a sine qua non of the former"* (emphasis added).

In fact, the Civil Code clearly provides that "[t]he ownership and the possession of a thing are distinct." La. Civ. Code Ann. art. 481. And, as Justice Dennis pointed out in his dissent to the first rehearing,

> "The right to possess is protected by the possessory action not merely for protection of the presumption of ownership inherent in possession, but also for protection of all rights attending possession. These rights include (1) present authority to detain and enjoy (until adverse ownership is proven), La. C.C. arts. 3421, 3422; (2) transferability for value or otherwise, La. C.C. 3441; (3) ownership of fruits gathered during possession and works built on the property possessed, La. C.C. arts. 485–486, 496–497; (4) reimbursement for expenses incurred by the possessor which inure to the owner's benefit, id., La. C.C. arts. 527–528; (5) and the right to maintain possession until the owner fully reimburses the possessor, La. C.C. 529."

Public Policy Considerations

According to our opinion on first rehearing, the strong public policy of the state to protect the wealth of its lands and minerals requires that all state lands be protected from contrary acquisition, and possession, since the possessory action was deemed to be nothing more than a prelude to ownership through acquisitive prescription, and resulted in the entitlement to certain fruits and revenues even in the event of ultimate eviction. That opinion's preoccupation with public policy, in our present view, is an inappropriate consideration in light of what we perceive to be controlling constitutional and statutory law. Nonetheless, our examination of the effects of permitting a possessory action against the state indicates that there is little basis for this concern. There is ample protection for the state's resources without stretching the existing law to exempt the state from the procedures designed by the Legislature to deal with questions of possession and ownership.

The Civil Code does provide that possession involves the "detention or enjoyment of a corporeal thing." La. Civ. Code Ann. art. 3421. As part of its enjoyment, the possessor is entitled to the ownership of fruits which he has gathered and to the reimbursement of his expenses for fruits he is unable to gather if evicted by the owner. La. Civ. Code Ann. art. 486. The ownership of the fruits, however, is limited to a "good faith possessor," which includes only one who "possesses by virtue of an act translative of ownership and does not know of any defects in his ownership." La. Civ. Code Ann. art. 486 and 487. Clearly, a simple squatter or bad faith possessor, who would be eligible to acquire ownership of other than state owned property by means of 30 years acquisitive prescription, would not be entitled to retain the fruits produced on the lands owned by the state (or any other owner if challenged before passage of the thirty year acquisitive period). Such a limitation on the acquisition of fruits certainly alleviates some fears that a possessor of state lands would be entitled to enjoy significant economic advantage at the expense of the state.

Furthermore, some of the state's more valuable resources, i.e., timber and minerals, would not be classified as fruits, that benefit which would accrue to the good faith possessor of property, state owned or otherwise. . . . Thus, a possessor in good faith, who may keep fruits, must return products to the owner on demand, but is entitled to reimbursement of his expenses.

. . . .

In this same vein, we reaffirm our determination in the original opinion that the state shall not be subject to the requirement of La. Code Civ. Pro. art. 3662(2) that it assert any adverse claim of ownership in a petitory action within 60 days of the judgment of possession. As we stated in the original opinion:

> This reason is based partly on the public policy consideration attending the Constitution's prohibiting the loss of state lands by acquisitive prescription. More pointedly, however, it is based on the constitutional proscription to the running of liberative prescription against the state, a provision which has been incorporated in our state constitutions since 1898. "Prescription shall not run against the state in any civil matter, unless otherwise provided in this constitution or expressly by law." La. Const. art. 12 § 13, La. Const. art. 19 § 16 (1921), La. Const. art. 193 (1913 and 1898).

> The sixty day period in La.C.C.P. art. 3662(2), within which the trial judge when asked must tell the loser in a possessory action to file a petitory action, fits indeed within the parameters of liberative prescription. This sixty (60) day period finds its source in the jactitory action, a jurisprudentially-created action which subsisted as a way of handling slander of title actions. *International Paper Co. v. Louisiana Central Lumber Co.,* 202 La. 621, 639, 12 So.2d 659 (1943); *Siegel v. Helis,* 186 La. 506, 172 So. 768 (1937) and cases cited therein at 172 So. at 771; *Packwood v. Dorsey,* 4 La. Ann. 90 (1849). In 1960 with the adoption of the Louisiana Code of Civil Procedure, the former jactitory action was merged with the former possessory action. 35 Tul.L.Rev. 541 (1961). That the sixty day period is a form of liberative prescription is evident from jurisprudential history of the jactitory action. *Siegel,* 172 So. [at] 771; *Packwood,* 4 La. Ann. 90.

Other Remedies

It has been suggested that similarly situated plaintiffs have numerous alternative actions in the event that this Court decides that a possessory action cannot properly be brought against the state. Among those suggested in brief are an action to remove a cloud from title; an action of nullity; an action in trespass; a declaratory judgment or similar proceedings under La.Code Civ. Pro. Ann. art. 3654; or a revendicatory action. The petitory action and an action of boundary have likewise been mentioned.

There is apparently some question as to whether the action to remove a cloud from title survived the 1960 enactment of the Code of Civil Procedure. Although this Court in *Walmsley v. Pan American Petroleum Corp.*, 244 La. 513, 153 So.2d 375 (1963), relied on introductory remarks before Title II, Real Actions, to conclude that the action was still viable, the decision has been much criticized. *Bordelon v. Haas Investment Co.*, 337 So.2d 904, 905 (La. App. 3rd Cir. 1976) (citing *Verret v. Norwood*, 311 So.2d 86 (La. App. 3rd Cir. 1975)). Furthermore, the action, if still valid, is generally brought by one who claims ownership of immovable property against another who has recorded an instrument which operates as a cloud on plaintiff's title. The desired judgment is the cancellation of the recorded instrument from the public records. *Giuffria Realty Co. v. Kathman-Landry, Inc.*, 173 So.2d 329 (La. App. 4th Cir. 1965) (citing *Daigle v. Pan American Production Co.*, 236 La. 578, 108 So.2d 516 (1958). . . .

An action of nullity, as exemplified in *Giuffria Realty Co. v. Kathman-Landry, Inc.*, 173 So.2d 329 (La. App. 4th Cir. 1965), contemplates a situation where plaintiff seeks to attack a title plaintiff himself established. In this case, Giuffria Realty sought the rescission of its purported sale to Salvador Giuffria. It hardly addresses plaintiff's predicament in the matter at hand.

Under the Louisiana Code of Practice, an action in trespass was employed to obtain damages such as resulted from cutting timber, removing dirt, or grazing of cattle by defendant. Such an action could therefore be proper in addition to the possessory action when the disturbance is "in fact." It would not be appropriate when the disturbance is "in law," as in this case.

In an action for a declaratory judgment or a concursus, expropriation, or similar proceeding, La.Code Civ.Pro.Ann. art. 3654 provides that the issue of ownership is presented, and that the judgment is rendered in favor of the party either entitled to the possession of immovable property in a possessory action, unless the adverse party proves title, or in favor of the party who proves better title, if neither is entitled to possession. Such actions which specifically incorporate the standards of a possessory action would not seem to be acceptable alternatives to those who object to the use of the possessory action with regard to matters involving the state.

The revendicatory action is available to the owner or person entitled to the possession for the recovery of *movables*. A.N. Yiannopoulos, La. Civil Law Treatise, Vol. 1 Property § 142 (1966). It is provided for in La. Civ. Code Ann. art. 526. According to Comment (b):

> In Louisiana, the revendicatory action for the recovery of immovable property is more specifically designated as *petitory action* and is governed by Articles 3651–3654 of the Louisiana Code of Civil Procedure.

Clearly, a revendicatory action is no alternative for the plaintiff in this case.

And, of course, it can not be maintained that a petitory action would be an appropriate remedy for plaintiff or others who would urge a possessory action against the state. La.Code Civ.Pro.Ann. art. 3651 provides:

> The petitory action is one brought by a person who claims the ownership, but *who is not in possession,* of immovable property. . . . (emphasis added).

Finally, although a boundary action may be an appropriate alternative to a possessory action in some cases, it would have only limited application. It requires "two contiguous lands" and thus could be utilized only when a plaintiff and the state own adjacent property with the disputed territory between the properties. In this case, the state claims that the disputed territory was the former bed and bottom of the Mississippi River, while plaintiffs contend that the property was formed by accretion, alluvion, dereliction or reliction. We are not dealing with two contiguous lands which have a disputed boundary, and we cannot properly employ the boundary action.

We therefore conclude that of the suggested alternatives to the possessory action by plaintiffs, only the action for a declaratory judgment might be appropriate. However, since the declaratory judgment would involve the issue of ownership of immovable property, the burden of proof would be on the adverse party to the plaintiff in possession (namely the state) to make out its title, just as is the case in the possessory action. Should both of these actions be denied the plaintiffs as objectionable to the state, they would seem to be left with no cause of action.

La. Civ. Code Ann. Art. 3422 and Acquisition of the Right to Possess

Although not addressed in our first rehearing opinion, an argument which perhaps more than any other prompted the first rehearing grant with a consequent first change in the result in this case, originated with the contention in the dissent by the Chief Justice that "the acquisition of the right to possess is itself a kind of prescription which cannot run against the state." This notion is founded on both the language of La. Civ. Code Ann. art. 3422 and the substance of La. Code Civ. Pro. Ann. art. 3658(2), which provide that a possessor for over a year acquires the right to possess and to maintain a possessory action. Proponents equate the one year period before acquisition of the right to possess or ability to bring a possessory action with a prescriptive period running against the state. Of course, prescription against the state is prohibited by both La. Const. art. 12, § 13 and art. 9, § 4(B). However, we can ascertain little foundation for this position in either the Civil Code or jurisprudence of this state.

We point out that the term, "right to possess," was not found in any French text, the Louisiana Civil Code of 1870, the Louisiana Code of Practice, or the Code of Civil Procedure. The term first appeared in Justice Tate's concurring opinion in the denial of an application for rehearing in Liner v. Louisiana Land and Exploration Co., 319 So.2d 766 (La. 1975) and was subsequently adopted by the redactors in a 1982 amendment to La. Civ. Code Ann. art. 3422. It was apparently devised in recognition of the "confusion [which] has resulted in Louisiana from the use of the word 'possession' in the Civil Code and in the jurisprudence to denote both physical control and the right to possess," the availability of a possessory action. Liner v. Louisiana Land and Exploration Co., 319 So.2d at 781. Thus, the "right to possess" is little more than a shorthand method of saying that one has acquired the right to bring a possessory action. It does not involve any other consequence in Louisiana law and was never intended to alter the civilian scheme of real actions for the protection of possession and ownership of immovable property.

According to La. Civ. Code Ann. art. 3422, "[p]ossession is a matter of fact." La. Civ. Code Ann. art. 3423 provides that the possessor "is considered provisionally as owner of the thing," a presumption which apparently commences immediately (without delays, prescriptive or otherwise). Likewise, as soon as possession commences, the possessor may be entitled to fruits and reimbursements of certain expenses. La. Civ. Code Ann. art. 486. Thus, the fact of possession and its attributes are not contingent upon the running of any period of time nor is possession a right acquired by the running of time. It either exists or does not exist without regard to any notion of prescription.

Even the availability of the possessory action, furthermore, is not always delayed one full year from the beginning of possession. According to La. Code Civ. Pro. Ann. art. 3658(2), the requirement of possession for more than a year prior to disturbance is not applicable when the possessor is "evicted by force or fraud."

It should also be noted that the history of La. Code Civ. Pro. Ann. art. 3658 supports our conclusion that, in connection with the required one year of peaceful possession, prescription is not involved. The source of art. 3658 is art. 49 of the Code of Practice, which in turn corresponds to the 1806 French Code of Civil Procedure art. 23, and the official comment to Article 3658 assures us that no change has occurred in the law with the article's incorporation in the Louisiana Code of Civil Procedure. French commentators have explained that the requirement of one year's actual possession for the availability of the possessory action is an emphasis on continuity, which expresses the quality of possession, and the period takes into account the agricultural cycle of preparation, planting and harvesting. Such a period is no prescriptive right, but a procedural assurance of the fact of undisturbed possession.

Decree

For the reasons expressed in our original opinion as well as those expressed hereinabove, the decree which we rendered in our original opinion is reinstated. The lower courts' judgments are affirmed except insofar as they "order [the state] to bring a petitory action against the plaintiffs to assert any claim of ownership that [the state] has to the property . . . within sixty (60) days after this judgment becomes executory or be precluded thereafter from asserting the ownership thereof."

ORIGINAL DECREE REINSTATED; JUDGMENT AMENDED; OTHERWISE AFFIRMED.

Notes and Questions

1. In his opinion on the second rehearing, Justice Calogero launches into the legal question at hand. The following excerpt from the court's original decision, *Todd v. State Dep't of Natural Resources*, 456 So.2d 1340 (La. 1983), details the factual and procedural background of the dispute:

> Turnbull Island was originally a peninsula-like section of land in West Feliciana Parish bordering Avoyelles, Concordia and Pointe Coupee Parishes, and around which the Mississippi River looped in its journey to the Gulf of Mexico. The Red River entered the Mississippi at the northwestern bend of the loop; the Atchafalaya River branched off from the southwestern turn of the River. The land became an island in 1831 when navigational problems for river traffic on the loop and the perceived ease in channelling through the land's narrow neck to the east, resulted in the excavation of Shreve's Cut-off. Thereafter the main channel of the Mississippi River bypassed the circular journey around the island. Through the years the water remaining along the northern edge of Turnbull Island, known originally as Upper Old River, formed a thalweg (a sort of a steep depression or descent) which came to be known as Sugar Mill Chute.

> The land between what is known as the 1845–47 meander line of Upper Old River to the south and the thalweg, Sugar Mill Chute, to the north, became the subject of the present controversy.

> Robert Todd and Charles Haynes, Jr. bought the eastern half of Turnbull Island on June 8, 1978 from A.B. Stevens, who reserved the timber rights. On September 10, 1978, the State of Louisiana halted Stevens' timber operations on the portion of Turnbull Island between the 1845–47 meander line and Sugar Mill Chute. With legislative permission to sue, plaintiffs brought a possessory action against the State of Louisiana. In their petition, they alleged that the property on which the timber operations had been halted was attached to Turnbull Island, having been formed by accretion, alluvion, dereliction or reliction, and that their ancestors in title had taken possession of the property through various acts of corporeal possession for one year prior to the disturbance. The plaintiffs sought judgment restoring possession, ordering the state to file a petitory action in the matter and awarding indemnification for loss resulting from the halting of timber operations.

> The state reconvened, claiming possession of the disputed tract as the former bed and bottom of the Mississippi River. They also filed exceptions of no cause/no right of action and one styled "peremptory exception of sovereign immunity." Of significance to this decision was the exception based on the property's being public and as such "not subject to alienation by the state of Louisiana." The exception went on to recite, "[c]onsequently the property is considered to be in the public domain and a possessory action

cannot be filed or prosecuted against the State since property in the public domain cannot be possessed by an individual for himself." The exceptions were referred to the merits.

After trial, the court overruled all of the state's exceptions, recognized the plaintiffs' right to possession of the disputed tract, reserved to Stevens his right to seek damages for losses resulting from the state's halting the timber operations, dismissed the state's reconventional demand for possession, and ordered the state to file a petitory action within sixty days.

In overruling the exception of no cause of action which had been based on the premise that a possessory action may not be brought against the State of Louisiana, the trial judge noted that the relief granted to a plaintiff in a possessory action merely recognizes his right to possession, maintains him in his possession, and does not determine ownership or matters pertaining to acquisitive prescription.

On the merits, after examining the nature of the land in dispute, the nature of the possession and the nature of the alleged disturbances, the trial judge found that plaintiffs had proven their right to be maintained in possession of the property. The trial court found the land in question had been formed by the excavation of Shreve's Cut-Off and accretion. Secondly, the trial judge determined that the plaintiff had proven possession of the land to which the area in dispute was attached, as well as possession of the disputed land itself. Finally this possession was shown to have been undisturbed for a year prior to the halting of the timber operations, and the evidence of occasional hunting on the property by members of the public was found not to constitute contrary possession by the state.

The Court of Appeal upheld the trial court's judgment favoring plaintiffs in this possessory action without addressing whether the land was or was not formed by accretion. The Court of Appeal noted that the latter concern more properly affects the question of ownership of the property and should be resolved in a later petitory action. However, the appellate court found that, indeed, possession of the disputed tract by the plaintiffs had been established, and that since title is not at issue in a possessory action, there is nothing inimical to the state's interest in allowing the possessory action. 422 So.2d 1353 (La. App. 1st Cir. 1982).

The Court of Appeal then reviewed and confirmed the acts of possession favoring the plaintiffs and denied the counterpart allegations by the state that *it* was in possession of the disputed area. We granted the state's application in this matter primarily to decide whether the lower courts were correct in allowing a possessory action to be maintained against the state.

Todd v. State, 456 So.2d at 1341–44.

2. The plaintiffs in *Todd v. State*, Todd, Haynes and Stevens (the timber estate owners), asserted that the property in question has been possessed by their ancestors through various acts of corporeal possession and that they had held and not lost the right to possess within the full year preceding the litigated disturbance in law — the halting of Stevens' timber operations. The State countered with the argument that the constitutional arrangements in La. Const. art. XII, sec. 13 & art. IX, sec. 4(b) vitiated Todd's possessory proceeding.

3. Review the principal rationales of the majority for allowing the possessory action against the State when a private thing is the object of possession. The majority emphasizes that the possessory action is concerned with the protection of possession, not acquisitive prescription. In particular, the court notes that the accrual of the right to possess is not equivalent to prescription. *Todd*, 474 So.2d at 437–38. How would you frame the counter argument? In effect, what does it mean to prevail in a possessory action?

4. Why would Todd, Haynes and Stevens, if successful in a possessory action, not be offered the relief made available by Article 3663(2) of the Louisiana Code of Civil Procedure? Compare the sixty-day mandate under penalty of preclusion to a form of liberative prescription.

Chapter 9

Acquisitive Prescription with Respect to Immovables

In Louisiana, we distinguish two distinct modes of acquiring ownership and other real rights in immovables by possession over time: ten-year acquisitive prescription, which requires both just title and good faith, and thirty year acquisitive prescription, which only requires meeting the requisite length of time for possession. La. Civ. Code arts. 3475 & 3486 (1982). This chapter focuses on acquiring *ownership* of immovables by acquisitive prescription. Chapter 14 addresses acquisitive prescription of other real rights, namely predial servitudes.

Before we explore the detailed rules governing acquisitive prescription, we present the scholarly and practical rationales offered in the literature to justify the operations of acquisitive prescription and its common law analogue, adverse possession.

A. Justifications for Acquisitive Prescription

Over the centuries, different policy justifications have emerged relative to an almost universally recognized legal principle that allows a person who possesses a thing for a designated period of time to become its owner, even though another person has formal title to the thing or, as we say in Louisiana, is the "record owner" of the thing. These rationalizations can be grouped into four general models: the administrative model, the developmental model; the limitations model; and the personhood model.

First, judges and scholars have contended for years that acquisitive prescription and adverse possession at common law serve the utilitarian purpose of providing a cost effective method to cure relatively innocent, run of the mill mistakes in the world of conveyancing—for example, mistakes made in copying a legal description in a deed or in surveying land. This rationale, which has been called the **administrative model**, is powerful. The legal system protects possessors who possess immovable property for a period of time in a reasonable belief they have become owner by virtue of an *act translative of ownership* (like an act of sale or act of donation). Acquisitive prescription cures errors in their own conveyancing documents or those of their predecessors in title. Thereby the legal system avoids costly battles over who has record title, conserves judicial resources, and protects persons who reasonably thought they had acquired ownership of the things they possess.

An additional benefit of rewarding good faith possessors with respect to immovables is that it encourages buyers and sellers and other persons acquiring real rights in immovables to use the public records system and employ professionals like abstractors, surveyors and lawyers to examine the chains of title available in public records and to determine boundary lines with scientific precision. When we examine the elements of ten year, good faith acquisitive prescription of immovables, we must ask whether these policy goals are always served by the decisions of our courts.

A more controversial rationalization for acquisitive prescription, especially for any form that does not require good faith or just title, seeks to reward persons who actively invest in and develop immovable property, albeit at the expense of absentee owners who fail to pay attention to their property or make productive use of it for significant periods of time. This rationale, which is also known as the **developmental model**, is rooted in deep and, at times, not fully articulated social norms. After a certain period of time, even though a thing might be owned by another person, a legal system may decide to reward active, industrious persons who add value to the thing through their acts of possession, or who exert their labor and invest time and energy in developing natural resources like land. Moreover, an absentee owner who allows another person to engage in the industrious use of his property for a long enough period of time is deemed to have waived his ownership rights. In Louisiana, the regime governing thirty year acquisitive prescription with regard to immovables reflects this development justification.

Another rationale for both ten and thirty year acquisitive prescription pertains to the social cost of resolving uncertain ownership claims after a long passage of time. From your study of torts or contracts, you have learned that all legal systems impose prescriptive periods, or statutes of limitations, with respect to certain kinds of claims because of concerns that once too much time has passed from the accrual of a claim, we lose confidence in the ability of courts to sort out the relevant facts because memories fade, documentary evidence is lost, and other kinds of evidence becomes less reliable. In short, at some point in time, all legal systems will disregard stale claims of any nature in the interest of providing repose. This rationalization for acquisitive prescription and adverse possession is called the **limitations model**.

Two conceptual challenges have been levied against the limitations rationale. First, in a legal system like Louisiana's, with a long-standing registry, the public records should contain a relatively accurate and complete picture of the record ownership of immovables and other real rights, thus alleviating concerns that competent evidence will become difficult and costly to obtain for decision makers over time. Second, unlike other statutes of limitations that simply declare that certain kinds of claims are barred after a period of time, acquisitive prescription and adverse possession sanction a change in ownership without any form of compensation to the formal title holder. Observing this anomaly, some property scholars have advocated that an adverse possessor, especially if in bad faith, should only be able to obtain ownership of the property that he possesses for the statutory period if he pays the formal title holder some form of compensation for the latter's loss.

A final rationale for acquisitive prescription is associated with the work of nineteenth century philosopher Georg Wilhelm Friedrich Hegel. It was promoted in the United States by none other than Unites States Supreme Court Justice Oliver Wendell Holmes. This justification, which has come to be called the **personhood model**, is grounded in the observation that persons who possess things for significant periods of time develop strong psychological attachments. These attachments are so strong that the possessors come to have certain expectations: that their possession will be honored by society and the legal system. Possessors will often exert considerable effort to protect their possession of things and might even engage in self-help. Such expectations eventually ripen into "reliance interests." Legal systems may endeavor to honor reliance interests because otherwise persons who have invested their time, energy and labor will be demoralized. Further, other members of the community eventually come to recognize persons who have created these reliance interests by possessing things over long periods of time as owners. Ignoring the interests of possessors and their acceptance by others could seriously destabilize a community's informal expectations about property entitlements.

These rationales are not mutually exclusive. They blend with and reinforce one another at the margins. Over the years, these rationales and their application in a variety of legal and social contexts have been the subject of extensive scholarship. *See, e.g.*, Lee Anne Fennell, *Efficient Trespass: The Case for Bad Faith Adverse Possession*, 100 N.W. L. Rev. 1037 (2006); Jefferey Evans Stake, *The Uneasy Case for Adverse Possession*, 89 Geo. L. J. 2419 (2001); Richard Posner, *Savigny, Holmes and the Law and Economics of Possession*, 86 Va. L. Rev. 535 (2000); John G. Sprankling, Understanding Property Law 449–51 (2000); John G. Sprankling, *An Environmental Critique of Adverse Possession*, 79 Cornell L. Rev. 816 (1994); Margaret Jane Radin, *Time, Possession, and Alienation*, Wash. U. L. Q. 739 (1986); Stewart Sterk, *Neighbors in American Land Law*, 87 Colum. L. Rev. 55 (1987); Richard Posner, Economic Analysis of Law § 3.10, at 70 (3d ed. 1986); Thomas Merrill, *Property Rules, Liability Rules and Adverse Possession*, 79 N.W. L. Rev. 1122 (1984–85). For a particularly lucid synthesis and critique of these rationales, see Joseph William Singer, Property 155–62 (3d ed. 2010). For a critique of the first century of debate among Anglo-American legal scholars about adverse possession at common law, see John A. Lovett, *Disseisin, Doubt and Debate: Adverse Possession Scholarship in the United States* (1881–1986) 5 Tex. A&M L. Rev. 1 (2018).

An exposition of the rationale for acquisitive prescription from the civil law cannon is found in the following excerpt from Gabriel Baudry-Lacantinerie and Albert Tissier's illustrious French civil law treatise:

Gabriel Baudry-Lacantinerie & Albert Tissier

28 Traité théorique et pratique de Droit Civil Nos. 27–32, at 16–22
(4th ed., 1924) (trans. La. State Law Institute)

§ II. The Bases of Prescription

27. The first impression . . . is that of spoliation: the owner is deprived of his ownership, the creditor of this creditor's right. But we know in fact that prescription is an institution necessary for the sake of legal stability. The redactors put it at the end of the code since prescription consolidates all the rights established by the preceding titles.

There would be no stability without prescription. Owners would never be sure that they will keep their property; debtors would never be sure that they will not have to pay twice.

The reason no one would be certain to keep his property is that the proof of ownership would often be impossible. In order to prove my ownership and thereby prevail in an action in revendication against a usurper, it does not suffice for me to show that I have acquired by a title translative of ownership, such as sale, exchange, donation inter vivos or through a testament; I must also prove that my author was owner, for he could transfer ownership to me only if he had it himself. *Nemo dat quod non habet.* To prove the title of my author, I must show the titles of everybody through whose hands the property has passed before he acquired it. If there is one person in the chain who was not owner, he could not transfer the full title and none of his successors could acquire it. Prescription simplifies all this. It eases the burden of proof by freeing the claimant from having to go back to an era when often no trace of his title can be discovered. All he has to prove is that he or his predecessors have been in possession for thirty years. Prescription also comes to the rescue of the owner who lost his documentary title. The function of prescription does not seem less legitimate in this case than in the first one.

We have also said that, without prescription, a debtor who has paid would never be safe against another claim for payment. Indeed, the loss of the receipt or its deliberate destruction after a certain time makes it impossible for the debtor to prove that he has already paid, if the creditor comes again and demands a payment. Here, too, prescription will substitute for the missing document.

Thus, on the one hand, prescription consolidates or strengthens legitimate ownership titles which are not sufficient in themselves, or it replaces a lost documentary title; on the other hand it protects the debtor who has paid against the claim of a dishonest creditor who knows that the receipt has been lost or destroyed. Thus it gives security to individuals by protecting their patrimony against unjust claims. Here it is correct to say that prescription rests partially on a presumption of ownership or discharge. Domat states it in this manner: "All types of prescription which cause a right to be acquired or lost are based on the presumption that the person who enjoys a right must have some just title, without which he would not have been allowed to enjoy it for such a long period; that he who ceases to exercise some right has been deprived of it for some just cause; and that he who has failed to claim his debt for a long time has either been paid or has recognized that nothing is owed to him." Prescription then appears as providing evidence to support situations which have existed a long time, the legitimacy of which is being contested.

28. But all human institutions have some weakness. Prescription is no exception. In some cases it will make a usurper prevail over the real owner; or it will discharge a debtor who has not paid his debt. In these cases the thirty-year prescription results in spoliation of the owner or of the creditor. Is it not a revolting injustice?

Let us not hasten too much to feel sorry for this owner or creditor, or to damn the possessor or the debtor who has enriched himself. First, we can at least say that the owner or creditor has been guilty of gross negligence. Why has the former waited thirty years without revendicating his property? Did this long silence not authorize the usurper to believe that the owner had renounced his right and thus sanctioned the usurpation by doing nothing about it? Is it not correct to say as did Roman law "Vix es enim ut non videatur alienare qui patitur usucapi?" And what about the creditor? How to explain his long inactivity? Should the debtor not have thought after a certain time that the creditor had renounced his right? And if charges on real property are involved, is it not reasonable that they disappear if the failure to exercise them for a long time shows that they are not important for entitled party?

On the other hand, after the long prescriptive period has run, the possessor or debtor who thinks that he will never be disturbed, no doubt bases his budgeting on his present resources. Moreover, the possessor acquiring by prescription may have made substantial improvements. Would it be just in all cases to honor the belated claim of the owner or creditor? "The law," says Troplong, "exploits his silence. It finds in it an element of amnesty in favor of the person who through thirty uninterrupted years of work, activity, and perhaps worry, has sufficiently expiated the violation of an unclaimed right."

29. At any rate, even if prescription seems to lead in some rare cases to results contrary to equity, if it constitutes what Justinian called "impium praesidium," it can easily be forgiven in exchange for the great services it renders to society. Without it there would be no security in transactions, no stability in private estates, no peace among individuals, no order in the state. These were the thoughts which inspired the spokesman of the government when he stated, in the exposé of the legislative motives: "Of all civil law institutions, prescription is the most necessary for social order." At times, it can injure equity. But, in a larger sense, Bigot-Préameneu is right in saying that "in general, justice is done; an individual interest which might possibly be hurt must give way to the necessity of maintaining social order."

This is the true and main foundation of prescription. The concept of presumed acquisition or discharge, as well as of the renunciation of the title holder of the prescribed interest, are only secondary and accessory motives. Domat wrote with regard to the predominant motive of social interest: "If there were no other reason favoring prescription than public interest in assuring the tranquility of possessors, it would be just in order to prevent a continuing uncertainty about ownership of things." Laurent expressed the same opinion: "after a certain lapse of time, possession should become the base of right. This represents more than a social interest; it is a question of existence. Hence society is entitled more than anybody else to oppose an individual, because society exists only where property is assured; and this does not happen unless possession is made secure. The title of the owner himself is, in its origin, nothing more than possession which society has sanctioned by giving it the authority of law. If ownership can be based on possession, it can be also acquired by possession against one who has ceased to possess."

We can say with Cujas: "Usucapio damno est dominis, bono reipublicae." Cicero correctly called it "finis solicitudinis as periculi litium." It is also essential not to allow rights to be exercised indefinitely. "Let us imagine the state of a community where rights 10,000 years old could be claimed! This would be the main cause of trouble in matters of property. There would not be a single person or family outside the reach of an action which could put their social standing in question. This permanent state of insecurity would cause a continuous social upheaval. How could individuals and the community persist in such anarchy? Anybody who complains to have lost a right by prescription should be answered that the same institution has protected the obligations contracted by him or by his ancestors centuries ago. This is the compensation for the loss of right which affects a creditor: it generates the general security which his debtor counterclaims."

In terms of its social utility, prescription can be compared with the rule of res judicata. Their function is analogous. There comes a moment when it is necessary to say the last word, where the uncertainty of the law is more burdensome than injustice. "Everything must end," says Troplong; "the state has an interest in seeing that rights are not held in suspense for too long." Thiers wrote similarly, "it is necessary to have a fixed term whereby that which exists will be declared legitimate by the very fact that it exists; without this litigation would spread all over the face of the globe."

30. To stress the importance of prescription in the field of immovables, we have said that it comes to the help of owners who otherwise could not present a complete and definitive evidence of their title. In our opinion, prescription is the normal form of evidence of ownership. We should note that French decisional law is based on a different idea and goes somewhat against the analysis we have suggested above. Aubry and Rau summarize it very neatly: "If the claimant seeking revendication shows an ownership title and the defendant shows none, the claimant should be considered as having sufficiently shown his title, provided it is prior to the possession of the defendant . . . If both parties produce ownership titles which come from the same author, the priority is determined by the order of inscription of the titles, or by their dates . . . Finally, if the claimant shows no title supporting his action and simply invokes either an old possession, or a presumption based on the state of the

thing or some other circumstances, the judge must determine the admissibility of this proof as a justification for the claim by classifying the possession of the defendant as exclusive and well characterized, or as merely an enjoyment the nature of which does not constitute a genuine possession. In the first case, the presumption of ownership in favor of the defendant must prevail, no matter how serious are the factual circumstances in favor of the claimant. In the second case, the judge must balance the presumptions invoked by the two parties and uphold or reject the claims depending on this comparative analysis."

We think that this decisional doctrine can be criticized strictly on principles. But it is established and this is not the place to discuss it. It cannot be denied that it has filled one of the greatest gaps in our legislation. In fact, in a good legislative system, prescription is manifestly insufficient as a proof of ownership, for it requires laborious search. Vigilant owners ought to have easier means of establishing their title. Decisional law grappled with these inconveniences and has no doubt done a workable job in organizing a system of proof. But this was, in our opinion, the task of the legislator.

31. Moreover, it is interesting to observe that in systems where land registers have absolute probative force, the reason for the institution of acquisitive prescription is substantially reduced and may even disappear. In legal systems which have land registers, a very delicate problem is to determine the possible effects of prescription outside the record in the books or in opposition to it. . . .

33. A question which has ceased to be interesting, but which in the past strained the subtlety of many writers, is whether prescription comes from civil law or from natural law. Cujas taught that it is of civil law origin and contrary to natural law and the jus gentium. Grotius, de Ferriére and Pothier held the same opinion.

The opposite conclusion was upheld especially by Puffendorf, Vattel, Brunemann, d'Argentré, Dunod. Troplong repeated it under the Civil code. It allowed aliens to benefit by prescription in the same manner as citizens. The *Parlement* of Paris had already sanctioned this rule in the 18th cent.

It is not necessary to go further into this well-worn topic. It suffices to have shown that prescription is an institution generally necessary, on imperative grounds in any legal system. Ordinarily it conforms with equity; it is always dictated by public interest. Although it appears to be rather an institution of civil law, its essential purpose makes it available to aliens as well as to citizens. This is no longer disputed in France: prescription is not a civil-law right *stricto sensu* in terms of Art. 11.

Question

1. Which of the contemporary models of adverse possession are most analogous to Baudry-Lacantinerie and Tissier's justifications for acquisitive prescription in the civil law? Try mapping the modern models to Baudry-Lacantinerie and Tissier's justifications.

B. Thirty Year Acquisitive Prescription

The foundational codal provision governing thirty year acquisitive prescription for immovable property provides:

Art. 3486. Immovables; prescription of thirty years

> Ownership and other real rights in immovables may be acquired by the prescription of thirty years without the need of just title or possession in good faith.

La. Civ. Code art. 3486 (1982). The proposition advanced in Article 3486 is quite stark. A person may acquire ownership of immovable property through thirty years of uninterrupted possession alone, unconnected to any claim of title or state of mind. Louisiana law has recognized this mode of acquiring ownership from the moment of codification. The Digest of 1808 (in its imperfect English translation) provided:

> **Art. 65.** After thirty years, all actions either personal or real are prescribed against; and the person pleading prescription in that case, is not obliged to produce any color of title nor can it be alleged against him that he acted knavishly.

> **Art. 66.** Immovable estates may also be prescribed for, after thirty years possession, though thus possessed without any title and knavishly.

La. Civ. Code arts. 65–66 p. 486 (1808). Indeed, many of the earliest cases decided by the Louisiana Supreme Court involved assertions of thirty year acquisitive prescription regarding land granted to early settlers by the French and Spanish colonial governments prior to the cession of the Louisiana territory to the United States.

Thing Subject to Acquisitive Prescription: Several other articles in Book III of the Louisiana Civil Code are also directly relevant to thirty-year acquisitive prescription. First, recall from our discussion of *Todd v. State*, 465 So.2d 712 (La 1985) that the thing must be susceptible of prescription. Accordingly, thirty-year acquisitive prescription will only apply to immovable property qualifying as a "private thing" and not otherwise excluded from the reach of acquisitive prescription by special legislation. La. Civ. Code art. 3485 (1982). As we learned in *Band v. Audubon Park Commission*, 936 So.2d 841 (La. App. 4 Cir. 2006), a private thing owned by a political subdivision of the state could theoretically be subject to acquisitive prescription, but a public thing, such as a public road or a public park, is not. *See also* La. Rev. Stat. § 9:5804 (1926, amended 1950) (explaining how a municipality can prevent the running of acquisitive prescription with respect to any immovable property).

Possibility of Constructive Possession: Second, recall that constructive possession is only available to one who possesses by virtue of a title. La. Civ. Code art. 3426 (1982); La. Civ. Code art. 3487 rev. cmt. (b) (1982). The following article addresses this point in the context of thirty- year acquisitive prescription:

Art. 3487. Restriction as to extent of possession

For purposes of acquisitive prescription without title, possession extends only to that which has been actually possessed.

La. Civ. Code art. 3487 (1982). This article effectively means that in the absence of any title describing the land claimed, the possessor must possess inch by inch or within enclosures. *See, e.g., Saunders v. Hollis*, 17 So.3d 482, 484 (La. App. 3 Cir. 2009). If, however, a possessor in bad faith relies on some kind of title, constructive possession is theoretically possible in the context of thirty-year acquisitive prescription. *See* La. Civ. Code art. 3426 rev. cmt. (c) (1982); La. Civ. Code art. 3488 rev. cmt. (c) (1982). In other words, an adverse possessor who possesses some portion of larger tract with corporeal possession and in reliance on a title could extend his possession to the limits of the title even though the title is defective or even though the adverse possessor did not commence possession in good faith. La. Civ. Code art. 3426 rev. cmt. (c) (1982).

Context Matters: The revision comments to Article 3487 underscore a theme that should be familiar by now: "Actual possession is determined according to the nature of the property." La. Civ. Code art. 3487 rev. cmt. (c) (1982). The particular acts that will suffice to establish possession in any given case are always context specific. As the decisions in this chapter vividly illustrate, certain kinds of seasonal acts of corporeal possession may be sufficient to possess swamps or woodlands within visible boundaries, whereas more definitive acts of possession may be required to establish possession of a vacant urban lot. *Compare Secret Cove, LLC v. Thomas*, 862 So.2d 1010 (La. App. 1 Cir. 2003), *with Mai v. Floyd*, 951 So.2d 244 (La. App. 1 Cir. 2006).

Absence of Vices of Possession: Article 3488 tells us that "[t]he rules governing acquisitive prescription of ten years apply to the prescription of thirty years to the extent that their application is compatible with the prescription of thirty years." La. Civ. Code art. 3488 (1982). For present purposes, the two most important rules for ten-year acquisitive prescription applicable to thirty-year acquisitive prescription include the following:

Art. 3476. Attributes of possession

The possessor must have corporeal possession or civil possession preceded by corporeal possession to acquire a thing by prescription.

The possession must be continuous, uninterrupted, peaceable, public, and unequivocal.

Art. 3477. Precarious possession

Acquisitive prescription does not run in favor of a precarious possessor or his universal successor.

La. Civ. Code art. 3476–77 (1982). Article 3476 of the Louisiana Civil Code provides a list of positive attributes of corporeal or civil possession that must be present to count for ten or thirty year acquisitive prescription. As the revision comments indicate, this \provision means that possession that is "discontinuous, interrupted, violent or equivocal is vicious and has no legal effect," La. Civ. Code art. 3476, rev. cmt (b) (1982). Put even more simply. "possession must be free of vices." The vices of possession are stated in Articles 3435 and 3436:

Art. 3435. Vices of Possession

Possession that is violent, clandestine, discontinuous, or equivocal has no legal effect.

Art. 3436. Violent, clandestine, discontinuous, and equivocal possession

Possession is violent when it is acquired or maintained by violent acts. When the violence ceases, the possession ceases to be violent.

Possession is clandestine when it is not open or public, discontinuous when it is not exercised at regular intervals, and equivocal when there is ambiguity as to the intent of the possessor to own the thing.

La. Civ. Code arts. 3435–36 (1982). Consider these provisions as you read the following decisions. In each instance, ask yourself whether the evidence was clear that the acquisitive prescription claimants proved that their possession was free of the vices of possession. Was the possession continuous and uninterrupted, or was it discontinuous? Was the possession peaceful, or was it violent? Was the possession public, or was it clandestine? Was the possession unequivocal, or was it equivocal. Or (worse yet) was the possession merely precarious? Which of these adjectival pairs is most important for assuring that the record owner has some meaningful notice that another person is possessing its immovable property with the intent to possess as owner?

Brunson v. Hemmler

989 So.2d 246 (La. App. 2 Cir. 2008)

PEATROSS, Judge. Plaintiffs, Robert Lee Brunson, Lydia Mae Brunson and Barbara G. Cannon, filed a Petition for Declaratory Judgment seeking to be declared the owners of certain disputed property. Defendants, C. Peck Hayne, Frank B. Hayne, III, Emily Hayne Walker Mehaffie, William B. Rudolf as Trustee of the Mary Hayne Bailey Rudolf Trust, the Administrators of the Tulane Educational Fund and the Rectors and Visitor of University of Virginia, disputed Plaintiffs' claim. After a bench trial, the trial court rendered a Declaratory Judgment in favor of Plaintiffs. Defendants appeal from this adverse judgment. For the reasons set forth below, we affirm the decision of the trial court.

Facts

The disputed property is approximately 60 acres in three tracts, approximately 20 acres each (hereinafter referred to as Tracts 1–3) A fourth tract of approximately 20 acres, (herein referred to as Tract 4), is located just east of the contested Tracts 1–3. Together, the four tracts make up the north half of the northeast quarter of

Section 19. While only Tracts 1–3 are at issue in this case, the entire 80-acre tract is the subject of much of the testimony.

Plaintiffs sought a declaratory judgment seeking to be recognized as the owners of the disputed property under the doctrine of acquisitive prescription. Defendants, as the record title owners of the disputed property, filed a reconventional demand with their answer. Defendants claimed ownership of the approximately 80 acres described above.

Discussion

Ownership of immovable property may be acquired by the prescription of 30 years without the need of just title or possession in good faith. C.C. art. 3486. . . .

Thus, in the case *sub judice,* Plaintiffs would have acquired the disputed property through acquisitive prescription if they established that they and/or their ancestors in title had possessed the disputed property within bounds for 30 years. As mentioned above, the trial court determined that Plaintiffs had done so and we cannot say that its conclusion was manifestly erroneous.

According to the many witnesses of Plaintiffs, Jule Gilley, Sr., Myrtle Shipley Gilley and their children moved to a location near the 80-acre tract in 1936, and, shortly thereafter, began using the entire 80-acre tract for farming activities.

All three Plaintiffs testified at trial that they were raised in the area. Mrs. Cannon and Mrs. Brunson grew up in the Gilley home near the disputed property and recalled from their early memories that the disputed property was used by their father, Mr. Jules Gilley, Sr., for crops and farming and that he fenced it. Mrs. Cannon and Mrs. Brunson testified that the property was used by Mr. Gilley, from approximately the time he moved with his family near the disputed property in 1936, and had been continuously used by him, or his lessees, and then by Plaintiffs and their lessees, until the current lawsuit.

Plaintiff Robert Brunson testified that he assisted Mr. Gilley in constructing a fence around the property in 1938. He also testified that the entire disputed area was used for pasture, except for about ten acres in the eastern tract which was used for crops, and that, over time, Mr. Gilley continued to clear the wooded areas. Plaintiffs' other witnesses confirmed that, at the time of suit, the disputed property remained under fence and continued to be farmed and maintained under Mr. Gilley's control, and then later, Plaintiffs' control.

In contrast, Defendants offered the testimony of Defendant Hayne who testified that he went hunting on the property while he was growing up and that 1965 was the last time he was on the property. He testified that he never came across any fences on the property or saw any people farming the disputed property. Furthermore, he testified that, at that time, the property was wooded and he had leased the disputed property to a third party for hunting purposes in the 1980s and renewed the lease in 1995 and again in 2005.

From our review of the record, we cannot find that the trial court was manifestly erroneous or clearly wrong in finding that Plaintiffs and their ancestors in title possessed the property for over 30 years and that the possession was continuous, uninterrupted, peaceable, public and unequivocal. The trial court, therefore, was within its great discretion in accepting the testimony presented by Plaintiffs to the effect that the fence enclosed the disputed property and that the said fence had existed for more than 30 years, regardless of the testimony of Defendant Hayne to the contrary. We, therefore, affirm the decision of the trial court.

The mere fact that a non-owner has physical possession of the land provides sufficient notice to the record owner and the public at large that a non-owner intends to possess the property for himself as owner. The nature of the possession must be such that it gives the owner of the property notice that his property is in jeopardy and cannot be covert. The intent to possess as owner cannot be covert and must be express. The record shows that Plaintiffs and their ancestors in title openly fenced and possessed the property.

Conclusion

For the foregoing reasons, we affirm the judgment of the trial court declaring Plaintiffs, Robert Lee Brunson and Lydia Mae Brunson to be owners of Tracts 1 and 3, and Barbara G. Cannon to be owner of Tract 2.

Notes and Questions

1. Which of the rationales for acquisitive prescription discussed earlier are most applicable to the court's reasoning in *Brunson v. Hemmler*, 989 So.2d 246 (La. App. 2 Cir. 2008)? How significant was it that the only defendant to testify about the use of the disputed sixty-acre tract by the record owners was one of the Payne defendants and that this person could only recall visiting the property for the last time in 1965? How could two of the defendants, the Administrators of the Tulane Educational Fund and the Rectors and Visitor of University of Virginia, have exercised possession of the disputed property? How highly did they value the disputed property? Which parties in this dispute had the strongest reliance interests in the sixty acres?

2. Identify the plaintiffs' acts of possession the court considered important in *Brunson*. The plaintiffs testified that they fenced and farmed the land or maintained it for grazing cattle. The fence built by the plaintiffs' father, Jules Gilley, marked the limits of his claim of possession. Observe that the court determined that the plaintiffs' possession was not afflicted with any of the vices of possession that are listed in Article 3435 of the Civil Code and reiterated in Article 3476 in a more positive light. *Compare* La. Civ. Code art. 3435 (1982), *with* La. Civ. Code art. 3476 (1982). Do you think the plaintiffs' acts of possession were sufficient to warn a reasonably diligent record owner that another person was possessing their property with the intent to become its owner?

3. Why did the plaintiffs in *Brunson* assert their acquisitive prescription claim in the form of a declaratory judgment action? In the following case, the record owner

of a much smaller, but still valuable parcel of land in a highly developed, suburban neighborhood of New Orleans brought a declaratory judgment action seeking judicial recognition that the defendant, a possessor, had not acquired any ownership interests in the land.

Charles Tolmas, Inc. v. Lee

903 So.2d 661 (La. App. 5 Cir. 2005)

DALEY, Judge. The plaintiff, Charles Tolmas, Inc., in Liquidation, filed a declaratory action against Calvin Lee (hereinafter referred to as Lee), deceased, seeking a judgment declaring that Lee had no ownership interests in a certain portion of land. Lee responded with Exceptions of Liberative and/or Acquisitive Prescription and No Cause of Action. The trial court ruled in favor of Lee, finding Lee acquired the property in question by thirty year acquisitive prescription. For the reasons that follow, we affirm as amended.

Facts

The parties owned property adjacent to each other on Metairie Road. The Tolmas property is at the corner of Metairie Road and Tolkalon Place and the Lee property is located on the intersections of Metairie Road, Fagot Street, and Metairie Court. In 1951, Lee built a building on his property very near its boundary with the Tolmas property. Lee operated a dry cleaning business in the building from the time the building was completed until sometime in the 1970s. After that time, the building was divided in two and the front portion of the building continued to house a dry cleaning business, while the back of the building was rented to various tenants. From the time the building was completed, customers and employees of the business used a triangular shaped area on the west side of the building as a parking area. This area is located on the right side of the building facing the building. In the late 1980s a member of the Tolmas family contacted a member of the Lee family in reference to the Lee family's use of the property on the west side of the building. In 1998, the declaratory action that forms the basis of this appeal was filed requesting a judgment declaring that the Lees had no ownership interest or rights in the property in question, the location of the property line separating the properties, and ordering that the encroachments be removed. A hearing was held on the Lees' Exceptions of Liberative and Acquisitive Prescription.

At the hearing the parties stipulated to a survey which depicted a triangular piece of land that was being used by the Lees. The survey identified a sign post base located approximately four feet from the Lee building. This post held the sign for Lee's Cleaners and was placed there in cement when the building was constructed. The parties also stipulated that the property in dispute is titled in the name of plaintiff.

The Lees presented several witnesses who testified as to the Lee family's use and care of the property in question. Peter Hagen, III testified that he became a customer of Lee's Cleaners in 1954. He explained that he always parked on the right side of the building. Mr. Hagen further testified that there was an area of concrete and shells on the right side of the building that had been there since the building was built. This area was used for parking. Mr. Hagen also testified that when parades passed on Metairie Road the Lees would rope off the area to the right of the building for friends and family to park. He explained that the Lees cut the grass in the area just to the right of the parking area. The grass on the Tolmas vacant lot farther to the right was not cut regularly and often contained high weeds. Mr. Hagen testified that the cemented portion and gravel portion of the parking lot, as well as the area of grass cut by the Lees had remained the same size over the years.

Lyndel Brauninger testified that her parents were friends of the Lees and patronized their dry cleaning business. Her earliest recollection of the building was in the early 1960s. She identified a photograph of her mother standing on the side of the building in the area that the Lees roped off for family and friends for parades. Ms. Brauninger also identified doors on the right side of the building that were used by employees and deliveries to the building. She testified that awnings had always been over these doors. Ms. Brauninger testified that the concrete parking area had always been there and was always the same size. She explained that it was easy to determine where the Lee property ended because the grass next to the Lee property was always very high.

Laura Greco testified that she had known Patrick Lee, son of Calvin Lee since she was a teenager. She patronized the Lee's dry cleaning business and attended parades there. Ms. Greco testified that the area between the building and the telephone pole on the right side of the building was used for parking for the business. In the late 1980s, Ms. Greco was a tenant in the Lee building. The front door of her shop was on the right side of the building.

Patrick Lee testified that Lee's Cleaners had doors on the right side of the building. The center door was used for deliveries and employee's entrance. The back door was used for ventilation. Mr. Lee testified that the sign pole had been there since the building was constructed and the cement and shelled parking area was always in the same area. He explained that there was a clear distinction between the Lee property and the Tolmas property because the grass around the parking area was always cut while the grass on the Tolmas property was always high.

The Lees submitted three depositions into evidence. Eighty-year-old Allen Lee testified that he is Calvin Lee's brother. He testified that the Lee's Cleaners sign and the parking area to the right of the building had been there since the cleaners opened. He further testified that the concrete parking area was poured around the same time the building was built. Allen's wife, Helen, testified that she married her husband in 1946. Mrs. Lee testified that the sign and parking lot had been there as long as the building was there. Sandra Lee, daughter of Helen and Allen, testified that the parking area and sign had been there as long as she remembered.

Eighty-four-year-old Oscar Tolmas testified that he had always lived in the New Orleans area. He had a law office two blocks from the property in question and passed this area four to five times a week. Mr. Tolmas testified that there was a concrete area on the property that connected the sidewalks on Metairie Road and Fagot Street when his family acquired the property in 1944. He testified that the family never developed their property on the corner of Metairie Road and Tolkalon Place and that he did not care if the cleaner's customers parked on the area. He further testified that members of the church across the street also parked on his property.

Mr. Tolmas testified that in 1987 or 1988 he noticed that there were businesses opening in the Lee building that put up awnings and planters. He viewed these as encroachments of the property and contacted the Lee family. Mr. Tolmas explained that this was the first time he saw activity he perceived as encroachments on the Tolmas property. He further testified that the concrete and shelled areas had increased in size since that time. Mr. Tolmas stated that he was unsuccessful in locating the survey of the property performed when the purchase was made. Surveys from 1985 and 1988 were admitted into evidence. They depict a triangular shaped concrete area and a gravel or shelled area alongside the building. A comparison of the surveys indicates that the shelled parking area is larger in the 1988 survey than it is on the 1985 survey. Mr. Tolmas testified that the 1985 survey accurately reflected the condition of the property in 1968 (thirty years before the declaratory action was filed).

Dr. Hyman Tolmas, Oscar's brother, testified that he had an office two blocks away from the property in question for 51 years. He estimated that he passed the property anywhere from two to five times per week. Dr. Tolmas then stipulated that the remainder of this testimony would be as Oscar testified.

After taking the matter under advisement, the trial court found that since the Lees purchased the property in 1951 until the present, possession of the Lees had been open, continuous, unequivocal and uninterrupted. The court concluded that the Lees had acquired ownership of the entire triangular shaped portion property extending from the rear corner of the Lee property diagonally to the utility pole by acquisitive prescription under Civil Code Article 3486. This timely appeal followed.

Law and Discussion

On appeal, appellants argue that the Lees' possession of the property was not sufficient to acquire the property through acquisitive prescription. They contend that in order to establish possession as owners sufficient to acquire the property, the Lees needed to construct some type of enclosure around the property they illegally possessed. They argue that the only type of enclosure erected by the Lee family was to rope off the area for parades. Appellants contend this was insufficient because this was not a permanent enclosure.

Appellants go on to argue that the only permanent encroachment on the property is the concrete area on the rounded corner where Metairie Road intersects with Faggot [sic] Avenue. Appellants contend that this concrete area was present when the Tolmases purchased the property based on the testimony of Oscar and Hyman Tolmas. Appellants argue that the Lee witnesses did not testify that the concrete was poured when the building was built, only that the concrete was "always there."

Appellants further argue that the placement of the shells on the Tolmas property and the erection of a sign were not sufficient to establish possession with intent to own.

Civil Code Article 3486 states: "Ownership and other real rights in immovables may be acquired by the prescription of thirty years without the need of just title or possession in good faith." The party asserting acquisitive prescription has the burden of proving that his possession was actual, adverse, corporeal possession that is continuous, uninterrupted, public, unequivocal, and within visible bounds. C.C. art. 3476. Whether or not disputed property has been possessed for 30 years without interruption for the purposes of acquisitive prescription is a factual determination that will not be disturbed on appeal in the absence of manifest error. *McKoin v. Harper*, 36,533 (La. App. 2 Cir. 1/31/03), 836 So. 2d 1260, *writ denied* 2003-0662 (La. 5/2/03), 842 So. 2d 1104. The necessity of a fence or a wall is not required to show adverse possession; possession is governed by the nature or use of the land. *Cheramie v. Cheramie*, 391 So. 2d 1126 (La. 1980).

All of the Lee witnesses testified that the area to the west side of the Lee building had been used for parking since the building was erected. Both Oscar and Hyman Tolmas agreed that the area to the west of the building had been used for parking since the building was erected. The Tolmases testified that they knew the area was being used for parking by the Lees, but they did not complain because they were trying to be neighborly. The Tolmases testified that the 1985 survey that identified the cement and gravel parking area depicted the property as it appeared in 1968, thirty years before the Petition for Declaratory Judgment was filed.

The testimony and evidence at the hearing established that the Lees had been openly and publicly using the cement and gravel parking area since the construction of the building in 1951. Members of the Tolmas family were aware of the Lees use of this land, but made no formal attempt to stop use by the Lees until the filing of this declaratory action in 1998, some 47 years after the Lees began using this land. The trial court awarded the Lees the entire triangular portion of land from the rear corner of the Lee lot to the utility pole as depicted on joint stipulation two. However, we find that this was in error.

A comparison of the 1985 and 1988 surveys indicate that the gravel parking area expanded between the time of the 1985 survey and the 1988 survey. Additionally, roping off the entire disputed area for the enjoyment of the Lee family and friends for parade parties is insufficient to establish adverse possession of the entire portion. The evidence established that the Lee's Cleaners sign was placed the time the building was built in 1951 and that the side of the building adjacent to the Tolmas property was used continuously by the Lee family for parking since the building was erected in 1951. The 1988 survey indicated that the gravel parking area increased in size sometime between 1985 and 1988. Although the Lee witnesses testified that the Lee family cut the grass adjacent to the parking area extending from the rear corner of the Lee property to the utility pole, this is not sufficient to establish adverse possession of the entire area. *See, Antis v. Miller,* 524 So. 2d 71 (La. App. 3 Cir. 1988). Thus, we find the trial court erred in finding the Lee family acquired the entire portion of land as depicted in stipulation two. However, we find no error in the trial court's finding that the Lees acquired the concrete and gravel parking area depicted in the 1985 survey by thirty years acquisitive prescription pursuant to C.C. art. 3486.

Accordingly, the judgment of the trial court is amended to state that . . . Lee acquired the concrete and shelled area depicted on the west side of the property, as shown in the "survey of a portion of ground located in front of Tokalon Place or Kostmayer Subdivision Jefferson Parish, La." dated September 18, 1985 by BFM Corporation that was attached to plaintiff's Exhibit Three, by thirty year acquisitive prescription. The judgment of the trial court is affirmed as amended.

AFFIRMED IN PART; AMENDED IN PART

Notes and Questions

1. How are the acts of adverse possession in *Charles Tolmas, Inc. v. Lee,* 903 So.2d 661 (La. App. 5 Cir. 2005), different than those in *Brunson v. Hemmler,* 989 So.2d 246 (La. App. 2 Cir. 2008)? Do you believe that the acts of possession by the Lees were sufficient to apprise the record owners, the Tolmas family, or the public at large that someone else was possessing the triangular shaped parcel of land with the intent to own it? Remember that Calvin Lee did not have title to the land in dispute, but he did own the adjacent lot. Also recall that Article 3487 of the Civil Code provides that "[f]or purposes of acquisitive prescription without title, possession extends only to that which has been actually possessed." La. Civ. Code art. 3487 (1982).

2. How did Lee prove his actual possession? The Tolmas family argued that Lee needed to enclose the land in dispute to give notice of his claim of possession and that Lee had never actually done this. How did the court respond to this argument? Notice that the court was not impressed by Lee's practice of roping off some of the parking area next to his building for Mardi Gras parades, nor, for that matter, with grass cutting, even though many of the witnesses located the property line by referencing the areas of cut and uncut grass. Why were these facts seemingly unimportant to the court?

3. Consider the sources of testimony in both cases. Possession is a question of fact. Where else might one look to determine if, in fact, Calvin Lee had adversely possessed the parking lot for thirty years?

4. In *Charles Tolmas, Inc.,* the plaintiff argued that Lee was merely a precarious possessor, tolerated on the property in dispute because of the plaintiff's spirit of good neighborliness. How, if at all, did the court respond to this argument?

5. A precarious possessor acquires no rights of his own based on his detention of property because he possesses for or on behalf of the person who gave him

permission to be on the property. La. Civ. Code art. 3437 (1982). According to Article 3477 of the Louisiana Civil Code, "[a]cquisitive prescription does not run in favor of a precarious possessor or his universal successor." La. Civ. Code art. 3477 (1982). Remember, however, that a possessor is generally "presumed to intend to possess as owner unless he began to possess in the name of and for another." La. Civ. Code art. 3427 (1982). In 2015, the Louisiana Supreme Court handed down a controversial decision that has injected considerable uncertainty into the analysis of precarious possession regardless of whether ownership of land or a servitude on land is claimed by acquisitive prescription. *See Boudreaux v. Cummings*, 167 So.3d 559 (La. 2015) (holding that a neighbor who uses a portion of his neighbor's land for a limited purpose such as access to a road is presumed to be possessing with the tacit or implied consent of the record owner). We feature the entire *Boudreaux* decision in the context of acquisitive prescription of predial servitudes. For a detailed exposition of the law of precarious possession, a critique of *Boudreaux*, and suggestions for reform, see John A. Lovett, *Precarious Possession*, 77 La. L. Rev. 617 (2017).

Keep in mind that a precarious possessor (other than a co-owner) who wishes to become an adverse possessor can begin the process of acquisitive prescription by giving actual notice of his intent to possess for himself *as owner*. Two articles of the Civil Code provide us with rules governing this process. The most directly relevant is Article 3478.

Art. 3478. Termination of Precarious Possession; commencement of possession

A co-owner, or his universal successor, may commence to prescribe when he demonstrates by overt and unambiguous acts sufficient to give notice to his co-owner that he intends to possess the property for himself. The acquisition and recordation of a title from a person other than a co-owner thus may mark the commencement of prescription.

Any other precarious possessor, or his universal successor, may commence to prescribe when he gives actual notice to the person on whose behalf he is possessing that he intends to possess for himself.

La. Civ. Code art. 3478 (1982). Article 3439 offers identical rules for the termination of precarious possession in other contexts:

Art. 3439. Termination of precarious possession

A co-owner, or his universal successor, commences to possess for himself when he demonstrates this intent by overt and unambiguous acts sufficient to give notice to his co-owner.

Any other precarious possessor, or his universal successor, commences to possess for himself when he gives actual notice of this intent to the person on whose behalf he is possessing.

La. Civ. Code art. 3439 (1982). Consider whether or not the requisite notice of intent to terminate precarious possession was given in the following case.

Memorial Hall Museum, Inc. v. University of New Orleans Foundation

847 So.2d 625 (La. App. 4 Cir. 2003)

ARMSTRONG, Judge. This case is a dispute over the ownership of certain land and the building thereon in New Orleans. The appellant is the Memorial Hall Museum, Inc. ("MHMI"). The appellee is the University of New Orleans Foundation ("UNO Foundation"). The trial court found that the property in question is owned by the UNO Foundation rather than by the MHMI. We agree with the trial court that the UNO Foundation owns the property in question. Therefore, we will affirm.

The MHMI argues that the property (informally referred to as the "Confederate Museum") was donated to its predecessor, the Louisiana Historical Association, or that it and/or the Louisiana Historical Association acquired title by acquisitive prescription. The UNO Foundation argues that the ownership of the property was not donated, that the MHMI did not acquire ownership by acquisitive prescription, and that, if title was acquired by the MHMI by acquisitive prescription, then the MHMI renounced that prescription. The trial court granted summary judgment in favor of the UNO Foundation as to all three issues and held that the ownership of the property was not donated, that there was no acquisitive prescription and, if there was acquisitive prescription, it was renounced. We agree with the trial court that ownership of the property was not donated and that title was not acquired by acquisitive prescription. We need not and do not address renunciation of acquisitive prescription.

The Howard Memorial Library Association ("HMLA"), the ancestor in title to the UNO Foundation, was organized in New Orleans in the late Nineteenth Century to administer the Howard Memorial Library in New Orleans. The library was housed on property in New Orleans. The library included a collection of materials related to the Confederacy. In order to house that collection, Frank T. Howard had constructed an annex next to the library. That annex, now known as the Confederate Museum, is the property at issue in the present case.

A group known as the Louisiana Historical Association ("LHA"), the predecessor to the MHMI, was seeking a place to house a collection of materials related to the Confederacy. Frank T. Howard decided to let the LHA use the annex building to house the LHA's collection. He gave a speech in 1891 in which he stated:

> It is with deep satisfaction that I perform the act of formally putting into your possession the Building, which, while it is an Adjunct of the Howard Memorial Library Association, is to be set apart forever for the use of your organization.

Mr. Howard wrote down the speech and gave it to the LHA.

Appellant MHMI argues that, by giving the speech, writing it down, and giving the writing to the LHA, Mr. Howard donated the ownership of the annex building to the LHA. We disagree. Mr. Howard did not say in the speech that he was donating the ownership of the building to the LHA. He spoke only of putting the LHA into "possession" of the building and of the building being for the "use" of the LHA. In short, Mr. Howard stated only that he would allow the LHA to use the building forever. The parties dispute as to exactly what rights, if any, Mr. Howard gave to the LHA. We need not, and do not, decide such issues. The present appeal concerns ownership of the property and it is apparent that Mr. Howard did not state that he was giving ownership of the annex building to the LHA. Thus, the trial court was correct in finding that ownership of the building was not donated to the LHA.

Because Mr. Howard's 1891 speech did not donate ownership of the property to the LHA, ten year acquisitive prescription is not applicable. See La. Civ. Code art. 3474 (1870).

As the LHA took possession of the property in 1891, thirty year acquisitive prescription could have begun running at that time, and the LHA could have acquired title as early as 1921, if the LHA openly, uninterruptedly and unequivocally possessed the property as owner for thirty years. La. Civ. Code art. 3475 (1870); La. Civ. Code art. 3500 (1870). However, there is a great deal of undisputed evidence that, far from unequivocally asserting ownership of the property, the LHA recognized that the HMLA was the owner of the property. In 1912, at a meeting of the LHA's Board of Governors, a committee appointed to investigate the status of the property concluded that the property belonged to the HMLA. At a March 4, 1931 meeting attended by the LHA and the HMLA members, an attorney retained by the LHA determined that the LHA had no legal claim to the property.

Appellant MHMI argues that a 1931 agreement, whereby the LHA allowed the HMLA to use part of the museum building, constituted an act of ownership by the LHA, recognized by the HMLA, and started the running of thirty year acquisitive prescription so that LHA acquired title to the property in 1961. We disagree. The LHA was given the right to use all of the building in 1891 and simply, in turn, gave some of that right to the HMLA in 1931. Both the LHA and the HMLA were of the understanding, in 1931, that the LHA had the right to use the entire building and so the fact that they entered into an agreement allowing the HMLA to use part of the building does not indicate that the LHA or the HMLA believed that the LHA was the owner of the building.

The MHMI points to a 1931 resolution of the LHA whereby the LHA "denied" the claim of HMLA to the property and thus, presumably, implied that the LHA owned the property. However, there is no evidence that this resolution was communicated to the HMLA or that there was any outward change in the routine of the LHA's use of the property. Thus, there is no evidence that the LHA began to openly and unequivocally possess the property "as owner" in 1931. Accordingly, not only is there no evidence that the LHA ever possessed the property openly and unequivocally as owner for any thirty year period, the evidence to the contrary is undisputed.

In sum, the property was not donated by Mr. Howard to the MHMI's predecessor, the LHA, and the LHA and the MHMI never acquired ownership of the property by acquisitive prescription. Therefore, the HMLA never lost ownership of the property until it conveyed ownership of the property, by deed, to the UNO Foundation. Consequently, the UNO Foundation is the owner of the property.

For the foregoing reasons, we affirm the judgment of the trial court.

AFFIRMED.

Notes and Questions

1. In *MHMI v. UNO Foundation*, 847 So.2d 625 (La. App. 4 Cir. 2003), the court distinguishes between the act of allowing another person to take physical possession of property and the act of transferring ownership. A precarious possessor—one who takes physical possession for or on behalf of another person—cannot acquire ownership by prescription without first giving notice to the person for whom he possesses. What notice did Memorial Hall Museum, Inc. (MHMI) claim that its predecessor, the Louisiana Historical Association (LHA), gave of its intent to possess as owner? Why were the 1931 agreement between the LHA and the Howard Memorial Library Association (HMLA) and the 1931 resolution of the LHA board both insufficient for purposes of giving notice of LHA's intent to possess as owner? The court further points out that the LHA interrupted any initial acquisitive prescription it might have begun by acknowledging the ownership of the HMLA in 1912 and again in 1931. Do you agree?

2. Notice that the court addressed the question of whether HMLA donated the building known as the "annex" to the LHA in 1891. Even if Frank T. Howard had stated in his speech of that year that he (or the HMLA) intended to transfer ownership of the building to the LHA, would his speech have been sufficient to constitute an effective donation? What formalities are required for an effective donation of immovable property? How is such a donation made effective against a third person? Is the UNO Foundation a third party in this case?

3. Even if MHMI had proven that the LHA had given effective actual notice of its intent to possess "the annex" as owner, can you think of any other impediments to a successful acquisitive prescription claim that the court did not consider? Is the annex a part of another building or is it a separate, free-standing building? If it is part of a building, what impact would Article 492 of the Civil Code have? *See* La. Civ. Code art. 492 rev. cmt. (a) (1979).

4. Louisiana has enacted a detailed framework allowing a person who takes possession of immovable property that has been declared or certified blighted, after an administrative hearing, in cities with populations over 300,000, to acquire ownership of the property through a three year acquisitive prescription without just title or good faith, if the possessor provides notice in the public records and at the actual location of the property of his intentions and complies with a host of other regulatory requirements. *See* La. Rev. Stat. § 9:5633 (2001, amended 2003, 2006, and 2011);

Ferrari v. Nola Renewal Group, LLC, 194 So.3d 1246 (La. App. 4 Cir. 2016). Because the regulatory framework for this three-year acquisitive prescription of blighted immovables is so complex, relatively few would-be adverse possessors have taken advantage of it. Moreover, owners have been successful with petitory actions against the prescriber. Difficult questions of liabilities and reimbursements also arise. In one recent decision, the court remarked that the blighted property acquisitive prescription statute "is complex and requires strict compliance, as the penalty for non-compliance results in the possessor losing all of his rights under the statute, as well as reimbursement of the money invested." *Moledoux v. Skipper*, 104 So.3d 585, 590 (La. App. 4 Cir. 2012), *writ denied*, 108 So.3d 85 (La. 2012). In *Moledeaux*, the court held, *inter alia*, that: (1) the trial court cannot bypass Section 5633(E)(4) of the statute, in contents and process, for purposes of evaluating expenditures for reimbursable items from the statutory list; (2) under Section 5633(D) the incumbent prescriber is shielded from tortious liability for the demolition of improvements on or after the date of his or her corporeal possession; and (3) Section 5633(E)(21) contemplates reimbursement for attorney fees. *Id.* at. 590–92.

C. Ten-Year Acquisitive Prescription for Immovables

At times, a transferee who takes possession of an immovable believes she is its owner but is not the owner of the property at all or may only own a part of it because of a defect in the conveyancing process. A mistake in the property description in the act of transfer may result in her possessing a strip of land that is not included in her record title. The property may have been previously owned by two or more persons, but only one of the co-owners executed the act transferring the property. In the case of a sale, the purported vendor may not have been the owner of the property at the time of the sale because the property had been previously conveyed to another person. This could occur because of an innocent mistake on the part of the purported vendor or because of outright fraud.

These kinds of title defects can go unnoticed for years. An unsuspecting transferee may take possession of immovable property, make expensive improvements on it and in other ways occupy it as owner without knowing of the defects. Ten-year acquisitive prescription is designed to cure these kinds of conveyancing errors and protect purchasers and other transferees who take possession of immovable property in a good faith belief that they are acquiring the property from a previous owner through a juridical act translative of ownership.

Ten-year acquisitive prescription allows a person possessing an immovable to acquire ownership or real rights in the immovable property when four requirements are met: (1) the claimant possesses the immovable for ten years; (2) by virtue of a just title; (3) the claimant's possession commenced in good faith; and (4) the thing itself is susceptible of acquisitive prescription. La. Civ. Code arts. 3473, 3475, 3482 (1982).

1. Ten Years of Possession

The ten-year acquisitive prescriptive period begins on the day after the possessor takes possession of the immovable as owner. *See* La. Civ. Code art. 3454 (1982) ("In computing a prescriptive period, the day that marks the commencement of prescription is not counted.") The ten years of possession can include corporeal possession, or civil possession preceded by corporeal possession by the prescriber or his ancestor. A person can take or continue corporeal possession through a precarious possessor. When possessing by virtue of a title, the possessor is deemed to be in constructive possession within the limits of the title.

We will detail the computation rules governing prescription along with rules governing interruption and suspension of prescription in the final portion of this chapter. For now, simply note that when a prescriptive period consists of one or more years, "prescription accrues upon the expiration of the day of the last year that corresponds with the date of the commencement of possession." La. Civ. Code art. 3456 (1982).

Consider the following example. Chauncey purchased a house and lot on February 3, 2000. His act of sale purported to transfer the entire house and lot. At the time of the purchase, he was unaware that the property was co-owned by three individuals and that he purchased from only one of the three owners. Chauncey moved into the house that same day and has been in possession adversely vis-à-vis the other two co-owners since his purchase. When he purchased the property, Chauncey acquired only a one-third interest in the property, but on February 3, 2010, at the end of the day, he became the owner of the entire house and lot. *See* La. Civ. Code art. 3484 rev. cmt. (b) (1982).

We have previously studied the attributes of possession that are elaborated in the second paragraph of Article 3476 of the Civil Code: possession must be "continuous, uninterrupted, peaceable, public and unequivocal." La. Civ. Code art. 3476 (1982). The same qualities of possession apply for a possessor to acquire ownership of an immovable or a real right in an immovable by acquisitive prescription. Crucially, though, the required length of possession is shorter only if *both* of the following two requisites, just title and good faith, are present.

2. Just Title

The Civil Code defines a just title for purposes of acquisitive prescription in a single article:

Art. 3483. Just title

A just title is a juridical act, such as a sale, exchange, or donation, sufficient to transfer ownership or another real right. The act must be written, valid in form, and filed for registry in the conveyance records of the parish in which the immovable is situated.

La. Civ. Code art. 3483 (1982). We recommend that you study the revision comments to this dense article, as they help illustrate the many components of a just title. An act constituting a just title would be a fully valid juridical act conveying ownership or establishing another real right, "if it had been executed by the true owner." La. Civ. Code art. 3483 rev. cmt. (b) (1982). A just title frequently originates from a person who honestly believes he is the owner of the property being conveyed, but who, for various reasons, is not the owner or does not own all of the property described in the act.

A just title must be a juridical act intended to have legal consequences. It must further be "*translative* of ownership or another real right, such as a sale, exchange, or donation." *Id*. rev. cmt. (b) (emphasis in original). An act *declarative* of ownership, like a judgment or partition, is not a just title. Nor is an act that transfers use of a thing, like a lease or loan. *Id*. Neither is an act that grants a contingent right to claim property, such as a mortgage.

Although the *translative* nature of the act is the most important requisite for a just title, the other requirements spelled out in Article 3483 should not be overlooked. The act must be "written." Thus, an oral transfer will not constitute a just title for purposes of ten-year acquisitive prescription of immovables. La. Civ. Code art. 3483 rev. cmt. (c) (1982). The act must be "in valid form." If the title is a sale of an immovable, it must be either an authentic act or an act under private signature. *See* La. Civ. Code art. 1839 (1984). If the title is a donation of an immovable, it must be in the form of an authentic act. La. Civ. Code art. 1541 (2008); La. Civ. Code art. 3483 rev. cmt. (c) (1982).

The 1982 revision of this article added the requirement that the act must be "filed for registry in the conveyance records of the parish in which the immovable property is situated." La. Civ. Code art. 3483 (1982). As the revision comments explain, this final requirement of recordation must be fulfilled *before* prescription can begin to run, even if the good faith possessor takes possession prior to recordation of the act. *Id*. rev. cmt. (d) (1982). Both possession and recordation of the just title must be in place before ten year acquisitive prescription can begin to accrue.

The concept of just title is also crucial in helping us understand how possession can be transferred from one possessor, a person called "the author" or "ancestor in title," to a subsequent possessor who wishes to "tack" his possession to that of his predecessor for purposes of combining periods of possession. As the comments to Article 3483 explain, tacking is allowed when the subsequent possessor possesses under a just title, whether that possessor is a "universal or particular successor." La. Civ. Code art. 3483 rev. cmt. (f) (1982). Tacking presupposes some kind of "juridical link" between the author and his successor. *Id*. In the case of a *particular successor*, the link is the act that specifically purports to transfer ownership of some particular property, like an act of sale, a donation inter vivos or mortis causa, or an act of exchange. In the case of a *universal successor*, the successor literally steps into the shoes of the author's own title; there really is no new title. The universal successor takes all the advantages and shortcomings of the author's title. *See generally* La. Civ. Code art. 3506(28).

Consider the following decision, which addresses all of the elements relevant to ten-year acquisitive prescription. Pay particular attention to the court's treatment of whether the land in controversy was subject to a claim of prescription in the first place and the interrelationship between just title and good faith when the act alleged to constitute a just title is a "quitclaim deed"—an act that transfers whatever interests the grantor may have in the property, without warranting that the grantor has good title to the property or has any title at all. Article 2502 of the Civil Code defines a quitclaim deed and addresses its effects:

Art. 2502. Transfer of rights to a thing

A person may transfer to another whatever rights to a thing he may then have, without warranting the existence of any such rights. In such a case the transferor does not owe restitution of the price to the transferee in case of eviction, nor may that transfer be rescinded for lesion.

Such a transfer does not give rise to a presumption of bad faith on the part of the transferor and is a just title for the purposes of acquisitive prescription. . . .

La. Civ. Code art. 2502 (1993). Study the revision comments to Article 2502 carefully. They provide useful insights into how courts might address quitclaim deeds in the context of ten year acquisitive prescription disputes. After your review of the revision comments study the decision below.

Cantrelle v. Gaude

700 So.2d 523 (La. App. 5 Cir. 1997)

GOTHARD, Judge. This is a property dispute between two neighbors in Lafitte. Plaintiffs, Patricia and Edward Cantrelle, Sr., began the action by filing suit in Jefferson Parish District Court seeking damages and injunctive relief. In the petition, the Cantrelles assert that defendants herein, Danny P. Gaude and Numa Marie Melancon, are trespassing on, and have blocked access to, a portion of plaintiffs' property causing damage and destruction to the property. . . . [P]laintiffs assert their ownership of the property by virtue of an act of sale dated September 21, 1990, Jefferson Parish Ordinance # 2934 adopted November 2, 1955, and through acquisitive prescription of ten and/or thirty years.

Defendants, Danny Gaude and Numa Melancon, filed an answer and reconventional demand in which they assert that the property in question is public property and seek damages for wrongful issuance of injunctive relief. . . .

. . . Evidence contained in the record shows that . . . Upperline Street, which intersects Shell Road and runs to Bayou Barataria, was dedicated as a public, forty-foot roadway by the original owner of the property, Isidore Fisher, in 1913. Levee Road, which runs along the bayou, begins at Upperline Street. . . .

The record also contains a survey of the area done in 1953 by Civil Engineer, H.E. Landry, which shows the heirs of Isidore Fisher re-subdivided the land at that time. . . .

In 1955, Jefferson Parish executed ordinance # 2934 which closed that part of Upperline Street "commencing at its southeastern intersection with the Shell Road, as shown on said [1953] plan, and ending at its northwestern intersection with the Public Levee and Road, also set out on the said [1953] plan, on the ground that same has actually been abandoned and is no longer needed for public use". That ordinance was never recorded in the Jefferson Parish records.

In 1975, Robert Gaude purchased land fronting Bayou Barataria on the opposite side of the former Upperline Street. . . .

In 1982 the Fisher heirs sold to Carmela Schieffler, by quitclaim deed, Lot 1 and;

> all of that portion of land which formerly constituted Upperline Street abutting Lot No. One (1) but which was retroceded to the owners of Lot No. One (1) by ordinance No. 2934 adopted by the Jefferson Parish Police Jury, November 2, 1995, closing that part of Upperline Street or Public Road situated in Barataria in the Isidore Fisher Subdivision # 1, commencing at its Southeastern intersection with the Western line of the Shell Road, and extending from that point to its intersection with the line of the public levee or road fronting on Bayou Barataria, all of the above as shown on map of H.E. Landry, Civil Engineer, dated November 4, 1953, having been actually abandoned and no longer needed for public use as a public road.

In 1990 Mrs. Schieffler sold the above property to her daughter and son-in-law, Patricia Schieffler and Edward Cantrelle, Sr., plaintiffs herein. . . . Thus, it appears that all of the former Upperline Street was included in the sale from the Fisher heirs to Schieffler. However, it appears that the Cantrelles only fenced the area subdivided as the original Lot 1 leaving the excess of the former Upperline Street, a strip of about 7 feet, open. Defendants have fenced their property up to the property line, thus creating the alleyway between the two adjacent properties. It is that alleyway which is the focus of this action.

It appears that both parties used and maintained the alleyway by cutting the grass until sometime in 1994 when Mr. Cantrelle blocked off the alleyway with a chain and no trespassing signs. He stated that his intent was to prevent motorcyclists from using it as an egress from Levee Road which ended at that point. That action apparently caused friction between the neighbors and the Cantrelles filed this suit to establish ownership of the alleyway. After a trial on the merits, the trial court divided the disputed land in half, giving each party 3 ½ feet of the alleyway.

In the dispute over the alleyway, the Cantrelles claim ownership. They argue that the 1955 ordinance abandoning a portion of Upperline Street is valid; therefore, the act of sale transferring the property to their ancestor in title, Mrs. Schieffler, is definitive of ownership. They further argue that the entire width of former

Upperline Street from Shell Road to the bayou, including the alleyway, was acquired by them in 1982 by virtue of the act of sale from Mrs. Schieffler. In the alternative, they argue that they acquired the entire portion of former Upperline Street, including the alleyway, by acquisitive prescription.

The defendants argue the ordinance was invalid and without effect since it was never recorded in the parish records. Therefore, the alleyway is public property, which they are entitled to use, and not the private property of the Cantrelles.

In order to resolve this dispute, we must first consider the validity of the 1955 ordinance. LSA-R.S. 48:701 provides:

> The parish governing authorities and municipal corporations of the state, except the parish of Orleans, may revoke and set aside the dedication of all roads, streets, and alleyways laid out and dedicated to public use within the respective limits, when the roads, streets, and alleyways have been abandoned or are no longer needed for public purposes.

> Upon such revocation, all of the soil covered by and embraced in the roads, streets, or alleyways up to the center line thereof, shall revert to the then present owner or owners of the land contiguous thereto. . . .

Recently the Louisiana Supreme Court has ruled that a formal act is necessary to revoke a statutorily dedicated public roadway. *State Dept. of Transp. v. Scramuzza*, 96-1796, 96-1820, 692 So.2d 1024 (La.4/8/97). The ordinance in question meets that requirement and evidences a determination by the police jury that the roadway is no longer needed for public purposes. Such a determination will not be disturbed absent an abuse of discretion. *Caz-Perk Realty, Inc. v. Police Jury of Parish of East Baton Rouge*, 207 La. 796, 22 So.2d 121, 122 (1945). Because no showing of an abuse of discretion has been made, we find that the ordinance in question effectively declared the road to be abandoned. That section of the roadway, although dedicated in 1913 as a public road by the owners of the land, was never actually constructed and was formally abandoned by parish ordinance in 1955.

We are not persuaded by defendants' argument that the failure to record the ordinance renders it invalid. Such failure speaks to its effect on third parties, not its validity. We recognize that the failure to record the ordinance in the parish conveyance office may not adversely affect the rights of third parties who rely to their detriment on public records. *Martin v. Fuller, on rehearing*, 214 La. 404, 37 So.2d 851 (1948). However, we do not find any such detrimental reliance in this case. On the contrary, should we invalidate the ordinance, the third party purchaser who relied on the ordinance for ownership would be harmed.

Normally, by operation of law, property abandoned in such a way would be divided equally between the contiguous land owners, giving the ancestors in title to both the plaintiffs and the defendants each 20 feet of the proposed roadway. LSA-R.S. 48:701. However, in this case it appears that the entire 40 feet was claimed by the plaintiffs' ancestors in title, the Fishers, who owned the property before it was subdivided. There is no indication in the record that anyone disputed that claim until the dispute over the alleyway at issue herein developed among the parties to this suit.

The ordinance revoking the dedication of the public road changed the character of the land from public to private property subject to acquisitive prescription pursuant to LSA-C.C. art. 3485. Therefore, we find no relevance in defendants' argument that public land is not amenable to acquisitive prescription. The issue is not whether the plaintiffs have acquired ownership of a forty-foot public roadway from the parish, but rather whether they have acquired ownership of a twenty-foot strip of land belonging to the contiguous land owner upon the abandonment of the public road.

. . . .

Possession

Possession for purposes of acquisitive prescription must be "continuous, uninterrupted, peaceable, public and unequivocal". LSA-C.C. art. 3476. With the exception of the alleyway, possession of the abandoned roadway by the Cantrelles is not disputed by the defendants. The area is fenced and used exclusively by Mrs. Schieffler and the Cantrelles. Evidence in the record shows that the possessor has been in peaceful possession of the property the entire time since the purchase of the property in 1982, with the exception of a period of about six months in which Mrs. Schieffler was too ill to live alone.

When one possesses under just title, possession as to any part of the immovable constitutes constructive possession as to those parts under such title that have not been actually possessed. LSA-C.C. art. 3426; *Harry Bourg Corp. v. Punch*, 94-1557 (La. App. 1 Cir. 4/7/95), 653 So.2d 1322. Thus, even though the alleyway has not been fenced, it has been constructively possessed by virtue of its inclusion in the title and the evidence that Mrs. Schieffler helped to maintain the alleyway as long as her health permitted.

Just Title

LSA-C.C. art. 3483 provides:

> A just title is a juridical act, such as a sale, exchange, or donation, sufficient to transfer ownership or another real right. The act must be written, valid in form, and filed for registry in the conveyance records of the parish in which the immovable is situated.

A title is just for purposes of acquisitive prescription when the deed is regular in form, is valid on its face, and would convey the property if executed by the owner. *O'Brien v. Alcus Lands Partnership Trust*, 577 So.2d 1094, 1097 (La. App. 1st Cir. 1991). The title relied upon by one seeking to establish ten year acquisitive prescription must sufficiently describe the property so as to transfer its ownership. One must be able to identify and locate the property from the description in the deed itself or from other evidence which appears in the public records. *Id.; Harry Bourg Corp. v. Punch*, supra. This is necessary because one cannot by the prescription of ten years acquire property not embraced within the title upon which the plea of prescription is founded. *Honeycutt v. Bourg*, 588 So.2d 1204, 1207 (La. App. 1 Cir. 1991); *Ensenat v. Edgecombe*, 95-0641, 95-0642 (La. App. 4 Cir. 5/15/96), 677 So.2d 138, 143.

The facts show that in 1982 the heirs of the original owner of the property sold, by quit claim deed to plaintiffs' ancestor in title, immovable property which included Lot One and;

> "all that portion of land which formerly constituted Upperline Street abutting said Lot No. One (1) but which was retroceded to the owners of said Lot No. One (1) by ordinance No. 2934 adopted by the Jefferson Parish Police Jury, November 2, 1995, closing that part of Upperline Street or Public Road situated in Barataria in the Isidore Fisher Subdivision # 1".

Thus, the quit claim deed is translative of title of the entire abandoned roadway including the alleyway at issue herein. Because title to the entire area vested in Mrs. Schieffler, it was transferred to the Cantrelles in the 1990 transfer.

Good Faith

The next issue for our consideration is whether plaintiffs are good faith possessors. Good faith is presumed by operation of LSA-C.C. art. 3481. LSA-C.C. art. 3480 defines good faith necessary for ten year acquisitive prescription as follows:

> For purposes of acquisitive prescription, a possessor is in good faith when he reasonably believes, in light of objective considerations, that he is owner of the thing he possesses.

That article became effective January 1, 1983, and is a codification of prevailing jurisprudence which provided that good faith of the possessor should be determined in light of objective considerations. *Phillips v. Parker*, 483 So.2d 972 (La. 1986). While the transference of property by quit claim deed may be suggestive of knowledge of title defects which may rebut the presumed good faith of the purchaser, it is not conclusive. The age and nature of the title defect, and other such factors bearing on the likelihood of discovery, are also relevant to the determination. *Id.*

The contiguous property owner was entitled to one-half of the revoked roadway at the time of abandonment of Upperline Street in 1955, by operation of law. LSA-R.S. 48:701. Thus the defect, inclusion in the title of the contiguous property owner's 20 feet of retroceded property, is not readily obvious as evidenced by the fact that even the property owner whose rights were originally infringed upon was apparently unaware of the infringement. Further, the property was purchased by Mrs. Schieffler, a widow who was unable to read or write. Mrs. Schieffler lived on the property until some time in 1989, when she was unable to continue living alone. Shortly afterward she transferred ownership of the property to her daughter and son-in-law, the Cantrelles. It appears that no title examination was made in either transfer. We find no evidence in the record which successfully rebuts the presumption of good faith afforded the titled owners by article 3481. Under these circumstances we find that the plaintiffs and their ancestor in title were in good faith for purposes of acquisitive prescription.

Considering the evidence presented and the applicable law, we find that the Cantrelles are the legal owners of the entire property described in the title filed in the parish records, including the alleyway at issue herein. However, our inquiry does not end at that determination. For the following reasons, we find that a predial servitude exists on the alleyway in favor of the defendants. . . .

Defendants further ask that this court condemn plaintiffs to pay all costs of proceedings in both the trial court and this court. Because we find valid legal arguments on both sides, we order each party to bear his own trial and appeal costs.

JUDGMENT REVERSED IN PART, AFFIRMED IN PART AND AMENDED.

Notes and Questions

1. In *Cantrelle v. Gaude*, 700 So.2d 523 (La. App. 5 Cir. 1997), the court held that the quitclaim deed granted by the Fisher heirs to Carmella Schieffler could serve as a just title for purposes of the plaintiffs' ten year acquisitive prescription claim. Do you see why? Would you want to know more about the transfer from Mrs. Schieffler to the Cantrelles?

2. A just title is a juridical act that has no apparent defects. It should look like an act that transfers ownership. If it purports to be an act of sale, for instance, it should show the names of the vendor and vendee, a description of the property, language of conveyance, and an effective date. The act may be defective and convey nothing, but it should have no defects *on its face*; it should not be *patently defective*.

3. In considering whether a person asserting ten-year acquisitive prescription has established a just title, courts examine juridical acts carefully. The act translative of ownership that a prescriber produces must describe the precise property that the claimant has possessed so that it can be identified and located from the description. The description must fully appear within the four corners of the deed, or the deed should refer to a map or plat so that the location of the property is clear. Otherwise, courts routinely hold that the act is not a "just title" and cannot support ten-year acquisitive prescription of the property claimed. *See, e.g., Hooper v. Hero Lands Co.*, 216 So.3d 965, 975–76 (La. App. 4 Cir. 2016) (determining "the language in the Hoopers' deed conveying without warranty 'all property . . . lying easterly [of Lot 26]' contains no definitive description of the land, and lacks boundary or property lines"); *Barrios v. Panepinto*, 133 So.3d 36, 38 (La. App. 4 Cir. 2014) (holding that defendants whose driveway and fence encroached on neighbors' property did not have "just title" for purposes of ten year acquisitive prescription defense because the legal description in their deed did not encompass the disputed eight-foot strip of land upon which the driveway and fence were situated, even though their act of sale included the improvements associated with their municipal address); *Jackson v. Herring*, 86 So.3d 9, 14 (La. App. 2 Cir. 2012) (finding that plaintiff could not

establish ten year acquisitive prescription because, even though she believed herself to be the owner of the property at issue, her deed to the lot did not cover the entirety of the property and particularly the portion where "an old red house" was located); *Hamel's Farm, L.L.C. v. Muslow*, 988 So.2d 882, 894 (La. App. 2 Cir. 2008) (observing that for an act to constitute a just title, the property claimed must be "identifiable from the description in the deed or from other evidence in the public records"); *Ryan v. Lee*, 870 So.2d 1137, 1140 (La. App. 2 Cir. 2004) (holding that a deed describing a different tract of land in a different township section from the one in controversy cannot be a just title for purposes of ten year acquisitive prescription); *McClendon v. Thomas*, 768 So.2d 261, 264–65 (La. App. 1 Cir. 2000) (determining that an act of sale that purported to transfer lot 170 in a mobile home subdivision could not constitute just title for purposes of establishing acquisitive prescription of lot 169, which plaintiff mistakenly occupied).

Did the quitclaim deed at issue in *Cantrelle* sufficiently describe the disputed property to constitute a just title? What could counsel for the defendant have argued?

4. In the end of the decision in *Cantrelle*, the court did provide some relief to the defendants who were unable to defeat the plaintiffs' claim of ten-year acquisitive prescription as to the entire alleyway in dispute. In that portion of the decision, the court held that the defendants were entitled to a predial servitude of passage across the entire alleyway giving them access to the public road known as Shell Road. *Cantrelle*, 700 So.2d at 529. Finding that the Gaude/Melancon property had no access to a public road once acquisitive prescription was complete, the court held that the defendants were entitled to claim a legal servitude of passage across the alleyway under Article 689 of the Louisiana Civil Code. We will discuss the legal servitude of passage for enclosed estates in Chapter 13.

5. In *Cantrelle*, the court analyzed whether the plaintiffs were good faith possessors in light of Article 3480 of the Civil Code and *Phillips v. Parker*, 483 So.2d 972 (La. 1986). We will study this provision and the *Phillips* case below. After you study the next section, reconsider whether the appellate court's analysis of the good faith issue in *Cantrelle* was adequate.

3. Good Faith

A person seeking to acquire ownership or other real rights in immovable property by ten-year acquisitive prescription must commence her possession in good faith. La. Civ. Code art. 3482 (1982). In the 1982 revision of the law governing acquisitive prescription, the legislature redefined good faith in several important ways. Note, however, that, as revised in 1979, Article 487 of the Civil Code, which defines good faith for purposes of accession, was not affected by the 1982 revision for acquisitive prescription. *See* La. Civ. Code art. 3480 rev. cmt. (b) (1982) (observing that for purposes of prescription, "good faith and just title are separate ideas, whereas for purposes of accession the two ideas are blended").

Article 3480 of the Civil Code defines good faith as follows:

Art. 3480. Good faith

For purposes of acquisitive prescription, a possessor is in good faith when he reasonably believes, in light of objective considerations, that he is the owner of the thing he possesses.

La. Civ. Code art. 3480 (1982). This definition expressly rejects certain prior decisions that had allowed a person to be in good faith under Article 3451 of the 1870 Civil Code when that person had only a *subjective* belief that he was the owner of the thing he possessed. In marked contrast, Article 3480 now adopts a *reasonable person* standard to determine good faith. *Id.* rev. cmt. (c). This does not mean, however, that a possessor's subjective belief that he is the owner of the property or the holder of a real right is irrelevant. If a possessor *subjectively knows* that he is not the owner of the thing as he begins to possess it, he certainly cannot be a good faith possessor. But subjective belief is no longer sufficient to qualify a possessor as being in good faith. His belief must also be reasonable in light of objective considerations.

Article 3480 establishes a two-step analysis for determining whether a possessor is in good faith. First, we ask whether the possessor subjectively believed that he commenced his possession as owner because he thought that he was acquiring the property from a previous owner. If the answer is affirmative, we then ask whether the possessor's belief was reasonable in light of objective considerations. Put differently, would a reasonable person in similar circumstances have thought he was acquiring possession as the owner? If the answer to the first question is negative, that is, if the possessor actually knew from the outset that he was not the owner, then there is no need to proceed to the second step of the analysis. Because good faith is presumed under Article 3481 of the Civil Code, the person opposing acquisitive prescription bears the burden of proof to show its absence. La. Civ. Code art. 3481 rev. cmt. (b) (1982).

When planning to acquire immovable property, a purchaser will often hire a lawyer or abstractor to conduct an examination of the public records to determine whether the vendor owns the property and can convey all of it free of encumbrances. Frequently, a title insurance company will provide this service directly to the purchaser or to the lender when the purchaser is borrowing funds to make the purchase. Before agreeing to insure the title, the title insurance company will conduct this kind of examination to be reasonably sure that no one can make a credible challenge to the purchaser's title or to the lender's mortgage. Must every purchaser of immovable property in Louisiana conduct an examination of the public records through a lawyer or title insurance company in order to claim the status of a good faith possessor?

Interestingly, the answer is no. Note that in *Cantrelle* a title examination was not performed for either the 1982 or the 1990 transfer at issue. A transferee of immovable property is not required to search the public records to determine the status of his transferor's title for purposes of establishing good faith; nor is he "charged with constructive knowledge" of what he would have found if he had undertaken a search of the public records. La. Civ. Code art. 3480 rev. cmt. (d) (1982). At the same time, however, the revision comments to Article 3480 also assert that a purchaser or transferee "who knows facts sufficient to excite inquiry" is "bound exceptionally to search the public records and is charged with the knowledge that a reasonable person would acquire from the public records." La. Civ. Code art. 3480 rev. cmt. (d) (1982). The seminal decision by the Louisiana Supreme Court in *Phillips v. Parker*, 483 So.2d 972 (La. 1986), presented below, resolved the confusion created by these seemingly conflicting statements.

Before you read the court's decision in *Phillips*, consider Article 3481 of the Civil Code:

Art. 3481. Presumption of good faith

Good faith is presumed. Neither error of law nor error of fact defeats this presumption. This presumption is rebutted on proof that the possessor knows, or should know, that he is not the owner of the thing he possesses.

La. Civ. Code art. 3481 (1982). In addition to clarifying that a possessor can still be in good faith if she makes a mistake in believing that she is the owner of the property because of some legal or factual misapprehension, this provision reinforces the idea that good faith is now based on a reasonable person standard. How does the record owner who is out of possession overcome the presumption that a prescriber is in good faith? He must prove either that the possessor actually knew that she was not the owner of the property at the commencement of her possession *or* that a reasonable person in the same objective circumstances should have known of the defect. *Id.* rev. cmt. (d).

Study revision comment (e) to Article 3481 before and after reading *Phillips*. The comment first states that "an acquirer of immovable property is not bound to search the public records unless he knows facts sufficient to excite inquiry," but then advises that in such a case, "the acquirer is charged with the knowledge that a reasonable person would acquire from the public records, and the presumption of good faith may be rebutted." La. Civ. Code art. 3481 rev. cmt. (e) (1982). In other words, when some red flag should warn a reasonable person of a problem, the acquirer is deemed to have "constructive" knowledge of what an examination of the public records would reveal.

But the same revision comment also offers that "[t]he same is true when an acquirer voluntarily undertakes to search the public records: he is also charged with the knowledge that a reasonable person would acquire from the public records, and the presumption of good faith may be rebutted." *Id.* Observe that this comment was published in conjunction with the promulgation of revised Article 3481 in 1982. In light of the court's decision in *Phillips v. Parker*, 483 So.2d 972 (La. 1986), is this statement still an accurate reflection of the law?

Phillips v. Parker

483 So.2d 972 (La. 1986)

LEMMON, Justice. This boundary action raises the question whether defendants were properly denied the status of good faith possessors of immovable property, for purposes of ten-year acquisitive prescription, simply because they obtained a title examination at the time of their purchase and the examining attorney failed to discover that the seller had already sold a portion of the property to another party. We conclude that, especially in the light of the 1982 revisions clarifying the Civil Code articles relating to acquisitive prescription, a party who obtains a title examination is not solely for that reason precluded from claiming the status of a good faith possessor in a plea of ten-year acquisitive prescription, but rather that the obtaining of a title examination and the information actually revealed by the examination are merely factors to be considered in the judicial determination of whether the presumption of good faith has been successfully rebutted.

Facts

In 1947 G.R. Weaver, plaintiff's and defendants' common ancestor in title, acquired a tract of land containing 2.55 acres. Weaver eventually built a camp on a small portion of the lakefront property. In 1955 Weaver agreed to sell two lakefront lots from the remainder of the tract to defendants and to the McCuller brothers, who were plaintiff's immediate ancestor in title. The tract was not subdivided and contained no visible boundaries.

On August 22, 1955, Weaver executed two cash deeds by which he sold one lot to defendants and one lot to the McCullers, each for the price of $750. When defendants went out to the property after the sale to mark off the lot, they learned that the property description in the deed did not describe the property they had intended to purchase, but instead described the part of the tract on which Weaver's camp was located. On advice of their attorney, defendants employed a surveyor, who surveyed the property defendants had intended to purchase, and an attorney, who examined the title to that property and expressed the opinion that Weaver had a good and valid title. Weaver then transferred to defendants by cash deed on October 7, 1955 the lot defendants had intended to buy, and defendants conveyed back to Weaver the lot purchased in error in August.

Defendants immediately cleared the property and built a camp. The following year they erected a fence in accordance with the survey, and they were in peaceful possession of the fenced property until 1982.

In the meantime the McCullers had conveyed their lot to plaintiff in 1972. When plaintiff desired to move a trailer onto her property in 1982, she discovered that the property described in her August, 1955 deed overlapped the property described in defendants' October, 1955 deed by thirteen feet. Her request that defendants remove the fence was apparently the first time that defendants learned that their fence was on plaintiff's property. [An accurate title examination at the time of Weaver's sale to defendants would have revealed the overlap, inasmuch as Weaver had already sold the thirteen-foot strip in question to the McCullers. The title examiner apparently either failed to find the recorded sale from Weaver to the McCullers or failed to check the measurements in the McCullers property description against the survey of the property defendants intended to purchase.]

In this ensuing boundary action, defendants filed an exception of ten-year acquisitive prescription, claiming to have possessed since 1956, in good faith and under just title, all of the property located within the fence. At trial the only disputed issue relative to defendants' plea of acquisitive prescription was their good faith. The title examiner testified that he did not recall finding the August, 1955 sale from Weaver to the McCullers. Apparently defendants relied completely on the title examiner's written opinion that Weaver had a good and valid title to the lot which they purchased in October 1955.

The trial court overruled the exception of prescription, concluding that the defendants were in "legal bad faith" because they obtained a title examination which did not reveal the defect in their title. The court further determined that plaintiff was the owner of the disputed strip and fixed the boundary accordingly.

The court of appeal affirmed. 469 So. 2d 1102. The intermediate court first noted that the doctrine of legal bad faith, under which an error of law (such as an erroneous conclusion as to ownership rights) precluded a finding of good faith for purposes of acquisitive prescription, had been legislatively overruled by La. C.C. Art. 3481 (enacted by Acts 1982, No. 187), which provides that neither an error of fact nor an error of law defeats the presumption of good faith. However, the court concluded that the 1982 Civil Code revisions did not affect the theory of law that a purchaser who undertakes a title search of the public records is charged with knowledge of the defects in title that a reasonable person would acquire from a search of the public records. Citing *Martin v. Schwing Lumber & Shingle Co.*, 228 La. 175, 81 So. 2d 852 (1955), the court held that because of this theory of constructive knowledge, based on the public records doctrine, the defendants were not in good faith once they had undertaken through their attorney a search of the public records which should have revealed the overlap in the property descriptions.

We granted certiorari to determine, especially in the light of the 1982 revisions, the validity of a theory of law which deems a party to be a bad faith possessor simply because he obtained a title examination, even though that party acted reasonably by employing an attorney to examine the title to the property he intended to purchase and then reasonably relied on the opinion of the title examiner that the seller had a good and valid title to the property.

The court of appeal (perhaps in reliance on some loose language in prior cases) has misconstrued the public records doctrine . . . It is therefore appropriate to review the public records doctrine and to analyze the effect of obtaining a title examination upon the determination of good faith under the 1982 Civil Code revisions.

The Public Records Doctrine

. . . The fundamental principle of the law of registry is that any sale, mortgage, privilege, contract or judgment affecting immovable property, which is required to be recorded, is utterly null and void as to third persons unless recorded. Redmann, *The Louisiana Law of Recordation: Some Principles and Some Problems*, 39 Tul. L. Rev. 491 (1965). When the law of recordation applies, an interest in immovable property is effective against third persons only if it is recorded; if the interest is not recorded, it is not effective against third persons, even if the third person knows of the claim. This principle is traceable to the decision in *McDuffie v. Walker*, 125 La. 152, 51 So. 100 (1909), in which the court held that the plaintiff, as purchaser of immovable property by recorded act, was entitled to recognition as owner in a petitory action against the defendant who had purchased the property seven years earlier and had immediately gone into possession, but had not recorded the deed. In response to the defendant's argument that the plaintiff had knowledge of the prior unrecorded sale, the court reiterated its decision in *Harang v. Plattsmier*, 21 La. Ann. 426 (1869) that actual knowledge is not the equivalent of registry, which is absolutely required in order for the sale to affect third persons.

Thus, the law of registry does not create rights in a positive sense, but rather has the negative effect of denying the effectiveness of certain rights unless they are recorded. The essence of the public records doctrine is that recordation is an essential element for the *effectiveness* of a right, and it is important to distinguish between *effectiveness* of a right against third persons and *knowledge* of a right by third persons. An unrecorded interest is not effective against anyone (except the parties). A recorded interest, however, is *effective* both against those third persons who have *knowledge* and those who do not have *knowledge* of the presence of the interest in the public records. From the standpoint of the operation of the public records doctrine, knowledge is an irrelevant consideration. Any theory of constructive knowledge which imputes knowledge of the contents of the public records to third persons forms no part of the public records doctrine.

Another element of the public records doctrine is the protection of third persons. La. R.S. 9:2722 provides that a third person is entitled to rely on the law of registry and is protected thereby. This protection of third parties has significance only when an interest which is required to be recorded is *not recorded*, because a third person under such circumstances can deal with the property in *reliance on the absence* of the interest from the public records, even if the third person has actual knowledge of the interest. Thus, the primary concern of the public records doctrine is the protection of third persons against *unrecorded* interests. The public records doctrine therefore has little applicability in the present case in which the claim of plaintiff's ancestor in title was recorded. [Because this protection against unrecorded claims has the result of inducing the recording of claims, prudent prospective purchasers or mortgagees will check the public records to determine if there are any sales, mortgages, privileges, contracts or judgments affecting the property in which he is interested.]

In the present case, the sale from Weaver to the McCullers included the disputed thirteen-foot strip, and recordation made the sale effective against third persons who thereafter dealt with that strip. Because of the recordation, plaintiff (as successor in title to the McCullers) had a superior title to the strip, and defendants did not obtain a valid title in their subsequent purchase from Weaver. The fact that defendants did not have *actual knowledge* of the recorded sale from Weaver to the McCullers did not bear one iota on the *effectiveness* of that sale. Moreover, as to the merits of the boundary action, defendants lost because the McCuller's recordation made the sale *effective* against any third persons who later dealt with that property and not because third persons (including defendants) had *constructive knowledge* of that recorded sale.

Title Examination and the Good Faith Possessor

The purpose of good faith acquisitive prescription is to secure the title of a person who purchases immovable property by a deed translative of title, under the reasonable and objective belief that he is acquiring a valid title to the property, and thereafter remains in peaceful possession of the property for more than ten years without any disturbance by the true owner. Acquisitive prescription plays an important social role by doing away with the insoluble problems that otherwise could arise if there was an unknown defect in the chain of title of a long-time possessor. 1 M. Planiol, Civil Law Treatise § 2645 (La. St. Law Inst. Trans. 1959). The redactors of the Civil Code therefore provided that a person who purchases immovable property under the required circumstances should eventually prevail in a title dispute with the owner who allows continuous, uninterrupted, peaceable, public and unequivocal possession for more than ten years without objection.

The law of registry is not involved in any way with the theory of acquisitive prescription that a party who reasonably believed he was acquiring valid title should be deemed to have a valid title after a certain period of possession in which the owner failed to object. The law of registry simply makes the true owner's recorded title effective against the good faith possessor until the period of time has elapsed by which the good faith possessor acquires a valid title by means of the required possession. The theory of constructive knowledge should also have no bearing on the determination from an objective standpoint of the good faith of a possessor of immovable property who claims acquisitive prescription. Nevertheless, inconsistent decisions prior to the 1982 revisions of the Civil Code imputed bad faith to certain possessors, irrespective of their objective good faith.

In the present case, the lower courts applied the theory of constructive knowledge to deprive defendants of the right to claim acquisitive prescription on the basis that they were not in good faith because their attorney failed to discover a prior sale by Weaver in the public records. If the constructive knowledge afforded by recordation of Weaver's sale to the McCullers would *absolutely* preclude a finding of good faith on the part of defendants who later purchased the same thirteen-foot strip from Weaver, then the theory of constructive notice would write ten-year acquisitive prescription completely out of the Code. Such a result is totally unacceptable. Equally unacceptable, from the standpoint of an objective determination of good faith, is the theory of constructive knowledge which precluded good faith possession only because the attorney employed by defendants examined the records and failed to find the prior sale. This result restricts good faith status to those possessors who purchased property without any attempt whatsoever to check the validity of the title, thereby penalizing a purchaser who employs a title examiner and rewarding one who doesn't. This theory places the purchaser in a dilemma, since it is imprudent in modern practice to purchase property without a title examination, but the obtaining of a title examination would forfeit any right to claim the status of a good faith possessor in the event of an ancient defect in title. The better approach, and the one we conclude is required by the clarification provided by the 1982 revisions, is that the good faith of the possessor should be determined by a consideration of all of the factors of the particular case relevant to the definition of good faith in the Civil Code, and not merely by any reference to the public records doctrine or to any theory of constructive knowledge. [Of course, the obtaining of a title examination and the knowledge actually obtained from the examination may be factors to be considered in the determination of good faith.]

La. C.C. Art. 3480, effective January 1, 1983, defines the good faith requirement in ten-year acquisitive prescription as follows:

> "For purposes of acquisitive prescription, a possessor is in good faith when he reasonably believes, in light of objective considerations, that he is owner of the thing he possesses."

The Comments to Article 3480 note that the definition of good faith was contained in former Article 3451 and that the new article changes the law. The Comments further note that while former Article 3451 was ambiguous and was sometimes construed as basing good faith on the subjective view of the possessor that he owned the thing possessed, the prevailing jurisprudence determined good faith in the light of objective considerations. *The new article codifies the prevailing jurisprudence.* The Comments also point out that the new article does not affect the public records doctrine and that any considerations involving a search of the public records should be addressed to the issue of whether the presumption of good faith in Article 3481 has been rebutted.

Even under the old law it was appropriate to determine good faith on the basis of objective criteria. Further, good faith is presumed under Article 3481, as it was under the old law. The legislative overruling of the doctrine of legal bad faith did change the law. See Comments to Article 3481. However, the problem is this case was not the application of the overruled doctrine of legal bad faith, but the misapplication of the theory of constructive knowledge to preclude the possessor (who was clearly in good faith on the basis of objective criteria) from claiming acquisitive prescription.

Perhaps the prior cases imputed knowledge of the public records to preclude good faith by possessors who obtained title examinations in order to prevent claims of good faith by purchasers to whom title defects had been privately communicated. Actual knowledge of a title defect at the time of purchase certainly precludes good faith. However, knowledge by a purchaser of title defects can be inferred from circumstances more relevant than the mere obtaining of a title examination. For example, a purchase by quit claim deed or at an extremely low price may be suggestive (but not conclusive) of knowledge of title defects which may rebut the presumed good faith of the purchaser. The age and nature of the title defect, and other such factors bearing on the likelihood of discovery, are also relevant to the determination. [Here, the defect was not as easily discoverable as the outstanding one-half ownership in *Martin v. Schwing Lumber & Shingle Co.*, 228 La. 175, 81 So.2d 852 (1955). To discover the defect, the examiner (assuming he found the sale from Weaver to the McCullers) had to calculate and lay out the measurements of the two properties sold by Weaver and probably should have required a survey of the McCullers' property. The point is that the difficulty in discovering the defect in this case enhances the likelihood that there was a deficiency in the title examination rather than a bad faith attempt to assert acquisitive prescription.]

The 1982 amendments, reiterating that good faith should be presumed and restricting to objective criteria the determination whether the presumption has been rebutted, have removed the questionable basis of prior decisions which imputed bad faith to certain possessors, regardless of their objective good faith, such as by imputing knowledge of the contents of the public records to those purchasers who employed title examiners or imputing errors of title examiners to their clients on the basis of agency. However, there was never any logical or compelling reason to deny a purchaser the status of a good faith possessor simply because the title examiner failed to discover a title defect. [Of course, if the attorney revealed to the purchaser that the seller's title was defective, the purchaser cannot claim good faith. *See Arnold v. Sun Oil Co.*, 218 La. 50, 48 So. 2d 369 (1949).] At worst, such a purchaser lacks objective good faith only as to the defects actually discovered in the title examination. As to defects that the purchaser's attorney failed to discover, the purchaser who relied on the seller's declaration and on the attorney's professional opinion should be in at least as good a position to claim the status of a good faith possessor, from the standpoint of objective criteria, as a purchaser who conducted no title examination. [Under decisions prior to the 1982 amendments, a purchaser of immovable property was not required to examine the public records in order to qualify as a good faith possessor. . . .]

Here, defendants' good faith was presumed by operation of La. C.C. Art. 3481. Neither the deed nor the evidence at trial suggested any reason for defendants to doubt that Weaver was the owner of the property. Weaver had built a camp on a portion of the property he was selling to defendants, and he represented that he owned the property that was being sold. When the August sale mistakenly described the lot on which Weaver's camp was located, defendants consulted an attorney and then followed the attorney's advice by obtaining a survey and a title examination. Defendants then reasonably relied on the professional opinion of the attorney they had employed for that purpose. Moreover, the defect was a simple overlap in a nearly contemporaneous sale (which had no survey showing the exact location relative to defendants' property) that the examiner could easily have missed. Both defendants and the examiner testified that they were unaware of the overlap, and the examiner also pointed out the bad condition of the records in that parish at the time. It would truly be a distortion of the term "good faith" to decide that defendants lacked objective good faith under these circumstances, inasmuch as a reasonable man under like circumstances certainly would have believed that the seller had a valid title.

We therefore conclude that plaintiff has failed to carry her burden of rebutting, on the basis of objective criteria, the presumed good faith on the part of defendants.

Accordingly, the judgments of the lower courts are reversed, and defendants' plea of ten-year acquisitive prescription is sustained.

Notes and Questions

1. In *Phillips v. Parker*, 483 So.2d 972 (La. 1986), G.R. Weaver was a common ancestor in title. When seeking to prove ownership against a person who derives his title from a common author, a party need only show that his title was recorded in the local parish conveyance records prior to the title of the competing transferee. La. Civ. Code art. 532 (1979); La. Civ. Code art. 3338 (2005).

Consider the following example. Edward sells twenty acres to Richard on Tuesday and then sells the same twenty acres to Faith on Thursday. If Faith files her act of sale before Richard, Faith will prevail in litigation against Richard. If Richard files his act of sale before Faith, he will prevail in litigation against Faith. Because both Richard and Faith received their titles from a common author, no further proof of ownership is needed as between the two of them. A different, and more stringent, level of proof is needed when a person claims ownership against a person who has acquired the right to possess and the parties do not share a common author. La. Civ. Code art. 531 (1979).

2. In the first portion of its legal analysis in *Phillips*, the court discusses what it describes as the *Public Records Doctrine*. Today that doctrine is largely codified in Title 22A of Book III of the Louisiana Civil Code. La. Civ. Code arts. 3338 *et seq.* (2005). In this portion of its opinion, the court held that, because the public records doctrine is a negative doctrine, the existence of instruments in the public records that might have informed the Parkers of the defect in their title did not give the Parkers actual or constructive knowledge of the defect. *Phillips*, 483 So.2d at 975–76. Although third parties can use the public records to help determine the ownership of an immovable and the presence of any contrary claims or interests with respect to the property, the availability of the public records does not charge an acquirer of immovable property or real rights in an immovable with knowledge of what could have been learned through a careful examination of those records. Consequently, the existence of information about a conflicting claim or interest in the public records by itself does not deprive an adverse possessor of good faith.

In the specific factual context of *Phillips*, the deed conveying the land at issue from the common author (Weaver) to the McCuller brothers (the immediate ancestor of Phillips in title) was properly recorded in the public records and discoverable by anyone who performed an examination of the public records, including the Parkers' attorney. Nevertheless, the court ruled in favor of the Parkers, holding that the Parkers could establish ownership of the disputed thirteen-foot strip of land through ten-year acquisitive prescription. It was indisputable that the Parkers had possessed the thirteen-foot strip of land with their camp since October 1955, continuously, peaceably, unequivocally and within a well-marked boundary (up to the fence that the Parkers erected one year after taking possession).

It was also undisputed that the Parkers possessed the strip of land in dispute pursuant to a just title—the deed used to correct the initial conveyancing mistake when Weaver first tried to sell the Parkers a lakefront lot in August 1955. It was a just title because it described all of the property that the Parkers thought they had acquired, but it was defective because it actually described more land than Weaver actually owned or could convey. In the end, then, the only issue left to determine was whether the Parkers were in good faith when they commenced their possession in October 1955. Why did the court find the Parkers to be in good faith?

3. The court in *Phillips* noted that the Parkers' title examiner and advising attorney made one of either two mistakes leading up to the October 1955 transaction between them and Weaver. He may have failed to find the August 1955 deed conveying a lot from the Weavers to the McCullers. Alternatively, even if he found the Weaver-McCullers deed, he may have failed to compare the measurements in the McCullers' property description with the survey of the property that the Parkers intended to purchase. *Phillips*, 483 So.2d at 974, n. 2.

It is easy to miss recent transactions when conducting a title search. Few clerks of court provide same day filing. Most documents submitted for recordation are eventually recorded, but some may be difficult to locate later. Louisiana laws allow courts to forego filing during war, which means that some recorded documents are not indexed. Even when filed, some documents cannot be located because of improper indexing or a spelling change in a name in a chain of title. Missing a transaction is not uncommon, which might explain the ubiquity of title insurance.

4. Note that the Parkers did not have to prove their good faith because it was presumed. Instead, the burden lay with Phillips as the record owner of the portion of the lot in dispute to prove that the Parkers were not in good faith. La. Civ. Code art. 3480 rev. cmt. (b) (1982). Phillips could have rebutted the presumption of good faith by showing that reasonable persons in the Parkers' circumstances should have suspected that their vendor was not the owner of all the property that he purported to convey or at least should have realized that further investigation of their vendor's title was necessary.

After the Parkers discovered the initial mistake in the property descriptions in the August 1955 transaction and their accidental purchase of the portion of Weaver's

2.55 acre lot where he had built his camp, was it reasonable for the Parkers not to take extra precautions in reviewing the property descriptions at the time of their October 1955 transaction with Weaver? Note that the Parkers hired both a surveyor and an attorney. Were they reasonable in relying on the opinions of these professionals? Should the Parkers' attorney or their surveyor have asked Weaver if he had recently sold any other portion of his original lot to anyone else? Should the failure of the attorney and the surveyor to "see what they ought to have seen" make the Parkers bad faith possessors?

5. Article 3482 of the Civil Code provides that "[i]t is sufficient that possession has commenced in good faith; subsequent bad faith does not prevent the accrual of prescription of ten years." La. Civ. Code art. 3482 (1982). The original cash deeds conveying Weaver's lots were executed in August 1955. The Parkers noticed an error and consulted an attorney and surveyor to correct the error. They believed that the property descriptions in the subsequent cash deed executed in October 1955 were accurate; and they took possession of the lot that they had originally intended to purchase from Weaver.

Suppose that two years after the Parkers took possession of their lot, they learned that the property description in their second deed was in error. If the defendants chose to ignore this new information and continued to possess the property, could they claim ownership by ten year acquisitive prescription in 1965 or in 1967?

6. In *Phillips*, the court refers at one point to the distinction between **constructive knowledge** of the public records (the knowledge that a person would have obtained had he or his agent conducted an accurate public records examination) and **imputed knowledge** (the knowledge that a principal is charged with having acquired based on the activities of his agent). *Phillips*, 483 So.2d at 978, n. 12–13. The court concluded that the Parkers should not be charged with constructive knowledge of what an accurate public records examination would have revealed because they reasonably relied on the advice of the professionals who examined the public records and surveyed the land before advising the Parkers that Weaver was the owner of the property he purported to convey in the second deed. Would the result have been different, however, if the Parkers' surveyor or attorney had discovered the title defect and simply failed to report the defect to the Parkers? Could they still be regarded as good faith possessors?

7. At least one commentator has argued that the Louisiana Supreme Court could have gone a step further in *Phillips* and adopted a rule imposing a duty on acquirers of immovable property to conduct a title examination. Under such a rule, the failure of a purchaser of immovable property to conduct an examination of the seller's title before completing the purchase would be a factor that weighs *against* a finding that the purchaser reasonably believed that he was acquiring the property from the actual owner in light of objective circumstances. Symeon Symeonides, *Error of Law and Error of Fact in Acquisitive Prescription*, 47 La. L. Rev. 429, 439 (1986). Would this amount to saying that a purchaser of immovable property who fails to conduct

a title examination should be presumptively regarded as possessing in bad faith? Do you think such a rule would be wise public policy?

8. In his law review article, Professor Symeonides describes the court's holding in *Phillips* as adopting a case-by-case, totality of the circumstances approach to good faith:

> The possessors' actual good or bad faith should be determined not by artificial fictions, but rather by evaluating, on a case by case basis, all of the surrounding circumstances, including the condition of the public records, the thoroughness of the particular title search, the competence and reputation of the title examiner, the type of title defect involved, the possibility of it being missed, and other similar factors. This is essentially the Supreme Court's approach in *Phillips*. . . .

Symeonides, 47 LA. L. REV. at 440–41. Is this kind of highly contextualized, multifactored approach workable or advisable? Should courts or the legislature adopt bright line rules of thumb or presumptions to shorten good faith deliberations?

Note that Professor Symmeonides also argued that, even though the court in *Phillips* never explicitly adopted a bright line rule making a title examination a factor weighing in favor of good faith, "the whole tenor of the opinion suggests that the court ascribes to the view that, if *conducted*, a title examination is an element that reinforces rather than weakens the possessor's claim of good faith." *Id.* at 441 (emphasis in original); *see also Phillips*, 483 So.2d 977 n. 7 (observing that "obtaining a title examination and the knowledge actually obtained from the examination may be factors to be considered in the determination of good faith").

* * *

Now consider a more recent decision involving ten year, good faith acquisitive prescription. Do you believe the court properly resolved whether the plaintiff, Nhut Van Mai, was in good faith in light of the objective circumstances in the following case?

Mai v. Floyd

951 So.2d 244 (La. App. 1 Cir. 2006)

LOVE, Judge, Ad Hoc. This appeal arises from a petition for declaratory judgment regarding a lot of immovable property sold by tax deed. Nhut Van Mai asserted that he owned the property via possession and acquisitive prescription. George Floyd asserted ownership based on a tax sale deed. The trial court found that Nhut Van Mai was in possession of the property, but that George Floyd owned the lot and dismissed the declaratory judgment. We find the trial court erred in declaring George Floyd the owner, reverse the judgment, and render.

Factual Background and Procedural History

On May 23, 2002, Nhut Van Mai ("Mr. Mai") filed a petition for declaratory judgment alleging ownership of "Addition to Roppolovilla, . . . Lot Ten (10), Square

Nine (9)" ("lot 10"), based upon possession and good faith, through successors of title, for ten years.

On June 19, 1984, Joseph and Lynn Campagna ("the Campagnas") sold "LOTS NINE (9) AND TEN (10), SQUARE NINE (9)" to Richard and Beulah Albert ("the Alberts"). The Alberts then sold lots nine and ten to Ali and Inggub Tabrizi ("the Tabrizis"), and Susan Zare ("Ms. Zare") on May 4, 1990. Ms. Zare sold her interest in the lots to the Tabrizis on July 17, 1991. Mr. Mai purchased the lots from Mr. Tabrizi, after he divorced Mrs. Tabrizi, on January 9, 1996. Mr. Mai operated the Premier Grocery Store ("Premier Grocery") on lots nine and ten. All of the above conveyances concluded without a title examination.

Raymond Floyd purchased lot ten of Mr. Mai's alleged property by tax sale in 1986. Raymond Floyd filed a petition for monition on April 26, 1996. The tax sale of lot ten was "confirmed and homologated" and "made perfect and complete" on June 20, 1996. In 1999, Raymond Floyd sold lot ten to his son George Floyd ("Mr. Floyd"). Mr. Floyd has paid and continues to pay the property taxes on lot ten.

In December 2001, Mr. Mai attempted to convey lots nine and ten to Ha Hoang ("Ms. Hoang"). While negotiating the purchase, Ms. Hoang's attorney performed a title examination, during which she and Mr. Mai discovered a previous tax deed conveying lot ten to Raymond Floyd. Ms. Hoang began operating the Premier Grocery in January 2002, and remains the "current operator." She redeemed lot nine from the State by paying over $ 15,000 around January 2005.

The trial court orally determined that Mr. Mai was in possession of lot ten, but held that Mr. Floyd was the owner and dismissed the petition for declaratory judgment. Mr. Mai's appeal followed.

Mr. Mai asserts the trial court erred by declaring Mr. Floyd the owner of lot ten as he and his predecessors in title "have enjoyed continuous, peaceful, uninterrupted possession of the property" for over ten years by maintaining and operating Premier Grocery. . . .

Declaratory Judgment

Courts "may declare rights, status, and other legal relations whether or not further relief is or could be claimed." La. C.C.P. art. 1871. [T]he existence of another adequate remedy does not preclude a judgment for declaratory relief in cases where it is appropriate." La. C.C.P. art. 1871. The result "shall have the force and effect of a final judgment or decree." La. C.C.P. art. 1871. Interested parties may use a declaratory judgment to determine their rights when it regards a "deed, will, written contract or other writing constituting a contract." La. C.C.P. art. 1872.

> When the issue of ownership of immovable property or of a real right therein is presented in an action for a declaratory judgment . . . the court shall render judgment in favor of the party:
>
> (1) Who would be entitled to the possession of the immovable property or real right therein in a possessory action, unless the adverse party proves

that he has acquired ownership from a previous owner or by acquisitive prescription; or

(2) Who proves better title to the immovable property or real right therein, when neither party would be entitled to the possession of the immovable property or real right therein in a possessory action.

La. C.C.P. art. 3654. Therefore, we must decide which party should prevail on a possessory action and if acquisitive prescription determines who owns lot ten.

Possessory Action

A possessory action is brought by the alleged possessor "when he has been disturbed, or to be restored to the possession or enjoyment thereof when he has been evicted." La. C.C.P. art. 3655. . . . The trial court found that Mr. Mai was in possession of lot ten and the issue in not appealed in this case.

Acquisitive Prescription

. . . . In the case *sub judice,* corporeal possession that is "continuous, uninterrupted, peaceable, public, and unequivocal" for ten years is mandated for prescription. La. C.C. art. 3476. Once proved, ownership boundaries are fixed according to "limits established by prescription rather than titles." La. C.C. art. 794.

Mr. Mai asserts that he has had "continuous, uninterrupted, peaceable, public, and unequivocal" possession for at least ten years. The tax sale occurred in 1986 during the Alberts' ownership: they sold the lots to the Tabrizis and Ms. Zare on May 4, 1990. If they were in good faith at the time of the conveyance, then Mr. Mai could tack on their ownership to his and become the owner of lot ten through the ten-year acquisitive prescription period. La. C.C. art. 3442.

The burden of proving bad faith remains with the party attempting to rebut the presumption of good faith. *Phillips v. Parker,* 483 So. 2d 972, 979 (La. 1986). Mr. Floyd avers that Mr. Mai was in bad faith because he stated that he was "happy" that he did not receive a tax bill for the property and that he knew he paid property taxes on his home and in Vietnam. However, this testimony does not address the central issue of Mr. Mai's good or bad faith at the time of conveyance. Mr. Mai testified that he and Mr. Tabrizi went to the tax assessor's office to check into whether delinquent taxes were owed on lots nine and ten. He was told that no taxes were due prior to his purchase. Additionally, the fact that no parties, prior to Ms. Hoang, conducted a title examination, which would have revealed the 1986 tax sale, does not create bad faith. *Ponder v. Jenkins,* 468 So. 2d 1275, 1278 (La. App. 1st Cir. 1985). The record is devoid of evidence as to bad faith on the part of the Tabrizis or Ms. Zare.

However, the record does document that the Premier Grocery has been operated without interruption for at least ten years. Mr. Floyd and Mrs. Floyd testified that Raymond Floyd attempted to sell lot ten to Mr. Mai. They also stated that Raymond Floyd and his attorney entered Premier Grocery on one occasion to inform the operators of lot ten's "true" owner. Mr. Mai was not at the store that day, but both Mr. Floyd and his mother testified that a woman became angry and ordered them out of Premier Grocery. However, Mr. Floyd and Mrs. Floyd testified that, to their knowledge, no further legal action or attempts to take corporeal possession of lot ten were taken. Accordingly, we find that Mr. Floyd failed to meet his burden of proving bad faith. In fact, the record demonstrates a lack of action by Raymond Floyd and Mr. Floyd. Thus, the trial court erred by declaring Mr. Floyd the owner of lot ten as Mr. Mai acquired ownership by acquisitive prescription.

Decree

Accordingly, we reverse the decision of the trial court and render.

Notes and Questions

1. In *Mai v. Floyd*, 951 So.2d 244 (La. App. 1 Cir. 2006), why did the plaintiff, Nhut Van Mai, file a declaratory judgment action seeking to establish his ownership of the lot in dispute (lot 10) by acquisitive prescription right away, as opposed to filing a possessory action first, which, if successful, could have put the onus on the defendant to bring a petitory action within sixty days of a judgment in the possessory action?

2. Do you agree with the court's determination that Mai was in good faith at the time he commenced his possession of lot 10 (and lot 9) in January 1996, even though he had not conducted a title examination prior to his purchase of the lots? What other factors seemed to be influential in the court's determination that Mai was in good faith?

3. For a detailed discussion of the Louisiana jurisprudence covering the good faith requirement for acquisitive prescription of immovables since the 1982 revision of the Civil Code, see John A. Lovett, *Good Faith in Louisiana Property Law*, 78 LA. L. REV. 1163, 1210–18 (2018). The author sums up his views about the role of good faith analysis in the context of acquisitive prescription in the following terms:

> What remains universally distinctive about all of these decisions, however, is the relatively microscopic level of analysis and the focus on objective reasonableness in light of all relevant circumstances. When the stakes are high, as they are in claims of ten-year acquisitive prescription with respect to immovables, the courts engage in relatively rigorous scrutiny, carefully searching for evidence of actual honesty and reasonable carefulness in the circumstances, even though possessors presumptively possess in good faith.

Id. at 1218. Do you agree?

D. Tacking and Transfer of Possession

Many of the acquisitive prescription decisions featured so far have referred to "tacking." Recall, for instance, the language in the previous decision in which the court stated that "[i]f they [the Tabrizis and Ms. Zare] were in good faith at the time of the conveyance, then Mr. Mai could *tack* on their ownership to his and become the owner . . . through the ten-year acquisitive prescription period." *Mai v. Floyd*,

951 So.2d 244, 247 (La. App. 1 Cir. 2006) (emphasis added). Tacking allows a possessor who acquires possession by title from a former possessor to connect or *cumulate* the time of possession of the former possessor with his own. This is crucial for a possessor who needs to satisfy the duration requirement of acquisitive prescription but has not possessed himself for the entire prescriptive period.

Tacking, however, requires a juridical link between the possessors. It is not available when two different possessors follow one another without any juridical link between them. Suppose, for example, that Bob began to possess a tract of land owned by Xavier and possessed the tract adversely and without any vices of possession for 25 years. One day, however, Bob abandoned his possession. The very next day Charles came along and began to possess adversely without any vices of possession and continued his possession for another 6 years. In this situation, Charles *cannot* tack his possession to that of Bob because there is no juridical link connecting their two possessions. Charles would have to possess for another 4 years, if he possessed in good faith and under just title; or another 24 years, if he lacked either just title or good faith.

Under the Louisiana Civil Code, the juridical link that allows a possessor like Charles to connect his possession to a previous possessor like Bob is supplied by the transfer of possession through either universal title or particular title.

1. Transfer of Possession by Universal or Particular Title

Article 3441 of the Civil Code offers the first important provision for understanding tacking:

Art. 3441. Transfer of Possession

Possession is transferable by universal title or by particular title.

La. Civ. Code art. 3441 (1982). Notice the two ideas inherent in this provision. First, possession may be transferred separate and apart from ownership. Remember that the Louisiana Civil Code regards ownership and possession as distinct property rights. La. Civ. Code art. 481 (1979). As we learned in *Todd v. State*, 474 So.2d 430 (La. 1985), possession is valuable in its own right, even when it does not lead to acquisitive prescription.

Second, Article 3441 makes plain that one of the core rights associated with possession lies in its transferability. By indicating that possession can be transferred through a universal or particular title, Article 3441 identifies the incumbent possessor as either a successor who takes by universal title (a "universal successor") or one who takes by particular title (a "particular successor"). The Civil Code defines these two types of successors in the following terms:

Art. 3506. General Definitions

(28) Successor.—Successor is, generally speaking, the person who takes the place of another.

There are in law two sorts of successors: the universal successor, such as the heir, the universal legatee, and the general legatee; and the successor by particular title, such as the buyer, donee, or legatee of particular things, the transferee.

The universal successor represents the person of the deceased, and succeeds to all his rights and charges.

The particular successor succeeds only to the rights appertaining to the thing which is sold, ceded or bequeathed to him.

La. Civ. Code art. 3506(28). What does this mean?

Suppose that Anne starts to possess a tract of land (Arpent Noir) as owner on October 3, 2001. She has just title and she is in good faith. Anne sells the land by authentic act to William on March 17, 2009, who also takes possession under just title and in good faith. On October 3, 2011, William can claim ten years of adverse possession and thus, establish acquisitive prescription. Under the Civil Code, William, who has acquired his title from Anne, can cumulate her possession with his own for purposes of meeting the ten-year requirement of possession for good faith acquisitive prescription.

In the example above, Anne transferred her possession of the land to William by particular title. Someone who buys a specific immovable property from a vendor is considered a particular successor. This type of successor succeeds the author with regard to the property rights sold, ceded or bequeathed by the act of transfer. *See* La. Civ. Code art. 3506(28). If Anne donated Arpent Noir to William during her lifetime by an authentic act, the act of donation would likewise transfer the property to William by particular title. If Anne died and specifically bequeathed Arpent Noir to William through a valid testament, William would be classified as a particular legatee of Anne, which also makes him a particular successor of Anne.

On the other hand, if Anne dies intestate and William is her sole heir, Anne's possession of the land would pass to William by universal title. As Anne's universal successor, William would represent Anne and stand in her shoes. Similarly, if Anne dies with a valid will that names William as her sole legatee and leaves him all of her property, William would be Anne's universal legatee and hence, her universal successor.

When possession is transferred by universal title, the transferee continues the possession of the transferor with all of its advantages and disadvantages. La. Civ. Code art. 936 (1977). The transferee's own good or bad faith and his awareness of the good or bad faith of the transferor are irrelevant. Consider Article 936 of the Civil Code which describes this continuation of possession:

Art. 936. Continuation of the possession of the decedent

The possession of the decedent is transferred to his successors, whether testate or intestate, and if testate, whether particular, general, or universal legatees.

A universal successor continues the possession of the decedent with all its advantages and defects, and with no alteration in the nature of the possession.

A particular successor may commence a new possession for purposes of acquisitive prescription.

La. Civ. Code art. 936 (1997). The universal successor continues the possession of the decedent, whether the decedent was in good or bad faith. But a particular successor gets to start a "new possession," regardless of the defects in her author's possession.

Suppose Paul takes possession of a tract of land (Arpent Vert) and continues in possession for twelve years until he dies, leaving Quentin as his universal successor. Quentin then lives on Arpent Vert for fifteen years before he dies, leaving Rochelle as his universal successor. Rochelle lives on Arpent Vert for more four years. Rochelle can claim thirty-one years of adverse possession. In this case of seamless successions by universal title, the successor inherits the good or bad faith of the author. So, we must ask whether Paul, the first possessor, was in good or bad faith when he took up possession. Quentin and Rochelle's good or bad faith does not matter for purposes of transferring possession to universal successors.

Of course, all of this falls apart if someone else takes possession of Arpent Vert for more than a year without Paul or Quentin or Rochelle's permission and, therefore, acquires the right to possess. La. Civ. Code art. 3442 rev. cmt. (c) (1982). The possession of the transferor cannot be tacked to the possession of the transferee if there has been an interruption of possession. La. Civ. art. 3442 (1982). Tacking also fails in the absence of a title, particular or universal, which evidences the transfer of possession between two successive possessors. *See* La. Civ. Code art. 3442 rev. cmt. (d) (1982).

2. The Mechanics of Tacking

For a better understanding of how tacking works we need to study three additional provisions in the Civil Code. First, consider Article 3442:

Art. 3442. Tacking of possession

The possession of the transferor is tacked to that of the transferee if there has been no interruption of possession.

La. Civ. Code art. 3442. In addition to stating the rule that tacking requires continuous, uninterrupted possession, this provision implies that tacking requires some kind of "juridical link" between two successive possessors. *Id.* rev. cmt (d).

According to Louisiana jurisprudence, a juridical link can be established by privity of contract or estate. In the seminal case of *Noel v. Jumonville Pipe and Machinery Co.*, 158 So.2d 179 (1963), the Louisiana Supreme Court explained:

Although it has been said that there is no definition of the word 'privity' which can be applied in all cases, as most generally defined, and in its broadest sense, 'privity' is the mutual or successive relationship to the same right of property, or such an identification in interest of one person with another as to represent the same legal right.

'Privity' is also defined as meaning a successive relationship to, or ownership of, the same property from a common source; a succession of relationship to the same thing, whether created by deed or by other act, or by operation of law; a succession of relationships by deed or other act or by operation of law; and is further defined as meaning a derivative kind of interest, founded on, or growing out of, the contract of another.

Id. at 184. In the example above, William can tack to Anne's possession whether he is her buyer or her heir because there is direct privity between the two persons. If William is Anne's buyer, there is privity of contract between Anne and William. If William is Anne's sole heir, there is privity of estate between Anne and William.

Article 3443 of the Civil Code adds a useful evidentiary rule for the resolution of tacking issues: "One who proves that he had possession at different times is presumed to have possessed during the intermediate period." La. Civ. Code art. 3443 (1982). A record owner should not be allowed to rebut this presumption of continued possession by pointing to simple gaps in corporeal possession; something more—either abandonment of possession or adverse possession by a third person that results in the loss of the right to possess—must be shown to overcome the presumption. La. Civ. Code arts. 3433, 3434 (1982).

The concept of a particular successor is crucial in one more context: it provides a mechanism to terminate precarious possession. As we saw earlier, "[a]cquisitive prescription does not run in favor of a precarious possessor or his universal successor." La. Civ. Code art. 3477 (1982). Recall Leroy Harper, the precarious possessor in *Harper v. Willis*, 383 So.2d 1299 (La. App. 3 Cir. 1980). In that case, the court determined that Harper could not prevail in a possessory action because he was a precarious possessor who was possessing on behalf of the true owners of the land. If Harper died intestate (or died testate but with only one named, universal successor—Leroy Jr.), his universal successor would step into his shoes as a precarious possessor. He would not be able to possess for himself and could not prescribe under of Article 3477.

But what if, rather than dying intestate, Harper sold his interests in the land he possessed to someone else. In that case, Harper's purchaser, a particular successor of a precarious possessor, could begin to prescribe in his own right. Article 3479 provides the alliterative authority for this result:

Art. 3479. Particular successor of precarious possessor

A particular successor of a precarious possessor who takes possession under an act translative of ownership possesses for himself, and prescription runs in his favor from the commencement of his possession.

La. Civ. Code art. 3479 (1982). We would reach the same result if Harper transferred his interests in the land he was possessing through a donation inter vivos or if he bequeathed those interests to a particular legatee. In any of those cases, the particular successor could begin to accrue possession for purposes of acquisitive prescription from the moment the particular successor acquires possession under an act translative of ownership. But note carefully that this particular successor would not be able to tack or to cumulate Harper's precarious possession with his own. *Id.* rev. cmt. (c).

3. Combining Different Qualities of Possession by Particular Title

By taking advantage of tacking, a possessor can cumulate either good faith or bad faith possession for purposes of acquiring ownership of an immovable by thirty-year acquisitive prescription. For purposes of acquiring ownership of an immovable by ten-year acquisitive prescription a possessor can cumulate two periods of good faith possession. But what if a subsequent possessor, whose own possession starts in bad faith, seeks to tack to his author's good faith possession? Is tacking allowed in that situation?

Consider the chart below, which presupposes that the author in possession has not possessed long enough to become the owner through acquisitive prescription in her own right:

Author in good faith conveys to acquirer in good faith.	Ten-year acquisitive prescription is available; and acquirer may cumulate author's possession.
Author in good faith conveys to acquirer in bad faith.	Only thirty-year acquisitive prescription is available; but acquirer may cumulate author's possession.
Author in bad faith conveys to acquirer in bad faith.	Only thirty-year acquisitive prescription is available; but acquirer may cumulate author's possession.
Author in bad faith conveys to acquirer in good faith.	Author's possession can be cumulated for thirty-year acquisitive prescription; or acquirer can maintain possession for ten years and gain ownership after ten years.

In the following decision, which of these scenarios does the court address? Do you agree with the majority's holding?

Bartlett v. Calhoun

412 So.2d 597 (La. 1982)

BLANCHE, Justice. This is a petitory action. The disputed property is a 300 acre tract of land located near the Black River in Catahoula Parish and owned at one time by W. C. Thompson and his wife. The Thompsons purportedly sold this tract to defendant, Stella Calhoun, on November 30, 1949. It appears from the record that thereafter the property was transferred by Ms. Calhoun to Grey Ramon Brown by act of sale dated December 10, 1949. Finally, in October of 1951, Ms. Calhoun re-purchased the property from Mr. Brown and it has remained in her possession since that date.

Plaintiffs, the alleged heirs of the Thompsons, filed this suit in 1977 seeking ownership and an accounting of revenue from the contested property. They challenge the validity of the November 30, 1949 act of sale, claiming that the Thompsons' signatures were forged.

Defendant moved for summary judgment, 404 So.2d 516 (La. App.), urging that because there was no issue as to a material fact, she was entitled to judgment as a matter of law. At the hearing on this motion, Ms. Calhoun contended that she had acquired the land in question by acquisitive prescription of ten years. Louisiana Civil Code article 3479, which sets forth the requisites for ten year acquisitive prescription, provides:

> Art. 3479. To acquire the ownership of immovables by the species of prescription which forms the subject of the present paragraph, four conditions must concur:
>
> 1. Good faith on the part of the possessor.
>
> 2. A title which shall be legal, and sufficient to transfer the property.
>
> 3. Possession during the time required by law, which possession must be accompanied by the incidents hereafter required.
>
> 4. And finally an object which may be acquired by prescription.

Plaintiffs argued that defendant, because of the alleged false signatures in the November 30, 1949 act of sale, was not in good faith. Defendant, in response to plaintiff's claim, urged that, even if she was in bad faith when she originally acquired the tract, she could take advantage of Grey Brown's (her transferee's) good faith, tack her subsequent possession to his, and own the property after the passage of ten years.

Both lower courts were of the opinion that the holding of *Liuzza v. Heirs of Nunzio*, 241 So.2d 277 (La. App. 5th Cir. 1970) was controlling in the instant case. When confronted with the identical issue, the court in *Liuzza* came to the following conclusion:

> In the very early case of *Devall v. Choppin*, 15 La. 566 (1840) the Supreme Court enunciated the proposition that if a successor showed that one of his authors was a possessor in good faith and had all the necessary ingredients for ten year prescription, he could acquire by such prescription even though he as well as an intermediary author possessed in bad faith. This interpretation has become the rule in our jurisprudence.

Accordingly, the trial and appellate courts held that, because Ms. Calhoun could rely on Grey Brown's good faith, it did not matter whether defendant was or was not herself in good faith. Concluding that plaintiff's challenge to Ms. Calhoun's plea of prescription did not bear on a material fact, summary judgment was rendered in favor of defendant. C.C.P. art. 966.

We granted writs to determine whether the lower courts' conclusion that defendant's status as a good or bad faith possessor was not a material fact was proper. In so doing, we re-evaluate the soundness of the jurisprudential rule which permits a bad faith possessor to tack his possession to that of his good faith author in order to acquire ownership by acquisitive prescription of ten years.

"Tacking", or the "joining of possessors", allows the present possessor to count, besides his own possession, that of his predecessor in order to prescribe. *M. Planiol*, Civil Law Treatise, Part 2, Sec. 2673 (12th Ed. La.St.L.Inst. trans. 1959). As a result, it is not necessary that the same individual possess the immovable during the entire period required for prescription. This joining, or tacking, of possessions is authorized by C.C. art. 3493, which provides:

> Art. 3493. The possessor is allowed to make the sum of possession necessary to prescribe, by adding to his own possession that of his author, in whatever manner he may have succeeded him, whether by an universal or particular, a lucrative or an onerous title.

By the word "author" this codal provision contemplates the person from whom another derives his right, whether by universal title or by particular title. C.C. art. 3494. Thus, it is imperative that a juridical link exist in order for a successor to acquire his predecessor's prescriptive rights. Though art. 3493 does not contain a separate provision for the universal successor as distinguished from the successor by particular title, we believe that a differentiation must exist due to the nature of these types of transfers.

The French commentators agree that the universal successor continues the deceased's possession and does not commence a new possession. 2 *Aubry & Rau*, Droit Civil Francais Nos. 218 (7th Ed. Esmein 1961), 2 Civil Law Translations at 365 (1966); *Baudry-Lacantinerie & Tissier*, Traite' Theoreque et Pratique de Droit Civil, Prescription Nos. 346, 347 (1924), 5 Civil Law Translations at 181 (La.St.L .Inst. trans. 1972). *See also Griffin v. Blanc*, 12 La. Ann. 5 (La. 1857). As noted by *Planiol*:

> The universal successor merely continues the deceased's possession (no. 2661). He succeeds to all of the latter's obligations as well as rights. It is thus not a new possession that begins but it is the deceased's possession that is transmitted to his heirs, with its virtues and its faults. *Planiol*, supra, Sec. 2674.

Because the universal successor's possession is nothing more than a continuation of the deceased's possession, he is bound by his author's good or bad faith and is powerless to alter the prescriptive rights transmitted to him. *Aubry & Rau*, Sec. 218, supra; *Planiol*, Sec. 2674, supra.

> For instance, the decedent possessed with just title and in good faith, an immovable belonging to another. He was thus in the process of prescribing ten to twenty years. His possession continues in favor of his heir with the same characteristics and the prescription will be completed at the end of ten or twenty years, commencing with the date when the decedent entered in possession. It is irrelevant that the heir is in bad faith at the moment when the possession is transferred to him.

> The effect of vices in the possession will be always the same as if the possession continued for the benefit of the decedent. It follows that vices incurable with respect to the decedent can not be cured by the heir. For instance, if the decedent was in bad faith from the beginning of his possession, his heir can prescribe only by thirty years although he is personally in good faith. *Baudry-Lacantinerie*, Sec. 348, *supra*.

Thus, it is evident that the provisions of C.C. art. 3482, which permit prescription to accrue after ten years as long as the possession is commenced in good faith, envisions only one possession and applies when property is transferred to a universal successor. *Baudry-Lacantinerie*, Sec. 351, *supra*. As far as the universal successor is concerned, it would be more accurate to leave out tacking and its connotations and describe the transaction as a mandatory substitution. Comment, "Tacking of Possession for Acquisitive Prescription", 8 La.L.Rev. 105 at 107–110 (1948).

Contrary to the universal successor, an individual who acquires by particular title commences a new possession which is separate and distinct from his author's possession. *Aubry & Rau*, Sec. 218, *supra*.

> . . . This type of successor commences a new possession, completely distinct from that of his grantor. Here we have two mutually independent possessions. *Baudry-Lacantinerie*, Sec. 350, *supra*.

Though the particular successor can cumulate his and his author's possessions, both must have all the statutory characteristics and conditions required for the completion of prescription. *Domat*, The Civil Law in its Natural Order, Sec. 2226 (2nd Ed., Cushing trans. 1861); *Aubry & Rau*, Sec. 218, supra; *Baudry-Lacantinerie*, Sec. 350, *supra*. The implications of this limitation on a particular successor's right to tack are fully explained by Planiol:

> Assuming that the preceding possessor was himself in the process of prescribing, several combinations may arise. If both of them were entitled to prescribe within from ten to twenty years, the new possessor would certainly have a right to consolidate the two possessions. The same result would obtain if neither of them was entitled to prescribe within these terms. In both cases, the thirty year period would be the only one available.

In these two cases, the two successive possessions of the successor and of his author may be added together. They are of the same nature and of the same quality.

But if it be assumed that the two successive possessors are not in the same position, from the standpoint of prescription — but one of them have a just title and being in good faith — complications arise. They are solved by this very simple rule: The years that apply to the thirty years prescription, which requires neither just title nor good faith, cannot be used in completing the prescription running from ten to twenty years. The latter prescription requires that both conditions exist. But, on the contrary, the years that have run in connection with this favored prescription may be counted in computing the thirty years prescription. All that it requires is possession.

EXAMPLES: Where the vendor is a possessor in good faith, and the purchaser is in bad faith. If the ten years prescription has not run in favor of the vendor, at the time of the sale, the purchaser cannot prescribe except upon the basis of thirty years, but he can count his author's years of possession.

Where the vendor was in bad faith but the purchaser in good faith, the latter can prescribe upon the basis of ten years but he cannot avail himself of his author's possession, because it applied solely to the thirty year period. In such a contingency, it might sometimes pay the purchaser to abandon his claim to the prescription of ten years in order to take advantage of the thirty years prescriptive period commenced by his author. This interest will come into play whenever the prescription has less than ten years to run before being completed. There is no doubt about the fact that he can then join his possession to that of his author to complete the thirty years. If the latter's possession would have applied to the shortened and privileged prescription it will a fortiori apply to the general prescription of thirty years.

Planiol, Sec. 2676, 2677, *supra*.

It is our opinion that this statement properly explains the restraints placed on a successor's right to join his possession with his author's possession for purposes of acquisitive prescription. Accordingly, any language to the contrary in previous opinions of this Court or of the courts of appeal must be disregarded. E.g. see *Liuzza v. Heirs of Nunzio*, supra; *Devall v. Choppin*, 15 La. 566 (1840); *Liquidators of Prudential Savings and Homestead Soc. v. Langermann*, 156 La. 76, 100 So. 55 (1924); *Brewster v. Hewes*, 113 La. 45, 36 So. 883 (1904); *Wheat v. Bayer and Thayer Hardwood Co. Inc.*, 15 La. App. 306, 131 So. 307 (1930); *Vance v. Ellerbe*, 150 La. 388, 90 So. 735 (1922); *Jackson v. D'Aubin*, 338 So.2d 575 (La. 1976).

Applying this civilian principle to the present case, it is evident that Ms. Calhoun's status as a possessor is essential to her claim of acquisitive prescription of ten years. Defendant, as a purchaser, is a successor by particular title. If she was in good faith when she re-acquired the property in 1951, she could cumulate the requisite ten years on her own, or tack her possession to that of her good faith author. On the other hand, if defendant was in bad faith she could not avail herself of Grey Brown's good faith and become owner of the land in question after the passage of ten years. Though she could still tack her possession to that of her author's for thirty year acquisitive prescription, the institution of this suit in 1977 would interrupt her possession and preclude her claim of ownership. *See* C.C. art. 3518.

However, both lower courts were of the opinion that defendant's status as a possessor did not present a material fact. As a result, it was never determined whether the pleadings, depositions, admissions of fact or affidavits established a genuine issue as to this material fact. This determination is to be made on remand.

Accordingly, the summary judgment rendered in defendant's favor is reversed, and the case is remanded to the district court for further proceedings in accordance with law.

MARCUS, Justice, dissenting. La. Civ. Code art. 3479 sets forth the conditions that must concur to acquire the ownership of immovables by acquisitive prescription of ten years. One of these conditions is "(g)ood faith on the part of the possessor." Article 3482 provides that "if the possession has commenced in good faith," subsequent bad faith "shall not prevent the prescription." Finally, art. 3493 provides that the "possessor is allowed to make the sum of possession necessary to prescribe, by adding to his own possession that of his author, in whatever manner he may have succeeded him, whether by an universal or particular . . . title."

Under the above articles, prescription accrues after ten years as long as possession commenced in good faith. Subsequent bad faith is of no moment. A possessor may add to his own possession that of his author in title to make the sum of possession necessary to prescribe. Hence, a bad faith possessor is permitted to "tack" his possession to that of his good faith author in title to acquire ownership by acquisitive prescription of ten years. This has been the law of this state since *Devall v. Choppin*, 15 La. 566 (1840). I see no compelling reason to change it at this time.

In the instant case, Ms. Calhoun originally acquired the property on November 30, 1949. It is alleged that she was in bad faith at the time of this sale. However, Grey Brown acquired the property in good faith by act of sale from Ms. Calhoun on December 10, 1949. In October of 1951, Ms. Calhoun repurchased the property from Mr. Brown and it has remained in her possession since that date. Since possession must be commenced in good faith, the prescription of ten years began to run when Mr. Brown acquired the property in good faith and by just title on December 10, 1949. As a subsequent possessor of the property, Ms. Calhoun is allowed to "tack" her possession to that of her author in title, Mr. Brown. Accordingly, Ms. Calhoun became the owner of the property by the acquisitive prescription of ten year on December 10, 1959. Hence, the trial judge correctly granted defendant's motion for summary judgment. The court of appeal was correct in affirming that judgment. I would affirm. Accordingly, I respectfully dissent.

Notes and Questions

1. Whose reasoning is most persuasive in *Bartlett v. Calhoun*, 412 So.2d 597 (La. 1982)? Justice Blanche's opinion for the majority? Or Justice Marcus in dissent? This decision was rendered at the height of the Civilian Renaissance in Louisiana. Notice the extent to which Justice Blanche's opinion relies extensively on French academic doctrine to reverse almost 140 years of prior Louisiana Supreme Court precedent. Is this kind of decision making typical of what you might expect from the highest court in one of Louisiana's sister states?

2. Here is one more commonsense rule to keep in mind when considering questions of tacking: tacking only applies when a possessor is attempting to link up his time of possession with that of a prior adverse possessor *who was not the true owner*. An adverse possessor seeking to establish ownership by acquisitive prescription is, by definition, attempting to use his and his author's possession to defeat the claims of a true owner who is not in possession of the immovable property in dispute. In the context of *Bartlett v. Calhoun*, this rule means that Stella Calhoun could in no case attempt to tack her possession, or that of her immediate predecessor in possession, to that of W.C. Thompson and his wife. Although the Thompsons certainly possessed the land in dispute, they possessed the land *as record owners*. In other words, an acquisitive prescription claimant can only tack back through the possession of adverse possessors. A record owner's possession cannot be cumulated by tacking.

3. From the discussion of Stella Calhoun's assertion of the right to tack a bad faith possession to that of a previous good faith possession for purposes of ten-year acquisitive prescription, one might assume that Stella Calhoun was ready to concede her bad faith. Yet, recall that the Louisiana Supreme Court remanded the matter to the trial court for further consideration and gave Calhoun the opportunity to prove that she was in good faith at the time she commenced her possession. Extensive litigation followed that remand. *See Bartlett v. Calhoun*, 430 So.2d 1358 (La. App. 3 Cir. 1983), *writ denied*, 438 So.2d 575 (1983); *Bartlett v. Calhoun*, 491 S0.2d 791 (La. App. 3 Cir. 1986), *writ denied*, 496 So.2d 328 (1986). For a discussion of the importance of *Bartlett v. Calhoun*, an analysis of contemporary criticism of the supreme court decision, a review of the subsequent litigation, and an explanation of how Stella Calhoun ultimately prevailed and established ownership of the land in dispute, see John A. Lovett, *Tacking in a Mixed Jurisdiction, in* Nothing So Practical as a Good Theory: Festschrift for George L. Gretton (Andrew J.M. Steven, et al, eds.) 162–76 (2017), *at* https://papers.ssrn.com/sol3/papers.cfm?abstract_id =3103308.

E. Boundary Actions and Boundary Tacking

In Louisiana, a nominate real action, which is distinct from the petitory action and the action for a declaratory judgment, governs boundary disputes between contiguous owners: the boundary action under Articles 3691 through 2693 of the Louisiana Code of Civil Procedure. La. Code of Civ. Proc. Arts 3691–3693. Title VI of Book II of the Civil Code provides a number of technical rules. *See generally* La. Civ. Code arts 784–96 (1977).

The right to bring an action to fix a boundary between contiguous lands is imprescriptible, which means that it can never be lost by the passage of time. La. Civ. Code art. 788 (1977). A boundary is generally defined as "the line of separation between contiguous lands" and a "boundary marker" is "a natural or artificial object that marks on the ground the line of separation of contiguous lands." La. Civ. Code art. 784 (1977). An action to ascertain and mark a boundary may be brought by an owner, by one who possesses as owner, and even by a usufructuary (although the action will usually not be binding on the naked owner). La. Civ. Code art. 786 (1977). A lessee may compel a lessor to bring a boundary action to protect the lessee's interest in the immovable property subject to the lease. La. Civ. Code art. 787 (1977).

A boundary may be fixed judicially or extrajudicially by written agreement between the parties, La. Civ. Code art. 789 (1977). In the judicial mode, the court will fix the boundaries according to the parties' ownership of the contiguous lands, or, if neither party can prove ownership, according to the limits established by possession. La. Civ. Code art. 792 (1977). When a party proves ownership through acquisitive prescription, the boundary is fixed according to the limits established by the possession of the parties rather than by titles. La. Civ. Code art. 794 (1977).

The second sentence in Article 794 of the Civil Code may be the most important, and frequently the most misunderstood, of the provisions found in Title VI:

Art. 794. Determination of ownership according to prescription

When a party proves acquisitive prescription, the boundary shall be fixed according to the limits established by prescription rather than titles. If a party and his ancestors in title possess for thirty years without interruption, within visible bounds, more land than their title called for, the boundary shall be fixed along these bounds.

La. Civ. Code art. 794 (1977). This provision allows a possessor who has title to some land, but who is actually possessing more land than his title describes, to cumulate his possession time to that of a predecessor in possession for purposes of thirty year acquisitive prescription, as long as some juridical link exists between the possessor and his authors and, most importantly, as long as both the ancestor and the succeeding possessor possessed within the same visible bounds. Article 794 creates an exception to the tacking requirement of strict privity of title—a juridical link describing all the property claimed by acquisitive prescription.

Suppose that Arnold owned three acres of land. Twenty-five years ago, Arnold sold this land to Bob with an act of sale that describes the three acres. At the time he purchased the land from Arnold, Bob erected a fence. But rather than enclose just the three acres described in the act of sale, Bob fenced in three-and-one-half acres—one-half acre more than his act of sale said he owned. He did this by intentionally or accidently placing his fence thirty feet farther east than the property description called for on the east side of his property.

Now suppose that Bob sold the land he owned to Cindy, who acquired the land in good faith and through an act of sale that was executed as an authentic act and recorded in the relevant public records; however, the act of sale used the same property description found in the act of conveyance from Arnold to Bob. When Cindy purchased the three acres from Bob, she only purchased ownership of the three acres described in that act. She did not purchase ownership of the additional one half acre fenced in by Bob. Although the act which Cindy purchased from Bob could not be considered a "just title" for purposes of ten year acquisitive prescription for the additional one-half acre because the half acre was not included in the act (*cf.* La. Civ. Code art. 3483 (1982)) that act would supply a sufficient juridical link to allow Cindy to tack her possession of the half acre to Bob's possession of it for purposes of thirty year acquisitive prescription. If Cindy continued to possess within the same "visible bounds" as Bob (up to the original fence) for another five years, she would succeed in establishing thirty year acquisitive prescription of the extra one-half acre not described in her act of sale under Article 794 of the Civil Code.

To understand another situation in which boundary tacking might come into play, imagine that in the hypothetical above Bob was a squatter—someone who took possession of the three-and-one-half acres enclosed by the fence without any title whatsoever. Now suppose that after fifteen years of uninterrupted adverse possession, Bob sold the land he possessed to Cindy by virtue of an act of sale that only described three acres, not all of the three-and-one-half acres that he possessed within the bounds of the fence. If Cindy purchased Bob's land in good faith, she could establish ownership of the three acres described in the act of sale after ten years of possession. Moreover, she could establish ownership of the *other one-half acre* after another fifteen years of possession within the visible bounds identified by the fence through boundary tacking under Article 794 of the Civil Code.

Read the following decision for an example of the challenges involved with establishing the visible bounds in the context of a boundary tacking claim under Article 794 of the Civil Code. Notice in particular the court's sensitivity to the specific characteristics of the land in dispute.

Secret Cove, L.L.C. v. Thomas

862 So.2d 1010 (La. App. 1 Cir. 2003)

PARRO, Judge. Secret Cove, L.L.C., the record owner of certain real property, appeals a judgment declaring that George Ronald Thomas and his wife, Audrey Lee Dykes Thomas (the Thomases), acquired ownership of a portion of that property by thirty-year acquisitive prescription. Based on our review of the facts and law, we affirm in part, vacate in part, and remand for amendment of the judgment.

Factual and Procedural Background

On April 28, 1997, Secret Cove, L.L.C. (Secret Cove), a corporation owned by Dr. Robert M. Hogan and his wife, Deborah Surgi Hogan (the Hogans), bought a tract of rural land in Section 35, Township 5 South, Range 13 East, St. Tammany Parish, containing approximately 216 acres. The property is south of Lock No. 2 and borders the western edge of the Pearl River Navigational Canal (the canal); the southern boundary of the property is the section line between Section 35 and Section 48. At the time of the purchase, a small portion of the property, between one and three acres in the extreme southeastern part of the tract adjoining the canal (the disputed property), was the site of a campground operated by the Thomases. The Thomases were and are the record owners of property in Section 48 that is immediately adjacent to and south of the disputed property. The disputed property, a narrow finger of land alongside the canal, extends perpendicularly from the section line northward into Section 35. After Secret Cove bought the property in Section 35, the Hogans attempted to obtain possession of the disputed property; however, the Thomases refused to leave. Eventually, this litigation between the parties ensued.

Secret Cove filed this suit as a petitory action on October 29, 1999, claiming ownership of and seeking possession of the disputed property, along with damages for trespass and lost revenues. The Thomases reconvened, claiming that they possessed the disputed property and that they and their family had possessed it continuously and openly since about 1957. They claimed that by virtue of thirty-year acquisitive prescription, they had acquired ownership of the disputed property.

Secret Cove presented evidence of its title, and the parties stipulated at trial that Secret Cove had valid record title to the disputed property. Therefore, the only issues at trial concerned the extent and nature of the Thomases' possession and whether it met the legal requirements for thirty-year acquisitive prescription. Following the trial, the court ruled in favor of the Thomases, finding they had continuous and open possession of the disputed property for thirty years, with the intent to own it and within certain described visible boundaries. The court concluded that although the Thomases' title over their property in Section 48 did not extend to the disputed property in Section 35, the possession of the disputed property by Jack J. Thomas, which began in 1957, could be tacked to that of his son, George Ronald Thomas. [In 1985, Jack J. Thomas and his wife sold a portion of the property in Section 48 to George and his wife to be used as a campground.] By tacking the father's possession to the son's possession, the court concluded the Thomases had reached the thirty years required for acquisitive prescription.

The judgment was signed July 9, 2002, maintaining the Thomases' plea of thirty-year acquisitive prescription and declaring them to be the owners of the disputed property. Secret Cove appealed, assigning as error the trial court's factual findings relative to visible boundaries; its conclusions that the nature and extent of the Thomases' possession satisfied the legal requirements for thirty-year acquisitive prescription; its signing of a judgment in which the eastern boundary line is described differently from the court's findings as set forth in its reasons for judgment; and its credibility determinations with respect to the witnesses who testified at the trial. . . .

Applicable Law

In Louisiana, the petitory action is available for the recovery of immovable property. A. N. Yiannopoulos, Property § 268, at 540, in *2 Louisiana Civil Law Treatise* (4th ed. 2001). The petitory action is brought by a person who claims ownership, but is not in possession, of immovable property, against another who is in possession or who also claims the ownership of that properly, seeking to obtain judgment recognizing the plaintiff's ownership. See LSA-C.C.P. art. 3651. Acquisitive prescription beyond title by possession to a visible boundary for a period of thirty years may be pleaded as a defense in a petitory action. *Cuthbertson v. Unopened Succession of Tate*, 544 So. 2d 1236, 1239 (La. App. 3rd Cir. 1989). In a petitory action, when one party relies on title and the other on acquisitive prescription, the party relying on title will prevail unless the adversary establishes his ownership by acquisitive prescription. *Pace v. Towns*, 33,071 (La. App. 2nd Cir. 4/5/00), 756 So. 2d 680. . . .

For purposes of acquisitive prescription without title, possession extends only to that which has been actually possessed. LSA-C.C. art. 3487. Actual possession must be either inch-by-inch possession or possession within enclosures. According to well-settled Louisiana jurisprudence, an enclosure is any natural or artificial boundary. LSA-C.C. art. 3426, comment (d), Revision Comments — 1982, citing A. N. Yiannopoulos, Property §§ 212–214, in *2 Louisiana Civil Law Treatise* (2d ed. 1980). The party who does not hold title to the disputed tract has the burden of proving actual possession within enclosures sufficient to establish the limits of possession with certainty, by either natural or artificial marks, giving notice to the world of the extent of possession exercised. *Conway v. Crowell Land & Mineral Corp.*, 93-1158 (La. App. 3rd Cir. 4/6/94), 635 So. 2d 544, 549–550, writ denied, 94-1198 (La. 7/1/94), 639 So. 2d 1166; *Hill v. Richey*, 221 La. 402, 420, 59 So. 2d 434, 440 (1952). . . .

Possession can be transferred by universal title or by particular title. LSA-C.C. art. 3441. When possession is so transferred, the possession of the transferor is tacked to that of the transferee if there has been no interruption of possession. LSA-C.C. art. 3442. Under these provisions, privity of contract or estate is an essential prerequisite to tacking of possession. *Brown v. Wood*, 451 So. 2d 569, 573 (La. App. 2nd Cir.), writ denied, 452 So. 2d 1176 (La. 1984).

Alternatively, under Louisiana Civil Code article 794, a title holder may acquire more land than his title calls for by possessing property beyond his title for thirty years without interruption and within visible bounds. Such a title holder may attain the thirty-year possessory period — which is necessary to perfect prescriptive title in the absence of good faith and just title — by "tacking" on to the possession of his ancestor in title. LSA-C.C. arts. 794 and 3442; *Brown*, 451 So. 2d at 572–73; *Falcone*, 691 So. 2d at 317. Under Article 794, the privity of title between the possessor and his ancestor in title need not extend to the property to which the possessor asserts prescriptive title; under this article, the juridical link, or written instrument that passes to the possessor from his ancestor in title need not encompass or include the particular property to which the possessor claims prescriptive title. *Brown*, 451 So. 2d at 572–73. In that sense, tacking under Article 794, which allows one to prescribe beyond title on adjacent property to visible boundaries, differs from tacking under Articles 3441 and 3442, which limit tacking for prescriptive purposes to the property described in title documents. *See Brown*, 451 So. 2d at 573.

. . . .

Discussion

The trial court provided extensive written reasons, summarizing the evidence supporting its judgment and explaining how that evidence met the legal criteria for adverse possession sufficient to acquire ownership of immovable property. We will not attempt to re-summarize that evidence. However, we will briefly examine those factors necessary to address the assignments of error.

Evaluation of Witnesses' Testimony

. . . .

Having examined the testimony and documentary evidence, we find no inconsistency, implausibility, or other indicia sufficient to establish that the trial court's conclusions concerning the witnesses were clearly wrong. While this court might have evaluated some or all of that testimony differently, the assessments are well within the trial court's purview and are not unreasonable. Therefore, this assignment of error is without merit.

Visible Boundaries

In two of its assignments of error, Secret Cove alleges the trial court erred in: (1) establishing visible boundaries when there are none on three of the four sides of the disputed property, and (2) determining the Thomases had acquired ownership of that property through thirty-year acquisitive prescription by finding visible boundaries and possession. The court stated that two of the boundaries are not in dispute, those being the section line on the south and the canal on the east. Although Secret Cove argues that a section line is not visible, various maps in evidence show that the section line is marked on the ground by concrete monuments set in place by the U.S. Army Corps of Engineers. Therefore, we find no error in the trial court's determination that one of the visible boundaries of the Thomases' possession is the section line.

As noted by the trial court, the most problematic "visible boundaries" involve the northern and western limits of the Thomases' possession. The court fixed these boundaries in accordance with a map or plat of survey by Billy C. Daniels, who surveyed the disputed property for the Thomases. The trial court set the northern boundary of their possession along the southern edge of a natural drainage feature, known to the Thomases as "Jessie Bayou," which drains into the canal from the swamp area to the north and west of the disputed property. Secret Cove argues there was no evidence to show possession to that point, but only that the Thomases conducted some activities involving a large sand pile just south of that waterway.

We disagree with this characterization of the evidence. Reverend William J. Harris, who is George Thomas's half brother, testified that George's father, Jack J. Thomas, had a sand and gravel business on the Thomas property in Section 48 and used the disputed property to stockpile the product. According to him, these piles extended from the section line "all the way up here to Jessie Bayou," right to the edge of it. In connection with the sand and gravel business, "the waterfront," which was what the Thomas family called the disputed property, was where barges were tied while the product was being loaded. He recalled that one of those barges got loose in 1957 and floated to the north until it ran aground at a sandbar at Jessie Bayou. The sand pile immediately to the south of Jessie Bayou is what remains of the sand and gravel that Rev. Harris off-loaded from that barge so it could be re-floated. After that year, the family used a bulldozer to clear and maintain the road "all the way back up here to Jessie Bayou."

Jack H. Thomas, George's brother, confirmed the location of the sand and gravel piles and said the road was kept open because his father "sold gravel from up there," and the buyers used the road to access the material. The sand and gravel business continued from the late fifties until the campground was built in 1967. Josephine Thomas, who is George Thomas's mother, confirmed that the family had used the waterfront property for "over fifty years," up to Jessie Bayou. She recalled that some of her husband's friends liked to camp there, because they had mentally handicapped children who could be allowed to play on the sand pile in safety. George Thomas testified that after the commercial campground was started in 1967, his father "always kept underbrush out of there, and he always kept that road cleared that runs along the canal." He also said that on the north end, the grassy area was always kept cleared, because "that's mainly where we picnicked and tent camped."

The surveys, aerial photographs, and topographic maps in the record clearly show the elevated sandy area just south of Jessie Bayou, although the waterway itself is not so clearly marked and is not named on the maps. However, there was consistent testimony concerning the existence of this natural boundary and the activities of the Thomas family up to that feature, including the sand and gravel operation, tent camping, picnics, road maintenance, and clearing of underbrush. This evidence supports the trial court's finding that the southern edge of Jessie Bayou is a visible boundary marking the northern limit of the Thomases' possession of the disputed property. Of course, there was evidence to the contrary from Secret Cove's witnesses. But the function of the trial court is to make a choice between conflicting versions of events, and this court cannot say, on the basis of the record in this case, that the trial court's choice of this boundary is clearly wrong.

Similarly, with respect to the western boundary, the record contains numerous references to a distinct difference in elevation between the disputed property and the swamp area lying immediately to its west. According to Daniels, "there's about a two-foot difference in height there," along which he drew the western boundary line on his survey. Another surveyor, Jeron Fitzmorris, confirmed that this difference was "visible as a natural distinction between high and low," and observed "by walking along in spots between the high and the low that it's a natural — it's sort of like a natural boundary as a river bank would be." Jack H. Thomas testified that at some point, his father had painted marks on some of the cypresses along the edge of the swamp "to keep people from running off into the swamp" where there was quicksand. Frank Thomas said the line between the "waterfront property" and the swamp was especially evident when the water was high, because then the disputed property "would be the only place that the land would be showing." Topographic maps confirm the existence of this natural feature distinguishing the area used by the Thomases from the "gum swamp" to its west.

Secret Cove's brief to this court states that the best legal definition describing what is required for a visible boundary is in *Rathborne v. Hale,* 95-1225 (La. App. 4th Cir. 1/19/96), 667 So. 2d 1197, 1201, *writ denied,* 96-0747 (La. 5/3/96), 672 So. 2d 692, where the court stated:

> An enclosure does not require a fence but it does require that the land possessed as owner may be established with certainty, either by natural or artificial marks, sufficient to give notice to the world of the character and the extent of the possession, as well as its full identity and its certain boundaries.

Applying this definition, we conclude that the visible boundaries recognized by the trial court, with the exception of the error concerning the canal on the east, are supported by the evidence and are sufficiently certain and identifiable to meet the legal criteria.

Possession

In the *Rathborne* case, the court ultimately concluded that although certain visible boundaries existed, the adverse possessor had not established by a preponderance of the evidence his requisite thirty years of "continuous, uninterrupted, adverse possession up to that boundary" with intent to own. *Rathborne,* 667 So. 2d at 1209. In the matter before us, the parties stipulated that the Thomases had been in continuous corporeal possession of the disputed property and had been using it as a campground since 1975. Therefore, it is their possession between October 1969 and 1975 that is crucial to the resolution of this case. To have legal effect, possession must be continuous, uninterrupted, peaceable, public, and unequivocal as to the intent of the possessor to own the property. See LSA-C.C. arts. 3435 and 3436. One who proves that he had possession at different times is presumed to have possessed during the intermediate period. LSA-C.C. art. 3443. The quality of possession required up to a visible boundary in a particular case depends upon the type of land in dispute. *Liner v. Louisiana Land and Exploration Co.* 319 So. 2d 766 (La. 1975); *Cuthbertson,* 544 So. 2d at 1239.

The land involved in this case is wild, undeveloped, rural property; the entire area is virtually uninhabited except for the Thomases to the south, and the disputed property is inaccessible except by boat or by a road through the Thomas property. The Thomases did not occupy the disputed property or any part of it on a continuous basis during these years; however, possession does not require them to inhabit the property or be constantly present on it. The evidence shows continuity of their possession during the years in question by clearing the underbrush, maintaining the road alongside the levee, and developing the campground area. Testimony of several witnesses revealed that the clearing for the campground, which began in 1967, continued during later years as the camping activity increased. The aerial photographs, as interpreted by experts for both sides, show clearing activity on both sides of the road in 1967, plus removal of ground vegetation and the presence of dirt piles along the canal. The large sand pile just south of Jessie Bayou is also clearly visible, as is the road leading to it. A 1971 photograph shows additional widening of the road and a possible "turn-around" area on the disputed property. By 1973, three trails can be clearly seen on the disputed property, leading from the road to the canal. A 1975 photograph shows extensive clearing and five small structures on the disputed property. By 1978, there were permanent structures on the disputed property, along with a number of boat docks.

The Thomases exercised possession as if they owned the disputed property-giving permission for their friends to use the property for camping, fishing, and picnicking; allowing people to use the road to access the sand pile near Jessie Bayou; selling or giving away the sand and gravel on the property; tying up boats and using the waterfront for recreation whenever they pleased; and eventually expanding their commercial campground to include the property. They took possession of the property peaceably and openly, and in all the years they used it until this suit was filed, there is no evidence that anyone ever questioned their right to use the property or tried to remove them from it.

Based on our review of the evidence in this case, we find a reasonable factual basis in the record for the trial court's finding that the Thomases possessed the disputed property as owners for thirty years. The evidence supports the conclusion that the nature and extent of that possession satisfied the requirements of acquisitive prescription. Furthermore, we find nothing in the record to convince us that the trial court's conclusion was manifestly erroneous. The trial court's application of the legal principles: of tacking under Louisiana Civil Code article 794 were also correct, thereby allowing the possession beyond the title of Jack J. Thomas to be added to that of his son to reach the requisite thirty years for ownership under acquisitive prescription. . . .

AFFIRMED IN PART, VACATED IN PART, AND REMANDED.

* * *

At times, assertions of boundary tacking under Article 794 of the Civil Code can create a legal quagmire. In the following case, the court of appeal was misled,

according to the Louisiana Supreme Court, by the argument that the Public Records Doctrine negated application of Article 794. Which court do you think is correct? The court of appeal or the Louisiana Supreme Court?

Loutre Land and Timber Co. v. Roberts
63 So.3d 120 (La. 2011)

CLARK, Justice. We granted certiorari to determine whether the court of appeal
erred in reversing the trial court's judgment and in recognizing the defendant as the
owner of a disputed tract of property. For the reasons that follow, we find the laws
on acquisitive prescription require reversal of the court of appeal's ruling, and we
remand for the determination of issues pretermitted on appeal.

Facts and Procedural History

The instant litigation involves a dispute over a tract of land that lies between two
contiguous pieces of property that are owned by two separate owners. The Marie
Wilson Morgan family owned an 80-acre tract that was described as the "Section 3
Tract" in a recorded deed dating back to 1943. As evidenced by the same recorded
deed, the Morgan family also owned twenty acres located adjacent to the Section 3
Tract, lying in the SW/4 of Section 2. The combined land is hereinafter referred to
as the "100 Acres." The Wilton A. Roberts family owned the tract of land that was
described as the "Section 10 Tract" in a recorded deed. Title to the Section 10 Tract
passed from Dorothy Harbour to Wilton A. Roberts and Rebecca Jane Roberts in
1964. Subsequently, Edward W. Roberts ("Roberts"), the defendant, inherited his
parents' interests in the property. The Section 3 Tract is immediately north of the
Section 10 Tract, and the "Ideal Boundary" between these two tracts is the governmental section line, separating the SE/4 of the SE/4 of Section 3 Tract and the NE/4
of the NE/4 of Section 10.

A fence, running from east to west, however, is located in the middle of the Section 10 Tract and has been present for well over thirty years. The amount of land
lying north of the fence to the Ideal Boundary is approximately 15 acres of property
and is hereinafter referred to as the "Disputed Tract." The record establishes (and
no one contests) that the Morgan family adversely possessed the Disputed Tract for
more than thirty years via actual acts of corporeal possession.

On July 29, 2002, the Succession of Marie Wilson Morgan ("the Succession")
sold the following land to Loutre Land and Timber Company ("Loutre") through a
full warranty deed, entitled "Act of Sale":

> The South Half of the Southwest Quarter of the Southwest Quarter
> (S-1/2 of SW-1/4 of SW-1/4) of Section 2, Township 16 North, Range 8 East,
> Franklin Parish, Louisiana, and the East Half of the Southeast Quarter
> (E-1/2 of SE-1/4) of Section 3, Township 16 North, Range 8 East, Franklin
> Parish, Louisiana, consisting of 100 acres, more or less, including all crop
> base acres.

Additionally, the deed transferred "all rights of prescription, whether acquisitive or liberative, to which said vendor may be entitled." Loutre paid the Succession $75,000.00. The deed was recorded on August 5, 2002.

After conducting a survey and confirming the Disputed Tract was included in the 1964 title he inherited from his parents, Roberts sought to obtain a quitclaim deed from the Succession ("the Quitclaim Deed") to recognize his right to the land. The Succession's attorney, Daniel Wirtz, indicated he believed the Succession had sold the Disputed Tract to Loutre and, therefore, had nothing to transfer to Roberts. However, on January 29, 2003, the Succession ultimately executed the Quitclaim Deed in favor of Roberts in exchange for $3,000.00. The Quitclaim Deed was recorded on February 27, 2003, and conveyed to Roberts the following property without warranty:

> Beginning at the northeast corner of Northeast Quarter of Northeast Quarter of Section 10, Township 16 North, Range 8 East, and running due west along the north line of said forty to the Northwest corner thereof, thence due south a distance of 15.50 chains, thence due east to the eastern boundary of said forty, thence due north a distance of 15.50 chains, to the northeast corner of said forty and the point of beginning, containing 32 acres, more or less, in the Northeast Quarter of Northeast Quarter of Section 10, Township 16 North, Range 8 East.

Subsequently, in June 2003, Roberts entered the Disputed Tract and "bush hogged" a path in an effort to erect a new fence to establish the boundary described in the Quitclaim Deed. In doing so, he destroyed pine seedlings that had been planted along the fence by Loutre and created ruts in the land. Loutre filed suit, contending it owned the Disputed Tract insofar as it tacked the possession of its ancestor, the Morgan family. In its petition for damages, Loutre asserted claims for trespass and property destruction. Roberts answered and filed a reconventional demand, arguing he owned the Disputed Tract and should be compensated for loss of rental income.

On October 7, 2004, Loutre filed a motion for partial summary judgment, asking the trial court to recognize the fence as the proper boundary. Finding Loutre to be the rightful owner of the property by virtue of acquisitive prescription, the trial court entered judgment in favor of Loutre on June 2, 2005. After a trial on the merits to determine the amount of damages, the trial court awarded Loutre $15,250.00.

Roberts appealed the grant of the partial summary judgment and the amount of damages. The court of appeal found there was a genuine issue of material fact regarding the intent of the Succession and Loutre as to what land was actually being transferred pursuant to the full warranty deed. Accordingly, the court of appeal found summary judgment was inappropriate and remanded the matter to the trial court to conduct a trial on the issue of intent. *Loutre Land and Timber Co. v. Roberts*, 42,918 (La. App. 2 Cir. 4/16/08), 981 So.2d 775, *writ denied*, 08-1422 (La. 10/31/08), 994 So.2d 535.

On remand, the trial court heard testimony and accepted evidence relative to the intent of the Succession and Loutre in executing the Act of Sale. The trial court ruled in favor of Loutre, finding the parties intended to convey all of the land north of the fence, including the Disputed Tract. Recognizing Loutre as the owner, it then awarded it $17,750.00 in damages. Both Loutre and Roberts appealed.

The court of appeal reversed the judgment of the trial court and remanded the case to fix the boundaries in accordance with the parties' surveys. *Loutre Land and Timber Co. v. Roberts*, 45,355 (La. App. 2 Cir. 8/4/10), 47 So.3d 478. In reaching this conclusion, the court of appeal held that the fact the Succession was the "ancestor in title" to both Roberts and Loutre placed the issue outside the scope of a typical boundary action when one party claims acquisitive possession and the other relies on title. Accordingly, it conducted an analysis under "something other than [Civil Code] Article 794" in order to rank the competing transfers. The court of appeal began by acknowledging the Morgan family's possession extended beyond thirty years and, thus, the Succession acquired the right to sell the property via acquisitive prescription. Next, the court of appeal recognized that Loutre continued the possession by virtue of planting the seedlings. Thus, it classified Roberts as an adverse possessor due to his act of bush hogging the land. Pursuant to La. Civ. Code art. 3654, then, Roberts was required to show "he had acquired ownership from a previous owner." Ultimately, by turning to the public records doctrine, the court of appeal found Roberts satisfied this burden. In particular, it found the Quitclaim Deed to Roberts specifically described the Disputed Tract while the Act of Sale to Loutre did not. As such, the deeds represented separate transfers of differently described immovables. Further, the court of appeal noted that Roberts was a third party to the transfer between the Succession and Loutre, and he could have concluded that the Succession intended to sell the 100 acres separate from the Disputed Tract. Under the law of registry, then, it determined Roberts' deed was superior to Loutre's deed. Finally, the court of appeal dismissed Roberts' claims for damages, finding no support in the record to justify an award.

Judge Moore dissented, finding La. Civ. Code art. 794 clearly governed and mandated a ruling different from that reached by the majority. He agreed that the Morgan family possessed the property for more than thirty years; therefore, the Succession acquired the right to sell it to Loutre. However, he disagreed that the public records doctrine had any relevance and opined that to the extent it could somehow trump acquisitive prescription, the doctrine would not work in favor of Roberts. Rather, the Act of Sale that conveyed 100 acres "more or less . . . together with all rights of prescription, whether acquisitive or prescriptive, to which said vendor may be entitled" clearly evidenced the intent by the Succession and Loutre to transfer all of the property north of the fence, including the Disputed Tract. Because (1) the Act of Sale conveyed the property to Loutre and (2) a quitclaim deed can only convey whatever interest the seller actually has in the property, the Succession had nothing to sell when it executed the Quitclaim Deed in favor of Roberts. Thus, nothing was transferred to Roberts. Additionally, Judge Moore believed the majority ignored the manifest error standard by failing to give credit to the trial court's credibility determinations that led it to find such intent indeed existed.

Loutre filed a writ application in this court, contending the court of appeal committed error. We granted certiorari to determine who is the rightful owner of the Disputed Tract. *Loutre Land and Timber Co. v. Roberts*, 10-C-2327 (La. 1/7/11), 52 So.3d 879.

Applicable Law

. . . .

In *Marks v. Zimmerman Farms, LLC*, 44,279, pp. 11–12 (La. App. 2 Cir. 5/20/09), 13 So.3d 768, 774–75, the Louisiana Second Circuit Court of Appeal succinctly explained tacking as it relates to La. Civ. Code art. 794:

> The legal principles which govern tacking under La. C.C. art. 794 are in some respects different and distinct from the principles which govern tacking under La. C.C. arts. 3441 and 3442. La. C.C. art. 794 deals with boundary prescription, strictly speaking, while La. C.C. arts. 3441 and 3442 provide general rules which refer in broader terms to acquisitive prescription of property, generally. *Brown v. Wood*, [451 So.2d 569 (La. App. 2 Cir. 1984), *writ denied*, 452 So.2d 1176 (La. 1984)].
>
> In *Brown v. Wood, supra*, this court noted that tacking under La. C.C. art. 794 is different from tacking under the general tacking provisions of La. C.C. arts. 3441 and 3442 in the following respect:
>
> Under Article 794, the privity of title between the possessor and his ancestor in title need not extend to the property to which the possessor asserts prescriptive title; under Article 794, the juridical link, or written instrument which passes to the possessor from his ancestor in title need not encompass or include the particular property to which the possessor claims prescriptive title. . . .
>
> Simply stated, under Art. 794 (old Art. 852), one may utilize tacking to prescribe beyond title on adjacent property to the extent of visible boundaries, but under the general prescriptive articles, Arts. 3441 and 3442, tacking may be utilized to prescribe only to the extent of title.

Discussion

The record establishes that the Morgan family corporeally possessed the Disputed Tract for more than thirty years, prior to the sale of the land to Loutre. [Several witnesses provided uncontradicted testimony that the Morgan family farmed and/or hunted on the land up unto the fence's boundary dating back to as early as 1959. Additionally, Roberts does not contest this finding of corporeal possession by the Succession.] The possession was continuous, uninterrupted, peaceable, public, and unequivocal. Thus, the Succession was legally entitled to sell the land. The

Succession then executed the Act of Sale with Loutre, transferring the 100 acres "more or less," "together with all rights of prescription, whether acquisitive or liberative, to which said vendor may be entitled." This full warranty deed, then, served as the juridical link. As explained above, the deed is not required to include the particular property to which the possessor claims prescriptive title, namely, the Disputed Tract. Rather, La. Civ.Code art. 794 allows a party to tack onto the possession of its ancestor in title if the possession occurs without interruption. If the combined possession spans thirty years, the party is entitled to have the boundary fixed along the visible bounds of the possession. Loutre, by planting the pine seedlings along the fence, continued the possession of the Succession, making the fence the proper boundary line. As such, the trial court correctly determined Loutre is the proper owner of the Disputed Tract. The inquiry ends after this straightforward application of La. Civ.Code 794.

The court of appeal, however, felt "something other than 794 must be considered" because the Succession was the seller to both parties. We find nothing in Louisiana's codal or jurisprudential authority to justify this assertion or to require an analysis under the public records doctrine. However, even if it could be argued that the Act of Sale to Loutre was required to include a specific description of the Disputed Tract, we find the language in the deed to be sufficiently particular. Namely, the Act of Sale conveys "more or less" the 100 acres together with all acquisitive prescription rights to which the seller was entitled. It is clear from the four corners of the deed that the Succession was selling all of its interests in the property.

Additionally, this exact issue of intent was decided by the trial court on remand. The Succession's attorney, Daniel Wirtz, unequivocally testified that the parties intended to convey all the land north of the fence, including the Disputed Tract. Roberts attempted to discount this testimony by suggesting Wirtz's memory of the sale was less than accurate. In particular, Roberts asserted the file on the matter had been destroyed; Wirtz could not correctly recall the amount of the consideration tendered in exchange for the Quitclaim Deed; and he could not remember who received the proceeds of the Quitclaim Deed. Furthermore, Roberts presented testimony in an attempt to show that the parties acknowledged the amount paid was $750.00 per acre for a total of $75,000.00. Thus, the parties must have intended to sell only the 100 acres. Ultimately, the trial court, after weighing the evidence and making credibility determinations, decided that both the Succession and Loutre intended to sell all of the property north of the fence. The court of appeal erred, then, by not giving deference to the trial court's factual finding on this issue without mention or application of the manifest error standard of review. Rather, the court of appeal simply noted ". . . [t]he Succession could have intended to sell the Disputed Tract and the 100 Acres separately to different parties." This speculation ignores the significant fact that a trial occurred to determine this very issue and a factual finding was made by the trial court.

Thus, we conclude that La. Civ. Code art. 794 does not require particular title to the Disputed Tract in order to convey the accompanying acquisitive prescription rights to that land. Rather, the continued possession of the land to the fence's boundary by the Succession and Loutre for over thirty years mandates a finding that Loutre owns the Disputed Tract. In fact, because the law operates in favor of Loutre in the absence of a particularized description of the land, the Act of Sale would have required a clause *excluding* the Disputed Tract if that had been the parties' intent. Even if the law could be read to require a deed's inclusion of all the land subject to transfer, the language of the Act of Sale was specific enough to effect a transfer of the Disputed Tract. Lastly, even if the language lacked specificity, the trial court made a factual determination that the parties intended to include the Disputed Tract, and, without a finding of manifest error or clear abuse, the court of appeal was not authorized to disturb that finding.

Decree

For the foregoing reasons, we reverse the ruling of the court of appeal and remand the matter to the court of appeal to rule on the assignments of error asserted by Loutre, which were necessarily pretermitted by the court of appeal's ruling. . . .

REVERSED AND REMANDED.

Notes and Questions

1. The controversy in *Loutre Land and Timber Co. v. Roberts*, 63 So.2d 120 (La. 2011) may have been caused by the fact that one prior landowner, the Succession of Marie Wilson Morgan (the Succession), executed in relatively short order two consecutive deeds that arguably conveyed the same land. The first deed, "the full warranty deed," entitled "Act of Sale," was executed by the Succession on July 29, 2002, and recorded by Loutre Land and Timber Company a few days later on August 5, 2002. The second deed, the "Quitclaim Deed," was executed on January 29, 2003, and recorded by Roberts on February 27, 2003. Loutre Land's full warranty deed was thus first in time and had priority over Roberts' quitclaim deed.

The confusion arose, however, because Loutre Land's full warranty deed did not describe the fifteen disputed acres lying in section 10, although it did purport to convey "all rights of prescription, whether acquisitive or liberative, to which said vendor may be entitled." Roberts' clever, but misleading, argument was that, under Louisiana's Public Records Doctrine, the full warranty deed did not convey the disputed acres in section 10 and that his quitclaim deed from the Succession conveyed this land to him. Was the Louisiana Supreme Court correct in concluding that the dispute between Loutre Land and Roberts was clearly governed by Article 794 and that "an analysis under the public records doctrine" was not required?

2. In some ways, the issue in this case is a reprise of the issue resolved by the Louisiana Supreme Court in *Phillips v. Parker*, 483 So.2d 972 (1986). Why do you suppose the court repeatedly has been required to address arguments that Louisiana's Public Records Doctrine should trump acquisitive prescription claims?

3. If the Morgan family had possessed the disputed property in section 10 within the fence for more than thirty years in its own right (as the court declares it did), was consideration of Article 794 even required in this case?

F. Computation, Interruption, Suspension, Effects and Renunciation of Prescription

1. Passage of Time and Legal Rights

The Louisiana Civil Code distinguishes between three different kinds of prescription: liberative prescription, prescription of nonuse and acquisitive prescription. La. Civ. Code art. 3445 (1982). Like common law statutes of limitation, *liberative prescription* is a mode of barring an action or extinguishing a claim due to the inactivity of the person who would otherwise be entitled to assert the action or claim. La. Civ. Code art. 3447 (1982). The Civil Code provides liberative prescription periods ranging from one to thirty years:

- **One Year**: La. Civ. Code art. 3492 (1992) (delictual action); La. Civ. Code art. 3493 (1983) (action for damages to immovable property).

- **Two Year**: La. Civ. Code 3493.10 (1999) (action arising due to damages sustained as a result of a crime of violence).

- **Three Year**: La. Civ. Code art. 3494 (1986) (action to recover compensation for services rendered, for arrearages of rent and annuities, on money lent, on an open account, to recover mineral royalties); La. Civ. Code art. 3496 (1983) (action by a client against an attorney to recover papers); La. Civ. Code art. 3496.1 (1988, amended 1992) (action against a person for abuse of a minor).

- **Five Year**: La. Civ. Code art. 3497 (1983, amended 2009) (action to annul testament, to reduce excessive donation, to rescind partition and warranty of portions, for damages for harvesting of timber without consent); La. Civ. Code art. 3497.1 (1984, amended 1990, 1997) (action to make executory arrearages relating to spousal support and contribution obligations); La. Civ. Code art. 3498 (action on instruments and promissory notes, whether negotiable or not) (1993).

- **Ten Year**: La. Civ. Code art. 3499 (1983) (personal action); La. Civ. Code art. 3500 (1983) (action against an architect or contractor on account of defects in construction, renovation or repair of buildings and other works); La. Civ. Code art. 3501.1 (1997) (action to make executory arrearages of child support).

- **Thirty Year**: La. Civ. Code art. 3502 (1983) (action for recognition of right of inheritance and recovery of whole or part of a succession).

The Civil Code offers detailed guidance as to when the liberative prescription period applicable to a particular cause of action begins to accrue. For example, a delictual action prescribes one year from the day the injury or damage is sustained. La. Civ. Code 3492 (1983). But the liberative prescription period for an action to recover damages to immovable property begins to run "from the day the owner of the immovable acquired, or should have acquired, knowledge of the damage." La. Civ. Code art. 3493 (1983). The Louisiana Revised Statutes house other important liberative prescription periods and detailed accrual rules. *See generally* La. Rev. Stat. 9:5601 *et seq.* In the context of discussing the distinction between public and private things, for example, we noted the two year liberative prescription for actions to recover damages when private property is damaged for public purposes. La. Rev. Stat. 9:5624 (1950, amended 1987).

Unlike liberative prescription, which operates to bar a person from bringing an action in court even though a natural obligation may remain, *peremption* destroys a right when the time period allotted for the existence of the right expires. *Compare* La. Civ. Code art. 3458 (1982), *with* La. Civ. Code art. 3447 (1982). Peremptive periods are sprinkled throughout the Louisiana Civil Code and the Louisiana Revised Statutes. In the context of lesion beyond moeity, we observed that an action to rescind the sale of immovable property or to recover profit must be brought within a *peremptive* period of one year from the date of the sale; otherwise, the right to bring the action is forever extinguished. La. Civ. Code art. 2595 (1993). An action against an attorney or a law firm for legal malpractice is subject to a one year peremptive period accruing from the date of the alleged act, omission or neglect at issue, or the date the act, omission or neglect should have been discovered, and a three year peremptive period running from the date of the alleged act, omission or neglect. La. Rev. Stat. 9:5605 (1990, amended 1992). Note that all the limitation periods in Section 5605 of Title 9 of the Revised Statutes are peremptive. *See Lewis v. Album,* 114 So. 3d 1155, 1158 (La. App. 5 Cir. 2013) (holding that the one year peremption began to run when the client knew or should have known of the alleged legal malpractice, which was at the time of the dismissal of his case); *Schonekas, Winsberg, Evans and McGoey v. Cashman,* 83 So. 3d 154, 158 (La. App. 5 Cir. 2011) (same). Unlike prescription, peremption need not be pleaded but may be supplied by the court. *Compare* La. Civ. Code art. 3452 (1982), *with* La. Civ. Code art. 3460 (1982). Most important of all, unlike prescription, peremption may not be renounced, interrupted, or suspended. *Compare* La. Civ. Code arts. 3449–51, 3462–72 (1982), *with* La. Civ. Code art. 3461 (1982).

Prescription of nonuse is a method of extinguishing a real right *other than ownership* due to a failure to exercise the right for a period of time. La. Civ. Code art. 3448 (1982). For example, when the owner of a dominant estate that is due a predial servitude of passage over a neighboring servient estate fails to use the servitude of passage in the prescribed manner for a period of ten years, the servitude will terminate. La. Civ. Code art. 753 (1977).

Observe that all of the various forms of prescription wield important redistributive effects on a person's patrimony. But only acquisitive prescription is a possession-based means of acquiring ownership or a real right in immovable property, whereas liberative prescription and prescription of nonuse either bar the enforceability of an obligee's rights or terminate a real right other than ownership.

2. Computation of Prescription

For purposes of understanding acquisitive prescription, it is essential to identify the point in time when the applicable prescriptive period starts and ends. The general rule applicable to any prescriptive period follows:

Art. 3454. Computation of time

In computing a prescriptive period, the day that marks the commencement of prescription is not counted. Prescription accrues upon the expiration of the last day of the prescriptive period, and if that day is a legal holiday, prescription accrues upon the expiration of the next day that is not a legal holiday.

La. Civ. Code art 3454 (1982). For purposes of acquisitive prescription, the applicable period starts to run on the day immediately after the possessor begins to possess. Note that because Sunday is always a legal holiday, if a prescriptive period would otherwise end on a Sunday, it will accrue by the end of the following Monday, unless that day is also a legal holiday. In that case, prescription will accrue at the end of the following Tuesday.

All official days of public rest, legal holidays, and half-holidays are listed in special legislation. La. Rev. Stat. 1:55 (as amended through 2016). Some legal holidays are location-specific. In Crowley, for example, the International Rice Festival may be a legal holiday, but in Monroe Mardi Gras is *not*.

3. Interruption, Suspension and Extension of Prescription

Articles 3462 through 3466 of the Civil Code govern the interruption of prescription and Articles 3467 through 3472 provide for the suspension of prescription. The difference between interruption and suspension is crucial. Compare the following two provisions:

Art. 3466. Effect of interruption

If prescription is interrupted, the time that has run is not counted. Prescription commences to run anew from the last day of interruption.

Art. 3472. Effect of suspension

The period of suspension is not counted toward accrual of prescription. Prescription commences to run again upon the termination of the period of suspension.

La. Civ. Code arts. 3466, 3472 (1982). Interruption and suspension are distinct. Under Article 3466, when prescription is *interrupted*, "the time that has run is wiped out, and prescription commences to run anew from the date of interruption." La. Civ. Code art. 3466 rev. cmt. (b) (1982). Suspension, on the other hand, is more like a "timeout." The clock of prescription temporarily stops, but once the suspension ends, prescription begins to run again from the point in time when it was initially suspended.

Modes of Interruption: The Civil Code identifies three different ways to interrupt prescription: (1) *natural interruption*; (2) *legal interruption*; and (3) *acknowledgment*.

Natural interruption is triggered by the loss of possession. It applies only to acquisitive prescription.

Art. 3465. Interruption of acquisitive prescription

Acquisitive prescription is interrupted when possession is lost.

The interruption is considered never to have occurred if the possessor recovers possession within one year or if he recovers possession later by virtue of an action brought within the year.

La. Civ. Code art. 3465 (1982). If a possessor abandons his possession or if a possessor is evicted by another before the right to possess has accrued, "prescription is interrupted upon the loss of possession." La. Civ. Code art. 3465 rev. cmt. (c) (1982). Once a possessor acquires the right to possess, possession can be lost when the possessor either manifestly abandons his possession or suffers eviction by another through force or usurpation. La. Civ. Code art. 3465 rev. cmt. (b) (1982). However, when a possessor is evicted by another, the right to possess will only be lost if the possessor does not recover possession within a year of the eviction or fails to file an action to recover possession within a year of the eviction. *See* La. Civ. Code arts. 3433–34 (1982). When prescription is interrupted, the time that has run is not counted. La. Civ. Code art. 3466.

The next method of interrupting prescription, *legal interruption*, occurs when a lawsuit is filed by a property owner against an adverse possessor asserting acquisitive prescription or when a lawsuit is filed by an obligee against an obligor with respect to some kind of liberative prescription. Legal interruption is governed by the following two articles:

Art. 3462. Interruption by filing of suit or by service of process

Prescription is interrupted when the owner commences action against the possessor, or when the obligee commences action against the obligor, in a court of competent jurisdiction and venue. If action is commenced in an incompetent court, or in an improper venue, prescription is interrupted only as to a defendant served by process within the prescriptive period.

Art. 3463. Duration of interruption; abandonment or discontinuance of suit

An interruption of prescription resulting from the filing of a suit in a competent court and in the proper venue or from service of process within the prescriptive period continues as long as the suit is pending. Interruption is considered never to have occurred if the plaintiff abandons, voluntarily dismisses the action at any time either before the defendant has made any appearance of record or thereafter, or fails to prosecute the suit at the trial.

A settlement and subsequent dismissal of a defendant pursuant to a transaction or compromise shall not qualify as a voluntary dismissal pursuant to this Article.

La. Civ. Code arts. 3462 (1982), 3463 (2018). Many complex and narrow controversies arise in the application of these two articles. It is generally useful to remember that "[i]ssues of interruption of prescription are determined as of the time of the filing of the suit sought to be dismissed, not as of the time of filing the exception based upon prescription." La. Civ. Code art. 3463 rev. cmt. (f) (1982).

For the minimum requirements governing the service of a law suit that is sufficient to interrupt prescription, *see* La. Civ. Code art. 3462 rev. cmt. (d) (1982) ("Service of process interrupts the running of prescription even though the process is defective and subject to exception, if it is sufficient to inform the person served of the legal demands made upon him from the described occurrence. . . . However, the proper person, as designated by law, must be served before service of process will interrupt the running of prescription.") (quoting *Conner v. Continental Southern Lines, Inc.*, 294 So.2d 485, 487 (La. 1974)). Note that if a lawsuit is brought before an incompetent court and process is served after the accrual of prescription, "prescription is neither interrupted nor suspended." La. Civ. Code art. 3463 rev. cmt. (c) (1982).

Article 3463 provides the general rule for how long interruption lasts (as long as the suit is pending) and how interruption may be undone (if the plaintiff abandons, voluntarily dismisses or fails to prosecute the lawsuit to trial). However, the revision comments provide much more detail on both subjects. *See* La. Civ. Code art. 3463 rev. cmt. (b) (1982).

For the effects of a dismissal with or without prejudice, see La. Code Civ. Proc. art. 1673 (as amended) ("A judgment of dismissal with prejudice shall have the effect of a final judgment of absolute dismissal after trial. A judgment of dismissal without prejudice shall not constitute a bar to another suit on the same cause of action."). *See also* La. Code Civ. Proc. art. 1671 (1997) (voluntary dismissal); *Sims v. Am. Ins. Co.*, 101 So.3d 1, 2, 7–8 (La. 2012) (holding that plaintiffs' dismissal with prejudice of a lawsuit filed in federal court after the defendant has made a general appearance of record is a voluntary dismissal for purposes of La. Civ. Code art. 3463).

The final mode of interruption—*acknowledgement*—applies to both acquisitive prescription and liberative prescription:

Art. 3464. Interruption by acknowledgment

Prescription is interrupted when one acknowledges the right of the person against whom he had commenced to prescribe.

La. Civ. Code art. 3464 (1982). Interruption by acknowledgement presupposes that the person making the acknowledgment has the capacity to alienate. *See* Robert E. Blum, *Prescription by Acknowledgement in Louisiana*, 14 Tul. L. Rev. 430 (1940). An acknowledgement may be oral or written, formal or informal, and express or tacit. La. Civ. Code art. 3464 rev. cmt. (e) (1982). An acknowledgment interrupting acquisitive prescription generally arises tacitly. For example, a person might grant a predial servitude over land to which she indisputably has record title but might except from the servitude an additional area that she possesses without a title but with the intent to acquire ownership through acquisitive prescription. This would result in an interruption of acquisitive prescription by acknowledgment. *W.J. Gayle & Sons, Inc. v. Deperrodil*, 300 So.2d 599, 606–07(La. App. 3 Cir. 1974).

Questions: If an adverse possessor remarks, "I *expect* that I owe Bro. Foscoe *a little rent* on this piece of land," should this constitute a tacit acknowledgement interrupting acquisitive prescription? *See Foscoe v. Mitchell*, 190 La. 758, 182 So. 740 (1938). Does an adverse possessor who is cutting timber and using a tramway on another person's land tacitly interrupt acquisitive prescription by making two payments to the other person in exchange for not filing suit? *See Bodcaw Lumber Co. v. Walker*, 17 La. App. 373, 136 So. 191 (1931).

Finally, note that the Louisiana Mineral Code contains detailed regulations concerning the interruption of prescription of nonuse with respect to mineral servitudes and other mineral rights. La. Civ. Code art. 3464 rev. cmt. (d) (1982). In general, the interruption by acknowledgment of the prescription of nonuse regarding mineral interests must be written and filed for registry to be effective against third parties. The acknowledgment must clearly express the intent of the landowner to interrupt prescription of nonuse and must identify the acknowledging party and the mineral servitude(s) acknowledged.

When Suspension Occurs and Between Which Classes of Persons: In contrast to interruption, suspension only tolls the running of prescription. It does not wipe out any previously accumulated prescriptive time. La. Civ. Code art. 3372 (1982). The temporary suspension of prescription occurs only when permitted by specific legislative authorization. *See* La. Civ. Code art. 3467 (1982) ("Prescription runs against all persons unless exception is established by legislation.").

The two most important suspension provisions for our purposes are Articles 3468 and 3469 of the Civil Code. Article 3468 declares that prescription runs against two vulnerable classes of people—absent persons and incompetents, including minors and persons who have been interdicted because of some mental or physical incapacity unless there is an express legislative exception:

Art. 3468. Incompetents

Prescription runs against absent persons and incompetents, including minors and interdicts, unless exception is established by legislation.

La. Civ. Code art. 3468 (1983). As the 1983 revision comments explain, this article represents a major change in the law. Prior to this revision, Louisiana law presumed that that prescription was suspended against minors and interdicts, unless an exception was established by legislation. *Id.* rev. cmt. (b). Now the presumption is the opposite: all forms of prescription—whether liberative, acquisitive or non-use—will run against absent persons and incompetent persons, including minors, unless a specific legislative exception is made. *Id.* rev. cmt. (c).

Question: Given that the Civil Code specifically provides that *ten year* acquisitive prescription runs against absent persons and incompetents, including minors and interdicts (La. Civ. Code art. 3474 (1982)) should we assume that thirty year acquisitive prescription also runs against the same classes of persons, especially since the "rules governing acquisitive prescription of ten years apply to the prescription of thirty years to the extent that their application is compatible with the prescription of thirty years"? La. Civ. Code art. 3488 (1982). *See Hooper v. Hooper*, 941 So.2d 726, 732 (La. App. 3 Cir. 2006) (observing that it is "understandable that ten-year acquisitive prescription might run against an incompetent, because its very nature requires good faith," and implying, without deciding, that thirty-year acquisitive prescription might *not* run against an incompetent person).

Article 3469 of the Civil Code lists the classes of persons to whom a temporary suspension of prescription is granted. It also provides the time interval for that suspension.

Art. 3469. Suspension of Prescription

Prescription is suspended as between: the spouses during marriage, parents and children during minority, tutors and minors during tutorship, and curators and interdicts during interdiction, and caretakers and minors during minority.

A "caretaker" means a person legally obligated to provide or secure adequate care for a child, including a tutor, guardian, or legal custodian.

La. Civ. Code art. 3469 (1982, amended 1988). Notice that the suspension of prescription in favor of minors and incompetent persons only governs their relationship with their fiduciaries. Article 3469 identifies these classes of persons and offers to minors and incompetents a limited form of immunity from prescription vis-à-vis persons assumed to be acting in their best interests. With respect to other persons (non-fiduciaries) no protection from prescription is offered. The same principle applies to spouses. Prescription is only suspended between the spouses during a marriage.

For an example of how suspension operates between spouses, see *Southern Natural Gas Co. v. Naquin*, 167 So.2d 434, 439 (La. App. 1 Cir. 1964) (observing that husbands and wives cannot prescribe against each other and therefore, the husband "could never have acquired any prescriptive title adverse to his wife"). For an example of a statutory suspension of acquisitive prescription applicable to alienable (private) immovable property owned by municipalities, see La. Rev. Stat. 9:5804 (1950).

Contra Non Valentem: Despite the clear language of Article 3467 of the Louisiana Civil Code, practitioners and courts have frequently resorted to the ancient maxim *contra non valentem non currit praescriptio* to allow a party unable to act to suspend the running of prescription. *See* Douglas Nichols, *Contra Non Valentem*, 56 La. L. Rev. 337 (1996). Although extra-codal in origin, the revision drafters acknowledge the relevance of this maxim based on equity and fairness. *See* La. Civ. Code art. 3467 rev. cmt. (d) (1982). In *Corsey v. State Dep't of Corrections*, 375 So.2d 1319 (La. 1979), the Louisiana Supreme Court reviewed the four basic situations in which the doctrine of *contra non valentem* is potentially applied:

> (1) Where there was some legal cause which prevented the courts or their officers from taking cognizance of or acting on the plaintiff's action; (2) Where there was some condition coupled with the contract or connected with the proceedings which prevented the creditor from suing or acting; . . . (3) Where the debtor himself has done some act effectually to prevent the creditor from availing himself of his cause of action . . . [; and (4)] Where the cause of action is not known or reasonably knowable by the plaintiff, even though his ignorance is not induced by the defendant.

Corsey, 375 So.2d at 1321–22.

Louisiana courts have more often deployed the maxim in cases involving liberative, as opposed to acquisitive, prescription. *See, e.g., Cyr v. Louisiana Intrastate Gas Corp.*, 273 So.2d 694, 697–98 (La. App. 1 Cir. 1973); *Colley v. Canal Bank & Trust Co.*, 159 F.2d 153, 154 (5th Cir. 1947). In *Keim v. Louisiana Historical Ass'n Confederate War Museum*, 48 F.3d 362 (8th Cir. 1994), the United States Court of Appeals for the Eighth Circuit was called upon to decide whether a Nebraska resident or a Louisiana association owned a Civil War flag. Applying Louisiana law, the court declined to toll the running of prescription on behalf of the Louisiana association, holding that *contra non valentem* did not apply:

> Nor does the Museum qualify under the doctrine of *contra non valentem agere nulla currit prescriptio*. ("No prescription runs against a person unable to bring an action.") *Aegis Ins. Co. v. Delta Fire & Cas. Co.*, 99 So.2d 767, 772 (La. Ct. App. 1957). Under this doctrine, the prescription period may be tolled where the plaintiff is unaware of his injuries or their cause because of some deception on the part of the defendant. Here, however, the Museum had sufficient notice of the flag's whereabouts and, therefore, its potential cause of action, more than ten years prior to the filing of this action, but instead chose not to pursue its claim. *See Henson v. St. Paul Fire & Marine Ins. Co.*, 354 So.2d 612, 615 (La. Ct. App. 1977), *affirmed and remanded*, 363 So.2d 711 (La. 1978) (prescription period begins to run when sufficient facts were known to the owner to enable him to commence an action to recover the property); *Aegis*, 99 So.2d at 786 (prescription is suspended from the date the movable is stolen until the plaintiff has sufficient knowledge of the cause of action upon which to act).

Keim, 48 F.3d at 365.

While Spanish law has remained unfavorable to suspension, in recent years the French legislature has codified the core of the *contra non valentem* maxim in Article 2234 of the French Civil Code:

> *Art. 2234. — La prescription ne court pas ou est suspendue contre celui qui est dans l'impossibilité d'agir par suite d'un empêchement résultant de la loi, de la convention ou de la force majeure.*

> *Art. 2234. — Prescription does not run or is suspended against a person who cannot act as a consequence of an impediment resulting from law, agreement or force majeure.*

French Civ. Code art. 2234 (loi no 2008-561 du 17 juin 2008).

For recent scholarship comparing Louisiana and French approaches to *contra non valentem*, see Benjamin West Janke & François-Xavier Licari, *Contra Non Valentem in France and Louisiana: Revealing the Parenthood, Breaking a Myth*, 71 La. L. Rev. 503 (2011); Benjamin West Janke, *Revisiting Contra Non Valentem in Light of Hurricanes Katrina and Rita*, 68 La. L. Rev. 497 (2008). It remains to be seen whether the Louisiana State Law Institute will produce a reform proposal codifying or modifying the doctrine of *contra non valentem* and whether the legislature would enact any such proposal.

Extension of Liberative Prescription: In 2013, the Louisiana Legislature added language to the Louisiana Civil Code expressly allowing an obligor to extend a liberative prescriptive period after it has begun to run but before it accrues:

Art. 3505. Acts extending liberative prescription

After liberative prescription has commenced to run but before it accrues, an obligor may by juridical act extend the prescription period. An obligor may grant successive extensions. The duration of each extension may not exceed one year.

La. Civil Code art. 3505 (2013). As Article 3505 stipulates, such extensions (or "tolling agreements" as they are often referred to by practicing lawyers) must be "express and in writing" and "may be interrupted or suspended during the period of extension." La. Civil Code arts. 3505.1 & 3505.4 (2013).

The policy rationale for the regulation of these prescription-extension agreements derives from their practical utility as they allow lawyers and their clients extra time to negotiate and settle a dispute rather than file suit to interrupt the running of a liberative prescription period about to accrue. La. Civ. Code art. 3505 rev. cmt. (c) (2013). The one-year time limit for such extensions, however, provides some check against the contractual freedom of the parties by preventing an obligor from granting "an excessively long or indefinite period of extension." *Id.* These extensions of liberative prescription must "be express and in writing" to avoid disputes about their existence. La. Civ. Code art. 3505.1 rev. cmt. (a) (2013). The form of writing required for a liberative prescription extension is flexible; an authentic act, an act under private signature or even an electronic transmission may satisfy the writing requirement. *Id*. rev. cmt. (b).

4. Effects of Accrual of Acquisitive Prescription

Upon accrual of acquisitive prescription, ownership retroactively vests in the adverse possessor who has established the passage of the requisite prescriptive period. The adverse possessor is deemed to have been the owner from the moment her possession began. This can have important effects on third parties. For example, if the true owner of immovable property grants a mortgage on the property while an adverse possessor is prescribing, the mortgage holder will not be able to foreclose on the property in the event of default by the true owner under the mortgage after prescription has accrued in favor of the adverse possessor. Conversely, after the accrual of prescription, the adverse possessor is entitled to the ownership of all fruits and products taken from immovable property while prescription was still running. A former landowner who cannot evict an adverse possessor has no claim for fruits or products taken from the land.

5. Renunciation of Acquisitive Prescription

Once a prescriptive period has run, the person in whose favor it has accrued may *renounce* the rights derived from the accrual of prescription if that person has the capacity to alienate. La. Civ. Code arts. 3449, 3451 (1982). With respect to acquisitive prescription and immovable property, renunciation is not, strictly speaking, an alienation of ownership; rather it is merely the abandonment of rights acquired as a result of the accrual of prescription. *See* La. Civ. Code art. 3449 rev. cmt. (d) (quoting 3 PLANIOL ET RIPERT, TRAITÉ PRATIQUE DE DROIT FRANCAIS, 748 (2d 3d Picard 1952)). An adverse possessor who renounces acquisitive prescription foregoes the benefits she has gained from prescription, as the law will retroactively consider her as never having had any rights to the property.

In contrast, a person who wants to surrender any advantages he might gain while prescription is still running does not renounce. Instead, he effects an acknowledgement that interrupts prescription and resets the prescriptive period to zero. *See* La. Civ. Code arts. 3449, 3464 (1982); *Carraby v. Navarre*, 3 La. 262 (1832).

Renunciation may be express or it may be tacit when the circumstances give rise to a presumption that the advantages of an accrued prescription have been relinquished. La. Civ. Code art. 3450 (1982). In all cases, however, renunciation of prescription must be unequivocal; the intent to renounce must be "clear, direct and absolute" and "made manifest either by words or actions of the party in whose favor prescription has run." *McPherson v. Roy*, 390 So.2d 543, 551 (La. App. 3 Cir. 1980). When renunciation involves immovables, however, it must be express and in writing. La. Civ. Code art. 3450 (1982).

Chapter 10

Vindicating Ownership: Petitory and Revendicatory Actions

Having studied possession—its fundamentals, its protection and its effects—and acquisitive prescription with respect to immovables, we return to ownership and address two questions. First, how does a purported owner of an immovable, or holder of a real right in an immovable, who is not in possession of the immovable, recover possession from someone currently in possession? Second, how does the owner of a movable regain its possession from someone who possesses or detains the thing?

The answer to the first question is provided in the Louisiana Code of Civil Procedure, the Civil Code and in jurisprudential rules governing **petitory actions** for the recovery of immovables and real rights. The answer to the second question is provided by case law covering **revendicatory actions** for the recovery of movables.

A. Petitory Actions for the Recovery of Immovable Property

We begin with three provisions in the Louisiana Code of Civil Procedure which define the petitory action, identify the plaintiff, and establish the requisite elements of a petitory action. Note from the outset that the status of the defendant as being *in possession* or *out of possession* of the property determines the burden of proof faced by the plaintiff.

Art. 3651. Petitory Action

The petitory action is one brought by a person who claims the ownership, but who is not in possession, of immovable property or of a real right therein, against another who is in possession or who claims the ownership thereof adversely, to obtain judgment recognizing the plaintiff's ownership.

Art. 3652. Same; parties; venue

A. A petitory action may be brought by a person who claims the ownership of only an undivided interest in the immovable property or real right therein, or whose asserted ownership is limited to a certain period which has not yet expired, or which may be terminated by an event which has not yet occurred.

B. A lessee or other person who occupies the immovable property or enjoys the real right therein under an agreement with the person who claims the ownership thereof adversely to the plaintiff may be joined in the action as a defendant.

C. A petitory action shall be brought in the venue provided by Article 80(A)(1), even when the plaintiff prays for judgment for the fruits and revenues of the property, or for damages.

Art. 3653. Same; Proof of Title; immovable

To obtain a judgment recognizing his ownership of immovable property or real right therein, the plaintiff in a petitory action shall:

(1) Prove that he has acquired ownership from a previous owner or by acquisitive prescription, if the court finds that the defendant is in possession thereof; or

(2) Prove a better title thereto than the defendant, if the court finds that the latter is not in possession thereof.

When the titles of the parties are traced to a common author, he is presumed to be the previous owner.

La. Code Civ. Proc. arts. 3651–53 (1960, amended 1981).

Pursuant to Articles 3651 and 3653 of the Code of Civil Procedure, the petitory action can be brought against either a person *in possession* of the disputed property or someone *not in possession* but who nevertheless claims ownership of the disputed property. Undoubtedly, the most controversial element of the regulatory framework for petitory actions pertains to the burden of proof facing a plaintiff *if the court finds that the defendant is in possession of the property.* La. Code Civ. Proc. art. 3653(1) (1960). The judicial decisions featured below will introduce you to the interpretive controversy surrounding this question. Before reading these decisions, though, consider the following two articles in the Civil Code, which were adopted in 1979, five years after the Louisiana Supreme Court's decision in *Pure Oil Co. v. Skinner,* 294 So.2d 797 (La. 1974):

Art. 531. Proof of ownership of immovable

One who claims the ownership of an immovable against another in possession must prove that he has acquired ownership from a previous owner or by acquisitive prescription. If neither party is in possession, he need only prove a better title.

Art. 532. Common author

When the titles of the parties are traced to a common author, he is presumed to be the previous owner.

La. Civ. Code arts. 531–32 (1979). These articles mirror almost word for word the language found in Article 3651 of the Code of Civil Procedure. Some courts and commentators interpret this match as a legislative endorsement of the court's interpretation of Article 3653(1) in *Pure Oil Co. v. Skinner*, 294 So.2d 797 (La. 1974). When you read *Pure Oil*, you will notice that the version of Article 3653 in place at the time of that decision had a slightly different formulation compared to the current contents of the provision. Be sure to identify the precise wording change in Article 3653 of the Code of Civil Procedure.

1. Proving Ownership from a Previous Owner or by Acquisitive Prescription

The plaintiff in a petitory action endeavoring to have a court recognize and enforce his ownership or a real right in an immovable confronts two options if the defendant is found to be in possession of the disputed property. La. Civ. Code art. 531 (1979); La. Code Civ. Proc. art. 3653(1) (1960, amended 1981). First, the plaintiff can attempt to prove that he or his ancestors in title acquired ownership through acquisitive prescription. If a long enough period of time has passed between the plaintiff's last possession or that of his ancestors in title, the plaintiff may be unable to obtain and offer sufficient proof of the requisite acts of corporeal possession and intent to possess as owner so as to establish that he or his ancestors in title acquired ownership by acquisitive prescription.

Because of these difficulties in proof, the plaintiff in a petitory action will have to turn to the alternative; he must prove that he has acquired ownership from "a previous owner." La. Civ. Code art. 531 (1979); La. Code Civ. Proc. art. 3653(1) (1960, amended 1981). Alas, for many disappointed plaintiffs in petitory actions, this is more easily said than done.

Proving acquisition of ownership from a previous owner under Article 3651 of the Code of Civil Procedure requires the plaintiff to establish "an unbroken chain of transfers from a previous owner" or title "good against the world." Louisiana courts have interpreted this standard of proof to mean that the plaintiff must show an unbroken chain of title back to a sovereign. Parts of Louisiana have been claimed by seven different sovereigns, including Great Britain, Spain, France, the United States, the West Florida Republic, Louisiana as a sovereign state, and the Confederate States of America. Despite our French and Spanish colonial past, it is only necessary to prove title back to 1812 — the year when Louisiana became a state. The Darby maps drawn up between 1808 and 1815 are considered authoritative with respect to land ownership as of 1812. William Darby was the surveyor commissioned by the U.S. Government to survey all the land within the boundaries of the state and to draw maps exhibiting the property lines of privately owned land and identifying the owners of that land.

To prove an unbroken chain of transfers, the current title holder must trace title to the property backwards through each previous record owner. This process involves identifying the document in the conveyance records of the parish where the property is located that transfers rights from the prior record owner to the subsequent record owner. An unbroken chain of titles back to a patent from a sovereign or back to 1812 proves title that is good against the world. As the following decisions reveal, the task of "making out one's title" is often fraught with difficulty.

Pure Oil Co. v. Skinner

294 So.2d 797 (La. 1974)

BARHAM, Justice. We granted writs (285 So.2d 541 (La. 1973)) to review the decision of the Court of Appeal on the issue of a plaintiff's burden of proof in a real action when defendant is the possessor of the property in controversy. Defendants, the relators in these cases, contended in their writ applications that the decisions of the Court of Appeal (284 So.2d 608, 284 So.2d 614 (La. App. 2d Cir. 1973)) conflict with that of the Third Circuit in *Deselle v. Bonnette*, 251 So.2d 68 (La. App. 3d Cir. 1971), wherein it was held that in a petitory action against a defendant in possession, a plaintiff must make out his title to the property in dispute without regard to the title of the party in possession.

The Court of Appeal in the instant cases held that respondents, the parties claiming title or ownership of the disputed land against adverse claimants in possession without a deed translative of title, did not have to prove a title good against the world but only had to prove better title than relators.

The issues in the instant cases were first presented for consideration in 1961 when The Pure Oil Company, which had oil, gas and mineral leases covering the disputed property from both claimants, instituted a concursus proceeding by depositing royalties attributable to the property in controversy in the registry of the court and citing both relators and respondents to assert their respective interests. Subsequent to the institution of the concursus proceedings, respondents instituted a boundary action against the relators and, by stipulation, the parties agreed that judgment rendered in the concursus proceedings would be determinative of the issues in the boundary action.

The one and one-half acres tract of land, the ownership of which is the subject of the controversy, is claimed under two chains of title. It was established in the lower courts to their satisfaction, and to ours, that neither respondents nor relators have valid record title to the property in dispute.

Code of Civil Procedure Article 3654 provides:

"When the issue of ownership of immovable property or of a real right is presented in an action for a declaratory judgment, or in a concursus, expropriation, or similar proceeding, or the issue of the ownership of funds deposited in the registry of the court and which belong to the owner of the immovable property or of the real right is so presented, the court shall render judgment in favor of the party:

(1) Who would be entitled to the possession of the immovable property or real right in a possessory action, unless the adverse party makes out his title thereto; or

(2) Who proves better title to the immovable property or real right, when neither party would be entitled to the possession of the immovable property or real right in a possessory action."

The record in this case establishes, and it is undisputed, that the relators have possessed the property in question since 1947. Therefore, it is clear that the burden of proof placed on respondents is greater than that provided in Code of Civil Procedure Article 3654(2), the burden of proving a better title. The statutory imposition of a higher burden of proof than simply proving better title when an adverse claimant is in possession of disputed land leads to the inevitable conclusion that respondents' burden was to "make out his title thereto." In other words, respondents were required to prove valid record title, to show title good against the world without regard to the title of the party in possession. C.C.P. Arts. 3653, 3654. See 2 A. Yiannopoulos, Louisiana Civil Law Treatise, § 137 (1967); 35 Tul. L. Rev. 541, at 547 (1961). This respondents have failed to do. The record reveals that there is a 16-year break in the title of the respondents from 1858, when an entry by Charles M. Cawthoon from the United States Government is recorded, to 1874, when conveyance of the subject property from Jeremiah Payne to Elizabeth J. Colvin was recorded.

Upon oral argument, in response to an inquiry by the Court, respondents contended that they had established acquisition of prescriptive title to the property in dispute prior to 1947, when relators entered into possession of the tract in dispute. The state of the record, however, does not support this contention of respondents and there is no holding by the lower courts to this effect. Respondents, therefore, have not established either valid record title or prescriptive title to the property in dispute.

Hutton v. Adkins, 186 So. 908 (La. App. 2d Cir. 1939), the case relied upon by the Court of Appeal for the holding that relators were required only to prove better title than respondent who was in possession without a deed translative of title, is hereby overruled.

The judgments of the lower courts are reversed and it is ordered, adjudged and decreed that there be judgment herein in favor of the relators ... decreeing that they are declared owners of the following described property. ...

It is further ordered that all costs are assessed against respondents, Henry Carl Skinner and Henry Carl Skinner, Jr.

REVERSED AND RENDERED.

SUMMERS and MARCUS, J.J., dissent and assign reasons.

SUMMERS, Justice (dissenting). The Skinners in these proceedings are the parties out of possession of the disputed lands. They are claiming title against the Simontons, the parties who have been in possession for more than one year. The trial court and Court of Appeal have found that the deed under which the Simontons are claiming is not translative of title. Apparently the majority agrees with this finding. I agree also, and I shall therefore consider the Simontons as mere possessors.

The only fault, if it can be considered such, in the chain of title asserted by the Skinners is a missing link between the original entry from the United States Government by Charles M. Cawthoon in 1858 and a deed from Jeremiah Payne to Elizabeth J. Calvin in February 1874, a period of sixteen years. However, as the trial judge found, "It is well known that prior to the creation of Lincoln Parish, as a parish, in the 1870s, that there are many missing deeds and records relating to title during that period of time, since Lincoln Parish was not, at that time, a parish at all, but was a part of either Union, Ouachita or Jackson Parishes."

After 1874 the links in the Skinner chain of title are complete. Their ownership was never brought into question until the Simontons enclosed the disputed one and one-half acres in 1947.

Since the concursus proceeding provoked these adverse claims between the Skinners and Simontons in 1961, the issues formed by the pleadings have assumed the character of a petitory action, with the Skinners, out of possession, claiming title against the Simontons, who are in possession but without semblance of title.

The first error committed by the majority is its decree that the Simontons are the owners of the property. In the posture in which the pleadings place the parties, the possessors can only be maintained in their right to possession, and, perhaps, be decreed entitled to the funds on deposit by virtue of the concursus proceedings. La. Code Civ. Proc. art. 3654. They assuredly cannot be decreed the owners of property when the majority has found that the possessors have no "valid" title.

Moreover, on the record before us, I would say that the Skinners have a title good and valid against the world. They have a complete and unbroken chain of title from 1874 to date. Their possession was disturbed in 1947 and, since these adverse claims were asserted in 1961 when this concursus proceeding was filed, there is no question of an adverse title in the Simontons acquired by the prescription of thirty years.

. . . .

More importantly, however, the majority is further in error when it imposes upon the Skinners, plaintiffs in a petitory action, who are out of possession, claiming title as against the Simontons who are possessors without title, the obligation "*to prove a valid record title, to show title good against the world without regard to the title of the party in possession.*" Under this stringent requirement the majority has held that the break in the chain of the Skinner title from 1858 to 1874 denies them the title requisite to maintain their petitory action.

The requirements of proof of title imposed upon a plaintiff in a petitory action were not changed by the enactment of Article 3654 of the Code of Civil Procedure. Under that article the possessor is entitled to be maintained in possession unless the adverse party "makes out his title" to the immovable or real right in question. Article 3653 (1) of the Code of Civil Procedure utilizes the identical language:

"To obtain a judgment recognizing his ownership of the immovable property or real right, the plaintiff in a petitory action shall:

"(1) Make out his title thereto, if the court finds that the defendant is in possession thereof; . . . ."

As the comments to Article 3653 make clear,

"When the defendant is in possession, this article makes no change in the law. The words 'make out his title' are taken from Art. 44 of the Code of Practice, and are intended to have the same meaning as given to them under the jurisprudence interpreting the source provision."

In addition, in a "Summary of Procedural Changes in Chapter 1" by Henry G. McMahon, appearing prior to the codal articles relating to real actions, this statement is found: "Art. 3653 makes no change in the burden of proof imposed on the plaintiff when the defendant is in possession." Article 44 of the Code of Practice of 1870, like the Code of Practice of 1825, declares "The plaintiff in an action of revendication must make out his title, otherwise the possessor, whoever he be, shall be discharged from the demand" (emphasis added).

It is not open to question, therefore, that the standards established by the jurisprudence interpreting Article 44 of the Code of Practice still govern the proof required of a plaintiff in a petitory action.

Considering the importance of land titles, it may be appropriate to recall the first principles established by this Court on the question before us. To do so, I quote from *Bedford v. Urquhart*, 8 La. 241, 245 (1835) as follows:

"At the threshold of this inquiry, we meet the question, whether the 44th article of the Code of Practice has introduced a new principle in relation to the petitory action, or whether it merely reasserts the well known maxim, 'that the plaintiff must recover by the strength of his own title, and not by the weakness of his adversary's.'

"'The plaintiff', says the Code, 'in an action of revendication, must make out his title, otherwise, the possessor, whoever he be, shall be discharged from the demand.'

"Pothier, in treating on this kind of action, adopts the rule, that the plaintiff in revendication, in order to succeed in his demand, must base it on some title of property; and such titles are said to be those, which are of a nature to transfer from one to another the ownership of the thing 'causae idonae ad transferendum dominium.' Among titles of that description, he enumerates an act of partition, by which it should appear that the thing sued for, fell to the share of the plaintiff in the succession of some of his relations.

". . . But when the title which the plaintiff exhibits, is anterior to the possession against whom the action is brought, and who on his part produces none, this title alone is sufficient. He, who by this title, sold or gave the property to the plaintiff or his author or predecessor, is sufficiently presumed to have been the proprietor and possessor, and to have transferred the possession and property. And further, even although it should appear that he who by the title which I produce, sold or gave me the property which I sue for, was not the owner, if I purchased in good faith having had reason to believe that he who sold or gave it to me, and of which I saw him possessed, was the owner, that title alone would suffice against a possessor who shows no title.' Pothier, Dom. de Pro. 323.

"We are of opinion, that the Code has not introduced any new principle on this subject. *It cannot be necessary in every petitory action, that the plaintiff should show title in himself good against the whole world, and perfect, in order to recover against a naked possessor.* He is bound to produce a title, as owner, causa idonea ad transferendum dominium, to repel the presumption of ownership, resulting from mere possession, and the date of his title ought to be anterior to the possession of the defendant.

"We have also the authority of Pothier, for assuming as a principle, that although regularly the action of revendication can be maintained only by the owner, it may sometimes be maintained by one who is not the real owner, but was in the way of becoming so, when he lost the possession. For he who was in possession in good faith, in virtue of a just title, and lost the possession before the period required for prescription, can recover it in a petitory action, from one who is in possession without title.

. . . Same, No. 292, 293."

Again in *Verdun v. Gilmore*, 128 La. 1063, 55 So. 675 (1911), the principles were repeated:

'It is a principle of law, so familiar as to have become trite, that a plaintiff in a petitory action must recover upon the strength of his own title, not upon the weakness of that of his adversary.' *Rowson v. Barbe*, 51 La. Ann. 347, 25 So. 139 at 140

"It is true that the rule thus stated is relaxed to the extent that, as against a mere trespasser, *a plaintiff in a petitory action is not required to exhibit a title 'good against the world'.* And the joint heir or owner may, perhaps, recover the whole of property, in which he has an undivided interest, from a mere possessor without title. Police Jury v. Robichaux, 116 La. [286,] 40 So. 705. But it is only when a plaintiff, seeking to recover property from a party in possession, exhibits at least *a better right than that of mere possession*, that the question of the defendant's title need be inquired into, since there is no reason why the possession of one person should be disturbed at the instance of another, who shows no better right to such possession. . . . (italics by the court)" (emphasis added).

The statement sometimes used that the plaintiff in a petitory action must make out his title "against the whole world" is explained early in our law by the decision in *Williams v. Riddle*, 10 Rob. 505 (La. 1845) where Mr. Justice Garland said:

"It has long been settled by this court, that a plaintiff in a petitory action must, to recover against a party in possession, claiming title also, not only show a better title than the defendant has, but he must show a title as good as any the defendant can oppose to him, whether it be vested in him or not. *Thomas v. Turnley*, 3 Robinson, 206. In the case referred to, and in others, we have said that the outstanding title must be a legal, subsisting one, and a better one than plaintiffs' to protect the defendant, and we have on various occasions intimated that, in fairness, it should be stated in the answer, so as to give the plaintiff notice, that he may be prepared to meet it."

As I understand this statement, it means that the defendant in a petitory action, who is in possession, may oppose to the plaintiff's title the title of any other (the whole world), and if he does, and if the title thus opposed to the plaintiff's is a better one than plaintiff's, defendant cannot be deprived of his possession by the plaintiff, the reason being that the better title opposed to plaintiff's has the superior right to dispossess the possessor. Therefore, the right is reserved by the law to the better title to bear against defendant's possession, and plaintiff's action must be dismissed.

When these principles are applied to the case at bar, it is readily apparent that the Simontons have not opposed the Skinners' title by the title of anyone else. They have only asserted their deed which is not translative of title and hence is no title at all. The Simontons have only the rights of possessors to assert against the title of the Skinners.

Cases that have been decided indicate that the burden upon the plaintiff in a petitory action is less where the defendant is a mere possessor than where defendant possesses by some semblance of record title. *Phelps v. Hughes*, 1 La. Ann. 320 (1846); *Glover v. Haley*, 118 La. 649, 43 So. 265 (1907); *Zeringue v. Williams*, 15 La. Ann. 76 (1860). *Bedford v. Urquhart*, 8 La. 241 (1835); *Gravenberg v. Savoie*, 8 La. Ann. 499 (1852); Young v. Chamberlin, 15 La. Ann. 454 (1860). The clear implication to be drawn from this rule is that the plaintiff in the petitory action need not establish a perfect title to prevail against the possessor.

The traditional rule to be applied here, and what is meant by "make out his title", is well expressed in *Smith v. Chappell*, 177 La. 311, 148 So. 242 (1933):

"A petitory action is one brought by an alleged owner of real estate who is out of possession against another having possession to determine owner-ship. The settled jurisprudence of this state is that a plaintiff in a petitory action, in order to recover, must rely on the strength of his own title and not on the weakness of that of his adversary. In order to maintain his suit, he carries the burden of proving title in himself. *The title of the defendant is not an issue until plaintiff has proved an apparently valid title in himself*" (emphasis added).

From this statement of the Court, supported by a long line of decisions, I conclude that "an apparently valid title" is all the Skinners had to prove to overcome the presumption of ownership arising from possession. Johnson, *Real Actions*, 35 Tul. L.

Rev. 541 (1961). By doing so the Skinners proved their right as owners to dispossess the Simontons. At this stage of the proceeding it was incumbent upon defendants to assert their title. Having failed to establish any title whatever, the "apparently valid" title of the Skinners was sufficient to entitle the Skinners to a decree of ownership and an order to the Simontons to deliver possession.

To impose the requirement of a title perfect against the whole world, when no better title is asserted to oppose the plaintiff's title in a petitory action, is virtually to require the impossible in some cases, as this case illustrates. Undoubtedly no complete chain of title can be established by the Skinners, for the deeds needed to complete the chain between 1858 and 1874 were lost. In many instances, as we all know, court houses have burned and the deeds needed to complete chains of title are nonexistent. The invalidity of the Skinner title upon which the majority relies is the sixteen-year break in the chain between 1858 and 1874. Otherwise the title is in all respects good and valid. In my view the Skinners have not only made out an "apparently valid" title, they have established a good, valid and perfect title against every title opposed to it.

To permit a possessor to occupy one's property for more than a year, and then compel the owner to come forth with a complete chain of title, perfect in all respects, to oust the possessor is entirely unsupported by the statutes or decisions of this Court. Such a rule is certain to create many problems seriously impairing stability of titles in this State.

I respectfully dissent.

Notes and Questions

1. From the moment the Louisiana Supreme Court decided *Pure Oil Co. v. Skinner*, 294 So.2d 797 (La. 1974), Louisiana judges, lawyers and commentators started to question the fairness and utility of the rule announced by the court: that when the defendant is in possession of the property in dispute in a petitory action, the plaintiff who seeks to prove that he acquired ownership from a previous owner (rather than by acquisitive prescription) must "show title good against the world without regard to the title of the party in possession." In his dissent, Justice Summers characterized this burden of proof as "virtually to require the impossible in some cases." *Id.* at 803. Is this burden of proof too high?

2. In *Pure Oil*, the Skinners could prove their title all the way back to 1874 and they could further show the chain of title from 1858 back to the sovereign. What eluded them was proof of how the title passed in the intervening sixteen year period from the last owner in 1858 to the new owner in 1874. Do you think that it is fair to require this level of proof for a plaintiff in a petitory action when the defendant in possession of the property, like the Simontons in *Pure Oil*, lacks any semblance of title and might even be described as a trespasser?

3. What countervailing arguments support Justice Barham's reading of Louisiana Code of Civil Procedure Article 3654(1), and by implication Article 3653(1), as it

stood at the time of the decision in *Pure Oil*? Why might it be problematic for courts to lessen the burden of proof for a plaintiff in a petitory action against a defendant in possession who lacks any semblance of title? Would this require courts to make too many value judgments about the quality of a defendant's purported title? What would be the harm, if any, of requiring a plaintiff in this situation to merely "prove a better title" than a defendant in possession?

4. Note that the specific provision of the Code of Civil Procedure at play in *Pure Oil* was Article 3654 because the plaintiff brought a concursus proceeding — an action to determine the appropriate party to whom mineral royalty payments were due. The Simontons — the "relators" in the concurcus proceeding — had been in possession of the property for a long time (since 1947). The Skinners, the "respondents" in the concursus proceeding, had title. Just as today, the requisites to prevail in an action under Article 3654 mirrored those of Article 3653.

5. In *Pure Oil*, the respondents, the Skinners, claimed in argument before the Louisiana Supreme Court that they had acquired ownership of the land in dispute through acquisitive prescription based on the alleged possession of their predecessors in interest between 1874 and 1947. The court, however, found no evidence to support this assertion. Nor did the record contain any findings by the lower courts on this issue. Why might the Skinners have failed to provide evidence to support this claim at trial?

6. In *Freeman Baptist Church v. Hillen*, 345 So.2d 74 (La. App. 1 Cir. 1977), a petitory action decided just three years after *Pure Oil*, the plaintiff church sought to vindicate its alleged ownership of a disputed three-acre strip of land, which it had recently purchased, against two trespassers who claimed oral permission to be on the property. Instead of seeking to establish ownership by acquisitive prescription at trial, the plaintiff relied on its claim of title, which it could trace back to a 1937 tax sale and, through a late proffer at trial, to a 1906 deed. The defendants who made no claim of ownership based their possession solely on the "sufferance of a third party whom [they] believe[d] to be owner." *Id.* at 75. The plaintiff argued before the court of appeal that Louisiana jurisprudence:

> recognizes a distinction between a mere possessor and one possessing with some semblance of title. In this respect, Plaintiff argues that where defendant is a trespasser (as Plaintiff alleges Defendants to be in this instance), plaintiff need establish only some color of title to prevail in a petitory action. In support of this position, Plaintiff cites and relies upon *Zeringue v. Williams, et al.*, 15 La. Ann. 76 (1860); *Taylor v. Williams*, 162 La. 92, 110 So. 100 (1926), and numerous other authorities.

Id. at 77. The plaintiff further argued that the defendants were only precarious possessors and therefore, could not adversely possess. The court of appeal ignored this latter fact, noting that the plaintiff had alleged the defendants' possession and thus, could not, without leave of court, amend its petition to convert the petitory action into a possessory action nor cumulate the petitory and possessory actions. *Id.*

Ultimately, the court of appeal affirmed the trial court's dismissal of the plaintiff's petitory action, holding that the plaintiff failed to make out its title under *Pure Oil* because the plaintiff could only trace its title back to the 1906 deed. The court further determined that the plaintiff could not introduce evidence of acquisitive prescription on appeal without having first offered such evidence in the trial court. *Id.* at 77–78.

Addressing the plaintiff's "final argument that the legislature could not have intended to enact a rule as harsh as the *Skinner* interpretation of Article 3653," Judge Landry, writing for the majority of the court of appeal, offered these words:

> Appellant correctly notes that *Skinner*, above, enables a trespasser to entrench himself on property and take advantage of a defect in the title of a record owner pursuant to a deed translative of title. We are fully mindful of the effects of *Skinner*, above. We note, however, that *Skinner*, above, expressly overruled *Hutton v. Adkins*, 186 So. 908, (La. App. 2d Cir. 1939), and that *Hutton*, above, involved a petitory action brought by a record owner against a trespasser. We find the instant case indistinguishable from *Hutton*, above. We note also the import of *Skinner*, to the effect that *Hutton*, above, was decided prior to the enactment of Article 3653, above, which the Supreme Court deems controlling.
>
> We seriously question the wisdom and practicality of the application of the rule laid down in *Skinner*, above, to an instance in which the record owner brings a petitory action against a trespasser or one possessing with no claim of recorded or prescriptive title. Nevertheless, the holding in *Skinner*, above, is clear and unmistakable. We apply it in this instance only because we must.
>
> For whatever comfort it may afford Appellant, it appears that Appellant need not rely solely on the strength of his recorded title to obtain relief against a trespasser. Other relief is available in the form of a possessory action or a claim of ownership based on either 10 or 30 years acquisitive prescription.

Id. at 78.

Judge Cole, writing in dissent, was no less blunt in stating his views of *Pure Oil*:

> Believing, as I do, that the majority holding in *Pure Oil Company v. Skinner*, 294 So.2d 797 (La. 1974), particularly as applied to the facts of this case, is an erroneous statement of law, and finding comfort in the fact that the civilian heritage of our law permits me to exercise my independent judgment without disrespect to my learned brothers of our highest court, I respectfully dissent.
>
> I find no valid bases in our law upon which to predicate the harsh jurisprudential rule of *Skinner* to the effect that a plaintiff in a petitory action, as against a mere squatter or trespasser, must establish a perfect title. Surely,

this is not what our Legislature intended when it enacted Article 3653 of our Code of Civil Procedure. And, as explained by Justice Summers in his well reasoned dissent to *Skinner*, historical interpretations do not substantiate a result which "is virtually to require the impossible in some cases." To the contrary, I agree with Justice Summers that the weight of our authorities only require such a plaintiff to prove "an apparently valid title." That burden was borne in the case now before us.

Id. at 78–79 (Cole, J., dissenting).

In *Freeman Baptist Church*, the plaintiff succeeded in proving title as far back as a 1937 tax sale. Tax sales are conducted by a government entity. Should tracing title back to a tax sale equate to tracing title back to the sovereign? Is a tax sale equivalent to starting a new chain of title from the sovereign?

Now consider a more recent decision addressing the burden of proof faced by a plaintiff in a petitory action.

Baker v. Romero

55 So.3d 1035 (La. App. 3 Cir. 2011)

KEATY, Judge. Plaintiff, Lyn Baker, appeals a judgment dismissing her petitory action against Defendants, Rogerist Romero and Carol Romero, and granting their possessory action on the basis that Baker did not meet her burden of proof regarding her claim of ownership of the subject immovable property while the Romeros established as a matter of law their right to possess the property. For the following reasons, we affirm.

Facts and Procedural History

According to a Cash Sale Deed (the Deed) recorded on July 26, 2006, Baker acquired the "right, title and interest" in a forty-foot strip of property located in the Toledo Bend Reservoir in Sabine Parish (the Property) from six of her relatives for the purchase price of $10. Shortly thereafter, Baker, through her attorney, mailed a certified letter to the Romeros, owners of land adjacent and contiguous to the Property, to inform them that she had recently acquired the Property and would be having it surveyed in the near future. This litigation ensued after the Romeros would not allow the surveyor hired by Baker to have access to the portions of the Property contained within the land that they owned.

Baker filed a Petition for Injunctive Relief against the Romeros, seeking to enjoin the Romeros from interfering with her exercise of ownership of the Property and specifically requesting that the Romeros be ordered to refrain from interfering with Baker's attempt to have the Property surveyed. Attached as Exhibit "A" to the petition was a description of the Property.

The Romeros filed an Answer and Reconventional Demand acknowledging that they would not allow Baker's surveyor on their property and claiming "possession and ownership of all property referenced herein," including the land which Baker claimed to own. More specifically, the Romeros asserted that they were the title owners and possessors of ten tracts of land as described in their own Exhibit "A," which they attached to their answer. The Romeros additionally asserted that they and their ancestors in title had possessed the Property without interruption for "much longer than" one year. The Romeros claimed that Baker had trespassed on the Property, and they requested that she and her agents, assigns, employees, and successors in title be prevented from using the Property and that they be awarded damages for the loss of use of the Property. In addition, the Romeros requested that the trial court render a judgment recognizing their right to possession of the Property.

Baker answered the Romeros' reconventional demand in the form of a general denial. Thereafter, she filed a motion for summary judgment seeking a judgment recognizing her as owner of the Property, ordering the Romeros to vacate the premises, and dismissing the Romeros' claims against her with prejudice. . . . The minutes further reflect that the Romeros agreed to allow Baker to survey the Property at her expense.

Baker filed a motion to amend and supplement her original petition. Therein, she stated that the Property had been surveyed and that a plat had been prepared and provided to the parties. According to Baker, the survey and plat reflected that the Romeros had and continue to trespass on land owned by her and that they had erected and/or moved structures onto the Property without her consent. Baker sought a judgment recognizing her as the owner of the Property and all structures placed thereon by the Romeros, both movable and immovable. Alternatively, Baker prayed that the Romeros be ordered to remove the structures at their expense. . . .

A bench trial took place on Baker's petitory action. In a written judgment, the trial court found that:

1. Plaintiff did not meet her burden of proof to establish ownership of the subject immovable property as a matter of law,

2. Defendants have been in statutory possession of the subject property since 1988, and

3. Plaintiff's Motion for Summary Judgment promptly and properly converted Defendants' possessory action pleaded in their Reconventional Demand to a viable and justiciable petitory action.

Accordingly, judgment was rendered in favor of the Romeros and against Baker dismissing her petitory action. The Romeros' possessory action was granted because the trial court found that they had established as a matter of law the right to possess the Property.

Baker is now before this court on appeal. . . .

Discussion

Louisiana Code of Civil Procedure Article 3651 defines a petitory action as "one brought by a person who claims the ownership, but who is not in possession, of immovable property or of a real right therein, against another who is in possession or who claims the ownership thereof adversely, to obtain judgment recognizing the plaintiff's ownership." . . .

In *Pure Oil*, 294 So.2d 797, the issue concerned the plaintiff's burden of proof in a petitory action when the defendant is in possession of the property in controversy. The supreme court held that those claiming title or ownership of disputed land in the possession of others are "required to prove valid record title, to show title good against the world without regard to the title of the party in possession. C.C.P. Arts. 3653, 3654." *Id*. at 799.

Badeaux, 382 So.2d 954, likewise involved a petitory action brought by a claimed owner of a tract of land against a person possessing the land; however, the defendant was found to have been a precarious possessor in that he possessed the land not on his own behalf but rather on behalf of and with the permission of another. *See* La. Civ. Code art. 3437. That being the case, the supreme court held that the plaintiff had met his burden of proof in his petitory action by proving that he had acquired the tract of land by thirty-year acquisitive prescription. *Id*. In doing so, the supreme court noted:

> "Although it be true that the plaintiff in a petitory action, must succeed on the strength of his own title, and not on the weakness of his adversary's yet, when the latter has no title at all, he cannot, as a trespasser, take advantage of any defect in the former's muniments of title. In such cases, a title apparently good, is all that is required to maintain the petitory action." *Zeringue v. Williams*[,] 15 La. Ann. 76 [(La. 1860)].

Id. at 956.

Assignment of Error Number One

Baker contends that the trial court erred in failing to make the Romeros the plaintiffs in the petitory action after they asserted possession and ownership of the Property in their answer and reconventional demand. In addition, she insists that the Romeros' possession claims were waived pursuant to La. Code Civ. Proc. art. 3657 when they made a claim of ownership of the Property. The Romeros counter that after the Property was surveyed, they acknowledged that they no longer had a claim of ownership and instead were claiming possession of the Property. Moreover, the Romeros claim that because Baker did not assert in the trial court that they should have been the plaintiffs in the petitory action, she should be precluded from asserting that argument for the first time on appeal.

In their answer and reconventional demand, the Romeros assert that they are the title owners of ten tracts of land and that they and their ancestors in title have possessed the Property for well over one year without interruption. Their prayer for relief requests that judgment be rendered recognizing their right to possession of the Property. Moreover, the Romeros stipulated at the June 19, 2009 hearing that they did not have title to the Property and were instead alleging good faith possession of the Property.

Ultimately, the Romeros did not claim ownership of the Property and thus did not waive their possession claims. In addition, because Baker did not allege in the trial court that the burden of proof in the petitory action should have shifted to the Romeros, she cannot make that argument for the first time on appeal. *See* Uniform Rules—Courts of Appeal, Rule 1-3; *Guilbeaux v. Times of Acadiana, Inc.*, 94-1270 (La. App. 3 Cir. 8/9/95), 661 So. 2d 1027, *writ denied*, 95-2942 (La. 3/29/96), 670 So.2d 1238. The trial court was correct in not making the Romeros the plaintiffs in the petitory action. Baker's first assignment of error lacks merit.

Assignment of Error Number Two

Baker next contends that the trial court erred in applying the *Pure Oil* standard and requiring that she prove title good against the world. She argued that the trial court should have instead . . . required that she prove title better than that of the Romeros, as was done in *Beaceaux*, 382 So.2d 954, a supreme court decision rendered after *Pure Oil*. The Romeros insist that the trial court properly and appropriately applied the *Pure Oil* standard . . . to this matter. In support of their argument, they rely on *Aymond v. Smith*, 476 So.2d 1081, 1084 (La. App. 3 Cir. 1985), wherein this court held that:

> When the defendant in the petitory action . . . is in possession, the plaintiff in the petitory action . . . must rely on the strength of his own title and not the weakness of that of his adversary, and the title of the defendant in the petitory action is not at issue until the plaintiff has proved valid title in himself.

Aymond, which was decided by this court eleven years after the supreme court handed down the *Pure Oil* decision . . . began as a possessory action brought by a plaintiff who claimed that the defendant had disturbed his possession of a one acre tract of land. In answer to the petition, the defendant denied the plaintiff's possession, claiming that he owned the land through title or thirty-year acquisitive prescription. We noted that, in claiming ownership of the disputed property, the defendant converted the possessory action into a petitory action in which he became the plaintiff with the burden of proving "ownership either by an unbroken chain of valid transfers from the sovereign or an ancestor in title common with the defendant or by acquisitive prescription" *Id.* (citations omitted). We further noted that "[i]f the plaintiff in the petitory action should fail and be unable to make out his title good against the world, his demands must be rejected and his case dismissed even if the defendant in the petitory action has no title to the property." *Id.* at 1084 (citing *Garrett v. Ernest*, 369 So.2d 713 (La. App. 1 Cir.), *writ denied*, 371 So. 2d 1340 (La. 1979); *Weaver v. Hailey*, 416 So.2d 311 (La. App. 3 Cir. 1982); *Crown Zellerbach Corp. v. Heck*, 407 So.2d 770 (La. App. 1 Cir. 1981); and *Osborn v. Johnston*, 308 So.2d 464 (La. App. 3 Cir.), *aff'd*, 322 So.2d 112 (La. 1975)).

Considering our prior decision in *Aymond*, we cannot conclude that the trial court erred in requiring Baker to prove title good against the world. Moreover, we agree that Baker's reliance on *Badeaux* is misplaced given the facts that the defendant in that petitory action was a precarious possessor who possessed the disputed property with the permission of its owner. Here, Mr. Romero testified that when he purchased the tract of land in 1987, he believed that he was getting all of the property within certain boundaries; there were no markers around the forty-foot strip, i.e., the Property now at the center of this litigation. Mr. Romero further testified that no one had ever given him any indication that they owned the Property until he got the letter from Baker in 2006 seeking to survey the Property which she claimed to have recently purchased. . . .

Assignment of Error Number Three

Finally, Baker asserts that even if she was the proper plaintiff in the petitory action and *Pure Oil* was properly applied, the trial court erred by reading into it a requirement that her title chain be traceable to a government transaction. The Romeros counter that the trial court properly applied the law of *Pure Oil* and *Aymond* and correctly held that the July 8, 1885 sheriff's tax sale deed upon which Baker relied was "not a transfer of title 'with a sovereign grant as its origin.'"

In dismissing Baker's petitory action and granting the Romeros' possessory action on the basis that they established their right to possess the Property, the trial court, referring to the burden established in *Pure Oil*, noted the Latin phrase "*Dura Lex, Sed Lex*" which means "the law is harsh, but it is the law." Nevertheless, the trial court recognized that although it had been heavily criticized, *Pure Oil* remained the law of this state and it was "duty-bound to apply it." Citing *Aymond*, the trial court reasoned that "[a] tax sale bespeaks prior *private* ownership, thus the evidentiary destination to a sovereign grant, the originating transfer upon which all title to the tract is founded, has not been reached." The trial court went on to state:

> Ownership back to a common ancestor in title, another route to prove ownership, does not apply here as Defendants claimed only possession of the subject tract, thus no possibility of a common author. The remaining alternative to prove ownership, acquisitive prescription, was neither pleaded nor argued and the court is prohibited from doing so *sua sponte.* La. Civ. Code art. 3452.

As noted by the trial court, Baker could have proven her claim of ownership of the Property through several routes other than by tracing her chain of title back to the sovereign, but for the reasons that it outlined, she was unable to do so. We are convinced that the trial court properly applied the law to this matter and that Baker simply failed to meet the requisite burden of proof.

Decree

For the foregoing reasons, the judgment of the trial court is affirmed in entirety. All costs of this appeal are assessed against the plaintiff, Lyn Baker.

Notes and Questions

1. In order to prove her claim of ownership, Lyn Baker, the plaintiff in *Baker v. Romero*, 55 So.3d 1035 (La. App. 3 Cir. 2011), was required to prove her title back

to a grant of land, or "patent," from the sovereign. Sometimes these original grants were unconditional; sometimes they were contingent on the grantee remaining in possession for a period of time and making improvements on or cultivating the land. These initial land grants were intended to promote agriculture and spur commerce. A tax sale is not a land grant or a patent from a sovereign. It is a contingent transfer of ownership from a person who failed to pay taxes to another person who has agreed to pay those taxes. Nevertheless, should a tax sale be allowed to provide the foundation for a petitory action?

2. Lyn Baker failed to offer proof of her title to the forty-foot strip of land in dispute back to a sovereign. Although her relatives conveyed to her their "right, title and interest" in the strip, the 2006 Cash Sale Deed could not demonstrate that she purchased the property from an actual owner. Baker paid her relatives only $10 for this strip of land. Does this raise any questions in your mind?

3. Notice the court's attention to the issue of whether Baker converted her lawsuit, initially styled a "Petition for Injunctive Relief," into a petitory action with the attendant burden of proof made under *Pure Oil Co. v. Skinner*, 294 So.2d 797 (La. 1974). What pleading specifically triggered the application of this burden of proof? Could Baker's attorney have avoided this in some way? Baker argued that *the defendants* assumed the burden of a plaintiff in a petitory action through their pleadings. How could the defendants have avoided this? What about plaintiff's argument that the defendants were not in possession of the disputed property as owners, but rather as precarious possessors? If this last argument had been successful, it appears the court might have only required Baker to show that her title was "apparently good" as set forth in *Badeaux v. Pitre*, 382 So.2d 954 (La. 1980). Why were the Romeros not found to be precarious possessors?

4. What happens when neither party is able to prove ownership of the disputed land in a petitory action or an equivalent proceeding under Article 3654 of the Code of Civil Procedure? In such a case the current possessor is generally left to continue in possession until he can prove ownership through acquisitive prescription or some other party proves ownership by tracing title back to a sovereign. *See e.g., Romby v. Zion Hill Baptist Church*, 327 So.2 538 (La. App. 2 Cir. 1976).

5. The *Pure Oil* standard for the burden of proof imposed on the dispossessed plaintiff in a petitory action when the defendant is in possession was known in medieval Europe as the *probatio diabolica* (diabolical onus or devil's proof) because it was so difficult to meet. Roman law addressed this issue through the Publician action (*actio Publiciana*), which is named after a praetor Publicius, possibly Quintus Publicius who was *praetor peregrinus* in 66 B.C. or shortly before.

Initially, the Publician action was granted to cure a vice in form, for example when a thing normally requiring highly ceremonial transfer formalities was delivered without the requisite form. The action employs a fiction in favor of the plaintiff by assuming that acquisitive prescription has begun to run, although the requisite time has not accrued. As the distinction between things requiring solemn formalities for transfer and things which could be transferred without formality waned, the Publician action was deployed by magistrate law to cover other kinds of cases, including when a plaintiff out of possession could not prove the ownership of his author. The Publican action is best understood as focusing on ownership rather than possession.

Several sister jurisdictions have embraced the Publician action by way of codification, jurisprudence or doctrine. For example, Article 894 of the Civil Code of Chile and Article 951 of the Colombian Civil Code, which have identical contents, explicitly elevate the Publician action into positive law:

Acción publiciana

Se concede la misma acción, aunque no se pruebe dominio, al que ha perdido la posesión regular de la cosa, y se hallaba en el caso de poderla ganar por prescripción.

Pero no valdrá ni contra el verdadero dueño, ni contra el que posea con igual o mejor derecho.

Publician action

The same action is granted, although ownership is not proved, to him who has lost regular possession of the thing, while having the opportunity to win it by way of prescription.

But it will not be allowed against the true owner nor against the person who possesses under equal or better right.

Código Civil de Chile art. 894 (1857, as amended); Código Civil Colombiano art. 951 (1873, as amended). In both jurisdictions, the Publician action, which is offered alongside the revendicatory action in the section governing the proper plaintiff in recovery proceedings, cures the harshness of the *probatio diabolica* in favor of a former possessor who has "lost regular possession of the thing" and who at this point cannot prove ownership through acquisitive prescription because it has not yet accrued.

In Louisiana, the Publician action has never been codified. Until *Pure Oil*, however, it subsisted in our jurisprudence. Recall the dissent in *Pure Oil* and Justice Summers' extensive quotation from *Bedford v. Urquhart*, 8 La. 234, *aff'd on rehearing* in 8 La. 241 (1835). After *Pure Oil*, a countering codification attempt by its detractors was deflected. In the late 1970s, a reform proposal offered by Professor A.N. Yiannopoulos and Fredrick T. Hass failed to gain approval in the Louisiana State Law Institute. An alternative version of Yiannopoulos and Hass' rejected proposal was offered in a law review article authored by Douglas Nichols in the mid-1990s:

One who claims ownership of an immovable against another in possession must prove that he has acquired ownership from a previous owner or by acquisitive prescription. *One who had possession of an immovable in good faith and under just title shall prevail against a possessor who has no title* [emphasis added]. If neither party is in possession, he need only prove better title.

Douglas Nichols, *Comment: The Publician Action*, 69 Tul. L. Rev. 217, 245 n. 186 (1994). What are the interests here that a legislator would need to ponder and weigh? Do you favor retaining the *Pure Oil* rule or re-introducing the Publician action into Louisiana law?

2. Titles Traced to a Common Author

The last paragraph of Article 3653 of the Code of Civil Procedure states that when the two litigants disputing ownership of immovable property, or a real right therein, trace their titles to a common author, this ancestor in title is presumed to be the previous owner. La. Code Civ. Proc. art. 3653 (1960, amended 1981); *see also* La. Civ. Code art. 532 (1979) (same). Rather than having to trace title to the sovereign, the plaintiff in this situation can prevail in a petitory action if he can prove that "his title is the *more ancient* from the common author." La. Civ. Code art. 532 rev. cmt. (a) (1979) (emphasis added). In other words, the transferee from the common author who first filed an act evidencing his acquisition of ownership, or a real right, in the conveyance records of the parish where the property is located will prevail, unless acquisitive prescription allows the other party to overcome this more ancient title. *Id*. rev. cmt. (b). Note, however, that this presumption in favor of the more ancient title from a common author applies only between the parties to the litigation. It has no *res judicata* effect on third persons who are not party to the litigation. *Id*. rev. cmt. (a).

3. Better Title When Neither Party Is in Possession

The second clause of Article 3653 of the Code of Civil Procedure allows proof of a better title in a petitory action when *neither party* is in possession of an immovable or real right therein. This may occur when the record owner cannot find evidence to prove his prior possession, or when the immovable was possessed so long ago that no record of possession exists. For example, forests, swamps, and inaccessible farmland may fall into disuse. Remember that a possessor of an immovable remains in possession until another person can establish that she is the owner. When ownership of an immovable is in dispute and no one is in possession, a plaintiff in a petitory action needs only prove better title than the defendant to be recognized as owner. La. Code Civ. Proc. art. 3653(2) (1960, amended 1981); La. Civ. Code art. 531(1979).

Nothing precludes a third party from proving better title than either the plaintiff or the defendant, but that third party would need to bring his own suit. As between the parties in the litigation, if neither is in possession, the plaintiff needs only prove better title than the defendant to be declared the owner of the immovable.

In *Griffin v. Daigle*, 769 So.2d 720 (La. App. 1 Cir. 2000), a partition document described the property boundaries with reference to the "public road" lying between and alongside the properties of the plaintiff and the defendant. Since the defendants had not shown they were in possession of the property, the court uses the "better title" standard. But what does "better title" mean?. According to the court, Louisiana jurisprudence has looked to the more ancient title in cases in which the title is traced back to a common author under Article 3653 of the Code of Civil Procedure and Article 532 of the Civil Code. However, when a transfer occurs simultaneously to both parties in an act of partition, the principle of "the more ancient title is the better title" does not come into play. According to the court, the analysis then proceeds in the following order: firstly, a comparison of the property descriptions and plats of survey, with primacy given to the plats; secondly, a distillation of the parties' intention from the entire language of the instrument; and, as a last resort, extrinsic evidence.

4. Proof of Title in Action for Declaratory Judgment, Concursus, Expropriation, or Similar Proceeding

Article 3654 of Code of Civil Procedure addresses the special case of someone other than the owner of an immovable, or a real right therein, initiating a proceeding to determine the owner or right holder. For example, in the context of an expropriation proceeding, a governmental entity or a private corporation with the power to expropriate may ask a court to identify to whom just compensation should be paid. Similarly, when an oil company has mineral royalties or other revenues to distribute, it may be uncertain to whom to make the payments. These persons, who do not claim to be either possessors or owners, may bring an action to have the ownership or possession of immovable property or real rights therein established.

The rules of proof are the same. The possessor is entitled to the relevant payment unless someone else proves ownership. A person proves ownership by proving either that he purchased from an owner or that he acquired ownership through acquisitive prescription. When none of the parties before the court has a right to possess, the person who proves better title gets the payment. See Louisiana Code of Civil Procedure article 3654 below.

> **Art. 3654. Proof of title in action for declaratory judgment, concursus, expropriation, or similar proceeding**
>
> When the issue of ownership of immovable property or of a real right therein is presented in an action for a declaratory judgment, or in a concursus, expropriation, or similar proceeding, or the issue of the ownership of funds deposited in the registry of the court and which belong to the owner of the immovable property or of the real right therein is so presented, the court shall render judgment in favor of the party:
>
> (1) Who would be entitled to the possession of the immovable property or real right therein in a possessory action, unless the adverse party proves that he has acquired ownership from a previous owner or by acquisitive prescription; or

(2) Who proves better title to the immovable property or real right therein, when neither party would be entitled to the possession of the immovable property or real right therein in a possessory action.

La. Code Civ. Proc. art. 3654 (1960, amended 1981). As previously noted, this provision was employed in *Pure Oil Co. v. Skinner*, 294 So.2d 797 (La. 1974).

B. Revendicatory Actions for the Recovery of Movables

Unlike the petitory action for immovables, a nominate real action expressly authorized by the Louisiana Code of Civil Procedure, the revendicatory action for recovery of movables bears no name and has no explicit statutory basis. It is an innominate real action grounded in French doctrine (*action en revendication*) and in the general language of Article 526 of the Civil Code:

Art. 526. Recognition of ownership; recovery of the thing

The owner of a thing is entitled to recover it from anyone who possesses or detains it without right and to obtain judgment recognizing his ownership and ordering delivery of the thing to him.

La. Civ. Code art. 526 (1979). *See also* La. Civ. Code art. 3444 ("Possession of movables is protected by the rules of the Code of Civil Procedure that govern civil actions.") (1982). Louisiana courts, however, have often used the term revendicatory action. *See, e.g., Dual Drilling Co. v. Mills Equipment Investments*, 721 So.2d 853, 856 (La. 1998).

The revendicatory action offers a dispossessed owner a convenient tool to recover possession of a movable and to have his ownership otherwise recognized. The action can be cumulated with various *personal* actions, including a delictual action, La. Civ. Code art. 2315 (1999), a quasi-contractual action grounded in unjust enrichment, La. Civ. Code art. 2298 (1995), and the quasi-contractual action brought by a person who made a payment or delivered a thing against a person who received a payment or thing not owed. La. Civ. Code art. 2299 (1995).

Remember that the owner of a lost or stolen thing is generally entitled to recover the thing from the thief or the finder. However, when a lost or stolen thing is sold by authority of law—for example, at a sheriff's sale, the transferee acquires ownership.

Art. 524. Recovery of lost or stolen things

The owner of a lost or stolen movable may recover it from a possessor who bought it in good faith at a public auction or from a merchant customarily selling similar things on reimbursing the purchase price.

The former owner of a lost, stolen or abandoned movable that has been sold by authority of law may not recover it from the purchaser.

La. Civ. Code art. 524 (1979). In civilian doctrine, a thing is *lost* when it is not in the possession of the owner and the owner did not intend to relinquish ownership. A person who finds a lost corporeal movable may be entitled to keep the thing if he makes a diligent effort to locate the owner and return the thing to the owner. La. Civ. Code art. 3419 (1982). A thing is considered "stolen" when a person (the thief) takes possession of a thing without the consent of the owner. La. Civ. Code art. 521 (1979). The thief cannot transfer ownership of the stolen thing. *Id.* ("One who has possession of a lost or stolen thing may not transfer ownership to another.").

The first paragraph of Article 524 balances the interests of a good faith purchaser who acquires a movable at a public auction or from a merchant who customarily sells similar things. It allows the original owner to recover the thing, but only upon reimbursing the good faith purchaser his purchase price. A purchaser with actual knowledge that the movable was a lost or stolen thing, or a purchaser confronted with circumstances that would have put a reasonably prudent person on notice to inquire about the transferor's ownership, is not in good faith and therefore, will not be entitled to reimbursement of the purchase price. *See* La. Civ. Code art. 523 rev. cmt. (b) (1979). According to Louisiana jurisprudence, the reimbursement requirement is triggered even when the seller is not a merchant, but uses a commercial agent to transact with a good faith purchaser. *See Southeast Equipment Co. v. Office of State Police*, 437 So.2d 1184 (La. App. 4 Cir. 1983).

A person who acquires a corporeal movable in good faith and for fair value from a person who obtained possession of the movable through means of fraud is entitled to retain ownership of the thing even though the title of her transferor may be subject to annulment because of a vice of consent. La. Civ. Code art. 522 (1979). *See also* U.C.C art. 2-403(1) (2003). Here the Civil Code protects the interests of the good faith purchaser for value and exempts him from any obligation to return the thing to the original owner. This is because, as between the two relatively innocent parties, the original owner is in the best position to avoid a loss by taking reasonable precautions to guard against fraud. *See* La. Civ. Code art. 522 rev. cmt. (c) (1979); *Trumbell Chevrolet Sales Co. v. Maxwell*, 142 So.2d 805, 806 (La. App. 2 Cir. 1962).

Under the revised law of acquisitive prescription a transferee who is in good faith and possesses for three years "under an act sufficient to transfer ownership," may acquire ownership. La. Civ. Code art. 3490 (1982). Compare La. Civ. Code 3506 (1970). By implication, a thief could not take advantage of this abbreviated prescriptive period because he would lack both good faith and an act sufficient to transfer ownership.

Finally, in order to prevail in a revendicatory action for the recovery of a movable, the plaintiff must prove his ownership. Article 530 of the Civil Code offers a scheme of presumptions in favor of possessors of corporeal movables:

Art. 530. Presumption of ownership of movable

The possessor of a corporeal movable is presumed to be its owner. The previous possessor of a corporeal movable is presumed to have been its owner during the period of possession.

>   These presumptions do not prevail against a previous possessor who was
>   dispossessed as a result of loss or theft.

La. Civ. Code art. 530 (1979). The provision first furnishes a presumption to the
current possessor. However, a similar presumption operates in favor of a previous
possessor for the time of his possession. Both presumptions are not available against
a previous possessor who was dispossessed in the wake of loss or theft. Possession
according to Article 530 of the Civil Code must be true possession. It cannot be precarious, equivocal, clandestine or based on fraud. *Id.* rev. cmt.

As the following decision illustrates, the revendicatory action is not subject to
liberative prescription because, as a general proposition, ownership exists independently of possession and may not be lost by non-use. La. Civ. Code art. 481 (1979).
In a revendicatory action, however, the defendant possessor can raise the defense
of acquisitive prescription. The following decision involves the renowned rhythm
and blues pianist and singer from New Orleans, Henry Roeland Byrd, affectionately
known as "Professor Longhair." Read the notes following the decision carefully to
understand the ultimate outcome of his heirs' efforts to vindicate Professor Longhair's property interests in several of his musical recordings.

Songbyrd, Inc. v. Bearsville Records, Inc.

104 F.3d 773 (5th Cir. 1997)

WIENER, Circuit Judge. Plaintiff-Appellant SongByrd, Inc. (SongByrd) appeals
from the district court's dismissal of its action seeking to recover from Defendant-
Appellee the Estate of Albert B. Grossman d/b/a Bearsville Records (Bearsville),
several master tapes recorded by a legendary New Orleans musician. Concluding
that (1) the district court improperly classified SongByrd's suit as a personal rather
than a real action, (2) real actions are imprescriptible under Louisiana law, and (3)
Bearsville has yet to establish that it gave SongByrd's predecessors-in-interest actual
notice of Bearsville's intent to possess the tapes for itself, we reverse the district
court's summary judgment ruling and remand for further proceedings consistent
with this opinion.

I

Facts and Proceedings

The late Henry Roeland Byrd, also known as "Professor Longhair," was an influential New Orleans rhythm-and-blues pianist and composer, and is widely regarded
as one of the primary inspirations for the renaissance of New Orleans popular
music over the last thirty years. His numerous hits included original compositions
such as "Tipitina" and "Go to the Mardi Gras," as well as his famous renditions of
Earl King's "Big Chief." After achieving modest commercial success as a local per-
former and recording artist in the 1940s and 1950s, Byrd fell on hard times during
the 1960s. His fortunes began to change for the better in 1970, however, when New
Orleans music aficionado Arthur "Quint" Davis, along with others, founded the
New Orleans Jazz and Heritage Festival ("JazzFest"). Needing talented performers

for JazzFest, Davis located Byrd in 1971 working in an obscure record store in New Orleans and transformed him into a perennial star attraction of the JazzFest and other venues from that time until his death in 1980.

Soon after Byrd's first performance at JazzFest, Davis, acting as the pianist's manager, and Parker Dinkins, an attorney, arranged for Byrd to make several "master recordings" at a Baton Rouge recording studio known as Deep South Recorders. These master recordings consist of four reels of 8-track tape which could be "mixed" to produce either demonstration tapes or final recordings suitable for the production of records, cassettes, and compact discs. According to SongByrd, several demonstration tapes produced from these master recordings found their way to Bearsville Records, Inc., a recording studio and record company located in Woodstock, New York and operated by Grossman. Impressed by the demonstration tapes, Grossman apparently arranged with Davis and Dinkins for Byrd and another New Orleans musician to travel to Bearsville's studio for a recording session.

For reasons that are unclear but not material to this appeal, the Bearsville recording sessions proved unsatisfactory. For equally unclear reasons, Davis and Dinkins wanted Grossman to be able either to listen to or play for others the full version of the Baton Rouge master recordings. In furtherance of this desire, Davis and Dinkins caused the four "master recording" tapes to be delivered to Grossman in New York. According to the as yet unrefuted affidavit of Davis, these tapes were delivered to Grossman, "as demonstration tapes only, without any intent for either Albert Grossman or Bearsville Records, Inc. to possess these aforementioned tapes as owner." Also for reasons as yet not explained by either party, the tapes remained in Grossman's possession for many years thereafter.

Acting on behalf of Davis and Byrd in 1975, Dinkins wrote two letters to Bearsville—the first addressed to a George James, the second to Grossman himself—requesting that Bearsville return the master recording tapes. Bearsville made no response whatsoever to Dinkins' letters (or at least has not introduced any evidence of a response). Dinkins, for reasons as yet unknown, did not press his request any further.

After Albert Grossman's death in the mid 1980s, Bearsville Records, Inc. was dissolved, but Grossman's estate continued to do business as "Bearsville Records." Even though it no longer signs artists or promotes their products, Bearsville Records still operates a recording studio which it leases to record labels and third parties; it also licenses a catalog of recordings by artists originally under contract with Bearsville Records, Inc. Acting in this latter capacity, Bearsville licensed certain of the Byrd master recordings to Rounder Records Corporation of Cambridge, Massachusetts (Rounder) for an advance against royalties.

In 1987, Rounder released *Professor Longhair, Houseparty New Orleans Style: The Lost Sessions,* an album that contained 11 songs or "tracks" made from Byrd's original Baton Rouge master recordings. This release garnered Byrd a posthumous Grammy Award for Best Traditional Blues Album of 1987. The liner notes of the Rounder album make hardly any reference to Bearsville and no reference whatsoever to the contractual agreement between Rounder and Bearsville. Bearsville Records also licensed certain of the master recordings to another record company, Rhino Records (Rhino). According to SongByrd's petition, Rhino released an album, titled "Mardi Gras in Baton Rouge," featuring seven tracks from the Baton Rouge master recordings.

In 1993, SongByrd, Inc. was incorporated and commenced business as successor-in-interest to the intellectual property rights of Byrd and his deceased widow, Alice Walton Byrd. In 1995, SongByrd filed this lawsuit in state court in New Orleans against Bearsville Records, Inc. SongByrd's "Petition in Revindication" sought a judgment (1) recognizing its ownership of the master recordings, (2) ordering return of the recordings, and (3) awarding damages. Bearsville timely removed the suit to federal court and subsequently filed a motion to dismiss . . . , asserting (a) lack of personal jurisdiction over Bearsville and (b) failure of SongByrd to state a cause of action because SongByrd's claims were barred by *liberative* prescription under Louisiana law. As both parties submitted affidavits and exhibits outside the pleadings, however, the district court correctly treated Bearsville's motion to dismiss as a motion for summary judgment. . . . Pretermitting the question of personal jurisdiction, the district court then granted the motion and dismissed SongByrd's case. The court held that SongByrd's action was barred by liberative prescription and also rejected SongByrd's argument that at all times Bearsville has been only a precarious possessor and therefore prescription has never commenced to run. SongByrd timely filed its notice of appeal from the district court's ruling.

II

Analysis

B. *Applicable Law* — Erie-*Bound*

1. *Special Louisiana* Erie *Considerations*

The basis of our jurisdiction, and that of the district court, to decide the instant case is diversity of citizenship, under which a federal court's obligation is to apply substantive state law. In Louisiana this obligation has special dimensions because of our unique Civilian tradition. We remain ever aware of the late Judge Rubin's caution to federal *Erie* courts applying Louisiana Civil law to steer clear of the common law principle of *stare decisis* and to apply instead the distinctly Civilian doctrine of *jurisprudence constante*:

> Because of the reviewing power of [Louisiana] appellate courts, the [Louisiana] trial judge may pay great respect to the decisions of these courts. He is not bound to do so, however, because the doctrine of stare decisis does not apply. Instead, each judge, trial and appellate, may consult the civil code and draw anew from its principles. Interpretation of the code and other sources of law is appropriate for each judge. The judge is guided much more by doctrine, as expounded in legal treatises by legal scholars, than by the decisions of colleagues. . . . Instead of *stare decisis,* the rule is one of

deference to a series of decisions, *jurisprudence constante*. [Alvin B. Rubin, *Hazards of a Civilian Venturer in a Federal Court: Travel and Travail on the Erie Railroad*, 48 La. L. Rev. 1369, 1372 (1988) (citations omitted) (emphasis in original)]

Emphatically elaborating on the proposition that *Erie* "does not command blind allegiance to [any] case on all fours with the case before the court," now-Chief Judge Politz wrote that:

If anything, this flexibility is even greater when a federal court sits as a *Erie* court applying the Louisiana civil law. In such cases, "*the* Erie *obligation is to the [Civil] Code, the 'solemn expression of legislative will.'"* *Shelp, 333 F.2d 431 at 439* (quoting the very first article of the Louisiana Civil Code). The Louisiana Supreme Court has taken great pains to "plainly state that . . . *the notion of stare decisis, derived as it is from the common law should not be thought controlling in this state.*" *Ardoin v. Hartford Acc. & Indem. Co., 360 So. 2d 1331, 1334 (La. 1978)*. While caselaw in the State of Louisiana is acknowledged as "invaluable as previous interpretation . . ." [*id. at 1335*], it is nonetheless properly regarded as "secondary information." *Id.* at 1334. [*Green v. Walker*, 910 F.2d 291, 294 (5th Cir. 1990)]

2. Prescription

The central issue in the instant appeal is whether plaintiff's action is time barred. The answer to this question depends on whether the applicable period of limitation — prescription in Louisiana; statute of limitations in the common law — is liberative or acquisitive. As shall be seen from our analysis of the pertinent provisions of the Louisiana Civil Code and from "legal treatises by legal scholars," the applicable type of prescription is acquisitive. And, as shall also be seen below, our analysis of Louisiana case law reveals that (1) this determination comports with implications of the most recent pronouncement of the Supreme Court of Louisiana, and (2) at the very least, the "jurisprudence" on point is *not* "constante," which frees us to pursue our own analysis of the Code, with the help of doctrinal writing.

C. Revindicatory Actions Are Imprescriptible

SongByrd contends that the district court erred when it determined that Song-Byrd's action seeking recognition of its ownership interest in the master recordings, return of those recordings, and damages, has prescribed under Louisiana law. The district court's memorandum order held that SongByrd's action had prescribed under *Louisiana Civil Code Articles 3499* and *3492* regardless of whether SongByrd's claims were based in contract, quasi-contract, or tort. In so doing, the district court implicitly characterized SongByrd's action as a "personal action" arising from these areas of law. This characterization of SongByrd's action constitutes the first and fundamental error committed by the district court and led to its first erroneous holding.

As explained by Professor A.N. Yiannopoulos in his treatise on Louisiana property law, actions seeking recognition of ownership or enforcement of the rights thereof, whether in movable or immovable property, are not *personal* actions; they are "*real* actions." Such real actions, otherwise known as "revindicatory actions," are expressly authorized by the Louisiana Civil Code. As the official comments to the Code make clear, there are two kinds of revindicatory action, depending on the object of the ownership interest that the plaintiff seeks to have recognized: (1) a "*petitory action*" for the recovery of immovable property (real estate), and (2) an "*innominate real action*" for the recovery of movable property (personalty). Further, any "incidental demand for damages made in an action for the recovery of an immovable [or a movable] does not affect the classification of the main demand as a real action."

It follows from this basic dichotomy that, as the Civil Code specifically provides liberative prescription periods for all manner of *personal* actions (including delictual, contractual and quasi-contractual actions), "liberative prescription does not bar *real* actions seeking to protect the right of ownership." The rationale for this distinction is that "under our Civil Code, ownership can never be lost by the failure to exercise it—only by the acquisition of ownership by another through possession sufficient to acquire it through an acquisitive prescription." Thus, it is well established in Louisiana that the petitory action (for the protection of immovables) is *not* barred by liberative prescription. The same rule applies to the revindicatory action brought to assert or protect the right of ownership in movable property because it, too, is a *real* action, not a personal one. On this point Professor Yiannopoulos' *Louisiana Civil Law Treatise* could not be clearer:

> An action that is grounded on a wrongful act, that is, an offense or quasi-offense, is subject to the prescription of one year and an action grounded on quasi-contract is subject to the prescription of ten years. *The revindicatory action [for the recovery of movable property] is imprescriptible;* however, such an object is without object when the defendant has acquired the ownership of a movable by the acquisitive prescription of three or ten years.

Despite this obvious truism of Civilian doctrine, a number of older Louisiana decisions overlooked or disregarded it and, just as the district court did here, applied either one-year or ten-year periods of *liberative* prescription on the erroneous assumption that the revindicatory action is personal in nature, either delictual or quasi-contractual.

Nevertheless, a 50-year old Louisiana Supreme Court case, *Faison v. Patout*, [212 La. 37, 31 So.2d 416 (1947)] appears to be the most recent pronouncement on point, and it supports our reading of the Civil Code and Professor Yiannopoulos' reading as well. In *Faison*, Mrs. Hypolite Patout executed a manual donation of her jewelry to her two daughters. Following the donor's death, one of her sons, Sebastian Patout, suggested to his sisters that it was unsafe for them to keep this jewelry in one sister's bedroom; so, with his sisters' permission, Sebastian put the jewelry in *his* bank safety deposit box. Sebastian died some twelve years later, whereupon his widow removed the jewelry from the safety deposit box and refused to give it to the sisters. In the sisters' suit to recover the jewelry, the trial court held, and the

Louisiana Supreme Court agreed, that the sisters were the true owners. More significant to our consideration today, the *Patout* defendants (children of Mrs. Hypolite Patout's sons) had pled liberative prescription under *Louisiana Civil Code article 3544* (1870). They contended that their aunts' action was personal and thus had prescribed because more than ten years had elapsed between the time the property left the aunts' possession and the time suit was filed. Rejecting this contention, the Supreme Court wrote:

> There might be some merit in a plea of prescription if Sebastian Patout had possessed the property *for himself and the other heirs,* and *adversely to [his sisters],* but the record convinces us that he was acting as depository for his two sisters, these plaintiffs, and that his possession of the property was for their benefit—for them, and *not in his own name or right.*
>
> Counsel for defendants is in error in his contention that the ten-year [liberative] prescription under article 3544 commenced to run in March 1931 [when Sebastian took possession of the jewelry]. [Acquisitive] prescription began to run when plaintiffs were first denied delivery of this jewelry in June 1942, after the death of their brother, Sebastian Patout, and this suit was filed in December 1942, about six months later.

In thus rejecting the defendants' plea of *liberative* prescription, the Louisiana Supreme Court clearly recognized that the concepts of *precarious* possession and *acquisitive* prescription applied to this action for the recovery of movable property, even though the court did not use these terms of art. The facts in *Faison* are closely analogous to the situation before us today, and the holding of the Louisiana Supreme Court in *Faison*—the most recent pronouncement by the highest court of the state—is instructive despite being non-binding due to the inapplicability of the common law doctrine of *stare decisis.*

In sum, even though some decisions of the Louisiana Supreme Court have treated actions for recovery of movables as personal (delictual and occasionally as quasi-contractual), other decisions of that court have found that such actions are properly considered to assert claims of ownership and therefore are subject only to *acquisitive* prescription. Despite its age, *Patout* is still the most recent Louisiana Supreme Court pronouncement on point, and it so held. But regardless whether the most recent pronouncement of the Louisiana Supreme Court supports our analysis of the Civil Code and that of Professor Yiannopoulos, there is simply no *jurisprudence constante* on the question. It follows, then, that our *Erie*-bound decision to follow the plain wording and indisputable structure of the Louisiana Civil Code and Professor Yiannopoulos' analysis is either supported by or at least does no violence to Louisiana's jurisprudence as a secondary source of law. To the extent that our decision today may constitute an "*Erie* guess," we take additional comfort in the observation that almost 60 years have passed since the Louisiana Supreme Court last applied liberative prescription to actions claiming ownership or possession of movable property—a span of years attributable at least in part, we assume, to the broad reliance in recent decades on Professor Yiannopoulos' doctrinal work on this subject.

As SongByrd's "Petition in Revindication" sought recognition of its purported ownership interest in the Baton Rouge master recordings and recovery of possession of those recordings, and only incidentally sought damages resulting from Bearsville's contravention of SongByrd's alleged ownership interest, we hold that, as a fundamental matter of Louisiana property law, SongByrd's action is not subject to liberative prescription.

D. Termination of Precarious Possession and Actual Notice

This foundational holding does not end our analysis in the instant case, however. In addition to its failure to characterize SongByrd's suit as a real action and its concomitant error in applying the rules of liberative prescription, the district court also missed the mark in its treatment of SongByrd's assertion that Bearsville was and is only a precarious possessor. To situate the concept of precarious possession in its proper Civilian context, we again return to basics. As Professor Yiannopoulos explains, a defendant in possession (such as Bearsville) may defend a revindicatory action for the recovery of movable property by (1) asserting some right, be it personal or real, to possess the movable, or (2) claiming that he is in fact the owner of the movable by virtue of, e.g., a transfer from the owner, *acquisitive* prescription, or some other mode of acquiring ownership. No such defenses have been proffered by Bearsville; but if, on remand, it should assert the defense of acquisitive prescription, the district court will have to address SongByrd's contention—made both in its original petition and in opposition to Bearsville's motion to dismiss—that Bearsville is and always has been nothing more than a precarious possessor.

Under the Civil Code, the concept of "precarious possession" is defined within Title XXIII of Book III, "Of the Different Modes of Acquiring the Ownership of Things," as "the exercise of possession over a thing with the permission of or on behalf of the owner or possessor." A precarious possessor is presumed to possess for another, but precarious possession may be terminated or converted to possession on one's own behalf in either of two specific ways. First, a precarious possessor who is a co-owner (or his universal successor) may terminate his precarious possession, and thus begin to possess for himself alone, only when he demonstrates his intent to possess for himself by "overt and unambiguous acts sufficient to give notice to his co-owner." Second, a precarious possessor who is *not* a co-owner is held to a higher standard and only "commences to possess for himself when he gives *actual notice* of this intent to the person on whose behalf he is possessing."

In the instant case, then, should Bearsville assert that it acquired ownership of the master recordings by acquisitive prescription of either three or ten years, pursuant to *Louisiana Civil Code Articles 3489–91*, it will have to overcome SongByrd's assertion, so far supported by Quint Davis' affidavit, that Davis and Dinkins delivered the master recordings to Bearsville intending only for Bearsville to possess the tapes precariously. Bearsville may, of course, assert that (1) it was never a precarious possessor, or (2) even if it was a precarious possessor initially, at some point it terminated its precarious possession and began to possess for itself. Either way, Bearsville will have the burden of proving facts sufficient to support such a defense.

It is the non-co-owner context in which we finally address the district court's alternative—and, strictly speaking, premature—holding that Bearsville's failure to respond to Dinkins' letters requesting return of the tapes in 1975 and its later licensing agreements with Rounder and Rhino, constituted "actual notice" sufficient to convert Bearsville's precarious possession as a matter of law. This ruling, we observe, is clearly inconsistent with Louisiana law.

We have not been able to locate (and Bearsville has not cited to us) a single Louisiana case that supports the novel proposition that alone either (1) a minimal, apparently clandestine action—such as entering into a contractual agreement with a third party to enjoy the fruits of a movable without directly informing the owner of the movable of that agreement—or (2) mere inaction in the face of a request for a return of the movable to its owner, can somehow constitute "actual notice" for purposes of terminating precarious possession of the movable of a non-co-owner. To the contrary, recent Louisiana cases concerning termination of precarious possession reflect that the notice burden imposed on precarious possessors in such instances is much more stringent. As one court put it,

> a possessor whose possession begins other than as an owner must do something to make generally known that he has changed his intent and he must prove specifically when he manifested to others his intent to possess as owner. Continued physical possession alone does not suffice to rebut the presumption that the possession remains precarious. The character and notoriety of the possession must be sufficient to inform the public and the record owners of the possession as owner. [*Hammond v. Averett*, 415 So.2d 226, 227 (La. Ct. App. 2nd Cir. 1982)]

We therefore conclude that actual notice sufficient to convert or terminate precarious possession cannot be based solely on either minimal and apparently clandestine actions such as those described above or on merely standing mute in the face of a direct inquiry or request for return of the property.

This is not to say, of course, that the defendant may not refer to these facts in a subsequent motion for summary judgment or a full evidentiary hearing should Bearsville eventually assert that at some point it began to possess the master recordings for itself and gave SongByrd's predecessors-in-interest actual notice of such an intention. Doubtless these facts and others will have to be considered by the trier of fact in resolving such an acquisitive prescription defense in general and the actual notice issue in particular. We simply hold today that the limited evidence presented to the district court on Bearsville's motion to dismiss-cum-summary judgment, on the ground of *liberative* prescription, was insufficient to determine that Bearsville satisfied the high burden of proof necessary to establish that it gave SongBrd's predecessors-in-interest *actual* notice of its intent thenceforth to possess for itself, converting its precarious possession to adverse possession for the purpose of *acquisitive* prescription.

III

Conclusion

For the reasons stated above, we reverse the district court's grant of summary judgment in favor of Bearsville and remand the case for further proceedings consistent with this opinion. On remand, the district court is free to address the personal jurisdiction question that it pretermitted in its summary judgment ruling, an issue which is not before us on this appeal and on which we express no opinion at this juncture.

REVERSED and REMANDED.

Notes and Questions

1. In *Songbyrd, Inc. v. Bearsville Records, Inc.*, 104 F.3d 773 (5th Cir. 1997), the basis for the accrual of federal jurisdiction was diversity of citizenship. 28 U.S.C. § 1332 (2018). Under *Erie Railroad Co. v. Tompkins*, 304 U.S. 64 (1938), a federal court exercising diversity jurisdiction must apply to state-based claims the substantive law of the forum state. In the core areas of Louisiana's private law, the *Erie* obligation unfolds within a civilian context. This may explain why in *Songbyrd*, Judge Wiener took such great care to distinguish the civilian concept of *jurisprudence constante* from the common law axioms of *stare decisis* and binding precedent. Using civilian tools for construing the law, Judge Wiener concluded that the revendicatory action was not subject to liberative prescription. Identify the rationales and sources invoked by the court in support of its determination.

2. Once the court in *Songbyrd* determined that the plaintiff's revendicatory action was imprescriptible, the court turned to the defendant's defense based on acquisitive prescription. A person who possesses a movable adversely to the owner can acquire ownership of the movable through either three or ten year acquisitive prescription. La. Civ. Code art. 3489 (1982). The three year acquisitive prescription for movables requires good faith and "an act sufficient to transfer ownership." La. Civ. Code art. 3490 (1982). Otherwise, the prescriptive period is ten years. La, Civ. Code art. 3491 (1982). For jurisprudence, see, for example, *Blanton v. Napier*, 209 So.3d 314, 320 (La.App. 5 Cir. 2016) (upholding trial court's finding of insufficient proof by purported prescriber because "[o]ther than her self-serving testimony that she 'told' everyone that the jewelry belonged to her, Mrs. Napier put forth no additional fact witnesses or physical evidence (*e.g.* an updated appraisal or insurance policy listing Mrs. Napier as the owner of the jewelry, or testimony from friends or acquaintances) to prove that she possessed the jewelry as owner"); *In Re Succession of Wagner*, 993 So.2d 709, 722–23 (La.App. 1 Cir. 2008) (holding that so

son lacked good faith required to acquire gold coins, which father purported to donate without the concurrence of his spouse because (1) son complied with the father's request to conceal the donation from his mother; and (2) son was aware that at least some of the coins were purchased with a check drawn on a community checking account).

3. Unlike Roman law, Louisiana law does not have a *lex Atinia*, which blocks prescription of stolen movables that have not been returned to the sphere of authority (*potestas*) of the true owner. Thus, even stolen things are susceptible of acquisitive prescription. *See Keim v. Louisiana Historical Association Confederate War Museum*, 48 F.3d 363 (8th Cir. 1995). However, the uncodified doctrine of *contra non valentem agere nulla currit prescriptio* ("no prescription runs against persons unable to bring action") might operate to suspend or toll acquisitive prescription from running until the true owner acquires sufficient knowledge of the thief's identity to bring a cause of action to recover the object of the theft. Alternatively, a thief who fails to reveal himself and the nature of his adverse claim to a stolen movable would be unable to assert acquisitive prescription because his possession would suffer from the vice of being "clandestine." La. Civ. Code art. 3435 (1982).

South Africa imposes significant hurdles when it comes to acquisitive prescription of movables. Not only must possession last for 30 years, but it must also be "open." *See* Section 1 of the Prescription Act 68 of 1969 ("a person shall by prescription become the owner of a thing which he has possessed openly and as if he were the owner thereof for an uninterrupted period of 30 years . . ."). The requirement of openness (*nec clam*) has been interpreted objectively to mean that the thing must be possessed openly not only vis-à-vis the general public, but also vis-à-vis the true owner. In other words, a claimant's possession must have come to the true owner's attention in the exercise of reasonable care. *See e.g., The University of Fort Hare v. Wavelengths* 256 (Pty) Ltd. (8605/2005) [2010] ZAWCHC 438 (2010) (rejecting a claim of acquisitive prescription in the case of a painting kept inside a claimant's private dwelling because (1) the true owner could not have ascertained that the painting was in the possession of the claimant and (2) the claimant's possession could not have created an impression in the world at large). For criticism in the literature, see Warren Freedman, *The Unholy Three: Acquisition of Ownership of Movables by Prescription—An Assessment of* University of Fort Hare v. Wavelength 25 (Pty) Ltd., 79 T.H.R.H.R. (Tydskrif vir Hedensdaagse Romeins-Hollandse Reg) 412 (2016). The author offers that, by its design, the court's strict approach to acquisitive prescription of movables in *University of Fort Hare* does not make clear what a person must do to satisfy the requirement of openness and that the court's approach is inappropriate for a bad faith possessor. *Id.* at 422. Moreover, under the facts of the case, while the claimant had developed a sense of personal attachment to the painting, the true owner did not even know that the painting was missing. *Id.* at 425.

4. In analyzing Bearsville's acquisitive prescription defense to Songbyrd's reven-dicatory action in *Songbyrd, Inc. v. Bearsville Records, Inc.*, 104 F.3d 773 (5th Cir. 1997), the federal courts in Louisiana had to determine whether Bearsville had been a true possessor or merely a precarious possessor of the master tapes. A precarious possessor who exercises physical control with the permission or on behalf of the owner or possessor cannot prescribe. La. Civ. Code arts. 3437, 3438, 3477 (1982). Precarious possession terminates, however, if the precarious possessor gives actual notice of his intent to possess for himself. La. Civ. Code arts. 3439 & 3478 (1982). Was the retention of the tapes by Bearsville in the face of the demand to return the tapes by Professor Longhair's legal representatives and Bearsville's confection of licensing agreements with third parties of sufficient "character and notoriety" to inform Professor Longhair, his representatives, and the public of Bearsville's intent to possess the tapes as owner?

5. Eventually, the U.S. Fifth Circuit court of appeal sent the case back to the U.S. District Court for the Eastern District of Louisiana to consider the factual issues connected with Bearsville's defense based on acquisitive prescription. The Fifth Circuit instructed that on remand the district court should address the issue of personal jurisdiction (the power of a court over the parties to the case) preter-mitted in the first round of litigation. *Songbyrd*, 104 F.3d at 781. The federal district court in Louisiana found that it lacked personal jurisdiction over the parties in Louisiana and transferred the case to the U.S. District Court for the Northern District of New York. *Songbryd, Inc. v. Estate of Grossman*, 23 F.Supp.2d 219, 221 (N.D. N.Y. 1998).

Applying New York state law, the federal district court in New York determined that Songbyrd's suit was time barred. *Id*. at 222–23. The U.S. Court of Appeals for the Second Circuit affirmed. *Songbyrd, Inc. v. Estate of Grossman*, 206 F.3d 172 (2nd Cir 2000):

> With the Northern District of New York properly regarded as the forum state after the valid transfer for lack of personal jurisdiction in Louisiana, there can be no doubt that New York's statute of limitations determines whether SongByrd's suit, alleging a wrongful conversion of a chattel in New York, is time-barred. See *Levy*, 871 F.2d at 10. The parties do not claim otherwise. Nor do they dispute that the relevant statute is the three-year limitations period for conversion and recovery of chattels. See N.Y. C.P.L.R. §214(3) (McKinney 1990). Their dispute concerns the time when SongB-yrd's cause of action accrued. The Estate contends, as the District Court ruled, that under New York law the limitations period for conversion begins to run at the time of the conversion. The District Court found that the con-version occurred when the Estate licensed the master recordings in 1986, well beyond the limitations period.
>
> Three decisions bear on the accrual issue. In *Sporn v. MCA Records, Inc.*, 58 N.Y.2d 482, 462 N.Y.S.2d 413, 448 N.E.2d 1324 (1983), the New York Court of Appeals ruled that the plaintiff had only a single cause of action

(for conversion) and that it accrued when the defendant began "commercially exploiting" the property as its own. . . .

In *Solomon R. Guggenheim Foundation v. Lubell*, 77 N.Y.2d 311, 567 N.Y.S.2d 623, 569 N.E.2d 426 (N.Y.1991), the Court of Appeals . . . rejected a requirement that the claimant to ownership exercise due diligence in locating its chattel, but acknowledged the New York rule that an owner, "having discovered the location of its lost property, cannot unreasonably delay making demand upon the person in possession of that property.". . . .

In *Hoelzer v. City of Stamford*, 933 F.2d 1131 (2d Cir. 1991), we . . . applied *Lubell* and ruled that under New York's demand-and-refusal rule, the City's claim was timely. . . . Although *Lubell* had involved a stolen chattel in possession of a good-faith purchaser, *Hoelzer* applied the *Lubell* demand-and-refusal rule to artwork that was not stolen and that was in possession of a custodian. Since New York used the demand-and-refusal rule to delay the accrual of the claim of the true owner even against a good-faith purchaser, *Hoelzer* understandably applied the rule to protect the true owner against a mere bailee who had not, prior to demand and refusal, acted to assert ownership.

Sporn bars SongByrd's claim. Like the possessor in that case, the Estate began using the master tapes as its own when it licensed portions of them to Rounder in 1986. . . . The conversion alleged by SongByrd occurred no later than that date. The demand-and-refusal rule, which functioned to delay accrual of the claim in *Lubell* and *Hoelzer* for the benefit of the true owner, normally provides some benefit to the good-faith possessor by precipitating its awareness that continued possession will be regarded as wrongful by the true owner. *See Ashton Hawkins et al., A Tale of Two Innocents: Creating an Equitable Balance Between the Rights of Former Owners and Good Faith Purchasers of Stolen Art*, 64 Ford. L. Rev. 49, 69–70 (1995). New York has not required a demand and refusal for the accrual of a conversion claim against a possessor who openly deals with the property as its own.

Even if a demand were required for accrual of SongByrd's claim, *Lubell* instructs that a plaintiff may not unreasonably delay in making a demand for property whose location is known. Byrd, either independently or through his agents, had known since the 1970s that the master tapes were in Grossman's possession, and the unanswered letters to Grossman in 1975 for return of the master tapes probably sufficed to alert him to Grossman's disregard of his ownership claim, thereby rendering any demand thereafter unreasonably delayed. In any event, his successors' delay in not making a demand in 1987, when Bearsville's licensing of the master tapes became well known in the music world as a result of the Grammy Award for Byrd's recordings, was clearly unreasonable.

> Where required, the demand-and-refusal rule "change[s] the charac-
> ter" of a good-faith possession before an action for conversion or recovery
> of a chattel can be maintained. . . . As in *Sporn*, however, no demand and
> refusal was needed here since the "character" of Bearsville's possession had
> changed by its actions in treating the master tapes as its own.

Songbyrd, 206 F.3d at 181–83.

6. The *SongByrd* decisions highlight the focus of the Erie doctrine upon intra-state
as opposed to interstate uniformity. Intra-state uniformity means that it should not
matter whether you file in the Erie court or a state court in a given state because both
courts will use the same substantive law to decide the case. The lack of inter-state
uniformity is a correlative consequence of the Erie obligation to the substantive law
of the state in which it sits. In *SongByrd*, it is illustrated by the different outcomes in
Louisiana and New York. Louisiana's acquisitive or positive prescription approach
asks whether a would-be adverse possessor has taken sufficient steps to begin to
possess as owner and deserves to be awarded with ownership through prescription. In turn, New York queries whether the true owner has been inexcusably passive in pursuing claims to recover his property. For an in-depth discussion of this
theme, see John. Lovett, *Professor Longhair's Legacy: A Comparative Perspective on
Revendicating Movables, in* NORTHERN LIGHTS: ESSAYS IN PRIVATE LAW IN MEMORY
OF PROFESSOR DAVID CAREY MILLER 31 (Douglas Bain, Roderick R.M. Paisley &
Andrew R.C. Simpson & Nicola J.M. Tait eds., Aberdeen Univ. Press 2018). In determining when to cut off an owner's claim to recover possession of a stolen movable,
which state's approach makes more sense: Louisiana's or New York's? Whose interests do Louisiana and New York, respectively, protect?

7. The case revolves around Professor Longhair's master tape recordings, which
are corporeal movables. The courts did not examine Professor Longhair's intellectual property rights in the recordings because the federal copyright act was only
amended to offer copyright protection to sound recordings in 1972, one year after
the master tapes were produced. In addition, Louisiana does not offer any "common law" copyright protection.

8. Do you agree with the proposition that, in Louisiana, *Erie* obligations are special? Is federal diversity jurisdiction a threat to Louisiana's civilian legal culture? *See
Alvin B. Rubin, Hazards of a Civilian Venturer in a Federal Court: Travel and Travail
on the Erie Railroad*, 48 La. L. Rev. 1369, 1381 (1988) (advising that, unless and until
diversity jurisdiction is abolished, "the lawyer who wishes the case tried by civilian
principles should shun diversity jurisdiction").

9. In light of the surprising diagnosis that actual data from federal judges deciding diversity cases under Louisiana law had never been collected, Dr. Puder designed
and conducted a survey of *Erie* judges' own perceptions of their duties when interpreting and applying the Louisiana Civil Code. The following excerpt describes his
project and findings.

Markus G. Puder, *Mixity Dynamics in Federal-State Frameworks: American Court-Structure Federalism and Louisiana's Codal Core*
77 Rabels Z (Rabel J. Comp. & Intl. Priv. L.) 251 (2013)

. . . .

III. Survey of Federal Judges Regarding *Erie* Courts and the La. Civil Code

The process for this research project—a "mail survey of specifically named persons"—involved three stages: design, execution, and analysis. In the design stage, a questionnaire was developed. It contains 35 questions, which ask the judges about their educational and professional background, the diversity litigation in their courts, the style and substance of attorney's oral and written arguments in their *Erie* case dossiers, and their *Erie* judgments. This "self-administered questionnaire" formed the central component in a mailer packet, which also contained a cover letter and a "notice of response" along with a stamped return envelope. Judges were invited to invest 40 minutes of their time, circle the letter for the choice offering the "best" answer to each question, and return the survey and notice of response. They were assured that their anonymity would be preserved.

Based on publicly available resources, 53 "Article III judges" currently sitting on the Fifth Circuit and the three U.S. District Courts in Louisiana—the Eastern District, the Middle District, and the Western District—were identified. A mailer packet was then sent to each judge. Upon receipt of a response, the judge's name was checked off on a tracking list and the return notice was separated from the survey. The field period spanned more than four months as the initial letter of request asked judges to respond within six weeks and the follow-up round offered the same time frame.

Twenty-one judges completed and returned their questionnaires. Three judges declined to participate in light of schedule constraints. Twenty-nine judges did not respond to the mailer. This yield translates into a basic response rate of 40%—a level of participation deemed sufficiently robust to carry this project into the data processing phase.

The completed survey forms were assigned a numeric identifier and the responses from the judges were extracted and entered into a database with the tools to capture, query, and present the information. The following synthesis of data trends traces the selection and flow of themes broached in the survey. . . .

1. Professional and Educational Background

Ten of the 21 judges who returned their surveys serve on the Fifth Circuit. Nine of the circuit judges returned their notice of response. They identify their base as Texas (five judges), Louisiana (three judges), and Mississippi (one judge). Eleven responses came from district court judges (seven for the Eastern District, three for the Western District, and one for the Middle District).

Seventeen judges look back to more than ten years of service as a federal judge. One judge has served for more than 35 years on the Fifth Circuit.

Eighteen judges are on their first federal judgeship. Before being called to the federal bench, these judges served in private practice or on state courts in and outside Louisiana. One appeals court judge held the position of city attorney in a major city. All district court judges were previously employed in Louisiana as judges or attorneys.

Asked about their educational background, eight judges report a civil law degree, seven a common law degree, and six a combination. Only one judge, who chose "combination," indicated unfamiliarity with the degree categories offered in the survey. All judges at the district court level hold civil law or combined degrees. Independent of degree programs, 16 judges characterize the range of courses in civil law methods and practice offered by their law school as excellent or adequate. Only five judges indicate that no coursework was offered.

2. Diversity Statistics

Most judges offer statistical information based on their own personal estimates or the clerk's figures. The proportion of diversity lawsuits in civil litigation at the district and circuit levels ranges from less than 25% to more than 50%. One judge reports the overall figure of 27% for the Fifth Circuit.

In terms of diversity cases lodged by Louisiana plaintiffs, ten judges report a share of less than 25%. The appeals court judge pinpoints the figure at 40%. Finally, most judges estimate the share of civil cases arriving by way of removal at less than 25%.

3. Style and Substance of Attorneys' Oral and Written Arguments

Judges are almost equally divided on the question of whether attorney's briefs and presentations in diversity cases differ from those offered in federal law cases. Relative to the authorities cited by attorneys in arguments based on the Louisiana Civil Code, three-quarters of the judges report that attorneys almost always rely on Louisiana court decisions. When attorneys invoke Louisiana Supreme Court jurisprudence interpreting the Louisiana Civil Code, they always or almost always argue that the court must follow these decisions. Attorneys do not attribute the same value to Louisiana lower court decisions.

With respect to federal jurisprudence prior decisions handed down by the Fifth Circuit appear with much higher frequency in attorneys' arguments than district court decisions. But most judges report that attorneys only at times argue that the court must follow these decisions.

Compared to jurisprudence, secondary sources like treatises and law review articles, according to all but one of the judges, play a minor role in attorneys' arguments before their courts. When attorneys argue the absence of a topical court decision interpreting the Louisiana Civil Code, two-thirds of the judges offer that they are then regularly urged to make *Erie* guesses rather than invoking their certification privilege.

4. *Erie* Judgments

Asked whether they considered it within their reviewing power to depart from a line of prior decisions of their own court after having resolved that these decisions did not properly interpret the Louisiana Civil Code, the district court judges, almost in unison, answer in the affirmative. Most judges from the Fifth Circuit do not deem such departure within their reviewing power. A couple of judges, however, refer to the en banc court. One judge offers that it sometimes depends on what the Louisiana courts have said in the interim. Except for two district court judges, all judges do not consider it within their reviewing power to depart from a line of prior decisions of the Louisiana Supreme Court. However, all but three judges do not extend the same commitment vis-à-vis decisions from the lower courts in Louisiana.

More than three-quarters of all judges report that they would distinguish the case at bar if departing from a line of prior decisions. According to one judge, a prediction of a different decision by the Louisiana Supreme Court in the case at hand would justify a departure. Yet another judge prefers to indicate overruling precedent and identify the pertinent rationales. According to more than three-quarters of the judges, their answers would not differ if only one relevant prior decision, as opposed to a line of decisions, were under consideration. All but three judges offer that the degree of influence by prior decisions does not vary with the title of the Louisiana Civil Code controlling the litigation. One circuit judge, however, calls out core areas of Louisiana's civilian heritage—immovable property, successions and donations, prescription and preemption, and pure tort. The judges report that in general, their decisions are only at times or rarely influenced by legal treatises or law review articles. The circuit judge, however, identifies an exception to this trend relative to those civilian titles in the Louisiana Civil Code that have been the subject of extensive scholarship produced by certain academics who have frequently appeared as experts before the courts.

If a question is not straight forwardly governed by the Louisiana Civil Code, most judges are guided in their decision process by a palette of authorities. All but one judge look to prior decisions of Louisiana courts; and one-third of the judges indicate doing so exclusively. One-half of judges add federal jurisprudence and codal or statutory analogues to the mix of authorities guiding their decision process. Two judges also include custom and equity.

Most judges identify Louisiana court decisions, especially those handed down by the Louisiana Supreme Court, among the authorities deemed as most influential to them. Several of these judges co-rank decisions by the Fifth Circuit. One circuit judge counsels against any ranking of authorities based on personal persuasions. In the absence of jurisprudential authority, more than two-thirds of all judges make an *Erie* guess in the majority of cases rather than certifying questions and propositions to the Louisiana Supreme Court. In the process of ascertaining whether or not to make the *Erie* guess, all but five of the judges endeavor to determine the validity of opinions potentially on point.

5. Miscellaneous Comments

More than one-half of the judges offer that federal diversity jurisdiction under *Erie* does not impact Louisiana's codal private law traditions. One judge, however, refers to the late Judge Rubin's diagnosis that civilian principles and diversity jurisdiction remain difficult to reconcile. Another judge calls out specific impact areas like torts and products liability. One judge indicates that the renaissance of interest in Louisiana's civil law heritage over the last decades has affected the *Erie* process — to the extent it has influenced Louisiana Supreme Court and Fifth Circuit precedents.

Half of the circuit judges report that the *Erie* process for Louisiana does indeed exhibit differences when compared to Texas and Mississippi. One judge offers that Louisiana judges on the Fifth Circuit emphasize the need to use the Louisiana Civil Code and not worry about state court precedents. This judge gives the Louisiana Civil Code more control than a judicially unexamined Texas or Mississippi statute.

IV. Validation of Survey Trends through Jurisprudence

Actual jurisprudence of the Fifth Circuit seems to mirror and validate the general trend lines revealed by the survey responses relative to the *Erie* process and Louisiana law. . . .

In *Dunbar* [*v. Seger-Thomschitz*, 615 F.3d 574 (5th Cir. 2010)], which features an action to quiet title to Oskar Kokoschka's painting *Portrait of Youth* (Hans Reichel) based on Louisiana's prescription laws, the Fifth Circuit offers a two-pronged reasoning for siding with the Plaintiff-Appellee. It first rejects the Defendant-Appellant's argument that federal common law doctrines (laches and unclean hands) should displace Louisiana's prescriptive periods to decide claims for the recovery of illicit works of art on their merits. After noting that "[n]o court has ever adopted . . . [any] form of special federal limitations period governing all claims involving Nazi-confiscated artwork," the Fifth Circuit diagnoses *sine ira et studio* that "as this case is brought under federal diversity jurisdiction, the application of state statutory limitation periods is controlled by *Erie*." In the absence of federally created causes of action and interstate or international implications of the controversy, according to the Fifth Circuit, the *Erie* protection for Louisiana's prescriptive periods stands.

With like verve, the Fifth Circuit rejects the Defendant-Appellant's argument of preemption under *American Insurance Association v. Garamendi* in light of an alleged conflict between Louisiana's prescription law and U.S. foreign policy articulated in the Terezin Declaration of the Prague Holocaust Era Assets Conference. This document urges "all stakeholders to ensure that their legal systems or alternative processes, while taking into account the different legal traditions, facilitate just and fair solutions with regard to Nazi-confiscated and looted art, and to make certain that claims to recover such art are resolved expeditiously and based on the facts and merits of the claims and all the relevant documents submitted by all parties." In a chiseled reasoning, the Fifth Circuit offers that unlike California's Holocaust Victim Insurance Relief Act, held in *Garamendi* to encroach on the President's dormant foreign affairs power, Louisiana's prescription laws do not pursue a specific policy objective other than regulating ownership claims to property within the state. Such exercise of state competence, according to the Fifth Circuit, remains "well within the realm of traditional state responsibilities."

[Discussion of SongByrd. Eds.]

V. Perspectives and Conclusions

In light of the small universe of eligible survey recipients, the input offered by each judge who returned a completed questionnaire, carries significant weight. Not so much meant to produce hard empirics but rather palpate the pulse of survey participants, the survey was not premised on any expectation of "right" responses.

. . . .

The comments offered by three judges at the end of the survey provide additional insights into their *Erie* postures and practices. Their words are echoed by a practitioner from a major New Orleans law firm.

> "I don't compartmentalize my cases in my head to be able to remember diversity from others. The bottom line is that I don't think federal judges should be pretending to be state judges and we should deeply respect the decisions of state courts, state treatises, law reviews, etc. on the meaning of state law." (Erie Survey, Database Counter #1)

> "The intersection of *Erie*, Federal court *stare decisis*, and La. *jurisprudence constante* can present an occasional enigma, but there are usually more ways than one to skin the cat in a principled manner." (Erie Survey, Database Counter #6)

> "The survey seems to imply that judges have discretion re: what is looked at in *Erie*. I believe this is dictated by law. We look at S. Ct. and then our [Fifth Circuit] precedent [and] intervening change or clarification in law in Louisiana." (Erie Survey, Database Counter #16)

> "The bottom line is that [federal] courts will apply the Civil Law and civilian concepts under the Erie-doctrine. Because Louisiana is the only Civil Law state, that it is important for clients to obtain sufficient knowledge or advice regarding those concepts if they are to do business, and do it well, in Louisiana."

. . . .

Notes

1. The late Judge Alvin Rubin vigorously advocated a clean repeal of diversity jurisdiction. Do you agree? Who would be in charge of suppressing federal diversity jurisdiction? Would this be constitutional? What would happen to the caseload of federal courts?

2. How do other federations organize their court structure? Law and Judicial Systems of Nations (World Jurist Ass'n 2002). In those jurisdictions, is a civil code always a sub-national document? Brazil's and Germany's civil codes are federal law. Conversely, Québec's civil code is provincial law. However, unlike the United States, Canada boasts a fully integrated court structure.

Chapter 11

Co-Ownership

A. Introduction

Previously we have focused on full, undivided ownership. However, ownership may be modified in Louisiana. The most elemental and common modification of ownership is called "co-ownership" or "ownership in indivision." Article 480 of the Louisiana Civil Code declares:

Art. 480. Co-ownership

Two or more persons may own the same thing in indivision, each having an undivided share.

La. Civ. Code art. 480 (1979). At its most basic level, co-ownership involves the concurrent sharing of ownership of the same thing between two or more persons. It assigns fractional shares to the respective co-owners. Before considering the technical rules for co-ownership offered by the Louisiana Civil Code, take a moment to study how the late-nineteenth-century French jurist Marcel Planiol described the workings and flaws of co-ownership. Notice not only the elegance of his metaphors for describing co-ownership but also his skepticism about the durability of a relationship between two or more co-owners.

Marcel Planiol, Treatise on the Civil Law
473–77 (La. Law. Inst. Transl., 1959) (footnotes omitted)

Definition. A thing belonging to several co-owners is in indivision when the right of each owner bears upon the whole (and not upon a given part) of the thing held in common. The share of each is therefore not a tangible share but a portion expressed by a fraction: a third, a fourth, a tenth. It is the right of ownership that is divided among them. The thing is not. It is held in indivision. The right of each co-owner must be pictured as striking every molecule of the thing and as there encountering the right of the other co-owners for the portions belonging to them.

Theoretically, there is no limit to the number of co-owners. As a matter of fact most indivisions exist between a small number of persons. The shares of each may be equal or unequal. If there be no inequality, they may be as numerous as may be wished (citations omitted).

How Indivision Ends. The state of indivision is terminated by partition which attributes to each owner a divided share in the thing instead of the undivided share he previously had. The tangible share which is attributed to each owner should be

of a value proportionate to that of the abstract share he had in the right of ownership applicable to the thing. The partition thus localizes the right of ownership.
The co-owner obtains things that are less than the total thing but which offer the
advantage of being clear cut ownerships, where the right of each is no longer limited
by the coexistence of competitive rights. Partition is therefore a juridical act whose
inherent function consists in terminating indivision by separating the thing into
shares or lots.

Perpetual Indivision. There are instances where the indivision is destined to
last forever and where application can never be made for partition. This is what is
known as forced indivision. The cases where perpetual indivision may arise, are,
theoretically speaking, exceptional and few in number. In fact, however, many
examples may be cited.

Most common examples of forced indivision always bear upon things which are
destined to the common use of several pieces of property. Such are:

(1) The narrow streets, passages, alleys and courts that are common to several
houses;

(2) The soil and certain parts of houses divided into stories by several owners . . .
and

(3) The walls, hedges and other party enclosures. This is distinctly the most frequently recurring example of things held in indivision in perpetuity. It will
be considered separately. . . .

Comparison of the Various Forms of Indivision. Under its original form, without
fixed duration, indivision offered nothing but disadvantages. It interferes with the
proper developments of property held in indivision. Every time one of the owners in
indivision proposes an innovation or an improvement he runs the risk of being met
by the resistance, the ill humor, the distrust of the others. And when this resistance
arises it is invincible, because the slightest change requires that all agree to it. One
of the co-owners cannot therefore, for example, change the mode of cultivation,
because he is bound to respect the rights of the others which are equal to his. "He
who has a companion has a master," said Loysel (*Institutes coutumières*, no. 379).
None of the co-owners can perform juridical acts alone (see as regards leasing, *Tribunal de la Seine*, Dec. 12, 1927, D.H. 1928. 159). Thus does the law earnestly desire
a partition which will make each owner free. This is why it will not permit that co-
owners agree to remain in indivision for more than five years.

Notes and Questions

1. According to Planiol, ownership in indivision is defined as an ideal, fractional
share that touches on "every molecule" of the co-owned thing. Each co-owner has a
right to the whole. This interest becomes localized only after a co-owners picks up
the magic wand of partition, which ends the state of indivision. Planiol offers that the
cumbersome governance rules for co-owners, especially those insisting upon unanimous consent of all co-owners with regard to use, management and development

decisions, are prone to generating stalemates and controversies. But is this always true? Can you think of situations where two or more co-owners of a thing cooperate happily, enjoying, managing and using a co-owned thing for many years?

2. Louisiana courts have traditionally shared Planiol's distrust of co-ownership, which they manifest by refusing to become deeply involved in disputes among co-owners. This posture of refusing to referee co-owner disputes suggests that ownership in indivision is an undesirable state of affairs that should be terminated if the co-owners cannot solve their conflicts by themselves. The law of ownership in indivision therefore offers partition as the way out. The codal restriction on the length of time that co-owners can contractually bind themselves to a co-ownership relationship also reflects this general antipathy towards co-ownership. *See* La. Civ. Code art. 807 (1990).

allowed
tolerated
not preffered

3. In the common law, "tenancy in common" comes closest to what we mean in Louisiana by "ownership in indivision." Both institutions confront similar issues. The rules developed by Louisiana courts and codified in our Civil Code to resolve these issues are generally quite intuitive.

B. Ground Rules for Owners in Indivision

Article 480 of the Louisiana Civil Code opens the door to "co-ownership" in Louisiana by providing that "[t]wo or more persons may own the same thing in indivision, each having an undivided share." La. Civ. Code art. 480 (1979). The detailed rules for "ownership in indivision" are offered in Articles 797 through 818 of Title VII of Book II. Added in 1990, this new title codifies the traditional doctrine and jurisprudence in Louisiana, which had previously been dispersed in other parts of the Civil Code as well as in case law.

Louisiana law contains another, more specialized form of co-ownership that can exist only between married persons—the regime of community property. Louisiana's community property regime is housed in Chapter 2 of Title VI of Book III of the Louisiana Civil Code (Articles 2334 to 2376) and in the Civil Code ancillaries under Title 9 of the Revised Statutes. The Louisiana Condominium Act, La. Rev. Stat. §9: 1121.101 *et seq.*, offers another important specialized piece of legislation for co-ownership.

When asked to resolve questions of co-ownership that are not precisely captured by the codal provisions governing indivision, courts may invoke principles from the law of ownership, successions, partnership and contract. *See Olson v. Olson*, 196 So.3d 19, 24–25 (La. App. 2 Cir. 2016) (holding that, under the provisions on distribution and division of partnership assets (Articles 2808 and 2833) and general principles of the law of obligations (Articles 2054 and 2055 of the Civil Code), a wife who did not make any claims pursuant to Article 806 of the Louisiana Civil Code was entitled to reimbursement of a shareholder debt owed to her, which she had utilized as the down payment for condominiums held in indivision with her husband).

1. Definition of Indivision

Article 797 of the Civil Code provides the foundational definition of co-ownership:

Art. 797. Ownership in indivision; definition

Ownership of the same thing by two or more persons is ownership in indivision. In the absence of other provisions of law or juridical act, the shares of all co-owners are presumed to be equal.

La. Civ. Code art. 797 (1990). Let us unearth some of the ingredients of this seemingly innocuous definition.

Ownership in indivision under Article 797 of the Louisiana Civil Code is real ownership. It includes all of the constitutive elements of ownership — the rights to use a thing, enjoy its natural and civil fruits, and dispose of the thing. For example, each co-owner has an equal, coextensive and correlative right to personally occupy and use all of the property according to its previous patterns. La. Civ. Code art. 802 (1990). Ownership in indivision also exhibits the other salient characteristics of ownership as the right that confers upon a person direct, immediate, and exclusive authority over a thing. *Id.* The characteristics of ownership operate *externally* vis-à-vis third parties but are curtailed *internally* as to the other co-owners because one co-owner generally cannot exclude fellow co-owners from using the co-owned thing in the absence of a specific agreement. *Id.* In one recent decision, the Louisiana Second Circuit Court of Appeal held that under Articles 800 and 802 a co-owner has the right to protect land he co-owns with others, independent of the wishes of the other co-owners and therefore, does not need to join his fellow co-owners in a trespass action against a levee board and its lessee who were allegedly trespassing on the co-owned land. *Whitlock v. Fifth La. Dist. Levee Bd.*, 164 So.3d 310, 318 (La App. 2 Cir. 2015).

Article 797 of the Louisiana Civil Code makes clear that the state of indivision operates among two or more persons. There is no limit on the number of co-owners who can own property in indivision. In fact, when immovable property has passed through several generations without a partition, the number of co-owners can be surprisingly large. Note that juridical persons as well as natural person can be co-owners.

Finally, observe that Article 797 of the Louisiana Civil Code facially refers only to the "thing" subject to ownership in indivision. Article 818 of the Civil Code, however, adds that the laws of ownership in indivision "apply to *other rights* held in indivision to the extent compatible with the nature of those rights." La. Civ. Code art. 818 (1990) (emphasis added). Such other rights may, for example, include servitudes and delictual claims.

2. Creation of Indivision

A co-ownership relationship can be created in numerous ways. Sometimes co-ownership arises as a matter of law, as in the case of intestate succession when the deceased dies without a will and is survived by two or more descendants of the same degree. La. Civ. Code arts. 880, 888 (1981). Indivision also results when a person has manufactured a new thing partly from his own materials and partly from materials of another, La. Civ. Code art. 513 (1979), or when a community property regime is terminated, La. Civ. Code arts. 2356 (1979), 2369.1 *et seq.* (1995).

Ownership in indivision may also come about as the result of a voluntary transfer of ownership; a sale, exchange, or a donation *mortis causa* or *inter vivos* may produce ownership in two or more persons. Should the law distinguish between and develop separate rules for co-ownership relationships that arise automatically or involuntarily and those that result from a voluntary exercise of will?

Can a co-ownership relationship come into being absent a clear juridical act or statement of positive law? The answer is no. *See, e.g., Troxler v. Breaux*, 105 So.3d 944, 947–50 (La. App. 5 Cir. 2012) (deciding that a male co-habitant failed to establish that a female co-habitant was unjustly enriched by purchases of items for a house they inhabited together or for deposits into a joint checking account). Absent an ownership interest acquired through a juridical act such as a joint purchase or a donation of a half interest from person to another, the principle of unjustified enrichment under Article 2298 of the Louisiana Civil Code provides the only recourse for such a co-habitant.

3. Division of Shares among Co-Owners

Article 797 of the Louisiana Civil Code states that "[i]n the absence of other provisions of law or juridical act, the shares of all co-owners are presumed to be equal." La. Civ. Code art. 797 (1990). The article offers a rebuttable presumption that the fractional interests among co-owners are equal when the law does not provide for a particular fractional interest or there is no juridical act establishing the fractions. Thus, a testator may allocate different interests to each legatee in her will. She might, for instance, bequeath her son a two-thirds interest and her daughter a one-third interest in the family home. Similarly, two friends who decide to purchase a cabin or camp together might agree to contribute different amounts to the purchase price and allocate their respective shares in proportion to their contributions.

Interesting questions arise concerning the nature of evidence required to rebut the presumption of equal ownership shares. Should a writing always be required if the co-owned thing is an immovable? Or should oral testimony be admitted in the case of an immovable acquired by several purchasers who failed to state the amount of their respective interests in the recorded act by which they acquired the immovable? For an illustration of the presumption that co-ownership shares are equal in the context of a valuable movable, a vintage WWII, "Stearman" airplane, see *Estate of Walker v. Peters*, 989 So.2d 241 (La. App. 2 Cir. 2008).

4. Right to Fruits and Products

Recall that under general principles of accession the ownership of a thing carries with it ownership of its fruits and products. La. Civ. Code arts. 483, 488 (1979). Fruits are yielded by a thing without diminishing its substance, La. Civ. Code art. 551 (1976). In contrast, products are derived from a thing as the result of diminishing its substance. La. Civ. Code art. 488 (1979). Article 798 of the Civil Code governs the rights of owners in indivision to the fruits and products of the co-owned thing.

Art. 798. Right to fruits and products

> Co-owners share the fruits and products of the thing held in indivision in proportion to their ownership.

> When fruits or products are produced by a co-owner, other co-owners are entitled to their shares of the fruits or products after deduction of the costs of production.

La. Civ. Code art. 798 (1990). The individual co-owner's share in the fruits and products generally mirrors the fractional ownership interest of each co-owner, but the active co-owner may deduct production costs. This deduction for production costs does not include a deduction for the co-owner's personal labor. Such a co-owner, however, may be entitled to recover personal labor costs pursuant to unjust enrichment or negotiorum gestio (the unauthorized management of the affairs of another). *See* La. Civ. Code art. 798 rev. cmt. (c) (1990) and La. Civ. Code arts. 2292–2305 (1995). Co-ownership law thus incentivizes co-owners to enter into management agreements. It discourages excessive expensing by an active co-owner to the disadvantage of absent co-owners. Consider the following hypothetical.

Problem: Three persons (Sally, the mother, and Ben and Caroline, her children) own a home in indivision: Sally owns one-half and Ben and Caroline each own one-quarter of the home. All three co-owners have agreed to convert the house into a duplex and rent out both units. As a duplex, the home generates $30,000 in rental income per year. A net annual revenue of $24,000 remains after property taxes and insurance premiums are paid. Ben, a gifted handyman, performs all the routine maintenance required for the rental property himself. His work includes regular exterior and interior painting, gutter cleaning and repair, maintaining the heating and air conditioning systems, and plumbing maintenance and repair. If Ben, Caroline and Sally had to pay someone to do all this work, it would cost them a total of $4,000 a year. What shares of the annual rent are Sally, Ben and Caroline each entitled to claim?

5. Liability of a Co-Owner

Pursuant to Article 799 of the Louisiana Civil Code, a co-owner is "liable to his co-owner for any damage to the thing held in indivision caused by his fault." La. Civ. Code art. 799 (1990). Although this article seems simple, it conceals two important questions. The first is whether a co-owner can be liable for fault not only if she takes some affirmative action with respect to the co-owned thing, but also if she fails to take action. In other words, does fault encompass only negligent actions or does it include omissions as well? Second, does "fault" under Article 799 entail a duty to maximize the economic interests of the other co-owners or does it merely involve a duty not to err when it comes to the use and enjoyment of a co-owned thing?

The common answer to these questions begins with the premise that the duties co-owners owe to one another are construed narrowly. Nothing in the Louisiana Civil Code indicates that co-owners are like partners of a formal partnership who owe fiduciary duties to one another or to the partnership. *Cf.* La. Civ. Code art. 2809 (1980). Nor are co-owners equivalent to married persons who owe one another fidelity, support and assistance. *Cf.* La. Civ. Code art. 98 (1897). Except when a co-owner acts in some administrative capacity (under an express agreement with fellow co-owners, under judicial direction, or as a "negotiorum gestor" or un-appointed manager for another person's property, La. Civ. Code arts. 2292, 2295 (1995)), the Louisiana Civil Code does *not* generally impose on any co-owner an affirmative duty to act as a prudent administrator of the co-owned thing.

Applying these general rules of thumb can be difficult. Recall the preceding problem involving the duplex and the three co-owners. What would happen if Sally, who owns one-half of the entire building, leased one unit in the duplex to her yoga teacher, Fred? Sally never discussed the lease with her co-owners, Ben and Caroline, and neither Ben nor Caroline signed the lease as lessors. Suppose that Sally charges Fred $3,000 per year to lease the apartment, although the unit has a fair market rental value of $15,000. If Article 799 of the Louisiana Civil Code is limited to actions actually undertaken, can Ben and Caroline argue that Sally is liable for not maximizing the rental value of the duplex? Are there other provisions of Title VII of Book Two that might be relevant? Consider Articles 801 and 805. La. Civ. Code arts. 801, 805 (1990).

Alternatively, if Sally lived in one of the units in the duplex by agreement among the co-owners and the house became infested with termites because Sally did not engage a termite inspector or otherwise take reasonable precautions to prevent a termite infestation, would she be liable under Article 799 of the Louisiana Civil Code? What would be the result if she was aware of a termite infestation but took no action to minimize the damage caused by the termites?

6. Right to Use versus Use and Management

Ownership in indivision and full ownership share many features. Co-owners may sell or encumber their individual interests to third parties or to other co-owners. They share not only the use of the property and the enjoyment of its fruits but also its costs. Crucially, however, the regime of co-ownership deviates from full, undivided ownership in several respects.

In certain situations, a co-owner's right to act with respect to a co-owned thing is governed by a **rule of unilateral action**. A co-owner may unilaterally use and enjoy a co-owned thing *without having to consult other co-owners or obtain their consent*. In other instances, a co-owner's actions are governed by a **rule of unanimous consent**. A co-owner cannot make certain decisions with regard to the use and management of the co-owned thing without obtaining the *unanimous consent of all of the co-owners*. A co-owner who violates a rule of *unanimous consent* may face unpleasant legal consequences. In certain, very limited situations, a co-owner who lacks the right to act unilaterally can escape the rule of unanimous consent by appealing to a court to establish the proper use of a co-owned thing. Although this third, and much smaller, **sphere of co-ownership regulation through judicial decision-making** has expanded somewhat in the last decade, it generally remains narrow.

Article 801 of the Louisiana Civil Code stakes out the general rule of unanimous consent, while Article 802 carves out the primary sphere of unilateral action. In the absence of an agreement and a pathway to partition, Article 803 of the Civil Code allows for judicial decision-making. Consider these articles and their inter-relationship:

Art. 801. Use and management by agreement

The use and management of the thing held in indivision is determined by agreement of all the co-owners.

Art. 802. Right to use the thing

Except as provided in Article 801, a co-owner is entitled to use the thing held in indivision according to its destination, but he cannot prevent another co-owner from making such use of it. As against third persons, a co-owner has the right to use and enjoy the thing as if he were the sole owner.

Art. 803. Use and management of thing in absence of agreement

When the mode of use and management of the thing held in indivision is not determined by an agreement of all the co-owners and partition is not available, a court, upon petition by a co-owner, may determine the use and management.

La. Civ. Code arts. 801–803 (1990).

Article 801 of the Civil Code mandates unanimous consent among all co-owners regarding *any change* in the use and management of a co-owned thing. *Cf.* La Civ. Code art. 802 (1990). Unanimity in use and management decisions may be difficult to achieve. Students are often surprised that the law of co-ownership does not impose a democratic decision-making regime, such as majority or super-majority decision-making. In many co-ownership settings, majority rule may operate informally, but, strictly speaking, under the law, use and management decisions are *not* subject to majority rule. A single co-owner, even one who owns a small fractional share, can effectively prevent a majority or super-majority of other co-owners from making a change in the use and management of the co-owned thing.

This veto power offered by Article 801 of the Louisiana Civil Code can allow a single co-owner to extract a high price for that person's consent, even when the change in use or management would benefit every co-owner by enhancing the value of the co-owned thing or by increasing the value of its fruits or products. Recall Planiol's diagnosis that "the resistance, the ill humor, the distrust of the others" will lead to "invincible" blockage. Perhaps one mollification of this harsh rule of unanimous consent is found in the fact that a co-owner's consent to the use and management of a co-owned thing does not always have to be expressed in writing; it can be construed from the circumstances. *See e.g., Estate of Walker v. Peters*, 989 So.2d 241, 245 (La. App. 2 Cir. 2008) (finding an implied agreement between co-owners regarding maintenance and upkeep of a vintage airplane based on the possession of the airplane).

In contrast to the rule of unanimous consent imposed on use and management decisions, Article 802 of the Louisiana Civil Code gives each co-owner a right to use the co-owned thing "according to its destination" as long as the co-owner does not interfere with the co-extensive rights of the other co-owners to use the co-owned thing. As illustrated in *Leblanc v. Scurto*, 173 So.2d 322 (La. App. 1 Cir. 1965), some courts will protect this *unilateral* right to use a co-owned thing with an injunction if it appears that the co-owner seeking the injunction plans to use the co-owned thing in a manner consistent with its ordinary and historical use. Courts have held that the unilateral right to use a thing "according to its destination" accrues independent of the size of a co-owner's fractional share. *See Butler v. Hensley*, 332 So.2d 315, 318 (La. App. 4 Cir. 1976) (on rehearing) (holding that co-owners cannot evict a fellow co-owner with a 1/15 share who has moved a trailer home onto an otherwise undeveloped tract of land).

Please note that a co-owner's right to use property held in indivision can be exercised rent-free. However, when a co-owner in possession actively prevents other co-owners who are out of possession from exercising their correlative right to use the thing according to its destination, the co-owner in possession may be charged rent. *Von Drake v. Rogers*, 996 So. 2d 608 (La. App. 2 Cir. 2008).

Relying on Articles 801 and 802 of the Louisiana Civil Code, courts favor the natural, ordinary or historical use of co-owned property. The concept of "destination" provides the line of demarcation between ordinary acts of *use* under Article 802, which *do not require the concurrence of all* co-owners, and *use and management* decisions under Article 801 (and substantive alterations or improvements under Article 804), which *do require unanimous consent*.

When one co-owner refuses to grant consent to a proposed change in the use and management of a co-owned thing, partition is the principal outlet for those co-owners who are unhappy. Through partition co-owners may *exit* from a situation in which unanimous consent becomes difficult or impossible to achieve.

When "partition is not available," Article 803 of the Louisiana Civil Code provides an alternative decision-making model for the use and management of a co-owned thing. That article gives stalemated co-owners access to court when the following two conditions are both present: (1) a use and management plan is not in effect; *and* (2) partition is not available. La. Civ. Code art. 803 (1990). In other words, a court will step into the breach and resolve a use and management dispute only when the parties have not otherwise entered into a valid use and management agreement, *and*, for some independent reason, such as an agreement not to partition, La. Civ. Code art. 807 (1990), or because the property cannot be partitioned without harming the ownership interest of one of the co-owners in some other thing, La. Civ. Code art. 808 (1990), partition is not otherwise available. In short, courts are not the general arbiters of use and management disputes among co-owners.

7. Disposition of Co-Owned Things

Article 805 of the Louisiana Civil Code provides a logical corollary to the distinction created by Articles 801 and 802:

Art. 805. Disposition of undivided share

A co-owner may freely lease, alienate or encumber his share of the thing held in indivision. The consent of all co-owners is required for the lease, alienation or encumbrance of the entire thing held in indivision.

La. Civ. Code art. 805 (1990). While a co-owner is free to lease, alienate or encumber his fractional share of the co-owned thing unilaterally, he cannot lease, alienate or encumber the entirety of the co-owned thing itself unless he obtains the unanimous consent of his fellow co-owners. The right to dispose of a co-owned thing thus straddles two spheres of co-ownership decision-making. For example, in *Brown v. Brown*, 121 So.3d 1242, 1245 (La. App. 2 Cir. 2013), the court held that a former wife, who co-owned a rental house with her former husband, proved that she no longer granted consent to the lease of the house to her former brother-in-law by seeking his eviction and was, therefore, entitled to evict the brother-in-law from the house.

Recall Sally, Ben, and Caroline from the hypothetical above. Suppose the home has not yet been converted into a duplex. Under Article 805 of the Louisiana Civil Code, Sally could donate her one-half share in the house to her friend, Fred, although Sally could not lease or sell the entire house to Fred without Ben and Caroline's consent. As the owner of one-half of the property, Fred could use any part of the house according to its destination. He may further enjoy a one-half share in the civil fruits produced if the house were rented out to tenants. But Fred may not exclude Ben or Caroline from any part of the house. Sally (or Ben or Caroline for that matter) could also lease out her share in the house, giving the lessee the right to use any part of the house. Sally's lessee, however, could also not exclude Ben or Caroline from the co-owned property.

8. Substantial Alterations or Improvements

Article 804 of the Louisiana Civil Code seeks to deter activist co-owners from taking unilateral actions that might have a significant impact on the co-owned thing by imposing legal consequences for substantial alterations and improvements to which the other co-owners have not consented:

Art. 804. Substantial alterations or improvements

Substantial alterations or substantial improvements to the thing held in indivision may be undertaken only with the consent of all the co-owners.

When a co-owner makes substantial alterations or substantial improvements consistent with the use of the property, though without the express or implied consent of his co-owners, the rights of the parties shall be determined by Article 496. When a co-owner makes substantial alterations or substantial improvements inconsistent with the use of the property or in spite of the objections of his co-owners, the rights of the parties shall be determined by Article 497.

La. Civ. Code art. 804 (1990). The general principle announced in the first paragraph is clear: *substantial* alterations and improvements to a co-owned thing are subject to the rule of unanimous consent. Implicit in this first paragraph is the notion that minor, insubstantial changes to a co-owned thing can be undertaken unilaterally. The second paragraph of the provision covers situations in which a co-owner breaches the rule of unanimous consent and makes a substantial alteration or improvement without obtaining express consent from the other co-owners.

Article 804 of the Louisiana Civil Code thus mandates a two-step analysis for *nonconsensual* alterations or improvements. First, determine whether the particular alteration or improvement is substantial. If it is not substantial, the analysis is over. However, if the alteration or improvement is substantial, Article 804 requires us to determine whether the active co-owner should be treated like a good faith possessor under Article 496 or a bad faith possessor under Article 497.

If the alteration or improvement is (1) consistent with the historical use of the property *and* (2) the active co-owner simply fails to secure the consent of his fellow co-owners, then Article 804 of the Louisiana Civil Code directs that we treat the active co-owner as a good faith possessor under Article 496 of the Louisiana Civil Code. As a result, the passive co-owners in this situation cannot demand demolition or removal of the alteration or improvement. In addition, the passive co-owners will be required to pay, at their option, either the cost of the materials and the workmanship, or their current value, or the enhanced value of property resulting from the alteration or improvement. La. Civ. Code art. 496 (1979).

However, if the active co-owner (1) makes an alteration or improvement that is "inconsistent" with the use of the property *or* (2) proceeds over the express "objections" from any of the other co-owners, then Article 804 of the Louisiana Civil Code treats the active co-owner as a bad faith possessor under Article 497. The passive co-owners now may demand demolition and removal of the alteration or improvement at the expense of the active co-owner. They may further obtain damages for any injury suffered. If, however, the passive co-owners elect to keep the alteration or improvement, and if the alteration or improvement is a *separable improvement* (such as a house, a barn, a carport), they must pay either the current value of the materials and workmanship of the separable improvement or the enhanced value of the improvement. La. Civ. Code art. 497, rev. cmt. (b). If the substantial alteration or improvement is inseparable and remains on the ground of the immovable, the passive co-owners may not owe any reimbursement to the active co-owners. Separability hinges on whether or not the alteration or improvement is merged with the soil.

Who decides how much a passive co-owner or active co-owner may have to pay in a dispute about substantial alterations and improvements—all co-owners, including the maker, or only the passive co-owners? Two commentators suggest that the active co-owner, *i.e.*, the maker of the substantial alteration and improvement, "should not be permitted to wear two hats" and, therefore, should not have a voice in valuation. Symeon C. Symeonides & Nicole D. Martin, *The New Law of Co-Ownership: A Kommentar*, 68 Tul. L. Rev. 69, 138–39 (1993). Louisiana courts tend to agree, holding that "[t]he choice of the method of compensation is at the option of the other co-owner." *Franklin v. Franklin*, 415 So.2d 426, 428 (La. App. 1 Cir. 1982). In a partition suit involving renovations made to a house by an active co-owner both before and after Hurricane Katrina in a "good faith" context, the court of appeal affirmed a trial court determination that the lowest possible reimbursement option was appropriate because the parties had not explicitly selected a valuation methodology on their own. *Gettys v. Gettys*, 247 So.3d 1133, 1136 (La. App. 4 Cir. 2018) (affirming reimbursement award in the amount of $48,476 for the "cost of materials and labor" the active co-owner had paid to renovate the property after Hurricane Katrina and no reimbursement for pre-Katrina repairs because the active co-owner was unable to prove any costs).

In *Lupberger v. Lupberger*, 805 So.2d 264 (La. App. 4 Cir. 2001), the court addressed substantial alterations made by an active co-owner in a "bad faith" context. It held that because the passive co-owner (an ex-wife) actually demanded the removal of improvements that had been secretly made by the active co-owner (her ex-husband) who then refused to remove them, the passive co-owner was *not* required to reimburse the active co-owner for the enhanced value of the co-owned property and could claim one-half of the enhanced value in the eventual partition. *Id.* at 271. The decision in *Lupberger* thus appears to permit a passive co-owner who demands the demolition and removal of nonconsensual alterations and improvements to evade the responsibility for reimbursement under Articles 804 and 497 of the Louisiana Civil Code, if the active, bad faith improver refuses to remove them, even though the passive co-owner will still benefit from the enhanced value of the immovable when it is eventually subject to partition. Perhaps the holding in *Lupberger* should be limited to the unique facts of this case—a partition of former community property.

Yet, it suggests that courts may be uncomfortable requiring passive co-owners to reimburse active co-owners for substantial alterations and improvements in "bad faith" contexts.

9. Preservation of the Thing and Expenses of Maintenance and Management

Article 800 of the Louisiana Civil Code furnishes each co-owner the prerogative to "take necessary steps for the preservation of the thing" without having to secure the "concurrence of any other co-owner." La. Civ. Code art. 800 (1990). It creates a co-owner right that clearly falls within the sphere of unilateral action. The difficulty in applying Article 800 lies in determining what is a "necessary step" to preserve a thing—as opposed to an act of administration or disposition, which is subject to the requirement of unanimous consent. In the context of Article 800, the revision comments speak of "conservatory acts" *See* La. Civ. Code art. 800 rev. cmt. (1990). Like a negotiorum gestor or un-appointed manager, a co-owner who takes appropriate action to preserve the co-owned thing can act alone. La. Civ. Code art. 800 rev. cmt. (1990); *cf.* La. Civ. Code art. 2292 *et seq.* (1995).

What then is a conservatory act? Articles 527 and 528 of the Louisiana Civil Code give us some idea by noting that while a "useful or luxurious" expense might add value to a thing, La. Civ. Code art. 528 rev. cmt. (b) (1979), a necessary expense is one incurred for the preservation of the thing or for the "discharge of public or private burdens." La. Civ. Code art. 527 (1979). Actions that have been held to be conservatory acts include payment of property taxes and assessments, *indispensable* repairs and maintenance, and payment of insurance premiums. La. Civ. Code art. 527 rev. cmt. (b) (1978).

Article 806 of the Louisiana Civil Code offers an active, intervening co-owner, who incurs necessary expenses, expenses for ordinary maintenance and repairs or necessary management expenses paid to third persons, a route to reimbursement from her fellow co-owners:

Art. 806. Expenses of maintenance and management

A co-owner who on account of the thing held in indivision has incurred necessary expenses, expenses for ordinary maintenance and repairs, or necessary management expenses paid to a third person, is entitled to reimbursement from the other co-owners in proportion to their shares.

If the co-owner who incurred the expenses had the enjoyment of the thing held in indivision, his reimbursement shall be reduced in proportion to the value of the enjoyment.

La. Civ. Code art. 806 (1990). Be careful to distinguish expenses that are not encompassed by Article 806. A useful or luxurious expense that adds value to a thing, but is not necessary for its preservation, will not be reimbursed. *Id.* rev. cmt (b). Likewise, an active co-owner cannot charge his fellow co-owners for his own labor or management activities in the absence of a management plan adopted by the co-owners or imposed by a court. *Id.* rev. cmt (c). This rule seeks to discourage co-owners from exploiting one another through excessive expensing. In fact, to win a reimbursement claim under Article 806, the active co-owner must prove that she incurred the expense and paid a third person. *See, e.g., Clark v. Simmons,* 167 So.3d 140, 143–44(La. App. 5 Cir. 2014) (holding that: (1) receipts that failed to show actual payment to third parties were insufficient to recover for renovations necessary to bring a co-owned bar, hall and house up to the building code; and (2) insurance invoices and self-generated spreadsheets that failed to show payment to third parties were insufficient to recover for insurance premiums).

Take note that a co-owner who does incur an expense eligible for reimbursement under the first paragraph of Article 806 of the Louisiana Civil Code but who also had exclusive enjoyment of the thing will see the amount of reimbursement subjected to a setoff that is equivalent to the value of that enjoyment. La. Civ. Code art. 806(2) (1990). Determining the value of exclusive enjoyment of a co-owned thing for purposes of Article 806(2) will essentially require a court to estimate the reasonable rental value of the thing. The resulting offset may end up cancelling out any potential reimbursement claim under Article 806(1). *See Succession of Sylvester,* 181 So.3d 250, 260–62 (La. App. 5 Cir. 2015) (holding that (1) the reimbursement owed to the wife for necessary expenses for property taxes and lawn care paid in relation to two properties co-owned with her late husband was subject to an offset under Article 806(2) as there were sufficient facts in the record indicating the properties had been used by the wife or her children to the exclusion of other co-owners after the husband's death; and (2) the value of this exclusive use far outweighed the wife's claim for reimbursement from the estate). Be mindful that the indirect rental charge mandated by Article 806(2) generally applies only in settings in which a co-owner has *exclusively* occupied the co-owned property. However, the setoff under Article 806(2) is subject to a margin of discretion. *Compare Clark v. Simmons,* 167 So.3d 140, 144 (La. App. 5 Cir. 2014) (reducing Article 806 reimbursement for taxes and utilities by 50% in light of the active co-owner's proportionate enjoyment of the property), *with Driscoll v. Mazaleski,* 95 So.3d 1140, 1147 (La. App. 4 Cir. 2012) ("Under these circumstances—a divided house co-owned by two parties, each of which has use of only his side—there is no reduction for enjoyment due under article 806."). For commentary on the subject of necessary expenses, see Symeon C. Symeonides & Nicole D. Martin, *The New Law of Co-Ownership: A Kommentar,* 68 Tul. L. Rev. 69, 152 (1993).

Are mortgage payments affecting the entire co-owned property necessary expenses subject to reimbursement and potential set-off if the active co-owner who made the payments is in possession of the property? The clear consensus is that they are not. *See Jackson v. Morton,* 232 So.3d 685, 687–88 (La. App. 5 Cir. 2017) (a mortgage is not an expense subject to reimbursement and citing numerous authorities); *Lupberger v. Lupberger,* 805 So.2d 264, 271 (La. App. 4 Cir. 2001) (a mortgage is not an expense whose payment is subject to set-off according to the value of the payor's enjoyment, but rather "a non-possessory right created over property to secure the performance of an obligation"). *See also Rocque v. Tate*, 631 So.2d 1385, 1386 (La. App. 5 Cir. 1994)). *But see Cahill v. Kerrins*, 784 So.2d 685, 690–91 (La. App. 2 Cir. 2001) (offering that, although mortgage payments are not necessary expenses, a co-owner who pays them may be entitled to contribution from the others without a reduction for the value of enjoyment).

What other expenses fit within the framework of Article 806 of the Louisiana Civil Code? *See Sork v. Sork*, 242 So.3d 640, 645–46 (La. App. 1 Cir. 2018) (determining that installation of granite countertops, reconfiguration of entry and doorway, procuration of new carpeting and shutters and paint jobs were not "necessary expenses" because they did not "appear to be clearly and obviously for the preservation of the home" and were not "ordinary maintenance and repairs" in the absence of any evidence they were "usual and routine").

* * *

The next four decisions address crucial questions raised by the general discussion above. When does one co-owner's attempt to use a co-owned thing amount to an attempt to change the destination of the thing and thus require unanimous consent of all the co-owners? *See Leblanc v. Scurto*, 173 So.2d 322 (La. App. 1 Cir. 1965). If one co-owner moves onto the property with the tacit consent of the others, is he enjoying the property exclusively? What events must occur before a co-owner out-of-possession is entitled to claim rent from a co-owner in exclusive possession of that property? *See Von Drake v. Rogers*, 996 So.2d 608 (La. App. 2 Cir. 2008). When can one co-owner demand access to a co-owned thing despite risks of harm to the interests of the other co-owners and when can a court intervene to establish a use and management plan? *See Succession of Miller*, 674 So.2d 441 (La. App. 1 Cir. 1996). Can a co-owner who wants to undertake an expense that does not qualify as ordinary maintenance and repair but may be necessary to preserve a thing ask a court to declare the expense reimbursable under Article 806 of the Louisiana Civil Code before he undertakes it? Or must the active co-owner take the risk of incurring the expense first and then seek reimbursement from his fellow co-owners later? *See Miller v. Seven C's Properties*, 800 So.2d 406 (La. App. 3 Cir. 2001).

LeBlanc v. Scurto

173 So.2d 322 (La. App. 1 Cir. 1965)

ELLIS, Judge. This appeal is before us challenging the correctness of a decision by the District Court of Terrebonne Parish which granted plaintiffs an injunction against defendant, enjoining and prohibiting the latter from in any way blocking a certain alley or interfering with the rights of plaintiffs to use the alley as a means of passage.

The plaintiff, Mrs. Santa Scurto LeBlanc, wife of Edward N. LeBlanc, is the owner of an undivided one-third interest in certain real property in Houma. Sam Scurto owns another one-third and Mrs. Antonia Mule Scurto, widow of Charles Scurto, owns the final one-third. While the latter co-owner was made a party defendant, it does not appear from the record that she took any part in defending the suit or that she is involved in the dispute. The common property is situated at the intersection of Barrow and Main Streets, fronting 67.1 feet on Main and 115 feet on Barrow. It is fully developed and occupied by several small stores and shops, among them a shoe shop of which defendant Sam Scurto is the proprietor.

On the south end of this property there is, and has been for at least fourteen years, a 12 foot alley opening into Barrow Street and dead ending some few feet east of the parties' east boundary. The passage has been used extensively by the Phillip Morris Furniture Company, the lessee of a store situated south of the litigants' property on property owned individually by Edward N. LeBlanc. Additional use was made of the alley by city garbage trucks.

On May 27, 1964, at about 9:00 A.M., defendant parked his car in this alley, effectively blocking it. Defendant did not often use the alley and claims to have done so on this occasion to facilitate the unloading of some parcels from his car into the shoe shop. Plaintiffs claim that defendant parked his car there in order to prevent them from using the alley and that such activity constitutes irreparable injury to their rights as co-owners to use the property.

It appears that the motive advanced by plaintiffs for the blocking of the alley is substantiated by the evidence. The testimony of Mrs. LeBlanc attributes to defendant statements to that effect. It is evident that there is considerable ill feeling between the parties and that the simple and infrequent blocking of the alley would not have led to the heated words and simple batteries which were freely exchanged between Mrs. LeBlanc and her brother, Sam Scurto, in the latter's shop while the alley was blocked. The record indicates that Sam Scurto acted as he did in an effort to persuade the LeBlancs to sell him their interest in the land and improvements occupied by his shoe store.

Regardless of the actual motives of the parties, this Court must determine the applicability of the injunctive process as between co-owners where one of the co-owners has acted to deliberately deny to the others the *equal* and *coextensive possession* of a designated portion of the common estate granted to each co-owner by the law of Louisiana.

It should be made clear at this point that plaintiffs are not seeking an injunction to prevent defendant from using the alley. No demand of that nature could be seriously proposed because of the obvious impossibility of protecting the equal rights of both parties by denying those rights to one. It is precisely this dilemma which impels the necessity of the provisions in our law giving to all co-owners a right to demand a partition of the property held in common.

What is sought by plaintiffs, and what was granted in the tribunal below, is an injunction prohibiting defendant from blocking the alley or interfering with the rights of plaintiffs to use the alley as a passageway. In other words, plaintiffs are before this Court seeking protection of their rights as co-owners, not a denial of those same rights to the defendant.

In determining whether or not injunctive relief is proper in cases of this nature, it is necessary to determine the use for which the common property is intended. In the case of on Stinson v. Marston, 185 La. 365, 169 So. 436, the Supreme Court recognized that:

> "The courts of this state have always recognized the right of a co-owner to use the property held in common *for the purposes for which it is destined,* such as the cultivation of farm lands of the sort involved in this controversy. Becnel v. Becnel, 23 La. Ann. 150; Toler v. Bunch, 34 La. Ann. 997; Moreira v. Schwan, 113 La. 643, 37 So. 542.
>
> ***
>
> The co-owner is further entitled to see that the property is preserved or maintained without deterioration; ***" (emphasis added).

Having established the use to which the common property is best suited, or is reasonably being put, the courts of this state will sanction injunctions between co-owners to prevent a waste of that property, or a denial of equal and coextensive possession by a co-owner. Thus, in *Cotton v. Christen*, 110 La. 444, 34 So. 597, the Court sanctioned an injunction between co-owners to prevent one from removing timber to the prejudice of the other, finding that such unauthorized removal was in the nature of a trespass on the rights of the other.

The alley in question was certainly used as an avenue of passage and not as a parking lot. There is evidence to indicate that the Phillip Morris trucks loaded and unloaded in an area which did not interfere with the passage. However, even if these trucks do block the alley, it cannot be said that the blocking is deliberate and no showing has been made that they have ever refused passage to defendant. The deliberate blocking of the alley by the defendant to satisfy his desire for revenge or to induce some action on the part of his co-owner cannot be sanctioned.

It is apparent, therefore, that injunction does lie as between the co-owners in the instant situation. In using the common property for spite, or even for parking an unreasonable length of time to unload parcels, the defendant has converted its use from passage to parking. By parking as did the defendant co-owner in the present case practically all day, plaintiffs co-owners have been deprived of equal and coextensive possession and use of the common property. This is in the nature of a waste of the property just as surely as the cutting of trees is a waste. Except in situations where a co-owner is entitled to be maintained in possession against attacks by a co-owner out of possession, either has the right to demand of the other equal possession and coextensive use of any given spot within the common estate. If the defendant co-owner wishes *exclusive* possession of the common property or any part thereof, his remedy is by suit for partition. He cannot legally prevent equal and co-extensive possession of the common property to his co-owner. The latter is entitled to be maintained in such possession. *Gulf Refining Co. v. Carroll*, 145 La. 299, 82 So. 277.

The defendant in this case has an equal right to an injunction against the plaintiffs to prevent them, or those tenants holding under them, from blocking the alley in such a manner as to destroy the equal and coextensive possession and use by all co-owners. However, such an injunction has not been sought by defendant. Such an action would clearly have defeated his purpose—the forcible filing of a partition suit by plaintiff or extra-judicial partition.

Counsel for defendant earnestly argues that even if plaintiffs sought to board up the windows and doors of the shoe shop, defendant would be without an injunctive remedy. While we do not propose to answer hypothetical questions, suffice to say that spiteful conduct on the part of a co-owner will not be tolerated on the pretense that he is simply exercising his equal and coextensive rights. Such conduct can be viewed in no other light than as constituting a waste of the property and a trespass on the rights of the co-owner.

The case of *Juneau v. Laborde*, 228 La. 410, 82 So.2d 693, is inapplicable in the instant situation because that was a suit by a co-owner out of possession to recover rents and revenues from the co-owner in possession. The court correctly reasoned that the former co-owner could not prevent the latter from cultivating the land, and that the remedy for the co-owner out of possession was to seek a partition of the property. In the instant case neither co-owner is out of possession. The object of the instant litigation is not an accounting but an injunction to prevent the spiteful and wasteful use by one co-owner of a particular piece of the common estate and to enforce plaintiffs' legal right to equal and coextensive possession and use of the passageway. If the defendant does not wish to remain in such possession with the plaintiffs co-owners, his remedy is by legal partition.

The decision of the lower court is affirmed.

Affirmed.

Notes and Questions

1. *LeBlanc v. Scurto*, 173 So.2d 322 (La. App. 1 Cir. 1965), features the classic rules for a co-owner's right to use a thing held in indivision. Every co-owner enjoys the right to use the thing according to its destination as long as the fellow co-owners are likewise not prevented from using the thing. A co-owner who wants to change the mode of use must secure the unanimous consent of the other co-owners. Otherwise, a co-owner who desires exclusive use must first end the indivision through partition. Does Sam Scurto, the unhappy defendant in this case, have any other alternative?

2. The underlying conflict in this case may have resulted from Sam's resentment that his brother-in law, Edward N. Leblanc, was allowing lessees to use the co-owned property to access an adjoining property he owned without compensating Sam. Sam, however, cannot change the use of the alley without the consent of both

of his co-owners, his sister Santa Scurto Leblanc and his apparent sister-in-law, Antonia Mule Scurto. Is this good public policy? Can you conceive of alternative governance models for things held in indivision?

3. The court's remedy for Sam's misbehavior in *LeBlanc* is an injunction. Why does the court get involved in this dispute at all? Would the outcome in *LeBlanc* change if Santa held a fractional share of one-tenth only? What would happen if Santa retaliated against Sam by having her tango band pull up chairs in the alley and rehearse for five hours every day?

4. According to the court, what is the ultimate remedy for a co-owner in the artificial state of indivision? Take a look at Article 808 of the Civil Code, which states that "[p]artition . . . is excluded when its use is indispensable for the enjoyment of another thing owned by one or more of the co-owners." La. Civ. Code art. 808 (1990). The court in *LeBlanc* does not mention this provision. Would it be applicable here? Was use of the alley indispensable to the enjoyment of another thing owned by one of the co-owners?

5. Finally, note the court's extensive discussion of the concept of "waste" in *Leblanc v. Scurto*. Waste can occur when one party in possession has a present right to use and enjoy a thing, while another person who is out of possession has a long-term interest that may be damaged if the present possessor acts in a way that extracts value from the thing in the short run. As we see in *Leblanc*, the prospect of waste can be a powerful concern for a court in many property contexts. *See generally* John A. Lovett, *Doctrines of Waste in a Landscape of Waste*, 72 Mo. L. Rev. 1209 (2007); Sally Brown Richardson, *Reframing Ameliorative Waste*, 65 Am. J. Comp. L. 335 (2016).

* * *

Von Drake v. Rogers
996 So.2d 608 (La. App. 2 Cir. 2008)

DREW, Judge. In this dispute between two brothers concerning a home they own in indivision, Eric Von Drake appeals a judgment denying his claim for fair rental value. We reverse and remand.

Facts

Eric Von Drake ("Eric") owns an undivided 1/3 interest in real estate located at 927 Madison Avenue in Shreveport. The property includes a family home where Eric lived for years with his now deceased parents and his two brothers, Edgar Rodgers ("Edgar") and Homer Rodgers ("Homer"). Edgar acquired Homer's interest, and accordingly now owns a 2/3 interest in the property. Edgar and his family live in a home on the property at issue.

Since their mother's death in January of 2002, there has been too much litigation between Eric and Edgar concerning this property, with most of the litigation having been instituted by Eric in a *pro se* capacity. Among the legal actions taken by the parties are. . . .

In the instant suit, Eric, now represented by counsel, filed suit against Edgar on September 22, 2006. He alleged that since February of 2002, Edgar had refused to allow him to occupy or use the home, and was thus liable to him for his share of the fair rental value of the home. Edgar made general denials in his *pro se* answer. The petition was later amended to add Angela as a defendant. In an answer to the amended petition, Edgar and Angela stated that Eric no longer had any legal interest in the property.

The trial court denied a motion for summary judgment filed by Eric. Following a trial on the merits, the court denied Eric's claims against Edgar and Angela. A motion for reconsideration or to reopen the case for the introduction of additional evidence was filed by Eric. It too was denied by the trial court. Eric has appealed.

Discussion

Demand for occupancy

The use and management of the thing held in indivision is determined by agreement of all the co-owners. La. C.C. art. 801. Except as otherwise provided in La. C.C. art. 801, a co-owner is entitled to use the thing held in indivision according to its destination, but he cannot prevent another co-owner from making such use of it. La. C.C. art. 802.

A co-owner in exclusive possession may be liable for rent, but only beginning on the date another co-owner has demanded occupancy and has been refused. *McCarroll v. McCarroll*, 96-2700 (La. 10/21/97), 701 So.2d 1280. *See Pelafigue v. Sudduth*, 01-807 (La. App. 3rd Cir. 5/15/02), 820 So.2d 583, *writ denied*, 2002–2157 (La. 11/8/02), 828 So.2d 1124.

In denying Eric's claim, the trial court concluded that there was no credible evidence of demand by Eric for fair rental value. Although we sympathize with the learned trial court for valiantly trying to make heads or tails of this mess, the correct standard should have been the demand for occupancy. Where one or more trial court legal errors interdict the fact-finding process, the manifest error standard is no longer applicable, and, if the record is otherwise complete, the appellate court should make its own independent *de novo* review of the record and determine a preponderance of the evidence. *Ferrell v. Fireman's Fund Ins. Co.*, 94-1252 (La. 2/20/95), 650 So.2d 742. Accordingly, we will conduct a *de novo* review of this record of fraternal strife.

In the early 1990s, Eric renovated a back room of the family home so he could live in it. Eric last lived at the family home in 1999, and resided in Dallas at the time of his mother's death. Even though he was living elsewhere, he kept some personal belongings in the back room.

Eric had a key to the house until Edgar changed the locks after their mother's death. Edgar did this allegedly because he was afraid that Eric would allow the keys to fall into the wrong hands out of spite. He explained that the basis of his fear was that Eric had attempted to convince their mother to change her will, and when she declined, he took her keys and Edgar did not know what Eric had done with the keys.

Edgar disputed Eric's claim that he had asked for a key and was refused. Edgar claimed that he did not know Eric wanted a key until he filed a partition for licitation. Nonetheless, a new key was never forthcoming, with Edgar holding the position that he would let Eric in when he requested it.

Eric claimed that he wrote to Edgar in March of 2002 to tell him that he wanted to move back into the home, but Edgar never responded. Eric also claimed that in May of 2002, Edgar would not allow him to enter the home, and Edgar would still not budge when Eric asked if he could enter to retrieve his personal belongings. Eric added that he called the police, but all Edgar did was cross his arms and refuse to let him in the house. Angela denied that Eric ever sent a letter or came to the property with the stated intention of wanting to move into the house. Angela testified that in January of 2002, Edgar told Eric to clean his room up and move in if he wanted, but Eric's response was that he was staying in Dallas.

What happened to Eric's personal belongings is another sore spot between the parties. Eric claimed that Edgar put his belongings in an outside storage room in 2004, and they were destroyed from exposure to the elements.

Edgar's version is that he asked Eric to move his items because the room was dirty, and when Eric delayed in doing this, Edgar moved them into the living room. Angela recalled that:

> ... when Eric learned that his belongings had been moved to the living room, he said he would return to retrieve his things, but he never did;

> .... Edgar then moved the items into an outdoor shed; and

> ... after Eric eventually appeared and examined his belongings, he left them in the yard.

Angela, Edgar, and Homer claimed that Eric came to the house in May or June of 2002 in order to be filmed for a music contest. Homer stated that he never heard Eric say at the time that he wanted to move into the house. There is also the claim that Eric came to the property in February of 2003, opened the gate, and walked around the yard. Edgar recalled that Eric came to the property in the spring of 2003 or 2004, but made no request to move in at the time.

There is no question that Eric did not have unrestricted access to his co-owned property. It was admitted as much by the other parties. According to Edgar, Eric was allowed on the property and came and went as he pleased until 2002, with the change in attitude prompted by Eric taking legal action against them. Eric was told that someone was always to be at the house if he came there, and he would be videotaped when in the house. They regarded Eric as being too unsafe and unworthy to enter the property. Edgar recalled that Eric's response to this plan was that he would not come to the house if he was going to be watched.

Edgar furthered testified that:

> . . . in the summer of 2005, Eric damaged the home's front and screen doors while attempting to enter the home, and left a notice stating that he wanted Edgar's family out of the house;
>
> . . . he told Eric, after he damaged the home, that he was in trouble; and
>
> . . . after this incident, he sought a restraining order against Eric.

Things were apparently quiet between the feuding parties until the following summer. In July of 2006, Eric decided that he would create his own passageway into the house by cutting a doorway in an exterior wall of the back room and installing a door. Eric claimed that he only wanted access to the back room, and his plan was to board up the door leading from that room to the rest of the house so that he would be isolated from Edgar's family. This back room apparently had a bathroom. In any event, a large, rectangular hole suitable for a door was cut in the wall. Eric claimed that he had a subcontractor do this, but asked him to leave before completing the job when a police officer would not remain at the scene and Eric became concerned for the worker's safety without police protection. Eric further claimed that when he returned to the home two weeks later to finish his project, Edgar would not let him in and told him there was a peace bond against him. Edgar denied telling Eric that a peace bond had been issued against him, but he told Eric that he would call the police if Eric returned to the house. Edgar repaired the hole in the wall, but eventually tore down the back room.

There was never an agreement between Edgar and Eric that Edgar would use the home to the exclusion of Eric. Although Eric may have had some inclination to exercise his rights as co-owner, no actual demand for occupancy can be construed from this record until Eric filed the instant suit seeking fair rental value for Edger's exclusive use of the property. Prior to then, many of his actions seemed to be mainly motivated by a desire to torment Edgar. Accordingly, Eric is entitled to 1/3 of the fair rental value of the house beginning on September 22, 2006. Things become a bit trickier when determining the fair rental value.

Stephanie Campbell testified as an expert in assessing the fair rental value of residential properties. On behalf of Eric, she calculated the house as having a conservative fair rental value of $550.00 per month. In reaching this figure, she compared the home at issue to rental homes that she had managed and she thought were comparable based upon similarities in size, construction type, and area. She based her estimate on a mere approximation of the exact size of the house. We question her valuation, as she never entered the home.

Edgar was questioned by Eric's counsel about a pleading that Edgar had filed in the Texas litigation. In that 2004 motion to dismiss, Edgar wrote that a fair amount for back rent would be based upon $375.00 per month. If Edgar intended to mean in that motion that Eric's 1/3 share was worth that much per month, that would give the entire house a fair rental value much higher than that even assessed by Campbell. We also recognize the context in which Edgar made that valuation; he was trying at the time to establish that the court lacked subject matter jurisdiction because the amount in controversy was less than the required amount.

Because the record is not adequate for this court to adequately assess the fair rental value of the home, we remand this matter to the trial court for a determination of the fair rental value of the home from September 22, 2006, until the date of partition. The amount determined should be rendered against Edgar alone. . . .

Conclusion

We reverse the judgment denying Eric Von Drake's claim for 1/3 of the fair rental value of the property. We remand this matter to the trial court for a determination of the fair rental value of the home from September 22, 2006, until the date of partition. All costs are to be split evenly between Edgar and Eric.

REVERSED and REMANDED.

Notes and Questions

1. In *Von Drake v. Rogers*, 996 So.2d 608 (La. App. 2 Cir. 2008), which involves a fraternal dispute, the court of appeals formulates additional rules for the right to use the thing held in indivision. In general, a co-owner's right to use a thing held in indivision is rent-free. However, a co-owner who occupies the property to the exclusion of the other co-owners may be liable for rent, albeit only from the date when an excluded co-owner demands occupancy and is refused. What findings does the record in *Von Drake* yield? Why does the court remand this case?

2. Common law courts use a similar test to determine whether one cotenant in common can obtain a share of rents and profits from property held in tenancy in common. They ask whether one cotenant has been "ousted" and "effectively excluded" from the common property. JOSEPH W. SINGER, PROPERTY 368 (4th ed. 2014). Ouster, however, requires more than exclusive possession by one cotenant. It requires "either an act of exclusion or use of such a nature that it necessarily prevents another cotenant from exercising his rights in the property." *Gillmor v. Gillmor*, 694 P.2d 1037, 1040 (Utah 1984). As the Utah Supreme Court put it, "when a cotenant out of possession makes a clear, unequivocal demand to use land that is in the exclusive possession of another cotenant, and that cotenant refuses to accommodate the other tenant's right to use the land, the tenant out of possession has established a claim for relief." *Id.* at 1040–41 Why do courts in both civil and common law jurisdictions require explicit proof of a demand for and a refusal to grant possession — or, put differently, clear communication of an intent to exclude — before awarding one co-owner a share of the rental value of a co-owned thing?

Succession of Miller

674 So.2d 441 (La. App. 1 Cir. 1996)

ARMSTRONG, Judge. This is an appeal from a judgment in a succession proceeding, authorizing the executor, Martin O. Miller II, to control access to the residence of the decedent, and the movables contained therein and elsewhere. Finding no error in the judgment of the trial court, we now affirm.

The decedent, Edna Kuntz Miller, died testate on August 22, 1994. One of her sons, Martin O. Miller II, was appointed executor pursuant to her statutory last will and testament. The decedent had been married once, to Martin O. Miller ("Mr. Miller"), who predeceased her. The couple had eight children born of the marriage, seven of whom survived her. The eighth child predeceased the decedent, but was survived by four children, all of whom survived the decedent.

At the time of the decedent's death, the seven surviving children each owned a one-sixteenth undivided interest, and the four children of the predeceased daughter, each a one-sixty fourth undivided interest, in a residence located at 24 Audubon Place, New Orleans, Louisiana, and the movables contained therein and elsewhere, by virtue of Mr. Miller's succession. Martin O. Miller II controlled the interest of one sister, Diane, who was an interdict, as her curator. The ownership interests of Mr. Miller's heirs was subject to the surviving spouse usufruct in favor of the decedent. Upon the decedent's death, they became owners in indivision of one-half of the property in question.

Because of concern about his personal liability as executor, on the advice of counsel, Martin Miller proposed a plan regarding access to the Audubon Place residence. He essentially gave the heirs two choices: (1) they could have access to the residence if they gave him reasonable notice, telling him how long they wanted access, access would be given only for a "reasonable time" and for a "legitimate purpose," and he or his designee would be present during the visit; or (2) the heirs could have unrestricted access to the house if they all released him from all personal liability. All heirs did not release him from liability so Martin Miller implemented the restricted access plan. The decedent's only other son, Pierre Valcour Miller ("Val Miller"), objected to the restricted access and filed a petition for injunctive relief, seeking to enjoin Martin Miller from interfering with his rights as a co-owner of the residence. The trial court denied relief. Approximately one week later, Martin Miller filed a "Motion To Determine Management of Property Held In Indivision."

At trial of the motion, Martin Miller testified that he was concerned about his personal liability should visitors to the residence, or heirs, remove movables from the residence or have an accident on the premises. The residence was appraised at $1,300,000.00 and, the contents, at $53,735.35. Martin Miller admitted that the Audubon Place residence and contents were insured for one million dollars and that all of the movables in the residence had been individually appraised. He said he had never refused anyone access to the residence under the plan and that Val Miller was the only heir who objected to the restricted access. Martin Miller also testified that there had been problems with Val Miller concerning the use of property co-owned by the heirs in Cameron and Vermilion parishes. He said Val Miller took two trailers and a bulldozer for personal use and had not returned them. He also said Val Miller had not been paying his share of the expenses to maintain this property. Martin Miller mentioned a check, in the amount of $1,130.75, from the State of Louisiana in reimbursement of money owed the late Mr. Miller's estate. Martin Miller said he sent the check to Val Miller for endorsement, with intentions of eventually sending it to all of the other heirs for signature. However, Val Miller would not sign the check, but instead, returned it to Martin. The check was eventually declared dead by the state. Martin Miller testified that the Audubon Place residence was listed for sale. A copy of an informational sheet from the real estate company was introduced into evidence.

A sister, Marian Miller Green, testified that she believed Martin Miller's restricted access policy was reasonable and that it would be chaos if everyone had unlimited access. She said it had been chaotic at the family-owned residence situated on the country property because one never knew how many people would be coming. Bed space was limited. On cross examination, she admitted there had been fewer beds than overnight visitors on only one occasion. She could not recall if Val Miller had been there on that occasion, nor could she recall Val Miller ever being associated with chaos.

Edward Rapier was the trustee of a trust established under the estate of the deceased daughter, Mildred Ann Miller Boulet, for Boulet's four children. Rapier said he agreed with Martin Miller's plan. He said as trustee he would not agree to hold Martin Miller harmless—it would violate his duty as a trustee.

Val Miller testified that he had tremendous sentimental associations with the Audubon Place residence. He lived there for twenty-two years and had continued to visit up to three times a week for thirty-three years until the death of his mother. Being a recovering alcoholic, he said is an extremely stressful time for him and it is being made more so by the actions of his brother in restricting his access to the residence. He believes as a co-owner, he has a right to unrestricted access to the home. He candidly admitted that he believed he has a right to take movables out of the residence without asking, possibly not returning the item(s) until another heir asks him to. However, he said he would agree not to take anything out of the residence and he would agree to hold Martin Miller harmless if he gave either himself or anyone else a key to the residence. He said he did not think he was legally required to get permission from the other co-owners before using the property.

Val Miller said he never interfered with the use of any of the Cameron or Vermilion Parish property by any of his co-owners. He introduced a letter into evidence wherein he requested that the co-owners voice any objection to his hosting a duck hunt bachelor party for his son at the country residence one particular fall weekend in 1993. He said one of his brothers-in-law drove the bulldozer into a canal years ago. He retrieved it after a period of time, intending to have it repaired, but discovered it would be too expensive. He still has the bulldozer in his possession and said none of the co-owners have ever asked for it. As for the two trailers, he said he uses those on the section of the country property he manages and that none of the co-owners has asked for them. He said he was not paying for the maintenance of the country property because he had paid the full cost of it for a period of time. As for the $1,130.75 check from the State of Louisiana, he said he did not feel it should have been simply endorsed by all heirs and negotiated as Martin Miller was attempting to do, rather, it should have been put through his father's succession. . . .

The trial court heard this evidence and rendered judgment "pursuant to Louisiana Civil Code Article 803," giving Martin Miller control of the keys and alarm code to the residence, and decreeing that the co-owners could have access to the residence only if accompanied by the executor or his designee, "upon reasonable notice, for a reasonable time, and for a legitimate reason related to the administration of the succession and disposition of the home and the movables contained therein."

Appellant Val Miller claims the trial court had no authority to issue the ruling it did.

The trial court rendered judgment, citing as authority, La.C.C. art. 803, which provides:

> When the mode of use and management of the thing held in indivision is not determined by an agreement of all the co-owners and partition is not available, a court, upon petition by a co-owner, may determine the use and management.

Val Miller argues that partition is available and, thus, C.C. art. 803 was not applicable. He cites La.C.C. art. 802 which states that a co-owner is entitled to use the thing but cannot prevent another co-owner from making use of it. He submits that La.C.C. art. 802 governs this case and that none of the co-owners can prevent him from using the property as Martin Miller is attempting to do. He argues that La.C.C. art. 803 is limited to a situation such as where the parties have agreed, in writing, not to partition property, for up to fifteen years, as provided for by La.R.S. 9:1112 and 9:1702.

Title VII of the Louisiana Civil Code, Ownership In Indivision, consisting of Articles 797 through 818, became effective in January 1991. There is scant jurisprudence interpreting these articles. La.C.C. art. 801 provides: "The use and management of the thing held in indivision is determined by agreement of all the co-owners." The codal scheme envisions, first, the co-owners agreeing among themselves how to manage the property held in indivision. Martin Miller submits that if, for some reason the co-owners cannot agree on the use and management of the property, and a partition has not yet been ordered, then La.C.C. art. 803 authorizes a court, upon petition by another co-owner, to determine the use and management of the property.

Martin Miller, as co-owner (and as executor), and all of the co-owners in indivision, including Val Miller, agreed to list the residence with a real estate agent for sale and, at the time of trial, it was on the market. If the residence sold, a partition would have been unnecessary. Given that situation, no co-owner had sought a partition as of the time of trial. A court order of partition by licitation would simply have resulted in the residence being offered for sale, as it already had been. Pending that sale, we believe a trial court could determine the use and management of the residence, in the absence of an agreement between the co-owners. The alternative would be infighting among the co-owners pending the actual sale. We find that, as a practical matter, a partition was "not available" because it would have been a needless expense and unnecessary judicial procedure. Because the co-owners could not agree on the use and management of the thing among themselves pending the sale of the residence, the trial court had the authority to make that determination pursuant to C.C. art. 803.

Val Miller next questions the reasonableness of the trial court's determination of use and management. At one point in his testimony, Val Miller said he believed he had a right to use the residence as he so desired and to remove movables and possibly keep them until another co-owner asked for them. However, he subsequently stated that he would agree not to remove any item from the residence. Val Miller also gave some emotional testimony about his sentimental attachment to the family residence, which he had lived in for twenty-two years of his early life and frequently visited for more than thirty years thereafter. Nevertheless, the trial court, heard the evidence, observed the demeanor of the witnesses, and determined what it felt was the best use and management of the residence under the circumstances. We cannot say the trial court erred.

For the foregoing reasons, we affirm the judgment of the trial court.

AFFIRMED.

Notes and Questions

1. *Succession of Miller,* 674 So.2d 441 (La. App. 1 Cir. 1996), highlights the relationship between two provisions of the Louisiana Civil Code: Article 802, which furnishes a coequal and coextensive right to each co-owner to use a co-owned thing, and Article 803, which opens the door to a judicial determination of use and management of a co-owned thing. The route to the courts becomes available only if: (1) the co-owners have not entered into a use-and-management agreement under Article 801; and (2) the exit route of partition is unavailable.

In *Succession of Miller,* why did Martin Miller suggest "restricted access" in the first place? How did the court get around the second requisite for judicial involvement and avoid recognizing Val Miller's right to equal and co-extensive use under Article 802 of the Louisiana Civil Code? What would a partition by licitation achieve in a case in which a valuable house held in indivision is listed for sale? Is Val liable to the other co-owners for the bulldozer allegedly damaged during the state of indivision?

2. Is this a well-reasoned decision or does the court arrogate too much discretion to itself? Methodologically, do you think that the court is properly filling a gap in the law, as permitted by Article 4 of the Civil Code? Or is this an excessively teleological reading of Article 803?

Miller v. Seven C's Properties, LLC
800 So.2d 406 (2001)

SULLIVAN, Judge. In this suit for declaratory judgment, a co-owner of immovable property seeks a determination that the repairs he proposes to make to the property's levee system are "necessary expenses" or "expenses for ordinary maintenance and repair" under La. Civ.Code art. 806, thereby entitling him to reimbursement from his co-owners in proportion to their share of ownership. The trial court dismissed the suit on exceptions of no cause of action, and the Plaintiff has appealed. For the following reasons, we reverse and remand.

Procedural History

Pierre Valcour Miller, individually and as the administrator of the estate of Max Kaplan, filed suit against several Defendants alleged to be his co-owners in indivision of certain immovable property identified as the "West Club District," the "Sweeney District," and the "Baker District," all located in Cameron Parish, Louisiana. Miller alleged that the levees surrounding these "districts" have been breached and/or are in need of maintenance and repairs to preserve their integrity and to prevent the encroachment of salt water. He prayed for a judgment declaring that:

> the co-owner making and paying the costs of those necessary maintenance and repairs [under La. Civ. Code art. 806] to the levees . . . including all costs of applying for and obtaining the necessary permits and mitigation required by the Corps of Engineers and any other regulatory bodies and/or agencies, may recover from his co-owners, as soon thereafter as said repairs have been completed and paid for, the costs expended in said repairs in proportion to a co-owner's ownership in the property.

Most of the Defendants filed exceptions of prematurity and of no cause of action. Three Defendants not excepting to the suit filed an answer denying, inter alia, that the proposed repairs were necessary. After a hearing, the trial court sustained the exceptions of no cause of action.

Opinion

Miller's petition for declaratory relief is based upon La.Civ.Code art. 806, which provides:

> A co-owner who on account of the thing held in indivision *has incurred necessary expenses, expenses for ordinary maintenance and repairs, or necessary management expenses paid to a third person, is entitled to reimbursement from the other co-owners in proportion to their shares.*

> If the co-owner who incurred the expenses had the enjoyment of the thing held in indivision, his reimbursement shall be reduced in proportion to the value of the enjoyment (emphasis added).

The comments to Article 806 indicate that it is a new provision, but that it expresses principles inherent in the Civil Code of 1870. The comments also refer to La. Civ.

Code arts. 527 and 528 for the definition of "necessary expenses" as distinguished from "useful and luxurious expenses." Under Article 527, "necessary expenses" are "incurred for the preservation of the thing and for the discharge of private or public burdens." As explained in Comment (b) to Article 528, "useful expenses" are those that result in an enhancement of value, but are not needed for the preservation of the property. Under Articles 527 and 528, an evicted possessor, whether in good or bad faith, may recover "necessary expenses," but only a good faith possessor may recover "useful expenses." Under Article 806, a co-owner may be reimbursed for both the "necessary expenses" and the "expenses for ordinary maintenance and repairs" that he has incurred. Article 806 also provides that a co-owner may be reimbursed for "necessary management expenses paid to a third person."

In granting the exceptions of no cause of action, the trial court reasoned that Article 806 must be strictly construed because it creates a new cause of action in derogation of the normal rights of co-owners. Because the article provides only for reimbursement of expenses already incurred, and because the expenses that are the subject of this suit have admittedly not yet been incurred, the trial court found that the petition failed to state a cause of action.

On appeal, Miller argues that the trial court erred in confusing whether the petition states a cause of action under Article 806, as opposed to a declaratory judgment under La. Code Civ. P. arts. 1871–83. He contends that an actual dispute exists between him and the other co-owners over the necessity of the repairs and that purpose of the declaratory judgment articles would be defeated if he were required to incur these substantial expenses while his right to reimbursement remains uncertain. Defendants reiterate their argument that there is presently no justiciable controversy under Article 806 because Miller has yet to incur any expenses. They further argue that Miller is not entitled to declaratory relief because the judgment he seeks will not end the controversy, as there will still be a dispute about the amount of the repairs, and because Miller is improperly using executory process to obtain an award of monetary damages in a declaratory judgment action.

Declaratory Judgment

La.Code Civ.P. art. 1871 provides that courts "may declare rights, status, and other legal relations whether or not further relief is or could be claimed" and that "the existence of another adequate remedy does not preclude a judgment for declaratory relief in cases where it is appropriate." . . . The purpose of the declaratory judgment articles is "to settle and afford relief from uncertainty and insecurity with respect to rights, status, and other legal regimes, and they are to be liberally construed and administered." La. Code Civ. P. art. 1881.

. . . .

Justiciable Controversy

As the supreme court explained in *American Waste & Pollution Control Co. v. St. Martin Parish Police Jury*, 627 So.2d 158, 161 (La. 1993) (citations omitted) (emphasis added):

Due to its nature, declaratory relief makes it possible to adjudicate a grievance at an earlier time than would otherwise be allowed. The purpose of the judgment is to settle and afford relief from uncertainty and insecurity, at times, before damages arise and the need for traditional remedies occurs. It is available to a party when the action meets the rules governing ordinary proceedings, and grounds for discretionary refusal to grant the declaration do not exist. Like actions for conventional judgments, basic to the exercise of procedures for declaratory relief, the action must present a justiciable controversy.

In *Abbott v. Parker*, 259 La. 279, 249 So.2d 908, 918 (1971), the supreme court offered the following considerations for determining when a justiciable controversy exists:

A "justiciable controversy" connotes, in the present sense, an existing actual and substantial dispute, as distinguished from one that is merely hypothetical or abstract, and a dispute which involves the legal relation of the parties who have real adverse interests, and upon which the judgment of the court may effectively operate through a decree of conclusive character. Further, the plaintiff should have a legally protectable and tangible interest at stake, and the dispute presented should be of sufficient immediacy and reality to warrant the issuance of a declaratory judgment.

After reviewing Miller's petition, we find that it does present a justiciable controversy. The record reflects that a real and substantial dispute exists among the co-owners as to the necessity of the levee repairs. If the proposed repairs are deemed to be "necessary expenses" or "expenses for ordinary maintenance and repairs," then the co-owners are obligated for reimbursement of those expenses under Article 806. Thus, a declaration as to the necessity of the repairs will determine the rights and obligations of the parties under the law.

Defendants argue that allowing Miller's suit to proceed amounts to an unauthorized use of executory process and that "there is no way at this stage to determine whether the proposed expenses are reasonable and necessary." We disagree. "A suit for declaratory judgment is an ordinary, not a summary proceeding. Accordingly, the procedures for a trial in an ordinary proceeding apply." *Bergen Brunswig Drug Co. v. Poulin*, 93-1945, p. 5 (La. App. 1 Cir. 6/24/94); 639 So.2d 453, 456 (citations omitted). Additionally, La. Civ. Code art. 1879 provides: "When a proceeding under Articles 1871 through 1883 involves the determination of an issue of fact, such issue may be tried and determined in the same manner as issues of fact are tried and determined in other civil actions in the court in which the proceeding is pending."

Thus, the trial court would determine whether or not the levee repairs are "necessary expenses" or "expenses for ordinary maintenance and repair" based upon evidence presented by all parties. Presumably, this evidence would address the present condition of the property, the type and extent, including the cost, of the proposed repairs, and the benefits to be derived therefrom. A declaratory judgment at this stage would end the present uncertainty as to the necessity of the repairs. A declaratory judgment would also prevent the possibility of one co-owner proceeding with the repairs, only to be denied reimbursement based upon a later finding that the repairs are not those contemplated under Article 806, while the other co-owners reaped the benefits of the improvements. If, as Defendants argue, a dispute would still exist as to the costs of repairs, that issue could be addressed in an application for supplemental relief, as discussed below.

Monetary Relief

Defendants also argue that the trial court did not err in dismissing the petition because it improperly seeks an award of monetary damages in a suit for declaratory judgment. . . .

In the present case, Miller prayed for a judgment declaring that he "may recover from his co-owners, as soon thereafter as said repairs have been completed and paid for, the costs expended in said repairs in proportion to a co-owner's ownership in the property." To the extent that this language represents a demand for monetary damages, the trial court was correct in disallowing it. However, we find that the trial court should not have dismissed the action, as it otherwise presents a claim for declaratory relief.

Decree

For the above reasons, the judgment of the trial court is reversed and the case remanded for further proceedings consistent with this opinion. Costs of this appeal are assessed to Defendants-Appellees.

REVERSED AND REMANDED.

Notes and Questions

1. *Miller v. Seven C's Properties, LLC*, 800 So.2d 406 (2001), offers the next installment in the saga of Pierre Valcour "Val" Miller and the property he inherited as a co-owner. This time, Val Miller brings a declaratory action (under Article 1871 *et seq.* of the Louisiana Code of Civil Procedure) against his co-owners. He asks the court to determine whether his proposal for repairs to the levee system surrounding the Cameron Parish property would qualify as "necessary expenses" or "expenses for ordinary maintenance and repair" under Article 806 of the Louisiana Civil Code. What did opposing counsel argue in light of the text of the provision? Note the use of the present perfect tense "has incurred" in the text of Article 806. Has Val already done anything to trigger reimbursement?

2. In terms of judicial policy, does this decision embody an ex ante judicial intervention in management disputes among co-owners? Does it judicially override Article 806 of the Louisiana Civil Code? Or does it restore common sense by protecting co-owners from unreasonable risks?

C. Termination of Precarious Possession and Acquisitive Prescription of Immovable Property by Co-Owners

We have already examined how a precarious possessor could terminate his status and begin to possess and prescribe in his own right. Under Articles 3439 and 3478 of the Louisiana Civil Code, a precarious possessor other than a co-owner, such as a lessee or depositary, must give actual notice of his intent to possess for himself to the person on whose behalf he is possessing. *See* La. Civ. Code arts. 3439, 3478 (1982). In cases like *Harper v. Willis,* 383 So.2d 1299 (La. App. 3 Cir. 1980), and *Memorial Hall Museum, Inc. v. UNO Foundation,* 847 So.2d 625 (La. App. 4 Cir. 2003), we saw that the actual notice requirement presents a high threshold. In this section, we turn our attention to how precarious possessors who are co-owners may acquire true possession and start to prescribe.

Recall that under Article 3437 of the Louisiana Civil Code a precarious possessor detains a thing "with the permission of" or "on behalf of" someone else, La. Civ. Code art. 3437 (1982). He thus lacks the crucial element of animus—the intent to possess as owner. La. Civ. Code art. 3424 (1982). We have already met various kinds of precarious possessors: lessees, depositaries, and borrowers in a loan for use. Co-owners must be added to the list. The ability of co-owners to terminate their status as precarious possessors is governed by a specially tailored set of rules.

A co-owner who engages in acts of use or enjoyment of the thing can be said to quasi-possess his fractional interest. At the same time, however, this co-owner precariously possesses the thing owned in indivision vis-à-vis the other co-owners. Under Article 3439 and 3478 of the Louisiana Civil Code, co-owners can only begin to possess for themselves if they demonstrate their intention by overt and unambiguous acts sufficient to give notice to their fellow co-owners. La. Civ. Code arts. 3439, 3478 (1982).

Why would a co-owner want to shed the attribute of precariousness? As we have seen, the incentives are manifold. Most significantly, under Article 3477 of the Louisiana Civil Code, a precarious possessor does not have the possession requisite for acquisitive prescription. Article 3478, which largely borrows the contents of Article 3439, sets the standard for the commencement of acquisitive prescription by a co-owner:

Art. 3478. Termination of precarious possession; commencement of prescription

A co-owner, or his universal successor, may commence to prescribe when he demonstrates by overt and unambiguous acts sufficient to give notice to his co-owner that he intends to possess the property for himself. The acquisition and recordation of a title from a person other than a co-owner thus may mark the commencement of prescription.

Any other precarious possessor, or his universal successor, may commence to prescribe when he gives actual notice to the person on whose behalf he is possessing that he intends to possess for himself.

Art. 3439. Termination of precarious possession

A co-owner, or his universal successor, commences to possess for himself when he demonstrates this intent by overt and unambiguous acts sufficient to give notice to his co-owner.

Any other precarious possessor, or his universal successor, commences to possess for himself when he gives actual notice of this intent to the person on whose behalf he is possessing.

La. Civ. Code art. 3478 (1982); La. Civ. Code art. 3439 (1982).

At first blush, the standard for termination of precarious possession applicable to the co-owner seems somewhat lighter when compared to the "actual notice" required of other precarious possessors. However, the demonstration "by overt and unambiguous acts sufficient to give notice" can be extraordinary because each co-owner may exercise all of the attributes of ownership. The language of the provision itself yields few insights into what types of acts are sufficient to meet this standard. Only from the second sentence in Article 3478(1) of the Louisiana Civil Code do we learn that the "acquisition and recordation of a title from a person other than a co-owner" could suffice. La. Civ. Code art. 3478(1)(cl.2) (1982).

The words "thus may mark" in Article 3478(1)(cl.2) of the Louisiana Civil Code signal the illustrative nature of this example. They suggest that a recorded act will not always constitute notice, as the provision does not declare "thus shall mark." In this light, a court must carefully examine the facts in each case to determine whether a sufficiently overt and unambiguous act has occurred. The occupation of an immovable by a co-owner may not alone amount to a hostile manifestation of the requisite intent to possess as owner. This is because Article 802 furnishes the right of full use to each co-owner. But a co-owner forcibly preventing the other co-owners from exercising their co-ownership rights may be sufficient to give notice. The decision, which follows, highlights that some courts are careful to preserve flexibility in determining whether a precarious possessor has engaged in sufficiently overt and unambiguous acts to give notice of his intent to possess co-owned property as its sole owner.

Franks Petroleum, Inc. v. Babineaux

446 So.2d 862 (La. App. 2 Cir. 1984)

HALL, Judge. In this concursus proceeding brought by the operator of producing gas units, the district court resolved the dispute between two sets of record co-owners, identified as the "Group A defendants" and the "Group B defendants", by holding that the Group A defendants had acquired full title to the properties involved by acquisitive prescription based on adverse possession by them and their ancestors for more than 30 years after notice of such adverse possession to the Group B defendants and their ancestors. From judgments recognizing the Group A defendants and those holding under them as entitled to the mineral and/or royalty interests involved, the Group B defendants appealed. Finding that the issues were correctly resolved by the district court in its comprehensive, studious reasons for judgment, we affirm.

On appeal, the appellants urge that the trial court erred in holding that a recorded ex parte judgment of possession sending the Group A defendants into possession of the properties involved constituted sufficient notice that their possession was as owners and adverse to the Group B defendants, and that the court erred in failing to find that the only actual notice of adverse possession was given in 1950, less than 30 years prior to the commencement of this litigation.

The property was acquired by C.C. Colvin and his brother, John A. Colvin, in 1874. The Group A defendants are the heirs of C.C. Colvin and his wife. The Group B defendants are the two children of one of the 10 children of John A. Colvin and his wife. The widow and all the other heirs of John A. Colvin executed quitclaim deeds of their interests in the properties to the Group A defendants in 1937 and 1938. The quitclaim deeds recited that C.C. Colvin purchased the interest of John A. Colvin in the property, and paid for the interest, but that the deed was lost or destroyed and was not recorded. The consideration for the quitclaim deeds was stated to be the consideration paid by C.C. Colvin to John A. Colvin and the vendors acknowledged that John A. Colvin received full payment.

The trial court correctly found that C.C. Colvin and then his heirs exercised full and complete possession of the property from as early as 1900 through the time this litigation was commenced by living on the property, farming it, growing timber, making timber sales, selling sand and gravel, having the property surveyed, marking boundaries, and the like. The trial court also correctly found that the evidence was insufficient to support any possession whatsoever by John A. Colvin or his heirs. These findings are not seriously questioned on appeal.

There is in evidence a timber deed dated in 1899 by which C.C. Colvin sold timber on the subject property. John A. Colvin signed as a witness to the timber deed.

In 1937, a judgment of possession was rendered in the Succession of C.C. Colvin and his wife, and was duly recorded, in which their heirs were recognized as the owners of the "whole interest in and to" the subject property.

In 1950 appellants were specifically told in a conversation with one of the C.C. Colvin heirs that John A. Colvin had sold his interest in the property, the deed was lost, and that they did not own any interest in the property. However, they had earlier knowledge that other heirs of John A. Colvin had quitclaimed their interest, and they were approached to sign papers to get the property "straight."

Subsequently, the heirs of C.C. Colvin partitioned the property, purporting in the recorded instrument to deal with the full interest in the property.

Appellants urge that the possession of their co-owners must be regarded as possession on behalf of all the co-owners of the property, and that such possession did not become adverse to them until they were given actual notice in the 1950 conversation, less than 30 years prior to their asserting their claim to title. Appellants particularly urge that the trial court erred in holding that the ex parte judgment of possession served as notice to them of the adverse nature of the possession of their co-owners.

Particularly applicable to the issues in this case are LSA-C.C. Arts. 3439 and 3478. . . .

These Civil Code articles were adopted by Act 187 of 1982, effective January 1, 1983. The provisions are new, but as noted in the comments thereto, do not change the law. See prior Articles 3512 and 3515.

The well-settled jurisprudential general rule is that an owner in indivision cannot acquire by prescription the rights of his co-owners in the property held in common. Possession by one co-owner is generally considered as being exercised on behalf of all co-owners. It is equally well settled that an exception to the general rule is recognized in those instances where the possessing co-owner gives notice to the other co-owners that he intends to possess as owner adversely and contrary to the common interest. Under such circumstances, one owner in common may prescribe against a co-owner provided such possession be clearly hostile and notice be given thereof. *Givens v. Givens*, 273 So.2d 863 (La. App. 2d Cir. 1973).

Under Civil Code Articles 3439 and 3478 and the jurisprudence, actual notice to other co-owners of the possessing co-owner's intent to possess for himself is not necessary. Actual notice is required in the case of other precarious possessors, but not in the case of co-owners.

In determining whether a particular case falls within the exception rather than the general rule, mere occupancy, use, payment of taxes, and similar acts of possession will not suffice to constitute notice of adverse possession to an owner in common. However, where a co-owner possesses under a recorded instrument apparently conveying title (even though the purported conveyance is invalid), the recorded instrument, together with the acts of possession, constitutes notice to other co-owners and the possession is then regarded as hostile to the interests of the other co-owners, rebutting the presumption that possession is for the benefit of all co-owners. *Givens v. Givens*, supra.

Civil Code Article 3478's provision that the acquisition and recordation of a title from a person other than a co-owner may mark the commencement of a prescription is illustrative, not exclusive. Recordation of an instrument translative of title is only one example of overt and unambiguous acts sufficient to give notice to co-owners.

A recorded instrument may constitute notice to co-owners even though it is not translative of title. Thirty years acquisitive prescription is founded upon possession, not a deed translative of title. The function of the recorded instrument is simply to serve as an overt manifestation that a co-owner exclusively possessing is doing so by virtue of his claim to exclusive ownership. It is objective evidence that he possesses adversely to those who may claim to be his co-owners. *Dupuis v. Broadhurst*, 213 So.2d 528 (La. App. 3d Cir. 1968). In *Dupuis*, a partition, not translative of title, coupled with active and open possession for 30 years, was held to negate the presumption that the possessing owner was possessing for other co-owners. Likewise, in *Minton v. Whitworth*, 393 So.2d 294 (La. App. 1st Cir. 1980), the language of a recorded partition was held to be a clear indication that the parties thereto considered themselves to be the owners of the full interest in the property and to constitute notice to co-owners that subsequent possession of the property was adverse and hostile to their interests.

A recorded invalid donation was held to constitute adequate notice in Givens, supra, and a simulated sale was given the same effect in *Detraz v. Pere*, 183 So.2d 401 (La. App. 3d Cir. 1966).

It was not error for the trial court to hold that the recorded ex parte judgment of possession which purported to send the C.C. Colvin heirs into possession of the "whole interest" in the subject property was an act of notice to the other record co-owners of the intended adverse possession of the C.C. Colvin heirs. *Boyet v. Perryman*, 240 La. 339, 123 So.2d 79 (1960), relied on heavily by appellants, is not applicable. That case held only that an ex parte judgment of possession does not purport to be a transfer of title and cannot serve as a basis for 10 years acquisitive prescription. It has no relevancy to the issue of notice of adverse possession as between co-owners and 30-years acquisitive prescription based on adverse possession.

Perhaps more significant than the judgment of possession are the declarations contained in the quitclaim deeds recorded in 1937 and 1938. The declarations serve as notice to the other co-owners that the C.C. Colvin heirs were possessing as owners for themselves and adversely to the John A. Colvin heirs under a lost or destroyed deed from John A. Colvin. This declaration was joined in by John A. Colvin's widow and all of his heirs except the appellants.

There is also evidence that the appellants were aware, prior to the 1950 conversation mentioned previously, of the claim by the C.C. Colvin heirs to full ownership of the property and their exclusive possession as full owners.

The intent of C.C. Colvin and his heirs to possess for themselves was demonstrated by overt and unambiguous acts sufficient to give notice to their co-owners, marking the commencement of acquisitive prescription more than 30 years prior to the commencement of this litigation. These acts included the actual physical acts of possession described earlier in this opinion, the timber deed by C.C. Colvin which was witnessed by John A. Colvin, the recorded declarations contained in the quitclaim deeds, the recitals of the recorded judgment of possession, and communications among the family which indicate an awareness on the part of appellants of their co-owners' intent to possess for themselves, all commencing or occurring more than 30 years ago. The judgment of the district court recognizing appellees' acquisition of the interests of appellants by 30-years acquisitive prescription is correct.

The appellants initially pled the invalidity of the quitclaim deeds on the grounds of lack of or insufficiency of consideration. Although this issue was not addressed in the trial court's reasons for judgment, the judgment rejecting in full appellants' demands for recognition of an ownership interest in the property had the effect of rejecting their claims in this respect. No formal specification of error is directed to this issue, but appellants, in brief, ask that the issue be decided on this appeal, and the plaintiff, in brief, has responded. Suffice it to say that the appellants have failed to demonstrate or establish that the consideration recited in the quitclaim deeds was not accurately stated or sufficient to support the transfers made in acknowledgment of the prior transfer by their ancestor for money consideration and to comply with the vendors' natural obligation to execute the disposition their ancestor and former owner had made. See LSA-C.C. Arts. 1758 and 1759.

For the reasons assigned, the judgment of the district court is affirmed at appellants' costs.

Affirmed.

Notes and Questions

1. In *Franks Petroleum, Inc. v. Babineaux*, 446 So.2d 862 (La. App. 2 Cir. 1984), a dispute about ownership of land is once again asserted in the context of a concursus proceeding in which the operator of producing gas units deposited mineral royalty funds into the registry of the court and invited all possible owners of the land and related mineral and royalty interests to assert their claims to those funds. *See* La. Code Civ. Proc. art. 4651 *et seq.*

2. Make a list of the facts assembled by the court that counted as overt and unambiguous acts required for the onset of prescription in Group A. Identify the recorded instruments before the courts. Recall that a quitclaim deed transfers a property interest without warranty of title and an ex parte judgment of possession recognizes the interest of the heirs in the estate of the deceased. Trace how the court's reasoning comports with the permissive phrase "thus may" in Article 3478(1) of the Louisiana Civil Code. Do we learn more about what type of title must be recorded? Does it have to be "translative"? Now turn to the "other acts" of possession present in the case.

3. The Louisiana Second Circuit Court of Appeal decision in *Franks Petroleum* builds on a long line of Louisiana jurisprudence that has its origin in *Succession of Seals*, 150 So.2d 13 (La. 1963). That case involved a purported transfer of 60 acres of land from one family member to another that turned out to be invalid under Louisiana community property law. In the wake of the invalid transfer, the prescriber, the purported transferee, began to engage with the land extensively: he paid off mortgages, paid property taxes, built houses and made other improvements, farmed the land, sold timber, fenced the land, granted mineral leases, sold off portions of the

land, and occasionally allowed relatives to live on the land rent-free. *Id*. at 217–18. The other co-owners, however, displayed indifference to the co-owned property in dispute until the land's extensive mineral value was discovered. Occasionally they stayed with the prescriber when they needed a place to live. The also made some minor improvements of their own. *Id*. at 21. Explaining its finding that the purported transferee had established acquisitive prescription of the co-owned land vis-à-vis his co-owners, the Louisiana Supreme Court commented:

> The genius of our law does not favor the claims of those who have long slept on their rights and who, after years of inertia, conveying an assurance of acquiescence in a given state of things, suddenly wake at the welcome vision of an unexpected advantage and invoke the aid of the courts for relief, under the effect of newly discovered technical error in some ancient transaction or settlement.

Id. at 21. Do you believe that the "sleeping on your rights" rationale for acquisitive prescription invoked by the court in *Succession of Seals* should apply in co-owner disputes as readily as in other kinds of acquisitive prescription cases? For more discussion, see John A. Lovett, *Precarious Possession*, 77 LA. L. REV. 617, 646–686 (2017) (discussing three types of paradigmatic disputes: (1) strangers; (2) contractual and legal status relationships; and (3) neighbors and members of close-knit communities).

4. As the decision in *Succession of Seals* established and as the decision in *Franks Petroleum* emphasized, co-owners or co-heirs can terminate precarious possession and begin to prescribe in their own right if they can show some written, recorded instrument that appeared to convey or declare title or ownership, even if that instrument was invalid, as long as additional acts of possession occurred after the recording of the instrument. Lovett, 77 LA. L. REV. at 666. Examples of recorded documents that have been found to give sufficient notice of adverse possession against co-owners, in conjunction with other acts of possession, include warranty deeds, simulated sales, acts of partition, and even a prohibited donation *omnium bonorum*. Lovett, 77 LA. L. REV. at 666–667. According to established jurisprudence, a recorded document of an attempted conveyance can still give notice of one co-owner's intent to possess for himself even if that conveyance was invalid. *Cockerham v. Cockerham*, 16 So. 3d 1264, 1269 (La. App. 2d 2009). However, a deed executed by a co-owner—rather than a non-owner—is not sufficient to put all owners of the property on notice. *Ebarb v. Unopened Succession of Sepulvado*, 241 So.3d 1103, 1114 (La. App. 3 Cir. 2018). Similarly, mere occupancy, use, and payment of taxes will not suffice to constitute "acts of ownership" amounting to a notice of adverse possession to co-owners. *Id.; Cockerham*, 160 So.3d at 1268–69.

5. **Problem**: Has a co-owner who has recently purchased an undivided interest in rural land proved an intent to possess for itself by "overt and unambiguous acts sufficient to give notice to [its] co-owner" in a possessory action based on the following facts: (1) three days after purchasing its undivided interest, the new co-owner sends a letter to a representative of one of the other co-owners and, on the same day, files

in the public records an "affidavit of possession;" (2) the affidavit of possession (a) elaborates upon the affiant's intention to possess as owner the entirety of the co-owned property, (b) lists the affiant's various acts of possession such as cleaning the property of garbage piles, cutting trails, posting 'no trespass' signs, repairing fences, placing a gate and lock to restrict access, destroying old deer hunting equipment, and attempting to restore electricity to and repair an old structure on the property, and (c) lists a number of unopened successions and persons against whom the affiant intends to possess with the objective of acquiring 100% of the property? *See Creek Williams Mgmt., L.L.C. v. Williams*, 223 So.3d 1194 (La. App. 2 Cir. 2017), *cert. denied*, 228 So.3d 1222 (La. 2017) (reversing summary judgment in favor of the affiant-plaintiff in the possessory action and remanding for trial).

6. The apparent "totality of the circumstances" approach adopted by Louisiana courts for purposes of determining whether notice has been given under Article 3478 of the Louisiana Civil Code is important for owners in indivision. Co-owners must guard not only against physical acts of possession on the part of a co-owner claiming acquisitive prescription but also check the public records for the presence of hostile instruments.

7. *Acquisitive Prescription, Co-Owners and Mental Incompetence*: In a complex decision, a Louisiana appellate court applied Article 3478 to determine whether a co-owner in physical possession of all of a 160-acre tract of land had acquired by prescription a one-sixteenth share in the land owned by his physically and mentally disabled brother. *Hooper v. Hooper*, 941 So.2d 726 (La. App. 3 Cir. 2006). In that case, the court ultimately held that the co-owner in possession (Billy) did not prescribe against his disabled brother (R.P.) because of the latter's mental incompetence. *Id.* at 731. As the court explained:

> The first conclusion that the facts of the case and the law compel is that no acts, however overt and unambiguous, could have sufficed as notice to R.P. Both the code articles and the jurisprudence show that the notice must be to the co-owner, not to the world in general as concluded by the trial court, and that there must be overt and unambiguous acts sufficient to give notice to a co-owner. *See Dunham v. Nixon*, 371 So. 2d 1288 (La. App. 3 Cir. 1979); *S. Natural Gas Co. v. Naquin*, s167 So. 2d 434 (La. App. 1 Cir.), *writ refused*, 246 LA. 884, 168 So. 2d 268 (1964). Long ago, in *John T. Moore Planting Co. v. Morgan's Louisiana & T.R. & S.S. Co.*, 126 LA. 840, 53 So. 22 (1908), our supreme court held that the notice must be enough so that the person in interest will have knowledge of it. The same decision explained that the outward acts of possession had to be of an unusually pronounced character so as to "let the owner know that a new order of things has begun." 53 So. 2d at 35. "In order for one co-owner or coheir to prescribe against the other, his possession must be clearly hostile to the rights of the other and, in such instances, it is necessary, in order to commence the running of prescription, that notice be given by the former to the latter of his intention to hold, animo domini, all of the common property." *S.E. Pub. Serv. Co. v.*

Barras, 246 So. 2d 298, 300 (La. App. 3 Cir. 1971) (quoting *Lee v. Jones*, 224 LA. 231, 237–38, 69 So. 2d 26, 28 (1953)). An adversely possessing co-owner must give notice to the other owner or owners in common that he intends to possess contrary to the common interest. *Id.*

In the present case, R.P. was mentally incapable of knowing the significance of adverse possession however pronounced, glaring, or hostile the acts manifesting Billy's intent to so possess might have been. Incompetent from birth, no act, however overt or unambiguous, would have served as notice to him. Appropriate notice to a legal representative would have been notice to him, but it was not until 1995 that a legal representative was appointed and qualified for him.

The plaintiffs point out that La. Civ. Code art. 3474 provides that prescription runs against incompetents. We acknowledge this article, but note that it refers to the ten-year acquisitive prescription provided for in La. Civ. Code art. 3473 and that La. Civ. Code art. 3488 makes the rules governing ten-year acquisitive prescription applicable to the prescription of thirty years only "to the extent that their application is compatible with the prescription of thirty years." It is understandable that ten-year acquisitive prescription might run against an incompetent, because its very nature requires good faith. La. Civ. Code art. 3475. Thirty-year acquisitive prescription requires no good faith. However, we need not reach the issue of whether the thirty-year acquisitive prescription runs against an incompetent, because we find that in this case, the prescription never began to run. Even if it could be said that notice was given to R.P., in this case Billy's possession was not demonstrably unambiguous. Louisiana Civil Code Article 3435 provides that equivocal possession has no legal effect. Additionally, La. Civ. Code art. 3436 provides that possession is equivocal "when there is ambiguity as to the intent of the possessor to own the thing." Planiol gives examples of the vice of being equivocal:

> Possession is equivocal when the acts of enjoyment can be explained in two ways. Most practical examples of equivocal possession come up in cases dealing with property in a state of indivision. Each of the co-owners has a right to perform acts of possession upon the totality of the thing. Such acts are ambiguous because they could be performed in virtue of the owner's partial ownership, as well as in virtue of exclusive ownership. As long as this ambiguity lasts his possession remains ineffective as against his co-owners. In order to dissipate this uncertainty it is necessary that he exclude his co-owners in some manifest manner.

1 M. Planiol, Traité élémentaire de droit civil 1 Pt. 2, at 350–351 (Louisiana State Law Institute trans. 1959).

Louisiana Civil Code Article 2452 provides that "[t]he sale of a thing belonging to another does not convey ownership." All agree that the 1958 deed did not convey ownership of the 160 acres to Billy. Nevertheless, "[t]he acquisition and recordation of a title from a person other than a co-owner may mark the commencement of prescription." La. Civ. Code art. 3478. Where one co-owner goes into continuous possession by reason of a deed translative of title, "even though the deed be invalid and the possession be in bad faith, the co-owner's possession ordinarily is then regarded as hostile to any claim of his co-owners and as normally rebutting any presumption that he was possessing for his co-owners as well as himself." *Cont'l Oil Co. v. Arceneaux*, 183 So. 2d 399, 401 (La. App. 3 Cir.), *writ refused*, 249 La. 66, 184 So. 2d 736 (1966).

However, the adverse title was not sufficient notice in the present case. To the contrary, by providing that R. P. retained the usufruct over his interest, the deed was probative of Billy's acknowledgment of R.P.'s usufruct, and, therefore, Billy's possession continued to be precarious. To explain, we repeat the definition of precarious possession in La. Civ. Code art. 3437: "The exercise of possession over a thing with the permission of or on behalf of the owner or possessor is precarious possession." Applying this article, if the deed could be said to have had the effect of changing the character of Billy's possession, it changed his possession only on behalf of R.P. as owner to one on behalf of R.P. as possessor. The acknowledgment of an adverse title in another establishes the intent to possess precariously. *Maddox v. Vanlangendonck*, 334 So. 2d 739 (La. App. 3 Cir. 1976). Thus, even if the attempted transfer of naked ownership could be regarded as probative of Billy's intent to commence possession for himself, that intent was negated by the instrument's reservation of the usufruct which included the right of possession in R.P. Because of that, Billy's possession was equivocal and continued to be precarious following that attempt to commence possession for himself.

It is certainly true that Billy's occupancy of the property and acts of possession for over thirty years were sufficient to establish acquisitive prescription adverse to a stranger. The defendants admit this. However, because Billy and his brother, R.P., were co-owners, the burden of proof of Billy's heirs was to establish the commencement of Billy's possession for himself, and, to establish this commencement, they had to show when and how Billy demonstrated by overt and unambiguous acts sufficient to give notice to his brother that Billy intended to possess for himself. Until he made such a demonstration he remained a precarious possessor and never commenced to prescribe. Billy's heirs failed to prove a change from precarious to adverse possession. Acquisitive prescription never began. The trial court erred legally in holding that it did.

Hooper, 941 So.2d at 731–33.

Do you believe the court in *Hooper* adequately distinguished Article 3474 of the Louisiana Civil Code, which provides that ten year acquisitive prescription runs "against absent persons and incompetents, including minors and interdicts," on the ground that this case involved thirty year, not ten year, acquisitive prescription? La. Civ. Code art. 3474 (1982). What about Article 3468, which provides generally that "[p]rescription runs against absent persons and incompetents . . . unless exception is established by legislation"? La. Civ. Code art. 3468 (1983). Ultimately, it appears the court chose to reject these arguments and to rest its holding in favor of the successors of the disabled brother (R.P.) on other grounds: above all, the failure of the possessing brother (Billy) to provide sufficient notice to R.P. of his intent to possess all of the family land for himself through overt and unambiguous acts under Article 3478. What in particular was wrong with Billy's acts that prevented them from meeting the standard set forth in Article 3478? Did the court set the bar too high for Billy and his heirs? Or was the court appropriately suspicious of their intentions?

D. Termination of Co-Ownership through Partition

The possibility of exiting the artificial state of ownership in indivision has permeated our discussion of its arguably cumbersome governance rules. We have seen the specter of exit loom in the background as a kind of ultimate antidote to the difficulty of managing co-owned property. Before we discuss partition in more depth, however, we observe that co-ownership may also terminate in other ways.

A co-owned thing may be lost or destroyed by natural causes. Assume that Andrea and Bob co-own a Persian cat named Georgina. One day the cat disappears in the bayou. Co-ownership terminates with the demise of the cat. When the loss or destruction of a thing has been occasioned by the fault of a third party, however, the co-owners may share a delictual claim under Article 2315 of the Louisiana Civil Code in indivision. Thus, if Georgina had been hit by a truck operated by a reckless driver, Andrea and Bob would share a claim against the driver in indivision. Indivision also can end when co-owners unanimously proceed to alienate an entire thing held in indivision—a disposition allowed by Article 805 of the Civil Code.

1. Availability of Partition

Article 807 of the Louisiana Civil Code states the rule that partition is generally available. But it also offers two important exceptions. Take a closer look at this important provision.

Art. 807. Right to partition; exclusion by agreement

No one may be compelled to hold a thing in indivision with another unless the contrary has been provided by law or juridical act.

Any co-owner has a right to demand partition of a thing held in indivision. Partition may be excluded by agreement for up to fifteen years, or for such other period as provided in R.S. 9:1702 or other specific law.

La. Civ. Code art. 807 (1990). The right to partition reflects the Romanist principle that co-ownership is a provisional state of affairs. If, as Planiol would say, "he who has a companion has a master," then no one should be compelled to remain shackled in co-ownership. The phrase "[a]ny co-owner" in Article 807 signals that the right to demand a partition is available to all co-owners, even a co-owner with a small fractional share. In the case of immovable property, however, a special procedure must be followed when a co-owner who holds only a small fractional share (fifteen percent or less) seeks to force a partition by auction or private sale. *See* La. Rev. Stat. 9:1113 (2003).

In some exceptional cases, however, co-owners may be prevented from exercising their right of partition. When partition is prohibited by law, as under Article 808 of the Louisiana Civil Code, the exclusion of partition may last indefinitely. A voluntary agreement not to partition, however, can endure only for a limited period of time.

Non-Partition Agreements. The Civil Code and the Revised Statutes provide that co-owners may agree to forego their right to partition property owned in indivision for up to fifteen years or up to ninety-nine years in the case of a nuclear electric generating plant. La. Civ. Code art. 807 (1990); La. Rev. Stat. § 9:1702 (1987, amended 2010). Why might co-owners agree not to partition their co-owned property?

Note that the right to exit ownership in indivision of a thing given or bequeathed may also be denied by a donor or testator. But the period for which partition is absolutely disallowed in this context may only last five years under Article 1300 of the Louisiana Civil Code. La. Civ. Code art. 1300 (1870). After the lapse of this five year period, co-heirs can petition a court for the right to partition by showing that they cannot agree among themselves on how to administer property inherited in common. *Id.* In no case, however, may a donor or testator bind donees or heirs to remain co-owners in perpetuity. La. Civ. Code art. 1299 (1870). This would conflict with the general rule stated in Article 807.

Keep in mind that courts have been emphatic in enforcing the general principle announced in Article 807 of the Louisiana Civil Code. In one recent case, a husband and wife who divorced entered into a community property settlement and partition agreement. They agreed that certain movable property in their community of acquets and gains would "remain owned in indivision in equal portions by the parties" and that, when one of the former spouses died, the property would then belong exclusively to the survivor. *Succession of Crute v. Crute*, 226 So.3d 1161. 1165–66 (La. App. 1 Cir. 2017). The trial court noted that this agreement was "somewhat unusual." *Id.* at 1172. The Louisiana First Circuit Court of Appeal found it to be unlawful. The court first declared that under Article 2369.8 a spouse "has the right to demand partition of former community property at any time" and that "[a] contrary agreement is null." *Id.* (quoting La. Civ. Code art. 2369.8 (1996)). However, as the agreement between the parties preceded the effective date of this provision, the court turned to basic principles of co-ownership law, which apply when former spouses have not yet partitioned community property:

> A juridical act is a lawful volitional act intended to have legal conse-quences. Black's Law Dictionary (10th ed. 2014). While an agreement between spouses is considered a juridical act, we note that such an act must be lawful. In the present case, Section (3(of the Partition Agreement violated the fifteen-year time limitation of Article 807 as it required Frank Crute to hold the property in indivision for the remainder of his life, an indeterminate amount of time. See La. C.C. art. 2347 comment (c).

Id. at 1173. The court further determined that the agreement constituted an *abso-lute nullity* under Article 2030 of the Civil Code because it violated "a rule of pub-lic order," emphasizing that: (1) "[l]imitations on the right to partition are to be strictly construed;" (2) "[a] co-owner's right to partition of a thing held in common is an incident of ownership and is absolute in the absence of an agreement excluding partition for no more than fifteen years;" and (3) "[t]he agreement not to partition by the spouses was indefinite and uncertain as to the duration in violation of the public policy of this state." *Id.* at 1173–74.

Are the statutory limitations on the length of agreements not to partition described above appropriate? Do they strike the "right" balance between preserving the status quo of indivision and offering an individual co-owner a way out if the co-ownership relationship proves to be an unhappy one? For findings with regard to durational limits for non-partition agreements in other jurisdictions, see Hanoch Dagan & Michael Heller, *The Liberal Commons*, 110 YALE L. J. 549, 618–20 (2001) (reporting that (1) France, Belgium and Japan limit non-partition agreements to only five years; (2) Swiss law places a thirty-year limit on agreements to restrain partition; (3) in Germany, agreements to restrain the alienation of co-ownership shares can last in perpetuity; (4) under Austrian and India law restrictions on par-tition may last indefinitely, but end upon the transfer of the property; and (5) in Hungary the right to exit is permanent and cannot be waived). Study the following provision of Louisiana law and characterize its contents.

La. Rev. Stat. 9:1112. Immovable property held in common; agreement not to alienate, encumber or lease

Persons holding immovable property in common may agree not to alien-ate, encumber, or lease the property held in common for a specific period of time, not to exceed fifteen years.

La. Rev. Stat. 9:1112 (1987). Does this statute cover agreements not to partition? What are the advantages and disadvantages of the agreements contemplated in the provision?

Limits on Partition Imposed by Law. Article 808 of the Louisiana Civil Code, which derives from the work of the influential, eighteenth-century Spanish jurist José Luis Febrero, who authored a seminal guide of the same name, provides that "[p]artition of a thing in indivision is excluded when its use is indispensable for the enjoyment of another thing owned by one or more co-owners." La. Civ. Code art. 808 (1990). Examples may include a common wall or staircase in an apartment building or common grounds in a subdivision.

In one of the few reported decisions involving the question of whether co-owned property may be susceptible to partition, the property consisted of seven burial plots owned by four siblings. *See Ben Glazer Co., Inc. v. Tharp-Sontheimer-Tharp, Inc.*, 491 So.2d 722 (La. App. 4 Cir. 1986). Citing the precursor to Article 808 of the Louisiana Civil Code (Article 1303 of the 1870 Civil Code), the court held that two burial plots already occupied by the deceased parents of the siblings were not amenable to partition "because their use is indispensable to all of the owners in paying respects to their parents" and because exhumation would violate the state's public policy of leaving final resting places undisturbed. *Id.* at 724. In this light, the court ordered that four of the seven plots be partitioned in kind, with one plot going to each heir, and the final plot be partitioned by licitation, with the proceeds distributed to the heirs. *Id.*

In the case that follows, the court of appeals deploys Article 808 of the Louisiana Civil Code in a context in which the "other thing" is a lessee's interest in a lease of immovable property. Is such an interest even a "thing" within codal notions? If so, is it the kind of thing protected by Article 808?

Ivanhoe Canal Corp. v. Bunn

694 So.2d 263 (La. App. 1 Cir. 1995)

FOGG, Judge. The salient issue in this suit for the partition by licitation of immovable property is whether LSA-C.C. art. 808 prevents the partition where one of the co-owners in indivision has a lease of adjacent, immovable property and contends it will be prevented from using the leasehold without continued access to the land and waterways which are the subject of the action for partition.

Since 1941, Texaco has leased a 20.14 acre tract of land located on a waterway known as the Ivanhoe Canal in St. Mary Parish (Ivanhoe Marine Base). The lease extends until the year 2021. Texaco uses the leased premises to support its oil and gas production and exploration activities in oil fields located over water in the East and West Cote Blanche Bay and Vermillion Bay areas. These operations are supported by vessels which operate out of the Ivanhoe Marine Base by means of the Ivanhoe Canal.

Adjacent to the Ivanhoe Marine Base is a thirty-two acre tract of immovable property (Milling Tract), through which the Ivanhoe Canal runs. Ivanhoe Canal Corporation (Ivanhoe), Patricia Bunn, Henry Haller, Jr., Margaret Crosby, the Succession of Clifford Webb, Madison Land Company, M.D.T. Partnership, the James Webb Trust, Dorthy Sharpe Milling, and Texaco, Inc. are co-owners of the Milling Tract.

Since 1950, Texaco has had a servitude of passage to use the Ivanhoe Canal across the Milling Tract; this servitude expired in September of 1991. Before expiration of the servitude, Texaco acquired an undivided ownership interest in the Milling Tract and has continued to use the Ivanhoe Canal across the Milling Tract pursuant to its rights as co-owner.

On April 1, 1993, Ivanhoe filed the instant action against the remaining co-owners, seeking a partition by licitation of the surface of the above described property. The trial court rendered judgment in favor of Ivanhoe. Texaco appeals that judgment, contending the trial judge erred in finding that LSA-C.C. art. 808 did not the exclude the partition.

LSA-C.C. art. 808 provides that "partition of a thing held in indivision is excluded when its use is indispensable for the enjoyment of another thing owned by one or more of the co-owners." Texaco contends the trial court erred in finding that its lease of the Ivanhoe Marine Base is not a "thing" and in finding that the use of the Milling Tract is not indispensable to Texaco's "enjoyment" of its lease. We agree.

Book II of the Louisiana Civil Code is entitled "Things and the Different Modifications of Ownership". Title I of that book is entitled "Things". The first article under Title I is Article 448, which provides that things are divided into common, public and private; corporeals and incorporeals; and movables and immovables. Private things are owned by individuals, other private persons, and by the state or its political subdivisions in their capacity as private persons. LSA-C.C. art. 453.

Rights and actions that apply to things are incorporeal immovables. Immovables of this kind are such as personal servitudes established on immovables, predial servitudes, mineral rights, and petitory or possessory actions. LSA-C.C. art. 470. This enumeration of incorporeal immovables is illustrative. See LSA-C.C. art. 470, Comment (b). Therefore, all rights and actions that have an immovable object are incorporeal immovable things.

A lease is a synallagmatic contract, by which one party gives to the other the enjoyment of a thing at a fixed price. LSA-C.C. art. 2669. The parties obligate themselves reciprocally, so that the obligation of each party is correlative to the obligation of the other. LSA-C.C. art. 1908. By the lease of the Ivanhoe Marine Base, Texaco's lessor is obligated to give Texaco use of the Ivanhoe Marine Base. This obligation is a thing; therefore, the lease is an incorporeal immovable thing.

Texaco further asserts that the trial court erred in determining that the use of the Ivanhoe Canal cross the Milling Tract is not indispensable to Texaco's "enjoyment" of its lease of the Ivanhoe Marine Base. The lease states that the leased premises will be used by Texaco to support its operations in the area. The operations which Texaco supports from the leased premises are Texaco's oil and gas production and exploration activities in oil fields located over water in the East and West Cote Blanche Bay and Vermillion Bay areas. These operations are supported entirely by vessels which operate out of the Ivanhoe Marine Base by means of a waterway known as the Ivanhoe Canal. Texaco's written lease and the testimony at trial establish that Texaco leased the 20.14 acre tract specifically to establish a marine base to use the Ivanhoe Canal. Texaco constructed a marine base to use the Ivanhoe Canal and the navigable water access it provides. Without the Ivanhoe Canal that marine base is useless to Texaco. As the trial court recognized, partition of the Milling Tract will force Texaco to build another marine base in another location and stop using its present marine base on the Ivanhoe Canal. The Ivanhoe Canal is, clearly, indispensable to Texaco's enjoyment of the lease of the Ivanhoe Marine Base.

The evidence reflects that only the Ivanhoe Canal is indispensable for the enjoyment of Texaco's lease of the property on which the Ivanhoe Marine Base is located. Therefore, pursuant to LSA-C.C. art. 808, partition of the Ivanhoe Canal is excluded. Partition of the remainder of the Milling Tract is, however, not excluded as the partition of that property has no bearing on the enjoyment of Texaco's lease.

For the foregoing reasons, the judgment of the trial court is amended to exclude the Ivanhoe Canal from the partition by licitation. In all other respects, the judgment is affirmed. Costs of this appeal are to be shared equally between the appellant and the appellees.

AMENDED, AND AS AMENDED, AFFIRMED.

Notes and Questions

1. When you review the facts in *Ivanhoe Canal Corp. v. Bunn*, 694 So.2d 263 (La. App. 1 Cir. 1995), distinguish between Texaco's lease and its operations under the servitude of passage across the Milling Tract. Identify the crucial move made by Texaco which enabled it to advance its argument under Article 808 of the Louisiana Civil Code. What exactly is Texaco's assertion?

2. Do you agree with the court's classification of the lease as an incorporeal immovable thing? What else could it be? Note that, as we have seen in our discussion of ownership of improvements made by someone other than the landowner, a lessee's rights under a lease can be given effect against third parties and successors, just like a real right, if the lease is recorded in the public records of the parish in which the leased immovable property is located. See La. Civ. Code arts. 2681, 2695, 2712, 3338(2). Is there any other language in Article 808 of the Louisiana Civil Code that should have drawn the court's attention? Even if the lease itself is an incorporeal "thing," are Texaco's rights in the lease things that are "owned" by Texaco? Does it make sense to think of Texaco as an owner of rights in the lease when the court in *Ivanhoe*, in addition to emphasizing the correlative "rights" of both parties, went out of its way to define a lease as "a synallagmatic contract, by which one party gives to the other the enjoyment of a thing at a fixed price."

3. Identify the thing that the court ultimately finds indispensable for Texaco's use of the lease. Why does the court restrict itself in its declaration as to what cannot be partitioned?

2. Methods of Partition

In Louisiana, partition of co-owned property may be accomplished either by judgment (*judicial partition*) or by agreement (*voluntary partition*). La. Code Civ.

Proc. art. 4601. The Civil Code appears to accord a preference to voluntary partitions by specifying in the first sentence of Article 809 of the Louisiana Civil Code that the "mode of partition"—whether it is a physical partition in kind, by sale or otherwise—"may be determined by agreement of all the parties." La. Civ. Code art. 809 (1990). Sometimes courts will recognize an exchange between co-heirs as a voluntary partition. *See Driscoll v. Mazaleski*, 95 So.3d 1140, 1145–46 (La. App. 4 Cir. 2012) (upholding a voluntary partition when an amended judgment of possession was signed after the original judgment of partition had been filed in the succession of the deceased father so that one son would take over the other son's interest in the property in exchange for the other son receiving alternative consideration from the succession). In practice, if co-owners agree in advance as to the mode of partition, they are likely to fare better than they would under a partition supervised by a court. Indeed, the Civil Code provides added protection for co-owners who enter into non-judicial partitions by allowing a co-owner to rescind a partition for lesion if he fails to receive at least seventy-five percent of the fair market value of the portion he should have received for his share. La. Civ. Code art. 814 (1990).

If the co-owners cannot reach a unanimous agreement on a partition plan, the second sentence of Article 809 of the Louisiana Civil Code provides that the co-owner who wishes to exit co-ownership can demand a judicial partition. La. Civ. Code art. 809 (1990). Article 4602 of the Code of Civil Procedure adds that partition must be judicial when a co-owner is "an unrepresented absentee, minor, or mental incompetent." La. Code Civ. Proc. art. 4602(1). The presence of one of these kinds of co-owners can impose further procedural safeguards in a partition proceeding. *See, e.g, Stewart v. Ogden*, 147 So.3d 1181, 1184–86 (La. App. 4 Cir. 2014) (holding that the absence of a co-owner does not automatically invalidate a partition or affect the shares of the other co-owners, but reversing trial court judgment in partition filed by majority co-owner because trial court failed to appoint a curator to represent interests of the absent minority co-owner). *See also* La. Code Civ. Proc. arts. 4623 and 5091. Note, finally, that pursuant to Article 817 of the Louisiana Civil Code the action for partition is imprescriptible. La. Civ. Code art. 817 (1990).

Louisiana law offers three methods of partition: (1) partition in kind; (2) partition by licitation; and (3) partition by private sale. La. Civ. Code arts. 810–11 (1990). Other methods are not available. *See, e.g., Lasseigne v. Baker*, 924 So.2d 1074, 1077–78 (La. App. 5 Cir. 2006) (denying the petitioner's assertion that he should have been allowed to purchase the defendants' interests for the value set by the court-appointed appraiser, because that option is not found in the Civil Code or the Code of Civil Procedure).

Article 810 of the Louisiana Civil Code and Article 4606 of the Code of Civil Procedure govern partition in kind. A **partition in kind** is a physical division of the thing subject to partition. Although the Civil Code appears to express a preference for this method of partition, the substantive prerequisites for a partition in kind tend to limit its availability. Article 810 offers the key provision:

Art. 810. Partition in kind

The court shall decree partition in kind when the thing held in indivision is susceptible to division into as many lots of nearly equal value as there are shares and the aggregate value of all lots is not significantly lower than the value of the property in the state of indivision.

La. Civ. Code art. 810 (1990). The provision establishes two requirements for partition in kind. First, the thing in indivision must be divisible into as many lots of roughly equal value as there are shares. Second, the aggregate value of the lots after the partition must not be significantly lower than the value of the thing in indivision before the partition. Article 4606 of the Code of Civil Procedure similarly declares that a partition in kind should be ordered "unless the property is indivisible by nature or cannot conveniently be divided." La. Code Civ. Proc. art. 4606 (1960). Notice how the statutory texts differ. The standard established by the Code of Civil Procedure appears to give a court a wider margin of evaluative discretion to choose the appropriate method of partition.

Conceptually, partition in kind represents what we might call a "property rule" approach to partition. It permits each co-owner to take his or her proportionate share of the actual thing held in indivision, rather than receive a proportionate share of the proceeds from a sale, just as an owner would in the case of an involuntary expropriation. Typically, before a court will order a partition in kind, it must be convinced by testimony that the aggregate value after partition is at least roughly equal to the pre-partition value. Once this finding has been made, the process involves dividing the property into lots of equal value and allocating them randomly. Consider the following jurisprudential explanation of why partition in kind is not suitable in a case in which property with valuable water frontage was held in indivision by four siblings:

> In this case, it is obvious that the major attribute of this lot is its 50-ft water frontage. To divide this lot into four lots with water frontage would give each lot only 12 1/2 feet of water frontage. Alternatively, to divide this lot into four lots with 32 1/2 feet depths, but two lots with water frontage of 25 feet each and two lots with street frontage of 25 feet each, would seriously diminish the value of all lots, particularly those with no water frontage. It seems impossible to submit this lot to partition in kind without seriously devaluing the property.

Lasseigne v. Baker, 924 So.2d 1074, 1077 (La. App. 5 Cir. 2006) (quoting from the trial court's reasons for judgment).

Article 811 of the Louisiana Civil Code and Article 4607 of the Louisiana Code of Civil Procedure govern partition by licitation and partition by private sale. Importantly, the party seeking partition by licitation or private sale has the burden of proving that the property cannot be partitioned in kind. In the course of *partition by licitation*, the thing is sold at a properly advertised and noticed public auction and adjudicated to the highest bidder. La. Code Civ. Proc. art. 4607 (1960). Thereafter, the proceeds of the sale are distributed pro rata to the co-owners according to their fractional interests. La. Civ. Code art. 811 (1990). The third method is *partition by private sale*. Article 811 appears to give courts discretion to avoid a public auction and instead order a private sale, which is far more likely to result in all co-owners receiving fair market value for their shares in indivision.

In contrast to a partition in kind, partition by licitation or partition by private sale offer what we might call a "liability rule" approach to partition. The co-owner is divested of his or her ownership interest in the thing. In exchange, he receives monetary compensation, much like a tort plaintiff receives in a successful tort suit or a condemnee receives in an expropriation proceeding. In response to criticism by scholars and advocates that this kind of forced partition may not be adequate for landowners who own rural land in highly fragmented shares of co-ownership, the Uniform Law Commission (also known as the National Conference of Commissioners on Uniform State Laws) has proposed an alternative solution under the Uniform Partition of Heirs Property Act (UPHPA) (2010). Below is the Uniform Law Commission's description of the UPHPA and its purpose:

> The Uniform Partition of Heirs Property Act addresses the issue of tenancy-in-common land ownership, a type of joint ownership without rights of survivorship. When there is no right of survivorship, the death of a tenant-in-common can trigger an action to partition the land to satisfy the deceased tenant's heirs. In a partition, the land is sold to satisfy tenant-in-common interests, often in a sale that does not meet market value. The Act establishes remedies for use in those partition actions involving heirs property. The remedies are designed to help those who own heirs property to maintain ownership of their property when possible or to insure at the very least that any court-ordered sale of the property is conducted under commercially reasonable circumstances that will protect the owners from losing substantial wealth upon the sale of their property.

Uniform Law Commission, Acts, Partition of Heirs Property Act, at http://www .uniformlaws.org/Act.aspx?title=Partition%20of%20Heirs%20Property%20Act. For more background and a thorough discussion of the problem of forced partition sales and their effect on African-American farm ownership in the United States, see Thomas W. Mitchell, *From Reconstruction to Deconstruction: Undermining Black Landownership, Political Independence, and Community through Partition Sales of Tenancies in Common*, 95 N.W. U. L. Rev. 505 (2001). *See also* Thomas W. Mitchell et al., *Class, Race, and the "Double Discount"*, 37 Fla. St. U. L. Rev. 589 (2010) (providing a deep analysis of factors that have contributed to the decline in African-American rural landownership). In recent years, the UPHPA has been enacted by at least eleven state legislatures and has been introduced in eleven more. *See* https:// www.uniformlaws.org/committees/community-home?CommunityKey=50724584 -e808-4255-bc5d-8ea4e588371d (last visited June 17, 2019). Is it time for Louisiana to enact a version of the UPHPA?

Perhaps in response to some of the same concerns that had motivated the Uniform Law Commission to develop the UPHPA, the Louisiana Legislature has created a statutory scheme that has the potential to override Article 811 of the Louisiana Civil Code when a co-owner who owns a small share in immovable property seeks to force partition by licitation or by private sale. Here is the full provision, which was enacted in 2003:

La. Rev. Stat. 9:1113. Partition of immovable property; minority interest; private sale; appraisal

A. If immovable property is susceptible of partition by licitation or private sale pursuant to Civil Code Article 811 and a co-owner or co-owners owning an aggregate interest of fifteen percent or less of the immovable property petition the court to partition the property, the court shall allow the remaining co-owners to purchase at private sale the petitioners' shares at a price determined by a court-appointed appraiser.

B.(1) Each remaining co-owner shall only be entitled to purchase a portion of the property being sold equal to his pro rata share. Each remaining co-owner shall have thirty days from the date the last defendant is served with the petition to partition or thirty days from receipt of written notice, sent by certified mail or commercial courier, from a co-owner waiving his right to purchase, whichever is earlier, in which to file a notice to exercise his option to purchase his pro rata share of the property being sold. The filed notice, which shall be served on all parties, shall be considered a fully binding contract to purchase the property.

(2) Upon the lapse of the thirtieth day, any co-owner who has failed to timely exercise his option to purchase the property shall relinquish his right to purchase his pro rata share. The relinquishment of the right to purchase shall inure to the benefit of the remaining purchasing co-owners, who shall then be entitled to purchase, by pro rata share, the shares made available by the co-owner who relinquished his right to purchase. Each remaining purchasing co-owner shall have an additional ten days from the previous deadline to file his notice to purchase the relinquished shares.

(3) The procedures provided in this Subsection shall continue until there are no outstanding forfeited shares; however, the court may use its discretion in rounding the shares of the co-owners to the nearest hundredth share.

(4) The initial calculation of the pro rata share in Subsection B of this Section shall be based on the percentage of ownership of potential purchasing co-owners, excluding the petitioning co-owners. When a potential purchasing co-owner relinquishes his right to purchase, the pro rata share shall be recalculated to include only the remaining purchasing co-owners, excluding the relinquishing co-owners. Once a purchasing co-owner relinquishes his right to purchase his pro rata share, he shall not be entitled to file any subsequent notice to purchase in the pending action.

La. Rev. Stat. § 9:1113 (2003). This statute effectively furnishes co-owners a right of first refusal to buy out a minority co-owner or minority co-owners who petition for partition by licitation or partition by private sale. The right of first refusal is triggered when the petitioning co-owner(s) hold an aggregate interest of fifteen percent or less of the immovable. How is this buy-out accomplished? What is the purpose behind this law? Does the statute achieve that purpose? Note that the window within which co-owners must take action to exercise their rights under this statute is not long. *Madden Contr. Co. v. Harris*, 113 So.3d 466, 471 (La. App. 2 Cir. 2013) (holding that co-owner waived the right to seek private sale under La. Rev. Stat. § 9:1113 by having waited almost two years to file motion for private sale).

3. Effects of Partition

Partition embodies the magic wand for localizing each co-owner's interest. Partition in kind makes each co-owner full owner of the part assigned to him or her; and partition by licitation or private sale allocates to each co-owner a share of the proceeds of the respective public auction or private sale that corresponds to his or her original share. Under Article 812 of the Louisiana Civil Code, real rights (like mortgages, liens, or servitudes) burdening the *entire thing* are not affected by a partition, regardless of whether the partition is in kind or by licitation. La. Civ. Code art. 812 (1990). Conversely, when a real right burdens the *fractional share* of a co-owner and a *partition in kind* occurs, that real right then attaches to the physical portion of the thing allotted to the person whose share was previously burdened. La. Civ. Code art. 813 (1990). After a *partition by licitation*, a mortgage, lien or privilege that burdened the co-owner's share before the partition attaches to that co-owner's share of the proceeds after partition. La. Civ. Code art. 815 (1990).

* * *

Consider the following decision. It reveals how, in practice, courts often order partition by licitation as the exit route from ownership in indivision even though the law, on its face, appears to favor partition in kind. In this case, partition by licitation has significant consequences for an asset other than the land held in indivision — a house built by one of the co-owners on the land held in indivision. Could the court have fashioned a partition that would have been more equitable to both of the respective co-owners?

Ark-La-Miss Timber Co., Inc. v. Wilkins

833 So.2d 1154 (La. App. 2 Cir. 2002)

STEWART, Judge. Ark-La-Miss Timber Co., Inc., ("ALM"), filed this suit for partition of 1,286 acres of land in Caldwell Parish. ALM and Paul B. Wilkins are co-owners of the property. Wilkins filed a reconventional demand to be recognized as separate owner of a log cabin located on the property. The trial court found in favor of Wilkins with regard to ownership of the cabin, but ordered that the property be partitioned by licitation. Wilkins appeals those portions of the judgment ordering partition by licitation and ordering him to pay all costs. In answer to the appeal, ALM seeks reversal of the finding that Wilkins owns the cabin. For the reasons expressed herein, we amend the trial court's judgment, and affirm as amended.

Facts

In 1983, Wilkins, Judge Ronald L. Lewellyan, and Quinton May purchased 1,286 acres of land in Caldwell Parish from International Paper for a total price of $525,000. Lewellyan and Wilkins later bought out May's share, and Lewellyan transferred his share to ALM, a land and timber management company of which he is president and sole shareholder. Consequently, Wilkins and ALM co-own the entire acreage. . . .

For purposes of this opinion and consistent with the testimony and evidence at trial, references may be made to the east half and the west half of the property.

The property is located in the Castor Creek flood basin. It is traversed by creeks and consists of bottomland hardwood areas and swampy areas. It is subject to flooding during rainy periods. Much of the land, particularly in the eastern half of the property, can be reached only by four-wheeler. The land is used primarily for recreational purposes, such as hunting and fishing, and for timber production. After purchasing the property, the parties sold timber, which was thinned or select cut from throughout the property, for $175,000.

In 1988, Wilkins built a log cabin on a ridge located on the west half of the property. Wilkins also had water and utilities connected to the cabin at his own expense. The cabin was regularly used by Wilkins, Lewellyan, and others over the years. At the time of trial, Wilkins was living in the cabin with his family.

The only legal route of access to the property is by way of a logging road built by International Paper in 1970. This road runs onto the west half of the property and then forks to the northwest and southeast. The northwest fork goes to the cabin and can generally be used for vehicular travel; the southeast fork goes into the east half of the property and includes a series of bridges built by the co-owners over the years. These bridges support four-wheeler travel only. The northwest fork has been better maintained over the years than the southeast fork, which has fallen into some disrepair due to areas and culverts that have been washed out and other areas that have become overgrown with foliage. The parties have regularly accessed the east half of the property by way of a private road owned by Plum Creek Timber Company. The Plum Creek road is located off Louisiana Highway 4 and runs into the northeast section of the property. However, the parties do not have any legal right to use this road, and Plum Creek denied a request by Wilkins made prior to trial to furnish a right of way.

The legal dispute arose when ALM filed a petition seeking a judicial partition. In answer, Wilkins stated that he too desired judicial partition of the co-owned property. He also asserted a reconventional demand to be recognized as separate owner of the cabin. The court appointed an expert, Merlin Smith, to survey the property and timber thereon and to provide a report as to his views on an equitable division of the property. Smith submitted his report to the court, but this report was not submitted as evidence at trial. Wilkins also commissioned Smith to perform a timber cruise of the property. The data from the cruise was used by Wilkins' expert appraiser to come up with a proposed equitable division of the property for trial purposes. . . .

On November 20, 2001, the trial judge rendered written reasons for judgment. The trial judge recognized Wilkins' separate ownership of the cabin. The trial judge noted that Wilkins built and paid for the cabin. In addition, the trial judge found no clear understanding between the parties as to any conveyance of an ownership interest in the cabin. In accordance with expert testimony, the trial judge valued the improvement at $69,500. While noting partition in kind to be favored under the law, the trial judge concluded it could not be done in a manner equitable to both parties. Two factors complicated a partition in kind. First was the presence of a road for vehicular access and a utility right of way on the west half of the property only. Second was the location of the cabin on the west half, the ownership of which necessitated a sale of the entire property and compensation of the cabin's value to its owner from the proceeds. The trial judge concluded that use of the same road by owners of the west half and east half would not be feasible due to problems that would arise in maintaining the road. A judgment in accordance with these reasons was rendered on January 7, 2002, ordering partition by licitation with proceeds of the sale to be attributed first to costs of the sale, then to payment of the value of the cabin to Wilkins, and then to be divided equally between ALM and Wilkins. Costs were assessed against Wilkins.

Wilkins filed a motion for a new trial contending that the property could be divided in kind with both parties having equal access and utilities, that the trial judge erroneously considered the separate ownership of the cabin in its analysis, that the judgment failed to appoint a notary as required by La. C.C.P. art. 4605, and that the judgment improperly assessed all costs to him. The trial judge granted the motion as to the notary issue and appointed a notary as required by law. The motion was denied as to all other issues raised. Wilkins then appealed the merits of the partition by licitation, the denial of the motion to supplement the record, and the assessment of costs to him. ALM answered the appeal to assert error as to the recognition of Wilkins' separate ownership of the cabin.

Discussion

Ownership of the Cabin

ALM argues that the trial court erred in failing to consider the presumption of La. C.C. art. 491 and the numerous exhibits showing payments over the years, including a one time payment of $10,000, of expenses associated with repair and maintenance of the cabin. ALM contends that the presumption and evidence requires reversal of the trial court's finding that Wilkins owns the house. We disagree with this contention.

La. C.C. art. 804 provides, in relevant part, "Substantial alterations or substantial improvements to the thing held in indivision may be undertaken only with the consent of all the owners." La. C.C. art. 491, referred to by ALM, sets forth the general principle that buildings or other constructions permanently attached to the ground may belong to a person other than the owner of the ground, but are presumed to belong to the owner of the ground absent a filed instrument evidencing separate ownership. However, a more specific provision governs ownership of improvements. La. C.C. art. 493 provides, in relevant part, "Buildings, other constructions permanently attached to the ground, and plantings made on the land of another with his consent belong to him who made them." Comment B of the Revision Comments of 1979 states:

> "(B) Buildings, other constructions permanently attached to the ground, and plantings made on the land of another with his consent, as by a lessee, a co-owner, a purchaser under a contract to sell, or a precarious possessor, belong to him who made them. Such separate ownership may be asserted toward third persons when it is evidenced by an instrument filed for registry in the conveyance records of the parish in which the immovable is located."

This provision governs ownership of the cabin between the co-owners, since the cabin was built by Wilkins with the consent and knowledge of ALM. Moreover, the testimony of the parties supports the factual conclusion that Wilkins is sole owner of the cabin.

Wilkins built the cabin in 1988. He testified that he asked Lewellyan if he had any objections to him building a camp on the land, and Lewellyan had none. Nothing in Lewellyan's testimony disputes this claim. Accordingly, we find that Wilkins built the cabin with co-owner consent.

Wilkins testified that he built the cabin at his own expense and spent about $78,000 on construction and an additional $4,000 getting utilities to the site. Wilkins was involved in every phase of construction and was on the building site every day. Both Wilkins and Lewellyan agreed that they met with another individual to select a building site that would not flood. However, Wilkins adamantly denied that he ever discussed granting Lewellyan or ALM an ownership interest in the cabin.

Wilkins testified that once the cabin was built, he gave keys to Lewellyan and others to use the cabin as they pleased. One individual with access to the cabin was Buddy Eikert. According to Wilkins, Eikert regularly used the cabin and paid two-thirds of the expenses associated with maintenance from 1989 through 1993. During this time, Lewellyan also used the cabin, but did not pay any of the expenses. Sometime in 1993, Eikert and Lewellyan had a falling out, so Eikert was no longer allowed on the land co-owned by ALM and Wilkins. Wilkins then began forwarding bills to Lewellyan with requests that he pay half of the expenses, such as insurance payments, utilities, and upkeep on the cabin. Thereafter, Wilkins and Lewellyan, through ALM, divided expenses associated with the cabin.

Lewellyan admitted that he paid no part of the costs associated with building the camp or establishing utility services. Nevertheless, he claims that Wilkins intended the camp to belong to both of them, despite the lack of any documentation showing an ownership interest on the part of either Lewellyan or ALM. Lewellyan used the camp and had a bedroom which he furnished. However, Lewellyan could not show that he contributed toward any expenses until 1993.

Lewellyan claimed that his ownership of the cabin derived from discussions wherein Wilkins mentioned giving him an additional forty acres due to his help in securing a case from which Wilkins made a substantial amount of money. Wilkins admitted discussing the possibility of giving Lewellyan an extra forty acres, possibly in the event of a partition, in gratitude for the case from which he profited. However, Wilkins denied that this possibility had anything to do with the cabin and testified that the discussion regarding the forty acres had not been mentioned in about fifteen years.

Lewellyan also bases his ownership claim on a $10,000 payment made by ALM to Wilkins in October 1996. However, nothing in the record relates this payment to the purchase of an ownership interest in the cabin. While Lewellyan testified that he believed the payment to be a settlement of all issues relating to cost and ownership of the cabin, the totality of the testimony indicates that the payment was to settle expenses associated with maintenance of the cabin and work done on the property.

Based on the evidence presented, we find no error in the trial court's recognition of Wilkins' separate ownership of the cabin. Wilkins built the cabin at his own expense and allowed others to use and enjoy it. In return, those using the cabin contributed to expenses associated with its maintenance. Neither the expenses paid by ALM since 1993 nor the payment of $10,000 establishes ownership of the cabin on the part of ALM or Lewellyan. This assignment of error by ALM is without merit.

Partition of the Property

Unless otherwise provided by law or a juridical act, no one may be compelled to hold a thing in indivision with another, and a co-owner has a right to demand partition of a thing held in indivision. La. C.C. art. 807; McNeal v. McNeal, 98-1586 (La. App. 3d Cir. 3/31/99), 732 So.2d 663.

The law generally favors partition in kind unless the property is indivisible by nature or cannot be conveniently divided. La. C.C.P. art. 4606; *Devco Inc. v. Richey*, 30,319 (La. App. 2d Cir. 2/25/98), 707 So.2d 161; *Marsh Cattle Farms v. Vining*, 30,156 (La. App. 2d Cir. 1/23/98), 707 So.2d 111, *writ denied*, 98-0478 (La. 4/24/98), 717 So.2d 1167. Property cannot be conveniently divided when the division would result in a diminution of its value, or loss or inconvenience to one of the owners. *Devco Inc. v. Richey, supra*; *Marsh Cattle Farms v. Vining, supra*; *Birdwell v. Jeffery*, 486 So.2d 1094 (La. App. 2d Cir. 1986). In kind division shall be decreed when "the thing held in indivision is susceptible to division into as many lots of nearly equal value as there are shares and the aggregate value of all lots is not significantly lower than the value of the property in the state of indivision." La. C.C. art. 810.

The party seeking partition by licitation bears the burden of proving that the property cannot be divided in kind. *Marsh Cattle Farms v. Vining, supra; Birdwell v. Jeffery, supra.* In addition, whether immovable property should be divided in kind or by licitation is a question of fact to be decided by the trial court. *Marsh Cattle Farms v. Vining, supra; Loupe v. Bybee,* 570 So.2d 31 (La. App. 3d Cir. 1990), *writ denied,* 572 So.2d 94 (La. 1991).

ALM sought partition by licitation. Wilkins sought partition in kind. Accordingly, the burden was on ALM to prove that the property could not be partitioned in kind. To meet this burden, ALM presented testimony to show that the property could not be partitioned in kind due to differences in the western and eastern halves which would preclude division into lots of nearly equal value and would result in a diminution in value and inconvenience to the owners. Wilkins produced evidence to prove that the property could be divided into lots of nearly equal value. It is apparent from the reasons for judgment that the trial judge determined that the property could not be conveniently divided due to inadequate vehicular access and the location of utilities and the cabin on the west half of the property. We cannot say that the trial judge was clearly wrong or manifestly erroneous in making this factual determination.

The evidence establishes that there is one route of legal access to the property. This is by way of a logging road built by International Paper in 1970. Testimony established that parts of the road and some culverts have been washed out. Where the road forks, the road along the western fork is suitable for some vehicular travel, but the road along the eastern fork is not. A series of creeks flows through the east section of the property. Wilkins and others built a series of bridges along the eastern fork of the road; however, these bridges are only suitable for use by four-wheelers. Moreover, many of the bridges are in need of repair, and the road is practically impassable during times of heavy rainfall.

The divisions proposed by Wilkins at trial placed the entirety of the road leading to the fork in the western half of the property. As such, the owner of the western half would possibly be compelled to grant a right of passage to the owner of the eastern half as provided in La. C.C. art. 694. Furnishing a right of passage would not necessarily alleviate the inconvenience of access associated with an in kind division. In *Hughes v. Heirs of Cain,* 268 So.2d 149 (La. App. 1st Cir. 1972), *writ refused,* 271 So.2d 259 (La. 1973), the court found division in kind to be inconvenient where landowners would acquire remote areas inaccessible except by crossing another's property. The court concluded that the situation would result in economic loss, inconvenience, and legal difficulties. Also, in *Doescher v. Powers,* 447 So.2d 1171 (La. App. 3d Cir. 1984), the court rejected an in kind division that would have required one owner to grant a right of way to the other owner. The court concluded that dividing the property so as to require a right of way would be an inconvenience to the owners that would prevent a partition in kind. The trial judge in the case sub judice concluded that it would not be feasible for the owners to use the same road due to problems that would certainly arise regarding routine maintenance and expenses. We agree.

Additionally, we find no error in the trial court's denial of Wilkins' motion to reopen and supplement the record with additional proposed divisions to address the access issue. This was a matter within the trial court's discretion, and we find no abuse of that discretion in this instance. Our review of the proffered evidence shows that the proposed divisions, would make the International Paper road the property line up to the fork. However, this would not alleviate the inconvenience that would result from the parties sharing the road, nor would it address the fact that the party receiving the west half of the property would have vehicular access, whereas the party receiving the east half would be largely limited to travel by way of four-wheelers on a road that has not been maintained.

In addition, utility lines are currently available only to the cabin located on the west half of the property. These were added by Wilkins when he built the cabin. Wilkins' separate ownership of the cabin is also a factor properly considered by the trial court in determining whether property cannot be conveniently divided. When property is divided in kind, lots of equal or nearly equal value are determined by experts and then drawn by chance by the co-owners. Neither the judge nor the experts can allocate a specific part to one of the owners. *Tri-State Concrete Company v. Stephens*, 406 So.2d 205 (La. 1981), *Marsh Cattle Farms, supra*. Under this procedure, Wilkins, who was living in the cabin with his family at the time of trial, would not be ensured of receiving the lot on which his cabin is located. His rights would then have to be determined under the Louisiana Civil Code articles pertaining to accession as it relates to immovables. In *Loupe v. Bybee*, supra, a residence on the property to be divided was a factor in finding that the property was not subject to division in kind. As stated in *Loupe v. Bybee, supra*:

It is not necessary to produce proof of the indivisibility of property in kind in order that it might be partitioned by licitation where the record shows that the nature and condition of the property is such that it cannot be conveniently divided in kind. *Kilbourne v. Hosea*, 19 So.2d 279 (La. App. 1st Cir. 1944).

Conflicting expert testimony was also presented to the trial court. ALM presented the testimony of Robert W. Lowe, Jr., who qualified as an expert real estate appraiser. Lowe's opinion was that the property could not be divided in kind or in equal value due to the presence of the utilities and cabin on the west half of the property and access issues, including the absence of legal access on the east side of the property and the condition of the International Paper road. Merlin Smith, who was the court appointed expert and who was hired by Wilkins to conduct a timber cruise, opined that the property could not be divided in kind without some diminution in value. Finally, Don Lockard, an expert real estate appraiser who testified on behalf of Wilkins, was of the opinion that the land could be divided into two parcels of nearly equal value. Lockard did not believe access and improvements to be factors that would significantly impact the market value of the property. It is within the trial court's broad discretion to determine the effect and weight of expert testimony. *Williams v. City of Monroe*, 27,065 (La. App. 2d Cir. 7/3/95), 658 So.2d 820, *writ denied*, 95-1998, 95-2017 (La. 12/15/95), 664 So.2d 451, 452. By concluding that the property could not conveniently be divided in kind, the trial court obviously gave greater weight and effect to some of the expert testimony. This was within the trial court's discretion.

Considering the conflicting expert testimony and other evidence at trial, we can find no error in trial court's determination that the property cannot be partitioned in kind. As such, we affirm the trial court's judgment ordering partition by licitation. . . .

Conclusion

For the reasons discussed, the judgment of the trial court is affirmed except as to that part of the judgment assessing all costs against Wilkins. That portion of the judgment is hereby amended to divide costs equally between the parties. Costs associated with this appeal are also assessed equally between the parties.

AMENDED IN PART, and AFFIRMED AS AMENDED.

Notes and Questions

1. In the first portion of the decision, *Ark-La-Miss Timber Co., Inc. v. Wilkins*, 833 So.2d 1154 (La. App. 2 Cir. 2002), the court discusses whether the trial court erred when it determined that Wilkins owned the cabin in sole and separate ownership. What are the legal rules for determining the ownership of improvements made to the land of another? Who is the maker and who owns the land in this case? Recall *Marcellous v. David*, 253 So.2d 383 (La. App. 3 Cir. 1971).

2. In the second portion of the decision, the court analyzes whether the trial court acted within its discretion when ordering partition by licitation rather than partition in kind. The decision of whether land should be divided in kind or by licitation is a question of fact to be decided by the trial court. *Lazarus Trading Co., LLC v. Unopened Succession of Washington*, 201 So.3d 989, 995 (La. App. 2 Cir. 2016). In general, courts enjoy great discretion as to the manner and conditions of effecting partition. La. Code Civ. Proc. art. 4605. When at least one owner is an absentee, property may be partitioned by licitation regardless of whether it is susceptible to partition in kind. La. Code Civ. Proc. art. 4621 (1960). *Madden Contr. Co. v. Harris*, 113 So.3d 466, 470 (La. App. 2 Cir. 2013).

3. What does Article 810 of the Louisiana Civil Code require for partition in kind? What does Article 4606 of the Code of Civil Procedure say? Notice how the court in *Wilkins*, after identifying both provisions, veers away from the arithmetic exercise laid out in Article 810. It frames the discussion in terms of the inconveniences associated with a partition in kind. Notice the two principal inconveniences suggested by the court if the division of the property into a western and an eastern half were ordered. First, only one legal and properly maintained access route, which comes from the west, would be available. Could this defect be cured by burdening the western half of the property with a servitude of passage in favor of the eastern half? Second, the western half would boast an improvement plus utility lines. The court hastens to explain that, in light of the draw of straws it believes is required

in partitions in kind, Wilkins, who owned the cabin separately from his fractional share in the land, would not be assured to receive the western half. *See generally* FRANK L. MARAIST, 1A LA. CIVIL LAW TREATISE: CIVIL PROCEDURE—SPECIAL PROCEEDINGS § 9.7, at 174 (2005). Could a creative court order some form of equalization to be paid to the recipient of the eastern half?

4. For examples of appellate court deference to trial court findings that partition in licitation is more practical, more efficient, and more just than partition in kind, see *Lazarus Trading Co., LLC v. Unopened Succession of Washington*, 201 So.3d 989, 995–96 (La. App. 2 Cir. 2016) (affirming the trial court's determination that 192 acres of rural land could not be partitioned in kind while maintaining present value of undivided property in case when the parcel was owned in indivision by 87 different owners, consisted of unimproved patchwork quilt of boundaries with center carved out, was crossed by various roads, highways and railroad, and included proposed lots that were only accessible by off road vehicle or were burdened with non-marketable existing trees); *Maxie v. Maxie*, 157 So.3d 1248, 1251–53 (La. App. 3 Cir. 2015 (upholding trial court's order of partition by licitation based on technical expertise in the record stating that: (1) the extant utility right of way and the overall topography of the twenty acres precluded a financially feasible partition in kind; and (2) a partition in kind would defeat the highest and best use of the acreage— timber growth and recreation); *Broussard v. Stutes Farms, L.L.C.*, 134 So.3d 226, 228–30 (La. App. 3 Cir. 2014) (affirming the trial court's determination that (1) the 120-acre and five-acre parcels used primarily for duck hunting were not susceptible to partition in kind due to the impossibility of dividing the land in a way that would allow both parties to hunt on the respective portions; and (2) even if such a division were possible, one portion would require a right of way over the other); *Mitchell v. Cooper*, 121 So.3d 736, 739–42 (La. App. 2 Cir. 2013) (affirming the trial court's decision to order partition by licitation of three commonly owned tracts in light of: (1) expert testimony as to size and shape of tracts, soil composition and impact of providing road division indicating that partition in kind would result in diminution in value; and (2) the fact of some of the co-owners owning substantial acreage in same area not being enough to establish unequal bidding power so as to require the partition be accomplished with the benefit of appraisal).

5. Immovables are not the only kind of property posing partition issues. In *Kite v. Kite*, 62 So.3d 313 (La. App. 3 Cir. 2011), one co-owner (Alan) filed a suit to partition a life insurance policy held in indivision with another co-owner (Jeffrey). Jeffrey objected arguing that a forced partition would compel him to cash-in the policy against his will and in violation of La. Rev. Stat. 22:912(E) ("No person shall be compelled to exercise any rights, powers, options, or privileges under any policy, contract, or education savings account depositor's agreement"). Alan countered that nobody can be compelled to hold a thing in indivision unless the law says otherwise. Judge Painter, writing for the majority, held that a life insurance policy is subject to partition as between the co-beneficiaries:

We find nothing in the insurance code preventing such an action. . . .

The insurance policy is attached to and made a part of the petition in the present case. Therefore, it is proper for us to consider the policy provisions in our determination as to whether a cause of action exists. The insurance policy at issue herein contains a partial surrender provision. There is nothing to prevent Alan from surrendering his fifty percent ownership in the policy and receiving half of the accumulated value, leaving the balance for Jeffrey. The policy provides that there is no surrender penalty after fifteen policy years, and we note that policy has been in effect well over fifteen years. This would not force Jeffrey to take any action and, therefore, would not violate La. R.S.22:912(E).

Kite, 62 So.3d at 315. What is the consequence of the majority holding? Once Alan has cashed in his portion of the policy, does this mean Jeffrey likewise has to cash out? Or can he not continue his portion in the policy and accumulate more value? According to the dissent written by Judge Genovese, a cause of action for a partition of a life insurance policy did not exist:

Life insurance policies are sui generis; thus, they are governed by the particular provisions of the Louisiana Insurance Code as opposed to the general provisions of the Louisiana Civil Code. . . . The majority opines that it "find[s] nothing in the insurance code preventing such an action" for partition. However, in my view, La.R.S. 22:912(E) . . . precludes an action for partition of an insurance policy.

Id. at 316. Are you more persuaded by the majority or the dissent? Is their disagreement ultimately one about statutory construction?

Other kinds of incorporeal property are also susceptible to partition. *See, e.g, Leblanc v. Elam*, 266 So.3d 935, 937–38 (La. App. 1 Cir. 2018) (holding that ex-wife's petition for partition of retirement benefits had not prescribed when petition alleged that post-divorce extrajudicial partition of community property did not include partition of retirement benefits because right to partition is imprescriptible under Article 817 of the Louisiana Civil Code).

Problem

Andrew Anderson and Beth Bergeron are the two adult children of Charles Anderson. Charles died in December 2015. In his valid will, Charles bequeathed a 2400 square foot house located at 214 Milagro Street in New Orleans to Andrew and Beth in undivided ownership and in equal shares. When Charles purchased the house ten years earlier, Charles took out a thirty-year, purchase money loan to buy the property. He secured the debt by granting a mortgage on the property to a local bank. Andrew is a free-lance writer and photographer. He lives in New Orleans, Louisiana. Beth is a cardiologist with a thriving practice in Metairie, Louisiana.

After Charles's succession was completed and Andrew and Beth jointly assumed the remaining mortgage indebtedness on the house, Andrew moved into the house. He set up a writing and photography studio for himself in the house. Moreover,

Andrew made substantial improvements to the kitchen and one of the bathrooms, using his own labor and paying for the materials and furnishings with his own savings.

Andrew also has a twelve-year old child, Denise, from a previous marriage. Andrew and his ex-wife have joint custody of Denise who spends approximately half of the week and every other weekend with Andrew in the house. Andrew has fitted out one of the spare bedrooms in the house for Denise, which she likes very much.

In the back of the house there is a separate unit, with its own separate entrance, a small kitchen and a separate bathroom. Andrew and Beth agreed to lease out this small unit to tenants (ideally, law students or medical students). They further agreed that they would use the rental income: (1) to pay the annual property taxes; (2) to cover the premiums on the insurance policies for the house; and (3) to continue paying down the mortgage indebtedness on the house (all of which are wrapped into a monthly escrow payment required by the bank).

Although the rental income derived from renting out the back apartment is not sufficient to pay all of the monthly mortgage note, insurance premiums and property taxes owed, it currently accounts for about 50% of those total expenses. Andrew and Beth agreed to split equally the responsibility for paying the additional amount owed to maintain the escrow balance with the bank. However, when Andrew has a slow month or two without much revenue coming in from his writing and photography, Beth has customarily paid the remaining amount owed to keep the escrow account in balance each month.

Recently, Beth has approached Andrew. She says that she and Andrew need to spend $60,000 immediately to replace the entire roof on the house, to switch out a number of deteriorated window frames, and to conduct some important electrical repairs. Beth asked a contractor to inspect the roof, windows and electrical wiring. Her contractor informed Beth that these repairs should be undertaken immediately to prevent a major failure should a storm or hurricane hit New Orleans and to reduce the risk of a fire in the house.

Andrew does not believe these repairs are necessary. He asked a contractor friend of his to inspect the house. Andrew's contractor has told him that the roof will last for another ten years at least, that the window frames are fine, and that the electrical wiring, though old, is still up to code.

Beth, who has substantial savings, could pay for all of the repairs herself. However, she insists that Andrew pay for half of the repairs. Andrew has very little savings as he used a good bit of his savings to pay for the materials and furnishings when the kitchen and bathroom in the house were renovated. Therefore, he does not want to undertake any of the repairs, let alone pay for them.

Andrew has come to see you for advice. Please advise Andrew with respect to the following questions:

(1) Is Andrew obligated to contribute $30,000 towards the repair of the roof, the window frames and the electrical wiring?

(2) If Andrew declines to make the requested contribution, what could Beth do in response? Conversely, what could Andrew do? What are the risks associated with those measures? Do you have any alternative suggestions for addressing this dispute?

(3) What will happen if Andrew (or for that matter Beth) demands a partition of the house? Keep in mind that Andrew would like to remain living in the house at Milagro Street. Given his current income, he could not afford such a nice house, which serves as his home office for his free-lance writing, as his photography studio, and as a home for his daughter Denise when she lives with Andrew. What will likely happen if a partition occurs? How will this affect your advice with respect to the other issues above?

Chapter 12

Usufruct

Usufruct ranks among the most distinctive institutions of Louisiana property law. It is rooted in Roman law and in the French Civil Code. In countries following the common law tradition, the closest analogue is the "life estate" which serves many of the same functions as the institution of usufruct. Life estates, however, have become less important in the United States because of the flexibility and versatility of the trust. In Louisiana, by contrast, the usufruct continues to play a vital role in contemporary property law.

This chapter overviews the structural role of the usufruct in Louisiana property law, surveys the ways to establish a usufruct and explores the general principles underlying the institution of usufruct. We also examine the day-to-day relationship between the usufructuary and naked owner—the two primary participants in a usufruct relationship.

Finally, this chapter asks you to assume the position of legal advisor tasked with the challenge of providing counsel to a usufructuary or naked owner who seeks guidance with regard to many specific problems implicating the law of usufruct. Despite the importance of several foundational judicial decisions interpreting the law of usufruct, this portion of the Civil Code tends to produce fewer reported judicial decisions than other parts of the Civil Code we have studied. Consequently, a Louisiana lawyer must be able to solve usufruct problems by construing the applicable articles of the Civil Code and as well as the pertinent revision comments, often without resort to extensive jurisprudential gloss. Further, a Louisiana lawyer must advise clients about the advantages and disadvantages of creating a usufruct relationship in the first place, as opposed to some other kind of property law relationship—for example, one governed by the law of co-ownership or trust. Therefore, this chapter frequently asks you to consider how someone's rights and obligations would be different if a co-ownership or trust relationship had been created rather than a usufruct.

A. Dismemberments of Ownership: The Place of Usufruct in the Civil Code

The institution of usufruct holds a distinctive place in the architecture of the Civil Code. As you recall, a personal right under Louisiana law is a right or legal power that a person has against another person to demand some kind of performance—usually to give something, do something, or not to do something—from that other person. We typically call the persons involved the obligee and obligor or the creditor and debtor. Personal rights are governed by the law of obligations.

A real right, on the other hand, is a right that a person has with respect to a thing, whether that thing is immovable or movable, corporeal or incorporeal. Real rights are the focus of property law. Recall that Article 476 of the Civil Code established our initial road map of real rights in Louisiana Law:

Art. 476. Rights in things

One may have various rights in things:

1. Ownership;

2. Personal and predial servitudes; and

3. Such other real rights as the law allows.

La. Civ. Code art. 476 (1978). Up to this point, we have been focused almost entirely on the first real right enumerated in Article 476: ownership. We have examined the kinds of things that are susceptible to private and public ownership, how one can acquire and voluntarily transfer ownership, how accession works as a cause and effect of ownership, how one can lose ownership to another through acquisitive prescription or protect ownership through real actions, and, finally, how ownership can be shared among multiple persons through ownership in indivision.

With this chapter we begin to examine the other real rights enumerated in Article 476—personal and predial servitudes and other real rights allowed by law. Many Louisiana lawyers speak of the "permissible dismemberments of ownership." La. Civ. Code art. 477 rev. cmt. (d) (1978). Louisiana law allows a person to take the constitutive elements of ownership outlined in Article 477 of the Civil Code—the right to use a thing, to enjoy its fruits, and to dispose of it (*usus, fructus* and *abusus*)—and reconfigure them in new forms to create real rights other than ownership. The remainder of this casebook discusses personal and predial servitudes as well as building restrictions (charges akin to predial servitudes).

Other kinds of real rights are recognized elsewhere in the Civil Code and in Louisiana law. These include the mortgage, certain recorded leases and mineral rights generally. The mortgage is governed by Title 22 of Book III of the Civil Code. *See* La. Civ. Code art. 3278 *et seq.* (1991). Although mortgages are occasionally addressed in this and subsequent chapters, they are primarily the subject of courses covering security devices under Louisiana law. While the contract of lease establishes only personal rights and obligations between a lessor and lessee, La. Civ. Code art. 2668 (2004), it acquires characteristics that make it function like a real right when it is recorded in the public records and becomes effective against a third party who acquires the property subject to the lease. La. Civ. Code art. 3338 (2005). With a few important exceptions, however, leases are addressed in courses specifically focused on sales and leases in Louisiana. Finally, mineral rights are classified as real rights under Louisiana law. La. Civ. Code art. 476 rev. cmt. (d) (1978). They are governed by the Louisiana Mineral Code. With a few important exceptions noted in this chapter, they are generally beyond the scope of this book.

Article 478 of the Civil Code is the first provision to invoke the institution of usufruct. It tells us that the right of ownership "may be subject to a resolutory condition, and it may be burdened with a real right in favor of another person as allowed by law." La. Civ. Code art. 478 (1979). That article continues by providing that "[t]he ownership of a thing burdened with a usufruct is designated as naked ownership." *Id.* The provision thus reiterates what has long been recognized under Louisiana law: that a person's ownership of a thing may be burdened by a usufruct and, when this happens, the ownership is temporarily reclassified as "naked ownership."

Title III of Book II of the Civil Code begins with two articles that situate the usufruct within the universe of real rights. Article 533 reiterates part of Article 476 by denoting two kinds of servitudes recognized under Louisiana law: personal and predial servitudes. La. Civ. Code art. 533 (1976). Article 534, however, provides the pivotal definition of a personal servitude and a further classification:

Art. 534. Personal servitude

A personal servitude is a charge on a thing for the benefit of a person. There are three sorts of personal servitudes: usufruct, habitation, and rights of use.

La. Civ. Code art. 534 (1976). The fundamental characteristic of a personal servitude under Louisiana law is that it gives *a specifically designated person* — whether a natural or juridical person — a set of rights *less than full ownership* with respect to a thing. This is what Article 534 calls "a charge for the benefit of a person." The rights in a thing less than full ownership given by a personal servitude belong to a person, *independent of whether that person owns or holds real rights in any other property.*

In contrast, a predial servitude creates rights in one immovable that benefit another immovable. Indeed, a predial servitude, as the following article indicates, creates rights that *benefit an estate*, not a person:

Art. 646. Predial servitude; definition

A predial servitude is a charge on a servient estate for the benefit of a dominant estate. The two estates must belong to different owners.

La. Civ. Code art. 646 (1977). An "estate" in this context means "a distinct corporeal immovable," usually a tract of land and its component parts, or a separate immovable such as a building or standing timber. *Id.* rev. cmt (b). Of course, an estate is an inanimate thing that cannot literally enjoy rights. When Louisiana lawyers refer to a predial servitude benefiting "an estate," they mean that the charges imposed by a predial servitude benefit *whoever happens to own the dominant estate* (a distinct corporeal immovable thing) at a particular moment in time. *Id.* rev. cmt. (c). Consequently, we say that a predial servitude benefits an estate, not a person. A personal servitude, by contrast, establishes rights that belong to the holder of the servitude, unrelated to any immovable property owned by that person.

Note that Article 534 declares that there are "three sorts of personal servitudes: usufruct, habitation and rights of use." La. Civ. Code art. 534 (1977). This chapter discusses the first of these servitudes—usufruct. Habitation and rights of use are addressed in subsequent chapters.

B. General Principles

1. Definition and Essential Characteristics

The Civil Code defines the usufruct in Article 535:

Art. 535. Usufruct

Usufruct is a real right of limited duration on the property of another. The features of the right vary with the nature of the things subject to it as consumables and nonconsumables.

La. Civ. Code art. 535 (1976). This deceivingly simple article encapsulates three distinguishing characteristics of a usufruct.

First, Article 535 clarifies that a usufruct is a real right, not a personal right like a lease or a license. This is significant because the rights of the usufructuary (the person who enjoys a usufruct) will continue to apply to the thing burdened by the usufruct, even if the ownership—that is to say, the naked ownership—of the thing changes hands. Put differently, because a usufruct is a real right, any transfer of the underlying thing will be *subject to the usufruct*. *See* La. Civ. Code art. 603 (1977, amended 2010). For criticism of the 2010 amendments to Article 603 of the Civil Code, and especially of the deletion of the phrase, "He [the naked owner] may also alienate or encumber the property subject to the usufruct," see A.N. YIANNOPOULOS, ED., LOUISIANA CIVIL CODE, Vol. 1, art. 603, Editor's Note (West Pamphlet ed. 2014).

Next, Article 535 declares that a usufruct is a real right of "limited duration." A usufructuary's right to use and enjoy a thing subject to a usufruct is temporally limited. Unlike the real right of ownership, which can last indefinitely and pass from one owner to another through voluntary or involuntary alienation or universal or particular succession, a usufruct in favor of a natural person must come to an end at some point in time: upon the death of the usufructuary or sooner. La. Civ. Code art. 607 (1976). Likewise, in the case of a usufruct granted in favor of a juridical person, the Civil Code requires that a usufruct terminate at a finite point in time no later than thirty years after it began. La. Civ. Code art. 608 (1976, amended 2010). It may end earlier—either at the time designated in the act creating the usufruct or at the dissolution of the entity constituting the juridical person. *Id*. This fundamental characteristic of limited duration also differentiates a usufruct from a right of use, which is "not extinguished at the death of the natural person or the dissolution of any other entity having the right, unless the contrary is provided by law or contract." La. Civ. Code art. 644 (1976). In short, the real right of usufruct, unlike the real right of ownership, must end at some finite point in time.

Finally, the last sentence of Article 535 tells us that the "features of the right," that is, the rights and obligations of the usufructuary and, by implication, those of the naked owner, "vary with the nature of the things subject to it as consumables and nonconsumables." Put differently, once you know that a thing is subject to a usufruct, you must always determine whether that thing is a consumable or a nonconsumable. In particular, the feature of the limited duration of a usufruct will interact with this final characteristic to generate different duties on the part of the usufructuary at the termination of the usufruct: the duty to act as a prudent administrator of nonconsumable things and the duty to account to the naked owner for the value of consumables. *See* La. Civ. Code arts. 538–539, 628–629.

We will have more to say about how to make this classification and its implications below. But for now, recognize that the features of a usufruct and the respective rights and obligations of the usufructuary and naked owner are controlled by the distinction between consumables and nonconsumables.

2. Advantages of a Usufruct

Before we engage in further analysis of the general principles of usufruct, we should address why someone might want to create this real right of limited duration in favor of one person burdening the property of another. Imagine yourself as a successful attorney considering writing your own will. You have a spouse or partner and several children, all of whom, for various reasons, might need some support in the years ahead. At the same time, you feel a strong charitable impulse to your law school alma mater. You would like your loved ones to have the use and enjoyment of your patrimony while they are alive, but ultimately you would like your patrimony to go to your alma mater. If you create a usufruct through your will, you can enable family members to use and enjoy your property during their lifetimes, but when the last usufructuary die, the usufruct will end and the naked owner, your alma mater, will become the unencumbered owner of the property.

Now imagine another situation. You are very sick. Your doctor has told you that you only have six months to live. You will be survived by a partner and two children. You want to leave your partner enough assets so that he or she will be financially secure, but you also want to provide for your children. What can you do? You could write a will allocating undivided shares of your assets among your spouse or partner and the children. You could give everything to your partner and ask him or her to leave something to your children at his or her death. Or, you can divide up your property and give some to your partner and some to your children. Creating a usufruct in this situation might accomplish your goals more readily than establishing a co-ownership regime or giving all your assets to one person with the hope that this person will be generous to another set of individuals. By creating a usufruct in favor of your partner, you can give that person a real right to use and enjoy certain assets during his or her life, or for a shorter period of time, but guarantee that the children will ultimately enjoy full ownership.

Consider another scenario. You have been hired to work away from your home for three years. You do not want to sell your home because you plan to return to it. You do not want to lease it to someone you do not know because you worry about collecting rent, paying taxes and making repairs. If you sell someone a usufruct over your home for three years, the usufructuary will be liable for ordinary maintenance and repairs, La. Civ. Code art. 577 (1976), necessary expenses for preservation and use of the property, La. Civ. Code art. 581 (1976), periodic charges such as property taxes, La. Civ. Code art. 584 (1976), and extraordinary charges. La. Civ. Code art. 585 (1976). You can enjoy your time away from home and not worry about collecting rent or any other responsibilities. As we shall see, your house sitter, if a usufructuary, will have a legal responsibility to return the house to you in good repair and otherwise account to you when the usufruct ends.

Usufruct is the civil law property institution that permits a temporal division of the building blocks of ownership. It allows one person, the usufructuary, to use and enjoy a thing for a limited period of time, while making sure that another person — the naked owner — will be able to enjoy full ownership of the thing once the specified period of time comes to an end. Although other legal institutions such as the trust can accomplish similar objectives, the usufruct remains an important property planning tool in Louisiana for many individuals and families. Usufructs are created every day through wills and other juridical acts. They also arise quite commonly as a matter of law.

3. Things Susceptible of Usufruct and Classification of a Usufruct

Two more preliminary matters require attention. First, the Civil Code is clear that a usufruct "may be established on all kinds of things: movable or immovable, corporeal or incorporeal." La. Civ. Code art. 544(2) (1976). Indeed, the only apparent limitation as to what can be the subject of a usufruct is that the thing be something capable of providing an economic advantage or other form of enjoyment to the usufructuary. *See* A.N. Yiannopoulos, 3 Louisiana Civil Law Treatise: Personal Servitudes § 1:4, at 10 (5th ed. 2011).

Second, despite the universality of the usufruct's reach, the usufruct is classified as an incorporeal thing. La. Civ. Code art. 540 (1976). As a real right the ususfruct is comprehensible to the understanding; it is not something that has a body and can be felt or touched. *See* La. Civ. Code art. 461 (1978) (listing "servitudes" as incorporeal things). If the object of a usufruct is an immovable, then the usufruct itself will be considered an *incorporeal immovable;* if the object is movable, then the usufruct will be an *incorporeal movable.* La. Civ. Code art. 540 (1977) (a usufruct is "movable or immovable according to the nature of the thing upon which the right exists"). Thus, a usufruct of a tract of land will be classified as an incorporeal immovable, while a usufruct of a bank account or shares of corporate stock will be classified as an incorporeal movable.

4. Establishment of Usufructs

The Civil Code provides for both *conventional* and *legal* usufructs. Conventional usufructs will be governed by the agreements that create them. When constitutive agreements are silent, they will be subject to the rules furnished by the Civil Code.

Art. 544. Methods of establishing usufruct; things susceptible of usufruct

Usufruct may be established by a juridical act either inter vivos or mortis causa, or by operation of law. The usufruct created by juridical act is called conventional; the usufruct created by operation of law is called legal.

Usufruct may be established on all kinds of things, movable or immovable, corporeal or incorporeal.

La. Civ. Code art. 544 (1976).

Usufructs can be created by an *inter vivos* juridical act such as a donation, sale or exchange during the grantor's life. La. Civ. Code art. 544 (1976). Although this is probably the least common way for a usufruct to come into being, it can occur when a property owner transfers ownership of a thing to another person but reserves for herself a usufruct. Conversely, instead of establishing personal rights through a lease, the owner can create a usufruct in favor of another for a period of time, but reserve for herself the naked ownership. We will see an example of such a *conventional usufruct* in *Bond v. Green*, 401 So.2d 639 (La. App. 3 Cir. 1981).

A conventional usufruct may also come into being through a juridical act *mortis causa*, that is, through a valid testament or will. La. Civ. Code art. 544 (1976). The *testamentary usufruct* is created by a testator who seeks to leave at his death a temporary dismemberment of ownership over some or all of his patrimony. Both a contractual and a testamentary usufruct are *conventional usufructs* under Article 544 because in both instances the usufruct comes into being as a result of the exercise of the will of the *grantor* of the usufruct.

The most common type of usufruct in Louisiana is the *legal usufruct*—a usufruct created by operation of law. La. Civ. Code art. 544 (1976). The legal usufruct came into Louisiana law directly from the French Civil Code. Some civil law countries, like Germany or Greece, do not provide for a legal usufruct; in those countries all usufructs are conventional. A.N. Yiannopoulos, 3 Louisiana Civil Law Treatise: Personal Servitudes § 1:6, at 12 (5th ed. 2011).

The Louisiana Civil Code currently provides for a number of circumstances under which a legal usufruct will automatically come into existence as a matter of law.

First, when one spouse "dies rich in comparison with the surviving spouse," the surviving spouse is entitled to claim a fraction of the deceased spouse's succession called the *marital portion*. La. Civ. Code art. 2432 (1979). This provision comes from Spanish law. *Id.* rev. cmt. (b). Louisiana courts have not established a "concrete test" to determine when this marital portion should be awarded. Instead, they compare the patrimonial assets of the deceased and the surviving spouse in relative terms. Courts commonly look for a patrimonial asset ratio of five to one or more to justify awarding the marital portion. *Id.* rev. cmt. (c). When it is awarded, the marital portion takes the form of a "usufruct for life" over the applicable portion of the deceased spouse's succession when the deceased spouse is survived by children. La. Civ. Code art. 2434 (1979). When there are three or fewer surviving children, the usufruct is over one fourth of the deceased's succession. In the presence of more than three surviving children, the usufruct is over a child's portion. *Id.* In no case may the marital portion exceed a million dollars. *Id.*

Next, Article 3252 of the Civil Code allows surviving spouses who find themselves "in necessitous circumstances" *and* who do "not possess in their own rights property to the amount of one thousand dollars" a usufruct of up to one thousand dollars from the succession of the deceased spouse until remarriage. La. Civ. Code art. 3252 (1870, amended 1979). Few surviving spouses will go to the trouble of fighting for this modestly endowed usufruct even if they qualify by need.

The third legal usufruct arising under the Civil Code applies to the estate of any person who is not married, or who is married but owns separate property, who has no children or other descendants, and who is survived by parents *and* siblings or his siblings' descendants. When these prerequisites are present, the "brothers or sisters or their descendants succeed to the separate property of the deceased subject to a usufruct in favor of the surviving parent or parents." La. Civ. Code art. 891 (1981, amended 2004). In other words, the *separate* property of the deceased will pass to the sibling or siblings or their descendants as naked owners, subject to a usufruct in favor of the surviving parent or parents. *Id.* If both parents survive the deceased, then their usufruct will be "joint and successive," meaning they will share the usufruct as co-usufructuaries until one parent dies; thereafter the remaining parent will enjoy the usufruct on his or her own until that parent's death. *Id.* This default rule for intestate successions only applies to "separate property." It does not apply to community property — property acquired by either the husband or wife as a result of the effort, skill or industry of either spouse, during their marriage in a community property regime. La. Civ. Code art. 2338 (1979).

Prior to 2016, former Articles 223 and 224 of the Civil Code provided that parents shall have during their marriage a usufruct over the property of their children until their children's majority or emancipation. La. Civ. Code art. 223 (1870). This *parental usufruct* did "not extend to any estate which the children may acquire by their own labor and industry." La. Civ. Code art. 226 (1870). In 2015, the Louisiana legislature suppressed the parental usufruct and enacted a new regime of parental administration of property of the child. The reform borrows from the law of usufruct without specifically using the specific term usufruct. *See* La. Civ. Code arts. 229–231 (adopted by La. Acts 2015, No. 260, § 1, eff. Jan. 1, 2016). For a brief discussion of the new provisions that allow for parents to administer a child's property, subject to court approval in some instances, see A.N. Yiannopoulos, 3 Louisiana Civil Law Treatise: Personal Servitudes §§ 7.23-7.28 (5th ed. 2011, 2017 Pocket Part).

A fifth kind of legal usufruct arises under La. R.S. 9:1426 (formerly La. Civ. Code art. 890.1 (1870)) in favor of a surviving spouse over recurring payments from a public or private pension plan, an annuity policy or plan, an individual retirement account, or Keogh plan, a simplified employee plan, or any other similar retirement plan, if the payments are considered to be community property. *See* A.N. YIAN-NOPOULOS, 3 LOUISIANA CIVIL LAW TREATISE: PERSONAL SERVITUDES § 7.1, at 429 (5th ed. 2011).

Article 891 establishes a *parental usufruct* for the separate property of a person (whether that person was previously married, was married at the time of death or was never married) who dies intestate survived by both a parent or parents and siblings (or their descendants), but without descendants of her own. La. Civ. Code art. 891 (1981, amended 2004). This article assumes that a person in this situation would want her separate property to be inherited by her siblings as the naked owners upon her death but would want her parents to have the use and enjoyment of her property for the rest of their lives as usufructuaries. Is this a reasonable assumption? Note that prior to the 1981 amendment of the Civil Code's intestate succession articles, the Civil Code provided for a very different result in this situation. The deceased's separate property was divided into two equal portions: one for the parents and the other for the siblings, if both parents survived the decedent; and in other proportions if only one parent survived. La. Civ. Code arts. 903–04 (1870). Why would the legislature replace a default rule that yielded a co-ownership relationship among the surviving parents and siblings of a deceased person without surviving children or other descendants with a parental usufruct across generational lines?

More than any other kind of usufruct found in Louisiana law, the final variety of legal usufruct authorized by the Civil Code largely accounts for the institution's continuing importance in the state. Article 890 is the source for what is called the *legal usufruct of the surviving spouse in community*, or, more simply, the *surviving spouse usufruct*:

> ### Art. 890. Usufruct of surviving spouse
>
> If the deceased spouse is survived by descendants, the surviving spouse shall have a usufruct over the decedent's share of the community property to the extent that the decedent has not disposed of it by testament. This usufruct terminates when the surviving spouse dies or remarries, whichever occurs first.

La. Civ. Code art. 890 (1996). Take careful note of the specific requirements and scope of this usufruct. It will only arise when three conditions are present: (1) a matrimonial regime of community property exists at the time of the decedent's death; (2) the deceased spouse is survived by descendants — children, grandchildren, or great grandchildren; and (3) the decedent dies intestate (without a valid will) or with a valid will that does not dispose of his or her share in the married couple's community property. A.N. YIANNOPOULOS, 3 LOUISIANA CIVIL LAW TREATISE: PERSONAL SERVITUDES §§ 7:3–:7 (5th ed. 2011).

If any one of these conditions is absent, then Article 890 will not apply. So, for instance, if the deceased divorced his or her spouse before death, the deceased has no community property at the time of his death. The former spouse is a co-owner of what was formerly community property and is entitled to his or her share as of the termination of the former community property regime. That share can be claimed through a community property partition. The divorced former spouse will have no claim to a usufruct interest over the decedent's share of the former community property at death. A.N. YIANNOPOULOS, 3 LOUISIANA CIVIL LAW TREATISE: PERSONAL SERVITUDES § 7:4, at 437 (5th ed. 2011).

Similarly, if a married couple has opted out of Louisiana's default community property regime and adopted a regime of separate property, or for other reasons their property is not subject to Louisiana's community property regime, then Article 890 will have no application to the surviving spouse's inheritance rights in an intestate succession. *Id.* § 7:4, at 436. Further, if the deceased spouse disposed of his share of the community property through a valid testament, the surviving spouse has no claim to a usufruct. *See, e.g., Succession of Sylvester,* 181 So.3d 250, 255–56 (La. App. 5 Cir. 2015) (decedent's surviving spouse could not claim an Article 890 usufruct because decedent's valid testament, executed prior to his second marriage to the surviving spouse, left "any and all things I may die possessed of" to the four children of his first marriage, thus demonstrating decedent's clear intent to dispose of not only all the property he owned at the time the testament was executed but also all of the property he acquired *after* the execution of the testament, including his share of the community property acquired during his second marriage). Finally, if a deceased spouse does not leave any descendants (whether by direct blood line or adoption), then the surviving spouse will acquire full ownership of the deceased's share of the community property. La. Civ. Code art. 889 (1981); *see also* A.N. YIANNOPOULOS, 3 LOUISIANA CIVIL LAW TREATISE: PERSONAL SERVITUDES § 7:5 (5th ed. 2011).

The existence of the legal usufruct of the surviving spouse in Louisiana represents a major policy decision by the legislature. In some civil law countries, particularly Germany and Greece, a surviving spouse is entitled to a forced share of the deceased spouse's estate *even if the deceased spouse dies testate,* or to a share of the deceased spouse's succession, along with certain classes of relatives, if the deceased spouse dies intestate. A.N. YIANNOPOULOS, 3 LOUISIANA CIVIL LAW TREATISE: PERSONAL SERVITUDES § 1.29, at 80–81 (5th ed. 2011).

In common law jurisdictions in the United States without a community property system, the rights of a surviving spouse to a share of a deceased spouse's property are roughly similar to the German model. When a spouse dies testate, most such "separate property" states allow the surviving spouse to claim a statutorily designated share of the decedent's estate and thus override the decedent's will if necessary. When a spouse dies intestate in these jurisdictions, a surviving spouse either takes all of the deceased spouse's property or shares the property with the descendants. *See* JOSEPH W. SINGER, PROPERTY § 9.3.1, at 396; § 9.7.2, at 420–21 (3rd ed. 2010).

Common law property states that have community property regimes like Louisiana follow the same basic German model in providing for the surviving spouse; they do not generally create life estates when a deceased spouse dies intestate. *Id.* § 9.3.1, at 401.

Louisiana is thus unique in its use of a usufruct model to balance the sometimes competing interests of a surviving spouse and surviving children. Professor Yiannopoulos summarizes the purpose of the legal usufruct of the surviving spouse in the following terms:

> The purposes of the usufruct of the surviving spouse, ever since its introduction into Louisiana law by Act No. 152 of 1844, have been to secure means of sustenance for the surviving spouse and to prevent partition or liquidation of the community to the prejudice of that spouse. As usufructuary of one half of the community property and owner of the remainder, the surviving spouse may continue to live in the family home and may also continue the operation of a community business unrestricted by the desires of the heirs of the deceased spouse.

A.N. YIANNOPOULOS, 3 LOUISIANA CIVIL LAW TREATISE: PERSONAL SERVITUDES § 7:3, at 10 (5th ed. 2011).

Professor Yiannopoulos's observation is instructive in several ways. First, it reveals a policy to protect the livelihood of the surviving spouse so that the spouse does not become dependent on the state or others for support. Second, it shows that under Article 890 of the Civil Code the surviving spouse will hold two property interests in the same property simultaneously. The surviving spouse will continue to own a one-half share of the former community property acquired during the marriage outright in full ownership. Moreover, by virtue of Article 890, the surviving spouse acquires a usufruct over the deceased spouse's share of the community property. The naked owners of the deceased spouse's one-half share of the community property will be the decedent's children or grandchildren — whether those children were born or adopted during the marriage between the surviving spouse and the decedent, or are children or grandchildren from another relationship or marriage. In sum, Article 890 produces a picture of property interests that may look like this:

Table 1: Property Interests in a Married Couple's Undisposed Community Property under Article 890

Surviving Spouse's One Half Share in Full Ownership	Usufruct of the Surviving Spouse
	Descendants' One Half Share in Naked Ownership

Remember, though, that Article 890 only applies to the decedent's share of the undisposed community property, not to his or her separate property; that is, property that the decedent acquired before or after the dissolution of the marriage, property that was acquired as a gift or inheritance to that spouse alone, and other property specifically defined as separate property. *See generally* La. Civ. Code art. 2341 (1979, amended 1981) (defining the different categories of separate property).

Finally, Professor Yiannopoulos's comment illuminates one of the primary policy concerns underlying the modern revision of the law of usufruct: the goal of protecting the integrity of the surviving spouse's interest in former community property as long as she wants to maintain possession and control over that property. Our examination of the specific rules governing the partition of property subject to a usufruct, will further illustrate this observation.

The legal usufruct of the surviving spouse should not be conflated with the testamentary surviving spouse usufruct permitted by Articles 1499 and 1514 of the Civil Code. The general rules governing all usufructs apply to the legal usufruct of the surviving spouse. Articles 1499 and 1514 of the Civil Code allow a testator to vary the rules governing a testamentary usufruct in favor of a surviving spouse to give the usufructuary more authority over property than in a legal usufruct. *Compare* La. Civ. Code art. 573.A(3) (1976, amended 2004, 2010), *and* La. Civ. Code art. 890 (1996), *with* La. Civ. Code arts. 1499, 1514 (1996, amended 2003).

5. The Usufructuary's Right of Enjoyment as Applied to Consumables and Nonconsumables

In many ways, a usufructuary enjoys the same practical rights to property subject to the usufruct that an owner would enjoy. A usufructuary may make use of the property and enjoy all of its fruits. La. Civ. Code art. 550 (1976). The primary difference between the rights of a usufructuary and the rights of an owner, however, is that the usufructuary, unlike an owner, generally does not enjoy the power to dispose of a thing subject to a usufruct, that is, to transfer or alienate ownership to another person or to encumber a thing (*abusus*). This very simple picture of a usufructuary's rights is complicated by two factors: (1) the distinction made between consumable and nonconsumable things outlined in Articles 536 through 537 of the Civil Code; and (2) the contractual and testamentary freedom accorded to persons who create conventional usufructs under Articles 545, 568 through 568.3, and 1499 of the Civil Code.

To see how this picture is complicated, first consider the Civil Code's definitions of consumable and nonconsumable things:

Art. 536. Consumable things

Consumable things are those than cannot be used without being expended or consumed, or without their substance being changed, such as money, harvested agricultural products, stocks of merchandise, foodstuffs, and beverages.

Art. 537. Nonconsumable things

Nonconsumable things are those that may be enjoyed without alteration of their substance, although their substance may be diminished or

deteriorated naturally by time or by the use to which they are applied, such
as lands, houses, shares of stock, animals, furniture and vehicles.

La. Civ. Code arts. 536–37 (1976). In most cases, the distinction between a consumable and nonconsumable thing is not difficult to appreciate.

Consumables are things that a person cannot practically enjoy or derive any economic benefit from unless the person actually depletes, diminishes or transforms them in the process of enjoying or using them. A loaf of bread is a perfect example. A person cannot enjoy the bread unless he consumes it, sells it or exchanges it with another person for money or some other thing. Similarly, a proprietor of a hardware store may have a store full of hardware merchandise, but cannot derive any economic benefit from that merchandise unless he sells it to customers for money or exchanges it with his suppliers for other merchandise. In each case, the loaf of bread or the hardware store merchandise is considered a consumable. Under the 1870 Civil Code, a usufruct over this kind of thing was called an *imperfect usufruct*. The 1976 revision of the law of usufruct suppressed that label in favor of the term *usufruct of consumables*. La. Civ. Code art. 536 rev. cmt. (b) (1976).

The list of consumable things provided in the text of Article 536 — "money, harvested agricultural products, stocks of merchandise, foodstuffs, and beverages" — is supplemented in the revision comments by an enumeration of other things that courts have classified as consumables, including promissory notes, certificates of deposit, negotiable instruments payable to the bearer, bales of cotton, and optional share accounts in a homestead association. *See* La. Civ. Code art. 536 rev. cmt. (c) (1976). We will analyze the seminal decision that classified bank stock as a nonconsumable, *Leury v. Mayer*, 47 So. 839 (La. 1908), below.

In contrast, *nonconsumables* are things that provide on-going enjoyment or economic benefits to the person because their use or enjoyment does not result in their depletion, diminishment or transformation into other things. Article 537 of the Civil Code lists as examples of nonconsumables "lands, houses, shares of stock, animals, furniture, and vehicles." La. Civ. Code art. 537 (1976). Thus, a tract of land, if it is managed responsibly, will continue to provide the usufructuary — and eventually the naked owner — with enjoyment and economic benefits year after year. Similarly, a usufructuary can continue to reside in a house year after year or rent the house out to obtain rental income as long as the house is kept in good repair.

A nonconsumable is a thing capable of providing long-term use and enjoyment to the usufructuary, including the production of natural and civil fruits, without any substantial diminution of the thing. Certain kinds of nonconsumables — in particular, corporeal movables such as equipment, vehicles and appliances that tend to wear out and lose their value over time — are subject to special rules that account for their unique characteristics. *See* La. Civ. Code arts. 568 and 569 (1976, amended 2010). Under the 1870 Civil Code, a usufruct over what is today considered a nonconsumable was called a *perfect usufruct*. La. Civ. Code art. 537 rev. cmt. (b) (1976).

This label has been suppressed in the current version of the Civil Code in favor of *usufruct of nonconsumables.*

Now consider how a usufructuary's basic rights and obligations are different depending on the classification of the thing subject to the usufruct:

Art. 538. Usufruct of consumable things

If the things subject to the usufruct are consumables, the usufructuary becomes owner of them. He may consume them, alienate or encumber them as he sees fit. At the termination of the usufruct he is bound either to pay to the naked owner the value that the things had at the commencement of the usufruct or to deliver to him things of the same quantity and quality.

Art. 539. Usufruct of nonconsumable things

If the things subject to the usufruct are nonconsumables, the usufructuary has the right to possess them and to derive the utility, profits and advantages that they may produce, under the obligation of preserving their substance.

He is bound to use them as a prudent administrator and to deliver them to the naked owner at the termination of the usufruct.

La. Civ. Code art. 538 (1976, amended 2010); La. Civ. Code art. 539 (1976).

If a thing subject to a usufruct is a *consumable*, the usufructuary enjoys complete freedom to use and enjoy the thing during the existence of the usufruct, including the rights to collect and keep all its fruits and to encumber or alienate the thing. Under Article 538, the usufructuary becomes the owner of a consumable thing. If the thing is something like food, the usufructuary can consume it. If the thing is money, he can spend it freely. If the thing is merchandise in a store, he can sell or exchange it. In addition to the right to use physically, occupy, possess and control the thing (*usus*) and the right to claim its natural and civil fruits (*fructus*), the usufructuary of a consumable thing is given the power of disposition (*abusus*).

There is one crucial limitation, however. At the end of the usufruct, the usufructuary or the usufructuary's succession must either pay the naked owner the value the consumables had at the commencement of the usufruct or deliver to the naked owner things of the same quantity and quality. La. Civ. Code art. 538 (1976). The usufructuary is not required to return consumables that remain at the end of the usufruct, but only to *replace* them or *reimburse* the naked owner for their original value. As the revision comments note, this duty constitutes an obligation "to account to the naked owner" for the value the consumables had at the commencement of the usufruct. *Id.* rev. cmt. (b). It imposes a personal obligation on the usufructuary or his succession but does not create in the naked owner any real right in the consumables.

The obligation of a usufructuary to pay the naked owner the original value of the consumables or to deliver things of similar quantity and quality may, at first blush, offer adequate protection for the long-term, residual interests of the naked owner. However, when the usufruct is for life, it will end once the usufructuary dies. Because the usufructuary will be deceased and because Louisiana succession law frees the successors of the deceased from any personal liability for the deceased person's debts in excess of its assets, *see* La. Civ. Code art. 1416 (1997, amended 2001), the naked owner may find it difficult to collect on this obligation if the estate of the decedent has been exhausted. *See also* KATHRYN V. LORIO, 10 LOUISIANA CIVIL LAW TREATISE, SUCCESSIONS AND DONATIONS §§ 6.2–6.5 (2nd ed. 2009) (explaining the limited liability of heirs and legatees under current Louisiana succession law).

The Civil Code protects the naked owner by giving him the right to demand that the usufructuary make an inventory of the things subject to the usufruct at the beginning of the usufruct as well as the right to demand some form of "security" from the usufructuary to guarantee that she will act as a prudent administrator of the property subject to the usufruct and fulfill all of her obligations as usufructuary, including the obligation to account to the naked owner with respect to consumables. *See* La. Civ. Code arts. 570–75. Indeed, the naked owner may prevent the usufructuary from taking possession of the property before the inventory is complete. La. Civ. Code art. 570 (1976). In addition, a court may appoint an administrator of the property if the usufructuary does not give security for the usufruct. La. Civ. Code art. 575 (1976).

The usufructuary's basic right with regard to a *nonconsumable* subject to a usufruct consists of two elements: (1) the right to use a thing—to physically occupy, possess and control it (*usus*); and (2) the right to claim its natural and civil fruits (*fructus*). The usufructuary thus has the right to possess and enjoy nonconsumables and derive "the utility, profits and advantages that they may produce," but she does not have the right of *abusus*. La. Civ. Code art. 539 (1976). For example, if the nonconsumable is a farm, the usufructuary can live on the farm, grow her own crops, sell them on the market and keep the revenue that she derives from their sale. She could also rent out the farm to a lessee and keep all the rental income. Crucially, the usufructuary will have *no obligation to account* to the naked owner for the value of these natural or civil fruits produced by the nonconsumable. Indeed, the right to enjoy these fruits is one of the core rights of a usufructuary. *See* La. Civ. Code art. 550 (1976) ("The usufructuary is entitled to the fruits of the thing subject to usufruct ...").

The one right that a usufructuary does not have with respect to a nonconsumable, however, is the power to alienate the thing, *unless* that power has been specifically granted to the usufructuary in the instrument creating the usufruct. La. Civ. Code art. 539 rev. cmt. (c) (1976); La. Civ. Code art. 569 (1976, amended 2010). The usufructuary cannot sell a nonconsumable to another person, donate it to someone else, exchange it for another thing, or encumber the thing itself (though he can transfer, lease or encumber the usufruct). As Article 539 declares, a usufructuary, unless otherwise authorized by the grantor, has an affirmative duty to "preserve [the] substance" of nonconsumable things and "to use them as a prudent administrator and to deliver them to the naked owner at the termination of the usufruct."

La. Civ. Code art. 539 (1976). Concomitant with the obligation to preserve the substance of nonconsumables and deliver them to the naked owner at the end of the usufruct is the duty to "use them as a prudent administrator." *Id.*

Essentially, this duty of prudent administration is a duty *not to commit waste,* not to use or transform the thing in a manner that allows the present user (the usufructuary) to claim a short term benefit while leaving the long term, residual interest holder (the naked owner) with an asset of substantially or entirely depleted value. *See also* La. Civ. Code art. 623 (1976) (providing that the usufruct "may be terminated by the naked owner if the *usufructuary commits waste,* alienates things without authority, neglects to make ordinary repairs, or abuses his enjoyment in any other manner") (emphasis added). This inherent tension between a usufructuary's general right to enjoy the use and the fruits of a nonconsumable and his duty to act as a prudent administrator can present difficult questions in the context of nonrenewable natural resources (like oil and gas) or very slowly renewing natural resources (like timber).

Compare the duty of a usufructuary to act as a prudent administrator with respect to a nonconsumable thing under Article 539 with the liability of a co-owner under Article 799 for damage caused to a thing owned in indivision through his fault. Recall that a co-owner does *not* have an affirmative duty to act as a prudent administrator of the co-owned thing unless he has expressly assumed that responsibility; the co-owner is only bound to avoid damage to the co-owned thing through his fault. La. Civ. Code art. 799 (1990). By contrast, a usufructuary is charged with the affirmative duty to prevent excessive wear and tear of nonconsumable things, to perform ordinary repairs, to pay for necessary expenses and to generally assure that a nonconsumable thing is as capable of producing value for the naked owner at the end of a usufruct (as it was for the usufructuary during the usufruct). *See generally* La. Civ. Code arts. 569, 577, 581, 584 and 585 (1976).

Now that we understand how a usufructuary's broad powers of use, enjoyment *and alienation* regarding consumable things complicate the simple picture of a usufruct-naked ownership relationship, we must complicate the picture further by appreciating that a grantor of a conventional usufruct may relieve a usufructuary of the duty to preserve the substance of a nonconsumable by giving the usufructuary the power to dispose of a nonconsumable. La. Civ. Code art. 568 (1976, amended 2010). In other words, a grantor of a conventional usufruct can allow a usufructuary to treat a nonconsumable as if it were a consumable, subject to certain limitations. *See* La. Civ. Code arts. 568.1–568.3 (2010). This power goes well beyond the inherent right of a usufructuary to dispose of corporeal movables that are gradually impaired by use, wear or decay. La. Civ. Code art. 568 (1976, amended 2010). A grantor's right to vary the rights of a usufructuary with respect to a thing subject to a usufruct originated in a late nineteenth century decision by the Louisiana Supreme Court, which held that a grantor can expressly grant to the usufructuary the power to dispose of a nonconsumable thing and thus convert a perfect usufruct (a usufruct of a nonconsumable) into an imperfect usufruct (a usufruct of a consumable). *Heirs of Michael v. Knox*, 34 La. Ann. 399, 1882 WL 8609 (1882).

The power to dispose of a nonconsumable, as if it were a consumable, can be enormously beneficial to a usufructuary whose usufruct includes a thing that might not be income producing but is expensive to maintain such as a house or tract of land. If the usufructuary enjoys the power to dispose of nonconsumables, she could sell the house or tract of land. The usufructuary's right of use and enjoyment will then attach to the proceeds of the sale, which, because it is a consumable, can then be spent by the usufructuary, subject to a duty to account to the naked owner. La. Civ. Code art. 539 rev. cmt. (c) (1976); La. Civ. Code art. 545 rev. cmt. (b) (1976); La. Civ. Code arts. 568.1, 616 (1976, amended 2010). A surviving spouse with the authority to alienate nonconsumables could sell a large family home and then purchase a smaller, more energy-efficient home. It is important to recognize, however, that the power to dispose of nonconsumables, as if they were consumables, must be expressly granted to the usufructuary in the instrument creating the conventional usufruct. La. Civ. Code art. 568 (1976, amended 2010). In contrast, a legal usufruct does not furnish this power to dispose of nonconsumables.

Many of the recent amendments to the law of usufruct under the Civil Code address specific problems that arise when the usufructuary has been granted this power to dispose of nonconsumables. We will examine these amendments in greater detail later in this chapter.

Consider the following decision. In this case, the court was called to determine whether shares of stock in a corporation were consumables or nonconsumables. Pay careful attention to the consequences of the court's classification choice.

Leury v. Mayer

47 So. 839 (La. 1908)

LAND, Justice. Plaintiff instituted this suit to be recognized as the owner of an undivided half interest in 20 shares of the capital stock of the Bank of Baton Rouge, represented by certificate No. 127 issued to the defendant, and for a partition by licitation of said shares and dividends accrued thereon.

Plaintiff is the only child of J.E. Leury and Hannah Leury, who were married in Baton Rouge on November 1, 1880. Plaintiff was born on November 4, 1881. Mrs. Leury died in Baton Rouge on August 17, 1893. On December 8, 1891, J.E. Leury acquired 20 shares of stock in the Bank of Baton Rouge, as evidenced by certificate No. 127. On October 27, 1893, a few months after the death of his wife, Leury transferred said certificate to the defendant.

The certificate was community property, and on the death of Mrs. Leury her undivided half interest therein was inherited by the plaintiff.

The defendant pleads the prescription of 3 and 10 years, and contends that the surviving husband, as usufructuary, had the legal right to sell the stock.

The last contention comes first in logical order, and is founded on the premise that the usufruct of shares of stock is an imperfect or quasi usufruct, under Rev. Civ. Code, arts. 534, 536, 549. The first article defines an imperfect usufruct to be one of the things which would be useless to the usufructuary, if he did not consume or expend them or change the substance of them, "as money, grains, liquors." Articles 536 and 549 provide that the imperfect usufruct transfers the ownership to the usufructuary, so that he may consume, sell, or dispose of them as he thinks proper, subject to the obligation of returning the same quantity, quality, and value to the owner, or their estimated price, at the expiration of the usufruct.

It is obvious that bank stock does not fall within the purview of article 534, Rev. Civ. Code, but represents an investment of money for the purpose of producing revenue. In such a case the usufructuary is entitled only to the fruits, as in the case of "rents of real property, the interest of money, and annuities." Articles 544, 545. The argument that in the case at bar the usufructuary had the right to sell the stock because it was not producing a revenue is not only unsound in law, but unsupported by the facts of the case. Within a few years the stock had doubled in value, and 60 days after the sale to the defendant the first dividend was declared. Since the date of the sale the defendant had collected $ 1,495 in dividends, or $ 47.75 for each share of the par value of $ 50. At the date of the trial below the stock was worth $ 317.76 per share.

The plaintiff's father was entitled to all the dividends declared up to the date of his death, January 30, 1896, though they may not have been collected by him. Article 547, Rev. Civ. Code.

It does not appear that J.E. Leury was ever confirmed and qualified as tutor of his minor son, Louis F. Leury. But even had the father qualified as tutor, he could not have sold at private sale the interests of his minor son in the stock in question without an order of court issued upon the advice of a family meeting. Act No. 21, p. 17, Laws 1890. Before the passage of this statute bonds and stocks belonging to minors or successions could not be sold except at public auction pursuant to an order of court.

The defendant's pleas of prescription are based on articles 3506 and 3509 of the Revised Civil Code. . . .

The judgment below recognized the plaintiff as the joint owner with the defendant of 20 shares of the capital stock of the Bank of Baton Rouge, as evidenced by certificate No. 127, together with the accrued dividends; and ordered that said interest in and to the said ownership in said bank be sold at public auction according to law for the purposes of effecting a partition between the plaintiff and the defendant, and referred the parties to a notary for the purpose of completing said partition, reserving their rights as against each other in any claim growing out of the above ownership in said bank; the same to be settled and determined in the partition.

The complaint of appellant is well founded as to the sale of the accrued dividends, amounting to $ 1,495.44, which have already been collected by the defendant. The only dividends which can be sold are such as have not been declared and paid by the bank. As already stated, the defendant is not accountable for dividends collected prior to the death of J.E. Leury, on January 30, 1896. The plaintiff further complains that the stock should not be sold because it is divisible in kind. The certify cate of stock originally issued was transferred to the defendant, who surrendered the same to the bank and obtained a new certificate. Defendant, in the court below, did not suggest that a division in kind of the shares might be effected by his surrender of the certificate and the issue of two certificates for 10 shares each. The court had no control of the certificate, and was not called upon by the pleadings to order its surrender to the bank and the issuance of other certificates. The bank was no party to the suit, and a division in kind could not have been made without the consent of the bank and the parties to the litigation. When property is indivisible by its nature, or when it cannot be conveniently divided, the judge is bound to order its sale at the instance of any one of the joint owners. Rev. Civ. Code, art. 1339. Nothing was left to the court but to order the sale of the interest in the capital stock represented by the original certificate, which had, as to the minor's interest therein, been illegally transferred and surrendered. The defendant might have made a division in kind practicable, but he did not offer to do so.

It is therefore ordered that the judgment appealed from be amended by restricting the partition sale to the stock plus dividends which have not been heretofore declared and paid, and by ordering the defendant to account in the partition for all dividends received by him on the stock in dispute since January 30, 1896; and it is further ordered that said judgment as thus amended be affirmed, and that plaintiff pay the costs of appeal.

Notes and Questions

1. *Leury v. Mayer*, 47 So. 839 (La. 1980), forces us to recognize the importance of the legal usufruct of the surviving spouse. Study the chronology of events and construct your own timeline. When J.E. Leury acquired the twenty shares of stock in the Bank of Baton Rouge in 1891, he was already married to his wife, Hannah; hence the stock was community property. When Hannah died two years later, survived by both her husband, J.E., and their son, Louis, Article 916 of the 1870 Civil Code, the predecessor of current Article 890, sprang into effect because Hannah apparently died intestate. Thus, as surviving spouse, J.E. held his one-half interest in the couple's community property outright as full owner and a usufruct over Hannah's one-half interest in the community property. Louis, as the sole descendant of Hannah, acquired naked ownership of Hannah's one-half interest in the community property.

2. The key issue in *Leury* was whether J.E. had the right to sell all twenty shares of stock in the Bank of Baton Rouge to the defendant, Mayer. If the court had determined that the shares of stock were consumables—if the usufruct had been declared to be "imperfect"—then J.E., as the functional owner, would have been acting within his rights when he sold the stock to Mayer, as long as he accounted

for the value of the stock at the termination of the usufruct. Why did the court conclude that J.E.'s usufruct over the stock was, in fact, a *perfect usufruct* and that the
stock was, to use the language of the current Civil Code, a nonconsumable thing?
Where in the Civil Code is this holding now codified?

3. Once the court in *Leury* concluded that the shares of stock were nonconsumables and J.E. Leury did not have legal authority to sell all of them to Mayer, it had
to find a way to remedy his improper action. The court's response was to engage in a
careful accounting of J.E.'s full ownership interest in one-half of that stock and J.E.'s
usufructuary interest in the other one-half, including the dividends (civil fruits)
produced by the stock. J.E. owned both his interest and its fruits as well as the fruits
from the interest owned by his son as naked owner. These he could transfer. He
could not transfer the naked ownership of the stock owned by his son. The other
crucial fact taken into account by the court was the date of J.E.'s death, January 30,
1896. Why is that particular date important to the holding of the court?

4. Notice that the court orders a partition of the stock certificate representing
twenty shares of the stock, with one-half going to Mayer and the other one-half to
Louis Leury. Are the dividends from the stock also split evenly? Make sure you can
articulate the reasoning behind the final accounting.

5. In another seminal decision, *Vivian State Bank v. Thomason-Lewis Lumber Co.*,
111 So. 51 (La. 1926), the Louisiana Supreme Court addressed the fate of a $10,000
certificate of deposit originally held by a married couple in a local bank as community property. After the husband's death, the certificate of deposit was owned one-
half outright in full ownership by the widow, while the other one-half interest was
owned by the couple's children as naked owners subject to the widow's usufruct.
The court held that the certificate of deposit was a consumable thing and thus, the
widow's usufruct was "imperfect" under the 1870 Civil Code. *Id.* at 53. In consequence, the widow's action in pledging the entire certificate of deposit as collateral
to secure a family business debt was fully authorized and effective. This meant that
the children could not later nullify the pledge when the debt went unpaid and the
bank seized the funds held pursuant to the certificate of deposit to satisfy the debt.
Id. at 52–53. Do you see why? The only recourse left to the children, who probably
saw a large part of their inheritance wiped out as the result of their mother's actions,
was to sue their mother (or her estate) at the termination of the usufruct.

What does *Vivian State Bank* teach us about the vulnerabilities of naked owners
to a usufructuary whose business affairs might be on a shaky footing? What might
you advise a testator about the risks of leaving a substantial portion of his or her
estate in usufruct? In *Vivian State Bank*, the court held that the certificate of deposit
was a consumable thing because the underlying funds could not be used unless they
were expended. Thus, ownership of the funds was entirely vested in the surviving
spouse. *Id.* at 52–53. Do you agree with this reasoning? Is it possible that the funds
invested in the certificate of deposit could be enjoyed in some other manner without being expended?

C. Limits on Contractual and Testamentary Freedom; Shared and Successive Usufructs

In general, the Civil Code casts the law of usufruct in terms of default rules. When a usufruct is created by operation of law, the default provisions of Title III, Chapter 2 of the Civil Code govern the relationship between usufructuary and naked owner throughout the usufruct. A grantor who establishes a conventional usufruct, however, is given wide berth to tailor the specific provisions of the usufruct to satisfy his wishes. Article 545 of the Civil Code states the general principle of contractual and testamentary freedom in broad terms:

Art. 545. Modifications of usufruct

Usufruct may be established for a term or under a condition, and subject to any modification consistent with the nature of usufruct.

The rights and obligations of the usufructuary may be modified by agreement unless modification is prohibited by law or by the grantor in the act establishing the usufruct.

La. Civ. Code art. 545 (1976). As noted above, one of the crucial modifications *allowed* by law consists in the grantor's freedom to relieve the usufructuary of the obligation to preserve the substance of the property subject to the usufruct. In effect, the grantor can give the usufructuary the power to dispose of the property even if the thing subject to the usufruct is a nonconsumable. *Id.* rev. cmt (b); La. Civ. Code art. 539 rev. cmt. (c) (1976). Before we study this important permissible modification in greater detail, though, we must appreciate that the law limits the grantor's contractual and testamentary freedom to deviate from the default rules that apply to a usufruct in certain crucial respects.

Recall that a usufruct is a real right of limited duration. La. Civ. Code art. 535 (1976). In the case of a usufruct granted in favor of a natural person, the usufruct must end at the death of the usufructuary. La. Civ. Code art. 607 (1976). Although a usufruct may be subject to a term shorter than the life of the usufructuary or a condition that could lead to termination before the usufructuary's death, a usufruct, by its nature, ends with the death of the usufructuary. A grantor cannot convert a usufruct into a heritable right that one person can transmit to another at death. La. Civ. Code art. 545 rev. cmt. (b) (1976); La. Civ. Code art. 607 rev. cmt. (b) (1976).

This seemingly clear rule about the limited duration of a usufruct is complicated by a series of articles that allow the grantor some margin of freedom. First, she has the ability to establish a usufructuary interest that is shared by more than one person and that lasts until the last of the usufructuaries dies. Second, she may create successive usufructs in favor of multiple persons. Consider the following three articles:

Art. 546. Usufruct in favor of successive usufructuaries

Usufruct may be established in favor of successive usufructuaries.

Art. 547. Usufruct in favor of several usufructuaries

When the usufruct is established in favor of several usufructuaries, the termination of the interest of one usufruct inures to the benefit of those remaining, unless the grantor has expressly provided otherwise.

Art. 548. Existence of usufructuaries

When the usufruct is established by an act inter vivos, the usufructuary must exist or be conceived at the time of the execution of the instrument. When the usufruct is established by an act mortis causa, the usufructuary must exist or be conceived at the time of the death of the testator.

La. Civ. Code arts. 546–48 (1976). Also consider the following article from Book III of the Civil Code that establishes an important limitation on donations *inter vivos* or *mortis causa*:

Art. 1520. Prohibited Substitutions

A disposition that is not in trust by which a thing is donated in full ownership to a first donee, called the institute, with a charge to preserve the thing and deliver it to a second donee, called the substitute, at the death of the institute, is null with regard to both the institute and the substitute.

La. Civ. Code art. 1520 (2001). Read together, these four articles establish the extent of a grantor's contractual and testamentary freedom with respect to the duration of the usufruct and the number of people who can be designated as usufructuaries. The best way to understand their meaning is to work through several hypothetical problems.

Problems

1. Suppose that Harold dies survived by his wife, Wendy, and his two children, Ann and Ben. In his will, Harold leaves a house that he acquired before his marriage (*i.e.*, his separate property) to Ann and Ben as naked owners, subject to a usufruct in favor of Wendy. Harold's testament further specifies that the usufruct will terminate if Wendy remarries. Is this condition valid? Why or why not?

2. Now suppose that, in his will, Harold also leaves $300,000 held in a savings account at a local bank to his wife, Wendy, subject to a usufruct in favor of his oldest child, Ann, from a previous marriage. In the will, Harold stipulates that both the funds in the savings account and the interest accruing on the funds in the account can be withdrawn by Ann for the purposes of paying for tuition and room and board at an accredited college or university in the United States. Harold also stipulates that the usufruct will terminate when Ann earns a bachelor's degree from an accredited college or university in the United States or reaches the age of 25, whichever occurs first. Are these conditions valid? Why or why not? Suppose that Ann uses all the interest that accrued on the savings account over a four year period. She also withdrew $100,000 of the funds originally held in the account at the commencement of the usufruct to pay for tuition and room and board at an accredited

university in Louisiana. Ann then graduated from that university at the age of 23. Upon graduation, what obligation, if any, does Ann owe to Wendy?

3. Same facts as in Question 2 above, but now suppose that Harold's will specifies that at the termination of Ann's usufructuary interest, Ben, his other child, will enjoy a usufruct under the same terms and conditions. Is this usufruct valid? Why or why not?

4. George, the owner of a farm in Avoyelles Parish, donated ownership of the farm to his grandson, Louis, subject to a usufruct in favor of his two sisters, Sally and Theresa. Is the usufruct valid? Why or why not? Assume that the usufruct is valid, that Sally dies on January 1, 2015, and that Theresa is still alive on that date. What interest does Louis have in the farm upon Sally's death? When will Louis be able to claim full, unencumbered ownership of the farm?

5. Same facts as in question 4, but now suppose that George comes to see you before executing his act of donation. He explains that he wishes to leave the naked ownership of his farm to his grandson, Louis, subject to a usufruct in favor of his sisters, Sally and Theresa. George also tells you that upon the death of either sister, he wants Louis to acquire a one-half, unencumbered interest in the farm. Can you help George accomplish this outcome? How will you revise the act of donation? *See* La. Civ. Code art. 547 rev. cmt. (d), *and* La. Civ. Code art. 541, rev. cmt. (b).

6. Ted, the owner of a large plantation in Ascension Parish, has died. In his will, he bequeathed ownership of the plantation to his alma mater, the University of Kansas, subject to a usufruct in favor of his eldest son, James. Ted's will further specified that upon James's death, the usufruct would continue in favor of James's children and grandchildren until their deaths. At the time of Ted's death, James had neither children nor grandchildren, but when James dies, he is survived by two children and three grandchildren. Will these children and grandchildren enjoy a usufruct over the plantation? Or will the University of Kansas own the plantation in full, unencumbered ownership?

7. Adam owned a house in Baton Rouge. Adam died testate. His will leaves a particular legacy of the house to his friend Carol, but declares that upon Carol's death, the ownership of the house shall pass to his cousin, David. Is the particular legacy of the house in favor of Carol valid? Why or why not?

Now consider the following case.

Succession of Goode

425 So.2d 673 (La. 1982)

LEMMON, Justice. This case involves the validity of a testamentary disposition. The issue is whether the contested legacy constituted a prohibited substitution.

The testator died in 1978, leaving no ascendants or descendants and being survived by a half-brother and the descendants of a predeceased half-sister. He left an olographic will, which provided for several specific dispositions, but no residuary legacy. The contested legacy provided as follows:

> "Fifth: All oil & gas royalty interest payments owned by me shall be paid to Pauline Egbert Parker for as long as she might live. After her death the amount of any payments shall be equally divided between my nieces and nephews and Linda Cosby Paine."[1]

After the will was probated, the opponents of the will filed a petition to annul the testament. The case was tried on stipulated facts, and the trial court held that the legacy was a prohibited substitution. The court of appeal affirmed. 395 So.2d 875. We granted certiorari to review those holdings. 401 So.2d 359.

C.C. Art. 1520 prohibits substitutions generally as follows:

> "Substitutions are and remain prohibited, except as permitted by the laws relating to trusts.

> "Every disposition not in trust by which the donee, the heir, or legatee is charged to preserve for and to return a thing to a third person is null, even with regard to the donee, the instituted heir or the legatee."

As noted in the Report by the Louisiana State Law Institute to Accompany the Proposed Louisiana Trust Code, a prohibited substitution must contain (1) a double disposition in full ownership of the same thing to persons named to receive it, one after the other, (2) a charge to preserve and transmit the thing, imposed on the first beneficiary for the benefit of the second, and (3) the establishment of a successive order that causes the thing to leave the inheritance of the burdened beneficiary and to enter into the patrimony of the substituted beneficiary. *See also Baten v. Taylor*, 386 So.2d 333 (La. 1979). Nevertheless, the disposition of a usufruct is not prohibited, nor is the disposition of successive usufructs. *See* C.C. Art. 1522 and 546.

In the present case the proponents of the will contend there was no express double disposition in full ownership and no express charge on the first beneficiary to preserve and transmit the property to a second beneficiary. They urge that we construe the testator's words as intending to separate his royalty interest in the property from the payments attributable to that interest, so that either (1) he intended to bequeath the payments to named beneficiaries by successive usufructs, while allowing the naked ownership of the royalty interest to pass by intestacy, or (2) he intended to bequeath a life usufruct to Pauline Parker and the naked ownership to the other named legatees.

On the other hand, the opponents contend there were no words such as "use", "usufruct", "naked ownership", "enjoyment" or "use and benefit" indicative of the testator's intention to create the institutions of usufruct and naked ownership. Further citing the principle that a testator is presumed to have intended to

---

1. Neither of the named legatees were heirs of the testator. There were six nieces and nephews.

dispose of all of his property, the opponents argue against construing the disposition as creating successive usufructs, while allowing the naked ownership to pass by intestacy.

When a landowner or servitude owner grants a mineral lease on property which is subject to a previously existing royalty interest and the lessee obtains production from the leased property, the royalty owner participates in the payments for minerals produced under the lease. See R.S. 31:80, codifying prior jurisprudence. But when the lease expires, the royalty interest remains in existence.

Although a layman, the testator (whose royalty income averaged more than $10,000 monthly) was undoubtedly aware of the difference between the royalty interest which he had acquired in one transaction and the payments he subsequently received, on account of that ownership, after the property was leased and production was obtained. Significantly, in drafting his will without benefit of counsel, he used the word "payments", and the deliberate use of that word suggests an intent to distinguish between the legal right he had originally acquired (royalty interest) and the income which subsequently flowed from that right. He could have left his royalty interest to Pauline Parker, thereby giving her both the right and the income currently flowing therefrom, but he chose to give her the royalty *payments*. While this disposition could reasonably be construed as a legacy of the royalty interest itself, it also could reasonably be construed as a legacy to Pauline Parker of the payments made on account of the royalty interest and a legacy to the other named legatees of the ownership of the royalty interest itself.

In interpreting testaments, courts should principally seek to ascertain the intention of the testator, without departing from the proper signification of the testamentary terms. C.C. Art. 1712. Furthermore, when testamentary language is subject to two reasonable interpretations, courts should choose the interpretation which validates the will rather than the one which invalidates it, as long as that interpretation does not violate the testator's intent.

Here, the testator clearly intended for Pauline Parker to receive the payments made on account of his royalty interest in the property until her death and for the other named legatees to receive the payments thereafter in equal proportions. The law permitted him to accomplish this intention by giving the usufruct to one and the naked ownership to the others. While his uncounseled language did not expressly provide for the establishment of the legal institutions of usufruct and naked ownership, neither did the language expressly provide that both sets of legatees were to receive the royalty interest in full ownership or that the first legatee was to preserve it for the other legatees. This disposition can therefore be interpreted with equal reasonableness as the bequest of a life usufruct of the royalty interest to Pauline Parker and of the naked ownership to the other named legatees, and that interpretation accords completely with the testator's apparent intent, while making the testament valid. Accordingly, we interpret the testamentary disposition as establishing the enforceable legal institutions authorized by C.C. Art. 1522.

In cases such as the present one, an appropriate solution is to give effect to the testamentary disposition by construing it as a valid usufruct-naked ownership legacy, rather than as a prohibited substitution, when the testator does not expressly outline all of the details of a prohibited substitution.[4] E. Nabors, *An Analysis of the Substitution-Usufruct Problem under Articles 1520 and 1522 of the Louisiana Civil Code*, 4 Tul. L. Rev. 603 (1930); A. Yiannopoulos, 3 Louisiana Civil Law Treatise-Personal Servitudes § 15 (2d ed. 1978). This interpretation achieves the laudable goal of validating testamentary dispositions, whenever the language may reasonably be construed so as to make the disposition valid and to achieve the testator's clear purpose, without frustrating the purpose of the prohibition against substitutions.[5] This interpretation also accords with Justice Dennis' suggestion in *Baten v. Taylor*, above, that pre-Trust Code jurisprudence concerning prohibited substitutions be reassessed in the light of the legislative amendments harmonizing substitutions with French doctrine and with the rule that penal and prohibitory laws should be strictly construed.

Accordingly, the judgments of the lower courts are reversed, and the petition to annul the probated testament is dismissed. Costs in all courts are assessed to the opponents.

CALOGERO, Justice, concurring. The majority opinion is correct in finding that there is not here a prohibited substitution. Presented with the tough job of interpreting the will to ascertain the intent of the testator, the majority in my view comes up with the more reasonable conclusion when it finds that the testator wanted his wife's sister-in-law (Mrs. Pauline Egbert Parker) to have the royalty interest payments for the rest of her natural life with the seven other legatees (six nieces, nephews, and one Linda Cosby Paine) enjoying the mineral interest, in particular the payments following Mrs. Parker's death, and the mineral interest in its entirety. It is the preferable interpretation of the will that Mr. Goode did not intend that there be usufructs spanning successively the life of Mrs. Parker and the lives of seven variously aged younger people, with the naked ownership of the mineral interest property at the usufructs' terminations devolving upon his legal heirs. Incidentally those

---

4. The author of this opinion points out that even if the testator intended the legacy as a disposition of the royalty interest in full ownership to both sets of legatees, Pauline Parker was not charged with the obligation to preserve the property and to return it to a third person, which is one of the essential elements of a prohibited substitution as defined by C.C. Art. 1520. In the author's view, a disposition by which a legatee is given full ownership of property for his life and charged to transmit the *residue* of the property at his death is a valid substitution which is not prohibited by C.C. Art. 1520, because it does not contain the essential charge to preserve and render. J. Tucker, *Substitutions, Fideicommissa and Trusts in Louisiana Law: A Semantical Reappraisal*, 24 La.L.Rev. 439, 489; A. Yiannopoulos, above; *Succession of Walters*, 261 La. 59, 259 So.2d 12 (1972), Barham, J., Concurring; *Crichton v. Succession of Gredler*, 256 La. 156, 235 So.2d 411 (1970), Sanders, J., Dissenting.

5. The purpose of the prohibition is to prevent attempts to tie up property in perpetuity. However, C.C. Art. 1482 accomplishes that objective by limiting capacity to receive gifts to persons conceived at the time of the donation or the death of the testator.

legal heirs are the six nieces and nephews and the testator's half-brother, respondent James Philip Goode, who was named in the will as executor and as custodian of the family heirlooms.

As I see it, the testator, in effect, gave Pauline Egbert Parker a legacy of revenues from specified property, a "kind of usufruct", one which, under La. C.C. art. 609, "terminates, upon the death of the legatee unless a shorter period has been expressly stipulated." Incidentally, La. C.C. art. 609 with its reference to a "kind of a usufruct" appears in § 5 of Chapter 2 of Title III (Personal Servitudes) a section relating to the *termination* of usufructs, not in the earlier sections (§ 1, § 2, § 3, § 4) of Chapter 2, Title III which govern the principles of usufruct and the rights and obligations of the usufructuary and the naked owner. As I interpret the codal articles there is no contemplation that the legacy of revenues, a "kind of usufruct", be governed by the articles relating to the obligations of a usufructuary of money and consumable things (La. C.C. art. 536 which appears in § 1 of Chapter 2 of Title III); neither is a return of the revenues at the end of the "kind of usufruct" contemplated. . . .

For these reasons I concur.

BLANCHE, Justice, dissenting. I respectfully dissent. The bequest containing the mineral interest created a double disposition in full ownership, as well as a charge to preserve and transmit.

The Mineral Code does permit the creation of a usufruct of a mineral right. R.S. 31:193. Thus, the payments generated by a mineral royalty may be distinguished from the interest that generates them. Therefore, Ronald Goode could have left the naked ownership of the mineral royalty to one and the payments it generated to another. The usufructuary, under such circumstances, would be entitled to all of the benefits of use and enjoyment that would have accrued to him if he were the owner of the right.

However, under the facts of this case, this writer is of the opinion that Ronald Goode intended to convey full ownership of the mineral royalty to the named legatees. Though C.C. art. 1713 requires a saving construction whenever possible, the language relied upon by the testator cannot be ignored. The language employed by Ronald Goode fails to support the conclusion that a usufruct was created. Absent are customary words such as "use", "usufruct", or "enjoyment", which suggest the existence of a usufruct. *See Succession of Thilborger,* 234 La. 810, 101 So.2d 678 (La. 1958).

Further, the law presumes that when a will is executed, the testator intends to dispose of his entire estate. *Carter v. Succession of Carter,* 332 So.2d 439 (La. 1976). The mineral royalty was Ronald Goode's major asset. He left no forced heirs and did not name a residuary legatee. These facts indicate that Goode, as a layman, intended to convey full ownership of the mineral royalty payments to Pauline Parker for her lifetime which, upon her death, would pass to the nieces, nephews and Linda Paine. To place a saving construction on the bequest by concluding that usufructs were created, this Court has not only stretched, but actually departed from, the language used by the testator. Based on the facts of this case, our reasoning in *Succession of Ledbetter*, 147 La. 771, 85 So. 908 (1920), ought to be controlling:

> "Article 1522 of the Code permits the giving of the usufruct property to one legatee and the naked ownership of the same property to another. *But if every substitution, by which property is given to one legatee during his life and at his death to another, is to be regarded as vesting a life usufruct in the one and the naked ownership in the other legatee, Article 1520, which prohibits such substitutions, must have lost its meaning*" (emphasis added).

Thus, if Ronald Goode was "undoubtedly aware" of the difference between the royalty and the payments that ownership generated, the surrounding facts and most reasonable construction of the language employed clearly reflect his total failure to express his knowledge of the legally permissible dismemberments of the right of ownership. Consequently, I find the bequest in dispute to contain a double disposition in full ownership.

Because the testator failed to create a usufruct in favor of the named legatees, any payments received by Ms. Parker during her lifetime are indistinguishable from the royalty that produces them. Consequently, the "payments" which are to be divided upon Ms. Parker's death are synonymous with the real right from which they are derived. Though there is no express charge placed upon Pauline Parker to preserve and transmit any payments she actually receives, future payments to the nieces, nephews and Linda Paine are dependent solely upon the preservation and transmission of the income producing interest. Thus, Ms. Parker is charged to preserve and transmit the royalty interest. Accordingly, the court of appeal was correct in its conclusion that the contested disposition constituted a prohibited substitution.

The strained interpretation of the contested bequest by the majority clearly hinders the objectives of C.C. art. 1520. The prohibition against substitutions prevents the testator from keeping property out of commerce and controlling the distribution of family wealth by altering the future order of succession. The bequest in dispute prevents the free alienation of the royalty interest and attempts to preserve the wealth generated by this real right. Though it is not likely that the existence and nature of mineral royalty interests were ever contemplated by the redactors of our Civil Code, the considerations which led to the prohibition against substitutions ought to apply with equal force to mineral interests.

WATSON, Justice, dissenting. The will contains what is clearly a prohibited substitution. This conclusion is pointed up by the difficult and strained interpretation by which the majority attempts to find otherwise.

I respectfully dissent for these reasons and also for the reasons assigned by Justice Blanche.

ON REHEARING

DIXON, Justice. [After reciting the facts, Justice Dixon noted that "the decedent's half- brother, James Philip Goode, Sr., resigned as testamentary co-executor and filed a petition to annul testament believing the following provision of the will was a prohibited substitution under C.C. 1520."] . . . . On original hearing this court was divided on the validity of the will's provision, and those upholding the provision were divided on which rights of ownership devolved to the nieces, nephews and Linda Cosby Paine. We granted rehearing to reconsider these questions.

In the interpretation of a legacy, our first task is to determine the intention of the testator. C.C. 1720. The trial court in written reasons found that the testator had attempted to make a bequest to Mrs. Parker during her lifetime and upon her death a bequest to other named legatees. This was considered to be a classic example of a prohibited substitution. The court of appeal, in examining the words of the testator, noted the absence of the terms "use" or "use and benefit" which would have suggested that a usufruct had been created, and determined that the testator was bequeathing a royalty interest and not merely payments made on account of a royalty interest. The court of appeal, therefore, also found a prohibited substitution.

Within the context of the Civil Code, the creation of a usufruct divides the rights of ownership between two or more persons for a period of limited duration. C.C. 535. The usufructuary generally has the right to the use of the property and to the fruits which it may produce, while the naked owner alone has the right to alienate the property. C.C. 561 directs that the rights of the usufructuary and the naked owner in mines and quarries are governed by the Mineral Code. Upon termination of the usufruct, the rights of the usufructuary and the naked owner are reunited.

As the Civil Code directs use of the Mineral Code only for the respective rights of the usufructuary and the naked owner, and not for the establishment or termination of a usufruct, the question of whether a usufruct has been created and when it will end must be determined under the Civil Code and relevant jurisprudence. However, our application of the Civil Code is clearer after examining the applicable provisions of the Mineral Code, R.S. Title 31.

Much of the difficulty in this case arises from the nature of the underlying asset (the mineral right) and the future payments which it generates (the royalty payments), and whether the two may be considered separately or are so united that they may not be distinguished. The opponents of the validity of the will's provision contend that the royalty payments are compensation for minerals removed from the ground; that the payments are only generated by the depletion of the asset. Under this reasoning, the payments are not fruits, but are compensation for the consumption of the asset itself. Under the Civil Code, a usufructuary is entitled only to the fruits. C.C. 550.

The Mineral Code does not divide the rights of the usufructuary and the naked owner consistently with the Civil Code concept of fruits. R.S. 31:16 describes the three basic mineral rights as the mineral servitude, the mineral royalty and the mineral lease. Mineral Code provisions concerning mineral rights are equally applicable to all three basic types of mineral rights. R.S. 31:80 defines a mineral royalty as the right to participate in the production of minerals from either land or a servitude owned by another; however, the owner of a royalty has no "executive rights," nor any rights to explore for or produce minerals. R.S. 31:81. Any benefit thus accruing to a royalty owner is contingent on the successful efforts of others.

A mineral royalty may clearly be the subject of a usufruct. In such a case, R.S. 31:193 provides:

> "One who has the usufruct of a mineral right, as distinguished from the usufruct of land, is entitled to all of the benefits of use and enjoyment that would accrue to him if he were the owner of the right. He may, therefore, use the right according to its nature for the duration of his usufruct."

While the comments to this article indicate that common sense requires the usufructuary have the rights of the owner to prevent the right from becoming lost, a royalty owner, and consequently the usufructuary of a royalty right, is prohibited by R.S. 31:81 from taking any direct action leading to the preservation of his right. This provision, applicable to mineral royalties, has the effect of merging into the usufructuary all of the rights of use and enjoyment of the naked owner.

With the exercise of the rights of use and enjoyment by the usufructuary, the minerals subject to the right become depleted, but the right itself is not diminished. The right to share in production remains. The usufruct of a mineral royalty is a usufruct of a nonconsumable though its value is dependent on a consumable resource—a resource which may be completely consumed during the term of the usufruct. But the attributes of ownership of the royalty right have been divided, and the naked owner stands ready to receive full ownership upon termination of the usufruct. The division of attributes of ownership of the royalty right is further clouded by the lack of rights and duties incumbent on a mineral royalty owner. Where there is a usufruct of a mineral royalty, the only readily apparent right is to receive royalty payments if and when production exists, with no corresponding duties.

Since there is so slight a difference between a full owner and a usufructuary of a mineral royalty, whether full ownership has been transferred or only a usufruct has been created is difficult to determine from analyzing the end result of any act of transfer or bequest. The language used in the transfer may be important in determining the intent.

The testator chose the word "payments" when describing the subject of his bequest. He did not choose the words "use" or "use and benefit" which would have clearly shown an intention to confer a usufruct on the named legatees. This is not, however, fatal to the validity of the bequest as a usufruct. What is required is a manifestation of the will of the testator to confer less than full ownership to the legatee. In bequeathing the "payments" rather than the "royalty interest," the testator fully described the benefits that would flow to a usufructuary of a mineral royalty. Since the case was submitted to the trial court on stipulated facts, there was no record developed below which would indicate the existence of any expertise of the decedent in the area of mineral rights. The stipulated facts are silent on the matter, but the death certificate filed into the record indicates the decedent was a retired independent oil operator. C.C. 1713, requiring a court to give a saving construction to a will whenever possible, encourages us to believe the testator understood the difference between a royalty payment and a royalty interest, and deliberately donated the payments and not the interest.

The testator again used the word "payments" when describing his bequest to the nieces, nephews and Linda Cosby Paine, who were to receive the payments, if any, upon the death of Mrs. Parker. Because of the identity of the language used, we find the same intent on the part of the testator, that is, to grant a usufruct of the mineral royalty to this second set of legatees. Successive usufructs are expressly provided for in the Civil Code in article 546. To hold otherwise strains the clear meaning of the words chosen by the testator. *See* C.C. 1712.

Finding successive usufructs in this will, where there is no mention by the testator of the disposition of the naked ownership and no residuary legatee, the naked ownership falls intestate. Under these circumstances, this is not an inconceivable result. At oral argument on the rehearing of this case, opponents of the validity of the will's fifth provision suggested that both at the time the will was written and at the time of death of the testator, the payments being received by the testator were around $300 per month and the royalty was not the substantial asset that it later became. It is not unreasonable that the testator did not make a specific bequest of a residual right in a depleting asset that may not have been anticipated to have any value at the death of his last niece or nephew many years later.[1] In any event, the slight prospect that the right would still have been valuable at a distant point in the future is not a sufficient basis for a present construction of the will that would completely ignore the testator's expressed intention to bequeath the payments to the named legatees.

Further, the lack of a termination point of the rights of the second set of legatees is not determinative of the kind of legacy they received under the will. C.C. 609 provides that:

> "A legacy of revenues from specified property is a kind of usufruct and terminates upon death of the legatee unless a shorter period has been expressly stipulated."

This article, read in conjunction with C.C. 547 providing that where there are several usufructuaries the termination of the interest of one usufructuary inures to the benefit of those remaining, fixes the termination of the usufruct granted to the second set of legatees at the death of the last remaining legatee, at which point the usufruct and the naked ownership will be reunited into full ownership, whether or not there is any value remaining in either.

---

1. That the testator may have believed that the payments would diminish over time may be inferred from the language of the bequest. With regard to Pauline Parker, the first usufructuary, the language used was: "*All* . . . payments owned by me shall be paid . . ." while the second set of legatees was to divide: ". . . the amount of *any* payments . . ." (emphasis added).

For the foregoing reasons, we hold that the fifth provision of the will of Ronald Bruce Goode creates successive usufructs[2] in favor of Pauline Egbert Parker, and, upon her death, in favor of the testator's nieces, nephews and Linda Cosby Paine. The naked ownership of the mineral royalty devolves to the intestate heirs.

The judgments of the lower courts are reversed, and the petition to annul the probated testament is dismissed, all at the cost of respondent, James Philip Goode, Sr.

CALOGERO, Justice, concurring in part, dissenting in part. I concur in the majority's finding no prohibited substitution, but disagree with the majority's conclusion that the naked ownership of the mineral royalty devolves in time, upon the testator's legal heirs. My reasons are more fully and ably expressed in the majority's original opinion and my concurrence thereto.

Notes and Questions

1. Ronald Bruce Goode's single page, olographic will created quite a significant legal controversy, sparking five separate opinions by justices of the Louisiana Supreme Court in the original hearing and then a brand new opinion by Justice Dixon on rehearing, which finally settled *Succession of Goode*, 425 So.2d 673 (La. 1982). Make sure you understand what was at stake in the matter:

- If the opponents had succeeded in striking down the contested legacy as a prohibited substitution, Goode's oil and gas royalty interests would have fallen into intestacy and the opponents, Goode's intestate heirs (his half-brother, James Phillip Goode, Sr., and descendants of a predeceased half-sister), would have acquired the oil and gas royalty interests in full ownership.

- If the contested legacy established a usufruct in favor of Pauline Parker, with the naked ownership of the oil and gas royalty interest payments held by Goode's "nieces and nephews and Linda Cosby Paine," his half-brother would have received nothing and the nieces and nephews would share their naked ownership with Ms. Paine, who was not a relative.

- If the contested legacy established successive usufructs in favor of Pauline Parker, and then in favor of Goode's "nieces and nephews and Linda Cosby Paine," the intestate heirs, as naked owners, would have to wait until all of the

---

2. The matter of security for the usufruct, though not before the court in this case, was mentioned in preceding dissenting and concurring opinions. Whether the payments bequeathed are considered legacies of revenues under C.C. 609 or as usufructs with the rights and obligations of the usufructuary and naked owner controlled by the provisions of the Mineral Code, there is probably no obligation on the legatees for either security or an accounting. Comment (d) to article 609 states that the legacies of revenues are only a "kind of usufruct" that does not transfer possession to the legatee but only a personal non-heritable right to receive the revenues. Such a bequest is considered a quasi-usufruct only for the purpose of limiting their duration, and as such these quasi-usufructs are not burdened with the obligations of a usufructuary. . . . Within the Mineral Code, R.S. 31:194, amended by 1975 La. Acts No. 589, § 2, expressly provides: ". . . a usufructuary of a mineral right is not obligated to account to the naked owner of the . . . mineral right for the production or the value thereof or any other income to which he [usufructuary] is entitled."

usufructuary interests in the oil and gas royalties terminated before they could claim full, unencumbered ownership. Although the nieces and nephews would enjoy successive usufructuary interests along with Ms. Paine, once Ms. Parker's usufruct terminated, Goode's half-brother could not claim his unencumbered ownership interest until after Ms. Paine and all the nieces and nephews had died.

2. In the end, which justice's interpretation of the will is most persuasive? What role does Article 609 of the Civil Code, which establishes a rule for the termination of a "legacy of revenues from specified property," play in the resolution of this dispute? *See* La. Civ. Code art. 609 (1976). A legacy of revenues allows the legatee to enjoy fruits and revenues derived from a thing, without any rights of possession or administration. La. Civ. Code art. 609, rev. cmt. (c) (1976).

3. In *Succession of Brown*, 69 So.3d 1211 (La. App. 3 Cir. 2011), a wife executed a donation inter vivos in favor of her husband granting him a "Non-Exclusive Usufruct" of their family home, which she had acquired before the marriage and which was her separate property. After she died intestate, her children from a former marriage filed a lawsuit asserting that the donation was invalid. The trial court agreed, stating that the donation of the usufruct was "void and meaningless." *Id.* at 1213. The Third Circuit Court of Appeal reversed, holding that, even though the word "non-exclusive" was a common law term meaning "capable of being divided or shared with others," the donation of the non-exclusive life usufruct was "legally permissible, valid and legally binding." *Id.* at 1214–15. The court explained:

> A non-exclusive life usufruct is simply a usufruct granted for life to a person which may be divided or shared with others. Neither our jurisprudence nor our Civil Code prohibit such a conveyance. Had Mrs. Brown chosen to do so, she could have granted the same or a similar type of usufruct to others, neither of which would have had exclusive or independent rights under the usufruct, with one and all having to share their respective legal rights under the usufruct.

Id. at 1215. If the usufructuary in this case, Mr. Brown, married someone else after the commencement of the usufruct, could he donate a one-half share in the usufruct over the home to his new wife? If so, when would her usufruct terminate?

4. A lawyer asked to draft an instrument that will allow multiple generations in a family to share in the wealth of a donor or testator over time must be aware that, in comparison to Articles 546 to 548 and 1540 of the Civil Code, the Louisiana Trust Code provides more flexibility for creating multi-generation, asset protection regimes. Under La. Rev. Stat. 9:1891(A), a settlor can create a class trust. The beneficiaries of the trust may consist of members of up to three generations (including great grandchildren, great grandnieces and great grandnephews), but, unlike Article 548 of the Civil Code, the Trust Code does not require that all beneficiaries be in existence at the time of the creation of the trust. Instead, only one member of any of the potential class of beneficiaries must be in being. Moreover, this person

in being does not have to be a member of the youngest possible generation. La. Rev. Stat. 9:1891 cmt. (a).

In short, Louisiana law has made it possible to create what some common law lawyers call "dynasty trusts" that can easily preserve assets and wealth within one extended family for more than one hundred years. Because legal title to all property in trust is held by the trustee, who can dispose of it within the terms of the trust, as long as the beneficiaries' interests are served, the property is technically not taken out of commerce. Now reconsider Article 1520 of the Civil Code concerning prohibited substitutions. Do you see the significance of the language "a disposition that is *not in trust* . . . is null"?

D. Divisibility and Partition of the Usufruct and Naked Ownership

As we learned in Chapter Eleven, any person who owns property in indivision with other co-owners has a powerful—indeed, imprescriptible—right to demand a partition of the co-owned property in the absence of an enforceable agreement not to partition and as long as use of the property is not indispensable for the enjoyment of another thing held in indivision. *See* La. Civ. Code arts. 807, 808 and 817 (1990). Three articles in the Civil Code (Articles 541, 542 and 543) address how usufruct and naked ownership interests can be held in undivided or divided shares and address their susceptibility to partition. Article 541 of the Civil Code governs the divisibility and susceptibility to partition of usufruct interests among multiple usufructuaries:

Art. 541. Divisibility of Usufruct

Usufruct is susceptible to division, because its purpose is the enjoyment of advantages that are themselves divisible. It may be conferred on several persons in divided or undivided shares and it may be partitioned among the usufructuaries.

La. Civ. Code art. 541 (1976). This article establishes that the usufructuary can alienate a portion of the usufruct, although not the property subject to the usufruct (unless specific authorization has been granted). Moreover, the grantor can create a usufruct over one mass of property in favor of more than one person. In addition, the article makes clear that joint usufructuaries may partition their usufructuary interests among themselves.

The revision comments elucidate these principles. When a grantor creates a usufruct in which the usufructuary interests take the form of "divided portions," rather than undivided interests, the termination of the interest of each beneficiary benefits the naked owner." La. Civ. Code art. 541 rev. cmt. (b) (1976). On the other hand, when usufructuary interests have been conferred in "undivided portions," the rule of Article 547, which we studied above, applies, and "the termination of one usufructuary's interest results in the accrual of that interest in favor of the remaining usufrucuctuaries." *Id.*

Consider the following hypothetical to understand the practical utility of Article 541 and its implications. Oscar grants two distinct, *divided* one-half usufructuary interests in Arpent Noir—one to his father, Abe, for life, and the other to his mother, Brenda, for life. Oscar grants the naked ownership to his two siblings, Carol and David. If Abe dies first, his usufructuary interest terminates completely and the naked owners, Carol and David, acquire full ownership of one-half of Arpent Noir, while Brenda's usufructuary interest will only burden "her" one-half of Arpent Noir. On the other hand, if Oscar had conferred *undivided* usufructuary interests to both Abe and Brenda, then, upon Abe's death, Brenda's usufruct would have absorbed Abe's usufructuary interest. In this case, the naked owners, Carol and David, would have to wait until Brenda died or Brenda's usufruct terminated for some other reason to become full owners (in indivision) of Arpent Noir. Return to Problem 5 in Part C above. Does this illustration help you answer that problem?

Note the rule in the second sentence of Article 541 of the Civil Code. It allows a usufructuary interest to be partitioned if it is held in undivided shares, thereby enabling a usufructuary, who might want a naked owner to be able to claim full, unencumbered ownership of an asset subject to a joint usufruct held by multiple usufructuaries, to bypass the delay required by Article 547. La. Civ. Code art. 541 rev. cmt. (b) (1976). Thus, in the hypothetical above, suppose that Oscar had only granted Abe and Brenda undivided, joint usufructuary interests, while granting Carol and David undivided naked ownership interests. Brenda wants Carol and David to enjoy a one-half full ownership interest in Arpent Noir upon either her or Abe's death. Brenda can partition her and Abe's undivided usufructuary interest into divided shares. When either she or Abe dies, Carol and David will become co-owners of a one-half interest in full ownership. When both of them die, the entirety of the mass of property subject to the usufruct will be co-owned by Carol and David in full ownership.

When considering Article 541 of the Civil Code, keep in mind that it is relatively uncommon for conventional usufructs to be created for the benefit of multiple usufructuaries. Among the legal usufructs, it is likewise uncommon, except for the parental usufruct established by Article 891 in favor of parents. Indeed, the usufruct pursuant to Article 890 in favor of the surviving spouse in community, which is by far the most common legal usufruct in Louisiana, establishes just one usufructuary. Thus, the rules under Article 541 may have more theoretical than practical application in most usufruct situations.

Article 542 of the Civil Code addresses the divisibility of the naked ownership interest but its practical applications may be similarly limited.

Art. 542. Divisibility of naked ownership

The naked ownership may be partitioned subject to the rights of the usufructuary.

La. Civ. Code art. 542 (1977). As the revision comments explain, "[w]hen the naked ownership of a thing is held by several persons in undivided shares and the usufruct by another person or persons, partition of the naked ownership in kind or by licitation may be demanded by any of the naked owners." *Id.* rev. cmt. (b). Importantly, though, such a partition of the naked ownership interest "does not affect adversely the interests of the usufructuaries, who continue to enjoy the things as if no change of ownership took place." *Id.* Revision comment (c) to Article 542 reviews the older jurisprudence that had disallowed partition of common elements as between co-usufructuaries or co-naked owners. The comment notes that current Articles 541 and 542 clearly allow for partition of common elements: usufructuary interests by co-usufructuaries holding undivided shares and naked ownership interests by co-naked owners holding undivided shares. La. Civ. Code art. 542 rev. cmt. (c) (1976).

Recognizing that several naked owners can partition their naked ownership interests pursuant to Article 542 subject to the usufructuary's continued enjoyment of the usufruct, what practical advantages could be gained by such a partition? How many potential buyers or lenders would realistically be interested in purchasing or taking a security interest in a divided naked ownership interest still subject to a usufructuary's right of enjoyment?

The final provision in the Civil Code concerning partition of usufructuary and naked ownership interests, Article 543, has very important practical implications for many usufructs, especially usufructs of the surviving spouse in community resulting from Article 890 of the Civil Code. Consider the text:

Art. 543. Partition of the property held in kind or by licitation

When property is held in indivision, a person having a share in full ownership may demand partition of the property in kind or by licitation, even though there may be other shares in naked ownership and usufruct.

A person having a share in naked ownership only or in usufruct only does not have this right, unless a naked owner of an undivided share and a usufructuary of that share jointly demand partition in kind or by licitation, in which event their combined shares shall be deemed to constitute a share in full ownership.

La. Civ. Code art. 543 (1976, amended 1983).

Consider a typical usufruct scenario under Article 890 of the Civil Code. Harold and Winifred, husband and wife, acquired their family home, a house and lot, during their marriage. The home is thus community property. Harold died intestate, survived by Winifred and the couple's two children, Andrew and Barbara. Upon Harold's death, Winifred owns one-half of the family home outright in full ownership. Andrew and Barbara become the naked owners of the other one-half interest, subject to Winifred's usufruct. How does Article 543 affect Winifred's rights as usufructuary and Andrew and Barbara's rights as naked owners?

If Winifred would like to liquidate her interest in the family home by selling the house, the first sentence of Article 543 allows her to take advantage of her one-half interest in full ownership and partition the family home, even in the face of Andrew and Barbara's opposition. After the likely partition by licitation, Winifred will be able to claim one-half of the proceeds outright as owner, while her usufruct will give her the right to enjoy the other half of the proceeds. Her usufruct is over consumables. In short, she could turn the family home into a funding vehicle for her retirement plans.

Conversely, because of the second sentence of Article 543 of the Civil Code, Andrew and Barbara will not, under any circumstances, be able to force a partition of the family home in which they share an undivided one-half naked ownership interest. Even if they need cash, they will not be able to force Winifred out of the family home through a partition by licitation or in kind, because they only have a "share in naked ownership." La. Civ. Code art. 543 (1976, amended 1983). Article 543 represents one of the clearest examples of how the last revision of the usufruct was designed to shore up protections for what the drafters perceived as particularly vulnerable usufructuaries—surviving spouses under Article 890 of the Civil Code.

The second sentence of Article 543 of the Civil Code can be helpful in situations involving multiple usufructuaries and naked owners. Suppose that Paul dies testate leaving his property to his four cousins subject to a joint usufruct in favor of his four aunts. One aunt is the parent of one cousin, another aunt is the parent of the other three cousins; the other two aunts are childless. The aunt with only one child may agree with her child to jointly demand partition of the property subject to the usufruct. This is because that child's one-quarter interest in naked ownership, when combined with the aunt's one-quarter interest in usufruct, creates a one-quarter interest in full ownership.

The 1983 revision comments and the Editor's note to revised Article 543 in the West pamphlet edition of the Civil Code detail the long jurisprudential battles over the source provisions of Article 543 and the debate about the retroactive and prospective applicability of the current provision. *See Smith v. Nelson*, 46 So. 200 (La. 1908); *Devillier v. Devillier*, 371 So.2d 1230 (La. App. 3 Cir. 1979); *Pasternack v. Samuels*, 415 So.2d 211 (La. 1983); *Cahn v. Cahn*, 468 So.2d 1176 (La. 1975). For a detailed discussion, see A.N. YIANNOPOULOS, 3 LOUISIANA CIVIL LAW TREATISE: PERSONAL SERVITUDES § 1:33 (5th ed. 2011).

E. Rights, Powers and Obligations of the Usufructuary and Naked Owner during the Usufruct

1. Introduction

After setting forth the general principles governing the real right of usufruct in Articles 535 through 549 of the Civil Code, Title III of Book II provides in Chapter 2,

Sections 2, 3 and 4, a long series of detailed rules governing the relationship between the usufructuary and the naked owner as well as their respective rights, powers and obligations during the existence of the usufruct.

Section 2 of Chapter 2, Title III, ("Rights of the Usufructuary") contains articles that establish:

- The usufructuary's rights to natural and civil fruits. (Articles 550–551)
- The allocation of rights to different kinds of corporate distributions and corporate voting rights as between the usufructuary and naked owner. (Articles 552–553)
- The commencement of the right to fruits and apportionment of civil and natural fruits between the usufructuary and naked owner. (Articles 554–556)
- The right of the usufructuary to possess and use the thing subject to the usufruct and the allocation of rights between the usufructuary and naked owner with regard to improvements and alterations of the property subject to the usufruct. (Articles 557–558)
- The allocation of rights between the usufructuary and naked owner with regard to accessory things, including alluvion and treasure discovered on the property subject to the usufruct. (Articles 559, 563–564)
- The allocation of rights between the usufructuary and naked owner with respect to trees, stones and material taken from land subject to a usufruct, and with regard to mines and quarries, and timberlands. (Articles 560–562)
- The right of the usufructuary to enjoy predial servitudes due to an estate subject to a usufruct. (Article 565)
- The right of the usufructuary to institute actions necessary to secure the possession, enjoyment and preservation of the usufruct. (Article 566)
- The right of the usufructuary to lease, alienate or encumber the usufruct and the consequences of such contracts. (Article 567)
- The limits to the usufructuary's right to dispose of nonconsumables and the power of the usufructuary to dispose of corporeal movables subject to gradual wear and decay. (Articles 568–569)

As you review those articles, keep in mind four important principles. First, one of the usufructuary's most basic rights is to enjoy all the fruits of the property subject to the usufruct. Consequently, the usufructuary will have no obligation to account to the naked owner for civil or natural fruits that accrue during the existence of the usufruct. Second, the usufructuary is required to manage all nonconsumables as a prudent administrator. This duty to act as a prudent administrator underscores many specific rules. Third, the usufructuary owns the consumables subject to the usufruct and enjoys much greater freedom of disposition with respect to them. However, the usufructuary must still "account" for the value of consumables at the end of the usufruct. Finally, a naked owner is ultimately entitled to receive nonconsumables at the termination of the usufruct without any unusual diminution in their substance.

Section 3 of Chapter 2, Title III, ("Obligations of the Usufructuary") contains articles that regulate the following topics:

- The usufructuary's obligations to provide an inventory and furnish security to the naked owner. (Articles 570–575)

- The usufructuary's standard of care with respect to the thing subject to the usufruct. (Article 576)

- The allocation of responsibility between usufructuary and naked owner for different kinds of repairs to the property subject to the usufruct. (Articles 577–580)

- The usufructuary's liability for expenses necessary for the preservation of the property subject to the usufruct. (Article 581)

- The usufructuary's right to abandon property subject to the usufruct for the purpose of releasing himself from the obligation of making certain repairs. (Article 582)

- The rights and obligations of the usufructuary and the naked owner when the property subject to the usufruct has been totally destroyed through accident, *force majeure* or age. (Article 583)

- The rights and obligations of the usufructuary and the naked owner with respect to periodic charges, such as property taxes, and extraordinary charges, such as road paving assessments. (Articles 584–585)

- The liability of the usufructuary for debts of the grantor, including estate debts and litigation expenses. (Articles 586–596)

- The liability of the usufructuary for the loss by nonuse of a predial servitude benefiting property subject to the usufruct or the acquisition of a servitude on the property subject to the usufruct as the result of acquisitive prescription by another. (Article 597)

- The responsibility of the usufructuary to inform the naked owner with respect to encroachments on immovable property subject to the usufruct. (Article 598)

- The rights and responsibilities of a usufructuary to use, replace, care for and dispose of a herd of animals. (Articles 599–600)

- The rights and obligations of the usufructuary with regard to the removal of improvements he has made to the property subject to the usufruct and set-off rights for improvements not removed. (Articles 601–602)

Section 4 of Chapter 2, Title III, ("Rights and Obligations of the Naked Owner"), the shortest section in Title III, contains only four articles addressing:

- The naked owner's right to dispose of the property subject to the usufruct. (Article 603)

- The naked owner's right to establish other real rights, such as predial servitudes, on the property subject to the usufruct. (Article 604)

- The naked owner's general duty not to interfere with the rights of the usufructuary. (Article 605)

- The naked owner's obligation not to make alterations or improvements on the property subject to the usufruct. (Article 606)

Although many of the provisions referenced above are straightforward, you should study all of them carefully before answering the hypothetical problems below. We also offer selected decisions from the jurisprudence to illustrate how some of these articles have been applied by the courts.

Problems

Oliver Linus was a farmer in St. Mary Parish, Louisiana. Four years ago, Oliver's wife Lucy passed away. Two years ago, Oliver died, survived by one son, Ned, who had moved away from home years ago. In his validly executed will, Oliver left all of his property to Ned, subject to a usufruct in favor of his niece, Ursula, who lived nearby and had taken care of Oliver in his last years. Ursula has very little property or wealth of her own. Oliver had been a resourceful man. His farm was full of animals, crops, trees and cabins that he rented out to visiting tourists. Please advise Ursula about her rights and obligations by answering the following questions.

1. Early this year, after taking possession of Oliver's farm as usufructuary, Ursula planted sugar cane on forty acres of Oliver's farm. She harvested the cane in the late fall of this year. Who is entitled to the sugar cane crop: Ursula or Ned? Is any reimbursement owed now or at the end of the usufruct?

2. Suppose that Oliver's will provided that Ursula's usufruct would terminate if she marries. Assume for purposes of this question only that in the late summer of this year, two months before Ursula was scheduled to harvest the sugar cane crop she had planted, Ursula married Victor. Who is entitled to the sugar cane crop still growing on the farm? Is any reimbursement owed by anyone? In addition to the articles referenced above, see also La. Civ. Code arts. 545 and 610 (1976).

3. Early this year, one of Oliver's cows gave birth to a beautiful new calf. Who is entitled to the calf? If it is Ursula, is she required to return the calf to Ned at the end of her usufruct? If she sells the calf, is she entitled to keep the proceeds for herself?

4. Early this year, Ursula decides to sell ten of the cows from Oliver's cattle herd to a slaughterhouse. Is Ursula entitled to the proceeds derived from the sale of the cows? Can she spend the proceeds? Or is she required to reinvest the proceeds in more cows? Must she account for the value of the cows at the end of the usufruct?

5. Early this year, Ursula sells 5,000 cubic yards of dense clay removed from the farm to the United States Army Corps of Engineers for $200,000 for use in the construction of new flood protection levees. Is Ursula entitled to the proceeds or is

Ned? Does it matter if the levees are in close proximity to the farm and will protect it from flooding?

6. Early this year, Ursula cuts down a 200-year-old cypress tree on the farm. She gives it to a carpenter who makes some furniture for Ursula out of the tree. Does Ursula owe Ned any reimbursement for the value of the cypress tree at the end of the usufruct? Who owns the furniture?

7. A navigable bayou runs through Oliver's land. Over the next ten years, 3,000 square feet of new alluvion is deposited in a bend in the bayou. Ursula builds a dock and fishing camp on the alluvion. At the end of the usufruct, who owns the newly formed alluvion? The dock? The fishing camp?

8. Ursula discovers a treasure chest filled with gold bullion buried on the other bank of the bayou across from the new alluvion. Archeologists establish that this treasure chest was left by a band of pirates affiliated with Jean Lafitte. Who is entitled to the treasure chest and gold bullion? Is your answer different if a visitor to the farm found the chest and bullion while he was staying in one of the cabins rented out by Ursula?

9. Ursula regularly rents out several of the cabins on the farm to visiting tourists, fishermen and hunters and rents out some of the vacant farmland to a tenant farmer. Who is entitled to the rental income from these leases? Does Ursula have any duty to account to Ned for the rental income now or at the termination of the usufruct?

10. During his lifetime, Oliver negotiated with a farmer who owned the neighboring farm and acquired a predial servitude of passage over that neighbor's farm to the nearest public road for the benefit of Oliver's farm. Who is entitled to use that predial servitude of passage? Ned? Ursula? Both of them? If Ursula fails to use the servitude of passage and it prescribes by nonuse, will Ursula be liable to Ned?

2. Hard Case: The Usufruct of Timberlands

Problem

Edna, an eighty-year-old widow, holds a usufruct over a 100-acre tract of wooded land in Iberville Parish. Fred, a seventy-six-year-old nephew of Edna, is the naked owner of this tract of land. The standing trees on this tract have never been subject to any kind of timber management program. Two years after the commencement of the usufruct, Edna hired a professional forester who advised her that the standing timber on the land would have a current market value of $400,000 if it was professionally harvested. Edna plans to harvest the timber by cutting down 80% of the standing trees, leaving the youngest 20% of the trees for future growth and reseeding the remaining land. Fred is upset. He believes that Edna's plan of action is unlawful and that if she goes ahead and harvests the timber, he should be entitled to some of the proceeds of the sale of the timber. Fred asks you for legal advice. Before formulating your advice to Fred, read the following decision of the Louisiana Supreme Court.

Kennedy v. Kennedy

699 So.2d 351, 357–60 (La. 1997) (ON REHEARING)

KNOLL, Justice. We granted rehearing in this case to revisit the issue of a usufructuary's right to harvest timber from a previously unmanaged tract of land. The facts of this case are laid out in detail in the original opinion. Helena Kennedy, the 91 year old usufructuary of a 143 acre tract of mature loblolly pine trees, sought a declaratory judgment authorizing a clear-cut on the tract. James Kennedy, the 70 year old naked owner, opposed the clear-cut.

Usufruct of Timberland

Ordinarily, the right of the usufructuary extends only to the fruits of the thing subject to the usufruct. La. Civ. Code art. 550. On account of their slow growth and high value, trees are usually considered to be capital assets rather than fruits. In the case of an ordinary tract of land, the usufructuary may cut trees only for his personal use or for the improvement or cultivation of the land. La. Civ. Code art. 560. The revision comments to Articles 551 and 560 suggest that the continuous production of a "tree farm" or "regularly exploited forest" may be regarded as fruits, and thus belong to the usufructuary.

However, we find that the designation of the timber as "fruits" or "products" is irrelevant in the instant case, since the right of a usufructuary to harvest trees from timberland is governed by a *specific* article, La. Civ. Code art. 562, which states:

> When the usufruct includes timberlands, the usufructuary is bound to manage them as a prudent administrator. The proceeds of timber operations that are derived from proper management of timberlands belong to the usufructuary.

La. Civ. Code art. 13 provides that where two statutes deal with the same subject matter, they should be harmonized if possible. However, if there is a conflict, the statute specifically directed to the matter at issue must prevail as an exception to the statute more general in character. *State ex rel. Bickman v. Dees*, 367 So. 2d 283, 291 (La. 1978). Article 562 is a new provision, added in the revision of the Civil Code articles on usufruct in 1976. It provides for a different disposition of the proceeds of timber operations on timberland than from cutting trees on ordinary land. Since Article 562 is specifically directed to timberland, it must be treated as an exception to the general rules of usufruct.

Two factual issues are raised under Article 562, namely, whether the tract is "timberland" and what constitutes "proper management" of that particular tract.

Timberland

Put simply, the central issue in the case *sub judice* is whether land containing valuable timber which has never been exploited or the subject of forestry management constitutes "timberland" for the purposes of the application of Article 562. Restated, does La. Civ. Code art. 562 require prior timber operations on the property for the land to be construed as "timberland"?

As noted by Justice Kimball in her dissent in our original opinion, this exact issue was considered by the drafters of the 1976 revision of the law of usufruct. The original draft of Article 562, prepared by the Louisiana State Law Institute, stated:

> If the usufruct includes lands that were *regularly exploited for timber* at the time of the creation of the usufruct, and if there is no provision concerning the use and enjoyment of the landowner's rights in timber, the usufructuary is entitled to *continue the operations* of the owner; but he has *no right to commence* timber operations without the consent of the naked owner (emphasis added).

This original version of the article was intended to adapt the "open mines" policy for the usufruct of minerals to the usufruct of timberlands. Nevertheless, upon a motion by Prof. Joseph Dainow, this draft of the article was rejected in favor of the more flexible "prudent management" standard found in Article 562 today. The language requiring regular exploitation or continuing timber operations was removed.

La. Civ. Code art. 11 provides that the words of a law must be given their generally prevailing meaning, and that words of art and technical terms must be given their technical meaning when a law involves a technical matter. "Timber" is defined by La. Civ. Code art. 562, Comment (c) as trees which, if cut, would produce lumber for building or manufacturing purposes. The term "timberland" is defined in Webster's Third New International Dictionary as "land covered with forest and especially with marketable timber."

The expert witnesses also supplied definitions of "timberland" as applicable to forestry operations. Mr. Lewis Peters, Mrs. Kennedy's forestry expert, defined "timberland" as "land that's capable of producing commercial forest products," while Mrs. Kennedy's other expert, Mr. Richard Freshwater defined "timberland" as "land with or without timber capable of growing timber in commercial quantities." Mr. Gary Wade agreed that "timberland" is "any land that has some type of timber growth on it, be it merchantable or not merchantable."

"Timberland" is distinguishable from land which has been regularly managed and exploited for timber, which is best defined by the term "tree farm." The defining characteristic of a "tree farm" as stated by this court is "the land's ability, through proper management techniques such as selective thinnings and plantings, to provide sustained yields." *Succession of Doll v. Doll*, 593 So. 2d 1239, 1249 (La. 1992). Mr. Peters noted that the term "tree farm" was "sort of like a trademark" and that "it's a designation that's given to landowners that apply and meet the requirements of the American Forestry Association whose . . . under whose umbrella the tree farm system was created." The 143 acre tract is not a "tree farm," as it has never been managed, and is unable to produce a sustained yield of timber in its present state.

Under both the general definition and under the technical definition supplied by the foresters, the 143 acre tract is "timberland." For this tract not to be classified as "timberland," this court would have to create an alternative legal definition or term of art, requiring that the tract be regularly managed or exploited for timber prior to the initiation of the usufruct, making "timberland" synonymous with "tree farm." We decline to do so, especially since this would substantively reenact the original version of La. Civ. Code art. 562, which had been rejected by the Louisiana State Law Institute.

Proper Management

The second issue before us is whether Mrs. Kennedy's plan to clear-cut the tract constitutes proper management or prudent administration of the tract. This is clearly an issue to be decided by the trier of fact. After a two day trial in which each party called two forestry expert witnesses, the trial court adopted the expert opinion of Mrs. Kennedy's forester, Mr. Lewis C. Peters, on the proper management of the tract.

Mr. Peters noted that the tract consisted of an even aged stand of mature and over mature loblolly pine, whose age was between sixty and seventy-five years. He testified that the life span of loblolly pine trees was between eighty and one hundred years. Mr. Peters stated that thirty acres in the southwest corner of the tract contained trees younger than those found on the remainder of the tract. Mr. Peters noted that undesirable hardwood species were beginning to succeed the pines on the tract, and he opined that because the tract had not been previously managed it would be difficult to rehabilitate.

Mr. Peters testified that the most prudent approach would be to harvest the merchantable timber on the majority of the tract, including the hardwoods, and replant the site with genetically superior seedlings. He stated that it would not be prudent to simply cut the larger pines since the smaller trees were the same age. He opined that the smaller trees were so old and suppressed that they would not respond to the removal of the larger trees. Mr. Peters outlined the risks associated with allowing the older pine trees to remain on the tract, noting that the trees were rapidly approaching the end of their life span, that they were vulnerable to insect attack, and that they could attract endangered species, thus preventing their harvest. Mr. Peters recommended that some hardwoods be left along watersheds and streams to prevent erosion and encourage wildlife. With respect to the thirty acre portion of the tract containing the younger trees, Mr. Peters recommended a selective cut of only the larger trees.

Obviously, what constitutes "proper management" of timberland will vary depending on the species, condition, size, location, age, and density of the timber on the tract. The trial court was presented with several expert opinions on the prudent administration of this particular tract, and was well informed about the several available alternatives. The trial court's acceptance of Mr. Peters' recommendations as the most prudent course of management of the property was reasonable, and we find no manifest error in its decision to accept Mr. Peters' expert opinion.

It is apparent from the findings of the trial court that prior to the initiation of the usufruct, the 143 acre tract had not been properly managed to provide sustained yields, and that selective thinnings and plantings on the tract would do little to rehabilitate the tract. Because the tract had been neglected for so long from a forestry standpoint, leaving some of the trees standing placed the entire stand of timber at risk of infection, infestation, destruction by the elements, and succession by less desirable species. These risks greatly outweighed any benefits that could accrue by leaving the smaller trees. The trial court reasonably concluded that the most prudent management of the tract called for a clear-cut of the majority of the tract, followed by replanting with genetically improved seedlings.

Had this tract been a properly managed "tree farm" prior to the initiation of Mrs. Kennedy's usufruct, it is unlikely that her plan to clear-cut the tract would be considered prudent. However, we recognize that under certain circumstances, such as those found in the present case, a clear-cut may be warranted. The prudent administrator/proper management standard is a flexible one, and we are unwilling to hold that as a matter of law clear-cutting will never constitute the proper management of timberland.

Accordingly, under Article 562, Mrs. Kennedy is entitled to the proceeds of the prudent management plan proposed by her foresters and approved by the trial court. The judgment of the court of appeal, limiting Mrs. Kennedy's timber activities to a selective cutting from the thirty acre stand of younger trees is reversed, and the judgment of the trial court is reinstated.

REVERSED.

JOHNSON, Justice, Dissenting. I respectfully dissent.

La. C.C. Art. 560 provides: **The usufructuary may cut trees growing on the land of which he has the usufruct and take stones, sand and other materials from it, but only for his use or for the improvement or cultivation of the land.**

This case presents an area of land that has not been improved or cultivated in many years. As a result, many of the trees have reached their prime and others are near maturity. It is evident that some type of maintenance is needed to preserve this land for both the naked owner and the usufructuary. When the parties cannot agree as to the management plan, the courts must approve a plan. In this case, the majority approved a clear cut plan.

The experts have testified that selective cutting of the timberlands is far more prudent.

This land is capable of producing commercial timber if properly maintained. The ecological aspects warrant a selective cutting and not a clear cut of the land. To follow the majority's plan would mean that the fruits of the land are being dissipated. **La. C.C. Art. 562** provides: **When the usufruct includes timberlands, the usufructuary is bound to manage them as a prudent administrator. The proceeds of timber operations that are derived from proper management of timberlands belong to the usufructuary.** The statute is clear that "timber operations should not deplete the substance of the land. The interests of the naked owner are protected by the prohibition of waste and by the obligations of the usufructuary to act as a prudent administrator and to preserve the substance of the property subject to the usufruct". See comments **La. C.C.P. Art. 562.**

A clear cut of the land will affect the substance of the property and therefore, deny the naked owner the protection that the statutes in this regard afford him. Clearly, prudent management of the land requires that it be selectively cut in order to preserve the substance of the land.

Notes and Questions

1. In *Kennedy v. Kennedy*, 699 So.2d 351 (La. 1997), the court interpreted Article 562 in a manner very favorable to the interests of the ninety-one-year-old usufructuary, Helena Kennedy. Helena acquired her usufruct over the 143 acres in question from her late husband, Walter Kennedy, who died in 1988. He left her the usufruct over the land, while leaving his cousin, James Kennedy, the naked ownership of the land. *Id.* at 352. In the original opinion in the case, the court noted that, at the time of the trial, "the value of the timber on the tract was estimated at $2,200–$2,500 per acre, and the value of the land itself, without trees or planted seedlings, was estimated to range from $200–$300 per acre." *Id.* What effect will the court's decision have on the prospects of James, the seventy-year-old naked owner, to realize some economic benefit from his naked ownership interest in the tract of land before he dies? Should the court have taken the respective ages of the usufructuary and naked owner into account?

2. If Walter, the grantor of the usufruct in *Kennedy*, had wanted to make sure that his cousin James would be able to profit from the valuable timber on his 143-acre tract of land, while at the same time, providing some security to his surviving spouse Helena, how else could he have crafted the usufruct?

3. If Walter had simply left Helena and James with equal undivided shares in the 143-acre tract of land and timber as co-owners, would James have been better off? What rights, if any, would Helena and James have had to harvest the valuable timber on the land as fellow co-owners?

4. Observe that in the course of her majority opinion on rehearing, Justice Knoll observed that the original draft version of Article 562 was "intended to adapt the 'open mines' policy for the usufruct of minerals to the usufruct of timberlands," but that this approach was rejected "in favor of the more flexible 'prudent management' standard found in Article 562 today." *Kennedy*, 699 So.2d at 358. In particular, that draft provision stated:

> If the usufruct includes lands that were *regularly exploited for timber* at the time of the creation of the usufruct, and if there is no provision concerning the use and enjoyment of the landowner's rights in timber, the usufructuary is entitled to *continue the operations* of the owner; but he has *no right to commence* timber operations without the consent of the naked owner (emphasis added).

Id. If the draft language had been adopted in the final version of Article 562, James Kennedy would likely have prevailed in his dispute with his aunt Helena. What policy arguments would have been advanced in favor of such an "open mines" approach to the usufruct of timberlands? Why were they rejected?

5. *Usufruct of Minerals*: Several articles in the Louisiana Mineral Code still apply the "open mines" policy mentioned in *Kennedy* to the rights of usufructuaries with regard to solid minerals and fugacious minerals such as oil and gas. *See generally* La. Rev. Stat. 31:188–196. The open mines doctrine in Louisiana originated in several older decisions predating the Mineral Code, most notably *Gueno v. Medlenka*, 117 So.2d 817 (La. 1960). In that case, the Louisiana Supreme Court held that, although a usufructuary does not have the right to explore for and withdraw oil and gas existing under land subject to a usufruct because such use of the oil and gas would alter the land's substance, a usufructuary was entitled to "the enjoyment and proceeds of mines and quarries in the land subject to the usufruct . . . *if they were actually worked* before the commencement of the usufruct." *Id*. at 819–20 (emphasis added).

In *Gueno*, the court further held that only the naked owner, and not the usufructuary, can open new mines on land subject to a usufruct and that the naked owner then enjoys the proceeds of those new mines exclusively. *Id*. at 822. At the same time, the naked owner cannot exercise his rights with respect to the minerals in a manner that would be detrimental to the usufructuary's rights of possession and use of the land. *Id*. at 823.

Finally, the court in *Gueno* held that the naked owner, not the usufructuary, has the exclusive right to execute mineral leases with respect to land subject to a usufruct. Therefore, the naked owner does not need the consent of the usufructuary to grant such leases. *Id*. at 824. Thus, the usufructuary is not a necessary party to a mineral lease executed by the naked owner. The usufructuary cannot prevent the naked owner's mineral lessee from entering the property to explore for minerals and reduce them to possession, as long as the lessee does not unreasonably interfere with the usufructuary's use of the land. *Id*. The court concluded that, when land with minerals is subject to a usufruct, the naked owner's rights with respect to those minerals are "coextensive and concurrent with, not subordinate to, the usufructuary's right of enjoyment and use." *Id*.

6. Several principles articulated in *Gueno* have now been codified in the Louisiana Mineral Code. Subject to certain important exceptions, when mineral rights are *not segregated* from the land subject to a usufruct, the naked owner will exclusively enjoy the mineral rights, including the right to search for and reduce minerals to possession and the right to benefit from mineral operations. *See* La. Rev. Stat. § 31:188 (1974) and La. Rev. Stat.§ 31:195 (1974, amended 1982). When mineral rights *are segregated* from the ownership of land, however, the grantor of a conventional usufruct can determine the rights of both the usufructuary and the naked owner; for example, by giving the usufructuary a conventional usufruct over the

mineral rights. *See* La. Rev. Stat. § 31:189 (1974) and La. Rev. Stat. § 31:193 (1974, amended 1975).

When a usufructuary has been granted a usufruct over mineral rights, he can explore for minerals and claim the benefits of mineral exploitation just as if he were the actual owner of the mineral rights. La. Rev. Stat. § 31:193 (1975). A usufructuary who has been granted a conventional usufruct of mineral rights under Article 193 of the Mineral Code will also generally enjoy the right to grant a mineral lease that extends beyond the duration of the usufruct because without this power the usufructuary of a mineral interest "could not care for the property properly" and satisfy his duty to act as a prudent administrator. A.N. Yiannopoulos, 3 Louisiana Civil Law Treatise: Personal Servitudes § 2:23, at 162 (5th ed. 2011) (citing La. Rev. Stat. § 31:118 (1974)).

The exceptions to the general principle that minerals and mineral proceeds are treated as products are found in Article 190 of the Mineral Code:

Art. 190. Usufructuary of land entitled to enjoyment of mines or quarries worked; exception

A. If a usufruct of land is that of parents during marriage, or any other legal usufruct, or if there is no provision including the use and enjoyment of mineral rights in a conventional usufruct, the usufructuary is entitled to use and enjoyment of the landowner's rights in minerals as to mines or quarries actually worked at the time the usufruct was created.

B. If a usufruct of land is that of the surviving spouse, whether legal or conventional, and there is no contrary provision in the instrument creating the usufruct, the usufructuary is entitled to the use and enjoyment of the landowner's rights in minerals, whether or not mines or quarries were actually worked at the time the usufruct was created. However, the rights to which the usufructuary is thus entitled shall not include the right to execute a mineral lease without the consent of the naked owner.

La. Rev. Stat. § 31:190 (1974, amended 1986).

Article 194 establishes that minerals and mineral proceeds will be treated as fruits and therefore, belong to the usufructuary. Moreover, the usufructuary will be relieved of any liability to account to the naked owner for the production of minerals or their value in two situations: (1) in the case of a legal or conventional usufruct that does not specifically grant the usufructuary rights to minerals, *when the mine or quarry is worked at the commencement of the usufruct*; or (2) regardless of whether there is an open mine or quarry, the usufruct is *either a conventional or legal usufruct in favor of the surviving spouse.* La. Rev. Stat. 31:194 (1974, amended 1975); *see also* A.N. Yiannopoulos, 3 Louisiana Civil Law Treatise: Personal Servitudes §§ 2:21-2:22 (5th ed. 2014).

Under the Mineral Code, the right to execute new mineral leases on land subject to a usufruct is reserved to the naked owner. So even a surviving spouse usufructuary will need consent from the naked owner to grant such leases on mines not opened at the commencement of the usufruct. La Rev. Stat. § 31:192 (1974). However, surviving spouses and other usufructuaries entitled to mineral rights may execute mineral leases on mines open at the beginning of the usufruct. *Id.*

3. Usufruct of Shares in a Corporation

Problems

Sally is an enterprising business woman from Abbeville. Twenty years ago, she established a business to provide eco-friendly swamp and bayou tours in the back country near Abbeville. She also sells her own line of Cajun seasoning, guide books and other tourism oriented products and services. The business was successful. By the time Sally passed away, her company, Sally Services, Inc., (SSI) employed fifty people and produced approximately $7 million in gross revenues. When Sally died two years ago, she owned 100% of the shares of the closely held corporation. She bequeathed the naked ownership in her shares to her niece, Nancy, subject to a usufruct in favor of her mother, Ophelia.

1. Last year, the corporation paid total dividends of $600,000 on the shares of stock owned by Nancy as naked owner and subject to Ophelia's usufruct. Who is entitled to these dividends? Does anyone owe reimbursement on these dividends?

2. This year, SSI declared a stock split and paid stock dividends instead of cash dividends. Who is entitled to the new shares of stock resulting from the stock splits and stock dividends: Nancy or Ophelia? Who is entitled to the cash dividends on the new shares of stock produced by the stock dividends and stock splits: Nancy or Ophelia?

3. At the next shareholders meeting of SSI, who will be entitled to vote the shares of stock that Sally previously owned?

4. One month ago, the Board of Directors of SSI voted to liquidate the corporation and distribute liquidation dividends to all of the shareholders. Who will be entitled to these liquidation dividends: Nancy or Ophelia?

4. The Power to Dispose of Nonconsumables

To understand a usufructuary's power to dispose of nonconsumables, we must return to Article 545 of the Civil Code, which sets forth core principles undergirding the institution of usufruct:

Art. 545. Modifications of usufruct

Usufruct may be established for a term or under a condition, and subject to any modification consistent with the nature of usufruct.

The rights and obligations of the usufructuary may be modified by agreement unless modification is prohibited by law or by the grantor in the act establishing the usufruct.

La. Civ. Code art. 545 (1976). As we noted before, one of the most important modifications *allowed* by law is that a grantor may relieve the usufructuary of the obligation to preserve the substance of the property subject to the usufruct. In other words, the grantor can give the usufructuary the power to dispose of the property even if the thing subject to the usufruct is a nonconsumable. *Id.* rev. cmt. (b); La. Civ. Code art. 539 rev. cmt. (c) (1976). When this power has been granted, the usufructuary's only obligation at the termination of the usufruct is to account to the naked owner for the value of the thing at the beginning of the usufruct. In other words, the thing subject to the usufruct will be treated as if it were a consumable.

Before answering the next set of problems, read the following excerpt from a law review comment published in 2012. It analyzes several of the important revisions to the rules governing the power to dispose of nonconsumables made by the Louisiana Legislature in 2010.

Adam N. Matasar, *The Usufruct Revisions: The Power to Dispose of Nonconsumables Now Expressly Includes Alienation, Lease and Encumbrance; Has the Legislature Fundamentally Altered the Nature of Usufruct?*
86 TUL. L. REV. 787, 788–89, 796–98, 798–811, 816, 818–19 (2012)

. . . . Over time, Louisiana Civil Code articles and case law have approached the usufructuary/naked-owner relationship equitably, imposing a modicum of mutuality between the parties. However, with each successive revision, the interplay between the usufructuary and naked owner has shifted. Consequently, the current revision reflects a continuing trend whereby the usufructuary is granted increasing authority.

The Louisiana Legislature most recently revised the law governing usufruct in Act 881, which became effective July 2, 2010. The revision, for the most part, retained the equitable characteristics that are integral to the very nature of usufruct. However, some revisions have resulted in Code articles that greatly expand the usufructuary's rights, decrease the naked owner's rights, and create a newborn legal landscape in which courts must create equitable outcomes with little to no jurisprudence to guide them. For example, article 568, which governs the usufructuary's power to dispose of nonconsumables, was expanded in Act 881 to include not only the power of alienation, but the powers of lease and encumbrance as well. This broad codification of the power to dispose of nonconsumables may have tilted the equitable balance of the relationship too far toward the usufructuary, and further legislative action and judicial activism seem inevitable to prevent misuse of this broadened power. . . .

III. The Usufruct Revisions

. . . .

A. Article 568: The Power to Dispose of Nonconsumables

Prior to the revisions, article 568 provided the only codification of the usufructuary's power to dispose of nonconsumables. This article codified a testator's ability to grant expressly to a usufructuary the power to "dispose of nonconsumable things" and unambiguously explained what the effect of such a "disposition" would be. As the 1976 revision comments indicate, article 568 was not intended to change the law, but was rather an effort to codify a principle elaborated by an early Louisiana Supreme Court decision, *Michel v. Knox* [34 La. 399 (1882)]. . . .

Thus, as the language from article 568 and the 1976 revision comments indicate, the legislative intent behind article 568 was to codify the finding of the court in *Michel*: a testator's desire to grant a usufructuary the power to dispose of nonconsumables is not contrary to law or morals. As indicated by comment (a), article 568 did "not change the law." But it would seem to have done just that, because article 539, with traditional civilian origins derived from articles 533 and 535 of the Louisiana Civil Code of 1870, clearly states that the usufructuary of nonconsumables is under the obligation of preserving those things' substance. However, article 545 declares that a "[u]sufruct may be . . . subject to any modification consistent with the nature of usufruct."

Code articles on the same subject matter must be read *in pari materia*, and every attempt should be made to give logical meaning to the Civil Code's many articles. Therefore, because article 545 permits testamentary freedom within the confines of public policy and the fundamental nature of usufruct, article 568 should be construed as a legislative codification that a testator may grant the usufructuary the power to dispose of nonconsumables without running afoul of public policy or the nature of usufruct. This conclusion is supported both by the requirement that the power to dispose is never to be presumed and must be expressly granted, as well as by the fact that regardless of this power, the usufructuary is still obligated to reimburse the naked owner for the value that the nonconsumable thing had at the moment of disposition. The "express" requirement indicates that the power to dispose is only conferred through a juridical act and is therefore only a reflection of the testator's will. Likewise, the reimbursement obligation ensures that despite the power to dispose, the equitability inherent in the usufructuary/naked-owner relationship will not be disturbed.

It is also helpful to compare the Louisiana Civil Code's provision of this power with other civilian codes. Both the German and Greek Civil Codes do not broadly recognize testamentary freedom, but rather expressly limit this freedom in the context of property law. Additionally, while the French Civil Code does not overtly limit testamentary freedom, it does not expressly grant such freedom either. . . .

While former article 568 clearly permitted the testator to grant the usufructuary the power to dispose of nonconsumables, it did not elaborate on what "dispose" meant. It was unclear whether a disposition included donations, leases, and mortgages, as the Greek Civil Code did, or whether a disposition was limited to onerous alienations. In response to this quandary, Act 881 revised article 568 in an effort to "clarify" the scope of the usufructuary's power to dispose of nonconsumables under article 568. Revised article 568 reads:

> The usufructuary may not dispose of nonconsumable things unless the right to do so has been expressly granted to him. Nevertheless, he may dispose of corporeal movables that are gradually and substantially impaired by use, wear, or decay, such as equipment, appliances, and vehicles, provided that he acts as a prudent administrator.
>
> The right to dispose of a nonconsumable thing includes the rights to lease, alienate, and encumber the thing. It does not include the right to alienate by donation inter vivos, unless that right is expressly granted.

There are two features of this article that have not changed as a result of Act 881's amendments. First, the power to dispose of nonconsumables is a right of the usufructuary that should never be presumed, but rather must be expressly indicated in the juridical act that creates the usufruct. The first sentences of both old and new article 568 clearly indicate that this is the case by stating that the power to dispose of nonconsumables must be "expressly granted" to the usufructuary. Thus, if the decedent merely granted the usufructuary the "greatest freedom that the law of usufruct permits," one could argue that the testament did not expressly grant the usufructuary the power to dispose of nonconsumables, and thus the usufructuary does not have that power.

The second unchanged aspect of article 568 is that even where the testator did not expressly grant the usufructuary the power to dispose of nonconsumables, the usufructuary will retain the power to "dispose of corporeal movables that are gradually and substantially impaired by use, wear, or decay, . . . provided that he acts as a prudent administrator." Thus, if the decedent died intestate, the decedent's surviving spouse would receive a legal usufruct over the decedent's estate. As a legal usufructuary possessed only with the default powers granted under the Civil Code, the surviving spouse could not alienate the decedent's house, but could legally sell the decedent's old car, provided that the sale could be shown to be an act of "prudent administrat[ion]" of the vehicle.

There are two distinct differences between the old and new iterations of article 568. This Comment is primarily concerned with the fact that while former article 568 merely dictated that a usufructuary may be granted the power to "dispose," revised article 568 "clarif[ies]" this right to include the power to alienate, lease, and encumber the nonconsumable. Further "clarifying" this right, article 568 also seeks to eliminate any ambiguity regarding the ability to donate the nonconsumable thing. It declares that the "right to dispose of a nonconsumable thing . . . does not include the right to alienate by donation inter vivos, unless that right is expressly granted." Hence, revised article 568 adequately resolves any ambiguity inherent in former article 568 by declaring that the power to dispose of nonconsumables includes powers of onerous alienation, lease, and encumbrance, but does not include the power to alienate gratuitously unless expressly conferred by the grantor of the usufruct.

Despite the fact that these additional powers of disposition are now included under article 568, the revision comments indicate that these powers always existed, because revised article 568 merely "clarifies" the rights inherent under former article 568. This statement attempts to resolve any ambiguity about the retroactivity of revised article 568 by declaring it a "clarification," and therefore interpretive and capable of retroactive application. Unfortunately, this revision comment, along with other comments in the revision, are not indicative of legislative intent. . . .

B. Article 568.1: Donation and Alienation

Despite the aforementioned problems created by the commenting process, the revisions did seek to create a more detailed and comprehensive scheme of the usufructuary's and naked owner's obligations and rights upon disposition of a nonconsumable. Revised article 568 does not mention what the usufructuary's obligations are upon disposition of the nonconsumable thing. Revised article 568 has instead eliminated any reference to the corresponding provision from former article 568 and has moved the substance of this provision, as well as the usufruct's attachment to the proceeds of the sale pursuant to *Michel,* to the more specific articles 568.1–568.3. The revised articles thus provide for differing obligations of the usufructuary depending on what method of disposition the usufructuary employs. Article 568.1 states, in part:

> If a thing subject to the usufruct is otherwise alienated by the usufructuary, the usufruct attaches to any money or other property received by the usufructuary. . . . If, at the time of the alienation, the value of the property received by the usufructuary is less than the value of the thing alienated, the usufructuary is bound to pay the difference to the naked owner at the termination of the usufruct.

As with other dispositions of property pursuant to articles 614–617, the usufruct attaches to the proceeds or other property received upon disposition. In addition, article 568.1 retains the equitable position of former article 568 in requiring the usufructuary to account for the entire value that the nonconsumable had at the moment of disposition, removing the ability of the usufructuary to prejudice the rights of the naked owners by selling the property for a below market value price.

This statutorily imposed default requirement that the usufructuary account for the full value that the property had at the moment of disposition seems to be sufficient protection for the naked owner's rights. However, the revision comment (a) to article 568.1 has inserted a curious addendum to this right and obligation of the usufructuary. This comment indicates that when a usufructuary has decided to exercise his right to dispose of nonconsumables, he may not sell the nonconsumable "for too low a price, and he is always subject to the obligation of acting as a prudent administrator. See Civil Code Article 576 and revision comment (b)."

This comment is curious because, as mentioned above, the naked owner has ample protection against the usufructuary for a sale price that is even one dollar below the value that the property had at the moment of alienation. The usufructuary is obligated under article 568.1 to account for any difference in the sale price to the naked owner at the termination of the usufruct. However, by inserting the "prudent administration" standard via a revision comment that was presented to the legislature, it may now be presumed that the legislative intent in drafting article 568.1 was to attach a prudent administration standard to the alienation of nonconsumables pursuant to such a grant of the power to dispose. This prudence standard would perhaps enable the naked owner to take immediate action to terminate the usufruct pursuant to article 623 and set aside any sale, as opposed to forcing the naked owner to wait until the termination of the usufruct before demanding an accounting.

The confusion surrounding this comment is increased by the fact that it is merely inserted into a revision comment, and not into a Civil Code article, thereby indicating legislative intent, but not necessarily acquiring the force of law. Whether the courts will entertain such an action to terminate a usufruct and set aside a sale pursuant to an article 623 abuse of enjoyment claim under the guise of this comment remains to be seen. However, perhaps a court should entertain such a claim. While the usufructuary is obligated to reimburse the naked owner for the nonconsumable's value when the usufruct terminates, this protection may prove to be illusory. If the usufruct terminates upon death of the usufructuary and if the naked owners are the successors of the usufructuary, then they would be reimbursing themselves out of the estate of the deceased usufructuary, which they likely stood to inherit. Furthermore, if the usufructuary spent the money received upon alienation of the nonconsumable, then the naked owners, even if not successors of the usufructuary, would be relegated to the position of unsecured creditors, forced to wait in line with the other creditors and limited to recovering whatever is left of the estate. As such, it would be in the naked owners' best interests to be able to intervene at an earlier time pursuant to article 623 and preserve their nonconsumable asset before it is too late.

In 2006, it appeared that the Louisiana Fourth Circuit Court of Appeal had an opportunity to examine the power to dispose of nonconsumables under former article 568 when a usufructuary's sale of immovable property pursuant to this grant was attacked as being well below the fair market value [*Yokum v. Van Calsem (Yokum I)*, 2005–0797, p. 3 (La. App. 4 Cir. 6/ 21/ 06); 935 So. 2d 736, 738]. The bulk of the opinion dealt with Louisiana Code of Civil Procedure articles regarding a requested preliminary injunction and the relationship between the required posting of security pursuant to such an injunction and the dispensation of the obligation of security in the act that established the usufruct. On subsequent appeal, the naked owners continued to assert that the sale should be rescinded [*Yokum v. Van Calsem (Yokum II)*, 2007–0676 (La. App. 4 Cir. 3/ 26/ 08); 981 So. 2d 725]. However, on appeal, the Fourth Circuit never reached that issue, but instead determined that the usufructuary only sold his interest in the property, namely the right of usufruct, and thus the naked owners did not become creditors of the usufructuary for the amount he received upon disposition, but rather remained naked owners of the property subject to the original usufruct. Accordingly, the purchasers were bound to furnish the property to the naked owners when the original usufructuary died.

Thus, this case illustrates two interesting points that deserve attention. The first is simply that a usufructuary with the power to dispose of nonconsumables should take care that the act of disposition clearly indicates what is being conveyed. If the act of sale between the usufructuary and the purchasers indicates—as did the act of sale between the usufructuary and purchasers in *Yokum v. Van Calsem*—that the usufructuary is transferring his interest in the property, then the usufructuary is merely disposing of his right under article 567, and the purchaser's rights in the property cease in conjunction with the termination of the original usufruct.

The second principle is a corollary to the first principle and is espoused in article 567 comment (b); namely, that there is a significant difference between a usufructuary disposing of his right as opposed to the property itself that is subject to usufruct. With the former, the usufructuary always has the right to lease, alienate, or encumber his right, regardless of whether the usufructuary has been granted the power to dispose of nonconsumables, whereas with the latter, the usufructuary may not dispose of the property subject to the usufruct without the express grant of the power to dispose. Thus, under article 568.1, it remains to be seen whether a naked owner can terminate a usufruct and set aside a sale under the guise of prudent administration or whether the naked owner will be bound by the usufructuary's decision to sell the nonconsumable, regardless of the sale price.

C. Article 568.2: Right to Lease

One of the most significant changes implicating the question of whether the revisions included a substantive change to the rights of usufructuaries and naked owners is found in articles 568 and 568.2 regarding the usufructuary's ability to enter into leases. Article 568 now expressly states that the right to dispose of a nonconsumable thing includes the right to lease the thing. Additionally, article 568.2 clarifies that the scope of this right means that the right to lease a nonconsumable thing pursuant to the power to dispose of nonconsumables includes the usufructuary's right to lease the nonconsumable beyond the duration of the usufruct. Upon termination of the usufruct, the usufructuary must account to the naked owners for the diminution in value of the property caused by the lease. Article 568.2 states:

> The right to dispose of a nonconsumable thing includes the right to lease the thing for a term that extends beyond the termination of the usufruct. If, at the termination of the usufruct, the thing remains subject to the lease, the usufructuary is accountable to the naked owner for any diminution in the value of the thing at that time attributable to the lease.

While the usufructuary has always been able to lease his own right, the Civil Code has been inordinately clear that the lease terminates when the usufruct terminates. Article 567 declares that the usufructuary may lease his right separately from the property itself, but that the contract embodying this lease "cease[s as] of right at the end of the usufruct." In accordance with this concept, the Louisiana Supreme Court firmly established this principle in 1937 under the seminal case of *Sparks v. Dan Cohen Co.*[, 175 So. 590, 593 (La. 1937)].

In *Sparks*, the plaintiffs, naked owners of a piece of immovable property, sought to terminate a lease entered into by their mother, the lessor, who had only a life usufruct over the property and who had recently died. The defendant-lessee of the property insisted that the lease should not terminate with the usufruct, but should continue for the duration of the term stipulated in the lease agreement. The defendant additionally claimed that the plaintiffs should be estopped from evicting the defendant because the plaintiffs unconditionally accepted the succession of the lessor-usufructuary, and thus inherited her obligation to warrant the possession of the lessee. The trial court ruled for the plaintiffs and terminated the lease.

On appeal, the Louisiana Supreme Court initially distinguished several cases cited for the defendant's proposition on the basis that sales and mineral leases conferred different rights than a residential lease, and thus were inapposite to the defendant's pleas. Significantly, the court relied on the predecessor to articles 567 and 2716 to hold that a usufructuary does not have the right to lease anything greater than his right of usufruct, and thus any leases entered into by the usufructuary cease immediately upon the termination of the usufruct. The court also held that the plaintiffs were not under an obligation to indemnify the lessee for the lessor's warranty of possession because the evidence indicated that the defendant was aware that the lessor was merely a usufructuary. Thus, the court also established the principle that the universal successors of a usufructuary-lessor are not under the obligation "to warrant and defend the lessee's right of possession [unless] the lessor claimed or pretended to be the owner of the leased premises."

However, what remains unclear following the revision and adoption of article 568.2 is what would have occurred in *Sparks* had the usufructuary-lessor been granted the power to dispose of nonconsumables. It is clear that in such a case, the lessees would likely be able to continue their possession because article 568.2 expressly assures that result. What is unanswered is whether the naked owners would also be obligated to warrant the possession of the lessees either if they were not successors of the usufructuary, or if they were successors, if the usufructuary did not claim to be the owner. Unfortunately, article 568.2 does not offer guidance on this subject.

However, it seems likely that the naked owners would have to warrant the possession of the lessee if the usufructuary represented that he had the power to dispose, because under article 568.2, the usufructuary's lease no longer terminates with the usufruct if the usufructuary has been granted this power. In *Sparks*, the court recognized that equitable principles only dictate that a lessor and his heirs or naked owners are under an obligation to warrant the lessee's possession if it would be reasonable for the lessee to assume the lessor had the legal authority to confer such obligations on others. This rule, which is similar to the equitable doctrine of estoppel, now arises due to the broadening of a usufructuary's rights to enter into leases that extend beyond the duration of the usufruct, thereby "binding" the naked owners to the usufructuary's obligation to warrant the lessee's peaceful possession under the lease.

Under the pre[-]revision approach of the *Sparks* court, the lessees could only maintain such a position if they were placed under the mistaken belief that the lessor was the full owner of the property, because only the full owner-lessor had the legal authority to compel others unilaterally to warrant the lessee's possession after the lessor's death. Conversely, a usufructuary with the power to dispose of nonconsumables under article 568.2 now has the legal authority to compel the naked owners to recognize a lease contracted by the usufructuary, even after the usufructuary's death. Thus, a court that utilizes the doctrine espoused by *Sparks* would likely enforce such a warrantability obligation against naked owners if the lessor represented to the lessees that he had been granted a usufruct with the power to dispose of nonconsumables. Although such an approach seems to be inequitable from the naked owner's viewpoint, it is [in] keeping with the court's equitable estoppel treatment of the lease arrangement in *Sparks* and approaches the dynamic from the point of view that the lessees are not in as good of a position to absorb the cost of such deception as are the naked owners.

This approach is also preferable from the viewpoint of judicial economy. The naked owners will probably already be embroiled in a contentious legal battle over the accounting of all the property that was subject to the usufruct. Thus, the resolution of further disputes over the warrantability of existing leases and diminution of the value of the property due to such leases will all be resolved in one judicial proceeding between the same two parties. If the approach taken were such as to require the lessees to litigate this position as well, then the lessees might be required to intervene with an interest in the accounting, which would further draw out and complicate an already difficult legal resolution during the final accounting when the naked owners are put into possession. As such, a court would likely enforce the warranty of habitability against either the naked owners or the usufructuary's heirs if the lessor represented to the lessees that he was a usufructuary possessed with the power to dispose of nonconsumables, because the lessees' argument that the law permits a usufructuary to contract leases that survive the termination of the usufruct would be reinforced by article 568.2.

Like *Yokum*, *Sparks* also indicates that a transferee of a nonconsumable thing, or any property for that matter, must be certain that the transferor not only has the authority to transfer real rights in the property, such as ownership, but also has actually conveyed those rights. Recall that in *Yokum*, the transferor was a usufructuary with the power to dispose of nonconsumables that failed to effectively transfer or dispose of anything greater than his right as usufructuary. Similarly, in *Sparks*, the transferor was a usufructuary, presumably without the power to dispose of nonconsumables, and so she could only grant a lease of his right as usufructuary. Thus, the law under both *Yokum* and *Sparks* is simple: upon entering into a lease or sale with a usufructuary, ensure both that the contract confers the rights that you expect to get and that the usufructuary actually has the authority to convey these rights. As succinctly stated by Marcel Planiol, "No one can confer greater rights than he has himself." [1 Marcel Planiol, *Treatise on the Civil Law* pt. 2, § 2809 (La. State Law Inst. trans., 1959)]

The Civil Code has another clearly enunciated instance of this principle (leases granted by a usufructuary terminate with the usufruct) that has not been amended to reflect the principle established by article 568.2. Louisiana Civil Code article 2716 unambiguously declares: "A lease granted by a usufructuary terminates upon the termination of the usufruct." Despite this tension between articles 2716 and 568.2, the more specific code article governs the situation over the more general code article. In this case, article 568.2 would be more specific because article 2716 merely deals with usufructuaries' leases in general, whereas article 568.2 deals with the specific situation of leases entered into by usufructuaries who have been granted the power to dispose of nonconsumables. Additionally, the more recent enactment of legislative will regarding a topic should govern. Because article 568.2 was enacted in 2010, and article 2716 was enacted in 2005, article 568.2 should control. . . .

D. Article 568.3: Requirement to Remove Encumbrance

Article 568 has been revised by Act 881 to provide that a usufructuary who has been granted the right to dispose of nonconsumables now expressly "includes the right[] to . . . encumber the thing." As with articles 568.1 and 568.2, the revision created a new article, 568.3, to detail the usufructuary's rights and obligations with regard to this power to encumber. Like articles 568.2 and 2716, there is an existing Code article that is in direct conflict with the granting of the power to encumber to the usufructuary. Article 711 expressly declares that usufructuaries "may not establish . . . any charges in the nature of predial servitudes."

An encumbrance is defined as "[a] burden or charge upon property," and a predial servitude is defined as "a charge on a servient estate for the benefit of a dominant estate." Thus, articles 568 and 711 plainly seem to conflict.

. . . .

Another issue raised by article 568.3 is the way in which the naked owners may now be "bound" by the contract entered into by a usufructuary, without any act of consent, despite their shared ownership of the property. The relationship between a usufructuary and naked owner could be considered a type of co-ownership, and in other co-ownership contexts, a co-owner may not encumber property without the consent of his other co-owners. Thus, while a co-owner may not bind the other co-owners to an encumbrance without their consent in other contexts, article 568.3 now makes it clear that a usufructuary possessed with the power to dispose of nonconsumables may bind the naked owners to the effects of such an encumbrance without the naked owners' consent.

Also, similar questions to those apparent in the lease context arise regarding the application of estoppel principles, in whether or not an encumbrance may be enforced against naked owners who are also a usufructuary's heirs. Under the court's reasoning in SPARKS, the naked owner-heirs would likely be obligors under the usufructuary's obligations, including any encumbrances, if the usufructuary represented that he was endowed with the power to dispose of nonconsumables.

Regardless of these conflicts, article 568.3 expressly requires the usufructuary to remove the encumbrance upon termination of the usufruct. Therefore, none of the inequitable concerns mentioned in reference to article 568.2 are present in article 568.3. However, as with the alienation context under article 568.1, the protection afforded to the naked owners under article 568.3's "remove the encumbrance" requirement will not adequately compensate the naked owners for their losses if the usufructuary's estate contains insufficient assets to discharge the encumbrance. In such a case, the property will either be sold to satisfy the encumbrance, and the naked owners will have lost their rights in the property, or the naked owners will be forced to discharge the encumbrance from their own patrimonies, and will be bound by the usufructuary's encumbrance without any mechanism of recompense.

Notes and Questions

1. If you were advising a client who wanted to create a usufruct relationship, would you recommend that the client give the usufructuary the right to dispose of nonconsumables? Why or why not?

2. Can a grantor of a usufruct give a usufructuary broader rights with regard to consumables than those set forth in the Civil Code's default rules? In a well-known, early twentieth century decision, the Louisiana Supreme Court held that, in addition to giving the usufructuary the power to dispose of a nonconsumable, a grantor could also, at least in the special circumstances of that case, relieve the usufructuary of the obligation to account to the naked owner for the value of consumable things at the termination of the usufruct. *In re Courtin*, 81 So. 457 (La. 1919).

In *In re Courtin*, a testator had instructed his executor that certain property be sold and invested in an interest bearing account. The testator further granted his sister a usufruct over the proceeds derived from the sale. In addition to the interest accruing from the principal, the sister was given the right to receive up to $40.00 per month from the principal amount invested in the account for the rest of her life. This would leave the naked owner with whatever portion of the principal remained at the end of the usufructuary's life. The court held that such a bequest was valid even though the usufructuary had the right to draw upon the principal amount invested in the account, without any obligation to account to the naked owner for the value the account had at the beginning of the usufruct. *Id.* at 459–60.

The strict limits imposed by the grantor on the usufructuary's right to draw on the principal provided some protection for the naked owner in *In re Courtin*. This may very well have justified the court's expansive holding in that case. Further, at the time of the decision, the 1870 Civil Code offered an additional safeguard for naked owners with respect to usufructs over sums of money by requiring usufructuaries to invest the sums "at interest on good security." La. Civ. Code art. 563(2) (1870). Today, however, no such limitations are imposed on a usufructuary. What protection, if any, does a naked owner have if a usufructuary is determined to expend all the consumables subject to a usufruct before his or her death? In light of *In re Courtin*, are there *any* meaningful limits to a grantor's testamentary or contractual freedom if a usufructuary is relieved of the obligation to account to the naked owner for consumables at the termination of the usufruct?

Problems

1. Georgia holds a testamentary usufruct over the family home where she and her late husband Edward resided during their marriage but which Edward had acquired before their marriage. Edward's children from a previous marriage, Jennifer and Ken, are the naked owners of the home. Edward's validly executed will gave Georgia the power to dispose of nonconsumables. Two years after the commencement of her usufruct, Georgia executed an authentic act donating the home to her only child, Lance, from a previous marriage. Is the donation valid? If Edward's will expressly gave Georgia the power to donate nonconsumables, what obligations, if any, will Georgia or her succession owe to Jennifer and Ken, upon the termination of her usufruct?

2. Peter has a usufruct over a fifty-acre undeveloped tract of land outside of Houma. Rebecca is the naked owner of the land. The grantor of the usufruct, Peter's late uncle Jack, expressly granted Peter the power to dispose of nonconsumables. Three years after the commencement of the usufruct, Peter sells the tract of land to Smart Guys, LLC, a real estate development firm, in which he shares a one-third interest. Smart Guys pays Peter $50,000 for the land, but other tracts of undeveloped land in the Houma area have recently been sold for $4,000 per acre. Is Peter's sale of the land to Smart Guys valid? Does Peter or his succession have any liability to Rebecca now or in the future?

3. Sam enjoys a usufruct for life over a commercial building in downtown Slidell. Theresa is the naked owner of the building. Sam leases the building for a term of five years to Apple, Inc., for use as an Apple Store. He does not obtain Theresa's consent to the lease. Apple promptly records the lease in the conveyance records of St. Tammany Parish. Sam dies in the third year of the lease. Theresa sends Apple a notice to vacate the premises immediately, unless it agrees to a new lease at a substantially higher rent. Assume that the grantor of the usufruct expressly gave Sam the power to dispose of nonconsumables. Will Theresa be able to evict Apple from the building? Will Apple be able to enforce the lease against Theresa and remain in possession of the building for the duration of the lease term? What remedies, if any, will Theresa have against Sam's succession?

4. Roberta enjoys the legal usufruct of the surviving spouse over her late husband Steve's community property interest in the family home that she and Steve acquired during their marriage. The naked owners of Steve's share in community are his two children from a previous marriage, Alexis and Bob. One year after the commencement of the usufruct, Roberta grants Iberia Bank a reverse annuity mortgage

(RAM) on the property. Two property scholars explain a RAM in the following terms:

> The *reverse annuity mortgage* (RAM) is a mortgage marketed to senior citizens who own their homes as a major source of wealth subject to little or no mortgage debt. For this group of elderly people, the RAM is designed as a way to provide a supplement to their retirement income while allowing them to remain in their homes. The concept behind the RAM is to pay the homeowner the value of her home overtime with monthly annuity payments. The RAM reverses the typical mortgage structure. Instead of a borrower making monthly payments to the lender until the loan is paid in full, the RAM has the lender make payments to the debtor until the limit of a pre-established credit line is reached. The credit line is typically around 75 to 80 percent of the equity value of the home.

Robin Paul Malloy & James Charles Smith, Real Estate Transactions 393 (4th ed. 2013). Did Roberta have the authority to grant the RAM to Iberia Bank? If Roberta had acquired a testamentary usufruct over Steve's one half share in community and Steve had granted Roberta the power to dispose of nonconsumables, would your answer be different? Under these facts, at the termination of the usufruct, what obligations, if any, will Roberta or her succession owe to Alexis and Bob?

5. Ordinary and Extraordinary Repairs; Prudent Administration

Disputes can easily arise between a usufructuary and a naked owner concerning maintenance and repair of valuable nonconsumable things subject to a usufruct such as buildings or tracts of land. The Civil Code contains a number of detailed articles addressing this subject. *See* La. Civ. Code arts. 577–583 (1976). The rules found in these articles are grounded in the fundamental obligation of a usufructuary to act as a prudent administrator of a nonconsumable thing subject to the usufruct and to deliver the nonconsumable thing to the naked owner at the termination of the usufruct. La. Civ. Code art. 540 (1976). At the same time, these rules take into account that the naked owner of the thing subject to a usufruct should be, as the residual property interest holder, responsible for very significant repairs that preserve the long-term capital value of the asset.

In *Walker v. Holt*, 888 So.2d 255 (La. App. 3 Cir. 2004), a worker was injured while delivering gas for his employer. The cause of the injury was a hole in the ground. The worker and his employer's worker's compensation carrier sued the parties who held property interests in the land—one individual named Smith who held a one-half interest in full ownership and a usufruct over the other one-half interest in the property and several individuals who shared a one-twelfth interest in naked ownership. They sought to recover damages for personal injury and to obtain reimbursement for money the insurer was required to pay the worker. In this case, the liability of the defendants turned on the question of whether the hole in the ground gave rise to an ordinary repair (for which the usufructuary was responsible) or an extraordinary repair (for which the naked owners, and presumably the owner of the other one half undivided share in full ownership, were responsible). The trial court found that the hole gave rise to an ordinary repair, within the meaning of La. Civ. Code arts. 577 and 578. Therefore, only the usufructuary was potentially liable. Affirming the judgment, the court of appeal explained:

> . . . Zurich assigns as error the trial court's holding that the "hole in the ground" was not an extraordinary repair and that the issue of whether defendants had notice of the hole in the ground is an issue for the jury. Article 578 defines extraordinary repairs as being "for the reconstruction or the whole or of a substantial part." We agree with the trial court that a hole in the ground is not an extraordinary repair, as defined by Article 578, that a naked owner would be obligated to repair. *See Succession of Crain*, 450 So. 2d 1374, (La. App. 1 Cir. 1984), where painting the interior and exterior of a house, repairing leak spots, removing glass mold in the kitchen, den and bedroom and resealing water leaks, replacing a frame of glass, erecting an iron post around an electrical substation, removing a small tree, and making repairs to an air-conditioning system were found to be ordinary repairs, and repairs to a dock, a boat slip, and a roof were found to be extraordinary repairs.

> We also find no error with the trial court's conclusion that Ms. Distefano, Ms. Campo, and Mr. Smith, Jr. did not have control of the property or a duty to inspect the property or knew, or should have known in the exercise of reasonable care, that the hole was present. Mr. Smith, Sr.'s usufruct of the Holt residence was a usufruct of a nonconsumable, La. Civ. Code art. 537, which gave him the right to possess the property and "to derive the utility, profits, and advantages" from it "under the obligation of preserving [its] substance." La. Civ. Code art. 539. As usufructuary, he is bound to use the property as a prudent administrator, La. Civ. Code art. 539, and is "answerable for losses resulting from his fraud, default, or neglect." La. Civ. Code art. 576.

> As the trial court discussed, Articles 577 and 578 address responsibility for ordinary and extraordinary repairs. In conjunction therewith, Article 579 provides that the naked owner may compel the usufructuary to make repairs for which he is responsible, *but* the usufructuary may not compel the naked owner to make extraordinary repairs. If extraordinary repairs are needed, the usufructuary's only recourse is to make the repairs and seek reimbursement from the naked owner. La. Civ. Code art. 579. The usufructuary, not the naked owner, is answerable for all expenses necessary for the preservation and use of the property subject to the usufruct. La. Civ. Code art. 581.

The rights and obligations of the naked owner are limited in comparison to those of the usufructuary. The naked owner can dispose of his naked ownership and the alienation or encumbrance of the property subject to the usufruct; however, he cannot affect the rights of the usufructuary. La. Civ. Code art. 603. Furthermore, the naked owner must not interfere with the rights of the usufructuary and may not make alterations or improvements to the property. La. Civ. Code arts. 605 and 606.

Consideration of the rights and obligations of the usufructuary and the naked owner leads to the conclusion that the usufructuary, not the naked owner, is obligated to maintain the property subject to the usufruct. Accordingly, we find no error with the trial court's conclusion that Ms. Distefano, Ms. Campo, and Mr. Smith, Jr. do not have a duty to inspect and maintain the property at issue.

Walker, 88 So.2d at 258–59.

Questions

1. Could the naked owners of the property at issue in *Walker v. Holt*, 888 So.2d 255 (La. App. 3 Cir. 2004), have required the usufructuary, Graham Smith, Sr., to repair the hole in the ground which caused Frederick Walker's back injury? *See* La. Civ. Code art. 579 (1976). If so, should the court have taken this into account in determining whether the usufructuary was liable to Walker? Should the court have considered the fact that Smith, Sr. himself also owned a one-half, undivided interest in the property? Does the holding in *Walker* impose an unreasonable burden on third persons who enter property subject to a usufruct and who suffer personal injuries while on that property due to a defect in a building or some other hazardous condition on the property?

2. In another recent decision, a court held that repairs necessitated by a fire that occurred on immovable property were extraordinary repairs and thus were the responsibility of the naked owner, not the usufructuary, to undertake. *Pidgeon v. Pidgeon*, 136 So.3d 819, 822 (La. App. 1 Cir. 2013). In the following case, which involved a sharp conflict between a usufructuary and a naked owner not related by blood, the court addressed significant questions regarding whether the usufructuary acted as a prudent administrator of the house subject to the usufruct.

Berthelot v. Pendergast

989 So.2d 798 (La. App. 5 Cir. 2008)

CHEHARDY, Judge. This appeal arises in a partition suit between a widow and her adult stepchildren, consolidated with a suit against the widow by one of the stepchildren. That stepchild appeals a judgment that dismissed the claim against the widow for failure to act as a prudent administrator of her usufruct of the family home. We affirm.

Facts

Victoria Pendergast was married to Harold A. Pendergast, Sr. and they resided at 2457 Roosevelt Boulevard in the Westgate subdivision in Kenner, a home they had purchased in 1973. Harold Pendergast, Sr. died testate in 1994. As surviving spouse in community, Victoria Pendergast was owner of a one-half undivided interest in the family home. In his will Harold Pendergast, Sr. bequeathed his one-half undivided interest to his children from his first marriage, Harold Pendergast, Jr. and Margaret Pendergast Adolph, and granted Victoria Pendergast a testamentary usufruct over their portion. The parties were placed in possession by judgment of possession in June 1994.

Ms. Pendergast continued to reside in the home for a decade after her husband's death. In May 2004, due to advanced age and infirmity, she went to live with her son from a former marriage, Joseph R. Berthelot, III. Mr. Berthelot informed Mr. Pendergast Jr. and Ms. Adolph that his mother wished to sell the property. In June 2004 the three met at the house to sign a listing agreement, but due to disagreement the meeting was aborted.

In December 2004 Mr. Berthelot, acting on behalf of his mother by power of attorney, filed suit against Harold Pendergast, Jr. and Margaret Adolph to force partition of the property. . . .

In May 2005 Margaret Adolph filed a separate suit against Victoria Pendergast, alleging Ms. Pendergast failed to act as a prudent administrator of the property by negligently allowing a leaking sewer line to progress into a serious foundation problem. . . . The suits were consolidated.

Despite attempts to confect a private sale, the property ultimately was sold at public auction for $54,000.00. The net proceeds of the sale, $50,595.56, were placed into the registry of the court.

By the time of trial, the issues in *Berthelot v. Pendergast* had been mostly resolved by the sale of the property, but the issues in *Adolph v. Pendergast* remained to be decided. It was undisputed that the parties each are entitled to their respective shares of the proceeds according to their ownership interests in the property. The issues were whether Ms. Pendergast, as usufructuary, was entitled to payment of her attorney's fees for the partition suit, and whether Ms. Pendergast was liable to Ms. Adolph for the serious structural damage to the property caused by its sinking foundation.

At trial on the merits, the testimony established that by the time the partition suit was filed in December 2004, the house had developed severe foundation problems. The slab was sinking so much in its center that it was almost bowl-shaped. This resulted in fracture of the slab, misalignment of doors, cracks in the walls, and large gaps at the bases of the walls.

Mr. Berthelot testified that after his stepfather's death, he made arrangements for repairs while his mother remained in the house. Among repairs done over a span of years were a new roof, a new air conditioning system, and replacement of the sewer line in 2003. Mr. Berthelot denied Ms. Adolph's allegation that the sewer line had been leaking for two years before it was repaired. He said as soon as he was told about the problem, which manifested in problems flushing the toilets, he contacted a plumber. The sewer line was repaired within two to three weeks.

Mr. Berthelot testified that in 1980, his mother and his stepfather had the home's foundation shored. A receipt entered in evidence that showed the house had been shored by the placement of pilings under the perimeter of the slab.

Mr. Berthelot also filed in evidence a summary of the water bills for the house from 2000 to 2006 that showed no significant differences in the amounts of monthly water usage.

While the litigation was pending, the parties attempted to negotiate a private sale of the property. They received two offers to purchase the home. The first, in February 2005, was for $75,000; it lapsed due to the parties' disputes over payment of certain items. Mr. Berthelot wanted Ms. Adolph to pay his attorney's fees for the filing of the partition suit. Ms. Adolph refused to do so, unless Mr. Berthelot was willing to waive his mother's rights as usufructuary.

Subsequently, they entered into a consent judgment, under which Ms. Adolph agreed to accept "the highest written offer to purchase the property at a private sale, or produce a higher written offer to purchase the property at private sale, on or before Friday, June 3, 2005." The agreement provided that any proceeds of the sale would be placed in the registry of the court.

The second offer, in June 2005, was for $60,000. Despite the consent judgment, that offer also fell through while the parties continued to bicker.

Mr. Berthelot had the house appraised in July 2005; the appraiser valued it at $ 81,000. In January 2006, the house was sold at public auction to Ms. Adolph's son for $ 54,000. As noted above, the net proceeds of the sale were deposited into the court registry.

Mr. Berthelot admitted that when he last saw the house, before it was sold at public auction in January 2006, there were cracks in the walls, the slab was caving in, the doors were hanging crooked, and walls were separating from the slab. He said the house had been in that condition for years, but it had gotten worse in the last couple of years.

Frank Fromherz, an expert in structural engineering, testified he was hired by Mr. Berthelot to inspect the house. He discovered the slab had a severe bowl-shaped deflection. There was a crack that could be felt under the carpet. Some of the walls were hanging from the ceiling, with space between the bottom of the walls and the slab.

Mr. Fromherz believed the cause was areal subsidence, a problem that has been observed in the New Orleans metropolitan area for the past 50 years. "Areal subsidence" is a term for the condition that results when the water table lowers and the lack of moisture causes soft surface soils to consolidate. Mr. Fromherz said that consolidation of soils was the cause of the settlement.

According to him, an open sewer line could accelerate the problem by washing away materials that could support the slab into the open pipe. If the sewer line was broken for an extended period, it could accelerate whatever settlement was occurring. He said it could not have caused a problem in only two or three weeks.

In addition, Mr. Fromherz said, there is a problem with the way the house is constructed. It should have had grade beams in the slab to support it, but the shape of the deflection makes it appear there is no grade beam under the slab.

Mr. Fromherz said the house was built 40 to 50 years ago, and this kind of subsidence takes 20 to 30 years. He said the shoring of the house 26 years ago explains why the middle is sinking and the edges are stable; the shoring was done on the perimeter, but the lack of grade beams across the center allowed the slab to continue to drop. The house has all its plumbing along the back wall, but the point of greatest settlement is at the middle of the slab, not toward the back. That is why he believed the sewer leak did not cause it.

Ms. Adolph testified her cousin, Norman Pendergast, handled her father's succession. When he met with them all to explain what had to be awarded, her stepmother was told she had to return the house in the same condition in which she had received it because she had the usufruct.

Ms. Adolph testified she had stayed in the home for the week before her father died. She did not see anything wrong with the house then. There definitely was no separation of the walls. After her father's death she visited her stepmother "fairly often," but eventually stopped going because she felt uncomfortable. She admitted that when she visited the house after her father died, she stayed in the front room and her visits were brief, so she was unable to say whether there was damage in the rest of the house.

When she went to the house for the meeting about selling it in 2004, it had been several years since she had been there. That was when she first noticed the damage to the house. She said it was "unbelievable" because when she was there before, there was no damage. She recalled a conversation with her brother, Harold, in which he told her "the base boards are coming up off the floor." That may have been a few months before the June 2004 meeting.

When Mr. Berthelot called to tell her he was moving his mother in with him, he told her there were some problems with the house. He said the house needed repairs and he didn't want to fool with it.

Ms. Adolph testified she didn't want to sign the paper to sell the house because she wanted Mr. Berthelot to waive the usufruct. She was willing to accept the $75,000 offer, but they could not come to an agreement. He indicated he was going to waive the usufruct, but only in return for her payment of his attorney's fees in the partition action. She did not feel she should have to do that. The same thing happened with the offer for $60,000.

Ms. Adolph testified that Allstate paid $3,279.15 on the claim for damage from Hurricane Katrina, but the money was not used to repair the hurricane damage.

She admitted she had no evidence to substantiate her allegation that the sewer problem began in 2001. She said she drew the conclusion because "the house went down so quick."

George Aldrete, an expert in shoring, testified as Ms. Adolph's expert witness. In June 2005, at the invitation of Ms. Adolph's son, Melvin Adolph, he wrote a proposal for shoring the house. The total cost of his proposal was $15,400.

Mr. Aldrete testified that sinkage is going on around Louisiana, particularly in Kenner and Metairie. The house has a floating slab, which is an earth-supported slab with no pilings. It has a center grade beam in the hall area. In his opinion, if the house had been shored 10 years before, the interior would not have been as damaged as it was by the time of the sale.

Mr. Aldrete did not attribute the damage in this case to subsidence. He said that to create this amount of damage there had to be kind of scouring under the slab; that is, water or something washing out the existing dirt and clay that supports the slab.

He said his company has leveled over 50% of the houses in the Westgate subdivision, but he had never seen damage this severe. According to him, in a case of subsidence the house will settle more or less uniformly. Here, however, the slab has actually become concave. He said the only way to explain it is that the material underneath was washed out. If it was a broken pipe around the outside wall, he said, it would show on the outer perimeter.

He said he is very familiar with the homes in the Westgate subdivision, because he lives in Westgate, and over 30 years he has done a hundred or so houses, so he knows where the grade beams are. He said you cannot see a grade beam unless you dig under the slab.

Upon being informed that the house was shored in 1980, with beams around the perimeter of the slab but not in the center, he still did not agree that would cause the slab to sink in a concave manner. He said the sinkage went almost all the way to the edge where the chain walls are, but the walls on the perimeter are not separated from the slab.

He agreed that a broken sewer line that was repaired within two to three weeks would probably not cause this extent of damage; it would take some time.

The district court rendered judgment denying attorney's fees to Ms. Pendergast in the partition action and denying Ms. Adolph's claim for damages in the prudent administrator case. In written reasons included within the judgment, the trial court found as follows.

With respect to the prudent administrator claims, the court found the testimony of Mr. Fromherz more convincing. The court concluded that the home's foundation problem resulted from areal subsidence, rather than from water or sewerage leaking from broken pipes. The court found the subsidence was not the result of Ms. Pendergast's neglect, and she did not fail to act as a prudent administrator.

As to whether the foundation repair was "ordinary maintenance" for which Ms. Pendergast as usufructuary was responsible, the court concluded the repair of the property's structural damage constitutes an extraordinary repair and, thus, was the responsibility of the naked owners rather than the usufructuary. The court also found that Ms. Pendergast is entitled to usufruct over the property's sale proceeds.

Finally, on the issue of whether Ms. Pendergast is entitled to attorney's fees from Ms. Adolph, the court ruled that the usufruct is testamentary and therefore a conventional usufruct. As such, La.C.C. art. 596 applies, which mandates that expenses of litigation between the usufructuary and the naked owner be borne by the person who incurred them.

Ms. Adolph filed a motion for new trial, citing newly-discovered evidence regarding existence of a center grade beam in the house's foundation. The trial court denied the motion for new trial because, first, Ms. Adolph failed to show she could not have obtained the new evidence prior to the trial and, second, even if the new evidence were considered, it did not change the court's opinion as to the cause of the damage to the house:. . . .

Liability as Prudent Administrator

Ms. Adolph argues that Ms. Pendergast failed to act as a prudent administrator because the house's foundation was severely damaged by major subsidence of the soil beneath the house. Ms. Adolph contends the subsidence was due to Ms. Pendergast's failure to repair broken plumbing beneath the slab. Alternatively, given the trial court's determination that the subsidence was areal subsidence and was not caused by broken plumbing, Ms. Adolph argues that Ms. Pendergast nonetheless had a duty to notify the naked owners of the foundation damage before the damage became severe.

The usufructuary is bound to use nonconsumable things as a prudent administrator and to deliver them to the naked owner at the termination of the usufruct. La.C.C. Art. 539. . . .

Considering these principles of law, we find no error in the trial court's ruling that the repairs were extraordinary repairs and thus were the responsibility of the naked owners. Similarly, we find no merit to Ms. Adolph's argument that Ms. Pendergast violated her duties as usufructuary by failing to make the repairs herself and then seeking reimbursement from the naked owners. Nor do we find merit to the contention that by failing to make the foundation repairs, then moving out of the house, Ms. Pendergast "abandoned" her usufruct.

We find no error in the trial court's determination, based on Mr. Fromherz's testimony, that there was "no maintenance activity which would have prevented the deflection of the slab." We interpret "maintenance activity" as meaning the "ordinary maintenance" that would be the responsibility of the usufructuary.

Similarly, we find no merit to the assertion that Ms. Pendergast violated her duty by failing to notify Ms. Adolph and Mr. Pendergast of the damage to the house. The testimony of both Mr. Pendergast and Ms. Adolph indicates that, in fact, they were aware of the problems some time before the 2004 meeting between the parties about selling the house. Further, as Mr. Fromherz testified, this type of damage occurs over a long period, from 20 to 30 years. Ms. Adolph did not carry her burden of proving that Ms. Pendergast failed to be a prudent administrator. . . .

For the foregoing reasons, the judgment is affirmed. Costs of appeal are assessed against the appellant, Margaret Adolph.

AFFIRMED

Problems

1. Louis enjoys a usufruct for life over a commercial building in downtown Bunkie. Esther is the naked owner of the building. Recently a tornado passed through Bunkie and caused major damage to the commercial building. The tornado destroyed the building's roof and left the building's back wall crumbled into a pile of bricks. The tornado also damaged most of the interior fixtures beyond repair. It will cost at least $400,000 to restore the building to its pre-tornado condition.

A. Who, if anyone, is obligated to make the repairs necessary to restore the building? Louis or Esther?

B. If Esther asks Louis to pay for these repairs, and he chooses to make them, does Louis have a right to demand reimbursement from Esther? If so, when?

C. If Louis asks Esther to make the repairs, and Esther makes them at her expense, is Esther entitled to any reimbursement from Louis? If so, when?

D. Can either Louis or Esther compel the other to pay for the repairs needed to restore the building?

6. Substantial Alterations or Improvements — Ameliorative Waste

Consider the following problem: Suppose Sheila, a surviving spouse, has a usufruct for life over a two-story residential building on Magazine Street in the Irish Channel neighborhood of New Orleans. Tom is the naked owner of the building. Sheila would like to undertake a complete renovation of the building, converting it into a state-of-the-art sound production studio for use in Louisiana's burgeoning music and film production industry. Sheila asks Tom to consent to her renovation plans, but Tom refuses. What recourse does Sheila have? Can she undertake the renovations without Tom's consent? If Sheila goes ahead and makes the renovations, what rights or obligations will Tom have at the end of his usufruct?

To answer these questions, study the contents of the revision comments to Article 558 of the Louisiana Civil Code. In addition, consider how your answer to this question might be different if the facts had arisen in France and a French court had been called up to apply Article 578 of the French Civil Code. To help you explore this second scenario, read the following excerpt from a recent law review article covering the subject.

Sally Brown Richardson

Reframing Ameliorative Waste, 65 Am. J. Comp. L. 335, 358–61 (2016).

III. Ameliorative Waste in Civil Law Jurisdictions Today

The Roman and English approaches that examined whether a material alteration to the property occurred are closely related to the approaches that remain in force today in civil law jurisdictions, which are derived from Roman law. Current civil law jurisdictions use as a default rule the Roman notion that usufructuaries cannot alter the purpose of the property they possess in usufruct. Some civil law jurisdictions have, like the common law, created more nuanced approaches that define material alteration as any change to the economic purpose of the property. Some jurisdictions have even placed additional caveats on a possessor's right to alter property, adopting a strict economic impact test.

A. France and Jurisdictions Based on the Code civil

As is well documented, the discovery of Justinian's Digest in the late eleventh century led to a reception of Roman law throughout Europe, and ultimately spawned a codification movement in the late eighteenth and nineteenth centuries. The most influential code was the Code Napoleon of 1804, which was based in large part on Roman law, as noted from both its structure and its substance. After its introduction to many European countries through the Napoleonic Wars, the Code Napoleon served as the basis for civil codes throughout Europe, including in Italy, Spain, and Germany. The Code Napoleon (or Code civil) was also implemented in French colonies in the western hemisphere and served as the basis for civil codes in Quebec, Louisiana, and throughout central America.

1. Usufructs

Usufruct law in France reflects the notion that "[n]either the usufructuary nor the [naked] owner can act as if he/she were the full owner. Each party must respect the interests of the other party while exercising his/her own rights." To balance this type of fiduciary relationship between the usufructuary and naked owner, the French Code civil places restrictions on the usufructuary's ability to alter property.

Article 578 of the French Code civil provides that "[u]sufruct is the right to enjoy things owned by another in the same manner as the owner himself, but on condition that their substance be preserved." In determining the right of *usus* possessed by the usufructuary, the Code civil contemplates that the usufructuary will use the property as a *bon père de famille*, a prudent administrator, which follows the Roman notion that a usufructuary use the property as a careful man.

Under these general obligations set forth for usufructuaries, a usufructuary cannot alter the property such that it injures the naked owner. French courts have strictly interpreted the *bon père de famille* standard and the preservation of the substance of the thing requirement, such that it is unlawful to alter the economic purpose of the property, even if doing so would not alter the actual constructions on the property.

For example, in *SARL Le Grand Verger v. Widow Cozon*, the Cour de cassation found that a usufructuary committed waste when she altered a residential building to a commercial building. In *Cozon*, a decedent left his house in usufruct to his widow and in naked ownership to Cozon. The widow-usufructuary leased the house to an individual who intended to turn the residential home into a commercial building for lodging and dining. The original lessee transferred his rights to Le Grand Verger.

Upon the death of the widow-usufructuary, the naked owner, Cozon, filed suit, claiming that the lease now held by Le Grand Verger was invalid because it altered the nature of the property from a residential home to a commercial enterprise. The Cour de cassation held that by transforming the country house into a commercial building, the widow-usufructuary altered the economic destination of the building and violated her duty to preserve the property. In summarizing the law concerning the duties of a usufructuary, the court stated, "the usufructuary should manage the object in due diligence, according to the purpose for which it was intended, on condition that the subject-matter is preserved and that he does not change the nature of the object under usufruct." The court went on to provide that by allowing a commercial lease, the usufructuary "establish[ed] and exploit[ed] a business in the accommodations which, until now, were intended to be used as a residential building, and by transforming a countryhouse into a commercial building, the [usufructuary] has changed the purpose of the building."

Most civil law jurisdictions with French heritage follow the same waste rules as France with regard to usufructs. For example, under the Spanish Códidgo Civil, usufructuaries have an obligation to maintain the form and substance of the thing. The Códidgo reiterates that the usufructuary can make alterations of the property subject to the usufruct, provided that he does not alter the form or substance of the property. As commentary on Spanish law provides, "the usufructuary cannot convert the *house into a warehouse*, or the *farm into a hotel. . . .* The fact that the alteration *enhances the value* of the property does not make a difference."

French courts have gone even a step further in examining allegations of waste to say that not only must a usufructuary retain the economic purpose of the property, but also any alterations must further some objective necessity and cannot have any additional economic impact on the property. In *Patrick v. Colette*, Colette had a right of use and habitation of Patrick's house. While occupying Patrick's house, Colette made a number of alterations to the house in what she claimed was an attempt to modernize the property, including installing a pergola in the backyard, pouring a concrete slab so as to extend the bathroom, and destroying a wall of the porch. Patrick asserted that these alterations were made without his consent, and that by essentially increasing the size of his house, Colette may have increased Patrick's overall property tax liability in the future. In response, Colette asserted that her alterations would likely increase the value of the home.

In examining what duties Colette owed to Patrick as a beneficiary of a right of use and habitation, the Cour d'appel de Bordeaux noted that the rights and duties of beneficiaries of rights of use and habitation are the same as the rights and duties of usufructuaries. Relying on article 578 of the Code civil and citing *Cozon*, the court stated that Colette had a duty to preserve the substance of the thing without making material alterations. According to the *Patrick* court, a material alteration is not only a change in the economic purpose of the property, but also a change that is not objectively necessary or that economically impacts the property beyond increasing its value. The changes made by Colette, while retaining the economic purpose of the property, were not objectively necessary, but instead were simply changes in aesthetic appearance. Moreover, the alterations likely would have extraneous economic impacts on the property by increasing the property taxes.

Colette argued that her alterations economically improved the property, but this allegation did not sway the court. In addition to questioning whether the alterations did increase the value, the court found that the real question at issue was whether Colette had made an alteration to the property.

The French interpretation of waste for usufructuaries places the question of material alteration at the center of the analysis and defines it as a change that alters the economic purpose of the property. In addition, at least some French courts take the analysis a step further to find that any alteration that economically impacts the property or is simply unnecessary is a material alteration that violates the usufructuary's duties.

Though most civil law jurisdictions based on the French Code civil do not allow for the usufructuary to make material alterations that alter the purpose of the property, Belgian law does provide two instances in which a usufructuary might substantially alter property. First, if there are socioeconomic factors outside of the usufructuary's control which require the property subject to the usufruct to be adapted to a new situation, then the usufructuary may make material alterations. Second, if the previous owner of the property used it in an "abnormal manner," then the usufructuary may significantly alter the property, but in doing so, the usufructuary must follow the *bon père de famille* standard.

Notes and Questions

1. As Professor Richardson observes elsewhere in her article, the problem of ameliorative waste arises when "two or more individuals have a predesignated, successive interest in the same piece of property, but at least one individual, the 'future owner,' does not currently possess the property" and when the current possessor "materially alters the property without the consent of the future, and that alteration *increases* the market value of the property." Sally Brown Richardson, *Reframing Ameliorative Waste*, 65 Am. J. Comp. L. 335, 336–37 (2016). Do you think the solution to the problem of ameliorate waste promulgated by Article 558 of the Louisiana Civil Code is superior or inferior to the solution found in French law?

2. The law of ameliorative waste has been the subject of several other articles, in addition to the article authored by Professor Richardson. See Jill M. Fraley, *A New History of Waste Law: How a Misunderstood Doctrine Shaped Ideas About the Transformation of Law*, 100 Marq. L. Rev. 861 (2017); Thomas W. Merrill, Melms v. Pabst Brewing Co. *and the Doctrine of Waste in American Property Law*, 94 Marq. L. Rev. 1055 (2011); Richard A. Posner, *Comment on Merrill on the Law of Waste*, 94 Marq. L. Rev. 1095 (2011); John A. Lovett, *Doctrines of Waste in a Landscape of Waste*, 72 Mo. L. Rev. 1209 (2007).

F. Termination of the Usufruct

The usufruct is a real right of limited duration. La. Civ. Code art. 534 (1976). Thus, unlike ownership or a predial servitude, a usufruct cannot last indefinitely. It must end.

A usufruct in favor of a natural person must end with the death of the usufructuary, although it can end earlier. La. Civ. Code art. 607 (1976). When a usufruct is established in favor of several usufructuaries, the termination of the interest of one usufructuary inures to the benefit of the remaining usufructuaries. La. Civ. Code art. 547. (1976). Thus, if a joint usufruct benefits two or more usufructuaries who happen to be natural persons and the usufruct is for their lives, the usufruct may continue as long as one of the usufructuaries is alive. Recall that a legacy of revenues from specified property "terminates upon death of the legatee, unless a shorter period has been expressly stipulated." La. Civ. Code art. 609 (1976).

The Civil Code identifies several other grounds for the termination of a usufruct. As you study this topic, recognize that in some cases, even though a thing subject to a usufruct may disappear, perish, or undergo some kind of transformation, the usufruct will nevertheless not terminate. Instead, according to the principle of *real subrogation*, it will attach to the thing that replaced the thing subject to the usufruct. For example, real subrogation occurs when property subject to a usufruct is sold or when insurance proceeds are collected because the thing subject to the usufruct has been damaged or destroyed. In either instance, the usufruct continues to apply to the proceeds from the sale or the insurance policy.

1. Termination of a Usufruct for Causes Other than the Death of the Usufructuary

Juridical Persons: When a usufruct is established in favor of a juridical person like a corporation or partnership, the usufruct will terminate either: (1) when "the juridical person is dissolved or liquidated," without being converted, merged, or consolidated into a successor juridical person; or (2), "[i]n any event, upon the lapse of thirty years from the date of the commencement of the usufruct." La. Civ. Code art. 608 (1976). This thirty-year maximum life of a usufruct does not apply to juridical persons acting in a "capacity as trustee of a trust." This once again illustrates the greater flexibility in estate planning that takes advantage of trust law. *Id.*

Terms and Conditions: When a usufruct is for a term or subject to a condition, the usufruct will terminate "upon the expiration of the term or the happening of the condition." La. Civ. Code art. 610 (1976). Thus, a usufruct granted to last as long as the usufructuary remains unmarried or pursues a college education will terminate when the usufructuary marries or completes the college education. The same principle can be seen at work when a usufructuary is charged to restore or transfer the usufruct to another person, as in the case of a successive usufruct established pursuant to Article 546. In that situation, the first usufructuary's right "terminates when the time for restitution or delivery arrives." La. Civ. Code art. 611 (1976).

A usufruct granted in favor of one person until a third person reaches a certain age is called a "usufruct for a term." La. Civ. Code art. 612 (1976). In such a case, "[i]f the third person dies, the usufruct continues until the date the deceased person would have reached the designated age." *Id.* For example, if a grantor established a usufruct in favor of his surviving spouse until his child reached the age of 24, and the child died unexpectedly at the age of 21, the usufruct would continue in favor of the surviving spouse until the child would have turned 24. If a grantor wishes to provide for a different outcome, he must expressly specify this intention in the instrument creating the usufruct. *Id.* rev. cmt. (b).

Loss, Extinction or Destruction: The destruction of the thing subject to the usufruct can trigger the termination of a usufruct. Article 613 of the Civil Code provides the operative rule:

Art. 613. Loss, extinction, or destruction of the property

The usufruct of non-consumables terminates by the permanent and total loss, extinction, or destruction through accident, *force majeure* or decay of the property subject to the usufruct.

La. Civ. Code art. 613 (1976, amended 2010) (emphasis in original). Article 613, however, must be read *in pari materia* with the next provision of the Civil Code, Article 614, which illustrates the principle of real subrogation:

Art. 614. Fault of a third person

When any loss, extinction, or destruction of property subject to a usufruct is attributable to the fault of a third person, the usufruct does not terminate but attaches to any claim for damages and the proceeds therefrom.

La. Civ. Code art. 614 (1976). Note that if the loss or destruction of a thing subject to a usufruct is "attributable to the fault of the usufructuary or naked owner, the usufruct continues to exist and the consequences of the loss are determined under the general rules of delictual obligations." La. Civ. Code art. 613 rev. cmt. (e) (1976). Moreover, Article 576 of the Civil Code specifies that the usufructuary is "answerable for losses resulting from his fraud, default or neglect." La. Civ. Code art. 576 (1976). Consider the following problem to understand how these two articles work together.

Problem

Mrs. Brown, a widow, is involved in a car accident while driving her Mini Cooper in downtown Shreveport. Mrs. Brown owns one-half of the vehicle, which she and her late husband purchased during their marriage, in full ownership. She has a usufruct over the other one-half of the vehicle. Her children, Edna and Frank are the naked owners of this one-half interest. The driver of the other car in the accident, Mr. Moon, was at fault and responsible for the accident. Although Mrs. Brown was unharmed, her Mini Cooper was completely destroyed. Mrs. Brown sues Mr. Moon and his insurance company for damages. Can Mr. Moon and his insurance company successfully assert that Mrs. Brown's usufruct has terminated and, therefore, Edna and Frank are persons that must be joined as parties to the lawsuit?

Enforcement of Encumbrances: When property subject to the ususfruct has already been encumbered prior to the creation of the usufruct and the encumbrance is enforced after the creation of the usufruct (for example, by foreclosure of a mortgage or execution of a lien), the usufruct will terminate. La. Civ. Code art. 620 (1976). Article 620 illustrates that real rights are always subject to temporal priority. If two real rights with regard to the same property compete, the real right established first in time will have priority. Temporal rank, in turn, is determined in light of the rules of registry. *Id*. rev. cmt. (b).

Consider the following example. George grants a mortgage on Blackacre to Bossier Parish Bank to secure a loan from the bank. He then grants a usufruct over Blackacre to Ursula, while retaining the naked ownership. Unable to repay the loan, George defaults on the underlying obligation to repay the loan. The bank forecloses on Blackacre. Whoever purchases Blackacre at the foreclosure sale, whether it is the bank or another party, will acquire ownership of Blackacre free and clear of Ursula's usufruct.

Conversely, a judicial sale of a usufructuary's interest by her creditors will deprive *her* of the enjoyment of the property subject to the usufruct but it will *not* terminate the usufruct. La. Civ. Code art. 620(2) (1976). In the example above, if Ursula falls behind on her own debts and *her* creditors obtain a judicial sale of *her* usufructuary interest in Blackacre, the purchaser will take her place and enjoy her usufructuary interest as long as the usufruct lasts. If Ursula's usufruct was for life, then the purchaser at the judicial sale could enjoy the usufruct until Ursula dies, unless the usufruct terminates for some other reason. Because relatively few individuals or juridical persons would be interested in purchasing a usufructuary's interest in property at a judicial sale, the rule in the second paragraph of Article 620 may be of more theoretical than practical value.

Prescription of Nonuse: Just like other kinds of servitudes, a usufruct will also terminate "by the prescription of nonuse if neither the usufructuary nor any other person acting in his name exercises the right during a period of ten years." La. Civ. Code art. 621 (1976). This prescription of nonuse applies regardless of whether the usufruct covers "an entire estate" or a "divided or undivided part of an estate." *Id.* Article 621 thus illustrates another of the basic differences between the real right of usufruct and ownership. Ownership of a thing is never lost by mere nonuse. *See* La. Civ. Code art. 481 (1979).

Confusion: A usufruct also terminates when the usufruct and the naked ownership of the thing subject to the usufruct "are united in the same person." La. Civ. Code art. 622 (1976). This article illustrates a basic principle of the law of servitudes: "no one can have a servitude on his own property." *Id.* rev. cmt. (b). A usufruct would not, however, terminate by confusion when the title resulting in the unification of the two interests is annulled on account of "some previously existing defect or some vice inherent in the act." *Id.*

Waste, Unauthorized Alienation, Neglect or Abuse: Article 623 of the Civil Code sets forth the circumstances under which a naked owner may ask a court to terminate the usufruct when the usufructuary fails to preserve the substance of a nonconsumable:

Art. 623. Abuse of the enjoyment; consequences

The usufruct may be terminated by the naked owner if the usufructuary commits waste, alienates things without authority, neglects to make ordinary repairs, or abuses his enjoyment in any other manner.

La. Civ. Code art. 623 (1976). When you read *Kimball v. Standard Fire Ins. Co.*, 578 So.2d 546 (La. App. 3 Cir. 1991), consider whether this article should have any bearing on the outcome of the case.

Article 624 of the Civil Code builds on Article 623 but gives a court a remedial option other than termination in the event that a usufructuary abuses the right of usufruct. It allows a court to protect the naked owner's interest and give the usufructuary some economic benefits from the usufruct by decreeing "that the property be delivered to the naked owner on the condition that he shall pay to the usufructuary a reasonable annuity until the end of the usufruct." La. Civ. Code art. 624(1) (1976). The article declares that the "amount of the annuity shall be based on the value of the usufruct." *Id.* A usufructuary who wants to avoid either termination of the usufruct or delivery of the property to the naked owner may "give security to insure that he will take appropriate corrective measures within a period fixed by the court." La. Civ. Code art. 624 (2) (1976).

Under Article 625 of the Civil Code, creditors of the usufructuary can likewise prevent the termination of the usufruct and the delivery of the property to the naked owner by "offering to repair the damages caused by the usufructuary and by giving security for the future." La. Civ. Code art. 625 (1976).

Renunciation: The last ground for termination of a usufruct other than by the death of the usufructuary arises through a voluntary act of renunciation by the usufructuary:

Art. 626. Renunciation; rights of creditors

A usufruct terminates by an express written renunciation.

A creditor of the usufructuary may cause to be annulled a renunciation made to his prejudice.

La. Civ. Code art. 626 (1976). The ability of a usufructuary to renounce his or her usufruct in the interests of a naked owner is significant. For altruistic or practical reasons, a usufructuary may wish to terminate the usufruct and allow the naked owner to become full owner. For example, the usufructuary may have ample assets of her own and would prefer that the naked owner of the subject property enjoy it in full ownership immediately. Or the usufructuary might lack the resources or expertise to manage a valuable nonconsumable. In this case, Article 626 must be read *in pari materia* with Article 582, which allows a usufructuary to release himself or herself from the obligation of making ordinary repairs "by abandoning the usufruct, or with approval of the court, a portion thereof." La. Civ. Code art. 582 (1976). Read together, these articles indicate that a usufructuary "may renounce the whole of the usufruct unilaterally [but needs the approval of the court to renounce] . . . a part thereof . . ." La. Civ. Code art. 626 rev. cmt. (c) (1976). Importantly, a renunciation must always be express and written, even if the usufruct applies to movables.

Now consider the following decisions to see how courts have applied the principles discussed above.

Bond v. Green

401 So.2d 639 (La. App. 3 Cir. 1981)

CUTRER, Judge. James and Ann Bond filed a rule to evict George and Mildred Green and J. B. and Freddie Powell from the following described property: . . .

The plaintiffs alleged that defendants were occupying the property without a lease and that the purpose of defendants' occupancy had ceased. In the alternative, the plaintiffs pleaded that, in the event it was determined that the defendants had a right to occupy the premises, the court should define the boundary of such occupied land. The defendants filed no pleading.

The trial court rendered judgment in favor of defendants, George and Mildred Green, recognizing that they had a usufruct over the following described property: . . .

The court further ordered the Greens to reimburse the plaintiffs, James and Ann Bond, for taxes previously paid in the amount of $ 24.89. The court ordered the Greens to pay taxes for 1980 and future taxes. Plaintiffs appealed. We affirm.

The issues presented on appeal are:

(1) Whether, under the facts, the Greens' usufruct had terminated; and

(2) If such usufruct is still in effect, whether the trial court erred in its designation of the extent of property subject to the usufruct.

Whether the Usufruct Terminated

The facts are generally undisputed. In 1966, George and Mildred Green sold to Lloyd Love a tract of land containing approximately 55 acres of land. The instrument by which the property was sold contained the following reservations:

"Vendors reserve unto themselves the usufruct of the house in which they now reside, the small house situated immediately on the west side of their residence and the yards surrounding the said residence."

Mrs. Green, 76 years of age, testified that following the sale to Lloyd Love in 1966, they continued to live in the larger of the two structures. She stated that at the time of the sale to Love, both structures were in bad shape or dilapidated. The Greens attempted to make repairs to the larger house where they resided. They changed the floor on the porch on two occasions. They installed bath fixtures and made other repairs, but the overall condition of the house could not be appreciably improved. The structural portions of the house had deteriorated to such an extent that the house could not be safely lived in.

The small house was not occupied and likewise was in a dilapidated condition when the sale was made to Love. The condition of this structure deteriorated to the point that it was falling down. Mrs. Green stated that in approximately 1976, she had her son-in-law remove the structures. This was done by pushing them down with a tractor. Mrs. Green explained the reason for removing the structures as follows:

"Q. What was the reason you tore the houses down?"

"A. The reason? Well, the termites got in the seals (sic) and ate the seals (sic). You know how termites will do. And the floors in the back of the house had fallen down about that far from the walls, and I didn't want the house falling down and injuring one of my grandchildren."

"Q. The termites had done great structural damage to the house."

"A. Yes. Both of them, as far as that's concerned."

After the removal of the structures, two mobile homes were moved on to the property and placed approximately in the location where the houses had been situated. The Greens occupied one mobile home and defendants, J. B. and Freddie Powell, daughter and son-in-law of the Greens, occupied the other.

Mrs. Green's daughter, Freddie Powell, testified that she and her husband moved a mobile home onto the property in order to assist her mother in caring for Mr. Green who was 76 years old. He had been sick for several years and was an invalid at the time of trial. The income of the Greens was limited to Social Security payments and food stamps ($439.00 per month). Mrs. Powell testified that the structures were old and literally had decayed and had become termite infested to the extent that they were falling down. She stated that at the time of the sale to Love, the structures were in very bad shape. She testified that her mother and father attempted to repair same but such repairs did not impede the continuing deterioration of the structures. She classified the larger house as not livable and a health hazard.

Lloyd Love testified that at the time he purchased the property both structures were in terrible shape. He stated that neither house was livable at that time. For this reason he attached no value to the structures when he purchased the property. Love stated that he wanted the Greens to have a place to live for the remainder of their lives, and had considered removing the structures and building a new house for the Greens to live in. Due to a financial problem, however, he could not carry out his intention. He stated that the Greens had his permission to remove the deteriorated structures.

Plaintiffs urge that, under the facts presented, the usufruct should be considered terminated on the ground that the property subject to the usufruct has been totally and permanently lost. Plaintiffs rely principally upon LSA-C.C. art. 613. This article reads as follows:

> "The usufruct of nonconsumables terminates by the permanent and *total loss*, extinction, or destruction through accident or decay of the property subject to the usufruct" (emphasis ours).

Plaintiff's position is without merit.

Article 613 terminates the usufruct if the total usufruct is lost through decay. In the case at hand, the usufruct extended to not only the two houses but the yards surrounding same.

The facts are undisputed that the two houses were in unlivable, decayed condition with no value at the time the usufruct came into existence. The attempts of the Greens to repair the structures proved to be an exercise of futility. The removal of these structures did not effectuate a total loss of the usufruct. This was a partial loss of the usufruct. The usufruct remained on the land or yards surrounding the structures.

Paragraph (d) of the Comment to article 613 explains this position as follows:

> "The *usufruct terminates only if the loss is total*. Thus, if the usufruct is established simply on a building, and this building is destroyed completely, the usufruct terminates. . . . *If the loss is only partial, the usufruct continues*

and is exercised on whatever remains of the thing. C.C. art. 614 (1870). Thus, if the usufruct is established "upon an estate of which the building is a part, the usufructuary shall enjoy both the soil and the materials.' . . . ." (emphasis ours).

Since the loss of the structures was due to decay of only a part of the usufruct, and not a loss of the total usufruct, the trial court correctly held that the usufruct continued on the remaining land.

Plaintiffs further urge that the Greens committed waste or neglected to make ordinary repairs or abused their enjoyment of the usufruct, and under LSA-C.C. art. 623, the usufruct terminates.

This position of the plaintiffs is likewise without merit. The facts clearly reflect that these structures were old and decayed. A usufructuary is not bound to restore property that has been destroyed because of age. LSA-C.C. art. 583 provides, in part, as follows:

"Neither the usufructuary nor the naked owner is bound to restore property that has been totally destroyed through accident or because of age."

Finally, the plaintiffs contend that the defendants' failure to pay the property taxes on the land they occupied entitled the plaintiffs, as naked owners, to terminate the usufruct. LSA-C.C. art. 584 places the obligation to pay the property taxes on the usufructuary but does not provide for termination of the usufruct upon failure to meet this obligation. That article reads:

"The usufructuary is bound to pay the annual charges imposed during his enjoyment on the property subject to the usufruct, such as property taxes."

This article clearly gives rise to an obligation on the part of the usufructuary to pay the taxes, but if the naked owner has paid the taxes he has only an action against the usufructuary for reimbursement, rather than a right to terminate the usufruct. We are buttressed in this opinion by the comments to that article. Comment (e) reads, in pertinent part, as follows:

"The naked owner, in order to avoid a tax sale of his property, may pay the taxes due by the usufructuary and bring against him an action for reimbursement. . . ."

Consequently, the trial judge was correct in ordering the Greens to reimburse the plaintiffs for back taxes. He also correctly concluded that the failure to pay the taxes was not a ground for termination of the usufruct. . . .

For the reasons assigned, the judgment of the trial court is affirmed. Plaintiffs are to pay all costs of this appeal.

AFFIRMED.

Notes and Questions

1. Could the defendants in *Bond v. Green*, 401 So.2d 639 (La. App. 3 Cir. 1981), George and Mildred Green, have successfully demanded that the naked owners,

James and Ann Bond, perform the repairs necessary to rebuild the houses at issue? If the Greens had paid for these repairs themselves, would they have been entitled to reimbursement?

2. In light of the court's ruling in *Bond*, what remedies do the Bonds have to recover for the unpaid property taxes associated with the property?

3. Assume that you had been the Bonds' attorney at the time they were contemplating purchasing the land subject to the Greens' usufruct. Further suppose that a title examination had revealed the existence of the Greens' usufruct and an inspection report for the property had documented the condition of the structures. What advice would you have given the Bonds about the proposed transaction?

2. Real Subrogation

Involuntary Changes in Form: Article 615 of the Civil Code explains the general principle of real subrogation. Real subrogation and its mechanics are further illustrated in Articles 616 through 618 of the Civil Code in the contexts of sale or exchange and insurance proceeds.

Art. 615. Change in the form of property

When property subject to a usufruct changes form without an act of the usufructuary, the usufruct does not terminate even though the property may no longer serve the use for which it was originally destined.

When property subject to a usufruct is converted into money or other property without an act of the usufructuary, as in a case of expropriation of an immovable or liquidation of a corporation, the usufruct terminates as to the property converted and attaches to the money or other property received by the usufructuary.

La. Civ. Code art. 615 (1976, amended 2010). Article 615 is only triggered when the property subject to the usufruct changes form involuntarily—without the voluntary participation of the usufructuary. The example given in its second paragraph is the easiest to understand. Suppose that Arpent Noir, a sugar cane farm, is subject to a usufruct in favor of Ellen and that the Louisiana Department of Transportation expropriates all of Arpent Noir for purposes of building a new state highway. Ellen's usufruct will not terminate; rather, the property that is subject to her usufruct will have changed form. After the expropriation is complete, Ellen's usufruct will apply to the money paid by the state as just compensation for the expropriation.

Voluntary Sale or Exchange: Article 616 of the Civil Code addresses a more common scenario—a change of form of property subject to a usufruct through a voluntary sale or exchange. It provides in pertinent part:

Art. 616. Sale or exchange of the property; taxes

When property subject to usufruct is sold or exchanged, whether in an action for partition or by agreement between the usufructuary and the naked owner or by a usufructuary who has the power to dispose of nonconsumable property, the usufruct terminates as to the nonconsumable property sold or exchanged, but as provided in Article 568.1, the usufruct attaches to the money or other property received by the usufructuary, unless the parties agree otherwise. . . .

La. Civ. Code art. 616 (1976, amended 1983, 2010). Article 616 offers an important clarification of the law because it tells us that, in the absence of an agreement to the contrary, all the proceeds of a sale or the property received as the result of an exchange (whether in the wake of a partition or an agreement between the usufructuary and the naked owner or a disposition by the usufructuary with the express power to dispose of nonconsumables) will be subject to the usufruct. The provision avoids drawing parties and courts into complicated disputes concerning the apportionment of sales proceeds or exchanged property between the usufructuary and naked owner. *See id.* rev. cmt (b) (1976). It thus helps to make the property subject to a usufruct far more marketable and liquid if the usufructuary has the power and the desire to sell or exchange that property.

Insurance Proceeds: Article 617 of the Civil Code, a short, but important, provision addresses the rights of the usufructuary and naked owner with respect to insurance proceeds:

Art. 617. Proceeds of insurance

When proceeds of insurance are due on account of loss, extinction, or destruction of property subject to usufruct, the usufruct attaches to the proceeds. If the usufructuary or the naked owner has separately insured his interest only, the proceeds belong to the insured party.

La. Civ. Code art. 617 (1976). Pursuant to Article 617, real subrogation takes place with respect to insurance proceeds, unless the usufructuary or the naked owner has separately insured his interest only. *Id.* When a pre-existing policy for the property is simply renewed after the commencement of the usufruct, the proceeds from that policy are subject to subrogation. They become consumables subject to the usufruct.

Security for Proceeds: Article 618 of the Louisiana Civil Code plays a pivotal role in providing some measure of protection for naked owners when a nonconsumable thing subject to a usufruct has been transformed as a result of a voluntary or involuntary transaction into a consumable. Consider the full text:

Article 618. Security for proceeds

In cases governed by Articles 614, 615, 616, and the first sentence of Article 617, the naked owner may demand, within one year from receipt of the proceeds by the usufructuary that the usufructuary give security for the proceeds. If such a demand is made, and the parties cannot agree, the nature of the security shall be determined by the court. This Article does not apply to corporeal movables referred to in the second sentence of Article 568, or to property disposed of by the usufructuary pursuant to the power to dispose of nonconsumables if the grantor of the usufruct has dispensed with the security.

La. Civ. Code art. 618 (1976, amended 2010).

Prior to 2010, Article 618 had allowed a naked owner to demand the "safe investment" of proceeds resulting from cases specified in its first sentence. By substituting the term "security" for "safe investment," the 2010 revision has raised a number of potentially problematic issues. For criticism of the recent revision of Article 618 and the substitution of "security" for "safe investment" in a variety of contexts, see A.N. YIANNOPOULOS, 3 LOUISIANA CIVIL LAW TREATISE: PERSONAL SERVITUDES §6.8 (5th ed. 2011) (noting uncertainty as to whether security will be required when the new requirement under Article 618 appears to conflict with dispensations of the obligation to provide security under Articles 573, 890, 1499 and 1514 of the Civil Code).

Compare the following two decisions to gain a better understanding of how Article 617 of the Civil Code can apply in both atypical and more typical situations involving insurance proceeds.

Kimball v. Standard Fire Ins. Co.

578 So.2d 546 (La. App. 3 Cir. 1991)

LaBORDE, Judge. On June 28, 1983, plaintiff, Bobbie Clark Kimball, filed suit against defendant, The Standard Fire Insurance Company of Hartford, Connecticut (Standard), seeking to collect fire insurance proceeds after a house purchased during her marriage to the late Guy W. Kimball was totally destroyed by fire. After the house burned, Michael H. Davis, who had been appointed provisional administrator of the Succession of Guy Kimball on June 24, 1980, gave notice to counsel for Standard that he intended to intervene in the suit on behalf of the succession. However, before a formal intervention was filed, Standard inadvertently sent a check directly to Mrs. Kimball's attorney and the check was cashed. Subsequently, on November 30, 1983, an intervention was filed by Mr. Davis and tried without a jury.

The trial court found that Mrs. Kimball was the only named insured under the fire insurance policy and that she did not intend to cover any interest other than her own insurable interest. Accordingly, the trial court determined that the Succession of Guy Kimball was not entitled to a share of the insurance proceeds and dismissed the intervenor's suit at intervenor's cost.

On appeal, intervenor argues that the trial court erred in failing to find that a portion of the insurance proceeds belonged to the Succession of Guy Kimball. After reviewing the trial record and appellate briefs, we find no error in law or manifest error in fact. Thus, we affirm the judgment of the trial court. Insofar as we are favored with its well-reasoned findings, we annex those reasons hereto. Costs of this appeal are to be paid by intervenor, the Succession of Guy W. Kimball.

AFFIRMED.

**Civil Suit Number 127,880 Bobbie Kimball Versus the Standard
Fire Insurance Company of Hartford, Connecticut Ninth Judicial District
Court Parish of Rapides State of Louisiana *Reasons for Judgment***

The plaintiff in this suit and her three children were the owners in indivision of the family home located at 200 High Country Drive in Pineville. This included a substantial two story brick and frame home which was the property of the plaintiff and her husband before his death, and thereafter of the plaintiff and his heirs.

The plaintiff's husband was murdered in the home on March 8, 19[79]. The plaintiff and two male friends were later charged in the murder of Guy Kimball. The plaintiff subsequently pled guilty to conspiracy to commit murder. She was being held in the Rapides Parish jail when the house was totally destroyed by fire on the afternoon of May 19, 1983.

Subsequent to the fire, a thorough investigation was done. The results tend to indicate that there is a very high probability that the fire was started and accelerated by means of arson. There were also strong indications that the home was unoccupied and had been unoccupied for a substantial period of time when destroyed. There are also reports that the home had been stripped of furnishings and fixtures prior to its burning.

Nonetheless, when the home burned on May 19, 1983, there was a policy of fire insurance in effect with The Standard Fire Insurance Company of Hartford, Connecticut covering the home and its contents. The policy covered the term June 3, 1982, to June 3, 1983. It was a renewal of a policy which had been in effect prior, but was renewed by Mrs. Kimball in her name alone. The premium was paid by her.

When the home burned, a claim was made on the policy. While the claim was being investigated, a sworn statement was taken from Mrs. Kimball in the parish jail, with her attorney, Eugene Cicardo, Sr., present. At that time Mrs. Kimball said that she alone had purchased the policy, but that the home was owned by herself and the late Mr. Kimball. The insurer was put clearly on notice of other potential ownership interests in the property, although the insurance was issued solely in Mrs. Kimball's name.

Subsequently, Mr. Michael Davis, who had been appointed the provisional administrator of the estate of Guy W. Kimball on June 24, 1980, gave notice to Mr. Edward Rundell, the attorney in Alexandria for Standard, that he intended to intervene in the insurance suit on behalf of the children who were owners in indivision with Mrs. Kimball in the house. A formal intervention was not at that time filed.

Standard, then at this juncture in the occurrence of events in the history of the suit, did a curious, unexplained and nonsensical thing. It mailed a check for $ 110,000.00 to Mrs. Kimball's attorney, Eugene Cicardo, Sr. No answer rationally explains why this payment was made or why it was made directly to the plaintiff, bypassing Standard's own attorney in Alexandria. The Court concludes that it was a mistake, suspicious, but not malicious. The insurer had nothing to lose through the intervention. It had nothing to lose in a concursus proceeding. It additionally had grounds for potentially avoiding payment on the policy; arson, vacancy. The payment appears not to have been incorporated in any settlement of the claim. Mrs. Kimball cashed the check, took the money and ran. She was not available for trial, and is apparently absent in violation of her probation terms.

The children of Bobbie Kimball and Guy Kimball have continued their intervention, bringing suit against Standard in an attempt to "raid" the proceeds of the claim payment to Mrs. Kimball. The theory of their right to do this is that they are owners in indivision with Mrs. Kimball as heirs of Guy Kimball. Since the whole of the destroyed property is insured, they claim that a proportion of the insurance policy reflective of their ownership interests is due to them.

In this suit this issue is greatly complicated by the unfortunate fact of the funds being gone. Mrs. Kimball has absconded with them, hence if monies are due to the intervenors under the insurance contract, the funds must come from Standard in excess of the policy payment previously made to Mrs. Kimball.

The Court determines that while the intervenors had an insurable interest in the insured property, that interest was not in fact insured. Mrs. Kimball by her actions showed an unequivocal intent not to insure the interests of the intervenors in the property, both before and after the loss. What is more, under the usufruct granted to Mrs. Kimball under LA. C.C. Article 890 it would appear that the intervenors had very little interest in the property. Their interest being an undivided partial one, subject to usufruct for life or until the remarriage of Mrs. Kimball, a woman in her low thirties. The Court feels that Mrs. Kimball was entitled to insure the full value of the property.

Although neither party cited this authority, the crowning blow seems to come from Article 617 of the Louisiana Civil Code which reads:

> "When Proceeds of insurance are due on account of loss, extinction, or destruction of property subject to usufruct, the usufruct attaches to the proceeds. If the usufructuary or the naked owner has separately insured his interest only, the proceeds belong to the insured party."

The usufruct of the house as community property subject to Article 890 would convert to a usufruct of insurance proceeds on insured property subject to usufruct. In a real sense, this intervention is a premature claim. Mrs. Kimball's Article 890 usufruct has metamorphosed into a usufruct of the insurance proceeds, a usufruct which does not terminate until her death or remarriage neither of which to the knowledge of the Court has occurred.

Additionally, the reasoning of the First Circuit enunciated in *Hartford Insurance Company of Southwest vs. Stablier*, 476 So.2nd 464, leads to a conclusion that the intervention should not prevail, although emotion and equity might suggest otherwise.

Therefore, the Court is led to the abiding conclusion that the intervention should be dismissed with court costs assessed to the intervenors.

Alexandria, Louisiana, this 2nd day of May, 1989.

Notes and Questions

1. After the disposition of the appeal in *Kimball v. Standard Fire Ins. Co.*, 578 So.2d 546 (La. App. 3 Cir. 1991), what rights, claims or remedies do the children of Guy Kimball have? Should Standard Fire have pursued a different course of action in this controversy? Should the attorney for Bobbie Clark Kimball, Eugene Cicardo, have turned over the insurance proceeds check to his client so readily when she was apparently still in jail after being charged for conspiracy in her late husband's murder? Did Cicardo have any alternative to the action he took in this case? What were his ethical duties in this situation?

2. Could the attorney or guardian representing the interests of Guy Kimball's children have taken any other steps to protect their interest in the property subject to the dispute? What actions could have been taken? Consider the relevance of La. Civ. Code art. 941 (1997).

3. Would it matter if Bobbie Clark Kimball had remarried a few years after Guy Kimball's death? Would a common law marriage trigger the termination of the usufruct under Article 890? Approximately a decade after the incidents described in the decision above, Bobbie Clark murdered another man named Michael Sievers, reportedly her "common law husband," by shooting him six times. Bobbie Clark is reportedly now serving a life sentence in a Louisiana penitentiary.

Johnson v. Laney

964 So.2d 418 (La. App. 4 Cir. 2007)

MURRAY, Judge. Defendants appeal the trial court's granting of summary judgment in favor of the plaintiff, Charmaine Johnson, declaring that Ms. Johnson's testamentary usufruct of her residence attached to insurance proceeds that were paid as a result of its damage by Hurricane Katrina, which rendered the house uninhabitable. For the reasons that follow, we affirm.

Facts and Proceedings Below

Defendants John A. Laney, IV, and Troy C. Laney are the plaintiff's grandchildren, the minor children of her son, John Laney, III, who died in 1986. Defendant Deborah Gambino is the mother of John A. Laney, IV, and defendant Julie Bonnano is the mother of Troy C. Laney. In his will, John Laney, III, bequeathed to his mother, Charmaine Johnson, the usufruct of the land and improvements located at 751 Filmore Avenue, where he was living with his mother at the time of his death. The naked ownership of the property was bequeathed to a trust for the benefit of Mr. Laney's two minor sons, naming their respective mothers as trustees. Ms. Johnson was living in the home until Hurricane Katrina struck on August 29, 2005. Because of the severe damage done to the home by the hurricane, Ms. Johnson now lives in Houston.

State Farm provided insurance coverage (both homeowner's and flood) for 751 Filmore Avenue. On January 23, 2006, Ms. Johnson filed a petition for declaratory judgment seeking to have the court declare that the insurance proceeds paid by State Farm to compensate for the loss of and/or damage to the home and its contents were subject to her usufruct. State Farm had issued four checks, one covering the building and one covering its contents under each of two policies—the flood policy and the homeowner's policy. All four checks were made payable to Ms. Johnson as usufructuary, Ms. Gambino as trustee for John A. Laney, IV, and Ms. Bonnano as trustee for Troy C. Laney. On May 1, 2006, the trial court ordered that these checks be endorsed by all payees and deposited into the registry of the court pending the resolution of the lawsuit.

Having filed an answer to the plaintiff's petition in April, the defendants on May 8, 2006, filed a "Reconventional and Third Party Demand." In the reconventional demand, defendants asserted that plaintiff is liable to them for violating the 1990 court-approved agreement that settled the succession of John Laney, III. In essence, defendants claimed Ms. Johnson had mismanaged funds in a certain "controlled" bank account of which she is usufructuary and they are the naked owners, and demanded that the trial court order that she render an accounting of her usufruct. Defendants also alleged that Ms. Johnson had abused her usufruct over movables, specifically firearms, located at 751 Filmore Avenue, by failing to file an insurance claim regarding their loss. Defendants further alleged that plaintiff's abuse of her usufruct is cause for the court to order that the usufruct be terminated or, alternatively, to order the usufructuary to post security to ensure she will take appropriate corrective measures within a period of time fixed by the court.[2] . . .

On June 9, 2006, Ms. Johnson filed a motion for summary judgment arguing that there was no genuine issue of fact regarding the claims raised in her original petition, that her usufruct attached to the insurance proceeds as a matter of law, and that therefore she was entitled to the State Farm checks deposited into the court's registry. On July 18, 2006, the trial court, after hearing the matter, rendered summary judgment in favor of the plaintiff, citing La. C.C. art. 617 as the basis for its holding that the plaintiff's usufruct attached to the insurance proceeds. The trial court then ordered that the funds be disbursed to Ms. Johnson, "who shall hold them in usufruct subject to the rights of the naked owners. . . ." Defendants appeal this judgment.

. . . .

Discussion

In the instant case, there are no facts in dispute. . . .

Thus, the sole issue before this court is whether, as a matter of law, the plaintiff's usufruct of 751 Filmore Avenue attaches to the proceeds of the homeowner's and flood policies covering the property. We hold that it does.

---

2. It is not completely clear from the reconventional demand which usufruct (the one over the bank account or the one over 751 Filmore Avenue, or both) defendants allege should be terminated.

La. C.C. art. 617, entitled "Proceeds of Insurance" states:

> When proceeds of insurance are due on account of loss, extinction, or destruction of property subject to usufruct, the usufruct attaches to the proceeds. If the usufructuary or the naked owner has separately insured his interest only, the proceeds belong to the insured party.

On appeal, the defendants argue that this article does not apply to the instant situation for two reasons: (1) the plaintiff failed to prove that the property subject to the usufruct was totally destroyed; and (2) the undisputed facts indicate that they separately insured their interest within the terms of Article 617. We address each argument in turn.

First, defendants argue that Ms. Johnson failed to introduce any evidence to prove that the insured movable and immovable property was lost, extinct or destroyed as required by Article 617. Citing La. C.C. art. 613 as authority, they further assert that "loss, extinction or destruction" as used in the Civil Code means "total loss, extinction or destruction." La.C.C. art. 613 states:

> The usufruct of nonconsumables terminates by the permanent and total loss, extinction or destruction through accident or decay of the property subject to the usufruct.

Contrary to defendants' argument, Article 613 does not purport to define the terms or phrase "loss, extinction or destruction" as used in the entire Civil Code. Instead, the legislature has qualified those terms as used in *that particular article* by including the adjectives "permanent and total." Plaintiff has never contended that Hurricane Katrina completely destroyed all the property subject to her usufruct, only that it damaged the house to the extent that it became uninhabitable. It is undisputed that the land upon which the house sits is still in existence. Therefore, Article 613 is not applicable to the instant situation, but Article 617 clearly is. Article 617 does not require the *total* loss or destruction of *all* the property subject to the usufruct, but rather the loss or destruction of at least some of the property, which loss is compensated for by insurance proceeds. Article 617's declaration that the usufruct attaches to the insurance proceeds in this circumstance comports with several other companion Code articles that determine what happens to the usufruct of property in other, similar circumstances. *See, e.g.,* La. C.C. art. 614 (When property is lost or destroyed by fault of a third person, the usufruct attaches to any claim for damages); La. C.C. art. 615 (When property changes form or is converted to money without any act of the usufructuary, the usufruct attaches to the new form of the property or to the money); La. C.C. art. 616 (When property is sold, the usufruct attaches to the proceeds of the sale). We therefore reject defendants' first argument.

Defendants next argue that they are entitled to a portion of the insurance proceeds because they separately insured their interest (the naked ownership of the property) within the terms of Article 617. However, defendants presented no evidence indicating that they separately insured their interest. They argue that the premiums for the insurance were paid from the principal amount in the so-called "controlled" bank account, which they claim is their "separate property." However, this assertion is contradicted by the written settlement agreement, which gives the plaintiff the usufruct over the account and the responsibility of paying the premiums. Moreover, defendants cite no authority for the proposition that their payment of the insurance premiums, even if such were proved, would equate to the separate insuring of their interest in the property.

The State Farm agent, Joseph Raymond, testified in his deposition that both the homeowner's policy and the flood policy in effect at the time of Hurricane Katrina were originally purchased by John Laney, III, during his lifetime. In 1990, pursuant to the agreement settling Mr. Laney's estate, Mr. Raymond changed the name of the "insured" on each policy to read:

> Charmaine R. Johnson, usufruct. This was a succession of John A. Laney, III, the property given to his mother. Please list as additional insureds the following: Deborah B. Gambino, trustee for John A. Laney, IV and Julie Raymond Bonnano, trustee for Troy C. Laney.

Mr. Raymond further testified that none of the four defendants had ever approached him about insuring their naked ownership interest in the property in question; nor had any of them ever requested that he do so or filled out an application for insurance on said property.

The defendants presented no evidence to contradict Mr. Raymond's testimony. Moreover, defendants cite no authority for the proposition that the mere inclusion of their names as additional insureds on the policies equates to the separate insuring of their naked ownership interest. Therefore, we reject defendants' contention that they separately insured their interest in the property.

Conclusion

Accordingly, for the reasons stated, we find no error in the trial court's granting of summary judgment declaring that the plaintiff's usufruct attaches to the insurance proceeds and ordering the disbursement of those funds to Ms. Johnson. We therefore affirm the judgment of the trial court, and remand the matter to that court for further proceedings consistent with this opinion.

AFFIRMED AND REMANDED

Question

1. In light of *Johnson v. Laney*, 964 So.2d 418 (La. App. 4 Cir. 2007), do you believe the Civil Code provided adequate tools for usufructuaries and naked owners to deal with the wave of property insurance claims in the wake of Hurricane Katrina?

Problems

1. Recall the commercial building and land in Bunkie belonging to Esther in naked ownership and subject to a usufruct in favor of Louis. A tornado that passed

through Bunkie destroyed the building. Suppose, however, that the building was insured under a general commercial property insurance policy issued by State Farm. The insurance policy lists both Esther and Louis as insured parties. The insurance premiums were paid by Louis. After investigating the property damage, State Farm determines that it owes $350,000 in proceeds with respect to the destruction of the building by the tornado.

A. Who is entitled to the insurance proceeds?

B. If Louis is able to claim the insurance proceeds, is he obligated to use them to restore the building to its pre-tornado condition? Or can he use the proceeds for his own purposes?

2. Same facts as in question 1 above, but suppose that the insurance policy had lapsed before the tornado hit and neither Louis nor Esther have enough money to restore the building. A developer named Isabel is willing to pay $400,000 in cash for the lot and the remains of the building. Isabel plans to build a casino in Bunkie on the property.

A. If Louis and Esther both agree to sell the property to Isabel, who will receive the proceeds of the sale?

B. If Louis receives the proceeds, does he incur any obligation to Esther with respect to the proceeds?

3. Consequences of Termination; Accounting

Once a usufruct has terminated for any of the reasons discussed above, the naked owner enjoys several important rights. As we know, these vary depending on the classification of the thing subject to the usufruct. When a usufruct of *nonconsumables* terminates for a cause other than the total and permanent destruction of the thing, full ownership is vested in the naked owner. La. Civ. Code art. 628 (1976). This reintegration of ownership requires the usufructuary or his heirs to deliver the nonconsumables to the naked owner, along with their accessories and any fruits produced since the termination of the usufruct. *Id.* If nonconsumables are lost or have deteriorated through the fault of the usufructuary, the naked owner is entitled to the value they otherwise would have had at the termination of the usufruct. *Id.* Of course, if nonconsumables are by their nature impaired through use, wear or decay (for example, appliances and vehicles), then the usufructuary is only obligated to return them to the naked owner in the condition they may be in at the termination of the usufruct. La. Civ. Code art. 569 (1976).

When a usufruct of *consumables* terminates, the usufructuary is required to deliver to the naked owner things of the same quantity or quality or to deliver the value they had at the commencement of the usufruct. La. Civ. Code art. 629 (1976). This same rule is articulated in Article 538 of the Civil Code. As illustrated by *Succession of Heckert*, 160 So.2d 375 (La. App. 4 Cir. 1964), the nature of the naked owner's rights against the usufructuary or his heirs will be characterized according to the classification of the thing subject to the usufruct. With respect to nonconsumables, the naked owner has an imprescriptible real right in the thing subject to the usufruct. In the case of consumables, the naked owner's right to things of the same quantity or quality or equivalent value takes the form of a personal right like that of any other creditor of the usufructuary.

Although most of these post-termination rules grant rights to the naked owner, Article 627 of the Civil Code gives the usufructuary an important right at this stage:

Art. 627. Right of retention

Upon termination of the usufruct, the usufructuary or his heirs have the right to retain possession of the property until reimbursement for all expenses and advances for which they have recourse against the owner or his heirs.

La. Civ. Code art. 627 (1978). What expenses or advances are contemplated by this provision? *See id.* rev. cmt. (c). Would a usufructuary's entitlement to retain possession include a right to fruits produced while waiting for reimbursement? *Id.* rev. cmt. (d).

Succession of Heckert

160 So.2d 375 (La. App. 4 Cir. 1964)

McBRIDE, Judge. John Earl Heckert and Anna I. Buch were married in 1912 and two children were born of the marriage, viz., John E. Heckert, Jr. and Mrs. Isabelle L. Heckert Hardie. The two children were of the full age of majority when their mother died intestate on July 24, 1938; her succession was opened in the Civil District Court for the Parish of Orleans, Docket No. 227-393; as per judgment therein rendered and signed August 8, 1938, Heckert was recognized as decedent's surviving husband in community and as such was sent into possession as owner of an undivided one-half interest in 710 shares of the capital stock of S. H. Kress and Company belonging to the community as represented by eight certain certificates issued therefor standing in his name, said certificates being described by number in the judgment; the two children were recognized as the sole heirs of their mother and sent into possession of the other undivided one-half of said shares, subject to the usufruct of their father thereon. Notwithstanding the change of ownership decreed by the judgment of possession, the stock certificates remained as originally issued in Heckert's name and possession and he collected the dividends.

Besides the 710 shares inventoried in the wife's succession, there were 300 other shares of the Kress stock which belonged to the community represented by three certificates for 100 shares each standing in Heckert's name. These shares, for some unknown reason, were not mentioned in the succession proceedings. However, Heckert likewise had possession of the uninventoried certificates and collected the dividends. Of course, the two children acquired an undivided one-half naked ownership in said 300 shares immediately upon the death of their mother under the doctrine of le mort saisit le vif. LSA-C.C. arts. 940, 941.

John Earl Heckert married his second wife, Eunice Knobloch, on August 4, 1939, in New York; it was then that his usufruct on the property derived by his children from the first wife's succession terminated by the operation of law. See LSA-C.C. art. 916. Heckert made no attempt to deliver to his children their portion of the 1010 shares of Kress stock on which his usufruct had existed, and the children made no demand on him therefor, but were content to permit him to retain possession of the certificates and to collect dividends.

Heckert departed this life on March 3, 1961, leaving a last will and testament which has been duly probated herein by which he bequeathed to his second wife, Mrs. Eunice Knobloch Heckert, the disposable portion of his estate and to his two children he left their legitime. Out of the 1010 shares of Kress stock of which Heckert had possession upon his first wife's death, only three certificates were found among his effects, these standing in his name as originally issued and being each for 100 shares. Two of said certificates (7154 and 7155) were among those inventoried in the first wife's succession and one certificate (7158) was one of those which had been omitted therefrom.

The record discloses that Heckert had 'donated' to his second wife at various times after their marriage 300 shares of the Kress stock which emanated from the first community, and that from time to time he had sold or otherwise disposed of 410 shares.

In the bank box of decedent and his second wife were found six certificates representing 400 shares, all issued to Mrs. Eunice Knobloch Heckert. Said shares were the subject matter of gifts to her by Heckert. . . .

The 'gift' of July 29, 1940 (Cert. H-1529) resulted from Heckert's surrender to the issuing corporation and cancellation of a certificate for 100 shares issued in his name which had been acquired during the second community. The last five mentioned certificates had been issued upon Heckert's surrender to the corporation and cancellation of three 100-share certificates which belonged to the first community and in which the two children had an undivided one-half interest.

Decedent's children (more than 21 years after the termination of the usufruct) have brought a suit against Mrs. Eunice Knobloch Heckert, in her individual capacity and also as decedent's testamentary executrix, attacking the donations inter vivos and mortis causa insofar as their interests derived from their mother in the donated shares of stock are concerned; they also plead that no gratuitous transfer of any of the stock could be made to the prejudice of their rights as forced heirs of their deceased father; alternatively, they allege that if the donations be decreed to be valid, then the value thereof must be ascertained and brought back into the mass of his succession in order to determine their legitime. They pray that they be decreed to be the owners of and entitled to have delivered to them 605 shares of the capital stock of S. H. Kress and Company or the value thereof. In summary decedent's two children are claiming:

(1) Stock which they were placed into possession of in their mother's succession 355 shares

(2) Their one-half interest in the 300 shares omitted from their mother's succession150 shares

(3) For the return of excessive donations 100 shares

Total   600 shares

Defendant, taking the position that what the two children by their suit are claiming is an accounting of the usufruct of their father on the property inherited from their mother, interposed the exception of ten years' liberative prescription provided by LSA-C.C. art. 3544 which reads as follows:

> 'In general, all personal actions, except those before enumerated, are prescribed by ten years.'

Upon said exception being overruled, defendant filed a voluminous answer, the contents of which need not be recounted. After a trial on the merits, there was judgment (the nature of which will be hereafter set out) in favor of plaintiffs and against Mrs. Eunice Knobloch Heckert, individually, as well as testamentary executrix, and she has perfected this appeal.

Appellant in this court, as the sole ground for reversal of the judgment, relies on her exception of ten years' liberative prescription which she reurges.

We do not construe the suit to be one for an accounting. Plaintiffs are merely demanding their share of the capital stock of S. H. Kress and Company which they acquired as the sole heirs of their deceased mother and also for their legitime in their father's interest in the 300 shares remaining in his succession and also for a reduction of excessive donations inter vivos to the second wife so that their legitime may be reserved.

Upon deciding the case, the trial judge assigned comprehensive and well-considered reasons for judgment which encompass the factual situation and the applicable law, and since we are in accord therewith, we quote and adopt as part of our opinion herein the following portion of said reasons:

> "The questions presented by the present action are: What property rights do the petitioners have in the three stock certificates standing in the name of John Earl Heckert, two of which certificates (7154 and 7155) were included in the inventory of the succession of Mrs. Anna Buch Heckert, and one of which certificates (7158) was omitted from the first wife's succession? What property rights do petitioners have in the six certificates standing in the name of Eunice K. Heckert? "A fundamental basis of respondent's defense to the present action is that the usufruct which the de cujus had in the stock

certificates was imperfect and that, therefore, there was a ten year prescriptive period for an accounting, such prescription running from the termination of the usufruct. However, such contention is not tenable under the law and jurisprudence of this state. The usufruct of the de cujus over the heirs' one-half of the first wife's succession is founded upon Civil Code Art. 916:

. . . .

"Since common stock in a corporation is not specifically mentioned in any of the Code articles dealing with usufructs, the controversy as to the type of usufruct must be settled by turning to jurisprudence and analysis of the facts.

"Civil Code Art. 534 indicates that if the usufructuary can enjoy the property to any extent without changing its substance, he has a perfect usufruct; and if the property would be totally useless unless consumed or expended, then the usufructuary has an imperfect usufruct. It is apparent to this Court that Mr. Heckert could have enjoyed the stocks to some extent without transferring or selling them, this by way of receiving the dividends. In *Leury v. Mayer*, 122 La. 486, 47 So. 839, the Court stated:

'It is obvious that bank stock does not fall within the purview of Article 534, Rev.Civ.Code, but represents an investment of money for the purpose of producing revenue. In such a case, the usufructuary is entitled only to the fruits, as in the case of 'rents of real property, the interest of money, and annuities.' Articles 544, 545. The argument that in the case at bar the usufructuary had the right to sell the stock because it was not producing a revenue is not only unsound in law, but unsupported by the facts of the case. ***'

"Respondent insists that the legislation dealing with transfer of stock, R.S. 12:501, et seq. (Act 215 of 1912), has nullified the holding of the Leury Case, supra. R.S. 12:501 provides:

'*** the person, firm or corporation, in whose name a certificate of stock stands, or to whom a certificate of stock is endorsed, whether in full or in blank and who has possession of said certificate shall be regarded as the legal owner thereof with full power to pledge, sell or otherwise dispose of said stock, and no person, corporation, firm nor transfer agent shall be responsible to any one claiming any interest in, or ownership of, said stock, or any part thereof, by virtue of any undisclosed or latent legal or conventional title or interest therein.'

"However, in the title of Act 215 of 1912 is found the following explanation of the purpose of the legislation:

'To protect corporations, persons, firms and transfer agents, dealing in or transferring stocks where the transferor has the possession of the stock transferred, and where the stock stands in the name of the person, corporation, or firm transferring it, or is endorsed over to said person, corporation or firm in full or in blank.'

"Thus, the Act was meant as a protective device for the benefit not of the transferor, but of the transferee. In other words, the transferee would be protected from actions on stocks where, on the face of the certificates or from the circumstances of the transaction, there is nothing to give the transferee notice of any latent defects in the transferor's title. Now, the answer to the question of whether this act broadens the powers or rights of the transferor, whatever might be his capacity or position, is answered by R.S. 12:525 (Act 180 of 1910, Sec. 2):

'Nothing in this Act shall be construed as enlarging the powers of an infant or other person lacking full legal capacity, or of a trustee, executor or administrator, or other fiduciary, to make a valid endorsement, assignment or power of attorney.'

". . . The above acts merely state that if the usufructuary does transfer the stocks without the permission of the naked owners, and the stocks stand in the name of the usufructuary, then the corporation is not liable to the naked owners for transferring the stocks. But, the usufructuary must still answer to the naked owners for the breach of fiduciary obligation. The holding of the *Leury* Case, supra, still stands as good law; Mr. Heckert's cancellations of the stocks representing the interests of the present petitioners was, therefore, a breach of his fiduciary obligation to the naked owners.

"Respondent has sought to apply the ten year prescription of Civil Code Article 3544 to petitioners' rights. However, the cases cited by respondent on this point all relate to the seeking of an accounting under an imperfect usufruct. *Cochran v. Violet*, 38 La. Ann. 525; *In re Jones*, 41 La. Ann. 620, 6 So. 180; *Burdin v. Burdin*, 171 La. 7, 129 So. 651. In fact, as relates to the property which was subject to a perfect usufruct in *Burdin v. Burdin*, supra, the Court said:

'*** The only piece of real estate situated in Louisiana, in which the children of the deceased Mrs. Elizabeth Franz Burdin have an interest is a certain piece of swamp land in the Parish of Iberville, which apparently was not inventoried in Mrs. Burdin's succession. Plaintiff does not allege that the defendant has denied her proportionate interest in this particular land, which she is at liberty at any time to assert and liquidate by the proper proceeding.'

"This quotation is cited to show that even though prescription may run on the right to an accounting under an imperfect usufruct, it cannot run as to rights of naked owners under a perfect usufruct. In an article by Leonard

Oppenheim entitled *The Usufruct of the Surviving Spouse*, 18 Tulane Law Rev., the author states:

'The usufructuary being a precarious possessor cannot prescribe against the naked owner, no matter how long he holds the things subject to the usufruct. ***" p. 217.

"This follows the codal provision of Civil Code Article 3510:

> "'Those who possess for others and not in their own name cannot prescribe, whatever may be the time of their possession. Thus, farmers, tenants, depositaries, usufructuaries, and all those generally who hold by a precarious tenure and in the name of the owner cannot prescribe on the thing thus held.'

"The law, as indicated by the above article, is that there can be no acquisitive prescription applied to a usufruct. As relates to the facts in the present case, were this Court to say that since the petitioners did not assert their rights to the stocks within ten years after the termination of the usufruct, their rights have prescribed; we would actually be saying that there can be acquisitive prescription under a usufruct. Such holding would be directly contrary to the clear and express provision of Civil Code Art. 3510. Any contention that the usufructuary's transferring the stock and converting it to money transforms the usufruct to an imperfect one is met by the holding of the court in *Wainer v. Wainer*, 210 La. 324, 26 So.2d 829, where, in effect, the Court held that when stock has been converted to money by the usufructuary, the usufruct does not thereby become an imperfect usufruct. "The stocks in the original succession were held in indivision after the termination of the usufruct of Mr. Heckert. Planiol, in TRAITE ELEMENTAIRE DE DROIT CIVIL, Vol. 1, part 2, No. 2497, says:

> 'A thing belonging to several co-owners in indivision when the right of each owner bears upon the whole (and not upon a given part) of the thing held in common. The share of each, therefore, is not a tangible share but a portion expressed by a fraction: a third, a fourth, a tenth. It is the right of ownership that is divided among them. The thing is not. It is held in indivision. The right of each co-owner must be pictured as striking every molecule of the thing and as there encountering the right of the other co-owners for the portions belonging to them.'

"The application of this principle leads to the conclusion that petitioners did not merely own a certain number of shares in the stock of S. H. Kress and Co., but actually owned one-half of each of the certificates, each representing a certain number of shares. Thus, when Mr. Heckert sold or otherwise transferred a certificate, he was transferring a piece of property, half ownership of which was vested in petitioners.

"'Based on this analysis the Court will determine petitioners' recovery as follows: From the original succession of Mrs. Anna Buch Heckert, petitioners received ownership of 505 shares of Kress stock, represented by the certificates in the inventory, and also the certificates numbered 7156, 7157 and 7158 which were inadvertently omitted from the inventory of that succession. In Mr. Heckert's succession there are only three certificates from that original succession still extant, these being numbered 7154, 7155 and 7158, representing in toto 300 shares. Since petitioners are due 505 shares, the Court must award them full ownership of the three extant shares in Mr. Heckert's succession. This leaves petitioners 205 shares short. Certificate number H-9983, Mrs. Heckert for 100 shares is dated December 17, 1942, the same date that certificate number 7153 was cancelled; therefore, the transaction would amount to an invalid donation of 50 shares belonging to petitioners, which shares must be returned to petitioners. Certificates numbered F-19232, F-19233, F-19234, and F-19235 are dated July 17, 1944, the same date that certificates numbered 9178 and 8438 were cancelled; therefore, this transaction would amount to an invalid donation of 100 shares belonging to the petitioners, which shares must be returned to petitioners. Since the donations to respondent were valid as to Mr. Heckert's one-half interest at the time they were made, this Court will only require that the number of shares, or their value, as pertains to petitioners' one-half interest be returned to petitioners. This leaves the petitioners 55 shares short, for which the Court will award a judgment in favor of petitioners and against respondent in her capacity as testamentary executrix of the Succession of John E. Heckert in the sum of $ 1,100.00, being the value of 55 shares on the date of death of Mrs. Anna Buch Heckert, said sum to be chargeable as a debt of decedent's separate estate or chargeable to his one-half of the community. . . .

The judgment appealed from does substantial justice, and, therefore,

It is affirmed.

Questions

1. In light of *Succession of Heckert*, 160 So.2d 375 (La. App. 4 Cir. 1964), did the adoption of La. Rev. Stat. 12:501 (1912) nullify the holding of *Leury v. Mayer*, 47 So. 839 (La. 1908)? Does liberative prescription apply to a claim for accounting brought by a naked owner at the termination of a usufruct of shares in corporate stock? Why or why not? In *Succession of Heckert*, who ultimately is liable for the mistakes made by John Heckert? Do John Heckert's children, John Jr. and Isabelle, share any responsibility for the problems that arose in this case?

2. Do you understand why Eunice Knobloch Heckert's plea of liberative prescription was rejected by the court in *Succession of Heckert*? Do you see any similarity between the court's reasoning here in *Succession of Heckert* and the reasoning of the

United States Fifth Circuit Court of Appeals in *Songbyrd, Inc. v. Bearsville Records*, 104 F.3d 773 (5th Cir. 1997)?

3. What effect does the law of ownership in indivision have on the allocation of rights among the respective parties after John Heckert's usufruct terminated in *Succession of Heckert*?

G. The Obligation to Give Security; The Legal and Testamentary Usufruct

In recent years, the Louisiana legal community has witnessed a lively debate over the question of when a usufructuary should be required to give security so as to assure a naked owner that the usufructuary will use the property subject to a usufruct as a prudent administrator and preserve the value of the things subject to the usufruct. Some of the controversy stems from piecemeal reform by the legislature inserting some rules in the law of usufruct (Title III of Book II) and others in the law of donations (Title II of Book III). The debate also reflects differing value judgments about the vulnerabilities of a typical usufructuary and a typical naked owner as well as the strained relationships that can arise when the surviving children of a decedent are not the natural or adopted children of the decedent's surviving spouse. As you review the following material, identify the underlying policy rationales that may explain the often confusing rules. Proceed deliberately and remember that the codal provisions addressing the obligation to provide security include a series of questions, each in turn triggering a conclusion or a further question.

The General Principle: We begin with the general rule established in Article 571:

Art. 571. Security

The usufructuary shall give security that he will use the property subject to the usufruct as a prudent administrator and that he will faithfully fulfill all of the obligations imposed on him by law or by the act that established the usufruct unless security is dispensed with. If security is required, the court may order that it be provided in accordance with law.

La. Civ. Code art. 571 (1976). Security is required to protect the naked owner's residual interests in the property subject to the usufruct. *Id.* The key question, however, is to determine when "security is dispensed with." *Id.*

Amount, Form, Delay and Failure to Provide: The next provision, Article 572 of the Civil Code, specifies that "[t]he security shall be in the amount of the total value of the property subject to the usufruct," unless otherwise increased or decreased by the court, but never in an amount "less than the value of the movables." La. Civ. Code art. 572 (1976). Why does the Civil Code exhibit this particular concern for the value of movables subject to a usufruct? Is it necessary? Immovables, like land and buildings, are always characterized as nonconsumables and therefore, a usufructuary must preserve their substance until the termination of the usufruct, unless the usufructuary has been granted the power to dispose of nonconsumables.

Neither Article 571 nor 572 of the Civil Code specify the form of the security that the usufructuary must provide, although the revision comments to Article 572 suggest that a usufructuary could, in the alternative, establish a surety contract to protect the naked owner's interest in the property subject to the usufruct. La. Civ. Code art. 572 rev. cmt. (b) (1976). Alternatively, a usufructuary could establish a special mortgage on other immovable property that is not subject to the usufruct. La. Civ. Code art. 572 rev. cmt. (b) (1976). The naked owner could then foreclose on this mortgage in the event the usufructuary breaches her obligations to act as a prudent administrator or to account to the naked owner at the termination of the usufruct for the value of consumables. *Id.* Regardless of the forms that the security can take, the obligation to provide security can be onerous and can significantly limit the freedom of a usufructuary to derive economic benefits from the property subject to the usufruct.

For a discussion of the considerable discretion that trial courts enjoy when setting the amount and form of security, see *In re Succession of Beard*, 147 So.3d 753, 764 (La. App. 1 Cir. 2014). *See also In re Succession of Beard*, 210 So.3d 310 (La, App. 1 Cir. 2016) (rejecting the arguments that (1) Article 572 mandates security in an amount greater than the value of one naked owner's interest; and (2) that the security cannot take the form of a promissory note signed by the usufructuary). For brief statutory guidance regarding the form of security that can be ordered by a court in the context of the legal usufruct of the surviving spouse, see La. Rev. Stat. § 9:1202 (2003) ("If security is owed to the naked owner by the usufructuary who is the surviving spouse, the court may order the execution of notes, mortgages, or other documents as it deems necessary, or may impose a mortgage or lien on either community or separate property, movable or immovable, as security.").

Even when a usufructuary is required to provide security, a usufructuary's delay in acting is not fatal to her interest. Rather, pursuant to Article 574 of the Civil Code, such a delay "does not deprive the usufructuary of the fruits derived since the commencement of the usufruct." La. Civ. Code art. 574 (1976). Article 574 implies that when a naked owner remains in possession of the property subject to the usufruct, his interests are adequately protected and therefore, he should be required to turn over to the usufructuary the fruits derived from the property subject to the usufruct since the inception of the usufruct. *Id.* rev. cmt (b). When the usufructuary delays in her obligation to provide security, however, the naked owner can postpone delivery of the property to the usufructuary. *Id.* rev. cmt. (c). Based on these policy concerns, Article 575 of the Civil Code declares:

Art. 575. Failure to give security

If the usufructuary does not give security, the court may order that the property be delivered to an administrator appointed in accordance with Articles 3111 through 3113 of the Code of Civil Procedure.

The administration terminates if the usufructuary gives security.

La. Civ. Code art. 575 (1976). Notice that even under this provision, the usufructuary's failure to provide security does not terminate the usufruct. Instead, it entitles the naked owner to ask a court to place the property subject to the usufruct in the hands of an administrator who can act as a prudent administrator. That person might be another relative, a trusted advisor, a trust department of a bank, or even the naked owner. La. Civ. Code art. 575 rev. cmt. (b) (1976). Once the property is in safe hands, Article 575 assumes that the administrator will collect and distribute fruits due to the usufructuary or perhaps even allow the usufructuary to use and enjoy the property subject to the usufruct in other ways.

Dispensations of Security-General Provision: Article 573 of the Civil Code specifies six situations when the usufructuary is automatically freed from the obligation to provide security. Articles 1499 and 1514 address security requirements arising in the context of a testamentary usufruct for a surviving spouse. Security may or may not be required depending on the relationship between the usufructuary and the naked owner and the status of the naked owner as a forced heir. Finally, a person who establishes a usufruct can, by exercising the contractual and testamentary freedom recognized under Article 545 of the Civil Code, expressly stipulate that the usufructuary will not be required to provide security. This freedom, however, is subject to the limitations set forth in Articles 1499 and 1514. *See* La. Civ. Code art. 573 rev. cmt. (b) (1976).

Consider the text of Article 573 carefully:

Art. 573. Dispensation of security

A. Security is dispensed with when any of the following occur:

(1) A person has a legal usufruct under Article 223 or 3252.

(2) A surviving spouse has a legal usufruct under Article 890 unless the naked owner is not a child of the usufructuary or if the naked owner is a child of the usufructuary and is also a forced heir of the decedent the naked owner may obtain security but only to the extent of his legitime.

(3) A parent has a legal usufruct under Article 891 unless the naked owner is not a child of the usufructuary.

(4) A surviving spouse has a legal usufruct under Article 2434 unless the naked owner is a child of the decedent but not a child of the usufructuary.

B. A seller or donor of property under reservation of usufruct is not required to give security.

La. Civ. Code art. 573 (1976, amended 2010). Article 573.A(1) of the Civil Code establishes two distinct categories of dispensation: (1) when married parents have a usufruct over the property of their minor, unemancipated children under Article 223 — a dispensation that is now meaningless in light of the repeal and revision of

Article 223 (1870); and (2) when a surviving spouse or minor children are left in necessitous circumstances and are entitled to a usufruct over $1,000 of the deceased spouse or parent's succession under Article 3252. Probably because of the relatively modest amounts of property involved, the dispensation of security with respect to these legal usufructs has spawned little controversy.

The dispensation under Article 573.A(2) of the Civil Code is far more significant because it applies in the common situation of a surviving spouse who acquires a usufruct over the deceased spouse's portion of the undisposed community property under Article 890 of the Civil Code. This provision, however, eliminates this dispensation and *re-imposes* the obligation to provide security in two specific situations that can arise when a surviving spouse acquires an Article 890 usufruct.

The first circumstance eliminating the dispensation from security arises when the naked owner, who under Article 890 of the Civil Code must be a descendant of the deceased spouse, is *not* the child of the usufructuary—that is, when the naked owner is a child of a prior marriage or relationship of the deceased spouse. Article 573.A(2) thus restores the obligation to provide security for the protection of the naked owner when a surviving spouse is a step-parent of the naked owner. This choice reflects the revision drafters' view that a usufructuary who does not share a blood or adoptive relationship with the naked owner may not have sufficient loyalty and concern for the naked owner and, therefore, should not be trusted to act in the naked owner's best interest. In short, Article 573.A(2) recognizes that the naked owner in a step-parent/step-child relationship may be vulnerable and require the protection of security. For an illustration of the powerful effect of this basic policy choice in the context of the law prior to the 2003 revision of these provisions of the Civil Code, see *In re Succession of Beard*, 147 So.3d 753, 762–64 (La. App. 1 Cir. 2014) (holding that a usufructuary who acquired what was considered a "legal usufruct" under the former version of Article 890 pursuant to the will of the usufructuary's deceased spouse was obligated to provide security because the naked owner demanding security was a child of the decedent's previous marriage). Is security required when the naked owner is a grandchild of the surviving spouse?

The second circumstance restoring the security obligation for a surviving spouse under Article 890 of the Civil Code occurs when the naked owner is a child of the usufructuary and also a forced heir of the decedent. Although the category of forced heirs under Louisiana law was considerably narrowed as a result of a controversial amendment to the Louisiana Constitution in 1995 and subsequent changes to the Louisiana Civil Code, Louisiana law still recognizes two distinct categories of forced heirs whose rights to demand security under Article 573.A(2) are protected: (1) "descendants of the first degree who, at the time of the death of the decedent, are twenty three years of age years or younger" and (2) "descendants of the first degree of any age who, because of mental incapacity or physical infirmity, are permanently incapable of taking care of their persons or administering their estates at the time of the death of decedent." La. Civ. Code art. 1493.A (1996, amended 2003).

Under Article 573.A(2), if a naked owner qualifies under either of these categories of forced heirs at the commencement of the usufruct, he or she can require the usufructuary to provide security to protect his or her *legitime*—the portion of the decedent's estate that is reserved to the forced heirs by law. *See* La. Civil Code art. 1494 (1996). The specific amount of the decedent's estate reserved for a forced heir is determined according to the number of forced heirs left at the decedent's death. If the decedent leaves only one forced heir, the forced portion or "legitime" will be one-fourth of the decedent's property; if the decedent leaves two or more forced heirs, the forced portion will be one-half of the decedent's estate, divided equally among the forced heirs. La. Civ. Code art. 1495 (1996). The second paragraph of Article 1495 sets forth an alternative method of calculating the forced portion when the decedent leaves more than four children who would otherwise qualify as intestate heirs but not all are forced heirs. *See Id.* rev. cmts. (c), (d).

The policy rationale behind this second restoration of the obligation to provide security in the case of a forced heir, even though the forced heir is a child of the usufructuary, is self-evident. The law wants to protect at least the forced portion of the decedent's estate from the imprudent administration of the property subject to the usufruct when the naked owner is a young person under the age of twenty-four or someone whose mental incapacity or physical infirmity is so severe that he or she could become a ward of the state if deprived of all of a deceased parent's estate.

Article 573 of the Civil Code further dispenses with the obligation to provide security in three other, less common situations. First, under Article 573.A(3), when a parent acquires a usufruct over the separate property of a deceased child under Article 891 of the Civil Code, the usufructuary is not required to provide security unless the naked owner, usually the sibling of the decedent, is not a child of the usufructuary. La. Civ. Code art. 573.A(3) (1976, amended 2004, 2010). In other words, when a parent acquires a parental usufruct, he or she will be spared from the obligation to provide security as long as the naked owners are also the children of that parent. Second, under Article 573.A(4), when a surviving spouse acquires a legal usufruct over the "marital portion" under Article 2434 of the Civil Code because a decedent spouse died rich in comparison with the surviving spouse, the surviving spouse will not be required to provide security unless "the naked owner is a child of the decedent but not a child of the usufructuary." La. Civ. Code art. 573.A(4) (1976, amended 2004, 2010). This dispensation mirrors the concern for step-children naked owners under Article 573.A(2).

Finally, under Article 573.B, when a usufruct is established by a person who reserves for himself a usufruct in the course of donating or selling property to another person during his lifetime, the usufructuary is not required to give security. La. Civ. Code art. 573.B (1976, amended 2004, 2010). Thus, the defendants in *Bond v. Green*, 401 So.2d 639 (La. App. 3 Cir. 1981), were not subject to the obligation to provide security.

Dispensations for the Testamentary Usufruct: Articles 1499 and 1514 of the Civil Code offer a specialized set of rules for dispensation of security when a decedent establishes a testamentary usufruct in favor of his surviving spouse. The testator may grant the surviving spouse a usufruct for life over separate and community property and also give the usufructuary the power to dispose of nonconsumables. Read Articles 1499 and 1514 *in pari materia*:

Art. 1499. Usufruct to surviving spouse

The decedent may grant a usufruct to the surviving spouse over all or part of his property, including the forced portion, and may grant the usufructuary the power to dispose of nonconsumables as provided in the law of usufruct. The usufruct shall be for life unless expressly designated for a shorter period, and shall not require security except as expressly declared by the decedent or as permitted when the legitime is affected. . . .

La. Civ. Code art. 1499 (1996, amended 2003).

Art. 1514. Usufruct of surviving spouse affecting legitime; security

A forced heir may request security when a usufruct in favor of a surviving spouse affects his legitime and he is not a child of the surviving spouse. A forced heir may also request security to the extent that a surviving spouse's usufruct over the legitime affects separate property. The court may order the execution of notes, mortgages or other documents as it deems necessary, or may impose a mortgage or lien on either community or separate property, movable or immovable, as security.

La. Civ. Code art. 1514 (1996, amended 2003).

Under Article 1499 of the Civil Code, when a decedent spouse grants his surviving spouse a testamentary usufruct, the surviving spouse will *not* be obligated to provide security unless either (A) the decedent's will expressly requires the surviving spouse to provide security, or (B) one of the exceptions provided in Article 1514 is present.

Article 1514 of the Civil Code creates the two narrow exceptions that re-impose the obligation to provide security in the context of a testamentary spousal usufruct. Both apply only when the naked owners are also forced heirs under Article 1493 and when the usufruct in favor of the surviving spouse affects the forced heir's legitime. First, a naked owner who is a forced heir may request security when he or she is *not a child of the surviving spouse*; that is, when the surviving spouse is a step-parent. Second, the naked owner who is a forced heir may request security to the extent that the surviving spouse's usufruct over the legitime *affects separate property* of the decedent. What might be the policy rationales for the restoration of security in these circumstances involving testamentary spousal usufructs?

Finally, note that a naked owner may always renounce the right to demand security even when the law otherwise requires it. La. Civ. Code art. 573 rev. cmt. (b) (1976). The naked owner's failure to demand security at the beginning of a usufruct does not forfeit his right to demand security later. Unless the right has been expressly renounced, the naked owner can demand that the usufructuary give security in the situations required by law or by the instrument establishing the usufruct at any time during the usufruct. To test your understanding of the basic rules governing the obligation to give security, answer the following problems.

Problems

1. George died intestate, survived by his wife, Wendy, and their healthy, competent, twenty-five-year-old daughter Caroline. At the time of George's death, George and Wendy owned a house, two cars, and $500,000 in savings. They acquired all of these belongings during their marriage. At his death, George also owned 10,000 shares of stock in IBM Corporation, which he had acquired before he married Wendy. Identify the property subject to a usufruct in favor of Wendy. Can Caroline require that Wendy provide security with respect to any of the property subject to Wendy's usufruct?

2. Same facts as in Question 1 above, but suppose that at the time of George's death, his daughter, Caroline, was only twenty-one years old. Can Caroline require that Wendy provide security now?

3. Same facts as in Question 1, but suppose that at the time of George's death, his daughter, Caroline, suffered from advanced Amyotrophic Lateral Sclerosis (ALS). Due to the disease, she was unable to care for herself or administer her property? Can Caroline require that Wendy provide security now?

4. Harold died intestate, survived by his second wife, Winona, and his healthy, competent, twenty-five-year-old son, Dave, his child from his earlier marriage with Trudy. At the time of Harold's death, Harold and Winona owned a house, two cars and $1,000,000 in savings, all of which they acquired during their marriage. At his death, Harold also owned 10,000 shares of stock in Exxon Corporation, which he had acquired before he married Winona. Identify the property subject to a usufruct in favor of Winona. Can Dave require that Winona provide security with respect to any of the property subject to Winona's usufruct?

5. Albert died with a valid will. He was survived by his wife Bernice and their two children Charles and Diana. At the time of Albert's death, Charles and Diana were healthy and competent. Charles was twenty-eight years of age and Diana was twenty-six years of age. Also at the time of Albert's death, Albert and Bernice owned a home, an RV and $400,000 in savings, all of which they acquired during their marriage. At his death, Albert also owned 10,000 shares in Pfizer Corporation, which he had acquired before his marriage to Bernice. In his will, Albert bequeathed all of his property, community and separate, to Charles and Diana, subject to a usufruct in favor of Bernice. Can Charles and Diana require that Bernice provide security with respect to any of the property subject to her usufruct?

6. Same facts as in Question 5 above, but suppose that at the time of Albert's death, Charles was twenty-five years old and Diana was twenty-three years old? Can

either Charles or Diana require that Bernice provide security with respect to any of the property subject to her usufruct?

7. Same facts as in Question 6 above, but suppose that Charles and Diana were both children of Albert's earlier marriage with Alice. Can either Charles or Diana require that Bernice provide security with respect to any of the property subject to her usufruct?

Chapter 13

Natural and Legal Servitudes

Natural and legal servitudes, alongside conventional servitudes, belong to the family of predial servitudes. Unlike a personal servitude, such as the usufruct, which confers a benefit on a person, a predial servitude creates a special kind of relationship between two different "estates." A predial servitude exhibits several essential characteristics.

A. The Essential Characteristics and Kinds of Predial Servitudes

Article 646 of the Civil Code opens with the foundational definition of a predial servitude in Louisiana law:

Art. 646. Predial Servitude

A predial servitude is a charge on a servient estate for the benefit of a dominant estate.

The two estates must belong to different owners.

La. Civ. Code art. 646 (1977). From this article and the Civil Code articles that follow, a number of essential characteristics of a predial servitude emerge.

First, a predial servitude embodies a *relationship between two different estates*. The word "estate" means some kind of "distinct corporeal immovable," usually a tract of land or a building, but also sometimes a "timber estate" or a part of a building such as an apartment unit. La. Civ. Code art. 646 rev. cmt. (b). A personal servitude of right of use typically involves just one estate (the servient estate) and confers an advantage to a particular natural or legal person. La. Civ. Code arts. 639–40 (1976). A true predial servitude requires two estates.

Second, the two estates connected by a predial servitude *must be owned by different persons*. If, for example, two neighboring estates in a relationship of charge and benefit are owned by the same person, a predial servitude cannot exist. A predial servitude *might* come into being later, if the two different estates fall into the hands of different owners. *See* La. Civ. Code art. 741 (1977) (providing for establishing a predial servitude by "destination of the owner"). Until the two estates belong to two different owners, a predial servitude cannot exist.

Third, a predial servitude *creates a "charge" on one estate (the servient estate).* This idea of "a charge" is subtle but significant. A charge on an estate can have either affirmative or negative attributes. If the charge gives the owner of the dominant estate "the right to do a certain thing on the servient estate," the servitude is "affirmative." La. Civ. Code art. 706 (1977). If the charge imposes on the owner of the servient estate "the duty to abstain from doing something on his estate," the servitude is "negative." *Id.* Often, the labeling of a predial servitude as affirmative or negative can appear to be a semantic trick because a predial servitude that allows the dominant estate owner to engage in some kind of activity on the servient estate (for example, a simple servitude of passage) will necessarily prohibit the owner of the servient estate from engaging in activities that would interfere with the dominant estate's owner's right to enjoy the servitude. Nevertheless, it is still important to identity the fundamental purpose of a predial servitude, particularly when it comes to determining whether the servitude has been extinguished by non-use. La. Civ. Code arts. 753–54 (1977).

Fourth, a predial servitude *confers a serious benefit for the dominant estate.* This requirement is expressed in the next article in the Civil Code:

Art. 647. Benefit to the dominant estate

There must be a benefit to the dominant estate. The benefit need not exist at the time the servitude is created; a possible convenience or a future advantage suffices to support a servitude.

There is no predial servitude if the charge cannot be reasonably expected to benefit the dominant estate.

La. Civ. Code art. 647 (1977). As we will learn, the distinction between a *predial* servitude, which establishes a benefit to a dominant estate, independent of whoever happens to be its owner, and a *personal* servitude of right of use, which creates an advantage for a particular person, depends largely upon whether or not the agreement clearly identifies a dominant estate that will benefit from the charge. Moreover, the benefit for the dominant estate has to be useful. Civilian scholars often call this the *"utility" requirement.* As Article 647 explains, the benefit to the dominant estate need not exist at the moment the predial servitude is created. The benefit or advantage might be one that is anticipated to arise in the future. The advantage or convenience contemplated by the creators of the predial servitude must, however, serve some "socially useful purpose." *Id.* rev. cmt. (b). The purpose could be economic or aesthetic, but completely whimsical benefits will not suffice to support a predial servitude. *Id.* Further, the possibility that an individual who owns the dominant estate will also receive some personal benefit does not prevent a particular charge from forming the basis for a predial servitude. *Id.* rev. cmt. (c).

Another characteristic of a predial servitude relates to the degree of *proximity* between the two estates. Although the two estates linked by a predial servitude need not be physically adjacent to one another, or even in close proximity, the two estates must be "so located as to allow one to derive some benefit from the charge on the other." La. Civ. Code art. 648 (1977). As you can see, this characteristic essentially restates the utility requirement. If two estates are so far apart physically that an alleged charge on the servient estate cannot realistically provide any advantage or benefit to the dominant estate, then the law will not recognize the existence of a predial servitude. Therefore, the two estates *must be close enough in proximity that some real benefit to the dominant estate is discernable.*

A sixth, crucial characteristic of a predial servitude is that it is **potentially perpetual.** In contrast to usufruct and habitation, which are real rights of limited duration, a predial servitude is not limited in time as matter of law. Unless the property owners that created a predial servitude established a time limit for the servitude in their constitutive agreement, a predial servitude can last indefinitely. The following provision states the principle that a predial servitude is *potentially perpetual* in duration. It also states a seventh, and crucial corollary characteristic of a predial servitude — its *inseparability from the land benefited or burdened by the servitude.*

Art. 650. Inseparability of servitude

A. A predial servitude is inseparable from the dominant estate and passes with it. The right of using the servitude cannot be alienated, leased or encumbered separately from the dominant estate.

B. A predial servitude continues as a charge on the servient estate when ownership changes.

La. Civ. Code art. 650 (1978). The importance of the notion of inseparability cannot be overstated. At Common Law, a special, colloquial expression captures the idea: easements, covenants and equitable servitudes "run with the land."

Imagine two contiguous tracts of land: Arpent Noir and Arpent Vert. The owners of each respective estate, Ann and Bob, agree that Bob's tract, Arpent Vert, will be subject to a servitude of passage in favor of Ann's tract, Arpent Noir. The servitude furnishes access to a public road that is adjacent to Arpent Vert. Assume that the servitude agreement is properly recorded. Now suppose that Ann sells Arpent Noir to Carolyn, and Bob conveys Arpent Vert to Dave. If Ann and Bob have established a true predial servitude, Arpent Vert (the servient estate) will be subject to a servitude of passage in favor of Arpent Noir (the dominant estate), even though the ownership of both tracts has changed hands and the new owners Carolyn and Dave have never directly contracted with each other to establish this relationship. The characteristic of inseparability — that both the burden and benefit of the servitude pass to the new owners of both the servient and dominant estate when their ownership changes — is one of the essential features of a predial servitude. By establishing a predial servitude and recording that agreement in the public records, Ann and Bob took what otherwise might have just been considered a contractual agreement, which only binds the two parties in direct privity of contract, and turned that agreement into a real right good against the world.

Yet another characteristic of a predial servitude (the eighth if you are still counting) is that it is **indivisible** when either the servient or dominant estate is divided by a juridical act of the relevant owner, through a sale or partition, or by some administrative action such as an expropriation or adjudication). Article 652 makes this *principle of indivisibility* explicit:

Art. 652. Indivisibility of servitude

A predial servitude is indivisible. An estate cannot have upon another estate part of a right of way, or of view, or of any other servitude, nor can an estate be charged with a part of a servitude.

The use of a servitude may be limited to certain days or hours; when limited, it is still an entire right. A servitude is due to the whole of the dominant estate and to all parts of it; if this estate is divided, every acquirer of a part has the right of using the servitude in its entirety.

La. Civ. Code art. 652 (1977). As the revision comments explain, "it follows from the principle of indivisibility that no predial servitude may be established on, or in favor of, an undivided part of an estate." La. Civ. Code art. 652 rev. cmt. (b) (1977). Pursuant to the second paragraph of Article 652 and Article 747 of the Civil Code, every acquirer of a part of the *dominant estate* retains the right to use the predial servitude as a whole, subject only to the caveat that no additional burden be imposed on the servient estate. La. Civ Code arts. 652, 747 (1977).

To understand the concept of indivisibility consider a predial servitude allowing the owner of the dominant estate to draw a specified amount of water from a well located on the servient estate. Once again assume that the original servitude agreement was recorded in the public records. If the dominant estate is divided into two new estates through an act of partition, the owners of both of the two new estates can enjoy the right to take water from the well, but the overall quantity of water taken cannot increase. The water taken must be apportioned among the owners of the two new estates because, as the revision comments to Article 652 explain, "the division of the dominant estate may not result in the placing of an additional burden on the servient estate." La. Civ. Code art. 652, rev. cmt. (c) (1977). Similarly, if a dominant estate that benefits from a servitude of passage is divided into two new estates, the owners of the two new estates are each entitled to use the servitude, but they must exercise it in the same location as established by the original servitude. *Id. See also* La. Civ. Code art. 747 (1977).

Interestingly, the Civil Code does not expressly address what happens when the *servient estate* is divided. Generally speaking, the servitude remains intact, subject to tailored exceptions. For example, a servitude of light is still due by each part of a divided servient estate to the dominant estate. However, if a servitude to draw water is localized on one of the divided parts of the servient estate, then the other parts not needed for the exercise of the servitude should be released from the servitude. *See generally* A.N. YIANNOPOULOS, 4 LOUISIANA CIVIL LAW TREATISE: PREDIAL SERVITUDES § 1.11 (4th ed. 2013).

Note that "[t]he use of a servitude may be limited to certain days or hours; when limited, it is still an entire right." La. Civ. Code art. 652 (1977). Thus, Samuel, who owns a servient estate, may grant a predial servitude of passage over the same gravel road to Adam (the owner of Blackacre) for the hours between midnight and 8:00 a.m, to Benjamin (the owner of Greenacre) for the hours between 8:00 a.m. and 4:00 p.m., and to David (the owner of Redacre) for the hours between 4:00 p.m. and midnight. Such an arrangement would be consistent with Article 652, as it does not embody a division into parts but rather gives each dominant estate an entire right. However, "[t]he advantages resulting from a predial servitude may be divided, if they are susceptible of division." La. Civ. Code art. 653 (1977). For example, "if a servitude of pasture of one hundred head of cattle exists in favor of an estate belonging to two owners, each of them may be apportioned the right to send to pasture fifty animals." *Id.* rev. cmt. (b).

The final, essential characteristic of a predial servitude is negative in character. Consider Article 651 of the Civil Code:

Art. 651. Obligations of the owner of the servient estate

The owner of the servient estate is not required to do anything. His obligation is to abstain from doing something on his estate or to permit something to be done on it. He may be required by convention or by law to keep his estate in suitable condition for the exercise of the servitude due to the dominant estate. A servitude may not impose upon the owner of the servient estate or his successors the obligation to pay a fee or other charge on the occasion of an alienation, lease or encumbrance of the servient estate.

La. Civ. Code art. 651 (1977, amended 2010). This important rule, known as the *in faciendo* rule or the *passivity principle*, means that *a predial servitude generally cannot impose affirmative duties on the owner of the servient estate*. Thus, the servient estate owner cannot be required by the predial servitude to perform certain acts for the benefit of the dominant estate. Similarly, the servient estate owner cannot be obligated to pay money to the owner of a dominant estate. This general rule, however, does not prevent a servitude agreement from requiring the servient estate owner to maintain his estate in a condition suitable for the operation of the servitude.

As the revision comments explain, "[t]his is a rule of public policy that may not be derogated from by juridical act, unless the law provides otherwise." *Id.* rev. cmt. (b). It is important to note, however, that the revised Civil Code has recognized a special category of real rights affecting immovable property that are an exception to this general rule prohibiting the imposition of affirmative duties. These special real rights are called *building restrictions*. *See* La. Civ. Code art. 775–783. (1977). As we will see in Chapter 16, building restrictions serve important purposes in connection with subdivision planning and maintenance.

Article 654 of the Louisiana Civil Code divides the realm of predial servitudes into three distinct sub-categories:

Art. 654. Kinds of predial servitudes

Predial servitudes may be natural, legal, and voluntary or conventional. Natural servitudes arise from the natural situation of estates; legal servitudes are imposed by law; and voluntary or conventional servitudes are established by juridical act, prescription, or destination of the owner.

La. Civ. Code art. 654 (1977). Natural servitudes exist, independent of any act of volition on the part of the owners of the estates, simply because of the physical relationship between the two estates. Natural servitudes are, therefore, neither created nor acquired. They exist as a matter of law.

Legal servitudes, as Article 654 makes clear, also exist as a matter of law. They are essentially limitations on ownership. La. Civ. Code art. 659 (1977). In fact, they are more purely creatures of law, because, unlike natural servitudes, their existence does not depend on any natural topographical relationship between the estates. Both kinds of servitudes "impose limitations on the content of ownership." La. Civ. Code art. 654 rev. cmt. (d) (1977).

Conventional servitudes are established either by title (through a constitutive instrument expressing the owners' intent to create the servitude), by acquisitive prescription or by destination of the owner. La. Civ. Code arts. 739–40 (1977). Conventional servitudes can also be created to negate or alter natural servitudes and legal servitudes that otherwise arise by operation of law. *See* La. Civ. Code art. 651 rev. cmt. (f) (1977); La. Civ. Code art. 729 (1977).

B. Natural Servitudes

Chapter 2 of Title IV (Predial Servitudes) of Book II of the Civil Code governs natural servitudes. Two articles address a servitude that establishes a particular relationship between two specific estates. The other two provisions describe the advantages any estate owner can enjoy with respect to running water that passes through the estate and the responsibilities this estate owner owes to the rest of the public with respect to that water.

Article 655 of the Civil Code establishes what is known in Louisiana as the natural servitude of drain:

Art. 655. Natural drainage

An estate situated below is the servient estate and is bound to receive the surface waters that flow naturally from a dominant estate situated above unless an act of man has created the flow.

La. Civ. Code art. 655 (1978, amended 2017). This provision addresses a common problem confronted by neighbors. Excess water that falls on or passes through one estate needs to drain downhill onto another estate. The servitude created by Article 655 gives the owner of a dominant estate ("the estate situated above") a real right to drain his estate and imposes on the servient state ("the estate situated below") an obligation to receive the surface waters that gravity impels downhill from the dominant estate. This legal obligation imposed on the lower elevation estate is significant because, in the absence of a personal or real right to drain an estate, the discharge of waters onto neighboring lands can amount to an unlawful act. *See Terrebonne Parish Police Jury v. Matherne*, 405 So.2d 314, 317 (La. 1981) ("An injunction preventing a landowner from diverting the natural drain of his property is not a taking or damaging of his property because he has no right to do anything to render the natural servitude of drain more burdensome upon the estates situated below. The parish governing authority was entitled to have the landowner's unlawful acts enjoined in order to prevent irreparable injury to its drainage project.")

1. Identifying the Dominant and Servient Estate

The natural drain servitude, which is limited to tracts of lands, can arise whenever there is any elevation differential between two tracts. The difference in elevation does not have to be dramatic. *See e.g., Broussard v. Cormier*, 154 La. 877, 882 (1923) (noting that a difference of only a few inches is sufficient to establish a natural servitude of drain so long as water flows from one estate to another). Whether one estate is higher than the other is a question of fact. Some courts focus on comparing the overall height of the estates. *See e.g., Poole v. Guste*, 262 So.2d 339, 344 (1972) (Summers, J., dissenting). Other authorities assert that the natural servitude of drain attaches to particularized points where one estate is higher than the other. A.N. YIANNOPOULOS, 4 LOUISIANA CIVIL LAW TREATISE: PREDIAL SERVITUDES § 2.2, at 62–63 (4th ed. 2013) ("In Louisiana's flatlands . . . relative overall elevation of two estates is not an easy matter to determine, even by scientific methods, and the most reliable guide remains the flow of waters. The existence of large estates and the possibility of reciprocal flows, which depends on slight differences in elevation, make overall height immaterial.").

2. Scope of the Charge

The servitude of drain only applies to surface waters that flow naturally from the dominant estate onto the servient estate. It does not apply to water flows resulting from human intervention. *See* La. Civ. Code art. 655 rev. cmt. (b) (1977). Underground waters must naturally reach the estate above before finding their way onto the estate below. Courts have refused to apply the servitude of drain to discharges of oil and salt water extracted from subterranean pools as the result of mineral exploitation. *See, e.g., McFarlain v. Jennings-Heywood Oil Syndicate*, 118 La. 537 (1907). Courts have also held that the availability of access to a public drainage system does not eliminate the right of an elevated estate to take advantage of a natural servitude of drain across a lower estate. A.N. YIANNOPOULOS, 4 LOUISIANA CIVIL LAW TREATISE, PREDIAL SERVITUDES § 2.2, at 65–66 (4th ed. 2013).

3. Rights and Duties of the Owners of the Two Estates

Article 656 of the Civil Code identifies the corresponding rights and duties of the owners of the servient and dominant estates:

Art. 656. Obligations of the owners

> The owner of the servient estate situated below may not do anything to prevent the flow of the water. The owner of the dominant estate situated above may not do anything to render the servitude more burdensome.

La. Civ. Code art. 656 (1977, amended 2017). Although the text seems to impose strict negative commands, the jurisprudence has infused these rules with a dose of elasticity. The owner of the dominant estate is bound to refrain from making the servitude more burdensome. This owner must exercise the servitude reasonably (*civiliter*). In agricultural and industrial settings in particular, however, the jurisprudence has relaxed somewhat the sweep of the prohibition against making the servitude more burdensome for the servient estate. Consider this excerpt from a late nineteenth century opinion:

> The owner of the lower lands of two adjacent estates can do no act which would impede the natural flow of waters on his lands, from those of the higher estate. The owner of the superior estate may make all drainage works which are necessary to the proper cultivation and to the agricultural development of his estate. To that end, he may cut ditches and canals by which the waters *running* on his estate may be concentrated, and their flow increased beyond the slow process by which they would *ultimately* reach the same destination.
>
> But the owner of the superior estate cannot improve his lands to the injury of his neighbor, and thus he will not be allowed to cut ditches or canals, or do other drainage works by which the waters running on his lands will be diverted from their natural flow, and concentrated so as to flow on the lower lands of the adjacent estate at a point which would not be their natural destination, thus increasing the volume of water which would by natural flow run over or reach any portion of the lower adjacent estate, or to drain over his neighbor's lands stagnant waters from his, and to thus render the servitude due by the estate below more burdensome.

Ludeling v. Stubbs, 34 La. Ann. 935, 937–38 (1882). Invoking the same interests in promoting the development of agriculture and industry, courts have also held that the owner of the dominant estate does not have the right to a specific drainage path over the estate below. Therefore, the servient estate owner may make works and constructions that concentrate the flow of water at a certain point on his estate, as long as the waters are removed from the dominant estate at the same speed as if the drainage occurred across the entire servient estate. *Darby v. Miller*, 1851 WL 3860 (La. 1851); A.N. Yiannopoulos, 4 Louisiana Civil Law Treatise: Predial Servitudes § 2.6 (4th ed. 2013).

Finally, the dominant estate owner does not have a statutory right to enter the estate below with workers and equipment to maintain the natural servitude of drain over the servient estate, even though Article 745 of the Civil Code gives a dominant estate owner such a right with respect to conventional predial servitudes. *See* La. Civ. Code art. 745 (1977). The absence of such a right in the Civil Code, however, does not preclude a dominant estate owner from requesting permission to enter the servient estate for such a purpose. *See Bransford v. Int'l Paper Timberlands Operating Co.*, 750 So.2d 424, 427 (La. App. 2 Cir. 2000).

Although Article 656 generally prohibits acts by the owner of the servient estate that would prevent the flow of the water from the dominant estate, courts have interpreted this command with some flexibility. In general, the owner of the servient estate does not have any obligation to engage in affirmative action. *See Bransford v. Int'l Paper Timberlands Operating Co.*, 750 So.2d 424 (La. App. 2 Cir. 2000) (refusing to impose damages for failure to clear beaver dams). On occasion, courts have required servient estate owners to undertake actions to preserve the utility of the natural servitude of drain. *See Brown v. Blankenship*, 28 So.2d 496, 498 (La. App. 2 Cir. 1946) (confirming the plaintiff's right to have the owner of the servient estate remove brush and obstructions that clogged a drainage ditch). *But see* A.N. YIANNOPOULOS, 4 LOUISIANA CIVIL LAW TREATISE, PREDIAL SERVITUDES§ 2.6, at 75 (4th ed. 2013) (criticizing courts for reading into Article 651 incidental services due by the owner of the estate below when natural processes are in play).

The owner of the estate below is generally barred from retarding or impeding the water flow even if such action would produce benefits for the servient estate. Thus, a servient estate owner cannot make constructions to protect the estate from rainfall or tidal overflow if these constructions would impound water flowing from the estate above. Should an exception from this prohibition be made for marshlands, especially considering the unique circumstances of coastal Louisiana where marshes are often exposed to strong tidal influences and storm surges? This question has been discussed in Louisiana jurisprudence and in French literature. *See Poole v. Guste*, 261 La. 1110, 262 So. 2d 339, 347 (1972) (Summers J., dissenting) (suggesting that owners of marshlands overflown by tides should have the prerogative to protect their property by means of dikes even if this causes a back-up of waters into the estate above). *But see* CHARLES DEMOLOMBE, TRAITÉ DES SERVITUDES 33 (1876) ("[T]he estates adjoining a marsh are bound to receive the waters that overflow as a result of rain; and . . . the owner[s] of lower lands . . . cannot free themselves of this [natural drain servitude] by means of works that cause the waters to back up into the higher estates or estates of the same elevation.").

In sum, the law governing the natural servitude of drain allows relatively little room for landowners seeking to block or dispose of surface waters—waters not running within a specific watercourse. Under English common law, and especially the so-called "common enemy doctrine," landowners enjoyed more freedom to deal with diffused surface waters. *See Butler v. Bruno*, 341 A.2d 735 (R.I. 1975). Some common law courts take an intermediate approach to the problem of drainage across neighboring estates, basing a landowner's liability on the reasonableness of his actions in the circumstances. *See Id.*

4. Termination of the Natural Servitude of Drain

The question of whether a servient estate can be freed from the obligations imposed under Articles 655 and 656 of the Civil Code has surfaced in various contexts. It is clear that the acquisition of either the dominant or servient estate by a third party does not terminate a natural servitude of drain because the servitude inures in the physical relationship between the two estates and thus is inseparable from the land. La. Civ. Code art. 650 (1977). However, if both the dominant and servient estates are acquired by the same person, the natural servitude of drain would terminate through confusion. La. Civ. Code art. 765 (1977).

If the owner of the dominant estate fails to exercise the natural servitude of drain, the servitude does not become extinct because prescription of nonuse does not against natural servitudes. La. Civ. Code art. 758 (1977). However, does Article 758 prevent a servient estate owner from acquiring a conventional servitude through acquisitive prescription based on operations or works contrary to the natural servitude of drain? The Louisiana Supreme Court has refrained from deciding whether a modification of a natural drain servitude by artificial works can change its nature and convert a natural servitude into a conventional one by way of acquisitive prescription. *See Poole v. Guste*, 261 La. 1110, 262 So.2d 339 (1972). Should the answer depend on whether the modification is material or innocuous?

5. Remedies for Breach of the Servitude of Drain

Roman law gave all estate owners the *actio aquae pluviae arcendae* ("action to ward off the water") (Dig. 39.3). This action allowed owners of agricultural estates to fend off influent rainwater if the natural efflux from neighboring estates was occasioned or changed through human works (*opus manu factum*) like water ditches or dams. However, this action was not available under Roman law when the works were created for agricultural purposes like plowing (*opera agri colendi causa facta*).

In Louisiana law, the owners of the estates have at their disposal two remedies — injunctive relief and damages. Injunctive relief is generally available as a matter of right. The jurisprudence has tailored this equitable relief to the civilian property context by curtailing the clean hands doctrine and the balancing of equities. *See Poole v. Guste*, 261 La. 1110, 262 So.2d 339 (1972). Courts generally prefer to issue injunctive relief in a prohibitory guise, but when a petitioner suffers an obstruction in the enjoyment of a real right, courts sometimes will issue a mandatory injunction requiring the defendant landowner to remove an obstruction. *See Richland Police Jury v. Debnam*, 92 So.3d 487 (La. App. 2 Cir. 2012).

When a landowner seeks damages for a breach of one of the obligations inherent in the natural servitude of drain, two issues have commonly arisen: (1) whether the liability standard should require fault; and (2) whether liberative prescription should run in one year or ten years. *See* A.N. YIANNOPOULOS, 4 LOUISIANA. CIVIL LAW TREATISE: PREDIAL SERVITUDES,§ 2.7 (4th ed. 2013). Sometimes, as we will see in *Adams v. Town of Ruston*, 193 So. 688 (1940), courts prefer to award monetary damages rather than issue injunctive relief if they believe the injunctive relief would create too much hardship for one of the parties in the servitude relationship. In one noteworthy decision, the Louisiana Supreme Court held that an action for injunctive relief brought against the State of Louisiana to remedy continued obstruction of the natural drainage that flooded the plaintiffs' adjacent lands had not prescribed because natural servitudes are imprescriptible under Article 758 of the Civil Code, but then decided that the difficulty of fashioning injunctive relief in the particular circumstances of the case would justify alternative relief in the form of monetary damages. *Garahan v. State through Dept. of Trans. and Dev.*, 579 So.2d 420, 422–23 (La. 1991).

6. Use and Extraction of Running Water

In addition to the natural servitude of drain set forth in Articles 655 and 656, Chapter 2 of Title IV contains two more provisions with specific rules for estates bordering on and crossed by running water. In contrast to the servitude of drain, Professor Yiannopoulos labels the riparian rights enjoyed by estate owners under Articles 657 and 658 of the Civil Code as sui generis real rights "part and parcel of the ownership of an estate fronting on or traversed by running water." A.N. YIANNOPOULOS, 4 LOUISIANA CIVIL LAW TREATISE: PREDIAL SERVITUDES§ 2.8, 85 (4th ed. 2013). One commentator notes that Yiannopoulos' "terminology is closer to that of the common-law authorities, but he does not say what distinction ought to be made in any given dispute between riparians *inter se* or between riparians and members of the general public, the state, or municipalities." James Klebba, *Water Rights and Water Policy in Louisiana: Laissez Faire Riparianism, Market Based Approaches, or a New Managerialism?*, 53 LA. L. REV. 1779, 1792 (1993).

With regard to an estate fronting on running water, Article 657 of the Louisiana Civil Code declares that "[t]he owner of an estate bordering on running water may use it as it runs for the purpose of watering his estate or for other purposes." La. Civ. Code art. 657 (1977). The use referenced in this article would typically apply to a riparian user engaged in farming or agricultural activities. The owner of an estate benefited by Article 657 would not, however, have the right to change the course of the running water that fronts on his estate because to do so would interfere with the rights of his neighbor on the opposite bank and his neighbors downstream. A.N. YIANNOPOULOS, 4 LOUISIANA CIVIL LAW TREATISE: PREDIAL SERVITUDES§ 2.8, 84–85(4th ed. 2013).

Article 658 of the Civil Code extends the use rights of the riparian owner to running water passing through the estate, and not merely bordering it. The provision also imposes some general responsibilities:

Art. 658. Estate through which water runs

The owner of an estate through which water runs, whether it originates there or passes from lands above, may make use of it while it runs over his lands. He cannot stop it or give it another direction and is bound to return it to its ordinary channel where it leaves his estate.

La. Civ. Code art. 658 (1977). One commentator interprets this article as allowing the riparian owner the right to "change the water's course within his estate as he sees fit," as long as he does not "stop the water or give it another direction" when it leaves the estate. A.N. Yiannopoulos, 4 Louisiana Civil Law Treatise: Predial Servitudes § 2.8, 84 (4th ed. 2013).

Notably, neither Article 657 nor 658 squarely addresses the extent of the riparian owner's right to draw water crossing his estate. *See* Klebba, *Water Rights and Water Policy in Louisiana: Laissez Faire Riparianism, Market Based Approaches, or a New Managerialism?*, 53 La. L. Rev. at 1798–1800 (1993) (discussing a reasonable use standard). The principle articulated in Article 658 that a landowner must return running water to its natural channel is reinforced by section of 218 of Title 38 of Louisiana's Revised Statutes:

§ 218. Diversion of natural drain prohibited

A. No person diverting or impeding the course of water from a natural drain shall fail to return the water to its natural course before it leaves his estate without any undue retardation of the flow of water outside of his enclosure thereby injuring an adjacent estate.

La. Rev. Stat. § 38:218 A. (2010, as amended 2016).

Louisiana jurisprudence has confirmed that if the water does not "run" across an estate, these provisions are not triggered. Whether or not water is running presents a factual issue determined at trial. In a case involving water in an oxbow lake created in the former channel of the Red River, which had abandoned its original course and opened up a new bed, Judge Domengeaux of Louisiana's Third Circuit Court of Appeals rejected the assertion of the riparian landowner defendant that it enjoyed a right to pump water out of the lake for irrigation purposes because evidence supported the district court's finding that the water in the lake was not running. *Verzwyvelt v. Armstrong-Ratterree, Inc.*, 463 So.2d 979, 984–85 (La. App. 3 1985) (affirming possessory judgment in favor of plaintiff-appellee who owned all the land underlying the water pursuant to La. Civ. Code art. 504 (1979) against defendant-appellant whose title extended only to the water's edge and whose pumping operations constituted a disturbance in fact).

Now, consider the three decisions below. They illustrate varying judicial approaches to enforcement of a natural servitude of drain. Notice how the disposition of each case seems to turn on the remedy sought by the plaintiffs and the court's assessment of whether the remedy sought is appropriate in each case.

Adams v. Town of Ruston

193 So. 688 (La. 1940)

PONDER, Justice. In this suit the plaintiff is seeking an injunction to restrain the Town of Ruston and its employees from causing or permitting waste water emptied from the town's swimming pool to flow across and damage his land.

The plaintiff owns a tract of land located in the town of Ruston. The town owns and operates a concrete swimming pool which has a capacity of between 450,000 to 500,000 gallons of water. The town owns the property on which the swimming pool is located. Between the town's property and the plaintiff's property there is a highway and a tract of land owned by Raymond Heard. There is a small branch or natural drain that runs through the town's property near the swimming pool across the property of Raymond Heard under the Dixie Overland Highway and across the plaintiff's property. Once a week during the summer the swimming pool is emptied into this ditch or natural drain from the swimming pool through a 14-inch outlet. It requires from an hour to an hour and a half to empty the water from the swimming pool. The point where the water enters the ditch is approximately 450 feet south of the plaintiff's south boundary line. The plaintiff instituted this suit seeking a judgment to enjoin the town of Ruston from emptying the water into the ditch or natural drain and permitting it to flow across and damage his land. The plaintiff alleged that if the town is permitted to continue discharging the water from the swimming pool it will damage him to the extent of total loss and thereby cause him irreparable injury. He alleged that the present value of his land is not less than $10,000 and that it has already been damaged by this water to an amount in excess of $5,000. The town answered the plaintiff's petition, the case was duly tried and the lower court rendered judgment rejecting the plaintiff's demands. The plaintiff has appealed.

The record does not show how many acres are contained in the plaintiff's land. The land was unimproved at the time the plaintiff bought it and no improvements have been placed on it. The plaintiff testified that when he purchased the property some twenty years ago that he could step across the ditch or drain, but that it is now from six to eight feet wide. He estimated that 75 per cent of the erosion that has taken place in the ditch since the pool was built has been caused by the water emptied from the swimming pool. A witness for the plaintiff testified that it was his opinion that the flow of water from the swimming pool across the plaintiff's property damages it. The mayor of the town of Ruston testified that the swimming pool was constructed in the year 1931 at a cost of $27,500 and that it is kept open and in operation about three and a half months each year. He testified that the pool is emptied on an average of about fifteen times per year. He further testified that the plaintiff has never made any complaint either to him or the town council of any injury or damage the water from the pool was causing his land until thirty days before this suit was filed and that that complaint was made in a letter from the plaintiff's attorney. A witness for the town, who is an Assistant Professor of Engineering at Louisiana Tech, testified that from scientific tests he had made the amount of water discharged from the swimming pool into the ditch each year is only one-tenth of the amount that flows through it from the natural drainage from rainfall. He testified from actual tests made by him that the water emptied from the swimming pool picked up and carried away only one-half of one cubic foot of soil and that on the basis of this experiment in a year's time the water from the swimming pool would erode seven and one-half cubic feet of soil which would only carry away seventy-five cubic feet of soil from the plaintiff's land in ten years.

The plaintiff contends that the natural drainage servitude imposed upon his property in favor of the defendant's property by Article 600, Revised Civil Code, is being made more burdensome by the discharge of the water from the swimming pool and that he is entitled as a matter of right to an injunction to protect his property from such additional injury and damage.

The record shows that when the swimming pool is emptied into the drainage ditch that the drainage ditch does not overflow but the water is confined solely within the ditch. From a preponderance of the testimony the damage caused the plaintiff is negligible which can be adequately compensated in money. While the natural servitude of drainage through plaintiff's property has been made slightly more burdensome on account of the water from the swimming pool flowing across the property, the damage is of such a negligible character that it would not entitle the plaintiff to an injunction as a matter of right. Under the doctrine laid down in the case of *Young v. International Paper Company*, 179 La. 803, 155 So. 231, 233, the question presented is one that addresses itself to the discretion of the court. In the case of *Young v. International Paper Company, supra*, the Court stated:

> "Plaintiff has asked for an injunction to abate the alleged nuisance. The trial court, under all of the facts before it, refused to grant the injunction. The granting of it was discretionary. Plaintiff's land is hardly susceptible now to any damage that the water may cause it, and, if such should occur, it may be easily compensated in money. To enjoin defendant from using the stream to take off its waste water, and thereby deprive it of its only means of doing so, is virtually to close down mills costing several millions of dollars to prevent some possible damage, of no particular moment, on land, which has but slight value, save possibly for mineral purposes."

In *City of Harrisonville, Mo., v. W. S. Dickey Clay Mfg. Co.*, 289 U.S. 334, 53 S.Ct. 602, 603, 77 L.Ed. 1208, it was said in a suit to enjoin the pollution of a creek by sewage from a city that:

> "Thus, the question here is not one of equitable jurisdiction. The question is whether, upon the facts found, an injunction is the appropriate remedy. For an injunction is not a remedy which issues as of course. Where substantial redress can be afforded by the payment of money and issuance of an injunction would subject the defendant to grossly disproportionate

hardship, equitable relief may be denied although the nuisance is indisputable. This is true even if the conflict is between interests which are primarily private."

The plaintiff can be adequately compensated for his damage and he is not entitled to an injunction herein.

The defendant urges in his answer that since the plaintiff has stood by for eight years and permitted the water from the swimming pool to be drained across his land that the plaintiff is estopped from claiming an injunction. Since we have arrived at the conclusion that the injury or damage is so negligible, it is unnecessary for us to consider this contention.

In the case of *McFarlain v. Jennings-Heywood Oil Syndicate*, 118 La. 537, 538, 43 So. 155, cited by the plaintiff, the demand was for damages and did not involve injunctive relief. *Ogden v. Police Jury of East Baton Rouge Parish*, 166 La. 869, 870, 118 So. 65, and *Chandler v. City of Shreveport*, 169 La. 52, 124 So. 143, cited by the plaintiff were cases where water was diverted to such an extent that the injury or damages were of an aggravated nature. In fact, they were of such nature that it practically destroyed the usefulness of the property over which the water flowed. Neither of the cases cited is authority to the effect that where the damage caused to the property is negligible and can be adequately compensated in damages that such causes irreparable injury and warrants the issuance of an injunction.

For the reasons assigned, the judgment is affirmed at appellant's cost.

Bransford v. Int'l Paper Timberlands Operating Co., Ltd.

750 So.2d 424 (La. App. 2 Cir. 2000)

WILLIAMS, Judge. The plaintiff, Camille S. Bransford, appeals a summary judgment rendered in favor of the defendant, International Paper Timberlands Operating Company, Ltd. ("IP Timberlands"). The district court found that the defendant did not have a duty to remedy naturally occurring conditions on its land that obstructed drainage and caused flooding of plaintiff's property.

For the following reasons, we affirm.

Facts

The plaintiff, Camille S. Bransford, and IP Timberlands own adjacent tracts of land in Webster Parish, Louisiana (referred to herein as the "Bransford Tract" and the "Timberlands Tract" respectively). Surface water from the plaintiff's land naturally drains across the defendant's property. In December 1991, the plaintiff, who is an elderly widow, gave to her son, James Bransford ("Bransford"), the power of attorney to manage her properties, including the Bransford Tract, which contains timber.

On and around the Bransford Tract, beavers had built dams which caused flooding in some areas of the property. In late 1995, Bransford began efforts to destroy and remove the beavers and their dams. During the summer of 1996, Bransford learned that flooding had also occurred on that part of the Bransford Tract contiguous to the Timberlands Tract. Subsequently, Bransford entered the Timberlands Tract and observed a beaver dam, which was apparently preventing drainage from plaintiff's land. Bransford did not attempt to dismantle the dam.

The plaintiff filed a petition for damages, alleging that the defendant's failure to remove beaver dams on its property caused flooding of plaintiff's land and the loss of timber. The case was removed to the United States District Court for the Western District of Louisiana, where the defendant filed a motion for summary judgment. Subsequently, the case was remanded to the 26th Judicial District Court, which held a hearing on the summary judgment motion.

For the purposes of the motion for summary judgment, IP Timberlands conceded that beaver dams built on its property had obstructed the natural drainage from the Bransford Tract, causing flooding of the plaintiff's land and damage to the timber. IP Timberlands does not dispute that there is a natural servitude of drainage between the two contiguous tracts of land, and that its parcel is the servient estate to the Bransford Tract.

Following the hearing on the motion, the trial court found that IP Timberlands did not have an affirmative duty to remedy conditions of a purely natural origin, and determined that such a duty would place an unreasonable burden on rural landowners. The district court granted the defendant's motion for summary judgment, dismissing plaintiff's claims. Consequently, the court did not address the defendant's prescription argument. The plaintiff appeals the judgment.

Discussion

The plaintiff contends the district court erred in granting the motion for summary judgment. Plaintiff argues that the defendant, as owner of the servient estate, is liable for damages due to its failure to remove beaver dams, which prevented drainage and contributed to flooding of plaintiff's dominant estate. . . .

A predial servitude is a burden on a servient estate for the benefit of a dominant estate, with each having different owners. LSA-C.C. art. 646. Generally, the owner of the servient estate is not required to do anything. His obligation is to abstain from doing something, or to permit something to be done, on his estate. He may be required by convention or by law to keep his estate in suitable condition for the exercise of the servitude due to the dominant estate. LSA-C.C. art. 651. A predial servitude may be a natural servitude, which arises from the natural situation of estates. LSA-C.C. art. 654.

Pursuant to the natural servitude of drainage, an estate situated below is bound to receive the surface waters that flow naturally from an estate situated above, unless the flow was created by an act of man. LSA-C.C. art. 655. The owner of the servient estate may not do anything to prevent the flow of water. The dominant estate owner may not act to render the servitude of drainage more burdensome. LSA-C.C. art. 656.

In the present case, the plaintiff's claim for damages is not based on the defendant's control of the beavers, but is based on the defendant's ownership of the servient estate, which is subject to a servitude of drainage for the benefit of the Bransford Tract. The defendant does not dispute the fact that the flooding of plaintiff's land was caused by beaver dams located on the Timberlands Tract.

In support of her argument that defendant is liable for damage caused by the flooding, plaintiff cites authority from another jurisdiction. In *Illinois Central R.R. Co. v. Watkins*, 671 So. 2d 59 (Miss. 1996), the railroad modified a natural drain and constructed a culvert to allow the flow of surface water. The culvert became obstructed by beaver dams, which prevented drainage and caused flooding of Watkins' land, damaging his crops. Watkins notified the railroad, which cleared the blockage. However, the culvert became blocked by beaver dams a second time and was cleared. Watkins sued for damages alleging that the railroad had negligently maintained its property. The court determined that the railroad had a duty to maintain its culvert, which became blocked by a dam, that the railroad knew of the condition and allowed it to remain, and that these facts supported the jury's finding that the railroad was negligent.

The factual situation in Watkins can be distinguished from that in the present case. Here, the defendant did not build a structure which modified or blocked the drainage area. Nor is there evidence that defendant was aware of the presence of beaver dams blocking the flow of water until being informed of this fact by Bransford after the flooding had occurred. Thus, the Watkins case does not provide persuasive authority for the plaintiff's argument.

In evaluating the defendant's codal duty as the servient estate owner, we must apply the provisions of the previously cited articles. Pursuant to Article 656, defendant was required to refrain from taking any action which would prevent the natural flow of water from the Bransford Tract. Article 651 obligated defendant to either abstain from doing something or permit something to be done on the Timberlands Tract, but defendant was "not required to do anything." The record shows that the defendant did not take any action to impede the natural flow of water from the plaintiff's land. Nor is there evidence that defendant refused to permit plaintiff's representative from acting in connection with the servitude.

The plaintiff contends that her property damage was caused by defendant's failure to remove the beaver dams from the Timberlands Tract. However, this court has previously provided for an award of damages only under circumstances in which the owner of the servient estate has acted directly to obstruct or interfere with the servitude of drainage. *See Tool House, Inc. v. Tynes*, 564 So. 2d 720 (La. App. 2d Cir.), *writ denied*, 568 So. 2d 1087 (La. 1990); *Cole v. Mott*, 351 So. 2d 1326 (La. App. 2d Cir. 1977). The record demonstrates that defendant did not act to prevent the flow of water from the plaintiff's land. Consequently, defendant is not liable for property damage caused by the flooding of the Bransford Tract.

The plaintiff also argues that the codal articles impose upon defendant the affirmative duty to remove naturally occurring obstructions which prevent the natural drainage from the Bransford Tract. We recognize that Article 651 provides that a servient estate owner may be required by convention or law to keep his estate in suitable condition for the exercise of the servitude. In addition, we are aware that in the case of *Brown v. Blankenship*, 28 So. 2d 496 (La. App. 2d Cir. 1946), this court affirmed a judgment ordering the owner of a servient estate to remove underbrush and other debris which accumulated over time and obstructed the natural drainage of water from the dominant estate.

However, in the present case, the plaintiff has not sought such injunctive relief. Thus, we will not address the issue of whether the defendant could have been compelled to remove the beaver dams which were preventing the natural drainage from the Bransford Tract. We note that in its brief, the defendant acknowledges that plaintiff would have been entitled to enter the Timberlands Tract in order to maintain the servitude of drainage by removing the obstructions.

Based upon this record, we cannot say the district court erred in granting the defendant's motion for summary judgment. The plaintiff's assignment of error lacks merit.

Conclusion

For the foregoing reasons, the district court's judgment granting the motion for summary judgment is affirmed. Costs of this appeal are assessed to the appellant, Camille Bransford.

AFFIRMED.

Richland Police Jury v. Debnam

92 So.3d 487 (La. App. 2 Cir. 2012)

BROWN, Chief Judge. Defendants, Donald and Joyce Debnam, appeal the judgment of the trial court . . . granting a preliminary injunction in favor of plaintiffs, Richland Parish Police Jury, Lester Wayne Johnson, M.D., R&B Planting Co., George B. Franklin & Son, Inc., Big Creek Farms Partnership, Ricky Goodman, Randy Swain, and Jerry Bell. For the reasons stated herein, we affirm the judgment of the trial court. . . .

Facts and Procedural Background

Defendants, Donald and Joyce Debnam, own 120 acres situated on the north side of Ruff Road in Richland Parish. Ruff Road runs east and west and forms the south boundary of the property. Cypress Creek runs in a generally north-south direction across their property. The Debnams constructed a dam, earthen works, and other structures on Cypress Creek adjacent to Ruff Road in an attempt to prevent the eroding and flooding of their property.

Plaintiffs, the Richland Parish Police Jury and numerous adjoining property owners, filed this suit for injunctive relief against defendants seeking to force them to remove the dams built on their land. Plaintiffs contend that the obstructions interfere with the natural flow of the creek and cause flooding to adjacent properties, causing damages to the surrounding landowners' crops and a parish-maintained roadway, Ruff Road.

The Police Jury had filed a prior suit in 2006 seeking to have the Debnams ordered to remove the dams then built on Cypress Creek. In that matter, the trial court ruled in favor of the Police Jury, but this court reversed that decision on appeal finding that there was an insufficient showing that the flooding alleged was solely caused by the obstructions on the Debnam property. We further concluded that there were multiple causes contributing to the damages alleged by the Police Jury, including the actions of the Police Jury itself. The Louisiana Supreme Court denied writs and defendants rebuilt their dams.

In the years that followed the first suit, the Police Jury has made modifications to the drainage system in the vicinity at issue, including the installation of new and larger culverts at Futch Road and Nicole Drive, and the clearing out of some obstructions in the W-27 canal north of the Debnam property.

Plaintiffs filed this current suit for injunctive relief on May 27, 2011. In response, defendants filed numerous exceptions. . . . Plaintiffs amended their petition on July 26, 2011, to demand a preliminary injunction. After a full evidentiary hearing on August 4, 2011, the trial court denied all exceptions and granted plaintiffs' preliminary injunction which prohibited the Debnams from erecting any new obstructions across Cypress Creek and ordered the removal of the then existing obstructions within 15 days, or should they not do so, for the police jury to remove the obstructions with the costs to be paid by defendants.

The Debnams filed a motion for appeal and requested a stay of all proceedings, which the trial court denied. Defendants then filed an application for a writ with this court to stay removal of the obstructions, which was granted on November 11, 2011.

Discussion

The Debnams' essential argument on appeal is twofold: that plaintiffs are not entitled to the relief sought, as their claim is barred by the doctrine of *res judicata*, and, that plaintiffs failed to show that they would suffer irreparable harm in the absence of the preliminary injunction.

The Debnams contend that plaintiffs failed to show that irreparable injury, a loss that cannot be adequately compensated in monetary damages, will result if the obstructions across Cypress Creek remain in place. They argue that since plaintiffs' petition for injunction demands various money damages, they can adequately value any damages that they may incur, and, thus, any harm is not irreparable. Plaintiffs assert, however, that defendants' obstructions are interfering with their natural servitude of drainage, and, as such, a showing of irreparable harm is not required.

A natural servitude of drainage is due by an estate situated below to receive the surface waters that flow naturally from an estate situated above. La. C.C. art. 655. The owner of the servient estate may not do anything to prevent the flow of water. La. C.C. art. 656.

La. C.C.P. art. 3601, the usual statutory grounds for the issuance of an injunction, provides in pertinent part that an injunction shall issue in cases where irreparable injury, loss or damage may otherwise result to applicant, or in other cases specifically provided by law. An injunction to protect a servitude, however, is authorized under *La. C.C.P. art. 3663*. Specifically, section 2 of that article allows a person injunctive relief to protect or restore possession of immovable property or of a real right in immovable property of which he claims ownership, possession, or enjoyment. A preliminary injunction brought pursuant to *La. C.C.P. art. 3663* does not require a showing of irreparable harm. *Monroe Real Estate & Development Co., Inc. v. Sunshine Equipment Co., Inc.*, 35,555 (La. App. 2d Cir. 01/23/02), 805 So. 2d 1200.

The general rule is that an injunction will only be issued in its prohibitory form, but when a defendant obstructs a plaintiff in the enjoyment of a real right, the latter may be entitled to a prohibitory injunction restraining the disturbance and also to a mandatory injunction for the removal of the obstruction. *Concerned Citizens for Proper Planning, LLC v. Parish of Tangipahoa*, 04-0270 (La. App. 1st Cir. 03/24/05), 906 So.2d 660; *Harris v. Pierce*, 73 So. 2d 330 (La. App. Orleans 1954).

The right to drain water from one's property over the lands of others is not a prerogative of ownership but a real right of servitude requiring a dismemberment of the ownership of others or a charge laid on their immovables. *Terrebonne Parish Police Jury v. Matherne*, 405 So. 2d 314 (La. 1981). When the owner of the servient estate does something to prevent the flow of the water, such as placing obstacles to drainage from the dominant through the servient estate, the remedy is a mandatory injunction ordering the owner of the servient estate to remove the obstacle. *Pool v. Guste,* 261 La. 1110, 262 So. 2d 339 (La. 1972); *Gaharan v. DOTD*, 566 So. 2d 1007 (La. App. 3d Cir. 1990).

A preliminary injunction in its prohibitory form seeks to preserve the status quo until a full trial on the merits and it may be issued upon a PRIMA FACIE showing by the applicant seeking the injunction. *Louisiana Granite Yard, Inc. v. LA Granite Countertops, L.L.C.,* 45,482 (La. App. 2d Cir. 08/18/10), 47 So. 3d 573, writ denied, 10-2354 (La. 12/10/10), 51 So. 3d 733; *Louisiana Gaming Corp. v. Rob's Mini-Mart, Inc.,* 27,920 (La. App. 2d Cir. 01/24/96), 666 So. 2d 1268. However, a mandatory preliminary injunction, so named because it orders the doing of something, requires the party seeking the injunction to show by a preponderance of the evidence at an evidentiary hearing that he is entitled to the preliminary injunction sought. *City of New Orleans v. Board of Directors of the Louisiana State Museum*, 98-1170 (La. 03/02/99), 739 So. 2d 748.

A trial court is afforded great discretion to grant or deny a preliminary injunction and its ruling will not be overturned absent manifest error. *Louisiana Granite Yard, Inc., supra.*

After a full evidentiary hearing on the preliminary injunction, during which witnesses, both lay and expert, testified and were cross-examined, and other evidence was introduced, the trial court found that the obstructions on the Debnams' property were blocking the natural drain of water from the plaintiffs' lands causing water to pool in the road ditches and on the plaintiff landowners' property. In particular, Fred Scott Franklin, a neighboring landowner, testified that he and his family had been farming the land off of Ruff Road for more than 50 years, and that up until the time that the Debnams built their dams and other obstructions across Cypress Creek the water from his land would naturally drain toward Cypress Creek to the W-27 canal. After the Debnams built the obstructions, Mr. Franklin testified that the water regularly backs up and floods his crops and other neighboring landowners' lands as well. The reason for this flooding, according to the testimony of Francis Markley Huey, a civil engineering, hydrology and drainage expert, is that the portion of Cypress Creek on the Debnams' property is the collection point for waters naturally flowing from the ditches on the east and west of Cypress Creek and from a high point approximately 1,000 feet south of Ruff Road. According to Mr. Huey, the waters that converge at this location have historically flowed north through Cypress Creek to where the W-27 canal is located. It was his opinion that the dams and other works built by the Debnams are obstructing the flow of Cypress Creek to the north and are a significant cause of the flooding and prolonged standing water.

Based upon the aforementioned testimony and our review of the record, a preponderance of the evidence supports the trial court's finding that the obstructions built by defendants to slow the flow of water through Cypress Creek are interfering with plaintiffs' natural servitude of drainage. In the decades prior to the construction of the impediments the area landowners rarely dealt with the flooding problems that they have since been dealing with on a regular basis. These obstructions infringe on plaintiffs' real rights and the trial court's issuance of a preliminary injunction was not erroneous. . . .

. . . .

Considering that the obstructions built by the Debnams are disturbing the possession and/or enjoyment of a real right, we find no reason to vacate the trial court's issuance of the preliminary injunction and instead will remand to the trial court for the furnishing of security.

Conclusion

For the foregoing reasons, the judgment of the trial court . . . granting a preliminary injunction in favor of plaintiffs is affirmed. . . .

Notes and Questions

1. In *Adams v. Town of Ruston*, 193 So. 688 (La. 1940), the Town of Ruston emptied its swimming pool fifteen times per summer into a drainage ditch that ran under a highway, crossed Heard's land and ran over Adams' undeveloped land. Adams petitioned to enjoin the Town. Characterize the source and quantities of the water flows in *Adams*. Is this the work of Mother Nature? Is the increase in flow appreciable?

Notice how the court distinguishes between a property rule remedy (injunctive relief) and a liability rule or delictual remedy (damages). Why does the Louisiana Supreme Court only afford Adams a right to the latter? What is the standard for granting injunctive relief? If the court had granted the prohibitory injunction, how would it justify its issuance?

2. In *Bransford v. Int'l Paper Timberlands Operating Co.*, 750 So.2d 424 (La. App. 2 Cir. 2000), the court had to decide whether the owner of the servient estate had a duty to remove dams built by beavers. The court refused to impose that duty and immunized the defendant from any liability in damages. Notice the court's language with regard to the potential availability of injunctive relief. How does this square with what the court did in *Adams*? How does this outcome fare in light of *Brown v. Blankenship*, 28 So.2d 496 (La. App. 2 Cir. 1946) and *Illinois Central R.R. Co. v. Watkins*, 671 So.2d 59 (Miss. 1996), cases cited in that opinion?

3. In *Richland Police Jury v. Debnam*, 92 So.3d 487 (La. App. 2 Cir. 2012), the Debnams constructed a dam, works and other structures to protect their property from flooding and erosion. The Richland Police Jury and other adjoining landowners who sought the removal of these constructions filed suit seeking injunctive relief. Exactly what type of injunctive relief was sought by the plaintiffs?

What was the Debnams' argument for why a preliminary injunction should not issue? How did the court respond? Compare Articles 3601 and 3663 of the Code of Civil Procedure.

What is the standard espoused by the court in *Richland Police Jury* with regard to the issuance of a mandatory preliminary injunction? What does the review of the record yield, according to the court?

4. ***Board of Commissioners of Southeast Louisiana Flood Protection Authority— East v. Tennessee Gas Pipeline Co.*, 850 F.3d 714 (5th Cir. 2017):** In July 2013, the Board of Commissioners of the Southeast Louisiana Flood Protection Authority— East ("the Board") filed a lawsuit against ninety-seven companies. These companies had dredged canals for the construction of oil and gas pipelines and conducting exploration-and-production activities in the wetlands southeast of New Orleans, an area identified as "The Buffer Zone." The Board claimed that acts and omissions of the defendants in connection with these canals, particularly their alleged failure to maintain the canal banks and to backfill the canals after their use ended, caused and would continue to cause weakening of the wetlands in the Buffer Zone. These acts and omissions, the Board contended, would lead to increased storm surges and raise flood protection costs to the Board and its constituent levee districts—The Orleans Levee District, the Lake Borgne Basin Levee District, and the East Jefferson Levee District.

One of the novel theories of liability raised by the Board concerned the natural servitude of drain. In particular, the Board alleged that the defendant companies had enjoyed "temporary rights of ownership" in the lands they dredged for the canals. When large storm surges occur as a the result of tropical storms and hurricanes, the Board argued, the rights of the defendant companies in the dredged canals constituted "dominant estates" under Article 655 of the Civil Code, while the Board's property was a servient estate because water naturally flowed from the defendants' dominant estates towards the Board's property. In this light, the Board continued, Article 656 (cl.2) of the Civil Code prohibited the defendants from doing anything to render the servitude of drain more burdensome for the Board's land.

In essence, the Board claimed that the defendants' activities associated with dredging canals and their failure to maintain and repair the canals altered the natural topography of the defendants' "lands" and thereby changed the locations, flowage patterns, and velocity of waters moving across the dominant estates and onto the servient estate. The cumulative impacts associated with these activities allegedly accelerated land loss on the dominant estates, leaving the coastal wetlands in the Buffer Zone more vulnerable to tropical storm surges and the natural servitude of drain more burdensome in violation of Article 656 of the Civil Code. The Board sought: (1) injunctive relief, in the form of abatement and restoration of coastal land loss, including backfilling and revegetating the canals; and (2) monetary damages for current and future expenses incurred by the Board.

Needless to say, the Board's lawsuit was highly contentious. In the summer of 2014, the Louisiana Legislature passed, and Governor Bobby Jindal signed, legislation specifically aimed at stripping the Board's authority to bring an action arising from or related to any permitted drilling and dredging activities in the state's coastal zone. 2014 La. Acts, SB 469, § 1 (enacting La. Rev. Stat. § 49:214.36(O)). The legislature also explicitly gave the new law retroactive effect with the apparent purpose of terminating the Board's litigation. *Id.* § 2. Eventually, after the lawsuit was removed from state court to federal court, all of the Board's claims were dismissed on the merits by the United States District Court for the Eastern District of Louisiana. *Board of Commissioners of Southeast Louisiana Flood Protection Authority— East v. Tennessee Gas Pipeline Co.*, 88 F.Supp.3d 615 (E.D. 2015). The district court addressed the Board's claim based on the natural servitude of drain as follows:

> Defendants argue that Plaintiff's natural servitude of drain claim fails as a matter of law because Plaintiff has not alleged that it owns property adjacent to property owned by any Defendants, or that the dominant and servient estates are "sufficiently close that water flows from a higher estate to another that is lower." In response, Plaintiff contends that, pursuant to Louisiana Civil Code Article 648, neither contiguity nor proximity of estates are requirements of a natural servitude of drain, and that, in fact, "[c]ourts interpret article 648's allowance liberally in finding servitudes of drain between properties miles apart."
>
> Plaintiff cites only two cases in support of its argument that the servient and dominant estates need not be contiguous. First, in *Young v. International Paper Co.* 179 La. 803, 155 So. 231, 232 (La. 1934), decided by the Louisiana Supreme Court in 1934, a landowner sued a paper mill operator located approximately eight miles upstream for emptying waste water

"into Stalkinghead creek [sic] — the chief medium of drainage for the city of Bastrop — [which] then enters Black bayou [sic], which traverses plaintiff's land." As a result, the plaintiff's land was flooded and some of his timber was destroyed. The legal basis for the lawsuit is not apparent from the opinion, which neither cites nor mentions the codal articles for natural servitude of drain. However, *Young* has been cited by scholars for the principle that damages due to interference with a natural servitude of drain are subject to a one year prescriptive period. *See* A.N. Yiannopoulos, 4 LA. CIV. L. TREATISE: PREDIAL SERVITUDES § 2:7.

In *Maddox v. Int'l Paper Co.*, 47 F.Supp. 829 (W.D. La. 1942), decided by the Western District of Louisiana in 1942, the owner of a fishing business filed a lawsuit pursuant to Article 2315 against a mill operator located thirty miles away for releasing waste material into a stream that fed directly into Bodcaw Bayou. Although the opinion suggests that the plaintiff's claim was for negligence, the *Maddox* court applied Article 660 and found, without further analysis, that the mill operator rendered a natural servitude of drain more burdensome on the plaintiff's estate. To reach this conclusion, the court cited the Louisiana Supreme Court's 1907 decision in *McFarlain v. Jennings–Heywood Oil Syndicate*, 118 LA. 537, 538, 43 So. 155 (1907), which involves a claim for interference of a natural servitude of drain between contiguous estates.

Both *Young* and *Maddox* are distinguishable from the instant case. First, there was no question in either case as to the relative positions of the dominant and servient estates because, in both cases, the plaintiff's estate was located downstream from the defendant mill operator. Here, in contrast, it is unclear whether the Defendants' estates are "situated above" the Plaintiff's estate, and Plaintiff does not so allege. Moreover, the plaintiffs in *Young* and *Maddox* suffered direct economic harm as a result of the upstream mill operators' activities. Here, Plaintiff alleges indirect economic harm to flood control structures over which it has a "usufructory" type of interest. The alleged harm at issue here is far more attenuated than the loss of physical property suffered by the landowner in *Young,* or the revenue loss suffered by the fisherman in *Maddox.* Additionally, as stated above, the plaintiff in *Maddox* appears to have sued for negligence, not natural servitude of drain, and the legal basis for the complaint in *Young* is unclear from the opinion. Moreover, in addition to the distinctions between *Maddox* and this case as noted above, *Maddox* is a decision from another federal district court and is therefore not binding on this Court.

Plaintiff additionally relies on *Poole v. Guste*, 261 La. 1100, 262 So.2d 399 (1972), to support its argument that a natural servitude of drain may exist on tidal lands. In *Poole*, the Louisiana Supreme Court was presented with the issue of whether a dominant estate had a servitude of drain into and through a canal constructed on the adjacent servient estate. Prior to

1916, surface water, including rainwater and "tidal overflow water" from a bordering canal and creek, flowed southeasterly across the dominant estate and into the servient estate. *Id.* at 340. In 1916, a canal was constructed on the servient estate, and until 1965 the surface water flowed into and down that canal. *Id.* at 341. In 1965, however, the owners of the servient estate constructed a levee that obstructed that flow of water through the canal. *Id.* The Louisiana Supreme Court determined that the servitude of drain at issue was "in part a natural servitude of drain, and in part a 'conventional' servitude of drain acquired by acquisitive prescription." *Id.* at 342. The Supreme Court explained that a conventional servitude of drain is the right of passing water collected in pipes or canals through the estate of one's neighbor, *Id.* (citing La. Civ. Code art. 714), and held that the servient estate was required to remove the levee so that the surface water from the dominant estate could, once again, flow into and through the canal. *Id.* at 344. In so holding, the Supreme Court expressly did not determine "[t]o what extent the servitude of drain from the [dominant estate] onto the [servient] estate at the bridge site is a natural servitude of drain under Article 660 . . ." *Id.* at 343–344.

Plaintiff contends that Poole establishes that a servitude may exist on tidal lands because, in that case, the drainage over the dominant estate included "tidal overflow" from a canal to the south and a natural creek to the west of the property. However, Poole does not assist the Court in determining whether a natural servitude of drain may exist with respect to "the violent wave action and storm surge that tropical storms and hurricanes transmit from the Gulf of Mexico." Moreover, as stated above, the Supreme Court did not address or analyze the extent to which the servitude at issue was a natural servitude of drain. In fact, it appears that the holding in Poole is directed at reinstating the right of passing water collected in a canal through the neighboring servient estate, i.e. a conventional servitude of drain. The Court notes, additionally, that Poole involved a dispute between contiguous estates, whereas here, the alleged dominant and servient estates are not adjacent.

Plaintiff cites no case law, nor can the Court locate any, where the Louisiana Supreme Court has found a natural servitude of drain under similar facts as the instant case. Plaintiff essentially urges this Court to expand Louisiana law by finding that a natural servitude of drain may exist between non-adjacent estates with respect to coastal storm surge. However, neither the codal articles nor the case law supports such a finding. If Articles 655 and 656 are to be expanded to include the circumstances presented in the instant case, such an undertaking must come from the legislature as the primary source of Louisiana law or from the Louisiana Supreme Court as a secondary source of law, not from a federal district court. *See Jefferson v. Lead Indus. Ass'n, Inc.*, 106 F.3d 1245, 1248 (5th Cir.1997) Having found no guidance from the civil code or the case law in support of Plaintiff's position, the Court is compelled to conclude that Plaintiff has not and cannot state a viable claim for natural servitude of drain.

Id. at 639–641.

The United States Fifth Circuit Court of Appeal affirmed. *Board of Commissioners of Southeast Louisiana Flood Protection Authority — East v. Tennessee Gas Pipeline Co.*, 850 F.3d 714 (5th Cir. 2017), *cert. denied*, 138 S.Ct. 420 (2017), in pertinent part:

> The explanation of the natural servitude claim contained in the complaint does little more than recite the legal requirements of such a claim. It does not name or describe the location of any of the relevant properties, and it does not explain the properties' relation to each other, other than by way of reciting the circumstances of any natural servitude claim. It does not specify which properties constitute the servient and dominant estates, and it therefore cannot allege that any particular property receives naturally flowing surface waters from any other. The Board says that Exhibits B through G to its claim exhibit a "wealth of specificity" on these questions, but the exhibits merely comprise a map indicating the location of the levee districts of the Southeast Louisiana Flood Protection Authority; the names and serial numbers of wells operated by Defendants; descriptions of the locations of wells subject to Defendants' dredging permits; and descriptions of the locations subject to Defendants' right-of-way permits. Because the Board does not argue that every single one of the hundreds of listed locations constitutes a dominant estate, it must intend only to allege that some of those locations are dominant estates. However, it has not made such an allegation. Another possibility is that its argument is that Defendants' actions have altered the flow of water into certain bodies of water, which in turn poses a storm surge risk to the lands the Board oversees. But this would hardly constitute "[a]n estate situated below . . . receiv[ing] the *surface waters* that flow naturally from an estate situated above," La. Civ. Code art. 655, and thus the district court properly dismissed the servitude of drain claim.

Id. at 730.

Not content to leave any rock unturned, the Louisiana legislature amended Articles 655 and 656 of the Louisiana Civil Code in 2017 to emphasize that in the context of a natural servitude of a drain the servient estate is the "estate situated below" and the dominant estate is the "estate situated above." La. Acts 2017, No. 105, § 1, eff. June 12, 2017. Would these amendments bar litigation similar to the lawsuit brought by the Board of Commissioners of the Southeast Flood Protection Authority-East if the two relevant estates were adjacent to or in much closer proximity to one another? Assume that the plaintiff in such a case could identify with specificity a particular estate near the open coast that had been degraded by the dredging of canals and that was subject to rapid inundation by "violent wave action and storm surge" caused by hurricanes and tropical storms. *See Board of Commissioners*, 88 F.Supp.3d at 640, n. 213.

C. Legal Servitudes

1. Limitations on Ownership

Immediately following the short chapter of the Civil Code addressing natural servitudes appears a much longer chapter: the law governing legal servitudes. The first section of this chapter, comprising Articles 659 to 672 of the Civil Code, bears the title "Limitations of Ownership." The linkage between the category of legal servitudes and mandatory limitations imposed on the rights of owners of immovable property is central to this part of Louisiana property law. Article 659 of the Civil Code provides a more precise definition of legal servitudes than the thumbnail reference in Article 654. Consider the text:

Art. 659. Legal servitude

Legal servitudes are limitations on ownership established by law for the benefit of the general public or for the benefit of particular persons.

La. Civ. Code art. 659 (1977). At first blush, this definition suggests that legal servitudes might not fit easily into the broader category of predial servitudes, especially as the definition implies that legal servitudes do not necessarily benefit a particular dominant estate. In truth, in some important examples of legal servitudes, there is no dominant estate. However, in other instances, the presence of a servient estate and a particular dominant estate, or at least several dominant estates, is apparent. Out of deference to German inspired ideas about servitudes, this new definition of legal servitudes emphasizes the functional purpose of legal servitudes: they limit the rights of owners of estates in order to provide benefits to the public at large or to certain members of the public, including, most importantly, neighboring property owners.

Articles 660 through 662 of the Civil Code establish legal servitudes that function as public safety regulations imposed on owners of buildings and walls. These servitudes protect neighboring property owners and people passing by from suffering injury as a result of disrepair of the buildings or walls. *See* La. Civ. Code arts. 660–662 (1977). Today these provisions are overshadowed by the law of delictual obligations and by municipal regulations. Indeed, in 1996, the legislature modified Article 660 to incorporate modern tort law principles of monetary liability tied to an owner's failure to exercise reasonable care with regard to his building when he has notice of its condition. *See* La. Civ. Code art. 660 (1977, amended 1996).

Articles 663 and 664 of the Civil Code are admonitory provisions that oblige a landowner not to build projections beyond the boundary of his estate and to keep his roof in repair so that rainwater does not fall onto a neighbor's ground. La. Civ. Code arts. 663–664 (1977). Although one can easily imagine the utility of these articles in the close confines of the Vieux Carré and older neighborhoods of New Orleans and other Louisiana cities in the nineteenth or early twentieth century, they have seldom been the cause of controversy or litigation.

2. The Levee Servitude

Article 665 of the Civil Code, commonly referred to as "the Levee Servitude," has been the subject of extensive litigation over the last one hundred years. It has recently been amended by the Legislature. The text of the article, however, is not particularly helpful in explaining the function of this servitude:

Art. 665. Legal Public Servitudes

Servitudes imposed for the public or common utility, relate to the space which is to be left for the public use by the adjacent proprietors on the shores of navigable rivers, and for the making and repairing of levees, roads and other public or common works. Such servitudes also exist on property necessary for the building of levees and other water control structures on the alignment approved by the U.S. Army Corps of Engineers as provided by law, including the repairing of hurricane protection levees.

All that relates to this kind of servitude is determined by laws or particular regulations.

La. Civ. Code art. 665 (1870, amended La. Acts 2006, No. 776). *South Lafourche Levee District v. Jarreau*, 217 So.3d 298, 308–11 (La. 2017).

One traditionally important consequence of the levee servitude, especially when read in light of a number of other constitutional and statutory provisions, concerns compensation to landowners when property is taken for purposes of levee construction and repair. Although both the United States and Louisiana constitutions require the payment of "just compensation" when property is taken for a public use or public purpose, riparian land in Louisiana has always been treated differently. From the establishment of the state in 1812 until 1898, the state and levee districts could use or destroy any riparian land for levee construction and repair without having to pay the landowner any compensation. John A. Lovett, *Comment: Batture, Ordinary High Water and the Louisiana Levee Servitude*, 69 Tul. L. Rev. 561, 562 (1994). This exception to the just compensation requirement has been justified with the argument that when riparian land bordering a navigable river or stream was severed from the sovereign in Louisiana and transferred to private owners, the state retained a servitude over that land for levee purposes. Thus, when the Louisiana Constitution began to provide some compensation for land "appropriated" under the levee servitude in limited portions of the state in 1898, this compensation was considered a kind of "gratuity" offered by the state to the effected landowners. La. Const. art. 313 (1898); *Taylor v. Board of Levee Com'rs of Tensas Basin Levee District*, 332 So.2d 495, 497 (La. App. 3d Cir. 1976). The Louisiana Constitution of 1921 extended the right of riparian landowners to receive this gratuitous compensation for appropriation under the levee servitude but batture was expressly excluded from this new compensation requirement. La. Const. art. 16. § 6 (1921). Finally, the Louisiana Constitution of 1974 limited the power of *appropriation* by requiring the state or its levee districts to pay a more generous level of compensation for the use or destruction of all privately owned riparian land, but still allowed uncompensated appropriations for batture. La. Const. art. VI, § 42 (1974):

> Lands and improvements thereon hereafter actually used or destroyed for levees or levee drainage purposes shall be paid for as provided by law. However, *nothing contained in this Paragraph with respect to compensation for lands and improvements shall apply to batture* or property the control of which is vested in the state or any political subdivision for the purpose of commerce.

Id. (emphasis added). *See also* La. Const. art. 1 § 4(E) (1974) ("This section shall not apply to *appropriation* of property necessary for levee and levee drainage purposes.) (emphasis added); La. Rev. Stat. § 38:281(1) (1985) ("Batture shall have the same meaning as that term was defined in the courts of this state as of the effective date of the Constitution of Louisiana.").

Consequently, both the Louisiana Supreme Court and the United States Supreme Court have recognized that neither the state nor a levee district is required to pay a private landowner any compensation for levee construction and repair, if the land taken or used pursuant to the historical levee servitude is defined as "batture" — the land between the ordinary low and ordinary high water mark of navigable rivers. *Eldridge v. Trezevant*, 160 U.S. 452, 468 (1896); *Dickson v. Board of Comm'rs*, 26 So.2d 474. 477–480 (La. 1946); *General Box Co. v. United States*, 351 U.S. 159, 166–67 (1956). Crucially, however, when a portion of a riparian tract is used or damaged for levee purposes and that land is *not* batture, which means that it lies landward of the ordinary high water mark, or when the land taken was never part of riparian tract at all, the landowner is entitled to just compensation for the appropriation. Lovett, 69 Tul. L. Rev. at 575–580 (discussing decisions reigning in the geographic scope of the levee servitude).

In *DeSamborg v. Bd. of Comm'rs for the Grand Prairie Levee District*, 621 So.2d 602 (La. 1993), *cert denied*, 510 U.S. 1093 (1994), a levee district used part of a riparian tract of land along the Mississippi River to acquire material to improve a levee but asserted that it was not required to compensate the landowners under the batture exception to the Louisiana Constitution. The Louisiana Supreme Court agreed, defining batture as "alluvial accretions annually covered by ordinary high water, the highest stage the river can be expected to reach annually in seasons of high water." *Id.* at 604. This definition allowed the defendant levee district to introduce statistical evidence of water level heights on the Mississippi River, rather than rely exclusively on evidence relating to physical characteristics of the land (like soil quality and vegetation) for purposes of determining the ordinary high water line. *Id.* at 611–12. The admissibility of this statistical averaging evidence in turn permitted the defendant levee district to prove that the ordinary high water line on the portion of the bank of the Mississippi River in dispute was eleven feet, rather than eight feet, above sea level. This increased the physical extent of riparian tract defined as batture, which the levee district could then use for levee construction and repair without paying compensation to the landowners. *Id.* at 613–14.

2006 Amendments. In 2006, in the wake of Hurricanes Katrina and Rita, the Louisiana legislature amended Article 655 by adding its current second sentence. This new codal language, along with contemporaneous amendments to the Louisiana Constitution, was designed to expand the general power of *appropriation* (the power of a levee district to take ownership of land immediately upon the filing of an act of appropriation by local officials and without the need for filing a judicial proceeding) to land that was not riparian at the time of severance from the sovereign and thus speed up the construction of new hurricane flood control systems. *See* **South Lafourche Levee District v. Jarreau, 217 So.3d 298, 305 (La. 2017)** (explaining the distinction between expropriation and appropriation under Louisiana law); *Taylor,* 332 So.2d at 497 ("A taking for levee purposes is characterized as an appropriation rather an expropriation."). This amendment to the Civil Code does not affect the constitutional "batture" exemption.

In *Jarreau,* the Louisiana Supreme Court specifically interpreted the contemporaneous amendments to Louisiana Constitution, art. VI, §42(A) and Art. I §4(G) enacted pursuant to Act. 853 of 2006. According to the court, these amendments limit compensation to *riparian* property owners whose land is taken, damaged or destroyed for construction, enlargement, improvement or modification of *hurricane protection projects* to the just compensation required by the Fifth Amendment of the U.S. Constitution: the fair market value of the property at the time of the appropriation. *Jarreau,* 217 So.3d at 307, 310–311. Riparian property owners who suffer an *appropriation* are thus no longer entitled to just compensation "to the full extent of loss," including lost profits and severance damages, as they otherwise would be entitled under La. Const. art. 1 §4(B)(5). *Jarreau,* 217 So.3d at 311. In other words, the court held that these amendments had the effect of merely reducing, but not eliminating, the damages owed to a riparian property owner for an appropriation of land for hurricane protection projects. *Id.* at 310–11. The court explained:

> [With these amendments] the legislature intended to preserve, yet restrict, the "gratuitous compensation" allowed for the appropriation of a levee servitude. If the legislature had intended to eliminate all compensation for an appropriation of a permanent levee servitude for a hurricane protection project, then it would have amended La. Const. art. VI, §42 and La. R.S. 38:301 to do so. The fact that it did not suggests that the legislature intended to treat property owners the same, allowing them compensation for the fair market value of their property, whether it was expropriated or appropriated for a hurricane protection project.

Id. at 311.

Is non-riparian land subject to the expanded levee servitude? In *Jarreau*, the Louisiana Supreme Court was not required to confront the issue of whether land that was *not riparian* at the time of severance from the sovereign could be subject to appropriation under the levee servitude because the landowner in that case did not contest the validity of appropriation by filing a petition in the district court. *Jarreau*, 217 So.3d at 307, n. 9. This was significant because several Louisiana judicial decisions rendered prior to the 2006 amendments to Article 665 had explicitly held that the levee servitude is not applicable to tracts that were non-riparian, and not subject to the levee servitude, at the time of severance from the sovereign. *Deltic Farm and Timber Co., Inc. v. Bd. of Com'rs for Fifth Levee District*, 368, So. 2d 1109. 112 (La. 3d Cir. 1989; *Delaune v. Board of Com'rs*, 87 So.2d 749, 752–53 (1956).

In a recently filed lawsuit, ***Plaquemines Dir & Clay Co., L.L.C. v. Plaquemines Parish Govt.***, No. 640082, Div. A., 25th Judicial District Court, the owner of a 600 acre tract of land that was allegedly non-riparian at the time of severance and continued to be non-riparian, has contested the right of a levee district to *appropriate* a significant portion of its property for the purpose of constructing a federal hurricane protection levee under the newly expanded version of Article 665. The landowner argues that if the levee district wants to acquire its property for purposes of constructing a hurricane protection levee, it must do so using its powers of *expropriation*, not appropriation, under La. Rev. Stat. § 38:351. This would require compliance with all the normal procedural and just compensation requirements for expropriation under Louisiana law. A final decision in this lawsuit will reveal the limits of the newly expanded Article 655.

3. Obligations of the Neighborhood (Articles 667–669)

Among the most important provisions under the heading of Limitations of Ownership are Articles 667 through 669 of the Civil Code. They establish the "Obligations of Vicinage" or the "Obligations of the Neighborhood." These provisions regulate what economists often call "spillover effects"—the negative impacts that one landowner's activities can have on a neighboring property owner's enjoyment of her property that usually fall short of an actual physical invasion of property under the law of trespass and that are not regulated by the natural servitude of drain.

Imagine a landowner who builds a factory on a semi-rural tract of land that is surrounded by farms, farm houses and small residential lots. Once constructed and operating, the factory regularly emits smoke and soot that pollutes the air in the neighborhood and leaves a fine residue on the land and structures of the neighboring property owners. The noise and odors emitted from the factory also upset the normal sensibilities of persons who reside nearby. The factory further causes vibrations that damage the structural integrity of nearby buildings. However, due to the microscopic size of the smoke and soot particles and the intangible nature of the smells, sounds and vibrations emitted by the factory, these emissions may not qualify as physical invasions covered by the law of trespass. Putting aside any relevant environmental or local land use regulations that may limit the emissions or activities of the factory, Articles 667 through 669 of the Civil Code can be invoked by the neighboring property owners if they sue either to shut down the factory or to obtain some form of monetary damages for the harm they may have suffered in the past or will suffer in the future as a result of the factory's emissions and activities.

Recall for the moment the foundational definition of ownership provided in Article 477 of the Civil Code:

Article 477. Ownership; content

Ownership is the right that confers on a person direct, immediate and exclusive authority over a thing. The owner of a thing may use, enjoy, and dispose of it *within the limits and under the conditions established by law.*

La. Civ. Code art. 477 (1979) (emphasis added). Perhaps more than any other part of the Civil Code, Articles 667 through 669 establish the most important "limits" and "conditions" with regard to the direct, immediate and exclusive authority of an owner declared in Article 477, at least with respect to immovable property.

Articles 667 through 669 of the Civil Code first appeared in Louisiana law as part of the Digest of 1808. They were modeled on Spanish laws (*Siete Partidas* and *Fuero Real*) and both Spanish and French doctrine (Febrero and Domat). Article 667, in particular, expresses the ancient maxim *sic utere tuo ut alienum non laedas* ("use your property so that you do not damage that of another"). For almost two hundred years, Articles 667 through 669 stood virtually unchanged in the various iterations of the Louisiana Civil Code. In 1996, however, Article 667 was amended as part of a major revision of the law of torts. *See generally* Frank L. Maraist and Thomas C. Galligan, Jr., *Burying Caesar: Civil Justice Reform and Changing Face of Louisiana Tort Law*, 71 Tul. L. Rev. 339 (1996). Prior to its amendment, the provision read as follows:

Art. 667. Limitations on use of property

Although a proprietor may do with his estate whatever he pleases, still he cannot make any work on it, which may deprive his neighbor of the liberty of enjoying his own, or which may be the cause of any damage to him.

La. Civ. Code art. 667 (1870). Act No. 1 of the First Extraordinary Session of the Louisiana Legislature of 1996 added an entirely new layer of legislative text to Article 667 so that it now declares:

Art. 667. Limitations on use of property

Although a proprietor may do with his estate whatever he pleases, still he cannot make any work on it, which may deprive his neighbor of the liberty of enjoying his own, or which may be the cause of any damage to him. However, if the work he makes on his estate deprives his neighbor of enjoyment or causes damage to him, he is answerable for damages only upon a showing that he knew or, in the exercise of reasonable care, should have known that his works would cause damage, that the damage could have been prevented in the exercise of reasonable care, and that he failed to exercise reasonable care. Nothing in this Article shall preclude the application of the doctrine of res ipsa loquitur in an appropriate case. Nonetheless, the proprietor is answerable for damages without regard to his knowledge or his exercise of reasonable care, if the knowledge is caused by an ultrahazardous activity. An ultrahazardous activity as used in this Article is strictly limited to pile driving or blasting with explosives.

La. Civ. Code art. 667 (as amended 1996). Curiously, Articles 668 and 669 of the Civil Code, the companions to Article 667, were not touched by the 1996 amendment. They still read as follows:

Art. 668. Inconvenience to neighbor

Although one be not at liberty to make any work by which his neighbor's buildings may be damaged, yet every one has the liberty of doing on his own ground whatsoever he pleases, although it should occasion some inconvenience to his neighbor.

Thus, he who is not subject to any servitude originating from a particular agreement in that respect, may raise his house as high as he pleases, although by such elevation he should darken the lights of his neighbor's house, because this act occasions only an inconvenience, but not a real damage.

Art. 669. Regulation of inconvenience

If the works or materials for any manufactory or other operation, cause an inconvenience by those in the same or in neighboring houses, by diffusing smoke or nauseous smell, and there be no servitude established by which they are regulated, their sufferance must be determined by the rules of the police, or the customs of the place.

La. Civ. Code arts. 668–69 (1870). There is no easy way to explain these provisions without considering the judicial decisions which have interpreted and applied them. Study the following decisions, along with the notes and questions. The first two decisions precede the 1996 amendment of Article 667. They allow you to gauge how Louisiana courts used the provisions to resolve conflicts between neighbors prior to the "Civil Justice Reform" movement. The next three decisions demonstrate how these provisions have been interpreted and applied after the 1996 revisions.

The Property Rule and Liability Rule Paradigm: As you review these decisions, pay attention to the form of relief sought by the plaintiffs. Is the plaintiff seeking an injunction to bar the defendant from engaging in the activity allegedly interfering with that person's enjoyment of the property? If so and if a court grants the plaintiff an injunction, a defendant will face one of several options: First, the defendant could simply stop engaging in the harmful activity altogether. Second, the defendant could make changes in the way he carries out the activity so as to eliminate the harmful effects of his activity. This remedial option is often called *abatement*. Third, the defendant could purchase the plaintiff's property to eliminate the basis for any further complaint. Finally, the defendant could acquire a servitude over the plaintiff's property permitting the defendant to continue the activity that causes the plaintiff harm and requiring the plaintiff and future owners of the plaintiff's property to tolerate the harmful effects of the defendant's activities. *See* La. Civ. Code art. 729 (1977) ("Legal and natural servitudes may be altered by agreement of the parties if the public interest is not affected adversely.").

An injunction is the default remedy most commonly used to protect one property owner's interests in being free from unlawful interferences with his property. Because injunctive relief protects the plaintiff's entitlement to use his property free from any interference unconditionally and gives the property owner the ability to set the price for any relinquishment of the right to enjoy his property free from interference, this type of injunctive relief has been called a "**property rule remedy**" in the context of nuisance litigation. The property owner is protected absolutely from unlawful interferences, and the defendant who is liable must either the invasive activity or pay the property owner a price set by private bargaining to eliminate the basis for liability.

The other form of relief typically sought in these situations is monetary damages. The plaintiff property owner will often seek monetary compensation for the harm and loss of enjoyment he has suffered in the past as a result of the defendant's activities or will suffer in the future if the defendant's activities are allowed to continue. This form of relief resembles what a plaintiff seeks when he has been injured by the *tortious* conduct of a defendant. If it is too late or too impractical to obtain an injunction to prevent the defendant from engaging in the harmful conduct, the plaintiff will seek compensatory damages for past and future harm. This form of relief is often called "**a liability rule remedy**," especially when it is awarded in lieu of injunctive relief *and the offending defendant is permitted to continue carrying on the activity that interferes with the plaintiff's enjoyment of his property*. In many cases, plaintiffs will seek to obtain both injunctive relief and compensatory damages — both a property rule and liability rule remedy.

Note, however, that, in certain cases, a plaintiff will only seek, or a court will only consider awarding, monetary relief for the past and future harm the plaintiff has suffered or will suffer as a result of the defendant's use of her property. In these situations, courts must decide whether, in effect, to set a *judicially determined* price for the defendant to be allowed to continue in the harmful use of her property. If a court awards this form of relief, the defendant in effect pays the plaintiff for a servitude allowing the defendant to engage in an activity that would otherwise be prohibited by the law governing the obligations of neighborhood. Whether courts should rely on this kind of *liability rule* remedy, particularly when it is prospective in nature, as opposed to a traditional *property rule* remedy in the form of an injunction, has been a highly controversial subject for decades in the United States.

The academic debate over the propriety of property rule and liability rule remedies dates back to a seminal decision handed down by the New York Court of Appeals and one of the most influential law review articles about property law in the last five decades. The decision was *Boomer v. Atlantic Cement Co.*, 257 N.E.2d 879 (N.Y. 1970), in which the New York Court of Appeals held that the owner of a cement factory could continue operations, despite its undisputed harmful effects on its neighbors, provided that the factory owner agreed to pay permanent damages to the neighbors in compensation for the long-term diminution in the value of their property). The article was *Guido Calabresi & Douglas Melamed, Property Rules, Liability Rules and Inalienability: One View of the Cathedral, 85 HARV. L. REV. 1089 (1972).*

The academic literature expounding the virtues of either a property rule or liability rule paradigm in many different property law conflicts is immense. For a brief overview, see John A. Lovett, *A Bend in the Road, Easement Relocation and Pliability in the New Restatement (Third) of Property: Servitudes*, 38 CONN. L. REV. 1, 9–16 (2005). For more scholarly commentary on the property rule versus liability rule debate, see Carol M. Rose, *The Shadow of the Cathedral*, 106 YALE L. J. 2175 (1997); James E. Krier and Stewart J. Schwab, *Property Rules and Liability Rules: The Cathedral in Another Light*, 70 N.Y.U. L. REV. 440 (1995); Henry E. Smith, *Property and Property Rules*, 79 N.Y.U. L. REV. 1719 (2004); Stewart E. Sterk, *Property Rules, Liability Rules and Uncertainty about Property Rights*, 106 MICH. L. REV. 1285 (2008).

When you study the decisions below, consider how the nature of the relief sought by the plaintiff in each case affects the elements that the plaintiff is required to prove in a claim arising under Articles 667 through 669 of the Civil Code. Also carefully consider whether the 1996 amendments to Article 667 changed the required elements necessary to obtain injunctive relief or monetary damages under the Obligations of Neighborhood. Which form of relief is now the easiest to obtain?

Finally, as you read the following decisions, pay attention to the court's tendency to employ common law conceptions and terminology in framing the issues. You will see that the judges use terms like "nuisance per se" and "nuisance in fact." Why are Louisiana jurists borrowing with such frequency from the common law in this area of property law? Is this appropriate or not?

Higgins Oil and Fuel Co. v. Guaranty Oil Co.

82 So. 206 (La. 1919)

PROVOSTY, Justice. The plaintiff holds an oil lease of a tract of land adjoining another tract of which the defendant holds a lease of the same kind. The plaintiff sunk a well on its tract, and was drawing oil from it by means of a pump at the rate of some 124 barrels a day, when defendant sunk a well on its tract approximately 400 feet from plaintiff's well. This well of defendant proved a nonproducer, and was abandoned. Through some underground communication it lets air into the radius affected by plaintiff's pump, thereby reducing the suction power of the pump, and as a consequence reducing markedly its production. By closing this dry well, which may be done with no trouble or expense by simply putting back the plug that has been taken out, the capacity of plaintiff's pump is at once restored. Defendant refuses to close it; and plaintiff brings this suit to compel defendant to do so, and also to recover the damages suffered up to now, and continuingly being suffered, as the result of the reduced production of the pump. The petition of plaintiff alleges these facts, and that, while plaintiff's pump is thus being prevented from working to its full capacity, the pumps which are being used by other parties on all the adjoining tracts of land are depleting the reservoir of oil which lies under the lands of that locality. And the petitioner further alleges as follows:

'That by permitting the said abandoned well to remain open does not in any way profit or aid the said Guaranty Oil Company, its lessee, the Nash Oil & Gas Company, in getting production from the producing well, Guaranty No. 2, and that the only effect of having the said well open is to injure petitioner without bringing about any advantage whatever to the said Guaranty Oil Company or the Nash Oil & Gas Company.'

Plaintiff does not allege that the underlying oil cannot be brought to the surface otherwise than by pumping, but that allegation is impliedly contained in the allegation which is made that every operator in that oil field is using a pump.

An exception of no cause of action was sustained below, and plaintiff has appealed.

The articles of our Code bearing upon the matter are the following:

'Art. 491. Perfect ownership gives the right to use, to enjoy and to dispose of one's property in the most unlimited manner, provided it is not used in any way prohibited by laws or ordinances.'

'Art. 505. The ownership of the soil carries with it the ownership of all that is directly above and under it.

'The owner may make upon it all the plantations, and erect all the buildings which he thinks proper, under the exceptions established in the title: Of Servitudes.

'He may construct below the soil all manner of works, digging as deep as he deems convenient, and draw from them all the benefits which may accrue, under the modifications as may result from the laws and regulations concerning mines and the laws and regulations of the police.'

'Art. 666. The law imposes upon the proprietors various obligations towards one another, independent of all agreements; and those are the obligations which are prescribed in the following articles.

'Art. 667. Although a proprietor may do with his estate whatever he please, still he cannot make any work on it, which may deprive his neighbor of the liberty of enjoying his own, or which may be the cause of any damage to him.

'Art. 668. Although one be not at liberty to make any work by which his neighbor's buildings may be damaged, yet every one has the liberty of doing on his own ground whatsoever he pleases, although it should occasion some inconvenience to his neighbor.'. . . .

The provision of article 667, that the owner may not make any work on his property 'which may be the cause of any damage to' his neighbor is found under the title 'Of Servitudes,' and hence apparently is one of the exceptions to which article 505 refers, and hence would seem to be a limitation upon article 505.

It is also apparently in direct conflict with the provision of article 491 that 'ownership gives the right to enjoy and dispose of one's property in the most unlimited manner.' The line of demarcation between what an owner may do with impunity and what he may not do without incurring liability is drawn by article 668 between what is a mere inconvenience and what causes a real damage. But that cannot be the meaning; for very evidently an owner cannot be debarred from the legitimate use of his property simply because it may cause a real damage to his neighbor. It would be contrary to the fundamental legal principle according to which the exercise of a right cannot constitute a fault or wrong, and, besides, every damage is real; and unreal damage cannot be a damage.

We cannot reconcile these contradictions, or gather the true meaning or scope of these articles, from the articles themselves, but, for ascertaining this true meaning, must resort to the works of Pothier and Toullier, whence these articles were derived by the framers of our Code.

Pothier, in his second appendix to his work on Partnership (Paris Ed. 1835) vol. 3, says:

At page 549:

'Neighborhood is a quasi contract which creates reciprocal obligations between the neighbors; that is to say, between the owners or possessors of contiguous estates.'

And at page 556:

'The laws of good neighborhood forbid me to cause anything to pass from my estate to that of my neighbor which may damage him; but they do not prevent me from depriving him of some convenience which he derives from my estate. For instance, if he derives light from my estate, I may, by raising a building on my estate, deprive him of this light.'

. . . .

Toullier, des Biens, Vol. 3, p. 207, No. 327, says:

'Independently of these special cases the law forbids, in general terms, all such use of one's property as may cause a real damage to the public or to individuals; and by damage we are to understand whatever loss or diminution we suffer in our property by the fault or the act of another.

'328. But the damage must be real. A simple inconvenience, or even the prejudice which might be caused to the neighbor by legitimate acts of ownership such as I have the right to exercise on my property, would not be a sufficient motive to cramp my liberty in the exercise of these rights, and to furnish ground of complaint to the neighbor, provided these acts are not dictated by a desire to injure the neighbor, without any usefulness to myself.

'Now, the desire to injure is not to be presumed in the person who does but use a right he has.

'For example, if in digging a well for my own utility I cut off the spring which was feeding the well of my neighbor, he has no right to complain.'

. . . . The Code Napoleon not containing a provision corresponding with the said proviso of article 668, Demolombe, basing himself upon the definition of ownership as giving the right to use, enjoy, and dispose of one's property in the most unlimited manner, and upon the principle that one who but exercises a right he has cannot be at fault, concludes that, even though what is done is simply for the purpose of injuring the neighbor, with no benefit to the owner, the neighbor has no right to complain; but the author adds that the contrary doctrine 'which is very ancient,' is generally admitted. Des Servitudes, Nos. 66 and 648.

Laurent, De La Propriete, vol. 6, [No. 140] says:

'It is then a settled principle that a person who uses his own right without infringing the right of another owes no reparation for the damage he may cause. But the application of that principle gives rise to more than one difficulty. If the owner who uses his right does it through malice, from a desire to injure, without any profit to himself, will he be held bound to repair the damage he causes, although he does not infringe any right? There is an ancient maxim inscribed in the Roman laws which says that we must not favor the perversity of men. Now, would it not be to encourage this perversity if a right were allowed to be used for the sole purpose of injuring another. Perhaps another maxim, equally inscribed in the Roman laws, will be invoked, according to which what one does in the exercise of one's own right cannot injure one, in this sense that the person acting is not held to repair the injury. But can it well be said that to exercise one's right for the sole purpose of causing injury is the exercise of one's right? Why are rights sanctioned by law? Because they are faculties which are necessary to enable us to fulfill our mission on this earth. Is it our mission, forsooth, to do evil for the mere pleasure of doing evil? And does the legislator owe protection to him who employs for doing evil a right which has been accorded to him as an instrument for intellectual and moral development? Conscience answers with the Roman jurisconsults: 'Malitiis hominum non est indulgendum.'

'And that has been the view taken by the courts. An owner constructs a building which cuts off his neighbor's light. In so doing he but exercises a right he has, and therefore owes no reparation of the damage he causes to the neighbor. But he does more; he erects in front and almost against the window of his neighbor, part of which is already masqued by the new building, a dummy chimney, beginning on the roof, resting on the rafters, at the extreme corner of the gable end of the building, and which cuts off all the light from the window. The court of Colmar ordered the suppression of the dummy chimney. It acknowledges that the owner can, in strictness, abuse of his property, but on one condition, that he does not do it for the purpose of injury. Rights are serious things and must be used seriously. Beyond that serious use there is no right but only wickedness, and justice cannot sanction an act prompted by malevolence.

'An owner constructing works on his land diminishes the volume of a spring the benefit of which his neighbor has been having. He is within his right. If he thereby causes an injury to his neighbor, the latter cannot complain; for he has not the absolute ownership of the waters. But, if it has been by malice that the works have been undertaken, for the sole purpose of injuring the neighbor, we have no longer the exercise of a right, but spitefulness, and he who abuses malignantly of his right ought to repair the damage he causes. This was the decision of the court of Lyons in the following case: A mineral spring spreads over several tracts. One of the owners sets up a pump for getting a larger quantity of the water, not for using it, but for pouring it, in pure waste, and, we will add, through spite, into a river. The court condemned him in damages, but without ordering the suppression of the pump. We think that in the latter connection the court was too conservative. From the moment that an act can be characterized as illicit the owner can no longer invoke any right of ownership; now an unlawful act should disappear.'

The treatment of the same matter by Baudry-Lacantinerie and Chauveau, des Biens, p. 159, No. 215 et seq., is as follows:

. . . The question of determining the point where an act begins or ceases to be injurious to the right of the neighbor is, no doubt, a very delicate one; it will be of absolute necessity to have recourse to an analysis, minute in its details, of the faculties, of the attributes, of the advantages which compose the right of ownership, to know if one of them is infringed upon, and thus to diagnose the injury to the neighbor's right. . . .

'222. On the contrary, in the extensive sense of the formula, an action in damages lies even though the owner be within the limits of his rights if he acts through malice, for the sole purpose of causing an injury to another, or even if, acting without any evil intention, he acts with great imprudence, and thereby causes injury to his neighbor. . . . Thus, an owner could not raise opposite the window of his neighbor a dummy chimney for no other purpose than to obstruct the opening and to deprive the neighbor of the little light which was left him by the new construction. In like manner an owner could not wickedly cut the source of a spring which comes out on his neighbor's property, not for the purpose of himself using the waters of the spring, but to pour them out in pure waste into a river. However, the mere inaction of an owner could not serve as a basis for a demand in indemnification, although the prejudice should result from this inaction. Thus an easy-going neighbor neglects to defend his property against the action of waters. The land is carried away little by little, and this brings on the collapse of the neighboring houses. This fact does not make the owner responsible, and he cannot be compelled to do anything to prevent the ruin of the houses. . . .

On the point of an owner not being allowed through pure spite or wantonness to do something on his property injurious to his neighbor, we find but one dissenting voice among the French law-writers and decisions. It is Demolombe, who, in his work on Servitudes (volume 12 of the Paris Ed. of 1859, at pages 139 and 140), says:

'No. 647. . . . Digging a well on one's own property, although it may cause the neighbor's well to go dry, is none the less a permitted act; this result is a purely fortuitous event; strictly speaking, it is less an actual damage the neighbor suffers as that he ceases to enjoy an accidental, casual, provisional profit, on which he had no right to depend. . . .

'No. 648. We must add, however, that generally a very important qualification is applied to that principle, which it is contended would be no longer applicable if the owner, in constructing on his land some work the effect of which is to deprive the neighbor of an advantage he has been enjoying, did so for no other purpose than to injure this neighbor with no benefit to himself.

'This modification, indeed, appears to be as ancient as the principle itself, and we invariably find it coupled with the principle in the works of the Roman jurisconsults (L. 1, paragraph 12, f. f. de aqua), and of our ancient authors [citing long list], and in the decisions of the courts [citing decisions].

'This modification, despite its traditional ancientness, appears to us to be inadmissible. . . .

'Legally no account can be required of him of his motives; there is here a bar which precludes the making of any allegation that he has acted from malice.' . . .

From these excerpts it is clear that cases like the present are not to be decided by the application of any broad or inflexible rule, but by a careful weighing of all the circumstances attending them, by diagnosing them, to use the expression of Baudry-Lacantinerie and Chauveau, with the aid and guidance of the two principles, that the owner must not injure seriously any right of his neighbor, and, even in the absence of any right on the part of the neighbor, must not in an unneighborly spirit do that which while of no benefit to himself causes damage to the neighbor.

Defendant does not contest the right of plaintiff to get out of its land all the oil it possibly can, and by means of a well, but contests plaintiff's right to do this by means of a pump, because a pump sucks the oil from under defendant's land. The argument is that plaintiff may appropriate the oil passing from defendant's land to plaintiff's, provided the oil passes, or flows, from the one tract to the other 'naturally,' that is, by gravity, and not as the effect of the use of artificial means.

So far as artificiality is concerned, we do not see the difference between a well and a pump; both are artificial; both cause the oil to flow from the neighbor's land; and both produce that effect by creating a vacuum which the oil from the neighbor's land comes in to fill. In both cases the oil flows from the neighbor's land by gravity. The fact that some of the oil which plaintiff's pump is producing may come from defendant's land can make no difference; for in the case of a flowing well so close to the boundary line that one-half of its product would to a reasonable certainty be known to be coming from the adjoining tract the owner of this tract would hardly, we imagine, claim either the ownership of one-half of the oil or the right to close the well; and the reason would be that an owner of land does not own the fugitive oil beneath it so as to have the right to follow it after it has left his land.

The analogy between the subterranean oil and subterranean or percolating waters is, we believe, near complete, . . . In the civil law the right to drain off by means of a deeper well the subterranean water of the neighbor is well settled, and apparently in the common law too. 20 A. & E. E. of L. 314. Judge Thornton, in his work on Oil and Gas (2d Ed.) p. 49, says that, if pumps could not be used, oil territory would be practically useless, and few wells would ever be drilled. And, of course, what is meant by this is that the neighbor cannot complain even though possibly or probably the oil under his land is being drained off by the pump.

All the operators in the oil field in question, including defendant, are using pumps; what good ground, then, could defendant have for denying plaintiff the right to do that same thing?

Plaintiff's right to operate this pump would appear, therefore, to be clear, and that defendant's well, or air pipe is seriously interfering with the operation of the pump is one of the facts alleged in the petition which for present purposes must be taken for true.

Were defendant leaving this well open for some purpose of utility other than the supposed utility of preventing the drainage of the oil from under defendant's land, a different case might perhaps be presented; but the allegation, which must be taken for true, is that leaving this well open is of no benefit to defendant. It will be noted that this action of defendant in leaving this well open has the effect not merely of preventing plaintiff from drawing the oil under defendant's land, but also from under plaintiff's own land; so that an unquestioned right of plaintiff is being interfered with.

Were this result brought about by the mere inaction of defendant, plaintiff could not complain. An owner is not bound to do anything to save his neighbor from loss. The only restriction upon him is that he abstain from doing anything that may cause a loss. In the present case defendant is not charged with mere inaction, but with the action of having bored this well and thereby opened a vent for the air to penetrate where it causes injury. Had defendant left things in their original condition, plaintiff would not be suffering. Defendant is causing this air to pass from its land to that of plaintiff. True, defendant is now merely passive or inactive; but the agency complained of was set in motion by defendant. Defendant alone is responsible for its beginning and its continuing: its activity is therefore that of defendant.

An owner has the perfect right to put down an oil well; but, when the well proves to be injurious to the neighbor, this brings about a complication—a complication which can be solved only by a consideration of all the attending circumstances . . .

The allegation is that the air is being let into a fissure or conduit through which it passes out of defendant's land into that of plaintiff and unto the radius affected by plaintiff's pump. Now if, knowing of this fissure, and knowing that any air let into it would go to plaintiff's land and paralyze plaintiff's pump, the defendant had sunk the dry well in question for the very purpose of its having that effect, would it not be plain that the defendant was not merely exercising its own right, but deliberately injuring the right of plaintiff. And what difference is there between sinking this dry well intentionally for that purpose and letting it remain open intentionally for that purpose.

In last analysis the case must turn upon whether plaintiff has the right to operate the pump in question, and whether, if plaintiff has that right, defendant may interfere with it with no benefit to itself, but simply to hinder plaintiff.

In the case supposed above of a well so near the boundary line as to be deriving one-half of its product from the adjoining land, we do not suppose there would be any dispute as to the right of the adjoining owner to interpose a partition between the two tracts of land so as to prevent the escape of oil from his land. Unquestionably he could build a wall for preventing the wild animals on his land from escaping; and oil comes much nearer forming part of the realty than the wild animals do. And if an owner may thus protect himself by means of a partition or wall, why not by any other kind of work on his land. So that, if defendant's action were limited to preventing the oil from escaping to plaintiff's land, we should be clear that plaintiff would have no good ground for complaining. But for all that is known, no oil is being drawn out of defendant's land, while to a certainty defendant is directly and seriously interfering with plaintiff's right to operate for oil and is doing so with no benefit to itself.

The judgment appealed from is therefore set aside, the exception of no cause of action is overruled, and the case is remanded for trial.

Notes and Questions

1. Justice Provosty's opinion in *Higgins Oil and Fuel Co v. Guaranty Oil Co.*, 82 So. 206 (La. 1919), is a landmark decision in Louisiana property law. Written almost

three decades before the establishment of the Louisiana State Law Institute and five decades before the appearance of English translations of French civil law treatises and in a period when knowledge of the French language and sources was waning in Louisiana, the opinion reawakened judges and lawyers to the relevance of French doctrine in Louisiana. Moreover, the opinion introduced the notion that a property owner engaging in activities that in normal circumstances would be considered a typical and unproblematic exercise of the right of ownership might, under certain circumstances, be engaged in an "abuse of right." *See generally* A.N. Yiannopoulos, *Civil Liability for Abuse of Right: Something Old, Something New*, 54 La. L. Rev. 1173 (1994). Justice Provosty's willingness to apply the French "abuse of right" doctrine to a dispute between two neighboring real right holders signaled a new departure for Louisiana law. Which of the French doctrinal writers appear to have been most influential on Justice Provosty's ultimate disposition of the case? Which of the cases decided by French courts seemed to him most directly relevant to the dispute between the two oil companies in *Higgins*?

2. At approximately the same time Justice Provosty brought the Abuse of Right theory to Louisiana jurisprudence, Louis Josserand, a Professor of Civil Law at the University of Lyon, popularized the same theory in France. Here is Josserand's statement of the central theme:

18. — *The case of Abuse of Property Rights* — Our jurisprudence constantly proclaims that property rights are capable of abuse and notably that the right holder's liability is triggered by his malicious use of it at the expense of a third party.

Our jurisprudence sets out this principle in a very general form for property imagined as a whole, in its universality; but it must be observed that decisions have invariably come about regarding one attribute of this right or another; it is not property as a whole with its powerful synthetic value that was diverted from its purpose, but only one of its countless linked prerogatives, in such a way that the abuse appears in a fragmented and specialized form.

LOUIS JOSSERAND, ON THE SPIRIT OF RIGHTS AND THEIR RELATIVITY (2d ed. 1939) (transl. David Lametti & Abby Shepard).

The doctrine of Abuse of Rights, under which a court may impose civil liability in the wake of antisocial or malicious exercise of otherwise legitimate rights, has been partially crystalized in Louisiana's *jurisprudence constante*. *See, e.g., Trushinger v. Pak*, 513 So.2d 1151, 1154 (La. 1987) (stating that to establish a claim for abuse of rights, a litigant must prove: (1) the exercise of a right with the predominant motive to cause harm; (2) the absence of a serious or legitimate motive for exercising the right; (3) the use of the right in violation of moral rules, good faith, or elementary fairness; or (4) the exercise of the right for a purpose other than in the original grant).

3. In *Higgins*, Justice Provosty asserts that Articles 667 through 669 of the Civil Code were derived by the drafters of the Digest of 1808 from the works of Pothier

and Toullier. Actually, the primary French source for these provisions is Jean Domat, *Les lois civiles dans leur order natural*, Book I, tit. XII, Sec. 2, nos. 8–10, 1 Ouvres de Domat 333–34 (ed. Remy 1828). For an English translation of Domat's doctrinal work in this area of the law, see DOMAT, THE CIVIL LAW IN ITS NATURAL ORDER, Vol. I, at 441–42 (William Strahan transl. 1853).

4. In *Higgins*, Justice Provosty also drew on American common law sources, particularly decisions involving neighboring landowners in conflict with one another over common pools of oil and gas beneath their lands. If the well sunk by the defendant, Guaranty Oil Co., had been producing paying quantities of oil or gas, would Justice Provosty have resolved the case any differently? What other solutions would be appropriate if the plaintiff, Higgins Oil and Fuel Company, had *not* been entitled to injunctive relief?

5. Justice Provosty's decision in *Higgins* has in turn influenced the development of mineral law in Louisiana. The revision comments to two important articles of the Louisiana Mineral Code cite *Higgins* and expound on its meaning. *See* La. Rev. Stat. § 31:8 cmt. (1974), and La. Rev. Stat. § 31:10 cmt. (1974). The second of these provisions, Article 10 of the Mineral Code, restates the basic principle of Article 667 of the Civil Cod in the context of minerals:

> A person with rights in a common reservoir or deposit of minerals may not may make works, operate, or otherwise use his rights so as to deprive another intentionally or negligently of the liberty of enjoying his rights, or that may intentionally or negligently cause damage to him. This Article and Article 9 shall not affect the right of a landowner to extract liquid or gaseous minerals in accordance with the principles of Article 8.

La. Rev. Stat. § 31:10 (1974). The comment to this article emphasizes that "[t]he applicability of the principle of Article 667 of the Civil Code to mineral matters in Louisiana is sustained in the case of *Higgins Oil & Fuel Co. v. Guaranty Oil. . . ."* *Id.*, cmt.

In a recent decision, a Louisiana court relied upon both Article 667 of the Civil Code and Article 10 of the Mineral Code to uphold a finding of civil liability against a chemical manufacturing company whose operations allegedly caused the contamination of an underground aquifer and thus damaged property owners who drew their water supply from the aquifer. *Thomas v. Wilbert & Sons, L.L.C.*, 217 So.3d 368, 388 (La. App. 1 Cir. 2017). The court concluded:

> Dow's negligence in contaminating the aquifer amount to violations of the duties set out by Civil Code Article 667 and the Mineral Code's article 10, which in turn constitute fault within the meaning of Article 2315 [of the Civil Code].

Id. Why did the court emphasize Dow Chemical's negligence in this case? What makes this holding different from the Louisiana Supreme Court's holding in *Higgins*? Was the court in *Thomas* influenced by the 1996 amendments to Article 667 of the Civil Code?

6. Note that both parties in *Higgins* were not the actual landowners but holders of mineral leases on the two adjacent tracts of land. Did Justice Provosty overlook these facts in applying Article 667 of the Civil Code to the dispute? Or does the court's decision indicate that the term "proprietor" can be read liberally to include not only owners of immovable property but also holders of real rights derived from those owners? We will return to a variation of this question when we encounter *Yokum v. 615 Bourbon Street, LLC*, 977 So.2d 859 (La. 2008).

7. Despite the novelty and erudition of Justice Provosty's opinion in *Higgins*, his particular "abuse of right" theory did not resurface prominently in Louisiana property law until the Louisiana Supreme Court handed down *Hero Lands Co. v. Texaco, Inc.*, 310 So.2d 93 (1975). In that case, the defendant acquired a right of way across a property owner's land and constructed a high pressure pipeline for the transmission of natural gas. The plaintiffs, a group of neighboring landowners, filed suit complaining that the right of way and the pipeline were located along the boundary between the plaintiffs' land and the neighboring servient estate. The plaintiffs sought monetary damages in an amount sufficient to compensate them for the allegedly diminished value of their property resulting, not from any negligence in the construction or operation of the pipeline, but from the defendant's decision to locate the pipeline in such close proximity to its boundary. In a per curiam decision, the Louisiana Supreme Court reversed a trial court decision dismissing the plaintiffs' claim and held that liability for damages in this situation could exist "even though [the defendant's] actions are prudent by usual standards." *Id*. at 97. Citing a decision from just a few years earlier, which involved the placement of a gas storage tank very close to a neighbor's property line and home, the court determined that the defendant's construction of such an inherently hazardous pipeline so close to the plaintiffs' properties could entitle the plaintiffs to damages for the reduced value of their properties. *Id*. at 98 (citing *Hilliard v. Shuff*, 256 So.2d 127 (1972)). Deploying what appeared to be a form of strict liability against a property owner who engages in what might be characterized as a legal, albeit potentially dangerous activity on his property under Article 667 of the Civil Code startled some observers of Louisiana law.

8. The following decision, which predated *Hero Lands* by several years, involved a less dangerous business—the operation of a horse stable. The geographic location of the defendant's stable, a dense urban neighborhood of New Orleans, created a classic situation calling for the application of the law governing the Obligations of Vicinage. Note the range of common law sources examined by Justice Summer's majority opinion for the Louisiana Supreme Court and Justice Barham's resistance to the use of these authorities in his concurring opinion.

Robichaux v. Huppenbauer

245 So.2d 385 (La. 1971)

SUMMERS, Justice. Plaintiffs are two neighboring property owners and two tenants all occupying dwellings near defendant Huppenbauer's horse stable located at 1618 Annette Street in the city of New Orleans. This suit was brought to permanently enjoin defendant from operating the stable or keeping horses on the premises. After trial, judgment was rendered enjoining defendant as prayed for. On appeal to the Fourth Circuit the judgment was affirmed. 231 So.2d 626. On defendant's application we granted certiorari limited to the contention that the Court of Appeal erred "in applying a positive injunction totally prohibiting defendant's operations, instead of limiting them in scope or manner." 256 La. 64, 235 So.2d 94.

Defendant uses the stable in connection with his business of providing horse drawn carriages for hire by tourists in the historic French Quarter or Vieux Carre Section of the city. The stables are about one mile from the French Quarter. These carriages are vestiges of a bygone era adding color and character to a section which is one of the city's outstanding attractions to visitors and tourists. Fifteen men are employed in the business of maintaining the horses at the stables and driving the carriages. The stable has been in operation for many years, even beyond the memory of the participants at the trial.

The lot, where the stable is located and where the horses are kept, has a frontage of 32 feet on Annette Street and runs 90 feet back into the block. All but 15 feet of this front portion is occupied by a dwelling house in which one of defendant's employees resides, the fifteen foot strip being used as a driveway. Behind this front portion the lot widens to 64 feet and extends back an additional 100 feet into the block. The horses are principally stabled, fed, washed and exercised on this 64 by 100 foot section.

For a short time prior to acquiring the stables in July 1968, defendant kept horses there under arrangement with the owner. When he acquired the property in August 1968, however, the Director of the Bureau of Public Health Sanitation, Charles J. Miramon, filed an affidavit charging violations of city ordinances regulating the harboring of rats and the removal of manure. At that time, according to Miramon, the stable did not comply with the standards prescribed by the Bureau, and it was a health menace.

Later, in September and October 1968, while these charges were pending in the Municipal Court, defendant's stable was inspected by James Bryant and Harold Clark, Sanitarians in the Bureau of Public Health, who found the stable free of any condition violative of the city's ordinances or their regulations. On the basis of these inspections, the charges were dismissed.

This suit for injunction was then filed and the case was tried on February 27, 1969, resulting in the injunction. Plaintiffs' petition charges that the use of the premises at 1618 Annette Street as a stable results in the deposit of manure on the lot which is responsible for nauseous odors, flies and insects and creates a stench, all of which infest the neighborhood and permeate the houses nearby.

At the trial, plaintiffs' witnesses, who lived very near the stable, some as close as four feet, testified that from eight to eighteen horses are kept there. Rats and flies, particularly horseflies, breed in the manure and urine deposited by the animals. These pests are prevalent on the lot and swarm onto the adjoining property endangering the health and destroying the peace and tranquility of plaintiffs' homes. Noxious odors remain in the neighborhood. At times the horses drop manure on the street and sidewalk as they move to and from the stable. And when it rains the manure runs from beneath the gate of the horse lot onto the sidewalk and into the gutters in front of the nearby houses. The departure and arrival of the carriages, waste disposal vehicles and the animals cause noises and disturb the plaintiffs' sleep and repose.

Plaintiffs rely upon Article 669 of the Civil Code to support their claim that the nuisance resulting from the stable should be abated. That Article must be read with Articles 666, 667 and 668. Article 666 declares that the law imposes upon the proprietors various obligations towards one another, independent of all agreements. Those obligations are prescribed in subsequent articles of the Code. Article 669, upon which plaintiffs rely, provides:

> If the works or materials for any manufactory or other operation, cause an inconvenience to those in the same or in the neighboring houses, by diffusing smoke or nauseous smell, and there be no servitude established by which they are regulated, their sufferance must be determined by the rules of the police, or the customs of the place.

Regrettably the present version of Article 669 deleted "the other different inconveniences which one neighbor may cause to another" which appeared in the corresponding article of the Code of 1808. If this omitted language had been incorporated in Article 669 we could say that all of the inconveniences complained of in this case are covered by Article 669. As it is, however, only one of the several grounds alleged as a basis for the injunction — nauseous smells — is mentioned in the Article. We would prefer to say that smoke and smell are merely illustrative, but in view of the omission in the present Code of any reference to "other inconveniences" serious doubt must be entertained that smoke and smell are mere illustrations of inconvenience. The implication from the change is that the Article's effect must be confined to smoke and smells. What the Article means, as we understand it, is that no servitude is imposed upon the neighboring properties insofar as smoke or nauseous smells are concerned, those matters being left to the regulation of the police or custom.

Thus, whereas Article 667 and the articles which follow impose reciprocal servitudes or restraints upon neighboring properties respecting the making of works which may damage a neighbor, Article 668 makes it clear that while the liberty to do what one pleases on his own ground does not mean that a neighbor may be damaged, some inconvenience may result to a neighbor from the use of one's property which the law does not reprobate. The Article illustrates by referring to buildings which impair a neighbor's light as being a mere inconvenience a property must expect to suffer from a neighbor's free use of his own.

In substance the Article relied upon only partially applies here — to nauseous smells — and then only to the extent of declaring that, as to this, no servitude is established by the Code on neighboring properties, resort being necessary to police regulation or custom to ascertain the extent to which nauseous smells must be endured. Cf. Planiol, Vol. 1, Nos. 2906, 2908; Aubry et Rau, Property § 194 et seq.

The principle is clearly stated in Aubry et Rau, supra, as follows:

> Although in principle it is not prohibited to cause nuisances to a neighbor by noise, smoke, gases, steam, radiation, tremors, dust or odor, such a damage becomes illegal when the source exceeds certain intensity. Until then no claim is possible for one cannot expect to live in a group without causing some inconvenience to neighbors.

Despite the apparent failure of these articles to deal explicitly with the standards to be followed in operations which may cause inconvenience to neighboring property or the failure of these articles to more comprehensively enumerate the "other inconveniences", they have nevertheless been employed by this Court together with the common-law theory of nuisance to grant relief where a use of property causes inconvenience to a neighbor.

The existence of a remedy under the city's health ordinances, as here, does not deprive the affected neighbor from bringing an action in damages before the Courts. *Pendoley v. Ferreira*, 345 Mass. 309, 187 N.E.2d 142 (1963); Aubrey et Rau § 194 et seq.

Thus the principle is enunciated in the cases that within reasonable limits the individual citizen has to submit to some annoyance and inconvenience from the legal exercise of the rights of others. Courts, therefore, will require strict proof that the activity carried on is of sufficient intensity, annoyance and inconvenience that he who causes it has created a nuisance which must be abated. *State ex rel. Violett v. King*, 46 La. Ann. 78, 14 So. 423 (1894).

Thus noxious smells, rats, flies and noise may constitute an actionable nuisance although produced and carried on by a lawful business, where they result in material injury to neighboring property or interfere with its comfortable use and enjoyment by persons of ordinary sensibilities. *McGee v. Yazoo & M.V.R. Co.*, 206 La. 121, 19 So.2d 21 (1944).

Nuisances by their nature are nuisances per se or at law, and nuisances per accidens or in fact. A nuisance at law or a nuisance per se is an act, occupation, or structure which is a nuisance at all times and under any circumstances, regardless of location or surroundings. Nuisances in fact or per accidens are those which become nuisances by reason of circumstances or surroundings.

In the case of a nuisance per se, the thing becomes a nuisance as a matter of law. Its existence need only be proved in any locality and the right to relief is established by averment and proof of the mere fact. But whether a thing not a nuisance per se is a nuisance per accidens or in fact depends upon its location and surroundings, the manner of its conduct, or other circumstances. In such cases, proof of the act and its consequences is necessary. *Borgnemouth Realty Co. v. Gulf Soap Corporation*, 212 La. 57, 31 So.2d 488 (1947). See also 39 Am.Jur., Nuisances, § 11; 66 C.J.S. Nuisances § 3.

A stable used for horses and other animals is not a nuisance per se. *Simonetti v. Carlton*, 17 Ala. App. 105, 82 So. 553 (1919). Whether any particular stable is or is not a nuisance is essentially a question of fact, in the determination of which, the stable's location, its construction, and the manner in which it is conducted are elements to be considered. *Hill v. Battalion Washington Artillery*, 143 La. 533, 78 So. 844 (1918); *Oehler v. Levy*, 234 Ill. 595, 85 N.E. 271 (1908); *Taulbee v. Miller*, 225 Ky. 516, 9 S.W.2d 296 (1928); *Francisco v. Furry*, 82 Neb. 754, 118 N.W. 1102 (1908).

Hence a stable in close proximity to a residence, in a residential section of the city, and kept in such a condition that it is unsanitary, and from which noxious and offensive vapors, fumes, smells, odors, and stenches arise during a period of twelve months, and enter into and spread and diffuse themselves over the adjoining residential property, is such a nuisance as will sustain an action. Simonett v. Carlton, supra.

The record satisfactorily demonstrates, and it is conceded, that the maintenance of defendant's stable is not prohibited by any law, property restriction or zoning regulation, and it is not a nuisance per se on this account. The record also supports the conclusion that the stable is a nuisance because of the manner in which it is operated. However, we have not been shown that it is impossible to maintain this horse lot and stable in such a manner as to free it from the complaints which the plaintiffs make, therefore we will not abate the business entirely. *Francisco v. Furry*, 82 Neb. 754, 118 N.W. 1102 (1908). Instead we will permit defendant to continue his operations under the following mandates, restrictions and injunctions:

> Spray ground and premises generally and thoroughly with a disinfectant and deodorizer, approved by the local health authorities, at such intervals as may be prescribed by those authorities.

> Dispense rat poison at strategic locations about stables, sheds and bins and renew weekly.

> Feed bins should be covered and so constructed as to deny rodents access to feed.

> Remove all manure and other waste daily.

> Limit the number of horses using the lot and stables to ten.

> Keep the premises properly drained to prevent water from standing there.

For the reasons assigned, this matter is remanded to the trial court where an injunction, mandatory and prohibitive, shall issue against defendant without delay in accordance with the mandates and restrictions enumerated above. The judgment, order and decree so issued shall prescribe compliance therewith by defendant within two weeks, failing in which he shall be subject to punishment for contempt of court, all in accordance with law. The right of plaintiffs to renew their complaints if compliance by defendant proves unavailing to abate the nuisance is reserved. *Tucker v. Vicksburg S. & P. R. Y. Co.*, 125 La. 689, 51 So. 689 (1910); *Hill v. Battalion Washington Artillery*, 143 La. 533, 78 So. 844 (1918).

BARHAM, Justice (concurring). I concur in the result which affords the defendant an opportunity to take corrective measures to abate the severe inconveniences caused the plaintiffs, his neighbors, because of his operation of a stable. However, I am of the opinion that the result should have been reached solely by the application of the civil law, more particularly Civil Code Article 669, without resort to common law authority or terminology. In *Reymond v. State Through Department of Highways*, 255 La. 425, 231 So.2d 375, at footnote 6, it was stated in dictum that Article 669 was the vehicle for defining the limits of the activities of man in use of property as they affect his neighbors. That article provides: "If the works or materials for any manufactory or other operation, cause an inconvenience to those in the same or in the neighboring houses, by diffusing smoke or nauseous smell, and there be no servitude established by which they are regulated, their sufferance must be determined by the rules of the police, or the customs of the place."

It was further stated in Reymond that although this article appears under a title and chapter dealing with servitudes, it does not in fact establish a servitude. That opinion pointed out, as has the majority here, that as originally adopted in our law (Article 17, p. 130, of our Code of 1808), it followed Domat by including, in addition to "smoke" and "nauseous smell", "the other different inconveniences which one neighbor may cause to another". Oeuvres completes de J. Domat, Book 1, Title 12, Section 2, No. 10 (ed. Remy 1835). Article 665 of our 1825 Civil Code and Article 669 of our present Code omit "the other different inconveniences". The majority here has concluded because of this omission that the article must be confined to "smoke" and "nauseous smell", and that we cannot treat these as being merely illustrative of the inconveniences which man need not suffer. After finding the Code article to be so limiting of application, the majority proceeds to resort to the common law to circumvent this very restrictive meaning which it has accorded the codal article.

I reiterate that Article 669 does not establish a servitude, for it does not provide for a dominant and a servient estate, and in fact, contrary to the servitude law, even provides redress for those in the same house and upon the same estate against their neighbors. 1 Pt. 2 Planiol, Treatise on the Civil Law (La. State Law Institute tr. 1959) No. 2906. However, I find the article vital and most functional in expressing the activities of men upon property they own, hold, occupy, or use which become impermissible by causing insupportable inconvenience to neighbors.

The majority's error in holding Article 669 of the Code of 1870 not to be illustrative because of the omission of the pertinent phrase from it and from corresponding Article 665 of the Code of 1825 results from failure to examine the *French* text of Article 665 of the 1825 Code. While the "other different inconveniences" is omitted from the English text of that article, the French text is the same as that of our 1808 Code, and contains the words: "*** et les autre differentes incommodites qu'un voison peut causer a l'autre ***." See 3 Pt. 1 Louisiana Legal Archives: Compiled Edition of the Civil Codes of Louisiana (1940), p. 385. It was stated in *Straus v. City of New Orleans*, 166 La. 1035, 118 So. 125 (1928):

"*** In fact the advantage of having access to both the French and English versions was pointed out in section 3 of chapter 29 of the Act of March 31, 1808, adopting the Digest [of the Civil Laws in Force in the Territory, referred to as the Civil Code of 1808], viz.:

"'That if in any of the dispositions contained in the said digest there should be found any obscurity or ambiguity, fault or OMISSION, both the English and French texts shall be consulted, and shall mutually serve to the interpretation of one and the other.'

"For the same purpose, it was provided in section 2 of the Act of April 12, 1824, p. 172, providing for the adoption and promulgation of the Code of 1825, that the English and the French version of each article should be printed opposite one another" (emphasis mine).

In *Chretien v. Theard*, 2 Mart.(N.S.) 582 (1824), it was said that the two texts of an article should be made to harmonize if possible, and that if one presented a more enlarged meaning or sense than the other, that version should be adopted, for in this way both texts could be given full effect.

We are required to hold that the 1825 Code, like the 1808 Code, included the "other different inconveniences" in the article. We need not inquire why the phrase was omitted from the English text in that Code, although the most obvious reason is that it was an error or oversight in translation. Reasonable men should agree that the 1870 Code, which is in English only, merely incorporated the English text of the 1825 article. The express language of the Legislature used in the Codes of 1808 and 1825 as well as our jurisprudence requires us, then, to find that "smoke" and "smell" as contained in the 1825 article were merely illustrative and that all other insufferable inconveniences were included; and that the 1870 text following the exact language of the English text of 1825 carries with it the same interpretation: That smoke and smell are merely illustrative and that we are required to exercise control over other inconveniences.

Moreover, our jurisprudence has established that our courts do have the power to protect neighbors from all insufferable inconveniences and not merely from those two named in Article 669, and the result reached by the majority holding here is the same. Among the many cases which have considered other inconveniences alleged to be insufferable to neighbors are *Froelicher v. Oswald Ironworks*, 111 La. 705, 35 So. 821 (1903) (noise, smoke, and odor); *Froelicher v. Southern Marine Works*, 118 La. 1077, 43 So. 882 (1907) (noise, steam, odors, vibrations); *Perrin v. Crescent City Stockyard & Slaughterhouse Co.*, 119 La. 83, 43 So. 938 (1907) (noisome gases and vapors); *Tucker v. Vicksburg, S. & P. Ry. Co.*, 125 La. 689, 51 So. 689 (1910) (soot, cinders, coal, and dust; air poisoned by gases; odors and vapors; noises including the screeching, rumbling, and bumping of the turntable); *Orton v. Virginia Carolina Chemical Co.*, 142 La. 790, 77 So. 632 (1918) (pollution of a stream with poisonous acid and the air with poisonous gases); *Dodd v. Glen Rose Gasoline Co.*, 194 La. 1, 193 So. 349 (1939) (flare burning waste gases and spreading heat, noise, sand, and impurities); *McGee v. Yazoo & M. V. R. Co.*, 206 La. 121, 19 So.2d 21 (1944) (smoke, gases, soot, cinders); *Devoke v. Yazoo & M. V. R. Co.*, 211 La. 729, 30 So.2d 816 (1947) (obnoxious smoke including gases, soot, and cinders). There are numerous other decisions from this court and the several Courts of Appeal which have considered many other by-products of men's activities for determining insufferable inconveniences to neighbors. Much of the jurisprudence has cited common law without resort to the Civil Code, a few cases have cited Article 669, and some cases have cited no authority. It is clear that the jurisprudence has constantly and consistently included the "other different inconveniences" even though our present Code article does not contain that phrase.

There is no question, then, that the words "smoke" and "smell" in our present Code article must be interpreted as being illustrative of the "other different inconveniences which one neighbor may cause to another". In accord with the *Chretien* and *Straus* cases, this court should prefer the French text of the 1825 article as more enlarged and inclusive than the English text, and realize that it was the intent of the redactors to carry into the 1825 Code the 1808 article unchanged. An obvious error of omission in the English version of the 1825 article was perpetuated when this version was adopted into our 1870 Code. We should therefore, in the instant case, grant the plaintiffs the relief sought under our Civil Code Article 669 according to "the rules of the police" and "the customs of the place", and need not resort to common law concepts or to the common law terminology of nuisance per se and nuisance per accidens.'

I concur in the result.

TATE, Justice (dissenting). I respectfully dissent.

The trial court, who saw and heard the witness, stated in his reasons for judgment that the "weight of the *believable* testimony" showed that the keeping of ten to sixteen horses in this thickly settled neighborhood created loathesome odor and stench and attracted flies and rodents. The court of appeal affirmed the trial court's issuance of an injunction which prohibited as a nuisance the continued operation of a stable on the premises.

The testimony shows that, even though the defendant complied with the (minimum) standards of the local health authorities, even though he removed manure and other waste (once) daily, even though he sprayed and poisoned, even though he covered his feed bins—in short, even though he met all those (minimum) requirements permitted by our limited injunction—nevertheless the maintaining of ten horses or so on the premises (surrounded by residences, some with people sleeping just four feet from horses) created intolerable stench and attracted rodents and flies which made the neighborhood unbearable.

The testimony of Charles Miramon, Director of the Bureau of Public Health Sanitation of the City of New Orleans, is of great interest. He noted that he himself had inspected the premises and, upon finding the conditions complained of, issued an order for the horses to be removed from the premises. He stated that he also filed affidavits for local criminal processing. "Unfortunately", he said, the prosecutions were dismissed, as (he stated) was usually the case with this local enforcement agency. He stated the stables were a "health menace" and a "rat harbor" and that the enterprise had no permit, as required by law, to maintain horses in those premises in the city.

Director Miramon further testified that it was the function of his office, under the State Sanitary Code, to issue permits for maintaining horses. However, he stated, "we could not issue such permits because we have found from experience that it is a false sense of security because unsanitary conditions usually arise whereby horses are maintained in thickly populated areas, and this was a thickly populated area."

I respectfully dissent from our modifying the injunction. In view of the strong evidence supporting these decrees of the previous courts, we should not disturb their considered judgment that the neighbors should have relief—that, because of the unavoidable intolerable stench, noise, and pest-attracting filth resulting from this stable, its continued operation on this narrow lot in this thickly settled neighborhood should be enjoined.

Notes and Questions

1. Note the disagreement among the justices about the proper interpretation of Article 669 of the Civil Code in *Robichaux v. Huppenbauer*, 245 So.2d 385 (La. 1971). Should this provision apply to the emissions other than the smells? Who has the better argument about the scope of Article 669? Justice Summers or Justice Barham? Is Article 669 really dispositive of the dispute? What principles seem to drive the majority opinion in this case?

2. Assuming that the defendant's operation of the horse stable was sanctionable in some manner, which remedy was more appropriate? Justice Summer's temporary injunction that gave the defendants a two week window to improve the conditions at the stables and perhaps re-start operations? Or Justice Tate's preferred remedy to permanently bar the defendant from operating the stable in its current location?

3. Is Justice Barham correct in scolding the majority opinion for its "resort to common law concepts or to common law terminology of nuisance per se and nuisance per accidens"? Could the majority have solved this case without resort to these authorities? Or did such borrowing give the majority some rules of thumb that are useful in disputes of this nature?

4. In the middle of the 1980s, the Louisiana Supreme Court decided another important "nuisance" case under the Obligations of the Neighborhood. *Rodrigue v. Copeland*, **475 So.2d 1071 (La. 1985)**. In this decision, the court enjoined Alvin Copeland, the founder and CEO of Popeye's Famous Fried Chicken, Inc., from erecting and operating an extravagant and noisy Christmas music-and-light display at his suburban New Orleans home because it attracted massive crowds and caused significant annoyance, inconvenience and even safety hazards to his residential neighbors. *Id.* In determining that Copeland's neighbors were entitled to a

mandatory injunction requiring Copeland to remove the most objectionable, over-sized and noisy elements of his Christmas display, the court found that the display caused "real damage" and not just "mere inconvenience" to the neighbors in light of "the character of the neighborhood, the degree of the intrusion and the effect of the activity on the health and safety of the neighbors." *Id.* at 1077. The *Rodrigue* court's formulation of factors relevant to application of Article 667 in the context of an action seeking injunctive relief has proven quite influential.

In the following decision, notice how, even after the 1996 amendments to Article 667 of the Civil Code, Louisiana courts remain attracted to this kind of multi-factor reasonableness test when they must decide whether to issue an injunction barring a defendant property owner from engaging in "troublesome" activities on his or her property.

Parish of East Feliciana v. Guidry

923 So.2d 45 (La. App. 1 Cir. 2005)

McCLENDON, Judge. Defendants appeal a trial court judgment enjoining them from operating a motocross track on their property based on the finding that such activities constitute a nuisance. For the reasons that follow, we affirm.

Factual and Procedural History

In 1997, Jeremy Guidry constructed a motocross track on his property in East Feliciana Parish ("Parish") for recreational use. Approximately one year later, he began to construct a larger track on his property. Mr. Guidry, who was employed by the sheriff's department and owned a trucking company, decided to operate this larger track as a commercial venture under the name, Midway Motocross. It opened for business on November 5 or 6, 1999. Later that month, Mr. Guidry and Midway Motocross were cited by the Parish Police Jury for violating the Parish's nuisance ordinance. In December of 1999, several of Mr. Guidry's neighbors wrote letters to Parish authorities complaining about the noise and dust generated by the motocross operation. Thereafter, the Parish Police Jury adopted a noise ordinance on April 18, 2000.

On May 25, 2000, the Parish filed a "Petition for Preliminary and Permanent Injunction" seeking to enjoin Jeremy and Amber Guidry from operating the Midway Motocross track on their property. It alleged that the dust, noise, and fumes generated by the operation of the track caused "serious and material discomfort to certain inhabitants of East Feliciana Parish and in particular those persons living on and/or owning property in proximity to the Guidry property." The Parish claimed that the Guidrys' motocross activities were a violation of both its nuisance ordinance and its noise ordinance and thus constituted a public nuisance *per se*. Thereafter, on June 21, 2000, various persons owning property surrounding the Guidrys' property filed a "Petition for Intervention" seeking to enjoin the motocross operation, alleging that it was a nuisance pursuant to La. C.C. arts. 667 and 669.

[After the trial court issued a preliminary injunction and other matters were disposed,] [t]he trial on the plaintiff's and intervenors' demand for a permanent injunction as well as the defendants' motion to dissolve the preliminary injunction began on July 24, 2002. . . .

Jeremy Guidry testified that when he first opened the track for business, he operated seven days a week from 9:00 a.m. until dark. Thereafter, he restricted the days of commercial operation to Thursday (12:00 p.m. until dark), Friday, Saturday and Sunday (10:00 a.m. until dark) with only recreational riding taking place on Monday, Tuesday, and Wednesday. The track began conducting races in July 2000. Only one race was held before the preliminary injunction went into effect. Approximately 100 motorcycles were entered in the race with 15 bikes racing per heat. He stated that once racing had begun, he would probably only operate the track every other weekend. He testified that on a non-racing weekend approximately 10 to 12 motorcycles would ride on the track with a fewer number using the track on weekdays. In an effort to reduce the noise generated by the track activity, he planted two rows of pine saplings eight feet apart and offered to construct an eight foot wooden fence. He also installed a sprinkler system to help keep the amount of dust down.

Intervenor, Joe Brown, owns the property next to Jeremy Guidry. He stated that he bought the property because of its rural, tranquil setting. It was his dream that he and his two daughters could each build their homes on the property. The area of his property that would be most suitable for building his home is adjacent to the Guidrys' track. However, he refuses to build his home until he knows that the track will not be allowed to operate. Although he had no problem with the recreational riding that took place on the Guidrys' property, he stated that there was a tremendous difference in the level of activity once the track became commercial. At the time of trial, Mr. Brown used the property for cattle farming and recreational purposes. However, while the track was operating he was unable to enjoy either hunting or fishing and had to limit the amount of time he stayed on the property. He stated that the noise generated by the track was "loud and irritating" and "sheerly aggravating." He described it as "a constant roar, almost like a deliberate aggravation, . . . an up and down constant roar, continuous, one after another." He averred that he was a person of normal health and agreed that the noise caused him emotional aggravation and stress.

Intervenor, Dennis Berthelot, owns the property next to Joe Brown. He testified that the noise on his property was about the same level as the noise on Mr. Brown's property. At the time of the preliminary injunction hearing, he and his wife were living in a trailer on their property. However, he subsequently built a home there prior to trial. He stated that while the track was operating, there was continuous motorcycle riding every day from 7:00 or 7:30 a.m. until dark. He could hear the noise from the track inside his trailer. He stated that the noise from the motorcycles was a "continuous revs of engines that, that go up to over eighty-five decibels down to zero and back up again continuously. . . . It's like a bumblebee in your ear that never goes away." He said that due to the noise he could not sit outside in the afternoons, fish in his pond, or deer hunt. He testified that he had to wear a Walkman or earplugs just to work in his garden. He and his family would leave their home on

Sundays to escape the noise. If the track is permitted to operate, he stated that he would not be able to live in his home. He claimed that the noise from the track was unbearable. Although he is a person of normal health and sensibilities, he maintained that the noise made him stressed and irritable and that he suffered stomach problems due to the stress.

Mr. Berthelot also claimed that he suffered due to the dust generated by the track. He maintained that the air was full of dust, which he did not want to breathe. He claimed that if the wind was blowing in his direction, everything in his yard would become covered with dust.

Mr. Berthelot's wife, Dena, also an intervenor, stated that she could live with the dust, however, she maintained that the noise was a nuisance. She claimed that they moved to the country for peace and quiet, but the noise they experienced from the track was nerve-racking and made her irritable. She claimed that she could hear the noise inside her trailer with the air conditioner and television running on some afternoons. However, she asserted that it was the noise outside that was truly intolerable. She claimed that it was the nature of the noise, not its level, that was frustrating. She said it was like having 50 chainsaws constantly running. She took a video on her property to document the noise, however, she testified that the noise recorded on the video is not nearly as loud as it is in "real life." She claimed that if the track is allowed to operate, even recreationally, she would be unable to live on her property.

The Berthelots' son, Steven, is also an intervenor. . . . When the trial for the permanent injunction was held, he was living in an apartment on the back of his father's home. He testified that the noise from the track was unbearable and that the dust was unbelievable. He maintained that he could hear the noise in his home even with the air conditioner and television running and that it was an aggravation. He claimed that the noise started early in the morning and continued until dusk. On some days, it continued for twelve or fourteen hours. Steven claimed that he could not watch television in his bedroom or barbecue in his backyard due to the noise.

Intervenor, George Remmetter, owns property approximately 1,500 to 2,000 feet away from the Guidrys' property. He testified that he bought his property in 1991 so that he could retire in peace and quiet. He stated that he heard "very, very loud noises" from the track that he described as "miserably, miserably annoying." He claimed that the noise caused him a great deal of stress and made both him and his wife irritable. . . . He claimed that the noise restricted his outdoor activities such as deer hunting. He could not stay on his deer stand any longer than fifteen minutes due to the extreme noise. . . .

Intervenor, Noelle Prescott, and several of her family members own a home on 135 acres near the Guidrys' property. They use it primarily as a retreat and for family gatherings. She described the noise from the track as a "constant buzz," "it will get loud and then it will drop . . . kind of like a dentist drill, it's more than noise, it's just this really persistent constant noise." She said that she can hear the noise inside the house, and that outside, it interferes with conversation. She stated that she and her family quit going to the property altogether because they could not relax outside, take nature walks, or fish in the pond due to the noise from the track.

Reverend Rufus Branch, also an intervenor, owns property approximately 750 feet from the Guidrys' property boundary. He stated that he could hear the noise from the track inside his home. He described the noise from the track as horrible and "very irritating" but stated that he considered the dust it generated a bigger problem. . . .

Steve Verret was accepted by the court as an expert in the field of industrial hygiene, which includes the measurement of sound. On April 2, 2000, he took sound level readings at thirteen locations along Joe Brown's and Dennis Berthelot's property boundaries using a Quest Model 215 Sound Level Meter. His report based on those readings was admitted into evidence. The report explained that the "numbers of operating motorcycles varied during the monitoring period from as few as one to as many as five to seven." Dennis and Steven Berthelot's testimony established that on the day the readings were taken, the activity and noise from the track was less than usual. Mr. Verret's report further stated that the noises were variable in loudness, in some cases reaching beyond the range of the Quest microphone. In those cases, he noted, "the highest noise level may not have been recorded."

Mr. Verret reported that the average readings taken from seven locations along the Berthelots' property boundary ranged from a low of 45 to a high of 58 decibels, while the maximum readings at those locations ranged from a low of 54 to a high of 69 decibels. The average readings taken at six locations along Mr. Brown's boundary ranged from a low of 55 to a high of 66 decibels, while the maximum levels recorded at these locations ranged from a low of 68 to a high of 85 decibels. He testified that the variations in readings were due to the character of the motocross noise, which constantly fluctuates up and down. He further testified that for every increase of 3 decibels, there is a doubling of the sound power level or noise. Therefore, the noise levels doubled more than seven times during the taking of the noise measurements.

At trial, Mr. Verret referred to recommendations published by the Environmental Protection Agency (EPA.). . . .

In his opinion, the noise level readings that he measured for his report would constitute an aggravation and a nuisance to persons of ordinary sensibilities. He stated that noise levels can affect blood pressure and cause nervous conditions and stress.

Mr. Verret discounted the sound barriers proposed by Mr. Guidry. He opined that an eight-foot fence would not be an effective barrier considering the waveform of sound and the height of the jumps on the track. As for Mr. Guidry's proposal to plant trees, he stated that it would require acres of trees, i.e., a veritable forest, before any reasonable amount of attenuation could be achieved.

Following the trial, the court took the issue of the permanent injunction under advisement. However, it denied the Guidrys' motion to dissolve the preliminary injunction. Thus, the preliminary injunction remained in effect pending a decision on the permanent injunction.

On August 27, 2003, the trial court issued written reasons for judgment. Therein, it concluded that the activities of the defendants constituted a nuisance that substantially interfered with the intervenors' enjoyment of their property and therefore must be enjoined. This ruling was memorialized in a judgment signed on September 24, 2003. From this judgment, defendants devolutively appeal. Defendants essentially argue that the trial court erred in finding that its track activities were a nuisance, because such a finding was not supported by facts that were clear and convincing.

Applicable Law

At the outset, we note that the intervenors, as neighboring property owners, requested injunctive relief based upon La. C.C. arts. 667 and 669. The Parish never alleged that it was a neighboring property owner. Rather, the basis for its request for injunctive relief was the violation of its "Noise Ordinance (Part II, Chapter 10[,] Article VI, Section 10-80 et seq.) and . . . Nuisance Ordinance (Part II, Chapter 10, Article V, Section 10-71 et seq.) of the Code of Ordinances of East Feliciana Parish." Importantly, Section 10-71 of the Parish's Nuisance Ordinance expressly states that "as used in this article, the term "nuisance" shall refer to the prohibitions contained in Articles 664 through 674 of the Louisiana Civil Code." Moreover, when there are several laws on the same subject matter, they must be interpreted in reference to each other. Thus, local nuisance ordinances must be construed in reference to the applicable civil code provisions. See *Hernandez v. Richard*, 2000-471, pp. 6–7 (La. App. 3rd Cir. 12/6/00), 772 So. 2d 994, 997–98. Accordingly, we now examine the pertinent civil code articles.

The corresponding rights and obligations of neighboring proprietors are principally governed by La. C.C. arts. 667–669. *Inabnett v. Exxon Corporation*, 93-0681 (La. 9/6/94), 642 So. 2d 1243, 1250. . . .

These articles place limitations on the rights of owners by setting out principles of responsibility that require an owner to use his property in such a manner as not to injure another. Louisiana Civil Code article 667 prohibits uses that cause damage to neighbors or deprive them of the enjoyment of their property, while La. C.C. art. 668 permits uses that merely cause neighbors some inconvenience. Louisiana Civil Code article 669 allows suppression of certain inconveniences if excessive under local ordinances or customs, and requires tolerance of lesser inconveniences. Together the three articles establish the following principles: (1) no one may use his property so as to cause damage to another or to interfere substantially with the enjoyment of another's property; (2) landowners must necessarily be exposed to some inconveniences arising from the normal exercise of the right of ownership by a neighbor; and (3) excessive inconveniences caused by the emission of industrial smoke, odors, noise, dust vapors, and the like need not be tolerated in the absence of a conventional servitude. Whether an inconvenience is excessive or not is to be determined in the light of local ordinances and customs. *Inabnet*, 642 So. 2d at 1250–51; *Barrett v. T.L. James & Co.*, 28,170, pp. 5–6 (La. App. 2nd Cir. 4/3/96), 671 So. 2d 1186, 1190–91, writ denied, 96-1124 (La. 6/7/96), 674 So. 2d 973.

The obligations of vicinage contained in articles 667–669 are legal servitudes imposed on the owner of property. These provisions embody a balancing of rights and obligations associated with the ownership of immovables. As a general rule, the landowner is free to exercise his rights of ownership in any manner he sees fit. He may even use his property in ways which occasion some inconvenience to his neighbor. However, his extensive rights do not allow him to do real damage to his neighbor. *Rodrigue v. Copeland*, 475 So. 2d 1071, 1077 (La. 1985).

Thus, the owner of property has a right to conduct thereon any lawful business not per se a nuisance, as long as the business is so conducted that it will not unreasonably inconvenience a neighbor in the reasonable enjoyment of his property. But every business, however lawful, must be conducted with due regard to the rights of others, and no one has a right to erect and maintain a nuisance to the injury of his neighbor even in the pursuit of a lawful trade, or to conduct a business on his own land in such a way as will be injurious or offensive to those residing in the vicinity. *Hilliard v. Shuff*, 260 La. 384, 256 So. 2d 127, 129 (1971), citing *Devoke v. Yazoo & M.V.R. Co.*, 211 La. 729, 30 So. 2d 816 (1947).

Hence, this court must determine whether the motocross operation is the type of inconvenience that neighboring proprietors must tolerate or whether it causes real damage to those neighboring proprietors and their right to enjoy their own premises. The extent of the inconvenience a property owner must tolerate without redress depends on the circumstances. *Barrett*, 28,170 at p. 6, 671 So. 2d at 1191. This analysis requires consideration of factors such as the character of the locality, the nature and degree of the intrusion, and the effect of the activity on the health and safety of the neighbors. *Rodrigue*, 475 So. 2d at 1077.

In *Robichaux v. Huppenbauer*, 258 La. 139, 245 So. 2d 385, 389 (1971), our supreme court stated that noxious smells, rats, flies and noise may constitute an actionable nuisance although produced and carried on by a lawful business, where they result in material injury to neighboring property or interfere with its comfortable use and enjoyment by persons of ordinary sensibilities. This test has also been applied by this court. In *McCastle v. Rollins Environmental Services of Louisiana, Inc.*, 415 So. 2d 515, 519 (La. App. 1st Cir.), writ denied, 420 So. 2d 449 (La. 1982), this court stated that the test of the right to an injunction against the maintenance of a nuisance is whether the alleged nuisance produces serious or material discomfort to persons of ordinary sensibilities in a normal state of health. In two of its more recent pronouncements, the supreme court granted injunctive relief because a defendant's activities constituted an unreasonable intrusion into the lives of his neighbors when considered in light of the character of the neighborhood, the degree of the intrusion and its effect on the use and enjoyment of their properties by his neighbors. *Diefenthal v. Longue Vue Management Corp.* 561 So. 2d 44, 57 (La. 1990); *Rodrigue*, 475 So. 2d at 1078.

To obtain injunctive relief under La. C.C. arts. 667–669, a party must prove irreparable injury under La. C.C.P. art. 3601 in addition to the necessary showing of real damage. *Rodrigue*, 475 So. 2d at 1078; *Salter v. B.W.S. Corp., Inc.*, 290 So.2d 821, 824–25 (La. 1974); *Day v. Warren*, 524 So.2d 1383, 1386 (La. App. 1st Cir. 1988). . . .

Analysis

With the foregoing precepts in mind, we find that the record herein provides a reasonable factual basis for the trial court's determination that the motocross operation has occasioned real damage, not mere inconvenience, upon the intervenors. Likewise, we conclude the record supports a finding that the intervenors will be irreparably harmed unless injunctive relief is granted. The defendants' motocross activities constitute "an unreasonable intrusion into the lives of [their] neighbors when considered in the light of the character of the neighborhood, the degree of intrusion and its effect on the use and enjoyment of their properties by [those] neighbors." *Rodrigue*, 475 So. 2d at 1078.

The record demonstrates that the affected area is a rural locale. Most of the intervenors testified that they bought property there in order to escape the city and enjoy the peace and quiet of country living. Many of them live on their property and actively pursue outdoor activities such as fishing, hunting, and gardening.

Mr. Verret testified that the ambient noise level for a rural community of this nature would be much lower than that of an urban community. He opined that the ambient noise level for the area at issue would probably be 35 to 45 decibels. He explained that an area with such a low ambient noise level would respond greatly to the introduction of an additional 10-decibel source into that community. However, the same 10 decibels would not have as much of an impact in an urban environment that had a higher ambient noise level. Because the community threshold was low, he stated that the noise produced by the track created a more significant intrusion.

The record indicates that the degree of this intrusion was extensive. Many of the intervenors testified that they could hear the noise within their homes and all of them stated that they were subjected to the noise outside. Mr. Verret took readings that reached a maximum of 85 decibels. However, he noted that some of the noise reached beyond the range of his microphone, thus he was unable to record any higher readings. Moreover, on the day the readings were taken, the number of operating motorcycles was less than usual. Had more motorcycles been operating, the sound levels would have measured even higher. Considering these facts, we note that the readings taken by Mr. Verret, in conjunction with the recommendations published by the EPA, support a finding that the level of noise normally generated by the track constituted an unreasonable intrusion into the lives of the intervenors.

Additionally, we find that the degree of the intrusion is not merely an issue of the level of the noise. We also find relevant the nature of the noise, as well as its persistence and duration. Many of the intervenors noted that the fluctuating character of the noise, which was likened to a chainsaw or dentist drill or buzzing bee, was particularly stressful. The intervenors further testified that the noise was constant and that it continued from the early morning hours until nightfall.

All of the intervenors testified that they were people of normal health and sensibilities. However, they maintained that the noise produced by the track made them stressed and irritable. Dennis Berthelot testified that he actually suffered stomach pains due to the stress. The intervenors claimed that they were unable to enjoy their property due to the noise from the track and many stated that they would not be able to live there if the track is allowed to operate.

Finally, Mr. Verret cast grave doubt on the effectiveness of Mr. Guidry's proposed sound barriers. While we recognize that Mr. Guidry did plant two rows of pine saplings, the evidence demonstrates this is woefully short of the forest of trees needed to achieve an appreciable amount of attenuation. Therefore, considering the foregoing, we cannot say that the trial court was clearly wrong in finding that the operation of the track occasioned real damage to the intervenors and that they were entitled to injunctive relief.

Decree

Accordingly, the judgment of the trial court enjoining defendants, Jeremy Guidry, Amber Guidry, and Jeremy Guidry d/b/a Midway Motocross, from operating a motocross track and related activities on their property and from creating or allowing others to create unreasonably excessive noise or dust by riding unmuffled or insufficiently muffled vehicles on their property is hereby affirmed. All costs of this appeal are assessed to defendants, Jeremy and Amber Guidry.

AFFIRMED.

GUIDRY, J., concurring in part and dissenting in part. I concur in part and dissent in part from the majority opinion. While I agree that the plaintiffs are entitled to some injunctive relief, I do not agree with the imposition of a complete injunction totally prohibiting all moto cross activity. Injunction is an equitable remedy and should be carefully designed to achieve the essential correction at the least possible cost and inconvenience to the defendant. *Hilliard v. Shuff*, 260 La. 384, 256 So. 2d 127, 129 (La. 1972). Other surrounding proprietors engage in various commercial and recreational activities on their property (such as running a dirt business or cutting hay or hunting) that, while not causing real damages, nonetheless occasion some inconvenience to their neighbors. I believe that the moto cross operation could likewise be conducted in such a manner. Accordingly, I believe that the injunction should have been modified to limit the number of days per month and the number of hours per day that the track could operate such that it would only cause the surrounding proprietors, at most, some inconvenience, rather than real damage. In my opinion, such a modified injunction would be the only way to strike a "fair balance" between the competing interests of these parties. See *Diefenthal v. Longue Vue Management Corp.*, 561 So. 2d 44, 57 (La. 1990). Therefore, I dissent from the majority opinion insofar as it affirms a total injunction prohibiting all moto cross activity. In all other respects, I concur.

Notes and Questions

1. Note that *Parish of East Feliciana v. Guidry*, 923 So.2d 45 (La. App. 1 Cir. 2005), was decided well after the 1996 amendments to Article 667 became effective. What effect might these amendments have had on the way the litigants approached this dispute?

2. Do you think the solution proposed by Judge Guidry in his concurring opinion would have struck a more fair balance between the interests of Jeremy Guidry and those of his neighbors?

3. The court was careful to note that a motocross track is not the kind of activity that can be characterized as a nuisance per se. This implies, that in some locations at least, a commercial motocross track would be a perfectly appropriate use for a large tract of land. Where could a motocross track be located so as not to cause unreasonable harm to its neighbors?

4. How important was it that the local parish authorities joined with Jeremy Guidry's neighbors in bringing suit to obtain a permanent injunction to close down the motocross track? Would the neighbors have succeeded if they had filed this action on their own?

5. *Parish of East Feliciana v. Guidry* involved motorcycle racing in a rural area of Louisiana. A decade later, a similar dispute arose in the context of a commercial automobile racetrack that opened in rural Union Parish. *Badke v. U.S. Speedway, LLC.* 139 So.3d 1117 (La. App. 2 Cir. 2014). Neighbors living in that rural community filed suit against the speedway seeking damages and a permanent injunction. Eventually 59 persons joined the lawsuit as plaintiffs. They claimed that the racetrack, which held commercial races on weekend evenings and practice races throughout the week, caused noise, which prevented the plaintiffs from enjoying their homes, and dust, which aggravated respiratory problems. The plaintiffs also contended that the racetrack reduced the value of their property. *Id.* at 119. As in *Guidry*, extensive testimony was offered by the plaintiffs to establish the nature of the alleged interference with the enjoyment of their property. The same industrial hygienist who testified in *Guidry* was a key witness. What outcome do you predict?

Rizzo v. Nichols

867 So.2d 73 (La. App. 3 Cir. 2004)

AMY, Judge. Plaintiffs, husband and wife, sought recovery for damage that occurred after the defendant changed the natural drainage of water across the plaintiffs' property. The trial judge determined that the defendant had notice that construction activities at this particular location would cause such drainage problems and that the defendant's activities were a cause-in-fact of the water damage to the plaintiffs' property. The trial judge awarded the plaintiffs actual damages as well as damages for inconvenience and mental anguish. From this judgment, the defendant appeals. For the following reasons, we affirm.

Factual and Procedural Background

According to the record, Jasper and Mary Rizzo, plaintiffs herein, moved into a house on Brooks Boulevard in Alexandria, Louisiana, in November 2001. At the time, and for several months thereafter, the Rizzos' property was located next to a vacant lot. Mr. Rizzo testified at trial that when it rained, the water that fell on his and the adjoining properties was channeled into a lower area that ran across the adjacent property and drained into the street. The record further indicates that Heath Nichols, defendant herein, purchased the vacant lot contiguous to the Rizzos' in June 2001. Mr. Nichols began construction of a duplex apartment shortly thereafter, whereupon the Rizzos' property allegedly began to flood. Mr. Rizzo filed the instant suit for damages on October 30, 2002, and a bench trial was held in the matter on April 29, 2003.

Mr. Rizzo testified at trial that until Mr. Nichols began construction on the duplex, his—Mr. Rizzo's—property never flooded after it rained. However, Mr. Rizzo noted, after construction, the natural drainage across Mr. Nichols's property was disrupted, and Mr. Rizzo began to have problems with standing water. He approached Mr. Nichols about the drainage problems, and he recalled that Mr. Nichols agreed to "look into it." Mr. Rizzo testified that he approached Mr. Nichols two or three more times after their initial conversation to repeat his request that he do something about the flooding, but Mr. Nichols took no further action. At trial, Mr. Rizzo advanced the theory that Mr. Nichols had built the duplex "up," at a higher elevation than the surrounding land, thereby causing Mr. Rizzo's property to be the low spot where water collected after a rain. Mr. Rizzo testified that the standing water had damaged the shed that stood behind his house and that he eventually had to install a catch basin at the back of his property to ameliorate the drainage problem.

The trial judge issued written reasons for judgment on June 20, 2003, in which he observed that the primary issue for determination in the matter was whether Mr. Nichols knew or was aware that construction on his property would cause damage and whether he could have prevented that damage by the exercise of reasonable care. The trial judge noted that Mr. Nichols admitted at trial that he had discussed the drainage issue with two plumbers but had not taken any action. As such, the trial judge concluded, Mr. Nichols had notice that his activities would cause damage to the Rizzos' property. The trial judge likewise concluded that the construction on Mr. Nichols's property was a cause-in-fact of the damage to the Rizzos' property. Accordingly, the trial judge awarded the Rizzos damages in the amounts of $2,175.00 for construction of a catch basin; $750.00 for repairs for water damage to the shed; $2,000.00 in inconvenience damages for the loss of use of the shed, loss of use of the yard, and standing water on the property; and $2,000.00 general damages for mental anguish. Mr. Nichols appeals the trial judge's findings.

Discussion

The present appeal involves the obligations of vicinage, set forth in Articles 667–669 of our Civil Code. . . .

In *Begnaud v. Camel Contractors, Inc.*, 98-207, pp. 5–6 (La. App. 3 Cir. 10/28/98), 721 So. 2d 550, 554, *writ denied*, 98-2948 (La. 2/5/99), 738 So. 2d 1, a panel of this court discussed the concept of reasonable care in context of vicinage as follows:

> Whether an owner of property is liable to his neighbors under the Civil Code Articles of vicinage, La. Civ. Code arts. 667–669, is a determination to be made by the trier of fact based upon the reasonableness of the conduct in light of the circumstances, and such an analysis requires consideration of factors such as the character of the neighborhood, the degree of intrusion privacy [sic] and the effect of the activity on the health and safety of the neighbors. *Barrett v. T.L. James & Co.*, (La. App. 2 Cir. 4/3/96); 671 So. 2d 1186, *writ denied*, 96-1124 (La. 6/7/96); 674 So. 2d 973.

A trial court's determinations in vicinage cases are reviewed by an appellate court pursuant to the manifest-error standard. *Begnaud*, 721 So. 2d at 554.

In the present appeal, Mr. Nichols argues that testimony elicited at trial establishes that he neither knew nor could have known that the construction activities on his property would cause flooding and damage to the Rizzos' property. Mr. Nichols maintains that although he knew that water stood on his property after a heavy rain, he did not know that said standing water would cause damage. In support of his assertion that he was unaware of the consequences of building on his property, Mr. Nichols points out that "standing water is common throughout the entire neighborhood" and that he "employed a reputable contractor, who built the duplex [on Mr. Nichols's property] in accordance with local codes and regulations."

According to the record of the proceedings below, Mr. Rizzo testified that he had informed Mr. Nichols of the drainage problem soon after construction began. Mr. Nichols's testimony confirmed that Mr. Rizzo had approached him during construction and that he had contacted two plumbers about remedying the situation. However, the record indicates that Mr. Nichols did nothing further to provide a solution to the disrupted drainage pattern occasioned by his activities. Instead, the record reflects that Mr. Rizzo installed a catch basin on his property in an attempt to remedy the situation.

Where an aggrieved party seeks recovery under the law of vicinage for damage occasioned by a neighboring landowner's activities, that party must demonstrate a causal link between the damage sustained and the neighboring landowner's action or inaction. *Haworth v. L'Hoste*, 95-0714 (La. App. 4 Cir. 11/30/95), 664 So. 2d 1335, *writ denied*, 96-408 (La. 3/29/96), 670 So. 2d 1235.

At trial, Mr. Elbert Wiggins, the previous owner of the Rizzos' property, testified that his land never flooded during the five years that he lived there; instead, he noted, water drained from his property through the lower-lying area that ran across the adjacent vacant lot, now owned by Mr. Nichols. Mr. Rizzo likewise testified that before Mr. Nichols began construction, his property never flooded, and water drained in the manner described by Mr. Wiggins. Mr. Rizzo introduced into evidence photographs of his land, taken before construction activities commenced next door, which showed the low-lying area on the adjacent property. He then introduced photographs of his property after construction began in which standing water covered substantial portions of his yard and surrounded his shed. Additional photographs, taken of Mr. Nichols's duplex after its completion, show that the duplex was built at a higher elevation than the surrounding land, as indicated by the dirt and sod sloping downward from the building to the level of Mr. Rizzo's property.

We find no manifest error in the trial judge's determination that Mr. Nichols knew that the activities on his property would cause damage to the Rizzos' property and that he could have prevented such damage by the exercise of reasonable care. Moreover, we find no manifest error in the trial judge's determination that the construction activities undertaken by Mr. Nichols disrupted the natural drainage of his and the Rizzos' respective properties and that these activities were the cause-in-fact of the Rizzos' damages. This assignment is without merit.

Damages

In addition to general damages, a plaintiff in a vicinage cause of action may recover damages for mental anguish, discomfort, irritation, anxiety, and loss of use and/or enjoyment of his property. *Branch v. City of Lafayette*, 95-298 (La. App. 3 Cir. 10/4/95), 663 So. 2d 216. A trial court is afforded great discretion in fixing damages in accordance with its factual determinations in a case, and an appellate court may not disturb such awards absent a clear abuse of this discretion. *Arnold v. Town of Ball*, 94–972 (La. App. 3 Cir. 2/1/95), 651 So. 2d 313. . . .

When we examine the record, we find that the trial judge did not abuse his vast discretion in awarding the Rizzos damages for the installation of the catch basin, for repairs to the shed, and for inconvenience. The evidence presented at trial clearly supports such awards. These assignments of error lack merit.

With respect to recovery for mental anguish, a panel of this court noted in *Begnaud* that such damages are appropriate:

(1) when property has been damaged by an intentional or illegal act; (2) where property is damaged by acts for which the tortfeasor will be strictly or absolutely liable; (3) when property is damaged by acts constituting a continuous nuisance; (4) when property is damaged at a time in which the owner thereof is present or situated nearby and the owner experiences trauma as a result [citations omitted].

Begnaud, 721 So. 2d at 555 (quoting *Kolder v. State Farm Ins. Co.*, 520 So. 2d 960, 963 (La. App. 3 Cir. 1987)).

Regarding the award of $2,000.00 for mental anguish, Mr. Nichols claims that such an award was inappropriate because the Rizzos failed to prove that any of the four considerations listed in *Begnaud*, above, were applicable.

Mr. Rizzo testified at trial that the standing water on his property kept him from venturing into his back yard and proved a breeding ground for mosquitoes. He also testified that the shed would often be unusable for a week's time after the water receded. Moreover, Mr. Rizzo testified that the condition of his property caused tension between him and his wife. Based upon our review of the record, we find no abuse of discretion on the part of the trial judge in awarding $2,000.00 to the Rizzos for mental anguish due to damage to their property. This assignment is without merit.

Decree

For the foregoing reasons, the judgment of the trial court is affirmed. All costs of this proceeding are assigned to the defendant-appellant, Heath Nichols.

AFFIRMED.

Notes and Questions

1. *Rizzo v. Nichols*, 867 So.2d 73 (La. App. 3 Cir. 2004), is the first decision to apply the three part, fault-based analysis imposed by the 1996 revision of Article 667 for the determination of whether a defendant can be "answerable for damages." Do you think the addition of this fault-based approach has made it significantly more difficult for an aggrieved proprietor to obtain damages under this provision? In *Rizzo*, the defendant's failure to exercise reasonable care was fairly obvious, but in a closer case, the new requirement to establish a lack of reasonable care might produce a different outcome.

Note the reference to *res ipsa loquitur* ("the thing speaks for itself") in the revised version of Article 667 of the Civil Code. Under this principle in tort law, the plaintiff can create a rebuttable presumption of the defendant's negligence by proving that: (1) the harm would not ordinarily have occurred without negligence; (2) whatever thing caused the harm was under the defendant's exclusive control; and (3) other plausible explanations as to how the harm occurred are not available. Could the plaintiff in *Rizzo* have appealed to *res ipsa loquitur* to prove his claim of damages as well?

A recent decision addressed the relevance of *res ipsa loquitor* in the context of a commercial property owner's claim seeking damages for flooding allegedly caused by constructions made by two neighboring commercial property owners. In that case, the court found that the plaintiff property owner failed to meet its burden of proof to establish liability for damages under Article 667 despite having asserted the relevance of *res ipsa loquitor*. *See Mitchell v. Aarons Rentals*, 218 So.3d 167, 175 (La. App. 1 Ci. 2017) (holding that the doctrine of *res ipsa loquitur* is inapplicable because the court was unable to draw a reasonable inference that the flooding of plaintiff's property could have been due to a cause other than the alleged negligent maintenance of drainage systems by the defendants).

2. In a case decided a few years later, the Second Circuit Court of Appeal distinguished *Rizzo* and held that a mobile home park owner was not liable under Article 667 of the Civil Code for damages arising from the overflow of several newly constructed oxidation ponds because the defendant had used reasonable care to prevent

runoff, silting and pollution by consulting experts, placing hay bales around the ponds and seeding levees to prevent damage to the plaintiff's property. *Taylor v. Haddox*, 968 So.2d 1200, 1203–04 (La App. 2 Cir. 2007). In another case, which involved water damage to a house allegedly caused by a neighbor's construction of a new house and saw a veritable "battle of the experts," the appellate court deferred to the trial court's finding that the plaintiffs simply failed to prove that the defendant's construction was the primary cause of the damage they sustained and therefore, the plaintiffs had no claim under Articles 2315, 656 or 667 of the Civil Code. *Fiebelkorn v. Alford*, 105 So.3d 110, 120 (La. App. 2 Cir. 2012).

3. It should be acknowledged, however, that the borderline between liability under Article 667 of the Civil Code and the articles establishing delictual liability under the Civil Code is often blurry. In a recent case, a jury was instructed that a defendant homeowner could be liable for damages to their neighbor for the faulty construction of a ten foot high retaining wall that separated the two properties and held dirt on the defendant's side of the wall and whose defects were likely to require significant remediation under either: (1) Article 2322 of the Civil Code, regarding damages owed by the owner of a building when caused by its ruin; (2) Articles 667 to 669 of the Civil Code governing obligations of the neighborhood; or (3) Louisiana Civil Code Article 670, covering encroaching buildings. After the jury returned a verdict in favor of the plaintiff for $340,000, the court of appeal affirmed, holding that it could not say the jury was clearly wrong in finding that the wall was structurally unsound due in part to the fault of the defendant homeowner. *Zaverri v. Husers*, 224 So.3d 389, 397 (La. App. 3 Cir. 2017).

3. *Ultrahazardous Activity*: Even though the revision of Article 667 of the Civil Code was designed in large part to eliminate the possibility that a property owner could be declared strictly liable for damages regardless of whether he knew of the hazard or exercised reasonable care, the revised provision did maintain strict liability for damages caused by an ultrahazardous activity. The legislature defined "ultrahazardous activity" quite narrowly by declaring that only two activities would qualify: "pile driving or blasting with explosives." La. Civ. Code art. 667 (1996).

In 2005, the Louisiana Supreme Court was called upon to determine the meaning of the term "pile driving." *Suire v. Lafayette City-Parish Government*, 907 So.2d 37 (La. 2005). After reviewing several pre-revision cases involving different kinds of activities similar to pile-driving, the court strictly interpreted the last sentence in Article 667. The court concluded that the defendant was not absolutely liable for damages to the plaintiff's house and patio after it pounded metal sheeting into the ground with a back hoe directly behind the plaintiff's house, even though the same conduct could lead to liability for damages under the negligence prong of Article 667 and expropriation theories. *Id.* at 48–51, 44, 58–60. *See also Millican v. River Road Construction, Inc.*, 924 So.2d 255, 257 (La. App. 5 Cir. 2006) (holding, based on *Suire*, that defendant could not be strictly liable for the installation of sheet piles that allegedly caused damage to plaintiffs' home).

In the following decision, the issue addressed by the Louisiana Supreme Court concerned the identity of a defendant as a lessor of immovable property. Should a lessor be liable for the actions of a lessee that allegedly violate the obligations of neighborhood set forth in Articles 667 to 669?

Yokum v. 615 Bourbon Street L.L.C.

977 So.2d 859 (La. 2008)

KIMBALL, Justice. We granted certiorari in this matter to review the Court of Appeal's ruling that Defendant in this matter, 615 Bourbon Street, L.L.C., as owner and lessor of the premises upon which its lessee operates the bar "The Rock," is not liable to the plaintiffs for the alleged excessive noise associated with the loud music played by the bar, and is therefore entitled to summary judgment. For the reasons that follow, we find that the Court of Appeal erroneously concluded under the facts of this case that the defendant/owner and lessor of this property cannot be held responsible for the actions of its lessee under Article 667 of the Louisiana Civil Code. Accordingly, the Court of Appeal's decision affirming summary judgment is reversed, and the case is remanded for further proceedings.

Facts and Procedural History

Peterson M. Yokum is the owner of and resides at the premises located at 723 Toulouse Street in the French Quarter in New Orleans, Louisiana, with his wife, Polly Elizabeth Anderson. The property located at 723 Toulouse Street is zoned "Vieux Carre Commercial District-2 Mixed Residential" ("VCC-2"). The entity 615 Bourbon Street, L.L.C. is the owner and lessor of the premises located at 615–617 Bourbon Street. On October 15, 2003, 615 Bourbon Street, L.L.C. executed a commercial lease of property with O'Reilly Properties, L.L.C. ("O'Reilly"), leasing the premises located at 615–617 Bourbon Street in New Orleans, Louisiana, to O'Reilly to be "used exclusively for legitimate, commercial, purposes . . .". Moreover, the lease between 615 Bourbon Street, L.L.C. and O'Reilly stated that "Lessee is obligated not to use same for any purpose that is unlawful or that tends to injure or depreciate the property, and such unlawful, injurious or depreciatory use shall, if not cured after 5 days notice, constitute a breach thereof. . . .". The lease also stated that as "additional consideration for this lease, Lessee agrees to maintain at all times during the term of this lease a valid liquor license for the leased premises and to pay all expenses incidental thereto." O'Reilly thereafter began operating the bar The Rock on the premises owned by 615 Bourbon Street, L.L.C.[2]

Plaintiffs, Mr. Yokum and Ms. Anderson, allege that they have been subjected to loud and ongoing live entertainment conducted at the bar known as The Rock, located at 615–617 Bourbon Street, beginning as early as 2003, which has prevented the proper quiet enjoyment of their home. . . . .

---

2. At oral argument of this matter, counsel for defendant indicated that the bar known as "The Rock" is no longer located on this premises.

Plaintiffs . . . thereafter filed a Petition for Damages and Declaratory and Injunctive Relief on July 20, 2005, in the Civil District Court for the Parish of Orleans, naming "615 Bourbon Street, L.L.C. d/b/a The Rock, Old Opera House, Inc. d/b/a Old Opera House and Willie Mintz" as defendants, and attaching the aforementioned letters as exhibits. In their petition, plaintiffs allege that defendant 615 Bourbon Street, L.L.C. d/b/a The Rock, located within the "Vieux Carre Entertainment District" ("VCE") "owns and operates a bar between the hours of 3:00 p.m. and 3:00 a.m. with live amplified music and entertainment at 615/617 Bourbon Street, New Orleans, Louisiana" with noises that "are sufficient to cause physical discomfort and annoyance to Peter Yokum and Polly Anderson, and any person of ordinary sensibilities, and constitute a nuisance."

Plaintiffs also allege in their petition that defendants have violated the municipal noise ordinances for the City of New Orleans, . . .

Plaintiffs further allege in their petition that 615 Bourbon Street, L.L.C. d/b/a The Rock and Old Opera House, Inc. d/b/a Old Opera House have violated La. R.S. 26:90(A)(14)(a) & 26:286(A)(14)(a), which plaintiffs state make it unlawful for a person holding a retail dealer permit under the alcoholic beverage control law to play live or recorded music which is so unreasonably intrusive or offensive as to interfere with the comfortable enjoyment of the property of a person.

Finally, and most relevant for purposes of the instant matter, plaintiffs assert in their Petition that defendants in this instance are in violation of Louisiana Civil Code articles 667 and 669, relating to nuisance. . . .

Defendant 615 Bourbon Street, L.L.C. filed . . . a Motion for Summary Judgment . . .

In addition to its alleged material facts not in dispute, defendant asserted in the memorandum in support of its Motion for Summary Judgment that plaintiffs' allegations of noise ordinance violations and the creation of a nuisance arise out of the operation of the business known as The Rock. Defendant further argued in its motion that "[t]he petition contains no allegations whatsoever which would impose liability upon 615 BOURBON STREET, L.L.C., in its capacity as lessor of the premises, and it is further submitted that liability, if any, would arise only out of the operation of La. Civil Code Articles 667 and 668." Defendant therefore asserted that "the issue is thus raised whether or not 615 BOURBON STREET, L.L.C., as lessor, has any liability whatsoever to its neighbors for the use of its premises by a lessee operating under permits issued by the governing authority, in this case, the City of New Orleans.". . . .

We granted certiorari in this matter to review the Court of Appeal's ruling that summary judgment in favor of defendant was appropriate because defendant 615 Bourbon Street, L.L.C., as lessor owner in this matter, is not the person actually responsible for the existence of the noise complained of, and therefore, there is no basis in law for holding the lessor/owner liable under Louisiana Civil Code article 667. We disagree with the Court of Appeal's reasoning, as our review of Louisiana law and its long-standing jurisprudence regarding this matter dictates a different conclusion. For the reasons set forth below, we find that the Court of Appeal's decision below was in error, and therefore reverse its ruling affirming summary judgment in favor of defendant, and remand the case to the trial court for further proceedings.

Discussion

Because the Court of Appeal affirmed summary judgment based upon its conclusion that defendant/lessor 615 Bourbon Street, L.L.C. is not responsible for the actions of its lessee under Louisiana Civil Code article 667, we must first examine article 667 and its application to owner lessors. From that determination, we must then decide whether summary judgment in favor of defendant 615 Bourbon Street, L.L.C. in this instance is appropriate. . . .

For purposes of the instant matter, our discussion focuses primarily on Louisiana Civil Code article 667, as we are faced with the issue of whether or not a "proprietor" owner and lessor can be responsible for the actions of its tenant/lessee. Article 667, originally enacted in 1808, was subject to the significant tort reform undertaken by the Louisiana Legislature in 1996. *See* Acts 1996, 1st Ex.Sess., No. 1, § 1. The language contained in Article 667 regarding strict or absolute liability for ultrahazardous activity was most heavily affected by the amendments, as this Court has so recognized. . . . *Suire v. Lafayette City-Parish Consolidated Government, et al.,* 04-1459, p. 13 (La. 4/12/05); 907 So. 2d 37, 49.

Notably, the 1996 amendments to article 667 also incorporated the requirement that a proprietor or landowner be responsible for damages to an aggrieved neighbor "only upon a showing that he knew or, in the exercise of reasonable care, should have known that his works would cause damage, that the damage could have been prevented by the exercise of reasonable care, and that he failed to exercise such reasonable care," thus shifting the absolute liability standard to a negligence standard similar to that set forth in La. C.C. art. 2317.1 and the 1996 amendments to Articles 2321 and 2322. The 1996 amendments to article 667 did not change WHO could be held liable under the article, namely, the "proprietor"; rather, it changed the theory of liability under which the proprietor could be held responsible. As a result, in order for a proprietor/landowner to be held responsible for damages allegedly caused by works or actions on his property, it must be shown that the proprietor/landowner knew or should have known that the "works" on his property would cause damage, and that the damage could have been prevented by the exercise of reasonable care.

The term "proprietor" as used in Article 667, while commonly interpreted to refer to landowners, "has been expansively interpreted by the courts to apply not only to a landowner, but also to a person whose rights derive from the owner." *Inabnet v. Exxon Corp.,* 93-0681, p. 12 (La. 9/6/94); 642 So. 2d 1243, 1251 (citing *Lombard v. Sewerage and Water Bd. Of New Orleans,* 284 So. 2d 905 (La. 1973) and Ferdinand F. Stone, *Tort Doctrine in Louisiana: The Obligations of Neighborhood,* 40 Tul.L.Rev.

701, 711 (1966)).[34] As mentioned previously, certain limitations are imposed upon proprietors through Article 667: "although a landowner may use and enjoy his property as he sees fit, Article 667 provides that he may not exercise his right in such a way as to cause damage to his neighbors." *State Through Dep't. of Transp. & Dev. v. Chambers Inv. Co.,* 595 So. 2d 598, 604 (La. 1992). Furthermore, this Court has also stated that "the proprietor is likewise responsible not only for his own activity, but also for that carried on by his agents, contractors and representatives with his consent and permission." *Id.*

Not only has the term "proprietor" been expanded from its traditional meaning of simply "landowner," the "work" to which Article 667 refers includes not only constructions but also activities that may cause damage. This Court stated in *Chaney v. Travelers Ins. Co.,* that "our view will not accept the proposition that a proprietor is responsible for damage to a neighbor for a 'work,' that is, a structure on his premises which harms his neighbor *without imposing a like responsibility for harmful activity.*" 259 La. 1, 249 So. 2d 181, 186 (La. 1971) (emphasis added). We further stated that "[i]t is not the manner in which the activity is carried on which is significant; it is the fact that the activity causes damage to a neighbor which is relevant." *Id.* Thus, we find that the alleged excessive noise emanating from the defendant's leased premises in this instance falls within the concept of "work" as contemplated by Louisiana Civil Code article 667, in that it is an activity that could be harmful to neighboring proprietors.[35]

Article 667, setting forth limitations imposed upon the *ownership* of land, is directly applicable to a proprietor landowner who may also be a lessor of its property, as the act of lease by the landowner is a right which is derived from ownership of the property. La. C.C. art. 2673 ("All things, corporeal or incorporeal, that are susceptible of *ownership* may be the object of a lease, except those that cannot be used without being destroyed by that very use, or those the lease of which is prohibited by law" (emphasis added).). Thus, because article 667 dictates, and this Court has previously established, that a proprietor/landowner can be responsible

---

34. "In these days of long term leases, complex mineral rights, and horizontal property divisions it would be a mistake to limit the word "proprietor" to its early nineteenth-century connotation, thus ignoring modern developments in property rights." Ferdinand F. Stone, *Tort Doctrine in Louisiana: The Obligations of Neighborhood,* 40 Tul.L.Rev. 701, 711 (1966).

35. *See also* Yiannopoulos, Predial Servitudes, 4 Louisiana Civil Law Treatise, §43 (West 2004): Limiting the meaning of the word "work" to constructions might thus be contrary to the intent of the redactors, and it would certainly be contrary to the pronouncements of an impressive Louisiana jurisprudence. While the literal interpretation of Articles 667 and 668 in the light of their historical derivation might leave room for the view that the word work means merely constructions, a teleological interpretation of the same articles leads to the conclusion that the word work ought to include acts. As a matter of policy, it is preferable to assert that Articles 667 and 668 apply to all situations in which constructions or activities cause unwarranted harm to property or persons. The contrary view would eliminate a most important basis of civil responsibility in the framework of vicinage.

for the works or actions on its property that may cause damage to neighboring proprietors, we find the Court of Appeal's reasoning in this matter erroneous. Merely because a proprietor/landowner utilizes his right as a property owner to lease his property to another does not eradicate his or her responsibilities and obligations, set forth above, as a landowner. Moreover, under the Court of Appeal's rationale, even an owner/lessor with full knowledge of the potentially harmful effects of the lessee tenant's activities on its property would have little or no responsibility to protect the public and his neighbors from his lessee tenant's harmful activities. As a result, the Court of Appeal's interpretation creates a virtual immunity for landowners, allowing them to remove themselves from potential liability for damages that arise out of the ownership of their property by simply establishing a lease on their property.

We therefore find the Court of Appeal was incorrect in its assertion that a mere lack of jurisprudence imposing liability upon an owner or proprietor for the actions of its lessee which cause damage out of a lessee's use of the premises equates to a finding that an owner is not responsible for the actions of its lessee. More specifically, as shown above, it is well-settled that a "proprietor," which at its very basic meaning is a landowner, can be responsible for damages for any "work" under Article 667 of the Louisiana Civil Code, which this Court has clearly stated includes not only constructions but also activities, performed on its land that may cause damage to neighboring proprietors.

We do not venture to specifically find that 615 Bourbon Street, L.L.C., as owner and lessor of the subject premises, is responsible for the alleged damages caused in this particular instance, as that issue is not specifically before the Court. As discussed above, we decide today only that the Court of Appeal was erroneous in its conclusion that a proprietor/landowner/lessor may not be responsible for the actions of its lessee under article 667 of the Louisiana Civil Code. Because we find that an owner lessor can be responsible for damages caused by its lessee tenant under article 667 of the Louisiana Civil Code, we therefore conclude the Court of Appeal was in error in affirming summary judgment in favor of defendant 615 Bourbon Street, L.L.C. . . .

Decree

For all of the above reasons, we find that the Court of Appeal incorrectly affirmed the trial court's grant of summary judgment in favor of Defendant 615 Bourbon Street, L.L.C. based upon the Court of Appeal's erroneous finding that there is no basis in law for holding a proprietor/owner/lessor liable under Article 667 for damages allegedly caused by its lessee. Louisiana law and jurisprudence have established that a proprietor, as landowner, can be responsible for those constructions or activities on its premises that may cause damage to its neighbors, whether the work or activities be performed by the proprietor itself or by one who maintains rights that derive from the ownership of the land, such as a tenant or lessee. . . . Accordingly, the decision of the Court of Appeal is reversed and the case is remanded to the trial court for further proceedings.

REVERSED AND REMANDED

Notes and Questions

1. In *Yokum v. 615 Bourbon Street*, 977 So.2d 859 (La. 2008), the Louisiana Supreme Court held that a lessor can be liable under Article 667 of the Civil Code for activities of its lessee when these cause real damage to a neighboring proprietor. Note carefully, however, that the Supreme Court did not reach the merits of the plaintiffs' claim in *Yokum*.

Do you think the plaintiffs would, or should, be able to establish liability under Articles 667 through 669 against 615 Bourbon Street, L.L.C. for the noisy operation of its lessee, O'Reilly Properties L.L.C.? Does it matter that the defendant's property is located in one of the most noisy entertainment districts in the United States? Does it matter that the plaintiffs' house, known as "Casa Hinard," has been continuously owned by Peterson Yokum's family for three generations (since the 1920s) and that is one of the oldest structures in all of New Orleans, dating back at least as far as 1797, and, in part, perhaps as far back as the 1720s? For the history of Yokum's French Quarter residence and the interesting life of Peterson Yokum, an accomplished portrait artist, see Angus Lind, *Creole Town House is One of the City's Oldest Buildings*, The Times-Picayune (April 4 2008).

After the decision in *625 Bourbon Street*, the Yokums continued to prosecute numerous lawsuits alleging violations of Article 667 of the Civil Code, municipal noise ordinances and state statutes against the proprietors of bars and music clubs in the vicinity of their French Quarter home. The Yokums have achieved mixed success in these lawsuits. *See, e.g., Yokum v. Pat O'Brien's Bar, Inc.*, 99 So.2d 74 (La. 4 Cir. 2012) (affirming trial court issuance of preliminary injunction to prohibit defendant from violating municipal noise ordinance and state statutes); *Yokum v. Nicholas S. Karno II, Inc.*, 126 So.3d 723 (La. App. 4 Cir. 2013) (affirming trial court's order that found operator of neighboring establishment liable for contempt and $1,000 civil fine for violating preliminary injunction requiring defendant to comply with municipal noise ordinance); *Yokum v. 544 Funky, L.L.C.*, 202 So.3d 1065, 1074–66 (La. App. 4 Cir. 2016) (affirming: (1) trial court's denial of permanent injunction requested under Articles 669 to 669 to enjoin nightclub from violating city noise ordinance and to require nightclub to institute policies to ensure level of noise emanating from nightclub did not exceed sound levels permitted by ordinance; and (2) trial court's finding that plaintiffs did not prove irreparable injury caused by nightclub's operations); *Yokum v. Funky 544 Rhythm and Blues Café*, 248 So.3d 723, 737–40 (La. 4 Cir. 2018) (affirming trial court finding that nightclub was not a nuisance under Article 667 and Article 2315 of the Civil Code).

2. The Supreme Court's decision in *Yokum* has had ramifications in other kinds of neighborhood disputes. According to a recent newspaper article, some New Orleans residents have begun to use the court's holding in *Yokum* as a tool to pressure landlords not to rent their properties to dangerous tenants. Richard A. Webster, *Mid-City residents use Louisiana Supreme Court ruling to evict nuisance neighbors*, The

Times-Picayune (May 25, 2013). The residents sent demand letters to lessors of residential property asserting that their lessees are drug dealers who create a criminal environment in the neighborhood. Citing *Yokum*, they demanded that the lessors evict the tenants known to be involved in the drug trade and screen potential tenants more carefully in the future. Reportedly, their demand letters have produced positive outcomes for the affected neighborhoods. *Id.*

3. *The proximity of neighbors under Article 667 through 669 of the Civil Code*: Another interesting fact in *Yokum* involves the degree of proximity between the neighbors. The plaintiffs' residence at 723 Toulouse Street and the defendant's property at 615–617 Bourbon Street are not adjacent to but around the corner from one another. Although the court in *Yokum* did not raise the issue of whether the two properties were situated in sufficient proximity to give rise to the obligations of neighborhood under Articles 667 to 669, this issue has been addressed in several other prominent decisions.

In *Barasich v. Columbia Gulf Transmission Co.*, 467 F.Supp.2d 676 (E.D. La. 2006), residents of various parishes in south Louisiana filed suit against oil and gas pipeline and production companies. They alleged that the long practice of dredging canals to install pipelines and gain access to and from drilling sites in the marshlands of Louisiana's coast has led to coastal erosion and the disappearance of more than one million acres of marshland and helped destroy the natural barrier which would have offered protection from hurricanes Katrina and Rita. Plaintiffs invoked Articles 667, 2315 and 2317 of the Civil Code. The federal district court dismissed the plaintiffs' suit for failure to state a claim under Louisiana law. In regards to liability under Article 667, the court found that the plaintiffs and defendants were not "neighbors" within the meaning of Article 667:

> The statute creates an "obligation of vicinage, a limitation on the use of property." *Butler v. Baber*, 529 So.2d 374, 377 (La. 1988). The statute applies only in the case of damage done to neighbors. *Id.* at 381 ("Fault under 667 is the damage done to neighboring property. . . ."); *see also Hero Land Co. v. Texaco, Inc.*, 310 So.2d 93, 97 (La. 1972) ("[Article 667] is a species of legal servitude in favor of neighboring property. . . ."). It has been used to create obligations between owners of adjacent properties, or properties that lay physically close to one another. *Inabnett v. Exxon Corp.*, 642 So.2d 1243, 1251 (La. 1994) ("The courts have referred to Articles 667–669 to determine the conduct which constitutes 'fault' under Article 2315 in the context of neighboring proprietors."); *see also Robicheaux v. Huppenbauer*, 245 So.2d 385 (1971) (owner of a horse stable could be enjoined from operation because "noxious and offensive vapors . . . diffuse themselves over the adjoining residential property"); *Chaney v. Travelers Ins. Co.*, 259 La. 1, 249 So.2d 181 (1971) (parish liable to homeowner for damage done to his home by vibration from heavy equipment used in canal digging nearby). The Court finds that the definition of "neighbor" under Article 667 does not contemplate the relationship plaintiffs assert. Plaintiffs ask for a finding of

liability between parties whose properties are hundreds of miles apart in many cases. If these parties could be held to be neighbors, the restrictive meaning of the statutory language would be eviscerated. Louisiana Civil Code article 11 requires courts, when interpreting the meaning of statutes, to give the words "their generally prevailing meaning." Plaintiffs have not suggested, and the Court is not aware of, any generally prevailing meaning of "neighbor" that could possibly apply to the relationship between a homeowner in Iberia Parish and an exploration company that dug a canal near the mouth of the Mississippi River.

The cases plaintiffs cite are unconvincing, because they all deal with relationships between property owners that are characterized by proximity. *See, e.g., Butler,* 529 So.2d 374 (oyster lessees could maintain action under Article 667 against mineral lessees whose dredging activities damaged plaintiffs' oyster beds); *Lombard v. Sewerage and Water Bd. of New Orleans,* 284 So.2d 905 (La. 1973) (plaintiffs could maintain action against a construction company whose activity while installing a drainage canal damaged homes immediately adjacent to the route of the canal); *Caldwell Country Club v. Dep't of Transp. and Dev.,* 438 So.2d 723 (La. Ct. App. 1983) (state agency's actions while excavating a creek caused excessive silt to be deposited on a neighboring golf course when it flooded, supporting recovery). Plaintiffs' Article 667 claim fails because they do not demonstrate that the "neighbor" referred to in Article 667 could be a party whose property is physically remote from that of the defendants. Moreover, as discussed *infra,* plaintiffs have not alleged that any individual defendant's actions were a cause-in-fact of any individual plaintiff's harms, further precluding recovery under Article 667.

Barasich, 467 F.Supp.2d at 690.

In *TS & C Investments, L.L.C. v. Beusa Energy, Inc.,* 637 F.Supp.2d 370, 383 (W.D. La. 2009), a putative class of plaintiffs consisting of businesses along Interstate 10 filed suit against several oil and gas drilling companies claiming they suffered economic losses as a result of an oil well blowout near Iberville Parish which damaged the highway, resulted in its temporary closure, and prevented vehicular traffic from reaching their places of business. *Id.* at 384. The federal district court dismissed the claims advanced by the putative plaintiffs under Article 667 of the Civil Code on two grounds. First, relying on *Barasich,* the court held that the class representatives were not "neighbors" within the meaning of Article 667 because nine out of the ten were located twenty miles away from the site of the well blow out. *Id.* at 38. Second, the court noted that the actual physical property damage was suffered by property adjacent to defendants' well (the interstate highway), and not by the plaintiffs' own property, which was next to the highway. *Id.* at 384. In the words of the court:

La. Civ. Code art. 667 should not be read to create a domino effect granting rights of recovery to neighbors of neighbors. Here, the neighbor who might argue recovery under La. Civ. Code art. 667 is the "owner" of Interstate 10, and not those businesses who might have been impacted by alleged damage to Interstate 10 from defendant's work on defendant's land.

TS & C Investment, 637 F.Supp. at 384.

Finally, in ***In re Katrina Canal Breaches Consolidated Litigation*, 647 F.Supp.2d 644, 648 (E.D. La. 2009)**, residents of St. Bernard Parish and the Lower Ninth Ward in Orleans Parish sought relief for damages caused by the breach of the Mississippi River-Gulf Outlet (MRGO) canal levee during Hurricane Katrina. The plaintiffs filed a class action suit against the United States claiming that the failure by the U.S. Army Corps of Engineers to properly design and maintain the levee system along the canal caused the destruction of their homes and businesses. *Id.* Noting that the closest plaintiff was located three miles away from the breached canal levee, the district court held that the plaintiffs could not be deemed "neighbors" for purposes of Article 667 of the Civil Code. *Id.* at 734. In particular, the court observed that "[a]lthough there is a paucity of guidance in the law as to the proximity required so as to be a 'neighbor' for purposes of art. 667, . . . the distance here is too attenuated for these plaintiffs to be so considered." *Id.* at 734. On appeal, the U.S. Fifth Circuit did not address the plaintiffs' claims under Article 667, as it found the government immune from suit on other grounds. *In re Katrina Canal Breaches Litigation*, 673 F.3d 381 (5th Cir. 2012).

4. Encroaching Buildings

The newest legal servitude recognized in the Louisiana Civil Code addresses a frequent problem that has troubled courts in Louisiana and other jurisdictions for centuries. Suppose, for example, that a landowner has constructed a building on her property; but, due to an innocent misapprehension about the precise location of the property line, the building rests at least in part on her neighbor's property. When the encroachment is discovered by the neighbor who suffered the encroachment, the two neighbors might bargain and reach an amicable solution. The owner of the encroaching building might purchase a small portion of the adjacent owner's land. Otherwise, if a negotiated solution cannot be reached and the owner of the property subject to the encroachment files a lawsuit, a court will face a harsh choice.

The law of trespass and the rules of accession could require a court to order the encroaching landowner to remove the encroaching portion of the building from her neighbor's land. Recall that Article 497 of the Civil Code seems to contemplate just such a result. *See* La. Civ. Code art. 497 (1979) ("When constructions, plantings or works are made by a bad faith possessor, the owner of the immovable may keep them or he may demand their demolition and removal at the expense of the possessor, and, in addition, damages for the injury he may have sustained."). Removal of the encroaching portion of the building at the request of the property owner who refuses to keep the building could be very expensive to the encroacher.

If the owner of the encroaching building can establish that she is a good faith possessor under Article 487 of the Civil Code, she might avail herself of the more generous accession rules established under Article 496 of the Civil Code. *See* La. Civ. Code art. 496 (1979) ("When constructions, plantings or works are made by a possessor in good faith, the owner of the immovable may not demand their demolition and removal. He is bound to keep them and at his option to pay to the possessor either the cost of the materials and of the workmanship, or their current value, or the enhanced value of the immovable."). Several problems, however, prevent ready recourse to Article 496. First, the person who constructs the encroaching building usually will not have an "act translative of ownership" describing the neighbor's property subject to the encroachment and, therefore, cannot be a good faith possessor under Article 487. *See* La. Civ. Code art. 487 (1979) ("For purposes of accession, a possessor is in good faith when he possesses by virtue of an act translative of ownership and does not know of any defects in his ownership."). Further, even if she did possess by virtue of such an act, Article 496, just like Article 497, seems to contemplate "constructions" or "works" that are entirely situated on someone else's land, not partial encroachments. Finally, even if Article 496 could apply to partial encroachments, it would seem to require partial ownership of the building by two different landowners—an awkward result to say the least.

Because of this gap in the law, Louisiana courts struggled with the problem of encroachments for decades. Relying upon equitable principles and the common law doctrine of "balancing the equities" in particular, some Louisiana courts refused to order the owner of the encroaching building to tear down the building when the encroacher acted in innocence and the complaining landowner had acquiesced in the encroachment for some period of time. In these cases, the courts restricted the complaining landowner to either a remedy in damages or a forced sale of the land occupied by the encroaching building. *See e.g., Porkorny v. Pratt*, 34 So. 706, 707 (La. 1903) (limiting acquiescing landowner to remedy in damages for a party wall that encroached a few inches onto the landowner's property); *Morehead v. Smith*, 225 So.2d 729, 734–36 (La. App. 2 Cir. 1969) (on rehearing) (granting landowner's demand for a forced sale of land taken in light of the good faith of the encroacher and the destruction of the entire building otherwise). Other courts refused to fashion this kind of equitable remedy and ordered demolition and removal of parts of encroaching buildings. *See Ensard v. Cangelosi*, 8 So.2d 673, 678–679 (La. 1942) (on rehearing) (ordering demolition and removal of a wall that encroached six inches on another's property).

In 1977, the legislature added Article 670 to the Civil Code, which codified the judicial decisions described above. Here is the text:

Art. 670. Encroaching building

When a landowner constructs in good faith a building that encroaches on an adjacent estate and the owner of that estate does not complain within a reasonable time after he knew or should have known of the encroachment, or in any event complains only after the construction is substantially completed the court may allow the building to remain. The owner of the building acquires a predial servitude on the land occupied by the building upon payment of compensation for the value of the servitude taken and for any other damage that the neighbor has suffered.

La. Civ. Code art. 670 (1977). As you can see, the application of this provision requires a court to consider a number of questions, including: (1) whether the encroaching building was constructed or maintained in good faith; (2) whether the would-be servient landowner complained within a reasonable time or waited to complain until after substantial completion of the building; (3) what the physical dimensions of the servitude under this provision should be; and (4) what the amount of compensation owed for the servitude claimed should be. In the following decision, Judge (later Justice) Knoll addresses all four of these issues. Identify her solutions.

Bushnell v. Artis

445 So.2d 152 (La. App. 3 Cir. 1984)

KNOLL, Judge. This suit involves a boundary dispute and a predial servitude between adjoining landowners in Allen Parish. The trial court determined that the plaintiffs owned a 15 foot wide strip of land between the homes, but awarded defendant a predial servitude because defendant's home encroached on the disputed land. As compensation for the predial servitude the defendant was ordered to pay plaintiffs $1500. The plaintiffs have appealed asking that defendant's home be demolished or, in the alternative, that the amount of compensation be increased. The defendant has answered the appeal seeking a reduction of the amount of compensation awarded. . . .

Facts

In 1965 Dallas Simeon sold the following described tract to the plaintiffs:

> The East one hundred five (105) feet off Lot Nine (9) of the Nixon Subdivision of Northwest Quarter Section Thirty-six (36) Township Six (6) South, Range Five (5) West of Louisiana Meridian. This tract is subject to a Fifteen (15) foot strip off the West side of said lot.

Mr. Simeon testified that the notary public who prepared the deed thought that the tract was subject to a 15 foot alley on the west side of the lot. No alley actually existed. Nonetheless, shortly after their purchase, plaintiffs erected a chain link fence which was offset twelve feet from their western boundary.

In 1977 Dallas Simeon sold defendant a fifty foot lot west of and adjacent to plaintiffs' land. There was no reference in defendant's deed to the fifteen foot strip of land described in plaintiffs' conveyance. Defendant constructed a brick home which encroaches approximately six feet onto the disputed fifteen foot strip.

Neither party to this appeal has contested that portion of the trial court's judgment which recognized plaintiffs' ownership of the fifteen foot strip of land.

Applicability of LSA-C.C. Art. 670

Plaintiffs urge that Art. 670 is not applicable because defendant was not in good faith when she constructed her home partially on plaintiffs' land. . . .

Plaintiffs base their argument on the definition of "possessor in good faith" found in LSA-C.C. Art. 487. We disagree. That article requires the good faith possessor to possess by virtue of an act translative of title. The opening language of Art. 487 restricts that definition of good faith solely "for the purposes of accession. . . ." Art. 670 does not appear in the same title of the Civil Code as Art. 487. Accordingly, the definition of good faith found in Art. 487 is not applicable to the provisions of Art. 670.

The trial court concluded, after listening to the testimony of the various witnesses, that the defendant's encroachment on the 15 feet in dispute was in good faith. The record fully supports this finding by the trial court. The defendant testified that she had always considered that her property extended to the fence which plaintiffs erected, and she was not aware that plaintiffs had offset the fence from the boundary. Defendant had maintained her yard up to plaintiffs' fence since 1966. Defendant constructed her home several years after she had moved to the property. During construction plaintiffs never complained to defendant about the location of her new home, and they did not commence this law suit until two years after construction was completed. This case does not approach the bad faith exemplified in either *Esnard v. Cangelosi*, 200 La. 703, 8 So. 2d 673 (1942) or *Barker v. Houssiere-Latreille Oil Co.*, 160 La. 52, 106 So. 672 (1925). The trial court's determination that defendant acted in good faith is reasonable and well supported by the record. Accordingly, we will not disturb this factual finding, therefore, the defendant is entitled to a predial servitude.

Extent of Servitude

LSA-C.C. Art. 670 was enacted in 1978 to empower the courts with discretionary authority to grant a predial servitude to landowners who constructed a building in good faith which encroached on an adjacent estate. This authority is premised on the provision that compensation be made to the adjoining landowner burdened by the servitude. *Thompson v. Hemphill*, 438 So. 2d 1124 (La. App. 2nd Cir. 1983).

In the case *sub judice* the defendant's home encroaches on plaintiffs' property for approximately six feet. The trial court awarded the encroaching landowner a predial servitude to allow a straight line boundary (of servitude) on a line 3 feet east of the east edge of defendant's roof from the rear of her lot south to the street.

The trial court's well reasoned opinion reflects sound reasoning in fixing the predial servitude. The trial judge stated:

> ". . . However, defendant must be allowed enough room to maintain and repair her building and keep noxious weeds from that part of her house.

> *In addition, it should be self evident that plaintiff and defendant have very poor relations with each other but seem destined to be neighbors. A straight boundary dividing their respective territory would seem more likely to eventually lessen their differences, rather than the possibility of a fence with right angle turns encompassing the immediate perimeter of defendant's house as a constant reminder to the parties and their successors of the problem which now is of such vital interest to them and which needs very badly to be put to rest."*

We therefore find that the predial servitude granted by the trial court under LSA-- C.C. Art. 670 was not error.

Compensation

In determining compensation for the predial servitude, the trial judge stated:

> *"Various land estimates are of record which are self explanatory. It must be remembered (and this court feels should be considered) that this is a taking of the surface in perpetuity and not a voluntary transaction, therefore normal front foot values found in area commercial transactions should not apply. It is the opinion of the court that the sum of $1500.00 would be a fair compensation for the servitude above described."*

The plaintiffs contend that compensation for the value of the servitude would include the value of the house placed on the encroaching land. They reason that the amount of the servitude is 15 feet and the total width of the lot that the house is on, is 50 feet. Therefore the servitude represents one-fourth the size of the entire lot. They place a value on the house and lot of $30,000 and arrive at a value of $6,000 for the servitude. The plaintiffs cite no authority for their method in arriving at the value of the servitude. Art. 670 does not provide a method to determine compensation. The defendant urges the value of the servitude to be between $453 and $500 which was an amount fixed by two appraisers. We find that the trial judge relied on sound reasoning in arriving at a value of $1,500 for the value of the servitude. In absence of manifest error, we will not disturb the trial court's factual determinations. *Canter v. Koehring Company* 283 So. 2d 716 (La. 1973).

The plaintiffs further contend that the trial court erred in denying damages for medical expenses and mental anguish. The trial judge as a trier of fact is in the best position to determine if damages were due the plaintiffs. In his written reasons it is obvious that the trial court was not impressed with this claim. The trial judge did not find any evidence that would support an award for personal injury against the defendant. We will not disturb the trial court's factual determinations where the record establishes that such finding is not clearly wrong or manifestly erroneous. *Arceneaux v. Domingue*, 365 So. 2d 1330 (La. 1978).

For the foregoing reasons the judgment of the trial court is affirmed. Costs of this appeal are assessed to the plaintiffs.

AFFIRMED.

Notes and Questions

1. **What constitutes a *building*?** Article 670 of the Civil Code applies to encroaching "buildings." Courts have shown flexibility in determining what constitutes a "building" for purposes of Article 670 of the Civil Code. In *Theresa Seafood, Inc. v. Berthelot*, 40 So.3d 132, 138 (La. App. 4 Cir. 2010), the court of appeal affirmed recognition of a servitude for encroaching portions of a dock, steel roofing covers and air conditioning compressors. Similarly, in *Atwood v. Hylan*, 685 So.2d 450, 453 (La. App. 2 Cir. 1996), the court held that a boathouse and pier encroaching on a privately held lakebed could be shielded from removal by the recognition of a servitude under Article 670.

In *Lakeside National Bank v. Moreaux*, 576 So.2d 1094, 1096 (La. App. 3 Cir. 1991), the court applied Article 670 of the Civil Code to a building and items exterior to the building's frame—a septic tank, its field lines, and underground air conditioning system pipes, which all were classified as integral parts and component parts of the building under Articles 465 and 466 of the Civil Code. The dissenting opinion in *Lakeside* stated that the court made an unwarranted extension of Article 670 by permitting a legal servitude for "things which were not in fact an integral and component part of the building itself, that is within the walls of the building itself." *Id.* at 1098. The dissent further noted that the underground septic tank, the field lines, and the air conditioning pipes are nonapparent, and, according to Article 739 of the Civil Code, are only amenable to being acquired by title. Thus, in the dissent's view, the court's holding "jurisprudentially allows for acquisition of a nonapparent servitude without title in direct contravention of the provision of La. C.C. Art. 739." *Id.* at 1099.

In *Thompson v. Hemphill*, 438 So.2d 1124 (La. App. 2 Cir. 1983), a trailer placed on a concrete slab encroached on adjacent property. The trial court granted a predial servitude under Article 670 of the Civil Code. On appeal, the Second Circuit found that the trial court erred, reasoning that, regardless of whether the trailer constitutes a "building," it was not proper to grant a predial servitude under Article 670 because the trailer was not permanently attached to the land and could be easily moved. *Id.* at 1128.

2. **Encroachment on servitudes?** Can Article 670 of the Civil Code authorize a servient estate owner to maintain a building that encroaches on a predial servitude? In *Creel v. Southern Natural Gas Co.*, 917 So.2d 491 (La. App. 1 Cir. 2005), one Louisiana appellate court answered this question in the negative. The dispute arose when the servient estate owners, the Creels, mistakenly built their house on land subject to a pipeline right of way held by the defendant, Southern Natural Gas (SNG). *Id.* Curiously, the predial servitude holder, SNG, argued that Article 670 should be applied to limit the Creels' tort claims against it based on detrimental reliance. The court ruled in favor of the Creels, observing:

> This article [670] is not applicable to the Creels' situation where the Creels' building encroaches on a servitude on their own land, rather than

encroaching on someone else's land. Application of this article to the instant situation would be non-sensical—the Creels would acquire a predial servitude on SNG's servitude on the Creels' land.

Id. at 500.

3. **Reasonable Time or Substantial Completion?** Article 670 of the Civil Code is meant to protect a property owner who, in good faith, constructs a building that encroaches on adjacent property from having to remove the encroachment. A court has discretion to award a predial servitude when the owner of the adjacent property fails to object to the construction "within a reasonable time after he knew or should have known of the encroachment, or in any event complains only after the construction is substantially completed." What result would you envisage if the encroaching building is a largely pre-fabricated structure that is erected quite quickly, before the adjacent owner has an opportunity to object? In *Pruitt v. Barry*, 551 So.2d 726, 732 (La. App. 1 Cir. 1989), the appellate court found that the adjacent owner timely complained of the encroachment and thus cut off the encroacher's right to claim a servitude under Article 670 as he objected nine days after the commencement of the construction of the aluminum building, even though construction was between 48% and 70% complete. The court refused to grant a servitude, reasoning that "the fact that the building could be substantially constructed, if not completely constructed, within a short period of time does not diminish the prudent and timely objection." *Id.* at 731–32. A dissenting opinion insisted that the phrase "*or in any event* complains only after the construction is substantially completed," literally interpreted, gave the trial court discretion to grant a servitude under Article 670, even if the adjacent owner objected within a reasonable time. *Id.* at 732 (Leblanc, J. dissenting). If a building can be quickly constructed and the objection by the adjacent owner has been given in a reasonably prompt manner, should the assumption that the encroachment can be just as quickly dismantled give a court pause before recognizing a servitude under Article 670? *See* A.N. Yiannopoulos, 4 Louisiana Civil Law Treatise, Predial Servitudes § 2.10, at 93 (4th ed. 2013).

4. In the next decision, the Louisiana Fourth Circuit addressed a particularly contentious neighbor dispute. Read the decision carefully to determine to what extent, if any, the house owned by the plaintiff, Dian Coleman Winingder, actually encroached on the property owned by the defendant, Sue Balmer. Do you believe that the court was justified in relying upon Article 670 of the Civil Code to resolve this case?

Winingder v. Balmer

632 So.2d 408 (La. App. 4 Cir. 1994)

WALTZER, Judge. . . . Plaintiff/appellee, Dian Coleman Winingder (Winingder), brought suit in September, 1989, for injunctive relief against her neighbor, Sue Ann Frances Balmer (Balmer), to restrain Balmer's proposed construction of a six foot high solid board fence along their common property line. At the time, Balmer was aware that her fence would be located, at various points, within four to six inches of Winingder's residence. The gravamen of Winingder's petition was that the close proximity of the fence to her residence would cause irreparable injury, including health and safety hazards to her family and physical damage to the improvements located on Winingder's property.

The trial court granted a temporary restraining order on September 29, 1989, which was dissolved on October 4, 1989 because of a procedural defect. Following dissolution of the restraining order, Balmer completed construction of the fence. Winingder filed First, Second and Third Amended Petitions, ultimately seeking injunctive and declaratory relief and determination of a servitude under LSA-C.C. Art. 667. Balmer filed an exception of no cause of action, which was granted by the trial court. On appeal, this Court held that the petition stated a cause of action under article 667.

Trial was held on December 14, 1992, and following the close of evidence, the trial judge ruled for the plaintiff. A judgment of January 12, 1993 granted plaintiffs a legal servitude under LSA-C.C. Art. 670 of 2.7 feet along the length of the common property line, awarded Balmer $18,000 as compensation, and ordered Winingder to pay the cost of moving the fence along the length of the servitude, each party to bear her own court cost. From that judgment, Balmer took a suspensive appeal by motion dated January 21, 1993.

Factual Background

The essential facts are not in dispute. Winingder, her husband and minor daughters have lived in the house bearing municipal number 1314 Webster Street since 1982. The house, built over eighty years ago, is located within inches of the common property line of the Balmer property, which bears municipal number 1324-26 Webster Street. At the time of Winingder's purchase, there was no fence along the common property line, except the remains of a broken down chain link structure.

Balmer purchased 1324-26 Webster Street in 1988. It adjoined the property on which her own home, bearing municipal number 1328 Webster Street, was located and where she had lived for more than fifteen years prior to her acquisition. Subsequent to her purchase, Balmer demolished the duplex and garage that constituted the improvements at 1324-26 Webster Street. Balmer was aware of the location of Winingder's home, and of the fact that it encroached on the common property line; she could also observe that Winingder's electrical utility box, air conditioning units and hot water heaters were located on the north side of her property adjoining Balmer's new acquisition, and that workmen engaged at the Winingder home had to cross onto the adjacent property in order to work on the north side of the house. Maintenance work was performed at Winingder's home on approximately a monthly basis, using the access through the Balmer property, with Balmer's knowledge and without complaint.

After Balmer's acquisition of the adjoining property, Winingder's husband initiated negotiations with Balmer seeking to achieve a mutually acceptable plan for development of Balmer's newly-acquired property, or in the alternative for purchase of a three foot strip of property along the common boundary line, but the negotiations were unsuccessful, and Balmer began construction of a solid wooden fence, six feet high, running the length of the common property line. This fence blocked off a rear window and a side window of the Winingder home, and blocked access to Winingder's utilities, hot water heaters and air conditioning units.

Plaintiff's witnesses at trial testified concerning certain specific categories of damage and hazard created by the position of the Balmer fence.

Restriction of Drainage

Ross D. Cashion, Jr., a semi-retired surveyor, testified as a graduate engineer and expert in the field of surveying immovable property. He surveyed the Winingder house and found the following encroachments along the north side of the property:

[1] The rear annex, or "carriage house", encroached on the adjacent lot by about two inches.

[2] The gutter line encroached on the north side.

Additionally, the Balmer lot had been built up above grade along her flower beds, within a space of about four feet north of the north property line of the Winingder property. Cashion offered the opinion that the board fence was so close to the Winingders' property line that the rain water from the side of the house was confined to drain through a very narrow strip of land between the fence and the building line. This confinement was so intense that it caused water to seep into the Winingder house. Prior to construction of the Balmer fence, water was fully free to spread out to the north as well as to the west, allowing for some cross drainage.

Cashion testified without contradiction that while boundary line fences are common in New Orleans, it is unusual to see a fence, particularly a board fence such as that installed by Balmer, constructed where there is a building along the property line.

Fire Hazard

Plaintiff qualified James Mazerat as an expert in fire inspections and safety programs. His expertise includes fire investigations, safety inspections and evaluations before and after fires concerning possible life safety or building code violations. He noted the following fire hazards created by the fence:

[1] According to the present floor plan, the Balmer fence denies egress through the rear laundry room window. The Winingder's first floor bath, bedroom and laundry room are located six steps below the main floor level. These rooms have two exits: through the south side of the bedroom and the north side laundry room window. Because the fence is within four inches of this window, a person attempting to flee a fire would be trapped in the laundry room or between the fence and the north wall of the house. Mazerat noted that a fire in any other part of the house would not be apparent to a person in those three lower level rooms until smoke effectively would deny them egress through the front of the house.

[2] The electrical panel is a major source of electrical house fires. The only access to the Winingders' panel is through the living room window. A workman working on the panel would be working in a confined area with energized wiring, and would not be able to avoid serious burns or other electrically-induced injury in the event of an electrical mishap because of the close quarters in which he would be working.

[3] To extinguish a fire on the north side of the house, to get to any small appliance, for example, that caught fire, the fire fighters would have to first tear down the fence.

[4] In case of a fire in the laundry room or lower level bathroom or bedroom, the fence would obscure the single window and the fire fighters would not know where to take down the fence to make entry into the house.

The fire hazard caused by the proximity of the Balmer fence constitutes an immediate danger, and is neither speculative nor remote. Such a condition clearly affects adversely the quality of life not only of Winingder, but also of her family members.

Balmer offered no evidence to contradict this testimony.

Structural Damage

Winingder offered the testimony of Edward R. Wedge, Jr., whose career includes experience as a draftsman, project manager, plant manager, and vice president of a large, regional architectural woodwork and building materials company. He has conducted two or three hundred investigations of exterior wood rot, decay, sinking and expansion, and was qualified by the trial court as an expert in the field of architectural woodwork.

Wedge examined the north wall of the Winingder home visually, and with a moisture meter, on a dry day. . . . The meter showed the wood on the north side of the Winingder carriage house below the level of the upper line of the fence to be fully saturated with water (a meter reading of thirty), in contrast to the area above the fence line, which was normal (a reading of between eight and ten). The area below the upper line of the fence was triple the Federal Housing Administration standard for the optimum moisture content for wood in this region. This saturated condition was caused, according to Wedge, by the fence's trapping humidity, leaves and mulch, all of which contribute to the saturation of the wood. . . .

Balmer offered no testimony to contradict Wedge's opinion.

Insect Damage

Joseph Azzarealo was called as an expert in structural entomology, specializing in urban pest management. . . . Azzarealo testified that the Balmer fence, in contact with the ground and only four inches from the north wall of the Winingder residence, creates "an ideal situation for termites to gain entry into a wooden structure."

He testified further that when the fence posts were dug, the chemical termite barrier that the Winingders had installed around their home was physically removed. The chemical barrier was also breached because of the debris that collects between the fence and the house wall, and which cannot be accessed for removal without taking down Balmer's fence. . . . The close proximity of the fence also encourages undetectable rodent burrows which further damage both the house and the chemical barrier surrounding it. In addition, the house cannot be inspected fully for termites annually as required for continuation of the standard termite control warranty contract. . . . The proximity of the fence is also a violation of the standard contract for termite control used by the Structural Pest Control Commission. Thus, if the Winingders were to go to the expense of removing the fence, retreating their home, and replacing the fence as Balmer insists along the property line, the contractual warranty for the termite service would be null and void.

Balmer introduced no evidence to contradict this testimony.

Applicable Legal Principles

Servitude under LSA-C.C. 670

The judgment of the trial court, granting a legal servitude in favor of the Winingder estate, and requiring payment by Winingder to Balmer of the value of the servitude and the cost of moving the Balmer fence and gate is authorized by article 670 of the Louisiana Civil Code, which provides in pertinent part: . . . .

. . . The trial judge fashioned a remedy consistent with the equitable background of article 670, to address the unusual situation created by the particular facts of this case, and the effect of such a remedy is strictly limited to those facts. These neighbors have substantial investments of money and of emotional energy in their respective homes; they share a common border, the bounds of which are undisputed, but which because of the position and encroachment of improvements, is and will continue, if unaffected, to remain a source of friction throughout the future. The trial judge, using the legal basis of the article 670 servitude, and equitable principles of article 21, recognized the equities favoring Mrs. Balmer by ordering compensation of approximately triple the value she paid for full ownership of the property on which the servitude was imposed. Mrs. Balmer remains in possession of this strip of property, and remains its owner, subject only to the servitude for which the Winingders are obliged to pay handsomely.

The encroachment by the Winingder house predates Balmer's acquisition of 1324-26 Webster Street. The encroachment appears on the survey of the property and the Winingders' windows and utilities were obvious to any interested observer. Balmer purchased her property with full knowledge of the nature and extent of these encroachments. Uncontroverted evidence was produced at trial that workmen at the Winingder home routinely gained access to the north side of the house by walking through the adjacent property, and neither Balmer nor her ancestor in title complained of this procedure. The record fully supports the trial court's implicit finding of Winingder's good faith and the need to establish a servitude. In *Bushnell v. Artis*, 445 So. 2d 152 (La. App. 3d Cir. 1984), the court of appeal affirmed a trial court's finding that:

"Defendant must be allowed enough room to maintain and repair her building and keep noxious weeds from that part of her house. . . .

Like the litigants in *Bushnell*, the Balmers and the Winingders are destined to remain neighbors. The trial court recognized the wisdom of providing a framework for that destiny that will require the least possible likelihood of necessitating further resort to the Courts. Merely to order removal of the offending fence pursuant to article 667 will not calm these turbulent waters. It is not difficult to imagine further difficulties should Mrs. Balmer reconstruct the fence at a distance of one or two inches to the north of the present fence. The trial judge chose a reasonable width for the article 670 servitude, which would allow access to the Winingders and to those having need to service the Winingder premises, while alleviating the fire hazard and moisture damage. The trial judge separated the "contending waters" of the Winingder and Balmer "oceans" with a device (the servitude) that operates not unlike the locks in a canal, to prevent the discord and disharmony attendant on the meeting of the oceans.

While the trial court's remedy under article 670 proceeds from an equitable background, plaintiff is not required to prove that she is a possessor in good faith as defined in Louisiana Civil Code article 487. Plaintiffs in *Bushnell* sought to defeat a similar article 670 servitude based on the defendant's lack of article 487 good faith, and relied on the defendant's lack of an act stating title to the portion of land representing the encroachment. The court held:

"Plaintiffs base their argument on the definition of 'possessor in good faith' found in LSA-C.C. 487. We disagree. That article requires the good faith possessor to possess by virtue of an act translative of title. The opening language of Art. 487 restricts that definition of good faith solely 'for the purposes of accession. . . .' Art. 670 does not appear in the same title of the Civil Code as Art. 487. Accordingly, the definition of good faith found in Art. 487 is not applicable to the provisions of Art. 670." *Bushnell v. Artis*, supra at p. 154.

The judgment granting Winingder's servitude implicitly finds plaintiff to have been in good faith. In the absence of manifest error, we will not disturb the trial court's factual determination of good faith within the context of LSA-C.C. 670 implicit in its rendition of judgment in Winingder's favor. *Canter v. Koehring Company*, 283 So. 2d 716 (La. 1973); *Rosell v. ESCO*, 549 So. 2d 840 (La. 1989).

Liability under LSA-C.C. 667

The trial court's finding that Balmer's fence constituted a violation of article 667 of the Civil Code is supported by the evidence. . . .

Our analysis of the legal consequences of Balmer's action in locating her fence on the property line, given the factual conclusions of the trial court, is guided by Justice Dennis' excellent summary of the relationship between articles 667 and 668 of the Louisiana Civil Code, and the distinction between "damage" and "inconvenience."

State through Dept. of Transp. and Development v. Chambers Inv. Co., 595 So.2d 598 (La. 1992). It is this distinction that controls the outcome of the case at bar.

. . . .

"Accordingly, in order to decide whether the State caused any damage to the claimant's right of ownership, we must determine whether the State's construction activities resulted in inconveniences that must be tolerated by the claimant under Article 668 or, rather, resulted in more serious inconveniences or interference that may be suppressed under Article 667. This is not always easy to determine. Broad language in certain court decisions might be taken to mean that there is no distinction between compensable and noncompensable damage, but the jurisprudence as a whole indicates that not all damage is recoverable under Article 667. In fact, as Professor Yiannopoulos has observed, "cases properly anchoring responsibility on this article either involve damage caused through fault or damage caused by constructions, by escaping dangerous substances, such as dammed water or sewage, and by ultrahazardous activities, such as dynamite blasting, spraying noxious chemicals, and pile driving operations by heavy equipment. No case has been found in which a landowner or other person was held liable under Article 667 for non-negligent acts and activities that were not ultrahazardous." Yiannopoulos on Servitudes, *supra,* Sec. 50, at 139–40, citing extensive authorities. For all other non-negligent acts, works, and activities that cause damage or inconvenience to neighbors, Professor Yiannopoulos recommends that the concept of abuse of right of ownership should be used to establish the line of demarcation between acts that constitute a lawful exercise of ownership and those that are forbidden by Article 667. *Id.,* citing D'Albora v. Tulane University, 274 So. 2d 825, 832 (La. App. 4th Cir. 1973); J. Cueto-Rua, *Abuse of Rights,* 35 La. L. Rev. 975 (1975), and other authorities. We are not prepared to say that, in all cases, a landowner must prove an abuse of right of ownership before he may suppress or recover for a violation of Article 667 by a neighbor. But we think that in a case, such as the present one, in which there is no allegation or evidence of personal injury or physical damage to property, it is consistent with the principles of the Civil Code and our jurisprudence to require proof of the presence of some type of excessive or abusive conduct to hold a landowner responsible under Article 667.

. . . .

In *Constance v. State, through Dept. of Transp. and Development*, 626 So. 2d 1151, 1157 (La. 1993), the Louisiana Supreme Court restated the *Chambers* conclusion:

"Where there is no allegation or evidence of personal injury or physical damage to property, a finding of liability under Article 667 'requires proof of the presence of some type of excessive or abusive conduct.'" (citing *Chambers.*)

Thus, it is not necessary always that plaintiff prove defendant's abuse of right. While the record reflects Balmer's total disdain for the difficulties and dangers caused by the placement of her fence on the property line, we need not reach the issue of abuse of right.[1]

Under the standard set forth in *Chambers Development Company*, in order to state a claim under the pertinent code articles, there must be a showing of personal injury or physical damage to property.

The evidence submitted by Winingder at trial supports both her deprivation of enjoyment and actual and likely future damages arising out of the location of Balmer's fence. The evidence adduced at trial shows that the Balmer fence presented a safety hazard, caused moisture damage to the house's structure, increased the likelihood of damage caused by termites and diminished the Winingder family's enjoyment of their home. These violations of the laws of vicinage give Winingder the right to amelioration of the damage and injunctive relief to forestall future damage not only to her property, but also to the lives and personal safety of her family members.

The record below amply demonstrates the unlikelihood of an amicable resolution of this conflict between neighbors. Balmer's total intransigence and unwillingness to modify the plans for her garden and garage indicate the necessity for a legal determination of Winingder's right to access to her utilities, and to removal of the fire hazard and cause of the deterioration of her home's north wall. The trial court fashioned a remedy consistent with the civilian law of servitudes and particularly designed to eliminate, to the greatest extent possible, the likelihood of future conflict. Under the specific facts of this case, we find that the court was not manifestly erroneous or clearly wrong in granting a servitude herein, and affirm the judgment of the trial court.

AFFIRMED

Notes and Questions

1. Professor Yiannopoulos has criticized the court's decision to apply Article 670 of the Civil Code in *Winingder v. Balmer*, 632 So.2d 408 (La. App. 4 Cir. 1994). Do you agree with his analysis (provided below) in regards to the applicability of Article 670 under these circumstances?

Article 670 of the Louisiana Civil Code authorizes the court to establish a servitude when a landowner erects in good faith a building that encroaches

---

1. Balmer's attitude is reflected in her suggestion in the reply brief, that the appropriate resolution of this matter would require Winingder's family home to be demolished and Mrs. Balmer to be awarded unalleged, unquantified and unproved damages. This suggestion is unsupported by the evidence or by the applicable law. Balmer has offered no proof of Winingder's bad faith in purchasing a property whose improvements encroach upon the adjacent property. Neither Balmer nor her ancestor in title complained of the position of Winingder's home or the passage of her workmen onto the adjacent property at any time prior to this litigation.

on the land of his adjoining neighbor. However, in *Winingder v. Balmer*, the court granted to a neighbor under that article a servitude of 2.7 feet along the length of the property line in the absence of any encroachment. The neighbor had erected a fence *on his own property* which, if left in place, would have caused irreparable injury to the adjoining neighbor, including health and safety hazards, as well as physical damage to improvements. Further, the court held that the fence constituted an abusive exercise of the right of ownership. Article 670 of the Louisiana Civil Code, however, does not support the grant of a servitude under the circumstances of this case. The removal of a fence that constitutes an abusive exercise of the right of ownership is a remedy provided by Article 667 of the Civil Code.

A.N. YIANNOPOULOS, 4 LOUISIANA CIVIL LAW TREATISE: PREDIAL SERVITUDES § 2:10, at 92–93 (4th ed. 2013) (emphasis in original). Is Professor Yiannopoulos correct in stating that the court held that Mrs. Balmer's fence amounted to an abuse of right? Does Mrs. Balmer's fence embody an abuse of right?

2. What was the exact extent and nature of the encroachment here? Apparently the main portion of Winingder's house itself did not encroach on the Balmer property, but the "rear annex" or "carriage house" encroached two inches on the Balmer property. Further, the gutter line encroached in some indeterminate amount. However, Mrs. Balmer's placement of her fence so close to the property line made it almost impossible for the Winingders to maintain their house in a safe condition.

3. Note that courts have, on occasion, expanded the size of the servitude under Article 670 to accommodate a building's prospective needs for maintenance and repair. *See, e.g., Bushnell v. Artis*, 445 So.2d 152, 155 (La. App. 3 Cir. 1984) (granting an additional three-foot servitude along one side of house for maintenance purposes); *Lakeside Nat'l Bank v. Moreaux*, 576 So.2d 1094, 1095 (La. App. 3 Cir. 1991) (approving a six-foot maintenance area on one side of a house).

4. *What constitutes "good faith" for purposes of Article 670?* Notice that Article 670 does not offer its own codal definition of good faith. Accordingly, it is not clear whether the owner of an encroaching building must have constructed his building in reliance of an act translative of ownership, must have conducted a survey prior to construction, or is denied good faith due to the existence of instruments recorded in the relevant public records indicating the existence of the actual boundary lines. As one of the authors of this casebook contends, however, the open-textured nature of "good faith" in the context of Article 670 is not necessarily problematic and may, in fact, be helpful:

All of these decisions applying Article 670 demonstrate that good faith in this context functions in a relatively straightforward, on-and-off manner. Rather than engage in complex, highly stylized determinations as to whether an owner acted reasonably in light of all the transactional circumstances, courts make quick, rough and ready determinations, largely focused on the simple question of whether the claimant knew he was encroaching when he started his construction project. It is true that courts often look at a number of objective facts—the presence of fences or other boundary markers, the degree of intrusion, the age of the encroachment, the neighbor's knowledge—to make an assessment about the reasonableness of the encroachment, but in the end their assessments are not highly complex. Courts also indulge in a generous presumption of good faith when they encounter the frequent problem of long-standing encroachments created by prior owners.

John A. Lovett, *Good Faith in Louisiana Property Law*, 78 LA. L. REV. 1163, 1179 (2018).

5. Common Enclosures

Landowners in Louisiana have the right to enclose their land with boundary installations ("enclosures"), including walls, fences, and vegetation. These enclosures may either be privately owned or held in indivision ("common"). Articles 673 through 688 of the Civil Code, originally derived from French (customary and codal) law and last revised in 1977 (Acts 1977, No. 514 § 1, eff. Jan 1, 1978), offer a series of rules for common enclosures. For a detailed *exposé des motifs* of the 1977 revision of the Civil Code provisions on this subject, see A. N. Yiannopoulos, *Common Walls, Fences, and Ditches: Louisiana and Comparative Law*, 35 LA. L. REV. 1249 (1975).

Common Walls. The Civil Code allows landowners to share what is called a "partition wall," or more colloquially, a "party wall," to maximize the space available for the interior of a building and to conserve land, labor and materials. The first landowner to build such a wall can place one-half of the width of the wall on his neighbor's land. However, the wall must be substantial, with its first floor of solid masonry, and it may not be wider than eighteen inches. It may not have more than three inches of plaster. If the wall meets these specifications, a landowner may encroach on a neighbor's property by up to a foot. La. Civ. Code art. 673 (1977); *see also* A.N. YIANNOPOULOS, 4 LOUISIANA CIVIL LAW TREATISE: PREDIAL SERVITUDES, § 4.1-4.24 (4th ed. 2013).

The initial encroachment by the person who constructs a party wall gives the neighboring landowner different options. First, the neighbor can ignore the wall. As long as he permits the intrusion, the neighbor bears no obligation with respect to the wall because it belongs to the landowner who built it. La. Civ. Code art. 673 rev. cmt. (f) (1977). Conversely, the neighbor can contribute to the cost of the wall. If the neighbor wishes to use a portion of the wall, the neighbor can pay one-half of the cost of building the wall and he then becomes a co-owner of that portion of the wall. The portion paid for becomes a common wall. La. Civ. Code art. 674 (1977). Finally, the neighbor can wait, and, at any time in the future, pay the current value of the wall, or of the portion he wishes to make common, and the wall, or the portion paid for, will become common. *Id.*

Walls straddling a boundary that separates two adjoining buildings are presumed to be common (up to the highest part of the lower building) unless there is proof to the contrary. La. Civ. Code art. 675 (1977). With regard to a private adjoining wall, the neighbor has a similar right to convert it into a common wall by paying the owner one-half of the current value of the wall (or of the part in which she is interested) plus one-half of the value of the corresponding soil. La. Civ. Code art. 676 (1977). Note that the neighborly prerogative to convert a wall from private to common and acquire co-ownership only applies to walls conforming to the criteria of the Civil Code for building material, height, and thickness.

Finally, the Civil Code provides specific rules governing the obligations and rights of the co-owners of a common wall. With regard to necessary repairs, the co-owners share in proportion to their interests. La. Civ. Code art. 678 (1977). A co-owner may only be relieved of his obligation for repairs if he abandons his right to use the wall in writing and if no construction of his is supported by the common wall. La. Civ. Code art. 679 (1977). The rights of co-owners of a common wall pertain to using it, making openings in it, and elevating its height. Every co-owner enjoys full use of a common wall but is barred from prejudicing its structural integrity and otherwise infringing on the rights of the neighbor. La. Civ. Code art. 680 (1977). Absent consent from the neighbor, a co-owner may not make any openings in a common wall. La. Civ. Code art. 681 (1977).

Article 681 of the Civil Code is of particular relevance for conventional servitudes as only apparent servitudes can be acquired by acquisitive prescription. *See* La. Civ. Code arts. 740, 742, 739 (1977). Because the rule in Article 681 requires neighborly consent for making an aperture in a common wall, openings in common walls embody "exterior signs" of *apparent* servitudes of light and view. Thus, in contrast to nonapparent servitudes of light and view arising out of a private wall, apparent servitudes of light and view in a common wall can, theoretically at least, be acquired by acquisitive prescription. *Palomeque v. Prudhomme*, 664 So.2d 88, 91 (La. 1995).

Finally, a co-owner has the right to elevate the height of a wall subject to its capacity to support the additional weight; however, this does not justify demolishing the structure and rebuilding a wall with the desired height. La. Civ. Code art. 682(cl.1) (1977); La. Civ. Code art. 682 rev. cmt. (b) (1977). If a common wall co-owner raises the height of the wall, this co-owner is solely responsible for the maintenance and repairs to the elevated portion. La. Civ. Code art. 682 (1977). The neighbor in turn still preserves the prerogative of converting the raised part from private to common by paying to the builder one-half of its then current value. La. Civ. Code art. 683 (1977).

Common Fences, Ditches, and Vegetation. The Louisiana Civil Code no longer distinguishes between lots in urban areas and rural fields but focuses on whether the land is enclosed or unenclosed. *See* La. Civ. Code art. 684 (1977).

A fence on a boundary will be presumed to be common unless there is proof to the contrary. La. Civ. Code art. 685 (1977). When adjoining lands are enclosed, a landowner may compel his neighbor to contribute to the expenses for the construction and repairs of common fences separating the lands. *Id*. Should the adjoining lands not be enclosed, this right accrues only to the extent prescribed by local ordinances. *Id*.

A ditch between two estates is presumed to be common unless there is proof to the contrary. La. Civ. Code art. 686 (1977). The adjoining owners are responsible for the maintenance of a common ditch. *Id*.

Trees, bushes, and other plants on a boundary line are presumed to be common unless there is proof to the contrary. La. Civ. Code art. 687 (1977). Vegetation situated on a boundary line may be removed by either of the adjoining landowners at his expense if it interferes with the enjoyment of his property. *Id*. If vegetation is located inside one estate ("separate vegetation"), the landowner may do with it as he pleases. However, a landowner may demand that the roots and branches of a neighbor's trees, bushes, or plants that extend over the boundary line and interfere with the enjoyment of his property be trimmed at the expense of the neighbor from whose estate the vegetation originates. La. Civ. Code art. 688 (1977).

Perspectives. The 1977 revision of the Civil Code with respect to the law governing common enclosures streamlined but preserved these servitudes. Independent of whether the number of landowners taking advantage of these servitudes has increased since the 1977 revision, local municipal ordinances (under the authority of La. Rev. Stat. 33:4751), zoning regulations, building restrictions, contractual arrangements by the parties, and modern technology obviate the need to invoke the codal rules in many neighbor disputes concerning common enclosures, common fences and vegetation. Consequently, reported cases are still scarce.

6. Right of Passage for Enclosed Estates

Our last legal servitude, the "Right of Passage," appears in Articles 689–696.1 of Book II of the Louisiana Civil Code. Louisiana law, just like the law of other states, has always endeavored to prevent the economic waste that would likely occur if parcels of land were left landlocked. An estate is "enclosed" when it lacks access to a nearby public road or utility. The nine articles in this portion of the Civil Code address this not infrequent problem.

Louisiana's right of passage for enclosed estates originates in provisions in the French Civil Code which themselves can be traced back to their Roman heritage. Roman law provided for a right of way across a private estate for family members to reach a tomb or a grave (*iter ad sepulcrum*). Curiously, Roman law did not have an analogue to Louisiana's right of passage for purposes of gaining access to public roads because of the institution of *limes*, which required openings between all tracts of land for agricultural and transportation purposes. Germanic law, however, recognized an even broader concept known as *uitweg* (exit, or literally, "way out") — a limitation on ownership that eventually broadened to include not only the obligation to allow one's neighbors a right of way to a church, a grave, a village or any other important location but also recognition that a plot situated on a public road should provide a means of access to a plot situated in back. *See generally* C. G. van der Merwe, *The Louisiana Right to Forced Passage Compared with the South African Way of Necessity*, 73 Tul. L. Rev. 1363, 1366–68 (1999). Today the German Civil Code speaks of a right of way by necessity (Notweg). BGB § 917.

The common law has also developed a number of doctrines which address the same problem. Terms such as "easements by necessity" or "easements implied by prior use" are used to describe how easements can be created without strict compliance with the statute of frauds. *See* Restatement (Third) Property: Servitudes §§ 2.11–2.15 (2000). Strictly speaking, the common law doctrine of easements by necessity is the closest analogue to the Louisiana right of passage. In this section, we will first review the legal framework for the right of passage and then, with our cases, focus on several interpretive problems posed by the applicable provisions in the Civil Code.

a. Entitlement to a Right of Passage, Scope and Constructions: Articles 689–691

The starting point for studying the right of passage is Article 689 of the Civil Code. Its current version provides:

Art. 689. Enclosed estate; right of passage

The owner of an enclosed estate that has no access to a public road or utility may claim a right of passage over neighboring property to the nearest public road or utility. He is bound to compensate his neighbor for the right of passage acquired and to indemnify his neighbor for the damage he may occasion.

New or additional maintenance burdens imposed upon the servient estate or intervening lands resulting from the utility servitude shall be the responsibility of the owner of the dominant estate.

La. Civ. Code art. 689 (1977, amended 2012). First, observe that Article 689 only establishes on behalf of the owner of the enclosed estate the right to "claim" a servitude over neighboring property. It does not create a conventional servitude, nor does it establish the location of the servitude. It merely gives the owner of the enclosed estate the right to *demand the establishment* of a servitude over the property situated between the enclosed estate and the nearest public road or utility. Put differently, a claim to a legal passage under Article 689 is not self-executing. *Smith v. Louisiana Dep't of Public Safety*, 620 So.2d 1172, 1189 (La. App. 1 Cir. 1992). A conventional servitude of passage comes into being when a particular right of way to a public road or utility is fixed either by agreement of the neighbors or by judicial decision. A.N. Yiannopoulos, 4 Louisiana Civil Law Treatise, Predial Servitudes § 5.3, at 282–83 (4th ed. 2013).

Nevertheless the right to demand a passage under Article 689 of the Civil Code is a powerful right. Indeed, the right of an enclosed estate owner to demand a passage

is imprescriptible. It cannot be lost by nonuse, even though the right of the intervening land owner to seek indemnification from the owner of the enclosed estate
"may be lost by prescription." La. Civ. Code art. 696 (1977).

Articles 690 and 691 of the Civil Code elaborate on the scope of a right of passage and the kind of constructions that can be erected on the right of way resulting
from a valid assertion of a right of passage under Article 689. Article 690 provides a
simple rule of proportionality:

Art. 690. Extent of Passage

The right of passage for the benefit of the enclosed estate shall be suitable
for the kind of traffic or utility that is reasonably necessary for the use of
that estate.

La. Civ. Code art. 690 (1977, amended 2012). Article 691 of the Civil Code similarly
declares that the owner of the enclosed (dominant) estate may "construct on the
right-of-way the type of road, utility, or railroad reasonably necessary for the exercise of the servitude." La. Civ. Code art. 691 (1977, amended 2012). For example,
the owner of an enclosed estate that consists of just a few acres and a single house
could reasonably demand a right-of-way of sufficient width to establish a modest
paved driveway, but not a sixty-foot wide access road capable of carrying industrial
traffic every day. Conversely, an enclosed estate that consists of 500 acres of heavily
wooded timberland might be entitled to a right-of-way sufficient to establish a serviceable logging road.

In *Elston v. Montgomery*, 70 So.3d 824, 827 (La. App. 2 Cir. 2011), the owners of
an enclosed rural estate in Bossier Parish sought to expand an existing servitude of
passage from 30 feet to 60 feet in order to accommodate a proposed subdivision. In
addition to invoking Article 690 of the Civil Code, plaintiffs advanced their claim
under Article 705, which, in the context of voluntary servitudes, similarly provides
that the extent of a servitude of passage "shall be suitable for the kind of traffic or
utility necessary for the reasonable use of the dominant estate." La. Civ. Code art.
705 (1977, amended 2012). In essence, the plaintiffs asserted that their servitude
should be expansive enough to serve the "highest and best use" they could envision
for their land. *Elston*, 70 So.3d at 832. Because much of the tract was located in a
flood zone and the local planning commission had not yet authorized the building
of a subdivision, the appellate court agreed with the trial court that the plaintiffs'
development plans were mere speculation and did not reflect the "actual needs" of
the enclosed estate as required by Article 690. *Id.* at 832–33 (citing *Davis v. Culpepper*, 794 So.2d 68 (La. App. 2nd Cir. 2001)).

What is an enclosed estate? The codal definition of an enclosed estate has changed
over time. In the nineteenth century, the proprietor of an estate was granted the
right to claim a servitude of passage for an indemnity as long as the estate had "no
way to the public road." La. Civ. Code art. 699 (1870); La. Civ. Code art. 695 (1825);
La. Civ. Code p. 136, Art. 46 (1808). In 1916, the legislature amended Article 699
of the Civil Code to allow a proprietor to claim a legal servitude if his estate "has

no way to a public road, a railroad, a tramroad or a water course." La. Acts No. 197 (1916). In 1977, the definition was further simplified and narrowed to include only estates lacking access to a public road. In 2004, the Louisiana legislature enacted a special statute to grant owners of enclosed estates accessible only by means of an extant waterway passing through neighboring property a right of passage over that waterway for purposes of gaining access to a publicly navigable waterway. La. Rev. Stat. 9:1254 (2004). For a detailed discussion of the legislative evolution of Article 689 and the various statutory iterations that complicated the interpretation of this provision, see A.N. YIANNOPOULOS, 4 LOUISIANA CIVIL LAW TREATISE, PREDIAL SERVITUDES § 5:2 (4th ed. 2013).

In 2012, the legislature expanded the definition of an enclosed estate in Article 689 of the Civil Code to include estates without access to a public road or *to a utility*. The legislature acted to overrule a controversial judgment handed down by the Louisiana Third Circuit Court of Appeal. In that case, the court had held that an enclosed estate owner only had a right to claim a right of passage for vehicular access to the nearest public road but *not* a right to erect or maintain water, telephone and electrical lines serving the enclosed estate. *See Perdue v. Cruse*, 38 So.3d 1235, 1240–42 (La. App. 3 Cir. 2010). *See also Aucoin v. Fell*, 779 So.2d 1087, 1089 (La. App. 3 Cir. 2001) (holding that there was no implied right to a utility right-of-way under Article 689). As a result of the 2012 amendments, the word "utility" was added to all of the relevant articles addressing rights of passage.

In general, the right to claim a passage across neighboring lands under Article 689 of the Civil Code is only available when an estate is truly "enclosed," that is, when it has "no access to a public road or utility." The fact that a parcel might not have direct access to the most advantageous or well-maintained public road does not suffice to qualify the estate as enclosed. In *Rockholt v. Keaty*, 237 So.2d 663 (La. 1970), the Louisiana Supreme Court addressed two issues: (1) whether an estate that literally borders an interstate highway could be deemed enclosed as it did not have a legal right to access that highway; and (2) where the right of passage should be properly located. Note that this decision pre-dates the 1977 revision of the Civil Code with regard to the right of passage.

Rockholt v. Keaty

237 So.2d 663 (La. 1970)

BARHAM, Justice. In this suit plaintiffs seek a right of passage over the defendant's property for their land which became landlocked as a result of an expropriation for Interstate 12 in East Baton Rouge Parish by the State of Louisiana through the Department of Highways. The plaintiffs originally owned a 35.521-acre tract, but after the expropriation in full ownership of a 300-foot strip through the tract, their property was left in two separated segments, a southern portion of 10.308 acres and a northern portion of 17.954 acres. It is the northern portion of the property which is involved in this litigation. This tract, trapezoidal in shape, is surrounded on the west by the lands of the defendant and by Keaty Place Subdivision, on the north by

Drusilla Place Subdivision, on the east by the land of Coastal Rentals Corporation, and on the south by the state highway, Interstate 12.

Relying upon Civil Code Articles 699 et seq., the plaintiffs alleged that their property was enclosed, and that they were entitled to a right of passage over the estate of their neighbor, the defendant Thomas S. Keaty, to the nearest public road. In their petition they recognized that Interstate 12 is the public road nearest to their property, but because it was a controlled-access highway, part of the National System of Interstate and Defense Highways, access to it had been denied in accordance with state and federal law. The right of passage sought is approximately 50 feet in width and crosses defendant's land at the corner bordering Interstate 12. This passage would give access not upon a public road but only to other property of plaintiffs at a point about 746 feet from Drusilla Drive, a public road. At the time of the filing of this suit there was no road on this other property to Drusilla Drive. However, this route is urged by plaintiffs to be the "shortest legally permissible and feasible passage to a public road" when cost, convenience, and practicality are considered.

The exception of no cause of action and the motion for summary judgment filed by defendant were sustained by the district court, and plaintiffs' suit was dismissed. On appeal taken by the plaintiffs the Court of Appeal affirmed the judgment of the district court. 226 So.2d 76. Both courts held that Article 699 of the Code is not applicable. They concluded that property is not "enclosed" within the meaning of the article when that property borders a highway, even though the highway is access-controlled and allows neither ingress nor egress. Both courts cited and relied upon the case of *English Realty Company, Inc., v. Meyer,* 228 La. 423, 82 So.2d 698 (1955).

Article 699 of our Civil Code granting private rights of way for roads of necessity (for authority, see Louisiana Constitution, Article 3, Section 37) reads:

"The owner whose estate is enclosed, and who has no way to a public road, a railroad, a tramroad or a water course may claim the right of passage on the estate of his neighbor or neighbors *to the nearest public road,* railroad, tramroad or water course and shall have the right to construct a road, railroad or tramway *according to circumstances and as the exigencies of the case may acquire* [require], over the land of his neighbor or neighbors for the purpose of getting the products of his said enclosed land to such public road, railroad, tramroad or water course, or for the cultivation of his estate, but he shall be bound to indemnify his neighbor or neighbors in proportion to the damage he may occasion" (emphasis supplied).

This article and its predecessors in our earlier Codes are based upon Code Napoleon Article 682. In 1881, however, the French article was amended to allow a right of passage also to the owner of an estate whose way to the public road was insufficient for the exploitation of his land. Planiol makes the following comment about the 1881 amendment:

"In order to solve certain difficulties created by the original draft of the law, the 1881 law made these two rulings: (1) An estate must be deemed to be enclosed, not only when it has no issue upon the public road, but if it has merely an insufficient issue ***. (2) The exploitation of the heritage of which the old law spoke must be deemed to apply to industrial exploitation as well as agricultural exploitation. These two solutions were however generally accepted before 1881." 1 Pt. 2 Planiol, Traite Elementaire de Droit Civil (Transl.La.State Law Institute, 1959), § 2920.

Planiol's comment is important for recognizing that the granting of the right of passage to enclosed estates for insufficient ingress and egress, as well as for no ingress and egress, was allowed prior to the 1881 amendment—that is, under the parent article of our Article 699. See 2 Fuzier-Herman, Code Civil Annote (1936), annotation under Article 682, pp. 208–209, cases Nos. 68, 71, 72, 79, 81, and 82.[2]

Article 699 of our Civil Code has also been amended, but for a different purpose. In 1916 the article was changed to include right of passage for lack of access to railroads, tramroads, or watercourses and the right to build a railroad or tramroad as well as a road. The amendment also added: "*** according to circumstances and as the exigencies of the case may acquire [require]." The purpose of this amendment was to allow construction of the proper facility needed in a particular case according to the circumstances and the exigencies of the case.

It is apparent that the French under their provision for passage from enclosed estates have from the beginning decided each case under its particular circumstances and have refused to reach for absolute legal pronouncements which would effect a restricted application of the law. We cannot be blind to the great change in the nature of land in our country and the needs of the people in regard to land since the adoption of our original provision. The open country and estates then in existence have rapidly disappeared, and the problems of access to estates for full utilization of them have become more complex. Additionally, estates surrounding enclosed lands may by the very nature and method of their development pose problems in affording access to the enclosed lands not foreseen or contemplated by the adopters of the Code article. The situation which brings this case to our attention—that is, the development of public roads, freeways, and expressways which necessarily deny access to abutting property owners—is of recent vintage.

Although the *English Realty Company* case said that the State had no right to deny abutting property owners access to a highway, it is now legislatively well settled that the State or its political subdivisions may deny such property owners access to certain public roads. See La.R.S. 48:301 et seq.; 23 U.S.C. 111. We also distinguish that case from the matter before us. The *English Realty* case cannot extend beyond

---

2. The general exploitation or use of the land was also anticipated under the original French article. We, too, have liberally construed the manner of use of an estate which requires passage. Littlejohn v. Cox, 15 La. Ann. 67 (1860).

the holding applicable to its particular facts. There the plaintiff purchased property *after* the building of an overpass and with knowledge of the limited accessibility afforded a portion of his property because of the highway construction. He then sold off various parcels of land until the remaining portion did not have adequate ingress and egress for a trucking business. The court in the *English Realty* case refused to let the plaintiff benefit from Article 699, holding that the enclosure was "*** not a direct consequence of the location of the land but of the act of the party seeking the relief".

In the instant case plaintiffs' property is enclosed by reason of the superior power of the State to expropriate property and to build non-access highways along and through the property of individuals. Our interpretation of Article 699 leads us to the conclusion that plaintiffs' property has become "enclosed" within the contemplation of the article because of expropriation and the construction of a non-access public road.

The argument is made that the compensation paid by the Highway Department in the expropriation suit fully compensated plaintiffs for their loss of ingress and egress, and that they should not be entitled to invoke Article 699. The loss of access was noted by the court in the expropriation suit, and some compensation for it was included in the amount awarded. Although we are not able to determine whether the award was for full compensation as though the parcel was totally landlocked forever, such a determination is not necessary. We are of the opinion that public policy would dictate that such land as is here involved, located in a desirable and strategic area, should not be taken out of use and commerce.

While Article 699 has been generally accepted as designed to benefit the landowner so he could produce profit for himself and obtain full utility of his land, it must now be deemed also to offer protection of public interest. As land becomes less available, more necessary for public habitation, use, and support, it would run contrary to public policy to encourage landlocking of such a valuable asset and forever removing it from commerce and from public as well as private benefit.

We have found enclosure as required by Article 699, and we must now determine whether the particular relief for passage sought by these plaintiffs is granted by law. The nature of the passage is governed "*** according to circumstances and as the exigencies of the case may acquire [require]". The right of passage granted is to "the nearest public road", subject to indemnification for damages occasioned to the neighbor or neighbors. Article 700 provides:

> "The owner of the estate, which is surrounded by other lands, has no right to exact the right of passage from *which of his neighbors he chooses*.

> "The passage shall be generally taken on the side where the distance is the shortest from the inclosed estate to the public road.

> "Nevertheless, it shall be fixed in the place the least injurious to the person on whose estate the passage is granted" (emphasis supplied).

The passage sought by the plaintiffs here is not to a public road but to other land of the plaintiffs on which there is no public road. The record reflects that there are numerous points of abutment where passage to a public road may be obtained, the shortest being a distance of approximately 125 feet. Plaintiffs contend that these latter properties are subject to building restrictions which would negate the possibility of obtaining passage across them, and that therefore the route here sought is the "legally" shortest and most feasible. We are not impressed with this contention. These restrictions alone would not be controlling of a landowner's right to obtain passage from enclosed land across neighboring property. We find (1) that plaintiffs do not seek passage to a public road as required by the Code and (2) that there are shorter, more direct, and more feasible routes of passage to public roads.

Under the express language of Civil Code Article 700 plaintiffs are not entitled to the relief sought against this defendant. The plaintiffs' right in regard to passage over the property of other abutting land-owners is not before us and must await adjudication in a suit to which these others are parties.

The judgments of the Court of Appeal and the district court are affirmed, but for the above stated reasons.

Notes and Questions

1. The Louisiana Supreme Court's decision in *Rockholt v. Keaty*, 237 So.2d 663 (La. 1970), has been cited many times by other courts for the general proposition that the law governing the right of passage must be interpreted in a practical and utilitarian manner and in light of contemporary social needs and recent developments. Indeed, the court clearly favors an interpretation of the relevant articles of the Civil Code that avoids property becoming permanently cut off from use and economic development. This explains the court's holding that the State's expropriation of some of Rockholt's land to build Interstate 12 in Baton Rouge, which left one portion of his land abutting the highway but without any legal access to a public road, justified recognition of Rockholt's right to a legal servitude of passage across neighboring land.

2. Given the utilitarian holding in the first part of the decision in *Rockholt*, do you think that the court's interpretation of Article 700 of the 1870 Civil Code, the predecessor of current Article 692 of the Civil Code, was equally well founded? Note the implication of the court's holding in the second part of the decision in *Rockholt* that the plaintiff will be required to seek recognition of a right of passage across one of the lots in Drusilla Place subdivision situated between Wesson Street and Rockholt's landlocked parcel. Where will the establishment of a servitude of passage likely cause the least injury to a neighboring property owner? Across one of these residential lots or across a narrow strip of defendant Keaty's property that abuts Interstate 12? What else could Keaty do with the corner of his property abutting Interstate 12? Would any of those potential uses be compatible with a servitude of passage?

3. Recent decisions continue to address the foundational question of whether a particular estate is, in fact, "enclosed" so that its owner may claim a right of passage

across neighboring lands. *See, e.g., Altemus v. Boudreaux*, 184 So.3d 142, 146 (La. App. 3 Cir. 2015) (holding that the trial court did not err in granting an alleged enclosed estate owner a 30 foot pedestrian servitude of passage over a wood trail crossing neighboring lands, even though the alleged enclosed estate was bordered by a public borrow canal on one side, because Article 689 requires access to a public road and "access to a waterway is irrelevant"); *Corley v. C & J Frye Properties, LLC*, 176 So.3d 439, 442–43 (La. App. 2 Cir. 439 2015) (holding that a parcel was enclosed even though its owner had permission to cross a neighbor's land because an area that might have furnished passage was "not developed as a road" and was periodically subject "to being inundated with water).

b. Locating and Relocating the Right of Passage; Compensation Owed to the Servient Estate Owner

Article 692 of the Civil Code governs the location of a right of passage. Its first part provides:

Art. 692. Location of Passage

The owner of the enclosed estate may not demand the right of passage or the right-of-way for the utility anywhere he chooses. The passage generally shall be taken along the shortest route from the enclosed estate to the public road or utility at the location least injurious to the intervening lands.

La. Civ. Code art. 692 (1977, amended 2012). Had this article been operative at the time *Rockholt* was decided, would the outcome of the second part of the court's decision have been any different?

In recent years, several decisions have addressed disputes over where to establish a right of passage arising under Article 689 of the Civil Code. Courts generally interpret Article 692 as requiring a two-step analysis. *See Davis v. Culpepper*, 794 So.2d 68, 72–73 (La. App. 2 Cir. 2001); *Cash Point Plantation Equestrian Ctr., Inc. v. Shelton*, 920 So.2d 974, 976 (La. App. 2 Cir. 2006). They will first decide which of the neighboring estates bordering an enclosed estate owes the servitude of passage. In making this determination, courts normally will choose the estate providing the shortest route to the nearest public road. But sometimes, especially when the estate providing the shortest route is covered by water or the costs of establishing the passage are exceptionally high, courts will establish the servitude over another estate even though it does not provide the shortest route. *Davis*, 794 So.2d at 74. Mere convenience for the enclosed estate owner, however, will not be sufficient to justify a deviation from the general rule. *Cash Point*, 920 So.2d at 979; *Avoyelles Parish v. U.S. Dep't of Interior*, 647 F.3d 570, 583 (5th Cir. 2011) ("exceptional circumstances are required before a court may depart substantially from the ordinary practice of fixing the shortest route to the nearest public road").

Once the appropriate servient estate has been chosen, courts "engage in a balancing test to determine where on the servient estate the passage should be located." *Davis*, 794 So.2d at 73. At this stage of the analysis, courts still tend to prefer the shortest distance to the nearest public road, yet they might establish a more circuitous or longer route to avoid obstructions like walls or other constructions or to steer clear of excessive construction costs. A.N. YIANNOPOULOS, 4 LOUISIANA CIVIL LAW TREATISE, PREDIAL SERVITUDE § 5:14 (4th ed. 2013). Other factors taken into account when considering how to minimize the injury to the intervening lands while minimizing expense for the owner of the enclosed estate include distance, existing roads, the degree of injury to the servient estate, practicality and cost. *Id.*

The decision featured below, *Dickerson v. Coon*, 71 So.2d 1135 (La. App. 2 Cir. 2001), is illustrative of the tensions inherent in these kinds of disputes. As you read the opinion, pay close attention to how the court resolved the other issue of damages in the case. Is the court's holding in this part of the decision still good law in light of the latest amendment to Article 689?

Finally, also consider the potential applicability of Article 695 of the Civil Code, which provides as follows:

Art. 695. Relocation of servitude

The owner of the enclosed estate has no right to the relocation of this servitude after it is fixed. The owner of the servient estate has the right to demand relocation of the servitude to a more convenient place at his own expense, provided that it affords the same facility to the owner of the enclosed estate.

La. Civ. Code art. 695 (1977). Like Article 748 of the Civil Code, which addresses the right of servient estate owners to relocate any kind of servitude at their own expense, Article 695 provides a landowner who is required to provide passage to an enclosed estate a unilateral right to relocate the servitude to "a more convenient place at his own expense" as long as the new location provides the same general level of access ("the same facility")—as the prior location. Does this provision offer sufficient protection to a neighboring landowner subject to a legal servitude of passage after the initial determination of its location has been made?

Dickerson v. Coon
71 So.3d 1135 (La. App. 2 Cir. 2011)

STEWART, Judge. The defendant, Joan Terry Coon, individually and as Independent Executrix of the Succession of Henson S. Coon, Jr. (hereafter "Coon"), appeals a judgment granting a right of passage in favor of the plaintiffs, Steven Ralph Dickerson and Marcia Jeanette Simmering Dickerson (referred to jointly as "Dickerson"). Coon asserts that the trial court committed manifest error in placing the servitude along the shortest route and in failing to award damages. We find no manifest error by the trial court in fixing the servitude along the shortest route, but we do find that the trial court erred in failing to award damages for the value of the timber that will have to be removed from Coon's land.

Facts

On March 11, 2008, Dickerson filed a petition seeking a right of passage for an enclosed estate described as follows:

> The Southwest Quarter of Northeast Quarter, Section 28, Township 17 North, Range 1 East, Ouachita Parish, Louisiana, containing 40 acres, more or less.

The nearest public road is Guyton Loop Road, part of which is located on neighboring property owned by Coon and described as:

> The Northeast Quarter of Southwest Quarter and Northwest Quarter of Southeast Quarter, Section 28, Township 17 North, Range 1 East, Ouachita Parish, Louisiana.

Dickerson asked that the right of passage be located along an existing logging road that begins at Guyton Loop Road and runs through Coon's land north of the road up to the southwest corner of his land. Alternatively, Dickerson asked the court to select the shortest route from Guyton Loop Road to the southwest corner of his property.

Dickerson attached to the petition plats and surveys detailing a 15-foot wide servitude over both the logging road and the shortest route. These two routes are in the same general area of the Coon property. According to calculations based on the attachments, the distance along the logging road is 2,433.67 feet, and the route contains 0.272 acres. The distance along the shortest route is 1,433.96 feet and contains 0.242 acres.

In answer, Coon asserted that the area of the logging road is the highest point of elevation on his land. He claimed that establishing a right of passage along the logging road would bisect the property and disturb the hunting club, which leases the acreage. Coon asserted that his acreage is used to grow timber, whereas the Dickerson acreage is at a lower elevation, subject to frequent flooding, and best described as a marsh for most of the year. Coon proposed an alternative right of passage along the north boundary of his westerly tract. Coon asserted that the boundary route would provide access to Dickerson's marshy acreage without bisecting his best land or disturbing the hunting club. Dickerson had previously rejected this route.

The main issues at trial concerned the location of the right of passage and damages, if any. That the Coon property was the servient estate and owed a right of passage for the benefit of Dickerson's enclosed estate was not disputed. The trial court recognized three possible options for location of the right of passage: (1) the shortest route; (2) the existing logging road; and (3) the border or west side/north side route proposed by Coon. After hearing the evidence and viewing the properties and areas of the proposed routes in person, the trial court ordered that the right of passage be fixed along the shortest route. The trial court found that the other two options had "pros and cons of equal weight" but that the first option, the shortest route, was clearly in line with the codal provisions governing rights of passage.

Judgment was rendered September 22, 2010, granting Dickerson the right of passage across the shortest route on Coon's land from Guyton Loop Road to the southwest corner of Dickerson's enclosed estate. The judgment did not mention any award of damages to Coon. Each party was ordered to bear its own costs and pay one-half the court costs.

Mr. Henson S. Coon, Jr., died on July 28, 2010. For purposes of the appeal, his wife, Joan Terry Coon, was appointed Independent Executrix for his succession and recognized as the defendant in lieu of the deceased.

Discussion

Location of the Right of Passage

The trial court's factual findings are subject to reversal if the appellate court finds that no reasonable factual basis exists for the findings of fact and determines that the record establishes that the trial court's findings are manifestly erroneous or clearly wrong. . . .

La. C.C. art. 689 permits the owner of an estate with no access to a public road to claim a right of passage over neighboring property to the nearest public road. The owner of the enclosed estate "is bound to indemnify his neighbor for the damage he may occasion." *Id.*

La. C.C. art. 692, which governs location of the right of passage, instructs that the owner of the enclosed estate may not demand a right of passage at the location of his choice. Rather, it "generally shall be taken along the shortest route from the enclosed estate to the public road at the location least injurious to the intervening lands." La. C.C. art. 692.

The use of "generally" in La. C.C. art. 692 indicates that there are exceptions to the shortest route requirement. The circumstances of each case will determine the location of the servitude. *Anderton v. Akin*, 493 So. 2d 795, 797 (La. App. 2d Cir. 1986), *writ denied*, 497 So. 2d 1014 (La. 1986). Upon determining which estate will be burdened with the right of passage, courts usually engage in a balancing test to determine where on the servient estate the right of passage should be located. *Davis v. Culpepper*, 34,736, p. 8 (La. App. 2d Cir. 7/11/01), 794 So. 2d 68, 73–74, *writ denied*, 2001–2573 (La. 12/14/01), 804 So. 2d 646, *citing Mitcham v. Birdsong*, 573 So. 2d 1294 (La. App. 2d Cir. 1991); *Roberson v. Reese*, 376 So. 2d 1287 (La. App. 2d Cir. 1979); C. Sherburne Sentell, III, Comment, *Fixing the Right of Passage from an Enclosed Estate: Deciding Where to Break Out Using Louisiana Civil Code Article 692*, 54 La. L. Rev. 1659, 1670 (1994).

However, departure from the general rule requiring location of the right of passage along the shortest route "must be supported by weighty considerations." A.N. Yiannopoulos, 4 La. Civ. Law Treatise, Predial Servitudes § 97, at 285 (3d Ed. 2004). While courts will normally grant a right of passage that is least injurious to the servient estate, other factors such as distance, degree of injury to the servient estate, practicability, and cost weigh in the decision of where to locate the right of passage. *Id.* at 285–86.

Instruction on fixing the right of passage is found in *Anderton*, 493 So. 2d at 798, which explains that while the right of passage should be fixed at the point least injurious to the servient estate, the matter of its location is not to be left to the "caprice or option" of the party who must grant the servitude. The court must also be mindful of the rights that the law affords the dominant estate owner. As such, a right of passage that is "extremely circuitous, impracticable, and expensive" should not be selected because it is less burdensome to the servient estate owner. *Anderton, supra, citing Wells v. Anglade*, 23 So. 2d 469 (La. App. 1st Cir. 1945), *citing Littlejohn v. Cox*, 15 La. Ann. 67 (La. 1860).

Coon argues that the trial court erred in fixing the passage along the shortest route rather than along the boundary route, which would be least injurious. Coon asserts that the evidence proves that both the logging road and the shortest route would be injurious. Both routes would divide the 55 acres north of Guyton Loop Road into about a 45-acre tract east of the servitude and a 10-acre tract west of the servitude. Also, either route would bisect the 55 acres at its crown (area of highest elevation), which Coon considers a prime area for building a house.

The possibility that grandchildren might one day build a house on the property and the concern that the passage dividing the property might prevent them from doing so was expressed by the defendants' son, Henson S. Coon, III, ("Henson") in his testimony and by the defendant, Henson S. Coon, Jr., ("Mr. Coon") in his deposition, which was introduced into evidence in lieu of his testifying. Coon's expert appraiser, A. J. Burns, Jr., agreed that fixing the passage along the shortest route or the logging road would bisect the property and diminish that area's desirability as a house site.

In his deposition, Mr. Coon stated that he inherited the land from his father, had owned it for 50 years, had harvested timber, and had leased it to a hunting club for the last 17 years. He recalled that when his father purchased the property, there had been a house site in the area of the logging road. His son Henson believed there may have been a home on the property about 100 years ago. Mr. Coon also recalled that the logging road was used for a while to access an oil well on the property. About five years before Dickerson bought the land, Mr. Coon had allowed a lumber company that was harvesting timber from what is now Dickerson's land to use the logging road.

We are not persuaded by the argument that the shortest route is injurious to Coon's land because it divides the 55 acres north of Guyton Loop Road at its crown and might prevent the use of that area as a home site. Coon has owned the property for over 50 years without residential development on it. There are no plans for future development. Mr. Coon and Henson merely expressed the desire that descendants might one day build a house on the property. If the servitude interferes with any future development, the servient estate has the right to demand relocation of the servitude to a more convenient location at his expense. La. C.C. art. 695. Also, nothing in the record shows that a passage along the shortest route would interfere with the hunting club which leases the Coon property.

Steven Dickerson testified that he purchased his property, which consists of 25 acres of wetland and 15 acres of timberland, in March 2008 for recreational purposes and for a timber investment. He estimated that he would need access to the property once per week to transport tools and materials either by foot, utility vehicle, or a light truck. He has no plans to erect a permanent structure or run utilities to the property. He requested the logging road because it was comparable to the shortest route, would require limited work to make passable, and no timber would have to be cleared. However, he had no strong objection to the shortest route even though it would require him to clear timber and bring in dirt to make a passage. He explained that the boundary route would require him to clear even more timber, to bring in even more dirt, and to contract engineering work to address an area where water collects along the route.

Darryl James Rayner, Jr., a dirt contractor and owner of R & R Dirt, L.L.C., testified as an expert in road maintenance and construction on behalf of Dickerson. Rayner prepared cost estimates for constructing a passable 15-foot wide servitude along the three proposed routes. Rayner testified that it would cost $997.50 to make the existing logging road passable and would require about 45 cubic yards of dirt to fill holes and shape the roadway. Construction of a passable roadway along the shortest route would cost $4,457.50, for excavation work, installation of a drainage pipe, and dirt work to fill the area of the roadway. Construction of a passable roadway along the Coon boundary route would cost $11,220.00, and would require the setting of two drainage pipes, excavation work, and 650 cubic yards of dirt for spreading and filling along the passage.

Gregory Hebert, a professional forester, testified as an expert in timber on behalf of Dickerson and conducted a timber assessment for the shortest route and the boundary route. He did not assess the area of the logging road because he did not expect there would be a need to remove much timber in an area where a passage already existed. He determined the value of the timber along the boundary route to be $643.60, and the value of the timber along the shortest route to be $291.43.

Considering cost and practicability, this court, if sitting as the trier of fact, may have selected the existing logging road which historically had been used as a passage and is in close proximity to the shortest route. However, we cannot conclude that the trial court's selection of the shortest route is unreasonable or that reversal is warranted. The law favors the shortest route, and departure from the general rule favoring the shortest route is not supported by "weighty considerations." The shortest route will provide direct access from the Dickerson's tract to the nearest public road. Making a passable roadway along the shortest route will involve considerably less expense than doing so along Coon's proposed boundary route. From our review of the record, we find the fixing of the right of passage along the shortest route to be neither manifestly erroneous nor clearly wrong.

Damages

Coon also argues that the trial court erred in failing to address and award damages. Coon seeks damages totaling $16,891.43 for a servitude along the shortest route.

The trial court's judgment is silent as to the issue of damages. When a judgment is silent as to a party's claim or demand, it is presumed that the trial court denied the relief sought. *TSC, Inc. v. Bossier Parish Police Jury*, 38,717 (La. App. 2d Cir. 7/14/04), 878 So. 2d 880. Based on this principle of law, we find that the absence of any mention of damages in the judgment equates to a denial of damages.

La. C.C. art. 689 provides that the owner of an enclosed estate who claims a right of passage over neighboring property is "bound to indemnify his neighbor for the damage he may occasion." This provision recognizes that the owner of the servient estate "may" receive "damage" requiring indemnification by the owner of the dominant estate. *Greenway v. Wailes*, 41,412, p.12 (La. App. 2d Cir. 8/1/06), 936 So. 2d 296, 303. The *Greenway* opinion explains that "damage" under La. C.C. art. 689 does not mean compensation based on the appraised value of the servient property as though the fixing of the right of passage is an expropriation or taking of the property. The right of passage is a legal servitude, a limitation on ownership established by law for the benefit of the general public or particular persons. La. C.C. art. 659. This limitation on ownership is for the "common utility" of adjacent properties and has been part of this state's policy regarding ownership of land since statehood. *Greenway, supra* at, 41,412, p.12, 936 So. 2d at 303, *and provisions cited therein*. Moreover, the right of passage for the enclosed estate "has been a limitation on ownership of immovables since our earliest civil code." *Id.*

The burden is on the owner of the servient estate to prove the amount of damage resulting from the servitude of passage. *Bailey v. McNeely*, 2005-629 (La. App. 3d Cir. 12/30/05), 918 So. 2d 1124. Burns, Coon's expert real estate appraiser, testified as to the damages he believed would be due for the "taking" or use of the right of passage. He valued the right of passage at $2,000 based on comparable sales of "rye grass and easements" and what he learned from talking to others who had negotiated such things. Next, he determined that the 55-acre tract, which he valued at $146,000, would suffer a 10 percent diminution in value when burdened with the right of passage. Thus, he assessed damages in the amount of $14,600. He likened these damages to severance damages. Burns believed that a right of passage along the shortest route, or even the logging road, would diminish the desirability of the area for building a house. Based on Burns' testimony and the timber value attributed to the shortest route by Dickerson's timber expert, Coon seeks damages in the amount of $16,891.43.

Dickerson's expert appraiser, Richard K. Moore, could not come up with any damages or calculate any loss to Coon's property from use of a right of passage along the shortest route, or even the logging route. He believed there to be enough acreage in the area of the crown to have a home site set back from the roadway. Thus, any damage from use of the right of passage would be minimal.

When expert testimony differs, the trial court must determine the more credible evidence. *ScenicLand Const. Co., LLC v. St. Francis Medical Center, Inc.*, 41,147 (La. App. 2d Cir. 7/26/06), 936 So. 2d 247. The effect and weight to be given to expert testimony depends on the underlying facts and rests within the broad discretion of the trial court. *Id.* In deciding to accept the opinion of one expert and reject the opinion of another expert, the trial court can virtually never be manifestly erroneous. *Id.; Fox v. Fox*, 97-1914 (La. App. 1st Cir. 11/6/98), 727 So. 2d 514, *writ denied*, 1999-0265 (La. 3/19/99), 740 So. 2d 119.

By denying damages, the trial court must have accepted the expert appraisal testimony offered by Moore and rejected Burns' testimony. This finding is supported by GREENWAY, SUPRA. Burns' assessment of damages was based on his view of the right of passage as a taking for which compensation is due rather than as the exercise of a limitation on ownership that already burdened Coon's property. The trial court could have reasonably credited Moore's opinion that there would be sufficient acreage for both a homesite and roadway in the area of the shortest route and that there would be no damage resulting from use of the right of passage. Also, Burns improperly valued the right of way by comparison with sales of easements. La. C.C. art. 689 refers to indemnification for damages that may be occasioned; it does not provide for compensation to the owner of the servient estate for the right of passage.

Though we find no error in the trial court's failure to award damages based on the testimony of Coon's appraiser, we do find that the record establishes damages in the amount of $291.43 based on the value of the timber that will have to be removed from the area of the servitude. We find that this amount, $291.43, should have been awarded to Coon, and amend the trial court's judgment accordingly.

Conclusion

For the reasons explained, we affirm the judgment of the trial court fixing the servitude of passage along the shortest route. We amend the judgment to award damages of $291.43 for the removal of timber in the area of the passage. Each party is to bear his own costs on appeal.

AMENDED IN PART, and AFFIRMED AS AMENDED.

Notes and Questions

1. Do you think that the trial court in *Dickerson v. Coon*, 71 So.3d 1135 (La. App. 2 Cir. 2011), made the right choice with regard to the location of the servitude of passage on Coon's estate for the benefit of Dickerson's enclosed estate? The court of appeal indicates that if it had been sitting as the trier of fact it might have selected the existing logging road. Do you agree? What about the boundary route preferred by the servient estate owner, Coon, which, as the court of appeal observes, appears to be the least injurious to the servient estate? Why not require the enclosed estate owner, Dickerson, to incur the approximate $7,000 in additional costs to construct a road on the boundary route?

2. If members of the Coon family do, in fact, later choose to develop their property by building a house and propose to relocate the servitude of passage, what will they have to prove under Article 695 of the Civil Code? Is it efficient to have Dickerson pay approximately $5,000 to build a road over the shortest route to a public road, only to have the Coons pay more later to relocate the road? Or will the Coons likely benefit from the construction of the road on their property at the expense of Dickerson?

3. In contrast to the formalism exhibited by the court in *Dickerson*, several other recent decisions have taken advantage of the flexibility inherent in Article 692 of the Civil Code and judicial doctrine in granting enclosed estate owners a right of passage along routes that were not technically the short route to a public road. *See, e.g., Phillips Energy Partners, LLC v. Milton Crow Limited Partnership*, 166 So.3d 428, 433–39 (La. App. 3 Cir. 2015) (locating an Article 689 servitude of passage on a route other than the shortest route due to environmental concerns, including the fact that "building a road on th[e] [shortest] route would require federal wetland mitigation, significant construction costs, and acquisition of other governmental permits, and on a route other than the one "least injurious to the servient estate" because that route was heavily wooded, crossed a steep incline and creek bed and raised other safety and maintenance concerns); *Corely v. C & J Frye Properties, LLC*, 176 So.3d 439, 443–45 (La. App. 2 Cir. 2015) (affirming trial court's fixing of a servitude of passage under Article 689 to run from an enclosed estate to another tract that was non-contiguous with the enclosed estate, and not the shortest route from the enclosed tract to another non-enclosed tract of land owned by the enclosed estate owner or to the public road, because the chosen route along a gravel road was not only the historic means of access, but also was already improved whereas the shorter, alternative route was not always conducive to passage due to flooding). *But see Corley* (Caraway, J. dissenting) 176 So.3d at 445–49 (contending that the majority erred in locating the servitude over the non-contiguous tract on numerous grounds, including that another tract contiguous to the enclosed tract also provided the most direct to another tract owned by the owners of the enclosed tract or to the public road).

4. *Compensation*: In the second part of the ruling in *Dickerson*, the court addressed the amount of damages, if any, Coon was entitled to receive under Article 689 of the Civil Code as indemnification for the imposition of a servitude of passage on her land. Relying on *Greenway v. Wailes*, 936 So.2d 296, 303 (La. App. 2 Cir. 2006), the court found that "damage" under Article 689 should not include compensation for a reduction in the appraised value of the servient property "as though the fixing of the right of passage is an expropriation or taking of the property." *Dickerson*, 71 So.3d at 1141. The court rationalized this approach by noting that the limitation on ownership imposed by Article 689 has been part of Louisiana law since statehood. It thus implied that compensation for any amount beyond the physical damages suffered by the servient estate would be a windfall to its owner. Do you agree?

In Act No. 739 of the 2012 Regular Session, the Louisiana Legislature amended the second sentence of Article 689. At the time *Dickerson* was decided that sentence read: "He [the owner of the enclosed estate] is bound to indemnify his neighbor for the damage he may occasion." La. Civ. Code art. 689 (1977). After the amendment, the second sentence declares: "He is bound *to compensate his neighbor for the right of passage acquired* and to indemnify his neighbor for the damage he may occasion." La. Civ. Code Art. 689 (1977, amended 2012) (emphasis added).

Recall that at the conclusion of its opinion in *Dickerson*, the court stated that Article 689 of the Civil Code "does not provide for compensation to the owner of the servient estate for the right of passage." *Dickerson*, 71 So.3d at 1142. Has the legislature's amendment of Article 689 effectively overruled the Second Circuit Court of Appeal's jurisprudence in *Dickerson* and *Greenway*? If so, should the legislature have used even more explicit language to indicate that the compensation owed should be based on a "takings" analysis? Note that under Article 670 of the Civil Code, the owner of an encroaching building entitled to a predial servitude on an adjacent estate owes "compensation for the *value of the servitude taken* and for any other damage that the neighbor has suffered." La. Civ. Code art. 670 (1977) (emphasis added).

c. When Enclosed Estate Owners Are Not Entitled to a Right of Passage: Articles 693 and 694

Although Article 689 of the Civil Code establishes a general entitlement in favor of the owner of an enclosed estate to claim a right of passage over neighboring property to the nearest public road or utility, the Civil Code also creates two specific exceptions to this rule in Articles 693 and 694. Article 693 was an innovation in the statutory scheme for rights of passage when it was adopted as part of the 1977 revision of the Civil Code. If the owner of an enclosed estate owner causes his own property to become enclosed by failing to reserve a conventional predial servitude at the time he alienates the intervening land, he will not be entitled to claim a right of passage over neighboring lands at all. Here is the text:

Art. 693. Enclosed estate; voluntary act

> If an estate becomes enclosed as a result of a voluntary act or omission of its owner, the neighbors are not bound to furnish a passage to him or his successors.

La. Civ. Code art. 693 (1977). Derived from similar provisions in the Greek and German Civil Codes, and based on older Louisiana jurisprudence, such as *English Realty Co., Inc., v. Meyer*, 82 So.2d 698 (La. 1955), Article 693 of the Civil Code is unsympathetic to an owner who encloses his property by alienating the part of his estate over which passage to a public road was previously exercised or could have been exercised without reserving a servitude of passage to guarantee access to the retained portion of his land. In this situation of "self-enclavement" the enclosed estate owner cannot claim a legal servitude under Article 689. Rather, he is left to seek a passage across his neighbors' property to a public road either by acquiring ownership of or a servitude across a neighboring parcel that does have access to a public road. The policy rationale behind this article derives from considerations of personal responsibility and the prevention of harm to innocent neighbors. If an owner is clearly responsible for his own self-enclavement by failing to secure a means of passage to a public road or utility when he transfers part of his estate to another person, the law should not require innocent neighbors to relinquish a servitude involuntarily. In this light, Article 693 of the Civil Code puts landowners on notice that they should be careful to retain a right of passage to a public road or utility when alienating or subdividing their land.

Despite its apparent clarity and candor, courts are cautious when applying Article 693 of the Civil Code, as it has the potential to leave parcels landlocked and limit their commercial or economic use. Compare *Griffith v. Cathey*, 762 So.2d 29, 36 (La. App. 3 Cir. 2000) (declining to apply Article 693 to deny a right of passage to a purchaser who knowingly or voluntarily acquires enclosed property), with *Spotsville v. Hebert & Murrell, Inc.*, 698 So.2d 31, 34 (La. App. 3 Cir. 1997) (applying Article 693 to preclude a vendor who sold the portion of his estate with access from claiming passage for his enclosed portion under Article 689).

Should universal or particular successors of the owner who encloses himself within the meaning of Article 693 of the Civil Code be similarly precluded from claiming a right of passage under Article 689? Note that the plain language of Article 693 suggests so. At least one recent, albeit unreported decision confirms this conclusion. *See Hayward v. Winston*, 2007 WL 1300811 (La. App. 1 Cir. 2007).

In what other circumstances might courts find that a voluntary act or omission has led to self-enclosure pursuant to Article 693 of the Civil Code? In one decision, the Louisiana Supreme Court held that Article 693 did not prevent an enclosed estate owner from seeking a right of passage over neighboring lands under Article 689 when the estate had become enclosed after the execution of an act of partition. ***Leblanc v. Thibodeaux*, 615 So.2d 295 (La. 1993).** At the time of the partition, the enclosed estate owner in *Leblanc* reserved a conventional servitude of passage across neighboring lands, but this servitude was later lost by non-use. *Id.* The court reasoned that Article 693 was "drafted primarily to address a vendor's voluntary act or omissions, where the vendor fails to reserve a right of passage after his land becomes enclosed as a result of *his sale* of adjoining property," that is, "where the enclosed estate's owner has caused his dilemma by selling off his access property." *Id.* at 299 (emphasis added). Because the owners of the enclosed estate had reserved a right of passage over neighboring land at the time the original act of partition was passed, the rules of self-enclavement under Article 693 did not apply to them or their successors. *Id.* at 298–99. As Justice Lemmon put it in his pithy concurrence:

> As the majority states, Article 693 was designed to prevent an owner from claiming passage across his neighbor's land when the enclosure results from the owner's voluntary act of selling or partitioning part of the property without reserving a right of passage. Here, plaintiffs reserved a right

of passage from the tract that would otherwise have become enclosed by the partition and did not voluntarily enclose themselves. The enclosure occurred ten years later when the servitude lapsed by operation of law.

In my view, the failure to use the servitude for ten years was not the type of voluntary act or omission contemplated by Article 693. Therefore, plaintiffs are entitled to claim passage under La. Civ. Code art. 689.

Leblanc, 615 So.2d at 300. Another court similarly refused to apply Article 693 of the Civil Code and instead granted an enclosed estate owner a right of passage under Article 689 when the estate at issue had become enclosed as the result of an alienation under the threat of expropriation, but the owner did not request a right of passage during the administrative procedure. *Bouser v. Morgan,* 520 So.2d 937, 939 (La. App. 3 Cir. 1987).

The Fourth Circuit Court of Appeals has held that Article 693 of the Civil Code does prevent an enclosed estate owner from claiming a right of passage under Article 689 when the owner lost the land providing access to a highway as the result of a sheriff's sale due to his failure to pay creditors. *Petrovich v. Trabeau,* 780 So.2d 1258, 1260 (La. App. 4 Cir. 2001). In this decision, the court found that the loss of the access land was "voluntary" because (1) the enclosed estate owner was requesting a right of passage across a parcel of land that did not have any connection with his own; and (2) he had earlier abandoned a thirty-foot right of passage across the land over which he later sought the right of passage as at that time he had acquired another, larger tract with access to a highway. *Id.* at 1259–61. For a critical discussion of the decision in *Petrovich,* see Scott D. Huffstetler, *Note, Don't Fence Me In: Louisiana's Fourth Circuit Expands "Voluntariness" under Louisiana Civil Code Article 693,* 63 La. L. Rev. 111, 122–25 (2002) (arguing that *Petrovich* expands Article 693 to apply not just to juridical acts, but also to "juridical facts"—an extension not warranted by the article's scope).

Unlike Article 693 of the Civil Code, Article 694 restates a principle that has always been part of Louisiana law. It was formerly expressed in Article 701 of the 1870 Civil Code. Although Article 694 can be viewed as an exception to the general right to claim a servitude of passage under Article 689, it is more generous to the enclosed estate owner in that it provides for a right of passage but does not require the enclosed estate owner to pay any indemnity to the owner of the servient estate. Rather, it grants the enclosed estate owner the right to a gratuitous passage. Here is the text:

Article 694. Enclosed estate; voluntary alienation or partition

When in the case of partition, or a voluntary alienation of an estate or of a part thereof, property alienated or partitioned becomes enclosed, passage shall be furnished gratuitously by the owner of the land on which the passage was previously exercised, even if it is not the shortest route to the public road or utility, and even if the act of alienation or partition does not mention a servitude of passage.

La. Civ. Code art. 694 (1977, amended 2012).

The best way to understand this provision is to consider a simple illustration. Suppose that Xavier owns a two-acre parcel of land that abuts State Highway 1 on the east. Xavier partitions his land and sells or donates the western half of the parcel to his brother Yves, but Xavier retains for himself the portion of the land abutting Highway 1. Even if the act of conveyance transferring the western half of the parcel from Xavier to Yves does not provide for a right of passage across the land still owned by Xavier for the benefit of Yves' land, Yves will be entitled to a right of passage over Xavier's land. Moreover, Yves will be able to claim this passage gratuitously—without paying any indemnity or damages to Xavier. What is more, Yves will be able to claim this gratuitous passage across Xavier's land even if it might be possible to establish a shorter passage to a public road over some other neighboring estate.

Whereas Article 693 of the Civil Code precludes the owner of an enclosed estate from claiming a right of passage when she is the *vendor, donor or transferor* of land over which passage to a public road was previously possible, Article 694 protects and grants a gratuitous right of passage to the enclosed estate owner who is a *vendee, donee or acquirer* of the enclosed estate. The underlying assumption here is that the original owner (vendor, donor or transferor) must have intended to confer a right of passage to his transferee and therefore, the law will imply such a grant and recognize the transferee's right to claim it gratuitously.

In the first decision below, *Stuckey v. Collins*, 464 So.2d 346 (La. App. 2 Cir. 1985), the court addressed a situation seemingly calling for the application of Article 694 of the Civil Code, However, the court held that the enclosed estate owner had the right to claim a right of passage under Article 689 over another neighboring estate. In the next decision, *Sceroler v. Rancher*, 808 So.2d 803 (La. App. 1 Cir. 2002), the court rigorously applied Article 694. Can you reconcile these two decisions or are they irreconcilable?

Stuckey v. Collins

464 So.2d 346 (La. App. 2 Cir. 1985)

HALL, Judge. Defendant, Richard Collins, appeals from a judgment granting plaintiff, Robert G. Stuckey, an unimpeded right of passage 30 feet in width across a narrow strip of defendant's property for access to a public road. On appeal, defendant urges that since plaintiff acquired his enclosed property by purchase from a vendor whose property had access to a public road, plaintiff is entitled to a LSA-C.C. Art. 694 gratuitous servitude across his vendor's property and, consequently, is not entitled to a LSA-C.C. Art. 689 servitude across defendant's property. Plaintiff argues principally that access across the vendor's property is impractical because the property which must be crossed to get to the public road is low and swampy and the construction of a road would be prohibitively expensive; on the other hand, a road already exists from plaintiff's property to and across defendant's land and is the shortest route to the road with the least inconvenience to adjoining properties.

Statement of the Facts

On November 16, 1981, Harvey Willis purchased a tract of land containing approximately 41.5 acres, and divided the tract into lots as shown on a recorded subdivision plat, a copy of which is attached to this opinion as an appendix [see below]. He then proceeded to sell several of the lots. One of these lots, Lot 3, was sold to plaintiff Robert Stuckey on December 10, 1981. Since the lot had no access to a public road, the deed conveying the lot granted a servitude of passage over Lot 1 which was still owned by Willis. Although the deed purportedly granted a passage all the way to Highway 148, the nearest public road, the narrow strip of land immediately adjacent to the highway was not owned by Willis, but by defendant Richard Collins.

Before Stuckey purchased Lot 3, Willis cleared a passage all the way to the highway. Collins did not protest this action apparently because Collins and Willis had discussed exchanging land owned by Collins, including the small strip adjoining the highway, for other land owned by Willis. This exchange never took place.

Stuckey used the passage both before and after purchasing Lot 3 in order to enter and exit his property. Although he testified that he knew Collins owned land near the highway, Stuckey stated that he did not know that Collins owned the strip across the front of the cleared passage. Stuckey became aware that Collins owned the strip when Collins decided to erect a barrier across the front of the passage in order to protect himself from what Collins perceived as a threat to his ownership of the land.

Collins and Stuckey agreed to make the barrier across Stuckey's passage one which could be opened and closed. Collins then erected two wooden posts on each side of the passage at the point where it joined the highway, and locked a piece of cable between the two posts. A key to the lock was given to Stuckey. The barrier was supposed to be temporary, and was to be removed when the land dispute was settled.

Stuckey eventually grew tired of locking and unlocking the cable, and took the cable down. However, Collins quickly replaced it. On March 11, 1983, Stuckey filed suit, and after trial, a judgment was rendered granting Stuckey an unimpeded passage across Collins's land at the disputed point. A motion for a new trial filed by Collins was denied and Collins appealed.

The Right of Passage

Under these facts plaintiff may be entitled to an Art. 694 gratuitous servitude across the land owned or formerly owned by Willis.[3] However, the evidence shows

---

3. The requirements of Article 694 are met to the extent that the original tract owned by Willis did border on the public road, and could theoretically have provided access from Stuckey's lot to the highway at the time the lot was purchased. At the present time, however, the applicability of Article 694 is questionable for two reasons. First, the article specifically provides that passage shall

that passage across that land is impractical if not impossible. The passage would have to cross an area that holds water, is boggy and swampy, and the construction of a road would "cost a fortune."

Langevin v. Howard, 363 So.2d 1209 (La. App. 2d Cir. 1978), writ denied 366 So.2d 560 (La. 1979), cited and relied on by appellant, holds that where an Art. 694 servitude is available, an enclosed owner is not entitled to an Art. 689 servitude across other land. We hold now, however, that where passage across the vendor's land is impossible or highly impractical, an enclosed owner, even though legally entitled to an Article 694 servitude across his vendor's property, may seek an Art. 689 servitude across a neighbor's land.

The instant case presents an exceptional situation. On the one hand, construction by Stuckey of an alternate passage would "cost a fortune"; on the other hand, the inconvenience to Collins of allowing Stuckey a right of passage is minimal since a road already exists, since only about 1/100 of an acre of Collins's land is affected, and since the affected land is located at an extreme corner of Collins's unfenced property.

Although the importance of not imposing a burden of forced passage on neighboring lands will be controlling in the majority of enclosure cases arguably falling under Article 694, the growing recognition of the importance of fully utilizing land dictates that a balancing of interests approach should be employed to a limited extent on a case-by-case basis. The Louisiana Supreme Court in *Rockholt v. Keaty*, 256 La. 629, 237 So.2d 663 (La. 1970), when discussing the policies behind Article 699 (now Article 689), stated:

> "As land becomes less available, more necessary for public habitation, use, and support, it would run contrary to public policy to encourage land-locking of such a valuable asset and forever removing it from commerce and from public as well as private benefit."

The court also noted:

> "It is apparent that the French under their provision for passage from enclosed estates have from the beginning decided each case under its particular circumstances and have refused to reach for absolute legal pronouncements which would effect a restricted application of the law."

A balancing of interests is apparent in French Civil Code Article 684 which, like Article 694 of the Louisiana Civil Code, addresses the situation in which an

---

be furnished by the owner of the land on which "the passage was previously exercised." In the present case passage from Stuckey's lot has never been exercised over the land of Willis. There is no previously existing road. Thus, strict adherence to the wording of the article arguably indicates the article's inapplicability to the situation at hand. See Fuller v. Wright, 464 So.2d 350 (La. App. 2d Cir. 1985), decided this day. Second, Willis no longer owns any of the lots sold from the original tract. Thus, the question arises whether the obligation of Willis to furnish passage to Stuckey was transmitted to Willis's successors.

estate becomes enclosed as the result of the division of a larger tract of land by sale, exchange, or partition. While both articles provide for passage over the lands which composed the original tract, French Civil Code Article 684 provides that when sufficient passage cannot be made over the lands which composed the original tract, Article 682 of the French Civil Code shall apply. Article 682 corresponds with Article 689 of the Louisiana Civil Code. Thus, under the French Civil Code, Article 682 rather than Article 684 is applied in the exceptional case in which sufficient passage may not be established over the divided lands. Similarly, under the facts of the present case, Article 689 of the Louisiana Civil Code should apply instead of Article 694; Article 694, even if otherwise applicable, provides an insufficient remedy.

In this case, the shortest and only practical route from plaintiff's property to the public road is across a narrow strip at the end of defendant's property which lies between the right of way granted by plaintiff's vendor and the public road. The road is in existence and was constructed and used for a period of time with the consent of and without interference by defendant. Inconvenience and damage to defendant is minimal. Construction of a road across the property formerly owned by plaintiff's vendor would be impossible or highly impractical and economically unfeasible. Under these circumstances, the trial court correctly granted plaintiff a servitude across the defendant's land under Art. 689.

Impediment to Passage

Under the facts of this case, plaintiff is entitled to the servitude without the impediment of the posts and cable erected by defendant. The cable serves no purpose other than as an impediment. An owner entitled to an Art. 689 servitude for passage to a public road may be subjected to some inconvenience where the servient estate owner has a fence and gate. *See Pittman v. Marshall*, 104 So.2d 230 (La. App. 2d Cir. 1958). But unlike the factual situation in *Pittman* where the plaintiff's estate was used for agricultural purposes, the Stuckeys' estate is being used as a place of residence. Because the route from the road to the Stuckeys' house is a quarter of a mile long and passes through a wooded area, visitors to the residence apparently have no way to directly alert the Stuckeys of their presence at the highway. Utility company employees who need to read meters or check lines are similarly hindered. Furthermore, Stuckey testified at trial that the ground near the cable had washed down to red clay which became very slick when rain fell. Once one stopped a vehicle in order to get out and open the cable, it was very difficult to get the vehicle moving again. Another factual difference between *Pittman* and this case is that the gates in *Pittman* served the necessary purpose of enclosing livestock. But here the posts and cable are not part of a fence and were erected, according to defendant's own testimony, simply to assert and delineate his ownership of the property crossed by the road, and serves no useful purpose. Under these circumstances, the impediment to use of the passage is unreasonable and is not warranted. See LSA-C.C. Art. 690.

Indemnity for Damages

Under LSA-C.C. Art. 689, plaintiff is bound to indemnify defendant for the damage occasioned. Damages were not made an issue at the trial of the case, probably because of the posture of the pleadings at the time the case went to trial. Defendant should not be precluded from claiming damages, and we will amend the judgment to reserve defendant's right to claim indemnification of any damages sustained.

Decree

For the reasons assigned, the judgment is amended to reserve defendant's rights to seek indemnity for damages sustained, and as amended, is affirmed.

Notes and Questions

1. The decision in *Stuckey v. Collins*, 464 So.2d 346 (La. App. 2 Cir. 1985), pivots on three crucial points. First, as a matter of law, the court created a new jurisprudential exception to a previous jurisprudential interpretation of the relationship between Articles 689 and 694 of the Civil Code. In *Langevin v. Howard*, 363 So.2d 1209, 1215 (La. App. 2 Cir. 1978), the Louisiana Second Circuit Court of Appeal had held that when a gratuitous servitude of passage under Article 694 is available, the owner of the enclosed estate is not entitled to a passage servitude under Article 689 across other land. But in *Stuckey*, the same court held "that where passage across the vendor's land is impossible or highly impractical, an enclosed owner, even though legally entitled to an Article 694 servitude across his vendor's property, may seek an Article 689 servitude across a neighbor's land." *Stuckey*, 464 So.2d at 348. Is this deviation from the rule in *Langevin* justified? What policy considerations would support the court in *Stuckey*? Note the court's discussion of the broad policy statements in *Rockholt v. Keaty*, 237 So.2d 663 (La. 1970) as well as source provisions from the French Civil Code.

This part of the court's decision in *Stuckey* can be seen as moving in the same direction as the common law's "reasonable necessity" test for the creation of easements by necessity set forth in Restatement (Third) of Property: Servitudes § 2.15 (2000):

§ 2.15 Servitudes Created by Necessity

A conveyance that would otherwise deprive the land conveyed to the grantee, or land retained by the grantor, of rights necessary to reasonable enjoyment of the land implies the creation of a servitude granting or reserving such rights, unless the language or circumstances of the conveyance clearly indicate that the parties intended to deprive the property of those rights.

Id. Is the Restatement's approach to easements by necessity broader or narrower than that of the Louisiana Civil Code? For a discussion of the historical development of the easement by necessity and the policy justifications offered at common law, see RESTATEMENT (THIRD) OF PROPERTY: SERVITUDES § 2.15, cmt. a (2000). For an intriguing cross-jurisdictional study of how different legal systems resolve the problem of landlocked parcels that proposes a novel solution combining elements of a liability rule and property rule approach, see Yun-Chien Chang, *Hybrid Rule: Hidden Entitlement Protection in Access to Landlocked Land Doctrine*, 91 TUL. L. REV. 217 (2016).

2. The two other pivotal points in *Stuckey* are addressed in footnote 3 of the opinion. As the court noted, passage to Stuckey's enclosed lot had never been exercised over the land of Willis — the land over which a gratuitous passage under Article 694 of the Civil Code might have been claimed. Thus, a literal reading of the language in Article 694 ("the land on which the passage was previously exercised") might have negated the possibility of a gratuitous passage over Willis' land anyway. As the court noted in *Stuckey*, jurisprudence supports this kind of literal reading of Article 694. *See Fuller v. Wright*, 464 So.2d 350, 352–53 (La. App. 2 Cir. 1985) (noting that for enforcement of a gratuitous passage under Article 694 "the right of passage must have been previously used or exercised"). In the next opinion, observe carefully how the First Circuit Court of Appeal addresses the same issue.

3. In footnote 3, the court in *Stuckey* further identified the interpretive problem created by the fact that none of the lots that originally comprised Willis' land was still owned by Willis. The question of whether, and under what circumstances, Article 694 of the Civil Code applies to *successors* of the landowner responsible for creating the enclosure is discussed below.

Sceroler v. Rancher

808 So.2d 803 (La. App. 1 Cir. 2002)

CLAIBORNE, Judge. This case involves a dispute about the plaintiffs' right to access a public road from their enclosed estates south of Denham Springs, Louisiana, and the validity of an alleged compromise agreement. The trial court articulated very detailed and well-written reasons for judgment in holding that plaintiffs were not entitled to a predial servitude under La. Civ. Code art. 689 but were instead entitled to one in the form of a gratuitous right of passage over the property of their donor according to La. Civ. Code art. 694. The trial court further held that the parties did not have an enforceable compromise agreement to settle their differences. It is from this judgment that plaintiffs appeal. For the following reasons, we affirm.

Facts and Procedural History

For many years, Larry W. and Nelda Rebecca McDonald (the McDonalds) owned an irregular-shaped tract of land in Livingston Parish, south of Denham Springs, Louisiana. The western boundary of the property was located adjacent to property owned by the defendants, Sheila and Vardie L. Rancher, Jr. (the Ranchers). The eastern boundary of the McDonald property was located along Henderson Road. Henderson Road always served as the public road access for the McDonald property because there was no other road adjacent to the property boundaries.

In 1988, the Ranchers decided to reserve ten acres of their property for their private residence and subdivide into lots and sell the remainder of their property located adjacent to the McDonald property. The Ranchers requested that the adjacent property owners, including the McDonalds, contribute towards the cost of building a road (Rancher Drive) along the common boundary line to serve as access for the subdivision to a nearby public highway, Harris Road. None of the adjacent landowners joined in the building of Rancher Drive, so the Ranchers proceeded to build the road approximately one foot inside the common boundary line thereby denying the adjacent property owners access to Rancher Drive. The Ranchers then dedicated Rancher Drive to Livingston Parish for use as a public road into the Ranchers' subdivision. As a condition of acceptance of the road into the parish system, the Ranchers were required, at considerable expense, to build the road so as to conform with parish road standards. The Ranchers sold eight residential lots with certain property restrictions; however, the Ranchers never sold the one foot "buffer zone" strip of land between Rancher Drive and the adjacent property owners.

On April 18, 1997, the McDonalds donated a portion of their property (approximately 2.93 acres) to their daughter and her husband, Donald Joseph Sceroler, Jr. and Pasha McDonald Sceroler (the Scerolers), to give them a place to build a family home near the McDonalds. On May 12, 1997, the McDonalds donated another portion of their property (approximately 10.24 acres) to their son, Larry Benard McDonald (Ben McDonald). The western boundaries of both tracts of donated land are adjacent to the Ranchers' narrow strip of land, approximately one foot away from Rancher Drive. Only the Sceroler tract adjoins (on the eastern boundary) the McDonalds' remaining property which has access to Henderson Road. Neither tract of donated land borders any public road. Ben McDonald's tract is separated by the Sceroler tract from the McDonald's remaining land with access to Henderson Road. Both tracts of donated property are vacant, unimproved pieces of pasture land with no bayous, creeks, woods, marshes, railroads or any other obstacles on the land. There are no roads, paths or trails on the donated tracts of land. At no time did the McDonalds access the property donated to their children from any location other than the area adjacent to Henderson Road. After the donations were made, both the Scerolers' land and Ben McDonald's land had no direct access to a public road.

Shortly after the donations in 1997, Ben McDonald and the Scerolers attempted to negotiate the sale of the one foot "buffer zone" strip of land owned by the Ranchers in order to gain access to Rancher Drive. The Ranchers were not willing to sell the strip of land without the same subdivision property restrictions that were required on the lots they had previously sold also encumbering all of the Scerolers' and Ben McDonald's property. The negotiations were unsuccessful, and the Scerolers filed suit against the Ranchers alleging that their property was enclosed and demanding access to the nearest public road, Rancher Drive.

Meanwhile, Ben McDonald continued to negotiate with the Ranchers in an attempt to purchase the one foot "buffer zone" strip of land. The Ranchers indicated their willingness to sell the strip of land provided the Scerolers and Ben McDonald were willing to subject the strip of land AND their respective tracts of land to the same restrictions imposed on the lots previously sold by the Ranchers.

Communications by letter and telephone conversations were ongoing between Ben McDonald's and the Scerolers' (plaintiffs') attorney and the Ranchers' attorney, concerning a possible compromise of the litigation. Plaintiffs' attorney wrote to the Ranchers' attorney on April 7, 1998, suggesting that "Ben and/or Pasha buy the strip of property bordering their land" and "by counter letter" assure the Ranchers that the property would not be used for any objectionable purpose. In a letter dated April 28, 1998, the Ranchers' attorney indicated that the Ranchers were willing to sell the "property in question" for $15,000 along with some proposed property restrictions to be "placed on the property conveyed." On May 11, 1998, in a letter to the Ranchers' attorney, plaintiffs' attorney accepted "the offer set out" in the April 28, 1998 letter and then indicated that he would have the proposed property description and "necessary conveyances" prepared. Then, by letter on June 17, 1998, plaintiffs' attorney wrote to the Ranchers' attorney enclosing "a draft of the Cash Sale between Ben McDonald and Vardie and Sheila Rancher." The letter stated: "as I understand it, Ben and the Ranchers have agreed to these terms and are ready to sign the deed." The last paragraph of the letter states: "if there are any terms that need to be changed, please let me know so that I can make the necessary changes. Otherwise, I look forward to hearing from you soon." After seeing the draft of the sale documents, the Ranchers notified their attorney that they would not sign the documents because the property restrictions were not encumbering all of the property that the Ranchers believed were a part of the agreement. On April 27, 1999, Ben McDonald and Pasha McDonald Sceroler filed suit for specific performance of the settlement agreement between them and the Ranchers. The two lawsuits were consolidated for trial which took place on June 18, 1999.

The trial court rendered judgment in favor of the Ranchers, dismissing plaintiffs' demands for access to Rancher Drive and for the sale of the one foot strip of property according to the alleged agreement. Plaintiffs appealed, arguing that the trial court erred in finding a gratuitous right of passage over their donor parents' property to Henderson Road instead of granting them access to the nearest public road, Rancher Drive. Plaintiffs also contend the trial court committed manifest error in finding an invalid compromise agreement.

Predial Servitude of Right of Passage

The question of what kind of passage the plaintiffs are entitled to is a question of law requiring *de novo* review. . . .

The facts surrounding the right of passage in this case are undisputed. The McDonalds donated property to plaintiffs without expressly giving plaintiffs a servitude of passage to allow access to Henderson Road. It is clear that both of the donated tracts of land are without access to a public road, except through the McDonalds' property. The nearest public road to both donated tracts of land is Rancher Drive, which can only be accessed by both tracts of land over the Ranchers' one foot strip of property. The McDonalds created this dilemma when they donated the enclosed tracts to the plaintiffs without leaving access to a public road. Prior to the donations, the land was not enclosed—the access to a public road was to Henderson Road. Plaintiffs did not create the enclosure, they merely *acquired* the enclosed property. Thus, if the plaintiffs are owners of a true enclave without access to a public road, they are not prohibited from seeking a right of passage by Article 693. See *Griffith v. Cathey*, 99-923, p. 10 (La. App. 3d Cir. 2/2/00), 762 So. 2d 29, 36, writ denied, 2000-1875 (La. 10/6/00), 771 So. 2d 85.

Article 694 is mandatorily applied when land becomes enclosed as a result of a voluntary alienation such as a sale, exchange, donation, subdivision or any other transaction that involves transfer of ownership. See A. N. Yiannopoulos, Predial Servitudes § 103, at 297–298, 4 Louisiana Civil Law Treatise (2d ed. 1997). Yiannopoulos observes, "in all cases, the right to demand a gratuitous passage is accorded to one who *acquires* an enclosed estate as a result of a voluntary alienation . . . of property." Yiannopoulos, Predial Servitudes § 103, at 297–298.

Although plaintiffs would clearly prefer to access the much closer public road (Rancher Drive) through the Ranchers' property, Article 689 only applies if the owner of the enclosed estate "has no access to a public road." If the owner of the enclosed estate is entitled to a gratuitous servitude of passage over "the land on which passage was previously exercised, even if it is not the shortest route to the public road," under Article 694, then technically Article 689 does not apply. The "access to a public road" is available over the land on which the passage was previously exercised. Thus, where a gratuitous passage is available under Article 694, an enclosed landowner is not entitled to an Article 689 servitude across a neighbor's land. See *Langevin v. Howard*, 363 So. 2d 1209, 1215 (La. App. 2d Cir. 1978), writ denied, 366 So. 2d 560 (La. 1979). Furthermore, the obligation of the McDonalds to furnish a gratuitous passage to Henderson Road arises as a result of a legal servitude in favor of the land on which the passage was previously exercised. Pursuant to the April 18, 1997 donation, the Scerolers became the owners of a portion of such land. Thus, the Scerolers, as owners of property burdened with a legal servitude of passage, are also obligated to grant Ben McDonald a gratuitous passage over their property to the McDonald's tract in order to access Henderson Road. See *Patin v. Richard*, 291 So. 2d 879, 883–884 (La App. 3d Cir. 1974). See also *Brown v. Terry*, 103 So. 2d 541, 547–548 (La. App. 1st Cir. 1958).

The trial court correctly concluded that unless the plaintiffs could show an exception to the general rule that they must avail themselves of the gratuitous right of passage over the McDonalds' property to Henderson Road, they may not compel their neighbors (the Ranchers) to provide them with access to the closer Rancher Drive, thereby burdening the Ranchers' property. The trial court noted in its reasons for judgment that Mr. McDonald had traveled his prior estate from "boundary to boundary" by tractor and all of it had access to Henderson Road. There was no testimony about any other road or any impediment to passage anywhere on the McDonald land, including that donated to the plaintiffs. We cannot say that the plaintiffs' property was without access to Henderson Road when that was the *only* way of accessing the property from a public road before the land was subdivided and donated to plaintiffs. The mere fact that a road or pathway did not actually exist on the ground does not change the fact that the property was accessed by way of Henderson Road in the past. Article 694 dictates that where a passage has been exercised in the past, the owner of the land upon which the right of passage was previously exercised is bound to furnish a gratuitous passage.

Likewise, we do not find the facts of this case to fit the jurisprudential exception outlined in *Stuckey v. Collins*, 464 So. 2d 346, 348 (La. App. 2d Cir. 1985), that where passage across the vendor's (or donor's) land is impossible or highly impractical, an enclosed owner, even though legally entitled to an Article 694 servitude across his vendor's (or donor's) property, may seek an Article 689 servitude across a neighbor's land. The trial court noted in its reasons for judgment,

> [t]here is no showing that a passage across the Larry McDonald land is impractical if not impossible. The Sceroler land is 300–400 feet from Henderson Road and the Ben McDonald land is approximately 1,000 feet. The exact distance is not known. There is no testimony about bayous, railroads, creeks, woods, canals or marshes which would render passage difficult or impossible.

The facts do not support the *Stuckey* exception.

We agree. Mr. McDonald testified that there were no obstacles on the vacant, unimproved tracts of land. Nothing blocked his passage onto the property in the past.

We conclude, as did the trial court, that plaintiffs must avail themselves of the gratuitous right of passage under Article 694 to Henderson Road through their donor's property. Thus, plaintiffs' first three assignments of error are without merit. . . .

Conclusion

For the foregoing reasons, the judgment of the trial court is affirmed. All costs of this appeal are assigned to plaintiffs, Donald Joseph Sceroler, Jr., Pasha McDonald Sceroler and Larry Benard McDonald.

AFFIRMED.

Notes and Questions

1. In *Sceroler v. Rancher*, 808 So.2d 803 (La. App. 1 Cir. 2002), the court applied the strict rule of interpretation set forth in *Langevin v. Howard*, 363 So.2d 1209 (La. App. 2 Cir. 1978), even though allowing the plaintiffs, Donald Sceroler and Pasha McDonald Sceroler, to claim a right of passage under Article 689 across the one-foot "buffer zone," which separated the plaintiffs' estates from Rancher Drive, would have necessitated only a very modest servitude across the Ranchers' property. What facts in this case justified the court's adherence to the *Langevin* rule? Was this reasonable?

2. Why did the McDonalds refuse to contribute to the construction of Rancher Drive in the first place? Why did the McDonald children (Pasha and her husband, Donald, and Larry Bernard McDonald, aka Ben McDonald) refuse to agree to the building restrictions sought by the Ranchers for inclusion in the compromise agreement that the parties came so close to executing?

d. The Rights and Obligations of Successors with Respect to Enclosed Estates and Neighboring Lands

One of the most difficult issues in connection with the legal servitude of passage imposed under Articles 689 through 696.1 of the Civil Code concerns the rights and obligations of successors to landowners. As we discussed earlier, Article 693, which prevents the owner of an enclosed estate who is responsible for his own self-enclosure from claiming a right of passage across neighboring land under Article 689, specifically provides that this prohibition also applies to the "successors" of that owner. La. Civ. Code art. 693 (1977). Article 694, however, is silent as to whether the right to claim a gratuitous passage across a transferor's estate also covers the successors of the original transferee and transferor. Several judicial decisions have addressed this problem, but their holdings conflict.

In a 1958 decision interpreting Article 701 of the 1870 Civil Code, the predecessor to Article 694, the First Circuit Court of Appeal was clear: when the owner of an estate sells off a portion of his estate that becomes entirely enclosed by the sale, the gratuitous right of passage creates a legal servitude which benefits and binds the two estates regardless of changes in ownership. *Brown v. Terry*, 103 So.2d 541, 546–47 (La. App. 1 Cir. 1958). The Third Circuit Court of Appeal reached a similar conclusion in the context of a partition. *Patin v. Richard*, 291 So.2d 879 (La. App. 3 Cir. 1974). In this case, a long, rectangular, beach front lot had been partitioned into three smaller lots and the owner of the beach front lot, which lacked access to a public road, claimed a gratuitous passage over the middle lot. *Id.* Both the middle lot and the enclosed lot had passed to successors. *Id.* The court nevertheless held that the enclosed estate owner was entitled to gratuitous passage over the middle lot under Article 701 of the 1870 Civil Code despite the changes in ownership since the original partition. *Id.* at 883–84. Based on these decisions, Professor Yiannopoulos contends that the "new owner of an estate that became enclosed as a result of partition or voluntary alienation may claim a gratuitous passage from a coparcener of his author, from the person who voluntarily transferred to his author the enclosed estate, or *from the universal or particular successor of those persons.*" A.N. Yiannopoulos, 4 Louisiana Civil Law Treatise, Predial Servitudes § 5:24, at 339 (4th ed. 2013) (emphasis added).

The question of whether the successor of the landowner is bound to provide an Article 694 gratuitous passage must likewise furnish a gratuitous passage was reopened in the following decision handed down by the Louisiana Supreme Court. What is the status of the law now? Is *Brown v. Terry*, 103 So.2d 541 (La. App. 1 Cir. 1958) still good law? Are successors of those who voluntarily alienate enclosed estates bound to provide gratuitous passage? Or are they shielded from that obligation by Louisiana's Public Records Doctrine?

Dallas v. Farrington
490 So.2d 265 (La. 1986)

LEMMON, Justice. This action seeks a declaratory judgment recognizing a servitude of passage in favor of plaintiffs' estate across contiguous property which had been owned by plaintiffs' vendor at the time of plaintiffs' acquisition and was later sold to the vendor's son. Naming both the vendor and his son as defendants, plaintiffs also seek to enjoin the son from interfering with their use of the servitude. The issues are (1) whether plaintiffs and their vendor established a conventional servitude which plaintiffs are entitled to enforce against the vendor's son and (2) whether plaintiffs are entitled, as owners of an enclosed estate, to demand a forced passage, with or without indemnity, across the vendor's son's land to the nearest public road.

Facts

In 1964 defendant Robert Farrington, Jr. owned a parcel of ground situated between La. Highway 30 and Bayou Des Familles and described as Plot 69 of Ida Plantation. Farrington proposed to resubdivide a portion of the property into eight lots which fronted on Roblaine Street, a proposed road extending from the highway to the bayou. . . .

Although the parish authorities tentatively approved the proposed resubdivision on February 24, 1965, the proposal was eventually rejected (at a time not disclosed in the record) because of the dead-end street.

On October 18, 1965, plaintiffs signed an agreement to purchase "Lots 2 and 3 of proposed subdivision of Plot 69, Ida Plantation". Farrington accepted the agreement which contained the following condition:

> "A further condition is the granting by seller without any restrictions or reservations whatsoever of a perpetual servitude to the buyer of the right to use Rob Lane Street as a means of ingress and egress to the property herein being purchased."

On December 20, 1965, Farrington executed an act of sale conveying Lots 2 and 3 to plaintiffs. The lots were described in accordance with the May 6, 1964 survey, although that resubdivision had never been completed. However, the survey was not attached to the act of sale, and there was no mention in the act of any servitude. Moreover, the act erroneously referred to Lots 2 and 3 as part of original Plot 68 (instead of 69).

On December 21, 1965, Farrington sold Lot 1 to James Fish. The act of sale described Lot 1 in accordance with a November 16, 1964 survey which showed only Lot 1 and the highway. The survey showed that the eastern boundary of Lot 1 coincided with the property line between Plots 68 and 69 of Ida Plantation, but did not show Roblaine Street or indicate that there was a street along the western side of Lot 1.

Shortly after the sale, plaintiffs placed a mobile home on the property and built a garage, with both buildings facing Roblaine Street. They immediately began using Roblaine Street for access from their home to the highway.

Several years later, Farrington applied for approval of a plan of resubdivision of his property in Plot 69 of Ida Plantation. . . .

The resubdivision was approved on January 28, 1971. Plaintiffs were never informed of the resubdivision, although they owned a portion of the property which became Lot 69E, and they continued to use Roblaine Street for access to their home. On March 22, 1973, Lots 69C and 69D of the resubdivided plot were rezoned from residential to commercial at Farrington's request.

On April 23, 1980, Farrington sold Lots 69C and 69D to his son, defendant Robert Farrington, III. The lots were described in accordance with the recorded resubdivision plan that had been approved in 1971. The act of sale recited a cash consideration of $5,000, and Farrington's son declared in the act that he was purchasing the lots as his separate property with separate funds derived as a gift from his father to him. On the very next day, Farrington executed an act of correction, amending the incorrect property description (Plot 68 to Plot 69) in the 1965 deed to plaintiffs. [The timing of the act of correction, in relation to the transfer (essentially without consideration) of Lot 69D, is suspicious, because Farrington at first declined to make the corrections. There are strong inferences of collusion to defeat plaintiffs' right to use Roblaine Street for passage.]

After Farrington's son took title to Lot 69D, he constructed a fence across the property and sent a letter through his attorney to plaintiffs, advising them to stop using the property for access to their home. Plaintiffs then instituted this action to obtain a declaratory judgment recognizing their right to a servitude of passage and an injunction restraining the obstruction of the servitude.

The trial court rendered a judgment recognizing the servitude on the mistaken basis that the act of sale had granted such a servitude. The court then granted a motion for a new trial and rendered judgment in favor of defendants, finding that a novation had occurred.

The court of appeal affirmed on other grounds. 465 So. 2d 763. The court correctly observed that the record did not support a finding that the plaintiffs and Farrington had intended at the time of the act of sale to extinguish Farrington's obligation in the purchase agreement to grant a servitude to plaintiffs for use of Roblaine Street as a means of ingress and egress. However, the court rejected plaintiffs' claim for enforcement of the conventional servitude allegedly established by the provision in the agreement to purchase, because conventional servitudes affecting immovable property must be in writing and must be recorded in order to affect third parties.

The court further denied plaintiffs' claim for a legal servitude of passage on the basis that the public records, at the time of Farrington's sale of Lot 69D to his son, did not show that Lots 2 and 3 constituted an enclosed estate, because of the error in the plot number (Plot 68 instead of Plot 69) and because of the absence of recordation of the May 6, 1964 survey. The court concluded that since it was impossible to determine from the public records that Lots 2 and 3 constituted an enclosed estate, Farrington's son acquired Lot 69D free of any obligation to recognize a legal servitude of passage in favor of plaintiffs. We granted certiorari, primarily to consider whether Farrington's son had a valid defense to a claim for a legal servitude of passage in favor of an enclosed estate on the basis that the public records did not disclose that the estate was enclosed at the time of the acquisition of Lot 69 D. 467 So. 2d 528.

Conventional Servitude

No conventional servitude was ever established. In the agreement to purchase, Farrington obligated himself as a condition of the sale to grant plaintiffs a servitude to use Roblaine Street for passage to their property, but the grant was omitted from the act of sale which transferred the property.

Contracts affecting immovable property must be recorded in order to affect third parties. La. R.S. 9:2721 and 2756. The public records doctrine is essentially a negative doctrine declaring that what is not recorded is not effective except between the parties, and a third party in purchasing immovable property is entitled to rely on the *absence* from the public records of any unrecorded interest in the property such as a sale or a grant of a servitude. *Phillips v. Parker*, 483 So. 2d 972 (La. 1986). Because recordation is essential for effectiveness against third parties, actual knowledge by third parties of unrecorded interests is immaterial. *McDuffie v. Walker*, 125 La. 152, 51 So. 100 (1909); Redmann, *The Louisiana Law of Recordation: Some Principles and Some Problems*, 39 Tul. L. Rev. 491 (1965). This principle of the law of registry applies here so that Farrington's son acquired the property free of any conventional servitude, irrespective of any actual knowledge that the father had obligated himself to grant a servitude, since actual knowledge outside the public records is immaterial. [In the present case, plaintiffs did not allege fraud on the part of Farrington's son in obtaining title to Lot 69D for the purpose of defeating Farrington's obligation to grant a servitude, nor did plaintiffs attack the sale from Farrington to his son as simulated.] A. Yiannopoulos, 4 *Louisiana Civil Law Treatise — Predial Servitudes* § 127 (1983).

Moreover, since Farrington is no longer the owner of the property originally designated as Roblaine Street, plaintiffs can no longer demand specific performance of Farrington's obligation to grant the servitude affecting that property. [The court of appeal noted that Farrington's obligation to grant a conventional servitude terminated when the act of sale from Farrington to plaintiffs was passed. Arguably, the obligation continued and could have been enforced by an action for specific performance as long as Farrington owed the property.] Perhaps plaintiffs may be entitled to damages from Farrington because of the breach of his personal obligation to grant a conventional servitude, but that relief was not demanded in the trial court. Inasmuch as this issue remains viable after plaintiffs' other demands have been rejected by this decision, the case will be remanded to the trial court to permit plaintiffs to plead and prove any right to damages.

Legal Servitude

A legal servitude is a limitation on ownership imposed by law. La. C.C. Art. 659. The legal servitude of passage in favor of an enclosed estate is a limitation imposed by law on the ownership of lands surrounding the enclosed estate. La. C.C. Art. 689. The law affords the owner of an estate which has no access to a public road the right to demand forced passage across his neighbor's land which offers the shortest and most convenient route to a public road, usually upon payment of indemnity fixed by agreement or by the court. However, if property becomes enclosed because of an alienation of part or all of the remainder of the estate, passage must be furnished gratuitously by the owner of the land over which passage was previously exercised, even if it is not the shortest route to the public road. La. C.C. Art. 694.

The court of appeal held that plaintiffs were not entitled to claim a legal servitude from Farrington's son because the public records at the time of Farrington's son's acquisition did not disclose that Lots 2 and 3 constituted an enclosed estate. We do not agree that the law of registry affects the *right of the owner* of an estate which is actually enclosed to claim passage across neighboring lands (although conceivably the *neighbor's right* to defend against a claim for a legal servitude or to obtain indemnity might be affected by the fact that the neighbor's action caused the estate to be enclosed).

At the time of their acquisition, plaintiffs' property was an enclosed estate with no access to a public road at the time of their acquisition. Plaintiffs therefore had the right to demand from Farrington the creation of a gratuitous conventional servitude of passage, since Farrington's sale to them had caused the property sold to become enclosed. La. C.C. Art. 694; A. Yiannopoulous, *supra*, at § 99. After Farrington sold Lot 69D and was no longer the owner of the property over which plaintiffs had been entitled to demand a conventional servitude under Article 694, plaintiffs were precluded by the public records doctrine from asserting against third persons the right to demand creation of a conventional servitude (just as they would have been precluded from asserting an unrecorded conventional servitude if one had actually been granted by Farrington). Perhaps plaintiffs at that time were entitled to a legal servitude under Article 689 from the owner of one of the surrounding estates, but that question became moot when plaintiffs (by the time of trial) had acquired other access to the public road.

The legal servitude of passage terminates upon termination of the enclavement, as when the owner of the enclosed estate acquires contiguous land that has access to a public road. A. Yiannopoulos, *supra*, at § 103. See also *Perry v. Webb*, 21 La. Ann. 247 (1869); *Pousson v. Porche*, 6 La. Ann. 118 (1851). Because forced passage across a neighbor's land is no longer the only means of access to a public road after such an acquisition, the purpose of the limitation on the ownership of the surrounding lands ceases, and the right to a legal servitude passes out of existence. As this court stated in the Pousson case, even an extreme inconvenience in passing over contiguous property acquired by the owner of the formerly enclosed estate does not warrant forcing a neighbor to yield a passage over his land.

In the present case plaintiffs eventually acquired Lot 1 (originally sold by Farrington to Fish), which was contiguous land having access to the highway. Since plaintiffs' estate after the acquisition of Lot 1 had access to a public road, there was no longer any entitlement to claim a right of passage over neighboring property.

Accordingly, the judgments of the lower courts are affirmed. The case is remanded to the trial court to allow plaintiffs an opportunity to plead and prove any right to damages based on Robert G. Farrington, Jr.'s breach of his obligation to grant plaintiffs a servitude of passage.

Notes and Questions

1. Professor Yiannopoulos has criticized the Supreme Court's decision in *Dallas*:

If the recorded act of sale provides for a gratuitous passage on the lands of the vendor, a purchaser of the enclosed estate may claim that passage against all successors of the vendor. However, if the act of sale is silent as to the gratuitous passage, the vendor may convey his property to a subsequent purchaser free of the legal obligation to furnish a gratuitous passage! This solution involves a misapplication of the public records doctrine and a misunderstanding of Article 694 of the Civil Code.

Article 694 imposes on the owners of lands which before the partition or alienation furnished access to a public road a *legal* obligation to provide, after the partition or alienation, a gratuitous passage to that road. The legal obligation, implied in partitions and alienation that result in the enclavement of lands partitioned or alienated, has been imposed on coparceners in favor of other coparceners and on transferors in favor of transferees in order to prevent claims for passage against neighbors under Article 689 of the Louisiana Civil Code. Indeed, coparceners in the case of partition, and transferors in the case of a sale or other alienation, should not be allowed to shift the burden of passage on their neighbors. The public records doctrine applies to acts which according to law must be filed for registry in order to have effect against third persons. This doctrine, however, does not apply to burdens imposed by law, including legal servitudes and legal obligations. The legal obligation imposed on coparceners and transferors of lands by Article 694 of the Civil Code should be enforced against subsequent purchasers without any recordation and without regard to the public records doctrine. In holding otherwise, the Louisiana Supreme Court apparently confused the *legal* obligation to provide a gratuitous passage under Article 694 of the Civil Code with the fixing of a *conventional* passage in compliance with that obligation.

A.N. Yiannopoulos, 4 Louisiana Civil Law Treatise, Predial Servitudes § 5:25, at 341 (4th ed. 2013) (emphasis in original).

Is Professor Yiannopoulos's criticism of the Supreme Court's decision in *Dallas* appropriate? What other factors might explain the outcome in *Dallas*? Was it the fact that the plaintiffs eventually acquired Lot 1 — a contiguous lot which provided ready access to Highway 30, so that their lot was no longer enclosed at the time the case was decided? Or, as the court of appeal held, was it because the defendant, Robert Farrington, III, had no means of knowing from the public records at the time he acquired Lot 69D (Roblaine Street) that Lots 2 and 3 constituted enclosed estates? In its reasoning the Supreme Court differed from the court of appeal, but notice the language in this crucial passage:

> After Farrington sold Lot 69D and was no longer the owner of the property over which plaintiffs had been entitled to demand a conventional servitude under Article 694, plaintiffs were precluded by the Louisiana public records doctrine from asserting against third persons the right to demand creation of a conventional servitude (just as they would have been precluded from asserting an unrecorded conventional servitude if one had actually been granted by Farrington).

Dallas v. Farrington, 490 So.2d 265, 270–71 (La. 1986).

Finally, consider the following statement from Judge Bouttall, a judge who dissented from the court of appeal decision in favor of Robert Farrington, III:

> In brief this is a situation where a land owner privately subdivided his tract of land and sold two lots, otherwise enclosed, fronting on a private road, Roblaine Street. Some years later he resubdivided the land, changing Roblaine Street into Lot 69D and sold it to his son who has refused to permit passage across the lot. Although I recognize the principle that third party purchasers should only be bound by the public record, I do not believe that this is the proper principle to apply in this case. I believe the controlling principle to be the right of passage expressed in Civil Code Article 701 as it read in 1964. . . .
>
> Regardless of the misdescription of the lots, there was no doubt in the minds of the parties at that time that the lots were otherwise enclosed and fronted on Roblaine Street which was to be used for the exercise of the right of passage. The right of passage was not included in the act of sale and so it is not a conventional servitude, but solely the legal servitude required in old Article 701. Indeed it is also required by new Article 694. Old Article 664 provides that the servitudes imposed by law are established for the utility of individuals, and old Article 666 imposes upon the proprietors of land various obligations toward one another, independent of all agreements. While such servitudes may be conventionally changed or altered, and while the owner of the subservient estate may change the place as in old Article 703, he cannot convey the land to others and destroy the legal servitude.

As noted in new Article 659, legal servitudes are limitations on ownership established by law.

Accordingly, I am of the opinion that the property formerly designated at Roblaine Street and now designated as Lot 69D is still subject to the legal servitude of passage of the owners of Lots No. 2 and 3. Accordingly, I would reverse the judgment of the trial court and enjoin interference with that right.

Dallas v. Farrington, 465 So.2d 763, 768–69 (La. App. 5 Cir. 1985).

Chapter 14

Conventional Predial Servitudes

A. Introduction

This chapter focuses on what Chapter 4 in Title IV of Book II of the Louisiana Civil Code labels "Conventional or Voluntary Servitudes." In contrast to natural servitudes, which result from the location of one estate in relation to another, and legal servitudes, which are established by rules of law, conventional servitudes can arise in three different ways, which are outlined in Articles 739 through 742 of the Louisiana Civil Code. La. Civ. Code arts. 739–742 (1977). First, and most commonly, conventional servitudes may be established "by title," which means that the owners of the dominant and servient estates agree to establish a servitude. La. Civ. Code arts. 739–740 (1977). Next, conventional servitudes may be the result of what Louisiana law calls "destination by the owner," which denotes a special kind of relationship between two estates that were at one time owned by the same owner or were part of a single estate. La. Civ. Code art. 741 (1977). Finally, conventional servitudes may be created by acquisitive prescription, but only when they are apparent. La. Civ. Code arts. 740, 742 (1977).

Articles 699 through 705 of the Louisiana Civil Code provide examples and descriptions of different types of predial servitudes. La. Civ. Code arts. 699–705 (1977). Read the following articles carefully as the cases below and our discussion will refer to all of the predial servitudes these articles describe:

- Article 699 (Examples of predial servitudes)
- Article 700 (Servitude of support)
- Article 701 (Servitude of view)
- Article 702 (Prohibition of view)
- Article 703 (Servitude of light)
- Article 704 (Prohibition of light)
- Article 705 (Servitude of passage)

B. Classification of Conventional Servitudes

The Civil Code sub-classifies conventional predial servitudes into two overlapping categories: (1) *affirmative* and *negative* servitudes; and (2) *apparent* and *nonapparent* servitudes.

1. Affirmative and Negative Servitudes

Most of the cases featured in this chapter involve affirmative servitudes. Negative predial servitudes have occasionally been controversial in Louisiana, particularly when used to restrict economic competition. The distinction between affirmative and negative servitudes relates to the nature of the charge imposed on the servient estate. Article 706 of the Louisiana Civil Code declares in this regard:

Art. 706. Servitudes; affirmative or negative

Predial servitudes are either affirmative or negative.

Affirmative servitudes are those that give the right to the owner of the dominant estate to do a certain thing on the servient estate. Such are the servitudes of right of way, drain, and support.

Negative servitudes are those that impose on the owner of the servient estate the duty to abstain from doing something on his estate. Such are the servitudes of prohibition of building and of the use of an estate as a commercial or industrial establishment.

La. Civ. Code art. 706 (1977).

An *affirmative predial servitude* exists when the owner of the servient estate must allow the owner of the dominant estate to do something on the servient estate. Consider the following examples: a predial servitude of passage gives the owner of the dominant estate the right to travel through the servient estate; a predial servitude of drain allows the owner of the dominant estate to drain waters across the servient estate; and a predial servitude of support furnishes the owner of the dominant estate the right to have buildings or other constructions rest on a wall of the servient estate. All of these examples embody affirmative servitudes because they permit the owner of the dominant estate to do something on the servient estate. The dominant estate receives an advantage over the servient estate it would otherwise not have.

A *negative predial servitude* imposes a restraint on the owner of the servient estate. The servient estate owner is no longer free to use his property in any way he chooses. Rather, the servient estate owner must refrain from engaging in some activity on the servient estate. A negative predial servitude may require, for example, the owner of the servient estate not to erect a second story on a building or not to open windows in its walls. *See, e.g.,* La. Civ. Code art. 701 (1977) (defining a servitude of view as including "the right to prevent the raising of constructions on the servient estate that would obstruct the view"); La. Civ. Code arts. 702, 704 (1977) (defining servitude of prohibition of view and servitude of prohibition of light as including rights to prevent or limit owner of servient estate in making openings in a building located on that estate).

The distinction between an affirmative and negative servitude may at times appear to be semantic. Consider a typical predial servitude of passage. The owner of the dominant estate will have the right to travel over a specified portion of the servient estate, thus rendering the servitude affirmative from the dominant estate owner's perspective. But the servient estate owner cannot erect any buildings, constructions or fences that would interfere with the dominant estate owner's right to travel over the portion of the servient estate burdened by the servitude. So from the perspective of the servient estate owner, the servitude of passage imposes a negative restriction.

Why does the distinction between affirmative and negative servitudes matter? For one thing, it helps determine the starting point for prescription of nonuse. Pursuant to Article 754 of the Louisiana Civil Code, prescription of non-use begins to run for affirmative servitudes from the date of their last use; it runs the date of an event contrary to the servitude for negative servitudes. La. Civ. Code art. 754 (1977).

2. Apparent and Nonapparent Servitudes

Pursuant to Article 707 of the Louisiana Civil Code, predial servitudes are also divided into *apparent* and *nonapparent servitudes*:

Art. 707. Servitudes; apparent or nonapparent.

Predial servitudes are either apparent or nonapparent. Apparent servitudes are those that are perceivable by exterior signs, works, or constructions; such as a roadway, a window in a common wall, or an aqueduct.

Nonapparent servitudes are those that have no exterior sign of their existence; such as the prohibition of building on an estate or of building above a particular height.

La. Civ. Code art. 707 (1977). This distinction, which turns on whether there is visible evidence of a charge on the servient estate, is essential for determining how a conventional servitude can be acquired. Article 739 declares that "[n]onapparent servitudes may be acquired by title only, including a declaration of destination . . . ." Under Article 740, "[a]pparent servitudes may be acquired by title, destination of the owner, or by acquisitive prescription." *Compare* La. Civ. Code art. 739 (1977) *with* La. Civ. Code art. 740 (1977). This means that non-apparent servitudes can only be created by voluntary agreement of the owners of two or more estates, whereas apparent servitudes can arise without express agreement between owners of separate estates. The distinction between apparent and nonapparent servitudes also has significant consequences in the law of sales, particularly in relation to the scope of the warranty against eviction implied in every sale under Article 2500. *See* La. Civ. Code art. 2500 (1993). Negative servitudes will always be classified as nonapparent servitudes because there is no visible sign of their existence on a servient estate. Affirmative servitudes can be either apparent or nonapparent, depending on the presence of exterior, visible manifestations of their existence.

3. Servitudes Intended to Restrain Competition

Regardless of the precise contours of a given conventional servitude, Article 697 of the Louisiana Civil Code declares that a servitude "may be established by an owner on his estate or acquired for its benefit." La. Civ. Code art. 697 (1977). This rule echoes the general principle under Articles 646 and 647 that in order for a predial servitude to exist, there must be a distinct "charge" on a servient estate and a "benefit" to a dominant estate. *See* La. Civ. Code arts. 646–647 (1977). When a negative predial servitude restricts economic competition for a business located on the dominant estate, what is the benefit to the dominant estate?

Article 706 of the Louisiana Civil Code expressly declares that negative servitudes are such as "prohibitions of building and *of the use of an estate as a commercial or industrial establishment.*" La. Civ. Code art. 706 (1977) (emphasis added). In recent years, a number of courts have confronted the question of whether negative servitudes can be used to restrict specific commercial activities from occurring on a servient estate—not for aesthetic purposes or to protect the dominant estate owner from interference with personal enjoyment of the estate, but for the primary purpose of shielding a business situated on a dominant estate from economic competition.

Professor A.N. Yiannopoulos took the position that agreements to restrict competition among businesses may take the form of personal obligations between the parties but should not be allowed through predial servitudes, burdening and benefitting the servient and dominant estates when they change ownership. A.N. YIANNOPOULOUS, 4 LA. CIVIL LAW TREATISE: PREDIAL SERVITUDES § 6.5, at 356–58 (4th ed. 2013). He contended that such agreements should not be enforceable as predial servitudes because they benefit a particular business owner, as opposed to an estate. *Id.* A pair of cases decided several decades ago reached conflicting results in largely fact-dependent decisions, without commenting on Professor Yiannopoulos' views. *Compare R & K Bluebonnet, Inc. v. Patout's of Baton Rouge, Inc.*, 521 So.2d 634, 635–36 (La. App. 1 Cir. 1988) (holding that a covenant prohibiting burdened property from being used as a "seafood restaurant" for five years was enforceable against successors as a negative predial servitude because two estates were involved and the covenant facially benefitted immediately adjacent property retained by the vendors of the burdened lot who operated a well- known seafood restaurant on the retained land), *with Mardis v. Brantley*, 717 So.2d 702, 710–711 (La. App. 2 Cir. 1998) (holding that covenants in deeds stating that a purchaser could not "sell" property for commercial purposes without the approval of the vendor and that appeared in some, but not all, sales of affected lots created only a personal obligation that the purchaser owed to the vendor and that was *not* enforceable by vendor's successors in interest as a negative predial servitude prohibiting commercial use of lots, because the covenants did not mention successors in interest and because the contracting parties did not clearly express an intention to create a predial servitude to benefit other property or estates owned by each vendor).

In common law jurisdictions, courts have become increasingly receptive to the use of restrictive covenants in restraint of trade. Moreover, such covenants have become a common feature of real estate development practice. Developers and business owners who invest large sums when establishing a particular enterprise on a parcel of land will, not surprisingly, want to assure that other nearby parcels (for example, parcels in the same retail shopping center) will not be used by direct business competitors. *See, e.g., Winn Dixie Stores, Inc. v. Big Lot Stores, Inc.*, 886 F.Supp.2d 1326 (S.D. Fl. 2012), *aff'd in part and reversed in part*, 746 F.3d 1008 (11th Cir. 2014) (addressing the attempt by a national supermarket chain to enforce a "grocery exclusive" clause in commercial leases against defendants who sought to open competing stores in shopping centers in Florida, Alabama, Mississippi, and Louisiana). Generally speaking, when future purchasers have notice, through the public records, of the existence of these use restrictions, common law courts have held that such covenants are enforceable against future owners of the burdened estates, as long as the restraint on trade or competition is not unreasonable. *See, e.g., Whitinsville Plaza, Inc. v. Kotseas*, 390 N.E.2d 243, 249–250 (Mass. 1979).

The Restatement of Property for this area of the law recognizes the utility of such covenants by declaring that "[a] servitude that imposes an *unreasonable* restraint on trade or competition is invalid." RESTATEMENT (THIRD) OF PROPERTY: SERVITUDES § 3.6 (2000). Consider the official comments to this provision of the *Restatement*:

a. *Historical note and rationale.* Land-use restrictions designed to protect a business against competition met with a hostile reaction in the Massachusetts court in the late 19th century. Justice Holmes initiated a line of decisions holding that the burden of covenants not to compete would not run with the land because the benefit did not touch or concern the land of the covenantee. In Virginia, the court adopted the same position, but then held that the covenant could be enforced in equity. The First Restatement of Property adopted this position — a covenant against competition was not a real covenant, and thus could not be enforced against a successor to the burdened land by a judgment for damages at law, but it could be enforced by injunction in equity.

Massachusetts has since overruled its old cases, and the predominant rule in the United States today is that stated in this section. The validity of covenants against competition is to be determined by the common law of unreasonable restraints on trade and competition and under statutory antitrust and competition laws. . . .

b. *Unreasonable restraints on trade and competition.* The common law of unreasonable restraints on competition looks to the purpose, the geographic extent, and the duration of the restraint to determine whether it is reasonable. Covenants against competition that are tied to a particular parcel of land are seldom unreasonable because the impact is limited to one piece of land. The owner is free to engage in the activity elsewhere. However, if the restricted land is extensive, or it is the only land available in a market area for a particular use, the restriction is unreasonable if it will tend toward a monopoly or substantially restrict competition in the relevant market.

RESTATEMENT (THIRD) OF PROPERTY: SERVITUDES § 3.6, comments (2000).

In the past two decades, perhaps reflecting developments in the rest of the United States, Louisiana jurisprudence has become more receptive to predial servitudes created for the express purpose of protecting the owner of a dominant estate from commercial competition. In the decision below, a Louisiana court addressed the question of whether this kind of negative, nonapparent servitude created by the owners of two adjacent estates and designed to limit commercial competition of a very specific nature could "run with the land" and whether it could be enforced by the successor of the original dominant estate owner.

RCC Properties, L.L.C. v. Wenstar Properties, L.P.

930 So.2d 1233 (La. App. 2 Cir. 2006)

DREW, Judge. Wenstar Properties, L.P., appeals from a judgment invalidating a predial servitude in favor of an estate owned by Wenstar. We reverse and render.

Facts

In 2002, AZT Winnsboro La., Inc., (AZT) sold a tract to Wenstar. A Wendy's restaurant is currently operating on the Wenstar property (the dominant estate). In the "Act of Cash Sale and Servitude," AZT, the vendor, granted to Wenstar, the vendee, a servitude in the following language:

> Vendor also grants to vendee a predial servitude in favor of the Property prohibiting the use of the property adjacent to the Property that is owned by Vendor and described on Exhibit A attached hereto and made a part hereof (hereinafter, Vendor's Adjacent Property) or any part or parcel thereof for a restaurant with a drive-thru pick-up window, the primary business of which is the sale of hamburgers, hamburger products or chicken sandwiches (or any combination thereof). For the purposes of this servitude and restriction, a restaurant has the aforesaid products as its primary business if fifteen percent (15%) or more of its gross sales, exclusive of taxes, beverage and dairy product sales, consists of sales of hamburgers, hamburger products or chicken sandwiches (or any combination thereof). This servitude and restriction shall burden Vendor's Adjacent Property for a period of twenty (20) years from the date of this act of sale; provided, however, that this servitude and restriction shall terminate at such time that the Property is no longer used as a Wendy's restaurant or if operation of a Wendy's restaurant ceases on the Property for a continuous period of three (3) months. . . .

In 2004, AZT sold the adjacent property (the servient estate) to R.C.C. Properties, L.L.C. R.C.C. subsequently received an offer to purchase this tract from Hannon's Food Service of Vicksburg, Inc., which intended to build a KFC (Kentucky Fried Chicken) franchise on the property. Hannon's agreed to purchase the property only if R.C.C. could obtain a satisfactory release of the servitude. . . .

In February 2005, R.C.C. filed a petition for a declaratory judgment asking the district court either to invalidate the servitude or declare it inapplicable to the

R.C.C. property. R.C.C. subsequently added Hannon's and Wendy's International, Inc., as defendants.

The court held a trial in July 2005 and heard testimony from several witnesses. Among the witnesses was Bobby Hannon, chairman of Hannon's, who explained that a KFC restaurant serves several types of chicken sandwiches and that any KFC built on the R.C.C. property would serve these sandwiches. Hannon also stated that "the deal would be off" as far as he was concerned if the servitude binding the property was found to be valid.

Edward Buchner, III, a certified public accountant from Vicksburg who handled Hannon's business, also testified. Buchner reviewed Hannon's sales figures for Hannon's KFC restaurants to determine what percentage of KFC restaurant sales, less taxes, beverages, and dairy, consisted of chicken sandwiches. For 2003, chicken sandwiches amounted to 1.77% of total sales; for 2004, the percentage was 1.81%, and for the first six months of 2005, the percentages were January— 1.91%; February—4.87%, March—14.18%, April—11.2%, May—10.8%, and June—6.7%.

Pete Subowicz, a field director for real estate for Wendy's International, testified that he negotiated this predial servitude with the original property owner when Wenstar acquired its Winnsboro property. He explained that deed restrictions limiting competition are a "pretty common standard" in the fast food industry. The servitude defined "primary business" as the sale of hamburgers, hamburger products or chicken sandwiches "if fifteen percent (15%) or more of its gross sales, exclusive of taxes, beverage and dairy product sales, consists of sales of hamburgers, hamburger products or chicken sandwiches (or any combination thereof)." In his view, a particular restaurant that wanted to locate on the servient estate would have to establish that its hamburger and chicken sandwich sales did not exceed 15%, as described above. In his view, that restaurant would have to establish that fact by submission of national sales records, then regional sales records and sales records of existing restaurants. Subowicz admitted that the existing predial servitude would not prohibit the construction of a KFC store provided the KFC owners could demonstrate that its sales of the proscribed sandwiches was less than 15%. Subowicz testified Wendy's International would never agree to the release of a predial servitude.

The court subsequently issued reasons for judgment stating its intent to invalidate the servitude in its entirety. The court stated, in part:

> This Court understands that predial servitudes are to be strictly construed, and any doubts as to the extent or exercise of rights created by such servitudes should be resolved in favor of the servient estate. This Court believes that this predial servitude is unclear and ambiguous. It is not clear as to what time period the chicken sandwich sales are to be measured. Is it one week, one month, one quarter or one year? It is also unclear how the determination is to be made. Does the owner of the dominant estate have

the right to examine the books and records on demand or must legal action be taken, or does the owner of the servient estate have a duty to provide those records on a weekly, monthly, quarterly, or annual basis? Since the servitude is silent as to both the time period and manner of showing compliance, this Court must determine the servitude to be ambiguous. Since servitudes are not favored and are to be strictly construed, any ambiguity is to be assessed against the dominant estate.

The court also noted that it did not consider the parol evidence presented by the parties regarding the intent when the servitude was negotiated and effected. On August 12, 2005, the court signed a judgment invalidating the servitude.

Discussion

In *Blanchard v. Rand*, 34,442 (La. App. 3/2/01), 781 So. 2d 881, *writs denied*, 01-0897, 01-0931 (La. 6/1/01), 793 So. 2d 193, 194, this court explained that a predial servitude is a real right burdening an immovable. To have a predial servitude requires two different tracts belonging to different owners. A predial servitude is due to the estate rather than the owner of the estate and is a charge on the servient estate for the benefit of the dominant estate. La. C.C. art. 646.

La. C.C. art. 697 provides:

Predial servitudes may be established by an owner on his estate or acquired for its benefit.

The use and extent of such servitudes are regulated by the title by which they are created, and, in the absence of such regulation, by the following rules.

A predial servitude restricting or prohibiting commercial use of property is a negative, nonapparent servitude which may be acquired only by title. La. C.C. arts. 706, 707, 739; *Mardis v. Brantley*, 30,773 (La. App. 2d Cir. 8/25/98), 717 So. 2d 702, 704, *writ denied*, 98-2488 (La. 11/20/98), 729 So. 2d 563. Once the document creating the servitude is recorded in the public records, the restriction is binding on subsequent owners who acquire the servient estate without further mention of the restriction in the act conveying the servient estate. *Mardis, supra.*

La. C.C. art. 730 provides:

Doubt as to the existence, extent, or manner of exercise of a predial servitude shall be resolved in favor of the servient estate.

La. C.C. art. 749 provides:

If the title is silent as to the extent and manner of use of the servitude, the intention of the parties is to be determined in the light of its purpose.

When a predial servitude is created by title, the intention of the parties to place a charge on one estate for the benefit of another estate, and the extent of the charge, must be expressed on the face of the title document and cannot be inferred or implied from vague or ambiguous language. *Mardis, supra.* Servitudes claimed under title are never sustained by implication; the title creating them must be express as to their nature and extent, as well as to the estate that owes them and the estate to which they are due. *Williams v. Wiggins*, 26,060 (La. App. 2d Cir. 8/17/94), 641 So. 2d 1068.

We disagree with the trial court's finding that the servitude was invalid because the method of measuring "primary business" described by the servitude was ambiguous. The servitude in favor of Wenstar's property is a conventional predial servitude. The original vendor, AZT, and purchaser of the dominant estate, Wenstar, clearly intended to create a predial servitude restricting the use of the servient estate still owned by AZT.

The instrument transferring the property to Wenstar was entitled "Act of Cash Sale and Servitude." The intent of the proprietor to create a servitude must clearly appear on the face of the document. *Blanchard, supra.* This instrument specifically stated a "predial servitude" was granted in favor of the property acquired by Wenstar. The "predial servitude" bound the adjacent property by prohibiting a certain use of the remaining property owned by AZT, the vendee. The title document clearly reflected the intention of the parties to create an obligation in favor of the dominant estate. *Blanchard, supra.* The extent of the charge on the servient estate is the prohibition against using the servient estate "for a restaurant with a drive-thru pick-up window, the primary business of which is the sale of hamburger products or chicken sandwiches (or any combination thereof)." The servitude is effective as written. The trial court erred as a matter of law in invalidating the servitude; therefore, we make a *de novo* review of the record.

Having found that the predial servitude is binding on the servient estate, we find that the trial court's concerns about the practical implementation of the servitude were perceptive. In particular, the method by which the "primary business" of the servient estate should be measured is unclear. The yearly totals of Hannon's KFC chicken sandwich sales for 2003 and 2004 were well underneath the 15% specification in the title, as was the average for 2005, but in three months of 2005, chicken sandwich sales approached 15% of Hannon's sales revenues.

Because the "primary business" measurement is related to the manner of use of the servitude, we look to the intent of the parties in creating the servitude. The trial court refused to consider parol evidence to determine that question. However, the intent of Wenstar and AZT in creating the servitude is apparent from the face of the title. Wenstar intended to prevent a competitor in the fast-food hamburger or chicken sandwich business from opening a restaurant next to the Wendy's. Toward that end, the servitude created by the parties defined the level of competition that would trigger the restriction.

Hannon's KFC sales figures, as recited at the hearing, showed that the revenues from chicken sandwiches sold at Hannon's other KFC restaurants never equaled or exceeded 15% of total restaurant sales. Although the future is uncertain, the only evidence presented showed that the "primary business" trigger in the servitude was never reached by the other Hannon's restaurants in the past. Interpreting the servitude in light of La. C.C. art. 730, the servitude does not prohibit the construction or operation of a KFC restaurant at this location.

We are not called upon to decide what result may obtain should the KFC, or any other restaurant, later have a revenue mixture that triggers the "primary business" measure in the servitude. We note that doubt as to the manner of exercise of a predial servitude is resolved in favor of the servient estate. La. C.C. art. 730. The intention of the parties in light of its purpose is used to determine manner of use of the servitude. La. C.C. art. 749. Considering the contingent nature of Hannon's agreement to buy the property from R.C.C. and Hannon's testimony that a valid servitude would result in the deal being off, it is unlikely that a decision will be necessary on how to determine 15% of the proscribed sales figures. . . .

As requested in R.C.C.'s pleadings, this decision is limited to the finding that a valid predial servitude exists in favor of the dominant estate. The trial court judgment, which declares the predial servitude (quoted above) "invalid and of no effect as to the entirety of the Servient Estate" is reversed.

Conclusion

For the above reasons, the judgment of the trial court invalidating the servitude is reversed. Costs of this appeal are assessed to appellee.

REVERSED AND RENDERED.

Notes and Questions

1. If you were to walk up to the property in question in *RCC Properties L.L.C. v. Wenstar Properties, L.P.*, 930 So.2d 1233 (La. App. 2 Cir. 2006), you might notice that a KFC or Burger King franchise is not located on the property. But you would have no way of knowing of the existence of the nonapparent negative servitude that effectively prevents the landowner from establishing a KFC or Burger King restaurant there. No visible evidence signals that the owner of the servient estate gave up its right to place a restaurant that sells hamburgers or chicken sandwiches on that lot. A casual observer may believe the lot is empty because the owner has no money to build on it or because the owner wants to provide green space for the city. A negative nonapparent servitude will have no outward or visible signs, but it will be evidenced by a recorded document in the parish conveyance records.

2. Notice that the restriction at issue in *RCC Properties* was only intended to be enforceable against the servient estate for a period of twenty years from the date of the act of sale of that estate. *Temporal limitations* on trade restriction covenants are a factor that courts in other jurisdictions weigh in favor of their enforceability.

In another case, a Louisiana appellate court held that a negative predial servitude, which prohibited the purchaser of a tract of land or its successors or assigns from using the tract and a planned office building as "an outpatient surgical center or a diagnostic center or any similar facility" without the written consent of the owner of the dominant estate or its successors or assigns (here, a large hospital), was enforceable against a new owner of the servient estate, even though the servitude did not contain any temporal limitation. *Meadowcrest Center v. Tenet Health System Hospitals, Inc.*, 902 So.2d 512, 515 (La. App. 5 Cir. 2005). The court noted that the original parties were "two independent corporations on equal footing," who entered into an "arms-length agreement for sale of real estate." *Id.* Further, the court observed that the restriction at issue did not "effectively" remove the property from commerce in violation of public policy of the state because: (1) uses of the servient estate other than as diagnostic or surgical centers were permitted; and (2) the dominant owner had in the past granted permission for such uses. *Id.* Finally, the court asserted that failure to enforce the servitude would undermine the viability of Article 706 of the Louisiana Civil Code, which expressly allows for negative servitudes prohibiting commercial or industrial uses. *Id.*

3. For a detailed discussion of how Louisiana and the mixed jurisdiction of Scotland have addressed the enforceability of these kinds of anti-competition covenants and other forms of trade restrictions as a matter of property law, see John A. Lovett, *Title Conditions in Restraint of Trade*, in VERNON V. PALMER & ELSPETH C. REID, MIXED JURISDICTIONS COMPARED: PRIVATE LAW IN LOUISIANA AND SCOTLAND 30–66 (2009). Professor Lovett summarizes his views with regard to recent developments in Louisiana law, in contrast to developments in Scotland, in the following terms:

> In all of these cases, the proximity test imposed by Scottish courts would have been met, but in none of the decisions do the judges wrestle with either traditional policy concerns about monopoly promotion or with traditional doctrinal requirements that servitudes should enhance the utility of the immovable itself—not the purely personal interests of the person who happens to be the owner at one moment in time. Instead, the courts defer to the customization choices and reliance interests of property owners and their vendees, as long as the original parties have provided notice of their choices by recording their agreements regarding trade restrictions in the public records. These decisions can be understood on one hand as simply evidence of the uncritical drift of Louisiana jurisprudence toward American common law norms which have grown increasingly receptive to treating "reasonable" covenants in restraint of trade as property interests. It may also mark the inevitable by-product of the decisive embrace of unlimited dismemberment of ownership by the Louisiana Supreme Court in *Queensborough Land [Co. v. Cazeaux*, 67 So. 641 (La. 1915).

Id. at 59–60. Do you agree that Louisiana judges should "wrestle" with traditional policy and doctrinal concerns in these cases? Do the decisions reflect an "uncritical drift" toward American common law norms? Or are these developments entirely positive?

4. For a thoughtful discussion of whether the current trend of Louisiana jurisprudence recognizing the enforceability of *predial* servitudes that restrict competition should be extended to noncompete clauses in commercial leases so that such

clauses could be directly enforced by a benefitted lessee against a violating lessee in the same shopping center, see Annie McBride, *Comment: The Need for Legislative Authorization of Noncompete Servitudes in Commercial Leases*, 61 Loy. L. Rev. 325 (2015) (arguing that, in light of Louisiana courts' traditional adherence to a numerus clausus of property rights, the Louisiana legislature should authorize by statute the enforcement of noncompete servitudes in commercial leases provided the servitudes are (1) fair, (2) reasonable, (3) reasonably likely to benefit the local economy, and (4) recorded in the relevant public records).

C. Conventional Servitudes Established by Title

When the owner of the servient estate agrees to give to the owner of the dominant estate a right to do something or agrees to refrain from some activity on the servient estate, the owner of the servient estate retracts certain prerogatives of full ownership with respect to the affected servient estate. Thus, under Articles 708 and 722 of the Louisiana Civil Code, the laws governing the alienation of immovable property apply to the establishment of a predial servitude, just as they would if full ownership of the servient estate was transferred. La. Civ. Code arts. 708 and 722 (1977).

As a consequence of this basic principle, a conventional predial servitude established by title will only benefit and bind third parties—successors of the original owners of the dominant and servient estates—if there is a signed writing memorializing the agreement to establish the servitude and this writing is filed for registry in the parish in which the affected immovable property is located. La. Civ. Code art. 1839 (1984); La. Civ. Code art. 2442 (1993, amended 2005). Note, however, that conventional predial servitudes established by destination of owner or by acquisitive prescription will also bind and benefit successors of the original owners of the servient and dominant estates even though there is no indication of their existence in the public records. This fact may explain why courts are sometimes reluctant to recognize predial servitudes created by destination of the owner or by acquisitive prescription.

When it comes to the use and extent of a conventional predial servitude established by title, Article 697 of the Louisiana Civil Code instructs us to look to the specific agreement that establishes the servitude. La. Civ. Code art. 697 (1977). If an agreement establishing a servitude does not address a particular issue relating to its use or extent, the default rules of Chapter 4 in Title IV of Book II of the Civil Code apply. For example, Article 700, which contemplates a servitude of support "by which buildings or other constructions of the dominant estate are permitted to rest on a wall of the servient estate," declares that "[u]nless the title provides otherwise, the owner of the servient estate is bound to keep the wall fit for the exercise of the servitude, but he may be relieved of this charge by abandoning the wall." La. Civ. Code art. 700 (1977) (emphasis added). Further, when the parties to an agreement creating a servitude address a particular issue, their agreement still cannot contravene mandatory principles of law governing all predial servitudes such as the prohibition on requiring the owner of the servient estate to engage in an affirmative action other than keeping his estate in suitable condition for the exercise of the servitude due the dominant estate. *See* La. Civ. Code art. 651 (1977, amended 2010).

Articles 744, 745 and 748 of the Louisiana Civil Code offer default rules with regard to the rights and obligations of the owners of the dominant and servient estates. *See* La. Civ. Code arts. 744 (1977) (giving dominant estate owner the right to make "works necessary for the use and preservation of the servitude"); La. Civ. Code art. 745 (1977) (giving the owner of the dominant estate "the right to enter with his workmen and equipment" and to "deposit materials," but subject to the obligation of "causing the least possible damage and of removing [material and debris] as soon as possible"); La. Civ. Code art. 748 (1977) (providing that owner of servient estate may do "nothing tending to diminish or make more inconvenient the use of the servitude" and granting a servient estate owner the right to relocate the servitude in certain circumstances). Several of our cases probe the extent to which these general rights and obligations can be modified by agreement of the parties.

1. Who Can Establish a Conventional Servitude

Articles 709 through 719 of the Louisiana Civil Code cover the question of who can establish a conventional servitude. La. Civ. Code arts. 709–713 (1977). A mandatary, or agent acting under a power of attorney, may burden the immovable with a predial servitude, but only when expressly authorized to do so. La. Civ. Code art. 709 (1977); La. Civ. Code art. 2996 (1997). A naked owner may establish a predial servitude, as long as the servitude does not interfere with the rights of the usufructuary or provided the servitude will take effect only after the usufruct is terminated. La. Civ. Code art. 710 (1977). In all other cases, the consent of the usufructuary is required. *Id.* As a rule, a usufructuary alone may *not* establish a predial servitude. La. Civ. Code art. 711 (1977). What if the usufructuary has been granted the power to alienate nonconsumables? *See* La. Civ. Code arts. 568, 568.1 (1976, amended 2010). Owners whose ownership is subject to a term, a revocatory condition, or a reservation of redemption, may establish a predial servitude, but the rights of the dominant estate will cease when the rights of the conditional owner of the servient estate end. La. Civ. Code arts. 712–13 (1977).

Suppose that Alberto donates land to a city with the revocatory condition that the city use the land to establish and maintain a baseball field. The city accepts the donation and builds the field. In addition, the city grants a nearby restaurant a servitude to use the parking lot attached to the baseball field for customer parking as long as the restaurant is in business. Eight years later, the city decides that it no longer wants to maintain the field. Once Alberto revokes the donation, the parking servitude will end when the land is returned to Alberto.

The rules governing co-owners and predial servitudes are consistent with the regime of indivision. According to Article 714 of the Louisiana Civil Code, co-owners must agree unanimously to burden the property in indivision with a servitude, but when only one co-owner purports to establish a servitude on the entire estate, the servitude is suspended until the consent of all co-owners is obtained. La. Civ. Code art. 714 (1977). Articles 715 through 718 offer rules for the different types of cases when one co-owner consents to the establishment of a servitude. They differ according to what exactly the servitude is to burden—the entire estate or the co-owner's fractional share in indivision. *See* La. Civ. Code arts. 715–18 (1977). Under Article 719, a successor to a co-owner who consented to a servitude is bound just as that co-owner unless the property was acquired through a partition by licitation. La. Civ. Code art. 719 (1977).

2. Interpretation Rules

Landowners wishing to establish conventional servitudes as well as their counterparts are sometimes frustrated by attorneys who are less than exact when drafting the pertinent documents. Articles 730 through 734 of the Louisiana Civil Code address this problem by providing a set of rules that guide the interpretation of written agreements allegedly creating predial servitudes. *See generally* La. Civ. Code arts. 730–34 (1977). In a typical controversy, a court may be asked to determine any of the following questions: (1) whether the contracting parties created a servitude or merely a personal obligation; (2) whether a servitude is predial or personal; or (3) where the servitude may be exercised, how it may be exercised, and whether it has terminated.

One of the most important provisions governing the interpretation of an alleged servitude is Article 730 of the Civil Code.

Art. 730. Interpretation of servitude

Doubt as to the existence, extent, or manner of exercise of a predial servitude shall be resolved in favor of the servient estate.

La. Civ. Code art. 730 (1977). This general rule of interpretation has been cited in hundreds of judicial decisions. Look for its appearance in the decisions that follow.

Civil law generally favors unencumbered ownership. Any departure from this instruction must be clear and unambiguous. A document purporting to create a predial servitude will be strictly construed so as to minimize the burden on the servient estate. The owner of the dominant estate will be allowed no greater rights than what the parties agreed to when establishing the servitude.

When questions arise as to what type of right the parties to an agreement intended to create, note that labeling is not always determinative. Indeed, as Article 731 of the Louisiana Civil Code instructs: "A charge established on an estate expressly for the benefit of another estate is a predial servitude although it is not so designated." La. Civ. Code art. 731 (1977). Further, when an act "does not declare expressly" whether the right granted by the servient estate owner is "for the benefit of an estate or for the benefit of a particular person," (*i.e.*, when it is not clear whether a servitude is predial or personal), Article 732 tells us that the nature of the right is determined in accordance with Articles 733 and 734. La. Civ. Code art. 732 (1977). These provisions declare:

Art. 733. Interpretation; benefit of dominant estate.

When the right granted be of a nature to confer an advantage on estate, it is presumed to be a predial servitude.

La. Civ. Code art. 733 (1977).

Art. 734. Interpretation; convenience of a person

When the right granted is merely for the convenience of a person, it is considered to be a predial servitude, unless it is acquired by a person as owner of an estate for himself, his heirs and assigns.

La. Civ. Code art. 734 (1977).

* * *

Consider how the courts have harnessed these interpretation guides in the following two decisions. Note that the first decision was rendered before the revision of Articles 730 through 734 of the Louisiana Civil Code. But the approach is essentially the same. In fact, the decision in *Burgas v. Stoutz* 141 So. 67 (La. 1932), is still considered to be a valuable precedent and is discussed in the revision comments. *See* La. Civ. Code art. 733, rev. cmt. (b) (1977). Can you see why the decision illustrates the approach articulated in Article 733? The second case was decided in 2015. But it involves an alleged predial servitude dating back to 1923. *Franks Inv. Co., LLC v. Union Pacific Railroad Co.*, 772 F.3d 1037 (5th Cir. 2014). Thus, the court invoked the 1870 Civil Code and topical pre-revision jurisprudence. The author of the dissenting opinion, which is provided below, Judge James L Dennis, previously served as Associate Justice on the Louisiana Supreme Court from 1975 to 1995.

Burgas v. Stoutz
141 So. 67 (La. 1932)

LAND, Justice. Mrs. Vincent Pizzolata owned a lot in Square 379, Seventh district of the city of New Orleans, bounded by Dublin, Apple, Belfast, and Dante streets. This lot was designated by the letter "X" on a plan of Adloe Orr, civil engineer, dated November 22, 1920, and formed the corner of Dublin and Apple streets. It measured 60 feet front on the former street and a depth of 90 feet on the latter street.

Thereafter, Mrs. Pizzolata subdivided lot "X" into lots "A" and "B," and another lot into lot "C," in a survey made by A. J. Oliveira, civil engineer, dated October 20, 1922. A later survey by the same engineer, dated February 25, 1929, and showing the location of lots "A" and "B," is filed in the transcript at page 55.

September 13, 1923, Mrs. Pizzolata sold lot "A" to the Security Building & Loan Association, and, on the same day, the association conveyed this lot to the plaintiff, Morris Burgas.

In the sale by Mrs. Pizzolata to the association, and in the sale by the association to plaintiff, the following stipulation appears: "It is distinctly agreed and understood between the parties hereto that the purchaser, its successors and assigns, shall have the privilege of using the paved driveway in the rear of the property hereinabove described, which paved driveway is part of Lot 'B' belonging to the vendors herein."

The above stipulation was recorded in the conveyance records of the parish of Orleans in the following language: "Purchaser (omitting "successors and assigns") has the privilege of using the paved driveway in the rear of the above property, which driveway is part of Lot B belonging to the vendor herein."

December 7, 1923, Mrs. Pizzolata sold lot "B" to the Fidelity Homestead Association. On the same day the homestead transferred this lot to Walter Clark. On August 20, 1925, Clark reconveyed the property to the homestead, and on the same day the homestead deeded the property to defendant, Henry L. Stoutz.

It is admitted that, at the date plaintiff purchased lot "A," together with the privilege of using the paved driveway on lot "B," Mrs. Pizzolata owned lots "A" and "B," and that the paved runways mentioned in the petition and shown on three photographs, marked "Plaintiff 5, 6, and 7," had been laid. Tr. 54.

It is also admitted that the runways were built by Mrs. Pizzolata prior to the time she disposed of either lot "A" or lot "B." Tr. 54.

It is further admitted that Henry L. Stoutz, defendant, had notified Morris Burgas, plaintiff, that he (Stoutz) was about to build a fence which would impair and destroy the use of the paved driveway. Tr. 54.

It was upon the receipt of this notification that the present suit for an injunction was brought by plaintiff. A preliminary injunction was issued, and, after hearing on the merits, was made permanent by judgment of the lower court, in which was fully recognized the right of plaintiff to use the driveway in dispute in this case, as delineated by red ink lines on a blueprint of survey made by A. J. Oliveira, civil engineer and surveyor, dated February 25, 1929, and in which was also reserved the right of plaintiff to claim whatever damage, loss, or injury that may have been occasioned to him by defendant herein.

From this judgment defendant has appealed.

1. Defendant attacks the recorded stipulation as to the right of passage granted to plaintiff on the ground that it is insufficient, as it does not state the length or width of same.

This particular ground of attack is without merit, since the paved runways are located as physical objects on the surface of lot "B," the property of defendant, as shown by photographs filed in evidence, and the length and width of same are easily ascertainable. That which can be made certain is considered in law as certain.

2. The second ground of attack by defendant is that a servitude of passage, a discontinuous servitude, cannot be acquired by destination de pere de famille, and parol evidence is inadmissible.

It is true that a right of passage is a discontinuous servitude, and can be established only by title. R.C.C., arts. 727 and 766.

The destination made by the owner is equivalent to title only with respect to continuous apparent servitudes, such as aqueducts, drain, view, and the like. R.C.C. arts. 727 and 767.

As the right of passage in this case depends upon contract, we must look to the terms of the contract in order to determine if they are sufficient to vest title in plaintiff.

In the original deeds from Mrs. Pizzolata to the Security Building & Loan Association, and from the association to plaintiff, Morris Burgas, the privilege of using the paved driveway on the property of the defendant is expressly granted to "the purchaser, its successors and assigns." Since the purchasers of lot "A," stipulating the servitude of passage over lot "B," owned by defendant, acquired it as owners of lot "A," and for their successors and assigns, it is clear that the right became real and is a predial servitude, and not a right merely personal to the individual and expiring with him. R.C.C. art. 757.

In the titles to lot "A" of the Security Building & Loan Association, and of plaintiff, Morris Burgas, as recorded, the servitude is granted only to "the purchaser," or the owner of the property. The acts establishing the servitude do not declare that the right is given for the benefit of an estate. It must then be considered, as declared in article 755 of the Civil Code, whether the right granted be of real advantage to lot "A," or merely of personal convenience to the owner.

As stated in article 756 of the Civil Code: "If the right granted be of a nature to assure a real advantage to an estate, it is to be presumed that such right is a real servitude, although it may not be so styled."

In our opinion, the right of passage over lot "B," granted to the purchasers of lot "A," is of real utility to the latter property, which is a 50-foot corner lot fronting on Apple street, and is not encumbered with a driveway; thereby giving to lot "A" more free space either for building or for flowers, or for a garden, and making the property more desirable and valuable. See map, Tr. p. 55 and photographs, Tr. p. 53.

It is also significant that the right of passage over lot "B" was not given to a named individual, but to "the purchaser," the owner of lot "A," thereby connecting the servitude with the property as a real advantage to it, and not as a mere matter of convenience to a particular person and terminating with him.

As the granting to plaintiff of the right of passage over lot "B" is of real benefit to lot "A," our conclusion is that such right is a real servitude.

Since the creation of a real servitude is a form of alienation, defendant contends that the recorded stipulation as to the right of passage over lot "B," owned by defendant, is too vague, uncertain, and indefinite in description to be a notice to a purchaser in good faith.

At the risk of repetition, we quote this recorded stipulation again, which is as follows: "Purchaser has the privilege of using the paved driveway in the rear of the above property, which driveway is part of Lot B belonging to the vendor herein."

The survey of lots "A" and "B," found at page 55 of the transcript, shows conclusively that there is but one paved driveway on lot "B," and that this driveway is indicated by a red line drawn next to lot "A," owned by plaintiff.

As the driveway consists of paved runways, as shown by the runways themselves in place, as well as by the photographs filed at page 53 of the transcript, it is idle for defendant to contend that the description of these runways as located "in the rear" of lot "A" is erroneous and misleading, since there is only one set of paved runways on lot "B," and this driveway is particularly described in the stipulation creating the right of passage as being "a part of Lot 'B.'"

Manifestly, this was sufficient recorded notice to have placed defendant on inquiry, and to have enabled him to have ascertained the true facts of the case before purchasing lot "B."

Besides, as held in *Schneidau v. New Orleans Land Company*, 132 La. 264, 61 So. 225, the law in this state has for many years been that an act of conveyance is effective against third persons as soon as deposited for record in the recorder's office. The original deeds in this case, deposited in the recorder's office, show conclusively that the servitude of passage over the driveway on lot "B" was granted to the purchaser, its successors and assigns, and was therefore a real servitude.

Under the circumstances of the case, we are of the opinion that it is unimportant that, in the chain of title from Mrs. Pizzolata to defendant, the servitude of right of passage in favor of lot "A," owned by plaintiff, is not mentioned, especially as plaintiff's title antedates that of defendant, and both have purchased from a common author.

Judgment affirmed.

Notes and Questions

1. When examining the original deeds to the property, the court in *Burgas v. Stoutz*, 141 So. 67 (La. 1932), noted the repeated use of the term, "the purchaser, its successors and assigns." This language satisfied the court that the right granted by Mrs. Pizzolata, the original common owner of both lots A and B, was a real right and more specifically, a predial servitude, and "not a right merely personal to the individual and expiring with him." *Id.* at 69. Study Article 734 of the Louisiana Civil Code, which has reproduced the substance of Article 757 of the 1870 Civil Code.

In *Burgas*, use of the driveway that had been constructed on lot B was intended not only for the immediate buyer of Lot A, but for all subsequent owners of that property. Hence, the real right established here was held to be a predial, and not a personal, servitude.

2. The court in *Burgas* noted that, while the original act of sale between Pizzolata and Burgas, which was "deposited in the recorder's office," referred to "the purchaser, its successors and assigns," the stipulation "recorded in the conveyance records" referred only to "the purchaser" of Lot A. This discrepancy may explain why the court looked to Article 756 of the 1870 Civil Code, the substance of which has since been partially reproduced in revised Article 733 of the Louisiana Civil Code.

In *Burgas*, the court determined that having use of the driveway on Lot B (the servient estate) conferred an advantage in favor of Lot A (the dominant estate). The servitude allowed the owner of this lot "more free space either for building or for flowers, or for a garden, and making the property more desirable and valuable." Thus, the servitude created a permanent benefit for the estate, as opposed to a mere convenience for a person. This helped to convince the court the servitude was predial and not personal.

3. In a more recent case, *Franks Investment Co., LLC v. Union Pacific Railroad Co.*, 772 F.3d 1037, 1046–48 (5th Cir. 2015), the United States Court of Appeals for the Fifth Circuit affirmed a federal district court decision holding that a 1923 deed, by which landowners sold a strip of land to a railroad and the railroad in turn conveyed three crossings across that strip of land to the landowners, created a *personal obligation* rather than a predial servitude. Crucial to the majority decision in *Franks* was the fact that the "crossing clause" in the deed did not bind the railroad and "its successors and assigns," whereas another clause in the same portion of the deed obligating the railroad to provide drainage outlets across the strip of land was binding upon the "successors and assigns" of the railroad. *Id.* at 1047.

Judge James Dennis authored a dissent in *Franks Investment Co.* His opinion reviews the facts, quotes the key passage from the majority opinion, and analyzes legal authorities under both the 1870 Civil Code and the Louisiana Civil Code in its current version. His opinion takes a somewhat more holistic approach to the interpretation of the ambiguous provision in the 1923 deed. Which interpretation do you find most convincing—the majority or the dissent?

Franks Investment Co., LLC v. Union Pacific Railroad Co.,

772 F.3d 1037, 1046–48 (5th Cir. 2015)

JAMES L. DENNIS, **Circuit Judge, dissenting:** At issue in this case is whether the owners of the Levy family plantation in Caddo Parish, Louisiana, who in 1923 deeded a strip of land bisecting the plantation to the Texas and Pacific Railway Company for railroad use, reserved a predial servitude of passage across the railroad's strip of land for the benefit of the plantation. The 1923 deed, in pertinent part, provides:

> It is understood and agreed that the said Texas & Pacific Railway Company shall fence said strip of ground and shall maintain said fence at its own expense and shall provide three crossings across said strip at the points indicated on said Blue Print hereto attached and made part hereof, and

the said Texas and Pacific Railway hereby binds itself, its successors and assigns, to furnish proper drainage out-lets across the land hereinabove conveyed.

The parties agree that the provision requiring the railroad to "provide three crossings across said strip" created a servitude of passage. (A servitude is a "charge laid on an estate." Art. 647.) [I agree with the majority that the 1870 Revised Civil Code of Louisiana, which was in effect in 1923, governs this case rather than the modern version. Hereinafter, unless specified otherwise, all citations to codal provisions refer to the 1870 code.] The parties dispute, however, whether the deed created a personal servitude (that is, a right of passage benefitting specific persons — here, the Levy family — and terminating with the lives of those persons) or a predial servitude (that is, a right of passage benefitting an estate — here, the Levy plantation — whoever may come to own it). The majority, however, rejects both positions in favor of a third option the parties did not raise: that the deed did not impose *any* charge upon an estate, but only imposed a *personal obligation* on the part of the Texas and Pacific Railway Company (which no longer exists and has been replaced as owner of the railroad strip by the appellant, the Union Pacific Railroad Company). For the reasons that follow, I respectfully dissent.

It should be obvious that, when the Levy family sold a strip of land to the Texas and Pacific Railway Company and included in the deed the reservation that the railroad "provide three crossings across" the purchased land at designated places, the parties intended to afford a *right to use* the crossings. There is no reasonable explanation why the Levy family would have reserved the right to crossings as a condition of the land sale if they would have been trespassers when stepping foot on the crossings. It is self-evident that the deed's provision of three crossings encompasses a right of passage across those crossings, and, under the Civil Code, "[t]he right of passage, or of way, *is a servitude*." Art. 722 (emphasis added); *see also* Art. 721 (stating that the right of passage is one of the "principal rural servitudes"). Thus, we must start from the premise that, unless shown otherwise, the parties intended to create what the Civil Code provides: a servitude. The question presented, as recognized and argued by the parties, is whether they intended for the servitude of passage to be predial or personal.

The deed does not say which sort of servitude was intended and, therefore, "he question whether the parties intended to create a predial servitude or another right is to be made in accordance with articles [755] through [757] of the Civil Code." A.N. Yiannopoulos, 4 *Louisiana Civil Law Treatise: Predial Servitudes,* § 6:28 (4th ed.). Article 755 instructs that the question turns on "whether the right granted be of real advantage to the estate, or merely of personal convenience to the owner." The next two articles elaborate. Article 756, the most critical article for our purposes, provides:

> If the right granted be of a nature to assure a real advantage to an estate, it is to be presumed that such right is a real servitude, although it may not be so styled.

Thus, for example, if the owner of a house contiguous to lands bordering on the high road, should stipulate for the right of passing through lands, without it being expressed that the passage is for the use of his house, it would be not the less a real servitude, for it is evident that the passage is of real utility to the house.

Article 757 provides that, "[i]f, on the other hand, the concession from its nature is a matter of mere personal convenience, it is considered personal, and can not be made real but by express declaration of the parties." It gives as an example "the right of walking and gathering fruits and flowers [in] a garden or park." Art. 757.

Here, there can be little doubt that the railroad crossings "assure a real advantage to an estate" (article 756) rather than provide a "mere personal convenience" to the original 1923 owners (article 757).

First, the benefit to the plantation estate is clear. Generally, plantation owners want access to their plantations, and more convenient means of access are preferred over less convenient alternatives. The railroad crossings here allow the owner of a plantation that has been divided by the railroad's strip to conveniently cross from one section of the estate to the other. Absent the crossings, a less convenient, circuitous path would be required. The crossings are a plain advantage. Moreover, without the railroad crossings, the land that has been divided by an intersecting railroad is rendered less accessible, and its value is consequently diminished. Put another way, the crossings served to increase and/or maintain the value of the Levy family's plantation. *See Burgas v. Stoutz,* 174 La. 586, 141 So. 67, 69 (1932) (holding that a servitude of passage was predial rather than personal because, *inter alia,* it had the effect of "making the property more desirable and valuable").

Second, it is clear that the benefit provided is *to the estate* itself rather than to an individual. *See State v. Cefalu,* 288 So.2d 332, 338 (La.1974) ("An examination of the grant reveals that it meets the basic requirement of predial servitudes—it is clearly of benefit to a dominant estate, namely the Cefalu tracts. The effect of the grant was to guarantee the Cefalu tracts direct access to each other. As a result it is clear that the Cefalu tracts were benefited."); *Plaisance v. Gros,* 378 So.2d 178, 179 (La. Ct.App.1979) (holding that the right of way contained in a 1906 deed was a predial servitude because it conferred "a real advantage to the then Dugas estate and not merely a personal convenience to the owner"). In fact, it is difficult to imagine a more plain benefit to an estate bisected by a railroad than passage over crossings affording the tracts "direct access to each other." *See Cefalu,* 288 So.2d at 338. In *Taylor v. New Orleans Terminal Co.,* 126 La. 420, 52 So. 562 (1910), for example, the Louisiana Supreme Court had little difficulty concluding that a railroad's contract to provide crossings afforded a predial, not personal, servitude: "The right followed the property and was not personal to the owner. The original owner acquired the right as a servitude for the benefit of the estate and not for his own benefit." *Id.* at 564.

Because it is clear that the railroad crossings provide a benefit to the estate, "it is to be presumed" under article 756 that they constitute a predial servitude. Thus, the question becomes, are there sufficient indicia in the record to rebut the predial presumption and rather find, as the Union Pacific Railroad Company argues, that the parties intended a personal servitude or, as the majority concludes, that the parties intended only a personal obligation?

Case law from Louisiana courts suggests that less-than-clear indications that a servitude may be personal rather than predial do not suffice to rebut the predial presumption under article 756. For example, in *Ogden v. Bankston,* 398 So.2d 1037 (La.1981), at issue was, as here, a 1923 property transfer. *Id.* at 1040. There, the terms of the act of sale provided a servitude of passage "to the vendor." *Id.* That the right of passage was granted, under the text of the document, "to the vendor" rather than to the estate might tend to suggest, of course, that the parties intended to create a personal right, that is, a personal servitude, for the vendor. However, the Louisiana Supreme Court, citing article 756, explained that such suggestion was insufficient to overcome the predial presumption: "Although the language creating the servitude in the 1923 act of sale recites that the passageway was granted 'to the vendor,' it is evident that the right of passage was a real benefit to the estate itself. For this reason, the servitude must be construed as a real right, not one which was personal to the grantee." *Id.* at 1041. In addition to *Ogden,* other similar cases include *Whitney National Bank of New Orleans v. Poydras Center Associates,* 487 So.2d 120, 123 (La.Ct.App.1986) ("It matters not that the language of the Act was couched in personal terms, for the right created was a real advantage to the dominant estate. . . ."), and *McLure v. Alexandria Golf and Country Club, Inc.,* 344 So.2d 1080, 1089 (La. Ct.App.1977) ("[D]efendant[] argu[es] that the servitude did not outlive Kaiser because it was given to 'vendor' and not to 'vendor, his heirs and assigns.' It has been specifically held that the addition of such language is not necessary for property rights in the nature of a servitude to pass to one's heirs.").

Here, there is a persuasive reason to find that the parties intended for the railroad crossings to be a predial servitude rather than, as the Union Pacific Railroad Company argues, a personal one. The 1923 deed states in its opening clause:

> This instrument made and executed by and between Louis Levy, resident of said parish and state [Caddo Parish, Louisiana], George W. Levy, Miss Julia Levy, Miss Fannie Levy, and Miss Carolina Levy, represented herein by Louis Levy, her agent and attorney in fact, *residents of the City of New York, and State of New York;* Aaron Levy, a resident of the Parish of Caddo and State of Louisiana, and Mrs. Annie Levy Dreyfus, wife of Leon Dreyfus, *resident of the City of London, in the Kingdom of Great Britain,* represented herein by Louis Levy, her agent and attorney in fact, parties of the first part, and the Texas & Pacific Railway Company, a corporation organized under the laws of the United States of America, whereof J.L. Lancaster and C.L. Wallace are Receivers, party of the second part.

(Emphasis added.) On one side of the 1923 transaction was the railway, and on the other side were a number of people, at least some of whom, importantly, resided outside Louisiana, in New York City and London. If the appellant was correct that the parties to this transaction intended for the railroad crossings to be a *personal* servitude, it would mean that the parties intended for the railroad crossings to benefit persons residing a world away. It is fantastical to presume, without evidence or expression, that persons residing in New York City and London had reserved the right of passage in Caddo Parish, Louisiana, as a matter of *personal* convenience similar to, e.g., the right of gathering fruits and flowers in a garden. *See* Art. 757. (Contrast, for example, *Deshotels v. Fruge*, 364 So.2d 258, 260–61 (La.Ct.App.1978), wherein the court found that a servitude was personal based on actual testimony about the beneficiary's personal reasons for desiring the servitude.) Based on the record in this case, the far more evident answer is that these persons in New York and London "acquired the right as a servitude for the benefit of the estate and not for [their] own benefit." *See Taylor*, 52 So. at 564 (holding that railroad crossings were a predial servitude); *cf. Gillis v. Nelson*, 1861 WL 3840 (La.1861) (stating, with respect to an irrigation servitude, that "the contract does not appear to us to be personal, for its object could only be for the advantage of the respective tracts of land").

To reach its contrary conclusion, the majority points to that part of the 1923 deed which states that "the said Texas and Pacific Railway hereby binds itself, *its successors and assigns,* to furnish proper drainage out-lets across the land hereinabove conveyed." (Emphasis added.) The majority explains:

> The problem for Franks is that Franks is trying to establish a predial servitude by presumption because the crossings clause does not expressly create a predial servitude, but the parties to the 1923 deed showed that they knew how to establish a predial servitude *expressly* in the drainage clause—not just in part of the same deed but in the very same sentence. Specifically, whereas the crossings clause binds only Texas & Pacific Railway Company to maintain fences and provide crossings (which does not necessarily establish a predial servitude), the drainage clause binds not only Texas & Pacific Railway Company but "itself, its successors and assigns," which is sufficient to create an express predial servitude.

Ante, at 1040.

Respectfully, I disagree that the "successors and assigns" language relating to the railroad's drainage obligations rebuts the predial presumption as to the right of passage. The drainage obligations are separate and apart—distinct—from the right of passage across the railroad crossings, and the railroad's agreement to bind itself and "its successors and assigns" to furnish drainage outlets across the land conveyed to it does not in any way add to or detract from the predial servitude of passage granted for the benefit of the Levy estate. Whether it was unusual for the railroad to bind itself, "its successors and assigns," in its obligation, or why it did so, is not a material issue in this case, but a matter that could vary widely depending on the company, the landowners, the terrain, and the particular circumstances involved.

Nothing in the Civil Code, other legislation, or custom prevented the landowners from obtaining *both* a predial right of passage in favor their estate across the railroad's estate and the railroad's obligation, binding on its "successors and assigns," to "furnish proper drainage out-lets across the land hereinabove conveyed."

The majority asks the wrong question: why did the parties "include the 'successors and assigns' language in the drainage clause"? *See ante,* at 1047. I see no reason for the plaintiffs to be required to explicate the drainage clause's meaning. The better question is, did the parties intend to create a predial servitude of passage across the railroad crossings even though they did not include "successors and assigns" language in *that* provision of the deed? For the reasons explained, the law gave them no reason to think that the absence of "successors and assigns" language indicated neither a predial or personal servitude but rather a personal obligation. The right of passage "*is a servitude,*" the Code says. Art. 722. In fact, the Code describes the right of passage as one of the "*principal* rural servitudes." Art. 721 (emphasis added). And the Louisiana courts have evinced no hesitation to construe rights of passage, including those over railroad crossings, to be predial servitudes. *See, e.g., Taylor,* 52 So. at 564. It was in the context of the Civil Code's articles on servitudes that the parties drafted the deed, and, when considered in that light, the addition of "successors and assigns" language with respect to the railroad crossings was not necessary. It was, rather, a reasonable omission. I suspect that, had the Levy family any way of knowing how this court would construe their deed nearly a century after it was written, they would be surprised to learn that, when they required railroad crossings as a condition for the sale of their land, they did not obtain a property right at all, but only a contractual right with one single railroad, meaningless against any other railroad that may succeed it.

In sum, under article 756, which provides the controlling rule of law in this case, this court must presume that the railroad crossings afforded in the 1923 deed constitute a predial servitude, and I do not believe that there is a reasonable basis to find that the presumption has been rebutted. On the contrary, there are persuasive reasons to conclude that the parties indeed intended to create a predial servitude for the benefit of the Levy family plantation. Therefore, I respectfully dissent from the majority's conclusion, argued for by none of the parties, that, as a matter of law, the deed created nothing more than a purely personal right of passage for the members of the Levy family as individuals and a personal obligation on the part of the Texas and Pacific Railway Company to allow such passage, and not a predial right for the benefit of the Levy plantation estate.

Notes and Questions

1. Do you agree with the following observation by Judge Dennis?

> If the appellant was correct that the parties to this transaction intended for the railroad crossings to be a *personal* servitude, it would mean that the parties intended for the railroad crossings to benefit persons residing a world away. It is fantastical to presume, without evidence or expression,

that persons residing in New York City and London had reserved the right of passage in Caddo Parish, Louisiana, as a matter of *personal* convenience similar to, e.g., the right of gathering fruits and flowers in a garden.

Franks Investment Co., L.L.C. v. Union Pacific Railroad Co., 772 F.3d 1037, 1051 (5th Cir. 2014) (Dennis J. dissenting). Or is the majority's observation that the 1923 deed used the language "itself, its successors and assigns" to refer to the obligations imposed on the railroad in the context of the drainage clause, but not the crossing clause, more persuasive?

2. If the language in the 1923 deed in *Franks Investment Co.* had created a personal servitude of right of use, and not a mere personal obligation as the majority held, would it have still been binding on the original railroad's successor? *See Sustainable Forests, L.L.C. v. Harrison,* 846 So.2d 1238 (La. App. 2 Cir. 2003) (featured *supra* in Chapter 15). What would the plaintiff in *Franks Investment Co.* have needed to prove for purposes of establishing an enforceable personal servitude of right of use under Articles 639 through 644 of the Louisiana Civil Code?

D. Conventional Predial Servitudes Acquired by Destination of the Owner and by Acquisitive Prescription

Although many predial servitudes are established by written agreement between the owners of two or more estates, it is important to realize that predial servitudes can also be created without a written agreement that is capable of being filed for registry in the public records. In this section, we address the two modes of creation of conventional predial servitudes that do not require an express written agreement: destination of the owner and acquisitive prescription. Keep in mind, of course, that predial servitudes can also come into existence as a matter of law, without any agreement between the owners of two estates and without application of the two doctrines discussed below, in the case of natural servitudes and legal servitudes.

1. Destination of the Owner

Under Article 741 of the Louisiana Civil Code, a servitude may be acquired by destination of the owner when two estates are owned by one person and then cease to belong to the same owner. Note that Article 741 distinguishes between *apparent* servitudes, which come into existence of right and *nonapparent* servitudes, which require the filing of a formal declaration.

Art. 741. Destination of the owner

Destination of the owner is a relationship established between two estates owned by the same owner that would be a predial servitude if the estates belonged to different owners.

When the two estates cease to belong to the same owner, unless there is express provision to the contrary, an apparent servitude comes into existence of right and a nonapparent servitude comes into existence if the owner has previously filed for registry in the conveyance records of the parish in which the immovable is located a formal declaration establishing the destination.

La. Civ. Code art. 741 (1977, amended 1978).

Consider the following hypothetical. A developer builds a three story building on a parcel of land he owns. He designs the roof to extend five feet beyond the edge of the building. The extended roof protects the building's windows from direct sunlight and reduces cooling costs. The view from the upstairs windows on the third floor of the building allows the owner to see for miles in any direction. Sometime after the building is erected, the developer decides to subdivide the land he owns into two separate estates. The footprint of the building the developer constructed is located entirely on the western parcel. Suppose, however, the surveyor who assisted the developer in the subdivision of the land established the boundary line between the western and eastern parcels only three feet from the side of the existing building so that the roof of the building actually extends two feet over the eastern parcel. After creating the two distinct estates, the developer sells the vacant eastern parcel as marked off by the surveyor.

While the two estates were owned by the developer, the building exhibited two features—the roof overhang and the view from the upstairs rooms—that arguably might give rise to predial servitudes. Under Article 741 of the Louisiana Civil Code, both features might embody "a relationship established between two estates owned by the same owner that would be a predial servitude if the estates belonged to different owners." La. Civ. Code art. 741 (1977). However, only the roof overhanging would be visible as an *apparent* servitude of projection or drip pursuant to Article 699 of the Civil Code. *See* La. Civ. Code art. 699 (1977). Thus, an apparent servitude of projection or drip would come into existence automatically when the two estates cease to be owned by the same person, unless the parties agree otherwise. La. Civ. Code art. 741 (1977). The right of the owner of the parcel featuring the building to enjoy the view out of the third floor window across the vacant lot next door *could* be protected by a non-apparent servitude of view. But in this case it is not evidenced by any exterior sign. Consequently, a non-apparent servitude of view across the vacant, eastern parcel would only come into existence by destination of the owner if "the owner has previously filed for registry in the conveyance records of the parish in which the immovable is located a *formal declaration* establishing the destination." La. Civ. Code art. 741 (1977) (emphasis added).

The person who purchases the vacant lot to the east of the building as marked off by the surveyor cannot demand that the roof overhang be removed because the overhang existed while the lots were owned by the same person and the overhang was visible prior to the sale. *See Alexander v. Boghel*, 4 La. 312 (1832). However, the purchaser of the vacant lot is not bound by a purported servitude of view. As its existence was not perceivable by an exterior sign, the *nonapparent* servitude would have come into existence only if the landowner had filed a formal declaration of destination in the parish conveyance records before he sold the vacant lot.

* * *

In the following decision, the court confronts a paradigmatic claim that a servitude of passage has been established through destination of the owner under Article 741 of the Louisiana Civil Code. Notice the court's careful review of the factual record and the court's response to the defendants' counter arguments based on the Louisiana Public Records Doctrine and Articles 689 and 694.

Naramore v. Aikman

252 So. 3d 935 (La. App. 1 Cir. 2018)

CRAIN, J. The defendants appeal a judgment recognizing a servitude of passage and permanently enjoining them from interfering with its use. The plaintiffs answered seeking an increase in damages and an award of attorney fees. We affirm.

Facts and Procedural History

This litigation involves several parcels of contiguous property located in Tangipahoa Parish, more particularly depicted in the appendix hereto. Plaintiffs Jerelean Arnold Naramore, Tammie Naramore Steib, and Craig Steib collectively own the 9.46–acre parcel identified on the appendix by Naramore's name. The adjacent 9.52–acre parcel to the east is owned by plaintiffs Carol Arnold Martinson and David Henry Martinson. Defendants Baynum and Kayla Aikman own a 1.767 parcel adjacent to the southwest side of the Naramore parcel. An asphalt road, West Sam Arnold Loop, is adjacent to the west side of the Aikman parcel. A gravel road extends from West Sam Arnold Loop through the southern boundary of the Aikman and Naramore parcels. The gravel road is located within an alleged servitude shown on the Bodin survey as the long rectangular area along the southern boundaries of the Aikman and Naramore parcels, and extending across the Martinson parcel into a tract owned by Ottis S. Arnold. The use of the gravel road, and more specifically the existence of the alleged servitude, is the origin of the dispute between the parties.

All of the above property (collectively the "Arnold property") was previously owned by Sam and Vivian Arnold, who acquired it in 1956. Although unclear when the gravel road was built, Sam and Vivian, along with their tenants, began using the road as early as 1960 to access the Arnold's home. The road was also used by the Worley family, the owners of property on the south side of the road, to access their property.

In the early 1980s, Sam and Vivian began transferring the property to their descendants. They first transferred the Martinson parcel to their daughter, Carol

Martinson, on March 25, 1980. The act of sale describes the Martinson parcel, along with the following:

> [A] servitude 0.45 chains in width in an East–West direction connecting the existing Public Road with servitude on property of Ottis Samuel Arnold in favor of Grace Louise Arnold Mapes, Ottis Samuel Arnold and Jerelean Avis Arnold Naramore as per plat and survey of Leey Mapes of record in COB____, page____, dated [.]

The referenced Mapes survey is dated March 20, 1979, and shows a servitude that is approximately the same in size and location as shown on the Bodin survey. The act of sale was recorded in the public records shortly after its execution, but the Mapes survey was not.

On April 28, 1982, Sam and Vivian conveyed to Jeffrey and Cynthia Arnold the 1.75 acres ultimately acquired by the Aikmans on August 13, 1993. The 1982 and 1993 conveyances do not mention the disputed servitude. On October 27, 1983, Sam and Vivian transferred the 9.46–acre parcel to Jerelean Naramore. That act of sale does not mention the servitude, but references the Mapes survey. Naramore transferred approximately four acres to her daughter, Tammie Steib, on May 29, 2008. That conveyance contained a survey identifying the gravel road.

The parties used the gravel road without any significant incidents until late 2010 or early 2011, when log trucks and other heavy equipment used the road in connection with timber operations on the Martinson parcel. Baynum objected and blocked further vehicular traffic beyond his driveway by parking a tractor on the road and pulling a large log across it. He later installed and locked a gate at the entrance to the road near West Sam Arnold Loop. Although he gave a key to some members of the Arnold family, confrontations continued. When efforts to amicably resolve the dispute failed, suit was filed on October 20, 2011.

The plaintiffs allege Sam and Vivian created a servitude of passage over the disputed strip to access all of the Arnold property, which the plaintiffs have continuously used for that purpose before and after their respective acquisitions. [The named plaintiffs are Jerelean Arnold Naramore, Tammie Naramore Steib, Craig Steib, LouAnn Naramore, Carol Arnold Martinson, David Henry Martinson, and Julie Faust Martinson.] Alleging the Aikmans prevented or interfered with use of the servitude, the plaintiffs requested a declaratory judgment recognizing the servitude, injunctive relief prohibiting the Aikmans from interfering with its use, and damages. Following an evidentiary hearing, the trial court issued a preliminary injunction on January 30, 2012, prohibiting the Aikmans from interfering with plaintiffs' use of the alleged servitude.

On May 8, 2013, Lynn and Winifred Worley, owners of the property south of the Aikman and Naramore parcels, filed a petitory action seeking recognition of their ownership of the portion of the Worley property allegedly subject to the servitude. The plaintiffs in this proceeding then amended their petition to include the Worleys as defendants. The two proceedings were consolidated, and the Worleys eventually entered a consent judgment recognizing the servitude along the boundaries described in the Bodin survey. . . .

Twenty witnesses, including three experts, testified at trial. The parties introduced numerous exhibits, including maps, surveys, and acts of sale reflecting the chain of title for each parcel. After taking the matter under advisement, the trial court ruled in favor of the plaintiffs. Relying, in part, on Louisiana Civil Code article 741 allowing for the creation of a servitude by "destination of the owner," the trial court found Sam Arnold created a servitude of passage used by the Arnold family to access the property for more than thirty years. In a judgment signed July 17, 2017, the trial court recognized the servitude of passage described in the Bodin survey, permanently enjoined the Aikmans from interfering with its use, and awarded $2,000.00 plus legal interest to Tammie Steib and Craig Steib, $1,000.00 plus legal interest to Jerelean Naramore and LouAnn Naramore, and $2,000.00 plus legal interest to Carol Arnold Martinson, David Martinson, and Julie Martinson. The Aikmans appeal, asserting multiple assignments of error, and plaintiffs answered the appeal, seeking an increase in damages and an award of attorney fees.

Discussion

The Aikmans contend the trial court erred (1) by declaring a servitude of passage and permanently enjoining the Aikmans from interfering with its use, (2) by denying a peremptory exception of prescription, and (3) by denying their motion for leave.

Servitude of Passage

Apparent servitudes may be acquired by title, destination of the owner, or acquisitive prescription. La. Civ. Code art. 740. Apparent servitudes are those perceivable by exterior signs, works, or constructions; such as a roadway, a window in a common wall, or an aqueduct. La. Civ. Code art. 707. Nonapparent servitudes are those with no exterior sign of their existence, such as the prohibition of building on an estate or of building above a particular height. *Id.* A servitude of passage is the right for the benefit of the dominant estate whereby persons, animals, utilities, or vehicles are permitted to pass through the servient estate. La. Civ. Code art. 705. Unless the title provides otherwise, the extent of the right and the mode of its exercise shall be suitable for the kind of traffic or utility necessary for the reasonable use of the dominant estate. *Id.*

Article 741 defines "destination of the owner" to be "a relationship established between two estates owned by the same owner that would be a predial servitude if the estates belonged to different owners." Article 741 further provides:

> When the two estates cease to belong to the same owner, unless there is express provision to the contrary, *an apparent servitude comes into existence of right* and a nonapparent servitude comes into existence if the owner has

previously filed for registry in the conveyance records of the parish in which the immovable is located a formal declaration establishing the destination. [Emphasis added.]

This article implicitly recognizes that when there is only one owner, there is no servitude, because no one can have a servitude on his own property. *See* Yiannopoulos and Scalise, 4 La. Civ. L. Treatise, *Predial Servitudes* § 6:38 (4th ed. September 2017 Update). But, when the single estate is divided, or two estates cease to belong to the same owner, an apparent servitude comes into existence of right unless the common owner disavows its existence. *See Phipps v. Schupp*, 09-2037 (La. 7/6/10), 45 So.3d 593, 601; Yiannopoulos and Scalise, at § 6:38.

Whether an apparent servitude has been created by destination of the owner is a factual determination reviewed under the manifest error-clearly wrong standard of review. *See Wong v. Alley Square I, L.L.C.*, 13–1958, 2014 WL 1778284, p.1 (La. App. 1 Cir. 5/2/14). . . .

The trial court heard from several witnesses, both fact and expert, familiar with the history of the property. Edward Murphy, an attorney accepted by the trial court as an expert in real estate title examination, researched the title and confirmed the property presently owned by the Aikmans, Martinsons, Steibs, and Naramore was previously owned by Sam and Vivian Arnold, who acquired it in 1956. The earliest indication of the road that Murphy found in the public records is a survey by C.M. Moore dated 1952, revised in 1958, and recorded August 3, 1959, which appears to show the roadway. Murphy confirmed the conveyances of the Martinson, Naramore, and Aikman parcels, and that the Mapes survey, referenced in the Martinson and Naramore transfers, was not recorded at the time of those transfers.

William J. Bodin Jr., a licensed civil engineer and surveyor, prepared the Bodin survey and described the servitude based on old maps, court records, and an onsite inspection. The oldest map cited by Bodin is a 1966 survey by Clifford Webb, apparently unrecorded, that shows a "0' LANE" along the northern boundary of the Worley property. On the western end of the disputed strip, Bodin placed the center of the servitude along the common boundary of the Worley and Arnold properties, with the southern half on the Worley property and northern half on what is now the Aikman, Naramore, and Martinson parcels. At its intersection with West Sam Arnold Loop, Bodin described the servitude as 29.7 feet wide. David Bickford, an employee of a surveying firm, went to the site and measured the servitude area and testified it was 29.7 feet wide. The gravel road itself, which Bickford measured as 12 feet wide, is also shown on the Bodin survey and lies entirely on the Aikman and Naramore parcels.

Recent photographs of the disputed strip show an open area bordered by trees in some stretches, with a gravel road running in an east-west direction. Maurice Jordan, the Tangipahoa Parish Engineer, testified the road is private and has never been adopted or maintained by the parish. Winifred Worley and her sister, Lynn Worley, described the origins of the road. According to Lynn, who was 77 at the time of trial, her uncle and Sam Arnold "put up that land" because they each needed access to homes built on the property. She described it as a "little country road" used to access the property for "years and years and years." Winifred, who was 84 when she testified, said Sam and Vivian "always used the road."

Erla Mae Perrilloux, a tenant of the Arnolds, lived at the end of the road from 1960 to 1962. She and her mother-in-law used the road for access. LouAnn Naramore, Jerelean's daughter, testified she used the road to access the property since the early 1960s. She never had problems using the road until Baynum put up the gate and locked it. Sam Naramore, Jerelean's son, testified he used the road for about 50 years as his only means to access the property. The servitude area, according to Sam, is correctly identified in the Mapes survey, which places it in the same approximate location as the Bodin survey.

David Martinson, who was 52 at trial, testified he used the servitude since he was old enough to walk. According to David, the servitude is the only access for the property, and there has never been a period of time when it was not used for that purpose. The Bodin survey correctly shows the location of the gravel road, which David estimated to be about 15 to 20 feet wide. There was not a gate on the road until Baynum installed one, which led to this litigation.

Tammie Steib, another daughter of Jerelean Naramore, lived in a house on the road from 1984 to 1990. She bought a piece of the Naramore parcel in 2008 that contains a residence where her daughter Robin now lives. She testified the cleared area of the servitude is about 30 feet wide, and the gravel road occupies about 20 feet of the servitude. She uses the road to access the property and never had significant problems until February 2011, when Baynum blocked the road just past the entrance to his driveway by putting a log across it and parking a tractor behind the log. Baynum later installed a gate, which he initially left open, but began locking in July 2011, forcing Tammie to park at the gate and walk in. After the preliminary injunction was signed, she had no problems with Baynum for about a year. In March 2013, Baynum began interfering again by digging trenches in the road and placing pipes across it.

Tammie's other daughter, Lisa Jenkins, used the road for access while she lived on the Naramore parcel from 2007 to 2014. Lisa testified the road has been there her whole life, and her family has always maintained it. In 2011, prior to the litigation, she purchased two loads of gravel that were placed on the road from her driveway to West Sam Arnold Loop. For the first four years she lived on the road, the Aikmans did not interfere with her use of it. Baynum then began blocking access to the road by placing logs across it and later by installing a locked gate. Baynum provided keys to Lisa, her husband, and Tammie Steib, but told them they were the only people who could use the road. Although Baynum's conduct improved after the preliminary injunction, he resumed obstructing the road by putting pipes across it and digging trenches in the road. After the contempt hearing, Baynum stopped interfering with the use of the road.

Other witnesses testified about their use of the servitude. Betty Faust used the road for several years beginning around 1970 to visit her grandmother who lived on the road. Jeffrey Wayne Murphy, a tenant, used the road to access the property on a daily basis from 1990 to 1992. Sam Galloway, another tenant, regularly used the road without any interference by the Aikmans from 1995 to 2001. Julie Martinson, David's wife, began using the servitude in 1998.

Baynum testified he bought his parcel in 1993 from Jeffrey Arnold, who told him there was no servitude across the property. His act of sale does not mention the servitude, and when he mortgaged the property, he was told his title was clear. According to Baynum, for the first two years of his ownership, nobody used the road, which he claimed went no further than his driveway. In late 2010 or early 2011, after a bulldozer crossed his property as part of a logging operation, he told the workers he did not want their equipment crossing his property. He pulled a log across the road and later installed the gate, but gave a key to any of the Arnolds who asked for one. After the preliminary injunction was issued, he put pipes on the road and cut ruts in it to discourage speeding. He does not believe the road is the only access to the Arnold property and has seen vehicles entering from Highway 22 to the north. The Aikmans called Walton T. Tate, an attorney accepted as an expert in real estate title examination, who testified he researched the Aikmans' title and found nothing in the public records indicating a servitude over their property.

On appeal, the Aikmans argue the public records do not sufficiently establish the servitude prior to the Aikmans' acquisition in 1993. Thus, under the public records doctrine, they maintain the servitude does not burden their property. Alternatively, the Aikmans contend the plaintiffs have access to their parcels through another servitude, which purportedly runs north and south along the east side of the Arnold property and connects to Highway 22. Neither of these contentions is material to the creation of a servitude by destination under Article 741.

It is undisputed Sam and Vivian Arnold previously owned all of the property presently owned by the Aikmans, Steibs, Martinsons, and Naramore. The record establishes a right of way was cleared and a road was constructed along the disputed strip in the late 1950s or early 1960s to provide access to the property. Since its construction, the road has been apparent and used on a regular basis by the Arnold family and their tenants for access. The construction and use of the road, which is perceivable by exterior signs, works, or constructions, created a relationship between the respective parcels now owned by the Martinsons, Steibs, Aikmans, and Naramore that allowed access to West Sam Arnold Loop. When Sam and Vivian conveyed a portion of the property in 1980 to the Martinsons, an apparent servitude of passage, extending along the visible right of way to West Sam Arnold Loop, was created in favor of the Martinson parcel. *See* La. Civ. Code arts. 707, 740–41; *Huy Tuyet Tran v. Misuraca*, 10–2183, 2011 WL 2617382, p.3 (La. App. 1 Cir. 5/6/11) (holding a servitude of passage was created by destination of the owner when property containing an apparent roadway was divided and sold). The subsequent conveyance of the Aikman parcel in 1982 likewise created a servitude along the same route in favor of the Naramore parcel.

The Aikmans' reliance on the public records doctrine is misplaced. The creation of the servitude was not dependent upon an express declaration in an act of sale, nor did it have to be identified in a survey recorded in the public records. A similar argument was rejected by the supreme court in *Phipps*, where the court explained:

> [T]he defendants maintain because Mr. Phipps could not refer to any "writing, title, survey, or other exterior sign that evidenced the common owner's intent to create an apparent servitude," the common owner did not intend to create a servitude by destination. The defendants concede that an express provision is not required to create a servitude by destination of the owner, but they contend had it existed, it would have shown the common owner intended for the driveway to serve 541 Exposition Boulevard. We find the defendants' argument is without merit, as La. C.C. art. 741 does not require an express provision in order for a servitude by destination of the owner to exist.
>
> Moreover, the common owner did not provide an express provision that a servitude by destination was not created when he sold 541 Exposition Boulevard. Under La. C.C. art. 741, the common owner must disavow the existence of a predial servitude when both estates cease to belong to him, or an apparent servitude comes into existence as of right.

Phipps, 45 So.3d at 601.

The act of conveyance by Sam and Vivian to the Martinsons does not contain an express disavowal of the existence of the servitude. To the contrary, the conveyance recognizes an east-west servitude, approximately 30 feet wide, "connecting the existing Public Road with servitude of Ottis Samuel Arnold," as set forth in the Mapes survey. Although that survey was not recorded at the time, it confirms the servitude described in the act of conveyance is, in fact, the servitude used for many years to access the Arnold property. While the failure to record the Mapes survey may have prevented the creation of a servitude *by title*, we cannot infer, as suggested by the Aikmans, an intent *to disavow* the servitude merely because the survey was not recorded.

The Aikmans erroneously rely on Louisiana Civil Code articles 689 and 694, governing enclosed estates, to argue the servitude should not be recognized because the plaintiffs purportedly have access to their property by another route, failed to offer any compensation for the servitude, or voluntarily enclosed their estates. The requirements of Articles 689 and 694 do not apply to the creation of a servitude by destination of the owner under Article 741. The plaintiffs did not have to prove their property was landlocked, nor do they have to compensate the Aikmans for a servitude created years before the Aikmans acquired their property.

The plaintiffs had to prove that when Sam and Vivian Arnold owned all the property, a "relationship" existed between the parcels that would have been a predial servitude if the parcels belonged to different owners; and when Sam and Vivian conveyed the parcels, they did not expressly disavow the servitude. *See* La. Civ. Code art. 741; *Huy Tuyet Tran*, 2011 WL 2617382 at p.3; *Jackson v. Jackson*, 00-2591 (La. App. 1 Cir. 3/6/02), 818 So.2d 192, 198. The record reasonably supports the trial court's conclusion the plaintiffs met that burden of proof. We find no manifest error in the trial court's factual determination that a servitude of passage was created by destination of the owner. We likewise find no error in the trial court's issuance of a permanent injunction prohibiting the Aikmans from interfering with the use of the servitude. This assignment of error is without merit.

Exception of Prescription

The Aikmans argue the trial court erred by denying a peremptory exception of prescription set for hearing at trial. Although the trial court's judgment does not address the exception, silence in a judgment as to any issue before the trial court is deemed a rejection of that demand or issue. The exception is thus deemed denied. *See Robertson v. Sun Life Financial*, 09-2275 (La. App. 1 Cir. 6/11/10), 40 So.3d 507, 510.

A predial servitude is extinguished by nonuse for ten years. La. Civ. Code art. 753. When the prescription of nonuse is pled, the owner of the dominant estate has the burden of proving he or some other person made use of the servitude during the period of time required for the accrual of the prescription, such that no continuous ten-year period of nonuse occurred. La. Civ. Code art. 764; *Claitor v. Brooks*, 13-0178 (La. App. 1 Cir. 12/27/13), 137 So.3d 638, 643, *writ denied*, 14-0198 (La. 4/4/14), 135 So.3d 1182. A predial servitude, such as a servitude of passage, is preserved by use by anyone, even a stranger, if used as appertaining to the dominant estate. La. Civ. Code art. 757; *Claitor*, 137 So.3d at 643. The phrase "appertaining to the dominant estate" means someone must use the servitude for the purpose of going onto the dominant estate for some legitimate purpose, either to see the owner or for something connected with the use of that property. *See Claitor*, 137 So.3d at 643; *Dupont v. Hebert*, 06-2334 (La. App. 1 Cir. 2/20/08), 984 So.2d 800, 806, *writ denied*, 08-0640 (La. 5/9/08), 980 So.2d 695; *Palace Properties, L.L.C. v. Sizeler Hammond Square Limited Partnership*, 01-2812 (La. App. 1 Cir. 12/30/02), 839 So.2d 82, 94, *writ denied*, 03-0306 (La. 4/4/03), 840 So.2d 1219. Partial use of a servitude constitutes use of the whole. La. Civ. Code art. 759. Therefore, using part of the area burdened with a predial servitude interrupts the prescription of nonuse as to the entire area. *Claitor*, 137 So.3d at 643–44. Whether a servitude is lost to nonuse is a factual determination subject to the manifest error-clearly wrong standard of review. *See Palace Properties, L.L.C.*, 839 So.2d at 89; *Grieshaber Family Properties, LLC v. Impatiens, Inc.*, 10-1216 (La. App. 4 Cir. 3/23/11), 63 So.3d 189, 194.

The Aikmans maintain no attempt was made to use the servitude until over ten years after their acquisition in 1993. According to the Aikmans, they permitted the plaintiffs, whom they characterize as precarious possessors, access "over their driveway" until the plaintiffs and their friends "became a nuisance."

Use of the servitude was well established at trial. A dozen witnesses testified the servitude was regularly used from as early as 1960 through the date of the trial, except when prevented by the Aikmans, to access the property currently owned by the Martinsons, Steibs, and Naramore. The record does not indicate any meaningful period when the servitude was not used by the Arnold family or their tenants. This use, some of which predated the Aikmans' acquisition by decades, was not reduced to acts of precarious possession just because the Aikmans allowed the use until it purportedly became a "nuisance." The plaintiffs were exercising, and preserving, a right vested years before the Aikmans' acquisition. The trial court did not err in denying the exception of prescription. . . .

Answer to Appeal

In an answer to the appeal, the plaintiffs seek an increase in damages awarded for Baynum violating the preliminary injunction. The trial court awarded $2,000.00 to the Steibs, $1,000.00 to the Naramores, and $2,000.00 to the Martinsons, plus accrued legal interest from date of judicial demand until paid. . . .

The evidence establishes Baynum violated the preliminary injunction by digging trenches in the road and placing small pipes across it. Those impediments, according to Baynum, were intended to discourage speeding, not to prevent use of the servitude, as evidenced by the fact his mother drove across the same road to get to her house. While the violations of the preliminary injunction caused some inconvenience, we do not find the limited damage evidence mandates greater awards. Because the awards are not abusively low, we will not increase them.

The plaintiffs also seek an award of attorney fees. Pursuant to Louisiana Revised Statute 13:461 1(1)(g), "[t]he court may award attorney fees to the prevailing party in a contempt of court proceeding." The legislature's use of the word "may" means an award of attorney fees is discretionary, not mandatory. *See Roper v. City of Baton Rouge/Parish of East Baton Rouge*, 16-1025 (La. App. 1 Cir. 3/15/18), 244 So.3d 450, —— (2018 WL 1324454); *Quality Environmental Processes, Inc. v. IP Petroleum Company, Inc.*, 16-0230 (La. App. 1 Cir. 4/12/17), 219 So.3d 349, 375, *writ denied*, 17-00915 (La. 10/9/17), 227 So.3d 833;. Appellate review of discretionary decisions is conducted under the "abuse of discretion" standard of review. *Id.* The record reflects Baynum's violations of the preliminary injunction were relatively minor. Under these circumstances, the trial court did not abuse its discretion in declining to award attorney fees. The answer to the appeal is denied.

Conclusion

The July 17, 2017 judgment is affirmed. All costs of this appeal are assessed to Baynum and Kayla Aikman.

AFFIRMED.

Notes and Questions

1. In *Naremore v. Aikman*, 252 So.3d 935 (La. 1 Cir. 2018), why was the Louisiana Public Records Doctrine inapplicable to the claim made by the plaintiffs that

a servitude had been established through destination of the owner? Why did the court go to the trouble of recounting so much of the written evidence and oral testimony of the various property owners in this decision?

2. What evidence helped the plaintiffs establish that the servitude of passage was apparent and was being used by the Arnolds at the time of the severance of their larger tract into smaller parcels? Did the court explore the interior state of mind of the property owners at the time of severance of the Arnold tract or was the court focused on objective facts? Notice that the plain language of Article 741 of the Louisiana Civil Code states that an "apparent servitude comes into existence *of right*" when the conditions for destination exist. La. Civ. Code art. 741 (1977). Are courts required to discern the intent of the common owner of the two estates when an exterior, visible sign points to an apparent servitude? Alternatively, is the common owner's intent only relevant when the common owner expressly provides that an apparent servitude should *not* come into existence once the two estates cease to belong to the same owner?

3. In a long-running case involving the claim that a servitude of passage had been created by destination of the owner over a small driveway that passed across a corner lot facing Audubon Park in New Orleans and complex issues relating to whether the claimant was entitled to a right of passage under Articles 689 or 694 of the Louisiana Civil Code, the Louisiana Supreme Court vacated a lower court decision, remanded the case for further proceedings and specifically directed the lower courts and the parties to address the *intention* of the common owner at the time of severance, even though the Civil Code does not seem to require such an inquiry. *See Phipps v. Schupp*, 45 So.3d 593, 601 (La. 2010) ("If the common owner provided the key to Mr. Botnick, who then gave it to the Phipps, then it would appear the common owner did intend for the driveway running through 543 Exposition Boulevard to serve 541 Exposition Boulevard."). This directive led to further confusion and litigation in the matter, without any apparent resolution in sight. *See Phipps v. Schupp*, 163 So.3d 3d 212 (La. 4 Cir. 2015) (reversing summary judgment and holding that: (1) public records doctrine, as interpreted by *Dallas v. Farrington*, 490 So.2d 265, 269–70 (La. 1986), precluded assertion of right to demand creation of gratuitous servitude of passage under Article 694; (2) factual questions remained regarding the existence and extent of the servitude allegedly created by destination of the owner under Article 741; and (3) if plaintiff's estate was not due a servitude under Article 741, the possibility remained that the claimant's estate was "enclosed" for purposes of claiming an indemnified right of passage under Article 689).

4. Controversy has arisen in the courts concerning "the question of whether a predial servitude may be created by destination when the owner of an estate establishes a relation between two parts of his estate that would be a predial servitude if those parts belonged to two different owners and the original owner transfers the ownership of one of those parts." A.N. Yiannopoulous, 4 Louisiana Civil Law Treatise: Predial Servitudes§ 6:38 (4th ed. 2013). Applying what Professor Yiannopoulous calls a "teleological interpretation" of Article 741 of the Louisiana Civil

Code, a majority of the Louisiana First Circuit Court of Appeal held that although the provision speaks of a relationship established between two estates owned by the same person, an owner may establish a servitude by destination between *two parts of the same estate. Huy Tuyet Tran v. Misuraca*, 10-2183, 2011 WL 2617382 (La. App. 1 Cir. 5/6/2011). The dissenting judge in that decision, Judge Guidry, noted that the former version of Article 741 and its French sources would have supported such a view but observed that the current version of Article 741 now refers explicitly to "two estates." Consequently he would not have found a servitude to have been created by destination in the absence of two distinct estates. *Id.* Notice that in *Naramore v. Aikman*, 252 So.3d 935, 943 (La. App. 1 Cir. 2018), the First Circuit Court of Appeal cited its own prior, unpublished decision in *Huy Tuyet Tran* for the proposition that a servitude of passage can be created by destination of the owner when property containing an apparent roadway is subdivided and sold to a third party.

5. At common law, the situation addressed by Article 741 of the Louisiana Civil Code is covered by the doctrine of easements implied from prior use or, as some courts and commentators suggest, from "quasi-easements." Two leading commentators on the common law of easements describe the doctrine in the following terms:

> Easements may be implied from a landowner's use of part of the landowner's property (the quasi-servient tenement) for the benefit of another part (the quasi-dominant tenement). Such use does not constitute a true easement because a landowner cannot obtain an easement in the landowner's own land. Rather, it is considered a quasi-easement, which may ripen into an easement upon the landowner's transfer of either the quasi-servient tenement or the quasi-dominant tenement. . . .
>
> Courts recognize the grant or reservation of an easement implied from quasi-easement when the claimant establishes the following elements:
>
> 1. Prior common ownership of the dominant and the servient estates
>
> 2. The common owner's apparent and continuous use of part of the land to benefit another part (quasi-easement)
>
> 3. Transfer of one of the parcels (severance)
>
> 4. Necessity at severance for the preexisting use to continue.

JON W. BRUCE & JAMES W. ELY, JR., THE LAW OF EASEMENTS AND LICENSES IN LAND §§ 4.15, 4.16, at 218–19, 222–23 (2019).

The *Restatement (Third) of Property: Servitudes* states the general rule in slightly different terms:

§ 2.12 Servitudes Implied from Prior Use

> Unless a contrary intent is expressed or implied, the circumstance that prior to a conveyance severing the ownership of land into two or more parts, a use was made of one part for the benefit of another part, implies

that a servitude was created to continue the prior use if, at the time of severance, the parties had reasonable grounds to expect that the conveyance would not terminate the right to continue the prior use.

The following factors tend to establish that the parties had reasonable grounds to expect that the conveyance would not terminate the right to continue the prior use:

(1) the prior use was not merely temporary or casual, and

(2) continuance of the prior use was reasonably necessary to enjoyment of the parcel, estate, or interest previously benefited by the use, and

(3) existence of the prior use was apparent or known to the parties, or

(4) the prior use was for underground utilities serving either parcel.

RESTATEMENT (THIRD) OF PROPERTY: SERVITUDES § 2.12 (2000). Do you believe either the general common law approach or the *Restatement (Third)* approach would be a useful model for Louisiana? Would either approach have helped avoid the protracted litigation in *Phipps v. Schuff*?

6. ***Underground Utilities***: Notice the Restatement's reference to the factor of whether, prior to severance into two separately owned parcels, one of the parcels was previously used for "underground utilities serving either parcel." RESTATEMENT (THIRD) OF PROPERTY: SERVITUDES § 2.12(4) (2000). This factor points to a common problem. In a recent decision, the Louisiana Third Circuit Court of appeal held that a predial servitude for an underground water line serving a landowner's residence was established by destination of the owner, even though the water line itself was buried and not visible, because the *water meter*, which serviced the residence and was located on the alleged servient estate, was visible and thus constituted an exterior sign of the servitude's existence at the time the commonly owned land was severed into two separately owned parcels. *Carpenter v. Guillory Investment, Inc.*, 266 So.3d 581, 586–87 (La. App. 3 Cir. 2019). The court in *Carpenter* also found the fact that the servient estate owner "had no particularized knowledge that the water meter on its property serviced the water line connected to the [alleged dominant estate]" was "inconsequential" because, under Article 741, "the current servient estate owner's knowledge is immaterial." *Id.* at 586. Should Louisiana follow the Restatement and adopt a presumption that underground utilities serving either of two parcels owned by a common owner are intended to remain in place and lead to the establishment of a predial servitude by destination of the owner unless the common owner expressly declares otherwise at the time of severance of the two parcels into separate ownership? What such a rule produce gains in efficiency?

2. Acquisitive Prescription

Pursuant to Article 740 of the Louisiana Civil Code *apparent* servitudes can also be established by acquisitive prescription. La. Civ. Code art. 740 (1977). *Nonapparent* servitudes cannot be acquired by acquisitive prescription because they cannot be openly possessed or enjoyed and thus the alleged servient estate owner would have no opportunity to notice and challenge the claimed possession or enjoyment. In accordance with Articles 739 and 741, non-apparent servitudes can only be acquired by title or by a declaration of destination filed for registry in the parish in which the immovable property is located. La. Civ. Code arts. 739, 741 (1977).

Because a servitude is an incorporeal real right, a person may enjoy a servitude by exercising quasi-possession. Yet a person claiming a servitude must still exercise the right with the intent to have it as one's own. Under Article 742 of the Louisiana Civil Code, the rules governing possession and acquisitive prescription of corporeal immovables apply by analogy to the quasi-possession of incorporeal immovables. La. Civ. Code art. 742. A quasi-possessor in good faith and under just title can acquire a servitude in ten years; a quasi-possessor without good faith or just title must quasi-possess for thirty years:

Art. 742. Acquisitive prescription

The laws governing acquisitive prescription of immovable property apply to apparent servitudes. An apparent servitude may be acquired by peaceable and uninterrupted possession of the right for ten years in good faith and by just title; it may also be acquired by uninterrupted possession for thirty years without title or good faith.

La. Civ. Code art. 742 (1977).

Consider the following hypothetical. Anne owns two hundred acres of land. A dirt road crosses Anne's land. Barbara, Anne's neighbor, owns two hundred acres of land immediately adjacent to Anne's tract. Suppose that Barbara has used the dirt road that crosses Anne's land to gain access to a nearby public road on a regular basis because it is more convenient than a dirt road on Barbara's land leading to a public road. Anne had never given Barbara permission to use the dirt road and Anne had never asked Barbara for permission to use it. What would be the result if, starting in 1980, Barbara used the dirt road described above for thirty years and her use was peaceable, continuous, open, public, and never challenged by Anne?

Until recently, most Louisiana lawyers and judges would have said that on these facts a servitude of passage burdening Anne's estate and benefitting Barbara's estate had come into existence because the servitude of passage was apparent and the quasi-possession by Barbara satisfied all of the general rules for thirty-year acquisitive prescription. Today, however, the outcome of a case like this might be more difficult to predict, particularly when the dispute is in essence between neighbors who know one another well. The law has become more complicated because of a controversial decision handed down by a divided Louisiana Supreme Court, a decision that was, oddly, "strictly limited to the facts" before the court. *Boudreaux v. Cummings*, 167 So.3d 559, 564 (La. 2015). *See* John A. Lovett, *Precarious Possession*, 77 La. L. Rev. 617 (2017) (discussing *Boudreaux* in light of the law of precarious possession).

Before we delve into *Boudreaux v. Cummings*, consider the following well-known and frequently cited Louisiana Supreme Court decision, which involves the alleged acquisition of servitudes of light and view. The defendant, celebrity chef Paul Prudhomme (1940–2015), played a prominent role in popularizing Cajun and Creole cuisine in the 1980s.

Palomeque v. Prudhomme

664 So.2d 88 (La. 1995)

MARCUS, Justice. On January 12, 1994, Dr. F.E. Palomeque filed a petition for injunctive relief to prohibit Paul E. Prudhomme from bricking over windows in the common wall between Dr. Palomeque's condominium at 422 Chartres Street and Prudhomme's property at 420 Chartres. Dr. Palomeque alleges that his condominium has acquired servitudes of light and view over Prudhomme's estate.

The properties at 420 and 422 Chartres Street were originally constructed in 1834 for Phillippe Auguste Delachaise as two buildings in a row of three, four-story brick buildings. There is no evidence as to how or when the buildings were reduced to their current state, but today the Prudhomme property at 420 Charters is but one story while the condominium building at 422 Chartres is two stories high. [A photograph from the Historic New Orleans Collection shows that as late as 1915, 420 Chartres was still four stories high while 422 was three stories. Thus, the upper floors of the buildings were destroyed sometime between 1915 and 1964.] On August 21, 1974, the Maison-Chartres Condominium Association acquired 422 Chartres and converted the building to condominiums with two units on the second floor. Architectural drawings by Leonard Reese Spangenberg, Jr., dated April 20, 1972 and created in anticipation of the condominium project, show ten windows in the common wall. At the time of trial there were only six functional windows. Two additional windows were apparent from the exterior but were sheetrocked over on the interior. Based on these discrepancies, the trial judge found that the windows were not pre-existing but rather were placed in the common wall as part of the conversion project in 1974.

In 1981 Paul Prudhomme purchased the one-story building at 420 Chartres, which now provides K-Paul's Restaurant with office space, a test kitchen and a garage facility. Prudhomme first applied to the Vieux Carre Commission ("Commission") for approval of a second story addition in 1985. This project requires the bricking up of the windows at 422 Chartres. The Commission granted a six month permit but no work was done until 1991, when, with Commission approval, Prudhomme began the process of strengthening the failing facade. The second floor facade was added at that time.

In July 1993, Prudhomme's architect met with Andrew McCollam and Dr. Palomeque, owners of the second floor units, regarding Prudhomme's plan to close the windows. No agreement was reached, and Prudhomme went forward with his efforts to obtain another permit. In the meantime, on September 20, 1993,

Andrew McCollam sold the front unit to Dr. Palomeque, who continued to oppose Prudhomme's efforts to enclose the second floor of 420 Chartres. A few days later the Commission approved the permit. Dr. Palomeque's action for injunctive relief followed.

A temporary restraining order was granted, and after a hearing, a preliminary injunction was granted. However, after a trial on the merits, the trial judge denied the permanent injunction and held that servitudes of light and view cannot be acquired by acquisitive prescription. Dr. Palomeque appealed. The court of appeal affirmed, finding that, even if acquisitive prescription were applicable, Dr. Palomeque did not have the requisite ten years of good faith. On application by Dr. Palomeque, we granted certiorari to review the correctness of that decision.

The issues presented for our consideration are: (1) whether servitudes of light and view can be acquired by acquisitive prescription; and (2) if so, whether servitudes were acquired in this case.

Apparent servitudes may be acquired by title, by destination of the owner, or by acquisitive prescription. La. Civ. Code. art. 740. Nonapparent servitudes may be acquired by title only. La. Civ. Code art. 739. Therefore, we must determine whether the servitudes of light and view are apparent or nonapparent servitudes.

Civil Code Article 707 defines apparent servitudes as those "that are perceivable by exterior signs, works, or constructions; such as a roadway, a window in a common wall, or an aqueduct." Non apparent servitudes are those "that have no exterior sign of their existence; such as the prohibition of building on an estate or of building above a particular height."

A window in a common wall is clearly an exterior sign of a servitude because a co-owner of a common wall may not make any openings in the wall without the consent of his neighbor. La. Civ. Code art. 681; A.N. YIANNOPOULOS, PREDIAL SERVITUDES § 135, at 390–91 (4 Louisiana Civil Law Treatise 1983) [hereinafter YIANNOPOULOS, PREDIAL SERVITUDES]. Thus, by definition, a servitude of light or view in a common wall is apparent and can be acquired by acquisitive prescription.[7] YIANNOPOULOS, PREDIAL SERVITUDES § 135, at 390–93. Nonetheless, Prudhomme argues that, even in a common wall, the servitudes of light and view cannot be

---

7. The trial judge's reliance on *Oldstein v. Firemen's Bldg. Ass'n*, 44 La. Ann. 492, 10 So.928 (1892), was misplaced. *Oldstein* is inapposite because it involved a private wall. In *Oldstein*, the neighbor had an imprescriptible right to make the private wall common by paying half of the value of the construction, but until he exercised that right, the wall was private and he had no right to demand the windows be closed.

Openings in a private wall are not exterior signs of a servitude because they are merely the exercise of a prerogative of ownership. The act of placing a window in a private wall is in no way adverse to one's neighbor. 1 Planiol & Ripert, Treatise On The Civil Law pt. 2, ch.4, no. 2958, at 743–44 (La. St. L. Inst. trans., 12th ed. 1939). Consequently servitudes of light and view in a private wall are nonapparent and can be established only by title or formal declaration of destination. *See* A. N. Yiannopoulos, *Creation of Servitudes by Prescription and Destination of the Owner*, 43 LA. L. REV. 57, 61–65 (1982).

apparent because they are equivalent to a prohibition against building, a nonapparent servitude. This argument is without merit. The servitudes cannot be equated. A servitude of prohibition of building is much more onerous in that it prevents the owner of the servient estate from building any constructions on his estate. With servitudes of light and view the owner of the servient estate may still build on his property; he is only prevented from raising constructions that would obstruct the light or view. This prohibition against obstructions is merely an accessory right to the servitudes of light and view. La. Civ. Code arts. 701, 703; *see also,* A. N. Yiannopoulos, *Creation of Servitudes by Prescription and Destination of the Owner,* 43 La. L. Rev. 57, 61–65 (1982).

Thus, we hold that the servitudes of light and view in a common wall are apparent servitudes which encompass the right to prevent the servient estate from building obstructions to the light and view. As apparent servitudes, the servitudes of light and view may be established by acquisitive prescription. La. Civ. Code art. 740.

This brings us to the second question presented: Did Dr. Palomeque acquire servitudes of light and view by acquisitive prescription of ten years. . . .

According to the Revision Comments [for article 742], this article was based on a combined reading of Articles 765 and 3504 and was intended to overrule all contrary jurisprudence. In 1982, the code article on just title was also amended. That article now requires that just title be written, valid in form and recorded in the conveyance records of the parish in which the immovable is situated. La. Civ. Code art. 3483.

Dr. Palomeque argues that these revisions to the law of predial servitudes are not applicable here and that under the pre-1977 law, he is not required to establish just title. Blanda v. Rivers, 210 So. 2d 161 (La. App. 4th Cir. 1968). This argument is without merit. Section 7 of Act No. 514 which enacted the 1977 revisions provides:

> The provisions of this Act shall apply to all predial servitudes, including those existing on the effective date of this Act; but no provision may be applied to divest already vested rights or to impair the obligation of contracts.

In order for a right to be vested it must be absolute, complete, unconditional, and independent of a contingency; the mere expectation of a future benefit or contingent interest in property does not create a vested right. *Tennant v. Russell,* 214 La. 1046, 39 So. 2d 726, 728 (1949); *Voelkel v. Harrison,* 572 So. 2d 724, 726 (La. App. 4th Cir. 1990), *writ denied,* 575 So. 2d 391 (La. 1991); *Matter of American Waste & Pollution Control,* 597 So. 2d 1125, 1130 (La. App. 1st 1992), *writ denied,* 604 So. 2d 1309, 1318 (La. 1992). On January 1, 1978, the effective date of Act No. 514, Dr. Palomeque's predecessors had been possessing these servitudes for approximately four years. The right to the servitudes was contingent on continued possession without interruption for six more years. Consequently, Dr. Palomeque had no vested right in these servitudes which would prevent the application of the 1977, or even the 1982, revisions.

Predial servitudes are in derogation of public policy because they form restraints on the free disposal and use of property. Therefore, servitudes are not entitled to be viewed with favor by the law and can never be sustained by implication. *Buras Ice Factory Inc. v. Dept. of Hwys. of La.*, 235 La. 158, 103 So. 2d 74, 80 (1958); *Gravolet v. Bd. of Commissioners*, 598 So. 2d 1231, 1234 (La. App. 4th Cir. 1992); *see also*, 1 Domat, The Civil Law In Its Natural Order, tit. XII, sec. 1, at 435 (Strahan, trans., Cushing ed., 2d ed. 1861). Any doubt as to the existence, extent or manner of exercise of a predial servitude must be resolved in favor of the servient estate. La. Civ. Code art. 730; *McGuffy v. Weil*, 240 La. 758, 125 So. 2d 154, 158 (1960).

Applying the revised law on acquisitive prescription of servitudes, Dr. Palomeque must establish that he has possessed the right for ten years in good faith and with just title. La. Civ. Code art. 742. The trial judge found that the windows were created in 1974. Based on the record, this finding is not clearly wrong. Thus, the ten years of adverse possession have been conclusively established. However, the requirement of just title is more problematic for Dr. Palomeque.

Just title is a juridical act sufficient to transfer ownership or another real right. It must be written, valid in form and filed for registry in the conveyance records of the parish in which the immovable is situated. La. Civ. Code art. 3483. As applied to servitudes, Article 3483 requires that the possessor have a title that would have established a servitude if it had been granted by the owner of the servient estate. YIANNOPOULOS, PREDIAL SERVITUDES § 137, at 396. As stated by Aubry & Rau, just title "is a title which as such—that means without regard to whether it comes from a true owner and a person competent to alienate—is appropriate for the purpose of conferring an ownership interest. In other words, any title the purpose of which is to transfer ownership is a just title, if it is legitimate as to its category and is in the form required to make it valid as such. . . ." Aubry & Rau, *Droit Civil Francais, in* 2 CIVIL LAW TRANSLATIONS § 218, at 359 (1966) (Emphasis Added).

Because Dr. Palomeque has no agreement with the servient estate, he argues that his titles to the two condominium units serve as just title for these servitudes. In setting forth the description of the properties to be conveyed in the acts of sale, the descriptions commence with the following standard language:

> *That Certain Piece Or Portion Of Ground, Condominium Parcels, Units And/Or Apartments, Common Elements And Limited Common Elements*, together with all the buildings and improvements thereon, and all the rights, ways, privileges, servitudes and appurtenances thereunto belonging or in anywise appertaining, situated on. . . .

This boilerplate language has been used in every deed transferring these condominiums since their development in 1974. The legal effect of this language is merely to transfer all rights which existed prior to the sale. With regard to servitudes, this is superfluous because predial servitudes run with the land and would be transferred regardless of the presence of this phrase.

Clearly, the language in question would be too ambiguous and imprecise to establish servitudes of light and view by title. Even if this language were used in an agreement with the servient estate, it could not establish servitudes of light and view. For a servitude to be created by title, the instrument must be express as to the nature and extent of the servitude. Because servitudes are so disfavored, an ambiguous agreement to establish a servitude is unenforceable. "Where the language is insufficient to convey ownership of property which belongs to the grantor, it cannot be sufficient to create just title in property which does not in fact belong to the grantor." *Williams v. Wiggins*, 26,060 (La. App. 2d Cir. 9/17/94), 641 So. 2d 1068, 1073.

Nonetheless, Dr. Palomeque argues that this language is sufficient to constitute just title for purposes of acquisitive prescription. We disagree. Even assuming this language could transfer a preexisting right, under no circumstance would this ambiguous language create a servitude. Therefore, it cannot suffice for just title. *Williams*, 641 So. 2d at 1073; *Eubanks v. State, Dept. of Trans. and Dev.*, 620 So. 2d 954, 959 (La. App. 3d Cir. 1993), *writ denied*, 629 So. 2d 351, 353 (La. 1993).

Moreover, "just title in acquisitive prescription is not required only as an element of showing good faith. It represents a separate condition. Hence it must exist in reality; the possessor's belief in its existence is insufficient, no matter how plausible." 2 Aubry & Rau, Droit Civil Francais §218, no. 311, at 363 (La. St. L. Inst. trans., 7th ed. 1961). Dr. Palomeque may not rely on his belief, no matter how justifiable, that the condominium association had a right to install windows in a common wall. He must show more than that; he must show a written, recorded act that would have created a servitude had it been granted by the owner of the servient estate. If this language were considered sufficient for the purposes of just title, the just title requirement would be rendered meaningless, resulting in the requirement of only good faith and ten years. . . . Lacking the requisite just title, the only way Dr. Palomeque could acquire servitudes of light and view is by accrual of thirty years of uninterrupted possession which he admittedly does not have.

Accordingly, we hold that the language in Dr. Palomeque's deeds is insufficient to constitute just title to a servitude under Civil Code article 3483. Having found that Dr. Palomeque lacks just title, we need not reach the issue of good faith.

Decree

For the reasons assigned, the judgment of the court of appeal is affirmed. All costs are assessed against Dr. F.E. Palomeque.

LEMMON, J., concurs and will assign reasons.

Notes and Questions

1. In *Palomeque v. Prudhomme*, 664 So.2d 88 (La. 1995), the court first classified the servitude of light and view allegedly burdening Prudhomme's estate as apparent. Had the court agreed with Prudhomme that the purported servitude was non-apparent, the court would never have reached the elements of either ten-year or thirty-year acquisitive prescription. Do you understand why the court classified

the alleged servitude as apparent? What different facts would have been needed for the court to characterize the servitude as nonapparent? Pay special attention to the architectural history offered by the court at the beginning of the opinion. Do you see why it was important for the court to note that the two adjacent buildings originally comprised "a row of three, four story brick buildings"?

2. Once the court had classified the alleged servitude as apparent, it addressed Dr. Palomeque's acquisitive prescription claim. Why did it fail? Why was Dr. Palomeque unable to assert thirty-year acquisitive prescription against Prudhomme?

3. Under the 1870 Civil Code, only servitudes that were *both apparent and continuous* could be acquired by acquisitive prescription or destination of the owner. *See* La. Civ. Code art. 740 rev. cmt (a)(1977). Servitudes that were classified as *discontinuous*, even if they were apparent, could not be acquired by acquisitive prescription or destination of the owner. Discontinuous servitudes were those that required the exercise of some human act; for example, a servitude of passage or a servitude to draw water from a well on another estate. Continuous servitudes were those that functioned without any exercise by man; for example, a servitude of aqueduct. The 1977 revision of the Civil Code provisions governing predial servitudes suppressed the distinction between continuous and discontinuous servitudes and explicitly modified the law to allow the acquisition of *apparent* predial servitudes by destination of the owner and acquisitive prescription without regard to their former characterization as continuous or discontinuous.

Because the new Article 740 of the Louisiana Civil Code was not given retroactive effect, quasi-possession of a servitude that would have been classified as discontinuous under pre-revision law (such as a servitude of passage) could not count toward a claim of acquisitive prescription until the effective date of the provision: January 1, 1978. As more than thirty years have now passed since that date, many servitudes previously deemed discontinuous have become potentially subject to acquisitive prescription claims. For more analysis of this significant change in the law, see Christopher M. Hannan, *Comment, Prescription Lenses: How Louisiana Courts Should Apply the Revised Articles Governing Thirty-Year Acquisitive Prescription of Apparent Servitudes*, 53 Loy. L. Rev. 937 (2007).

* * *

Now consider the Louisiana Supreme Court's controversial decision in *Boudreaux v. Cummings*. Pay attention to the three major opinions authored by Justices Clark, Knoll and Weimer. Identify the legal sources, facts, and policy concerns that seem to be most important to each justice.

Boudreaux v. Cummings
167 So. 3d 559 (2015)

CLARK, Justice. We granted certiorari to determine whether the lower courts erred in recognizing the plaintiff as the owner of a predial servitude over land owned by the defendant. For the reasons that follow, we find the laws on acquisitive prescription and precarious possession require reversal of the court of appeal's ruling. Accordingly, we reverse and render judgment in favor of the defendant.

Facts and Procedural History

The plaintiff, John Boudreaux (hereinafter referred to as "Boudreaux"), filed suit against the defendant, Paul Cummings (hereinafter referred to as "Cummings"). In the lawsuit, Boudreaux sought recognition of a predial servitude/right of way by virtue of acquisitive prescription and a permanent injunction prohibiting Cummings from interfering with his use of the right of way. Specifically, Boudreaux avers that since at least 1948, he and his ancestors in title have been using a pathway and gate to cross the neighboring property that belongs to Cummings and his ancestor in title, the Weills. Testimony established that Boudreaux, his family, and farmers employed by Boudreaux used the right of way to transport farm equipment, to get to and from town for personal errands, and for convenient access to the adjacent road. In 1969, the Weills asked Boudreaux to move the right of way. Boudreaux acquiesced in the request and continued to use the pathway until 2012, when Cummings locked the gate and prevented Boudreaux's use.

Based on the foregoing, Boudreaux alleges that he adversely possessed the predial servitude for thirty years and is entitled to ownership thereof.

Cummings filed a motion for summary judgment, contending that Boudreaux was a precarious possessor. As such, he argues acquisitive prescription never began to run in Boudreaux's favor. The trial court denied the motion for summary judgment, finding genuine issues of material fact remained. The matter went to trial on July 8, 2013. The trial court found precarious possession was irrelevant to a discussion of ownership of an incorporeal immovable, such as a predial servitude. The trial court rendered judgment in favor of Boudreaux, ruling that the Boudreaux estate acquired a right of way over the Cummings estate by way of acquisitive prescription.

Cummings appealed. The court of appeal affirmed the judgment. *Boudreaux v. Cummings*, 13–1291 (La.App. 3 Cir. 6/11/14), 138 So.3d 797. In affirming, the majority held that, under the manifest error standard, there was adequate evidence for the trial court to conclude that Boudreaux was using the right of passage on his own behalf, rather than as a precarious possessor. The court of appeal cited to record testimony regarding Boudreaux and his family's use of the right of way for over thirty years and found that the Weills' awareness of the use was "sufficient to show the elements of acquisitive prescription [had] been met." Judge Amy dissented, finding Boudreaux had permissive use of the passage and, therefore, could not satisfy the requirements to prove ownership by acquisitive prescription.

Cummings filed the instant writ application, contending the lower courts erred. We granted certiorari to determine whether a predial servitude was established by acquisitive prescription. *Boudreaux v. Cummings*, 14–1499 (La.11/7/14), 152 So.3d 163.

Applicable Law

When reviewing courts find that a reversible error of law was made in the lower court, appellate courts are required to re-determine the facts *de novo* from the entire record and render a judgment on the merits. *Rosell v. ESCO,* 549 So.2d 840 (La.1989).

Louisiana Civil Code Article 740 provides: "Apparent servitudes may be acquired by title, by destination of the owner, or by acquisitive prescription." Louisiana Civil Code Article 742 provides: "The laws governing acquisitive prescription of immovable property apply to apparent servitudes. An apparent servitude may be acquired by peaceable and uninterrupted possession of the right for ten years in good faith and by just title; it may also be acquired by uninterrupted possession for thirty years without title or good faith."

Louisiana Civil Code Article 3437 defines precarious possession as "the exercise of possession over a thing with the permission of or on behalf of the owner or possessor." "Acquisitive prescription does not run in favor of a precarious possessor or his universal successor." La. Civ.Code art. 3477. Excluding a co-owner, any precarious possessor or his universal successor may commence to prescribe when he gives actual notice to the person on whose behalf he is possessing that he intends to possess for himself. La. Civ.Code art. 3478.

Discussion

Standard of Review

Despite the court of appeal's statement to the contrary, a review of the record indicates the trial court did not make a factual finding as to whether Boudreaux was a precarious possessor. Rather, the trial court found that precariousness does not apply to incorporeal immovables. However, the Louisiana Civil Code clearly states that the laws of acquisitive prescription of immovable property apply to apparent servitudes. La.Civ.Code art. 742. Precariousness, or the lack thereof, is a legal concept relevant to acquisitive prescription, and is, thus, applicable to apparent servitudes, such as the right of way over Cummings' land. See La.Civ.Code art. 3477. Accordingly, the trial court legally erred, necessitating a *de novo* review by this court.

Nature of the Possession

In resolving this matter, we must first determine whether Boudreaux was a precarious possessor of the predial servitude. If he was possessing precariously, the second step of the analysis tasks this court with ascertaining whether Boudreaux gave actual notice to the landowner (either Cummings or his ancestor in title) that he (or his own ancestor in title) was beginning to possess on his own behalf so as to commence the accrual of the acquisitive prescription period. See La.Civ.Code art. 3478.

Boudreaux asserts that his possession of the right of passage is presumed to be on his own behalf, pursuant to La.Civ.Code art. 3427, which provides, "[o]ne is presumed to intend to possess as owner unless he began to possess in the name of and for another." Thus, it is the landowner's duty to show that such use was merely an accommodation. Boudreaux argues that Cummings' failure to object to his use of the right of way does not amount to consent by the landowner, *i.e.*, precarious possession.

Conversely, Cummings contends Boudreaux was merely using the right of way with his or the Weills' permission in a gesture of neighborly accommodation. Thus, acquisitive prescription could not run in Boudreaux's favor absent a showing of actual notice of his commencement of adverse possession.

We disagree with Boudreaux's characterization of the scenario as equating a "failure to object" with "permission." However, we do find support in the law for implied or tacit permission being the basis of precarious possession. The pre–1982 version of Louisiana Civil Code art. 3490 provided:

> *The circumstances of having been in possession by the permission or through the indulgence of another person, gives neither legal possession nor the right of prescribing.*
>
> Thus, those who possess precariously, that is, by having prayed the master to let them have the possession, do not deprive him thereof, but, possessing by his consent, they possess for him. [Emphasis added].

Professor A.N. Yiannopoulos, in the Civil Law Treatise on Predial Servitudes, explained that the French article, on which the Louisiana article was based, more accurately translates as "acts that are the exercise of a prerogative, and *those of simple tolerance,* cannot be the foundation of either possession or prescription." [4 A.N. Yiannopoulos, Louisiana Civil Law Treatise, Predial Servitudes, § 139, (3d ed. 1997)] (Emphasis added). Yiannopoulos further explained in his discussion of precarious possession:

> Such a possessor may acquire neither ownership nor a servitude by prescription.
>
> Thus, one who uses a servitude of passage by virtue of a lease granted to him by the owner of the dominant estate may not acquire by prescription the servitude of passage for himself; and one who uses an aqueduct with the express or *tacit permission* of the owner of the estate on which the aqueduct is located may not, by prescription, acquire a servitude of aqueduct. *The owner of the estate on which the passage of aqueduct is located may tolerate certain invasions in the spirit of good neighborhood or in the pursuit of his own interests; in neither case is he presumed to have consented to a servitude. Moreover, the person who encroaches on the rights of the landowner with his express or tacit permission does not have the intent to acquire a servitude; he implicitly recognizes that the ownership of the estate is unencumbered and prescription does not run in his favor.*

Article 3490 of the Louisiana Civil Code of 1870, corresponding with Article 2322 of the French Civil Code, declared *that acts of simple tolerance could not be the foundation of either possession or prescription.* The purpose of this provision was to maximize the use of immovable property in the general interest. *If acts of simple tolerance were to be considered as acts of adverse possession, landowners would be compelled to object to innocent or occasional invasions for fear that their lands would be burdened with predial servitudes.*

Id. (Emphasis added).

Yiannopoulos further opined that while Article 3490 was not produced in the 1982 revision of the Louisiana Civil Code, he believed its absence was merely because the provision is "self-evident." *Id.* Moreover, Professor Symeon C. Symeonides explained the change in the law on precarious possession as follows:

> The articles of the old law dealing with precarious possession were spread out in three different parts of the Code and were quite repetitive. They could be found in the chapter on possession, [old articles] 3433, 3441, 3445–3446; in the subsection on the ten-year acquisitive prescription, [old articles] 3489–3490; and in the subsection on the causes which prevent acquisitive prescription, [old articles] 3510–3515. The new law is far more concise but still regulates precarious possession in two different parts of the Code, first in the title on possession, [new articles] 3428–3429, 3437–3440, and then in the title on prescription, [new articles] 3477–3479.

[Symeonides, *One Hundred Footnotes to the New Law of Possession and Acquisitive Prescription*, 44 La. L. Rev. 69, 81 (1983).]

Symeonides, like Yiannopoulos, is of the opinion that the changes in the Civil Code regarding precarious possession were merely for organizational purposes, and not substantive changes. As such, we find the concept of implied permission as it relates to precarious possession is still a viable theory of our civilian law. Accordingly, even in the absence of express permission, tacit permission can be presumed under the limited circumstances where "indulgence" and acts of "good neighborhood" are present. As applied to the instant case, we find that Cummings' neighborly act of tolerance (and that of his ancestor in title, the Weills) cannot be, and is not, the foundation of adverse possession needed for the purposes of acquisitive prescription. Rather, Boudreaux was possessing the right of passage precariously.

Deconstructing the requisites of acquisitive prescription further bolsters our holding. Louisiana Civil Code article 742, as referenced above, provides "the laws governing acquisitive prescription of immovable property apply to apparent servitudes." Therefore, the attributes of possession are applicable. The possessor must intend to possess as owner and must take corporeal possession of the thing. La.Civ .Code art. 3424. The possession must be uninterrupted and free of vices, *i.e.,* continuous, public, peaceable, and unequivocal. La.Civ.Code arts. 3435 and 3476. The possession must be *adverse;* it must be an *unauthorized* use that infringes on the ownership of the servient estate. [4 A.N. Yiannopoulos, Louisiana Civil Law Treatise, Predial Servitudes, § 138, (3d ed. 1997)] (Emphasis added). One who merely exercises a right has nothing to prescribe. *Id.* With these governing principles in mind, we find support for the conclusion that Cummings' awareness of Boudreaux's use and his allowance thereof marks Boudreaux's use as an authorized use that cannot be characterized as adverse under the circumstances.

Further, we address the contention that Boudreaux's acquiescence in the request to move the gate is somehow dispositive of the issue. Mr. Cummings relies on this act to show that Mr. Boudreaux complied with his request, revealing his status as a permissive user. Mr. Boudreaux, though, relies on the act to show that he owned the right of way and as the owner of the dominant estate, he was merely fulfilling his codal obligation of accommodating the servient estate. See art. La.Civ.Code art. 748 ("if the original location has become more burdensome for the owner of the servient estate . . . he [the owner of the servient estate] may provide another equally convenient location for the exercise of the servitude which the owner of the dominant estate is bound to accept.") With legal explanations supporting both sides of the issue, we do not find this fact offers any definitive resolution to the underlying issue of ownership of the right of way, and, is, thus, irrelevant to our analysis.

Having concluded that Boudreaux and/or his ancestor in title began his possession precariously, the second step in the two-fold analysis instructs us to determine whether actual notice was ever given to the landowner, be it Cummings or the Weills, that Boudreaux intended to possess for himself so as to authorize the commencement of the prescriptive period. La.Civ.Code art. 3478.

Louisiana Civil Code Article 3438 provides: "A precarious possessor, such as a lessee or a depositary, is presumed to possess for another although he may intend to possess for himself." Thus, by virtue of his status as a precarious possessor, Boudreaux is presumed to have possessed on behalf of Cummings, regardless of whether he intended to possess for himself. As such, testimony or evidence beyond Boudreaux's intent is required to terminate his precariousness. Boudreaux must have given actual notice of his intent sufficient to alert the landowner that his property was in jeopardy. *Delacroix Corp. v. Perez*, 98–2247, p. 10 (La.App. 4 Cir. 11/8/00), 794 So.2d 862, 869, *writ denied*, 00–3245 (La.1/26/01), 782 So.2d 635, citing *Armstrong v. Armstrong*, 493 So.2d 253 (La.App. 3 Cir.), *writ denied*, 496 So.2d 353 (La.1986). Apart from the continued use of the right of way, we find nothing in the record that indicates actual notice was given to the landowner that Boudreaux intended to change the nature of his possession. Accordingly, we find Boudreaux never terminated his precarious possession by giving actual notice to Cummings or his ancestor in title, thereby preventing the commencement of acquisitive prescription.

Our holding today is strictly limited to the facts before us. We recognize the validity in both parties' arguments and admit the ownership of the right of passage was not a clear cut determination. However, La.Civ.Code art. 730 clearly states "[d]oubt as to the existence, extent, or manner of exercise of a predial servitude shall be resolved in favor of the servient estate." This court has declared that "servitudes are restraints on the free disposal and use of property, and are not, on that account, entitled to be viewed with favor by the law." *Cont'l Grp., Inc. v. Allison,*

404 So.2d 428, 440 (La.1981), citing *Parish v. Municipality No. 2,* 8 La.Ann. 145, 147 (1853), cited with approval in *Buras Ice Factory, Inc. v. Department of Highways,* 235 La. 158, 103 So.2d 74 (1958).

Conclusion

For the foregoing reasons, we find Boudreaux was a precarious possessor of the predial servitude, who never gave actual notice of his intent to possess on his own. Accordingly, acquisitive prescription could not and did not run in his favor. We reverse the court of appeal's judgment and render judgment in favor of Cummings.

REVERSED AND RENDERED.

KNOLL, J., dissenting. This case requires the Court to determine whether or not John Walter Boudreaux ("Boudreaux") possessed the real right at issue as "owner," thereby acquiring by acquisitive prescription of thirty years a predial servitude of passage, or whether he exercised this real right merely as a "precarious possessor"—that is, "with the *permission* of or on behalf of" Paul Christopher Cummings ("Cummings") and his ancestors in title, the Weills. In my view, the majority opinion eviscerates the well-established burden-shifting structure laid out in our Civil Code, allowing Cummings to prevail based simply on an assertion of "neighborliness," despite his failure to put on any *evidence* that Boudreaux used the passage way with "*permission*" as required by the Louisiana Civil Code article 3437. Accordingly, I respectfully dissent from the majority opinion and would affirm the District Court's judgment recognizing Boudreaux has obtained a predial servitude of passage by thirty years acquisitive prescription.

The party asserting acquisitive prescription bears the burden of proving all facts that are essential to support it. [*St. John Baptist Church of Phoenix v. Thomas,* 08–0687 (La.App. 4 Cir. 12/3/08), 1 So.3d 618, 623 (quoting *Phillips v. Fisher,* 93–928 (La.App. 3 Cir. 5/6/94), 634 So.2d 1305, 1307).] Because Boudreaux is the party asserting acquisitive prescription, he bears the burden of proving all the facts that are essential to support it, including possession for the requisite number of years. [*EOG Resources, Inc. v. Hopkins,* 48,577 (La.App. 2 Cir. 11/27/13), 131 So.3d 72, 80.] However, as the Third Circuit explained in *Town of Broussard v. Broussard Volunteer Fire Dept.,* 357 So.2d 25 (La.App. 3 Cir.1978), interpreting the predecessor of Louisiana Civil Code 3427, "The possessor is aided in this burden by a presumption that he possessed as owner." [In *Town of Broussard,* the Third Circuit was interpreting former La. Civ.Code art. 3488. According to 1982 Revision Comment (a) to La. Civ .Code art. 3427, "This provision reproduces the substance of Article 3488 of the Louisiana Civil Code of 1870. It does not change the law." Former La. Civ.Code art. 3488 provided: "As to the fact itself of possession, a person is presumed to have possessed as master and owner, unless it appears that the possession began in the name of and for another. "] Under Louisiana Civil Code article 3427, "One is presumed to intend to possess as owner unless he began to possess in the name of and for another." The 1982 Revision Comment (d) to article 3427, however, provides that the presumption set forth in this article does not arise "[w]hen it *is shown* that the possession was begun for another." (emphasis added). If the presumption does arise, the opponent of the plea of prescription—here, Cummings—then bears the burden of rebutting this presumption, which he may do by *proof* that the proponent's possession *was precarious*. According to Louisiana Civil Code article 3437, "The exercise of possession over a thing with the permission of or on behalf of the owner or possessor is precarious possession. "If Cummings *proves* Boudreaux's possession was "with the permission of or on behalf of the owner," only then does a presumption arise under Louisiana Civil Code article 3438: "A *precarious possessor,* such as a lessee or a depositary, is presumed to possess for another although he may intend to possess for himself." (emphasis added). Should this presumption arise, Boudreaux could rebut it under Louisiana Civil Code article 3439, provided he presented proof that he has given "actual notice of [his intent to possess for himself] to the person on whose behalf he is possessing." (emphasis added).

Applying this burden-shifting framework, the threshold question is whether or not the presumption of ownership found within this article arises at all. According to Revision Comment (d) of Louisiana Civil Code article 3427, "When it *is shown* that the possession was begun for another, the presumption set forth in this article *does not arise*." (emphasis added). In positive terms, the presumption of ownership does arise *absent a showing* that the possession was begun for another. Therefore, the initial question is whether there is a positive showing on the record that Boudreaux's "possession was begun for another." Although Cummings strenuously *asserts* that Boudreaux began his possession with the permission of the Weills, neither the evidence nor the testimony at trial supports this assertion. While witnesses, including Boudreaux and his wife, agreed that the Weills and the Boudreauxs had a good relationship and some witnesses, including Boudreaux's wife, testified the Weills knew about Boudreaux's gate and his use/maintenance of the access road and did not object, no one testified that the Weills had ever granted Boudreaux permission to use the property. In fact, Boudreaux explicitly denied ever receiving the Weills' permission: "I never got any permission from him. We just used it."

Rather than put on evidence to rebut Boudreaux's testimony, Cummings called no witnesses of his own. The only exhibits he entered into evidence were grainy aerial pictures of the tract of land and a Tobin survey of the property from 1985. The sole episode to which Cummings points to support his argument that Boudreaux was permissively using the disputed strip of land is Boudreaux's agreement in 1969 at the request of Mr. Weill to move the location of the gate, which granted Boudreaux access to the Weills' property, closer to the Vermillion River. As the majority acknowledges, however, this evidence does not offer any support for Cummings' argument that Boudreaux's "possession was begun for another" because this episode could just as easily be interpreted as evidence of Boudreaux's intent to possess as owner. [Indeed, Boudreaux and Weill's interaction during this episode is perfectly consistent with what the Code would require if Boudreaux actually owned a right of passage across Weill's property. Under Louisiana Civil Code article 748,

The owner of the servient estate may do nothing tending to diminish or make more inconvenient the use of the servitude.

If the original location has become more burdensome for the owner of the servient estate, or if it prevents him from making useful improvements on his estate, he may provide another equally convenient location for the exercise of the servitude which the owner of the dominant estate is bound to accept. All expenses of relocation are borne by the owner of the servient estate.

Here, according to Boudreaux and to his wife, Weill proposed a location for the gate that was closer to the Vermillion River, Boudreaux accepted this proposed location, and Weill paid for some of the expenses of rebuilding the gate. In order for Cummings to prove Boudreaux was not entitled to the presumption of ownership, it would seem logical that he should have to make a showing that Boudreaux's actions were somehow inconsistent with those required of the holder of the right which Boudreaux seeks to acquire.]

Given the complete absence of evidence showing Boudreaux's "possession was begun for another" or with the permission of the Weills, the presumption of ownership must arise in Boudreaux's favor. Although the presumption alone is enough to shift the burden of proof to Cummings, [See 2 La. Civ. L. Treatise, Property § 320 (4th ed.) ("Article 3427 declares that one is presumed to intend to possess as owner unless he began to possess in the name of and for another. A person who exercises factual authority over property may rely on this presumption and opt not to introduce any evidence as to his intent to possess as owner.")] Boudreaux put on ample evidence in support of the presumption. Numerous witnesses testified that Boudreaux mowed the tract of land and maintained the property. Likewise, witnesses testified the Boudreauxs used the passage continuously for various purposes, including hauling farm equipment, making visits to the doctor, going to vote, running errands, etc. Keith Melebeck entered into an agreement in 1999 — an agreement which endured till Cummings locked Boudreaux's gate in 2012 — to mow the road for Boudreaux in exchange for Boudreaux's permission to keep mowing equipment on Boudreaux's property. Melebeck testified that Boudreaux told him during this period that the strip has "been a right of way for a hundred years, that they've been using [it] since, you know, since their family owned the property." In 1980, when Boudreaux feared the Weills' sale of another piece of property might hinder his ability to use the passage adjacent to his own property, Boudreaux appeared at a meeting of the Abbeville Harbor and Terminal District (the "Terminal District") to express his concerns about road construction that might obstruct his access to the passage on the Weills' property. Joseph Schexnaider was a registered civil engineer who worked for the Terminal District to whom the Weills sold a piece of property for the construction of the Port of Vermillion. Consistent with Boudreaux's own testimony, Schexnaider testified that he was present at this meeting with Boudreaux and that Boudreaux "was concerned whether the roads we were building were going to be public or private, and, in either case, would he still be allowed access to go ahead and go through the [Weills'] property and access his property as he had been doing before we got there." In response to a question from Cummings' counsel about whether he ever questioned the Terminal District as to whether or not he had access to the Weills' property, Schexnaider responded, "No. He didn't question us whether he had access or not. He told us that he had access, and he was concerned about being able to reach that access point through the port property." Indeed, in 1980, soon after the amendment to Louisiana Civil Code Article 740 which would have allowed the Boudreaux's right of use to begin prescribing, Boudreaux's interests in using the property were adverse to the Weills' interests in selling property that would potentially encumber its use. This evidence strongly supports Boudreaux's position that, regardless of the Weills' knowledge, Boudreaux was using this property for his own benefit—possessing the right for himself without interruption.

Because Cummings failed to prove that Boudreaux was not entitled to the presumption of ownership, the burden shifted to Cummings to rebut the presumption, which he must do by *proof* that Boudreaux's possession was precarious. Although Cummings asserts that Boudreaux and the Weills were good neighbors and that Boudreaux and Cummings also were on neighborly terms prior to litigation, Cummings put on *no evidence* whatsoever that Boudreaux's possession was begun with the permission of the Weills or of Cummings. The majority's decision to countenance Cummings' unsupported *argument* is gravely misguided and severely jeopardizes the law on acquisitive prescription in this state by allowing any property owner to avoid prescription by simply *arguing* that his opponent's use of the property was allowed in the spirit of neighborliness. Not only is this contrary to the plain language of article 3437 and its definition of a precarious possessor as one who possesses with "permission," but its effect would also negate the 1977 revision to article 740, which made discontinuous apparent servitudes susceptible to acquisitive prescription, by making it virtually impossible for a person to be able to prove the elements of acquisitive prescription with respect to such a real right.

At its core, this case concerns a problem of proof. According to the plain language of article 3437, Cummings had to prove that Boudreaux possessed the property between 1978 and 2008 "with the permission" of Cummings and his ancestors in title. Cummings failed to meet his burden. Therefore, Boudreaux should prevail on his action to obtain recognition of his right of passage. Accordingly, I would affirm the judgments of the lower courts.

WEIMER, J., concurring. The opinion articulates the correct legal standards to apply to this vexatious dispute between neighbors. Both explicit permission and tacit permission deriving from acts of "good neighborhood" by an owner can defeat the claim of someone who contends he benefits from adverse possession so as to acquire a servitude of passage upon the owner's property. *Boudreaux v. Cummings*, No. 14–1499, slip op. at 7 (La.3/17/15). Given the legal standards, I write to emphasize certain facts. Most notably, I respectfully disagree with the dismissal by both the opinion and the dissents of certain extensive record evidence regarding the placement of the gate. The sole basis for rejecting the record evidence of collaboration in the placement of the gate is the view that such collaboration is not dispositive of Mr. Boudreaux's status as a permissive user because the collaboration could just as easily be interpreted as evidence that Mr. Boudreaux, as owner of the right of way and of the dominant estate, was merely fulfilling his codal obligation of accommodating the servient estate. *See,* La. C.C. art. 748. However, while the interactions between Mr. Boudreaux and Mr. Weill during this episode may be consistent with what the Civil Code would require if Mr. Boudreaux *actually owned* a right of passage across Mr. Weill's property, the fact is that a right of passage is a discontinuous apparent predial servitude and Louisiana did not provide for acquisitive prescription of this right until the 1977 revision of Louisiana Civil Code article 740 went into effect on January 1, 1978. *See,* La. C.C. art. 740, Revision Comments (a). Because Mr. Boudreaux's possession of the right of passage could not have begun to become effective until 1978, his actions in 1969 with respect to the placement of the gate simply *could not* be interpreted as evidence of Mr. Boudreaux's intent to possess as owner. In other words, Mr. Boudreaux cannot avail himself of the presumption that his possession of the passageway was with the intent to possess as owner at a time when the law did not allow him to acquire a servitude of passage by acquisitive prescription.

Far from being irrelevant and non-dispositive, I find the record evidence regarding the collaborative nature of the gate's placement, its construction, and its later use to be direct and relevant evidence that Mr. Boudreaux used the passageway with "permission" as required by La. C.C. art. 3437, regardless of whether that evidence was adduced on direct or cross examination. Further, I find that the evidence of neighborly acts on the part of the successive property owners (Mr. Weill and Mr. Cummings) effectively rebuts any presumption that might otherwise arise from the fact of Mr. Boudreaux's possession, notwithstanding Mr. Boudreaux's self-serving protestation of his clandestine intent to possess as owner.

Mr. Boudreaux testified that when he moved to the property in 1969, he "rebuilt the fence." Mr. Boudreaux admitted much more than the rebuilding of the fence was accomplished because he worked collaboratively with the landowner:

> Me and Mr. Bob Weill [Cummings' ancestor in title] got together, and the fence was in bad repair, and he allowed me to clear some trees on him and on me and to rebuild the fence, which he gave me part of the material to help me build the fence. And he also asked me to move the gate a little further to the east, toward the end of his property closer to the river, which I did.

Presumably, the clearing of trees "on him" and "on me" referred to clearing trees on Mr. Weill's land and on Mr. Boudreaux's land, respectively. In any event, the quoted testimony indicates that establishing a passageway in 1969 was a collaborative effort between Mr. Boudreaux and Mr. Weill because Mr. Weill even supplied materials. Thus, because this gated access point was established in 1969 and the passage beyond the gate has remained there to this day, the circumstances of its establishment were collaborative and, therefore, indicative of both permission and acts of "good neighborhood," rather than of adverse possession.

Physical possession of a thing, such as land, the Civil Code informs us, involves as a general proposition "physical acts of use, detention, or enjoyment over a thing." La. C.C. art. 3425. More specifically, for purposes of acquisitive prescription as claimed by Mr. Boudreaux here, "[t]he possession must be continuous, uninterrupted, peaceable, public, and *unequivocal*." La. C.C. art. 3476 (applicable to prescription of ten years in good faith and under just title) (emphasis added); *see also* La. C.C. art. 3488 (generally rendering the "rules governing acquisitive prescription of ten years appl[icable] to the prescription of thirty years"). The Code further emphasizes that "[p]ossession that is . . . equivocal has no effect," (La.C.C. art. 3435) and "[p]ossession is . . . equivocal when there is ambiguity as to the intent of the possessor to own the thing." La. C.C. art. 3436.

The facts recounted above about the origin of the passageway between the Weill and Boudreaux properties indicate the passageway was constructed with the permission of Mr. Weill, at a place designated by Mr. Weill, and even with some materials supplied by Mr. Weill. Given these facts, Mr. Boudreauxs possession was, at best, equivocal. As to this point, Comment (e) to La. C.C. art. 3476 dispels any doubt: "**The exercise of possession over a thing with the permission of . . . the owner . . . is precarious possession.**" (Emphasis added.) Precarious possession defeats the possibility of acquiring a servitude through acquisitive prescription: "Acquisitive prescription does not run in favor of a precarious possessor. . . ." La. C.C. art. 3477.

Therefore, Mr. Boudreaux's possession began as precarious possession because it originated from Mr. Weill's consent. The record reflects no change in the permissive nature of Mr. Boudreaux's use of the passageway. Indeed, by Mr. Boudreaux's own admission, the passageway continued to be used by explicit permission and as an act of "good neighborhood" on behalf of Mr. Weill, as follows.

Mr. Boudreaux testified to having used the passageway to "bring tractors and combines across there and harvest my rice." Significantly, Mr. Boudreaux also testified using the passageway to assist with farming on Mr. Weill's property as follows: "I would go back across there when he was harvesting his rice and help him." In fact, according to Mr. Boudreaux, the passageway was used for the benefit of both himself and Mr. Weill, because "the Duhon boys" who harvested Mr. Weill's land also "harvested my [Mr. Boudreaux's] crop with their combines."

To reiterate, the opinion utilizes has identified the correct legal standard for evaluating these facts. Explicit permission and tacit permission deriving from acts of "good neighborhood" by an owner can convey no more than equivocal possession (La.C.C. art. 3476) and, in turn, precarious possession gains no foothold for acquisitive prescription. La. C.C. art. 3477. The concept of acquisitive prescription is ancient, and the rationales for preventing permissive and neighborly uses to allow the user to wrest away ownership rights have also been long recognized. As Planiol noted:

The Ancients said of prescription that it was the patroness of the human species. . . . Acquisitive prescription . . . plays an important social role. Without it no patrimony would be safe from unforeseen revindications. It is certain that there are times when prescription may avail a possessor without title and in bad faith. It would then afford a shield to a spoliator. But such instances are of rare occurrence. And it would happen even more infrequently that the owner despoiled through prescription had not been guilty of negligence. Why did he remain for such a long time without performing an act of possession as regards his thing or without laying claim to it? A sufficient delay is allowed him within which to learn of the usurpation committed against him and in which to protest against it.

M. PLANIOL, TREATISE ON THE CIVIL LAW § 2645 at 571–572 (La.St. L.Inst. Trans.1959).

Here, Mr. Weill was not "guilty of negligence" in disregarding his property. *Id.* Nor can it be said Mr. Weill "remain[ed] for such a long time without performing an act of possession as regards his thing or without laying claim to it." *Id.* Rather, in the spirit of being a good neighbor, Mr. Weill permitted and even aided Mr. Boudreaux in constructing the passageway. As Mr. Boudreaux admitted, rather than being used adversely, the passageway was frequently used as a means for maintaining good relations between the adjacent property owners:

Q. [Cummings' counsel] You considered yourself a good neighbor of the Weills?

A. [Mr. Boudreaux] We always got along well with the Weills.

Q. And Mr. Weill would have thought the same, you think, of you?

A. Yes. He and his wife came drink [sic] coffee often.

. . . .

Q. [Boudreaux's counsel] When the Weills came drink [sic] coffee at your house, how did they get to your house?

A. [Mr. Boudreaux] Sometimes-sometimes they actually walked. Because Mr. Weill and his wife liked to exercise, and they would walk a lot. Sometimes they would park on the right of way and walk, and sometimes they would come down the public road.

Q. Did they pass through that gate that you were talking about?

A. Sometimes they did, yes.

Our venerable Civil Code generally encourages moral conduct and deters immoral conduct. Consider the consequences of a determination that one is engaged in a bad-faith breach of an obligation ["An obligor in bad faith is liable for all the damages, foreseeable or not, that are a direct consequence of his failure to perform." La. C.C. art. 1997.] or is a bad-faith seller in a redhibition action. [La. C.C. art. 2545 . . . .] The Civil Code increases damages in those situations. [*Compare* La. C.C.

art. 1997 with Article 1996 . . . *Compare* La. C.C. art. 2545 with Article 2531 . . .] The law of lesion beyond moiety reflects a moral component by protecting a seller of an immovable from falling prey to a buyer whose price is out of line with certain market standards. ["The sale of an immovable may be rescinded for lesion when the price is less than one half of the fair market value of the immovable." La. C.C. art. 2589.] The denial of spousal support to one who is at fault for the demise of a marriage also has a moral component. The Civil Code further reflects a moral component in recognizing natural obligations.

By comparison, the law of acquisitive prescription allows the taking of another's property even if done in bad faith. Such departure from what could be considered moral conduct exists to serve other societal purposes, including quieting titles to property which has been abandoned and keeping property in production, and reflects a populist philosophy.

To balance what could be perceived a departure from moral underpinnings, the Civil Code mandates that possession be public and unequivocal, not silent and clandestine. *See* La. C.C. arts. 3435 and 3436.

The Civil Code does not contemplate depriving an owner of full enjoyment of property simply because the owner has acted as a good neighbor in allowing use of the property. Had Mr. Boudreaux wished to depart from the neighborly use allowed him by Mr. Weill and by Mr. Cummings, the Civil Code afforded him such a procedure. Under La. C.C. art. 3478, a "precarious possessor, or his universal successor, may commence to prescribe when he gives actual notice to the person on whose behalf he is possessing that he intends to possess for himself." Mr. Boudreaux adduced no evidence of having given such notice to Mr. Weill. Mr. Boudreaux did not unequivocally manifest an intent to possess, as owner, the passageway on Mr. Weill's land, either when sharing a neighborly cup of coffee or in a more conspicuous setting.

In conclusion, from my review of the relevant Codal articles and of the principles on which those articles are based, I find the adage that "no good deed goes unpunished" has yet to be incorporated into Louisiana's law of acquisitive prescription. Allowing a neighborly use of one's property is instead encouraged by the Civil Code, which does not deprive an owner of a property right for having acted as a good neighbor. Thus, I respectfully concur.

HUGHES, Justice., dissents for the reasons assigned by KNOLL, J. and CRICHTON, J.

CRICHTON, J., dissenting. Boudreaux unwaveringly declared he was never given permission to use the passageway, and he and his ancestors in title always used the passageway as if it was their own. From an evidentiary standpoint, Boudreaux's unambiguous declaration of his intent to possess as owner coupled with the legal presumption that he was possessing as owner caused the burden to shift to the defendant, Cummings, to marshal sufficient evidence to chip away, if not to erode, this presumption. This ultimately led to what I believe to be and, more importantly, what the trial court believed to be, a preponderance of evidence favoring Boudreaux.

Cummings failed to present even a scintilla of evidence, instead engaging in mere argument, leaving the trial court with only one choice.

Accordingly, based on this record, I respectfully dissent and would affirm the lower courts.

Notes and Questions

1. Compare the three lengthy opinions in this case and the legal authorities upon which they primarily rely. Justice Clark's opinion invokes Article 3490 of the 1870 Civil Code and commentary from a treatise authored by Professor Yiannopoulos, who drew attention to comparable rules offered in the French Civil Code. Justice Clark further relies upon a law review article authored by Professor Symeonides. In the key passage of his opinion, Justice Clark states:

> As such, we find that the concept of implied permission as it relates to pre-carious possession is still a viable theory of the civil law. *Accordingly, even in the absence of express permission, tacit permission can be presumed under the limited circumstances where "indulgence" and acts of "good neighborhood" are present.* As applied to the instant case, we find that Cummings' neigh-borly act of tolerance (and that of his ancestor in title, the Weills) cannot be, and is not, the foundation of adverse possession needed for the purposes of acquisitive prescription. Rather, Boudreaux was possessing the right of passage precariously.

Id. at 563 (emphasis added). Is it appropriate for the court to articulate an impor-tant presumption that is not stated directly in the current text of the Louisiana Civil Code? In a previous decision, Justice Dennis noted: "It is the function of the legis-lature to formulate new legal presumptions." *Illinois Central Gulf R.R. Co. v. Inter-national Harvester Co.*, 368 So.2d 1009, 1013 (La. 1979). Did Justice Clark's majority opinion formulate a new presumption or simply restate an old one?

Justice Knoll's dissenting opinion stresses the clear textual language found in Articles 3427 and 3437 of the Louisiana Civil Code and the accompanying revision comments. Note Justice Knoll's stern warning near the conclusion of her dissent:

> The majority's decision to countenance Cummings' unsupported *argument* is gravely misguided and severely jeopardizes the law on acquisitive pre-scription in this state by allowing any property owner to avoid prescription by simply *arguing* that his opponent's use of the property was allowed in the spirit of neighborliness. Not only is this contrary to the plain language of article 3437 and its definition of a precarious possessor as one who pos-sesses with "permission," but its effect would also negate the 1977 revision to article 740, which made discontinuous apparent servitudes susceptible to acquisitive prescription, by making it virtually impossible for a person to be able to prove the elements of acquisitive prescription with respect to such a real right.

Id. at 568. Is her fear justified?

Justice Weimer's opinion begins by labelling the case as "a vexatious dispute between neighbors." Id. at 568. Why is this important? If the parties had not known each other at all, would the outcome have been different? His opinion also quotes from the revision comments to Article 3476 of the Louisiana Civil Code and emphasizes that Boudreaux' possession of the alleged servitude of passage was, "at best, equivocal." Id. at 570 (quoting La. Civ. Code art. 3476 rev. cmt (e)). He also cites passages from Planiol. Does Justice Weimer's opinion embrace the presumption stated by the majority opinion, which speaks of "tacit permission" arising in cases "where 'indulgence' and acts of 'good neighborhood'" are present? Id. at 563. Or is Justice Weimer simply arguing that the defendant Cummings rebutted the traditional presumption under Article 3427 of the Louisiana Civil Code that a possessor is presumed to possess with the intent to own?

2. Commentary criticizing the decision in *Boudreaux* appeared quickly. *See* 4 A.N. Yiannopoulos Louisiana Civil Law Treatise: Predial Servitudes §6.36 n. 2 (4th ed. 2013, Supp. 2018–19) (cautioning that the majority holding in *Boudreaux* "should not be read broadly and should not be read to equate permission with a landowner's awareness and failure to object to a disturbance or eviction"); Andrew M. Cox, Boudreaux v. Cummings: *The Louisiana Supreme Court Presumes Away the Right to Acquire a Servitude of Passage*, 90 Tul L. Rev. 973, 984 (2016) (suggesting that faulty reasoning in *Boudreaux* "looms dangerously over the right to prescribe a servitude of passage"); Cody J. Miller, Boudreaux v. Cummings: *Time to Interrupt an Erroneous Approach to Acquisitive Prescription*, 77 La. L. Rev. 1143 (2017) (arguing that *Boudreaux* strayed from proper civilian analysis and left the law unclear).

3. One of the authors of this casebook has also criticized the majority opinion in *Boudreaux*. Professor Lovett advances a new approach to the conflict between the assertion of ownership or predial servitudes by acquisitive prescription and the defense of precarious possession when the parties are neighbors or members of the same close-knit community. Consider the following excerpt from his article:

John A. Lovett, *Precarious Possession*
77 La. L. Rev. 617, 618–19, 621–22, 686–94, 699 (2017)

Introduction

The institution of acquisitive prescription has startling transformative power. A person who commences possession of immovable property in good faith and with a just title can acquire ownership that is good against the world after just ten years of uninterrupted possession. Even more remarkable is that a possessor who does not commence possession in good faith or who lacks a just title can still acquire ownership of an immovable after 30 years of uninterrupted possession. Finally, a person who merely uses another person's land in a limited manner can acquire a real right in the form of an apparent servitude through either ten or 30 years of quasi-possession.

According to several Louisiana jurists and commentators, the venerable institution of acquisitive prescription in Louisiana is now under threat. The source of that threat is a recent decision of the Louisiana Supreme Court [*Boudreaux v. Cummings*] . . . .

To address whether precarious possession is actually undermining the institution of acquisitive prescription, this Article takes a step back and looks at a broad range of precarious possession cases decided in the last 50 years in Louisiana. This broader review reveals that almost all precarious possession disputes fall into one of three different relational contexts. The first involves parties who are more or less strangers to one another. In the second, parties find themselves connected to one another through a contractual relationship or by virtue of some special legal status, typically a co-ownership or family relationship, or some other sui generis special relationship. The third context involves parties who are neighbors and know one another relatively well or who are at least members of the same relatively small or tight-knit community. . . .

III. The Future of Precarious Possession

Many Louisiana lawyers and jurists must now be wondering what to make of the three judicial opinions that emerged from the Louisiana Supreme Court decision in *Boudreaux*, particularly in light of the majority opinion's statement that "[o]ur holding today is strictly limited to the facts before us." On the one hand, courts might follow the majority opinion and begin to ignore what up until now had been, at least according to Justice Knoll (and also Professor Hargrave), the Civil Code's relatively well-understood burden-shifting structure regarding possession. In that event, courts may well accept assertions of tacit permission summarily, without demanding much proof of such permission and without taking into account the specific relational context of an acquisitive prescription claim or possessory action. The defense of precarious possession could then end up swallowing the general principle that possessors are presumed to possess as owners, especially in the context of acquisition of servitudes by neighbors. If courts follow this path, Justice Knoll may well be right that *Boudreaux* "severely jeopardizes the law on acquisitive prescription in this state."

On the other hand, this unfortunate outcome could be avoided if lawyers, judges, and jurists treat *Boudreaux* as a cause for reflection and as an occasion to begin a new conversation about acquisitive prescription and precarious possession in Louisiana. As this Article explains, even though Justice Knoll and Justice Weimer each reached a different conclusion about the ultimate issue in *Boudreaux*, both of their opinions model a relational approach to the kind of complex factual dispute that can arise in a paradigmatic neighbor or close-knit community case. But before turning to a detailed reconsideration of *Boudreaux*, this Article offers new jurisprudential tools that could help Louisiana courts make sense of the most difficult precarious possession cases they are likely to confront.

A. New Jurisprudential Tools to Analyze Neighbor and Close-Knit Community Cases

Louisiana courts have generally applied the traditional presumptions of possession and precarious possession in cases that fall into the stranger and contractual or legal status categories in a consistent and principled manner. As Part II.A demonstrates, when confronted with a stranger case, courts are hesitant to find that an adverse-possession claimant is a precarious possessor as long as it is clear the possessor and record owner have had little or no relationship with each other over the years. In these situations, the baseline presumption provided by article 3427 of the Civil Code—that a possessor is presumed to possess as owner—is usually applied vigorously unless clear evidence demonstrates that the claimant's possession began with the permission of or on behalf of another person.

Conversely, as Part II.B shows, courts confronted with cases that clearly fall into the second paradigm—cases in which the parties have a contractual or legal status relationship with each other—are appropriately attentive to the likelihood that the possessor began to possess precariously. In these cases, the presumption of article 3438—that precarious possessors are presumed to continue possess on behalf of another even though they may intend to possess for themselves—serves as the foundational presumption. As our jurisprudence teaches, however, application of article 3438 does not mean that a record owner will always prevail in such a case. Sometimes, particularly in the context of acquisitive prescription claims involving co-owners, a claimant will be able to "[demonstrate] by overt and unambiguous acts sufficient to give notice to his co-owner that he intends to possess the property for himself" so that acquisitive prescription can begin to run. In general, though, Louisiana courts do not need new rules to handle cases falling into either of the first two categories discussed in Part II. Rather, they simply must continue to demonstrate sensitivity to the distinct relational contexts that these kinds of cases present.

In true neighbor or close-knit community cases, however, the jurisprudential authority is less clear, and as the cases discussed in Part II.C demonstrate, courts are much more likely to struggle. Further, when the nature of the right claimed is a predial servitude, courts will often have difficulty distinguishing quasi-possession that has been adverse from simple toleration granted by a record owner, especially when the record owner asserts that he has tacitly permitted the claimant to use his property in the spirit of being a good neighbor. Yet, as in *Boudreaux*, when a possessor—claimant has used his neighbor's property for a long period of time and appears to have organized his relationship to his own land or to his community in reliance on continued access to or use of the record owner's land, strong equitable justifications weigh in favor of recognizing his claim as well.

1. The Presumption of Sharing

Given the difficulty of cases falling into the third category of possession and acquisitive prescription disputes, Louisiana should consider developing an additional presumption—a presumption of sharing that would apply specifically at the outset of a relationship between a possessor and record owner who are practicing, inhabiting, engaged neighbors or members of the same close-knit community. Stated simply, this presumption would provide that when one neighbor uses a fellow neighbor's property or when a member of a close-knit community uses another community member's property, that use takes place with the implied permission of the owner. This presumption could be adopted as a jurisprudential rule by Louisiana courts, or it could be expressed in a new Civil Code article. In either format, it would provide a useful complement to the two existing presumptions found in articles 3427 and 3438 of the Civil Code by aligning judicial decision-making with the fundamental values that inform property law and by enhancing the predictability of judicial decision-making in this area.

One justification for a new presumption of sharing can be found in the scholarship of Gregory Alexander and Eduardo Peñalver, who have written powerful pieces about how property law can be understood as an institution that serves the goal of promoting human flourishing. For Alexander and Peñalver, property law is not solely a utilitarian machine designed to produce economic efficiency and wealth maximization, although these are among the many desirable, incommensurable values that property law can and should promote. Drawing on Aristotle, Aquinas, and other philosophers working in the Aristotelian tradition, Alexander and Peñalver argue that because humans are essentially social beings who thrive only through and because of their relationships with other people and through human community, property law must also be understood as serving social values. Property law should thus facilitate the development of human capabilities that are necessary for individuals to be able to choose and pursue their own projects from a meaningful set of options while also helping to sustain families, friendships, and communities—the very social networks that make human flourishing possible.

One particular aspect of Alexander and Peñalver's "human flourishing" theory of property law that is directly relevant to precarious possession is their insight that an individual must have some property to develop and practice one of the essential Aristotelian ethical virtues—what might be called "the virtue of sharing." Describing why Aristotle believed that private ownership must form a crucial part of any property system, Alexander and Peñalver observe,

> Another reason [Aristotle] gives in favor of private property is that it promotes friendship. Aristotle's thinking here seems to be that through proper education individuals will learn that property, though privately owned, is to be shared with friends. Relatedly, private ownership facilitates the exercise of such virtues as generosity and moderation. His point here ties in with the one just raised. Aristotle means to say that the possibility of generosity depends upon the existence of some degree of private rights. Generosity presupposes a voluntary act of sharing, so that the owner must willingly transfer to someone else the power to use and enjoy the resource. And her own act can only be voluntary and therefore praiseworthy, if she was entitled not to share.

This insight explains why article 2232 of the French Civil Code declared that acts of "mere toleration" cannot lead to prescription and why Louisiana courts have been hesitant in neighbor cases like *Boudreaux* to allow a possessor—claimant to acquire ownership or real rights whenever owners make plausible arguments that they merely consented to the claimant's use or possession in a spirit of neighborly cooperation. Louisiana courts intuitively recognize the importance of encouraging neighbors and members of the same community to share their property with each other to build the bonds of friendship and reciprocity that make community possible.

Adopting a presumption of sharing will thus encourage courts to reveal more fully the likely bases of their decision-making in these difficult neighbor cases. In neighbor cases, judges would no longer feel the need to manipulate the existing presumptions in the Civil Code to find a way of stating an important normative value that they likely bring to bear in most neighbor cases already. In short, adoption of a presumption of sharing would promote another important systemic virtue—the virtue of judicial transparency.

A final reason to adopt a presumption of sharing is that the presumption would enable courts to visualize neighbor and close-knit community cases not only from the point of view of the possessor, which is the focus of Louisiana's two existing presumptions, but also from the point of view of the record owner. In other words, this new presumption would help judges and lawyers become more fully conscious of what this Article contends. They already do so subconsciously in these cases—approaching these disputes in their full relational complexity. Unlike the existing codal presumptions that are focused solely on the state of mind of the claimant—possessor, the presumption of sharing directs courts and lawyers to consider equally the state of mind of the other party, the neighbor who contends that she was merely practicing the Aristotelian virtues of friendship and sharing. By openly directing courts' attention to the true owner's perspective, the new presumption would thus bring to the surface the kind of analysis that courts appear inclined to engage in regardless, as the *Boudreaux* case itself demonstrates so clearly.

2. Indicia of Giving or Renunciation

Any useful presumption in law should be capable of being rebutted. This capability is certainly true for the presumption of sharing. Louisiana must recognize, therefore, that at any point during the existence of a long-term relationship between two neighbors or members of the same close-knit community, the presumption of sharing could be overcome by clear signs that the parties have reached a new equilibrium, a new explicit or implicit understanding about the property at issue. To determine whether the presumption of sharing has been overcome, courts should be directed to employ several specific factual criteria. These criteria, which should be called "indicia of giving or renunciation," could be spelled out in a new Civil Code article or articulated jurisprudentially. Either way, they would serve to channel judicial discretion in difficult neighbor and close-community cases in a useful manner.

The underlying assumption in this scenario is that property relationships are not static. The reasonable expectations and assumptions of parties in a long-term property relationship can and do evolve. At some point, the presumption that a neighbor is sharing her property with another neighbor to whom she has granted some kind of access evaporates, especially when it becomes obvious that the passive neighbor has actually given away, renounced, or abandoned all or a portion of her property or her right to exclude others from that property.

In some ways, this reasoning may sound like a restatement of the "negligent owner" rationale for adverse possession and acquisitive prescription noted earlier. This Article's intention, however, is not to encourage courts to make simplistic or conclusory statements about a record owner's passivity. Instead, courts should focus on the way in which the neighbor relationship between the possessor—claimant and the record owner is transformed. After all, as Baudry-Lacantinerie and Tissier remarked, acquisitive prescription is a legal institution that has startling transformative power. Courts should therefore be asking if and how property relationships potentially affected by acquisitive prescription have themselves been transformed.

With these factors in mind, this Article offers the following indicia of giving or renunciation: (1) the physical extent and intrusiveness of the claimant's use or corporeal possession of the record owner's property; (2) any investments or improvements made by the claimant to the record owner's property in reliance on an implicit promise of continuing access to or use of the record owner's property; (3) any changes made by the claimant to other property the claimant owns or to the claimant's other life projects, economic or otherwise, made in reliance on continued access to or use of the record owner's property; (4) the degree to which the record owner's own actions have signaled an intention to maintain agenda-setting authority for the property or, conversely, whether those actions or non-actions have signaled a de facto abandonment or renunciation of the property; (5) community perceptions regarding the rights of the parties with respect to the property involved; (6) the length of time beyond the 30-year prescriptive period the claimant has used or possessed the record owner's property; and (7) the existence or absence of any acknowledgements by the possessor—claimant of the record owner's authority.

A potential objection is that these criteria are too subjective and vest too much discretion in judges in neighbor and close-knit community cases involving precarious possession. Yet the work that Louisiana courts must do to resolve precarious possession defenses in these cases is already subjective, as the three divergent opinions in *Boudreaux* and the inconsistent results in other neighbor disputes reveal. Reasonable judges will always bring their own moral and normative perspectives to bear on these kinds of cases. If courts were to acknowledge the presumption of sharing explicitly and then focus their analysis on whether that presumption has been rebutted with regard to the indicia of giving or renunciation, the results of neighbor or close-knit community cases would actually become more consistent and predictable. At a minimum, courts would be more likely to give full attention to the specific relational facts that these criteria implicate when they address precarious possession in the neighbor and close-knit community context.

B. Reconsidering *Boudreaux*

With the preceding new analytical framework in place, this Article now reconsiders the dilemma presented by the difficult factual dispute in *Boudreaux*. First, this Section analyzes the three contrasting opinions that emerged in *Boudreaux*. It then demonstrates how the new jurisprudential tools offered—the presumption of sharing and the indicia of giving or renunciation—could be used to resolve the same factual dispute. . . .

2. Resolving *Boudreaux* with New Jurisprudential Tools

If another court were to examine the facts presented in *Boudreaux* in light of the rebuttable presumption of sharing and the indicia of giving or renunciation introduced above, an even more satisfactory solution might be possible. The court would first recognize that initially the relationship between Boudreaux and the record owners would be governed by the presumption of sharing. Yet facts relating to the parties' on-going relationship might also reveal that over time the presumption had been rebutted. For instance, Boudreaux's extensive use of the right of way to move heavy equipment across the Weill-Boudreaux farm could weigh in favor of rebuttal under criteria (1). The work that Boudreaux performed to maintain and relocate the right of way and the work that Boudreaux performed on the gate could weigh in favor of rebuttal under either criteria (2) or (3). The fact that Boudreaux used the right of way not just to move farm equipment but to access a public road and to reach the nearest town where his community life was based could weigh in favor of rebuttal under criteria (3) as well. The absence of any clear signals by the Weills or Cummings that they were maintaining their agenda-setting authority, other than the Weills' request to relocate the gate, could also point to rebuttal under criteria (4). Any facts pertaining to community perceptions about Boudreaux's rights to use the path across the Weill-Cummings property could have been interpreted under criteria (5). Finally, the 60-year history of uninterrupted use of the right of way could itself weigh in favor of rebuttal under criteria (6). In the end, a decision using this kind of analysis might well have persuaded the Louisiana Supreme Court to affirm a finding that Boudreaux had obtained a servitude of passage by acquisitive prescription even though the Weills initially benefitted from a presumption of sharing.

Questions

1. Do you think the Louisiana Supreme Court or the Louisiana legislature should make a fresh start on the subject of acquisitive prescription of servitudes and precarious possession? Do you believe Professor Lovett's framework offers a workable solution? Can you imagine other approaches?

3. Expropriation; St. Julien Doctrine

As this casebook demonstrated in Chapter 6, certain entities that function as common carriers, such as power companies, pipeline companies and telecommunication companies, have long enjoyed the power to expropriate either ownership of immovable property or servitudes. When a servitude is expropriated, the owner of the immovable property is entitled to compensation for the property interest taken: damages for the reduction in value of the immovable property resulting from the interference caused by the servitude. *See e.g.*, La. Rev. Stat. Ann. 48:218 (1977) (detailing the compensation regime for the expropriation of a right-of-way by the Louisiana Department of Transportation and Development); A.N. YIAN-NOPOULOS, 4 LOUISIANA CIVIL LAW TREATISE: PREDIAL SERVITUDES § 6:44 (4th ed. 2013).

Although servitudes may not be created by estoppel in Louisiana, *Ryan v. Monett*, 666 So.2d 711 (La. App. 4 Cir. 1995), a judicially created doctrine, once known as the St. Julien Doctrine, "allowed entities having the power of expropriation to acquire servitudes by unopposed use and possession of another's land for some public purpose." YIANNOPOULOS, *supra*, § 6:44, at 470. Under this doctrine, the entity occupying the land acquired the servitude immediately, without any prescriptive period running, as long as the occupation occurred with the knowledge, consent or acquiescence of the owner. Once the servitude was acquired, the owner could not sue for damages or for the removal of any works, but only for the value of the servitude taken, and only if he brought an action within ten years.

In *Lake, Inc. v. Louisiana Power and Light Co.*, 330 So.2d 914, 918 (La. 1976), the Louisiana Supreme Court prospectively overruled the line of decisions establishing the St. Julien Doctrine. The court reasoned that pursuant to civilian principles the only kind of servitude that could be acquired by a method other than title was an apparent and continuous servitude — one visible by exterior signs and not requiring a positive act of man. Soon after this decision, however, the Louisiana legislature enacted a statute (Act No. 504 of 1976), which, in substantial part, resurrected the St. Julien Doctrine. Consider the statute:

La. Rev. Stat. § 19:14

A. In any case where the state or its political corporation or subdivision has actually, in good faith believing it had authority to do so, taken possession of privately owned immovable property of another, and constructed facilities upon, under, or over such property with the consent or acquiescence of the owner of the property, such owner shall be deemed to have waived his right to contest the necessity for the taking and to receive just compensation prior to the taking, but he shall be entitled to bring an action for such compensation, to be determined in accordance with the provisions of R.S. 19:9, for the taking of his property or interest therein, the just compensation to be determined as of the time of the taking of the property, or right or interest therein, and such action shall proceed as if the state, its political corporation, or subdivision had filed a petition for expropriation as provided for in R.S. 19:2.1.

B. In the case where any expropriating authority referred to in R.S. 19:2, other than the state or its political corporations or subdivisions, has actually, in good faith believing it had the authority to do so, taken possession of privately owned immovable property of another and constructed facilities upon, under, or over such property with the consent or acquiescence of the owner of the property, it shall be presumed that the owner of the property has waived his right to receive just compensation prior to the taking, and he shall be entitled only to bring an action for judicial determination of whether the taking was for a public and necessary purpose and for just compensation to be determined in accordance with R.S. 19:9, as of the time of the taking of the property, or right or interest therein, and such action shall proceed as nearly as may be as if the expropriating authority had filed a petition for expropriation as provided for in R.S. 19:2.1.

C. The provisions of Subsection A of this Section shall apply only to privately owned immovable property over which the state or its political corporation or subdivision has exercised actual possession in good faith for ten years and has completed construction of facilities upon, under, or over such property. The provisions of this Section shall not be deemed to authorize the acquisition of any interest in privately owned immovable property adjoining such facilities, including but not limited to a servitude, right of use, or any right of passage across or access to the private immovable property adjoining such facilities.

La. Rev. Stat. § 19:14 (1976, amended 2007, 2012).

How do Subsections A and B differ? Subsection A provides that when the state or its political corporations or subdivisions (1) take possession of privately owned immovable property of another, (2) in good faith, believing that it had the authority to do so, and (3) construct facilities "upon, under or over" the property, (4) with the consent or acquiescence of the landowner, then a presumption will arise that the landowner "is *deemed to have waived* his right to contest the necessity for the taking and to receive just compensation *prior* to the taking." La. Rev. Stat. § 19:14(A) (emphasis added). At this point, the landowner's only remedy vis-à-vis the state or a political corporation or subdivision will be an action for just compensation to be determined, by statutory formula, at the time of the taking. *Id.*

Under subsection B, however, the landowner's remedy against a private corporation with the power to expropriate is somewhat broader when the same four factual predicates exist. In cases governed by this provision, the landowner is deemed to have waived only "his right to receive just compensation prior to the taking" and, therefore, can still contest "whether the taking was for a public and necessary purpose." La. Rev. Stat. § 19:14(B).

Subsection (C), which was added in 2007, engrafts additional requirements of actual possession for ten years and completion of construction to the other four prerequisites applicable to the assertion of rights under Subsection (A) by the state or political subdivisions of the state (such as levee districts). La. Rev. Stat. § 19:14(C). How is this different from ten-year acquisitive prescription of servitudes under Article 742 of the Louisiana Civil Code? Why do these additional requirements not apply to claims of servitude acquisition by common carriers under subsection B? Why did the legislature make it easier for common carriers to acquire servitudes over privately owned land without formal expropriation proceedings?

In most cases involving the application of the St. Julien Doctrine or La. Rev. Stat. § 19:14, the entity exercising the right to acquire a servitude will not own a nearby dominant estate. Consequently, the servitude acquired will be for the benefit of a juridical person and therefore, will be characterized as a right of use, which is a limited personal servitude. Pursuant to Article 645 of the Louisiana Civil Code, the rules governing usufruct and predial servitudes generally apply to rights of use to the extent their application is compatible. La. Civ. Code art. 645 (1976).

E. Rights and Duties of the Parties to the Servitude

1. Accessory Rights

Article 743 of the Louisiana Civil Code declares that when a servitude is established the owner of the dominant estate also acquires all the rights that are necessary for the use of the servitude. La. Civ. Code art. 743 (1977). In reference to the civiliter principle, the provision further notes that these rights "are to be exercised in a way least inconvenient for the servient estate." *Id.* Article 744 gives the owner of the dominant estate the right to "make at his expense all the works that are necessary for the use and preservation of the servitude." La. Civ. Code art. 744 (1977). Consider how the court addresses both provisions in the following decision, which also briefly addresses acquisitive prescription of servitudes.

Ryan v. Monett
666 So.2d 711 (La. App. 4 Cir. 1996)

PLOTKIN, Judge. Elizabeth H. Ryan appeals a preliminary injunction that permits Alexandra Monett to maintain four window unit air conditioners on the side of her building at 2708 Coliseum Street that extend beyond the property line onto appellant's adjacent property at 2700 Coliseum Street. We amend the injunction to require appellee to remove these air conditioners, and we remand for further proceedings.

Ryan and Monett own adjacent estates at 2700 and 2708 Coliseum Street, respectively. Both lots contain buildings that were constructed over a century ago. The foundation of the building at 2708 Coliseum was built on the boundary between the estates. On March 21, 1958, a predecessor in title to Ryan executed a document that purported to create a servitude of overhang, which document states:

> [Ryan's predecessor in title] hereby recognizes the existence of a servitude of overhang over his said property in favor of the said adjoining property more particularly described hereinafter, to the extent of one foot (1′) by the cornice of the main building of said property and eight inches (8″) by the roof thereof, and does therefore hereby grant, donate, confirm, transfer and deliver, in favor of said adjoining property, a servitude of overhang to the extent hereinabove mentioned over and above his said property, the same to be continued in full force and effect in favor of said adjoining property for as long as the aforesaid building designated as Municipal No. 2708 Coliseum Street, New Orleans, Parish of Orleans, State of Louisiana, shall continue in existence as presently located, but to terminate upon the removal thereof;

Monett acquired 2708 Coliseum in December 1971 and reacquired it for use as rental property in March 1993 by dation en paiement from Mary Hart and her husband George O. Lillich Jr. Ryan owns and resides at 2700 Coliseum.

On March 7, 1995, Ryan sought an injunction to compel Monett to remove four air conditioners that extended over the property line and to remove a spout that had been added to a gutter of 2708 Coliseum that drained onto a garden at 2700 Coliseum. Ryan also sought damages from trespass by Monett's workers. On April 25, 1995, the trial judge, after reviewing the pleadings and affidavits, issued a preliminary injunction that required Monett to relocate the spout to its original position, to give reasonable notice to Ryan when Monett's workers would enter Ryan's yard, and authorized Monett to maintain no more than four window unit air conditioners that extended over the property line. The preliminary injunction is appealed only with regard to the air conditioners.

The trial judge stated the following in his reasons for judgment:

> Since these homes were built prior to the lifetime of the present litigants, it is obvious that predial servitudes exist in favor of the property at 2708 Coliseum Street and that these predial servitudes have been acquired by prescription in excess of thirty years.
>
> (. . .)
>
> With respect to the location of the window units projecting onto the plaintiff's property, the Court cites CC Article 647 for the proposition that a servitude may exist although the benefit need not exist at the time the servitude is created and that a possible convenience or a future advantage suffices to support a servitude.
>
> In other words, air conditioning units did not exist at the time the property at 2708 Coliseum Street was erected. Nevertheless, the fact that the

house was located on the property line, has continued to exist beyond ten years and that the window units are necessary in order to enjoy the property at the present time means that the servient estate—2700 Coliseum Street—must accept the overhang of the air conditioning units.

Also, CC Articles 743 and 744 provide for the accessory rights and necessary works in order to use the servitude.

On appeal, Ryan contends that the judge erred in the application of Civil Code articles 647, 743–744, and the law of acquisitive prescription.

A charge on 2700 Coliseum Street to tolerate the overhang of existing window unit air conditioners from the adjacent property for the benefit of 2708 Coliseum Street would be an apparent, affirmative predial servitude, which can only be acquired by title, destination of the owner, or by acquisitive prescription. See La. C.C. arts. 646, 697, 706–707, 740. Because there has been no allegation of common ownership that might implicate destination of the owner, we must consider only whether any such servitude has been created by title or by acquisitive prescription and, if created, not extinguished by nonuse.

The only "title" that is purported to have created a servitude is the March 21, 1958 agreement. A conventional servitude may be created by any juridical act sufficient to establish a real right in immovable property. See La. C.C. art. 708; see also A.N. Yiannopoulos, Louisiana Civil Law Treatise vol. 4, Predial Servitudes § 112 (1983). Because we interpret this agreement as not intending to create a servitude that would encompass the air conditioners, it is not necessary to decide, nor can it be determined from the record, whether this agreement is a juridical act sufficient to establish a real right in immovable property, or whether the effectiveness of this agreement against third persons was maintained in accordance with the public records doctrine.

A document purporting to create a predial servitude is interpreted in accordance with both the general rules of contract construction as well as in accordance with specific rules of construction for instruments that purport to create servitudes. Yiannopoulos, supra, § 128. A court must determine the intent of the parties, resolving any doubt as to the existence, extent, or manner of exercise of the purported servitude in favor of the servient estate. La. C.C. arts. 697, 730, 749, 2045, 2057. Assuming that the March 21, 1958 instrument validly created a servitude, it is clear, by reading the unambiguous language in favor of the servient estate, that this servitude was intended only to authorize the roof to extend eight inches, and the cornice to extend a foot, over the property line.

Neither do we agree with the trial judge that air conditioners were a future benefit intended by the parties and authorized by Civil Code article 647, nor that air conditioners are authorized by Articles 743 and 744 as necessary or accessory rights to this servitude. Article 647 provides in part: There must be a benefit to the dominant estate. The benefit need not exist at the time the servitude is created; a possible convenience or a future advantage suffices to support such a servitude.

Without deciding whether an overhanging air conditioner can be considered a future advantage under Article 647, the precise language of the instrument, which defines the type and extent of overhang to be permitted, does not permit the inference that the parties intended any future advantage. Articles 743 and 744 provide:

Art. 743. Accessory rights

Rights that are necessary for the use of a servitude are acquired at the time the servitude is established. They are to be exercised in a way least inconvenient for the servient estate.

Art. 744. Necessary works; cost of repairs

The owner of the dominant estate has the right to make at his expense all the works that are necessary for the use and preservation of the servitude.

Window unit air conditioners cannot be considered necessary under Article 743 to the continued overhang of the roof and the cornice. Moreover, the owner of the dominant estate is free to install a central air conditioning unit on the other side of the property, obviating entirely the need for window units and causing less inconvenience to the servient estate. Likewise, Article 744 does not authorize air conditioners, which are not necessary to the use and preservation of the overhanging roof and cornice.

Apparent predial servitudes may also be created by acquisitive prescription and extinguished by nonuse. See La. C.C. arts. 740, 742, 753; see also Yiannopoulos, supra, §§ 134, 163. The trial judge found it obvious that, because the building at 2708 Coliseum had existed on the property line for more than a century, predial servitudes must have been acquired by prescription. The trial judge may be correct that some servitudes have been acquired; however, the question to be resolved is whether a servitude permitting the overhang of the air conditioners has been acquired by prescription. The record is insufficient to support the finding that such a servitude has been acquired. . . .

. . . The only evidence regarding the length of time the air conditioners have been in place is the following: By affidavit, Lillich stated that air conditioners were there when he began to manage the property in 1983, although he conceded that particular window units may have been replaced between 1983 and 1993; and from photographic evidence, it is apparent that four air conditioners are still there.

Assuming without ruling that this possession suffices for purposes of acquisitive prescription, we find the appropriate prescriptive period to be thirty years. Although no evidence has been presented to rebut the presumption of good faith, neither has any evidence been presented to establish just title. Monett suggests that after a century just title must be present, but cites no authorities supporting the presumption of just title. The only "title" appearing in evidence is the instrument dated March 21, 1958. This document on its face does not purport to describe or convey any property right that would authorize the placement of the window units. Without just title, the soonest this servitude could be created by prescription appears from the only evidence before this Court to be some time in the year 2013, if prescription had not been interrupted by the filing of this suit.

Monett contends that "cooling system platforms" were in place as early as 1971. It is not necessary to decide whether these suffice to commence possession for the purpose of acquisitive prescription; this still would not establish thirty years uninterrupted and peaceable possession.

Monett also contends that when the original owners built these houses over a century ago, a servitude was created. Monett claims that Ryan was aware that the building at 2708 Coliseum was built on the property line when she purchased 2700 Coliseum and suggests that Ryan should be barred by Civil Code article 670 from complaining of this "encroachment" because a reasonable time has passed. The trial judge appears not to have accepted Monett's argument under Article 670. In essence, Monett asserts that Ryan should be estopped from bringing this suit by her own acts and the acts of her predecessors in title. Estoppel, however, is not one of the methods enumerated in the Civil Code for the creation of a predial servitude, and resort to equity under the facts of this case is neither authorized by the Code nor appropriate under the circumstances.

Instead, the trial judge articulated his decision on the basis of acquisitive prescription; Civil Code articles 647, 743–744; and the notion that the addition of window unit air conditioners might be the justifiable growth in use of an existing servitude. We find the record insufficient to support the conclusion that a servitude, which would permit Monett to extend window unit air conditioners over the property line onto Ryan's estate, was created by either convention or by acquisitive prescription. Even if we assume the existence of an underlying servitude of some sort, we cannot find that Monett has acquired the additional right to extend window units over the property line before acquisitive prescription has accrued. Additional rights cannot be acquired by use except by acquisitive prescription. See Yiannopoulos, supra, § 136.

Accordingly, we amend the injunction to require Monett to remove all window unit air conditioners that extend over the property line between 2700 and 2708 Coliseum Street within thirty days after any final judgment in these proceedings, and we remand for further proceedings in accordance with this opinion. All costs of this proceeding are assessed to appellee.

Notes and Questions

1. The court in *Ryan v. Monett*, 666 So.2d 771 (La. App. 4 Cir. 1995), reminded the litigants that the servitude on Ryan's estate in favor of Monett's estate allowed for a roof overhang and a cornice. It did not contemplate that Monett was to have the use of all the airspace from the ground up to the cornice. How are the air conditioners, which do not extend as far out as the overhang, a greater use of Ryan's property than the overhang?

2. The court in *Ryan* provided two reasons for rejecting Monett's argument that the air conditioners were "necessary" either "for the use of a servitude" (Article 743)

or "for the use and preservation of the servitude" (Article 744). Can you articulate those reasons?

3. Do you agree with Judge Plotkin's rationales for not applying Article 670 of the Louisiana Civil Code in favor of Monett? Would the decisions in *Bushnell v. Artis*, 445 So.3d 152 (La. App. 3 Cir. 1984), and *Winingder v. Balmer*, 632 So.2d 408 (La. App. 4 Cir. 1994) have been helpful to the court in Ryan?

4. Does a servitude of passage include an accessory right of the dominant estate owner to park vehicles on the servient estate? In *Garner v. Holley*, 968 So.2d 234 (La. App. 2 Cir. 2007), a Louisiana court held that it did not: "A servitude of passage is for the benefit of a dominant estate whereby persons or vehicles are *permitted to pass through* a servient estate. La. CC art. 750 (emphasis added). This statute is unambiguous and we find no reason to expand it to allow vehicles to park on, and not pass through, a servient estate." *Id.* at 239.

Two weeks after *Garner*, the House of Lords, then the highest court in the United Kingdom, reached the opposite conclusion in the Scottish case of *Moncrieff v. Jamieson*, 2007 UKHL 42, 2008, SC (HL) 1. As Professor Kenneth Reid observes, the difference in outcomes is explained more by the particular facts of *Moncrieff* rather than different doctrinal foundations of the law of servitudes in Louisiana and Scotland:

> If the contrast is fascinating, it is also misleading. In *Moncrieff*, the land fell so steeply that it was impossible to take a vehicle from the road, over which the servitude was exercisable, on the dominant land and to the house on that land. Unless parking was allowed on the road, it would be necessary, after depositing luggage and passengers near the house, to turn round and park some distance away at the top of a steep hill. In these unusual circumstances, the House of Lords concluded, not without hesitation, that in the absence of a right to park "the proprietor's right of vehicular access would effectively be defeated". By contrast, the vehicles in *Garner* could be parked elsewhere. It should not be supposed, therefore, that accessory rights are more easily established in Scotland than in Louisiana. On the contrary, the doctrinal basis identified for such rights in Louisiana seems less limiting and more flexible than its counterpart in Scotland.

Kenneth G.C. Reid, *Predial Servitudes, in* VERNON V. PALMER & ELSPETH C. REID, MIXED JURISDICTIONS COMPARED: PRIVATE LAW IN LOUISIANA AND SCOTLAND 1, 11 (2009) (footnotes omitted). Would a Louisiana court faced with facts similar to those presented in *Moncrieff v. Jamieson* find that a servitude of passage burdening a steeply sloped servient estate implies a right to park vehicles on that estate as well? What Civil Code articles would be most relevant to a Louisiana court's analysis?

Disputes as to whether servitudes of passage grant dominant estate owners an implied right to park vehicles continue to arise. *Compare 1025 Conti Condominiums, LLC v. 1025 Bienville, LLC*, 183 So.3d 724, 729–30 (La. App. 4 Cir. 2015) (affirming the trial court's determination that a vaguely worded predial servitude of passage and access did not grant the dominant estate owner a right to park on the alley and courtyard burdened by the servitude); *with Ventura v. McCune*, 184 So.3d 46, 50 (La. App. 5 Cir. 2014) (reversing summary judgment and holding that the language in an act creating a "servitude of passage as a private lane" and explicitly describing the servitude as "an extension of . . . Rue Chardonnay," a public street, granted both neighboring owners facing the private lane a right to park on the 50′ × 100′ piece of land described as the private lane in the same manner and to the same extent as on Rue Chardonnay).

2. Rights and Obligations of the Dominant Estate Owner

Under Article 744 of the Louisiana Civil Code, the owner of the dominant estate has the right "to make at his expense all the works that are necessary for the use and preservation of the servitude." La. Civ. Code art. 744 (1977). In the same vein, Article 745 grants the owner of the dominant estate additional rights related to the construction and repair of works needed for the use and preservation of the servitude:

Art. 745. Right to enter into the servient estate

The owner of the dominant estate has the right to enter with his workmen and equipment into the part of the servient estate that is needed for the construction or repair of works required for the use and preservation of the servitude. He may deposit materials to be used for the works and the debris that may result, under the obligation of causing the least possible damage and of removing them as soon as possible.

La. Civ. Code art. 745 (1977).

Because this right of entry for purposes of facilitating the use and conservation of the servitude might inconvenience the owner of the servient estate, the owner of the dominant estate is bound to cause the least possible damage and to remove any materials or debris after the work is completed. Thus, Article 745 of the Louisiana Civil Code once again illustrates the civiliter principle, which permeates the law of servitudes: the servitude must be exercised in a way that engenders a minimum of disturbance or inconvenience to the owner of the servient estate.

* * *

Compare the following two decisions *Ryan v. Southern Natural Gas Co.*, 879 F.2d 162 (5th Cir. 1989), and *Terrebonne Parish School Board v. Columbia Gulf Transmission Co.*, 290 F.3d 303 (5th Cir. 2002), in which the United States Fifth Circuit Court of Appeal confronted the problem of whether owners of coastal marshland in Louisiana have any recourse against servitude holders when canals constructed pursuant to those servitudes eventually widen and cause considerable damage to the rest of the servient estate. Note that in the first case, the defendant, Southern Natural Gas Company, appeared to hold a right of use — one of the personal servitudes enumerated by Article 534 of the Louisiana Civil Code. Because a right of use servitude is subject to the rules governing predial servitudes to the extent their application is compatible with a right of use servitude (La. Civ. Code art. 645 (1976)), the court looked to the rules governing conventional predial servitudes. In the second case, the court identifies the defendants as owners of two separate dominant estates, thus indicating that conventional predial servitudes were involved.

Ryan v. Southern Natural Gas Co.
879 F.2d 162 (5th Cir. 1989)

DAVIS, Circuit Judge. Southern Natural Gas Company (SNG), which was granted a servitude to property owned by appellees' ancestors, challenges the district court's judgment against it for the loss and deterioration of approximately 330 acres of marshland. The district court found that the marsh damage was due to appellant's failure to dam a pipeline canal it constructed on plaintiffs' property. Because the servitude agreement absolved SNG from the obligation to dam the canal, appellant owed no duty to appellees to do so. We therefore reverse and render the judgment entered by the district court.

I.

In 1956, SNG obtained a servitude agreement from several ancestors of the plaintiffs/appellees (collectively the "Harrisons"). Pursuant to the written agreement, SNG constructed a pipeline canal on two portions of the Harrisons' land, which we refer to as the southern strip or strip I and the northern strip or strip II. The agreement required SNG to backfill the pipeline canal in the northern strip and allowed the canal in the southern strip to be left open. The agreement specifically prohibited SNG from backfilling the southern strip.

Consistent with its contractual obligations, when SNG built the pipeline canal in 1956, it did not backfill or dam that part of the canal running through the southern strip. In 1978, the Harrisons' attorney wrote to SNG complaining that erosion had taken place along the spoil banks of the canal in the southern strip, causing it to widen beyond the right-of-way. The Harrisons also complained that failure to dam the southern part of the canal was allowing the tide to flow into and out of the canal and marsh, resulting in saltwater damage to a large area of the marsh beyond the right-of-way. The Harrisons requested that SNG dam or plug the canal. SNG refused.

In 1986, the Harrisons filed this action to recover for (1) land lost due to erosion and widening of the canal and, (2) "extended marsh loss" allegedly caused by the change in the ecological makeup of the marshlands because of increased tidal flow in and out of the canal. The Harrisons sought damages under theories of negligence, strict liability and breach of the servitude agreement. The district court found that the Harrisons' contract claim had prescribed, but allowed the Harrisons to recover from SNG under a negligence theory; the court found that SNG's negligent failure to dam the canal caused the canal banks and the marshland top soil to erode. The court awarded the Harrisons damages both for the loss of thirty-nine acres of land due to the widening of the canal and for the cost of stabilizing the surrounding marshland to prevent further deterioration.

SNG appeals the adverse judgment against it; the Harrisons, by way of cross-appeal, contend that the trial court erred in finding that SNG was not strictly liable for the loss.

II.

The initial issue confronting us is whether the servitude agreement between SNG and the Harrisons absolved SNG of any duty to dam the canal.

When a servitude is established by contract, the extent and mode of using the servitude is regulated by the contract. *See Ogden v. Bankston*, 398 So. 2d 1037, 1040–41 (La. 1981). A written agreement is the law between the parties and must be interpreted and enforced according to its terms. La. Civ. Code art. 1983; *Massie v. Inexco Oil Co.*, 798 F.2d 777, 779 (5th Cir. 1986) (applying Louisiana law). The duty of SNG to plug or backfill the pipeline canal in question was defined by its contract with the Harrisons:

> The Grantee [SNG] is given the right to use the right of way granted above for the purpose of constructing a canal or ditch, ... and which canal or ditch may, at [SNG's] option, be left open insofar as [the southern strip] is concerned. ... The canal or ditch constructed by the Grantee will not be backfilled upon completion of construction at any other time by [SNG]. ...

The plain words of the contract gave SNG the option to leave the canal "open." This obviously gave SNG the right to refrain from damming the canal. The Harrisons argue that irrespective of the language of the contract, article 745 of the Louisiana Civil Code ["The owner of the dominant estate has the right to enter with his workmen and equipment into the part of the servient estate that is needed for the construction or repair of works required for the use and preservation of the servitude. He may deposit materials to be used for the works and the debris that may result, under the obligation of causing the least possible damage and of removing them as soon as possible."] establishes a general duty by the servitude owner to avoid unreasonable damage. We disagree. Any duty imposed on the servitude owner by article 745 is subject to the provisions of the written servitude agreement between the parties.

Article 697, Louisiana Civil Code, makes it clear that the duty imposed on the servitude owner by article 745 to avoid unreasonable damage to the ... [servient] estate is subject to the provisions of the instrument creating the servitude: "The use and extent of such servitudes are regulated by the title by which they are created, and, in the absence of such regulation, by the following rules." Also, article 774 (the predecessor article to article 745), which was in effect in 1956 when the servitude was created, explicitly recognized the ability of the parties to contractually alter the duty owed by the servitude owner. We conclude therefore that any duty SNG had under article 745 did not include the duty to dam the canal because SNG was relieved of that specific duty under the servitude agreement.

We reach a similar conclusion with respect to the Harrisons' claim under Louisiana Civil Code article 667, which imposes a strict duty on proprietors to avoid work on their property that may cause damage to their neighbors. Assuming without deciding that the relief afforded by article 667 is available to the Harrisons, as the owners of the . . . [servient] estate, against SNG, the servitude owner, we know of no reason the parties cannot contractually modify the duty SNG would owe the Harrisons under that article. Article 729 of the Louisiana Civil Code provides: "Legal and natural servitudes may be altered by agreement of the parties if the public interest is not affected adversely." Thus article 667 cannot be the source of any duty upon SNG to dam the canal when the parties dispensed with that duty in their agreement. *See Butler v. Baber*, 529 So. 2d 374, 382 (La. 1988) (Dennis, J. concurring).

The Harrisons call our attention to an SNG memo, written around the time the servitude agreement was executed, in which the SNG representative stated, "I was greatly surprised that we were able to talk Captain Harrison out of making us construct several dams or plugs, which I believe would have cost us at least $25,000." The Harrisons argue that this memo tags SNG with culpability in declining to place dams in the canal when it fully expected it would be required to do so. But in our view, this memo is more detrimental than helpful to the Harrisons' position. It demonstrates that the contracting parties turned their attention to whether SNG would be required to construct dams in the canal and SNG was successful in negotiating an agreement that relieved it of this responsibility.

Our conclusion that the servitude agreement relieved SNG of any duty to dam the canal resolves this case and makes it unnecessary for us to discuss the remaining issues. Accordingly, the judgment of the district court is reversed and the case is remanded for entry of a take-nothing judgment in favor of SNG.

REVERSED and REMANDED.

Notes and Questions

1. Please note that in *Ryan v. Southern Natural Gas Co.*, 879 F.2d 162 (5th Cir. 1989), the plaintiffs, the Ryans, were not a party to the original contract creating the servitude but were nonetheless bound by it. This case thus illustrates one of the fundamental characteristics of a predial servitude: its inseparability from the dominant and servient estates. Pursuant to Article 650 of the Louisiana Civil Code, a predial servitude "is inseparable from the dominant estate and passes with it" and "continues as a charge on the servient estate when ownership changes." La. Civ. Code art. 650 (1977, amended 2004). A predial servitude thus binds all subsequent owners of both estates, unless it terminates. Here, the Ryans' estate, the land originally owned by Captain Harrison, was burdened by a limited personal servitude of right of use. As noted in the beginning of this chapter, the Civil Code's rules applicable to predial servitudes govern a right of use to the extent those rules are compatible with a right of use. La. Civ. Code art. 645 (1977). This means that even though the defendant, Sothern Natural Gas Co., did not own a dominant estate, the right of use still continued to burden the servient estate even after its ownership changed hands.

2. The Harrisons called the court's attention to the default rules in Chapter 4 of Title IV of the Louisiana Civil Code as these might have brought them some relief. But the court refused to apply these provisions. Does this seem to be a fair result? Consider Article 743 ("Rights that are necessary for the use of the servitude are acquired at the time the servitude is established. *They are to be exercised in a way least inconvenient for the servient estate.*"). La. Civ. Code art. 743 (1977). What principle does this provision codify?

3. Should the court in *Ryan* have given more consideration to the SNG memorandum in which an SNG employee expressed surprise that they were "able to talk Captain Harrison out of making us construct several dams or plugs . . ."?

Terrebonne Parish School Board v. Columbia Gulf Transmission Co.
290 F.3d 303 (5th Cir. 2002)

WIENER, Circuit Judge: Plaintiff–Appellant the Terrebonne Parish School Board (the "Board"), as owner of a servient estate, appeals from the district court's summary judgment that the Board's causes of action against the two owners of separate dominant estates—Defendants–Appellees Koch Gateway Pipeline Company ("Koch") and Columbia Gulf Transmission Company ("Columbia")—have prescribed. Concluding that genuine issues of material fact exist with regard to prescription of the Board's possible causes of action under Louisiana's law of delict (tort) and contract, we reverse the district court's grant of summary judgment and remand.

I.

Facts and Proceedings

Shortly after Louisiana gained statehood, Congress extended to Louisiana a policy of reserving, from among the public lands in newly created states, the sixteenth section of every township for the support of education. This policy created a patchwork of reserved section sixteen lands ("sections sixteen") throughout each such state, as a result of uniform surveying according to the township-and-range system. (A township is six miles square and contains thirty-six sections, which are one mile square; thus each section sixteen is five miles distant from the nearest other sections sixteen, one in each of the four contiguous townships.)

Title to sections sixteen in Terrebonne Parish passed from the United States to the Board sometime during the nineteenth century. The Board-owned section sixteen that is located in Township 18 South, Range 13 East, Terrebonne Parish, Louisiana, and which contains about 641 acres, is the subject of this case and is hereafter referred to as "Section 16 (18–13)."

Before the events at issue here, much of Terrebonne Parish, including Section 16 (18–13), consisted of floating freshwater marsh. Typically, this kind of marsh comprises "marsh mats" that are as much as a foot thick and literally float several feet above the silt and clay bottom, unattached by roots.

Section 16 (18–13) is now traversed by two pipelines that exist pursuant to conventional (contractual) servitude agreements granted by the Board. The first was constructed pursuant to a "standard form" agreement executed by the Board in 1957 in favor of Koch's ancestor in interest. This servitude agreement (the "Koch Agreement") reads in part as follows:

> That for and in consideration of THREE HUNDRED SIXTY SIX AND 60/100 ($366.60) Dollars . . . Grantor does hereby Grant and Convey unto United Gas Pipeline Company . . . a right of way and easement one hundred feet in width to construct, maintain, operate, repair, replace, change the size of and remove pipe lines and appurtenances thereto, including the right at its election to lay such pipe line or lines in open ditches or canals not to exceed forty feet in width, which may be filled in or left open at the option of Grantee. . . .
>
> . . .
>
> TO HAVE AND TO HOLD unto Grantee, its successors and assigns, so long as the rights and easements herein granted, or any of them, shall be used by, or useful to Grantee for the purposes herein granted, with ingress to and egress from the premises, . . . for the purposes of construction, inspecting, repairing and replacing the property of Grantee herein described. . . .
>
> . . .
>
> [S]aid Grantor shall not obstruct or permit to be constructed any house, structures or obstructions, on or over, or that will interfere with the maintenance or operation of, any pipe line or appurtenances constructed hereunder, and will not change the grade over such pipe line.

Koch's pipeline canal was dredged and its pipeline built in 1958.

In 1964, Columbia entered into negotiations with the Board to build the second pipeline across Section 16 (18–13). During negotiations, however, Columbia built its pipeline. When, in 1965, this trespass was discovered by the Board, it and Columbia negotiated a servitude agreement using a somewhat different standard form (the "Columbia Agreement"). In return for $685.20, the Board granted Columbia

> a servitude, right of way and easement to construct, lay, maintain, operate, alter, repair, remove, change the size of, and replace a pipe line and appurtenances thereto, including but not limited to fittings, tie-overs, valves, corrosion control equipment and other apparatus. . . .
>
> . . .
>
> [S]aid Grantors shall not construct nor permit to be constructed any house, structures, or obstructions and shall not plant nor permit to be planted trees on or over, or that will interfere with the construction, maintenance or operation of any pipe line or appurtenances constructed hereunder, and will not change the grade over such pipe line.

> The right of way granted herein shall be 100 feet wide. . . . It is understood and agreed that Grantee shall not be required to backfill the open flotation ditch excavated during construction.
>
> It is hereby understood that the Grantee, its successors and assigns, shall not be obligated to pay Grantors or any subsequent owner of [Section 16 (18–13)] any damages resulting from the construction of the [pipeline], such damages having been anticipated and paid in advance at the time of execution of this instrument.

Koch and Columbia have continuously maintained the pipelines, often using the canals to do so. Both concede, however, that they have not maintained the canals or their banks.

The Board contends that, at least partly as a result of the servitude holders' failure to maintain the canals or their banks, the canals have widened and their banks have been breached. The Board asserts that the Koch canal has widened to an average width of 70 feet, almost double the 40–foot limit specified in the Koch Agreement; and that the Columbia canal has widened beyond the specified 100–foot right of way, to an average width of 135 feet. Koch and Columbia (collectively, "the defendants") object that there is no record evidence for these statistics, but a scaled satellite photo tends to support the Board's assertion. There is also causation evidence suggesting that breaches in the canals' banks have exposed the floating marsh to tidal surges, which have washed away, and continue to wash away, the light organic soil necessary for the marsh mats to cohere. The record suggests that this erosion may occur slowly—and vertically—from the water bottom up, causing the marsh mats to thin out and eventually disappear. Now, argues the Board, where there was once healthy marsh, there is open water.

The Board sued several entities that operated on its sections sixteen, filing the instant action in state court in October 1999 against Columbia and Koch jointly, and seeking either the physical restoration of Section 16 (18–13) or compensatory damages. The Board's petition contains explicit tort and contract claims, the latter including an innominate property argument. The defendants removed to the Eastern District of Louisiana and later moved for summary judgment.

The district court granted summary judgment to the defendants. It held, in contract, that the servitude agreements did not require Columbia and Koch to continue to maintain the canals' banks; therefore any contractual claim had prescribed. In tort, the district court reasoned that failure to maintain a canal is not conduct that can support a claim under a continuing tort theory. The district court also held that the Board's "failure to hire an expert or investigate the erosion at the time it became aware of the damage does not prevent prescription from commencing." Apparently viewing the defendants' liability as arising out of discontinuous violations, the court held that prescription of the Board's delictual (tort) claims began to run when it learned of the damage to various of its sections sixteen. As the Board "was aware of the erosion of Section 16 in or before 1985," the district court reasoned, it cannot now maintain an action with respect to Section 16 (18–13). This timely appeal followed.

I.

Analysis

Even though the district court approached this case as largely implicating tort claims, it actually involves equal or greater questions of contract and property rights. To review the district court's ruling, we must consider procedural and delictual issues, but the Louisiana law that governs this case is chiefly the civil law of servitudes—a mixture of contract interpretation and suppletive (gap-filling) rules of property law. . . .

C. Substance

Substantive analysis of this case requires first that we touch on the distinction between contract and delict (or tort) under Louisiana law. To paraphrase Planiol, contractual fault consists of violating a contractual obligation; delictual fault is an act between juridical strangers that violates some duty imposed by law, not by contract, and that requires reparation. [*See State ex rel Guste v. Simoni, Heck & Associates,* 331 So.2d 478, 490 (La.1976) (Summers, J., dissenting) (quoting 2 M. PLANIOL, TREATISE ON THE CIVIL LAW, Nos. 873–74 at 485–86 (11th ed. La .State.L.Inst.trans.1939)).] The parties here are juridical acquaintances. The Board, Columbia, and Koch's predecessor decided to burden one estate for the benefit of two others. These decisions created conventional predial servitudes that the parties memorialized in servitude agreements. [*See* LA. CIV.CODE ANN. art. 646 (West 1980) (defining "predial servitude").] The proper place to begin analyzing this case is thus the servitude agreements themselves. Then we shall turn to obligations supplied or imposed by the Civil Code.

1. Contract

When there is a contract, it is law between the parties and must be performed in good faith and enforced according to its terms. When, as here, the contract creates a conventional predial servitude, the mode of use of the servitude is regulated by the contract. [*See Ogden v. Bankston,* 398 So.2d 1037, 1040 (La.1981).] If, however, the contract is silent on a non-essential question, like the mode of use, Louisiana's law of conventional obligations in general and predial servitudes in particular supplies the answer, filling in the blanks. [*See* LA. CIV.CODE ANN. art. 697 (West 1980) ("The use and extent of such servitudes are regulated by the title by which they are created, and, in the absence of such regulation, by the following rules.").]

The parties dispute two aspects of their contractual relationship: (1) whether the Board *released* Koch and Columbia from liability for marsh erosion; and (2) whether the contract imposes any *duties to maintain* the canal or its banks—stated differently, any duties to protect the servient estate against damage resulting from use of the servitude.

a. Release

[In this portion of the decision, the court determined that standard-form release agreements obtained from the Board by Koch and Columbia's ancestor in title only released the original grantee, United Gas, and its successors, from claims for damages resulting from the pipeline's *initial construction* and did not address any erosion damages that might result from a released party's act or omission decades after the pipeline's construction. Eds.]

b. Continuing Contractual Duty to Maintain

The parties also debate whether the servitude agreements require Columbia and Koch to maintain the banks of the canals so as to prevent widening and breach. Although the district court stated that it granted the motion for summary judgment "only as to prescription of the claims," this characterization overlooks its own explicit ruling that the servitude agreements did not impose a continuing duty to maintain the canals. This ruling flowed in turn from the court's understanding of *St. Martin v. Mobil Exploration & Producing U.S. Inc.*, 224 F.3d 402 (5th Cir.2000), in which we affirmed a trial court's conclusion that such a duty existed. In that case, the servitude agreement provided that

> Grantor does hereby convey to [Grantee], its successors and assigns, the right and servitude to dredge, construct, maintain and use a canal having a width of 65 feet. . . . Grantee is also given the right to deposit spoils within a distance of 150 feet on each side of the banks of the canal, but shall do so in such manner as to cause as little interference as possible to drainage.

Despite the implication from this language that the canal was meant to drain, we held that the agreement imposed a duty on Grantee to maintain the banks of the canal so as to prevent further marsh erosion. We also concluded, from the agreement's statement that the rights it created would exist until leases expired, that the ten-year prescriptive period in contract did not apply, and that the landowner's right to enforce the canal owner's duty to maintain the canal lasted for the length of the servitude.

In the instant case, the district court distinguished *St. Martin* on the ground that here "[t]here is no language regarding the continuing obligations of the defendants in either of the contracts." Therefore, reasoned the court, *St. Martin v. Mobil* did not apply, and the Board lacked a viable claim in contract. We agree with this distinction only in part, disagreeing in part as well.

One basis for this distinction, advanced on appeal by Koch and Columbia, is that the agreement in *St. Martin v. Mobil* was a *canal* servitude, unlike these agreements, which specify *pipelines*, not canals. This argument is an oversimplification. Each agreement at issue here grants a right of way and easement for a "pipe line and appurtenances thereto." The Koch Agreement specifically states that this grant "includ[es]" the right to lay the pipeline in "open ditches or canals." The Columbia Agreement specifically states that the "Grantee shall not be required to backfill the open flotation ditch excavated during construction." Both agreements provide that the Board "will not change the grade over such pipe line," so that the right to change the grade along the pipeline rests with Koch and Columbia, not the Board.

Both Koch and Columbia concede that they continue to use the canals to inspect and maintain the pipelines. We harbor no doubt, then, that if the Board were to try to fill in the canals, Koch and Columbia would cry foul, and rightly so. We therefore view the canals not merely as vestiges of the pipelines' original construction that have no relevance to the parties' continuing relationship, but rather as "appurtenances" to the pipelines and essentials to their use. The canals are part and parcel of these conventional predial servitudes.

The more meaningful distinction between this case and *St. Martin v. Mobil* is found in the answer to the question whether the servitude agreements *require* that the canals be maintained. We agree with the district court that the language in these agreements is much less explicit and more ambiguous than the language in the *St. Martin v. Mobil* agreement. As a matter of contract interpretation alone, the mere grant of a *right* to maintain a canal does not necessarily impose the *duty* to maintain it or to take other steps to prevent the canals from widening and the surrounding marsh mat from eroding. But neither do the agreements clearly contemplate that the canals will widen; nor do they either explicitly or implicitly permit Koch and Columbia simply to stand by and let this happen while continuing to use the canals in connection with their use of the pipeline servitudes.

Indeed, on this point each agreement contains an internal contradiction: Each specifically allows the grantee to keep the canals open and bars the Board from regarding; but the Koch Agreement gives the grantee the right to dig a canal "not to exceed forty feet in width," and the entire width of each servitude is only one hundred feet. The parties variously contend that these provisions resolve the marsh-erosion question one way or the other, but in light of what the summary-judgment evidence tells us about the delicate hydrology of floating marshes, we view these provisions as being in internal conflict, to whatever extent they bear on the question. This conflict suggests that the parties either did not anticipate erosion damage in drafting and signing the agreements or did not intend the explicit language of the agreements to resolve the liability question one way or the other.

This case, therefore, does not at all resemble *Ryan v. Southern Natural Gas Co.*, 879 F.2d 162 (5th Cir. 1989), on which Columbia relies heavily. As here, the landowner in *Ryan* sued the pipeline servitude owner for damages caused by the erosion of marshland and the widening of a pipeline canal. We held that language of the servitude agreement governed the parties' relationship, "reliev[ing the pipeline owner] of any duty to dam the canal," and therefore the landowner could not recover either in tort or in contract, at least on the servitude agreement itself. The best factual support for our *Ryan* holding was *not* the servitude agreement's provision (as in the Koch Agreement here) that the pipeline canal could be left "open," but rather, as the district court noted, the pipeline owner's signature on and the landowner's acceptance of a "letter agreement" that bound the former to pay the latter $400 per acre of land encroached on by the canal in the event that it widened. [*Ryan v. Southern*

Natural Gas Co., 1987 WL 19044, at *2 (E.D. La.).] The intent of the *Ryan* parties, as evidenced by this letter agreement, precluded recovery by the *Ryan* plaintiffs on the servitude agreement, irrespective of the underlying legal theory advanced. *Ryan* is therefore clearly distinguishable from the instant case, as there is no provision in either the Koch Agreement or the Columbia Agreement—or any side agreement—that demonstrates how the parties intended to treat claims of marsh erosion.

As we do not understand the pertinent kind of erosion to have been within the parties' contemplation for release purposes, it should come as no surprise that we do not interpret the servitude agreements themselves as determining whether Koch and Columbia have a continuing duty to prevent marsh-erosion damage. Therefore, under Louisiana law, our task shifts from plain-wording contract interpretation to application of the Louisiana Civil Code's suppletive rules for immovable property, which—together with relevant case law—come into play when issues are not explicitly disposed of in the writings of the parties. [Given our uncertainty as to whether the Board had notice of erosion in Section 16 (18–13), which we discuss below, we do not accept, for summary-judgment purposes, Koch's and Columbia's arguments that the Board acquiesced in a course of performance that evinces the intention of the parties with respect to marsh erosion.]

c. Louisiana's Suppletive Law—Conventional Servitudes

Civil Code article 697 establishes that when the parties creating a conventional servitude do not specify the use and extent of that servitude, Louisiana's suppletive rules of property law apply. Because the district court did not apply any of them, we shall address them only to the extent necessary to determine whether the district court correctly granted Koch and Columbia summary judgment on the basis of prescription.

One principle of servitude jurisprudence is that ambiguity in a servitude agreement must be construed in favor of the servient estate [La. Civ. Code Ann. art. 730 (West 1980)]—here, the interests of the Board. As the Louisiana Supreme Court has reasoned:

> Predial servitudes are in derogation of public policy because they form restraints on the free disposal and use of property. Therefore, servitudes are not entitled to be viewed with favor by the law and can never be sustained by implication. Any doubt as to the existence, extent or manner of exercise of a predial servitude must be resolved in favor of the servient estate.

[*Palomeque v. Prudhomme,* 95–0725, 7 (La.11/27/1995), 664 So.2d 88, 93 (citations omitted).] This principle militates in favor of our interpretation of the servitude agreements and suggests that they do not govern marsh-erosion claims.

Another well-established rule of servitude law is that the dominant estate owner—here, each defendant—must not "aggravate" the condition of the servient estate. [*See* LA. CIV.CODE ANN. art. 743 (West 1980) ("Rights that are necessary for the use of a servitude are acquired at the time the servitude is established. They are to be exercised in a way least inconvenient for the servient estate."); LA.

CIV.CODE ANN. art. 745 (West 1980) ("The owner of the dominant estate . . . may deposit materials to be used for the works and the debris that may result, under the obligation of causing the least possible damage."); *Duet v. Louisiana Power & Light Co.,* 169 F.Supp. 184, 186 (D.La.1958):

> It is settled in Louisiana . . . that one having an easement or servitude on another's land is bound to use that easement or servitude in such manner as not unreasonably to injure the right of the owner of the servient estate, and that if the owner of the easement or servitude uses it in a negligent, unauthorized, or unreasonable manner, the owner of the servient estate may maintain an action for damages resulting from such use.

. . . A.N. YIANNOPOULOS, 4 LOUISIANA CIVIL LAW TREATISE: PREDIAL SERVITUDES § 156 (West 1997) ("The owner of the dominant estate may not make a use of the servitude that aggravates the condition of the servient estate."); *id.* § 152 ("The propositions that the owner of the dominant estate may only use the servitude within the limits established by title or possession and that he cannot make changes in the manner of use of the servitude that aggravate the condition of the servient estate are self-evident and do not require legislative affirmation.").] As Professor A.N. Yiannopoulos has observed, the duty not to aggravate the condition of the servient estate, "correlative of the real right of servitude, is not grounded on negligence"; and, absent an express contractual exoneration for marsh erosion damages, "to the extent that the damage to the servient estate was caused by abuse of right, the damage should be compensable."

Furthermore, the duty not to aggravate the servient estate is a continuing duty. This is the lesson of *Lewis v. Sohio Petroleum Co.,* 532 So.2d 754 (La. 1988), in which the Louisiana Supreme Court evidently found merit in a claim similar to the one advanced by the Board, tersely reversing a summary judgment that the plaintiff's causes of action had prescribed. *Lewis* involved a canal servitude agreement that provided that the canal "shall not be more than sixty-five feet wide." In 1957, the canal exceeded its permissible width by thirty feet. When the landowner sued, in 1985, the intermediate appellate court affirmed summary judgment on the ground that the plaintiff's claims had prescribed. The Louisiana Supreme Court, however, granted certiorari, reversed the summary judgment, and remanded the case to the district court with instructions to refer the exception of prescription to the merits. *Lewis,* 532 So.2d at 754 (La.). From this result, we conclude that the life of the duty of a servitude owner not to aggravate the condition of the servient estate by allowing a canal to widen is coextensive with the life of the servitude. When such a duty exists, it is continuous.

Whether and to what extent the defendants' use of the canals caused the deterioration of the Board's property and aggravated the servient estate are questions to be determined in the light of this case's particular circumstances. [YIANNOPOULOS, PREDIAL SERVITUDES, *supra,* § 156. *See also Chevron U.S.A., Inc. v. Common L.P.,* 1999 WL 1021831 (E.D. La.) ("[C]ourts should take into account the situation of the estates, the agreement of the parties, the needs of the dominant estate at the time of the creation of the servitude, and the prejudice sustained by the owner of the servient estate."). This is a fact-intensive inquiry best left to the district court or jury.] As the district court made no factual findings on this point, even a *de novo* appellate review of this issue would be improvident. It is enough for us to conclude that it was improper for the district court to grant summary judgment on the basis that, because the contracts did not expressly impose a continuing duty, any contract claim had prescribed.

d. Damages Recoverable; Prescriptive Period

Even if the district court determines, on remand, that Koch and Columbia are under a continuing duty not to aggravate the servient estate, effectively rendering prescription irrelevant for liability purposes, prescription may nevertheless matter when it comes to damages. [*See R.J. Reynolds Tobacco Co. v. Hudson*, 314 F.2d 776, 781 (5th Cir.1963) (stating that where alleged offense was a continuing tort, parties may recover for the damages sustained within the applicable prescriptive period before suit was filed).] The prescriptive period governing a claim for aggravation of a servient estate is not yet well established in Louisiana.

When adjudicating a claim for which state law provides the rule of decision, federal courts are bound to apply the law as interpreted by the state's highest court; but if the state's highest court has not spoken on a particular issue, we must make an "Erie guess" and determine as best we can what the highest court of the state would be most likely to decide. The district court's task on remand will be to "attempt to predict state law, not to create or modify it." In making that attempt, a federal court "may look to the decisions of intermediate state courts for guidance." Indeed, "a decision by an intermediate appellate state court is a datum for ascertaining state law which is not to be disregarded by a federal court unless it is convinced by other persuasive data that the highest court of the state would decide otherwise."

Only one intermediate appellate Louisiana court has ruled on the length of the prescriptive period for a claim of aggravation to the servient estate. In *Stephens v. Int'l Paper Co.*, 542 So.2d 35 (La. App. 2 Cir. 1989), the court held that the duty not to aggravate the servient estate was a "general duty rather than a specific contractual duty or obligation assumed by the owner of the servitude," making the action *ex delicto* and thus prescriptable in one year, rather than *ex contractu* and thus prescriptable in ten years. This distinction — between general legal duties and specific contractual ones — is foundational for the distinction in Louisiana between delictual and contractual actions:

> The classical distinction between "damages ex contractu" and "damages ex delicto" is that the former flow from the breach of a special obligation contractually assumed by the obligor, whereas the latter flow from the violation of a general duty owed to all persons.

[*Davis*, 149 So.2d at 254.]

The *Stephens* court, however, may have misapplied this fundamental principle, and the district court may be persuaded that if the Louisiana Supreme Court were to consider this issue, it would adopt the opposite rule. For even though the servitude agreements here do not expressly impose on the grantees an affirmative duty actively to prevent the canals from widening, the duty to avoid aggravating a servient estate is not one that is owed to all persons under the law, but is one that is owed only to the servient estate holder by the grantee as a result of the conventional (contractual) relationship of the parties. Here, the parties are not neighbors, and the property interests involved here are not two contiguous but separately owned estates that have reciprocal obligations of vicinage. The fact that, as imposed here, the duty to avoid aggravation is supplied by the Civil Code and is also applicable to all servitudes may not mean that the parties' relationships and the duties they owe each other are general. Rather, as we observed at the outset, this case arises out of free choices to enter into conventional relationships.

When faced with this issue, the Louisiana Supreme Court might determine that ten years is the appropriate prescriptive period for an action by the grantor of a servitude against the grantee for aggravation of the servient estate. If it did so, that conclusion would be bolstered by the fact that prescription of the servitude itself for nonuse is a ten-year prescription [LA. CIV.CODE ANN. art. 753 (West 1980).]: A coextensive prescription period for damage to the servient estate by the neglect of the dominant estate holder would be logical. On remand, the district court should address whether, for damages-calculation purposes, the Board's cause of action for aggravation of its servient estate is governed by a prescriptive period of one year or of ten years.

2. Delict (Tort)

[In this portion of the decision, the court analyzed the defendants' assertion of prescription in relation to the plaintiff's claims arising in tort, the doctrine of *contra non valentum*, questions of actual notice and constructive notice, and the dispute between the parties as to whether this case involves a continuing tort. The court concluded that the district court erred in granting summary judgment in favor of the defendants on all of these issues. Eds.]

Conclusion

We agree with the district court that the servitude agreements here at issue do not expressly impose on Columbia and Koch the duty to prevent the canals from widening and eroding adjoining marshland. Whether, in the absence of an express contractual duty, the suppletive law of Louisiana might here impose such a duty remains to be resolved, as does the question whether such a duty might in turn render the failure to maintain canal banks a continuing tort. Because this case presents several genuine issues of material fact—not the least of which implicate actual or constructive knowledge of damage and its causation—with respect to prescription as well as duty, in tort and in contract, summary judgment was not providently granted. We remand this action for further proceedings consistent with this opinion.

REVERSED and REMANDED; MOTION DENIED.

Notes and Questions

1. In *Terrebonne Parish School Board v. Columbia Gulf Transmission*, 290 F.3d 303, 315–17 (5th Cir. 2002), the court held that the holder of a pipeline servitude, in the absence of any contrary language in the servitude agreement, has a duty *not to aggravate the condition of the servient estate* by allowing a pipeline canal dredged under the authority of the servitude agreement to widen beyond the specified width of the canal or the servitude itself. Are you convinced by the court's reasoning that the decision in *Ryan v. Southern Natural Gas Co.*, 879 F.2d 162 (5th Cir. 1989) is distinguishable from the situation in *Terrebonne Parish School Board*?

2. In yet another decision, the United States Fifth Circuit Court of Appeal determined that the holder of a pipeline servitude acquired by expropriation was also subject to the continuing duties imposed by Articles 743 and 745 of the Louisiana Civil Code to use that servitude in a manner that does not unreasonably injure the rights of the servient estate owner and not to aggravate the condition of the servient estate. *Rose v. Tennessee Gas Pipeline Co.*, 508 F.3d 773, 778 (5th Cir. 2007).

3. In recent years, disputes between landowners and private companies holding right-of-way servitudes that grant the servitude holder the right to dredge a canal in connection with construction, operation and maintenance of a pipeline or for purposes of navigation have become more frequent as marsh erosion caused by the widening canals has been recognized as a threat to the survival of Louisiana's working coast. For the assertion that knowledge of the potential harms caused by canals date as far back as 1925, see generally Oliver A. Houck, *The Reckoning: Oil and Gas Development in the Louisiana Coastal Zone*, 28 Tul. Envtl. L. J. 185, 194–210 (2015) (reviewing the history of oil and gas canal construction and operation in Louisiana).

In 2015, landowners owning 20,000 acres of land in Southeastern Louisiana filed a significant lawsuit against multiple pipeline companies that held right-of-way servitudes on the land owned by the plaintiffs. The servitudes authorized the construction and operation of pipelines and dredge canals. In 2017, after removal of the suit to federal court, the United States District Court for the Eastern District of Louisiana found that: (1) the servitude holders had an implied duty to maintain the canals constructed pursuant to certain of the servitude agreements; (2) the servitude holders breached this duty; and (3) the breach caused damage to the plaintiffs. *Vintage Assets, Inc. v. Tennessee Gas Pipeline Co., LLC*, CV 16-713, 2017 WL 3601215, at *7 (E.D. La. Aug. 22, 2017) (Milazzo, J.). On appeal, however, the federal district court ruling was vacated for lack of subject matter jurisdiction because there was not complete diversity of citizenship between the plaintiffs and defendants. *Vintage*

Assets, Inc. v. Tennessee Gas Pipeline Co., LLC, 18-30688, 2018 WL 6264375, at *1 (5th Cir. Oct. 2, 2018).

Because its decision was not vacated on the merits, however, the federal district court's reasoning may still enjoy persuasive authority in subsequent state court proceedings. It is noteworthy that the federal district court in *Vintage Assets* distinguished between two types of servitude agreements at issue in the case—those specifying that "open ditches or canals" were "not to exceed 40 feet in width" and those that did not contain "not to exceed" measurements for the canals or rights-of-way. With regard to the first set of servitudes, the court observed:

> Each allows the canals to be left open but contemplate a maximum width of the canals and rights-of-way. Three of the agreements prevent Plaintiffs from regrading the area over the pipelines. Just as in *Columbia Gulf*, the agreements are ambiguous as to Defendants' duty to maintain the canals and, indeed, evidence a failure to contemplate the effects of erosion.

Vintage Assets, 2017 WL 3601215, at *6. After reviewing the decision in *Terrebonne Parish School Board v. Columbia Gulf Transmission Co.*, the court concluded with respect to these agreements:

> It is well settled, though, that Louisiana's suppletive law on servitudes imposes "a continuing duty to refrain from injuring or aggravating a servient estate." The question of first impression before this Court then becomes whether the duty to refrain from aggravating the servient estate encompasses a duty to maintain canals and canal banks from eroding the servient estate. This Court finds that it is self-evident that allowing a canal to widen such that it encroaches on the servient estate or erodes the servient estate into open water constitutes aggravation. Accordingly, pursuant to suppletive law Defendants have a duty to maintain the canals and canal banks to prevent erosion, and therefore aggravation, of the servient estate.
>
> There is no dispute that defendants did not maintain the canals at issue and allowed the canals to widen to widths far exceeding that set forth in the servitude agreements. Indeed, some of the canals have widened into open water. Defendants do not dispute these facts. Accordingly, this Court holds that Defendants had a duty to maintain the canals, and that duty was breached. Plaintiffs are entitled to judgment on their claims for breach of the 1953, 1958, 1964 and 1970 contracts.

Id. at *7 (citations omitted). However, because the "no measurement contracts" also gave the defendants the right to leave the canals open, the court held that these agreements were comparable to those at issue in *Ryan v. Southern National Gas Co.* and therefore, absolved the defendants of any obligation to backfill or dam those canals. *Vintage Assets*, 2017 WL 3601215, at *7. In due course, Louisiana state courts may soon be called upon to confront the difficult interpretative issues raised by *Ryan*, *Terrebonne Parish School Board* and now *Vintage Assets*.

3. The Servient Estate Owner

The most significant obligation imposed on the owner of the servient estate is one of noninterference with the use of the servitude. Article 748 of the Louisiana Civil Code articulates this obligation:

Art. 748. Noninterference by the owner of servient estate

The owner of the servient estate may do nothing tending to diminish or make more inconvenient the use of the servitude.

If the original location has become more burdensome for the owner of the servient estate, or if it prevents him from making useful improvements on his estate, he may provide another equally convenient location for the exercise of the servitude which the owner of the dominant estate is bound to accept. All expenses of relocation are borne by the owner of the servient estate.

La. Civ. Code art. 748 (1977).

The content of the first paragraph of this provision complements the civiliter principle. While the owner of the dominant estate is bound not to make the servitude more burdensome, the owner of the servient estate likewise may do nothing tending to diminish or inconvenience the dominant estate owner's right to exercise the servitude. What happens if the owner of the servient estate agrees to make the works necessary for a servitude at his own expense and then changes his mind? Consider the following scenario.

Suppose Bruce owned a piece of property next to a public road. Carol, his neighbor, asked him for a servitude of passage so she could build a private dirt road across his land. Bruce did not mind giving Carol some right to cross his land, but he worried that Carol would not take good care of the road. She might build a shoddy road and not make the necessary repairs. Bruce was also afraid that Carol's construction of the road would damage his yard. In the act establishing the conventional predial servitude, Bruce therefore agreed to build the road in exchange for the payment of a sum of money and to maintain the road himself. Bruce was happy with this arrangement, but after he died his children no longer wanted to be bothered with road repairs. What alternatives do they have? One solution is provided by Article 770 of the Louisiana Civil Code. This provision allows Bruce's children to free themselves of the obligation to maintain the road by abandoning ownership of the road to Carol. As the new owner, Carol will be responsible for repairs and other matters concerning the road. *See* La. Civ. Code art. 770 (1977) ("A predial servitude is extinguished by the abandonment of the servient estate, or the part on which the servitude is exercised. It must be evidenced by a written act. The owner of the dominant estate is bound to accept it and confusion takes place."). Can you see any downsides to this solution? What recommendations would you make to Bruce's children before they abandon the servient estate to Carol under Article 770?

Confronted with disputes about the extent of the use and exercise of conventional predial servitude, Louisiana courts typically state that they will analyze the contractual agreement between the original parties to determine the intended scope of the servitude:

> [T]he use and extent of a predial servitude are regulated by the title by which they are created and in the absence of such regulation, they are governed by the rules set forth in LSA-C.C. arts. 698 through 774. It is only where the title does not specify the extent of the right and the mode of its exercise that the extent of the servitude of passage is subject to interpretation based on what is suitable for the kind of traffic necessary for the reasonable use of the dominant estate.

> Thus, when a predial servitude is created by contract, courts have found that the title by which the servitude was created regulated the use and extent of such a servitude. Furthermore, only if the title was silent as to the extent and manner of use of the servitude have the courts resorted to an examination of the intent of the parties to determine the purpose of the servitude. When the title provides the exact dimensions of the area affected by the servitude, that contract must be given full effect. The owner of the servient estate may not, by unilateral action, effectively take over the unused areas of the servitude by establishing permanent structures thereon.

Dupont v. Hebert, 984 So.2d 800, 807 (La. App. 1 Cir. 2008), *writ denied*, 980 So.2d 695 (La. 2008) (citations omitted).

In the two cases below, consider the scope of the servitude, the intended use by the dominant estate owner and the types of "interferences" tolerated by the courts.

Hymel v. St. John the Baptist Parish School Board
303 So.2d 588 (La. App. 4 Cir. 1974)

SCHOTT, Judge. Plaintiffs instituted these injunction proceedings to prevent defendant from interfering with their use of a right-of-way. In answer defendant denied it impeded the use of the servitude. After trial plaintiffs were awarded a judgment for only part of the relief they sought and they have appealed.

Plaintiffs are the owners of a tract of ground in St. John the Baptist Parish. This tract which they cultivate as sugar cane farmers is directly to the rear of a smaller tract owned by defendant which has constructed and is operating a public school on the tract. Plaintiffs and defendant derive their respective titles from a common ancestor in title, Willie Hymel. When Willie Hymel sold the smaller tract to the defendant in 1963, he reserved a servitude in the following words:

> "There is hereby reserved by vendor for himself, his heirs, successors, and assigns, a right of way 25 feet in width along the westerly line of the above property to afford ingress and egress in favor of the property situated south of the herein conveyed property."

The Succession of Willie Hymel later sold to plaintiffs the rear tract together with the servitude.

A surveyor employed to examine the situation noted on a plot of survey the location, dimensions and elevations of various encroachments on the right-of-way. They consisted of a chain-link fence across the width of the servitude in the front, an overhang of the school roof, encroaching on the right-of-way by 1.7 feet in the front and increasing to 2.9 feet in the rear for a distance of 70 feet and at a height of 9.5 feet above ground level; three drop inlets, extending from 2 inches above the natural ground to 11 inches above, all connected with an underground drainage pipe on the east side of the right-of-way near the school building and on the west side a drainage ditch 3 feet wide and 3 feet deep extending entirely along the length of the property line, located entirely within the right-of-way and 1 foot inside the line. Other testimony established that school automobiles were regularly parked on the front portion of the right-of-way.

Plaintiff, Lynn Hymel, testified that the right-of-way is not used constantly but is used to some extent; that the amount of use fluctuates with the various agricultural seasons, such as planting time, cultivation time and harvest time; that the vehicles using the passage are cane cutters, about 13 feet in height and 10 feet in width, cane haulers or trailers about the same size and tractors of various sizes including one used as a three row tractor with draw boards and having a width of at least 20 feet; that all of the right-of-way is necessary for plaintiffs' use; and that various obstacles in the right-of-way prevent two of his vehicles from passing abreast on the servitude from the front of the school building to the rear.

The trial court, recognizing plaintiffs' right-of-way, permanently enjoined defendant from interfering with plaintiffs' peaceful use of it as follows:

"(a) The barrier fence across the entire right of way is to be removed.

(b) The parking of vehicles on and across said right of way is to cease and said vehicles are to be parked elsewhere.

(c) The building overhang is to remain as is and defendant school board is not required to remove same, provided that said plaintiff shall have no interference and peaceful use of said right of way subject to said use bearing in mind that the safety of the school children shall be accorded by plaintiffs in the use of said right of way and specifically at no time shall two vehicles, namely, canecutters pass side by side.

(d) That in accordance with (c) supra the defendant school board is to abandon (by covering up) or remove and cover up said drainage devices currently in use or on said right of way with an end in view to separate defendants property from the right of way with a small ditch or swale in order to afford drainage.

(e) Furthermore, it is ordered adjudged and decreed that the defendant school board strongly consider the installation of a fence separating their property from the right of way in question in order to afford a workable solution with plaintiffs use of their right of way and to afford the maximum degree of safety to the school children.

Each party is to bear his own respective court costs."

Plaintiffs appeal from sub-section (c) and (d) of this judgment and from that portion taxing costs. They specify errors in that the trial judge did not order the removal of the overhang, in that he exceeded his authority in enjoining them from using the right of way as they see fit, and in not taxing court costs, including the expert witnesses' fee against the defendant.

In denying plaintiffs' prayer that defendant be ordered to remove the overhang the trial judge gave the following reasons:

> "As far as the building overhang, it is not of such a degree that would warrant removal. The evidence preponderates that said right of way can be used without same impeding said use. The court will not order the overhand removed. To do so would cast an unreasonable burden upon a situation of which the free use of the servitude can be had without forcing removal of the overhang."

Our discussion of the problem begins with LSA-C.C.Art. 777 which provides:

> "The owner of the estate which owes the servitude can do nothing tending to diminish its use, or to make it more inconvenient.

> "Thus he can not change the condition of the premises, nor transfer the exercise of the servitude to a place different from that on which it was assigned in the first instance.

> "Yet if this primitive assignment has become more burdensome to the owner of the estate which owes the servitude, or if he is thereby prevented from making advantageous repairs on his estate, he may offer to the owner of the other estate a place equally convenient for the exercise of his rights, and the owner of the estate to which the servitude is due can not refuse it."

Defendant contends that under this article plaintiffs have the burden to prove that the overhang has diminished the use of the servitude or made it more inconvenient and that they failed to carry this burden. Defendant relies on evidence which demonstrated that the servitude was used only sparingly and at particular times of the year for the passage of agricultural vehicles and that with the removal of the other impediments, plaintiffs will experience no difficulty whatsoever in the passage of their equipment through the right-of-way. While it may be that two of the larger vehicles may not pass abreast of each other in the area where the school building is located, the testimony is that there is never an occasion when two such vehicles must pass abreast because the servitude is so sparingly used.

On the basis of these facts and the rationale in *Kaffie v. Pioneer Bank & Trust Company*, 184 So.2d 595 (La. App. 2nd Cir. 1965), *Appeal after Remand* 204 So.2d 54 (1967), *Writ Refused*, 251 La. 685, 205 So.2d 605 (1968), defendant contends that a result in its favor is clearly indicated. We do not agree and hold that the trial court erred in this part of his judgment.

When the right-of-way "is the result of a contract, its extent . . . is regulated by the contract." C.C.Art. 722. It is only where the contract does not designate the width of the right-of-way that its extent is subject to interpretation based upon previous use of the servitude. C.C.Art. 780. Pursuant to these articles there could hardly be any doubt that plaintiffs are entitled to clear passage at ground level for the full width of 25 feet. Nor is there a sound basis for a distinction as to encroachments above ground level.

While the Civil Code provides that ownership of the soil carries with it ownership of all that is directly above it, Art. 505, we have no codal authority for the proposition that a right of passage or right-of-way confers the right to all that is above the soil. It seems that Art. 722 in defining right-of-way as a servitude by virtue of which one has the right to pass on foot or in a vehicle or to drive beasts or carts through the estate of another implies that the right-of-way does include something above ground level, at least sufficient to accommodate such things as carts and vehicles.

The expressed purpose of the right-of-way in this case was to provide plaintiffs' ancestor with ingress to and egress from the property to the rear of defendant's property. The uncontroverted evidence is to the effect that plaintiffs' property was always used for sugar cane production and that plaintiffs' sugar cane cutter and their trailer used for hauling the cane are 13 feet high. These are precisely the vehicles and cart spoken of in C.C.Art. 722. Plaintiffs' ancestor reserved a 25 foot right-of-way to accommodate his equipment and they are now being made to suffer a reduction of their right-of-way. Surely this is a clear cut violation of the spirit if not the letter of the law embodied in the Codal Articles cited.

The trial court's reasoning that the overhang "is not of such a *degree* that would warrant removal" is not consistent with C.C.Art. 777 which provides that the owner "can do *nothing tending to diminish*" the servitude's use. The word "tend" means to move or extend in a certain direction or to be disposed or inclined. It cannot be said that defendant's construction of their overhand well below the height of plaintiffs' equipment is not even inclined to diminish plaintiffs' use of the servitude, when as a fact plaintiffs are prevented from using from 6.8% of the right-of-way on one end of the overhang to 11.6% on the other end for a distance of 70 feet.

We therefore conclude that there is no basis for permitting defendant to construct any obstacles within the 25 foot roadway at such height which might impede the passage of any equipment regardless of its height, and plaintiffs are entitled to an order to defendant to remove the encroaching overhang.

As to the remainder of paragraph (c) of the judgment, it limits the plaintiffs in the use of the right-of-way by requiring that it cannot be used in any way detrimental to the safety of the school children and specifically at no time shall two vehicles, namely cane cutters, pass side by side. There was no issue raised herein that plaintiffs were using the servitude in any manner which may create a hazard to the school children. As a matter of fact, their testimony evidences the reverse situation. Plaintiffs, being fearful that they may in some fashion damage either the school board property and presumably thus endanger the children, have hesitated to use the property in full, and have been using other means of egress and ingress to their farmlands because of these considerations. Although we appreciate the concern of the trial judge, we believe the inclusion of the vague restriction of use without regard to safety of the school children goes beyond the pleadings and the issues of this case. Likewise, the restriction against two vehicles passing side by side has no basis in the pleadings or the evidence. Even so it would be inconsistent with the nature of plaintiffs' right-of-way to impose limitation on its use not found in the contract which created it.

Finally, the trial judge's concern that defendant's removal of the overhang would be "an unreasonable burden" is not supported by any evidence as to the scope or cost of such work.

Accordingly, the judgment appealed from will be amended so as to delete the entirety of paragraph (c) and to order defendant to remove that part of the overhang of its building which encroaches upon plaintiffs' right-of-way.

While plaintiffs appealed from paragraph (d) of the judgment they specify no error in this connection and we are unable to perceive any inconvenience or harm suffered by plaintiffs from that portion of the judgment. . . .

Accordingly, paragraph (c) of the judgment appealed from is reversed and there is judgment in favor of plaintiffs, ordering defendant, St. John the Baptist Parish School Board, to remove that portion of the overhang of its building which encroaches upon plaintiffs' right-of-way. Paragraph (d) of the judgment is affirmed and all other respects the judgment is affirmed, except that all costs including the fee of plaintiffs' expert and the costs of this appeal are to be taxed against defendant.

Reversed in part, affirmed in part.

Toups v. Abshire

979 So.2d 616 (La. App. 3 Cir. 2008)

EZELL, Judge. In this matter, Earl Toups appeals the decision of the trial court refusing to order the removal of alleged encumbrances on his servitude of passage over the land of Wade and Melinda Abshire. For the following reasons, we affirm the decision of the trial court.

Mr. Toups owns an enclosed estate with no access to a public road. The land has a thirty-foot wide by one-hundred fifty-eight foot long servitude of passage running over the southern thirty feet of the property of the Abshires. The servitude was created in a 1974 partition of a previous, larger estate. Located on the servitude is an approximately seventeen-foot wide crushed limestone road. The area encumbered by the servitude also serves as the only access point for the Abshires to a public road.

In 2003, disputes arose between the Toupses and the Abshires regarding the use of the thirty-foot servitude. At that time, a stipulated judgment was signed by the parties ordering the Abshires to remove speed bumps placed by them on the road, setting the speed limit on the road at ten miles-per-hour, and declaring that Mr. Toups could widen the road at his expense if he deemed necessary, with the restriction that the expansion could be in a southernly direction only. This judgment was not appealed.

After the stipulated judgment was entered, the Abshires removed the existing speed bumps, but the Toupses and their guests disregarded the speed limit set by the judgment. The parties remained confrontational, resulting in this present suit wherein Mr. Toups sought to have alleged encumbrances on the servitude removed, namely a drainage ditch running along the road, a culvert placed by the Abshires where their driveway meets the road, and a fence running along the servitude. After hearing the testimony of the parties and examining the property in question, the trial court ruled that the Abshires had not encumbered the reasonable use of the servitude and that due to the constant speeding along the road, two speed bumps were ordered to be placed at either end of the Abshires' property to enforce the speed limit set by the stipulated judgment. From this decision, Mr. Toups appeals.

Mr. Toups asserts two assignments of error on appeal. His first assignment of error is vague and unclear as to what alleged error he wants corrected by this court, but he seems to claim that the trial court erred in failing to have alleged impediments to the full use of the thirty-foot servitude removed. His next assignment of error, that the trial court erred in preparing and signing an ex parte judgment regarding the installation of speed bumps, was not briefed and, therefore, need not be addressed. Uniform Rules—Court of Appeal, Rule 2-12.4.

Mr. Toups apparently believes that he is entitled to use the entirety of the thirty-foot servitude as he sees fit, unencumbered by the Abshires in any way, shape or form. We disagree. Louisiana Civil Code Article 705 (emphasis added) describes the conventional servitude of passage, or right of way, and the general parameters of its use:

> The servitude of passage is the right for the benefit of the dominant estate whereby persons, animals, or vehicles are permitted to pass through the servient estate. *Unless the title provides otherwise, the extent of the right and the mode of its exercise shall be suitable for the kind of traffic necessary for the reasonable use of the dominant estate.*

"The owner of the servient estate may do nothing tending to diminish or make more inconvenient the use of the servitude." La. Civ. Code art. 748. *See also* La. Civ. Code art. 651. However, the dominant estate must exercise its rights "in a way least inconvenient for the servient estate." La. Civ. Code art. 743.

The issue of whether any alleged encumbrances made the use of the servitude more inconvenient for the Toupses was an issue of fact. *See Cathcart v. Magruder,* 06-986, 06-987, 06-988 (La. App. 1 Cir. 5/4/07), 960 So.2d 1032. Therefore, we will review this decision using a manifest error standard of review. *Stobart v. State through Dept. of Transp. and Dev.,* 617 So.2d 880 (La. 1993).

As trier of fact, the trial court ruled in favor of the Abshires, finding that the installation of the culvert, fence, and driveway did not restrict Mr. Toups's use of the servitude. To the contrary, the trial court found that the roughly seventeen-foot wide limestone road was wide enough for Mr. Toups to reasonably use for his tractor and trailers, even when hauling the seventeen-foot blade. The trial court found that the biggest problem for Mr. Toups in accessing the right-of-way was nothing done by the Abshires, but rather a ditch owned by Mr. Toups and a pole placed by him to mark the property line. These findings are supported by the record before this court. Accordingly, we can find no manifest error in the trial court's decision.

The same considerations apply to the trial court's determination that the installation of speed bumps was required to protect the Abshires' child from speeders using the right of passage. The record established that the Toupses and their guests frequently violated the ten mile-per-hour speed limit established in the stipulated judgment, posing a potential threat to the Abshires' young child, and that because of the isolated location of the lots in question, local law enforcement could not police the area with any kind of regularity. We agree with the trial court that the speed bumps in no way render the passage unsuitable for the kind of traffic necessary for the reasonable use of the Toups's estate and are, in fact, necessary to enforce the stipulated judgment agreed to by Mr. Toups. Again, there is no manifest error in this ruling.

For the above reasons, the decision of the trial court is hereby affirmed. Costs of this appeal are assessed against Earl Toups.

AFFIRMED.

GENOVESE, Judge, concurring in part, dissenting in part. I concur in the majority opinion except for the "speed bumps" issue from which I respectfully dissent. There is no legal authority for the trial court to order traffic control devices, i.e., speed bumps, when ruling upon the rights, duties, and obligations of the parties in a servitude of passage case. Traffic control is not the function of the trial court in a servitude of passage case. The result of this case creates an intriguing issue as to liability, *vel non,* for potential personal injury and/or property damage sustained by a motorist traversing these speed bumps in the use of this servitude?

I would affirm the trial court except for the court-ordered speed bumps which I would reverse and order removed.

Notes and Questions

1. In *Hymel v. St. John the Baptist School Board,* 303 So.2d 588 (La. App. 4 Cir. 1974), Willie Hymel and the school board clearly created a predial servitude. In the act of sale by which Hymel sold a tract of land to the school board, he reserved a right of passage "for himself, his heirs, successors, and assigns." Moreover, the act established the width of the servitude at twenty-five feet and its location "along the

westerly line" of the servient estate. The act even noted the purpose of the servitude: "to afford ingress and egress." Why would the school board later deny that it had impeded the use of the servitude? Do you think that the appellate court in *Hymel* was unconcerned about the safety of the children who attended the school?

2. Disputes about gates, fences and other encroachments erected by a servient estate owner on land burdened with an affirmative predial servitude are common. Courts sometimes attempt to balance the needs of the servient estate owner to make such constructions for purposes of security or safety with the needs of the dominant estate owner to exercise the servitude conveniently. In other instances, as we can see in *Hymel*, courts will interpret and enforce conventional servitude agreements strictly, especially when the original agreement establishing the servitude specifies the precise dimensions or location of the servitude.

In *Thiels v. Dennis*, 29 So.3d 715 (La. App. 3 Cir. 2010), a court held that a servient estate owner must remove not only the gates across a fifty-foot-wide servitude of passage but also the brick columns erected on the servitude that narrowed its width to eleven feet. In *Dupont v. Hebert*, 984 So.2d 800, 808 (La. App. 1 Cir. 2008), a court, relying on *Hymel*, held that a servient estate owner's construction of "a fence, a concrete slab, a wooden building, and a levee for his turtle pond within the 20-foot servitude of passage" constituted an unauthorized encroachment on the servitude and, therefore, his "turtle farm's constructions" had to be removed. Why was the court more willing to consider the needs of the servient estate owner and tolerate the servient estate owners' installation of the speed bumps in *Toups v. Abshire*, 979 So.2d 616 (La. App. 3 Cir. 2008)?

4. Servitude Relocation

The second paragraph of Article 748 of the Louisiana Civil Code grants the owner of the servient estate a powerful right to relocate a servitude if the original location has become "more burdensome" for the servient estate owner or "prevents him from making useful improvements on his estate," as long as the new location proposed by the servient estate owner is "equally convenient" to the dominant estate and the expenses of relocation are borne by the servient estate owner. La. Civ. Code art. 748 (1977). Louisiana doctrine and jurisprudence have recognized the significance of this right.

In *Denegre v. Louisiana Public Service Comm'n*, 242 So.2d 832 (La. 1970), the servient estate owners sought to relocate several conventional servitudes providing railroad rights of way across their property so that the potential of the servient estate for commercial development could be enhanced. The railroad carriers had no objection, but the dominant estate owners (adjoining property owners and customers of the railroads) objected. Following a hearing, the public service commission denied the requested relocation on the ground that the public's transportation interests would be adversely affected. A district court and a majority of the Louisiana Supreme Court affirmed. *Id.* at 834–36. Justice Albert Tate, Jr., a towering figure associated with the civil law renaissance in Louisiana, wrote a separate concurrence to underscore the right of a servient owner "to secure judicial adjudication under Civil Code article 777 [the predecessor of Article 748 of the Louisiana Civil Code] for a relocation to a less burdensome place on his property." *Id*. at 838. Putting aside the public and administrative law issues, Justice Tate articulated the competing interests under Article 777:

> The petitioner bought property subject to a railway servitude and therefore of lessened industrial value. He seeks to greatly enhance the property's value by relocating the trackage. The opponents' predecessors sold the property at a lesser price because of these tracks. They are not enthusiastic about this windfall to result to the petitioner if he can secure the relief sought. More-over, if the petitioner's property becomes available for industrial use, their own adjacent property loses the relatively greater value it has because of its unique availability for industrial use in the vicinity.

Denegre, 242 So.2d at 837–38 (Tate, J., concurring). Justice Tate recognized that Article 777 of the 1870 Civil Code required a court to make a utilitarian determination about the social value of the respective stakes which could very well upset the expectations and reliance interests of dominant estate owners.

Justice Tate also corrected "erroneous dicta" in the majority decision seem-ingly limiting application of Article 777 of the 1870 Civil Code to servitudes estab-lished by destination of the owner, judgment, or prescription—a result that would have rendered the provision meaningless for other conventional servitudes. Cit-ing Planiol, Tate explained that the "plain intent of [Article 777] is to permit the court to displace the site of the previous servitude, even if established by agreement or judgment, when the servitude is localized at a place too burdensome upon the encumbered estate." *Denegre*, 242 So.2d at 838–39. In summary, Tate concluded:

> Thus, all conventional servitudes are created subject to the possibility of judicial modification in the future.
>
> This is in accord with fundamental civilian principles. The interests of society are furthered by the free use of the land by private owners for its most advantageous social utility. The full ownership of land is favored, as against restrictions upon its use imposed decades or even centuries in the past; provided that no prejudice is caused to property rights conferred by conventional agreement of the parties or predecessors in title.

Denegre, 242 So.2d at 839. Fully chastened by Justice Tate's mini-treatise, the entire court, in a brief per curium opinion on rehearing, recalled its previous statement appearing to preclude the application of Article 777 of the 1870 Civil Code to con-ventional servitudes in general.

In subsequent decisions, the Louisiana Supreme Court continued to grapple with the difficult balancing required for the relocation of servitudes. In one case, the court rejected a servient estate owner's request to relocate a servitude for a private navigational canal, reasoning that under Article 777 of the 1870 Civil Code the alternative proposal for the canal route was not only "less convenient but more dangerous" than the original. *Discon v. Saray, Inc.*, 265 So.2d 765, 771 (La. 1972). In another case, the court approved a request by a servient estate owner to relocate a servitude of passage along a rustic, tree-lined, mile-long road, servicing an otherwise enclosed riverside estate, because the relocation facilitated the servient owner's plans to create a residential subdivision. *Ogden v. Bankston*, 398 So.2d 1037 (La. 1981). The servient estate owner had sought the relocation because the original placement of the road prevented ten lots in the proposed subdivision from having a "full" or typical depth of about 150 feet, which would have reduced the developer's profit margin. Justice Dixon, writing for the majority, approved the relocation:

> Yet, under C.C. 777, it is clear that the primitive assignment of the servitude has in fact become more burdensome. When the servitude was originally created in 1923, it is doubtful that the owner of the servient estate contemplated the use of his rural property as a suburban neighborhood. *The potential for development arose when circumstances changed*: it cannot be doubted that the existence of a country lane prevents an altogether different imposition upon the owner of property when it runs through a residential subdivision rather than over rural undeveloped land.

Id. at 1044 (emphasis added). Do you think that changed circumstances should justify relocation of a conventional predial servitude?

The South African decision below enunciates a rule that allows a servient estate owner to relocate a servitude unilaterally at his own expense. Notably, the rule deviates from the common law of England and much of the United States. Permitting unilateral relocation has been accepted not only in many mixed jurisdictions around the word but also in the RESTATEMENT (THIRD) OF PROPERTY: SERVITUDES §4.8(3) (2000). Should the owner of the servient estate always be allowed to move the location of the servitude if the requisites of Article 748 of the Louisiana Civil Code have been established?

Linvestment CC v. Hammersley

(634/2006) [2008] ZASCA (The Supreme Court of Appeal of South Africa, 28 February 2008) (footnotes omitted)

HEHER JA: The issue in this appeal, simply stated, is whether the owner of a servient tenement can, of his own volition, change the route of a defined right of way registered against the title deeds of his property.

The appellant is the registered owner of Portion 136 of the Farm Driefontein, registration division FS, Province of KwaZulu-Natal, in extent 25,0912 hectares held under Certificate of Consolidated Title No T66117/2004.

The first respondent is the registered owner of the Remainder of Sub 3 of the Farm Driefontein No 1389, KwaZulu-Natal, in extent 20,9085 hectares held under

Deed of Transfer No T19322/1992 and Deed of Transfer No T28469/1998. The second respondent, her husband, apparently resides on this property.

The appellant's property is subject to two registered servitudes in favour of the first respondent's property . . . The two servitudes are so located as to constitute a continuous strip of land over which the rights can be exercised.

In its declaration in the High Court the appellant, as plaintiff, made the following allegations:

1. The plaintiff had given notice to the first defendant of its intention to amend the course of the servitudes from that shown on the diagrams to [another route over the plaintiff's property].

2. The plaintiff had tendered all costs of amending the registration of the servitudes, including the costs of sonable.

5. The present servitudes constituted undue inconvenience to the plaintiff.

6. The substitution of the proposed servitudes for the present servitudes would not excessively inconvenience the defendants.

7. The plaintiff is entitled to a declaration which will permit it to substitute the proposed servitudes for the existing servitudes.

In the premises the appellant claimed an order declaring that it was entitled to substitute the proposed servitude route for the existing route.

The respondents pleaded that they were under no obligation to accept the alternative route and that the declaration sought was not competent in law since the defined route could only be changed by mutual consent.

For the purposes of adjudication by the High Court the parties agreed that the appellant's averments relating to the unreasonableness of the respondents' refusal, the undue inconvenience to the appellant of the existing route and the absence of excessive inconvenience to the first respondent of the proposed route, were not placed in issue.

The parties agreed that the question of whether the declaration was competent in law was to be tried as an issue separated in terms of Rule 33(1) according to a stated case containing the facts set out in paragraphs [2] to [6] of this introduction.

The High Court (Madondo AJ) answered the question in favour of the respondents and ordered the appellant to pay the costs.

With leave of the court *a quo* the appellant appealed to this Court against the whole of the judgment and the order made.

Mr Gorven, who appeared for the appellant, conceded that the established law is against his client. In *Gardens Estate Ltd v. Lewis* this Court said (*per* De Villiers AJA):

'A further question between the parties is: Did the Gardens Estate Syndicate have the right to deviate the pipe-line as it did in 1902? In my opinion it

had no such right. A definite servitude having originally been constituted,
it could only be altered by mutual consent. . . .

The first step in determining the nature and extent of a registered condition
is to examine its terms. In the present instance we are concerned with servitudes
of rights of way which are precisely defined in relation to the remainder of the
servient tenement by reference to surveyors' diagrams and leave no room for
uncertainty. . . .

In the event of his failing to persuade us of the correctness of his initial submission, Mr Gorven based an argument on s 25 (1) of the Constitution of the Republic
of South Africa. He contended that the effect of refusing to allow the appellant to
move the servitude to a more convenient place, was to restrict the free use of the
land over which the servitude presently extends; thereby it deprived the appellant of
a right to property.

But that cannot be so. The appellant acquired and, no doubt, paid for the property in the knowledge (actual or implied) that its right of ownership was limited by
the servitude. It is deprived of nothing by the proper interpretation of the servitude.
And if it had been a party to the agreement constituting the servitude, it would
have suffered no deprivation of its rights but only a limitation to which it had freely
consented.

The conclusion reached in *Gardens Estate Ltd v. Lewis* is also in accordance with
existing principle. As the law stands, once the servitutal rights of the parties are
unambiguously circumscribed by the terms of their agreement, a court will not
order a departure from such terms in order to bring about a lessening of the burden
on the servient property: *pacta sunt servanda* — *Van Rensburg en andere v. Taute en
andere* — except in the case of constitutional violations: *Barkhuizen v. Napier*.

Selikowitz J summarised the existing state of the law in *De Witt v. Knierim*:

'Whilst our law apparently seeks to promote the *bona fide* development by
an owner of his agricultural land and to optimise its utilization in the public interest, it also recognises and enforces the principle that once a right
has been given to another the grantor cannot either directly or indirectly
reappropriate it.'

That, however, is what the appellant seeks to do. . . .

The attempt of appellant's counsel to introduce the rule that servitudes must be
exercised *civiliter modo* as a means of justifying his client's attempt to remove the
right of way to a route more convenient to it, is misconceived. As Van den Heever J
pointed out in *Penny v. Brentwood Gardens Body Corporate*.

'Civility is not in law synonymous with a waiver of one's rights. . . .

According to existing principle, therefore, the conclusion which this Court
reached in *Gardens Estate Ltd v. Lewis* would appear to be unassailable. But the
judgment is founded on the unstated premise that the law expounded by Voet correctly reflected the common law of South Africa. The refinements brought about to

Roman-Dutch law in the century between the publication of Voet's Commentary and the occupation of the Cape in 1806 are not always readily ascertainable. Whether the relevant authorities were available to the judges in 1920 may be doubted since there exists evidence that that law, in so far as it related to the subject of relocation of servitudes, was, by 1806, no longer consistent with the inference which was properly drawn from *Voet* 8.3.8 in *Gardens Estate Ltd v. Lewis*.

In order to appreciate the force of the evidence some reference to history is necessary. After the kingdom of Holland threw off the French yoke early in the 19th century, an attempt was also made to replace French law which had applied there since 1809. A decision was taken to compile a new, indigenous code of law. A commission was appointed under the chairmanship of Prof J M Kemper of Leiden for this purpose. It completed a draft by 1816. The southern (Belgian) part of the country was, however, dissatisfied with the emphasis that it placed on Roman-Dutch law, and preferred instead a system closer to the French Code Civil. The committee published a revised draft in 1820 which also found no favour in the south. Hahlo and Kahn describe this draft as 'a distillation of pure Roman-Dutch law in its final stage of development'.

The Seventh Title of the revised draft is of particular significance in the present context.

> 1188. The owner of the servient tenement may not do anything by which the use of the servitude is rendered less useful or convenient.
>
> He may therefore not change the condition of the property, nor transfer the exercise of the servitude to or impose it upon any part of the property other than that on which it was originally laid.
>
> Nevertheless, when the original institution has become more burdensome to him, or hinders him in carrying out any necessary or useful repair, he may offer to those entitled to the right of servitude another equally good and convenient for their exercise, at his cost; an offer so made cannot be refused.

There is nothing in this passage, or, indeed, in the compilers' treatment of the nature of servitudes in Part 1 of the Seventh Title, to suggest an intention to draw a distinction between servitudes generally and specifically created. If art 1188 was, as it appears to have been, an authoritative statement of the Roman-Dutch private law at the date of the British occupation of the Cape, it contained principles which should have been applied in *Gardens Estate v. Lewis*. That it was apparently overlooked certainly justifies a reconsideration of the issue. . . .

The question of mitigating the burden of servitudes has been addressed in many systems of law, usually in statute or code. Although Kemper's draft was, for reasons which Prof de Vos explains, not adopted as the codified law in Holland, in 1838 a Burgerlijk Wetboek was adopted which contained many elements of the Napoleonic Code, including art 701. In the 19th century, Laurent [*Principles de Droit Civil Francais*, 2 ed (1876) para 277.], discussing art 701 of the French Code, said that that article dealt with mutability of title and commented:

'As the needs of the properties change, and society being concerned that servitudes do not hamper the changes which become necessary, the law must permit interested parties to modify the exercise of the servitude'.

According to Prof Meijers, (writing in the middle of the 20th century) the right of relocation of a defined servitude is 'recognized by most foreign codes' including Switzerland, Italy and Greece, subject to the duty of the servient owner to prove that the dominant owner's right of enjoyment would not thereby be reduced.

The Belgian Civil Code and the German BGB are to similar effect.

Scots law is discussed *in extenso* by Cusine and Paisley. There is apparently an unresolved dichotomy of authority between that which favours sanctity of contract and that which would allow a right to relocate on the grounds of manifest convenience to the servient owner and absence of detriment to the dominant proprietor. The authors debate the arguments for and against the respective views. Within the same legal environment, an instructive comparative survey ['A New Way: Servitude Relocation in Scotland and Louisiana' by John A Lovett 9 *EDIN LR* 352 (2004–5).] traces the progress of the law from the common Roman roots of Scotland and the state of Louisiana until the 21st century, showing how the tide is turning from strict adherence to contractual rights toward a utilitarian power of relocation that is judicially controlled or to legislative intervention having similar effect.

Even from this brief, and necessarily superficial, survey it is apparent that widespread civilised practice favours a flexible approach to the relocation of servitudes. If that flexibility is soundly based I think we would be wrong to adhere blindly to an inference drawn from the views of Voet expressed at the end of the 17th century, albeit affirmed as late as 1920 by this court.

I am persuaded that the interests of justice do indeed require a change in our established law on the subject. The rigid enforcement of a servitude when the sanctity of the contract or the strict terms of the grant benefit neither party but, on the contrary, operate prejudicially on one of them, seems to me indefensible. Servitudes are by their nature often the creation of preceding generations devised in another time to serve ends which must now be satisfied in a different environment. Imagine a right of way over a farm portion registered fifty years ago. Since then new public roads have been created providing new access to the dominant tenement, the nature of the environment has changed, the contracting parties have long gone. Why should a present owner, on no rational ground, be entitled to rely on his *summum ius* derived from the alleged sanctity of a contract or a grant or prescriptive acquisition to which he was not privy. Properly regulated flexibility will not set an unhealthy precedent or encourage abuse. Nor will it cheapen the value of registered title or prejudice third parties.

But even if the dominant and servient tenements still remain in the ownership of the original contracting parties, the opportunity for relocation should not be excluded if the circumstances prevailing at the time of the original agreement have changed and the dominant owner no longer possesses any acceptable reason to subject the servient property to the strict terms of the grant. It seems to me that, in such a case, the respective interests of the parties can fairly be regulated by reliance on the concepts of convenience and prejudice which I have introduced into the order.

In line with the extensive international trend of legal development in this respect, I therefore propose that, in circumstances falling within the problem posed by the stated case, the law be developed to ensure that injustice does not result. . . .

I would make the following order:

1. The order of the court *a quo* is set aside and replaced by the following—

    'It is declared that if the owner of a servient tenement offers a relocation of an existing defined servitude of right of way the dominant owner is obliged to accept such relocation provided that:

    (a) the servient owner is or will be materially inconvenienced in the use of his property by the maintenance of the *status quo ante*;

    (b) the relocation occurs on the servient tenement;

    (c) the relocation will not prejudice the owner of the dominant tenement;

    (d) the servient owner pays the costs attendant upon such relocation including those costs involved in amending the registration of the title deeds of the servient tenement (and, if applicable, the dominant tenement).'

2. The parties are ordered to pay their own costs in both courts.

Notes and Questions

1. In *Linvestment CC v. Hammersley*, (634/2006) [2008] ZASCA, the Supreme Court of Appeal of South Africa examined current South African law and decided that the law required further development. Identify the two major factors supporting the path forward charted by the court.

2. South Africa, like Scotland, Louisiana and Quebec, is also a mixed jurisdiction; however, its civil law base is uncodified. Note the court's reference to Louisiana law in *Linvestment*. Louisiana updated its law of servitudes in 1977, whereas South Africa's law on the subject of servitude relocation dates back to the 1920s and perhaps even to 1806.

3. For a more detailed discussion of servitude relocation in the United States, Scotland and Louisiana, see John A. Lovett, *A Bend in the Road, Easement Relocation and Pliability in the New Restatement (Third) of Property: Servitudes*, 38 CONN. L. REV. 1 (2005); John A. Lovett, *A New Way: Servitude Relocations in Scotland and Louisiana (A Comparative Mixed Jurisdiction Analysis)*, 9 EDIN. L. REV. 352 (2005). For a recent Louisiana judicial decision featuring Article 748 of the Louisiana Civil Code, see *Welch Planning and Zoning Comm. of East Baton Rouge Parish*, 220 So.3d 60, 64–68 (La. App. 1 Cir. 2017) (finding that a developer of a new subdivision on

a servient estate violated the principles underlying the article when it unilaterally relocated a thirty foot wide right-of-way benefitting three enclosed residential lots because the new rights-of-way provided by the developer over public roads were only twenty feet wide and thus diminished the utility of the servitude to the dominant estate).

4. Under the traditional common law majority rule in the United States, neither a servient estate owner nor a dominant estate owner can relocate or modify an easement unless the other party consents to the relocation or modification or such a right has been specifically reserved in the instrument creating the easement. JON W. BRUCE & JAMES W. ELY, JR., THE LAW OF EASEMENTS AND LICENSES IN LAND § 7.13 (2019); LEONARD A. JONES, A TREATISE ON THE LAW OF EASEMENTS §§ 343, 345, 352 (1898). Pursuant to Section 4.8(3) of the *Restatement (Third) of Property: Servitudes*, however, a servient estate owner may seek judicial approval to relocate an easement:

> Unless expressly denied by the terms of an easement, as defined in § 1.2, the owner of the servient estate is entitled to make reasonable changes in the location or dimensions of an easement, at the servient owner's expense, to permit normal use or development of the servient estate, but only if the changes do not
>
> (a) significantly lessen the utility of the easement,
>
> (b) increase the burdens on the owner of the easement in its use and enjoyment, or
>
> (c) frustrate the purpose for which the easement was created.

RESTATEMENT (THIRD) OF PROPERTY: SERVITUDES § 4.8(3) (2000). This nakedly utilitarian solution to the deadlock that often arises when an easement holder rejects a servient estate owner's request to change the location of an easement for purposes of facilitating the development or safe enjoyment of the servient estate has divided the courts that have confronted this issue since the promulgation of Section 4.8(3).

A number of state courts, including several supreme courts, have adopted strong versions of Section 4.8(3). *See Roaring Fork Club, L.P. v. St. Jude's Co.*, 36 P.3d 1229, 1237–39 (Col. 2001) (holding, however, that servient estate owners cannot engage in self-help and must, in the absence of easement holder consent, apply for a declaratory judgment to obtain judicial approval to relocate an irrigation easement); *MPM Builders, LLC v. Dwyer*, 809 N.E.2d 1053, 1057–59 (Mass. 2004) (emphasizing that, in light of a proper construction of section 4.8(3), the servient estate owner may not resort to self-help and must seek a declaratory judgment before making any alteration). Other courts have likewise adopted Section 4.8(3), but limited its application to easements when locations have not been previously defined by the instrument creating the easement, a subsequent agreement, or subsequent conduct. *See, e.g., Lewis v. Young*, 705 N.E.2d 649, 653–54 (N.Y. 1998); *Stanga v. Husman*, 694 N.W.2d 716, 718–20 (S.D. 2005); *St. James Village, Inc. v. Cunningham*, 210 P.3d 190, 193–96 (Nev. 2009).

A number of courts have also flatly rejected the *Restatement* approach. *See, e.g., Alligood v. Lasaracina*, 122 Conn. App. 473, 476–78, 999 A.2d 836, 839 (App. Ct. 2009) (invoking "uniformity, stability, predictability and judicial economy"); *AKG Real Estate, LLC v. Kosterman*, 717 N.W.2d 835, 842–47 (Wisc. 2006) (rejecting the application of the "impossibility of purpose doctrine" under *Restatement* § 7.10(1), the "changed conditions doctrine" under *Restatement* § 7.10(2) and the "unilateral relocation rule" under *Restatement* § 4.8(3) and agreeing with the proposition that "parties need not include a provision in an express easement to prevent unilateral modification or relocation" because "the rule is that the owner of the servient estate cannot unilaterally modify an express easement"); *Herrin v. Pettergill*, 538 S.E.2d 735, 736 (Ga. 2000) (explicitly rejecting Section 4.8(3)). As reported decisions in many other states have not addressed relocation disputes since the advent of the new Restatement rule, it appears that the traditional common law rule of mutual consent still governs in these states.

In 2018, the Uniform Law Commission (also known as the National Conference of Commissioners on Uniform State Laws), formally constituted a Drafting Committee to prepare the Easement Relocation Act. Building on the Restatement, the Draft Easement Relocation Act offers a detailed mechanism for a servient estate owner to obtain judicial approval of a proposed easement relocation. For a committee draft and discussion documents, see https://www.uniformlaws.org/HigherLogic /System/DownloadDocumentFile.ashx?DocumentFileKey=674e546e-a9e5-dfa0 -7654-a2ccf2922455&forceDialog=0.

F. Extinction of Conventional Predial Servitudes

We have already seen that conventional predial servitudes, when they have been filed for recordation in the parish conveyance records, are enforceable by and against all subsequent owners of the dominant and servient estates. This binding effect may last in perpetuity. The Louisiana Civil Code, however, provides for seven different means of extinguishing a conventional predial servitude.

1. Destruction of the Dominant or the Servient Estate

The Louisiana Civil Code distinguishes between the permanent and total destruction of the dominant estate (or of a part of an estate burdened with a servitude) and temporary conditions that make it impossible to exercise the servitude on an estate. Articles 751 and 752 define the consequences of this distinction:

Art. 751. Destruction of dominant or of servient estate

A predial servitude is extinguished by the permanent and total destruction of the dominant estate or of the part of the servient estate burdened with the servitude.

La. Civ. Code art. 751 (1977).

Art. 752. Reestablishment of things

If the exercise of the servitude becomes impossible because the things necessary for its exercise have undergone such a change that the servitude can no longer be used, the servitude is not extinguished; it resumes its effect when things are reestablished so that they may again be used, unless prescription has accrued.

La. Civ. Code art. 752 (1977). Destruction of an estate—the situation contemplated by Article 751—means that either the dominant estate or the portion of a servient estate subject to the servitude vanishes physically or otherwise becomes permanently inaccessible. This could occur in a number of situations; for example, when land is swept away by a sudden change in the course of river, when land is permanently inundated as the result of rising seas or a storm surge, or when land is expropriated by the state or a political subdivision for use as a public facility. In these situations, the entire dominant estate or the part of the servient estate that hosts the servitude could disappear or no longer be capable of being used by the dominant estate owner. The servitude would thus no longer serve any purpose and the utility requirement of Article 647 of the Louisiana Civil Code would fail. Hence, the servitude would be extinguished. A.N. YIANNOPOULOS, 4 LOUISIANA CIVIL LAW TREATISE § 8.2, at 510 (4th ed. 2013).

Conditions that might render a servitude temporarily impossible to use—the situation contemplated by Article 752 of the Louisiana Civil Code—include the drying up of a well, a road becoming impassable because of overgrown vegetation, ruts or holes, or the collapse of a supporting wall on a servient estate burdened by a servitude of support. In these situations, a servitude holder could theoretically resume using the servitude after the temporary condition rendering the servitude impossible to use is corrected. *See* La. Civ. Code art. 751 rev. cmt. (b) (1977). Hence, the servitude is not extinguished; it subsists until the servitude may be exercised once again. Of course, some time may pass while the parties determine who is responsible for correcting the impediment to use or while repairs are underway. If too much time passes, the servitude may be extinguished by prescription of non-use. *See* La. Civ. Code art. 752 (1977) (a servitude "resumes its effect when things are reestablished so that they may again be used, *unless prescription has accrued*") (emphasis added).

Under Article 753 of the Louisiana Civil Code, predial servitudes are generally extinguished by nonuse for a period of ten years. La. Civ. Code art. 753 (1977). However, if the owner of the dominant estate is prevented from using the servitude by a material obstacle that he cannot prevent or remove, Article 755 declares that prescription of nonuse is suspended for a period of up to ten years. La. Civ. Code art. 755 (1977); La. Civ. Code art. 752, rev. cmt. (b) (1977). Thus, for example, if a road becomes impassible because of some condition of the road, but the road could have been fixed by the owner of the dominant estate, prescription is not suspended and the servitude may be extinguished.

2. Prescription for Nonuse

Prescription of nonuse, one of three kinds of prescription under the Louisiana Civil Code, is a mode of terminating a real right other than ownership as a consequence of a failure to exercise the right for a period of time. La. Civ. Code arts. 3448, 3445 (1982). All conventional servitudes are subject to prescription by nonuse. In contrast, Article 758 declares that prescription of nonuse does not run against natural servitudes. La. Civ. Code art. 758 (1977). The Civil Code does not make an express declaration regarding the applicability of prescription of nonuse to legal servitudes. However, as legal servitudes arise as a result of an inherent relationship between two nearby estates, logic dictates that, just as with natural servitudes, they are not subject to prescription of nonuse. A.N. YIANNOPOULOS, 4 LOUISIANA CIVIL LAW TREATISE § 8.4, at 516 (4th ed. 2013). In the law of enclosed estates, this proposition is confirmed by Article 696, which provides that the right to seek indemnity against the owner of an enclosed estate that claims a right of passage under Article 689 is subject to a ten year liberative prescription, but which also notes that "this prescription has no effect on the right of passage." La. Civ. Code art. 696 (1977).

Articles 753 and 754 of the Louisiana Civil Code govern the length and the onset of prescription of nonuse in the law of conventional predial servitudes.

Art. 753. Prescription for nonuse

A predial servitude is extinguished by nonuse for ten years.

La. Civ. Code art. 753 (1977). Prescription of nonuse frees the servient estate from the burden of the servitude when the servitude has not been used or enforced by the owner of the dominant estate or by someone on his behalf for more than ten years. A special set of rules applies to prescription of nonuse because the exercise of a servitude requires cooperation between the owner of the servient estate and the owner of the dominant estate.

When prescription of nonuse is applied to predial servitudes, the codal distinction between affirmative and negative servitudes plays a central role:

Art. 754. Commencement of nonuse

Prescription of nonuse begins to run for affirmative servitudes from the date of their last use, and for negative servitudes from the date of the occurrence of an event contrary to the servitude.

An event contrary to the servitude is such as the destruction of works necessary for its exercise or the construction of works that prevent its exercise.

La. Civ. Code art. 754 (1977). For an affirmative servitude, prescription begins to run from the date it was last used. Each use of the servitude interrupts prescription and any counting has to begin anew. *See* La. Civ. Code art. 3466 (1982). For negative servitudes, prescription commences with an event contrary to the exercise of the servitude.

* .* *

Recall that in *Naramore v. Aikman*, 252 So. 3d 935, 944–45 (La. App. 1 Cir. 2018), the court rejected a defense of prescription of nonuse in a case involving a servitude of passage established by destination of the owner. That decision reviewed the basic principles of prescription of nonuse. Now consider the following case involving a conventional predial servitude in which the parties chose to establish a shorter prescriptive period. Should the owner of the dominant estate lose a servitude in the circumstances described below?

Ashland Oil Co., Inc. v. Palo Alto, Inc.

615 So.2d 971 (La. App. 1 Cir. 1993)

LOTTINGER, Chief Judge. This is an appeal by Ashland Oil Company Inc. and International Minerals and Chemical Corporation of a judgment terminating their pipeline right of way. The trial court found, on Palo Alto's reconventional demand, that the servitude had not been used within the 12-month prescriptive period provided for in the contract. Appellants seek to have their servitude enforced and the public records reformed to erase a survey error indicating that the servitude did not completely traverse Palo Alto's lands.

Facts

In 1980, James Lawn, an employee of Ford, Bacon & Davis Construction Company, acting as agent for Ashland Oil Company and International Minerals and Chemical Corporation (joint venturers, both hereinafter referred to singularly as Ashland), began negotiating with the landowners along a 26 mile long route for a pipeline right of way, from Agrico Chemical Company's plant near Donaldsonville to Ashland's plant near Plaquemine.

Ashland's plant . . . would produce methanol. The plant could produce approximately 100 million gallons per year when Ashland purchased it, but it was determined that a pipeline feeding carbon dioxide (CO_2) to the plant could boost production to 130 million gallons per year.

During negotiations with Palo Alto's president, Arthur Lemann, Jr., Mr. Lawn learned that any right of way across Palo Alto's lands would be conditioned upon an agreement restricting use of the pipeline to the transportation of CO_2, and that there would be a shortened term for the prescription of non-use of 12 months, as opposed to La. Civil Code article 753's 10-year prescriptive period.

After haggling over the price, the parties agreed to the servitude and confected an agreement providing that the servitude granted to Ashland was:

> [A] non-exclusive right of way and servitude to construct, lay, maintain, operate, repair, remove and replace below ground, one single pipeline . . . for the transportation of carbon dioxide in either its gaseous or liquid state, through lands which [Palo Alto] owns, situated in the Parishes of Iberville and Ascension. . . .

Following the grant of servitude language, were numbered conditions for use of the servitude, the sixth of which provided:

> This agreement shall be null and void and of no effect if [Ashland] shall fail to construct, complete and put into actual operation said pipeline described herein across said right of way within twenty-four months from the date hereof. . . . It is further agreed and understood that after the said pipeline shall have been constructed and put into operation, should [Ashland] fail to use the same for the purposes herein provided for a period of twelve consecutive months, then and in that event the within right of way agreement shall be terminated. . . .

The Allemania plant and pipeline were used as planned until July, 1984, when methanol production became unprofitable for Ashland. The plant was mothballed and the pipeline was pressurized with nitrogen to prevent its corrosion during the time it was unused.

However, in order to prevent the 12-month prescriptive period from accruing, Ashland had crews at the Agrico and Allemania plants run CO_2 through the line on an 11-1/2 month basis, beginning in April, 1985. The CO_2 was fed into the line at Agrico and run through it under pressure to Allemania, where it was simply vented into the atmosphere. This procedure was repeated in two additional years, until Ashland began selling Agrico's CO_2 to Georgia Gulf via the pipeline in 1988 and, later, again began to produce methanol in January, 1989.

Ashland, additionally, visually inspected the route of the right of way to ascertain that no encroachments or potentially disruptive activities occurred on or near the servitude and pipeline. Ashland considered these activities, and the nitrogen injections, maintenance in compliance with the language of the servitude grant. Ashland contends that all of these activities sufficiently constitute the specified "use" of the pipeline such as would interrupt the running of the 12-month prescriptive period. . . .

Discussion

It has long been the law in this state that to use a servitude, so as to interrupt prescription, requires one to use it in the manner contemplated by the grant of the servitude. *Continental Group, Inc. v. Allison*, 404 So. 2d 428, 437–438 (La. 1981) (on rehearing), *cert. denied*, 456 U.S. 906, 72 L. Ed. 2d 163, 102 S. Ct. 1753 (1982); *Lynn v. Harrington*, 193 La. 877, 192 So. 517, 518 (1939); *Goldsmith v. McCoy*, 190 La. 320, 182 So. 519, 523 (1938); *Louisiana Petroleum Co. v. Broussard*, 172 La. 613, 135 So. 1, 2 (1931). Reference must therefore be made to the object of the grant, not for the purpose of determining whether there has been a breach of any obligation, but to determine whether there has been such use as to interrupt prescription. 135 So. at 2–3. . . .

Accordingly, in *Broussard*, the Court stated that in the case of a mineral servitude, where the exploiting, though begun, has been stopped or abandoned at a depth at which there was no reasonable hope of discovering minerals in paying quantities, the use is not such as to interrupt prescription. 135 So. at 3. In *Goldsmith*, the Court concluded that geophysical exploration of the premises for the purpose of determining the indication of minerals underlying the surface will not interrupt prescription. 182 So. at 523. In *Harrington*, the Court did find that prescription had been interrupted where a mineral lessee drilled carefully, taking numerous core samples for testing, and stopped drilling only when he had reached the frontiers of geological knowledge circa 1938. The Court specifically noted that the well "was not drilled as a mere gesture by the mineral owners to preserve a servitude, but by the owner of a mineral lease under an obligation to substantially develop with due diligence." 192 So. at 518.

It is important to note, that although these decisions were based on former La. Civ. Code articles 796–800 (repealed in 1977), the articles relied upon pertained to use of a servitude that was less than allowed or called for in the title creating it. Thus, they applied where the **manner** of use was inconsistent with a broadly or generally worded grant of a servitude. See La. Civ. Code article 759, Comments (b) and (c); La. Civ. Code article 761.

We can see, therefore, that Ashland erroneously relies upon the following language, found in Professor Yiannopoulos' treatise on predial servitudes in 4 Louisiana Civil Law Treatise 449:

> If the title does not establish an exclusive manner of use, the use of the servitude in a different manner from that which is designated or appropriate ought to interrupt the prescription of nonuse.

Ashland asserts that this language supports its contention that any use of the pipeline involving the running of CO_2 from one end of the pipeline to the other is use of the servitude comporting with the object of the grant of the servitude. However, this sentence must be read in conjunction with the sentence preceding it, wherein Professor Yiannopoulos states:

> The use of a servitude for over ten years in a manner different from that which is appropriate for the servitude ought to result in extinction of the original servitude by nonuse, **if the title establishes an exclusive manner of use** (emphasis added).

Id.

In this case the title did establish an exclusive manner of using the pipeline; it is "for the **transportation** of carbon dioxide in either its gaseous or liquid state, through lands with [Palo Alto] owns" (emphasis added). The servitude is not used, as Ashland asserts, merely by running CO_2 through the line. This would be "a mere gesture by the [pipeline] owners to preserve a servitude," *Lynn v. Harrington*, 192 So. at 518, which practice has been repudiated in our law. Thus, we find, as did the trial court, that Ashland did not use its servitude for at least twelve consecutive months between July, 1984, and January, 1989. This finding compels the conclusion, under the contract, that the servitude was prescribed for nonuse.

This determination obviates consideration of Ashland's third, fourth, and fifth assignments of error, and we pretermit them.

Conclusion

Therefore, the judgment of the trial court is AFFIRMED at appellants' costs.

AFFIRMED.

FOIL, Judge, Dissenting. I disagree with the majority in this case. The majority affirms the trial judge in holding that the servitude ended because of prescription, in that it was not used in the manner contemplated by the grant of the servitude. Ashland, the servitude owner, in 1980, at the outset of the servitude, transported CO_2 through the pipeline servitude to its plant to produce methanol. Ashland stopped producing methanol at the plant in 1984. From that time until 1989, Ashland ran CO_2 through the line approximately once each year to keep the servitude alive, but the CO_2 was merely vented into the atmosphere at the end of the line rather than used to produce methanol. Ashland began producing methanol again in 1989.

The servitude agreement stated the servitude would terminate if Ashland failed to use it "for the purposes herein provided" for a period of 12 consecutive months. The purposes of the servitude specified in the contract of servitude were to "lay, maintain, use, and to transport gas through the lands" of Palo Alto. There was no requirement that Ashland was to continue producing methanol in order to keep the servitude alive.

I would reverse the trial court's finding that the servitude had prescribed, and remand the case for further proceedings.

Notes and Questions

1. Note that in *Ashland Oil Co., Inc. v. Palo Alto, Inc.*, 615 So.2d 971 (La. App. 1 Cir. 1993), the contracting parties agreed to a one-year period for prescription of nonuse instead of the codal ten year prescriptive period. Should such a short prescriptive period be allowed as a matter of public policy?

2. Ashland stopped using the pipeline to support its methanol production plant in Allemania in July 1984, but it resumed normal operations in January 1989. Why do you think that Palo Alto, the servient estate owner, waited until at least 1989 to assert that the servitude had been extinguished by nonuse?

3. The court considered Ashland's running CO_2 through the pipeline to be a "mere gesture" insufficient to preserve the servitude. What does the court say about Ashland's other activities, including visual inspections of the pipeline route and maintenance of nitrogen in the pipeline? Are these activities sufficient use of the servitude to prevent the running of prescription?

4. Would Ashland have had better luck if it had invoked Article 759 of the Louisiana Civil Code? This provision declares that "[a] partial use of the servitude constitutes use of the whole." La. Civ. Code art. 759 (1977). In *Phipps v. Schupp*, 45

So.3d 593, 603 (La. 2010), the Louisiana Supreme Court relied on this article to hold that plaintiff Phipps had not lost his right to bring a possessory action to protect his interest in a servitude of passage allegedly acquired through destination of the owner because he had continued to walk across the passageway even though vehicular access was blocked. Is pumping CO_2 through a pipeline without any industrial need a more or less significant partial use than walking across a driveway meant for vehicular access?

5. Consider the relevance of Article 761 of the Civil Code to the dispute between Ashland Oil Co. and Palo Alto, Inc.:

Art. 761. Use of accessory right

The use of a right that is only accessory to the servitude is not use of the servitude.

La. Civ. Code art. 761 (1977). In another case, *Palgrave v. Gros*, 829 So. 2d 579 (La. App. 5 Cir. 2002), the court considered whether prescription of nonuse terminates a servitude of passage that gave the dominant estate owners the right to cross the servient estate to launch boats on a bayou bordering the servient estate. The dominant estate owners contended that prescription had been interrupted because they had exercised the servitude by walking up and down the right of way. The court rejected this argument:

The servitude in this case granted the Palgraves the right of ingress and egress to the bayou and the right to bring their boats in and out of Bayou Barataria. At trial, Mrs. Palgrave admits that since the granting of the servitude, she and her husband have not brought a boat onto the servient estate as authorized by the servitude. . . .

[A]ppellants contend that their actions in walking across the servient estate is a use of the servitude sufficient to interrupt prescription. In support of their position, the Palgraves submitted a list of numerous occasions when they visited the property during the period from 1990 when the location of the servitude was designated until the year 2000 when this suit was instituted. Based on our review of the record before us, we find no merit in appellant's argument that their actions in walking across the property constituted a use of the servitude.

La. C.C. art. 761 provides that the use of a right that is only accessory to the servitude is not use of the servitude. In this case, the purpose of the servitude was to allow the Palgraves ingress and egress through the property to bring their boats to Bayou Barataria. Even assuming that they walked across the property, this action does not constitute a use of the servitude unless they also attempted to bring a boat across the property to access the bayou. The passage is merely accessory to the right of ingress and egress to enter the bayou. See Revision comment (b) to La. C.C. art. 761.

Palgrave, 829 So.2d at 583–84.

In *Broomfield v. Louisiana Power and Light Co.*, 623 So.2d 1376 (La. App. 2 Cir. 1993), the court similarly held that a utility company's acts of clearing trees on the right of way included in a sixteen-foot wide utility servitude did not constitute use of the servitude under Article 761 of the Louisiana Civil Code. As the court explained:

> The Revision Comments to article 761 give an example that is precisely on point:
>
>> [I]f one who has the servitude of drawing water from the well of his neighbor passes over the servient estate and goes to the well without drawing any water during the period required for prescription, he will lose the servitude because the passage is merely accessory to the right of drawing water.
>
> The fundamental flaw in LP & L's position is that, as the district court found, there has been no exercise, upon the servient estate, of the principal right to transmit electricity since 1972. Without this, LP & L's claim to have exercised the accessory right of clearance is as unavailing as for the water-drawer in the Comment. Performing some acts on the servient estate will not block prescription unless the servitude right is also exercised thereon.

Id. at 1379. In light of the reasoning in *Palgrave* and *Broomfield*, was the pumping of carbon dioxide through the pipeline located on Palo Alto's land by Ashland Oil merely an "accessory use" of the servitude or was it use for the actual purpose for which the servitude was established?

6. In *Palgrave v. Gros*, 829 So.2d 579 (La. App. 5 Cir. 2002), the court also considered whether the owners of the dominant estate in that case had been prevented from using the servitude of passage. If they had been prevented from using the servitude by some obstacle over which the dominant estate owners had no control, prescription of nonuse would have been suspended as set forth in Article 755 of the Louisiana Civil Code:

Art. 755. Obstacle to servitude

> If the owner of the dominant estate is prevented from using the servitude by an obstacle that he can neither prevent nor remove, the prescription of nonuse is suspended on that account for a period of up to ten years.

La. Civ. Code art. 755 (1977). Thus, if some legal or physical impediment, such as an injunction or a temporary inundation, prevents the dominant estate owner from exercising the servitude, prescription of nonuse will be suspended for a period of up to ten years. However, if the obstacle could be removed by the dominant estate owner—either through physical or legal action—prescription will continue to run. A.N. Yiannopoulos, 4 Louisiana Civil Law Treatise: Personal Servitudes § 8.6, at 521 (4th ed. 2013). In *Palgrave*, the court applied these principles as follows:

> Appellants contend, however, that they were prevented from exercising the servitude because of the obstacles placed on the property by the Gros. . . .

La. C.C. arts. 744 and 745 provide that as owners of the dominant estate, the Palgraves had the right to make repairs for use and preservation of the servitude at their expense. La. C.C. art. 755 provides that prescription will be suspended where the owner of the dominant estate is prevented from using the servitude by an obstacle that he can neither prevent nor remove.

At the hearing on defendants' exceptions, Mrs. Palgrave testified that she and her husband were unable to use the servitude because of several obstacles which prevented transporting or launching a boat from the designated area. Mrs. Palgrave stated that a tree and other debris on the property, including parts of an old boat, prevented their access to the property. She introduced several photographs which depicted these obstacles on the property. Appellants contend that it was not possible to launch a boat from the servitude due to these obstacles, and thus prescription did not commence to run. Alternatively, they argue that prescription was suspended while the obstacles prevented use of the servitude.

However, the Palgraves failed to introduce any evidence to show that they attempted to remove the obstacles on the servient estate. Although the law allows the owners of the dominant estate to make repairs and remove obstacles for the use and preservation of the servitude, there is nothing in the record to show that appellants were prevented from entering the property to remove the obstacles. In fact, the testimony produced at the hearing indicates that the Palgraves did not request that the Gros remove the obstacles. Under these circumstances, we fail to find that the Palgraves were not prevented from using the servitude due to the obstacles on the property, and prescription commenced to run from the creation of the servitude.

Palgrave, 829 So.2d at 583. Put differently, in *Palgrave* the court held that because the dominant estate owners failed to take any informal action on their own to remove the debris which impeded their access to the boat launch and failed to take any legal action to make the servient estate owners clear the debris, they could not prove that they confronted an insurmountable obstacle that would have suspended the running of prescription of nonuse.

7. Article 756 of the Louisiana Civil Code refines the "obstacles doctrine" further by distinguishing, for purposes of suspension, between two particular situations and subsequent responsibilities.

Art. 756. Failure to rebuild dominant or servient estate

If the servitude cannot be exercised on account of the destruction of a building or other construction that belongs to the owner of the dominant estate, prescription is not suspended. If the building or other construction belongs to the owner of the servient estate, the preceding article applies.

La. Civ. Code art. 756 (1977). If a construction necessary for exercise of a servitude and belonging to the owner of the dominant estate is destroyed (for example, a bridge), the dominant estate owner must repair and use it to preserve the servitude. In the dominant estate owner fails to make the necessary repairs and put the construction to use by exercising the servitude within ten years, the servitude will terminate. If, however, the construction that has been destroyed belongs to the owner of the servient estate, prescription is suspended for up to ten years provided the owner of the dominant estate cannot compel the owner of the servient estate to rebuild it. La. Civ. Code art. 756 rev. cmts. (b) and (c) (1977). Otherwise, prescription of nonuse will continue to run unless the dominant estate owner interrupts prescription by filing suit. *Id*. rev. cmt. (c).

8. In *Palgrave v. Gros*, 829 So.2d 579 (La. App. 5 Cir. 2002), one of the dominant estate owners admitted that she did not use the right of way to bring boats in and out of Bayou Barataria. She might have exercised her right of servitude, however, by allowing a neighbor or friend to embark upon these activities. According to Article 757 of the Louisiana Civil Code, her right would have been preserved even if a stranger had used the servitude:

Art. 757. Sufficiency of acts by third persons

A predial servitude is preserved by the use made of it by anyone, even a stranger, if it is used as appertaining to the dominant estate.

La. Civ. Code art. 757 (1977). What does the phrase "as appertaining to the dominant estate" mean?

In *Palace Properties, L.L.C. v. Sizeler Hammond Square Ltd. Partnership*, 839 So.2d 82 (La. App. 1 Cir. 2002), the court of appeal discussed the general public's use of a servitude of passage over two estates which had created a short cut from one major highway to another. Although the trial court had found that use of the servitude by "innumerable members of the public" benefitted the dominant estate by improving the value of that property, and therefore, interrupted the prescription of nonuse, the court of appeal reversed:

The public use of this roadway was not for the purpose of going onto the Palace property for any reason connected with that property. Rather, the public use of C. M. Fagan Drive served the purpose of carrying vehicles and people past and through the Palace property to get somewhere else. Such travel was *not purposive use* of the servitude of passage for the benefit of the dominant estate.

Id. at 95 (emphasis added). Is the concept of "purposive use" helpful in interpreting Article 757?

9. When the prescription of nonuse is asserted by a servient estate owner in a lawsuit, that owner does not carry the burden of proof. Instead, Article 764 of the Louisiana Civil Code provides an alternative burden of proof:

Article 764. Burden of proof of use

When the prescription of nonuse is pleaded, the owner of the dominant estate has the burden of proving that he or some other person has made

use of the servitude as appertaining to his estate during the period of time
required for the accrual of the prescription.

La. Civ. Code art. 764 (1977). This sensible rule takes account of the likelihood that
the dominant estate owner will usually be the party best positioned to marshal evidence of prior use of the servitude and show interruption of prescription of nonuse.
If the burden of proof with respect to prescription of nonuse was placed on the servient estate owner, that owner would often find itself in the awkward predicament
of having to prove a negative—that the servitude has not been used—at least with
respect to affirmative servitudes.

10. Pursuant to Article 762 of the Civil Code, use of a servitude by a co-owner
will prevent prescription of nonuse from running:

Art. 762. Use by co-owner

If the dominant estate is owned in indivision, the use that a co-owner
makes of the servitude prevents the running of prescription as to all.

If the dominant estate is partitioned, the use of the servitude by each
owner preserves it for his estate only.

La. Civ. Code art. 762 (1977).

11. Recall that partial use of a servitude constitutes use of the whole. As Article
761 of the Louisiana Civil Code makes clear, however, use of an accessory right does
not constitute use of the servitude. La. Civ. Code art. 761 (1977). Further, use of the
servient estate beyond what is contemplated in the title establishing the servitude
does not create additional rights except by acquisitive prescription:

Art. 760. More extensive use than title

A more extensive use of the servitude than that granted by the title does
not result in the acquisition of additional rights for the dominant estate
unless it be by acquisitive prescription.

La. Civ. Code art. 760 (1977).

11. Keep in mind that disputes about prescription of nonuse are highly fact-
intensive. Courts may be reluctant to terminate a conventional predial servitude
unless it is clear that the dominant estate owner has failed to use the servitude for
the purpose specified in the agreement establishing the servitude. *See, e.g., Thompson v. FRF Properties*, 229 So.3d 598, 605–06 (La. App 4 Cir. 2017) (reversing the
trial court's determination that a servitude of passage had terminated by prescription of nonuse and holding that: (1) the testimony by the dominant estate owner's
tenant that he saw individuals drive their vehicles onto and park on both strips of
the shared driveway established use of the servitude; and (2) this use was sufficient
to interrupt prescription, even though the users did not use the driveway to access
the rear of property, as any partial use of an area burdened with a predial servitude constitutes use of the whole); *Willow Chute Farms, LLC v. Roos*, 184 So.3d 266,
271–72 (La. App. 2 Cir. 2016) (affirming the trial court's finding that a personal

servitude of passage had not prescribed by nonuse as the holder demonstrated that a lessee and others had used the servitude over a gravel road for fishing, hunting, and hauling hay).

3. Confusion

Pursuant to Article 646 of the Louisiana Civil Code a predial servitude is a "charge established on a servient estate for the benefit of a dominant estate," and the "two estates must belong to different owners." La. Civ. Code art. 646 (1977). As we saw in the context of destination of the owner, when two estates that might be in a service relationship are owned by the same person, a predial servitude cannot come into being until the two estates cease to belong to the same owner. When the ownership of a servient estate and a dominant estate linked by a predial servitude becomes united or merged in one person, Article 765 declares that confusion terminates the servitude:

Art. 765. Confusion

A predial servitude is extinguished when the dominant and the servient estates are acquired in their entirety by the same person.

La. Civ. Code art. 765 (1977). If the owner of one estate acquires only a part of the other estate or merely an interest in indivision, however, confusion does not take place. *Id.* rev. cmt. (b). Similarly, under Article 768 of the Louisiana Civil Code, there is no confusion when one estate is owned as separate property of a spouse and the other is owned as community property. The servitude continues to exist. La. Civ. Code art. 768 (1977). Further, a predial servitude is not extinguished by confusion immediately when a successor who owns one estate is seized with possession of the other. Rather, pursuant to Article 767, the servitude continues until the successor has "formally or informally accepted" the succession of the complementary estate; if the succession is renounced, the servitude remains. La. Civ. Code art. 767 (1977). Finally, once a predial servitude is extinguished by confusion, Article 769 declares that it ceases to exist and can only be reestablished in the way that new servitudes are created. La. Civ. Code art. 769 (1977).

4. Abandonment of the Servient Estate

When the owner of the servient estate tires of enduring the servitude, she can abandon the servient estate in its entirety or abandon the part subject to the exercise of the servitude.

Art. 770. Abandonment of servient estate

A predial servitude is extinguished by the abandonment of the servient estate, or of the part on which the servitude is exercised. It must be evidenced by a written act. The owner of the dominant estate is bound to accept it and confusion takes place.

La. Civ. Code art. 770 (1977). After the abandonment of a servitude, which must be in writing, the owner of the dominant estate now owns the entire servient estate or the portion of the estate upon which the servitude was exercised. Confusion takes place and the servitude is extinguished.

5. Renunciation by the Owner of the Dominant Estate

Pursuant to Article 771 of the Louisiana Civil Code, a servitude terminates upon renunciation by the owner of the dominant estate:

Art. 771. Renunciation of servitude

A predial servitude is extinguished by an express and written renunciation by the owner of the dominant estate.

La. Civ. Code art. 771 (1977). A renunciation of a predial servitude by the owner of the dominant estate must be express and in writing. Renunciation is never presumed. Nevertheless, any written agreement that has the clear effect of renouncing a servitude can result in termination. *See Mars Beach, LLC v. McQuirter*, 234 So.3d 98, 910, 913 (La. App. 1 Cir. 2017) (holding a written boundary agreement that seeks to "convey, transfer, and quitclaim any and all rights, title and interest which [the transferor] may have or had to the movable or immovable property" was sufficient to constitute an express, written renunciation of any predial servitude that may have existed on the alleged servient estate).

We have noted that, under Article 762 of the Louisiana Civil Code, "the use that a co-owner makes of the servitude prevents the running of prescription as to all." La. Civ. Code art. 762 (1977). In contrast, Article 772 declares that "[a] renunciation of a servitude by a co-owner of the dominant estate does not discharge the servient estate, but deprives him of the right to use the servitude." La. Civ. Code art. 772 (1977).

6. Expiration of Time or Happening of a Condition

Conventional predial servitudes by title are governed by the agreement between the parties. Article 773 of the Louisiana Civil Code provides that, when a servitude is established under a resolutory condition or for a term, it is extinguished when that condition is met or when the term ends. La. Civ. Code art. 773 (1977).

7. Dissolution of the Right of the Grantor

Finally, under Article 774 of the Louisiana Civil Code, a servitude can be extinguished by the dissolution of the right of the grantor. La. Civ. Code art. 774 (1977). This old civil law doctrine means that "when the title of the grantor is subsequently declared nonexistent or is annulled for defects," a previously granted predial servitude terminates. La. Civ. Code art. 774 rev. cmt. (c) (1977). "[T]he declaration of nullity clearly results in the cancellation of all real rights granted by the person whose title is annulled." *Id.*

G. Protection of Servitudes

We conclude this chapter with a short discussion of how servitudes may be protected. The principal proceedings for the protection of ownership and possession include the petitory action and the possessory action. Because these proceedings are designed primarily for the protection of possession and ownership of corporeal immovable property, their application to *incorporeal* immovable property such as a predial servitude has raised interesting debates in the courts and the commentary.

Article 3651 of the Code of Civil Procedure confirms the availability of a petitory action to a person who claims a real right in immovable property, including a servitude. La. Code Civ. Proc. art. 3651 (1960, amended 1981). As we already know, one of the most contentious issues related to a petitory action concerns the burden of proof thrust upon the plaintiff. As in any petitory action, the plaintiff's burden of proof will hinge on the status of the person interfering with the property right at issue—here the servitude.

Consider the following example. Alberto, who owns Blackacre, grants Claudia, who owns neighboring Greenacre, a servitude of passage across a paved road bisecting Blackacre. Alberto sells Blackacre to David, who loathes car traffic. David closes off access to Blackacre by changing the access code for lifting and lowering the ingress and egress barriers. If Claudia institutes a petitory action against David, would a court classify David as being in or out of possession of the servitude?

This hypothetical illustrates that the normal rules applicable to petitory actions with respect to corporeal immovables must be adapted because David is the owner of Blackacre, the servient estate, and cannot exercise a servitude over property he owns. To determine the requisite burden of proof, a court must therefore inquire whether David is in possession of Blackacre, the servient estate.

Now consider a variation. David has not blocked off the passage across Blackacre but Berta, the owner of Redacre, which likewise adjoins Blackacre, claims this servitude as hers and changes the access code for the barrier to shut out Claudia. Now, when Claudia brings a petitory action against Berta, the question will be whether or not Berta is in possession of the servitude.

A possessory action in the context of a servitude will focus on the acquisition and retention of the right to quasi-possess the servitude. Importantly, the existence of the servitude right as such will not be at issue. Recall that Article 3421(2) of the Louisiana Civil Code confirms the amenability of a real right, such as a servitude, to possession analysis. La. Civ. Code art. 3421(2) (1982). When someone exercises a servitude with the intent to have it as his own, we speak of quasi-possession and apply, by analogy, the rules governing possession of corporeal things. Quasi-possession is exercised by means of material acts and constructions on the servient and dominant estates. This interpretation is preferable to deploying the rules governing the presence and cessation of use under Article 754, which is predicated upon the distinction between negative or affirmative servitudes. La. Civ. Code art. 754 (1977).

Moreover, for a plaintiff to prevail in a possessory action with respect to a servitude, the quasi-possession must be quiet and without interruption for more than one year prior to the disturbance. In *Louisiana Irrigation and Mill Co. v. Pousson*, 262 La. 973 (1972), the court had to decide whether the plaintiff, who used a canal irregularly to send water to farmers only when they grew rice and demanded water, lost his right to quasi-possess the servitude after a usurpation by the defendant who used it to pump water on his tract for longer than a year. The majority held that the plaintiff suffered an eviction. *Id.* at 976–82. In light of the nature of the servitude, which was to be exercised only when the farmers made a demand, the dissent disagreed. *Id.* at 987–94.

In addition to the challenge of properly construing continuous quasi-possession of a servitude, a question has arisen as to whether a possessory action does indeed effectively protect the exercise of a servitude. Suppose that a plaintiff in a possessory action is successful in having a court restore or maintain quasi-possession of a servitude. The defendant can still file a petitory action and prevail if she proves that she owns the underlying, allegedly burdened, estate and that the estate is not subject to a charge in the form of a servitude. Because ownership is presumed to be free from such burdens and the owner would not be required to prove a negative, it may ultimately fall to the party asserting the servitude to establish his claim to the servitude. This could only be done by establishing that the servitude was created by title or created by destination of the owner or by acquisitive prescription through quasi-possession over time if the servitude is apparent. Professor Symeonides has explored the dilemma of a plaintiff in a possessory action who has satisfied the requisites of the action, but remains ultimately disadvantaged when the litigation is continued. He focuses on a decision by the Louisiana Supreme Court, *Kizer v. Lilly*, 471 So.2d 716 (La. 1985), as a test case for his proposals.

Symeon Symeonides, *Developments in the Law, Property*
46 La. L. Rev. 655, 675–680 (1986)

The Hypothetical Aftermath of Kizer

. . . .

The question about the burden of proof is more difficult. In a very thoughtful concurring opinion in *Kizer*, Justice Lemmon tentatively addressed this issue, and suggested that, in a subsequent (negatory) action [in which the plaintiff seeks a judgment declaring his ownership to be free of burdens, such as servitudes or other real rights], the plaintiff would have to prove "that he owns the immovable property free of the claimed servitude," i.e., "that no servitude has been established by title, by destination, or by acquisitive prescription." This statement sounds inherently logical, but upon closer examination some qualifications might be necessary.

The first question is whether, in the negatory action, the plaintiff should have to prove *ownership* of the part of the land over which the claimed servitude is exercised. The reason this question is asked is because the direct objective of a negatory action is to determine the existence or nonexistence, validity, and scope of the claimed servitude, rather than the ownership of the underlying land. Yet, for obvious reasons, title to such land must be a prerequisite for bringing the negatory action. A person who does not assert title to the allegedly servient estate should have no right or standing to complain about burdens thereon. But title and ownership may be two different things. A title may be a "perfect" title, in which case it is ownership, or according to the old expression "good against the world," or it may be something less than perfect, i.e., merely a "just title" or a "better" title. It is submitted that, in a negatory action, the plaintiff's burden should not be to prove perfect title or ownership, but rather a "better title" as this term is used in Civil Code article 531 and Code of Civil Procedure article 3654. The reason has to do with the defendant's lack of possession and title. The defendant, i.e., the person exercising the claimed servitude, is in quasi-possession of the incorporeal thing we call a servitude, but is *not* in possession of the corporeal immovable over which the claimed servitude is exercised. A person exercising a servitude of drawing water quasi-possesses the servitude, but does not possess the land on which the well is located. This distinction may be more difficult to detect in a case like *Kizer* involving a servitude of passage which is exercised through acts similar or identical to acts by which corporeal property is possessed. The distinction is nevertheless important, and the very fact that Mrs. Kizer claimed only quasi-possession of the servitude rather than possession of the strip of land over which the passage was exercised is, at least, an implicit acknowledgment that she did not [intend to] possess the strip itself. If a true petitory action, or an action for a declaratory judgment, were to be brought against Mrs. Kizer, the plaintiff's burden of proof would be to prove "better title" rather than ownership. There is no reason why this burden should be increased in a negatory action where, after all, the ownership of the strip is not even the primary issue. A "better title" should suffice, and, in this case, any title by the plaintiff is a "better title", simply because, by definition, the defendant has no title at all. The reason the defendant cannot have title to the strip is because, if he had such a title, he could not claim a servitude in the first place. *Neminem res sua servit* (One cannot have a servitude on his own land).

The second question is whether, after having proved his title, i.e., prima facie ownership of the [allegedly servient] estate, the plaintiff should also have to prove that the estate is not in fact servient, or, as Justice Lemmon put it, "free of the claimed servitude." An affirmative answer to this question would mean that the plaintiff would be required to prove a negative proposition. In an 1822 case, Justice Porter resolved the similar question of the burden of proving the USE of a servitude for purposes of the prescription of nonuse by placing the burden on the owner of the dominant rather than the servient estate. Citing a provision of the *Siete Partidas*, Justice Porter said that "where the affirmative involves a negative, the burden of proof is thrown on the opposite party, because a negative cannot be proved." This solution was subsequently codified in what is now article 764 of the Civil Code and should apply by analogy here, supported also by the general civilian principle that ownership is presumed to be free of burdens. Thus, the burden of proving that a servitude came into existence should rest with Mrs. Kizer, not Mr. Lilly. This solution is supported by the weight of doctrinal authority, including Yiannopoulos, Planiol and Ripert, and Aubry and Rau. According to these authorities, because ownership is presumed to be free of burdens, the burden of proving the existence of the claimed servitude rests with the defendant rather than the plaintiff in the negatory action. Aubry and Rau, as well as Planiol and Ripert, state expressly that "[i]t is the same when the defendant obtains judgment in a possessory action that maintains him in the possession of the servitude."

If this analysis is accepted, Justice Lemmon's misgivings about "the effect and the value of the judgment that a plaintiff receives in a possessory action to maintain possession of a servitude" become more understandable, and so does the reluctance of some other members of the court and of the lower courts to allow the possessory action in the first place. For, IF this plaintiff is later sued in a negatory action he can draw virtually no procedural advantages from his prior victory in the possessory action. The contrast with a similarly situated possessor of corporeal property is obvious. As Professor Yiannopoulos explains:

> A possessor of a corporeal immovable who has satisfied the requisites of Article 3658 of the Code of Civil Procedure will remain in possession unless the owner of the immovable proves his ownership in a petitory action. In contrast, the possessor of a servitude who has satisfied the requisites of Article 3658 of the Code of Civil Procedure will eventually be evicted unless he proves the existence of the servitude. This is not an odd proposition. The possessory action protects the possession of an immovable, whether corporeal or incorporeal, and presupposes the existence of the thing possessed. The existence of a corporeal immovable is hardly ever in dispute but the existence of an incorporeal immovable must be proven by the plaintiff who claims that he is entitled to its possession.

Whatever the reasons and need for a different treatment between possessors and quasi-possessors, its detrimental effects on the efficiency of the system should not be disregarded. It would certainly be more efficient if both questions, that is, the quasi-possession of the servitude and its existence, could be resolved in one proceeding. Two solutions come to mind, but there are certainly more and probably better ones. The first, is to merge the possessory action for the protection of a servitude into the confessory action, that is, the innominate real action that seeks a judgment declaring the existence of the claimed servitude, rather than its mere exercise in fact. This solution would, in effect, amount to a compulsory waiver of the possessory action and a requirement that the person claiming the servitude prove its existence at the outset, in order to have any chance for judicial protection. This solution must be rejected because, among other things, it reduces to zero the effect of quasi-possession, thus depriving the plaintiff of an important tactical weapon. The second solution is to merge the defense to the possessory action into the negatory action. Unlike the previous solution, this one does not essentially deprive the defendant of the options he has under the current system. The defendant could, as under the present system, defend the possessory action either by denying the plaintiff's quasi-possession, or by denying the existence of the servitude and asserting his own title, in which case he converts the action into a negatory one and judicially confesses the quasi-possession of the plaintiff. The difference lies in the fact that, under this tentatively suggested solution, the defendant would *have to* assert his title, if, after having denied the plaintiff's quasi-possession, the plaintiff was able to prove its exercise for the requisite year. The fact that, as suggested earlier, the defendant need only prove title rather than ownership, explains why the suggested solution does not put the defendant in a worse position that he is under the current law. If he has a title, he would prevail, unless the plaintiff proves the existence of the servitude. If he has no title, he is not a proper object of judicial solicitude, and, in any event, he would not prevail even under the current scheme. To recapitulate, the suggested solution would work as follows: A person exercising a servitude would have the same options in protecting its enjoyment as he has under the current law. He could file either the confessory action, in which case he has the burden of proving the existence of the servitude, or he could file a possessory action, in which case he has the burden of proving quasi-possession of the servitude for a year preceding the disturbance. In the latter situation, his opponent, the defendant, must assert and prove his title, and if he fails to do so he should be precluded from litigating the issue in a subsequent proceeding against the same plaintiff. If the defendant proves his title, the burden would shift back to plaintiff who would have to prove the existence of the servitude. The difference between this solution and the current system is that a defendant who is defeated on the issue of quasi-possession of the servitude is forced to initiate the discussion of—though not to prove—the servitude's existence in one and the same proceeding rather than waiting to do so in a second proceeding. Since, as explained earlier, the burden of proving the servitude's existence remains with the plaintiff, the defendant's positions remains essentially the same, while the system's efficiency is enhanced.

Notes and Questions

1. Professor Symeonides' article expands our menu of real actions. In Louisiana, a "confessory action" is an innominate real action in which the plaintiff seeks a judgment declaring the existence of the claimed servitude. Conversely, a "negatory action" is an innominate real action in which the plaintiff seeks a judgment declaring his ownership to be free of burdens.

2. What does Professor Symeonides see as the potential inefficiency posed by the current system? What does he propose in the alternative?

3. Professor Yiannopoulos offers the following observations:

> A survey of Louisiana jurisprudence indicates that predial servitudes are frequently protected by an action for mandatory or prohibitory injunction. Injunctive relief may be grounded on Article 3601 of the Code of Civil Procedure, Article 3663 of the same Code, or on the substantive provisions of the Louisiana Civil Code governing servitudes.

A.N. YIANNOPOULOS, 4 LOUISIANA CIVIL LAW TREATISE: PREDIAL SERVITUDES § 9.16, at 585 (4th ed. 2013). Yiannopoulos adds that "Louisiana courts have declared that an action for injunctive relief in case of interference with a right of servitude is 'neither petitory nor possessory in nature.'" *Id.* at 589 (quoting *James v. Buchert*, 144 So.2d 435, 440 (La. App. 4 Cir. 1962)).

Chapter 15

Limited Personal Servitudes: Habitation and Right of Use

The 1976 Revision of the Louisiana Civil Code made significant changes to the law of servitudes. These included establishing the new category of limited personal servitudes, which are a species of real rights conferring *on a person* certain specified advantages of use or enjoyment over an immovable. Borrowed from Germany and Greece, limited personal servitudes fill an intermediary position between predial servitudes, which are charges in favor of an estate, and usufruct, which furnishes a right of full enjoyment over immovables or movables in favor of a person, not an estate. There are two subspecies of limited personal servitudes: (1) habitation (Articles 630 through 638); and (2) rights of use (Articles 639 through 645). In the words of the redactor "[t]he notion of limited personal servitudes is sufficiently broad to accommodate not only habitation [a nominate limited personal servitude] but all real rights that confer on a person a specified use of an immovable less than full enjoyment." A.N. YIANNOPOULOS, 3 LOUISIANA CIVIL LAW TREATISE: PERSONAL SERVITUDES § 8.2, at 520–23 (5th ed. 2011).

Habitation gives a natural person a tightly circumscribed real right to dwell in the house of another person for a limited period of time. La. Civ. Code art 630 (1976). Functionally, it resembles a usufruct, but it confers a narrower right limited to a particular house. It does not allow the holder of the right of habitation to enjoy any civil fruits of the house.

A right of use is quite different than a right of habitation n in that it offers the right holder the same kind of advantages furnished by a predial servitude, with the crucial difference that it benefits a person rather than a particular dominant estate. In addition, unlike habitation, a right of use may benefit a juridical person as well as a natural person. La. Civ. Code art. 641 (1976). Finally, and quite significantly, a right of use gives the holder a transferable, heritable and thus *potentially permanent* real right to use an estate for a specified purpose. La. Civ. Code arts. 639, 643, 644 (1976).

A. Right of Habitation

The right of habitation embodies the most narrowly defined real right enumerated in the Louisiana Civil Code. Article 630 of the Louisiana Civil Code offers its definition:

Art. 630. Habitation

> Habitation is the nontransferable real right of a natural person to dwell in the house of another.

La. Civ. Code art. 630 (1976). Unlike a usufruct or a right of use, a right of habitation cannot be transferred, alienated, let, or encumbered. La. Civ. Code art. 637 (1976). However, just like a usufruct, right of habitation is not heritable. In other words, it cannot be bequeathed to or inherited by another person. It must end at death. *Id.* Just as with a usufruct, "the right of habitation terminates at the death of the person having it unless a shorter period is stipulated." La. Civ. Code art. 638 (1976). Further, because a legal entity, like a corporation or partnership, is not a natural person and cannot "dwell in the house of another," a legal entity cannot hold a right of habitation. *Cf.* La. Civ. Code art. 630 (1976).

To understand these rules, consider the following hypothetical. Jennifer owns two houses facing each other on State Street in New Orleans. In two separate valid donations inter vivos, Jennifer transfers ownership of both houses to her niece Mary subject to two different servitudes for the benefit of her sister Kim and her brother Larry. Mary gives her sister Kim a right of habitation over the house on the west side of the street (House A) and she gives Larry a usufruct over the house on the east side of the street (House B). In some ways, the rights of Kim and Larry are similar. They both will enjoy the right to live in the respective houses. Both of their real rights will terminate at death, unless Jennifer specified a shorter duration or some other event occurs that gives rise to termination of their respective real rights. Neither Kim nor Larry will be able to bequeath their interests to another person. However, there are some crucial differences as well. Kim, the holder of the right of habitation, will *not* be able to alienate, lease, or encumber House A. In contrast, Larry, as a usufructuary, would be able to lease, alienate or encumber his usufructuary interest, although all such contracts would cease to have effect at the termination of his usufruct. *See* La. Civ. Code art. 567 (1976). If Larry had been given the power to dispose of nonconsumables, his rights to lease, alienate or encumber House A would be even broader. *See* La. Civ. Code arts. 568, 568.1-568.3 (1976, amended 2010). Further, Jennifer could give her alma mater, Loyola University, a usufruct over either house, but could not give Loyola a right of habitation.

In general, the title creating a right of habitation determines the scope, terms and conditions of the limited personal servitude. La. Civ. Code art. 632 (1976). For example, the owner of a house may give a natural person a right to live in the entire house for the rest of that person's life *or* for a shorter period of time. La. Civ. Code art. 638 (1976). The owner of the house may also grant a natural person an exclusive right of habitation that entitles that person to the exclusive use of the entire house or a right to dwell in just part of the house, for example a bedroom, with permission to use other rooms, like the kitchen or a living room. La. Civ. Code art. 634 (1976). The instrument or title establishing the right of habitation governs the rights of the parties, but "[i]f the title is silent as to the extent of habitation, the right is regulated in accordance with Articles 633 through 635." La. Civ. Code art. 632 (1976).

In *Barret v. Barrett*, 5 So.2d 381 (La. App. 2 Cir. 1941), Ellen Barrett, a 65-year-old, unmarried woman, sold a lot in Shreveport, Louisiana, along with its "large, dilapidated, old house," to her nephew Rufus Barrett. As part of the bargain, she reserved a right of use and habitation (what today would be called a right of habitation) in a new residence that her nephew promised to build on the lot. The agreement between the parties was filed in the conveyance records of the parish, but it did not specify the extent of Ellen's right in the new house promised by Rufus. After Rufus demolished the old house and built the new residence consisting of three bedrooms, a kitchen, a bathroom and a living room, he reserved one of the three bedrooms for his aunt and offered "to furnish to her all of the necessities of life so long as she lives." *Id*. at 382. Ellen was not happy with this arrangement and sued her nephew. She claimed that in consideration for transferring her property to him she was supposed to receive a right of habitation in an entire and separate three-bedroom house.

Affirming a trial court judgment in favor of Rufus, the court of appeal held that Ellen did not reserve an exclusive right of use for an entire three-bedroom house. Noting that at no point in time had Ellen objected to her nephew's undertaking, the court agreed with the trial judge's conclusion that "[i]t is beyond all reason for the court to conclude that they [Rufus's family] put all of their resources into a home that they could not occupy for years." *Id*. at 382. The dispute in *Barrett* illustrates the importance of clarifying the expectations of the parties with regard to the extent of exclusive occupation the holder of a right of habitation will be entitled to enjoy. These expectations should be carefully addressed in the writing establishing the real right.

When a writing does not specify the extent or limitations on the rights of the person enjoying a right of habitation, those rights are governed by Articles 633 and 634 of the Louisiana Civil Code:

Art. 633. Persons residing in the house

A person having the right of habitation may reside in the house with his family, although not married at the time the right was granted to him.

Art. 634. Extent of right of habitation

A person having the right of habitation is entitled to the exclusive use of the house or of the part assigned to him, and, provided that he resides therein, he may receive friends, guests, and boarders.

La. Civ. Code arts. 633, 634 (1976). Pursuant to these provisions, a person with the right of habitation may invite friends, family members and even boarders into his home. He may invite family members, including a new spouse and children, to share the home or part of the home subject to the right of habitation, even though he was not married at the time he acquired the right. Conversely, he may exclude others from the dwelling subject to the right of habitation.

Articles 635 and 636 of the Louisiana Civil Code govern the duties imposed on the holder of the right of habitation. Just like a usufructuary of a non-consumable thing, the holder of a right of habitation must act as a prudent administrator of the dwelling subject to the right of habitation. At the termination of the right he must deliver the dwelling to the residual owner:

Art. 635. Degree of care; duty to restore the property

A person having the right of habitation is bound to use the property as a prudent administrator and at the expiration of his right to deliver it to the owner in the condition in which he received it, ordinary wear and tear excepted.

La. Civ. Code art. 635 (1976). *Cf.* La. Civ. Code arts. 539 (1976). Similarly, just like a usufructuary, the holder of a right of habitation is responsible for ordinary repairs, taxes and other annual charges.

Art. 636. Taxes, repairs, and other charges

When the person having the right of habitation occupies the entire house, he is liable for ordinary repairs, for the payment of taxes, and for other annual charges in the same manner as the usufructuary.

When the person having the right of habitation occupies only a part of the house, he is liable for ordinary repairs to the part he occupies and for all other expenses and charges in proportion to his enjoyment.

La. Civ. Code art. 636 (1976). *Cf.* La. Civ. Code arts. 577, 584 (1976).

Article 637 of the Civil Code identifies a distinctive feature of the right of habitation compared to the right of use:

Art. 637. Nontransferable and nonheritable right

The right of habitation is neither transferable nor heritable. It may not be alienated, let, or encumbered.

La. Civ. Code art. 637 (1976). Unlike a usufructuary, the holder of the right of habitation cannot transfer his or her right to another person and cannot lease it out to another person. *Compare* La. Civ. Code arts. 556, 567 (1976) *with* La. Civ. Code art. 637 (1976). In other words, a right of habitation can *only be enjoyed* by the natural person who acquires the right in the first instance.

Despite the narrow scope of the right of habitation, it is nevertheless a real right. If the instrument establishing a right of habitation is recorded in the conveyance records of the parish in which the house is located, the right will be enforceable against third parties. Further, a person who has inherited a right of habitation through a donation mortis causa can enforce the right against persons who acquire ownership of the house after it has been sold as a result of a partition by licitation. This is true even if the testament creating the right of habitation is not recorded in the public records. *Crozat v. Louisiana Coastal VII, LLC*, 830 So.2d 319, 324–27 (on rehearing) (La. App. 4 Cir. 2002).

Why might a property owner create a right of habitation? A person who owns land and a house, for instance, might decide to sell the property to another person but reserve for himself the right to live in the house for the remainder of his life. Such an arrangement may provide a mortgage interest deduction for a family member with a greater income. Alternatively, a homeowner may wish to generate cash by transferring the ownership of the home to someone else but reserving for himself a right of habitation. This may be more attractive than selling one's home and moving into an apartment because the landowner can generate cash without rendering himself homeless. A right of habitation can also result from a testament. A testator may make a specific bequest of a home to one or more legatees but give another natural person—a spouse, a family member, a loved one—a right of habitation in that home.

In re Succession of Firmin, 938 So.2d 209 (La. App. 4 Cir 2006), which follows below, features a right of habitation that resulted from a testament. The specific issue raised in the case involves the responsibility of the holder of a right of habitation to pay either the principal or interest portion of a mortgage note for the house. Interestingly, this important subject is not addressed by any of the codal provisions discussed above. Note that the testator in this case used the language "use and habitation" to describe the right he left to his surviving spouse, but the court properly interpreted this to mean that the testator intended to create what the current Louisiana Civil Code calls a right of habitation.

In re Succession of Firmin
938 So.2d 209 (La. App. 4 Cir. 2006)

TERRI F. LOVE, Judge. This case arises from a dispute in a succession proceeding regarding the payment of the mortgage debt on a home. The issue on appeal is which of the parties is responsible for payment of the interest on the mortgage note as between the wife of the decedent, who was left the "use and habitation" of the property, and the succession. We affirm the trial court's judgment in holding that the decedent's wife is not required to pay the interest on the mortgage debt.

Factual Background and Procedural History

Albert P. Firmin died testate on February 2, 2003, leaving his wife, Valerie Bosworth Firmin ("Mrs. Firmin"), full ownership of all his "household furniture and belongings, appliances, and miscellaneous personal effects" and "use and habitation" of the house in which they resided at 24 Chatham Drive, New Orleans. The home is encumbered by a mortgage. Additionally, the will provided for the creation of a trust, for the benefit of Mr. Firmin's two major daughters from a previous marriage, to which he left "the balance of all the property of which I die possessed" subject to "the right of use and habitation of my home" and the other "special legacies set forth in Article I." He appointed his sister Henrynne Louden ("Executrix") as his executrix and trustee.

Testamentary language directs that Mrs. Firmin have "use and habitation" of the home for as long as she may live, provided that she not vacate the premises for over six months, and that she care for the property as a prudent administratrix, making all reasonable repairs, paying taxes and maintaining both fire insurance and "extended coverage insurance." She has resided in the home from the date of Mr. Firmin's death.

On July 9, 2003, Mrs. Firmin filed a Motion to Compel Executrix to Pay Mortgage on the Family Home; the Executrix filed a motion in opposition on October 2, 2003. The Executrix then filed a Petition for Partial Possession and Motion and Incorporated Memorandum to Require Legatee to Accept or Renounce Legacy. In response, Mrs. Firmin claimed that she was neither under a legal nor a testamentary obligation to pay the mortgage notes. The Executrix alleged that Mrs. Firmin must either pay the mortgage in order to maintain her right of habitation of the property or relinquish her use of the property. Mrs. Firmin asserted that the Louisiana Civil Code does not require a holder of the right of habitation to pay fees associated with either usufruct or ownership.

After a hearing, the trial court issued a judgment denying the Motion to Force Valerie Firmin to Pay the Mortgage, Reimburse the Succession for Mortgage Payments Already Made and in the Alternative for Rent. The trial court found there existed no legal authority to require Mrs. Firmin to pay the mortgage or to pay rent.

After the issuance of judgment, the Executrix filed a memorandum asserting that under the doctrine of limited liability to legatees, succession debts are charged against the encumbered property itself. Thus, she contends that if Mrs. Firmin accepted the legacy, she would be required to pay at least the interest portion of the mortgage notes without any right to reimbursement from the succession or the owners of the home. According to the Executrix, failure to pay the interest on the mortgage notes would require Mrs. Firmin to renounce her right of habitation. The Executrix also sought reimbursement from Mrs. Firmin for the mortgage notes paid by Mr. Firmin's succession. Mrs. Firmin's Reply Memorandum alleged that the Executrix did not differentiate between the responsibilities of universal and particular usufructuaries' and legatees such as herself, and that the decedent's debt does not attach to particular legatees. Additionally, she argued that the testamentary language specifically does not require a legatee to pay the mortgage debt.

The trial court issued its Final Judgment denying the motion to force Mrs. Firmin to pay the mortgage, and further denied the Executrix's motion for a new trial. The Executrix's timely appeal followed.

The Executrix asserts that Mrs. Firmin, as a person with the right of "use and habitation," has an affirmative obligation under the Louisiana Civil Code to pay the interest due on the mortgage while she enjoys exclusive use and habitation of the property. The Executrix does not appeal the trial court's judgment that Mrs. Firmin is not liable for the principal on the mortgage. If Mrs. Firmin does not pay the interest, the Executrix argues that the person must be required to terminate her use and habitation of the property.

. . . .

Rights of Habitation and Use

Mr. Firmin's will explicitly directs that the legatee be granted "the right of use and habitation" of the home in which they had resided, subject to the conditions that she not vacate the premises in excess of six months, and that she care for the property as a prudent administratrix. Mr. Firmin included in the will that Mrs. Firmin "shall be responsible to make all reasonable repairs, pay all taxes, and keep the improvements located on the property covered with adequate fire and extended coverage insurance." The right of habitation is a "nontransferable real right of a natural person to dwell in the house of another." La. C.C. art. 630. This right is "regulated by the title that establishes it." La. C.C. art. 632. Thus, Mrs. Firmin's right of habitation is governed by the above mentioned testamentary language which explicitly delineates her rights and responsibilities.

The Louisiana Supreme Court "has indicated that the function of the courts is to carry out the intention of the testator and effect should be given to all language contained in the will if possible." *Succession of Bel*, 377 So.2d 1380, 1383 (La. App. 4th Cir. 1979). Mr. Firmin's will specified the legatee's financial responsibilities concomitant to "use and habitation." These are substantially similar to those obligations provided for in the Louisiana Civil Code, including responsibilities for reasonable repairs and taxes on the property. La. C.C. art. 636.

Furthermore, the will details the formation of a trust, comprising the balance of the estate, in favor of Mr. Firmin's major daughters. The care in drafting and attention to detail further supports Mrs. Firmin's assertion that Mr. Firmin intended only to bequeath to her the limited rights of use and habitation. *See Succession of Cottrell v. Quirk*, 05-841, pp. 2–3 (La. App. 3 Cir. 2/1/06), 921 So.2d 1235, 1238.

The rights of both use and habitation are limited rights, providing for less than full enjoyment of immovable property. The right of use grants a personal servitude over the specified use of an estate. La. C.C. art. 639.

In *Aucoin v. Fontenot*, 304 So.2d 754, 757 (La. App. 3 Cir. 1974), the court differentiated between a right of use and that of a usufruct, reiterating then La. C.C. art. 638, which stated, "the person who has the right of use can neither transfer, let, nor give his right to another." This distinction is further emphasized in the 1976 Revision Comments to the Louisiana Civil Code. La. C.C. art. 632 Revision Comments — 1976 paragraph (b), provides that the "right to receive the fruits of a house and to sell and dispose of them freely, would be a right of usufruct. . . ." The legatee does not possess these rights in conjunction with habitation; these rights are held by the trust. Furthermore, the Revision Comments — 1976 state that "[i]f a juridical act confers advantages that exhaust the utility of the property, it establishes a usufruct rather than a right of use." La. C.C. art. 639 Revision Comments — 1976 (b).

The Executrix argues that taken together these testamentary rights of habitation and use give rise to an affirmative obligation that the legatee pay the interest portion on the home mortgage. She further argues that the Louisiana Civil Code articles that analogize the rights and obligations of habitation to that of a usufruct. La. C.C. arts. 631, 635, 636.

The Executrix relies on paragraph (b) of the Revision Comments—1976 to La. C.C. art. 630 for the proposition that where the Louisiana Civil Code articles on habitation are silent, then the right of habitation is governed by the code articles on usufruct. La. C.C. art. 630 defines the term "habitation" as the "nontransferable real right to dwell in the house of another." Paragraph (b) of the Revision Comments—1976 to La. C.C. art. 630 states that habitation is a charge on property in favor of a person and therefore, the personal servitude of habitation is "akin to usufruct," which is also a charge on property in favor of a person. The language does not connote, as the Executrix asserts, that where the Louisiana Civil Code articles on habitation are silent, the articles on usufruct apply.

The Executrix relies on La. C.C. art. 632 to support her position because it states that "[t]he right of habitation is regulated by the title that establishes it." Additionally, "[i]f the title is silent as to the extent of habitation, the right is regulated in accordance with Articles 633 through 635." The Revision Comments—1976 to La. C.C. art. 632 state in paragraph (b) that if an agreement exceeds the limits on the rules governing the right of habitation, then another right is created. Paragraph (b) further states that, if, for example, a person is given the right to receive the fruits and dispose of the fruits of a house in addition to the right of habitation, then a usufruct is created, and all of the laws concerning usufruct would be applicable to the right to receive and dispose of the fruits.

The Executrix interprets paragraph (b) as applying the laws of usufruct relating to paying the mortgage on the family home because the will did not dictate who should pay the mortgage. This is without merit. La. C.C. art. 632 states that only when the title establishing the extent of the right of habitation is silent, the right is regulated in accordance with La. C.C. articles 633 through 635, which are contained in the chapter of the Louisiana Civil Code on the right of habitation, not in the chapter on usufruct. If Mr. Firmin's will had granted Mrs. Firmin rights that exceeded those of habitation such that a usufruct was established in favor of Mrs. Firmin, the provision in paragraph (b) relating to the laws of usufruct would become operative. Mr. Firmin's will did not establish a right beyond that of habitation. Therefore, the provision in paragraph (b) relating to the law of usufruct is inapplicable in this case.

La. C.C. art. 636 states the obligations of a person with the right of habitation. If the person occupies an entire house, that person is liable for "ordinary repairs, for the payment of taxes, and for other annual charges *in the same manner as the usufructuary*" (emphasis added). Therefore, the articles on usufruct provide instruction on the manner in which a usufructuary is required to make ordinary repairs, to pay taxes, and to pay annual charges.

The manner in which a usufructuary is liable for ordinary repairs is set forth in La. C.C. arts. 577–583. The manner in which a usufructuary is liable for the payment of taxes and the payment of annual charges is set forth in La. C.C. art. 584, which provides that the usufructuary is required to pay the annual charges, such as property taxes, that are imposed while the usufructuary enjoys the use of the property. Paragraph (d) of the Revision Comments — 1976 to article 584 makes it clear that the annual charges to which La. C.C. art. 584 refers are "annual public charges." There is nothing in La. C.C. arts. 577–583 or in La. C.C. art. 584 that refers to mortgage payments. Thus, these articles are not applicable in this case. Mrs. Firmin's obligations relating to the repair of the family home and the payment of taxes and annual charges on the home are governed by the provisions of Mr. Firmin's will and the provisions of La. C.C. art. 636.

Obligations of a Usufructuary

If the Louisiana Civil Code articles relating to use and habitation could be analogized to those rights and obligations created by usufruct, the legatee would not be responsible for the interest on the mortgage debt. The Executrix relies on the language of Louisiana Civil Code articles relating to habitation to assert that it imparts usufructuary obligations on the legatee. *See generally* La. C.C. arts. 630–636. However, the provisions on usufruct mortis causa do not support this argument.

La. C.C. art. 587 states "the position of a usufructuary relative to the payment of the debts of the succession depends on whether the usufruct is universal, under universal title, or under particular title. The usufruct . . . of individually determined things is under particular title." The legacy of a right of use and habitation is of an individually determined thing. Moreover, a legatee of a usufruct is not liable for the debts of the succession, although she "may discharge the indebtedness." La. C.C. art. 588 Revision Comments — 1976 (c). The Revision Comments — 1976 further explain "[t]hese debts must be paid by the universal successor of the grantor, be he the naked owner or a third person." La. C.C. art. 588 cmt (b).

The case at bar is distinguishable from *Succession of Crain,* 468 So.2d 778 (La. App. 1 Cir. 1985), relied on by the Executrix. In *Crain,* the will confirmed a legal usufruct, and thereby expressly assigned all of the rights and obligations detailed in the Louisiana Civil Code to the legatee. *Id.* However, in this instance, even if Mrs. Firmin were considered to be in the position of a usufructuary, she is a particular legatee. Under both the reasoning of the Louisiana Civil Code and Louisiana case law, the universal successor and the naked owner are liable for the debts of the estate. *See Succession of Dougart,* 30 La. Ann. 268 (La. 1878).

In taking the position that Mrs. Firmin is required to pay the mortgage interest on the family home, the Executrix also cites La. C.C. art. 586 in support of her contention. La. C.C. art. 586, which is contained in the chapter of the Louisiana Civil Code on usufruct, not the chapter of the code on right of habitation, clearly states that "[w]hen the property subject to the usufruct is burdened with a mortgage . . . the usufructuary *may* discharge the indebtedness and may claim reimbursement only for the capital he has expended" (emphasis added). Even if La. C.C. art. 586 were applicable to Mrs. Firmin's right of habitation, that article would not obligate her to pay the mortgage interest that accrues during her occupancy of the family home. Paragraph (c) of the Revision Comments—1976 to La. C.C. art. 586 states that "the usufructuary has the *right* to discharge the indebtedness" if the property subject to a usufruct is burdened with a mortgage (emphasis added). The right to discharge the mortgage does not create an obligation.

The Executrix also relies on La. C.C. art. 592 to support her argument that Mrs. Firmin is obligated to pay the interest portion of the mortgage payment while she occupies the family home. La. C.C. art. 592, which is in the chapter of the Louisiana Civil Code on usufruct, not the chapter on habitation, provides that a usufructuary is entitled to be reimbursed without interest at the termination of the usufruct for succession debts paid by the usufructuary. La. C.C. art. 592 further provides that if the usufructuary does not advance the funds to pay a debt, then the naked owner may advance the funds, "for which the usufructuary shall pay interest during the period of the usufruct." The naked owner also has the right under La. C.C. art. 592 to sell a part of the property subject to the usufruct to pay the succession debts, if the usufructuary does not pay the debts.

Paragraph (c) of the Revision Comments—1976 to La. C.C. art. 592 states that a usufructuary is not permitted to return the property subject to a usufruct to the naked owner burdened with interest accrued during the term of the usufruct. Thus, if Mrs. Firmin had been granted a usufruct over the family home, she could not simply allow the mortgage to remain unpaid such that the property would be burdened at the termination of the usufruct with mortgage interest that had accrued during the term of the usufruct. Paragraph (c) is not applicable in the case *sub judice*. The right of usufruct is a broader right than that of habitation, and the obligations of a usufructuary may be more burdensome than those of a person with a right of habitation. The Louisiana Civil Code articles on habitation do not require Mrs. Firmin to pay interest on the mortgage on the family home and those articles do not connote the incorporation of the provisions of La. C.C. art. 592 into the Civil Code provisions on habitation.

Debts of the Succession

The Executrix relies on Section 3 of Chapter 13 of the Civil Code, Responsibilities of Successors Among Themselves, La. C.C. art. 1420 *et seq.,* in support of her argument that the legatee must pay the mortgage debts. She argues that under the theory of limited liability of successors, estate debts are charged against the property itself and its fruits and products, and not to the successors personally. *See* La. C.C. art. 1428 Revision Comment—1997. However, the legatee does not possess civil fruits of the succession, which are defined, in La. C.C. art. 551 Revision Comments—1976(c), as "revenues derived from a thing by operation of law or by reason of a juridical act, such as rentals, interests, and certain corporate distributions."

The mortgage on a family home is a debt of the succession, and the payment of succession debts are governed by the Louisiana laws governing successions and the administration of successions. La. C.C. art. 1422, for example, provides that "when a decedent has encumbered property to secure a debt, the debt is presumptively charged to that property and its fruits and products." As noted, Mrs. Firmin has only the limited rights of use and habitation; the fruits of the property belong to the trust.

Accordingly, Mrs. Firmin's "use and habitation" of the home does not require her to pay interest on the mortgage note. Mrs. Firmin's rights are more limited than those of a usufructuary. Accordingly, we affirm the trial court's ruling that there is no legal authority to force Mrs. Firmin to pay interest on the mortgage note.

Decree

For the reasons assigned above, we affirm the decision of the trial court.

AFFIRMED.

Notes and Questions

1. Does the court's holding in *In re Succession of Firmin*, 935 So.2d 209 (La. App. 4 Cir. 2006), strike a fair balance between the interests of the holder of the right of habitation, Valerie Firmin, and her stepdaughters, who hold the residual interest in the house? Will the stepdaughters have an opportunity to derive any income from the house in order to pay the mortgage interest? Commentators believe that the court in *Succession of Firmin* reached a fair outcome in holding that when property subject to a right of habitation is burdened by a mortgage the person with the right of habitation should not be required to pay anything and that principal and interest should be paid by naked owners or universal successors of the grantor. A.N. Yiannopoulos, 3 Louisiana Civil Law Treatise: Personal Servitudes § 8.11, at 546 n. 1 (5th ed. 2011).

2. Notice that the court determined that Albert Firmin's will "did not establish a right beyond that of habitation." *In re Succession of Firmin*, 938 So.2d at 214. If Albert's will had granted Valerie Firmin a usufruct, rather than simply a right of habitation, would she have been obligated to pay either the principal or interest portion of the monthly mortgage note on the house, or none of it at all? If Valerie had paid some portion (or all) of the monthly mortgage note during the existence of the usufruct, would she have been entitled to any reimbursement from her stepdaughters, the residual legatees of Firmin's estate? Which provisions of the Louisiana Civil Code are applicable to this determination: Article 584, Articles 587–588, Article 590, Article 592, or other provisions?

3. What considerations might have motivated Albert Firmin to grant his second wife, Valerie Firmin, a right of habitation, rather than a usufruct in his will? If you had been Albert Firmin's lawyer, what advice would you have given him if you had assisted him with the drafting of his will?

4. In light of the decision in *In re Succession of Firmin*, how would you counsel a homeowner today who is considering donating his house to one person (perhaps a loved one or family member), subject to a right of habitation in favor of another person, if the house has already been encumbered by a mortgage to secure a loan and a

substantial principal indebtedness remains? What advice would you give the donee or legatee who is to receive ownership of the house subject to the right of habitation? Should that person accept or renounce the gift or legacy?

5. In a subsequent proceeding involving the same parties, the Louisiana Fourth Circuit Court of Appeal addressed the rights of Valerie Firmin and her late husband's succession concerning the same house subject to the right of habitation after it was destroyed by Hurricane Katrina. *In re Succession of Firmin*, 38 So.3d 445 (La. App. 4 Cir. 2010). In that case, Mrs. Firmin contended that she should be awarded use of the proceeds from the insurance policy covering the family home after it was destroyed by the hurricane, particularly since neither she nor her late husband's succession wanted to repair the house or could afford to do so. *Id.* at 450. The Louisiana Fourth Circuit Court of Appeal, however, disagreed. It first focused on the specific nature of the bequest granting Mrs. Firmin the right of habitation, noting that "Mr. Firmin's will stipulated that if Mrs. Firmin did not specifically live in the family house for a period of six months, the conferred right of use and occupancy would cease." *Id.* at 451. Next, it observed that "the executrix [of the succession] offered Mrs. Firmin use of the insurance proceeds to repair the family house for her to occupy it," but then observed that Mrs. Firmin did not accept the offer. *Id.* In light of these factors, the court of appeal affirmed "the trial court's determination that Mrs. Firmin could not be granted the use of the insurance proceeds in lieu of fulfilling the occupancy requirement stipulated by Mr. Firmin in his will." *Id.* If Mrs. Firmin had been granted a testamentary usufruct, rather than a right of habitation, would the Louisiana Civil Code have supported her claim to be able to use the insurance proceeds for other purposes? *See* La. Civ. Code arts. 617–618 (1976). What does this episode reveal about the comparative flexibility of a usufruct and a right of habitation?

B. Right of Use

Unlike the right of habitation, the limited personal servitude of right of use is transferable and heritable, unless prohibited by contract or by law. La. Civ. Code arts. 643-44 (1976). Moreover, a right of use can be established in favor of either a natural person or a legal entity. La. Civ. Code art. 641 (1976). The right of use is a heritable right. Therefore, it is not extinguished by the death of a natural person in whose favor it is established or by the dissolution of a legal entity enjoying the right, unless the contrary is provided by law or by contract. La. Civ. Code art. 644 (1976). Like the right of habitation, however, the right of use confers a use less than full enjoyment. La. Civ. Code art. 639 (1976).

A recent decision by the Louisiana Third Circuit Court of Appeal illustrates the importance of the temporal flexibility and heritability of a limited personal servitude of right of use. *Roy v. Bordelon*, 164 So.3d 367 (La. App. 3 Cir. 2015). In *Roy*, two married couples conveyed two contiguous tracts of land and reserved "any and all hunting rights on the property." The underlying land was later subject to a foreclosure proceeding and, as a result, was conveyed to subsequent purchasers, the defendants in the lawsuit. All of the deeds specifically referenced the hunting rights originally reserved by the Roys. All deeds were recorded in the public records. In time, a dispute arose between the Roys, who had reserved the hunting rights, and the subsequent purchasers of the underlying tracts of land. In particular, the subsequent purchasers acknowledged that the reservation of hunting rights in favor of the Roys created limited personal servitudes in the nature of a right of use. Nevertheless, they contended that, because the original acts of sale did not specifically reserve the hunting rights for heirs and assigns, the rights of use were only personal to the Roys and not heritable. *Id.* at 370–73. Writing for the majority of a five-judge en banc panel of the court of appeal, Judge Marc Amy rejected this argument, noting that Article 644 of the Louisiana Civil Code does not require such a designation. *Id.* at 375. Judge Amy more fully explained his reasoning as follows:

> Article 644 instead positively anticipates that such a right 'is not extinguished at the death of the natural person or at the dissolution of any other entity having the right unless the contrary is provided by law or contract." In this case, the parties have pointed to no other law or contract that would undermine heritability by the vendor's successor.
>
> In contrast, it is important to remember that the Roys, as the original vendors, did not reserve the hunting rights by lease. That reservation was accomplished, instead as a right of use on the respective properties. Simply, the defendants seek the return of a component of the ownership of the property that was never acquired by their ancestors in title. That component was dismembered and retained by the vendors at the time of the original 1980 transfers to the Bordelons. In this instance, the conveyances did not include a mechanism by which the rights of use would revert to the defendants. Rather, La. Civ. Code art. 644 provides that a right of use is heritable "unless the contrary is established by law or contract." The defendants have pointed to no such law applicable to the facts established at trial nor to any contract that would undermine the heritability characteristic described in La. Civ. Code art. 644. Thus, the trial court appropriately designated the right of use as heritable under the facts of this case.

Roy, 164 So.3d at 375–76. Elsewhere in the decision, the court of appeal also affirmed the trial court's determination that the reservation of hunting rights gave the original vendors and their heirs and assigns, a right to have a reasonable number of invitees engage in hunting activities on the land for reasonable durations of time. *Id.* at 376–77.

A more typical scenario in which a right of use will be deployed arises when a utility company needs to acquire a right of way to erect utility lines. Because it may not own, or want to own, a distinct corporeal immovable in the vicinity that could serve as a dominant estate benefitted by a predial servitude, the utility company may instead acquire a personal servitude of right of use. Such a servitude will often include not only a right to place wires or cables on the servient estate directly contiguous with the building or immovable being served, but also a right to place wires, pipes or other facilities that serve a broader customer base throughout the neighborhood. Pipeline companies engaged in the transmission of oil, gas or other fluids will regularly have similar interests. Instead of acquiring a predial servitude that favors a distinct corporeal immovable estate, they will chose a right of use for the purpose of constructing, operating and maintaining one or more pipelines that will be located in a particular right of way across a servient estate.

Quite frequently a utility company will acquire a limited personal servitude of right of use across various servient estates from a landowner who subdivides his land for the purpose of a residential or commercial development. In such a case, the right of use will be marked on the plat of the subdivision filed in the conveyance records of the parish in which the servient estates are located. Once evidence of the right of use is filed in the conveyance records, all future owners of the servient estates will be bound. Because a right of use is transferable and heritable, particular and universal successors of the holder of the right of use may also enjoy it, in the absence of contrary language in the title creating the right of use. *See* La. Civ. Code arts. 643–44 (1976).

Suppose that ABC Power Company (ABC) agrees with Matthew to provide electrical service to Matthew's property. ABC obtains from Matthew the right to place electricity-transmission wires on his property to enable it to provide the service. Their agreement is filed in the conveyance records of the parish where Mathew's property is located. Now suppose that ABC is acquired by MNO Power Company (MNO) and that their agreement transfers all of ABC's servitudes, rights of way and rights of use to MNO. MNO now has a right to exercise the limited personal servitude of right of use on Matthew's property that ABC acquired before being sold to MNO. Further, suppose that Matthew next sells his land to Brenda. Brenda must now allow MNO to exercise the right of use on the land she acquired from Mathew.

This example illustrates the vast practical utility of a right of use. By allowing juridical persons such as power companies, telecommunications companies and pipeline companies to acquire a transferable and temporally unlimited real right in the nature of a limited personal servitude of right of use, the revised Louisiana Civil Code codified the holdings of a number of Louisiana judicial decisions which had gradually recognized that the specified list of real rights less than full ownership in the Civil Code of 1870 (usufruct, use, and habitation) did not prohibit the recognition of what we now call a limited personal servitude of right of use. *See* A.N. Yian-nopoulos, 3 Louisiana Civil Law Treatise: Personal Servitudes § 8.2-8.4, at 520–529 (5th ed. 2011) (tracing the evolution of limited personal servitudes of right of use in other civil law jurisdictions as well as in Louisiana).

Article 640 of the Louisiana Civil Code provides that "[t]he right of use may confer only *an advantage* that may be established by a predial servitude." La. Civ. Code art. 640 (1976) (emphasis added). Book II, Title IV describes the kinds of predial servitudes permitted by law. Because right of use servitudes generally bestow the same advantages as predial servitudes, they are often confused with one another.

Remember that predial servitudes cannot, generally speaking, impose affirmative obligations on the owner of a servient estate. La. Civ. Code art. 651 (1977). Can a right of use granted to a natural person or legal entity entitle that person or entity to receive affirmative services from the owner of a servient estate? In *Wagner v. Alford*, 741 So.2d 884 (La. App. 3 Cir. 1999), which follows, the court addresses this difficult question. In all of the decisions we discuss, pay special attention to how courts distinguish predial servitudes from personal servitudes.

Wagner v. Alford

741 So.2d 884 (La. App. 3 Cir. 1999)

AMY, Judge. The plaintiff condominium owners filed a petition for declaratory judgment seeking enforcement of a purported personal servitude establishing rights on the adjacent resort property. The defendant real estate company filed a reconventional demand alleging that the plaintiffs breached an oral agreement wherein the plaintiffs were to be given title to an adjoining condominium unit in exchange for assisting the defendant's purchase of additional condominiums. The defendant maintained that the plaintiffs breached this agreement by failing to satisfy the contract in full. The lower court found for the plaintiffs in both respects. We reverse the lower court's determination as it relates to the purported servitude and affirm that portion relating to the reconventional demand.

Factual and Procedural Background

The plaintiffs in this matter, W.L. and Nina Wagner, purchased a condominium located in the Fairway Villas Condominium Association in 1990. This condominium complex is adjacent to Toro Hills Resort, a hotel and golf facility in Sabine Parish, Louisiana. Stephen Alford, one of the defendants in this matter, testified that, as early as the 1980s, he was part of a partnership that owned three units at the complex. Afterwards, Rael, Inc., a company in which Alford is the sole stockholder, purchased property in the condominium facility. At the time the parties first bought property in the complex, the Toro Hills facility was owned by Toro Investment Corporation.

Mrs. Wagner testified that, after the 1990 purchase of their condominium, services such as garbage collection, sewerage, water, cable television, and telephone services were provided through the hotel. Alford also testified that, as a condominium owner, his services too were provided through the resort for a monthly fee ranging from an estimated amount as low as $50.00 to $75.00 per month. This fee also included maintenance, parking, and privileges at the golf course.

Mrs. Wagner testified that, as negotiations began for the sale of Toro Hills by Toro Investment Corporation, she and her husband, along with Alford, sought to protect the above-listed services. Mrs. Wagner testified that she, along with Alford, confected a "Service Agreement" listing the services they wanted to safeguard. Her testimony indicates that she and her husband presented their copy of the service agreement to George Gouffray, an employee of Toro Investment Corporation who acted as manager of Toro Hills, and that his staff retyped the agreement. The agreement, which was an exhibit at trial, is written on Toro Hills letterhead and provides, the following:

To: Mr. & Mrs. Wagner

From: George Gouffray—Toro Investment Corp.

Subject: Service Agreement

Date: February 22, 1996

Per our conversation today, please see below the details of the service agreement Toro Hills Resort/Toro Investment Corporation will honor with Mr. & Mrs. Wagner, Condo 4A and 4B.

Services—

1) Present level of services not to be diminished

a. Garbage pickup

b. Sewerage & Water

c. Cable TV & Telephone

d. Upkeep & Maintenance of property

e. Four parking spaces maintained

f. Lifetime golf membership & privileges for family members.

g. Use of personally owned golf cars on golf course

h. Use of all facilities on 265 acres more or less included but not limited to tennis courts, pools, recreation rooms at no additional charges

i. One-half price for motel rooms

j. One-half price for guests golf green fees

k. One-half price for guests golf cart fees

Monthly fee for services will be $75.00 not to increase unless agreed by owner 4A and 4B. Services to be binding on all future owners of property.

The agreement contains the signatures of Mr. and Mrs. Wagner and Gouffray, who signed in his capacity as President of Toro Investment Corp. Gouffray testified that he did not recall the portion of the agreement regarding future owners of the property. Instead, Gouffray stated as follows: "As long as we owned the property, that they could have that agreement." The record indicates that the service agreement was filed with the Clerk of Court for Sabine Parish on July 10, 1996.

In February 1997, Toro Hills, both the hotel and golf facilities, was sold to Alford's company, Rael, Inc. Gouffray's deposition testimony indicates that, during negotiations, he attempted to incorporate the service agreement into the sale of the property, but that Alford refused to buy the property if the agreement was part of the sale. Gouffray stated that he informed the Wagners of Alford's refusal to consider the agreement and that the sale was ultimately completed without the inclusion of the agreement.

Alford testified that following Rael's purchase of Toro Hills, the services outlined in the service agreement were provided for approximately one year. At some point, however, he ceased accepting the $75.00 monthly payments from the plaintiffs. Alford stated that he did not feel that the agreement was valid or binding against Rael and that he stopped accepting the $75.00 payments as he had put together two service packages from which condominium owners could choose and that the plaintiffs never made a choice between the options. He admitted that the new packages presented to the Wagners would result in a higher monthly fee than the $75.00 fee discussed in the original service agreement. The record reveals that many of the services listed in the agreement ultimately ceased to be provided.

In June 1997, the plaintiffs filed a petition for declaratory judgment requesting the court to declare the service agreement binding and enforceable against Rael. Subsequently, Rael filed a reconventional demand against the Wagners asserting that they were indebted to Rael for $49,000.00, the purchase price of the Wagners second condominium at Toro Hills. Thus, Rael asked the court to recognize Rael as the true owner of the condominium or, in the alternative, order the plaintiffs to reimburse the purchase price to Rael.

Following a trial, the lower court ruled in favor of the plaintiffs in both actions. With regard to the declaratory judgment, the court found that the recorded service agreement constituted a valid personal servitude, specifically, a right of use. As for the reconventional demand, the trial court concluded that the plaintiffs had completed the work necessary for receipt of the condominium and that the portion of the oral agreement that had not been completed had been agreed to by the plaintiffs under duress.

The defendants appeal both portions of the lower court's judgment assigning the following as error:

1. The Trial Court erred by upholding the service agreement as a valid personal servitude.

2. The Trial Court erred by denying the reconventional demand of defendants and failed to recognize defendant as the correct owner of condominium Unit 4A.

Discussion

Service Agreement

The defendants assert a variety of deficiencies that arguably prevent the service agreement from being considered a personal servitude. First, they maintain that the agreement was not created by either authentic act or act under private signature and, thus, cannot now be considered a properly confected right of use. They also contend that the plaintiffs have failed to prove that the person entering into the alleged servitude, George Gouffray, had authority to enter into this type of agreement. Further, the defendants maintain that the agreement is invalid as a servitude as it is vague as to the nature and extent of the servitude and, additionally, it requires that the servient estate, in this case Toro Hills, perform services for the plaintiffs which is contrary to the nature of a predial servitude. The plaintiffs continue to argue that the service agreement created a personal servitude of right of use in their favor.

The Louisiana Civil Code provides for two types of servitudes, personal and predial. La. Civ. Code art. 533. A personal servitude, the type at issue, "is a charge on a thing for the benefit of a person. There are three sorts of personal servitudes: usufruct, habitation, and rights of use." La. Civ. Code art. 534. It is the right of use with which we are now concerned.

Article 639 of the Louisiana Civil Code explains that: "The personal servitude of right of use confers in favor of a person a specified use of an estate less than full enjoyment." Only those advantages that may be provided by a predial servitude are permissible rights of use. La. Civ. Code art. 640. Further, "[a] right of use is regulated by application of the rules governing usufruct and predial servitudes to the extent that their application is compatible with the rules governing a right of use servitude." La. Civ. Code art. 645. It is when we turn to the rules pertaining to predial servitudes that we encounter problems with the lower court's determination that the "service agreement" acts as a servitude. Although recorded and arguably created by an act under private signature, we do not conclude that the service agreement is consistent with the articles pertaining to predial servitudes.

La. Civ. Code art. 651 relates to the types of obligations that may be imposed by predial servitude upon the owner of a servient estate, in this case, the Toro Hills property. It provides as follows:

> The owner of the servient estate is not required to do anything. His obligation is to abstain from doing something on his estate or to permit something to be done on it. He may be required by convention or by law to keep his estate in suitable condition for the exercise of the servitude due to the dominant estate.

When applying Article 651 to the services listed in the agreement at issue, the lower court concluded that the services were permissible under the statute. The judge explained as follows in his reasons for ruling: "Further, any acts of maintenance required towards the upkeep of the golf, tennis, pool, and recreation room facilities are acts ordinarily occasioned by the golf course and hotel." We conclude that this reasoning was erroneous.

The portions of the service agreement that we find necessarily run afoul of Article 651 are those related to garbage collection, the provision of utilities, property maintenance, and reduced prices for resort services. These services do not relate to the plaintiffs' right of use of the servient *estate*. Rather, they relate solely to resort services to be provided for the plaintiffs. Furthermore, we note that, arguably, some of these services such as garbage collection and maintenance of the property do not involve the servient estate at all, but, rather, would involve employees of the defendant traveling onto the plaintiffs' property to perform the services. These types of services are more akin to personal obligations than rights of use.

Thus, we consider the remaining provisions of the service agreement. Those portions relating to lifetime golf membership at the golf facilities, use of personally owned golf carts on the course, and general use of Toro Hills facilities are closer to the traditional type of rights of use, *i.e.*, they allow the plaintiffs to do certain things on the servient estate. While these things *may* be properly transferred as rights of use, they were not created by a traditional method in this case. Rather, they are labeled as services, are listed with a variety of "services" we have concluded are not proper rights of use, and are conferred to the plaintiffs only upon the payment of a monthly fee. Without payment of this fee, any right would be properly withheld and, thus, a servitude has not been conferred. Given the peculiar nature of the agreement, we cannot be certain that a servitude was intended.

La. Civ. Code art. 730 provides that "doubt as to the existence, extent, or manner of exercise of a predial servitude shall be resolved in favor of the servient estate." We note that the wording of the agreement leaves doubt in several regards. Although the parties involved in the agreement may have enjoyed a common understanding of the services, those subsequently interpreting the agreement may have differing opinions as to the meaning of the terms. For example, rather than precisely defining the required services, the agreement contains general statements regarding the provision of sewerage, water, cable television, and telephone. This type of statement could be open to varying interpretations absent a complete factual background. Further, as referenced above, even those portions of the agreement relating to more traditional rights of use are contained in a "service agreement" requiring a monthly charge. La. Civ. Code art. 730 requires that these types of uncertainty be resolved in favor of the defendant. Thus, we reverse the lower court's determination that the service agreement created a personal servitude of right of use. Finding the agreement deficient to constitute a servitude, we need not reach the defendants' remaining arguments as they relate to the service agreement. . . .

Decree

For the foregoing reasons, the decision of the lower court is reversed as it relates to the service agreement and affirmed with regard to the reconventional demand. All costs of this appeal are to be divided equally between the plaintiffs, W.L. and Nina Wagner, and the defendants, Stephen R. Alford and Rael, Inc.

AFFIRMED IN PART; REVERSED IN PART AND RENDERED.

COOKS, Judge, concurring in part and dissenting in part: . . . I disagree with the majority's position relating to the validity of the "Service Agreement" for two reasons. First, La. Civ. Code art. 645 does not require in every instances that a right of use fits the definition or conditions of a usufruct or predial servitude. The article specifically declares such right of use shall be regulated by the rules applicable to usufructs and predial servitudes to *the extent that their application is compatible.* The majority opinion makes no reference to the latter and, in fact, ignores the more expansive language found in the article. When a conflict occurs or the rules just do not fit, article 645 does not require that we vitiate the parties' undertakings. The service agreement in this case granted plaintiff a right of use albeit a non-traditional one. Times are "a changing" and the kinds of "understandings and undertakings" between contracting parties are too. The redactors of the code were not short-sighted—they envisioned the day when a right of use might not be compatible with the rules applicable to usufruct and predial servitude. That day has come in this case; and, nothing in the civil code prevented the trial judge from finding the at issue agreement to provide the noted services valid.

Second, I vehemently disagree with the majority's finding that the remaining services, though akin to the those typed as rights of use, do not establish a servitude because for some reason they cannot surmise what the parties intended. I have read the "Service Agreement" carefully and it is very clear to me what the parties intended. There is nothing ambiguous or confusing in the document; and, there is nothing I find "peculiar" about it; it's pretty straightforward. In expressing their intent, the parties were not required to use legal jargon. I know what they meant to do, they knew what they meant, and even Alford does not deny that he had the same understanding. He acquired the property knowing the agreement existed, after it was recorded in the public record.

DOUCET, C.J., dissenting. The record herein contains the Declaration Establishing a Condominium Regime Under the Provisions of LSA-R.S. 9:1121.101, et seq., and Establishing the Covenants and Restrictions of the Fairway Villas Condominiums. The provisions thereof are sufficient to establish servitudes for ingress and egress, support, maintenance and repair of the units as well as for utilities including electric power, gas, hot and cold water, and garbage and sewerage disposal. In light of the provisions of that document, I would render declaratory judgment finding the existence of a servitude for those purposes. As a result, I respectfully dissent from the majority herein.

Notes and Questions

1. Why do you suppose Judge Cooks disagreed so "vehemently" with the majority opinion authored by Judge Amy in *Wagner v. Alford*, 741 So.2d 884 (La. App. 3 Cir. 1999)? Is it because the defendant, Rael, Inc., and its principal owner, Stephen Alford, both had actual and constructive notice of the contents of the "service agreement" executed by Toro Investment Corporation and recorded in the conveyance records of Sabine Parish?

2. Should agreements like the one at issue here, if executed in writing and recorded in the public records, be deemed unenforceable because they are novel in nature? If the service agreement had been granted in exchange for a single lump-sum payment by the Wagners (say $5,000.00), rather than a monthly service fee of $75.00, would the court have been more likely to enforce the service agreement as a right of use or predial servitude? Should this make a difference? What else might the Wagners have done to protect their rights under the agreement?

3. Can a personal servitude of right of use impose *negative* restrictions on a servient estate — for instance, a prohibition against using the property for some particular commercial or industrial purpose? Can a right of use prohibit any kind of development at all? *See* La. Civ. Code art. 640 rev. cmt (a) ("It is *only advantages* that may become the object of a predial servitude that may also be stipulated in the form of a right of use servitude.") (emphasis added). *See also id.* rev. cmt (b) (listing rights granted in the form of a right of use).

In several specific statutes, the Louisiana Legislature has authorized the creation and enforcement of a real right by a juridical person that does not own a dominant estate in the vicinity of the affected servient estate. These negative limited personal servitudes address very particular situations. *See* La. Rev. Stat. § 1271 (establishing the Louisiana Conservation Servitude Act); La. Rev. Stat. § 1272(A) (defining a "conservation servitude" as "a non-possessory interest of a holder in immovable property imposing limitations or affirmative obligations the purposes of which include retaining or protecting natural, scenic, or open-space values of immovable property. . . ."); La. Rev. Stat. § 1252(A)-(B) (providing that the owner of immovable property "may create a perpetual real right burdening the whole or any part thereof of that immovable property, including, but not limited to, the façade, exterior, roof, or front of any improvement thereon to any corporation, trust, community chest, fund or foundation, organized and operated exclusively for religious, scientific, literary, charitable, educational, or historical purposes" and making such a right "binding on the grantor, his heirs, successors, assigns, and all subsequent owners of the immovable property, regardless of the fact that the grantee does not own or possess any interest in a neighboring estate or the fact that the real right is granted to the grantee and not to the estate of the grantee"). If the Louisiana Legislature has recognized the need for specific statutory authorization in the cases of conservation servitudes and "façade servitudes" for ecological or historic preservation purposes, what does this reveal about the general scope of a limited personal servitude in the nature of a right of use?

* * *

The following decision, though brief, addresses the consequences of characterizing an agreement giving a juridical person a right of way across a particular tract of land as a right of use rather than a predial servitude. Notice that the parties who created the original 1963 agreement at issue purported to create an "easement for the construction and maintenance of a forest road." This decision thus illustrates the problems that can result when lawyers use common law terminology that does not fit within Louisiana's civil law framework for property.

Sustainable Forests, L.L.C. v. Harrison

846 So.2d 1283 (La. App. 2 Cir. 2003)

DREW, Judge. Sustainable Forests, L.L.C. ("Sustainable"), appeals a judgment recognizing its "forest road" right of passage across defendants' land, but prohibiting members of Sustainable's lessee, Grand Bayou South Hunting Club, from using the road. Noticing *sua sponte*, the peremptory exception of no right of action which had been denied by the trial court, we sustain the exception and grant Sustainable leave to amend its suit.

Facts and Procedural History

Sustainable brought this action against Jack Keith Harrison and Leisa Miller Harrison (the "Harrisons") to prevent the Harrisons from interfering with Sustainable's use of a road right-of-way across their rural tract of land. The Harrisons objected to the use of the road by hunters crossing their tract in Section 3 to access Sustainable's land in Section 4. The hunters possessed hunting leases from Sustainable.

Sustainable characterized its suit as a possessory action and sought injunctive relief. Sustainable's petition asserts as the basis of its claim, a 1963 road grant (hereinafter the "Servitude Deed") from the Harrisons' predecessor-in-title, Olan B. Davis, to Sustainable's predecessor-in-title, International Paper Company ("IP"). The Servitude Deed described the property now owned by the Harrisons and identified, on an attached plat, a 12-foot right-of-way. The Servitude Deed granted IP "an easement for the construction and maintenance of a forest road across" the Davis tract in Section 3.

Sustainable's petition next asserts a 1998 deed (hereinafter the "1998 Deed") from IP to Sustainable conveying the land in Section 4 along with many other tracts of land. Sustainable claimed that on the basis of these title instruments, IP and Sustainable had been in open and continuous possession of the servitude of passage across the Harrison Tract.

In response to the suit, the Harrisons filed certain exceptions, including the exception of no right of action. The Harrisons pointed out to the court that IP's 1998 Deed to Sustainable did not specifically describe the 12-foot right-of-way. Therefore, it was urged that the ownership right of the disputed servitude remained in IP. The ruling on the exception was deferred to the trial of the case, and at the close of trial was rejected by the trial court.

After the bench trial, the Harrisons prevailed, nevertheless, on the merits of their defense concerning the limited scope of the "forest road" created by the 1963 Servitude Deed. Citing the Civil Code articles for the interpretation of predial servitudes, the trial court found that at the time of the 1963 transaction, IP acquired the road for its timber operations in Section 4 and not for hunting leases on that property. The trial court concluded:

> Therefore, the term "forest road" would not have included hunters. The only way that hunting rights could be included would be by more specific language or by acquisitive prescription.

The trial court also found that there was insufficient evidence supporting Sustainable's alternative claim of acquisitive prescription under Civil Code Article 760 of an expanded use of the servitude across the Harrisons' tract.

Sustainable now brings this appeal.

Discussion

The resolution of this dispute begins with the characterization of the right which was created by the Servitude Deed. The 1963 instrument is entitled "Grant of Roadway Easement." It grants to IP "an easement for the construction and maintenance of a forest road across" the land of Harrison's predecessor-in-title, Davis. The agreement further twice references the right as a right-of-way. The 1963 instrument additionally provided that a one-year period of non-use, instead of the usual ten-year prescription of non-use, would result in the extinction of the servitude.

Most significantly and overlooked by the parties and the trial court, the Servitude Deed does not describe a dominant estate; it only describes a servient estate. There is nothing in the public records describing IP's land in Section 4 as the dominant estate. From the descriptions of Sustainable's land acquired from IP and the Harrisons' tract as set forth in the petition, and as shown on the plat exhibit in the record, the IP/Sustainable tract is not contiguous to the Davis/Harrison tract. Therefore, although contiguity is not necessary for the creation of a predial servitude (La. C.C. art. 648), its absence in this case may explain why there is no dominant tract described in the 1963 instrument.

In the absence of a description of a dominant estate in the title instrument, this conventional right of passage and access in favor of IP falls within the category of personal servitudes, which the Civil Code defines as a "right of use." La. C.C. arts. 639, et seq. In 1963, when the servitude was created, such right of use, although not expressly addressed in the Civil Code, had been recognized in the jurisprudence as a real right. *Simoneaux v. Lebermuth & Israel Planting Co.*, 155 La. 689, 99 So. 531 (1924). The right of use may confer only an advantage that may be established by a predial servitude, such as this right of passage. La. C.C. art. 640. The right of use is a transferable right which the initial grantee may convey to others. La. C.C. art. 643. Nevertheless, the right of use is not a predial servitude because of the absence of a dominant estate, and the distinction between these separate rights is critical in this case.

The 1998 Deed from IP to Sustainable describes large tracts of land, including a large tract in Section 4, which apparently is the land to which the disputed road provides access. The 1998 Deed, however, does not describe IP's right to the personal servitude created in the 1963 Servitude Deed. For this reason, Harrison pled the exception of no right of action in the trial court. The trial court denied the exception, however, apparently in reliance upon the principle set forth in Civil Code Article 650, which is applicable to predial servitudes. Article 650 provides, in pertinent part:

> A predial servitude is inseparable from the dominant estate and passes with it. The right of using the servitude cannot be alienated or encumbered separately from the dominant estate.

Under Article 650, since [sic] a prior recorded grant of a predial servitude for a right of passage evidences the dominant estate status of a tract listed therein, the predial servitude's benefit is an accessory and passes with the sale of the dominant estate without mention of the prior grant of the predial right of passage. Nevertheless, when the right of passage is granted as a right of use to a juridical person, there is no dominant estate from which the principle of Article 650 may thereafter operate. The person who owns the right of use may convey that right by a deed identifying either the initial deed of origin of the right of use or a description of the land burdened by the right of use, which in this case would be a description of the 12-foot portion of the Harrisons' tract.

In this case, IP has not conveyed its right of use created by the 1963 Servitude Deed to Sustainable. Sustainable's assertion of those two recorded instruments as the basis for its suit therefore demonstrates its lack of right to assert the right of passage across the Harrisons' tract. The exception of no right of action assumes that the petition states a valid cause of action for some person and questions whether the plaintiff in the particular case has a legal interest in the subject matter of the litigation. *Louisiana Paddlewheels v. Louisiana Riverboat Gaming Commission*, 94-2015 (La. 11/30/94), 646 So. 2d 885, 888. Pursuant to La. C.C.P. arts. 927 and 2164, we choose to notice the peremptory exception, which was rejected by the trial court, and render judgment in this matter on that basis. Moreover, in accordance with La. C.C.P. art. 934, since the grounds for Sustainable's no right of action may be removable depending upon the scope of Sustainable's purchase agreement with IP, our judgment sustaining the exception shall allow Sustainable thirty days from the finality of this judgment to amend its suit and allege its title to the right of use.

Finally, while Sustainable has characterized this action as a possessory action in which title is normally not the issue (La. C.C.P. art. 3661), such characterization does not change our view regarding Sustainable's lack of a legal interest in the subject matter of this litigation. The jurisprudence holds that even though the grantee of a servitude or other real right possesses both for himself and the landowner, he also possesses in another sense for himself alone and may bring a possessory action against the landowner from whose ownership his right is derived. *Parkway Development Corp. v. City of Shreveport*, 342 So. 2d 151 (La. 1977); *Faust v. Mitchell Energy Corp.*, 437 So. 2d 339 (La. App. 2d Cir. 1983). This is somewhat of a different slant upon the more traditional possessory action which pits a possessor of land against another possessor or record title holder of the land. To the contrary, this suit centers on the scope of the original 1963 title instrument. Moreover, the record does not show that Sustainable's intermittent use of the road for over one year prior to this suit was sufficient adverse possession to the Harrisons, who also had the use of the road during the same period. Sustainable's possessory action is against the admitted landowner whose tract is burdened by the asserted servitude as alleged in its petition and therefore rests upon the 1963 Servitude Deed and its 1998 Deed from IP. Finding that the 1998 Deed did not convey the disputed right of use, we hereby grant the peremptory exception of no right of action subject to Sustainable's right to amend under La. C.C.P. art. 934.

Decree

With costs of this appeal assessed equally to both parties, the peremptory exception of no right of action is GRANTED, and this matter is REMANDED for Sustainable's right to amend.

Notes and Questions

1. In *Sustainable Forests, L.L.C. v. Harrison*, 846 So.2d 1283 (La. App. 2 Cir. 2003), the plaintiff, Sustainable Forests, L.L.C., which claimed to have a real right burdening the tract of land owned by the defendants, the Harrisons, brought a possessory action against the Harrisons. If Sustainable Forests had proved that it had a right of use or predial servitude burdening the Harrison tract, would a possessory action have been an appropriate procedural mechanism to protect their quasi-possession rights in the right of use or predial servitude? *See* La. Code Civ. Proc. art. 3655 (1981); La. Civ. Code arts 3421, 3440 (1982).

2. At the end of the day, the most important issue in *Sustainable Forests* concerned the nature of the right-of-way acquired in 1963 by International Paper Company, the predecessor-in-interest of Sustainable Forests. What is the primary lesson of this case for the practicing attorney? What should International Paper and Sustainable Forests have done in 1998 to avoid the problems that subsequently arose between Sustainable Forests and the Harrisons?

3. What is the significance of the appellate court's decision in *Sustainable Forests* to grant the defendants' peremptory exception of no right of action "subject to Sustainable's right to amend"? What actions must Sustainable Forests undertake? What agreements must it obtain to file an amended petition? What would be the Harrisons' likely response?

4. In a subsequent case, the Louisiana Second Circuit Court of Appeal relied upon *Sustainable Forests* to determine whether a utility servitude agreement created by a development company over its property benefitted another tract of land owned by another development company as a predial servitude or whether it granted a right of use in favor of the City of Shreveport. *St. Andrews Place, Inc. v. City of Shreveport*, 914 So.2d 1203 (La. App. 2 Cir. 2005):

> In the case *sub judice*, the trial court applied La. C.C. arts. 731–34 to determine that the Original Servitude placed a charge on one estate (Southern Trace) for the benefit of another estate (St. Andrews/Country Club Estates). We feel the trial court's interpretation of these codal articles was misplaced. Here the Original Servitude document on its face designates that the benefit is for the City, and it failed to express that it is a charge for the benefit of *another estate*; it only described a *servient estate*. *See Sustainable Forests, L.L.C. v. Harrison* . . . Louisiana C.C. art. 732 applies to cases where the act does not express that the charge is to benefit a person. In this instance, the Original Servitude document does express that the charge is to benefit the City. Thus we find the rules specified in La. C.C. arts. 733 and 734 are not applicable in

this case. Further, there is no evidence to indicate Southern Trace and the City intended to make St. Andrews/Country Club Estates as the dominant estate to effect a predial servitude. To the contrary, the document itself is the best evidence, and it declares that the right granted was for the benefit of the City. *See Sustainable Forests, supra*, where this court found a similar omission to be a critical deficiency. In the absence of a description of a dominant estate in the Original Servitude, we find this conventional right of passage and access in favor of the City falls within the category of personal servitudes, which the Civil Code defines as a "right of use." La. C.C. art. 639, *et seq.*

Id. at 1210 (emphasis in original, footnotes omitted). In light of this finding, the court concluded that the City of Shreveport, as opposed to the owner of the purported dominant estate, was the only entity that had authority to renounce the servitude. *Id*. at 12.

5. Recall our discussions of the law of predial servitudes and Article 743 of the Louisiana Civil Code, which declares in relation to predial servitudes: "Rights that are necessary for the use of a servitude are acquired at the time the servitude is established. They are to be exercised in a way least inconvenient for the servient estate." La. Civ. Code art. 743 (1977). Article 642 offers a similar yet subtly different provision in the law governing the right of use:

Art. 642. Extent of the servitude

A right of use includes the rights contemplated or necessary to enjoyment at the time of its creation as well as rights that may later become necessary, provided that a greater burden is not imposed on the property unless otherwise stipulated in the title.

La. Civ. Code art. 642 (1976). Article 642 of the Louisiana Civil Code contemplates two kinds of rights not specifically covered by the granting document: (1) those *necessary* to enjoyment *at the time the right of use is created*; and (2) those that may *subsequently become necessary*. The recognition of these rights, however, must not result in a greater burden on the property subject to the right of use unless the title provides otherwise. Does the proviso clause apply to both sets of rights—those necessary at the time of creation *and* those that subsequently become necessary—or just the latter?

A contentious and novel dispute featuring Article 642 of the Louisiana Civil Code was recently decided by the Louisiana Supreme Court in WT Offshore, LLC v. Tex. Brine Corp., 2019 La. LEXIS 1582, *reh'g recalled*, 2020 La. LEXIS 212. The case involves a larger replacement pipeline that was routed adjacent to a smaller original pipeline constructed pursuant to a right of use. In 1979, Texas Brine Corporation, LLC (Texas Brine) entered into a "Salt and Underground Storage Lease" with the predecessors of W&T Offshore, LLC (W&T) to utilize certain land for conducting salt mining operations. The lease granted Texas Brine a limited personal servitude of right of use "to construct, operate and maintain a pipeline for the transportation of brine over and across" the leased property. The initial pipeline, which was installed in 1980, was 14 inches in diameter and 6.7 miles long. In 1993, W&T acquired a 23.66% co-ownership interest in the land burdened by the right of use. Many years later, after the original pipeline had begun to leak, Texas Brine installed a replacement pipeline, which was 18 inches in diameter, roughly 7 miles long, and eight feet away from the original pipeline. All co-owners except W&T had previously agreed to the replacement project.

In the litigation that followed between Texas Brine and W&T, their various actions were ultimately consolidated. Texas Brine sought declaratory and injunctive relief asserting that the construction and operation of the replacement pipeline was authorized by the original lease as well as the agreement with the other co-owners. W&T likewise asked for injunctive and possessory relief, damages for trespass, and damages for bad faith.

The district court held for Texas Brine, granting it full injunctive and declaratory relief while dismissing all of W&T's claims. *W&T Offshore, L.L.C. v. Tex. Brine Corp.*, C-128742 C/W C-128754 (Jan. 27, 2017). On appeal, the Louisiana First Circuit held that Article 642 of the Louisiana Civil Code allowed Texas Brine to construct and install a replacement pipeline. *W&T Offshore, L.L.C. v. Tex. Brine Corp.*, 250 So.3d 970 (La. App. 1 Cir. 2018). The replacement pipeline, the court held, could be located eight feet away from the original pipeline in order to allow for continuous production and transportation of salt brine over the servient estate. *Id.* at 979–80. However, the court held that installation of an 18-inch, as opposed to a 14 inch, replacement pipeline constituted a trespass on the servient estate because Texas Brine failed to obtain consent from all of the co-owners of the servient estate. *Id.* at 980–81. Therefore, W&T was entitled to trespass damages against Texas Brine. Both Texas Brine and W&T Offshore filed petitions for a writ of certiorari which were granted. *W&T Offshore, L.L.C. v. Tex. Brine Corp.*, 253 So.3d 788 (La. 2018).

In a brief per curiam opinion, the Louisiana Supreme Court reversed the court of appeal and reinstated the judgment of the district court with regard to the trespass claim and damages, but emphasized that its holding was limited to the precise and narrow facts before it. *W&T Offshore, L.L.C. v. Tex. Brine Corp.*, 1919 La. LEXIS 1582. Justice Weimer wrote a vigorous dissent. He offered that the majority's opinion represented an unduly broad interpretation of Article 642 of the Louisiana Civil Code and that it failed to resolve doubts about the extent, manner or exercise of a servitude in favor the servient estate owner as mandated by Article 730 of the Civil Code. Moreover, Justice Weimer cautioned that the majority's opinion would allow right of use holders unlimited opportunities to expand the width, scope or extent of such servitudes to the detriment of servient estate owners. Finally, according to Justice Weimer, the majority's opinion would destabilize title to land and create uncertainty throughout Louisiana. A few months later, the Louisiana Supreme Court wanted W&T's application for a rehearing, but subsequently recalled its order (as improvidently granted) and denied W&T's application for a rehearing. *W&T Offshore, L.L.C. v. Tex. Brine Corp.*, 2020 La. LEXIS 212.

6. The final provision in the law governing the right of use reminds us again of the connection between the limited personal servitude of right of use and predial servitudes.

Art. 645. Regulation of the servitude

A right of use is regulated by application of the rules governing usufruct and predial servitudes to the extent that their application is compatible with the rules governing a right of use servitude.

La. Civ. Code art. 645 (1976). Recall that Judge Cooks based her dissent in *Wagner v. Alford*, 741 So.2d 884, 890 (La. App. 3 Cir. 1999), on this provision. She noted that Article 645 of the Louisiana Civil Code requires application of the rules of usufruct and predial servitudes "*only to the extent that their application is compatible.*" *Id.* (emphasis in original). She further pointed out that "[w]hen a conflict occurs or the rules just do not fit, Article 645 does not require that we vitiate the parties' undertakings." *Id.* Finally, she praised the foresight of the codal redactors, observing: "they envisioned the day when a right of use might not be compatible with the rules applicable to usufruct and predial servitude." *Id.*

More recently, a decision by the Louisiana Supreme Court decision invoked Article 645 of the Louisiana Civil Code to suggest, albeit in dictum, that a right of use granted in favor of a juridical person, just like a usufruct granted for the benefit of a juridical person, terminates upon the lapse of thirty years from the date of the commencement of the usufruct. *Faulk v. Union Pacific Railroad Company*, 172 So.3d 1034, 1048 (La. 2015) (citing both Articles 645 and 608 as well as former articles 612 and 628 of the 1870 Civil Code). An opinion by the Office of Attorney General reached a similar conclusion. *See* La. Atty. Gen. Op. No. 12-0166, 2013 WL 191348, at *3, n. 10 (April 29, 2013).

The dictum in *Faulk* has not received any endorsement from property law scholars in Louisiana. It is true that a right of use is, just like a usufruct, granted in favor of a person, not an estate. But in most respects a right of use is functionally much closer to a predial servitude than to a usufruct. A right of use typically gives its holder a limited right to engage in a *narrowly circumscribed use* of an estate less than full enjoyment, whereas a usufruct furnishes the usufructuary a much broader set of rights, closer in many respects to ownership. As the revision comments to Article 639 of the Louisiana Civil Code explain, because a right of use "confers advantages less than full enjoyment," in this crucial respect "it resembles a predial servitude." La. Civ. Code art. 639 rev. cmt (b) (1977). Furthermore, recall that a predial servitude is potentially perpetual in duration. That is one of its crucial characteristics. If the court's dictum in *Faulk* proves to be an accurate statement of the duration of rights of use in Louisiana, thousands upon thousands of rights of use held by power companies, telecommunication companies, pipeline companies, and other juridical persons, not to mention rights of use held by governmental entities like levee districts or the United States Army Corps of Engineers that undergird Louisiana's complex flood control system, will be in jeopardy.

* * *

As Article 643 of the Louisiana Civil Code and the decision in *Sustainable Forests* instruct, a right of use can be transferred from one beneficiary to another, but is not automatically transferred when the person benefited by a right of use conveys a particular parcel of land. The servient estate, however, does remain burdened by a limited personal servitude of right of use when *its* ownership changes as the result of a sale or some other voluntary transfer of ownership, assuming the instrument creating the servitude was recorded in the conveyance records of the parish where the immovable property is located. In the case below, the court reminds the owner of the servient estate that he is bound to permit the exercise of a limited personal servitude of right of use granted by his ancestor in title. Also notice the court's discussion of the argument that the personal servitude had terminated because of nonuse.

McCormick v. Harrison

926 So.2d 798 (La. App. 2 Cir. 2006)

PEATROSS, Judge. This appeal by Plaintiff, Dr. George M. McCormick, II, arises from the denial of McCormick's petition to terminate a servitude that Defendant, Donald Harrison, claimed to exist in his favor. For the reasons stated herein, we affirm.

Facts

This is a dispute over a servitude of use for a private horse racetrack in Bossier Parish. Harrison owns a two-acre tract in Bossier Parish that he purchased from Danny and Susan Payne. When the Paynes acquired the property in 1993 from Gilbert and Nancy Ciavaglia and Plum Hill Training Center, Inc., the Paynes acquired the following rights:

> As additional consideration, Vendor grants to Vendee a non-exclusive servitude of usage of a 5/8 mile horse race track located in the East Half (E1/2) of Section 27, T19N, R12W, Bossier Parish, Louisiana, which servitude shall include the right to gallop and exercise at all reasonable times, a maximum of fifteen (15) horses stabled at Vendee's barn located on the above described track (sic) of land; provided that Vendee shall pay Vendor $ 100.00 per month maintenance fees for any month that any of Vendee's horses are exercised on said 5/8 mile track.

The 1995 deed conveying the property from the Paynes to Harrison included this language:

> Included in this transfer are all of vendor's rights under that certain non-exclusive servitude of usage of a 5/8 mile horse track located in the East half (E1/2) of Section 27, Township 19 North, Range 12 West, Bossier Parish, Louisiana, as set forth in the Cash Deed from Gilbert A. Ciavaglia et al. to Danny W. Payne et al., recorded under registry number 561809, Conveyance Records of Bossier Parish, Louisiana.

The horse track described in the 1993 and 1995 deeds is located on McCormick's property, a much larger tract immediately to the northeast of Harrison's tract. McCormick purchased this tract from Lifeline Nursing Company ("Lifeline") in September 2004. Lifeline purchased the tract from the Ciavaglias in 1999. Neither the plaintiff's deed nor the deed from the Ciavaglias to Lifeline mentioned the horse track or the servitude.

From the time when Harrison purchased his property in 1995 until 1999 when the Ciavaglias sold the track to Lifeline, Harrison exercised his horses on the track. Harrison paid the Ciavaglias $100 for each month he used the track; the payments were made at irregular intervals. After the Ciavaglias sold the property containing the track to Lifeline, Harrison did not use the track because Lifeline objected to Harrison's use of the track.

When Lifeline sold the property to McCormick, Harrison decided to use the track. Without contacting McCormick, on October 26, 2004, Harrison's employee exercised a horse on the track without interference. On October 28, 2004, Harrison's employee attempted to use the track, but McCormick's son arrived and asked him to leave. The employee complied, but the next day Harrison's employee returned to exercise another horse on the track, accompanied by a deputy sheriff. McCormick or his representative again asked Harrison's employee to leave, and that was the last time Harrison tried to use the track. Harrison did not attempt to pay McCormick $100 for the use of the track at any time; he testified that he was asked to leave, not to pay $100. It is not clear from the evidence adduced at trial whether the horse that Harrison trained at the track was stabled at Harrison's barn.

In December 2004, McCormick filed a rule to show cause in the district court asking for a declaratory judgment to decide the parties' rights to the track. Specifically, McCormick asked the court for a judgment declaring that the servitude was extinguished. Harrison answered the rule and brought a reconventional demand asking for damages because of McCormick's refusal to allow Harrison to use the track.

At trial, the parties disagreed about the condition and usefulness of the track. McCormick, who had been a horse trainer for many years, said that the track was unusable and "totally unsafe for horse or rider" because a previous owner of the property had plowed over the track and had brought up subsurface rocks. Harrison, also an experienced horseman, agreed that the track was unsuitable for running horses, but said that the track was "fine for a horse that you're just breaking or colts to be broke and go on."

After considering the evidence, the court signed a judgment on September 2, 2005, incorporating reasons for judgment. The court concluded that the servitude held by Harrison was a personal servitude that was still in existence. The court declared that Harrison was entitled to continue to use the track so long as he paid McCormick $100 per month, in advance, for the use of the track. The court also held that Harrison did not owe McCormick for the month of October 2004. Finally, the court denied Harrison's demand for damages. McCormick took a suspensive appeal.

Discussion

The trial court found the servitude established by the Paynes' deed to be a personal servitude of right of use, and we agree with that characterization. By use of the terms "vendor" and "vendee," the parties made clear their intent that the servitude ran in favor of persons and not estates. La. C.C. arts. 533, 534, 639; *Sustainable Forests, L.L.C. v. Harrison*, 37,152 (La. App. 2d Cir. 5/22/03), 846 So. 2d 1283. Limited personal servitudes are real rights that confer on a person limited advantages of use or enjoyment over an immovable belonging to another. *Swayze v. State, DOTD*, 34,679 (La. App. 2d Cir. 9/17/01), 793 So. 2d 1278, *writ denied*, 01-3136 (La. 2/1/02), 808 So. 2d 342, *citing* Yiannopoulos, 3 *Civil Law Treatise* § 223 (4th Ed. 2000). Such rights are transferable. La. C.C. art. 643.

Right of use servitudes are regulated by the rules governing usufruct and predial servitudes to the extent that these rules are compatible with the servitude of right of use. La. C.C. art. 645. Doubt as to the existence, extent or manner of exercise of a servitude must be resolved in favor of the estate claimed to be burdened by the servitude. La. C.C. art. 730; *St. Andrews Place, Inc. v. City of Shreveport*, 40,260 (La. App. 2d Cir. 11/4/05), 914 So. 2d 1203; *Mardis v. Brantley*, 30,773 (La. App. 2d Cir. 8/25/98), 717 So. 2d 702, *writ denied*, 98-2488 (La. 11/20/98), 729 So. 2d 563.

A servitude may terminate in several different ways. For example, if that part of the servient estate that is burdened with the servitude is permanently and totally destroyed, the servitude is extinguished. La. C.C. art. 751. Although there was some evidence through McCormick's testimony that the horse track was in an unusable condition, the trial court accepted Harrison's testimony that the track remained useful for a limited purpose. A servitude may also end due to nonuse for a period of ten years. La. C.C. arts. 752–756. In this case, less [sic] than ten years had elapsed since Harrison used the track prior to his attempts to use it during McCormick's ownership.

In brief, McCormick urges that the servitude terminated because Harrison did not pay McCormick $100 for the use of the track in October 2004. Again, the evidence shows that, in October, Harrison used the track one day without interference and thereafter attempted twice to use the track only to be turned away. The evidence does not show that Harrison or his employee offered to pay for the use of the track, nor does the evidence show that McCormick or his representative demanded payment of the $100. The agreement creating the servitude specifies only that "Vendee shall pay Vendor $100.00 per month maintenance fees for any month that any of Vendee's horses are exercised on said 5/8 mile track." The agreement *does not* specify when or where payment is to be made.

We find no support in the civil code for the argument that a right of use servitude terminates upon the failure of the holder of the right to pay an installment. We have considered La. C.C. art. 749, which provides:

If the title is silent as to the extent and manner of use of the servitude, the intention of the parties is to be determined in the light of its purpose.

This article, however, is intended to govern the scope of the servitude itself. The manner and place of payment for the servitude or right of use, at least in this instance, are not closely related to the purpose of the right, so the purpose of the right does not provide guidance for resolving this dispute.

Instead, the allowable delay for making the payment may be examined under the law of obligations. La. C.C. art. 1777 provides:

A term for the performance of an obligation may be express or it may be implied by the nature of the contract.

Performance of an obligation not subject to a term is due immediately.

La. C.C. art. 1778 provides:

A term for the performance of an obligation is a period of time either certain or uncertain. It is certain when it is fixed. It is uncertain when it is not fixed but is determinable either by the intent of the parties or by the occurrence of a future and certain event. It is also uncertain when it is not determinable, in which case the obligation must be performed within a reasonable time.

Under the terms of the right of use, the holder of the right is entitled to use the track, but must pay the owner for each month when the track is used. We construe the nature of the contract to imply a monthly term for payment; the intent of the parties, as best as may be determined, was that the owner would be paid monthly in those months when the payor used the track. The specific time for payment—in particular, whether payment should be made at the beginning or the end of the month—however, is not determinable.

We note that the trial court's judgment provides that, prospectively, the maintenance fee must be paid *in advance* of Harrison's exercise of his use of the track. This portion of the trial court's ruling was not appealed and, therefore, we will not review this finding. In any event, we conclude that, although Harrison was able to use the track once in October, twice later that month the owner refused to allow him the use of the track. The obligation of the owner of the track was to allow the holder of the right of use to exercise his right without interference. Cf. La. C.C. art. 748. Since McCormick refused to allow Harrison to use the track in accordance with the terms of the right of use, McCormick lost the right to demand that Harrison pay for October because McCormick did not fully perform his obligation. La. C.C. art. 1758(B)(1). Thus, we reject McCormick's argument that the servitude was extinguished by Harrison's failure to pay.

Conclusion

For the foregoing reasons, the judgment of the district court is affirmed at the cost of George M. McCormick, II.

AFFIRMED.

Notes

1. Remember that the court in *Wagner v. Alford*, 741 So.2d 884, 888 (La. App. 3 Cir. 1999), stated that "[w]ithout payment of this fee, any right would be properly withheld and, thus, a servitude has not been conferred." In *McCormick v. Harrison*, 926 So.2d 798 (La. App. 2 Cir. 2006), the court was not concerned with the monthly $100 maintenance fee required for the right of use holder to use a horse track. Is a periodic payment dispositive of whether an agreement creates a personal servitude or a predial servitude or something other than a real right like a license or a lease? Would Judge Amy, the author of the Third Circuit Court of Appeal decision in *Wagner*, have found a personal servitude of right of use under the facts in *McCormick*?

2. Once it is determined that the parties have created a personal servitude of right of use, as opposed to a predial servitude, it may still be necessary to determine the scope of the right of use and the existence of other accessory rights related to the right of use. In *St. John the Baptist Parish v. State Dep't of Wildlife and Fisheries*, 943 So.2d 1209, 1212–15 (La. App. 5 Cir. 2006), the court first determined that St. John the Baptist Parish had acquired a personal servitude of right of use entitling it to construct a drainage canal in a 150-foot strip across a servient estate. The court then confronted the status of certain private hunting camps that had initially been established by private clubs immediately adjacent to the canal with the permission of the original landowner, then donated by the clubs to the parish, and finally leased back by the parish to the clubs. The court finally decided that these hunting camps had to be removed when ownership of the servient estate passed to the State of Louisiana, which planned to create a wildlife refuge on the property, because they were not necessary to the enjoyment of the parish's right of use regarding the canal. As the court explained:

> A right of use includes the rights contemplated or necessary to enjoyment at the time of its creation as well as rights that may later become necessary, provided that a greater burden is not imposed on the property unless otherwise stipulated in the title. La. C.C. art. 642. Rights that are necessary for the use of a servitude are acquired at the time the servitude is established. La. C.C. art. 743. They are to be exercised in a way least inconvenient for the servient estate.

> Upon review of the record, we find that the camp buildings and related club activities are not necessary to the Parish's enjoyment of its servitude. Accordingly, the trial court erred in issuing a permanent injunction against DWF, prohibiting it from removing, destroying or dismantling the camps and related structures located within the Parish servitude and in finding that the Parish is within its rights of servitude to enter into leases of the existing camp buildings.

Id. at 1215. What does this decision add to our understanding of Article 642 of the Civil Code? Are the private camp buildings leased to the hunting clubs by the parish similar to or distinguishable from the replacement pipeline at issue in the litigation between W&T Offshore and Texas Brine discussed earlier?

* * *

The final case in this chapter demonstrates how the State of Louisiana expropriated private property and made it available to the United States Department of Veterans Affairs without a violation of the Louisiana Constitution by transferring a personal servitude of right of use. Recall that Article I, Section 4(H)(1) of the Louisiana Constitution forbids the sale or lease of expropriated property to another person, if the property is not held by the expropriating entity for at least thirty years without first offering the property for sale to the owner at the time of the expropriation. La. Const. Art. I, § 4(H)(1) (1974, amended 2006, 2010). Do you think the court of appeal decision below, which held that the State did not violate this constitutional prohibition through its acquisition and novel transfer of a right of use, is consistent with the spirit of the Louisiana Constitution?

2400 Canal, LLC v. Board of Supervisors of Louisiana State Mechanical and Agricultural College

105 So.3d 819 (La. App. 4 Cir. 2012)

LEDET, Judge. This is an action for mandamus, declaratory relief, and damages. The plaintiff, 2400 Canal, LLC ("2400 Canal"), is the former owner of property located at 2400 Canal Street in New Orleans (the "Property"), which was expropriated by the Board of Supervisors of Louisiana State University Agricultural and Mechanical College (the "Board"). The stated purpose of the expropriation was to facilitate the construction by the United States Veterans Affairs (the "VA") of a new hospital on the site, the new VA Medical Center hospital ("VAMC"). Thereafter, 2400 Canal commenced this action against the Board and its president, John Lombardi. In its petition, 2400 Canal alleged that the Board violated its constitutional rights under La. Const. Art. I, § 4(H)(1) by leasing the Property to the VA without offering it, as the original owner, a right of first refusal to purchase the Property at current fair market value. The Board and Mr. Lombari responded by filing peremptory and dilatory exceptions. From the trial court's judgment sustaining the exceptions and dismissing the action, 2400 Canal appeals. Noticing on our own motion 2400 Canal's lack of a cause of action under La. Const. Art. I, § 4(H)(1), we affirm the trial court's judgment in this case. We, however, dismiss the appeals in the two consolidated cases.

La. Const. Art. I, Section 4(H)(1) provides:

> Except for the removal of a threat to public health or safety caused by the existing use or disuse of the property, and except for leases or operation agreements for port facilities, highways, qualified transportation facilities or airports, the state or its political subdivisions shall not sell or lease property which has been expropriated and held for not more than thirty years without

first offering the property to the original owner or his heir, or, if there is no heir, to the successor in title to the owner at the time of expropriation at the current fair market value, after which the property can be transferred only by competitive bid open to the general public. After thirty years have passed from the date the property was expropriated, the state or political subdivision may sell or otherwise transfer the property as provided by law.

Factual and Procedural Background

In March 2010, the Board filed a petition to expropriate the Property. In its petition, the Board stated that, pursuant to La. Const. Art. VII, § 14(C), the City of New Orleans, the Board, and the State of Louisiana, through the Division of Administration, (the "State") had entered into a Cooperative Endeavor Agreement ("CEA") to acquire the property necessary for the construction of the VAMC. The Board further stated that the purpose of the expropriation was "for [the] public and necessary purposes of the VA Medical Center [VAMC]."

In September 2011, the parties settled the expropriation action by entering on the record a confidential compromise agreement. Under that agreement, 2400 Canal agreed to "forever release and discharge" the Board from "any and all liability and responsibility for any . . . amount and all claims and causes of action that it may have or may have had arising out of or in any manner associated or connected with any events, facts, transactions or occurrences alleged or that could have been alleged in this matter." Following the settlement, 2400 Canal contended that it learned of the Board's intent to lease the Property to a third party, the VA, in violation of its constitutional rights under La. Const. Art. I, § 4(H)(1).

In November 2011, 2400 Canal filed the instant action, which it styled as a "Petition for Writ of Mandamus, For Declaratory Relief and For Damages," against the Board and its president. The principal relief it requested was the nullification of the Right of Possession, Use, and Occupancy Agreement, dated February 17, 2010, entered into between the Board, the VA, and the State (the "Use Agreement"). According to 2400 Canal, the Use Agreement was an illegal lease because it violated 2400 Canal's constitutional rights under La. Const. Art. I, § 4(H)(1). In its petition, 2400 Canal prayed for three types of relief: (i) an order nullifying the alleged lease (the Use Agreement), (ii) an order requiring the Board to offer the Property to 2400 Canal for its current fair market value, and (iii) damages.

In response, the Board and its president (the defendants) filed multiple exceptions. As to the Board, the defendants asserted a peremptory exception of res judicata based on the compromise agreement and dilatory exceptions of unauthorized use of a summary proceeding and improper cumulation of actions. As to the Board's president, the defendants asserted peremptory exceptions of no cause and no right of action.

Following a hearing, the trial court sustained all of the exceptions and dismissed the action. . . . .

Agreeing with the defendants, the trial court found, based on the compromise agreement, that res judicata barred re-litigating the claims and issues raised in this action. In so finding, the trial court reasoned:

> The compromise agreement contained a full and complete release of *all claims* and causes of action that 2400 Canal *had or may have* in connection with the expropriation of its property. Plaintiff's Writ of Mandamus seeks to enforce its constitutional rights under Article I Section 4(H)(1) of the Louisiana Constitution of 1974 by classifying the Right of Possession, Use and Occupancy Agreement between the LSU Board, VA and the State of Louisiana as a *lease* and seeking nullification of same. LSU asserts that the Right of Possession, Use and Occupancy Agreement is not covered by this constitutional provision. Plaintiffs argued that res judicata could not apply to the instant action for constitutional violations since La. R.S. 19:147 limited their defense of an expropriation to a Motion to Dismiss and did not encompass its allegations of constitutional violations for expropriating its property and "leasing" it to the VA, without extending the right of first refusal to plaintiff as original owner. This argument has no merit in the context of the instant action where the plaintiff has compromised *all claims and causes of action* that 2400 Canal *had or may have* in connection with the expropriation of its property.

From that decision, 2400 Canal appeals.

Discussion

The relevant facts in this case are undisputed; hence, the appeal is limited to legal questions. . . .

In deciding an exception of no cause of action a court can consider only the petition, any amendments to the petition, and any documents attached to the petition. . . . The grant of the exception of no cause of action is proper when, assuming all well pleaded factual allegations of the petition and any annexed documents are true, the plaintiff is not entitled to the relief he seeks as a matter of law; any doubt must be resolved in the plaintiffs' favor. *Kuebler v. Martin*, 578 So.2d 113 (La. 1991).

Applying these precepts, we find based on our review of the petition and the documents attached to it—the Expropriation Petition and the Use Agreement—that 2400 Canal lacks a cause of action. In its petition, 2400 Canal alleged the following:

- 2400 Canal, LLC acquired the immovable property at 2400 Canal Street *via* auction from the City of New Orleans in February of 2006.

- On or about March 10, 2010, BS [the Board] filed a Petition to Expropriate the immovable property at 2400 Canal Street (see Exhibit "A").

- Upon information and belief, BS [the Board] has leased the property that it expropriated to a third party, specifically, the Veterans' Administration, on February 17, 2010, *via* a Right of Possession, Use and Occupancy Agreement executed between the Board of Supervisors of Louisiana State University A&M

College, United States Department of Veterans Affairs and the State of Louisiana, through the Division of Administration, Office of Facility Planning and Control (see Exhibit "B").

- The Right of Possession, Use and Occupancy Agreement [the Use Agreement] is apparently for a hospital and is an illegal lease of property expropriated. [*See* La. Const. Art. I, § 4(H)(1).]

- Prior to leasing the property, BS [the Board] failed to offer the property to 2400 Canal for fair market value.

- As a result of the defendant's actions, BS [the Board] has violated 2400 Canal's constitutional rights.

Although 2400 Canal alleges in its petition that the Use Agreement is an illegal lease, this is a legal conclusion that we cannot consider in deciding an exception of no cause of action. Legal conclusions asserted as facts are not considered well-pled factual allegations for purposes of an exception of no cause of action. . . .

Under Louisiana law, a lease is distinguishable from a right of use. *Eagle Pipe and Supply, Inc. v. Amerada Hess Corp.*, 10-2267, pp. 16–17 (La. 10/25/11), 79 So.3d 246, 262; *Richard v. Hall*, 03-1488, pp. 17–18 (La. 4/23/04), 874 So.2d 131, 145. The Louisiana Civil Code defines a lease as "a synallagmatic contract by which one party, the lessor, binds himself to give to the other party, the lessee, the use and enjoyment of a thing for a term in exchange for a rent that the lessee binds himself to pay." La. C.C. art. 2668. The Civil Code defines a right of use as a personal servitude. La. C.C. art. 534. The Civil Code further provides that "[t]he personal servitude of right of use confers in favor of a person a specified use of an estate less than full enjoyment." L C.C. art. 639. By its terms, the Use Agreement is governed by Louisiana law, abs otherwise controlling federal law.

The distinction between a lease and a right of use, as indicated in the Civi' is that a right of use is a real right and a lease is a personal right. "Louisia' all leases as personal contracts. Louisiana does not make a taxonomic? tion between leases of movables and leases of immovables, as does th law, under which a lease of real property creates an estate in land wh personalty creates only a personal right." *General Elec. Capital Corp.* ' *Health Care, Inc.*, 950 F.2d 944, 950 (5th Cir. 1991). In sum, a leas able from a real right, such as a right of use, because "[a] lease of re personal rights, rather than real rights." Peter S Title, *2 La. Prac.* ed. 2011) (citing *Prados v. South Central Bell Tel. Co.*, 329 So. 2 rehearing)).

As noted, 2400 Canal labels the Use Agreement as a lease the Board violated its constitutional right under La. Const ing the Property to the VA without first offering it a rig Agreement, which is attached to the petition as Exhib references that are relevant to the issue of whether thi'

- "Grantor [The Board] hereby grants to Grantee [the VA], and Grantee hereby accepts from Grantor, an irrevocable right of possession, use, and occupancy for the Premises. . . . Grantee shall pay to Grantor during the Term rental of ONE dollar ($1.00) per year. Additional consideration for this right of possession, use, and occupancy is VA's plan to construct the new VAMC in close proximity to the new University Medical Center."

- "Grantor will not obtain any property interest in any improvements placed upon the property by Grantee. During the term or upon the expiration or termination of this Agreement, all improvements made by the Grantee shall remain the property of the United States of America."

- "Grantee shall be responsible for paying all real property taxes (if any) duly assessed against Grantee's interest in the land and Building comprising the Premises."

- "This Agreement does not constitute a transfer of fee simple title ownership in the Premises to Grantee [the VA], but is rather a right of possession, occupancy, and use."

The above quoted provisions of the Use Agreement belie 2400 Canal's label of this agreement as a lease. The Use Agreement, by its terms, confers real rights on the VA; hence, it is not a lease. *See Richard*, 03-1488 at pp. 17–18, 874 So.2d at 145 (noting that "[u]nder the civil law concept, a lease does not convey any real right or title to the property leased, but only a personal right.") Although the Use Agreement refers to the VA's payment of "rental" of one dollar per year, "if the right intended to be conveyed has the attributes of a real right such as a personal servitude or a limited personal servitude of use, then the contract is not a lease, even though the parties used terms like 'rent' or "lease.'" La. C.C. art. 2668, Official Revision Comment (d). Such is the case here.

On appeal, 2400 Canal also contends that the Board violated La. Const. Art. I, § 4(H)(1) by selling the Property pursuant to an Act of Exchange and Amended Act of Exchange. It emphasizes that the Act of Exchange expressly states that it may be deemed to be a credit sale. Although 2400 Canal attached copies of the Act of ⸀change and the Amended Act of Exchange as exhibits to its appellant brief, nei-⸀ of these documents were introduced into evidence in the trial court. "Appellate ⸀ are courts of record and may not review evidence that is not in the appel-⸀rd, or receive new evidence." *Denoux v. Vessel Mgmt. Servs., Inc.*, 07-2143, ⸀'21/08), 983 So.2d 84, 88; *see also Triss v. Carey*, 00-0608, p. 3 (La. App. 4 ⸀781 So. 2d 613, 615; *Argence L.L.C. v. Box Opportunities, Inc.*, 07-0765, ⸀ Cir. 3/13/08), 980 So.2d 786, 789 n. 3. "Evidence not properly and ⸀ and introduced [in the trial court] cannot be considered, even if it ⸀ in the record." *Denoux, supra.* Given that 2400 Canal failed to ⸀ct of Exchange or the Amended Act of Exchange into evidence ⸀documents are not part of the record on appeal and cannot ⸀t.

Accordingly, we find that the Use Agreement is not a lease and that 2400 Canal therefore lacks a cause of action against either defendant under La. Const. Art. I, §4(H)(1), which by its express terms applies solely to the sale or lease of expropriated property.

Decree

For the foregoing reasons, the appeals in 2012-CA-0221 and 2012-CA-0222 are dismissed. The judgment of the trial court in 2012-CA-0220 is affirmed.

AFFIRMED IN PART, DISMISSED IN PART

Notes and Questions

1. In *2400 Canal, LLC v. Board of Supervisors of Louisiana State Mechanical and Agricultural College*, 105 So.3d 819 (La. App. 4 Cir. 2012), the court distinguishes the right of use, a *real right* in immovable property in favor of a person, from *personal rights resulting from a contract of lease* "by which one party, the lessor, binds himself to give the other party, the lessee, the use and enjoyment of a thing for a limited term in exchange for a rent that the lessee binds himself to pay." La Civ. Code art. 2668 (2004). Is the court's distinction just a ruse to allow the defendant to avoid complying with the protections supposedly afforded private property owners by La. Const. art. I, §4(H)(1)? Or is there a material distinction between the two rights? What rights does the owner of a personal servitude of right of use enjoy that a lessee does not?

2. Is the court's ruling in *2400 Canal* in favor of the state explainable by some other factor? Was it credible for the property owner, 2400 Canal, LLC, to complain it had no idea that the property subject to expropriation by the state was going to end up in the control of the Department of Veterans Affairs? Should 2400 Canal, LLC, have taken this into account when it entered into a settlement agreement with the state?

3. The distinction between a lease and a right of use can be difficult to discern. At times, the distinction arises from the means chosen to establish the right. In one of the decisions cited by the court in *2400 Canal*, the Louisiana Supreme Court addressed whether an oral agreement through which the owner of a commercial recreational development gave another company duck hunting rights on the owner's property for a season was a lease or personal servitude of right of use to determine whether the latter company was immune from liability under Louisiana's Recreational Use Immunity Statutes (RUS), La. Rev. Stat. §§ 9:2791 & 2795. *Richard v. Hall*, 874 So.2d 131 (La. 2004). According to the court,

> The duck lease at issue before us cannot be classified as a right of use. Personal servitudes affecting immovable property which are created by agreement between the parties must be in writing. . . . It is undisputed that the duck lease at issue was an oral agreement and was not in writing.
>
> More importantly, the duck lease did not convey any real rights to SSI. The duck lease was not a charge on the property in favor of SSI. It more

closely resembles a contract whereby the lessors undertook the obligation to furnish to SSI the enjoyment of duck hunting on Lock Leven for a certain period of time in consideration of the $10,000 which SSI promised to, and did, pay. The three elements of lease are present: the price was $10,000, the consent between the lessors and SSI, and the thing, namely, the right to hunt ducks on Loch Leven, which is an incorporeal. [. . .]

We note with approval that the First Circuit Court of Appeal has held that an oral agreement whereby an owner for fixed consideration gave another the right to trap on his land is a contract of lease; the object of the lease was the right to trap. *Defilice v. Autin*, 159 So. 648, 649–50 (La. Ct. App. 1 Cir. 1935). . . .

Id. at 145–46. If the duck lease in *Richard v. Hall* had been created by a written agreement, would it still have been characterized as a lease? How significant was it that the permission to hunt was given for one year only?

4. Finally, recall that when written and filed for registry in the public records of the parish in which leased immovable property is located, a lease can function like a real right. *See* La. Civ. Code art. 2681 (2005) (stating that the lease of an immovable is effective against third parties when filed for recordation in the manner prescribed by legislation). *See also* La. Civ. Code arts. 2711-12 (2005); La Civ. Code art. 2711, rev. cmts. (b) and (c) (2005); La. Civ. Code art. 3338(2). In light of these provisions, if the lease in *Richard v. Hall*, 874 So.2d 131 (La. 2004) had been written *and recorded*, would the result have been different? Compare *Richard* with *Roy v. Bordelon*, 164 So.3d 367 (La. App. 3 Cir. 2015).

Chapter 16

Building Restrictions

A. History and Controversy

Building restrictions are the newest form of real rights expressly recognized in the Louisiana Civil Code. La. Civ. Code art. 775 rev. cmt (a) (1977). In common law jurisdictions they are also known as conditions, covenants, and restrictions (CC&Rs). Initially, building restrictions were a creature of Louisiana jurisprudence. In time, piecemeal statutes recognized their existence. In 1977, the legislature finally codified building restrictions in the Civil Code. Today, building restrictions establish mutually enforceable restraints on the use and improvement of immovable property. They can also be used to impose affirmative duties on immovable property owners. As Article 775 of the Louisiana Civil Code provides, however, for such restraints and duties to be enforceable, building restrictions must be established "in pursuance of a general plan" that is "feasible and capable of being preserved." *Id.*

Art. 775. Building restrictions

Building restrictions are charges imposed by the owner of an immovable in pursuance of a general plan governing building standards, specified uses, and improvements. The plan must be feasible and capable of being preserved.

La. Civ. Code art. 775 (1977). Intended to promote uniformity of use and design and to preserve the lasting aesthetic and monetary value of property within the land area affected, building restrictions are a ubiquitous feature of property ownership in Louisiana. Many residential subdivisions and mixed-use developments built over the last sixty years have included building restrictions.

Building restrictions usually originate when the owner of a sizable tract of land who decides to subdivide the land for a particular form of development has a vision of how the development should appear and function. She will typically use a set of building restrictions to realize what she envisages. By making all of the lots in the proposed development subject to the building restrictions, the developer can also assure prospective purchasers that their neighbors will build houses, or other kinds of structures, of a certain size and quality. She can further carefully control other aspects of the development; for instance, the kinds of animals or plantings that will be permitted, the paint colors that may be chosen, the use and nature of outbuildings that may be constructed on a lot, the kinds of vehicles that may be parked in a driveway, and even what types of businesses owners may conduct from their homes. Although the developer could try to effectuate her vision through predial servitudes benefitting certain dominant estates and correspondingly burdening other servient estates, there are inherent limits as to what predial servitudes can accomplish. In short, the invention of building restrictions has allowed land developers to overcome the limitations of predial servitudes. *See* John A. Lovett *Creating and Controlling Private Land Use Restrictions in Scotland and Louisiana: A Comparative Mixed Jurisdiction Analysis*, 2008 (2) Stellenbosch L. Rev. 231 (reviewing the practical necessity for and historical development of building restrictions in Louisiana and Scotland).

Building restrictions are "incorporeal immovables and real rights likened to predial servitudes" in favor of the owners of the lots in the area affected. La. Civ. Code art. 777 (1977). Unlike predial servitudes, however, building restrictions can impose on owners of affected parcels "affirmative duties that are reasonable and necessary for the maintenance of a general plan." La. Civ. Code art. 778 (1977). In this respect, building restrictions avoid the codal prohibition against predial servitudes imposing affirmative obligations on the owner of a servient estate. *See* La. Civ. Code art. 651 (1977, amended 2010). Because affirmative obligations can be imposed through building restrictions, a homeowner's association, for instance, can collect annual fees from the owners of parcels subject to the building restrictions. It can use those fees to maintain commonly used infrastructure, facilities and amenities like roads, parks and recreational facilities such as golf courses, swimming pools, tennis courts, or club houses..

The communities that result from a regime of building restrictions or CC&Rs are often called "common interest communities" (CICs). The *Restatement (Third) of Property* defines a "common interest community" as:

> a real estate development or neighborhood in which individually owned lots or units are burdened by a servitude that imposes an obligation that cannot be avoided by nonuse or withdrawal
>
> (a) to pay for the use of, or contribute to the maintenance of, property held or enjoyed in common by the individual owners, or
>
> (b) to pay dues or assessments to an association that provides services or facilities to the common property or to the individually owned property, or that enforces other servitudes burdening the property in the development or neighborhood.

Restatement (Third) of Property: Servitudes §6.2(1) (2001). This definition reflects the importance for a planned community to be able to impose affirmative obligations on its constituent members through CC&Rs. It further highlights the centrality of the community's need to collect dues or assessments to maintain commonly owned assets and pay for services to members of the community. Common interest communities include not only planned communities of single-family homes but also condominiums and cooperatives. Condominium regimes, in particular, share many traits with building restrictions in that they impose detailed rules on the use and occupancy of the condominium units in a particular building. They also provide for the financing, maintenance and regulation of common elements such as hallways, elevators, parking garages, and shared heating and cooling equipment.

CICs play an important role in terms of social organization in the United States. The Community Associations Institute and its Foundation for Community Association Research counted 344,500 CICs in the United States as of 2017, and approximately 70 million persons (about 24 percent of the total U.S. population) living in some form of CIC. For Louisiana, the number of CICs comes to somewhere between 1000 and 2000, with an estimated 400,000 people living in such communities. *See* COMMUNITY ASSOCIATION INSTITUTE, NATIONAL AND STATE STATISTICAL REVIEW FOR 2017, *at* https://foundation.caionline.org/wp-content/uploads/2018/06 /2017StatsReview.pdf; 2017 COMMUNITY ASSOCIATION FACT BOOK FOR LOUISIANA 12, *at* https://foundation.caionline.org/wp-content/uploads/2018/08/LA2017.pdf.

Almost every U.S. state has adopted a statutory regime for organizing common interest communities. Some are based on the Uniform Common Interest Ownership Act (1982, amended 2008). These statutes typically require a declaration of rules that govern the community. Moreover, these rules must be disclosed to purchasers who acquire property in a CIC. Typically, a homeowners association, to which all property owners must belong, enforces the restrictions set forth in the declaration and collects the assessments used to maintain the commonly owned elements and facilities. In Louisiana, the Louisiana Homeowners Association Act, La. Rev. Stat. § 9:1141.1 *et seq.*, provides the detailed rules governing common interest communities in which property owners are required to belong to a homeowners association. Similarly, the Louisiana Condominium Act, La. Rev. Stat. § 9:1121 *et seq.*, governs the establishment and operation of condominium regimes. At present, a committee of the Louisiana State Law Institute is drafting new legislation that aims to incorporate many elements of the Uniform Common Interest Ownership Act into Louisiana law. The drafters hope that these efforts will result in legislation: the Louisiana Planned Community Act.

The purposes behind building restrictions and CC&Rs have not always been benign. Some of the first attempts in the early twentieth century to establish real rights of the kind we would today describe as building restrictions were motivated by the desire to achieve racial segregation in housing. *See, e.g., Queensborough Land Co. v. Cazeaux*, 67 So. 641 (La. 1915). For a detailed discussion of *Queensborough Land* and its legacy, see John A. Lovett, *Commercial Title Conditions in Scotland and Louisiana, in* MIXED JURISDICTIONS COMPARED: PRIVATE LAW IN LOUISIANA AND SCOTLAND 30–66 (Vernon Palmer and Elspeth Reid, eds.) (Edinburgh University Press 2009).

Building restrictions and CC&Rs can also facilitate economic segregation. Minimum square footage requirements, obligations to use certain kinds of building materials, prohibitions against mobile or modular homes, prohibitions against the kinds of vehicles that can park in driveways all can serve to separate the more affluent from the less wealthy, reinforce perceived social class boundaries and diminish the motivation of the more affluent to support public services. When a subdivision has its own golf course and clubhouse, its homeowners may be less likely to support a public park. Some scholars believe the extensive use of building restrictions or CC&Rs to create privately governed communities can curtail individual autonomy, undermine community trust, and lead some homeowners associations to engage in petty or tyrannical enforcement actions. Paula A. Franzese, *Privatization and Its Discontents: Common Interest Communities and the Rise of Government for "the Nice"*, 37 Urb. Law 335 (2005). Others view the private ordering that building restrictions and CC&R regimes facilitate as beneficial because they create a wider array of options for households seeking to enter the homeownership market and because private governance may be more efficient than public regulation. Robert C. Ellickson, *Alternatives to Zoning: Covenants, Nuisance Rules and Fines as Land Use Controls*, 40 U. Chi. L. Rev. 681 (1973); Robert C. Ellickson, *Cities and Homeowners Associations*, 130 U. Pa. L. Rev. 1519 (1982); Clayton P. Gillette, *Courts, Covenants and Communities*, 61 U. Chi. L. Rev. 1375 (1994).

A vast literature has been generated to explain the rise of CICs, evaluate their benefits and harms, and investigate the degree of deference that courts should show to these privately constituted rules and to the decisions made by the private associations enforcing the rules. Some scholars have even explored the appropriation and adaptation of the CC&R-CIC model by certain public regulatory bodies. *See, e.g.,* Gregory S. Alexander, *Dilemmas of Group Autonomy, Residential Associations and Community*, 75 Cornell L. Rev. 1 (1989); Henry Hansmann, *Condominium and Cooperative Housing, Transactional Efficiency, Tax Subsidies, and Tenure Choice*, 20 J. Leg. Studies 25, (1991); Evan McKenzie, Privatopia: Homeowners Associations and the Rise of Residential Private Government (1994); David Callies et al, *Ramapo Looking Forward: Gated Communities, Covenants and Concerns*, 35 Urb. L Rev. 177 (2003); Lee Anne Fennell, *Contracting Communities*, 2004 U. Ill. L. Rev. 829; Steven Siegal, *The Public Role in Establishing Residential Communities*, 38 Urb. Law. 859 (2006); Paula Franzese & Stephen Siegal, *Trust and Community: The Common Interest Community as Metaphor and Paradox*, 72 Mo. L. Rev. 1111 (2007); Hannah Wiseman, *Public Communities, Private Rules*, 98 Geo. L.J. 697 (2010). Although the merits of CICs will continue to be debated, their growing importance in U.S. property law cannot be ignored. Further, as Professor Lee Ann Fennell observes: "While this form of ownership is plainly thriving, significant numbers of these communities have become hotbeds of litigation and acrimony." 2004 U. Ill. L. Rev. at 831. The judicial decisions featured below highlight some of these themes.

B. Creation, Modification and Termination of Building Restrictions

1. Creation of Building Restrictions

Building restrictions spring into existence most typically when a landowner or developer files a Declaration of Building Restrictions in the conveyance records of the parish where the affected immovable property is located. Occasionally, of number of owners of immovable property in an area that has already been developed or subdivided will come together and agree to establish a building restriction regime by executing a juridical act that submits all of their properties to the regime. *See, e.g., Diefenthal v. Longue Vue Foundation*, 865 So.2d 863, 786–88 (La. App. 4 Cir. 2004). Article 776 of the Civil Code authorizes both methods for creating a building restriction regime:

Art. 776. Establishment

Building restrictions may be established only by juridical act executed by the owner of an immovable or by all the owners of the affected immovables. Once established, building restrictions may be amended or terminated as provided in this Title.

La. Civ. Code art. 776 (1999).

Typically, the landowner who subdivides a tract of land and records a subdivision plan, including a declaration of building restrictions, establishes a set of mutually enforceable rules that govern and benefit every lot in the development and bind all subsequent owners of immovable property in the development. It is crucial to understand that even when these building restrictions do not reappear in all of the subsequent acts that convey ownership of individual lots within an affected area, the subsequent purchasers and transferees of those lots will still be bound by the original set of restrictions recorded in the conveyance records of the parish at the time the original subdivision occurred, as long as those building restrictions are expressly included in or incorporated by reference in the original act of sale of each lot in the subdivision. In general, the initial act of conveyance of a lot from a developer who establishes building restrictions will include or reference the recorded building restrictions, thus binding *all* subsequent owners of the affected lots, whether they acquire the lots by purchase, exchange, succession or donation, unless the building restrictions are amended or terminated. Consequently, attorneys advising potential purchasers of immovable property should always search the chain of title of the immovable property for the existence of building restrictions that will affect the property. Attorneys may want to provide clients with copies of any building restrictions affecting the property and discuss their impact before their clients proceed with a real estate transaction.

2. Modification, Amendment and Termination of Building Restrictions

Article 780 of the Louisiana Civil Code declares that "[b]uilding restrictions may be amended, whether such amendment lessens or increases a restriction, or may terminate or be terminated, as provided in the act that establishes them." La. Civ. Code art. 780 (1977, as amended 1999). Thus, if the act establishing the building restrictions describes the manner in which the restrictions may be amended, modified or terminated, then the procedures prescribed in the declaration must be followed. In most planned community documents used by developers today, the declaration of building restrictions will include detailed rules on amendment and termination of the restrictions governing the community.

If the declaration of building restrictions makes no provision for the amendment or termination of the restrictions, however, the remainder of Article 780 of the Louisiana Civil Code provides the methods for amendment and termination.

Art. 780. Amendment and termination of building restrictions

Building restrictions may be amended, whether such amendment lessens or increases a restriction, or may terminate or be terminated, as provided in the act that establishes them. In the absence of such provision, building restrictions may be amended or terminated for the whole or a part of the restricted area by agreement of owners representing more than one-half of the land area affected by the restrictions, excluding streets and street rights-of-way, if the restrictions have been in effect for at least fifteen years, or by agreement of both owners representing two-thirds of the land area affected and two-thirds of the owners of the land affected by the restrictions, excluding streets and street rights-of-way, if the restrictions have been in effect for more than ten years.

La. Civ. Code art. 780 (1977, as amended 1999). Article 780 provides three distinct amendment and termination regimes. For purposes of determining which rules apply, the affected property owner must first know how long the restrictions have been in effect.

If the restrictions have been in effect for *fewer than ten years*, modifications and terminations are not allowed at all. *Id*. If the restrictions have been in effect for *at least ten years, but not yet for fifteen years*, a modification or termination requires the "agreement of both [1] owners representing two-thirds of the land area affected and [2] two-thirds of the owners of the land affected by the restrictions, excluding streets and street rights-of-way . . .". *Id*. In this intermediate stage, two measurements must take place. The proponents of the change or termination must first determine the area of the land affected and obtain the consent of the landowners of two-thirds of that land area. Next, the number of owners of all the affected land must be calculated and then two-thirds of these owners must agree to the change. Both tests must be met. When the restrictions have been in effect for *at least fifteen years*, the law relaxes the requirements for amendment and termination by providing "owners representing more than one-half of the land area affected by the restrictions, excluding streets and street rights-of-way . . ." must agree to the proposed modification or termination. La. Civ. Code art. 780 (1977, as amended 1999). Thus, at this later stage in the life of building restrictions, only the land area affected is taken into account, and only the owners of more than one-half of that area must agree to the proposed change or termination.

The following example illustrates the operations of Article 780 of the Louisiana Civil Code. Suppose that six landowners own properties in a 100-acre subdivision. Landowner 1 owns thirty acres, landowner 2 owns twenty acres, landowner 3 owns twenty acres, landowner 4 owns ten acres, landowner 5 owns ten acres, and landowner 6 owns ten acres. If the building restrictions have been in effect for at least ten years, but not yet fifteen years, owners of two-thirds of the affected land area and two-thirds of the landowners must agree to make modifications. Landowners 1, 2, and 3 own two-thirds of the land, but could not make modifications unless one other landowner agrees to the modification. At least four landowners, two-thirds of six, must agree.

If the building restrictions have been in effect for at least fifteen years, owners of more than half of the affected land must agree to make modifications. Because landowners 1, 2, and 3 own more than half of the land, they could agree to make modifications that would be binding on all six landowners, whether the amendment increases or lessens a restriction.

Even when building restrictions include provisions for their amendment, controversies still arise. For example, the amendment provisions of a building restriction regime may call for a vote of the majority of the owners but might not explain exactly what constitutes a vote or how the vote is to be counted. *See Levier v. Jeff Davis Bancshares, Inc.*, 244 So.3d 504, 507 (La. App. 3 Cir. 2018) (determining that a written document signed by the majority of affected lot owners which permitted commercial use of three lots in an otherwise residential-use-only subdivision constituted a valid amendment because, according to the generally prevailing meaning of the word, a "vote" reflects approval or disapproval of a proposal, but does not require a notice or a hearing on the matter).

3. Termination of Building Restrictions by Prescription or by Abandonment

Building restrictions can be terminated in the same manner in which they are amended. They can also be extinguished by prescription or by abandonment. Pursuant to Article 781 of the Louisiana Civil Code, an individual lot owner can free a lot from a particular building restriction if that owner can prove that a "noticeable violation" of the restriction continued for two years without being challenged by the other owners in the affected building restriction regime.

Art. 781. Termination; liberative prescription

No action for injunction or for damages on account of the violation of a building restriction may be brought after two years from the commencement of a noticeable violation. After the lapse of this period, the immovable on which the violation occurred is freed of the restriction that has been violated.

La. Civ. Code art. 781 (1977). The two-year prescriptive period established in Article 781 can be interrupted, however, by an enforcement action. Litigation over alleged violations of building restrictions is relatively common because benefitted property owners and homeowners associations are often concerned that if a noticeable violation goes uncontested for too long, the restriction will become unenforceable in the future, at least with respect to the lot where the violation occurred.

Crucially, the person seeking to enforce a building restriction—the owners of other properties subject to the building restriction regime or, quite commonly, the homeowners or property owners association that has been granted the power to enforce the restrictions in the original declaration—can bring an action for injunctive relief without having to prove irreparable injury:

Art. 779. Injunctive relief

Building restrictions may be enforced by mandatory and prohibitory injunctions without regard to the limitations of Article 3601 of the Code of Civil Procedure.

La. Civ. Code art. 779 (1977). A property owner who violates a building restriction can also be liable for damages, grounded in theories of contractual or delictual responsibility. *Id*. rev. cmt. (d).

Violating a building restriction in an insignificant or a surreptitious manner, such as holding an occasional business meeting at a home or selling puppies from a recent litter, although technically in violation of a restriction against engaging in a business, will normally not trigger the two-year prescriptive period. A *noticeable* violation is thus one that is ongoing, visible and obvious to neighbors who have a right to enforce the building restrictions. The determination of whether an alleged violation is "noticeable" is a question of fact that will turn on the circumstances of the individual case.

Note, however, that a noticeable violation by one property owner for a period of two years frees only that owner's particular property from enforcement of the specific restriction violated. It does not liberate the property from other building restrictions. Moreover, one noticeable violation occurring on a single lot also generally does *not* free other property owners from the relevant restriction. *See* La. Civ. Code art. 781 rev. cmt. (d) (1977) ("Prescription of one type of restriction on a particular lot does not free that lot from other restrictions nor other lots from restrictions of the type that has been violated, unless, of course, there has been a general abandonment of the restrictive plan or of particular restrictions.")

When neighbors allow *pervasive* violations to continue unabated, reflecting little interest in enforcement, a court may find that the *entire general plan*, or at least the particular restriction that has gone unenforced, has been abandoned. In other words, a landowner will not be required to adhere to a building restriction when other landowners in the same building restrictions regime have not been required to do so.

Art. 782. Abandonment of plan or of restriction

Building restrictions terminate by abandonment of the whole plan or by a general abandonment of a particular restriction. When the entire plan is abandoned the affected area is freed of all restrictions; when a particular restriction is abandoned, the affected area is freed of that restriction only.

La. Civ. Code art. 782 (1977). Note, though, that while the pervasive violation of one building restriction may indicate the abandonment of that restriction, it does not necessarily signal the abandonment of the entire general plan.

C. Enforcement of Building Restrictions

In disputes over building restrictions courts have typically been asked to decide: (1) whether a true general plan exists to justify the recognition of a building restriction regime; (2) whether some particular action or inaction by an affected landowner constitutes a violation of a building restriction; (3) when a violation of a restriction becomes "noticeable" so as to start the two-year liberative prescription period; and (4) when, if ever, building restrictions are abandoned or terminated. The cases featured in this section address these litigation themes.

Most of the time, the person seeking to enforce a building restriction is another landowner whose land is similarly restricted or affected by the building restriction or a homeowners association or other body charged with the duty to enforce the restrictions by the original act of declaration. Property owners whose property is not restricted by a particular restriction but who benefit from the building restriction regime may also sue to enforce the restriction. *See* La. Civ. Code art. 779 rev. cmt. (c) (1977). Accordingly, in a community regulated by building restrictions, any owner of property whose interests are negatively impacted by a noticeable violation of a restriction may obtain injunctive relief without having to prove irreparable injury. Moreover, depending on the nature of the violation, negatively impacted owners may also sue the violator for damages and breach of contract. They may further invoke Articles 667 to 669 of the Civil Code. La. Civ. Code art. 779 rev. cmt. (d) (1977).

Pursuant to Article 775 of the Louisiana Civil Code, building restrictions are enforceable only when they support a general plan "governing building standards, specified uses, and improvements." La. Civ. Code art. 775 (1977). "In the absence of a general plan, any restriction on the use of land may be only a personal obligation or a predial servitude." La. Civ. Code art. 775 rev. cmt. (c) (1977). Personal obligations and predial servitudes may entitle the complainant to a different form of relief.

Article 783 of the Louisiana Civil Code makes clear that the law favors the freedom to use one's land as one chooses. Building restrictions are thus strictly construed to limit their application.

Art. 783. Matters of interpretation and application

Doubt as to the existence, validity, or extent of building restrictions is resolved in favor of the unrestricted use of the immovable. The provisions of the Louisiana Condominium Act, the Louisiana Timesharing Act, and the Louisiana Homeowners Association Act shall supersede any and all provisions of this Title in the event of a conflict.

La. Civ. Code art. 783 (1977, as amended 1999). Note that this provision references the Louisiana Condominium Act, La. Rev. Stat. §9:1131.1 (1983) *et seq.*, the Louisiana Timesharing Act, La. Rev. Stat. §9:1121.101 (1979) *et seq.*, and the Louisiana Homeowners Association Act, La. Rev. Stat. §9:1141.1 (1999) *et seq.* When these special purpose statutes apply, their provisions supersede the codal regime for building restrictions. Several portions of the Louisiana Homeowners Association Act are particularly important in this respect.

The **Louisiana Homeowners Association Act**, La. Rev. Stat. §9:1141.1 (1999) *et seq.*, defines a "Homeowners association" as "a nonprofit corporation, unincorporated association, or other legal entity, which is created pursuant to a declaration, whose members consist primarily of lot owners, and which is created to manage, or regulate, or both, the residential planned community." La. Rev. Stat. §9:1141.2(5) (1999) (emphasis added). Under the Act, a "residential planned community" or a "planned community" is defined as "a real estate development, used primarily for residential purposes, in which the owners of separately owned lots are *mandatory members* of an association by virtue of such ownership." La. Rev. Stat. §9:1141.2(7) (1999) (emphasis added).

The Louisiana Homeowners Association Act allows a homeowners association to enforce building restrictions, impose fines for non-compliance, and "have a privilege upon the lot and improvements thereon of an owner in the subdivision who fails to pay charges, or fees, or dues imposed . . ." La. Rev. Stat. §9:1145 (1979). The statute also applies to "existing and future residential planned communities whose declarations have been duly executed and filed for registry." La. Rev. Stat. §9:1141.3 (1999).

Unlike Article 783 of the Louisiana Civil Code, the Louisiana Homeowners Association Act takes a liberal position with respect to the interpretation and application of building restrictions.

§ 1141.4 Building restrictions; matters of interpretation

The existence, validity, or extent of a building restriction affecting any association property shall be liberally construed to give effect to its purpose and intent.

La. Rev. Stat. §9:1141.4 (1999). Instead of favoring freedom of use of the underlying immovable property, this statute requires courts to interpret any ambiguity in a document governing a covered residential planned community in a manner that gives effect to the purpose and intent of a building restriction.

For example, in one recent case, a court addressed an alleged violation of a building restriction prohibiting the parking or temporary storage of boats and campers "in front of any homes." *Fashion Plantation Estates Prop. Owners Ass'n v. Sims*, 209 So.3d 384, 385 (La. App. 5 Cir. 2016). In reversing a trial court judgment in favor of the defendant property owner, the court of appeal chided the trial court for failing to take account of the purpose and intent behind a building restriction on property regulated by a homeowners association as mandated by La. Rev. Stat. § 9:1141.4. *Id.* at 388. Moreover, the court of appeal "liberally" construed the scope of the words "in front of" in the parking restriction to mean that the area where the defendant's boat was parked—"next to the garage door (between the garage door and the side line of the lot), but in front of the farthest to the right wall of the home that faces the street with a decorative in lay"—was actually "in front of" the defendant's home and thus constituted an actionable violation of the building restriction. *Id.*

In similarity to Article 780 of the Louisiana Civil Code, the Louisiana Homeowners Association Act also provides detailed rules for creating, amending or terminating building restrictions. La. Rev. Stat. § 9:1141.6. However, just as with Article 780, these rules apply only when the documents creating a residential planned community governed by a homeowners association or property owners association are silent as to these matters. La. Rev. Stat. § 9:1141.6.B (1999). Rather than focus on the amount of time the building restrictions have been in effect, the voting rules under the Louisiana Homeowners Association Act are keyed to the nature of the proposed change in the restriction. Thus, three-fourths of the owners of the lots governed by the association must agree to *establish* a new building restriction for the community. *Id.* § 9:1141.6.B(1). Two-thirds of the lot owners must come together to make a building restriction *more onerous* or to *increase* its impact *Id.* § 9:1141.6.B(2). Only one-half of the lot owners must find agreement to make a building restriction *less onerous*, to *reduce* its impact, or to *terminate* it. *Id.* § 9:1141.6 B(3). Quite innovatively, Section D of the Louisiana Homeowners Association Act allows a property owner to decline to be covered by a subsequent change to the building restrictions approved by the requisite number of lot owners, but only if the non-consenting landowner acts within thirty days of the pertinent vote. La. Rev. Stat. § 9:1141.6 D.

The Louisiana Homeowners Association Act does not apply to commercial or industrial developments governed by building restrictions. Thus, until the legislature adopts new legislation for commercial, industrial or mixed-use CIC's, the codal regime for building restrictions applies to non-residential building restriction regimes as well as residential building restriction regimes that do not impose mandatory homeowner association membership.

In the case below, carefully trace the court's understanding of the general plan for the subdivision.

Head v. Gray

938 So.2d 1084 (La. App. 2 Cir. 2006)

CARAWAY, Judge. Owners in a subdivision brought this action to enjoin the use of a manufactured home on a neighbor's lot based upon a recorded building restriction. The building restriction which was part of the general plan for the residential development was directed against temporary structures, including mobile homes. Defendants' home, which was designed in two sections for placement on a permanent foundation, was ordered to be removed from the subdivision by the trial court. Finding doubt as to the extent of the building restriction, we reverse.

Facts

Cypress Point Subdivision adjoins Cypress Bayou Reservoir in Bossier Parish. In July 1977, the Estate of W.B. Jacobs, Inc. ("Jacobs, Inc.") subdivided the land comprising the subdivision. As a part of this process, Jacobs, Inc. declared and recorded protective covenants and building restrictions (hereinafter "Covenants") governing the use of subdivision property. The disputed restriction, labeled "Temporary Structures" (Restriction # 8, *infra*), provides that no "mobile home" shall be placed or used on a subdivision lot.

Richard and Cinder Mutter now occupy Lot 8, Cypress Point Subdivision. The Mutters own a home manufactured by Franklin Homes, Inc. The Mutters' home was previously in another subdivision nearby for a period of time but was not secured on a foundation there and its roof was apparently never finished. On a date not specified in the record, the Mutters had the home moved to the Cypress Point lot. The structure's two sections were then completely assembled and attached to the foundation.

Thereafter, a group of Cypress Point lot owners brought this action for injunctive relief against the owner of Lot 8, Adolphus Lee Gray, and the Mutters claiming a violation of the Covenants by the Mutters' construction of their modular/ mobile home on the lot. Plaintiffs asked the court to prohibit the defendants "from allowing the placement of said mobile home or manufactured home in said subdivision. . . ." Plaintiffs subsequently filed an amended petition recognizing that the Mutters had already placed and assembled the home on the site and seeking an injunction for its removal.

None of the parties testified at trial. However, Russell Foster testified that his modular home was placed on a lot next to Lot 8 in August 2003. The structure was placed on the concrete foundation one section at a time by a crane and attached to the foundation and bolted together. Although he characterized the home as a permanent dwelling, he acknowledged it could be moved like any other permanent home. Foster also identified photos of various lots with outbuildings, sheds, metal garages, motor homes and other temporary structures which were allegedly out of compliance with the building restrictions.

Photographs showing the transport and assembly of the Mutters' home were also submitted into evidence. This home was comprised of rectangularly-shaped sections, approximately 75 feet long by 15 feet wide. The interior length of each module was exposed so the two sections could be fastened together on site to complete the unified structure. The sections were framed with wooden studs and rafters like a site-built dwelling and the pitch of the roof line produced some attic space. The home sections comply with the same building codes applicable to site-built homes.

After completion of construction, each module is put on a separate, wheeled chassis that permits transportation from the factory. This road chassis is removable and does not furnish any structural integrity to the completed unit. The assembled home is not equipped with wheels.

The foundation for the Mutters' home consisted of a concrete footing poured around the perimeter for the 75 × 30 home. Along the centerline of the foundation where the two sections are joined, a series of cement cinder block piers support the structure.

At the close of trial, the court concluded that the placement of the Mutters' home was prohibited by the Covenants and signed a judgment granting a permanent injunction against the placement of the home in the subdivision. It is from this judgment that defendants appeal.

Discussion

II.

. . . Doubt as to the existence, validity, or extent of building restrictions is resolved in favor of the unrestricted use of the immovable. La. C.C. art. 783. *See generally Tri-State Sand & Gravel, L.L.C. v. Cox*, 38,217 (La. App. 2d Cir. 4/7/04), 871 So.2d 1253, *writ denied*, 2004-1357 (La.9/24/04), 882 So.2d 1144. The words of a contract must be given their generally prevailing meaning. La. C.C. art. 2047. Words of art and technical terms must be given their technical meaning when the contract involves a technical matter. *Id.* The law favors the free and unrestrained use of immovable property, and it follows that any doubt as to the interpretation of a servitude encumbering property must be resolved in favor of the property owner. *McGuffy v. Weil*, 240 La. 758, 125 So.2d 154 (1960). The intention of the proprietor to establish a servitude must clearly appear from the title document. *McGuffy v. Weil, supra*, citing *Noel Estate v. Kansas City Southern & Gulf Ry. Co.*, 187 La. 717, 175 So. 468 (1937). From these principles, if the instrument purporting to create a building restriction is susceptible to two or more reasonable interpretations thereby creating ambiguity and doubt as to the subdivider's intent, the interpretation that least restricts the property will apply regardless of an actual intent for a greater restriction.

There are various provisions in the Covenants for this subdivision which should be reviewed in order to place the disputed "Temporary Structures" restriction in context. We consider the following restrictions of the Covenants relevant for our interpretation of the disputed provision:

> 1. LAND USE AND BUILDING TYPE. No lot shall be used except for residential purposes. No building or structure shall be erected, altered, placed, or permitted to remain on any lot other than one single family dwelling, private garage, carport, and associated lakeshore structures. No garage apartments shall be erected on any lot. . . .

2. DWELLING SIZE. The habitable heated area of the main structure, exclusive of open porches and garages, shall be not less than 1200 square feet.

* * *

4. LOT AREA AND WIDTH. No dwelling shall be erected or placed on any lot having a width of less than 65 feet at the minimum set back line. . . .

* * *

8. TEMPORARY STRUCTURES. No structure of any temporary character, trailer, mobile home, tent, shack, barn, or other similar outbuilding shall be placed or used on any lot at any time as a residence either temporarily or permanently.

. . . .

From a jurisprudential context, it is noteworthy that closely similar versions of the language of Restriction # 8 have been the subject of a rich history of dispute in Louisiana and other states. See, *Smith v. DeVincent*, 322 So.2d 257 (La. App. 2d Cir. 1975), and cases from other states cited therein; *Jackson Square Towne House Homes Ass'n, Inc. v. Mims*, 393 So.2d 816 (La. App. 2d Cir. 1981); *Mitchell v. Killins*, 408 So.2d 969 (La. App. 2d Cir. 1981); *Webb v. Johnson*, 95-1518 (La. App. 3d Cir. 4/3/96), 671 So.2d 1120; *Ritter v. Fabacher*, 517 So.2d 914 (La. App. 3d Cir. 1987); *Mouille v. Henry*, 321 So.2d 377 (La. App. 3d Cir. 1975). These cases suggest that the language and phraseology of Restriction # 8 have some common source, possibly evolving from an early formulary. With changing contexts for employing the restriction, some alteration in its language and differing schemes envisioned for individual subdivision plans, disputes have arisen.

Most of these cases, including our initial review of language closely similar to Restriction # 8 in *Smith*, deal principally with the issue of whether the use of "trailer" alone in early versions included the concept of mobile home. As *Smith* points out, cases in other states gave conflicting answers to that question. Some of the above cases also discussed the degree of permanent attachment or immobilization in situations where the chassis, wheels and tongue/tow bar were removed from a mobile home and the remaining structure was placed on piers and other such foundations. Finally, the *Smith* case had to address the phrase, "used on any lot at any time as a residence either temporarily or permanently." Unlike the present Covenants, which make clear that "residential purposes" is an overriding restriction on the lots in Cypress Point Subdivision, the limited set of covenants in *Smith* had no such general restriction. Therefore, the *Smith* court was restrained to conclude, rather anomalistically, that while the defendants' mobile homes were included within the meaning of the word "trailer" as used in the restriction in that case, the defendants were not required to remove their mobile homes/trailers from the subdivision because of the lack of a clear building restriction prohibiting their placement in the subdivision. The owners in *Smith* were only enjoined from using their mobile homes as residences within the subdivision. The court concluded:

If this subdivider had intended to prohibit the placement of trailers (or mobile homes), temporary structures, even barns, sheds or outbuildings on the subdivided property, as well as to prohibit their 'use' as a residence, the restrictions should have and could have been phrased so as to expressly and unequivocally provide.

Presented here is an example of imprecise draftsmanship and our ruling herein should serve as notice to those who would restrict either or both the structures on their property and the uses which may be made of permitted structures to be precise in drafting restrictive covenants.

Smith, supra at 263.

In contrast to the limited set of restrictions in *Smith,* our later ruling in *Mitchell, supra,* involved subdivision covenants with a "residential purposes" restriction almost identical to Restriction # 1 of the present Covenants and a "Re-location of Buildings" restriction which required every residence to be constructed on site. This court therefore affirmed the mandatory injunction granted by the trial court in *Mitchell* for removal of a mobile home immobilized in the subdivision. The "temporary structure" restriction in *Mitchell* was identical to the disputed restriction central to the *Smith* ruling. Yet, because the entire set of restrictions for each subdivision differed, the outcomes of the two cases using the very same restriction were different.

Smith and *Mitchell* demonstrate the importance of considering the entire framework for the subdivision's "general plan" which is identified in the Civil Code definition for building restrictions under Article 775. As the Civil Code further provides, "[e]ach provision in a contract must be interpreted in light of the other provisions so that each is given the meaning suggested by the contract as a whole." La. C.C. art. 2050. Accordingly, we first examine the overall context or "general plan" for the Cypress Point Subdivision as reflected in the above quoted restrictions.

Restriction # 1 of the Covenants begins with a general prohibition against uses other than for "residential purposes." More significantly, the second sentence specifically limits the subdivision lots, listing the "single family dwelling, private garage, carport, and associated lakeshore structures" as the *only* structures permitted on them. This would arguably prohibit certain things listed in Restriction # 8, such as an "RV trailer," "tent," "shack" and "barn," from use as a structure on the lots since these are not generally understood as structures for the accommodation of a "single family dwelling." Thus, the limitation of Restriction # 8 is in many respects already addressed by the broad limitation of Restriction # 1. Nevertheless, it adds explanation by addressing "outbuildings" of a "temporary character," so as to make it more than superfluous.

The next important contextual feature of these Covenants is the consistent use of the term "placed" as it pertains to buildings and structures. Most of the quoted restrictions discuss an allowance for structures to be "placed" on a lot, and three of them specifically use "placed or erected" as contrasting verbs. This indicates that a house with a pier-and-beam structure built long before the advent of mobile homes and modern manufactured housing could be brought in and "placed" on the same foundation which the Mutters constructed for their home. Such house might have a roof pitch and attic space like the Mutters' home so that its aesthetic features would be virtually the same. Unlike the "Re-Location of Buildings" restriction in *Mitchell,* which required every residence in that subdivision to be constructed on site, the Covenants for Cypress Point do not prevent a home built elsewhere from being moved and placed in the subdivision.

A third feature of these building restrictions is their lack of specific limits on aesthetic features. Aesthetic considerations play a small part in these Covenants when dealing with square footage for the homes and minimum setback lines. The Covenants do not however attempt to specify particular construction features, such as brick veneer or roof material or pitch, that might have a more pronounced aesthetic impact on the subdivision and tend indirectly to restrict the use of manufactured housing. See, *Travosos v. Stoma,* 95-1568 (La. App. 3d Cir. 4/3/96), 672 So.2d 1070, *writ denied,* 96-1633 (La. 9/27/96), 679 So.2d 1343. Thus, any objections by the plaintiffs that might relate to the aesthetic features of the Mutters' manufactured home gain no support by affirmative or negative duties set out in the Covenants so as to sanction an injunction for the home's removal.

Last, before considering the meaning and scope of the term "mobile home," the context of Restriction # 8 must be reviewed. This restriction expresses certain general concepts that do not relate to the Mutters' home. First, the restriction is labeled "Temporary Structure" and its language speaks of a "temporary character" for the listed structures. This is aimed as a restriction on the way the building is built. The Mutters' home rests on a foundation like any other pier-and-beam home that might have been constructed on site. That concrete foundation may be considered as permanent in that it is embedded in the ground and cannot be removed without destroying its structure. The fact that an assembled manufactured home is placed on a foundation and may be disassembled and removed does not mean that the Mutters' home is a "temporary structure" with a "temporary character." It is more reasonable to characterize this home, like any pier-and-beam home constructed on site, as permanent in nature. Restriction # 8 also concludes its specific listing of structures with the phrase "or other similar outbuilding," reflecting a use restriction. Unquestionably, every structure identified in Restriction # 8 can be used as an outbuilding, or a structure separate in its identity and use from the principal "single family dwelling" of each residential lot. The Mutters' manufactured housing, however, is not being used as an outbuilding. Thus, the general expressions within Restriction # 8 — "temporary" "outbuildings" — arguably define its prohibitory focus, and the Mutters' home does not fall within that focus.

Plaintiffs' position is that Restriction # 8 must be interpreted literally, that "no mobile home . . . shall be placed or used" on Cypress Point lots, and that this interpretation controls without regard to any other contextual expressions in the restriction itself or in the Covenants. They also maintain that the meaning of "mobile home" includes within its scope the Mutters' double-wide manufactured structure.

From our review of the law and jurisprudence, we find various expressions attempting to define the term mobile home. For example, in 1975, two years before these Covenants were drafted, the Third Circuit Court of Appeal in *Mouille, supra,* considered Webster's definition for mobile home as "a trailer that is used as a permanent dwelling." *Mouille* at 378. At the same time of that ruling, La. R.S. 51:911.22, which was included in Louisiana's Uniform Standards Code for Mobile Homes, provided a definition as follows:

> (5) "Mobile home" means a factory-assembled structure or structures equipped with the necessary connections and made so as to be readily movable over roads and highways as a unit or units, which exceeds eight body feet in width or is thirty-two feet or more in body length and is designed for occupancy with or without a permanent foundation. It may consist of one or more units which can be telescoped when towed and expanded later for additional capacity, or may consist of two or more units, separately towable but designed to be joined into one integral unit.

Act 281 of 1974. Later, this definition in the Revised Statutes was amended several times. At one point, "mobile home," "manufactured home" and "manufactured housing" were used together in La. R.S. 51:911.22 and said to be interchangeable. Act 576 of 1984. The present version of the statute defines mobile home differently from manufactured home. La. R.S. 51:911.22. Finally, in our law pertaining to highway regulations, La. R.S. 32:1 has its own definition of "mobile home" placing emphasis on the "trailer or semitrailer" design of the structure which "is equipped for use as a conveyance on highways."

At trial, the Mutters attempted through expert testimony to raise distinctions between a mobile home and a manufactured or modular home. The mobile home was said to have a permanent chassis that forms a part of its structure, while the Mutters' home was moved on a separate transporter/trailer and lifted into place onto a permanent foundation. An executive of the company that built the Mutters' home testified that the modular home was built to the same building codes as a pier-and-beam constructed home. The building standards for a mobile home were said to be different. Also, the testimony discussed the legal requirement for a mobile home to have a vehicle identification number for transport as a vehicle while no such requirement applied to the Mutters' home.

Noteworthy distinguishing features of the Mutters' home are its roof pitch and attic space. The photos of the home as it was moved on a trailer into the subdivision reveal that its roof was incomplete with only a lower, temporary roof covering each home section. The lower roof obviously allowed for easier transport along the highway. Once at its destination, a steeper roof with rafters was added to each section, and a gabled roof with attic space comprised the finished structure. Foster's manufactured home located next door had an even steeper roof since his modular home units were designed to accommodate an upstairs living area.

Contrary to the plaintiffs' argument, the term "mobile home" does not have such a generally prevailing meaning as to clearly include all forms of manufactured housing, hence the need to detail the scope of its meaning as illustrated by varying definitions in our statutes. Another reasonable and narrower interpretation might recognize the mobile home's origins as a trailer with a tow bar, comprising a single self-contained living area and designed to sit on its own axle. Our ruling in *Smith* had little difficulty recognizing that the single unit mobile home in that case was essentially a "trailer," which was the only term utilized in the early version of the "temporary structure" restriction which *Smith* addressed. The court observed:

> By whatever name, these homes convey to reasonable minds a rather elongated structure (10 to 14 feet in width by 40 to 80 feet in length), capable of being towed on the highways, with axles and wheels attached to the frame of the structure. The very name mobile or trailer conveys this meaning. The overall appearance, as distinguished from exterior decor, of one mobile home is not grossly dissimilar to another, and in the eyes of reasonable men, they all "look alike." We also take note that occasionally they may be immobilized on a particular location, but nonetheless, remain capable of being mobilized without too much effort and expense. They are not so much "constructed" or "assembled" even in a small part on the location the owner desires but are "connected" to sewerage and utilities. Indeed, one of their greatest selling points is their complete containment, ease of connection, and mobility.

Smith v. DeVincent, supra at 263.

The Mutters' home was assembled; its roof and attic constructed; and its remobilization would now require much effort and expense. Though double-wide trailers requiring assembly existed at the time of *Smith* (see Act 281 of 1974), this court's definitional description plainly suggests that modern manufactured housing units designed for placement on a foundation by a crane and requiring roof construction would not be included in its 1975 view of the trailer/mobile home.

Moreover, as seen by the detailed definitions for "mobile home" utilized in the above Louisiana statutes, careful drafting avoids the question of whether a mobile home with a permanent foundation is still to be considered a *mobile* home. That question is reasonable, and the question raises doubt. In the *Mitchell* case, the subdivision restrictions were clear that an immobilized mobile home would not be considered as an acceptable permanent residence because they further provided that every residence also be constructed on site. Other restrictions specifying aesthetic features of a residence could also effectively prevent most manufactured housing in a subdivision if that is indeed a goal for the subdivision plan.

In summary, we determine that issues exist in the Covenants creating reasonable doubt under Civil Code Article 783 as to the extent of the application of these building restrictions for Cypress Point Subdivision. There is doubt as to the meaning and scope of the term "mobile home." Mobile structures are allowed to be "placed" in the subdivision with no requirement that every residence be "erected" on site. Most significantly, even if the term mobile home may be broadly construed to include all forms of manufactured and modular housing, the context of Restriction # 8 suggests a limited interpretation for its application. That interpretation of Restriction # 8 prevents the placement on a lot of such manufactured housing with a less than permanent foundation for use as an outbuilding serving the main dwelling. Such an interpretation by a third party viewing the public records and reading these Covenants is reasonable, whether or not it is the only interpretation that can be understood for Restriction # 8. It thus becomes the interpretation the law mandates for the most free and unrestrained use of the immovable.

Conclusion

The permanent injunction issued by the trial court is reversed. Costs of appeal are assessed to appellees.

REVERSED AND RENDERED.

Notes and Questions

1. Note how the court in *Head v. Gray*, 938 So.2d 1084 (La. App. 2 Cir. 2006), stated at the outset that the building restrictions were part of the general plan for the residential development. The court also noted that the defendant's home was placed on a permanent foundation. What was prohibited by the building restriction? Did the defendant's actions violate that building restriction?

The court examined the intent of the building restriction at issue by exploring the general plan of the subdivision and by interpreting each provision in light of the general plan as shaped by an understanding of the other provisions. It narrowly construed the language of the restriction to permit the manufactured home to remain in the subdivision. It noted the relevance of Article 783 of the Louisiana Civil Code: "[d]oubt as to the existence, validity, or extent of building restrictions is resolved in favor of the unrestricted use of the immovable." La. Civ. Code art. 783 (1977, amended 1999). Do you agree with the court's reasoning? Would you expect the same outcome had the subdivision been a planned residential community governed by the Louisiana Homeowners Association Act?

2. The court identifies differences among mobile homes, trailers, manufactured homes and modular homes. It considered outbuildings, sheds, motor homes and metal garages. Can these things be easily categorized for purposes of a building restriction prohibition? What criteria would you use to describe these items if you were drafting a set of building restrictions for a client who is a developer?

3. The court in *Head* cites to *Smith v. DeVincent*, 322 So.2d 257 (La. App. 2 Cir. 1975), which admonished drafters of building restrictions to be more precise in

their language. Often drafters will base their clauses on what others have done, adding only slight modifications to particularize the restriction. Consequently, almost identical restrictions appear in a large number of general plans. Additionally, drafters will respond to a court decision by adjusting the language of a restriction to achieve the interpretation sought by their clients. When drafting these restrictions for Jacobs, Inc. in July 1977, could the lawyer have anticipated and avoided this dispute? What was the subdivider's original intent?

4. Consider Restriction No. 4 in *Head*: "No dwelling shall be erected or placed on any lot having a width of less than 65 feet at the minimum set back line. . . ." A setback refers to the distance of a structure from a property line. Building restrictions frequently impose setbacks to influence the character of the neighborhood. When building restrictions impose large setbacks, a developer typically presumes that purchaser of lots in a residential planned community value privacy and lots of green space around their homes. In *Lakewood Prop. Owners' Ass'n v. Smith*, 231 So.3d 822, 826–27 (La. App. 4 Cir. 2017), the court of appeal affirmed a trial court determination that a car port had to be removed because it could not be made compliant with a five-foot setback from side interior lot lines established under a building restriction regime governing a residential development in New Orleans.

* * *

The case below involves mobile homes placed in a subdivision. Note the variety of arguments raised by the defendant.

Chambless v. Parker

867 So.2d 974 (La. App. 2 Cir. 2004)

PEATROSS, Judge. This appeal arises from a denial of Defendant Sheila Parker's ("Parker") motion for summary judgment and grant of Plaintiffs' Robert and Collene Chambless, Jerry and Marilyn Moses and Hollis Faulk ("Plaintiffs"), motion for summary judgment. Parker now appeals the judgment of the trial court. For the reasons stated herein, we affirm.

Facts

In July 2000, Parker purchased two lots (Lots 10 and 11) in the "Frost Estates," a subdivision in Ouachita Parish. Parker purchased the lots with the intent of renting out mobile home slots. In late August or early September 2000, Parker had placed four mobile homes on the properties and had leased some of them for residential occupancy. On October 27, 2000, Plaintiffs filed suit against Parker alleging that, according to the building restriction found in the deeds from the original landowner to the first vendees of Lots 10 and 11, the owner of the land could have no more than one residence on the land and the land could not be used for anything other than a residential purpose. The restriction found in the original deeds provided that:

> Said property shall be used for residential purpose only and only one residence shall be constructed thereon, the same to cost not less than $10,000.

This restriction was not in the deeds given to Parker by her predecessor in title when she purchased the land; however, the building permits she received from the Ouachita Parish Clerk of Court's office state that she should make herself aware of possible deed restrictions. In their lawsuit, Plaintiffs sought to enjoin Parker from using Lots 10 and 11 for any commercial purposes, other than what is consistent with the restriction found in the deeds. . . .

Discussion

Building Restrictions

Parker argues that the subdivision does not meet the requirements of La. C.C. art. 775, because the building restriction in the deeds is not part of a general development plan; and, thus, it cannot be enforced. We do not agree.

The property owners in the subdivision have the right to bring enforcement actions to prohibit any use of the property that does not comport with the general plan of development. See La. C.C. art. 779 and comments thereafter. Courts in Louisiana have held that, in order for a building restriction to be enforced, however, it must be part of a general development plan. See *R And K Bluebonnet, Inc. v. Patout's of Baton Rouge, Inc.*, 521 So.2d 634 (La. App. 1st Cir. 1988). Building restrictions constitute real rights only in the framework of subdivision planning. *Ezell v. Vaughn*, 496 So.2d 534 (La. App. 1st Cir. 1986). *Ezell v. Vaughn*, 496 So.2d 534 (La. App. 1st Cir.1986). In *Murphy v. Marino*, 60 So.2d 128 (La. App. 1st Cir.1952), the court held that, in order to find that a general development plan existed, the restriction had to be applied to at least a particular part of the subdivision, known to each purchaser and thereby, by reference or implication, forming a part of his contract with the subdivider. In *Richard v. Broussard*, 378 So.2d 959 (La. App. 3d Cir.1979), the court found that a building restriction did not exist because the original landowner did not have an orderly subdivision plan. The court, in *Richard, supra*, found that formal planning of a subdivision, platting by a surveyor, subdividing lots from the beginning and an evident scheme or plan of the subdivision would show that a general development plan existed.

The fact alone that restrictive covenants are inserted into individual acts of sale does not establish that they were not intended to pursue a general plan of development for the subdivision. *Gwatney v. Miller*, 371 So.2d 1355 (La. App. 3d Cir.1979). In addition, Louisiana law does not require that the restriction exist in every deed in the lots of a subdivision in order for a general development plan to exist. On the contrary, Louisiana law provides that a general development plan can exist even if only ***most of the deeds*** of lots in a subdivision contain the restriction. La. C.C. art. 775 cmt. e provides, in pertinent part:

> When restrictions are imposed by stipulations inserted in individual acts of sale, care should be taken to impose uniform restrictions on ***most, if not all,*** individual lots in the subdivision. Omission to make the restrictions uniform or to insert them in a ***substantial number of sales*** may be taken to indicate absence of a general development plan. (Emphasis added.)

As real rights, building restriction clauses are not rights that are personal to the vendor. *Five N Company, L.L.C. v. Singer A & P Remainder Trust*, 97–2165 (La. App. 1st Cir.11/6/98), 721 So.2d 1066, *writ denied*, 98–3051 (La.2/5/99), 738 So.2d 4. Building restrictions inure to the benefit of all other property owners under a general plan of development: such restrictions are real rights running with the land. *Blessey v. McHugh*, 94–0555 (La. App. 1st Cir.7/27/95), 664 So.2d 115. Once a building restriction has been imposed upon the land by a properly recorded act which transfers the property, the restrictions affect future assigns and vendees, even if the building restriction is later omitted in subsequent deeds. *Clark v. Reed*, 122 So.2d 344 (La. App. 2d Cir. 1960); *McGuffy v. Weil*, 240 La. 758, 125 So.2d 154 (1960). Moreover, the fact that no subdivision plat was of record when the building restriction was created does not affect the validity of the restrictions. *Fitzwater v. Walker*, 281 So.2d 790 (La. App. 3d Cir.1973).

Building restrictions are a means of insuring the lasting aesthetic and monetary value of property. *4626 Corp. v. Merriam*, 329 So.2d 885 (La. App. 1st Cir. 1976), *writ refused*, 332 So.2d 800 (La. 1976). The owners of lots in a subdivision with building restrictions expect those restrictions to be enforced.

In the case *sub judice*, there were eighteen lots established in the subdivision. Of those eighteen lots, the deeds in thirteen of the lots contained the restrictive language. Even though not all the deeds contained the restriction, **most** of the deeds did contain it, including the deeds to Lots 10 and 11. The restrictive language in the deeds to each of the thirteen lots was exactly the same. An orderly subdivision plan was established by Benton Frost in 1963. Mr. Frost formerly planned his subdivision, had it platted by a surveyor and subdivided his land into lots from the beginning. The plat of this subdivision was filed into the Plat Book in the Ouachita Parish records in 1963. In reviewing the layout of the lots in the subdivision and the characterization of each lot, we conclude that a general plan of development was established by Mr. Frost. Since the restriction was inserted in pursuance of a general development plan, there is no doubt that the restrictive language in the deeds to the owners of these lots was a building restriction. We find that Parker's land is subject to a valid building restriction and is enforceable in this subdivision. Parker's first assignment of error is without merit.

Building Restriction Abandonment

Parker asserts that, even if this court finds that an enforceable building restriction exists in this case, the restriction has been abandoned due to a number of violations of it that have taken place in the subdivision that have not been enforced. We find no merit in this assertion.

After a plaintiff seeking an injunction enforcing a building restriction has established a violation of the restriction, the burden shifts to the defendant of the restriction to prove its abandonment. *Harrison v. Myers*, 25,902 (La. App. 2d Cir. 6/22/94), 639 So.2d 402. La. C.C. art. 782 cmt. b provides, in pertinent part:

Abandonment of the entire restrictive plan is ordinarily predicated on a great number of violations of **all or most restrictions.** Upon abandonment of the **entire plan** all restrictions fall, and the use of the property is free for all purposes. Abandonment of a particular restriction is predicated on a *sufficient number of violations* of that restriction in relation to the number of lots affected by it. Thus, if a restriction requires that a building should face a certain street, or should be erected a number of feet from the property line, **only violations on property subject to the same restrictions are considered in determining the question of abandonment.** When the violations are **sufficient in number** to warrant the conclusion that a particular restriction has been abandoned, the **property is freed of that restriction only** (emphasis added).

In deciding whether there has been abandonment, the court must decide what the subdividers intended the scheme or plan to be and then inquire into alleged violations to determine whether the plan has been disrupted. *East Parker Properties, Inc. v. Pelican Realty Co.,* 335 So.2d 466 (La. App. 1st Cir. 1976), *cert. denied,* 338 So.2d 699 (La. 1976).

Whether a waiver or relinquishment of a restriction has occurred by common consent or universal acquiescence depends upon the facts of each case. *Lakeshore Property Owners Association, Inc. v. Delatte,* 579 So.2d 1039 (La. App. 4th Cir. 1991), *writ denied,* 586 So.2d 560 (La. 1991). The character, materiality, number of the violations and their proximity to the objecting residents are all factors to be considered in determining if a restriction has been abandoned by acquiescence. *Harrison, supra.* Insubstantial, technical or infrequent violations of a restriction, which are not subversive to the general plan or scheme, weigh little towards establishing an abandonment. *Id.* Further, in order to find that abandonment in a subdivision has occurred, the property owner against whom abandonment is asserted must have known of the alleged violations or have had a duty to know. *Schwab v. Kelton,* 405 So.2d 1239 (La. App. 1st Cir. 1981), *writ denied,* 407 So.2d 749 (La. 1981).

The intended general development plan in the instant case was that of a residential subdivision. Two of Parker's alleged violations of the building restriction in the subdivision are not violations at all. It is not a violation of the building restriction to have a mobile home on a lot owner's property if that is the owner's residence and the only residence on that property. Further, the issue of mobile homes and mobile home parks in surrounding neighborhoods is irrelevant. The only possible technical violation of the building restriction is that of the lot owner who Parker alleges is operating a commercial welding service. Parker has not shown that Plaintiffs even knew of this alleged welding service and has not submitted any other evidence to show that there are any other violations of the building restrictions occurring in the subdivision. As Louisiana law sets forth, one technical violation of the restriction is not enough to establish that the building restriction, which is enforceable against everyone living in the subdivision, has been abandoned. We find that the building restriction has not been abandoned and summary judgment is appropriate; and, therefore, Parker's third assignment of error is without merit.

Residential or Commercial Use of Property

Parker contends that the mobile homes on her lots are residential and not commercial; and, therefore, they do not violate the building restriction. We do not agree.

The building restriction provides that the use of the property should be for residential purposes only and that only one residence may exist on each property. Parker cites both *Vienna Bend Subdivision Homeowners Association v. Manning*, 459 So.2d 1345 (La. App. 3d Cir. 1984), and *Concord Estates Homeowners Association, Inc. v. Special Children's Foundation, Inc.*, 459 So.2d 1242 (La. App. 1st Cir. 1984), in support of her argument that she is not violating the building restriction. We find that those cases are inapplicable to the case *sub judice*. Both of those cases dealt with homes for mentally challenged individuals operated by nonprofit corporations in subdivisions that contained restrictions similar to the restriction in this case. The courts in both cases found that the use of those homes was not for commercial activity. The use of both those homes was through nonprofit corporations.

In contrast, in the instant case, Parker rented mobile home slots for profit. Parker has already rented four mobile homes slots and has ten total available mobile home slots open to rent on Lot 10. This is a commercial use of the property and it violates the building restriction not only because it is a commercial use, but also because more than one residence exists on the property. Parker is in violation of the building restriction; and, consequently, her last assignment of error is without merit. Finally, since we find that the restriction in the deed to Parker's lots is a building restriction that is enforceable and has not been abandoned, we pretermit discussion of Parker's assignment of error concerning predial servitudes.

Conclusion

For the foregoing reasons, the judgment of the trial court granting Plaintiffs' Robert and Collene Chambless, Jerry and Marilyn Moses and Hollis Faulk, motion for summary judgment and denial of Defendant Sheila Parker's ("Parker") motion for summary judgment is affirmed. Costs of this appeal are assessed to Sheila Parker.

AFFIRMED.

Notes and Questions

1. Sheila Parker's lawyers devised several arguments in support of her claims in *Chambless v. Parker*, 867 So.2d 974 (La. App. 2 Cir. 2004). First, Parker argued that, because the restrictions were not included in her deed, they did not bind her. The court, however, determined that inclusion of the restrictions in each deed was not necessary, stating that "[o]nce a building restriction has been imposed upon the land by a properly recorded act which transfers the property, the restrictions affect

future assigns and vendees, even if the building restriction is later omitted in subsequent deeds." *Id.* at 978.

Next, Parker argued that the building restrictions did not form part of a general plan and therefore, were unenforceable. After reviewing the layout of the lots and the restrictions applicable to each lot, the court disagreed. It found that the subdivision consisted of eighteen lots and that the original deeds to thirteen of those lots contained the building restrictions. The court concluded that this was sufficient to create a general plan. *Id.* at 979. Do you agree there was a general plan that was "feasible" and "capable of being enforced" within the meaning of Article 775 of the Louisiana Civil Code? Is the court's conclusion defensible in light of the general instruction in Article 783 that all "doubt as to the existence, validity, or extent of building restrictions is resolved in favor of unrestricted use of the immovable"?

Parker next argued that the restrictions had been abandoned. As this was a factual inquiry, the court considered evidence as "to the character, materiality, number of violations and their proximity to the objecting residents." *Id.* at 979. In this light it determined that a general abandonment of the plan did not occur. *Id.* at 980. Do you agree that an abandonment had not occurred?

As a last resort, Parker argued that her use of the land conformed to the building restrictions. Her tenants, after all, used the mobile homes as their residences. The court rejected this final argument as well finding that Parker's activities violated the building restrictions in two different respects and distinguishing two other decisions involving group homes run by non-profit corporations. *Id.* at 980. Do you agree with the court's conclusion that Parker's activities were commercial in character and violated the building restrictions?

* * *

In the two enforcement cases below, the defendants argue that a building restriction no longer applies to their lot because the violation at issue has continued for more than two years. In the first case, other more fundamental issues relating to the enforceability of the building regime were also raised.

Cosby v. Holcomb Trucking, Inc.
942 So.2d 471 (La. 2006)

VICTORY, Justice. We granted this writ application to determine whether the court of appeal erred in reversing a trial court determination that this action to enforce a building restriction had not prescribed. After oral argument, we requested further briefing on whether the applicable building restrictions form part of a general plan as required by Louisiana Civil Code Article 775. Upon further review of the record and the applicable law, we reverse the judgment of the court of appeal and reinstate the judgment of the trial court on the original grounds upon which this writ was granted. The trial court's determination that this action was filed within the two-year time period because the violations of the building restrictions were not noticeable until 2001 was not manifestly erroneous.

Facts and Procedural History

In 1982, William Monroe King, Jr. and his wife Shirley Martin King developed Wedgewood Acres Subdivision ("Wedgewood Acres") in rural Livingston Parish. Contemporaneously with that development, the Kings established building restrictions for Wedgewood Acres, and on December 15, 1982, they filed the restrictions in the Livingston Parish public records.

Two years later, the Kings, along with other family members, Darron and Michele King, developed four rural tracts of land adjoining Wedgewood Acres along Ben Fuglar Road (the "Front Lots") in Livingston Parish. As part of that development, the Kings established a building restriction agreement expressly stating that with the exception of the set-back restrictions, "[a]ll other restrictive covenants shall be exactly as provided in the restrictive covenants for Wedgewood Acres Subdivision as per said [recorded] restrictions." On May 22, 1984, the Kings filed this second restrictive covenant agreement in the Livingston Parish public records.

The provisions of the restrictive covenants pertinent to the present case are:

1. All tracts are hereby designated as residential, and they shall be used for none other than residential purposes. No building shall be erected, altered, placed or permitted to remain on any tract, other than one single-family dwelling, not to exceed two and one-half stories in height, with the usual and appropriate out buildings, enclosed barns, and private garage and/or carports designed to house no fewer than two automobiles.

* * *

7. No house trailers, buses, commercial vehicles or trucks shall be kept, store [d], repaired, or maintained on any lot, servitude or right-of-way in any manner which would detract from the appearance of the subdivision. No structure of any temporary character, trailer, basement, tent, shack, or other out-building shall be allowed on any tract for a prolonged period of time so as to detract from the appearance of the subdivision, unless approved by developer.

* * *

16. No building or structure shall be used to operate any commercial activity on any tract, and no commercial activity shall be conducted from any lot in this subdivision, unless approved by developer.

In 1985, Harry and Joyce Holcomb acquired Lot "P" in Wedgewood Acres, but never built on the property. On January 9, 1985, William M. King, Jr., individually, executed an authentic act wherein he: (1) "grant[ed] permission to [Harry H. Holcomb, Jr.] to enter through public access and park on his premises his truck used in his profession;" (2) permitted him to "maintain this truck for normal maintenance but cannot enter into commercial maintenance in any form;" and (3) allowed him "to construct and maintain a permanent structure for the housing of this truck as long as it is built to other subdivision restrictions and does not detract in any manner from the appearance of the subdivision. Detraction from the general appearance of the subdivision shall be determined by the developer." In exchange, Holcomb agreed "not to haul loads in excess of 50 thousand pounds into Wedgewood Acres except pre-sold loads to other landowners."

Subsequently, on June 18, 1992, the Holcombs exchanged Lot "P" for one of the Front Lots on Ben Fugler Road. Harry Holcomb testified no search of the Livingston Parish public records was made prior to the exchange. In 1993, the Holcombs constructed a home on the newly exchanged lot and approximately four years later, they constructed a 40×40 steel outbuilding 1 on their lot for use in connection with their trucking company, Holcomb Trucking, Inc. [At no time did the plaintiffs object to the Holcombs' construction of the outbuilding. Similarly, they did not complain about Joyce Holcomb's use of the Front Lot property to park her school bus.] Traditionally, the Holcombs serviced their vehicles at a shop they leased in Livingston Parish. After the construction of the steel building on their lot along Fugler Road, they terminated this shop lease and started bringing trucks onto their Fugler Road lot for maintenance and service. He testified that none of the trucks are regularly parked at the residence and only general maintenance and minor vehicle repairs, i.e., oil changes, truck lubrication, and brake adjustments, are conducted in the shop. Additionally, the Holcombs also regularly use pressure washers to wash down at least one truck per weekend outside the shop on their property.

On February 20, 2002, eight of the Holcombs' neighbors filed these proceedings, alleging the Holcombs keep, store, repair and maintain one or more commercial vehicles and operate a commercial business on their property in violation of the 1984 restrictive covenants. The neighbors further claimed the continuing disturbance to the neighborhood caused by the Holcombs' trucking business violates the provisions of La. C.C. art. 667. On June 30, 2002, after this litigation began, Holcomb obtained and recorded a document in which William M. King, Jr. declared that the exemption Holcomb originally obtained on January 9, 1985, from the commercial activity provisions applicable to Wedgewood Acres, was applicable to his lot on Fugler Road. In that document, King further stated, in an effort to "clarify" the earlier agreement, that Holcomb was permitted to: operate his trucking business; bring in trucks and trailers for Holcomb, Inc. for cleaning and maintenance; maintain the outbuildings needed to operate the trucking business; have third parties deliver parts and materials for the operation of the business; and, engage in any other activities needed for the operation of the trucks and trailers.

The Holcombs responded to the petition with peremptory exceptions of no right of action and prescription. After conducting a contradictory hearing at which evidence was introduced, the trial court overruled the peremptory exceptions. After a trial on the merits on the defendants' violation of the building restrictions, the trial court granted a preliminary injunction, prohibiting the Holcombs from bringing commercial vehicles or trucks on their property in the Front Lots and from engaging in commercial activity on the property, excepting specified business communications. [The excepted business communications included conducting communications from their home by telephone, mail, email, and internet. Eds.]

The Holcombs appealed, seeking review of several issues, including the trial court's denial of their peremptory exception of prescription. Applying article 781, the appellate court found no reasonable factual basis for the trial court's finding the Holcombs' activities were not noticeable and apparent to the public until the spring of 2001 and reversed the trial court's denial of the Holcombs' peremptory exception of prescription. *Cosby v. Holcomb*, 03-2423 (La. App. 1 Cir. 12/17/04), 890 So.2d 35 (unpublished opinion). Accordingly, it found the plaintiffs' suit filed on February 20, 2002, "over four years after 'the commencement of a noticeable violation'" was time-barred and the Holcombs' property was freed of the pertinent restrictive covenants that had been violated. *Id.* We granted the plaintiffs' writ application. *Cosby v. Holcomb*, 05-0470 (La.5/6/05), 901 So.2d 1078.

Discussion

In 1977, the Louisiana Legislature enacted a new Title V of Book II of the Louisiana Civil Code regulating building restrictions. Accordingly, Articles 775–783 of the Louisiana Civil Code now define and govern building restrictions. Because prior to 1977 the Civil Code did not specifically address building restrictions, these new articles generally codified the existing jurisprudence.

Building restrictions are defined as "charges imposed by the owner of an immovable in pursuance of a general plan governing building standards, specified uses, and improvements." La. C.C. art. 775. "The plan must be feasible and capable of being preserved." La. C.C. art. 775. "The law is clear that building restriction clauses constitute real rights, not personal to the vendor, and inure to the benefit of all other grantees under a general plan of development, and are real rights running with the land; and that the remedy of the other grantees to prevent a violation of the restrictions by another is by injunction." *Oakbrook Civic Ass'n, Inc. v. Sonnier*, 481 So.2d 1008, 1010 (La. 1986) (citing *Edwards v. Wiseman*, 198 La. 382, 3 So.2d 661 (1941))....

When this case was filed and argued to the lower courts and to this Court, there was no dispute that the building restrictions constituted a general plan of development which was properly filed and which gave constructive knowledge of its contents to all prospective purchasers. The defenses presented by the Holcombs in their peremptory exceptions were that a certain plaintiff had no right to pursue an action based on the restrictive covenants applicable to the Front Lots, and that the plaintiffs' actions had prescribed. On appeal, the only issues raised by the defendants other than the above issues, were that King granted them a waiver from the restrictive covenants and that the trial court erred in granting an injunction if the injunction was based on La. C.C. arts 667, 668 and 669. *Sua sponte,* this Court asked the parties to brief the issue of whether the restrictive covenants constituted a general plan in light of *Le Blanc v. Palmisano*, 43 So.2d 263 (La. App. Orl. 1949), which held that a restrictive covenant did not run with the land because whether or not property could be used for commercial purposes was "contingent entirely upon the caprice" of the developer.

After further review, we find that this appellate court case is not dispositive and that the mere fact that certain restrictions can be waived by the developer does not *ipso facto* make the restrictive covenants unenforceable as such. For instance, in an analogous case, we explained as follows:

> There is a conflict in the circuit courts as to whether a building restriction requiring approval of construction plans by a neighborhood committee, when no guidelines or very general guidelines for approval are provided, is enforceable in this state. The Fourth and Third Circuits have held that such restriction is unenforceable because it is too vague, indefinite and ambiguous. *Lake Forest, Inc. v. Drury,* 352 So.2d 305 (La. App. 4 Cir. 1977), *writ denied,* 354 So.2d 199 (La. 1978); *Community Builders, Inc. v. Scarborough,* 149 So.2d 141 (La. App. 3 Cir. 1962). The Second Circuit and the First Circuit, until the instant case, have upheld such a provision, determining the validity of the enforcement by the reasonableness of the committee's actions. *Jackson Square Towne House Homes Ass'n, Inc. v. Mims,* 393 So.2d 816 (La. App. 2 Cir. 1981); *4626 Corp. v. Merriam,* 329 So.2d 885 (La. App. 1 Cir.), *writ refused,* 332 So.2d 800 (La. 1976). The majority of the states which have considered the issue have held that covenants requiring submission of plans and consent before construction are valid and enforceable, even though they vest the approving authority with broad discretionary powers, so long as the authority to consent is exercised reasonably and in good faith.

> We think that the applicable rule in the instant case should be that where the power is granted to a committee to approve or disapprove the erection of a building based on a standard of whether it conforms to the harmony of external design and location in relation to the surrounding structures and topography, such a standard is not ambiguous and is enforceable, provided that the authority is exercised reasonably and in good faith.

Oakbrook, supra at 1011–12.

While the restrictions in *Oakbrook* dealt with the discretion to approve of construction plans by a neighborhood committee, and some of the restrictions in this case arguably deal with the discretion to approve of certain types of commercial activity by the developer, the relevant issue in both cases is whether the fact that certain of the restrictions are not absolute and are subject to the discretion of a third party negates the finding of a general plan. In *Oakbrook,* this Court found that as long as the discretionary power is exercised reasonably and in good faith and is based on a standard that is unambiguous, the restrictions were enforceable.

In this case, plaintiffs' complaint is that the Holcombs are bringing commercial trucks onto their property and servicing them there. Section 7 of the building restrictions provides that "[n]o ... commercial vehicles or trucks shall be kept, store[d], repaired, or maintained on any lot, servitude or right-of-way in any manner which would detract from the appearance of the subdivision." This restriction is not subject to the discretion of the developer at all, therefore whether it constitutes part of a general plan is not at issue. Section 16 also appears to have been violated by the Holcombs' servicing of their trucks on their property. Section 16 provides that "[n]o building or structure shall be used to operate any commercial activity on any tract, and no commercial activity shall be conducted from any lot in this subdivision, unless approved by developer." There may be disagreement on whether the phrase "unless approved by developer" applies to both phrases in this sentence, or just the second phrase. However, whatever commercial activity may or may not be allowed based on the discretion allowed the developer, there is no doubt that such commercial activity cannot include keeping, storing, repairing, or maintaining commercial vehicles or trucks in such a manner as would detract from the appearance of the subdivision. Thus, not only did no party allege to the lower courts or to this Court that the building restrictions did not constitute a general plan, the activity complained of in this case, servicing and maintaining commercial trucks on the property in a manner which detracts from the appearance of the subdivision, was not subject to the discretion of the developer in any event and is strictly prohibited. Thus, we need not consider this issue further.

The only issue assigned as error in this case, and the reason we granted this writ, is whether the court of appeal correctly applied the appropriate standard of review in reversing the trial court's factual determination that this case had not prescribed. La. C.C. art. 781 provides:

> No action for injunction or for damages on account of the violation of a building restriction may be brought after two years from the commencement of a noticeable violation. After the lapse of this period, the immovable on which the violation occurred is freed of the restriction that has been violated.

As stated in this Official Comments to this Article, "[t]his prescription does not merely bar actions for the enforcement of building restrictions as sui generis real rights; it extinguishes the real right itself in the same way that the prescription of nonuse extinguishes the right of a servitude." La. C.C. art. 781, Official Revision Comments (b).

The plaintiffs filed this suit on February 21, 2002. Six witnesses testified at trial regarding the time of the commencement of a noticeable violation. Wayne Cosby, who lives behind and two lots to the east of the Holcombs, testified that he first noticed the trucking business operations in the spring or early summer of 2001 when he noticed trucks being pressure washed on the Holcombs' property. Stan McDonald, who lives four houses down from the Holcombs, testified that in the late spring of 2001, he first heard a truck being pressure washed. A few weeks after that, he was forced off to the side of the road because of an advancing commercial truck. Subsequently, he asked a driver of one of the trucks what he was doing and the driver said, "we have a shop down there where we get our trucks worked on."

He testified that he never noticed any trucking business activity before 2001. Carl Williams, who lives three houses down from the Holcombs, testified that he first noticed the trucks being serviced on the property in April of 2001 when he noticed a truck being pressure washed. After that, he began noticing more activity, such as "banging on the tire . . . changing tires, and stuff like that."

Harry Holcomb testified that "immediately after the shop was finished" in September of 1997, he began using the facility for the repair and maintenance of the company's eighteen-wheel trucks. Mr. Holcomb offered documentary evidence to establish that commercial tire companies came to the lot several times in 1997 and 1998 to repair and install tires on the eighteen-wheelers. Mr. Holcomb testified that he does not house his eighteen-wheelers at the shop; however, on average, an eighteen-wheeler is washed on the property once every week, and an oil change is done every month. He indicated that although oil changes take place within the confines of the shop, the trucks are washed outside of the building and that this takes between two and three hours. However, on cross-examination, he acknowledged that in his pre-trial deposition he testified that he did not begin to use the shop for servicing his trucks "until the last 18 months or two years." William King, who is the Holcombs' friend but who does not live in the same neighborhood, testified that Mr. Holcomb worked on some vehicles in his driveway in 1997. Randolph Hall, who lives next door to the Holcombs, testified that after the shop was built in 1997, Mr. Holcomb brought a truck to his home "most every week;" but later testified that the truck activities were no longer frequent. Further, on cross examination, he testified that he does not know exactly when the defendants started these operations, and that if Mr. Holcomb testified in his pretrial deposition that he started this activity only within 18 months or two years before his deposition, he would agree with that too.

In its written Reasons for Judgment, the trial court ruled:

> The Court finds that plaintiffs became aware that the defendants were operating a trucking business out of their residence sometime in early 2001. The defendants testified that although he had been in the trucking business for 35 years, he had not run the business from the Ben Fugler Road residence during that entire time. Defendant further testified that he built a shop on his property but did not use it to bring trucks in right away.

> Plaintiffs testified that they only noticed the trucking company activity and noise from washing the trucks on weekends in the year 2001. Prior to 2001, plaintiffs testified that they heard or saw nothing that would indicate a trucking company was operating in the shop on Ben Fugler Road. Carl Williams testified that he was planting flowers in April 2001 when he noticed the sound of the pressure washer and banging. Other neighbors testified that they had been in the shop and not noticed a trucking business being operated there.

It appears that the trucking business was first noticed to be active sometimes in April 2001. Suit was filed February 20, 2002. Accordingly, plaintiffs
suit has not prescribed.

Reviewing the record and the trial court's factual findings under the manifest
error standard, the court of appeal concluded:

> Taking into account the testimony and documentary evidence in the
> record, we find no reasonable factual basis for a finding that the Holcombs'
> activities were not noticeable and apparent to the public until the spring of
> 2001. There is testimony from two witnesses, one of whom lives next door
> to the Holcombs, that the Holcombs had been using their shop for repair
> and maintenance of eighteen-wheelers since late 1997. Thus, the two-year
> peremptive period found in Article 781 began to run at that time, over four
> years after "the commencement of a noticeable violation." La. Civ. Code
> art. 781. Accordingly, the plaintiffs' cause of action for injunctive relief was
> perempted at the time of the filing of suit. Moreover, pursuant to Article
> 781, the Holcombs' property is freed of the pertinent restrictive covenants
> that had been violated.

Cosby v. Holcomb, supra, 890 So.2d 35.

Under the manifest error standard of review, a factual finding cannot be set aside
unless the appellate court finds that it is manifestly erroneous or clearly wrong.
Smith v. Louisiana Dept. of Corrections, 93-1305 (La.2/28/94), 633 So.2d 129, 132. . . .

Here, three witnesses testified that they did not notice the trucks coming onto
the Holcombs property to be serviced until the spring of 2001. This provides a reasonable factual basis for the trial court's finding that a noticeable violation first
occurred in 2001 and therefore, the case has not prescribed. While Mr. Holcomb
testified that some commercial truck activity occurred on his property beginning in
1997, he also testified that he really did not begin to use the property for this activity until 18 months before his deposition testimony. Further, while two witnesses
testified that trucking activity began on the property before 2001, the trial court
evidently discredited this testimony and believed the testimony of the other witnesses instead, finding that a noticeable violation of the building restrictions did not
occur until 2001. This is a typical case where there were two permissible views of the
evidence and the fact finder chose one. Generally, credibility determinations are the
sole province of the trial court. Thus, the court of appeal erred in substituting its
judgment for the judgment of the trial court.

Decree

For the reasons stated herein, the judgment of the court of appeal is reversed, the
judgment of the trial court is reinstated, and the case is remanded to the court of
appeal for consideration of the remaining assignments of error consistent with the
reasoning of this opinion.

REVERSED AND REMANDED TO THE COURT OF APPEAL.

KNOLL, Justice, dissenting. With all due respect to my colleagues, I dissent. In my view the building restrictions in this case fall far short of a real right running with the land. The building restriction's prohibition against the operation of commercial activity on the tract, as well as the proscription against the storage, repair or maintenance of commercial vehicles or trucks, was left entirely to the whim or caprice of the developers which renders a general plan ineffective, and ignores the requirements of LA. CIV.CODE ANN. art. 775.

The majority skirts this issue and frames the issue as to whether the commercial activity "detracts from the appearance of the subdivision, [which] was not subject to the discretion of the developer in any event and is strictly prohibited." I find resolving the issue in this manner troubling and an incorrect approach to this case. While the issue of whether the building restrictions constituted a general plan was not raised in the lower courts, in my view we cannot engage in a proper analysis on any issue raised concerning building restrictions unless the building restrictions constitute a valid general plan that is a real right running with the land. The majority's feigned attempt to analyze this case under an "appearance of the subdivision" is internally inconsistent when the alleged offending appearance is commercial activity that is prohibited by the building restrictions unless allowed at the whim of the developers. I find this approach unreasonable and ignores the dictates of LA. CIV.CODE ANN. art. 783, which requires us to resolve doubt as to the existence, validity or extent of building restrictions in favor of the unrestricted use of the immovable.

The existence of a general plan that is "feasible and capable of being preserved" is a threshold requirement for the creation of building restrictions as *sui generis* real rights. LA. CIV.CODE ANN. art. 775. Without such a plan, building restrictions are simply not *sui generis* real rights. *See McGuffy v. Weil*, 240 La. 758, 125 So.2d 154 (1960). Failure to provide for the uniformity of the restrictions may vitiate a general development plan. *See Murphy v. Marino*, 60 So.2d 128 (La. App. 1 Cir. 1952).

In *Murphy,* the court stated:

> It is our understanding of the law that in order to create a binding covenant running with the land in a subdivision, and enforceable by any purchaser of property therein, there should be a uniform plan of restriction applicable to the subdivision as a whole, or to a particular part of the subdivision, known to each purchaser and thereby, by reference or implication, forming a part of his contract with the subdivider. . . .

Murphy, 60 So.2d at 130. *See also Richard v. Broussard,* 378 So.2d 959 (La. App. 3 Cir. 1979) (finding a building restriction did not exist because the original landowner did not have an orderly subdivision plan); *Herzberg v. Harrison,* 102 So.2d 554 (La. App. 3 Cir. 1958) (holding that "[b]uilding restrictions are valid and enforceable where inserted in deeds in pursuance of a general plan devised by the ancestor in title to maintain certain building standards"); *In re: Congregation of St. Rita Roman Catholic Church,* 130 So.2d 425 (La. App. 4 Cir. 1961) (restrictions on 40 percent of the lots does not constitute a general plan).

Particularly germane is *LeBlanc v. Palmisano,* 43 So.2d 263 (La. App. Orl. 1949). In *LeBlanc,* property owners in the Claiborne Gateway Subdivision sued the defendant, requesting injunctive relief to prohibit him from erecting a tourist court on property he owned in the subdivision in violation of a title restriction or covenant running with the land. The particular restriction at issue provided:

> No building shall be constructed to cost less than two thousand dollars. No commercial property shall be permitted to be constructed or occupied as such on this property except by written consent of the [developer] Claiborne Avenue Extension Realty Company, Inc.

In its affirmation of the trial court's denial of the plaintiffs' application to restrain the defendant from erecting commercial buildings on the property, the appellate court stated:

> The law is clear that building restriction clauses constitute real rights, not personal to the vendor, and inure to the benefit of all other grantees under a general plan of development, and are real rights running with the lands; and that the remedy of the other grantees to prevent a violation of the restrictions by another is by injunction. *Queensborough Land Company v. Cazeaux et al.,* 136 La. 724, 67 So. 641, . . . *Edwards v. Wiseman,* 198 La. 382, 3 So.2d 661, 663.

> In our opinion, however, a casual reading of this restriction indicates that it is not a covenant running with the land, but is a personal covenant between the vendor, Claiborne Avenue Extension Realty Company, Inc., and Henry M. Rahders, the predecessor in title of defendants.

> . . . . *Whether or not certain property in this subdivision shall be used for commercial purposes is contingent entirely upon the caprice of the Claiborne Avenue Extension Realty Company, Inc., and, therefore, this covenant did not run with the land for the benefit of the purchasers or grantees of property in this subdivision.*

LeBlanc, 43 So.2d at 265–66 (emphasis added).

In the present case, two of the building restrictions at issue closely parallel the covenant found unenforceable in *LeBlanc* because the restriction did not constitute a general plan governing building restrictions for the subdivision. The two provisions William M. King, Jr., his wife, and other family members adopted for Wedgewood Acres and the Front Lots on Fugler Road state:

7.

> No house trailers, buses, commercial vehicles or trucks shall be kept, store [d], repaired, or maintained on any lot, servitude or right-of-way in any manner which would detract from the appearance of the subdivision. No structure of any temporary character, trailer, basement, tent, shack, or other out-building shall be allowed on any tract for a prolonged period

of time so as to detract from the appearance of the subdivision, *unless approved by developer.*

* * *

16.

No building or structure shall be used to operate any commercial activity on any tract, and no commercial activity shall be conducted from any lot in this subdivision, *unless approved by developer* (emphasis added).

. . . .

Although contained in one numbered paragraph of the building restriction, paragraph 7 contains two separate restrictions. First, the opening sentence addresses house trailers, buses, commercial vehicles or trucks and states they "shall [not] be kept, store[d], repaired, or maintained on any lot, servitude or right-of-way in any manner which would detract from the appearance of the subdivision." Then, the concluding sentence considers a structure of any temporary character, trailer, basement, tent, shack, or other out-building and provides that they "shall [not] be allowed on any tract for a prolonged period of time so as to detract from the appearance of the subdivision, unless approved by developer." Considering the separate topics contained in paragraph 7, it is evident from a clear reading of the provision that it is only the latter provision that the developer may exempt.

No such interpretation is needed for the provision of paragraph 16 of the building restriction. Clearly, with the approval of the developer, a building or structure, as provided in paragraph 16 of the building restrictions, may be used to operate a commercial activity on any tract in this subdivision.

Clearly, the same holding in *LeBlanc* is applicable here. Whether or not certain property in the Front Lots may be used for commercial purposes as contemplated in paragraph 16 is contingent entirely upon the caprice of William M. King, Jr., his wife, Shirley Martin King, and the two other family members who developed the Front Lots on Fugler Road. Similarly, as provided in the second sentence of paragraph 7, the developer may allow a temporary structure, trailer, basement, tent, shack, or other out-building. Considering the provisions of LA. CIV.CODE ANN. art. 775, these provisions of the building restrictions failed to constitute real rights because they did not foster the development of this property in pursuance of a general plan capable of being preserved. Therefore, these covenants did not run with the land for the benefit of the purchasers or grantees of property in this subdivision.

It cannot be denied that the provisions of Paragraph 1 ("All tracts are hereby designated as residential, and they shall be used for none other than residential purposes,") and the opening sentence of Paragraph 7 ("No house trailers, buses, commercial vehicles or trucks shall be kept, store[d], repaired, or maintained on any lot, servitude or right-of-way in any manner which would detract from the appearance of the subdivision.") conflict with paragraph 16 which clearly gives the developer the right to approve a commercial use of the property. Such a conflict, however, calls into operation the general rules of construction.

Even if the words are fairly explicit, it is our duty to refrain from construing them in such a manner as to lead to absurd consequences. *Texaco v. Vermilion Parish School Board,* 244 La. 408, 152 So.2d 541 (1963); *National Roofing and Siding Co. v. Giaise,* 434 So.2d 85 (La. App. 5 Cir. 1982), *writ denied,* 435 So.2d 443 (La. 1983). When a literal interpretation will produce absurd consequences, the court may consider all pertinent facts and circumstances, including the parties' own conclusion of the instrument's meaning, rather than adhere to a forced meaning of the terms used. LA. CIV.CODE ANN. art. 2046; *Kendrick v. Garrene,* 233 La. 106, 96 So.2d 58 (1957); *Cardos v. Cristadoro,* 228 La. 975, 84 So.2d 606 (1955).

Considering the irreconcilable difference created in this building restriction as regards commercial activity and giving recognition to the dictates of LA. CIV .CODE ANN. art. 783 to resolve doubt as to the existence, validity, or extent of building restrictions in favor of the unrestricted use of the immovable, I conclude these building restrictions relative to commercial activity do not constitute a general plan as required in LA. CIV.CODE ANN. art. 775. As provided in paragraph 16, the developer may approve commercial activity on any tract despite the declaration in paragraph 1 that "[a]ll tracts are ... designated as residential." Thus, I find the plaintiffs may not enforce the provisions of paragraphs 1 and the first sentence of paragraph 7 pertaining to commercial trucks and vehicles, as they do not constitute a real right.

Building restrictions are a means of insuring the lasting aesthetic and monetary value of property. They involve a scheme or plan of which all prospective purchasers are aware. *Chambless v. Parker,* 38,276 (La. App. 2 Cir. 3/3/04), 867 So.2d 974, 978; *4626 Corp. v. Merriam,* 329 So.2d 885 (La. App. 1 Cir.), *writ denied,* 332 So.2d 800 (La. 1976). A cursory reading of the building restrictions in the present case would have alerted any prospective purchaser that the developer reserved the right to approve any of the subdivision lots for commercial use. In this regard, I further find the majority's reliance on *Oakbrook Civic Ass'n v. Sonnier,* 481 So.2d 1008 (La. 1986), misplaced and factually distinguishable. Although this Court approved the use of neighborhood committees to approve certain construction plans in *Oakbrook,* in the present case the Kings reserved to themselves, in the restrictions, the option of granting a variance for commercial use, which reservation clearly negated a finding of a general plan as required by the pertinent provisions of the civil code. This vastly differs from the procedure approved in *Oakbrook.*

For the foregoing reasons, I would affirm the court of appeal on other grounds, dismiss the plaintiffs' action based upon the violation of building restrictions, dissolve the preliminary injunction granted in the trial court, and remand the matter to the trial court for consideration of the issues related to the plaintiffs' contention that they are also entitled to damages and the issuance of an injunction grounded on the law of nuisance.

Notes and Questions

1. In *Cosby v. Holcomb Trucking, Inc.*, 942 So.2d 471 (La. 2006), the majority opinion accepted the trial court's factual finding that the building restrictions were established pursuant to a general plan and that Harry Holcomb's violations of those restrictions were not noticeable until 2001. In her dissent, Justice Knoll asked a more fundamental question: Did the building restrictions actually establish a general plan in light of the provisions allowing the developer to approve certain types of temporary structures as well as certain commercial activity in contradistinction to the pertinent restrictions? Justice Knoll concluded that the developer's ability to waive certain restrictions rendered the building restrictions void. Who do you think is correct?

2. Note the majority's reliance in *Cosby* on *Oakbrook Civic Ass'n, Inc. v. Sonnier*, 481 So.2d 1008, 1011–12 (La. 1986). In that case the court held that when building restrictions grant an *architectural control committee* the power to approve or disprove the erection of a building by determining whether the proposed structure is in harmony with the rest of a development, the building restrictions are still valid, as long the committee exercises its discretion reasonably and in good faith. Was the developer's discretion in *Cosby* cabined in a similar way? Do you think *Oakbrook Civic Ass'n* was correctly decided? Should an architectural control committee, whose members may or may not have architectural expertise and whose members may change over the years, have broad power to decide what kinds of building plans are consistent with the developer's original vision?

3. In *Mulberry Ass'n, Inc. v. Richards*, 369 So.2d 185 (La. App. 4 Cir. 1979), the court was asked to determine "whether use of a residence for a 'law office' violates a building restriction which stated that 'the use of said property shall be limited to residential purposes.'" *Mulberry Ass'n*, 369 So.2d at 185. After considering a similar case, *Woolley v. Cinquigranna*, 188 So.2d 701 (La. App. 4 Cir. 1966), which involved a field manager for a brush manufacturer who had engaged in advertising and interviewed salesmen in his home and who had stored merchandise in his garage, the court in *Mulberry Ass'n* concluded that the lawyer who maintained his office in his home violated the building restriction and that this violation could be enjoined, without a showing of irreparable injury, by any owner of property in the subdivision. *Mulberry Ass'n*, 369 So.2d at 186.

The majority opinion in *Mulberry Ass'n* provoked a strong dissent by Judge Redmann, who contended that the "residential uses" restriction should not apply to home occupations:

> "Residential purposes" has, from time immemorial, been understood in this metropolitan area to include home occupations such as professional practice. Zoning ordinances in this area (while not overriding narrower restrictive covenants) have always allowed home professional practice in the most restrictive residential areas. . . . One can well sympathize with neighbors' desire for the extension of their homes' privacy, tranquility and

security throughout their whole subdivision. But a limitation of land use to "residential purposes", especially more than 30 years ago, did not express that desire to the extent that plaintiff urges today. It did not say then and therefore does not mean now that a lawyer or a doctor may not practice his profession in his home, any more than it said or means that a professional artist may not paint or that a professional writer may not write in his own home."

Id. at 187. Do you agree with the majority or Judge Redmann? How would a court interpret a similar restriction today? Is the activity of a lawyer writing a brief in his or her home office a commercial use of the house? Should characterization of the activity depend on whether the homeowner maintains a separate office elsewhere?

4. In *Bayou Terrace Estates Home Owners Ass'n v. Stuntz*, 97 So.3d 589 (La. App. 1 Cir. 2012), a homeowners association sought to enjoin Jessica Stuntz from providing art lessons and painting portraits, for which she was paid, in her home. The association relied on the following building restriction:

all Lots shall be used solely for single family residential purposes, and no more than one single family residence shall be built upon any Lot. The use of a Lot for other forms of residential use or for commercial, institutional, medical, retail, religious or commercial storage uses of any kind is strictly prohibited.

Id. at 591–92. Mrs. Stuntz argued that she was "carrying on her profession in her home and . . . not operating a business, trade, industry, or commercial enterprise as generally understood." The appellate court, however, affirmed the trial court's determination that her art lessons violated the restriction. *Id.* at 593.

Addressing Stuntz's claim that she had been giving art lessons in her home since she moved into the subdivision in October 2006 and that therefore, the residential use restriction had prescribed under Article 781 of the Louisiana Civil Code, the court looked for a noticeable violation—an activity on the lot which is obvious and apparent. *Id.* at 594. Although Stuntz made her neighbors aware of her art lesson business when she handed out postcards in the subdivision, maintained a website and placed a sign in her yard advertising her business, the court nevertheless held that these activities were insufficient to trigger the two-year prescriptive period under Article 781. *Id.*

In light of *Stuntz*, can a professional artist paint in her house with the intent to sell her work? Could a homeowner sell puppies from a litter born at his house? Could a child of a homeowner sell girl-scout cookies? What other kinds of home occupations could neighbors attack relying on a "residential use only" restriction?

5. In *Edwards v. Landry Chalet Rentals, LLC*, 264 So.3d 754, 757–58 (La. App. 2 Cir. 2018), the court of appeal cited *Chambless v. Parker* and held that a trial court did not commit a manifest error when it found that the repeated, short-term

vacation rental of a lakefront house by the defendant, a limited liability company, constituted commercial use in violation of a building restriction prohibiting commercial use of the property. The defendant had begun leasing the six-bedroom, five-bath house immediately after purchasing the property. *Id.* at 755, 757–58. Moreover, the defendant had advertised the property on a vacation rental website and insured the property using a commercial insurance policy that provided coverage for "loss of rents" and "business liability." *Id.* at 758. Given the clear holding in *Edwards* prospective real estate investors interested in taking advantage of the apparent market demand for short term vacation properties should be aware of the existence of building restrictions prohibiting commercial uses.

If a homeowner occasionally rented out a spare bedroom in her home through an online platform such as Airbnb, while continuing to reside in the rest of the home, would that activity violate a building restriction prohibiting commercial use?

6. Hostility to short-term vacation rentals is not limited to CICs consisting of stand-alone, single family homes. In recent years, many condominium associations have also adopted by-laws to prevent condominium units from being rented for short-term vacation use. Although technically not regarded as building restrictions, condominium by-laws (when adopted pursuant to the governing documents establishing a condominium regime and in conformity with the Louisiana Condominium Act, La. Rev. Stat. § 9:1121.101 *et seq.*) are enforceable just like building restrictions. Condominium by-laws have been used to enjoin unit owners from engaging in short-term rentals. *See, e.g., New Jax Condominiums Ass'n v. Vanderbilt New Orleans*, LLC, 219 So.3d 471, 478–80 (La. App. 4 Cir. 2017).

* * *

Hidden Hills Community, Inc. v. Rogers

869 So.2d 984 (La. App. 3 Cir. 2004)

GREMILLION, Judge. In this case, the plaintiff, Hidden Hills Community, Inc., appeals the judgment in favor of the defendant, Frank Rogers, Jr., finding that he was not in violation of their restrictive covenant. Rogers also appeals the trial court's failure to grant his exceptions of no right of action and/or no cause of action. He asserts the peremptory exception of prescription and abandonment for the first time on appeal. For the following reasons, we reverse and remand.

Factual and Procedural Background

Hidden Hills is a community surrounding a lake. The developers of Hidden Hills adopted a set of restrictions and affirmative duties in order to maintain the community in the manner it deemed fit and recorded them in the records of the Clerk of Court for the Parish of St. Landry. Article 17 of the Restrictions provides that lots must be kept "reasonably neat and clean." In September 2001, Hidden Hills filed a Petition for Declaratory Judgment seeking to enforce the above restriction and to have the trial court determine if Rogers' property was "reasonably neat and clean" in accordance with the subdivision restrictions. It further sought to assess Rogers with a $200.00 per day fine in accordance with the rules. Rogers filed an Exception of No Right of Action urging that Hidden Hills did not have the authority to bring the lawsuit. The trial court dismissed the exception. After a trial on the merits in February 2003, the trial court found that Rogers' "presentation in his decoration and landscaping do not violate the covenants as written." Hidden Hills thereafter filed a Motion for New Trial, which was denied. Hidden Hills now appeals.

Issues

Hidden Hills' sole assignment of error is that the trial court committed manifest error in finding that Rogers' property did not violate the Act of Amended Restrictions of its community. We shall review the trial court's decision in that regard. Rogers assigns as error the trial court's failure to grant his peremptory exception of no right of action. However, since he failed to file an answer to appeal, we need not address this assignment pursuant La. Code. Civ. P. art. 2133.

Prescription

Rogers urges, for the first time on appeal, that Hidden Hills' claims against him have prescribed and/or been abandoned pursuant to La. Civ. Code arts. 781–782.

La. Civ. Code art. 781 states:

> No action for injunction or for damages on account of the violation of a building restriction may be brought after two years from the commencement of a noticeable violation. After the lapse of this period, the immovable on which the violation occurred is freed of the restriction that has been violated.

Rogers claims that the suit is prescribed because several of the residents had begun noticing his unusual manner of decoration as early as 1998. To wit, he states:

1. Bobby Broussard testified that in 1998 he was aware that his home was colored a light pastel, he had noticed bones on the trees, his sidewalks had been painted in a striped fashion, the bottom of his house was painted in a checkerboard fashion, and he had items hanging from his trees.

2. Alvin Guidroz testified by the time he finished construction on his house in 1997, Rogers had life rafts, resin plastic chairs painted florescent colors and umbrellas and different colored carpet on his lawn.

We disagree and do not find these things were enough to qualify as the commencement of a noticeable violation. We hold that bright and unusual paint choices as well as fluorescent painted lawn chairs do not meet the standard of not "reasonably neat and clean." The testimony below reveals that the massive accumulation of various objects in Rogers' yard did not become a noticeable violation until late 2000, when the residents of the community began to report it to the Hidden Hills Board of Directors as a violation of the covenant. This assignment of error is dismissed as being without merit.

. . .

Reasonably Neat and Clean

We will not set aside a trial court's finding of fact in the absence of error or unless it is clearly wrong. *Rosell v. ESCO,* 549 So.2d 840 (La. 1989) . . . .

A restrictive covenant is a contract and, as such, is subject to the general rules governing contracts. "When the words of a contract are clear and explicit and lead to no absurd consequences, no further interpretation may be made in search of the parties' intent." La. Civ. Code art. 2046. "The words of a contract must be given their generally prevailing meaning." La. Civ. Code art. 2047. Restrictive covenants are governed by La. Civ. Code arts. 775 et seq. as they are building restrictions. . . .

Further, "[b]uilding restrictions may impose on owners of immovables affirmative duties that are reasonable and necessary for the maintenance of the general plan." La. Civ. Code art. 778. The affirmative duty in question under the "MAINTENANCE" heading of the Rules and Restriction and/or by-laws of Hidden Hills Community, Inc., states:

> Lots, both occupied and unoccupied, are expected to be kept in a reasonably neat and clean condition, with grass not to exceed 18 inches in height. Upon complaint by other members, the offending member's lot may be mowed or cleaned at the direction of a member of the board and charges for the work shall be presented for payment to the offending property owner.

After reviewing the evidence, particularly the photographs, we find that the trial court's finding that Rogers' property was "reasonably neat and clean" was not reasonable. WEBSTER'S NEW COLLEGIATE DICTIONARY 212 (10TH ED. 1993) defines "clean" as "free from dirt or pollution." It is synonymous with words such as "immaculate," "spotless," and "unsullied." WEBSTER'S COLLEGIATE THESAURUS 140 (1976). It is in contrast with words such as "grubby," "messy," "slovenly," and "foul." *Id.* "Neat," on the other hand, is defined as "free from irregularity," and "marked by tasteful simplicity." WEBSTER COLLEGIATE DICTIONARY 775 (10TH ED. 1993). When used as an adjective, it means, "plain, pure, unadulterated, undiluted and unmixed," or "manifesting care and orderliness." Webster's Collegiate Thesaurus 545 (1976). It is synonymous with words such as "orderly," "shipshape," "tidy," "trim," "uncluttered," and "well-groomed." *Id.* Words that contrast "neat" are "disheveled," "disorderly," "sloppy," "slovenly," "unkempt," "untidy," "lax," and "remiss." *Id.*

Bobby Brousssard testified that he began building a home in the Hidden Hills subdivision in 1997, three houses down from Rogers' home. He stated that, at the time his house was completed, in 1998, Rogers' home was colored a light pastel, and there were multi-colored rings in Mardi Gras colors around his trees and bushes. However, he stated that, later that year, Rogers began hanging bones from trees, painting stripes on his sidewalk and a checkerboard pattern on the bottom of his house. By mid-1999, Broussard testified he began hanging more items from trees and placing toilets on his lawn. Broussard, who is President of the Hidden Hills Landowner Association, testified that he began receiving complaints from neighbors in late 2000. He stated that the board had a meeting on March 23, 2001, and Rogers was served on March 25, 2001, with a notice of the violations giving him thirty days to remove boards which were restricting the right of way and lines that were in the lake. Broussard testified that the boards were removed from the lake, but the lines were back on June 6, 2001, and the boards were back in a right of way on June 7, 2001.

Broussard testified that none of the items hanging from the trees have been removed and that, in fact, Rogers has added to the collection with jugs, flags, streamers, and concession stand looking items. He then reviewed with counsel a series of pictures depicting the conglomeration of objects that Rogers has placed on his property.

Frank Rogers, Jr., testified that he bought the lot in Hidden Hills in June 1986, and began "decorating" his property sometime in 1997, beginning with painting the bottom portion of his house several different colors. However, at this time, the front of his house remained yellow with green shutters. Rogers testified that, over the years, he began "touching up a little bit here and there with a lot of different colors." He testified that the white plastic bleach jugs he has hanging from string between trees are birdhouses, although he has not cut out any holes for the birds. He further testified that, since the institution of the lawsuit, he has added more political signs, jugs, surveyor tape, and triangular banners typically used at car dealerships. He also testified that he has around four or five displays of bundled up empty chlorine bottles strung together hanging from the trees, which he says serve as birdhouses. Rogers has also added a peanut machine, a cash register machine, TVs, pieces of ladders, non-working satellite dishes, snow cone advertisements, a sign that says "rice and gravy," and cow skulls with deer horns and bull horns in them or a telephone sitting on top.

Deanna Cobb, Rogers' immediate next-door neighbor, testified that she has lived in the house next door since 1997. She stated that Rogers' property began to substantially change sometime in November 2000. Cobb testified that Rogers painted his shrubs assorted colors, painted rings around the trees, and painted animal horns and hung them from the trees. He continued adding items to the exterior of his property such as: dishwashers, weedeaters, lawnmowers, squirrel traps, vacuum cleaners, and telephones strung from the trees. Cobb testified that the next thing to occur, following her March 2001 complaint to the board, was a "plastic explosion," which included long pieces of triangular banners, plastic bottles hung from trees, flagging tape banners, political signs, food signs, real estate signs, home loan signs, PVC pipe, rope, television sets, computer monitors, and a plastic grandfather clock. She also noted a screen door suspended in the air, and a glove six or seven feet high in the air on PVC pipe with the middle finger pointing toward her property. Cobb testified that there are in excess of one thousand jugs on Rogers' property, and that he runs his sprinklers all night which cause the jugs to hit each other and make noise all night long.

Alvin Guidroz, who lives across the lake from Rogers' property, testified that he purchased his lot in 1995, and started building in 1997. He stated that, at this time, Rogers' home was neat and well kept, through to 1998. Guidroz testified that, after he moved into his house, he started noticing little changes here and there but nothing to be concerned about. However, he testified that it escalated to the hundreds of jugs, tapes, and assorted sundry items.

While the testimony in this case is brief, the photographic evidence tells the story. Rogers' property evidences thousands of plastic chlorine bottles hung in every which way on his property, brightly painted shrubs, hundreds of political signs, banners, caution tape, and flagging hanging everywhere. It can only be called a veritable junkyard, but brighter and more noticeable as many of the items, such as the white plastic jugs, are suspended from lines run across the trees.

The definition of neat referred to by the trial court, was "clean and in good order; trim, tidy." WEBSTER'S NEW WORLD DICTIONARY 905 (3RD ED. 1994). Using this definition, the trial court found that Rogers' property was "reasonably neat and clean" and not in violation of the covenant. We disagree with our learned colleague. Not only do we find that the property is not "clean and in good order: tidy, trim," we find that it is not "immaculate," "spotless," nor "unsullied." To the contrary, it is "grubby," "messy," "slovenly," and even "foul." The property is certainly not "free from irregularity" or "marked by tasteful simplicity." It is not "plain, pure, unadulterated, undiluted, and unmixed" nor does it "manifest care and orderliness." It is, on the other hand, "disheveled," "disorderly," "sloppy," and "unkempt."

Further, we find that the term "reasonably neat and clean" is not ambiguous in the context used. In drafting the restrictive covenants, the redactors clearly meant to prohibit certain uses to one's property. It would be virtually impossible to draft a set of covenants that would consider all conceivable offending uses of property, notwithstanding the fact that no one would have dreamed up this instant offending use of property.

We acknowledge that "one person's trash is another person's treasure," however, a reasonable person cannot claim that the Rogers' property is neat and clean. He argues that the term "neat and clean" actually describes his property and argued at oral argument that the jugs and other objects are strung in a geometrical manner which should be pleasing to the eye. In a word, that is absurd. Accordingly, we reverse the trial court's finding that Rogers' property was not in violation of the restrictive covenant. We shall not address the penalty assessment, but shall remand this case to the trial court for a determination whether a penalty should be assessed under the restrictive covenants and, if so, how much.

Conclusion

The judgment of the trial court finding that the defendant-appellee, Frank Rogers, Jr., did not violate the plaintiff-appellant's, Hidden Hills Community, Inc., restrictive covenant is reversed and this matter is remanded to the trial court for a determination of the penalty assessment. All costs of this appeal are assessed to Rogers.

REVERSED AND REMANDED.

Notes and Questions

1. Addressing the issue of prescription, the court in *Hidden Hills Community, Inc. v. Rogers*, 869 So.2d 984 (La. App. 3 Cir. 2004), discounted the landowner's past "decorations," including bones on trees, striped sidewalks and umbrellas and different colored carpet on his lawn. Rather, the court determined that the defendant's violations of the "reasonably neat and clean" building restriction became noticeable at the time the neighbors began to make complaints. Do you agree that the prescriptive period started to run only after the neighbors reported a violation to the homeowners association, as opposed to the point in time when the offending behavior began?

2. What do you think of the Mardi Gras rings around the bushes, resin plastic chairs painted with florescent colors, or the gallon jug bird houses hanging from trees without any openings for the birds to enter? was the court imposing its own standards for tidiness on the homeowner? Or was Rogers just expressing his own unique artistic vision through his home and lawn decoration? Where is the line between the freedom to use one's property as one wishes and a regime that protects neighbors' reasonable expectations about standards of cleanliness? Would you prefer to live in a community with or without building restrictions?

3. What happened in *Hidden Hills* to the standard of deference with regard to the trial court's findings of fact? A trial judge usually lives locally and knows the character of the community. Was the trial court clearly wrong in failing to find that the yard was a mess? Would you argue that Rogers' geometric patterns were neat?

4. Keep in mind that in many building restriction enforcement actions, a property owner in a CIC who has clearly violated one of the restrictions will typically argue that the restriction should not be enforceable because either: (1) the property owner, or a predecessor-in-interest, clearly violated the restriction some time ago, thus triggering the two year liberative prescription period found in Article 781 of the Louisiana Civil Code; or (2) the restriction was abandoned more generally under Article 782. As *Hidden Hills* and the other cases above demonstrate, however, courts are often reluctant to find a noticeable violation or an abandonment. *See also Bagley v. Lake Bruin Landing and Marina, L.L.C.*, 248 So.3d 613, 619–20 (La. App. 2 Cir. 2018) (affirming the trial court's finding that the building restrictions of the subdivision that limited each lot to single residence and prohibited the use of temporary structures and trailers had not been waived or abandoned based on actions of the previous property owner's guests and friends who had parked trailers and constructed electric cords, septic tanks, water lines and patios on the lot). Can you see why? For a contrary result, see *Aucoin v. Copper Meadows Homeowners Ass'n*, 269 So.3d 859, 867–68 (La. App. 3 Cir. 2019) (determining the presence of a

noticeable violation for more than two years before the enforcement action was filed in light of evidence, including testimony, sufficient to support findings that: (1) Mr Aucoin had parked his truck, with a trailer attached, outside his home overnight during the week as well as on weekends and holidays; (2) Copper Meadows had to have known about this conduct because it attempted to fine the Aucoins without ultimately imposing the fine).

5. Liberative prescription questions have also arisen in connection with actions brought by homeowners associations seeking to enforce the affirmative obligation to pay assessments established pursuant to a building restriction regime. In *Brier Lake, Inc. v. Jones*, 710 So.2d 1054, 1062–63 (La. 1998), the Louisiana Supreme Court held that a homeowner's obligation to pay assessments to the association, when created solely through a building restriction, is subject to the two-year liberative prescription period of Article 781 of the Louisiana Civil Code, as opposed to the general ten-year liberative prescription period for personal actions established under Article 3499. According to the court, the homeowner who had failed to pay assessments was, therefore, not liable for assessments that had been due for over two years at the time the homeowners association's enforcement action was filed. *Id.* at 1066.

Although the Louisiana Homeowners Association Act, La. Rev. Stat. § 9:1141.1 *et seq.*, was adopted to overrule other aspects of the *Brier Lake* decision, no portion of that act addresses the subject of liberative prescription and the efforts of homeowners association to collect unpaid assessments. For a detailed discussion of this issue and a cogent argument in favor of the continued application of *Brier Lake* in this context, see *Southern Trace Property Owners Ass'n v. Williams*, 210 So.3d 835, 845–47 (La App. 2 Cir. 2016) (J. Caraway, dissenting).

Index